D0782490

The Advanced Professional Pastry Chef

The Advanced
Professional
Pastry Chef

Bo Friberg

with Amy Kemp Friberg

WILEY

JOHN WILEY & SONS, INC.

Library of Congress Cataloging-in-Publication Data is available upon request.

ISBN 13: 978-0-471-35926-5

ISBN-10: 0-471-35926-2

Printed in the United States of America

Book design by Richard Oriolo

10 9

CONTENTS

Preface   vii

Acknowledgments   xiii

Chapter 1   Decorated Cakes   3

Chapter 2   Wedding Cakes   67

Chapter 3   Individual Pastries   93

Chapter 4   Plated Desserts   129

Chapter 5   Frozen Desserts   203

Chapter 6   Light and Low-Calorie Desserts   267

Chapter 7   Charlottes, Custards, Bavarian Creams, Mousses, and Soufflés   321

Chapter 8   Modernist Desserts   373

Chapter 9   Holiday Classics and Favorites   423

Chapter 10   Chocolate Artistry   505

Chapter 11   Sugarwork   569

Chapter 12   Marzipan Modeling   633

Chapter 13   Advanced Decorations   665

Chapter 14   Basic Recipes   749

Appendix: Weights, Measures, and Yields   805

Index   828

PREFACE

The decision to become a pastry chef may be a one-time occurrence, but the realization of that goal continues throughout one's career. A good chef is constantly evolving — trying new things, learning different techniques, and improving his or her skills. The old saying "it's best to leave well enough alone" does not apply in our field. Rather than being content with something that is just good enough, we must always strive for improvement to stay competitive. We learn from our failures as well as our successes, and many of us share both with others in our profession. I have always offered all of my knowledge to my colleagues and my students while continuing to learn, experiment, and work on new projects. The idea of continually looking for an original way to prepare a recipe or trying a fresh approach with a classic dessert presentation, for example, was the impetus behind the three revisions of *The Professional Pastry Chef* over the last 18 years, and now the creation of this new volume.

When the time came to revise *The Professional Pastry Chef, Third Edition*, it was clear that we needed to divide the text into two volumes. The first of the two books was *The Professional Pastry Chef, Fourth Edition: Fundamentals of Baking and Pastry*. The fundamentals volume contains recipes for yeast breads, flatbreads, cookies, basic individual pastries and decorated cakes, breakfast breads, doughs, ice creams, sauces, syrups, fillings, custards and puddings, plated desserts, and an introduction to chocolate work and decorating. This book, *The Advanced Professional Pastry Chef*, contains some revised material from the third edition which reflects industry trends, suggestions from students and colleagues, and my own improvements, plus dozens of new recipes, photographs, and templates. As in the companion volume, here too you will find chapters on decorated cakes, plated desserts, and individual pastries, but in this book the recipes are more complex. Further, this text features a much more comprehensive chocolate section, as well as chapters dedicated to the more specialized areas of pastry such as wedding cakes, frozen desserts, light desserts, modernist desserts, holiday classics, sugarwork, marzipan, and advanced decorating techniques.

While the majority of the recipes in this book are aimed at the more experienced chef who has mastered the fundamentals, many simple and easy-to-prepare recipes are included as well—most notably in the chapters for light desserts, frozen desserts, and holiday classics and favorites, as these chapters are not included in the companion volume, meaning that all of my recipes for these desserts are found here.

Many culinary schools have implemented advanced pastry courses for the same reason that the third edition of my book became two volumes: There is simply too much information required for today's pastry chef to fit all of it into a single class or a single book. As the field of baking and pastry grows to new heights, advanced techniques are becoming more and more important.

Over the past few decades the general public has become much more educated about all types of food preparation, and the interest in dining out has never been higher. More importantly, from our perspective, the public's never-ending love of sweets has created an increased demand for top pastry chefs. Today, more consumers than ever before consider dessert to be a "must have" when dining out. What was once often an afterthought or an optional part of the meal has become an important source of revenue for restaurateurs. With desserts in many fine restaurants priced at the same level as first course selections, it is no longer enough to simply place a slice of cake or a serving of custard on a plate and accompany it with a pool of sauce—no matter how good the combination may taste. When the customer has made the kind of monetary investment required for an evening out in an upscale restaurant today, he expects us to put on a bit of a show at the end of the meal. To create a dessert of this caliber, it is necessary for the plate to be finished to order, with the pastry chef artfully arranging several prepared components together with complementary sauces and/or decorating syrups, and garnishes made of sugar, chocolate, or tuile paste, for example. Today's dessert menus are often every bit as elaborate as the menus for the other courses, and they generally recognize the pastry chef that heads the department. Although this book covers much more than just recipes for desserts to be served after a meal, that element is undoubtedly the most important subject for a restaurant pastry chef to master.

As a teaching guide, this book may be used alone for an advanced course or it can be combined with *Fundamentals of Baking and Pastry* for a class that covers the full spectrum of the field. Both volumes share the same design and the easy-to-multiply or -decrease yields and portions that proved to work so well in the third edition. The recipe introductions, chef's tips, informational sidebars, and the new procedural photographs in this volume all reflect my teaching philosophy: I believe we learn best when it is clear not only what steps to take to accomplish the goal, but why the steps must be completed in a particular sequence.

Before You Use This Book

Certain ingredient information is standard throughout the book. Please note the following conventions:

- Salt used in these recipes is common granulated table salt. If you prefer another type of salt, such as flaked kosher salt, you may substitute the same amount by weight without adjustment. For volume measures, however, such as measuring by the teaspoon or tablespoon, the amount must be modified. This type of kosher salt has larger crystals that do not pack together as tightly, so a measurement of kosher salt weighs less than an equal volume of table salt. Four tablespoons of table salt weigh approximately 65 grams, whereas 4 tablespoons of flaked kosher salt weigh about 35 grams, making kosher salt much lighter. You therefore need to substitute almost twice as much kosher salt for table salt when measuring by volume.

- Butter is always specified as "unsalted butter." Salted butter can be substituted if the salt in the recipe is reduced by about ⅕ ounce (6 g) for every pound of butter. However, you cannot substitute salted butter if the recipe contains little salt or if the main ingredient is butter.

- The number of eggs specified in each recipe is based on 2-ounce (55-g) eggs (graded large). If you use eggs of a different size, adjust the number accordingly. For convenience in kitchens where a supply of separated egg yolks and whites is available, a volume measure is given when yolks or whites are used independently. The quantity of yolks, whites, and whole eggs per cup has been rounded to twelve, eight and four, respectively, for these measures.

- Raw eggs: When egg yolks, whites, or whole eggs are included in a recipe in which they are not cooked, e.g. in a mousse or gelatin-fortified cake filling, they are first heated to at least 140°F (60°C) to pasteurize them. This is done using different procedures depending on the recipe; often it involves whisking a hot syrup into the eggs or whipping the eggs over a bain-marie with another ingredient. Because eggs contain a large amount of protein, they are an ideal breeding ground for bacteria, especially salmonella. Inadequate cooking or unsanitary use or storage of eggs can lead to food-borne illnesses. U.S. Department of Agriculture (USDA) guidelines state that pasteurization is complete when the egg is heated to 140°F (60°C) and ideally is held there for 2 to 3 minutes. (Pasteurization is defined as heating a liquid to a preset temperature for a specified period of time in order to destroy pathogenic bacteria.) Only fresh and freshly cracked eggs should be used in uncooked dishes. Frozen and precracked egg products should be reserved for use in dishes where they will be completely cooked, such as for baked items.

- Yeast is always specified as "fresh compressed yeast." To substitute dry yeast for fresh, reduce the amount called for by half. Dissolve the dry yeast in the warm liquid called for in the recipe, adding a small amount of sugar if the liquid is water rather than milk. If the recipe calls for cold liquid rather than warm, warm a portion of the liquid and use this to dissolve the yeast. "Fast rising" yeast (which is usually used dry, combined with the flour in a recipe) should be avoided. It is treated with conditioners that accelerate the yeast and give the chef less control. Furthermore, it impairs the flavor of baked goods in most cases.

- Gelatin is called for as unflavored powdered gelatin. To substitute sheet gelatin, see page 817.

- The unsweetened cocoa powder called for in the recipes in this book refers to the alkalized (Dutch process) type, preferred for its darker color and smoother flavor, and also because it dissolves more easily. Natural cocoa powder, which is somewhat acidic, may be substituted provided it is used in a recipe that contains a sweetener. However, it should not be used to sift on top of a pastry or to coat a truffle because it can be bitter eaten alone.

- Both metric and U.S. units are given throughout. However, to avoid unmeasurable fractions, metric amounts have been rounded to the nearest even number. The equivalent for 1 ounce, for instance, is given as 30 grams rather than 28.35 grams.

- When 1 ounce or less of an ingredient, dry or liquid, is needed, the quantity is always given in teaspoons or tablespoons and is based on an exact measurement. Hedges like "scant" or "heaping" are not used in this book.

- Avoid the temptation to convert ingredients into cups and tablespoons. Weight measurements are used in professional recipes for better accuracy, and a good scale can be purchased inexpensively. Make certain that your scale (old or new) is properly calibrated.

- Sheet pans are the standard American size. Full size is 16 x 24 inches (40 x 60 cm), and half size is 12 x 16 inches (30 x 40 cm). Both have a 1-inch (2.5-cm) slightly slanted border.

- In some recipes, instructions are given to spread a batter (most often a sponge batter) over a sheet of baking paper set on the work surface and then to drag the paper onto a sheet pan. This is done to facilitate spreading the batter evenly without the long sides of the sheet pan getting in the way, as the standard industry sheet pans in the United States have 1-inch (2.5-cm) sides. Readers throughout Europe and in other countries where regular sheet pans contain raised sides only on the short ends may eliminate this step.

- Some recipes in this text include instructions for making templates. Thin cardboard is one possibility; it is readily available and easy to work with. If sprayed on both sides with food lacquer, the templates can be cleaned and used several times. However, untreated cardboard templates are intended for one-time use only. A sturdier and more practical template can be made from $\frac{1}{16}$-inch (2-mm) plastic. These take a bit more effort to construct, but they can be used over and over. I prefer the laminated type of plastic since it will lie perfectly flat and will not tear (this is the type often used to cover office files or documents), but polyurethane sheets also work well.

- Any recipe in this book can be scaled up or down in direct proportions as long as it is not multiplied or divided by any number greater than four. In calculating ingredients that do not divide straight across, e.g. to divide in half a recipe calling for 3 eggs or $1\frac{1}{3}$ cups of a liquid, round the number up (using 2 eggs or $5\frac{1}{2}$ ounces of liquid for the examples given).

- When a weight yield is given for baked goods (for example, four 1-pound 4-ounce [570 g] loaves), it relates to the product before being baked. As a general rule, 10 percent of the weight of any item is lost in steam during the baking process. When a large amount of liquid is part of the ingredients (such as for bread), up to 2 ounces (55 g) for every pound (455 g) of dough will expire.

- A properly calibrated thermometer is of great importance both for safe food handling and to obtain desired results whenever the exact temperature of the ingredients determines the outcome. Refer to page 630 for instructions on how to calibrate a thermometer.

- When white flour is used in recipes in this book, cake flour, bread flour, or high-gluten flour is specified. All-purpose flour, pastry flour, and the dozens of other specialty white flours are not used. Many recipes combine cake flour and bread flour to create the desired protein content. If you do not have cake flour or bread flour, all-purpose flour may be substituted with a good result in most cases. When high-gluten flour is unavailable, bread flour may be used instead. The protein content of cake flour is generally around 7 percent. Bread flour has a protein content of approximately 12 percent, and high-gluten flour about 14 percent. When cake flour and bread flour are combined in equal amounts, they essentially create all-purpose flour, which has a protein content of approximately 9 to 10 percent. All of these protein percentages vary depending on the manufacturer.

- Recipes in this text (with a few exceptions) do not call for chocolate with a specific ratio of sugar to cocoa mass, as in semisweet chocolate or bittersweet chocolate, for example. Instead, either sweet dark chocolate or unsweetened chocolate is specified, and often the two are combined to create the desired ratio of sugar to cocoa mass, giving the chef greater control over the intensity of the chocolate flavor. Most brands of sweet dark chocolate contain approximately equal proportions of sugar and cocoa mass. Semisweet chocolates usually contain about 60 percent cocoa mass and bittersweet chocolates 70 percent. These numbers vary by manufacturer and can range from 48 to 72.5 percent. If a recipe calls for both sweet and unsweetened chocolate, either semisweet or bittersweet chocolate may be substituted for the combined weight.

- Any recipe in this book can be scaled up or down in direct proportions as long as it is not multiplied or divided by any number greater than four. When scaling up or down more than four times, adjustments become necessary. When dividing a recipe more than four times, increase any yeast, salt, and spices by ten percent. When multiplying a recipe more than four times, decrease these ingredients by ten percent. Other modifications that must be made are increasing or decreasing the duration of kneading, mixing, whipping, and baking. In calculating ingredients that do not divide straight across, e.g. to divide in half a recipe calling for 3 eggs or 1⅓ cups of a liquid, round the number up (using 2 eggs or 5½ ounces of liquid for the examples given).

For questions, updates, and information please visit my web site at www.ChefBo.com.

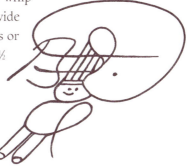

Bo Friberg

ACKNOWLEDGMENTS

In the three years it took to complete this book and its companion volume, *The Professional Pastry Chef, Fourth Edition: Fundamentals of Baking and Pastry*, many friends in the industry helped and contributed in various ways. The first person I would like to thank is my ever-so-patient and loving wife, Amy. Without her full-time commitment, neither of these books would have been published.

Though there are too many names to list all of them here, I would like to say a sincere thank you to the following people whose contributions stand out:

- Chefs Jacques Pepin, Hubert Keller, and Rick Rodgers, for their kind endorsements of the first volume. Also, Chef Jacquy Pfeiffer of the French Pastry School in Chicago for his endorsement of this volume.

- Hatsuo Takeuchi and Elaine Fiener of Demarle, who contributed the two most famous of Demarle's inventions — the Silpat and the Flexipan — for recipe testing throughout both volumes.

My two favorite chocolate manufacturers, Felchlin of Schwyz, Switzerland, and El Rey of Caracas, Venezuela, for their supplies of fantastic chocolate as well as their hospitality during my visits to their factories. Thank you specifically to Hans Baumann, owner of Swiss Chalet Fine Foods, the distributor of Felchlin chocolate, and to Felchlin's corporate pastry chef, Stephan Iten, both of whom took such good care of me in Switzerland. In Caracas, thank you to Jorge Redmond Schlageter, president and owner of El Rey, for not only arranging for me to tour his chocolate empire, but for taking the time to invite me for dinner.

Leo Kollener, my former colleague of many years, for his help and advice on the templates and photography.

Don Harwerth, a former student who owns a busy bakeshop and deli in St. Louis, for dropping everything at a moment's notice and flying to New York to assist me with a photo shoot.

Amy Peeples, Michelle Raluy, Rochelle Foles, and Lara Bice for their help with typing and research.

The whole gang at St. Honoré Restaurant and Bakeshop in Caracas, Venezuela, especially Morris Harrar and his family, as well as Roberto Zinn, director of City Grill, for their hospitality during my stay in Venezuela.

The faculty of Centro de Artes Culinarias Maricu in Mexico City, where I have taught seminars over the years but have always come away with more knowledge than when I arrived. The entire crew is wonderful but especially so the owner, Chef Maricú Ortiz.

And last, but not least, at John Wiley & Sons, Inc., Andrea Johnson in the production department, who contributed far more than could have been expected and whose assistance was invaluable, and Jeff Faust in the creative services department for their extra effort on this book as well as on *Fundamentals of Baking and Pastry*, and for their always helpful and professional demeanors.

The Advanced Professional Pastry Chef

Apple Wine Cake 9

Apricot Cream Cake 12

    CONTEMPORARY APRICOT CREAM CAKE 13

Black Currant Cake 14

    CRANBERRY MOUSSE CAKE 16

Caramel Cake 17

Charente Bavarois Cake 19

    CHARENTE BAVAROIS MODERNE 20

Chestnut Puzzle Cake 22

Chocolate and Frangelico Mousse Cake 24

    CONTEMPORARY CHOCOLATE AND FRANGELICO MOUSSE CAKE 26

Chocolate Ganache Cake 27

Chocolate Mousse Cake with Banana 29

    CHOCOLATE-BANANA MOUSSE CAKE NOUVELLE 30

Chocolate Truffle Cake with Raspberries 31

Dark Chocolate Shingle Cake 32

Dobos Torte 34

Gâteau Malakoff 36

Gâteau Mocha Carousel 38

Harlequin Cake 40

Lemon Chiffon Cake 42

    LEMON CHIFFON FRUIT BASKET CAKE 44

Mocha Cake 45

    CLASSIC MOCHA CAKE 47

Opera Cake 47

Parisienne Chocolate Cake 49

Queen of Sheba Cake 50

Raspberry Cake 52

    RASPBERRY CAKE NOUVELLE 53

    BLACKBERRY CAKE 54

Sicilian Macaroon Cake 55

Strawberry Bagatelle 58

Strawberry Kirsch Cake 61

Tropical Coconut Cake 63

Decorated Cakes

By definition, a cake is a sweet baked good usually containing flour, sugar, liquid, and fat. Other typical ingredients are flavoring agents, eggs, and other leaveners, such as baking powder or baking soda. Cakes are generally categorized by their main ingredient or flavoring — for example, cheesecake, chocolate cake, or raspberry cake — or by their method of preparation — mousse cake, chiffon cake, flourless cake, and so on.

Sponge cakes are almost always a component of assembled decorated cakes. Baking sponge cake and variations thereof is a basic skill every baker or pastry chef must master. Not having a properly made sponge affects not only the taste of the cake but also its final appearance, as it will be harder to decorate attractively. Sponge cakes are classified by their preparation method, such as the *creaming method* or the *foaming method*.

Sponge cakes are made from the three ingredients no baker can do without — eggs, sugar, and flour — although some sponges contain butter as well. Classically made sponge cakes (génoise in French) do not contain baking powder or baking soda; their volume and light texture come solely from the air whipped into the eggs.

Formula Balance in Sponge Cakes

An extremely heavy or rich sponge contains equal parts eggs, sugar, and flour. In other words, for every 8 ounces (225 g) eggs (approximately 4), such a sponge cake contains 8 ounces (225 g) sugar and 8 ounces (225 g) flour. This ratio is the formula for a standard pound cake. A medium-bodied mixture contains 5 ounces (140 g) each flour and sugar for the same 8 ounces (225 g) eggs. In the lightest and most common type of sponge cake, the sugar and flour weights are 4 ounces (115 g) each per 8 ounces (225 g) eggs. The sugar and flour ratio can be altered slightly in individual formulas, such as 3 ounces (85 g) sugar and 4 ounces (115 g) flour, or vice versa. If butter is used, the amount is generally about one-fourth the weight of the sugar or flour, and it is added at the end.

Sponge Cake Ingredients

In any sponge formula, the weight of the eggs is always the basis for determining the quantity of the remaining ingredients. Whole eggs, entirely or in part, may be replaced with egg yolks or egg whites. More egg yolks result in a denser sponge with finer pores. Increasing the amount of egg whites produces a lighter sponge with a larger pore structure. Increasing the yolk content in an already heavy sponge cake can have a detrimental effect. The yolks reduce the available water content, making it difficult for the sugar to dissolve. The eggs should be shelled as close as possible to the time of making the sponge. Eggs that have been shelled and left overnight should not be used for sponges. Both egg whites and egg yolks are available pasteurized, ready to use, and packaged in convenient refrigerator cartons (such as the type milk and juice come in). These products are becoming increasingly popular in the industry not only for their health and sanitation advantages but also because they are efficient to use, reducing labor, spoilage, and breakage.

A fine grade of granulated sugar, such as castor sugar, is preferable for use in a sponge cake to ensure that the sugar dissolves easily. The proper amount in relation to the other ingredients is also important, as discussed above. Too little sugar, in addition to affecting taste and color, can make the cake tough by throwing the formula off balance; in actuality, the problem is too much flour. This condition also causes the crust to darken unfavorably and gives the sponge a dense texture.

The flour itself must have a good ratio of starch and protein. Some gluten (a high percentage of which is found in bread flour, for instance) is necessary to bind and hold the structure, but too high a percentage makes the batter rubbery and hard to work with and results in a tough and chewy sponge. A flour high in starch, such as cake flour, produces a light and tender sponge, but the structure may collapse partially when baked. To provide greater control over the finished product, I prefer to adjust this ratio myself in individual recipes by combining both bread and cake flours in the proper proportions rather than using premixed all-purpose flour.

Pure starches, such as potato starch and cornstarch, can be used to weaken the gluten, but no more than half the weight of the flour should be replaced. Cocoa powder, which also contains no gluten, is usually added for flavor rather than as a means to reduce the gluten strength.

Flour for sponge cakes should always be sifted. If you use unsweetened cocoa powder or any other dry ingredient, sift it in with the flour. You must be careful, when adding the flour to the batter, not to break the air bubbles you just whipped in. Fold in the flour with a rubber spatula or your hand and turn the mixing bowl slowly with your other hand at the same time to combine the ingredients evenly. Never stir the flour into the batter or add it with the mixer.

Butter is added to a sponge cake not only for flavor but to improve the quality of the finished sponge. The cake develops a finer pore structure as the batter becomes heavier. Butter also extends shelf life.

Butter can be added to a sponge in an amount up to two-thirds the weight of the sugar. The butter should be melted but not hot. It is always added last, after the flour is completely incorporated. Otherwise, the butter will surround any small lumps of flour, which you won't be able to break up without losing volume.

Chopped nuts or chopped candied fruit may be added to a sponge cake without changing the formula, provided it is a fairly heavy sponge, such as one made using the creaming method. The pieces should be coated with a portion of the flour and incorporated when the flour is added or they will settle on the bottom of the cake as it bakes. This problem is amplified in light sponge batters. Chopped nuts do not absorb much moisture and therefore do not have the same effect on the batter that ground or finely crushed nuts do (see below). Almond or hazelnut paste may also be added without any reformulating; however, in this case, the butter is generally left out. The almond or hazelnut paste is first softened and worked free of lumps by incorporating egg white. The egg yolks are whipped as directed in the recipe, then folded into the nut paste mixture quickly and smoothly without causing lumps or losing volume.

Ideally, ground or finely crushed almonds and other nuts, which add both flavor and structure to sponge cakes, should be of a consistency fine enough to allow them to be sifted with the flour. If this is not possible, the nuts should be thoroughly combined with the flour by hand. The flour must be reduced accordingly, as the fine structure of the nuts acts as a binding agent in the same way flour does. Decrease the weight of the flour by 1 ounce (30 g) for every 3 ounces (85 g) ground nuts added. The quantity of ground nuts added cannot be greater than the weight of the sugar in the recipe.

Unsweetened cocoa powder may be substituted for cake flour in an equal weight. No more than 3 ounces (85 g) cocoa powder should be used per 1 pound (455 g) flour in the total recipe. Sift in the cocoa powder with the flour. Melted unsweetened chocolate can be added (not substituted) at a ratio of no more than 5 ounces (140 g) per 1 pound (455 g) flour. Melted sweet chocolate may be added at the same rate, but the sugar should be decreased by 2 ounces (55 g) for this amount. Fold the warm (but not hot) chocolate into a portion of the batter to temper it, then fold this into the remaining batter. The batter must not be too cool or it will be difficult to incorporate the chocolate. Using this method, the best results are achieved with cakes containing a chemical leavening agent rather than with traditional egg-leavened sponges.

Baking a Sponge Cake

A sponge cake batter of the genoise type, which does not contain chemical leaveners, should be divided into prepared pans and baked immediately, or the air bubbles will start to break. Pans should be buttered and floured with a combination of 4 parts melted butter to 1 part flour by volume. By brushing this mixture on the pans, you need to handle them only once. A pan spray may be used instead. With some lighter mixtures, such as two-way and chiffon batters, it is advantageous to butter and flour or spray the bottom of the pan only, or to line it with a circle of baking paper; this allows the sponge to stick to the sides, thereby preventing it from shrinking as it bakes.

The latest tool for baking sponges and other cake bases is the Flexipan cake mold. Just as with the Silpat baking mats made by the same company to replace baking paper, Flexipans are convenient in that they do not require greasing and flouring. You do not need to adjust your oven temperature and baking time when using Flexipans; however, as is true in all situations, you may need to make alterations according to the type of oven you use, how full it is, and so on. The Flexipan performs in the same way as a conventional pan, so if you know your oven tends to run hot, for example, make your usual modifications. Ideally, Flexipans should be placed on a perforated sheet pan when using an oven with grill-style racks or, when baking directly on the hearth in a deck oven, on a regular sheet pan. Sometimes it is necessary to double-pan when using a deck oven. To unmold the baked cakes, invert the cake in the pan, pick up two sides of the Flexipan, and gently peel the form away from the cake.

The oven should be around 400°F (205°C) for a typical cake pan or cake ring measuring 10 × 2 inches (25 × 5 cm). The deeper and wider the cake pan, the lower the heat should be. On the other end of the scale, if you are baking a ¼-inch (6-mm) sheet for a roulade, the oven should be at 425°F (219°C), or the sheet will dry out as it bakes and be difficult (or impossible) to roll. To test a sponge for doneness, gently press down in the center with your finger; the sponge should spring right back and not leave any indentation.

In most cases, you should not unmold any sponge before it is at least partially cooled. Store it covered or wrapped in plastic. If you do not need to reuse the pans, leave the cakes in the pans, turn them upside down to store, and unmold as needed. When sponge cakes or sheets are refrigerated, the skin on top becomes soft; it must be removed before the layers are used. Sponge cake freezes exceptionally well, even for weeks, if wrapped properly; both the professional baker and the home cook should always have sponge cake in the freezer for creating a last-minute dessert.

Using Powdered Gelatin in Cake Fillings

Many of the layered cakes in this chapter use unflavored gelatin powder to thicken the filling so the cakes can be cut attractively without the filling oozing out. Gelatin powder is first softened by sprinkling it over a cold liquid, usually water, and allowing it to stand for two or three minutes. The surface area of the liquid must be large enough to allow all the gelatin to become wet and absorb the liquid. Do not stir at this point, or the gelatin may form lumps. The mixture is then heated until the gelatin dissolves completely. This actually occurs at 86°F (30°C), but it is necessary to heat it to a higher temperature, about 100°F (43°C), or the gelatin would set up almost immediately. If you do not have a thermometer and are unsure of the temperature, heat the mixture until it is warm to the touch — just a little higher than body temperature.

In fact, it is not absolutely necessary to heat gelatin to any particular temperature in order for it to work properly; warming gelatin simply facilitates the dissolving process. Depending on its use — and, more specifically, how it will be mixed with the other ingredients — a higher or lower temperature can be preferable. In the glaze on the Black Currant Cake, for example, the dissolved gelatin is heated to a fairly low temperature so that it will set up quickly and not run down the sides after it is spread over the cakes. Because the glaze does not contain whipped cream, it can be reheated if it sets up before you are ready to use it, without damaging the glaze. The other ingredients in the glaze are stirred into the dissolved gelatin in this case because a relatively small amount of gelatin is used, and it is important that none is left clinging to the sides of the bowl or pot in which it was dissolved. Also, because there is no cream in the glaze, it is not necessary to temper the heated gelatin before mixing it with the remaining ingredients.

On the other hand, in the recipe for Chocolate Cognac Cream, the instructions call for quickly mixing the dissolved gelatin into a small portion of the filling to temper it before adding it to the remaining filling. In this instance, the gelatin should be heated until it is a bit warmer because it is added to a large amount of cold whipped cream, causing it to lose heat, and you need time to mix the gelatin in thoroughly before it sets up. If the dissolved gelatin is added directly to the cold cream, it might start to set up (lump) before it is completely incorporated. And because of the cream, you cannot reheat the filling to melt the lumps, as you can with the glaze discussed above. In this particular filling, melted chocolate, which is a thickening agent in itself, is added at the same time; this causes the filling to set up more rapidly.

Adding gelatin that is too hot to a filling containing whipped cream will cause too much of the cream to melt — a small amount of melting cannot be avoided — which decreases the volume of the filling and results in an overly firm, dense finished product. Although it is better to heat gelatin a little too hot than to have the filling lump because of cold gelatin, in most instances, any temperature above 130°F (54°C) is considered too hot. If you are unsure and do not have a thermometer available, dip your finger into the liquid. If you cannot keep it there comfortably, the liquid is too hot and must be allowed to cool before it is used. If the gelatin mixture is accidentally heated to the boiling point, discard it and start over. Gelatin that boils forms a skin after it cools and loses some of its ability to thicken.

The same problems associated with adding gelatin that is too hot to a cream filling also occur when a whipped cream filling containing gelatin must be reheated due to the gelatin lumping or setting up prematurely: The cream melts and deflates, and the filling loses volume. Because the same amount of gelatin is now contained in a smaller amount of filling, the texture will be too firm and much less appealing. It is therefore important that the forms that will be used to contain the filling are prepared before the filling is made, or at least before the gelatin is added. Stainless steel cake rings, either solid or adjustable, are ideal, although plastic strips made of acetate or polyurethane may be used instead in most cases. You need a strip 34 inches (85 cm) long to make a round frame 10 inches (25 cm) in diameter. If you use cake rings that are not made of stainless steel, line them with strips of plastic or baking paper.

BLOOM

The term *bloom* refers to the strength of the set gelatin, which is measured by the gelatin manufacturer using a gellometer, invented by a French scientist named Bloom — hence the term. A gellometer is a calibrated rod (like a thermometer) with markings from 50 to 300 bloom; 225 to 250 bloom is the average reading for most set gelatin products. The tool is dropped into the set gelatin from a predetermined height to obtain a reading. Sometimes the word *bloom* is used to describe the process of softening the gelatin in a cold liquid before it is dissolved. These are two distinct meanings. (The word *bloom* is also used to describe the grey streaks that appear on improperly tempered chocolate, but that meaning has nothing to do with gelatin.)

Using Sheet Gelatin in Cake Fillings

Most brands of sheet gelatin weigh $\frac{1}{10}$ ounce (3 g) per sheet. Gelatin sheets, like the powder, must be softened in a liquid before they can dissolve. However, sheets can be softened in virtually any amount of liquid as long as they are submerged. The amount of liquid need not be specified because, as they soften, the sheets always absorb the same amount: approximately 2 teaspoons (10 ml) per sheet. Once they are soft, the sheets are melted in a pan or a bain-marie.

To use sheet gelatin in a recipe that calls for powdered gelatin, substitute an equal amount by weight, remembering that each sheet weighs $\frac{1}{10}$ ounce (3 g), or calculate the exchange based on 1 sheet replacing each 1 teaspoon (3 g) powdered gelatin. Submerge the sheets in cold water and leave to soften. Remove the sheets without squeezing out any of the water that they have absorbed. Melt the sheets and add to the recipe as directed, omitting the water that would have been used to soften the gelatin powder. If the recipe calls for softening the gelatin in a liquid other than water — wine, fruit juice, or milk, for example — use this liquid instead of water for softening the gelatin sheets. If necessary, add enough water to the liquid so that the sheets are just covered. Instead of lifting the sheets out of the liquid once they have softened, melt the sheets in the flavored liquid and add the entire mixture to the recipe. It is not necessary to make adjustments in the water added to the recipe to offset the water absorbed by the gelatin sheets unless you are using as much as 3 ounces (85 g) or 28 sheets (84 g) in a single recipe. When using such a large amount of sheet gelatin in a recipe specifying powdered, calculate the total amount of water absorbed by the sheets and compare that to the water specified for softening the powdered gelatin. Add the amount of water needed to make up the difference instead of omitting the water as directed above.

To substitute powdered gelatin in a recipe that calls for gelatin sheets, use an equal weight of powder softened and then dissolved in as much cold water as the sheets would have absorbed (2 teaspoons/10 ml per sheet). For example, if the recipe calls for 6 sheets softened gelatin, substitute 18 g powdered gelatin, softened in the same amount of water that the sheets would have absorbed — in this case, 2 ounces (60 ml).

After softening, sheet gelatin, like powdered, must be heated until completely dissolved. As with powdered gelatin, the sheets must never be boiled, as boiling reduces the strength of the

Powdered and Sheet Gelatin Equivalencies and Substitutions
- Unflavored gelatin powder and gelatin sheets can be substituted for one another in equal weights.

- 1 sheet of gelatin (most brands) weighs $\frac{1}{10}$ ounce (3 g).

- 1 tablespoon (15 ml) unflavored gelatin powder weighs just under $\frac{1}{3}$ ounce (9 g).

- 1 ounce (30 g) unflavored gelatin powder measures 3 tablespoons plus 1 teaspoon (50 ml) by volume.

- A consumer packet or envelope of unflavored gelatin powder weighs $\frac{1}{4}$ ounce, or just over 7 grams, and is equivalent to $2\frac{1}{2}$ teaspoons (12.5 ml) by volume.

Substituting Unflavored Gelatin Powder in a Recipe That Uses Sheet Gelatin

Recipe calls for	Use
5 sheets gelatin	½ ounce (15 g) or 5 teaspoons (25 ml) unflavored gelatin powder
1 sheet gelatin	$\frac{1}{10}$ ounce (3 g) or 1 teaspoon (5 ml) unflavored gelatin powder

Substituting Sheet Gelatin in a Recipe That Uses Unflavored Gelatin Powder

Recipe calls for	Use
1 ounce (30 g) unflavored gelatin powder	10 sheets gelatin
3 tablespoons (45 ml) unflavored gelatin powder	9 sheets gelatin
1½ teaspoons (7.5 ml) unflavored gelatin powder	1½ sheets gelatin

gelatin and causes a skin to form, which is impossible to incorporate without creating lumps.

Many tropical fruits — raw papayas, pineapples, guavas, kiwis, mangoes, passion fruits, and figs, to list the best known — contain an enzyme that prevents gelatin from setting up partially or totally by dissolving its protein structure; their presence in a recipe that depends on gelatin can adversely affect the outcome. However, the enzyme is destroyed if the fruit is heated to at least 175°F (80°C), so these fruits do gel normally if they are cooked first.

Apple Wine Cake   yield: 2 cakes, 10 inches (25 cm) in diameter

If the seventeen steps involved in making this cake are more than you want to tackle, try this simpler version instead; like the original, it is both unusual and refreshing. Omit the jelly rolls, use all four sponge layers, and double the amounts of apples, raisins, and poaching liquid. Divide the fruit mixture in half after cooking, reserving the most attractive apple wedges for decorating the cakes. Assemble the cakes as described in the main recipe, placing the second sponges on top of the cream filling and brushing them lightly with poaching liquid before refrigerating the cakes. Decorate the tops of the cakes with the reserved apple wedges and raisins (instead of jelly roll slices), arranging the apples in concentric circles, as is done in the layer inside. Brush the apple wedges with apricot glaze and continue as directed in the main recipe.

1 recipe Almond Sponge batter (page 795)

3 pounds 8 ounces (1 kg 590 g) Delicious, pippin, or Granny Smith apples (about 8 medium)

3½ cups (840 ml) muscat or Riesling wine

½ cup (120 ml) maple syrup

1 tablespoon (15 ml) lemon juice

1 cinnamon stick

⅔ cup (160 ml) plus ¼ cup (60 ml) Calvados

4 ounces (115 g) dark raisins

2 Short Dough Cake Bottoms (page 792), 10 inches (25 cm) in diameter

4 ounces (115 g) apricot jam

Calvados Wine Filling (recipe follows)

8 ounces (225 g) smooth raspberry jam

1 cup (240 ml) heavy cream

2 teaspoons (10 g) granulated sugar

1 recipe Apricot Glaze (page 774)

6 ounces (170 g) sliced almonds, toasted and lightly crushed

1 recipe Mousseline Sauce (page 338)

Florentina Twists (page 690)

1. Line the bottom of a cake pan, 10 inches (25 cm) in diameter, with baking paper (or grease and flour the bottom, leaving the sides uncoated).

2. Pour a little more than half of the almond sponge batter into the pan and spread to even the surface. Pour the remainder of the batter onto a sheet of baking paper and spread it into a rectangle measuring 20 × 15 inches (50 × 37.5 cm). Drag the paper onto a sheet pan.

3. Bake both sponges at 400°F (205°C). The sheet takes approximately 8 minutes to bake and the round cake takes about 18 minutes; when done, the tops of the cakes spring back when pressed lightly in the center. Immediately transfer the thin sheet to a second (cool) sheet pan. Let both sponges cool completely.

4. Peel and core the apples, then cut them lengthwise into wedges (not slices) no more than ½ inch (1.2 cm) thick at the widest point. To prevent oxidation, drop the apples into a bowl of acidulated water as you work.

5. Combine the wine, maple syrup, lemon juice, cinnamon stick, and ⅔ cup (160 ml) Calvados in a saucepan. Heat the liquid to boiling, then add the raisins and the apple wedges. Simmer, occasionally stirring gently, until the apples are soft but not falling apart, from 10 to 20 minutes depending on the ripeness of the fruit. Set aside and let cool.

6. Trim the skin from the top of the round sponge cake. Slice the cake horizontally into 4 thin layers; reserve 2 layers for another project or use them to make the simpler version of this recipe described in the introduction.

7. Place the short dough cake bottoms on cardboard cake rounds for support. Divide the apricot jam between them and spread evenly to cover the short dough. Place 1 sponge layer on each. Place a 10-inch (25-cm) stainless steel cake ring snugly around each sponge. (If cake rings are not available, secure strips of acetate or polyurethane around the sponges instead.)

8. Remove the cinnamon stick from the apples and raisins and discard it. Strain off the liquid. Reserve 1 cup (240 ml) poaching liquid for the Calvados wine filling. Brush some of the remainder over the sponge cakes to moisten them lightly. Discard the remainder of the liquid, unless you are making the variation.

9. Arrange the apple wedges in concentric circles on top of each sponge, dividing the apple-raisin mixture evenly.

10. Divide the Calvados wine filling between the cakes. The filling should be just starting to thicken when you pour it into the rings. Refrigerate the cakes until the filling is set, approximately 2 hours.

11. Invert the thin sponge sheet onto a sheet of baking paper, then peel the paper off the back of the sponge (see Chef's Tip). Cut the sponge in half lengthwise and transfer 1 piece to a second sheet pan. Spread the raspberry jam over the entire surface of both sponges. There should be just enough jam to make the surface sticky. Roll the sponge sheets lengthwise, following the instructions for Yule Logs (sees Figures 9-9 and 9-10, page 454). Place the jelly rolls in the freezer for at least one hour (longer is fine), to make them firm and easier to cut.

12. Remove the cake rings or plastic strips from the round cakes. Trim away any excess short dough to even the sides of the cakes (see Figure 1-7, page 32).

13. Whip the heavy cream and the sugar to stiff peaks. Ice the tops and sides of the cakes with a thin layer of whipped cream.

14. Cut the jelly rolls into thin slices, approximately ⅛ inch (3 mm) wide. Starting at the edge of the cakes, arrange the slices in concentric circles to cover the tops of the cakes. Place the rounds in each circle between those in the previous row to cover as much of the surface as possible.

15. Brush apricot glaze over the jelly rolls on top of the cakes. Cover the sides of the cakes with sliced almonds (see Figure 1-1, page 18).

16. Cut the cakes into the desired number of servings. Flavor the mousseline sauce with the remaining ¼ cup (60 ml) Calvados.

17. Presentation: Place a slice of cake off-center on a dessert plate. Pour a pool of mousseline sauce in front of the dessert and place a Florentina Twist so it leans against the cake.

CALVADOS WINE FILLING yield: 3 pounds 8 ounces (1 kg 590 g)

Once this filling starts to set up, it cannot be softened by reheating, so do not make it until you are ready to assemble the cakes.

2½ tablespoons (22 g) unflavored gelatin powder

1 cup (240 ml) strained liquid from poaching the apples (Step 8 above), chilled

4 egg yolks (⅓ cup/80 ml)

¼ cup (60 ml) or 3 ounces (85 g) light corn syrup

5 cups (1 L 200 ml) heavy cream

¼ cup (60 ml) Calvados

1. Sprinkle the gelatin over the chilled poaching liquid and set aside to soften.

2. Beat the egg yolks lightly just to blend them.

3. Heat the corn syrup to boiling. Whisk the corn syrup into the egg yolks in a thin stream and continue whisking until the mixture is light and fluffy.

4. Whip the cream to soft peaks. Fold the whipped cream into the yolk mixture. Add the Calvados to the softened gelatin mixture. Place over a bain-marie and heat until the gelatin is dissolved; do not overheat. Rapidly mix the gelatin into a small part of the cream mixture; then, still working quickly, stir this into the remainder.

Apricot Cream Cake yield: 2 cakes, 10 inches (25 cm) in diameter (Color Photo 9)

This is a refreshing dessert to keep in mind during peak apricot season in July and August. It is perfect when you need something you can prepare ahead, as the cakes can be made through Step 3, covered, and refrigerated for up to five days or frozen for two to three weeks. While Cointreau can be relatively expensive, and in many instances it wouldn't matter if you used a less expensive orange liqueur, in this filling you can tell the difference, so avoid using a substitute unless you must.

2 Short Dough Cake Bottoms (page 792), 10 inches (25 cm) in diameter

4 ounces (115 g) smooth apricot jam

1 Chiffon Sponge Cake I (page 797), 10 inches (25 cm) in diameter

Apricot Whipped Cream (recipe follows)

1½ cups (360 ml) heavy cream

1 tablespoon (15 g) granulated sugar

6 ounces (170 g) sliced almonds, toasted and lightly crushed

Dark chocolate shavings

Apricot wedges

Apricot Sauce (page 303)

Mint leaves

1. Place the short dough bottoms on cardboard cake rounds for support. Divide the jam between them and spread evenly to cover the short dough.

2. Trim the skin from the top of the sponge cake, leveling the top at the same time. Cut the sponge horizontally into 4 thin layers. Place 1 layer on each short dough bottom. Place stainless steel cake rings, 10 inches (25 cm) in diameter, around each sponge, setting them on top of the short dough. If cake rings are not available, secure strips of acetate or polyurethane around the sponges.

3. Divide the apricot whipped cream between the rings and spread it evenly. Place the remaining cake layers on top of the filling. Refrigerate the cakes for at least 2 hours to set the filling.

4. After the filling is set, remove the rings or plastic strips from the cakes. Trim the short dough around the base of the cakes to make the sides even (see Figure 1-7, page 32).

5. Whip the heavy cream and granulated sugar to stiff peaks. Ice the top and sides of the cakes with the whipped cream, using just enough to cover the sponge. Place the remaining whipped cream in a pastry bag with a No. 6 (12-mm) plain tip and reserve in the refrigerator.

6. Cut a circle, 6 inches (15 cm) in diameter, from the center of a cardboard cake circle that is 10 inches (25 cm) in diameter. Set aside.

7. Cover the sides of the cakes with the crushed sliced almonds (see Figure 1-1, page 18).

8. Cut or mark the cakes into the desired number of pieces. Place the doughnut-shaped template on top of one cake, setting it gently so it does not leave a mark. Sprinkle the shaved chocolate over the top to cover the center of the cake. Carefully remove the template and repeat with the second cake.

9. Pipe a rosette of the reserved whipped cream at the edge of each slice; top each rosette with an apricot wedge.

10. Presentation: Place a slice of cake off-center on a dessert plate. Pour a small pool of apricot sauce in front of the slice. Place a mint leaf next to the sauce.

APRICOT WHIPPED CREAM yield: 4 pounds (I kg 820 g)

1 pound 4 ounces (570 g) ripe apricots

6 egg yolks (½ cup/120 ml)

½ cup (120 ml) or 6 ounces (170 g) light corn syrup

2 tablespoons (18 g) unflavored gelatin powder

½ cup (120 ml) cold water

3 cups (720 ml) heavy cream

½ cup (120 ml) Cointreau

¼ cup (60 ml) apricot juice

2 ounces (55 g) apricot puree

1. Wash and stone the apricots, then cut them into chunks ¾ inch (2 cm) in size. If you must use apricots that are not fully ripe, poach them first in plain poaching syrup (see recipe and instructions, page 789).

2. Whip the egg yolks until they are blended.

3. Bring the corn syrup to a boil; whip the hot syrup into the egg yolks in a thin stream. Continue to whip until the mixture is cooled and has a light, fluffy consistency.

4. Sprinkle the gelatin over the cold water and set aside to soften.

5. Whip the cream until soft peaks form. Fold the cream into the egg yolk mixture.

6. Add the Cointreau and apricot juice to the softened gelatin mixture. Place over a bain-marie and heat until the gelatin is dissolved; do not overheat.

7. Remove about one-quarter of the cream mixture and rapidly mix the gelatin into it. Working quickly, stir this into the remaining cream. Fold in the apricot puree and chunks.

8. If the filling has not started to set up, wait a few minutes and mix again before using in the cakes to prevent the apricot chunks from sinking to the bottom of the filling.

VARIATION
CONTEMPORARY APRICOT CREAM CAKE
yield: 2 cakes, 10 inches (25 cm) in diameter (Color Photo 4)

You can give the apricot cream cake a more modern look by replacing the crushed almonds on the sides of the cakes with strips of decorated sponge sheets.

Omit the short dough cake bottoms, apricot jam, and sliced almonds from the ingredient list. Replace them with 1 Ribbon-Pattern Decorated Sponge Sheet (page 672), made with the chocolate ribbons formed lengthwise in a wavy pattern. You will have quite a bit of ribbon sponge left over, but it is not practical to make less than one sheet at a time. Leftover sponge can be kept for several weeks in the freezer if wrapped well.

1. Cut 2 strips lengthwise from the ribbon sponge sheet, each 2 inches (5 cm) wide. Place 2 cake rings, 10 inches (25 cm) in diameter, on cardboard cake circles (or use 10-inch/25-cm cake pans if cake rings are not available). Line the inside of the rings or pans with strips of acetate, polyurethane, or baking paper. Line the sides with the ribbon sponge strips, placing the striped side against the plastic or paper.

2. Trim the skin from the top of the chiffon sponge cake, then

CHEF'S TIP

The sponge must fit snugly, or the filling will run out and mar the appearance of the cake. Trim the sponge to fit as needed; if the sponge is too small, make a cut from the outside to about halfway toward the center, then open it to create an open wedge. This makes the sponge larger so that it fits tight against the sides.

cut the cake into 4 layers. Place 1 layer of sponge inside each ring, making sure it fits snugly against the ribbon sponge and the side.

3. Divide the apricot whipped cream between the rings and spread it evenly. Place the remaining cake layers on top of the cream filling. Refrigerate the cakes for at least 2 hours to set the filling.

4. Continue as directed in the main recipe, but do not ice the sides of the cakes in Step 5 and omit Step 7.

Black Currant Cake yield: 2 cakes, 10 inches (25 cm) in diameter (Color Photo 12)

This is a cake to choose when you're looking for something out of the ordinary. It is not the quickest, I admit, but the results are worthwhile. The black currants give the filling a rich dark purple color and impart a distinctive tangy flavor not found in any other fruit.

Black currants are quite rare in the United States; when people speak of currants, they are usually referring to the dried Zante grape. In fact, over the years, a few of my students who were unfamiliar with fresh black currants have attempted to make the puree for this recipe using the almost black, dried grapes. They usually catch on in Step 2, however, when they try to pass the sticky paste through a strainer with little or no success.

2 Short Dough Cake Bottoms (page 792)

4 ounces (115 g) smooth apricot jam

1 Cocoa Almond Sponge (page 796)

¼ cup (60 ml) Black Currant Puree (recipe follows)

¼ cup (60 ml) crème de cassis

Black Currant Mousse (recipe follows)

Black Currant Glaze (recipe follows)

Fresh black currants for garnish

Granulated sugar

Apricot Sauce (page 303)

Chocolate Sauce for Piping (page 681)

Fanned fresh apricot halves or other fruit in season

Mint sprigs

1. Place the short dough cake bottoms on cardboard cake rounds for support. Divide the jam between them and spread evenly to cover the short dough.

2. Trim the skin off the top of the sponge cake, leveling it at the same time. Slice into 2 layers and set them on the jam.

3. Combine the black currant puree with the crème de cassis. Brush the mixture over the sponges, allowing all the liquid to soak in.

4. Place stainless steel cake rings, 10 inches (25 cm) in diameter, around the sponge layers, setting them on top of the short dough. If cake rings are not available, secure strips of acetate or polyurethane around the sponges instead. Divide the black currant mousse between the cakes. Refrigerate for at least 2 hours to set the filling.

5. When the cakes are completely set, carefully run a thin knife dipped in hot water around the inside of the rings, then remove the rings; or simply peel away the plastic. Trim away any short dough that protrudes outside the sponge to make the sides even (see Figure 1-7, page 32).

6. Pour half of the black currant glaze over 1 cake and quickly spread it with a metal spatula to cover the entire surface. Do not pour the glaze straight down in one spot, or it will make a hole. Repeat with the second cake.

7. Refrigerate the cakes for a few minutes to set the glaze. If any glaze has run down the sides, cut it away with a knife. Warm a metal spatula and use it to smooth the sides of the cakes.

8. Using a thin knife dipped in hot water, slice the cakes into the desired number of serving pieces, usually 12 per cake. (Let the warm knife melt through the glaze, then cut.)

9. Roll the black currants in granulated sugar to coat them. Place one at the edge of each slice. If necessary, attach them to the cake by touching a hot metal skewer or heated knife-tip to the glaze to melt it, then setting the currant on top.

10. Presentation: Place a slice of cake off-center on a dessert plate. Pour a pool of apricot sauce in front of the slice and decorate it with chocolate sauce for piping (see pages 682 to 685). Place a fanned apricot half on the opposite side of the plate and place a mint sprig next to the apricot.

BLACK CURRANT MOUSSE yield: 4 pounds (1 kg 820 g)

B ecause it sets fairly quickly, do not make this filling until you are ready to use it.

3 cups (720 ml) heavy cream

2 tablespoons (18 g) unflavored gelatin powder

¾ cup (180 ml) cold water

6 egg whites (¾ cup/180 ml)

6 ounces (170 g) granulated sugar

8 ounces (225 g) white chocolate, melted

1½ cups (360 ml) Black Currant Puree (recipe follows)

1. Whip the cream to soft peaks. Reserve in the refrigerator.

2. Sprinkle the gelatin over the water and set aside to soften.

3. Combine the egg whites and sugar. Heat the mixture over simmering water until it reaches 140°F (60°C), whipping constantly to prevent the egg whites from cooking on the bottom. Remove from the heat and immediately continue whipping until the mixture is cold and forms stiff peaks.

4. Stir the white chocolate into the black currant puree.

5. Place the softened gelatin mixture over a bain-marie and heat until dissolved. Do not overheat.

6. Rapidly add the gelatin mixture to the currant puree (be sure that the puree is no cooler than room temperature). Gradually fold this mixture into the reserved meringue. Fold into the reserved whipped cream.

BLACK CURRANT GLAZE yield: enough to cover the tops of 2 cakes, 10 inches (25 cm) in diameter

1 tablespoon (9 g) unflavored gelatin powder

¼ cup (60 ml) cold water

½ cup (120 ml) simple syrup

¼ cup (60 ml) Black Currant Puree (recipe follows)

1. Sprinkle the gelatin over the water and let sit until softened. Place the gelatin mixture over a bain-marie and heat until dissolved. Do not overheat.

2. Stir in the simple syrup and the currant puree and use as soon as the glaze shows signs of thickening. Should the glaze thicken too much before it can be applied, reheat to ensure a smooth surface on the cakes.

BLACK CURRANT PUREE yield: approximately 2 cups (480 ml)

2 pounds (910 g) fresh or frozen black currants (see Note)

1 cup (240 ml) water

4 ounces (115 g) granulated sugar

1. Combine the currants with the water and granulated sugar in a skillet. Cook over low heat until the currants start to soften, about 5 minutes.

2. Puree the mixture, then pass the puree through a strainer. Divide as follows:

- ¼ cup (60 ml) to use in assembling the cakes
- ¼ cup (60 ml) to use in the glaze
- Approximately 1½ cups (360 ml) remaining, to use in the mousse

NOTE: If using black currants in heavy syrup, strain and reserve the syrup before weighing the currants. Substitute 2 cups (480 ml) syrup for the granulated sugar and water.

VARIATION

CRANBERRY MOUSSE CAKE yield: 2 cakes, 10 inches (25 cm) in diameter

If black currants are not available or if you want to make a dessert especially suitable for the holiday season, you can alter the recipe in the following ways:

- Substitute Cranberry Puree (directions follow) for the Black Currant Puree.
- Use whole cranberries instead of currants to decorate.
- Replace the crème de cassis with cranberry juice.
- Serve the cake with Cranberry Coulis (page 243) instead of Apricot Sauce.

Cranberry Puree yield: approximately 2 cups (480 ml)

1 pound (455 g) fresh or frozen cranberries

½ cup (120 ml) water

6 ounces (170 g) granulated sugar

I. Set aside the number of berries you need for decoration.

2. Combine the remaining cranberries, the water, and the granulated sugar in a saucepan.

3. Cook over low heat until the berries start to soften and split, about 5 minutes.

4. Puree the mixture, then pass the puree through a strainer. Use as directed.

Caramel Cake yield: 2 cakes, 10 inches (25 cm) in diameter (Color Photos 6 and 14)

Simply switching the sponges around a little makes this cake interesting and unusual. If you do not already have the sponges on hand, instead of making two separate sponges, make the full almond sponge recipe, divide the batter in half, and add 1½ ounces (40 g) unsweetened cocoa powder to one half.

As a variation, try serving this cake with Bitter Chocolate Sauce (page 413) instead of the sweeter (but oh-so-good) caramel sauce.

1 Almond Sponge (page 795), 10 inches (25 cm) in diameter

1 Cocoa Almond Sponge (page 796), 10 inches (25 cm) in diameter

2 Short Dough Cake Bottoms (page 792), 10 inches (25 cm) in diameter

4 ounces (115 g) smooth apricot jam

¾ cup (180 ml) Plain Cake Syrup (page 789)

Caramel Cream (recipe follows)

1½ cups (360 ml) heavy cream

1 tablespoon (15 g) granulated sugar

6 ounces (170 g) sliced almonds, toasted and lightly crushed

Dark chocolate shavings

Fortified Caramel Sauce (recipe follows)

Chocolate Sauce for Piping (page 681)

Sour Cream Mixture for Piping (page 727)

I. Trim the skin and ⅛ inch (3 mm) off the tops of the almond and cocoa sponges, leveling them at the same time; cut each sponge horizontally into 2 layers.

2. Using a plain cookie cutter, approximately 5½ inches (13.7 cm) in diameter, cut a circle from the center of all 4 layers. Place the center circles from the light sponge inside the rings from the dark sponge and vice versa.

3. Place the short dough bottoms on cardboard cake rounds for support. Spread the apricot jam evenly on top. Place one of the dark sponge rings with a light center on top of the jam on each short dough round. Brush the sponges with half of the cake syrup. Place stainless steel cake rings around both cakes, fitting them snugly around the sponge layer and setting them on top of the short dough. If cake rings are not available, use strips of acetate or polyurethane to make a frame around the sponges.

4. Divide the caramel cream between the cakes and spread it out evenly. It should be thick enough to hold its shape as you spread it. If it does not, wait until the cream thickens a little more before using. Place the remaining sponge layers on top of the cream. Brush the remaining cake syrup over the sponges. Refrigerate the cakes for about 2 hours to set the cream.

5. Whip the heavy cream and sugar to soft peaks. Remove the cake rings or plastic strips from the cakes. Trim any excess short dough from the bottom of the cakes to make the sides even (see Figure 1-7, page 32). Ice the top and sides of the cakes with the whipped cream.

6. Cover the sides of the cakes with the sliced almonds (Figure 1-1).

FIGURE 1-1 **Pressing crushed almonds onto the side of the Caramel Cake**

7. Place the cookie cutter used in Step 2 in the center of one of the cakes and sprinkle the shaved chocolate around the outside of the cake. Repeat with the second cake. Cut the cakes into the desired number of slices, usually 12 per cake.

8. Presentation: Place a slice of cake off-center on a dessert plate. Pour a pool of caramel sauce in front of the slice. Decorate the sauce with chocolate sauce for piping and sour cream mixture for piping (see pages 682 to 685).

CARAMEL CREAM yield: 3 pounds 2 ounces (1 kg 420 g)

12 ounces (340 g) granulated sugar

1 cup (240 ml) hot water

4 teaspoons (12 g) unflavored gelatin powder

⅓ cup (80 ml) cold water

3½ cups (840 ml) heavy cream

1. Caramelize the sugar to a light brown color (see directions on page 612). Add the hot water and cook out any lumps. Let cool completely. If too much water evaporates while the caramel cooks, it will be too thick when it is cold and difficult to combine with the cream. If this happens, add just enough water to return the caramel to a syrupy consistency.

CHEF'S TIP

It is important to caramelize the sugar dark enough not only to color the filling but also to give it a rich caramel flavor with just a hint of bitterness. When caramelizing sugar for a caramel sauce, the sugar should be cooked only until golden, not brown, since you want a light caramel color for appearance and a flavor that is not bitter.

2. Sprinkle the gelatin over the cold water and set aside to soften.

3. Whip the cream to soft peaks. Fold in the cooled caramel.

4. Place the softened gelatin mixture over a bain-marie and heat until dissolved. Do not overheat. Rapidly mix the gelatin into a small portion of the cream, then quickly add that mixture to the remainder of the cream.

FORTIFIED CARAMEL SAUCE **yield: approximately 3 cups (720 ml)**

This rich caramel sauce is meant to be served hot. It is quite thick when cooled, even just to room temperature. If the sauce is to be used to mask a plate, for example, thin it with water to the desired consistency, or use Clear Caramel Sauce (page 328). Fortified Caramel Sauce is perfect for serving with ice cream or with apple or pear tarts.

1 pound (455 g) granulated sugar
⅓ cup (80 ml) water
1 teaspoon (2.5 ml) lemon juice

2 tablespoons (30 ml) glucose *or* light corn syrup
1½ cups (360 ml) heavy cream, warmed
2 ounces (55 g) unsalted butter

1. Place the sugar, water, and lemon juice in a small saucepan. Bring to a boil. Brush down the sides of the pan with a clean brush dipped in water. Add the glucose or corn syrup. Cook over medium heat until the syrup reaches a golden amber color.

2. Remove the pan from the heat and add the heavy cream carefully. Stand back as you pour in the cream, as the mixture may splatter (warming the cream minimizes this problem). Stir to mix in the cream. If the sauce is not smooth, return the pan to the heat and cook, stirring constantly, to melt the lumps.

3. With the pan off the heat, add the butter. Keep stirring until the butter melts and the sauce is smooth.

Charente Bavarois Cake **yield: 2 cakes, 8 inches (20 cm) in diameter**

This cake evolved from the Charente Bavarois dessert on page 332. I modified the filling slightly to make it possible to slice the cake into clean attractive servings. For a slightly different and more contemporary look, use a ladyfinger comb to distribute the ladyfinger batter as shown in the procedure photos on page 20. A ladyfinger comb is a tool 22 inches long x 4 inches wide (55 x 10 cm) with half-sphere indentations on one of the long sides and pointed notches on the other

Ladyfinger Batter (recipe follows)
Bavarois Filling (recipe follows)

Marble Mirror Glazes (recipe follows)

1. On a sheet of baking paper, draw 3 strips, 2 inches (5 cm) wide × 18 inches (45 cm) long, spacing them about 2 inches (5 cm) apart. On a second sheet of paper, draw 2 circles, 7½ inches (18.7 cm) in diameter. Invert each paper onto a full-sized sheet pan.

2. Place the ladyfinger batter in a pastry bag with a No. 3 (6-mm) plain tip (alternatively, a ladyfinger comb may be used to distribute the batter). Pipe the batter onto the pan within the drawn lines for the strips, piping it crosswise between the lines in one unbroken back-and-forth line, the full length of each strip. Divide the remaining batter between the drawn circles and spread it out evenly within the lines.

3. Bake both sheets at 425°F (219°C) for about 10 minutes. Do not overbake; when the sheets just start to turn golden, they are done. Immediately slide each baking paper onto a cold sheet pan to prevent the sponge sheets from drying out as they cool.

4. Line the sides of 2 cake rings, 8 inches (20 cm) in diameter by 2 inches (5 cm) high, with plastic strips. Trim 1 long side of each ladyfinger strip to make the strips 1¾ inches (4.5 cm) wide.

(You will need approximately 25 inches/62.5 cm to line each ring, depending on the thickness of the sponge.) Line the rings with the ladyfinger strips, placing the top (contoured) side next to the plastic and the trimmed (flat) long sides next to the bottom of the pans. Make sure the strips fit snugly. Place the circles in the rings, trimming them as needed to fit tightly within the lined sides. Cover and reserve the lined rings while preparing the filling.

5. Divide the bavarois filling evenly between the rings and spread the tops to make them flat. Refrigerate the cakes until the filling is set, a minimum of 2 hours, preferably a bit longer.

6. Remove the cake rings and the plastic strips from the sides. Spoon some of the clear glaze on top of 1 cake. Place a small pool of each of the tinted glazes on top of the clear glaze. Use a spatula to carefully spread the glaze and marble the two colors together where they meet. Repeat with the second cake. Return the cakes to the refrigerator until the glaze sets.

VARIATION
CHARENTE BAVAROIS MODERNE

In Step 2, instead of piping the batter out as directed, first spread enough batter within each of the drawn circles to make 2 rounds approximately ½ inch (1.2 cm) thick. Spread the remaining batter ½ inch (1.2 cm) thick on a full-size sheet pan lined with baking paper or a Silpat, spreading it the full length of the pan; the batter will not cover the width (see Procedure 1-1a). Starting at the long edge of the pan where the batter meets the side, pull the comb though the batter crosswise to the long edge of the pan closest to you (see Procedure 1-1b). This creates a pattern that looks like the batter was piped out of a pastry bag in straight lines, one next to the other. Bake the sheet and the rounds as directed in Step 3. Trim one long side of the baked ladyfinger sheet to make it

PROCEDURE 1-1a **Spreading ladyfinger batter over a Silpat**

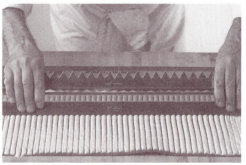

PROCEDURE 1-1b **Pulling a ladyfinger comb through the batter**

PROCEDURE 1-1c **Cutting a 1¼-inch (3.1-cm) wide strip from the baked sheet**

PROCEDURE 1-1d **Using a strip to line a cake ring**

even. Starting from this trimmed edge, cut the sheet crosswise into strips 1¼ inches (3.1 cm) wide (see Procedure 1-1c). Use the strips to line the cake rings in Step 4, mitering the short edges where they meet (see Procedure 1-1d). You will have some leftover strips for another project.

Because the ladyfinger strips are trimmed on both long sides, they do not have the contoured (fluted) edge that is produced when using a pastry bag. By cutting strips just 1¼ inches (3.1 cm) wide you make a clean straight edge on the top that looks great as the cake filling covers it, creating a thin band of exposed filling parallel to the top of the ladyfinger strip (see Color Photo 4 as an example). To create this same contemporary look without a ladyfinger comb, pipe the batter as directed and then trim both sides of the baked ladyfinger strip to make it 1½ inches (3.7 cm) wide. You will not achieve the same precise lines created by the comb, but the result is still attractive and up to date.

LADYFINGER BATTER

yield: 3 strips, 2 × 18 inches (5 × 45 cm), plus 2 rounds, 7½ inches (18.7 cm) in diameter

3 egg yolks (¼ cup/60 ml)	3 ounces (85 g) granulated sugar
1 whole egg	2 ounces (55 g) cake flour, sifted
4 egg whites (½ cup/120 ml)	

1. Whip the egg yolks and whole egg by hand just to combine. Cover and reserve.

2. Whip the egg whites until frothy. Gradually add the sugar and continue to whip until stiff peaks form. Spoon about one-third of the whites into a separate bowl. Fold the egg yolk mixture into the remaining whites. Fold in the flour. Fold in the reserved egg whites.

3. Immediately pipe or spread the batter into the desired shape.

4. Bake at 400°F (205°C) for approximately 10 minutes.

BAVAROIS FILLING yield: 7 cups (1 L 680 ml)

2½ ounces (70 g) dried currants	6 egg yolks (½ cup/120 ml))
¾ cup (180 ml) port wine	¼ cup (60 ml) simple syrup
¼ cup (60 ml) Cognac	2 cups (480 ml) heavy cream
2 tablespoons (18 g) unflavored gelatin powder	4 egg whites (½ cup/120 ml)
	4 ounces (115 g) granulated sugar

1. Macerate the currants in one-third of the port, preferably the day before but at least several hours before proceeding with the recipe.

2. Add the Cognac to the remaining port. Sprinkle the gelatin over the mixture and set aside to soften.

3. Whip the egg yolks for 1 minute. Bring the simple syrup to a boil and gradually pour it into the egg yolks in a thin stream while whipping rapidly. Continue whipping until the mixture has a light and fluffy consistency. Reserve.

4. Whip the cream to soft peaks. Set aside in the refrigerator.

5. Combine the egg whites and sugar in a bowl. Set over simmering water and heat to 140°F (60°C) while whipping constantly. Remove from the heat, continuing to whip as you move the bowl, and whip until the meringue is cold and holds soft peaks.

6. Combine the yolk mixture and whipped cream. Fold in the meringue. Heat the gelatin and wine mixture to dissolve the gelatin. Quickly add all of the gelatin to about one-quarter of the cream mixture to temper it. Still working quickly, add this to the remaining cream. Fold in the macerated currants, including the port.

MARBLE MIRROR GLAZES yield: 1¼ cups (300 ml)

2 teaspoons (6 g) unflavored gelatin powder	3 ounces (85 g) granulated sugar
¼ cup (60 ml) plus ⅓ cup (80 ml) cold water	2 teaspoons (10 ml) raspberry syrup
⅓ cup (80 ml) white wine	2 teaspoons (10 ml) orange syrup

1. Sprinkle the gelatin over ¼ cup (60 ml) of the cold water.

2. Combine the wine, sugar, and remaining ⅓ cup (80 ml) water and heat to dissolve the sugar; do not boil. Remove from the heat, add the gelatin, and stir until the gelatin dissolves.

3. Stir the raspberry syrup into one-quarter of the glaze. Stir the orange syrup into one-quarter of the glaze and leave half of the glaze plain and clear. Reserve all three glazes separately to use as directed in the main recipe.

Chestnut Puzzle Cake yield: 2 cakes, 10 inches (25 cm) in diameter (Color Photo 7)

This challenging cake is one of the desserts I made on the PBS television series *Cooking at the Academy*. Unfortunately, I think I made it look too easy. Do not feel bad if your cake does not look like the photograph on your first try. Just as some of my viewers learned the hard way — this cake takes practice before you can complete it comfortably. Perhaps I should have posted a warning: "For professionals only. Do not try this at home." I received numerous letters, not to mention phone calls, from people trying to find their way out of the puzzle. However, they did not have this book to guide them.

This is the showy kind of dessert that will have your customers and friends oohing and aahing even before they discover how delicious it is, trying to figure out how you managed to get the cake layers to go in alternate directions. With this reward in mind, I assure you it is well worth the effort to make two different sponges and two flavors of buttercream, then go through all the steps to assemble them. You can simplify the presentation by omitting the berries, the tulip, and the chestnut, and instead decorate the sauce with Sour Cream Mixture for Piping (see page 727 for the recipe and pages 682 to 685 for design ideas).

3 pounds (1 kg 365 g) Vanilla Buttercream (Swiss Method; page 753)	¼ cup (60 ml) water
8 ounces (225 g) unsweetened chestnut puree, softened	6 ounces (170 g) sliced almonds, toasted and lightly crushed
8 ounces (225 g) sweet dark chocolate, melted	8 ounces (225 g) shaved light chocolate
2 Chiffon Sponge Cake I (page 797), 10 inches (25 cm) in diameter	Piping Chocolate (page 543), melted
2 Chocolate Chiffon Sponge Cake I (page 797), 10 inches (25 cm) in diameter	Strawberry Sauce (page 186)
½ cup (120 ml) Frangelico liqueur	Candied chestnuts (optional)
	Miniature Tulip Crowns (page 717; optional)
	Wild strawberries or other small strawberries

1. Flavor 1 pound 12 ounces (795 g) of the vanilla buttercream with the chestnut puree. Flavor the remaining buttercream with the melted dark chocolate. Set the two buttercreams aside.

2. Cut about one-third off the top of both plain sponges and reserve for another use. Slice the remaining two-thirds of each plain sponge horizontally in half.

3. Trim just enough off the top of the chocolate sponges to make the tops even, then cut the sponges into 3 layers each. (You need 5 layers of sponge cake, ¼ inch (6 mm) thick, 3 chocolate and 2 plain, for each cake.) Cover 2 of the chocolate layers and reserve.

4. Place 2 of the remaining chocolate layers on cardboard cake circles for support. Combine the Frangelico with the water and brush or spray some of this mixture over the layers to moisten.

5. Reserve 6 ounces (170 g) of the chestnut buttercream to use for decoration. Spread a layer of the remaining chestnut buttercream, ⅛ inch (3 mm) thick, evenly over each of the chocolate layers on the cardboard circles.

6. Place a plain sponge layer on the buttercream on each cake. Brush or spray some of the Frangelico mixture on top to moisten. Spread another ⅛-inch (3-mm) layer of the chestnut buttercream on top.

7. Continue layering, alternating another chocolate and plain layer on each cake and brushing or spraying each sponge with the Frangelico mixture before spreading a ⅛-inch (3-mm) layer of chestnut buttercream on top. You should end with plain sponges as the top layers. Do not brush these with the Frangelico mixture. Place the cakes in the refrigerator until the buttercream is completely set.

8. Using a thin chef's knife or pointed serrated knife dipped in hot water, cut a cone-shaped piece from the top of each cake, 8 inches (20 cm) in diameter at the top of the cake and approximately 2 inches (5 cm) in diameter at the bottom (Figure 1-2). Place one hand flat on the cake and use a knife or spatula to help you remove the cone by inverting it onto your hand. Place the cone flat side down on a cardboard. Repeat with the second cake. Set the two cone-shaped pieces aside.

9. Ice the inside of the crater and the remaining top edge of each cake with a layer of chocolate buttercream ¼ inch (6 mm) thick (Figure 1-3).

10. Place the reserved chocolate sponges flat on top of each cake. Place cardboard cake circles on top and invert the cakes so the uncut chocolate layers are now on the bottom.

11. Gently press the top around the hole in and down so it touches the bottom of the cake and you have a cone-shaped crater again (Figure 1-4). Repeat with the second cake.

FIGURE 1-2 Cutting a cone-shaped piece from the layered sponges

FIGURE 1-3 Icing the inside and the top edge after removing the cone-shaped piece

FIGURE 1-4 After inverting the cake so the uncut sponge layer is on the bottom, pushing the ring of chocolate sponge down and inside the cake to create a new cone-shaped crater

Decorated Cakes 23

To Make a Single Cake

If you are making only one cake, you can speed the process by making 1 recipe Chiffon Sponge Cake I and baking one-third of the batter in a prepared 10-inch (25-cm) cake pan. Sift 1½ ounces (40 g) unsweetened cocoa powder over the remaining batter, carefully fold it in, and bake in a second prepared pan. Trim the tops to level them, then cut the plain sponge into 2 layers and the cocoa sponge into 3 layers. Working the cocoa batter twice decreases the volume and produces a slightly denser sponge, but you will save time.

12. Ice the new craters with a layer of chocolate buttercream ¼ inch (6 mm) thick. Replace the cones in the craters.

13. Trim the sides of the cakes to make them even. Ice the tops and sides of the cakes with just enough chocolate buttercream to cover the sponge. Cover the sides of the cakes with the crushed almonds (see Figure 1-1, page 18).

14. Using a plain round cookie cutter, 5 inches (12.5 cm) in diameter, mark a circle in the center of each cake. Place the reserved chestnut buttercream in a pastry bag with a No. 3 (6-mm) plain tip. Pipe a spiral on top of each cake, inside the circle only, starting in the center and piping the rings next to one another (see example in the Meringue Noisette recipe, Figure 14-2, page 782).

15. Sprinkle shaved chocolate around the piped circles on top of the cakes. Refrigerate the cakes until the buttercream is firm. Cut the cakes into the desired number of serving pieces.

16. Place the piping chocolate in a piping bag and pipe a scalloped line of chocolate across the lower part of as many dessert plates as you expect to need. Reserve the plates until time of service.

17. Presentation: Place a slice of cake off-center on a prepared dessert plate. Pipe strawberry sauce on the plate, filling in the chocolate border. Place a candied chestnut in a tulip crown, if you are using them, and place in front of the cake slice. Arrange a few strawberries in the sauce and next to the chestnut. Try to serve the cake at room temperature, as buttercream tastes best when it is soft.

CHEF'S TIP

If you are having second thoughts about cutting the cone out of the cakes as described, try placing an instant-read meat thermometer or a metal skewer in the center of the cake, sticking it into the cardboard. Use it to guide the tip of your knife evenly around the bottom. You will not get the desired 2-inch (5-cm) hole in the bottom, but you will at least get an evenly cut cone.

Chocolate and Frangelico Mousse Cake

yield: 2 cakes, 10 inches (25 cm) in diameter (Color Photos 11 and 14)

In common with the previous recipe, this cake is layered with fillings that do not conform to the flat, horizontal norm. In addition to the unusual look of the cut slices, the combination of hazelnuts and chocolate is a tried-and-true palate-pleaser. I have made this cake on many occasions in a slightly simplified and lighter version, replacing the chocolate rounds with fresh raspberries and substituting raspberry sauce for the mousseline and chocolate sauces. It is not as rich, and it's a timesaving alternative when raspberries are in season. A second variation with a contemporary finish follows the recipe.

1 Sponge Cake (page 794), 10 inches (25 cm) in diameter

2 Short Dough Cake Bottoms (page 792), 10 inches (25 cm) in diameter

4 ounces (115 g) red currant jelly

1/3 cup (80 ml) Plain Cake Syrup (page 789)

Dark Chocolate Cream (recipe follows)

Frangelico Cream (recipe follows)

Shaved light chocolate

1¼ cups (300 ml) heavy cream

1 teaspoon (5 g) granulated sugar

Chocolate Rounds (page 520), 1 inch (2.5 cm) in diameter

½ recipe Mousseline Sauce (page 338)

2 tablespoons (30 ml) Frangelico liqueur

½ recipe Chocolate Sauce (page 413)

Seasonal fruit

Mint leaves

1. Slice the sponge into 3 layers. Reserve the top layer for another use.

2. Place the short dough bottoms on cardboard cake circles for support. Divide the red currant jelly between them and spread evenly to cover the short dough. Place the sponge layers on top of the jelly. Brush the cake syrup on top.

3. Check the consistency of the dark chocolate cream. If it seems too thin to hold its shape, stir it until it thickens. Divide the chocolate cream equally between the cakes and spread it into a high dome shape on each one.

4. Place stainless steel cake rings, 10 inches (25 cm) in diameter, snugly around the sponges. If you do not have cake rings, secure strips of acetate or polyurethane around the sponges. Place the cakes in the refrigerator until the chocolate cream is set, but do not leave them longer than 3 hours.

5. Make certain that the chocolate cream is set, then divide the Frangelico cream between the cakes. Spread it evenly over the chocolate dome, adding more around the sides so the tops of the cakes become level (Figure 1-5). Refrigerate the cakes until the fillings are set, about 2 hours. If desired, at this point the cakes can be stored in the refrigerator for several days, or frozen, well wrapped, for 1 or 2 weeks, to finish as needed. Refrigerate the chocolate shavings as well to make them easier to put on the cakes.

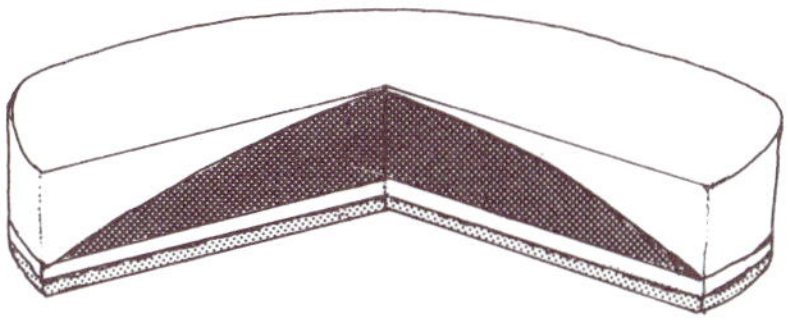

FIGURE 1-5 **The configuration of the two fillings in the Chocolate and Frangelico Mousse Cake**

6. Remove the rings or plastic strips from the cakes. Trim any short dough that protrudes outside the sponge layer to make the sides of the cakes even (see Figure 1-7, page 32).

7. Whip the heavy cream and sugar to stiff peaks. Ice the sides of the cakes with a thin layer of whipped cream. Place the remaining whipped cream in a pastry bag with a No. 6 (12-mm) plain tip and reserve in the refrigerator.

8. Center a round template, 7 inches (17.5 cm) in diameter, on top of 1 cake. Use a spatula to pick up the chilled chocolate shavings and gently pat them onto the side of the cake. Still using the spatula, sprinkle additional shavings over the top of the cake. (If you were to use your hands, the shavings would melt as you touched them; wearing food-handling gloves will eliminate the problem.) Carefully remove the template and repeat with the second cake.

9. Mark or cut the cakes into the desired number of serving pieces. Pipe a cherry-sized mound of the reserved whipped cream on each slice on the exposed cream just next to the shaved chocolate. Place a chocolate round on each mound so the rounds stand vertically.

10. Flavor the mousseline sauce with the Frangelico liqueur and place a portion of the sauce in a piping bottle. Place a portion of the chocolate sauce in a separate piping bottle.

11. Presentation: Place a slice of cake in the center of a dessert plate. Pipe pools of chocolate sauce and mousseline sauce next to each other in front of the dessert. Swirl the sauces together where they meet (Color Photo 11). Place a small piece of fruit and a mint leaf behind the cake.

DARK CHOCOLATE CREAM yield: 2 pounds 6 ounces (1 kg 80 g)

2½ teaspoons (8 g) unflavored gelatin powder

¼ cup (60 ml) cold water plus ⅓ cup (80 ml) water at room temperature

3 cups (720 ml) heavy cream

¼ recipe Swiss Meringue (page 782)

¼ cup (60 ml) crème de cacao liqueur

4 ounces (115 g) sweet dark chocolate, finely chopped

1. Sprinkle the gelatin over ¼ cup (60 ml) of cold water and set aside to soften.

2. Whip the cream to a very soft consistency; it should fall in soft mounds, not peaks, when dropped from the whisk. If overwhipped, it is likely to break when you add the rest of the ingredients. Fold the cream into the meringue.

3. Place the softened gelatin mixture over a bain-marie and heat until dissolved. Do not overheat. Stir in ⅓ cup (80 ml) water, the crème de cacao, and the chocolate. Keep stirring until all of the chocolate melts.

4. Rapidly add this mixture to a small amount of the cream mixture. Still working quickly, stir this back into the remaining cream mixture. If the filling is not thick enough to hold its shape, mix it a little longer.

FRANGELICO CREAM yield: 2 pounds 10 ounces (1 kg 195 g)

4½ teaspoons (14 g) unflavored gelatin powder

½ cup (120 ml) cold water

3½ cups (840 ml) heavy cream

2 ounces (55 g) granulated sugar

½ cup (120 ml) Frangelico liqueur

1. Sprinkle the gelatin over the cold water and set aside to soften.

2. Whip the cream and sugar to very soft peaks.

3. Place the softened gelatin mixture over a bain-marie and heat until dissolved. Do not overheat. Add the liqueur. Rapidly stir the gelatin into a small part of the whipped cream. Then, still working quickly, stir this mixture into the remaining cream.

VARIATION

CONTEMPORARY CHOCOLATE AND FRANGELICO MOUSSE CAKE

To produce a striking nouvelle finish using ribbon sponge sheets instead of sliced almonds to cover the sides of the cakes, follow the recipe and instructions with the following changes. Because these cakes have a thin layer of sponge around the outside, they will be slightly larger in diameter, approximately 10¼ inches (26.2 cm).

- Omit the short dough cake bottoms and the currant jelly and replace with 1 Ribbon-Pattern Decorated Sponge Sheet (page 672). You can form the ribbons in whatever direction you wish: horizontal, vertical, diagonal, or curved. One ribbon sheet is actually enough for up to 6 cakes, but it is not practical to make a partial sheet, and the extra can be frozen for another use.

- Slice the sponge cake into 2 layers rather than 3 in Step 1. Place the cake layers on cardboard cake circles for support. Brush with syrup and spread the chocolate cream on top as directed. Wrap strips of acetate or polyurethane (or use adjustable stainless steel cake rings) loosely around the sponge cakes. Cut strips, 2 inches (5 cm) wide, from the ribbon sheet. Place the ribbon sponge strips with the striped side against the plastic or cake rings, fitting them between the rings and the sponge cake layers on the cardboard cake circles. Tighten the plastic collars or cake rings so they fit snugly.

- Continue as directed (there will be no short dough crust to trim in Step 6), omitting icing the sides of the cakes and covering them with chocolate shavings.

Chocolate Ganache Cake yield: 2 cakes, 10 inches (25 cm) in diameter (Color Photo 2)

When you read through this book, you will find that I use this versatile chocolate ganache filling in half a dozen recipes, varying the percentage of chocolate, adding different flavorings, and molding the filling in several shapes. The filling is quick and easy to prepare, and any leftovers can be stored in the refrigerator for weeks. Using the surplus filling is, in fact, the reason I started making this cake.

To make two smaller cakes, 7 inches (17.5 cm) in diameter, make half the quantity of both the chocolate sheet batter and the filling. Spread the batter into 2 rounds, each 7 inches (17.5 cm) in diameter. Bake the cakes and trim them to fit inside cake rings 7 inches (17.5 cm) in diameter. Continue as directed, adjusting the number of butterfly garnishes as needed.

½ **recipe Baked Chocolate Sheet batter (page 355; see Step 2)**

1 ounce (30 g) bread flour

1 Ribbon-Pattern Decorated Sponge Sheet (page 672), 15 × 22 inches (37.5 × 55 cm), made with diagonal stripes

Chocolate Ganache Filling (recipe follows)

Unsweetened cocoa powder

Cookie Butterflies (page 695; see Note)

Edible flowers

1. Set a stainless steel cake ring, 10 inches (25 cm) in diameter, on a sheet of baking paper. While turning the ring, repeatedly fold in the edges of the paper to secure it on the bottom of the ring (Figure 1-6). (This is the same method used to secure the opening of the paper used in savory cooking when baking food in parchment.) Repeat with a second ring (see Chef's Tip).

2. Make the chocolate sheet batter, sifting the 1 ounce (30 g) bread flour into the batter at the end when folding in the egg white. Divide the batter evenly between the cake rings. Bake immediately at 375°F (190°C) for approximately 12 minutes or until baked through. Let cool.

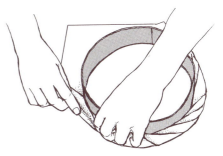

FIGURE 1-6 **Securing a base of baking paper on a cake ring by pleating the paper tightly against the sides of the ring**

If you do not have cake rings for baking the chocolate sheet batter, bake it in 2 cake pans, 10 inches (25 cm) in diameter, instead. The cake pans can also be used for assembly instead of rings. Line the sides of the pans with strips of acetate or baking paper. Invert the cakes to unmold, being extremely careful not to damage the tops.

3. Cut lengthwise strips from the ribbon sponge, 1¾ inches (4.5 cm) wide. The stripes will run diagonally on the cakes.

4. Run a knife around the inside of the chocolate cakes to loosen them, then remove the cake rings. Clean the rings and place them on cardboard cake circles for support. Line the inside of the rings with strips of acetate or baking paper. Place the ribbon sponge strips inside the rings so that the striped sides are against the rings. Peel the baking paper from the chocolate sponge layers (trim to fit if needed) and place 1 layer inside each ring.

5. Divide the ganache filling between the cake rings and smooth the tops to make them even. Take extra care here because the cakes will not be iced but simply dusted with unsweetened cocoa powder to finish. Place cardboard circles on top of the rings to cover the cakes. Chill in the refrigerator for a minimum of 2 hours to set the filling.

6. Remove the cake rings and peel away the plastic or paper strips. Sift cocoa power lightly over the tops of the cakes. Using a knife dipped in hot water, cut each cake into the desired number of servings. Wipe the knife clean and dip it into hot water after each cut. Place a butterfly at the edge of each slice, gently pressing it into the cake so it will stick.

7. Presentation: Make a stencil with a round opening 6 inches (15 cm) in diameter and attach it to a bottomless pie tin (see page 692 for instructions). Place the stencil against the base of a dessert plate. Sift unsweetened cocoa powder lightly over the stencil. Carefully remove the stencil. Place a slice of cake in the center of the cocoa round. Place an edible flower on the cocoa next to the slice.

NOTE: The cake in Color Photo 2 is made to be cut into 12 portions, and the larger butterfly was used for decoration. However, because this cake is so rich, you can easily cut it into 14 or even 16 servings, in which case you should use the smaller butterfly template when you make the decorations.

CHOCOLATE GANACHE FILLING yield: 10 cups (2 L 400 ml)

1 pound 12 ounces (795 g) sweet dark chocolate

6 ounces (170 g) unsweetened chocolate

5 cups (1 L 200 ml) heavy cream

8 egg yolks (⅔ cup/160 ml)

3 ounces (85 g) granulated sugar

½ cup (120 ml) or 6 ounces (170 g) honey

⅓ cup (80 ml) Frangelico liqueur

I. Chop the sweet and unsweetened chocolates into small chunks. Melt the chunks in a bowl set over simmering water. Set aside, but keep warm.

2. Whip the heavy cream until soft peaks form.

3. Whip the egg yolks with the sugar for about 2 minutes; the mixture should be light and fluffy. Bring the honey to a boil, then gradually pour it into the egg yolks while whipping. Continue whipping until cold. Fold in the reserved chocolate and the Frangelico liqueur. Quickly stir in the whipped cream until blended.

Chocolate Mousse Cake with Banana yield: 2 cakes, 10 inches (25 cm) in diameter

This is a great do-ahead cake. Although the cakes cannot be frozen because of the bananas, they can be refrigerated for up to three days after completing Step 5. Finishing each cake as needed goes quickly after that point. Chocolate Mousse Cake with Banana makes an elegant substitute for the ordinary chocolate mousse station at a brunch or luncheon buffet. The banana flavor combines well with chocolate, and the banana looks interesting in the cut slice. Alternatively, I have made this cake several times without bananas (when I found out that the bananas I intended to use were more suitable for banana bread), and it is delicious that way as well. If you have a little more time or have a ribbon sponge sheet in the freezer, try the variation.

1 Cocoa-Almond Sponge (page 796), 10 inches (25 cm) in diameter, *or* 1 Chocolate Chiffon Sponge Cake I (page 797), 10 inches (25 cm) in diameter

2 Short Dough Cake Bottoms (page 792), 10 inches (25 cm) in diameter

4 ounces (115 g) red currant jelly

½ cup (120 ml) Plain Cake Syrup (page 789)

5 medium-size ripe bananas

Chocolate Cognac Cream (recipe follows)

1½ cups (360 ml) heavy cream

1 tablespoon (15 g) granulated sugar

6 ounces (170 g) sliced almonds, toasted and lightly crushed

Dark Chocolate Figurines (page 545)

1. Trim the skin from the top of the sponge cake, cutting it level at the same time. Slice the cake into 2 layers.

2. Place the short dough bottoms on cardboard cake circles for support. Spread the jelly on top in a thin, even layer.

3. Place the sponge layers on the jelly. Brush the cake syrup over the sponges. Place stainless steel cake rings snugly around the sponge cakes. If cake rings are not available, secure strips of polyurethane or acetate around the sponges.

4. Peel the bananas and slice them in half lengthwise. Bend the halves carefully to accentuate the natural curve (they will break slightly, but the breaks are unlikely to show in the finished cakes). Make 2 circles of banana on each cake, placing the slices with the cut sides against the sponge. Place the first circle close to the edge of the sponge and the second smaller circle about 2 inches (5 cm) away from the first, toward the center.

5. Spread the chocolate Cognac cream on top of each cake in a smooth, even layer. Refrigerate the cakes until the cream is set, 1 to 2 hours.

6. Whip the heavy cream with the sugar until stiff peaks form.

7. Remove the rings or plastic strips. Spread a thin layer of whipped cream on the sides of the cakes. Cover the sides with the almonds (see Figure 1-1, page 18). Cut or mark the cakes into the desired number of servings.

8. Place the remaining whipped cream in a pastry bag with a No. 7 (14-mm) plain tip. Pipe a mound of whipped cream at the edge of each slice. Decorate each mound with a chocolate figurine.

CHOCOLATE-BANANA MOUSSE CAKE NOUVELLE

yield: 2 cakes, 10 inches (25 cm) in diameter (Color Photo 4)

The elegant look of this finished cake makes it well worth the extra steps. One ribbon sponge sheet is enough to make up to six cakes, but it doesn't make sense to make less than half of the recipe at a time. Besides, the leftover sheet can be stored in the freezer, well covered, for weeks and can be used for many other projects. For a different look, finish the tops of the cakes with a spiral of whipped cream piped to cover the entire surface; you will need twice as much cream and sugar. Decorate with chocolate shavings instead of chocolate figurines.

1 sheet (½ recipe) Ribbon-Pattern Decorated Sponge Sheet (page 672; see Chef's Tip)

1 Cocoa-Almond Sponge Cake (page 796), 10 inches (25 cm) in diameter, *or* 1 Chocolate Chiffon Sponge Cake I (page 797), 10 inches (25 cm) in diameter

Plain Cake Syrup (page 789)

5 medium-size ripe bananas

Chocolate Cognac Cream (recipe follows)

1 cup (240 ml) heavy cream

1 tablespoon (15 g) granulated sugar

Dark Chocolate Figurines (page 545)

1. Place 1 stainless steel cake ring, 10 inches (25 cm) in diameter, on top of each of 2 cardboard cake circles measuring 12 inches (30 cm) in diameter. Cut strips lengthwise from the ribbon sheet, making them 2 inches (5 cm) wide. Line the cake rings with the strips of ribbon sponge. (Although not absolutely necessary, it is always a good idea to line the rings with strips of baking paper or acetate first to prevent the sponge from sticking to them.)

2. Trim the skin from the top of the almond or chocolate sponge and slice it into 2 layers. Place 1 layer inside each of the rings, adjusting the rings or trimming the cakes as needed for a snug fit. Brush cake syrup over the top of each sponge.

3. Continue with Steps 4 and 5 in the master recipe (page 29).

4. Remove the cake rings and the paper or acetate strips, if used. Cut or mark the cakes into the desired number of servings.

5. Whip the heavy cream and the sugar to stiff peaks. Place in a pastry bag with a No. 7 (14-mm) plain tip. Pipe a large mound of whipped cream at the end of each slice. Decorate each mound with a chocolate figurine.

CHEF'S TIP
To create different patterns, try dragging the trowel in a wavy pattern when you make the ribbon sheet, or use a wide-notched trowel and drag it crosswise instead. When the strips are cut lengthwise, the stripes will appear vertically on the cakes.

CHOCOLATE COGNAC CREAM yield: 8 cups (1 L 920 ml)

Do not make this filling until you are ready to use it.

4 teaspoons (12 g) unflavored gelatin powder

⅓ cup (80 ml) cold water plus ½ cup (120 ml) warm water

2½ cups (600 ml) heavy cream

¼ recipe Swiss Meringue (page 782)

¼ cup (60 ml) Cognac

7 ounces (200 g) sweet dark chocolate, melted

1. Sprinkle the gelatin over the cold water and set aside to soften.

2. Whip the cream to a very soft consistency. Fold the cream into the Swiss meringue.

3. Place the softened gelatin mixture over a bain-marie and heat until dissolved. Do not overheat. Stir in ½ cup (120 ml) warm water, the Cognac, and the melted chocolate.

4. Rapidly add this mixture to a small amount of the cream mixture. Then, still working quickly, stir this combination into the remaining cream mixture.

Chocolate Truffle Cake with Raspberries   yield: 2 cakes, 10 inches (25 cm) in diameter

At first glance, Chocolate Truffle Cake with Raspberries may appear too rich, too expensive, and too time-consuming for anything other than a very special occasion. But considering that this dessert keeps fresh for up to four days and that each cake can be cut into 16 servings, the time and expense are certainly justified. Also, the number of steps can be decreased by omitting the chocolate collar and leaving the sides of the cake plain (take extra care when icing the sides, in this case). If you make the cakes more than one day ahead, do not put the raspberries on the top until you are ready to serve or display the cakes. Before you add the raspberries, use a blowtorch to carefully soften the ganache so that they stick.

½ **recipe Japonaise Meringue Batter (page 781)**

½ **recipe Chocolate Sponge Cake batter (page 795)**

4 **pounds (1 kg 820 g) Ganache (page 770)**

½ **cup (120 ml) brandy**

¼ **cup (60 ml) simple syrup**

2 **Short Dough Cake Bottoms (page 792), 10 inches (25 cm) in diameter**

5 **pints (2 L 400 ml) raspberries**

Dark coating chocolate, melted

Raspberry Sauce (page 173)

Sour Cream Mixture for Piping (page 727)

Powdered sugar

1. Pipe the Japonaise meringue batter into 2 circles, 10 inches (25 cm) in diameter, using the procedure for Meringue Noisette (see Figure 14-2, page 782). Bake at 300°F (149°C) for approximately 30 minutes or until golden.

2. Divide the chocolate sponge cake batter between 2 greased and floured cake pans, 10 inches (25 cm) in diameter. Bake at 375°F (190°C) for about 15 minutes or until the cakes spring back when pressed lightly in the middle. Set aside to cool.

3. Warm the ganache to soften it to a thick, saucelike consistency.

4. Combine the brandy and the simple syrup.

5. Place the short dough bottoms on cardboard cake circles and cover with a thin layer of ganache. Place the Japonaise circles on top. Spread another thin layer of ganache over the Japonaise.

6. Trim the top of the sponge cakes to make them level, then cut them horizontally into 2 layers, each about ¼ inch (6 mm) thick. Place 1 sponge layer on each cake, on top of the ganache. Brush with the syrup mixture. Arrange one-quarter of the raspberries evenly over each sponge.

7. Place cake rings, 10 inches (25 cm) in diameter, around each sponge, or make collars out of acetate or polyurethane strips. Don't worry if the short dough bottom and the Japonaise are larger than the collars; you will trim the excess later.

8. Reserve 1 pound (455 g) of the ganache and pour the remainder evenly over the raspberries. You may have to warm the ganache slightly to pour it.

9. Place the second sponge layers on top of the ganache and press down gently so they stick. Brush the cakes with the remaining syrup mixture. Refrigerate to set.

10. Remove the cake rings or plastic collars and trim the short dough and Japonaise as needed to make the sides even (Figure 1-7).

FIGURE 1-7 **Trimming the excess short dough and Japonaise from the base of the Chocolate Truffle Cake to make the sides even**

11. Warm the reserved ganache to give it a nice shine. Ice the top and sides of the cakes with the ganache. Immediately, while the ganache is still sticky, arrange the remainder of the raspberries on top of the cakes, starting at the edge and making concentric circles next to each other.

12. Measure and cut out 2 strips of polyurethane or acetate as wide as the cakes are high and the exact length of their circumference. Place 1 of the strips on a flat surface and spread just enough of the dark coating chocolate evenly on top to cover the plastic. Because this has to be done quickly, it is impossible to avoid spreading some of the chocolate beyond the plastic, so be certain the surface around the plastic is clean.

13. Before the chocolate hardens, pick up both ends of the chocolate-covered plastic and position it around the cake so that the chocolate sticks to the cake. Repeat with the second cake. Refrigerate the cakes for a few minutes.

14. Place a portion of the raspberry sauce in a piping bottle.

15. Carefully pull the plastic away from the chocolate. When cutting the cakes into the desired number of pieces, first melt through the chocolate layer with a hot knife.

16. Presentation: Place a cake slice in the center of a dessert plate. Pipe a pool of raspberry sauce on the plate at the tip of the slice. Place a small amount of the sour cream mixture in a piping bag and pipe it into the sauce to decorate (see pages 682 to 685). Sift powdered sugar lightly over the cake and onto the serving plate in front of the slice.

Dark Chocolate Shingle Cake yield: 2 cakes, 8 inches (20 cm) in diameter

Because it is just about impossible to slice this unusual-looking cake into servings without ruining the look of the carefully placed decorative chocolate shingles, it is a great choice for a birthday celebration or any other occasion where the cake is presented whole. If the cake must be displayed in individual portions, cut the cakes in Step 4 and then arrange the shingles on each slice, keeping the pattern within the cuts. This will not produce as dramatic a finish, but the servings will still look impressive.

If you prefer not to use the chocolate spray or you do not have time to make and apply it, the cakes will look fine — and taste just as good — with a light dusting of cocoa powder over the shingles instead.

Bittersweet Chocolate Sponge (recipe follows)

Vanilla-Scented Gianduja Cream Filling (recipe follows)

1 recipe Chocolate Glaze (page 774)

Chocolate Shingles (page 532)

Chocolate Solution for Spraying (page 557)

1. Trim the tops to even all 4 sponges. Cut each in half horizontally. Spread a layer of gianduja cream, ½ inch (1.2 cm) thick, over 1 of the 8-inch (20-cm) layers. Top with a second 8-inch (20-cm) layer. Spread a layer of gianduja cream, ½ inch (1.2 cm) thick, over the top. Place a 6-inch (15-cm) layer in the center on top of the cream. Add another layer of cream and top with a second 6-inch (15-cm) sponge. Repeat with the remaining sponge layers to form the second cake; you will not use all of the gianduja cream at this point.

2. Ice the tops and sides of the assembled cakes with the remaining gianduja cream, making as smooth a dome shape on each as possible. Place the cakes in the freezer to set for approximately 30 minutes. (If the cakes will not be finished right away and are only to be prepped to this point, cover and refrigerate instead.)

3. Remove the cakes from the freezer and use a heated spatula to smooth the surface of the cream. Place the cakes on an icing rack and cover with the chocolate glaze.

4. Begin to layer the shingles around the base of the cake, placing them side by side in an even row. Continue by making a second row of carefully spaced shingles, overlapping the first row halfway. Repeat until the cake is fully covered, arranging 4 or 5 shingles in a circle to cover the top. Repeat with the second cake. Return the cakes to the freezer for 30 minutes.

5. Spray the shingles with the chocolate mixture to create a rich velvet finish.

BITTERSWEET CHOCOLATE SPONGE

yield: 2 layers, 8 inches (20 cm) in diameter, and 2 layers, 6 inches (15 cm) in diameter, or 1 full sheet (16 × 24 inches/40 × 60 cm), approximately ¾ inch (2 cm) thick

1 pound 6 ounces (625 g) granulated sugar	1 tablespoon (15 ml) vanilla extract
4 ounces (115 g) unsweetened cocoa powder	8 ounces (225 g) bread flour
3 cups (720 ml) boiling water	8 ounces (225 g) cake flour
1 cup (240 ml) vegetable oil	2½ teaspoons (10 g) baking soda
5 eggs	2 teaspoons (10 g) salt

1. Line the bottoms of 2 round cake pans, 8 inches (20 cm) in diameter, and 2 round cake pans, 6 inches (15 cm) in diameter, with baking paper.

2. Place the sugar in a mixer bowl. Sift the cocoa powder over the sugar. Using the whip attachment, mix the two together thoroughly. Gradually add the boiling water and mix until smooth. Incorporate the oil, eggs, and vanilla. Mix at medium speed for about 3 minutes.

3. Sift together the bread flour, cake flour, baking soda, and salt. Gradually incorporate the dry ingredients into the egg mixture. Continue to mix at medium speed until the batter is well combined and smooth, scraping down the bowl once or twice as needed.

4. Divide the batter between the prepared cake pans (or spread evenly over a sheet pan lined with baking paper).

5. Bake at 375°F (190°C) for approximately 30 minutes or until the centers of the cakes spring back when pressed lightly. Set aside to cool.

VANILLA-SCENTED GIANDUJA CREAM FILLING   yield: approximately 10 cups (2 L 400 ml)

It is best not to make this filling until you are ready to use it.

4 ounces (115 g) milk chocolate

1 pound 4 ounces (570 g) gianduja chocolate

1 quart (960 ml) heavy cream

2 tablespoons (30 ml) vanilla extract

6 ounces (170 g) hazelnuts, toasted and coarsely crushed

1. Chop both chocolates into small pieces. Place in a bowl over a bain-marie and stir constantly until melted. Be careful not to overheat. Set aside.

2. Whip the heavy cream with the vanilla extract to the consistency of a thick sauce.

3. Place approximately one-quarter of the cream in a separate bowl and, stirring vigorously with a spoon, add the melted chocolate to the smaller amount of cream to temper.

4. Working quickly, stir in the remaining cream, then add the hazelnuts. Continue to stir until the mixture is thick enough to hold its shape.

Dobos Torte   yield: I cake, 10 inches (25 cm) in diameter, or 12 servings (Color Photos 3 and 8)

For the chef, a perfectly prepared Dobos torte, one of the most popular classic cakes all over the world, is a great show of talent. Spreading hot sugar over a thin sponge layer is impressive in itself, but cutting the layer into precise pieces before the sugar hardens and cracks is even more of an accomplishment. Dobos torte is not a practical cake, however, because you must make many thin sponges. I use only 6, but Hungarian cookbooks refer to anywhere from 8 to 12. Also, the caramelized sugar topping will not look as good the next day, which is why this recipe makes one cake only. If you need two cakes, it is possible to prepare two caramelized tops at once, provided you are fairly experienced. Spread the sugar over both pieces before cutting the first one.

1 recipe Dobos Sponge batter (page 799)

¾ cup (180 ml) Plain Cake Syrup (page 789)

¼ cup (60 ml) Frangelico liqueur

2 pounds (910 g) Chocolate Buttercream (page 752)

7 ounces (200 g) granulated sugar

⅓ cup (80 ml) water

½ ounce (15 g) or 1 tablespoon (45 ml) unsalted butter

1. Draw 2 circles, 10 inches (25 cm) in diameter, on each of 3 sheets of baking paper. Invert the papers and place them on perfectly even sheet pans.

2. Divide the sponge batter equally among the 6 circles. Spread the batter out flat and even within the markings.

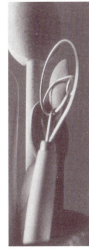

History of the Dobos Torte

Budapest, Hungary, has always been famous for both its architecture and its culinary achievements. Its pastries were heavily influenced by nearby Vienna. József C. Dobos was born in Hungary in the mid-nineteenth century; his father was an accomplished chef, presiding in the kitchen of Count Rákóczi. József Dobos opened a gourmet delicatessen in Budapest, where he sold previously unheard-of imported gourmet products, such as special cheeses and champagne. He invented the showy Dobos torte in 1887 and found a way to package and ship the cake to foreign countries. The Millennium Exposition in 1896 featured a Dobos Pavilion at which his creation was baked and served to the crowds. Dobos published the original recipe for his torte in 1906; by this time, of course, many had copied his idea. Before his death in 1924, Dobos published four cookbooks, the best known being The Hungarian-French Cookbook. In 1962, the Hungarian Chefs and Pastry Chefs Association held a celebration to commemorate the seventy-fifth anniversary of the creation of the Dobos torte, and a 6-foot (1.8-meter) Dobos torte was paraded through the streets of Budapest.

3. Bake immediately at 425°F (219°C) for approximately 8 minutes or until just baked through. Set aside to cool.

4. Invert the papers and peel the paper from the sponge rounds. Select the best-looking layer and set it aside. Using a cake ring 10 inches (25 cm) in diameter, or a cardboard cake circle of the same size, trim the 5 remaining sponge layers (they usually spread a bit in the oven) and level the tops, if necessary. Trim the reserved layer to make it 9½ inches (23.7 cm) in diameter, cover, and set it aside to use as the top (see Chef's Tip).

5. Combine the cake syrup and Frangelico liqueur (this amount of syrup and liqueur is sufficient if you apply it with a brush, but you will need to double both to use a spray bottle effectively). Place a 10-inch (25-cm) sponge layer on a cardboard cake circle. Brush or spray some of the cake syrup mixture on top.

6. Reserve 2 ounces (55 g) chocolate buttercream (about ½ cup/120 ml). Using some of the remaining buttercream, spread an even layer on top of the sponge layer with cake syrup, making it ⅛ inch (3 mm) thick. Continue layering the remaining sponges, brushing or spraying them with the cake syrup mixture and spreading a ⅛-inch (3-mm) layer of buttercream between each layer. Use all of the buttercream, but take care not to get any on the sides of the cake. Spread the buttercream just to the edge each time; the sides of the cake are not iced so that the many thin layers remain exposed. Press down lightly on the top of the cake with the bottom of a flat cake pan or sheet pan. Run a metal spatula around the side of the cake, holding it at a 90-degree angle and pressing firmly, to remove all excess buttercream. Refrigerate the cake until the buttercream is set.

7. Taking the usual precautions for cooking sugar, combine the sugar and water in a small, heavy saucepan. Cook the sugar to the amber stage — just before it turns light brown or caramelizes. Remove from the heat and quickly stir in the butter. Using an oiled palette knife, immediately spread the caramel over the top of the reserved sponge layer (see Chef's

CHEF'S TIP

By trimming the top layer to a smaller diameter than the whole cake, the caramelized pieces will fit perfectly on top. If left untrimmed, they would protrude outside the circumference of the cake.

Spread a small amount of vegetable oil on top of a sheet of baking paper and set it next to your work area. This is a great help (and a must, if you are making two cakes) to allow you to quickly re-oil the palette knife and chef's knife as you spread the caramel and cut the top sponge layer.

Tip). Quickly, before the caramel hardens, use a thin, oiled chef's knife to cut the sponge into 12 wedges.

8. Cut the cake into 12 servings. Place the reserved buttercream in a pastry bag with a No. 3 (6-mm) plain tip. Pipe a rope of buttercream along 1 cut edge of each slice. Placing 1 wedge on each slice of cake, arrange the caramelized sponge wedges on top of the buttercream lines, setting each one at an angle, to create a fan pattern.

Gâteau Malakoff   yield: 2 cakes, 10 inches (25 cm) in diameter, 12 servings each

The name *Malakoff* is given to various culinary items, including a type of Neufchâtel cheese. The best-known of the sweets, however, is the Charlotte Malakoff. The source of this title is unclear. Some research indicates that Malakoff was a noble Russian family who lent their name to the creation, but others say the term comes from the town of the same name in north-central France. The French town of Malakoff was named for the fortress of Malakhov, captured by the French during the Crimean War. (Are you confused yet?) A third possibility is that a French general, le duc de Malakoff, took a liking to this pretty, maraschino-flavored dessert, and it was named for him.

In any event, this cake is a variation of the classic Charlotte Malakoff recipe. I have added rum and left out the nuts traditionally included in the filling.

½ recipe Ladyfingers batter (page 801)

2 Short Dough Cake Bottoms (page 792), 10 inches (25 cm) in diameter

5 ounces (140 g) smooth strawberry jam

2 Cocoa-Almond Sponges (page 796), 10 inches (25 cm) in diameter

¾ cup (180 ml) Plain Cake Syrup (page 789)

¾ cup (180 ml) simple syrup

½ cup (120 ml) light rum

Maraschino Cream (recipe follows)

8 ounces (225 g) Ganache (page 770)

Whipped cream

1. Place the ladyfingers batter in a pastry bag with a No. 4 (8-mm) plain tip. Pipe the batter onto sheet pans lined with baking paper to make approximately 120 ladyfingers, each 1½ inches (3.7 cm) long. Bake at 425°F (219°C) for about 8 minutes or until golden brown. Let cool and reserve.

2. Place the short dough cake bottoms on cardboard cake circles for support. Spread the jam evenly to cover the short dough.

3. Trim the skin and about ¼ inch (6 mm) from the top of the sponge cakes. Slice each cake into 2 layers. Place 1 layer on each short dough cake bottom. Brush the sponges with cake syrup. Place a stainless steel cake ring snugly around each sponge; make collars from strips of polyurethane or acetate if cake rings are not available.

4. Combine the simple syrup and rum. Pour this mixture over the base of a half-sheet pan. Reserve 72 of the most attractive ladyfingers to use in decorating. Place the remaining ladyfingers in the rum syrup on the pan and let them soak about 5 minutes to fully absorb the liquid.

5. Top each of the sponge cakes with one-quarter of the maraschino cream and spread it evenly within the rings.

6. Arrange the soaked ladyfingers flat side down on the cream in a spoke pattern, making a circle 1 inch (2.5 cm) from the edge of the cake. Work quickly so the filling does not set up.

7. Divide the remaining maraschino cream between the cakes and spread it evenly over the ladyfingers. Place the remaining sponge layers on top of the cream and press down gently to make the tops even. Brush the sponges with the remaining cake syrup. Refrigerate the cakes at least 2 hours to set the filling.

8. Run a thin knife around the inside of the rings to free the cakes, then remove the rings. (If using plastic strips simply peel them away.)

9. Heat the ganache until liquid and glossy. Spread the ganache over the top of the cakes, using just enough to cover the sponge. As soon as the ganache starts to harden, use the back of a chef's knife to score lines every ½ inch (1.2 cm). Turn the cake 45 degrees and repeat to create a diamond pattern.

10. Ice the sides of the cakes with whipped cream. Cut each cake into 12 servings. Stand 3 ladyfingers upright on the side of each slice. If the ladyfingers are taller than the cake, trim one end and place the cut end at the base of the cake.

MARASCHINO CREAM yield: 7 cups (1 L 680 ml)

Because you cannot reheat this filling to soften it, do not make it until you are ready to use it in the cakes.

4 teaspoons (12 g) unflavored gelatin powder	3 ounces (85 g) granulated sugar
⅓ cup (80 ml) cold water	½ cup (120 ml) dry white wine
5 cups (1 L 200 ml) heavy cream	⅓ cup (80 ml) maraschino liqueur *or* kirschwasser
4 egg yolks (⅓ cup/80 ml)	

1. Sprinkle the gelatin over the cold water and set aside to soften.

2. Whip the cream to soft peaks. Reserve in the refrigerator.

3. Whip the egg yolks and sugar until just combined. Whip in the wine and maraschino liqueur. Place over simmering water and heat to about 140°F (60°C), whipping the mixture to a thick foam in the process. Remove from the heat and continue whipping until cool. Fold the yolk mixture into the reserved whipped cream.

4. Place the softened gelatin over simmering water and heat to dissolve. Working quickly, add the gelatin to a small portion of the cream mixture, then rapidly mix this into the remaining cream mixture.

Gâteau Mocha Carousel yield: 2 cakes, 10 inches (25 cm) in diameter (Color Photos 10 and 14)

Any variation on traditional horizontal cake layers makes for an impressive, professional-looking presentation. Other examples are Chocolate Triangles (page 98) and Chestnut Puzzle Cake (page 22). To achieve the desired outcome with any of these pastries, it is extremely important that the sponges are thin and are cut precisely. The narrow strips used for this cake must be placed on top of the ganache while it is still sticky so they adhere and remain standing straight when the filling is added. To help prevent the strips from sliding, it is a good idea to fill in all of the sponge circles partway before filling the outside circle to the top. If the vertical layers lean every which way in the set filling when the cake is sliced and served, the distinctiveness and elegance of the intended effect is greatly diminished.

½ recipe Japonaise Meringue Batter (page 781)	Ground coffee
1 recipe Cocoa-Almond Sponge batter (page 796)	Marzipan Coffee Beans (page 640) *or* candy coffee beans
8 ounces (225 g) Ganache (page 770)	1 recipe Mousseline Sauce (page 338)
Mocha Whipped Cream (recipe follows)	¼ cup (60 ml) Kahlúa liqueur
¼ cup (60 ml) Plain Cake Syrup (page 789)	Fanned apricot halves
2½ cups (600 ml) heavy cream	Mint leaves
1 ounce (30 g) granulated sugar	

1. Draw 2 circles, 10 inches (25 cm) in diameter, on a sheet of baking paper. Invert the paper on a sheet pan. Place the Japonaise meringue batter in a pastry bag with a No. 3 (6-mm) plain tip. Pipe the batter in a spiral within each circle, as described in the recipe for Meringue Noisette (see Figure 14-2, page 782). Bake at 275° to 300°F (135° to 149°C) until golden brown, about 35 minutes.

2. Line the bottom of a cake pan, 10 inches (25 cm) in diameter, with baking paper (or grease and flour the bottom, but not the sides). Pour about one-third of the cocoa sponge batter into the pan and spread it out evenly.

3. Pour the remaining batter onto a sheet of baking paper and spread it to make a rectangle slightly smaller than the size of the paper (24 × 16 inches/60 × 40 cm) by leaving a border approximately ¼ inch (6 mm) all around. Drag the paper onto a sheet pan (see Figure 9-22, page 481). Immediately bake both sponges at 400°F (205°C). The round cake will take about 15 minutes; the sheet will take about 10 minutes. Let the sponge cakes cool completely. Cut the thin chocolate sheet lengthwise into strips 1 inch (2.5 cm) wide.

4. Warm the ganache to soften it. Place the Japonaise bottoms on cardboard cake circles for support; divide the ganache between them and spread it evenly. Place stainless steel cake rings, 10 inches (25 cm) in diameter, on the ganache. Do not be concerned about Japonaise that protrudes outside the rings; it will be trimmed later.

5. Stand the sponge strips on the ganache in 5 evenly spaced concentric circles, starting at the outside against the ring on each cake.

6. Place the mocha whipped cream in a pastry bag with a No. 6 (12-mm) plain tip. Pipe the cream between the

FIGURE 1-8 Piping the mocha whipped cream between the sponge rings in the Gâteau Mocha Carousel

sponge circles (Figure 1-8). Spread the excess evenly over the tops with a spatula.

7. Trim the skin off the top of the 10-inch (25-cm) chocolate sponge, cutting the top even at the same time, if necessary. Slice the sponge into 2 layers. Place 1 on top of each cake and press gently to be sure the layers stick to the mocha cream. Brush cake syrup over the sponges. Refrigerate the cakes until the cream is set, about 2 hours.

8. Remove the cake rings. Trim away any excess Japonaise that protrudes outside the sponge to make the sides even (see Figure 1-7, page 32).

9. Whip the heavy cream and sugar to stiff peaks. Ice the top and sides of the cakes with a thin layer of whipped cream. Place a portion of the remaining whipped cream in a pastry bag with a No. 6 (12-mm) flat, plain tip. Pipe vertical lines on the sides of the cakes, working from the bottom to the top and placing the lines next to one another. Use a palette knife to make the top edge even all around each cake.

10. Mark or cut the cakes into the desired number of pieces. Place the remaining whipped cream in a pastry bag with a No. 6 (12-mm) star tip. Pipe a rosette of cream at the edge of each slice. Sprinkle ground coffee very lightly on the whipped cream inside the piped rosettes. Place marzipan or candy coffee beans on the rosettes.

11. Flavor the mousseline sauce with the Kahlúa and place a portion of the sauce in a piping bottle.

12. Presentation: Place a slice of cake in the center of a dessert plate. Pipe mousseline sauce in front of the dessert in a half-circle. Sprinkle ground coffee in a narrow band along the round edge of the sauce. Place a fanned apricot half and a mint leaf on the other side of the cake.

MOCHA WHIPPED CREAM yield: 3 pounds (1 kg 365 g)

Do not make this filling until you are ready to use it.

4½ teaspoons (14 g) unflavored gelatin powder

½ cup (120 ml) dry white wine

4 egg yolks (⅓ cup/80 ml)

½ cup (120 ml) or 6 ounces (170 g) light corn syrup

1 quart (960 ml) heavy cream

⅓ cup (80 ml) Kahlúa liqueur

¼ cup (60 ml) Coffee Reduction (page 754) *or* 1 teaspoon (4 g) mocha paste

1. Sprinkle the gelatin over the wine and set aside to soften.

2. Beat the egg yolks just until combined. Heat the corn syrup to boiling and whip the hot syrup into the yolks, continuing to whip until the mixture has cooled and has a light, fluffy consistency.

3. Whip the cream to soft peaks and combine with the yolk mixture.

4. Add the Kahlúa and coffee reduction to the softened gelatin mixture. Place over a bain-marie and heat until dissolved. Do not overheat. Rapidly combine this mixture with a small amount of the yolk and cream mixture. Still working quickly, combine with the remaining cream.

Harlequin Cake yield: 2 cakes, 10 inches (25 cm) in diameter

Reflecting the contrasting pattern of the harlequin's clown costume, the title Harlequin, or *Arlequin* in French, is given to many culinary specialties. Harlequin food items range from canapés to roasts, casseroles, and an abundance of sweets. They are so named either for being colorful or for exhibiting a marked contrast between two colors — most often black and white. The most famous of these sweets is the classic soufflé Harlequin, which contains vertical layers of chocolate and vanilla. Other pastries comprise multiple flavors and components reminiscent of the patches on Harlequin's costume.

1 Ribbon-Pattern Decorated Sponge Sheet (page 672)

1 Devil's Food Cake Layer (page 393), 10 inches (25 cm) in diameter

White Chocolate Bavarian Filling (recipe follows)

½ recipe Chocolate Cognac Cream (page 30)

½ cup (120 ml) heavy cream

10 ounces (285 g) marzipan, untinted or chocolate-flavored

Powdered sugar

Dark coating chocolate, melted

Piping Chocolate (page 543), melted

Candied violets

Raspberry Sauce (page 173)

Orange Sauce (page 278)

Sour Cream Mixture for Piping (page 727)

1. Place 2 stainless steel cake rings, 10 inches (25 cm) in diameter, on a sheet pan lined with baking paper. (If cake rings are not available, line the sides of 2 cake pans with strips of polyurethane or acetate.) Cut lengthwise strips from the ribbon sponge sheet, making them 2 inches (5 cm) wide. Place the sponge strips inside the rings with the striped sides against the rings.

2. Trim the skin from the top of the devil's food cake to make it level. Cut the cake into 2 layers. Trim the sides to fit, then place 1 layer inside each cake ring.

3. Divide the white chocolate Bavarian filling between the cakes and smooth to make the tops level. Place the cakes in the refrigerator while making the chocolate Cognac cream.

4. Divide the chocolate Cognac cream between the cakes, on top of the Bavarian filling, and spread the tops level. Refrigerate to set, approximately 2 hours.

5. When the fillings are completely set, remove the rings from around the cakes (or invert the cakes to remove them from the cake pans, turn right-side up, and remove the plastic strips). Whip the cream to stiff peaks and ice the tops of the cakes.

6. Divide the marzipan into 2 pieces. Using powdered sugar to prevent them from sticking, roll them out 1 at a time into circles about 12 inches (30 cm) in diameter and ¹⁄₁₆ inch (2 mm)

About the Harlequin Figure

The original Harlequin was one of the principal characters in the Italian commedia dell'arte, a comic theater popular throughout Europe from the mid-sixteenth through the eighteenth centuries. Harlequin's earliest costume had colorful rags and patches on a peasant shirt and trousers, and his role was that of a wild and comic servant. Later, as the character developed, he became a faithful valet noted for his patience and good spirits, and his costume became a tight-fitting one-piece suit decorated with triangular or diamond shapes either in numerous bright colors or in black and white, and he wore a black half-mask.

thick. Place the marzipan rounds on cardboard cake circles and spread a thin layer of melted dark coating chocolate on top. Use just enough to cover the marzipan circles evenly.

7. Using a guide, trim each round into an even circle slightly smaller than the top of the cakes (save the trimmings for rum balls or chocolate-flavored marzipan).

8. Cut the marzipan circles into the same number of slices you plan to cut the cakes into (see Note). Slide the cuts, chocolate-side up, all at once onto the top of the cakes (as shown in Figure 1-9, page 53), or pick the pieces up 1 at a time and reassemble on the cakes.

9. Cut between the marzipan pieces to slice the cakes into serving pieces. Be sure to clean the knife after each cut. Pipe the melted piping chocolate decoratively on top of each slice. Place a small piece of candied violet at the wide end of each piece.

10. Presentation: Place the raspberry and orange sauces into separate piping bottles. Place a slice of cake off-center on a dessert plate. Pipe small pools of raspberry sauce and orange sauce next to each other in front of the slice. Pipe a line of sour cream mixture where the sauces meet. Using a wooden skewer, swirl the three together in a circular pattern (see Figure 13-18, page 685).

NOTE: If the cakes are not to be precut, the chocolate marzipan tops should be cut the same size as the cakes and placed on the top whole.

WHITE CHOCOLATE BAVARIAN FILLING yield: 4¹⁄₂ cups (1 L 80 ml)

This delightful silky-smooth filling is easy to make, provided you heed the following two warnings: Whip the cream just until soft peaks form, and do not overheat the white chocolate. To ensure that the chocolate does not get too hot, do not walk away when melting it; stay with it and stir it constantly to speed the process. Remove the chocolate from the bain-marie while a few unmelted chunks remain and continue to stir off-heat until they melt. The chocolate should be warm but not hot. Ignoring these cautions will cause the filling to separate and become grainy, and you will have no choice but to start over. Lastly, do not make the filling until you are ready to use it, because it thickens quite fast.

1¹⁄₂ cups (360 ml) heavy cream	4 ounces (115 g) granulated sugar
1 tablespoon (9 g) unflavored gelatin powder	4 egg whites (¹⁄₂ cup/120 ml)
¹⁄₄ cup (60 ml) cold water	6 ounces (170 g) white chocolate, melted
1¹⁄₂ tablespoons (14 g) pectin powder (see Note)	2 ounces (55 g) pistachio nuts, blanched, skins removed, and chopped

1. Whip the heavy cream to soft peaks. Do not overwhip. Cover and refrigerate.

2. Sprinkle the gelatin over the cold water and set aside to soften.

3. Combine the pectin powder and granulated sugar in a mixing bowl. Stir in the egg whites. Place the bowl over simmering water and heat, stirring constantly with a whisk, to 140°F (60°C). Remove from the heat and immediately whip the mixture until it has cooled completely and has formed stiff peaks.

4. Place the gelatin mixture over a bain-marie and heat until dissolved. Quickly stir the gelatin into the melted white chocolate, then quickly stir the chocolate mixture into one-third of the meringue mixture to temper it. Still working quickly, add this to the remaining meringue. Stir in the reserved whipped cream. Fold in the chopped nuts.

NOTE: Use regular canning pectin. If it is unavailable, increase the gelatin by 1 teaspoon (3 g) for a total of 1 tablespoon plus 1 teaspoon (12 g). Increase the cold water by 1 tablespoon (15 ml) and the granulated sugar by 1 ounce (30 g).

Lemon Chiffon Cake yield: 2 cakes, 10 inches (25 cm) in diameter (Color Photo 13)

This cake comes from one of my first notebooks, which I still refer to from time to time. The book is starting to show its age after all these years by getting a little rough around the edges, but so, I might add, is the author of this book. Back when I started, one had to earn the right to copy a particularly good recipe or a certain shop specialty like Lemon Chiffon Cake. To obtain a really top-secret recipe, some apprentices would try to figure it out one ingredient at a time, observing closely, checking the scale after the boss was through, even counting the eggshells in the garbage! Usually, nothing was written down to copy; it was all memorized. Even in the cases where the recipe was on paper, one ingredient was often intentionally left out or changed in such a way that the recipe would work only if you knew the code.

I often tell my students that if they were to take with them just one recipe from my class, it should be the Lemon Chiffon Cake. Not only is this cake inexpensive to produce, it can be made up in advance through Step 3 and stored for several days in the refrigerator or for weeks in the freezer, so it is perfect for banquets. Its refreshing light taste makes it appropriate for use on a lunch or brunch buffet and, with the addition of a sauce, it can be transformed into an elegant plated dessert. The chiffon filling is simplicity itself to make. It is important to use finely grated lemon zest, which will give the filling a better flavor and texture than coarsely grated or, worse, zested lemon zest. If a fine grater is not available, coarsely grate or zest the lemon, then use a chef's knife to mince the zest very fine, as one would chop parsley.

If you do not have time to make either glaze, substitute shaved chocolate sprinkled lightly over the center of the cake within the rosettes of whipped cream.

¼ cup (60 ml) lemon juice

½ cup (120 ml) Plain Cake Syrup (page 789)

1 Chiffon Sponge Cake I (page 797), 10 inches (25 cm) in diameter

Lemon Chiffon Filling (recipe follows)

1 quart (960 ml) heavy cream

2 tablespoons (30 g) granulated sugar

⅔ cup (160 ml) Pectin Glaze (page 776) *or* Lemon Mirror Glaze (recipe follows)

Chocolate Transfer Squares (page 521)

Lemon slices

Piping Chocolate (page 543), melted

Raspberry Sauce (page 173)

Sprigs of lemon mint

1. Add the lemon juice to the cake syrup and set the mixture aside.

2. Trim the skin from the top of the sponge cake and level the top if necessary. Slice the cake into 2 layers. Place the layers on cardboard cake rounds for support. Brush the lemon-flavored cake syrup over the sponges. Place a stainless steel cake ring, 10 inches (25 cm) in diameter, snugly around each sponge, or secure a strip of polyurethane or acetate around each to form a collar.

3. Divide the lemon filling between the sponge layers and spread it evenly within the rings. Cover the cakes and refrigerate until the filling is set, about 2 hours.

4. Remove the cake rings or plastic strips. Whip the heavy cream and sugar to stiff peaks. Spread a layer of cream ¾ inch (2 cm) thick on the top of each cake and ice the sides with just enough cream to cover the sponge. Reserve the remaining cream in the refrigerator.

5. Cover the top of the cakes with a thin layer of pectin or lemon glaze. When the glaze is set, cut or mark the cakes into the desired number of pieces. Place a chocolate square on the side of each slice; it should stick to the cream.

6. Place the remaining whipped cream in a pastry bag with a No. 6 (12-mm) star tip. Pipe a rosette of cream at the edge of each slice. Place a small wedge of sliced lemon on each rosette.

7. Pipe a large S of piping chocolate on the base of as many dessert plates as you will need. Place a portion of the raspberry sauce in a piping bottle.

8. Presentation: Pipe enough raspberry sauce into the bottom loop of the S on a prepared plate to fill the loop. Place a slice of cake in the top loop next to the sauce. Place a sprig of lemon mint in front of the cake.

LEMON CHIFFON FILLING yield: 2 pounds 6 ounces (1 kg 80 g)

5 teaspoons (30 g) finely grated lemon zest

1 cup (240 ml) lemon juice

2 tablespoons (18 g) unflavored gelatin powder

½ cup (120 ml) cold water

6 egg yolks (½ cup/120 ml)

¾ cup (180 ml) or 8 ounces (225 g) light corn syrup

3 cups (720 ml) heavy cream

1. Stir the grated lemon zest into the lemon juice. Set aside.

2. Sprinkle the gelatin over the cold water and set aside to soften.

3. Start whipping the egg yolks at medium speed on a mixer. Place the corn syrup in a small saucepan and bring to a boil. Lower the mixer speed and pour the hot syrup into the whipped egg yolks in a thin, steady stream. Increase the mixing speed and continue whipping until the mixture is light and fluffy.

4. Whip the heavy cream to soft peaks. Combine the egg yolk mixture, whipped cream, and lemon juice with the zest.

5. Place the gelatin mixture over a bain-marie and heat until dissolved. Do not overheat. Place about one-quarter of the cream mixture in a separate bowl and rapidly mix in the dissolved gelatin. Quickly mix this into the remaining cream mixture.

LEMON MIRROR GLAZE yield: 1 cup (240 ml)

1 tablespoon (9 g) unflavored gelatin powder

¼ cup (60 ml) cold water

½ cup (120 ml) strained lemon juice

¼ cup (60 ml) simple syrup

¼ teaspoon (1.25 ml) Tartaric Acid Solution (page 629)

1. Sprinkle the gelatin over the cold water and let sit until softened. Place the gelatin mixture over a bain-marie and heat until dissolved. Do not overheat.

2. Stir the lemon juice, simple syrup, and tartaric acid solution into the gelatin mixture.

CHEF'S TIP
This glaze can be made in a larger
quantity as a mise en place item;
simply melt the amount needed
each time.

3. Use the glaze on the cakes as soon as it shows signs of thickening. If the glaze becomes too thick to pour into a smooth, even layer, warm it before using to avoid ruining the appearance of the cakes.

VARIATION

LEMON CHIFFON FRUIT BASKET CAKE

ÿield: 2 cakes, 10 inches (25 cm) in diameter (Color Photo 4)

You can produce an entirely different finish and a refreshing, less rich cake by omitting the whipped cream, lemon glaze, and chocolate squares, and decorating the sides of the cakes with ribbon sponge sheets and the tops with a colorful arrangement of fresh fruit instead. You can cut the ribbon sponge so that it covers the entire side of each cake or so that it comes just halfway up the side, as shown in Photo xx. You will not need a full ribbon sponge sheet, but it is not practical to produce a partial sheet. Should you have leftover ribbon sponge on hand, this is a good place to use it.

1 Ribbon-Pattern Decorated Sponge Sheet (page 672)	1 recipe Lemon Chiffon Filling (page 43)
¼ cup (60 ml) lemon juice	¾ cup (180 ml) heavy cream
¼ cup (60 ml) Plain Cake Syrup (page 789)	2 teaspoons (10 g) granulated sugar
1 Chiffon Sponge Cake I (page 797), 10 inches (25 cm) in diameter	Fresh fruit
	Pectin Glaze (page 776)

1. Place 2 stainless steel cake rings, 10 inches (25 cm) in diameter, on cardboard cake rounds for support. Line the sides of the rings with strips of ribbon sponge cut 1¾ inches (4.5 cm) wide, or strips cut about half that width if you want the sponge to cover just half of the filling.

2. Add the lemon juice to the cake syrup.

3. Trim the skin from the top of the sponge cake and level the top at the same time. Cut the sponge into 4 thin layers. Reserve 2 layers for another use. Place each of the remaining layers in the bottom of a lined cake ring, trimming as needed so that the sponges fit snugly. Brush the lemon-flavored cake syrup over the sponges.

4. Divide the filling between the cake rings or cake pans. Cover the cakes and refrigerate until the filling is set, about 2 hours.

5. Whip the heavy cream and sugar to stiff peaks. Place in a pastry bag with a No. 8 (16-mm) star tip. Reserve in the refrigerator.

6. Remove the cake rings. Decorate the tops of the cakes with fresh fruit. Brush the pectin glaze over the fruit and the top of the cakes. Pipe rosettes of whipped cream next to the fruit.

Mocha Cake yield: 2 cakes, 10 inches (25 cm) in diameter

When I was teaching at the California Culinary Academy in San Francisco, I always tried to make a new and impressive dessert for each student graduation luncheon. These celebrations took place every two months and totaled about 300 people, including students and guests, so the possibilities were somewhat limited. A few times, I simply created a showier presentation of an old favorite, as was the case with both Cappuccino Mousse with Sambuca Cream in a Chocolate Coffee Cup (page 328) and Strawberries Romanoff (page 183). For the graduation where we served the following recipe, the students had requested a classic mocha cake. While it certainly is a good old-fashioned cake, I felt it needed a facelift.

As you look through this recipe, you will see it is actually a scaled-down version of Chestnut Puzzle Cake (page 22), using one less sponge layer and a simplified method to remove the center. You must still make both a chocolate and a plain sponge, but at least you have to worry about one flavor of buttercream only. The presentation described here can be replaced by serving the cake with chocolate sauce or mousseline sauce flavored with a hint of cinnamon, if you wish.

2 pounds 12 ounces (1 kg 250 g) Vanilla
    Buttercream (Swiss Method; page 753)

1 tablespoon (15 ml) mocha extract *or* 3
    tablespoons (45 ml) Coffee Reduction
    (page 754)

1 Chiffon Sponge Cake I (page 797), 10 inches
    (25 cm) in diameter

1 Chocolate Chiffon Sponge Cake I (page 797),
    10 inches (25 cm) in diameter

½ cup (120 ml) Kahlúa liqueur

¼ cup (60 ml) water

4 ounces (115 g) sliced almonds, toasted and
    lightly crushed

Chocolate Figurines (page 545)

Espresso coffee powder

½ recipe Mango Coulis (page 244)

1. Flavor the buttercream with the mocha extract or coffee reduction. Reserve 4 ounces (115 g) to use in decorating. Set the buttercream aside.

2. Trim the skin from the top of both sponge cakes, leveling the tops at the same time. Cut each sponge into 4 thin layers. Place 2 of the chocolate layers on cardboard cake rounds, cover, and set aside.

3. Place 1 plain layer on each of 2 cardboard cake rounds. Combine the Kahlúa and the water. Brush or spray some of this mixture on top of the sponge layers to moisten. Spread a thin, even layer of buttercream, approximately ⅛ inch (3 mm) thick, over each sponge. Place the 2 remaining chocolate sponges on top. Brush or spray with the Kahlúa mixture, then top each with another thin layer of buttercream. Top with plain sponge layers. Press the assembled cakes together lightly. Brush or spray the Kahlúa mixture over the cakes. Place in the refrigerator until the buttercream is set.

4. Dip a sharp, pointed knife (a cake knife or an 8- to 10-inch/20- to 25-cm chef's knife) into hot water. Cut out a cone-shaped piece by holding the knife at a 45-degree angle and cutting a circle around the perimeter of one cake about ½ inch (1.2 cm) away from the side at the top, angling down to about 2 inches (5 cm) from the side at the bottom (see Figure 1-2, page 23). Move the knife up and down as you cut; dip the knife back into the hot water if you feel any resistance. Remove the cut piece by lifting it out with the knife and inverting it onto your hand. The inverted piece should be approximately 6 inches (15 cm) at the top and 9 inches (22.5 cm) at the bottom. Place this piece on a cardboard cake circle. Repeat with the second cake.

If you are making only one cake and do not
have sponges on hand, rather than making two
kinds, you can save time by doing the following: Make ½ recipe of the plain sponge batter
and pour half of it into a prepared 10-inch (25-
cm) cake pan. Sift 3 tablespoons (24 g)
unsweetened cocoa powder over the remaining batter and fold it in very carefully. Place this
batter in a second prepared pan and bake the
sponges as directed. After they have cooled,
cut each sponge into 2 layers. Because you
work the chocolate sponge batter twice, it will
be a little denser and lower in volume. Be
careful when slicing it in half, as it may be quite
thin.

5. Ice the flat ring around the top of each cake and the area inside the cut with a layer of buttercream ⅛ inch (3-mm) thick (see Figure 1-3, page 23).

6. Place a reserved chocolate sponge layer flat on top of each cake. Place a cardboard cake round on top of each. Invert the cakes so the new chocolate layers are on the bottom.

7. Gently press the cut rings in and down so they touch and adhere to the bottom of each cake (see Figure 1-4, page 23).

8. Ice the newly formed craters with a layer of buttercream ⅛ inch (3-mm) thick. Set the cut-out pieces inside the craters. Trim the sides of the cakes to make them even (see Note).

9. Ice the top and sides of the cakes with just enough buttercream to cover.

10. Lightly mark the top of the cakes in quarters to identify the center. If necessary, stir the reserved 4 ounces (115 g) buttercream to make it smooth. Place in a pastry bag with a No. 3 (6-mm) plain tip. Starting in the center of 1 cake (where the lines cross), pipe a spiral of buttercream; make it 5 inches (12.5 cm) in diameter, with each ring of buttercream touching the previous one. (You can first mark the tops with a 5-inch/12.5-cm cookie cutter if you are not sure where to stop, or just count 7 to 8 rings of buttercream.)

11. Cover the sides of each cake as well as the undecorated portion of the tops with crushed almonds (see Figure 1-1, page 18). Refrigerate the cakes until the buttercream is set, approximately 1 hour.

12. Cut the cakes into the desired number of serving pieces. Use a small skewer to make an indentation in the center of the almond-covered portion of each slice; insert a chocolate figurine in each.

13. Make the template on page 188 and attach it to a paper plate or a disposable pie tin that fits within the base of your serving plates (see page 692 for more information). Position the template over the base of each dessert plate and sift coffee powder over the top. Decorate as many plates as you expect to need.

14. Place the mango coulis in a piping bottle.

15. Presentation: Place a slice of cake on one of the prepared plates, positioning it diagonally on the coffee powder lines. Pipe 5 or 6 dots of mango coulis, each about ½ inch (1.2 cm) in diameter, on the exposed portion of the plate.

NOTE: It is impossible to press the top part of the cakes into the bottom without deforming and possibly even cracking the sides of the cakes. Consequently, the finished cakes will probably be closer to 9½ inches (23.7 cm) than 10 inches (25 cm) in diameter.

CLASSIC MOCHA CAKE yield: 1 cake, 10 inches (25 cm) in diameter

To make the classic version of mocha cake, cut a 10-inch (25-cm) vanilla sponge into 3 or 4 layers. Follow the directions given in the main recipe to assemble the cake through Step 3. Use all of the sponge layers. Ice the top and sides of the cake in the conventional fashion. Cover the sides with toasted sliced almonds. Chill the cake to set the buttercream before cutting it into the desired number of pieces. Place the reserved buttercream in a pastry bag with a No. 7 (14-mm) star tip. Pipe a rosette of buttercream at the end of each slice and decorate each with a chocolate figurine. Sprinkle ground coffee lightly over the center of the cake within the rosettes.

Opera Cake yield: 2 cakes, 8 inches (20 cm) square (Color Photos 46 and 47)

This classic French cake, which is just as often made into individual pastries (see Opera Slices, page 106), is comparable to a simplified version of Marjolaine. Both combine the well-loved flavor combination of chocolate, coffee, and almonds. Color Photo 46 shows Opera Cake dressed up with bubble-wrap chocolate decorations as well as sheets of chocolate imprinted with musical notes (using transfer sheets) to reflect the opera motif. It also features the more conventional embellishments of gold leaf and artistically arranged fresh fruit. All of these are optional for the presentation. The traditional finish calls for covering the top of the cake with chocolate glaze, leaving the sides exposed to show off the multiple layers. Lacy filigree designs are piped over the glaze as well as the word *Opera*.

Opera Sponge (recipe follows)

4 ounces (115 g) dark coating chocolate, melted

Coffee Syrup for Opera Cake (recipe follows)

1 pound 8 ounces (680 g) Ganache (page 770)

1 pound 12 ounces (795 g) Vanilla Buttercream (Swiss Method; page 753)

1 tablespoon (15 ml) mocha extract *or* 3 tablespoons (45 ml) Coffee Reduction (page 754)

12 ounces (340 g) marzipan, untinted

½ recipe Opera Glaze (recipe follows)

Chocolate transfers (optional)

Chocolate decorations (optional)

Fresh fruit (optional)

Powdered sugar

1. Remove the baking paper from the sponge sheets. Rub the skin from the top of the sponge layers and remove if it comes away easily. Cut each sheet across into 3 equal pieces, 8 × 9 inches (20 × 25 cm) each.

2. Invert 2 of the sponge rectangles and brush a thin layer of melted chocolate over the bottom sides. Allow the chocolate to set up, then place the pieces, chocolate-side down, on corrugated cardboard cake sheets for support.

3. Brush coffee syrup over the sponge layers on the cardboard sheets. Soften the ganache if needed, divide it between the cakes, and spread it evenly. Top each cake with a second sponge layer, pressing lightly to make certain the sponges adhere to the ganache. Brush coffee syrup over the sponge layers.

4. Flavor the buttercream with the mocha extract or coffee reduction. Set aside a small amount (approximately 4 ounces/115 g) and divide the remainder between the cakes. Spread the buttercream to make an even layer on each cake. Place the remaining sponge pieces on top of the buttercream on each cake, again pressing lightly to be certain they are secure. Brush coffee syrup over the tops of the sponges. Spread a thin layer of the reserved buttercream on top.

5. Roll out half of the marzipan to approximately ⅛ inch (3 mm) thick and slightly larger than the cakes. Place the marzipan sheet on top of 1 cake. Place a piece of baking paper on top, then place an inverted sheet pan or a sheet of cardboard on the paper. Invert the cake so that the marzipan layer is on the bottom against the paper. Leave it upside down.

6. Repeat Step 5 with the remaining marzipan and the second cake. Place both cakes in the refrigerator until they are thoroughly chilled.

7. Remove the cakes from the refrigerator and turn them right-side up. Adjust the viscosity of the opera glaze as necessary. Working on 1 cake at a time, pour enough of the glaze onto the marzipan to allow you to spread it in a thin layer covering the marzipan; do not glaze the sides. Refrigerate the cakes until the glaze is firm.

8. Using a sharp knife dipped into hot water and held at a 90-degree angle, carefully trim the sides of each cake, removing the excess marzipan as well as a thin layer of the cake itself, to make the cakes approximately 8 inches (20 cm) square. Reserve the scraps for another use, such as rum balls.

9. Decorate the sides of the cakes with chocolate transfers as shown in the color photos, if desired, or leave the sides uncovered to display the layers. Decorate the top of the cakes with chocolate decorations and/or fresh fruit. Sift powdered sugar lightly over the tops.

OPERA SPONGE yield: 2 sheets, 10 × 24 inches (25 × 60 cm) each

10 ounces (285 g) unsalted butter, at room temperature	10 egg whites (1¼ cups/300 ml), at room temperature
10 ounces (285 g) granulated sugar	6 ounces (170 g) cake flour, sifted
10 egg yolks (⅞ cup/210 ml), at room temperature	4 ounces (115 g) finely ground almonds (almond meal)
1 teaspoon (5 ml) vanilla extract	

CHEF'S TIP
To make ½ recipe, or one Opera Cake, spread the batter evenly over a half-sheet pan (12 × 16 inches/ 30 × 40 cm) lined with baking paper and bake as directed. Cut two 8-inch (20-cm) squares from one side, then cut the remaining 4- × 16-inch (10- × 40-cm) strip in half across; use those 2 pieces as the center layer when assembling the cake.

1. Measure and draw a line lengthwise 9 inches (22.5 cm) away from and parallel to a long side on each of 2 sheets of baking paper measuring 24 × 16 inches (60 × 40 cm). Invert the papers onto sheet pans and set aside.

2. Cream the butter with half of the sugar to a light, fluffy consistency. Beat in the egg yolks, a few at a time, together with vanilla extract.

3. Whip the egg whites until foamy. Gradually add the remaining sugar and whip until soft peaks have formed. Carefully fold the whipped egg whites into the yolk mixture.

4. Combine the cake flour with the ground almonds. Gently fold the flour and almond mixture into the egg mixture.

5. Divide the batter evenly between the prepared sheet pans, spreading it within the marked area on each to make sheets measuring 9 × 24 inches (22.5 × 60 cm).

6. Bake at 425°F (219°) for about 10 minutes or until baked through. Let cool.

COCOA OPERA SPONGE

To make a cocoa-flavored sponge, replace 1 ounce (30 g) of the cake flour with 1½ ounces (40 g) unsweetened cocoa powder, sifted with the remaining flour. Add in Step 4.

COFFEE SYRUP FOR OPERA CAKE

yield: 1½ cups (360 ml), enough for 2 cakes, 8 inches (20 cm) square

¾ cup (180 ml) strong brewed coffee

¾ cup (180 ml) simple syrup

2 tablespoons (30 ml) coffee-flavored liqueur

1. Combine all the ingredients.

2. Use as directed in the Opera Cake recipe.

OPERA GLAZE yield: 1¾ cups (420 ml)

8 ounces (225 g) sweet dark chocolate, chopped

5 ounces (140 g) unsalted butter, at room temperature

3 ounces (85 g) or ¼ cup (60 ml) light corn syrup

4 teaspoons (20 ml) coffee-flavored liqueur

1. Melt the chocolate over a bain-marie. Add the butter, stirring until fully incorporated.

2. Remove from the heat and stir in the corn syrup and the liqueur.

3. Cool, stirring occasionally, until the glaze has thickened slightly before using it on the cakes.

Parisienne Chocolate Cake yield: 2 cakes, 10 inches (25 cm) in diameter

An exceptionally light, delicious chocolate and nut combination, this cake is inexpensive and quick to produce, but it does require advance planning because the Crème Parisienne should be made one day ahead in order to whip properly (or, in a pinch, it should chill at least 6 hours before whipping). Failing this, substitute Chocolate Cream (page 766). Double the recipe and heed the caution about overwhipping the cream.

The same consideration applies, to a lesser degree, when working with the Crème Parisienne. You must take into account that, as you spread the cream back and forth while icing the cakes, the friction continues the whipping process (the same phenomenon occurs as you force whipped cream through the small tip of a pastry bag). If the cream is whipped too far initially, a smooth, attractive finish will be impossible to achieve.

¾ cup (180 ml) light rum

¼ cup (60 ml) simple syrup

1 recipe Crème Parisienne (page 768)

2 Hazelnut-Chocolate Sponges (page 800), 10 inches (25 cm) in diameter

Shaved dark chocolate

¼ cup (60 ml) Frangelico liqueur

1 recipe Mousseline Sauce (page 338)

Chocolate Sauce for Piping (page 681)

Chocolate Cigarettes (page 516)

Fresh fruit

1. Combine the rum and the simple syrup.

2. Whip the Crème Parisienne to stiff peaks.

3. Trim the skin from the top of the sponges and level them, if necessary. Slice each sponge into 3 layers. Brush the bottom layers with one-third of the syrup mixture. Spread a layer of Crème Parisienne, ¼ inch (6 mm) thick, on top. Place the second layers on the cream. Repeat the procedure, adding more syrup, filling, and the remaining sponge layers. Brush the remaining rum syrup on the top of the cakes. Ice the tops and sides of the cakes with a thin layer of Crème Parisienne. Place the cakes on cardboard cake rounds for support.

4. Place approximately half of the remaining cream in a pastry bag with a No. 6 (12-mm) flat star tip. Pipe vertical strips of buttercream on the sides of the cakes, each next to the other, working from the bottom to the top. Smooth the top edge of each cake with a spatula.

5. Place the remainder of the Crème Parisienne in a second pastry bag with a No. 4 (8-mm) plain tip (unfortunately, you cannot put a round tip on the outside of a flat one, as would otherwise be the sensible thing to do). Pipe lines, ½ inch (1.2 cm) apart, on the tops of the cakes, first in one direction, then at a 45-degree angle, to create a diamond pattern.

6. Cut the cakes into the desired number of servings. Sprinkle shaved chocolate lightly over the tops of the cakes and place in the refrigerator until needed. Combine the Frangelico liqueur and the mousseline sauce. Place a portion of the sauce in a piping bottle and reserve it as well as the remaining sauce in the refrigerator.

7. Presentation: Place a slice of cake in the center of a dessert plate. Pipe a pool of mousseline sauce at the tip of the slice so it runs evenly on both sides. Decorate the sauce with chocolate sauce for piping (see pages 682 to 685). Lean a chocolate cigarette against the slice and place a piece of seasonal fruit on the side.

Queen of Sheba Cake yield: 2 cakes, 10 inches (25 cm) in diameter

There are countless variations of this classic French chocolate cake, but you would be hard put to find *Reine de Saba* in a French pastry shop or on a restaurant menu; this is a dressed-up version of what is typically more of a homemaker's specialty in France and other parts of Europe. The flavor of the Queen of Sheba cake base — a combination of chocolate and ground hazelnuts — is similar to the famous Sacher torte. The decoration used here, however, is more elaborate.

4 ounces (115 g) Short Dough (page 791)

Dark coating chocolate, melted

Queen of Sheba Cake Base (recipe follows)

½ cup (120 ml) orange juice

3 tablespoons (45 ml) orange liqueur

2 pounds (910 g) Ganache (page 770)

14 ounces (400 g) Vanilla Buttercream (Swiss Method; page 753)

Powdered sugar

10 ounces (285 g) marzipan, untinted

Hazelnuts, toasted and crushed

1. Roll out the short dough to ⅛ inch (3 mm) thick. Using a fluted cookie cutter 1 inch (2.5 cm) in diameter, cut out 2 to 3 dozen cookies — one for each serving of cake. Place the cookies on a sheet pan lined with baking paper. Using a No. 2 (4-mm) plain pastry tip, cut 3 holes, evenly spaced, in the center of each cookie.

2. Bake the cookies at 375°F (190°C) until golden brown, about 10 minutes. Let the cookies cool, then place them next to each other and streak melted coating chocolate over the tops, applying the chocolate in just one direction.

3. Trim the skin from each cake base, leveling the tops at the same time. Slice each cake into 2 layers. Combine the orange juice with the orange liqueur. Brush some of the mixture over the bottom cake layers.

4. Reserve 10 ounces (285 g) of the ganache and mix the remainder with the buttercream. Spread a layer of the ganache mixture on the bottom cake layers, making it ¼ inch (6 mm) thick. Invert the remaining cake layers and place 1 on top of each ganache layer. Brush the remainder of the orange juice mixture over the top cake layers. Ice the top and sides of the cakes with the ganache mixture, using just enough to cover the sponge. Reserve the remainder for decorating.

5. Using powdered sugar to prevent it from sticking, roll out half of the marzipan to a circle ¹⁄₁₆ inch (2 mm) thick and slightly larger than 10 inches (25 cm) in diameter. Place the marzipan on a cardboard cake circle, 12 inches (30 cm) in diameter or any size slightly larger than the cakes. Leaving the marzipan in place on the cardboard, use a guide 10 inches (25 cm) in diameter to cut out a circle the same size as the tops of the cakes. Carefully slide the marzipan circle onto the top of one of the cakes (see Figure 1-9, page 53). Place the cardboard circle on top of the cake and invert the cake. Press down firmly to even the top of the cake. Repeat the entire procedure to make a marzipan circle for the second cake.

6. Warm the reserved ganache until it is liquid. Turn the cakes right-side up and spread ganache on top of the marzipan in a layer just thick enough to cover. Let the ganache sit for a few minutes to set, then use the back of a chef's knife to mark a diamond pattern by making parallel marks every ½ inch (1.2 cm); turn the cakes a quarter-turn and repeat. Cover the sides of the cakes with crushed hazelnuts (see Figure 1-1, page 18). Refrigerate the cakes until the ganache and buttercream are firm.

7. Mark or cut the cakes into the desired number of serving pieces. Place the remaining ganache and buttercream mixture in a pastry bag with a No. 6 (12-mm) plain tip. Pipe a small mound, the size of a cherry, at the edge of each slice. Place one of the cookies at an angle on each mound. This cake should be cut when it is well chilled, but it tastes better at room temperature.

QUEEN OF SHEBA CAKE BASE yield: 2 cake layers, 10 inches (25 cm) in diameter

1 pound (455 g) sweet dark chocolate	12 eggs, separated and at room temperature
½ cup (120 ml) dark rum	8 ounces (225 g) almond paste
1 pound (455 g) unsalted butter, at room temperature	10 ounces (285 g) bread flour
1 pound (455 g) granulated sugar	7 ounces (200 g) hazelnuts, toasted and finely ground

1. Line the bottom of 2 cake pans, 10 inches (25 cm) in diameter, with baking paper (or use pan spray, but do not spray the sides).

2. Melt the chocolate. Stir in the rum and set aside, but keep warm.

3. Beat the butter with 8 ounces (225 g) sugar until light and fluffy.

4. Gradually mix the egg yolks into the almond paste. Mix them in a few at a time or you will get lumps. Stir the yolk mixture into the butter mixture. Add the melted chocolate rapidly and mix until completely incorporated.

5. Whip the egg whites to a foam. Gradually add the remaining 8 ounces (225 g) sugar and whip to stiff peaks. Carefully fold the egg whites into the chocolate mixture in 3 portions.

6. Sift the flour and mix with the nuts. Fold into the batter. Divide the batter equally between the prepared pans.

7. Bake at 350°F (175°C) for about 50 minutes, making sure the cakes are baked through. Let the cakes cool completely. Cut around the sides with a thin knife and unmold.

Raspberry Cake yield: 2 cakes, 10 inches (25 cm) in diameter

I use this gorgeous cake primarily as a buffet item, as the flower design of the marzipan looks so impressive presented whole. To serve Raspberry Cake as a plated dessert, use the presentation suggested for Lemon Chiffon Cake (page 42). Raspberry Cake tastes good with a number of fruit sauces; raspberry and lemon sauces together are an especially nice combination.

You will find several other cakes in this text that start with a thin short dough or meringue layer on the bottom; this is a traditional European method. The contrast between the crisp, dry base and the soft sponge and cream filling is pleasing to the palate. A classic example is the famous Swiss specialty, Zuger Kirsch Torte.

2 Chiffon Sponge Cake I (page 797), 10 inches (25 cm) in diameter	8 ounces (225 g) Vanilla Buttercream (Swiss Method; page 753)
2 Short Dough Cake Bottoms (page 792), 10 inches (25 cm) in diameter	5 ounces (140 g) sliced almonds, toasted and lightly crushed
4 ounces (115 g) raspberry jam	8 ounces (225 g) marzipan, untinted
½ cup (120 ml) Plain Cake Syrup (page 789)	Powdered sugar
Raspberry Cream (recipe follows)	Shaved dark chocolate
2 pints (960 ml) raspberries	Raspberries

1. Trim the tops of the sponge cakes to level them, then slice each cake into 2 layers.

2. Place the short dough cake bottoms on cardboard cake rounds for support. Divide the jam between them and spread evenly to cover the short dough. Place 1 layer of sponge cake on each jam-covered base. Brush cake syrup over the layers. Place stainless steel cake rings around the cakes, setting them on top of the short dough. If cake rings are not available, secure strips of acetate or polyurethane around the cakes.

3. Pour one-quarter of the raspberry cream on each cake. Spread it evenly within the rings.

4. Arrange whole raspberries, stem-side down, over the cream in 3 evenly spaced concentric circles. Start the first circle about ½ inch (1.2 cm) from the cake ring. Use both hands to put the berries on the cakes quickly, before the remaining cream sets up.

5. Divide the remaining cream filling between the cakes, pouring it over the raspberries; spread out evenly. Place the remaining cake layers on top of the cream and press down lightly to make the tops level. Brush the remaining cake syrup over the top cake layers. Refrigerate the cakes until the filling is set, about 2 hours.

About Raspberries

Wild raspberries were discovered in Greece as early as the first century A.D., at which time they were especially plentiful on the island of Crete. Today, of course, the fruit is cultivated all over the world, but wild raspberries are still found in Greece and other parts of Europe, as well as within the United States. Because of their uniform petite size and bright red color, raspberries are popular for decorating and garnishing cakes, pastries, and tarts. Raspberry sauce, or coulis, is used extensively in the pastry kitchen, and raspberries are also used in fruit salads, ice creams, and sorbets. Fresh raspberries, previously available during the summer only, are now obtainable year-round due to imports from New Zealand and Chile. The price, of course, is higher when the fruit is imported. Frozen raspberries can be used with good result to make sauce and sorbet. Refrigerate raspberries in a single layer to prevent them from becoming moldy.

6. Remove the rings or plastic strips. Trim away any short dough that protrudes outside of the cake layers to make the sides even (see Figure 1-7, page 32). Spread a thin layer of buttercream over the top and sides of each cake. Cover the sides of the cakes with crushed almonds, gently pushing them into the buttercream (see Figure 1-1, page 18).

7. Roll out the marzipan to $\frac{1}{16}$ inch (2 mm) thick, using just enough powdered sugar to prevent it from sticking. Make sure there is no powdered sugar underneath when you finish, as part of the bottom side will be visible in the final presentation. Texture the marzipan with a waffle rolling pin.

8. Cut out 2 circles of marzipan the same size as the tops of the cakes. Place the marzipan circles on cardboard rounds and cut circles 3 inches (7.5 cm) in diameter from the centers. Reserve the centers for another use.

9. Mark the marzipan rings into the desired number of slices for each cake. Cut through the marks from the center of the rings, stopping 1 inch (2.5 cm) from the edge so the pieces remain attached at the outside edge of the rings. Roll back the cut edge of each marzipan wedge toward the outside of the rings.

10. Carefully slide the rings onto the tops of the cakes (Figure 1-9). Cut between the rolled marzipan pieces to divide the cakes into serving pieces. Cover the exposed centers of the cakes with shaved chocolate. Place the remaining buttercream in a pastry bag with a No. 6 (12-mm) plain tip. Pipe a small mound of buttercream on the flat portion of marzipan at the edge of each piece. Top each mound with a whole raspberry.

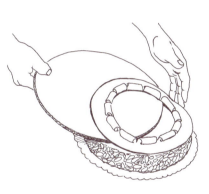

FIGURE 1-9 Siding the marzipan ring into place on top of the Raspberry Cake

VARIATION

RASPBERRY CAKE NOUVELLE yield: 2 cakes, 10 inches (25 cm) in diameter (Color Photo 4)

You can give the cakes a contemporary air by using ribbon sponge sheets on the sides and leaving out the short dough bases, as shown in Color Photo 4. If you have a partial ribbon sheet left over from another project, this is even easier. One sheet is enough to cover the sides of approximately six cakes, so if you make a sheet specifically for this recipe, you will have quite a bit left. You can use the extra for the variations of Apricot Cream Cake (page 13), Chocolate Mousse Cake with Banana (page 30), or Lemon Chiffon Cake (page 44).

To make this variation, omit the short dough cake bottoms, raspberry jam, and the toasted almonds from the ingredient list. Place the stainless steel cake rings around the cakes directly on top of cardboard cake circles for support instead of the short dough bases in Step 2 (or make 10-inch/25-cm collars from strips of acetate or polyurethane). Cut strips lengthwise from the ribbon sponge, 2 inches (5 cm) wide. Place the sponge strips inside the rings or collars with the striped side facing out. Trim the sponge cake layers so they fit snugly inside the rings. Place one layer of sponge inside each ring and continue as directed, cutting the top sponge layers thin enough so they fit just below the top edge of the ribbon sponge. Do not ice the sides of the cakes in Step 6.

RASPBERRY CREAM yield: 3 pounds (1 kg 365 g)

Do not make the filling until you are ready to use it in the cakes.

5 teaspoons (15 g) unflavored gelatin powder	3 ounces (85 g) granulated sugar
½ cup (120 ml) cold water	½ cup (120 ml) dry white wine
3 cups (720 ml) heavy cream	¼ cup (60 ml) raspberry liqueur
3 egg yolks (¼ cup/60 ml)	½ cup (120 ml) strained raspberry puree
2 whole eggs	

1. Sprinkle the gelatin over the cold water and set aside to soften.

2. Whip the cream to soft peaks. Cover and reserve in the refrigerator.

3. Whip the egg yolks, whole eggs, and sugar until just combined. Add the wine and raspberry liqueur and whip over simmering water until the mixture reaches 140°F (60°C). Remove from the heat and continue whipping until the mixture has cooled and has a light, fluffy consistency, about 15 minutes.

4. Fold the yolk mixture into the reserved whipped cream. Stir in the raspberry puree.

5. Place the gelatin mixture over a bain-marie and heat until dissolved. Do not overheat. Quickly add the gelatin to a small portion of the cream mixture. Then, still working quickly, stir this mixture into the remaining cream.

VARIATION

BLACKBERRY CAKE yield: 2 cakes, 10 inches (25 cm) in diameter

Substitute whole blackberries for the raspberries inside the cakes and in the decoration. In the cream filling, substitute ½ cup (120 ml) heavy cream for the raspberry puree and Chambord liqueur for the raspberry liqueur. Pureed blackberries are not used in the filling because they create an unappetizing grey color when combined with the remaining ingredients.

Sicilian Macaroon Cake yield: 2 cakes, 10 inches (25 cm) in diameter

The prospect of making short dough, meringue, and sponge layers might give you second thoughts about the practicality of this cake. True, plenty of slice-and-fill cakes can be prepared in less than half the time, but if you are looking for something special, Sicilian Macaroon Cake is both unusual and delicious.

½ recipe Japonaise Meringue Batter (page 781)

1 tablespoon (5 g) ground cinnamon

½ recipe Almond Sponge batter (page 795; see Step 2)

Dark coating chocolate, melted

2 Cocoa Short Dough Cake Bottoms (page 792), 10 inches (25 cm) in diameter

4 ounces (115 g) red currant jelly

Macaroon-Maraschino Whipped Cream

(recipe follows)

¼ cup (60 ml) orange juice

2 tablespoons (30 ml) maraschino liqueur

Small Almond Macaroons (recipe follows)

2 cups (480 ml) heavy cream

1 tablespoon (15 g) granulated sugar

5 ounces (140 g) sliced almonds, toasted and lightly crushed

Shaved dark chocolate

1. Draw 2 circles, 10 inches (25 cm) in diameter, on baking paper and invert the paper on a sheet pan. Place the Japonaise meringue batter in a pastry bag with a No. 4 (8-mm) plain tip. Pipe the batter in a spiral within each of the circles as described in the Meringue Noisette recipe (see Figure 14-2, page 782). Bake at 300°F (149°C) until the meringue is dry, about 45 minutes.

2. Line the bottom of a cake pan, 10 inches (25 cm) in diameter, with baking paper (or grease and flour the bottom, but not the sides). Sift the ground cinnamon with the flour when you make the sponge batter. Pour the batter into the pan. Bake at 400°F (205°C) for about 15 minutes or until done.

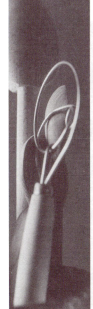

How Sicilian Cake Got Its Name

Now what does Sicily have to do with this cake? you may wonder. After all, the majority of Italian almonds are grown in the north, especially in the Piedmont-Lombardy region, which is famous for its almonds, amaretti cookies, and the well-known almond liqueur *Amaretto di Saronno*. Nor is maraschino liqueur Sicilian; its main ingredient, the marasca cherry, is grown primarily in the Trieste area, in the northeast corner of Italy. How this cake came to be called Sicilian goes way back in history. Sicily has, at one time or another, hosted every great civilization of the Mediterranean region; the Romans, Arabs, Greeks, Vikings, and, more recently, the Spanish and French have all laid claim to it at one time or another. In fact, this beautiful and much sought-after island has belonged to Italy for a little more than a century. All of these cultures contributed to what are now considered indigenous Sicilian foods. When the Romans took charge in the early sixth century, they introduced wheat and other grains. The fertile soil in the valleys gave Sicily the nickname "Grain Bowl of the Roman Empire." When the Arabs conquered the island in the ninth century, they introduced rice, planted citrus trees and date palms, and, much more importantly, brought with them their spices — saffron, cloves, and cinnamon — which were important to trade at the time and helped make Sicilian seaports, such as Palermo and Catania, notable trade centers. Then, in the tenth century, the Greeks planted olive trees and grapevines, but it is the gift of Arabian spices that provides the surprising answer: The cinnamon-flavored sponge is what gives this cake its Sicilian title.

About Cinnamon

Cinnamon was once a commodity of great value and, together with two other important spices — nutmeg and clove — was the reason for much human bloodshed over time. The spice made its way to Europe over the ancient and dangerous spice route. Beginning in the ninth century, the Arabs kept their source of Ceylon cinnamon a highly guarded secret for many hundreds of years. They tried to discourage competitors from finding alternate sources by telling other traders, such as the Dutch and Portugese, stories of monsters inhabiting the countries that the Arabs suspected might contain the spice. That cinnamon grows wild throughout Ceylon was not known elsewhere before the fourteenth century.

The most widely used cinnamon today is the *Cinnamomum cassia* variety that originated in Burma. The other type, *Cinnamomum zeylanicum,* is native to Ceylon, now Sri Lanka. Both types are derived from the bark of an evergreen laurel tree. Because of a then poorly prepared Chinese product, cassia was once known as an inferior imitation of *Cinnamomum zeylanicum,* but today you would be hard put to tell the difference between the two in ground form. Ceylon cinnamon has a slightly milder aroma than cassia and is lighter in color; the quills (the curled strips of bark) are thinner and have a smoother, round appearance.

Preparation and marketing of both kinds is simple: Thin shoots or young branches are cut when the bark is easy to separate from the wood. The shoots are trimmed to about 4 inches (10 cm) long. A slit is cut on two sides of the bark, and the piece is carefully separated into two long strips; these are immediately placed back on the stick so they retain their shape. The pieces are then set aside for about six hours to let the bark ferment. In the next step, the thin outer skin is scraped off to expose the inner bark, which is the part we call *cinnamon*. The strips are dried for a short time, then formed into quills, which, as they dry and contract, tighten into hard sticks. Cinnamon sticks keep indefinitely in a dry place.

The flavor of cinnamon makes a wonderful addition to many types of desserts and, because of the natural affinity of the two flavors, especially fruit desserts containing apple. Warm apple desserts, such as apple pie, turnovers, crisp, and apples *en croûte* are particularly pleasing with an accompaniment of cinnamon-flavored custard sauce or cinnamon ice cream. Cinnamon is used in many cookie recipes, spice cakes, and poaching syrups. Cinnamon sugar is widely used to top breakfast and Danish pastries.

3. Brush melted coating chocolate on 1 side of the Japonaise layers. Place the short dough bottoms on cardboard cake rounds for support. Divide the red currant jelly between the short dough bottoms and spread it evenly. Place the Japonaise layers on top, chocolate side up.

4. Put stainless steel cake rings, 10 inches (25 cm) in diameter, on top of the Japonaise and press lightly to seal. If you must use rings that are not stainless steel, line the inside with baking paper, acetate, or polyurethane strips to prevent the metal from staining the filling. As soon as the macaroon-maraschino whipped cream filling begins to thicken, divide it equally between the cakes.

5. Trim the top of the sponge to make it even, then cut it into 2 layers. Place the layers on top of the cream on each cake. Combine the orange juice and maraschino liqueur; brush the mixture over the sponge layers to moisten. Refrigerate the cakes until the cream is set, about 2 hours.

6. While the cakes are chilling, dip the macaroons halfway in melted dark coating chocolate.

7. Remove the cake rings and the paper or plastic strips. Trim the sides of the cakes so that the short dough and Japonaise are even with the filling (see Figure 1-7, page 32). Whip the heavy cream and sugar to stiff peaks. Ice the top and sides of the cakes with a thin layer of the cream, saving some for decoration.

8. Cover the sides of the cakes with the crushed almonds (see Figure 1-1, page 18). Place a plain cookie cutter, 6 inches (15 cm) in diameter, in the center of each cake. Sprinkle chocolate shavings inside the cutters, using just enough to cover the cream. Mark or cut the cakes into the desired number of servings.

9. Place the remaining whipped cream in a pastry bag with a No. 5 (10-mm) plain tip. Pipe a small mound of cream at the edge of each slice. Place a macaroon on each whipped cream mound.

SMALL ALMOND MACAROONS yield: about 100 cookies, 1 inch (2.5 cm) in diameter

Macaroons are a cross between a cookie and a confection. They can be served as is or dipped part-way in melted coating chocolate.

2 pounds (910 g) almond paste

1 pound (455 g) granulated sugar

6 to 8 egg whites (¾ to 1 cup/180 to 240 ml)

1. Place the almond paste and sugar in a mixer bowl. Using the paddle at low speed, blend in 1 egg white at a time, being careful not to get any lumps in the batter. Add as many egg whites as the batter will absorb without becoming runny; the number will vary depending on the firmness of the almond paste and, to some degree, the size of the egg whites. Beat for a few minutes at high speed to a creamy consistency.

2. Place the batter in a pastry bag with a No. 6 (12-mm) plain tip. Pipe the batter into mounds, just slightly smaller than 1 inch (2.5 cm) in diameter, onto sheet pans lined with baking paper or Silpats. The cookies will bake out slightly, so do not pipe them too close together.

3. Bake the cookies, double-panned, at 410°F (210°C) for about 8 minutes or until light brown.

4. Let the macaroons cool attached to the baking paper. To remove them from the paper, turn them upside down and peel the paper away from the cookies rather than the cookies off the paper (Figure 1-10). If they are difficult to remove, brush water on the back of the paper, turn right-side up, and wait a few minutes, then try again. For long-term storage, place the cookies in the freezer still attached to the baking paper.

FIGURE 1-10 **Peeling the baking paper away from the baked almond macaroon cookies with the cookies turned upside down**

MACAROON-MARASCHINO WHIPPED CREAM yield: 3 pounds 12 ounces (1 kg 705 g)

This is a good opportunity to use up leftover or dry macaroons. If you make macaroons fresh just for this cake, bake the macaroons for the filling at a lower temperature until they are dried all the way through to prevent them from falling apart when they are mixed with the cream.

10 ounces (285 g) dry Small Almond
    Macaroons (preceding recipe)

½ cup (120 ml) maraschino liqueur

2½ tablespoons (23 g) unflavored gelatin
    powder

½ cup (120 ml) cold water

1 quart (960 ml) heavy cream

6 egg yolks (½ cup/120 ml)

3 ounces (85 g) granulated sugar

⅓ cup (80 ml) milk

1. Cut the macaroons in half. Place in a bowl and add the maraschino liqueur, tossing the pieces to coat evenly. Set aside.

2. Sprinkle the gelatin over the cold water and set aside to soften.

3. Whip the heavy cream to soft peaks. Cover and reserve in the refrigerator.

4. Whip the egg yolks and sugar just to combine. Add the milk, set the bowl over a bain-marie, and continue to whip until the mixture reaches 140°F (60°C) and is light and fluffy. Remove from the heat and whip until the mixture has cooled completely. Fold into the reserved whipped cream.

5. Place the gelatin mixture over a bain-marie and heat to dissolve. Rapidly add the gelatin to a small portion of the cream. Still working quickly, add this mixture to the remaining cream. Fold in the soaked macaroon pieces.

Strawberry Bagatelle yield: 2 cakes, 8 inches (20 cm) square

Bagatelle *aux fraises* is a classic French cake that is always made in a square shape. It is composed of two sponge cake layers filled with a thick layer of Diplomat cream (or Bavarian cream) and strawberries cut in half lengthwise and arranged so that their cut sides are visible at the circumference of the finished cake. The sides of the cake are left unadorned to expose the strawberry layer. The bagatelle is topped with pale green marzipan and traditionally decorated with a twisted rope of green and pink marzipan. *Fraise* is the French word for "strawberry," and this cake is also known as *Fraisier* and *Le Fraisier* as well as simply *Bagatelle*.

½ recipe Almond Sponge Batter (page 795)

½ cup Plain Cake Syrup (page 789)

2 pounds (910 g) medium-size ripe
    strawberries, washed and hulled

Vanilla Bean–Lemon Verbena Bavarian
    Cream (recipe follows)

6 ounces (170 g) Vanilla Buttercream (Swiss
    Method; page 753)

1 pound (455 g) marzipan, tinted pale green

Powdered sugar

4 ounces (115 g) marzipan, tinted pale pink

1. Immediately after making the sponge batter, spread it into a rectangle measuring 14 × 24 inches (35 × 60 cm) on a sheet pan lined with baking paper. Bake at 400°F (205°C) just until baked through, about 10 minutes. Allow the sponge to cool.

Making Your Own Cake Frames

If necessary, prepare 2 frames, 8 inches (20 cm) square, as follows: Cut 4 strips of thick corrugated card-board, each 2 inches wide and 16 inches long (5 × 40 cm). Score the center of each piece crosswise (cut it halfway through). Bend the pieces at a 90-degree angle and place 2 pieces on each of 2 cake circles, 12 inches (30 cm) in diameter, to form a square on each. Tape the corners of the squares together and tape the outside edges of the squares to the cardboard circles to attach them and to prevent the filling from running out when the cakes are assembled. Line the sides inside the frames with strips of baking paper or acetate.

2. Line 2 cake frames, 8 inches (20 cm) square, with strips of baking paper or acetate. If you do not have frames of this size, follow the instructions for "Making Your Own Cake Frames" above.

3. Trim 1 long and 1 short edge of the baked sponge sheet to make the edges even. Starting where the trimmed edges meet, cut out 2 squares, 8 inches (20 cm) each. Cover the squares and set aside to use as the tops of the cakes. Use the remaining sponge to cover the bottom of the cake frames by cutting and fitting the pieces together. Be sure the sponges fit snugly against the sides of the frames. Brush cake syrup over the sponges, cover, and set aside.

4. Select approximately 36 of the best-looking, most evenly sized strawberries. Ideally, none of the berries should be more than 1 inch (2.5 cm) tall. If necessary, trim the bottom (wide end) of any strawberries that are too large, cutting evenly so they will stand straight. Choose 4 of the roundest (fattest) strawberries and cut these into quarters lengthwise. Slice the remaining select-ed berries in half lengthwise. Slice the leftover strawberries in half lengthwise as well and reserve each group separately.

5. Make the Bavarian cream and immediately (it should be quite liquid) pour ¾ cup (180 ml) over the sponge base in each cake frame. The Bavarian cream layer should be about ¼ inch (6 mm) thick. Place the cakes in the freezer for a few minutes to set the cream. Reserve the remain-ing Bavarian cream at room temperature.

6. As soon as the cream is firm, quickly arrange the strawberries on top of the filling as fol-lows. Begin by fitting the quartered berries into the corners of the frames, stem ends down. Next, arrange the nicer halved berries, evenly spaced, stem ends down, by firmly placing their cut sides flat against the sides of the frames (see Figure 1-11, page 62, as an example). You do not want any space where the cream filling can run between the flat sides of the berries and the frame. Still working quickly, distribute the remaining halved berries over the cream, flat side down. Pour the reserved Bavarian cream into the frames, dividing it evenly; the cream should com-pletely cover the strawberry layer. If the cream becomes too thick to pour, warm it very gently over a bain-marie, stirring constantly. Take care to deflate the minimum amount possible of the air that has been whipped in.

7. Place the reserved sponge cake squares on the cream layers and press down gently to make the tops of the cakes flat and even. Brush cake syrup over the sponge on each cake. Cover the cakes and refrigerate until the filling is set, at least 4 hours but no longer than 12 hours, or the strawberries will bleed and stain the filling.

8. Remove the cake frames, but leave the baking paper or acetate strips on the sides of the cakes to prevent the sponge from becoming dry. Spread a thin film of buttercream over the top of each cake.

9. Reserve 4 ounces (115 g) of the green marzipan. Using powdered sugar to keep it from sticking, roll out half of the remaining green marzipan to just over ⅛ inch (3 mm) thick and into a square just slightly larger than the top of the cakes. Turn the marzipan over and texture the top with a marzipan rolling pin. Invert the sheet, roll it up on a dowel, and unroll it over the top of one cake. Place a sheet of baking paper on top of the cake and cover with an inverted sheet pan. Invert the assembly so that the cake is upside down and the marzipan is against the baking paper. Refrigerate for a few minutes to set the buttercream, but no longer than 30 minutes or the marzipan may become sticky. Repeat to top the second cake with marzipan.

10. Leaving the cakes upside down, trim the marzipan evenly along each edge. Invert to set the cakes right side up.

11. Using powdered sugar to keep it from sticking, roll half of the remaining green marzipan into a thin rope 28 inches (70 cm) long, by rolling it against the table. Using half of the pink marzipan, make a second rope the same size as the first. Place the ropes next to one another and twist them together by placing one hand flat at each end and quickly moving your hands in opposite directions. Arrange the two-tone rope around the top edge of the cake (see Chef's Tip), trim the ends, and pinch the seam together to hide it. Repeat to make a rope for the second cake. Sift powdered sugar lightly over the tops of the cakes, remove the paper or plastic strips, and present immediately.

CHEF'S TIP
If the ropes do not stick to the tops of the cakes, use a small brush to lightly brush water along the top edges of the cakes to make the marzipan sticky.

NOTE: For a different look, omit making the marzipan ropes (you will need only 12 ounces/340 g green marzipan to cover the tops of the cakes). Use the pink marzipan to make 1 rose and 2 ribbons for each cake. Place the roses and ribbons on a marble slab and use a torch to lightly caramelize the edges. Place a rose in a far corner on each cake and arrange the ribbons in a curved line on either side of the roses so they fall toward the center of the cakes.

VANILLA BEAN–LEMON VERBENA BAVARIAN CREAM yield: 2 quarts (1 L 920 ml)

If fresh lemon verbena is not available, substitute dried, increasing the amount slightly. If neither is available or if you prefer not to use the herb, increase the vanilla to two beans. Cut the beans in half lengthwise, scrape out the seeds, and add both the seeds and the pod halves to the milk in Step 1. Scald the milk and allow the mixture to steep as directed. Omit Step 3. Remove and discard the vanilla bean pods in Step 5 before whisking the hot milk into the yolk mixture. With either version, do not make this filling until you are ready to use it, as it must be used immediately.

1 ounce (30 g) fresh lemon verbena leaves	2 cups (480 ml) heavy cream
2¾ cups (660 ml) whole milk	8 egg yolks (⅔ cup/160 ml)
2 tablespoons plus 2 teaspoons (24 g) unflavored gelatin powder	8 ounces (225 g) granulated sugar
1 vanilla bean	

1. Finely chop the verbena leaves. Pour 2 cups (480 ml) milk into a saucepan, add the verbena, and bring to scalding. Remove from the heat, cover, and set aside to steep for 30 minutes.

2. Sprinkle the gelatin powder over the remaining ¾ cup (180 ml) milk; let soften.

3. Strain the steeped milk and discard the verbena leaves. Cut the vanilla bean in half lengthwise and scrape out the seeds. Add the seeds to the verbena-flavored milk; reserve the pod halves for another use.

4. Whip the heavy cream until soft peaks form. Cover and reserve in the refrigerator.

5. Whip the egg yolks and sugar together until light and fluffy. Warm the infused milk to the scalding point. Gradually whisk the hot milk into the egg yolk mixture. Place over a bain-marie and heat, stirring constantly until the custard is thick enough to coat a spoon; do not boil. Remove from the heat.

6. Warm the milk and softened gelatin mixture to dissolve the gelatin. Stir this into the custard. Let cool until just slightly over body temperature, then quickly stir the custard into the reserved whipped cream.

Strawberry Kirsch Cake yield: 2 cakes, 10 inches (25 cm) in diameter

This cake signifies the arrival of spring in many European countries — or, I should say, it did in the past: This has changed in recent years because flying in fresh strawberries from the other side of the equator during the winter months has become less expensive. I suppose this is a change for the better, but it sure takes some of the romance out of many pastries. When I lived in Sweden, it used to be that we got the first fresh strawberries (usually from Italy) in April and then, as the spring oh-so-slowly made its way north, our Swedish strawberries were ready to pick at the end of June — just in time for the midsummer festivities. As soon as this cake was put into the display case, all the customers would change their mind from whatever they had come into the *konditori* to buy in the first place.

Some shops made the cakes in long strips (40 to 80 inches/1 to 2 meters) that were displayed whole in a showy fashion. These were then cut to order and priced by the centimeter. In this variation, the buttercream and almonds were omitted from the sides. You may want to leave them off the round cakes as well to save time and effort. If so, pay extra attention to the edges of the sponge when brushing or spraying the kirsch syrup. This cake should not be frozen because the strawberries will lose their texture and look unpleasant when thawed.

1 Chiffon Sponge Cake I (page 797), 10 inches (25 cm) in diameter

2 Short Dough Cake Bottoms (page 792), 10 inches (25 cm) in diameter

4 ounces (115 g) strawberry jam

⅓ cup (80 ml) simple syrup

¼ cup (60 ml) kirschwasser

2 pounds (910 g) medium-size strawberries, stems removed (about 50)

Kirsch Whipped Cream (recipe follows)

Vanilla Buttercream (Swiss Method; page 753)

5 ounces (140 g) sliced almonds, toasted and finely crushed

10 ounces (285 g) marzipan, untinted

Powdered sugar

Piping Chocolate (page 543), melted

Strawberry Sauce (page 186)

Sour Cream Mixture for Piping (page 727)

Small sprigs of mint

1. Trim the skin from the top of the sponge cake, leveling it at the same time. Slice the sponge into 4 thin layers.

2. Place the short dough cake bottoms on cardboard cake rounds for support. Divide the jam between them and spread evenly to cover. Place 1 sponge layer on the jam on each cake bottom. Combine the simple syrup with the kirschwasser. Brush or spray some of the mixture over the sponge layers to moisten. Place a stainless steel cake ring, 10 inches (25 cm) in diameter, snugly around each cake. If you must use rings that are not stainless steel, line them with strips of acetate, polyurethane, or baking paper to prevent the metal from discoloring the filling.

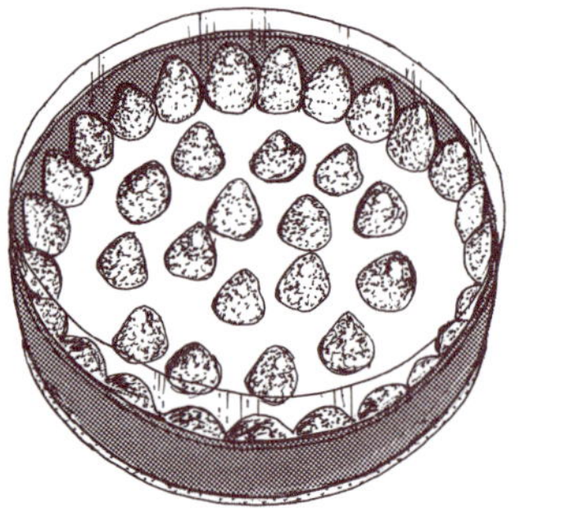

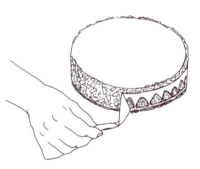

FIGURE 1-11 Strawberry halves placed on top of the sponge cake with the cut sides against the cake ring and the whole strawberries arranged in the center

3. Cut enough strawberries in half lengthwise (pick the nicest-looking ones) to line the inside of each ring; you will need approximately 32 halves per cake. Place them stem-end down with the cut sides against the rings. Divide the remaining whole strawberries between the cakes, placing them evenly over the sponges, points up (Figure 1-11).

4. Divide the kirsch whipped cream between the cakes. The cream should be just starting to set up before you pour it over the strawberries; if it is too thin, it will run between the cut strawberries and the ring, ruining the appearance of the cakes. Place the remaining sponge cake layers on top of the cream filling on each cake. Brush or spray the remaining simple syrup mixture over the sponge layers. Refrigerate the cakes until the filling is set, at least 2 hours.

5. Remove the rings and the paper or plastic strips. Trim away any excess short dough to make the sides of the cakes even (see Figure 1-7, page 32). Cut 2 new strips of baking paper wide enough to cover the strawberries on the sides of the cakes, leaving the top and bottom sponges exposed. Wrap the paper strips around the strawberry layers, making sure you do not cover the sponge on either the top or the bottom. Make a mark on the cardboard rounds where the ends of the paper meet so you will be able to find them easily later.

FIGURE 1-12 Removing the strip of baking paper after icing the sides of the cake to reveal the cut strawberries and the filling layer in the center of the cake

6. Ice the tops and the sides of the cakes, including the protective paper, with a thin layer of vanilla buttercream. Cover the sides of the cakes with crushed almonds (see Figure 1-1, page 18), getting as few as possible on the paper strips. Carefully pull off the paper strips (Figure 1-12). Do not refrigerate the cakes before removing the paper.

7. Roll out half of the marzipan to ⅛ inch (3 mm) thick, using powdered sugar to prevent it from sticking. Place the marzipan on a cardboard cake round and cut out a circle the same size as the top of the cake. Repeat to make a marzipan circle for the second cake. Carefully slide the circles onto the tops of the cakes (see example in Figure 1-9, page 53).

8. Cut or mark the cakes into the desired number of serving pieces. Decorate the top of each slice with the piping chocolate.

9. Place a portion of the strawberry sauce in a piping bottle.

10. Presentation: Place a slice of cake off-center on a dessert plate. Pipe a round pool of strawberry sauce next to the slice. Decorate the sauce with the sour cream mixture (see pages 682 to 685). Place a mint sprig next to the sauce.

About Kirschwasser

I have seen the word *kirschwasser* used incorrectly on products that are actually liqueurs. *Kirsch* is the German word for "cherry" and *wasser* means "water." True kirschwasser is a spirit and is not sweet. It is a colorless brandy distilled from the juice of a small black cherry found in the southern part of Germany. Kirschwasser is also known as *kirsch;* however, kirsch liqueur is a different product. If you substitute a kirsch liqueur for the kirschwasser mixed with simple syrup to moisten the sponge layers, replace the simple syrup with water.

KIRSCH WHIPPED CREAM yield: 7 cups (1 L 680 ml)

Do not make the filling until you are ready to use it.

2 tablespoons (18 g) unflavored gelatin powder

1 cup (240 ml) dry white wine

5 cups (1 L 200 ml) heavy cream

4 egg yolks (⅓ cup/80 ml)

4 ounces (115 g) granulated sugar

¼ cup (60 ml) kirschwasser

1. Sprinkle the gelatin over half of the wine and set aside to soften.

2. Whip the cream to soft peaks. Cover and reserve in the refrigerator.

3. Whip the egg yolks and sugar until just combined. Add the remaining wine and the kirschwasser and whip over a bain-marie until the mixture reaches 140°F (60°C) and is light and fluffy. Remove from the heat and whip until cool. Fold the yolk mixture into the reserved whipped cream.

4. Place the gelatin mixture over a bain-marie and heat until dissolved. Do not overheat.

5. Rapidly mix the gelatin into a small part of the cream and egg yolk mixture. Still working quickly, mix this into the remaining cream.

Tropical Coconut Cake yield: 2 cakes, 8 inches (20 cm) in diameter

Chocolate pairs easily with many flavors, and the combination of coconut and chocolate used here is a natural. This nouvelle and trendy-looking cake evolved from the Chocolate Coconut Tropicana Pastries (page 100). When assembling the cake, take care not to get any chocolate mousse filling on the plastic liner above the ribbon sponge when leveling the mousse. The best way to accomplish this task is to use the flat side of a plastic scraper.

Experiment by trying different flavors and colors in the mirror glaze or, rather than creating a marbled pattern, cover the cakes with just one flavor of glaze, such as raspberry or orange.

1 Ribbon-Pattern Decorated Sponge Sheet (page 672)

1 recipe Rum-Scented Chocolate Mousse (page 101)

Coconut Cream Filling (recipe follows)

Coconut Mirror Glaze (recipe follows)

1 cup (240 ml) heavy cream

2 teaspoons (10 g) granulated sugar

Chocolate Figurines (page 545) *or* other chocolate decorations

About Coconut

The coconut palm grows throughout the temperate part of the globe. Its value to people wherever it flourishes cannot be described better than in the old Hawaiian proverb: "He who plants a coconut tree plants vessel and clothing, food and drink, a habitat for himself, and a heritage for his children." It has, in fact, been called the tree of life. Ropes and fishing nets are made from the fibers surrounding the coconut shell, the leaves are made into mats and used as roofing material, the trunk is used as timber, the coconut flesh and liquid are nourishing, the shells can be used to make bowls, and the tiny shoots of the palm can be prepared and eaten as a vegetable.

Although the name suggests otherwise, the coconut is not a nut but a drupe (stone fruit) belonging to the same family as plums, apricots, and peaches. The name *coconut* comes from a Portuguese word, *coco*, meaning "goblin" or "frightening spirit," in reference to the three indentations on the bottom of the coconut shell, which are said to resemble a small face. Each coconut palm contains about 20 nuts at a time; each takes approximately one year to ripen. Because the trees flower and bear fruit continuously, the fruits can be harvested all year.

Fresh coconuts are relatively inexpensive and are available year round. In most grocery stores in the United States, fresh coconuts are almost exclusively marketed with their thick leathery skin and fibrous coating removed. In choosing a whole coconut, pick one that feels heavy for its size. You should be able to hear a sloshing sound from the liquid inside when you shake the coconut. To extract the meat, first puncture one or all three of the eyes on the end. Drain the milk; then, using a mallet or hammer, firmly tap the shell all around to loosen the meat inside. Break the coconut open using the same tool and remove the meat from the shell. Pry the meat away from the shell, then use a vegetable peeler or a sharp knife to remove the brown skin from the meat.

Before they are opened, coconuts keep in the refrigerator for up to a month, depending on how fresh they were at the time they were purchased. Once opened, the meat and the coconut milk should be used within a week or frozen for longer storage. Packaged coconut meat is available in many forms: flaked, shredded, grated, and ground.

1. Place 2 cake rings, 8 inches in diameter × 2 inches high (20 cm × 5 cm), on a sheet pan lined with baking paper. Line the inside of the rings with plastic strips 2 inches (5 cm) wide. The ends of the strips should overlap slightly.

2. Cut strips of ribbon sponge 1¾ inches (4.5 cm) wide and use them to line the inside of the rings, fitting them snugly against the sides with the striped side of the sponge strips against the plastic. Cut 2 rounds from the remaining ribbon sheet, making these just slightly smaller than the inside of the rings. Place 1 round in the bottom of each ring.

3. Divide the chocolate mousse filling between the sponge rounds and spread it in an even layer. Place the cakes in the refrigerator to set while you make the coconut filling.

4. Fill the rings to the top with the coconut filling. Refrigerate at least 2 hours to set the filling.

5. Spoon the plain portion of the coconut mirror glaze over the top of the cakes, spreading it evenly. Spread the chocolate-flavored portion on top (quickly, before the plain glaze sets) and blend the two together slightly to achieve a marbled look. Chill for a few minutes to set the glaze.

6. Carefully remove the rings and plastic strips (you may need to run the tip of a knife around the inside perimeter of the ring or plastic strip to release the coconut filling that sits above the sponge strips). For plated service, cut the cakes into the desired number of servings. Whip the heavy cream with the sugar to stiff peaks. Using a No. 6 (12-mm) tip, pipe a rosette of whipped cream at the wide end of each slice. Decorate with chocolate figurines or other chocolate decorations. If the cakes are to be presented whole, space 8 rosettes evenly around the perimeter of each cake.

Coconut Products

Coconut Cream — The term is used to refer to two different products. The first, sweetened coconut cream, is a liquid distilled from coconut, sugars, and various thickeners. Originating in Puerto Rico, coconut cream was first known as Coco Lopez, named after its creator, Don Ramon Lopez-Irizarry; it is still produced under this brand name. Coconut cream is often used in cocktails, such as the piña colada. The term *coconut cream* is also used to refer to the thicker portion of canned coconut milk that, being higher in fat content, naturally rises to the top of the liquid.

Coconut Milk — Unsweetened coconut milk, exported mainly from Thailand, is available canned. It is usually sold in grocery stores specializing in Asian food products or in the Asian food section of the supermarket.

Coconut Oil — Oil made by processing the dried meat of a coconut after it has been sweetened and shredded.

Desiccated Coconut — A term used for ground dried coconut. Desiccated means "dried." A desiccant is a drying agent. Dried coconut is made from the white portion of the coconut kernel after the brown skin is removed. After the coconut is processed and dried, it is sorted into various grades of coarseness, the finest of which is labeled *macaroon coconut*. My experience over the years using desiccated coconut in different countries and different brands/suppliers in the United States is that the amount of moisture coconut absorbs can vary greatly depending on how fine it was ground and how dry it is. In many recipes, that factor, in turn, affects the consistency of the dough or paste. It is often necessary to adjust the amount of moisture in the recipe until you achieve a satisfactory result.

COCONUT CREAM FILLING yield: 3 cups (720 ml)

Do not prepare this filling until you are ready to use it.

¼ cup (60 ml) unsweetened coconut milk

3 tablespoons (45 ml) light rum

3 teaspoons (9 g) unflavored gelatin powder

1 cup 240 ml) heavy cream

1 cup (240 ml) Coco Lopez

1. Combine the coconut milk and the rum. Sprinkle the gelatin over the top and set aside to soften.

2. Whip the heavy cream to soft peaks.

3. Add the Coco Lopez to the gelatin mixture. Heat just enough to dissolve the gelatin, being careful not to overheat. Quickly stir in one-third of the reserved whipped cream, followed by the remaining cream.

COCONUT MIRROR GLAZE yield: approximately ½ cup (120 ml)

1½ teaspoons (5 g) unflavored gelatin powder

¼ cup (60 ml) cold water

2 tablespoons (30 ml) Coco Lopez

2 tablespoons (30 ml) simple syrup

1 teaspoon (5 ml) chocolate liqueur

1. Sprinkle the gelatin over the cold water and set aside to soften.

2. Add the Cocoa Lopez and simple syrup to the softened gelatin. Heat to dissolve the gelatin.

3. Divide the glaze into 2 equal portions. Stir the chocolate liqueur into 1 portion. Use immediately as directed.

Wedding Cake Logistics   72   Wedding Cake Assembly and Decoration   84

Cake Size Calculations   80   Suggested Wedding Cake Combinations   89

Wedding Cakes

Without question, a wedding cake is one of the most important creations a pastry chef will ever compose. An elaborate wedding cake is truly a work of art; some cakes require days, or even weeks, of advance planning and preparation. With the multitude of potential combinations of cake flavor, filling, icing, decoration, and assembly style to choose from, a selection of recipes for specific decorated wedding cakes can, and certainly do, fill a book by themselves. Furthermore, as a wedding cake is a personal choice for each bride and groom, I feel that the experienced pastry chef, whenever possible, should create a unique cake for each couple — one that reflects their taste, the style of the reception, their budget, and the season. With this in mind, instead of a recipe and assembly instructions for a set cake — a five-tier, stacked, square-layer devil's food chocolate cake filled with fresh raspberries and white chocolate mousse, iced with vanilla buttercream, and decorated with marzipan roses, for example — what you will find here, instead, are what I call *wedding cake logistics* — what you need to know to take recipes for cake bases, fillings, buttercream, and decorations from other chapters in this book and put them together to create a spectacular wedding cake.

Traditional Wedding Cakes of Different Cultures

GREAT BRITAIN

The style of the tiered English wedding cake has without doubt influenced wedding cakes around the world. Today's typical British wedding cake is similar to that first eaten in the nineteenth century: a rich, dark cake made with candied fruits and brandy, covered with a layer of jam, and finished with multiple layers of royal icing. Pillars made from pastillage and ornaments fashioned from gum paste in baroque, gothic, or floral styles are traditional. It is interesting that the fruitcake is still so popular, as it was created so the dessert could be kept for a long time in an era without refrigeration. People still joke about the life span of fruitcake, and it is documented that one couple, having saved the top tier of their cake, as is traditional, continued to "enjoy" it for 28 anniversaries.

History of the Wedding Cake

The history of the wedding cake is interesting, at least to a professional pastry chef. Long before any type of cake was eaten at a wedding celebration, the custom of showering the bride with *far*, a type of wheat, which was a symbol of prosperity, was common. As early as 100 B.C., Roman bakers began to use this wheat to make small, sweet cakes that were served at wedding ceremonies. The custom of tossing something at the bride, however, was one that the guests were still attached to. Rather than throwing the small cakes at the bride (thank goodness), the practice of breaking a cake over the bride's head, after the groom had eaten from it, became the norm. It was believed this would ensure fertility in the marriage. The bride and groom as well as the guests then gathered and ate the broken pieces, signifying good luck and abundance. This practice began with the patrician elite of Rome and was referred to as *confarreatio*, or "eating together." This term gave us the word *confetti*, which is also often thrown at weddings. *Bryd ealy*, or "bride's ale," an old-fashioned wedding beverage, is the origin of the word *bridal*.

The early Anglo-Saxons ate small, dry crackers at their marriage celebrations. Huge baskets of these crackers were set out, and guests took them home after the ceremony — a bit like today's custom of giving party favors. The poor received any crackers that were left over. Later in history, wedding guests began to bring small, richly spiced buns to the ceremony. These were stacked in a large mound on a table. The bride and groom then kissed over the tower of buns, assuring a lifetime of prosperity if they could do so without toppling the pile.

In England in the 1660s, under the reign of King Charles II, a French chef visiting London reportedly saw a tower of wedding buns and was appalled at the disarray. Inspired to create something more beautiful, he arranged the cakes in tiers, which he held together with simple icing. The English reportedly thought this idea excessive, but by the end of the century, tiered cakes were widely accepted and were found at most weddings. Sometime later, the tiers of frosted sweet buns were transformed into large fruitcakes, which were traditionally encased in royal icing.

In the early nineteenth century, a sweet known as *bride's pie* came into fashion. Bride's pies were filled with sweetbreads, mincemeat, or even simple mutton. Each pie was baked with a glass ring hidden inside— which, we are told, portended the marriage of the woman who found it in her piece of pie. Bride's pies lost favor in the late nineteenth century, when wedding cakes in the style we know today became popular. Both the French and the English claim to have invented the modern tiered wedding cake.

Another English tradition that remains in favor today is baking small charms inside the cake layers. Each charm has a special meaning: It is believed that a person who finds a thimble in their slice of cake will be blessed; a coin signifies great fortune; a bell equals betrothal; a horseshoe signifies good luck; and a wishbone means wishes will come true.

More modern cakes are now being made in England along with the old-fashioned variety. These modern cakes often contain a sponge cake base in chocolate, vanilla, or lemon paired with a wide variety of custards and other fillings and finished with buttercream icing.

AUSTRALIA AND SOUTH AFRICA

The wedding cakes of these countries, in the areas that were colonized by England, are similar to traditional British wedding cakes. The Australian wedding cake is a fruitcake, typically decorated with white icing, although pastels are sometimes seen. The cake may be tiered, stacked, or displayed on multilevel stands. Octagon, square, or horseshoe shapes are common alternatives to rounds. Intricate sugar and gum paste flowers often decorate Australian cakes, as do royal icing ornaments, string work, and embroidery. Another more modern cake is known as a *mud cake;* this is covered with rolled chocolate and decorated with flowers or abstract designs.

South African cakes closely follow the British and Australian tradition, usually starting with dense, soaked fruitcake that is covered with rolled fondant. As with Australian cakes, the fondant may be delicately tinted and covered with intricate, lifelike flowers made from gum paste. The addition of royal icing "wings" gives South African cakes their distinction. The wings are made by piping royal icing designs onto a flat or curved surface. After the ornaments harden, they are applied to the sides of the cake, creating a three-dimensional appearance.

UNITED STATES

Without doubt, the American wedding cake is a product of British tradition. Although today the cake is most often sponge cake rather than fruitcake, the formal tiered and often columned style definitely reflects British ancestry.

American wedding cakes, in the past, were almost exclusively white sponge cake, filled and iced with either true buttercream or its commercial alternative — an icing made from shortening and confectioners' sugar. Today, all styles and flavors of wedding cakes are found in the United States and, quite often, the flavor of the cake varies from tier to tier. Popular alternatives to basic sponge cake are enriched chocolate or butter cakes, carrot cake, and cheesecake. The trend of covering the cake with rolled fondant in addition to icing it with buttercream is growing in North America, as it is in Australia. Decorating wedding cakes with fresh flowers and fruits is also quite popular and more economical than the labor-intensive gum paste or sugarwork flowers used traditionally.

Novelty cakes often reflect the theme of the wedding or the interests of the bride and groom. After seeing some of my marzipan figures, one customer had me decorate her cake with nearly two dozen marzipan lions, tigers, elephants, and monkeys — the bride and groom were going on an African safari for their honeymoon. Another couple wanted marzipan sailboats encircling each layer — they had their ceremony at a yacht club. The strangest request I had came from a couple who specified two large pink marzipan pigs (wearing running shoes!) on the top tier, one marzipan cat hidden in some fresh flowers on the middle tier, and 16 marzipan crocodiles, nose to tail, around the bottom tier. Even after inquiring discreetly about this idiosyncratic combination, I never did fully understand its significance.

Dictated by the fashion of the day, influenced greatly by media and whim, wedding cake trends in America change quickly. Still, it is doubtful that the traditional British-influenced cakes will ever disappear.

FRANCE

Vastly different from the British style is the traditional French wedding cake known as *croquembouche*. Loosely translated, the name means "crack" or "crunch in the mouth," referring to the hard caramel used to hold the cake together.

A croquembouche is made of dozens or sometimes hundreds of small profiteroles filled with vanilla pastry cream that are stacked around a metal cone in layers. Each profiterole is dipped into hot liquid caramel as it is placed. The final cake, after the form is removed, has the shape of an inverted cone. It is placed on a nougatine base and may be decorated with golden Jordan almonds, candied violets, marzipan, pulled sugar flowers, or draped with spun sugar. For serving, individual profiteroles are broken off and given to the guests to eat. Humidity can harmfully affect the crunch and holding power of the caramel, so the cake should be assembled the day it is to be served and as close to serving time as possible. This makes a croquembouche less practical than many cakes, but it is a lovely alternative for couples who desire something different from the typical tiered wedding cake, and many find its texture and heritage appealing.

SCANDINAVIA

Traditional Swedish, Danish, and Norwegian weddings always feature a *kransekaka* (Swedish) or *kransekager* (Danish), a cake composed of concentric rings of baked macaroon paste. The rings (typically eighteen of them) are stacked to form a tall inverted cone, generally about 2 feet 8 inches (80 cm) high, that is held together and decorated with royal icing. The cakes are sometimes made in a cornucopia or horn of plenty shape, with candies and small pastries flowing from the open end. These are then known as *overflodigshorn* in Denmark or *överflödighetshorn* in Sweden. Traditionally, both styles of cake are topped with a miniature bride and groom or a pair of doves, plus crisscrossed national flags and marzipan roses.

A similar showpiece is made from the same macaroon paste piped into large curved S shapes, half rings, and curlicues that are then assembled into a tall, multitiered decorative tower. These again are decorated with national flags plus fresh sugar paste or marzipan flowers. In some cases, the tower is set on top of an actual cake to be served, or it may be for decorative purposes only.

These styles of almond-paste cake are also served in Scandinavia to celebrate anniversaries, birthdays, and christenings. For anniversaries, each ring of the *kransekaka* signifies a year of marriage. Should a couple be celebrating a fiftieth anniversary, two cakes are made with twenty-five rings each.

Princess cakes, covered with untinted marzipan, are also a popular choice for weddings in Sweden.

BELGIUM

The traditional Belgian wedding cake is made of sponge cake with as many as ten tiers, none of which touch another. The bottom layer is the largest, with progressively smaller layers, supported through the center, placed above one another. Legend has it that the support used in olden times was a broomstick; today a rod or dowel is used. The cakes are iced and decorated elaborately with fresh flowers. In 1859, Queen Victoria's daughter had a Belgian-style wedding cake; the bottom layer was rumored to be 9 feet (2 m 70 cm) in diameter. The upper layers of larger cakes such as this are usually for show only, made from pure sugar or Styrofoam, elaborately decorated. The pyramid design of this type of cake can be seen in the cakes of many other regions as well, including Scandinavia.

ITALIAN

Italian wedding cakes are beautifully and elaborately embellished. One traditional style features separated tiers of filled sponge cake wrapped in tinted marzipan. The marzipan is generally colored to a soft rose or light brown shade and is decorated with royal icing piped into intricate designs featuring lace and net patterns, drop loops and tiny dots.

One cake, known as *Sacripantina,* is filled with sponge cake layers that are brushed generously with Marsala and layered with coffee-flavored zabaglione that has been mixed with crushed macaroons.

Large fruit tarts are sometimes served at wedding celebrations. These are made with a thin layer of sponge cake in the bottom and displayed on tiered cake stands.

San Francesco is the name of a dome-shaped cake made with alternating layers of thin sponge cake, fresh raspberries, pastry cream, and baked meringue sheets. The cake is iced with whipped cream and decorated with crumbled meringue and fresh raspberries. As it would be difficult to make a single large cake in this shape, multiple cakes are prepared and displayed on individual stands of varying heights.

Another style of Italian wedding cake, a specialty of Sicily, is made in the same way as the dessert cassata. This cake consists of layers of liqueur-soaked genoise filled with a mixture of sweetened ricotta cheese, candied fruits, and shaved chocolate. It is covered with pale green marzipan and decorated with piped whipped cream or meringue.

Profiteroles are sometimes used on Italian wedding cakes in a style similar to gâteau Saint-Honoré.

Contemporary Wedding Cakes

Cakes classified as *modern* are generally defined by their relative simplicity in comparison to traditional cakes. Modern cakes are usually iced with whipped cream or buttercream or covered with rolled fondant, modeling chocolate, or marzipan. Decorations may be made from pastillage, chocolate, or marzipan; cascades of fresh fruit, flowers, or both are currently popular. As with trends in savory cooking, modern cakes take advantage of the freshest bounty of the season, using fresh ripe fruits for fillings and decoration. Also, not being bound by tradition, wedding cakes may take unusual forms reflecting the hobbies or the favorite dessert of the couple being married.

Modern cakes frequently offer new interpretations of the classics. For example, one recipe for a modern gâteau Saint-Honoré begins with a layer of puff pasty on the bottom covered with a thin layer of chocolate buttercream. White genoise layers moistened with rum and filled with rum custard and whipped cream follow. The last layer is made up of profiteroles filled with rum custard. The layers are wrapped in rolled fondant and stacked.

Modern Swedish Princess cakes may be baked in square pans and layered rather than being made as traditional single-layered dome-shaped cakes. Conventional Princess cakes are filled with strawberry jam, custard, and whipped cream and covered with a layer of pale green marzipan. A modern Princess cake might be filled with raspberry, lemon, or apricot mousse, and it is often covered in white marzipan.

Modern Japanese wedding cakes tend to be fantastic — many as high as 10 feet (3 m) tall and with special effects, such as smoke and recorded music that plays as the bride and groom cut into the cake. Decorations are simple, and the color of the cake is usually either pure white or white with pale decorations. These cakes are of the European style, with graduated layers separated by tall columns. It is rare that these cakes are eaten — usually the only edible portion is a small section that the bride and groom cut into to feed one another. In some cases, even this small section is left out and, instead, a slot is built into the back of the cake where the bride and groom can insert a knife during photographs. The remainder of the cake is made of Styrofoam covered with elaborate royal icing decorations. Guests are served a sheet cake plated by the waitstaff in a side room. These gigantic cakes belong to the hotel or property where the reception takes place. The inventory of wedding cakes in these reception halls can be huge, and the cakes are used over and over again.

Wedding Cake Logistics

SALES AND DESIGN

As discussed previously, a wedding cake is not only a unique, decorative, edible composition, it is also a personal statement made by the bride and groom. The cake should reflect the taste of the couple, and it should complement the overall tone of the celebration. When selling and designing a cake, you will find it helpful to learn a bit about the rest of the plans for the reception so you can help the couple select a wedding cake that will have the appearance they are looking for, one that will taste delicious, please as many of the people involved as possible, and be practical and realistic for you to produce.

While the wedding cake is ultimately consumed as dessert, and it is certainly important that it taste wonderful and be ample enough to feed all of the guests, the significance of the cake's appearance sets it far apart from everything else in the dessert category — even the fanciest dessert served at a top restaurant. A wedding cake is generally on display throughout the wedding reception. This means that it is often studied by a hundred people or more over a period of several hours, and it is usually second only to the bride and groom as the favorite photo subject for the day. Not only the professional wedding photographer but also, in my experience, many of the guests take pictures of the cake as well — of the cake by itself, of guests posed next to it, and of the cake cutting and accompanying toasts. With all of this scrutiny, the finishing work must not only be beautiful to start with, it must hold up under whatever conditions are present. You must, therefore, ask about timing, temperature, display, serving procedure, and so on when you meet with the bride and groom so you can avoid any potential problems.

DATE AND TIME

The initial data you need from a wedding cake client are the date and time of their wedding. There is no point in talking for an hour about cake flavors and design details only to realize that you are already fully booked for the time slot they have in mind. The wedding cake business is definitely seasonal and, with rare exceptions, weddings take place almost exclusively on weekends. Although the temptation to take on as much business as possible during the busy time is understandable, it is crucial to be realistic as to how many finished cakes you are able to produce on a given day or over a weekend.

Once you have established that you are available on the date and at the time the cake will be needed, consider the season. What fresh fruits are available? If it is the middle of the summer, will the reception location be air conditioned? A cake filled with whipped cream or covered with a chocolate glaze is simply not a practical choice for a hot day in a non-air-conditioned space or a reception held outdoors. If the reception is to be held late in the evening, determine if the cake will be sitting out for a long period. When a daytime party takes place outdoors, you must specify a shady spot for the cake table (ask if there will be a tent or at least a large umbrella), and you have to consider insects. If the wedding is scheduled on a holiday or on a holiday weekend, deliveries from your regular suppliers may be affected, and traffic considerations may affect your delivery of the finished cake as well. If you are decorating the cake with fresh flowers, be aware of their seasonal availability as well as the price fluctuations that occur in the flower market around holidays such as Christmas, Easter, Mother's Day, and, especially, Valentine's Day. Wholesale flower prices for roses generally double in the two weeks before Valentine's Day.

NUMBER OF GUESTS OR SERVINGS

The next thing to find out is the number of guests expected; you should know this before you start to discuss the specifics of the cake. At the planning stage, the client will give you an estimate. Try to get high and low figures to work with; this encourages the client to give the matter some thought and to be more specific instead of just throwing out a round number. It is not reasonable to expect an exact guest count until about two weeks before the event. Base your initial price on the estimated number of guests, and ask the client to let you know should it look like the number is going to change considerably before the final count is due. If the estimate is 100 people and the guarantee 110, your plans will probably not be much affected. However, if two weeks before the wedding the count rises to 150 people, you may wish you had found out sooner. I usually explain that, as RSVPs come in, it is helpful to let me know as soon as possible if it looks like the total number of guests will differ more than about 10 percent from the estimated number. If not, I just need the final count two weeks before the wedding.

You will probably want to establish a minimum for your wedding cake business. This may be a dollar minimum for a finished cake, or it may be a minimum number of servings (the size of the cake). Figure this out ahead of time and let your client know your policy if it sounds as if it will be an issue. This should also be stated in your contract, so you don't end up trying to make a three-tier wedding cake to serve twenty people (or if you do, you will be paid enough to make your time worthwhile).

It is not uncommon for clients to think they do not need to order cake for everyone who will attend, their rationale being that some people skip dessert and some people leave the party early. While both of these can be true, it is also true that some people eat two or three slices if

DIETARY RESTRICTIONS

Some clients have special dietary restrictions, and they may ask about having a cake prepared without dairy products, or perhaps without wheat, or sugar, or alcohol. This last request is easy enough, but unless you are already experienced in specialized quantity baking and you have successful, tested recipes, I would not recommend taking the others on for a wedding cake. If the bride or groom breaks out in hives from strawberries, a strawberry cake obviously doesn't make sense. But if they are worried because they have one friend who they think might not eat dairy products, I would assure them that this person is probably used to checking with the server before they consume something.

In cases of special dietary needs, advise the clients to discuss their concerns with the caterer or banquet manager; an alternate dessert can most likely be set aside for the guest in question. On this note, when you are delivering a cake but will not be present when it is served, it is helpful to tell the person who will be on site (again, the wedding coordinator, banquet manager, or caterer) about the ingredients in the cake so he or she can answer potential questions from guests. You certainly don't have to supply the exact recipe; information about nuts, nut oils, chocolate, berries, or anything unusual that is not readily visible will probably suffice.

FINISH AND DECORATION

Once you and the client have decided on the cake flavor and filling, you need to determine what the cake will look like. I present photographs of cakes to the client and point out and discuss the differences in the styles:

Shape — round layers versus square or, less commonly, heart-shaped.

Assembly — the difference between a stacked cake and a cake in which the tiers are separated with pillars.

Finish — the look of a buttercream finish as compared to a cake finished with a glaze; a cake wrapped with marzipan, rolled fondant, or modeling chocolate; various styles of piping on and around the tiers; how buttercream decorations compare with those made from chocolate or sugarwork; and the multitude of possibilities using fresh fruit and flowers.

Clients do not necessarily have to see the exact cake they want. By discussing their preferences as they look at the different cakes, you can determine, for example, that they like square layers better than round, that they prefer the cake layers stacked rather than separated with pillars, that they like simple beaded piping around the tiers and think a lot of piping on the sides is "too fussy," and that they love the look of fresh flowers. This is basically everything needed to create what they want, and, using this information, you can offer the bride and groom a custom wedding cake. A design based on the couple's likes and dislikes will be more meaningful than simply copying the latest fad off the cover of a wedding magazine, and it is also much more likely that they will be satisfied in the long run, as no two cakes are ever going to look exactly alike. (If they *do* want the latest hot trend off the magazine cover, hopefully this will come up in the do-you-have-anything-particular-in-mind stage and not after you have reviewed your entire portfolio.)

Any ideas you can suggest to personalize the cake are great. For example, if the couple mentions that their linens are going to be embroidered with tiny purple flowers, suggest tiny purple flowers on a background of white buttercream on the sides of the cake. Or offer to duplicate the lace pattern of the bride's dress on the cake by using a delicate, lacy, filigree piping. If the invitations, placecards, and menu cards are to be printed with a monogram, suggest an icing monogram for the top of the cake.

Once you have determined the components of the design, describe to the client how you will put them together. If you are good at drawing, a simple sketch is a nice touch. This is the time to factor in the number of people expected so that you can estimate how many tiers are needed, and to consider significant external conditions. Make alternate suggestions, if needed, based on an ingredient being out of season, or if the cake the client wants is not appropriate to the weather, and so on. If you are not comfortable with a request or idea, explain why in a way that shows that you want to produce the best possible product. Do not undertake something you have never done before, or have doubts about the success of, just because the clients have their hearts set on it.

Clients occasionally present a photo from a book or a magazine showing a cake that makes no sense outside of a photography studio. To a nonprofessional, a cake decorated with spun sugar or other delicate caramel garnishes may look great in the picture, but the decoration will never hold up for the time required. You need to be able to explain why certain things will and will not work under various conditions, and you must do so in a professional manner.

FLOWERS

More and more wedding cakes are decorated with fresh flowers. Flowers in many forms, from the table centerpieces to the bride's bouquet, are a big part of most weddings. When flowers are used on the wedding cake, they should complement those used in the decor. The best solution is to have the cake flowers provided by the florist hired by the bride and groom. Even if you have enough wedding cake business to justify going to the wholesale flower market yourself, when the cake flowers come from the same source as those in the other decorations, many potential problems are avoided. You will not have to spend a lot of time pinning down what "pinkish lavender" really means to that bride, for example, and if the florist ends up making a change or substitution at the last minute, the cake flowers will still match.

If the customer chooses fresh flowers for the cake decoration, explain that the flowers should be provided by the florist and offer to contact the florist to explain what is needed. Depending on how your pricing is set up, the florist may bill either you (if the flower expense is already factored in) or the client.

In most cases, the flowers used on a wedding cake are not actually eaten. With the exception of pansies or rose petals pressed into the buttercream, large, whole flowers are removed when the cake is cut and served. While the flowers need not be edible, they must not be poisonous (like lily of the valley), and they must not have been sprayed with anything inedible. If flower stems are inserted into the cake, cover them in plastic wrap first. If you intend the flowers to be eaten, be sure the person who will be cutting and serving the cake knows this.

While I recommend getting the flowers from the florist, you must put them on the cake yourself. If you are providing the cake, you are the one responsible for finishing it, and you are the one who will look bad if the florist is late and the cake isn't ready on time, or if the flowers are placed incorrectly. When you contact the florist to discuss the type of flowers needed, find out if the florist's delivery time coincides with your setup time (it usually does), or make arrangements to get the flowers the day before.

YOUR PORTFOLIO

You should create a portfolio to display and sell your work. As you are getting started in business, it is fine to show examples from books and magazines, provided you can actually produce what you are showing and you do not try to pass it off as your own work. As you create more cakes, take pictures as often as you can; people want to see what they are buying. The old adage "a picture is worth a thousand words" is true. Because the cake is almost always finished at the reception location, take a camera with you on deliveries. Another idea is to ask the photographer hired by the bride and groom if he or she is willing to sell you a picture of your cake to display in your portfolio. Many times, photographers are happy to send you a picture free of charge or for a small fee, especially if their name is on the photo. An alliance with a professional photographer can become a good source for referrals for both of you. Talk to a photographer with whom you work frequently about helping you put a portfolio together; he or she may be willing to sell you a nice photo album at a reasonable price.

PRICING

The wedding cake is a big part of the overall wedding budget, and there are several ways to structure the pricing. Because each cake ends up a little different from all the others, you usually need to start with a base price to which you can add extras once you know what will be required. Use your recipes and labor cost to come up with a starting price for your average cake base with a buttercream filling and icing. Don't forget to factor in cardboard cake rounds and squares, plastic plates and pillars if you use them, dowels, and any other hardware you need to complete the cake. If you are including delivery and setup, work this in also. Add your profit margin, then use the total as your starting price. You can price by the serving or by the whole cake based on the tier combinations that you are going to use (see suggestions on pages 89 to 91). All other decorations — fresh flowers, pulled sugar, marzipan flowers and figures, gold leaf, chocolate, marzipan or fondant wrapping, chocolate glaze, and whatever else you offer — can be priced separately, usually per serving.

If you offer a special cake stand, you may charge a separate rental fee for its use, and you may want to get a separate refundable deposit. Anything that you expect to be returned to you should be labeled with your name and telephone number and should be specified in your contract. The bride and groom are not going to be thinking about your cake stand after the wedding. Tell the person in charge at the reception location if you expect any hardware to be saved. Plan to pick it up yourself, don't expect it to be washed, and don't expect it to be there if you wait three weeks to go back for it.

PAYMENT

You should get an initial deposit when you are hired. Fifty percent of the total based on the estimated number of guests is reasonable. Recalculate the balance when you know the final number of guests. You should receive the balance before the day of the wedding. The bride and groom are not going to be available at the time you will be setting up the cake. This is a busy day for them, and it is much better if the payment is handled ahead of time. Specify the payment schedule in your contract.

STORAGE

A wedding cake is generally completed over several days. Consider how you will store the cake layers, buttercream, and decorations during the preparation stages, and determine storage for the iced layers or assembled stacked cake as well.

TRANSPORTATION AND SETUP

Transporting a wedding cake to a reception location requires the utmost care. Getting the cake where it needs to go, and having it ready on time, is just as important as how it looks and how it tastes. Under no circumstances should you attempt to transport a fully assembled cake that is displayed on a stand or has pillars between the tiers. Provided it is relatively small, you can sometimes move an assembled stacked cake if you secure the layers by inserting vertical skewers through the finished cake before you add the final decorations. In most cases, however, each tier should be packed separately, the cake should be assembled on the table where it will be displayed, and the finishing work should be done on site. You must have a large flat surface, such as the back of a station wagon or van, to transport the tiers. If you are delivering cakes during the summer months, the vehicle must have air conditioning.

Probably the biggest concern in moving the layers is making sure that nothing can mar the sides of the cake. The bottom tier is usually placed on a board or platter larger than the base itself, so it has a bumper, but the other tiers are set on cardboard cake rounds or squares that are the same circumference as the cakes themselves. Give each of these a bumper as well by attaching the cake cardboard to a larger cardboard with loops of tape; place each layer in a sturdy box that just holds the larger cardboard without any room for it to slide. Pack the boxes of cake in such a way that they will not shift in the car. Cover the boxes as completely as possible; any dust or dirt particles floating in the air will stick to the soft buttercream and be impossible to remove without leaving a mark. Even after taking these precautions, bring extra buttercream, piping bags, spatulas, and decorations so you can make repairs as needed.

Before the wedding day, contact the person in charge at the facility where you will be delivering and confirm the following:

- the time you plan to arrive

- where you should park to unload

- where the cake will be displayed

- the time you need to be finished preparing the display

Confirm that the cake table will be set up and draped with linen when you get there. Bring with you anything needed for setup and cleanup, such as scissors, towels, tape, a stepladder, and so on. Do not assume that these things will be available to you when you get there. Be sure everything is tidy when you are finished; don't leave behind empty cake boxes, flower buckets, or other refuse for someone else to clean up. Leaving a mess or not arriving on time will negatively affect potential referrals.

DELIVERY TIME

The completion time for setting up the cake may depend on whether or not the ceremony and reception are held in the same location. Basically, the cake must be ready (and you must be cleaned up and gone) before the guests start arriving at the location. Find out how this applies to the event. If the cake is to be displayed where the guests will see it as they come in, you will need to finish sooner than if the cake is to be displayed in another area. Also, many couples complete their formal photography prior to the ceremony. Having the cake ready at this time can help the photographer get the shots he or she needs.

SERVING

Different reception locations and caterers have different polices on cutting and plating the cake. Some prefer to take the cake in the back, out of sight of the guests, to cut it after the bride and groom have cut their first piece. I think it is preferable to cut and plate the cake where it is displayed, which saves time and eliminates the risk of damaging the cake when it is moved.

Be sure the cake plates, forks, and napkins are ready. To cut and serve the cake you will need a platter or bowl in which to place the flowers or other decorations, a serrated knife, a presentable container of very hot water (a wine bucket is a good choice), a few cloth napkins, a small pair of pliers, and a spatula or cake server.

The first step is to remove the top tier and set it aside if it is to be saved. Leave the cake top or floral decorations on the top tier. Also set aside the cake knife or server used by the bride and groom to cut the cake. These are usually heirlooms or keepsakes and should not be used to serve the remainder of the cake. Next, remove the flowers or other decorations from the entire cake. If greenery is decorating the table around the cake, remove this as well so it will not be in the way. Arrange the cake plates in several medium-high stacks on your left (or on your right if you are left-handed). Place the hot water container on your right. Place the serrated knife in the water. Using the spatula, remove the first tier of cake and set it on the table in front of you. If there are supports in the cake, such as straws or wooden dowels, pull these out using the pliers (don't stick your fingers in the cake). This layer will probably be small enough that you can simply cut it into wedges. Keeping the spatula in your left hand, cut the slices and transfer them to the plates as you cut. A second person should be there to remove each plate as soon as you place cake on it. With several stacks of plates, you can cut and plate quickly. For most cakes, you should dip the knife into the water frequently between cuts and wipe it clean on a cloth napkin. Continue removing one tier at a time, working from top to bottom. As you get to the larger layers, begin each one by cutting a circle parallel to the outside edge about 3 to 4 inches (7.5 to 10 cm) toward the center. Slice the resulting ring into the desired size portions, then cut another ring, and so on. When you are left with a small round center, cut this into wedges.

To slice square layers, begin by making a cut parallel to the edge of the cake closest to you, cutting a section that is as wide as the desired length of the servings. Then, cut across this section to slice the portions.

Cake Size Calculations

CALCULATING TIER SIZES AND RECIPES

The following table lists the number of servings you can plan on per tier from the average cake. Very rich cakes, such as cheesecake and chocolate decadence cake, yield more servings than a lighter cake, as the pieces can be cut smaller. These figures are based on round tiers that measure 3 to 4 inches (7.5 to 10 cm) in height after being filled and iced.

Round Tier Size	Estimated Number of Servings
5 inches (12.5 cm)	6
6 inches (15 cm)	8
7 inches (17.5 cm)	10 to 12
8 inches (20 cm)	12 to 14
9 inches (22.5 cm)	16 to 20
10 inches (25 cm)	24 to 28
12 inches (30 cm)	36 to 42
14 inches (35 cm)	48 to 64
16 inches (40 cm)	72 to 84
18 inches (45 cm)	92 to 108

Putting together the best combination of tier sizes to produce both the correct amount of cake and a balanced presentation requires careful calculation. Following are some successful combinations. These totals assume that the top tier will not be served; if it will be served, increase the total accordingly.

Tier Combination	Estimated Number of Servings
6, 9, and 12 inches (15, 22.5, and 30 cm)	52 to 62 (6-inch/15-cm layer not served)
6, 10, and 14 inches (15, 25, and 35 cm)	72 to 92 (6-inch/15-cm layer not served)
6, 8, 12, and 14 inches (15, 20, 30, and 35 cm)	96 to120 (6-inch/15-cm layer not served)
6, 10, 14, and 16 inches (15, 25, 35, and 40 cm)	144 to 176 (6-inch/15-cm layer not served)
6, 10, 14, and 18 inches (15, 25, 35, and 45 cm)	164 to 200 (6-inch/15-cm layer not served)

CAKE PAN CAPACITIES (VOLUME)

Once you have determined the size of the cake tiers, you will need to scale the recipe to produce the layers. The best way to proceed will depend, in part, on your equipment — the size of your mixers and ovens — and on the particular recipe; some recipes can be multiplied more successfully than others. In general, the easiest way to compare the yield of a particular recipe to the number of portions desired is to consider the capacity or volume of the cake pans the batter will fill.

Example: The recipe you want to use yields 2 layers, 10 inches (25 cm) each. In other words, the batter will fill 2 cake pans measuring 10 × 2 inches (25 × 5 cm) each. You want to make a three-tier cake consisting of tiers measuring 6, 10, and 14 inches (15, 25, and 35 cm) in diameter. This means you need to make enough cake batter for 2 pans, 6 inches (15 cm) each; 2 pans, 10 inches (25 cm) each; and 2 pans, 14 inches (35 cm) each, because each finished tier will contain 2 layers of cake.

Using the chart below, you can calculate that your initial recipe makes 18 cups (4 L 320 ml) batter: a pan measuring 10 × 2 inches (25 × 5 cm) holds 9 cups (2 L 960 ml) batter; 2 × 9 cups (2 L 960 ml) = 18 cups (4 L 320 ml). By adding the volume of the pans you want to fill, you will determine that you need 65 cups (15 L 600 ml) batter.

- One 6-inch (15-cm) tier requires 2 layers, 6 inches (15 cm) each — 2 × 3.5 cups (840 ml) = 7 cups (1 L 680 ml)

- One 10-inch (25 cm) tier requires 2 layers, 10 inches (25 cm) each — 2 × 9 cups (2 L 160 ml) = 18 cups (4 L 320 ml)

- One 14-inch (35-cm) tier requires 2 layers, 14 inches each — 2 × 20 cups (4 L 800 ml) = 40 cups (9 L 600 ml)

The total needed is 65 cups (15 L 600 ml).

Sixty-five cups (15 L 600 ml), the amount needed, divided by 18 cups (4 L 320 ml), the yield of your recipe, equals 3.61. This means that you need to multiply your recipe by this amount. In this case, you would probably multiply the recipe by 3.5 or 4.0 rather than 3.6 to keep the measurements easier to work with. In general, it is better to make more batter than you think you will need rather than less. If you have some left after filling your pans, bake it separately. Before you begin preparations, make sure you will be able to fit the batter in your mixer and that all of the pans will fit into your oven at the same time. You may need to bake the cake in batches.

When you scale recipes up or down, keep notes on your yield, baking time, and successes and failures, so you have a reference when refining your calculations next time.

The volume listed for pan sizes below takes into consideration that you do not want to fill the pan to the top with batter. The appropriate amount of batter also varies depending on the type — less for a dense cake such as carrot cake, more for a light sponge. Therefore, technically, these numbers do not list the precise volume of each pan; they tell you the amount of batter that can be baked in a pan of that size.

Pan Size	Volume (allowing for expansion in the oven)
5 inches (12.5 cm) in diameter × 2 inches (5 cm) high	2½ cups (600 ml)
6 inches (15 cm) in diameter × 2 inches (5 cm) high	3½ cups (840 ml)
7 inches (17.5 cm) in diameter × 2 inches (5 cm) high	5 cups (1 L 200 ml)
8 inches (20 cm) in diameter × 2 inches (5 cm) high	6¾ cups (1 L 620 ml)
9 inches (22.5 cm) in diameter × 2 inches (5 cm) high	8½ cups (2 L 40 ml)
10 inches (25 cm) in diameter × 2 inches (5 cm) high	9 cups (2 L 160 ml)
12 inches (30 cm) in diameter × 2 inches (5 cm) high	13 cups (3 L 120 ml)
14 inches (35 cm) in diameter × 2 inches (5 cm) high	20 cups (4 L 800 ml)
16 inches (40 cm) in diameter × 2 inches (5 cm) high	28 cups (6 L 680 ml)
8-inch (20-cm) square × 2 inches (5 cm) high	7 cups (1 L 680 ml)
10-inch (25-cm) square × 2 inches (5 cm) high	11 cups (2 L 640 ml)
12-inch (30-cm) square × 2 inches (5 cm) high	14½ cups (3 L 480 ml)
14-inch (35-cm) square × 2 inches (5 cm) high	22½ cups (5 L 400 ml)

APPROXIMATE AMOUNTS OF CAKE SYRUP, FILLING, AND BUTTERCREAM NEEDED FOR VARIOUS SIZES

The table above will help you determine how much cake batter to make. The following table will help you calculate the quantities required for the other components of the cake. The amount of buttercream required can vary quite a bit depending on the type of piping used for decoration. It is always good to keep notes of what worked and what didn't so you can adjust next time.

Tier Combination	Syrup	Filling	Buttercream (for 2 coats plus decoration)
6, 9, and 12 inches (15, 22.5, and 30 cm)	4 cups (960 ml)	5 cups (1 L 200 ml)	5 quarts (4 L 800 ml)
6, 10, and 14 inches (15, 25, and 35 cm)	6 cups (1 L 440 ml)	7 cups (1 L 680 ml)	6 quarts (5 L 760 ml)
6, 8, 12, and 14 inches (15, 20, 30, and 35 cm)	7 cups (1 L 680 ml)	8 cups (1 L 920 ml)	7 quarts (6 L 720 ml)
6, 10, 14, and 16 inches (15, 25, 35, and 40 cm)	9 cups (2 L 160 ml)	10 cups (2 L 400 ml)	9 quarts (8 L 640 ml)
6, 10, 14, and 18 inches (15, 25, 35, and 45 cm)	10 cups (2 L 400 ml)	12 cups (2 L 880 ml)	10 quarts (9 L 600 ml)

TO CALCULATE THE CIRCUMFERENCE OF A CIRCLE

A circumference is the distance measured around the perimeter of a circle. You may want to calculate the circumference of a cake if you want to cut strips of paper to line the sides of a cake pan or if you are making a chocolate band to wrap around the tier of cake, for example. The mathematical formula used to find the circumference is to multiply the diameter of the circle (the distance measured across the circle) by 3.1415926. The Greek letter π (pi) represents this number. For baking purposes, multiplying by 3 and adding a bit will suffice, as we usually need a little overlap at the edges.

CAKE ORDER FORM/CONTRACT

The best approach is to have a form to fill out as you talk with your client. Not only does it make you look much more professional than if you were to write the information on scrap paper, it helps assure that you ask all the necessary questions to get the information you need, plus it helps you use your time more efficiently. The order form can also be used as a contract. Following is a sample you can copy and modify for your business. Once you have a form that works well for you, you can store it in your computer and print copies as needed. Always give a copy to the client.

I. Chèvre Cheesecake in a Cocoa-Nib Florentina Cup with Port-Poached Pears

(top left) 2. Chocolate Ganache Cake **(top right) 3. Dobos Torte** **(clockwise from top left) 4. Lemon Chiffon Fruit Basket Cake, Contemporary Apricot Cream Cake, Chocolate-Banana Mousse Cake Nouvelle, and Raspberry Cake Nouvelle**

(clockwise from top left) **5. Chocolate Triangles (variation) 6. Caramel Cake   7. Chestnut Puzzle Cake**

(clockwise from top left) **8. Dobos Torte   9. Apricot Cream Cake   10. Gâteau Mocha Carousel   11. Chocolate and Frangelico Mousse Cake   12. Black Currant Cake   13. Lemon Chiffon Cake**

(top) **14. From top left: Chocolate and Frangelico Mousse Cake, Caramel Cake, Gâteau Mocha Carousel, and Chocolate Decadence Cake** (bottom left) **15. White Chocolate and Pistachio Mousse with Chocolate Lace (optional presentation)** (bottom right) **16. Petite Chocolate and Brandied Cherry Pastries**

17. Assorted pastries including Othellos, Princess Pastries, Chocolate Triangles (4th, 5th, and 6th from the left), and Macaroon Bananas (2nd from the right)

18. (from left to right) Chocolate-Filled Macadamia Morsels, Miniature Palm Leaves, Three Sisters, Strawberry Hearts, Brandy Pretzels, Almond Doubles, Hazelnut Cuts

(clockwise from top left)
19. Marjolaine 20. Baklava with Mascarpone Bavarian and Cherry Sauce 21. Caramel Boxes with Caramel–Macadamia Nut Mousse 22. Caramelized Apple Galette in Phyllo Dough with Kumquat Sauce 23. Blueberry Pirouettes

(clockwise from top left) 24. Chocolate Bread Pudding with Cookie Citrus Rind 25. Chocolate-Banana Tart with Almond Ice Cream and Spun Sugar 26. Chocolate Ganache Towers 27. Dessert Sampling Platter 28. Date-Stuffed Saffron-Poached Pears with Chardonnay Wine Sauce 29. Cherry Basket wth Cherry Compote and Black Pepper

Business Name

Business Address

Business phone number, fax number, and e-mail address

Today's Date _____   Wedding Date _____

Bride's Name _____

Groom's Name _____

Address _____

_____

Daytime Phone Number _____   Evening Phone Number _____

Fax Number _____   E-mail Address _____

Expected Number of Guests _____

Ceremony Time and Location _____

Reception Time and Location _____

Time the Cake Must Be Set Up _____

Contact Person at Reception Location _____

Contact Person's Phone Number _____

Florist's Name _____   Phone Number _____

Photographer's Name _____   Phone Number _____

Cake Flavor I _____   Filling _____

Cake Flavor II _____   Filling _____

Layer Shape: Round, Square, or Heart (circle one) _____

Icing _____

Pillars or Stacked (If stacked, layers centered or justified to one side; circle one) _____

Description of Design and Decorations: _____

_____

Special Requests, Allergies, Concerns: _____

_____

Date the Final Guest Count Is Required (2 weeks prior to wedding) _____

Estimated Total Cost $ _____   50 percent deposit $ _____

Balance (due no later than 1 week before the wedding) $ _____

Customer's Signature _____

Pastry Chef/Salesperson's Signature _____

FIGURE 2-1 Sample cake order form/contract

Wedding Cake Assembly and Decoration

These are general assembly and decorating directions to use as a starting point; you will want to customize them according to your own style and preferences.

ASSEMBLY USING A CAKE STAND

1. Place the cake plates from the stand on top of cake cardboards (use the heavy, double-lined variety) and trace around them with a pen. If the stand has a supporting pillar that goes through each tier (Figure 2-2), mark this spot on each cardboard as well.

2. Draw a second line, ⅛ inch (3 mm) inside the circles. If you do not have a compass, use the cake plates as a guide (draw part of the way, move the plate, draw a bit more, etc., until you end up where you started).

3. Using a sharp utility knife, cut out the smaller circles. Cut a space for the center support(s), if applicable.

4. Trim the skin from the top of the sponges, leveling them at the same time. Check the bottoms and cut off the crust if it is too dark; this is usually the case on larger sizes.

FIGURE 2-2 A wedding cake made using a stand with a central supporting column

5. Place your cut cardboards on top of the corresponding sponges and cut straight down, trimming the sides of the sponge to fit the cardboard exactly.

6. Cut the cakes into 2 or 3 layers each. Place 1 layer on the cardboard, then fill and stack the layers. As you layer the sponges and filling, it is a good idea to brush the sponge with a mixture of cake syrup and a liqueur that complements the flavor of the filling to ensure the cake remains moist. This is especially important if you cut each sponge into only 2 layers.

7. To make sure the buttercream is smooth and contains no air bubbles, soften it (over hot water, if necessary), then place in the mixer with the paddle attachment. Stir on low speed for about 10 minutes.

8. Unless the buttercream is applied to the cakes in a very thick layer, it is impossible to apply buttercream without getting cake crumbs in it. For this reason, you must first apply a *crumb layer* or *crumb coat* of buttercream. Ice the top and sides of the cakes with a thin layer of buttercream just as carefully as if you were icing the final layer. Place the cakes in the refrigerator long enough to harden the buttercream and glue the crumbs in place.

9. Remove 1 layer at a time from the refrigerator and place it on the corresponding cake stand plate, attaching the cardboard to the plate with a piece of tape rolled into a loop, sticky side out.

10. Place the layer on a cake-decorating turntable and ice the top and sides with buttercream in a perfectly even layer. This process would be difficult as well as time-consuming if the cake were the same size as the cake plate. However, because the stand is slightly wider than the cake (this is why you made the cardboards slightly smaller in Step 2), it is easy to fill in the space and make the sides even simply by holding the spatula against the cake stand, straight up and down, while rotating the turntable (see Procedure 2-1). Ice all of the layers in the same manner. Because the turntable will be too large to follow this procedure for the smallest layer(s), turn the turntable upside down and use the bottom as a base on which to place these layers.

11. If the layers are to be decorated with the classical drop-loop pattern — which can be done quickly and simply or made as complicated as you wish — it is essential that the pattern come together evenly. You do not want the last loop to be one-quarter the size of the others, especially if you are decorating the top following the pattern on the sides, in which case it will be even more evident. To prevent this, check the pattern and the remaining space to be decorated when you are about three-quarters of the way around the layer, then either increase or decrease the size of the loops gradually and make them come out even. Alternatively, evenly mark the top edge of the cake very lightly before piping to show where the loops must begin and end. Cover these marks when you decorate the top.

PROCEDURE 2-1 Icing a cake tier with butter-cream with the cake on a turntable; holding the spatula vertically to fill in the space between the cake plate and the cake cardboard while rotating the turntable; the tier has already been iced with a crumb coat

12. The tops of the cakes are usually decorated with a simple pearl pattern piped around the edge and a rosette piped where the ends of each loop meet. The cakes can then be decorated with flowers, either fresh or made of buttercream or marzipan.

ASSEMBLY OF A STACKED CAKE

1. Trim corrugated cardboard cake sheets to make circles or squares, each slightly smaller than the sponge layers. Use a sharp utility knife to cut precisely and evenly. It is essential that you use the thick grade of corrugated cardboard, not just to ensure proper support for the cake but to avoid having the cardboard warp. To make a disposable base, cut out 2 extra cardboards, one about 1 inch (2.5 cm) smaller and one 3 inches (7.5 cm) larger than the piece cut for the base tier of the stacked cake.

2. Decorate the largest cardboard as appropriate — with a doily or by wrapping it in a smooth layer of decorative embossed foil. If you use doilies, do not attach them with staples. Staples can come loose easily and work their way into the cake. Glue the smaller extra cardboard in the center underneath the decorated cardboard to elevate it slightly. You can, of course, place the cake on top of one of the cake plates from a traditional cake stand, use a suitable platter, or use a cake pedestal, in which case you do not need to make this base.

3. Cut hollow pipes of clear plastic, $\frac{1}{2}$ to $\frac{3}{4}$ inches (1.2 to 2 cm) in diameter, into lengths just slightly longer than the height of the cake layers. The pipes should not show in the finished cake (Figures 2-3 and 2-4). In general, you need 4 pipes to support each of the larger layers and 3

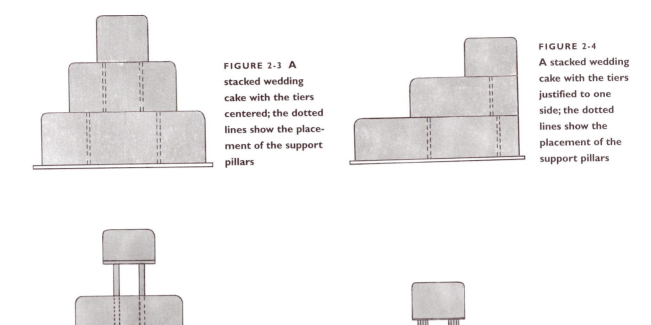

FIGURE 2-3 A stacked wedding cake with the tiers centered; the dotted lines show the placement of the support pillars

FIGURE 2-4 A stacked wedding cake with the tiers justified to one side; the dotted lines show the placement of the support pillars

FIGURE 2-5 A tiered wedding cake with visible support columns

FIGURE 2-6 A combination stacked and tiered wedding cake

pipes to support each of the smaller sizes. Make certain that all of the supports used for each layer are exactly the same height, or the cake will lean. Alternatively, you can make the support pillars longer (Figure 2-5) or use a combination of pillars that are not visible and pillars that are (Figure 2-6).

4. Fill and layer the cakes and ice with the crumb layer, as described in the directions for assembly using a cake stand. When the crumb layer is chilled, place the layers, one at a time, on the turntable and ice the tops.

5. A nice way to decorate the sides of a stacked cake is to pipe vertical lines of buttercream on the sides, using a No. 5 (10-mm) flat star tip. Pipe the strips next to one another, making sure you cover the cardboard at the bottom at the same time; pipe from the bottom to the top. Another option is to leave about ¼ inch (6 mm) between the strips, then fill in the space later with a series of small dots, made using a No. 3 (6-mm) plain tip. (Space the dots evenly from top to bottom, with the bottom dot covering the cardboard.)

6. A third popular option is to decorate the cakes with a basketweave pattern; see "Making a Basketweave Pattern," at right.

7. Level any buttercream that sticks above the edge on the top. Holding the spatula at a 45-degree angle against the cardboard, do the same on the lower edge of the cake. Decorate the top of the layers with a pearl pattern piped with a No. 3 (6-mm) plain tip.

8. When all of the layers are iced and decorated, place the bottom layer on the base made

Making a Basketweave Pattern

This design can be made with any type of piping tip, but it looks best made with a flat tip (plain or star). If you do not have one, you can flatten the end of a regular tip yourself.

1. Start by piping a vertical line close to one edge of the item you are decorating. (In the case of a round cake, you can start anywhere on the side.)

2. Pipe horizontal lines on top of the vertical line, leaving a space between them the same size as the width of the lines. The length of the horizontal lines should be 3 times the width, and the ends must line up evenly.

3. Pipe a second vertical line, one line-width from the first one, just slightly overlapping the ends of the horizontal lines.

4. Pipe more horizontal lines between the first rows, going over the second vertical line. Repeat alternating vertical and horizontal lines until finished (Figure 2-7).

FIGURE 2-7 The consecutive steps in piping a basketweave pattern in buttercream

Rose Design

Figure 2-8 shows rose designs that can be piped out using piping chocolate or royal icing on top of a cake covered with marzipan or fondant. Enlarge the designs as needed.

FIGURE 2-8 Rose designs that can be piped onto a wedding cake that has been covered in marzipan or rolled fondant

Making a Chocolate Ornament for the Top of a Cake

If the bridal couple does not have a family heirloom for the top of the cake and does not have any other specific idea for the top, you may want to suggest this pretty chocolate ornament. The decoration can be made of 3 or 4 pieces joined together. These instructions can be used to make the ornament from royal icing as well.

1. Pour melted coating chocolate or tempered dark chocolate into a round 4 inches (10 cm) in diameter and ⅛ inch (3 mm) thick. If making the ornament with royal icing, make the base from white chocolate or cut out a round of pastillage. Set the base aside to harden.

2. Copy the larger design in Figure 2-9. The drawing as shown is the correct size; the smaller drawing is used to show how the first two pieces will look after they are joined.

3. Place a sheet of acetate or baking paper on top of the drawing and secure it so it will not shift. Trace over the drawing using piping chocolate; pipe the lines a bit thicker than the drawing to make the ornament more durable. Also, the chocolate lines tend to warp slightly if they are not thick enough. Carefully move the acetate or paper to the side and repeat to make 2 or 3 more figurines (making 1 or 2 spare pieces is a good idea, as they are fragile).

4. Chill the figurines and the base for a few minutes so the pieces will hold together quickly when you attach them.

5. Wear food handling gloves to prevent fingerprints on the chocolate. Determine the placement of the figures on the base; they should be evenly spaced. For 3 figurines, divide the base (by eye) into 3 equal wedges. Four figurines will go at the 12, 3, 6, and 9 o'clock positions, as if the base were the face of a clock. If you feel the need, use a knife to make a light mark indicating the positions. Pipe a few drops of chocolate where 2 of the figures will be attached to the base (see Note); also pipe a drop of chocolate on 2 of the figures at the points where they meet (shown in the illustration). Carefully attach 2 figures to the base and hold them until they are secure. Attach the remaining figure(s) in the same way.

FIGURE 2-9 The template used to create a chocolate ornament for the top of a wedding cake; joining the first two pieces of the ornament

Note: If the figurines are made from white chocolate or royal icing, use white chocolate to assemble the ornament. Alternatively, you can use royal icing to assemble a royal icing ornament, but it will take much longer to dry, and you will need to support the pieces until the icing is hard and dry.

earlier, attaching it with loops of tape so it will not slide. Push the plastic pipes into the cake, spacing them evenly and placing them so that the next layer will fit securely on top. Stack the remaining layers with pipes in between in the same way. Finish decorating the cake as desired.

Although you could stack enough cakes to serve a wedding party of 400 to 500 guests if the layers were supported properly, it would be a very expensive cake and not really practical, as it would take a long time to serve. A better option is to make a smaller cake for display and the cake-cutting ceremony and to make up the remainder of the servings from sheet cakes with the same flavors of sponge, filling, and buttercream. The sheet cakes can be cut and plated ahead of time and be ready to serve from the kitchen. This is also a good option to suggest to a customer who has a more typical guest count of 100 to 200 people as a way of reducing cost.

Suggested Wedding Cake Combinations

As stated earlier, customers rarely choose a predetermined combination of cake, filling, icing, and decoration. To spark your imagination, following are some successful combinations. Refer to the tables to determine the quantities you will need of each component relative to the number of servings required. Then use the information that explains how to multiply the recipes to make the quantities needed.

LEMON VERBENA–RASPBERRY CAKE

Cake base	Lemon Chiffon Sponge Cake I (page 797)
Brush the cake layers with	Plain Cake Syrup (page 789) flavored with lemon zest and vanilla bean
Fillings	Lemon Curd (page 772); Quick Bavarian Cream (page 774) flavored with lemon verbena; fresh raspberries
Icing	Vanilla Buttercream (Swiss Method; page 753)
Decorations	small fresh berries, fresh flowers, Fondant Ornaments (page 676)
Serve with	Raspberry Sauce (page 173; optional)

GIANDUJA CAKE

Cake base	Hazelnut-Chocolate Sponge (page 800)
Brush the cake layers with	Plain Cake Syrup (page 789) flavored with Frangelico
Fillings	Crème Parisienne (page 768) made with gianduja chocolate
Icing	Chocolate Buttercream (Italian Method; page 752)
Decorations	Gianduja Chocolate Shavings (page 531); Chocolate Figurines (page 545)

MOCHA CAKE

Cake base	High-Ratio Sponge Cake (page 800)
Brush the layers with	Plain Cake Syrup (page 789) flavored with Coffee Reduction (page 754)
Fillings	Chocolate Buttercream (page 752) flavored with Coffee Reduction (page 754); Ganache (page 770)
Icing	Rolled Fondant (page 592)
Decorations	Piped Chocolate Figurines (page 545); Chocolate Ornament for Wedding Cake (page 88)
Serve with	Crème Anglaise (page 754; optional)

PRINCESS CAKE

Cake base	Chiffon Sponge Cake I (page 797)
Brush the cake layers with	Plain Cake Syrup (page 789) flavored with vanilla extract
Spread with	strawberry jam
Fillings	Quick Bavarian Cream (page 774); Chantilly Cream (page 765); seasonal berries
Icing	thin layer Vanilla Buttercream (Swiss Method; page 753)
Cover layers with	natural-colored marzipan
Decorations	Marzipan Roses (page 651); Marzipan Leaves (page 644)
Serve with	Strawberry Sauce (page 186; optional)

TROPICAL COCONUT-MANGO CAKE

Cake base	High-Ratio Sponge Cake (page 800), made with unsweetened coconut milk substituting for the whole milk in the recipe
Brush the cake layers with	Plain Cake Syrup (page 789) infused with fresh ginger
Fillings	Vanilla Buttercream (Swiss Method; page 753) flavored with mango puree
Icing	Chocolate Buttercream (Italian Method; page 752) made with white chocolate substituting for the sweet dark chocolate in the recipe

Decorations	Mango Wafers (page 725); Caramelized Macadamia Nuts (page 625)
Serve with	Mango Coulis (page 244; optional)

TIRAMISU CAKE

Cake base	Ladyfinger Sponge (page 21)
Brush the layers with	Plain Cake Syrup (page 789) flavored with espresso
Fillings	Vanilla Buttercream (Swiss Method; page 753) flavored with mascarpone cheese
Icing	Vanilla Buttercream (Swiss Method; page 753)
Decorations	Ladyfingers (page 801); fresh flowers

Almond Truffles — 95

Battenburg — 96

Chocolate Triangles — 98

Chocolate Coconut Tropicana Pastries — 100

Hazelnut Nougat Slices — 102

Macaroon Bananas — 104

Noisette Rings — 105

Opera Slices — 106

Othellos — 107

Petite Chocolate and Brandied Cherry Pastries — 109

Petits Fours Glacés — 111

Petits Fours Glacés with Frangipane and Apricot Filling — 114

Petits Fours — 115

PETITS FOURS SECS

Almond Doubles — 117

Brandy Pretzels — 117

Chocolate-Filled Macadamia Morsels — 118

Hazelnut Cuts — 119

Hazelnut Flowers — 120

Macaroon Candies — 121

MACAROON FIGURES — 121

Miniature Palm Leaves — 122

Strawberry Hearts — 122

Three Sisters — 123

Viennese Petits Fours — 124

Princess Pastries — 125

Walnut-Orange Tartlets — 126

Individual Pastries

The words *pastry* and *pastries* have broad meanings. The first encompasses everything from a dough or batter, to the name of any baked item that includes a crust, to an individual dessert; it is also part of our professional title, as in *pastry chef* or *pastry cook*.

This chapter features recipes for the types of pastries most often served as part of a buffet assortment or on an afternoon pastry tray, or offered for sale in a pastry shop. For the most part, these sweets are meant to be eaten with the fingers, although some of the larger selections can certainly be served as a plated dessert by adding an appropriate sauce and garnish.

Most of the recipes contain multiple components. Individual pastries often include premade elements, such as a short dough crust, a sponge, or a meringue base topped with layers of fillings such as frangipane, ganache, buttercream, lemon curd, or jam. Many are decorated with or dipped into chocolate or fondant, both for flavor and decoration and to preserve the pastry by sealing it from the air. It is essential

How to Dip Pastries in Chocolate

1. Set up your workstation as follows: If you are right-handed, always work from left to right. Place the cut pastries on a tray on your left; melted coating chocolate or tempered chocolate in front of you; several sheets of baking paper to your right to use for blotting excess chocolate; and sheet pans lined with baking paper on your far right to hold the finished pastries. Your left hand should pick up an undipped pastry as your right hand sets the dipped item down on the tray.

2. For the most part, a pastry to be covered completely in chocolate is set on top of a dipping fork (there are exceptions). If only the base and sides are to be covered, insert the dipping fork into the side of the pastry (Figure 3-1).

3. Lower the pastry into the chocolate; cover it fully or partially, lift it out of the chocolate, and allow the excess chocolate to drip back into the bowl (Figure 3-2).

4. Scrape the base of the pastry against the side of the bowl (Figure 3-3).

5. Blot the pastry on a sheet of baking paper (Figure 3-4).

6. Place the pastry on the tray reserved to hold the finished pieces (Figure 3-5). Remove the dipping fork as shown if it has been inserted into the side of the pastry — you will leave a mark; this is unavoidable — or simply slide the fork out if it is underneath the pastry. For pastries in which only the base and sides are covered (as shown in the illustration), you may steady the pastry by placing your finger on top as you remove the fork. This is not possible when the entire pastry is covered with chocolate and a fork has been inserted. In this case, press the bottom of the pastry firmly against the sheet pan as you pull the fork out.

For pastries in which only the top portion is dipped in chocolate, simply hold the base with your fingers, dip the top in the chocolate, and then make a few up and down motions and perhaps a small scrape against the side of the bowl to remove excess chocolate; these are not blotted on paper. When the pastry is held with your fingers, it is important not to leave fingerprints, which will happen if you hold the pastry too close to the chocolate. This is even more difficult to avoid with small, thin pastries, such as those made in barquette molds. If you have trouble holding this type of pastry with your fingers, try using a dipping fork, or even a paring knife, inserted into the bottom of the barquette at an angle. This will provide a convenient handle and make the pastries easier to manage. Simply pull the knife or fork out after setting the pastry, chocolate-side up, on the tray. You may need to use a finger on your free hand to steady the pastry as you pull out the knife or dipping fork; do not press down to free the tool or you will break the crust.

FIGURE 3-1 Inserting a dipping fork partway into the side of a pastry

FIGURE 3-2 Letting excess chocolate drip back into the bowl after dipping the bottom and sides of the pastry into melted chocolate

FIGURE 3-3 Scraping the pastry against the side of the bowl to remove excess chocolate from the bottom

FIGURE 3-4 Blotting the pastry on a piece of baking paper

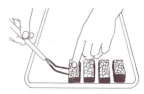

FIGURE 3-5 Removing the dipping fork after placing the dipped pastry on a paper-lined sheet pan, touching the topping rather than the chocolate coating if necessary to steady the pastry

that all of the base elements are of the highest quality and that great care is taken in assembly. Individual pastries should look neat, elegant, and uniform. A sloppy appearance, uneven layers, smeared fillings, overly thick piped decorations, and unevenly cut portions have no place here. When applying the final touches — piping a design on top of a petit four, dipping a pastry into chocolate or fondant — you must work neatly and with precision, or your previous efforts and diligence will be lost.

General guidelines for dipping pastries into chocolate are on page 94. Instructions for the application of fondant are found on pages 678 to 679, and decorating techniques are covered in Chapter 13. Coating chocolate or tempered chocolate may be used according to your preference and situation. If a pastry is to be dipped or coated only partially with chocolate, coating chocolate is acceptable in most situations, as the flavor of the pastry itself will be more pronounced. See pages 511 to 514 for instructions on tempering chocolate. Both types of chocolate may need to be thinned depending on the degree of coverage desired for a particular item. Use cocoa butter to thin tempered chocolate and soybean oil or a commercial thinning agent for coating chocolate.

Almond Truffles yield: 30 pastries, 2¼ × 1¼ inches (5.6 × 3.1 cm) each

These are among the best production-oriented pastries in this book. The chocolate coating seals in the moisture of the ganache and the almond filling, and together with the crisp short dough, the combination makes a pleasing tidbit indeed.

You might want to consider doubling the recipe, as making a half-sheet really doesn't take much longer, and, due to the magic of numbers, the larger pan produces 70 pieces, giving you a bonus of 10 pastries. In Step 5, cut the half-sheet into 10 strips lengthwise, and in Step 7, cut each strip into 7 equal slices.

If stored covered in a cool location, Almond Truffles will keep for one week with no loss of quality. If you must refrigerate them, finish the pastries through Step 6 only. They can then be refrigerated, well wrapped, without negative effects, or frozen for several weeks. Finish them as needed.

10 ounces (285 g) Short Dough (page 791)

2 ounces (55 g) smooth apricot jam

2 pounds 4 ounces (1 kg 25 g) Frangipane Filling (page 769), soft

12 ounces (340 g) Ganache (page 770)

Tempered sweet dark chocolate or dark coating chocolate, melted

Light coating chocolate, melted

Candied violets (optional)

Blanched pistachios (optional)

1. Roll out the short dough to ⅛ inch (3 mm) thick. Line the bottom of a quarter-sheet pan (8 × 12 inches/20 × 30 cm) with baking paper. Place the dough in the pan and trim the edges so only the bottom of the pan is covered. Save the short dough scraps for another use.

2. Spread the jam evenly over the dough, then spread the frangipane filling evenly on top.

3. Bake the sheet at 375°F (190°C) for about 30 minutes or until the filling is baked through. Let cool.

4. When completely cold, preferably the next day, cut around the inside edge of the pan to loosen the cake; then cut off the skin and level the top. It is easiest to do this by leaving the sheet in the pan and using a serrated knife held parallel to the top of the cake; use the edge of the pan

CHEF'S TIP

If the pastry does not separate
easily from the pan, do not force
it. Instead, warm the bottom of
the pan using a blowtorch, or
place a hot sheet pan on the outside of the inverted pan and wait
a few seconds. The heat will soften
the fat in the short dough, which
is making it stick, and the pan can
then easily be removed.

as a guide for your knife. Unmold onto an inverted sheet pan or a cardboard cake sheet (see Chef's Tip).

5. Invert the sheet again so it is now right-side up. Trim 1 long side. Measure from this edge and cut lengthwise into 6 equal strips; they should be approximately 1¼ inches (3.1 cm) wide. Separate the strips slightly.

6. If necessary, soften the ganache, then place it in a pastry bag with a No. 8 (16-mm) plain tip. Pipe the ganache in a long rope down the center of each strip. The ganache should be soft enough to stick to the frangipane, but it should still hold its shape. Refrigerate until the ganache is firm.

7. Using a thin, sharp knife, trim the short ends, then cut each strip into 5 equal slices, approximately 2¼ inches (5.6 cm) long.

8. Dip each slice into tempered chocolate or melted dark coating chocolate as described on page 94; however, unlike the example shown in the illustration, dip the entire pastry in the chocolate.

9. Streak thin lines of light coating chocolate over the tops for decoration. Add a small piece of candied violet or a half of a blanched pistachio as further decoration if desired. Attach these with a small dot of chocolate.

Battenburg yield: 48 pastries, approximately 1 × 1¾ inches (2.5 × 4.5 cm) each

I dug out this old-fashioned classic to add a bit of extra color to the buffet table. The idea is similar to rainbow pastries, another old-timer that never seems to go out of style, but here the color is added to the frangipane filling rather than to the buttercream. Battenburg pastries are quick and easy to prepare. The base, made through Step 5, can be kept for up to one week if stored, well covered, in the refrigerator. Wait until close to serving time to wrap the strips in marzipan and slice, as the marzipan gets soft and sticky from the moist air in the refrigerator (and the condensation after it is removed), even when the pastries are well covered. Battenburg may be served standing up or lying flat, depending on your needs, but avoid placing the slices in paper cups, which will mask some of the colorful pastry.

½ recipe or 2 pounds 5 ounces (1 kg 50 g)
  Frangipane Filling (page 769)

Red, yellow, and green food coloring

4 ounces (115 g) Vanilla Buttercream (Swiss
  Method; page 753)

Powdered sugar

8 ounces (225 g) marzipan, untinted

1. Line 3 quarter-sheet pans (12 × 8 inches/30 × 20 cm) with baking paper (see Chef's Tip).

2. Divide the frangipane filling into 3 equal portions. Tint the portions pale pink, pale green, and pale yellow. Spread the batter perfectly even within the 3 prepared pans.

3. Bake at 400°F (205°C) for approximately 20 minutes or until the center of the cakes springs back when pressed lightly. Let the cakes cool completely.

4. Run a knife around the inside edge of the pans to loosen the sheets. Place a sheet pan or a sheet of cardboard over the tops, then invert the pans to unmold the frangipane sheets. Peel away the baking papers. Cut the skin from the tops and level them at the same time, if necessary.

About Marzipan Rolling Pins

Marzipan rolling pins look quite different from the better-known wooden rolling pins used for dough. Although some marzipan pins have handles just like conventional rolling pins, the majority of these decorating tools are hollow plastic tubes, open on each end. The tubes have a textured surface that creates a pattern when they are rolled over a sheet of marzipan. The two most common pins are one that marks a pattern of fine parallel lines, which is sometimes called a *tread rolling pin* or *ribbon rolling pin,* and a pin that produces a checkered, or waffle, design.

In addition to their use for marzipan, the pins can be used to texture and decorate sheets of modeling paste, rolled fondant, pastillage, and even short dough and some cookies.

5. Reserve one-third of the buttercream. Spread half of the remaining buttercream on top of the pink cake; it should be about ⅛ inch (3 mm) thick. Top with the yellow cake. Spread the remaining buttercream over the yellow cake. Place the green cake on top. Press down firmly to secure. Place the assembled 8- × 12-inch (20- × 30-cm) cake in the refrigerator. Chill until the buttercream is firm.

6. Trim 1 long side of the cake to make it even. Starting from this side, cut the cake lengthwise into 4 strips, each 1¾ inches (4.5 cm) wide.

7. Using powdered sugar to prevent it from sticking, roll out the marzipan to ⅛ inch (3 mm) thick and as wide as the length of the strips. Use a marzipan rolling pin to texture the top of the marzipan (see "About Marzipan Rolling Pins," above). Trim the short side of the marzipan sheet nearest you to make it even. Invert the marzipan. Spread a thin film (not a layer) of the reserved buttercream on the back (the nontextured side that is now on top) of the marzipan. Place a cake strip at the trimmed edge and roll the strip 1 complete turn to encase it in marzipan. Cut the strip free; repeat to encase the 3 remaining cakes. Reroll the marzipan as needed. Refrigerate the strips just long enough for the buttercream to become firm.

8. Trim the short ends, then cut each strip of cake into 12 slices. Ideally the pastries should be used immediately. If you must store the finished pastries, keep them tightly wrapped in a cool place. Do not refrigerate the cakes once you have enclosed them in marzipan.

CHEF'S TIP

If quarter-size sheet pans are not available, line 2 half-sheet pans (16 × 12 inches/40 × 30 cm) with baking paper. Cut out 2 strips of corrugated cardboard measuring 1 × 12 inches (2.5 × 30 cm). The pieces should fit snugly across the width of the pans. Wrap aluminum foil tightly around the cardboard strips. Place 1 strip across the center of each pan, dividing the pans in half. Portion the tinted batters into 3 of the 4 spaces and spread it level. Place a small weight in the empty section, against the cardboard, to hold the strip in place.

Chocolate Triangles

yield: 24 pastries, 3¼ × 3¾ inches (8.1 × 9.5 cm) each (Color Photos 5 and 17)

Chocolate Triangles, or Chocolate Points, as they are also known, are a must for inclusion in any well-rounded selection of French pastries. Not only does their radical change of layer direction make them eye-catching, the shape is also interesting, and they add height to the display. The size of the finished triangles is really an optical illusion, as I demonstrate to my students. I leave one strip of cake as it appears at the end of Step 3 (before cutting it in half diagonally) and finish it in the same way as the triangle, icing this piece with buttercream, covering it with marzipan, and applying the coating chocolate. When the two strips are later sliced and displayed next to one another, the students cannot believe that they started out (and actually are) the same size, except that they watched it happen.

While the flat rectangular shape is not as intriguing as the triangle, it, too, is a classic French pastry configuration and can be made up using various flavors of sponge and filling (one example is the recipe for Opera Slices, page 106). The triangles may also be made with another flavor of sponge and/or a different filling. Color Photo 5 shows the triangle pastries made with both chocolate and vanilla buttercream.

1 Cocoa-Almond Sponge (page 796), ¼ × 14 × 24 inches (6 mm × 35 cm × 60 cm)	Powdered sugar
1 cup (240 ml) Plain Cake Syrup (page 789)	10 ounces (285 g) marzipan, untinted
1 pound 6 ounces (625 g) Chocolate Buttercream (page 752)	Tempered sweet dark chocolate or dark coating chocolate, melted
	Light coating chocolate, melted

1. When the sponge sheet is cold, cut it crosswise into 4 equal strips, leaving the baking paper attached. Invert 1 sponge strip and peel the paper from the back. Brush or spray some of the cake syrup over the sponge to moisten. Spread a layer of buttercream ⅛ inch (3 mm) thick on top.

2. Pick up a second sponge sheet, holding it by the paper, and invert it on top of the buttercream, lining up the edges evenly on 1 long side. Peel the paper from the back. Brush or spray with cake syrup and spread a layer of buttercream on top.

3. Add the remaining 2 sponge sheets in the same way, adding cake syrup and layering buttercream between them. Refrigerate until the buttercream is firm.

4. Trim the uneven long side of the layered sponge sheets. Cut in half lengthwise to create 2 strips, 14 inches (35 cm) long and approximately 2¾ inches (7 cm) wide.

5. Place 1 of the strips at the very edge of the table with the layers running horizontally. Using a long serrated knife dipped in hot water and using the table edge as your guide, cut the strip in half diagonally, making 2 triangles (Figure 3-6). Move the cut strip away from the table

Sponge Sheets for Triangle Pastries

Ideally, the sponge sheet should be made ahead and either frozen or refrigerated to allow you to easily brush or scrape the skin from the top. This important step should be done before you cut the sponge strips or the skin will come away from the sponge after you layer the sheets with buttercream, ruining your pastries. If the sponge is freshly baked, use the edge of a knife to carefully scrape away as much of the skin from the top as will come away easily.

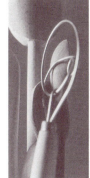

Making Professional-Looking Triangle Pastries

You should not expect the triangles to come out perfect on your first try, as more than one thing can go wrong. First, and most important, the batter for the sponge sheet must be spread in a thin, even layer, and the sponge strips must be layered with the buttercream in the same way. Keep in mind that the finished pastry will be the same height as the width of the strips before making the diagonal cut, and the base will be twice as wide as the height of the strip. Therefore, if the layers are too thick, the pastries will be large and awkward-looking. Next, if the triangles are too cold when you apply the chocolate, it will set up too quickly, leaving an uneven surface, and the coating will be too thick, making it difficult to slice the pastries without breaking the chocolate.

edge and tilt the top piece toward you (Figure 3-7). Tilt the bottom piece in the opposite direction so the layers in both pieces run vertically (Figure 3-8).

6. Arrange the triangles so the 2 long uncut sides are back to back, with the layers running vertically (Figure 3-9). Place a dowel about 2 inches (5 cm) behind the strips and tilt the back piece onto the dowel.

7. Spread a ¼-inch (6-mm) layer of buttercream on the back piece (Figure 3-10). Use the dowel to pick that piece up and put it back into place with the buttercream in the middle (Figure 3-11). Lightly press the 2 pieces together with your hands (Figure 3-12). Transfer the cake to 1 side of an inverted sheet pan topped with baking paper.

FIGURE 3-6 **Cutting the layered sponge and buttercream rectangle into two triangles**

FIGURE 3-7 **After moving the cut strip away from the table edge, tilting the top piece so that what was the long side is now the base; the layers of this piece now run vertically rather than horizontally**

FIGURE 3-8 **Tilting the second piece in the opposite direction so that the long side is now the base and the layers on this piece now run vertically rather than horizontally**

FIGURE 3-9 **Turning the first piece around so that the two pieces are back to back with the layers of both pieces running vertically**

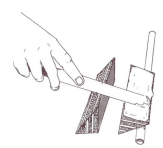

FIGURE 3-10 **Spreading a layer of buttercream over a triangle after resting the piece on a dowel**

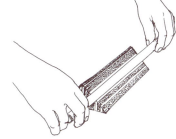

FIGURE 3-11 **Using the dowel to return the iced piece to its original position**

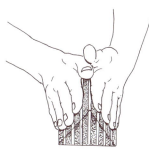

FIGURE 3-12 **Lightly pressing the halves together**

8. Repeat Steps 5 through 7 with the second cake, placing the finished triangle on the same sheet pan. Ice the 2 exposed sides of the triangles with a thin film of buttercream.

9. Using powdered sugar to prevent it from sticking, roll out the marzipan to $^1\!/_{16}$ inch (2 mm) thick, approximately 7 inches (17.5 cm) wide, and twice as long as 1 strip. Cut in half crosswise.

10. Roll 1 piece of marzipan up on a dowel and unroll it over a triangle. Press the marzipan in place with your hands. Trim the excess marzipan even with the bottom of the cake on the long sides (do not worry about covering the ends or trimming the marzipan on the ends at this time). Cover the second cake with marzipan in the same way.

11. Working on 1 cake at a time, spread a layer of tempered chocolate or melted dark coating chocolate over the marzipan just thick enough to prevent the marzipan from showing through; if the chocolate layer is too thick, the cake will be difficult to cut. Keep spreading the chocolate back and forth until it starts to set up. Repeat with the second cake.

12. Decorate both cakes by streaking light coating chocolate crosswise over the dark chocolate. Refrigerate the cakes just until the buttercream is firm. (If you need to refrigerate them longer, make sure they are well covered.)

13. Trim the ends and cut each triangle into 12 slices approximately $1^1\!/_8$ inches (2.8 cm) wide using a thin, sharp (or serrated) knife dipped in hot water.

Chocolate Coconut Tropicana Pastries

yield: 16 pastries, 3 × 1¾ inches (7.5 cm × 4.5 cm) each

These pastries are made in a contemporary style in which the sponge sheet used to line the sides of the molds is cut slightly shorter than the height of the finished pastries so a portion of the top layer of filling is exposed on the sides. Another example of this idea can be seen in Wine Foam and Blackberry Bavarian Greystone (Color Photo 74). For this design to work to its best advantage when two layers of filling are used, it is important that the filling used on the bottom (in this recipe, the chocolate mousse) does not protrude above the sponge. Thus, even if you have a bit of filling left over, do not add too much to the forms. It is quite possible that you will have more filling than you need, as the amount required to fill the forms will vary depending on the thickness of the sponge sheets used to line the sides and the bottom of the forms — which, in turn, affects the capacity of the molds.

For a different finish, cover the top of the pastries with a thin layer of Coconut Mirror Glaze (page 65) either instead of or in addition to the decoration specified in the recipe. If you use both the mirror glaze and a rosette of whipped cream, use a No. 3 (6-mm) tip to pipe the cream so the rosette will be small enough to reveal the glaze all around it on top.

1 Ribbon-Pattern Decorated Sponge Sheet (page 672)	1 recipe Coconut Cream Filling (page 65)
Rum-Scented Chocolate Mousse (recipe follows)	¾ cup (180 ml) heavy cream
	2 teaspoons (10 g) granulated sugar
	16 Chocolate Figurines (page 545)

I. Line the inside of 16 tubes, 1¾ inches in diameter by 3 inches tall (4.5 × 7.5 cm), with plastic strips measuring 3 × 6¼ inches (7.5 × 15.6 cm); baking paper may be substituted, if necessary. The strips should overlap slightly inside the tubes.

2. Cut 16 strips of ribbon sponge 2 inches (5 cm) wide and long enough to line the tubes (approximately 6 inches/15 cm); the sponge should fit tight against the inside of the tubes with the edges pressed together but not overlapping. Place the sponge strips in the tubes with the decorated side against the lining. Stand the tubes on end on a sheet pan lined with baking paper.

3. Use a plain cookie cutter approximately 1½ inches (3.7 cm) in diameter to cut out rounds from the remaining sponge. Place one in the bottom of each tube.

CHEF'S TIP

If the coconut filling sticks to the plastic it will create a ragged surface rather than the smooth shiny surface desired. If this happens as you peel away the plastic from the first pastry, place the remaining pastries in the freezer for 15 to 30 minutes and the plastic will become easy to remove.

4. Place the chocolate mousse filling in a pastry bag and pipe it into the tubes, filling them up to but not above the sponge strip. Be careful not to get any chocolate filling on the plastic above the sponge. Set aside in the refrigerator so the chocolate filling will become firm while you prepare the coconut filling.

5. Place the coconut filling in a pastry bag and pipe into the tubes, filling them to the top. Use a palette knife to spread the filling level on top of each one. Refrigerate for at least 2 hours or, preferably, a bit longer to set the coconut filling.

6. Carefully remove the tubes, then peel away the plastic (see Chef's Tip).

7. Whip the heavy cream and the sugar to stiff peaks. Place in a pastry bag with a No. 6 (12-mm) star tip. Pipe a rosette on each pastry and stand a chocolate figurine in the rosette.

RUM-SCENTED CHOCOLATE MOUSSE yield: 6 cups (1 L 440 ml)

5 ounces (140 g) sweet dark chocolate	2 tablespoons (30 ml) dark rum
3 ounces (85 g) unsweetened chocolate	3 egg whites
1¼ cups (300 ml) heavy cream	⅓ cup (80 ml) light corn syrup

1. Chop both chocolates and melt together over a bain-marie. Set aside, but keep warm.

2. Whip the heavy cream with the rum to not-quite-soft peaks.

3. Whip the egg whites to a foam. Bring the corn syrup to a quick boil and pour it into the egg whites in a thin, steady stream while whipping at medium speed. Turn the mixer to high speed and continue whipping until the meringue is thick and completely cooled.

4. Quickly stir one-third of the whipped cream into the warm chocolate. Add the remaining cream and then, still working quickly, stir in the meringue.

Hazelnut Nougat Slices yield: 30 pastries, 3½ × 1½ inches (8.7 × 3.7 cm)

Hazelnut Nougat Slices are fairly tall pastries; they appear quite elegant when cut precisely and evenly, with straight sides. Take great care, therefore, when cutting them. The familiar cautions to use a steady hand and a good knife, and to watch what you are doing, certainly apply here. If the pastries are cut at an angle, not only will they look clumsy and amateurish, they may even fall over on the display tray. To cut cleanly through the pâte à choux screen, use a thin, sharp chef's knife. Dipping the knife into hot water between strokes will warm the knife, making it easier to slice through the cream, and it will also ensure that you do not leave any residue on the pâte à choux. Hazelnut Nougat Slices can also be served as a plated dessert: Cut the sheet into squares measuring 2 × 2½ inches (5 × 6.2 cm) and serve with a fruit sauce, such as strawberry or orange.

½ recipe Chiffon Sponge Cake II batter (page 798)

½ recipe Pâte à Choux (page 783)

¼ cup (60 ml) Plain Cake Syrup (page 789)

¼ cup (60 ml) Frangelico liqueur

5 ounces (140 g) smooth apricot jam

Hazelnut Nougat Cream (recipe follows)

1½ cups (360 ml) heavy cream

1 tablespoon (15 g) granulated sugar

Powdered sugar

1. Line the bottom of a half-sheet pan (16 × 12 inches/40 × 30 cm) with baking paper. Spread the sponge cake batter evenly on top. Bake at 400°F (205°C) for about 10 minutes or until the cake springs back when pressed lightly in the center.

2. Make 2 copies of the template shown in Figure 3-13, enlarging them 200 percent. Align and tape 2 of the long sides together. Cut a piece of baking paper to the same size as the sponge

FIGURE 3-13
The template used as a guide to pipe the pâte à choux screen for Hazelnut Nougat Slices

cake. Place the baking paper on top of the template and tape the edges to hold the 2 pages in place.

3. Place the pâte à choux in a pastry bag with a No. 1 (2-mm) star tip. Pipe the pâte à choux onto the paper following the template.

4. Bake at 400°F (205°C) until the pâte à choux is golden brown and dry enough to hold its shape once removed from the oven, about 15 minutes.

5. Cut the reserved sponge free from the sides of the pan, invert onto a cake cardboard, remove the baking paper, and turn it right-side up. Cut off the skin and, if necessary, level the top at the same time. Slice the sponge horizontally into 2 layers.

6. Combine the cake syrup and the Frangelico. Brush half of the mixture over the bottom sponge layer, then spread the apricot jam over it. Place the top layer on the jam, then brush the remainder of the cake syrup mixture over the top layer.

7. Cover the top of the cake with the hazelnut nougat cream. Refrigerate until the cream is set, about 2 hours (see Chef's Tip).

8. Whip the heavy cream and granulated sugar to stiff peaks. Spread the whipped cream evenly on top of the hazelnut cream. Place the pâte à choux screen on top of the whipped cream; lightly press it into place.

9. Trim the 2 long sides of the sheet to make them even. Use a thin, sharp knife to cut the sheet lengthwise into 3 strips. Cut each strip into pieces measuring 1½ inches (3.7 cm) wide. Sift powdered sugar lightly over the slices.

CHEF'S TIP

Once the pâte à choux screen is placed on the whipped cream, the pastries should be cut and served within a few hours; otherwise, the pâte à choux becomes soft, detracting from the flavor and making it difficult to slice the pastries neatly. The pastries may be prepared through Step 7, however, and stored in the refrigerator for 1 or 2 days before finishing.

HAZELNUT NOUGAT CREAM yield: 8 cups (1 L 920 ml)

4½ teaspoons (14 g) unflavored gelatin powder
⅓ cup (80 ml) cold water
4 cups (960 ml) heavy cream

1 teaspoon (5 ml) vanilla extract
10 ounces (285 g) Pastry Cream (page 773)
½ recipe Hazelnut Paste (page 778) or 4 ounces (115 g) commercial hazelnut paste

1. Sprinkle the gelatin over the cold water and set aside to soften.

2. Whip the heavy cream and vanilla to soft peaks.

3. Gradually add a small amount of pastry cream to the hazelnut paste to soften it, then mix it with the remaining pastry cream. Mix this combination into the whipped cream.

4. Place the gelatin mixture over a bain-marie and heat until dissolved. Do not overheat. Rapidly add the gelatin to a small part of the cream mixture, then quickly mix this combination into the remaining cream. Allow the filling to thicken slightly before using.

Macaroon Bananas yield: 20 pastries, 4 × 1 inch (10 × 2.5 cm) each (Color Photo 17)

I am somewhat surprised that I rarely see these pastries in either shops or cookbooks. They were a standard item in many German pastry shops when I first picked up the idea back in the 1960s. With *banana* stylishly scripted on top, Macaroon Bananas are a great way to add variety to a fancy French pastry assortment. They are easy to pick up and eat with your hands, and they taste even better one or two days after they are made, when the macaroon has absorbed some moisture from the banana. If you cannot obtain red bananas or finger bananas, use small yellow bananas cut to size as is shown in the illustration. You may have to do some mitering in this case.

½ recipe Small Almond Macaroons batter (page 57)

6 ounces (170 g) Vanilla Buttercream (Swiss Method; page 753)

4 ounces (115 g) smooth red currant jelly

10 ripe red bananas or large ripe finger bananas

Tempered sweet dark chocolate or dark coating chocolate, melted

Piping Chocolate (page 543), melted

I. Place the macaroon batter in a pastry bag with a No. 8 (16-mm) plain tip. Use a small amount of batter to fasten a sheet of baking paper to a sheet pan so the paper will not move as you pipe. Pipe the batter into 20 slightly curved cookies, 4 inches (10 cm) long, holding the pastry tip close to the paper so the batter comes out wider and flatter than the opening of the tip.

2. Bake immediately, following the instructions in the macaroon recipe. Let the cookies cool completely.

3. Invert the paper and peel it away from the cookies. Place the cookies flat side up on a sheet pan. Press down lightly, if necessary, to flatten the cookies so that they do not wobble.

4. Place the buttercream in a pastry bag with a No. 2 (4-mm) plain tip. Pipe a border of buttercream around the cookies, ⅛ inch (3 mm) from the edge.

5. Place the red currant jelly in a pastry bag made from baking paper. Pipe a small line of jelly inside the frame of buttercream.

6. Peel the bananas and cut them in half lengthwise; do not use overripe or bruised bananas.

7. Place a banana piece, flat side down, on each of the cookies, bending it slightly to fit the curve of the cookie, if necessary (Figure 3-14). Press the banana down lightly to be sure it is

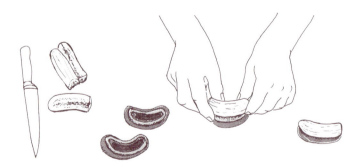

FIGURE 3-14 **Placing cut bananas on top of inverted macaroon cookies after piping buttercream and red currant jelly on the cookies**

FIGURE 3-15 **Coating the macaroon banana pastries with melted chocolate**

firmly attached. No banana should protrude beyond the macaroon. Trim the banana to fit, if necessary. Refrigerate just until the buttercream is firm.

8. Place a cake cooling rack over a sheet pan lined with baking paper. Arrange the pastries on the rack in straight rows, curved side toward you.

9. Starting with the pastry in the upper right-hand corner and working right to left, back to front, to avoid dripping chocolate on the bananas once they are coated, spoon the tempered chocolate or melted coating chocolate over the bananas (Figure 3-15). Be sure the top and sides of each pastry are completely covered in chocolate. When the chocolate has hardened, use a thin, sharp knife to cut the pastries off the rack.

10. Place the piping chocolate in a piping bag and cut a very small opening in the tip. Write the word *banana* on each pastry. Macaroon bananas will keep for a few days, covered, in a cool place, and for up to 1 week if refrigerated. To protect the chocolate from moisture in the refrigerator, place the pastries in a box and wrap the box in plastic.

CHEF'S TIP
If you do not have time to write on each pastry, simply streak either dark or light coating chocolate (or tempered sweet dark or milk chocolate) diagonally over the pastries.

Noisette Rings yield: 35 pastries, 2¾ inches (7 cm) in diameter

The combination of rum-flavored almond paste and crunchy hazelnuts on a short dough cookie tastes as good as it is simple. The size of the rings is easily adjustable to make a smaller buffet-sized serving, or simply cut these in half before dipping. Keep in mind that there is no decoration other than the crushed nuts, so it is essential that they be coarse enough to stand out under the chocolate coating. For the same reason, it is equally important that the chocolate is thinned sufficiently. Thinning the chocolate also keeps its flavor from becoming overpowering.

1 pound 4 ounces (570 g) Short Dough (page 791)

8 ounces (225 g) hazelnuts, toasted, skins removed, coarsely crushed

¼ cup (60 ml) dark rum

¼ cup (60 ml) water

1 pound (455 g) almond paste

Dark coating chocolate, melted, or tempered sweet dark chocolate

Soybean oil or a commercial thinning agent if using coating chocolate; cocoa butter if using tempered chocolate

1. Roll out the short dough to ⅛ inch (3 mm) thick. Using a fluted cutter, cut out 35 cookies, 2¾ inches (7 cm) in diameter. Place the cookies on sheet pans lined with baking paper or Silpats. Using a fluted cutter, 1 inch (2.5 cm) in diameter, cut a circle from the center of each cookie. Remove the small circles of dough, cover, and reserve for another use together with the other leftover dough. Bake the cookies at 375°F (190°C) for about 10 minutes or until light brown. Set aside to cool.

2. Sift the crushed nuts to remove the powder and any very small pieces. Save these for another use and reserve the coarse pieces.

3. Add the rum and enough water to the almond paste to make it just soft enough to pipe; the amount of water required will vary depending on the consistency of the almond paste. Place the mixture in a pastry bag with a No. 6 (12-mm) plain tip. Holding the bag straight above the cookie to prevent the cookies from sliding sideways, pipe a ring of almond paste onto each. If the cookies slide, the almond paste is probably too firm (see Chef's Tip, page 123).

4. As soon as you finish piping the paste, invert the cookies into the crushed hazelnuts and press gently to make the nuts stick and to flatten the almond paste slightly. Do not wait too long to do this, or the almond paste will form a skin and the nuts will not stick. Use your fingers to reshape the almond paste circles so they are even all around.

5. Thin the coating chocolate with enough soybean oil so the hazelnuts will show through the coating — approximately 2 parts chocolate to 1 part oil by volume. If using tempered chocolate, thin it by adding enough cocoa butter to achieve the correct consistency.

6. One at a time, hold the cookies upside down and dip them into the chocolate, covering all of the almond paste as well as any short dough that is visible on the top. Move them up and down a few times above the bowl to allow as much chocolate as possible to fall back in the bowl and to prevent the chocolate from running out around the pastry before it hardens. Place the dipped pastries on pans lined with baking paper. Noisette rings should not be refrigerated, but if you have no choice, be sure they are well wrapped.

Opera Slices yield: 24 pastries, 3½ × 1¼ inches (8.7 × 3.1 cm)

1 recipe Opera Sponge batter (page 48)	Powdered sugar
1 recipe Coffee Syrup for Opera Cake (page 49)	12 ounces (340 g) marzipan, untinted
1 pound 2 ounces (510 g) Ganache (page 770)	½ recipe Opera Glaze (page 49)
1 pound 6 ounces (625 g) Vanilla Buttercream (Swiss Method; page 753)	Piping Chocolate (page 543)
2 teaspoons (10 ml) mocha extract or 2 tablespoons (30 ml) Coffee Reduction (page 754)	Candied rose petals or violets

1. Line the bottoms of 2 half-sheet pans (12 × 16 inches/30 × 40 cm) with baking paper. Divide the cake batter between the pans and spread it out evenly. Bake at 425°F (219°C) for about 10 minutes or until baked through. Let cool.

2. Once the sponge cakes are completely cool (preferably the following day), invert the sheets, remove the baking paper, turn right side up, then rub off as much of the skin from the tops as will come away easily. Slice each sheet lengthwise into 3 equal strips.

3. Place 2 sponge strips on a cardboard cake sheet or on an inverted sheet pan. Brush coffee syrup generously over the sponges. Soften the ganache if needed to make it spreadable, then divide it between the 2 sponge strips and spread it out evenly. Top each strip with a second sponge layer, pressing the sponge lightly to make sure it sticks to the ganache. Brush coffee syrup over the sponge layers.

4. Flavor the buttercream with the mocha extract or coffee reduction. Set aside about 2 ounces (55 g) of buttercream, divide the remainder evenly between the 2 strips, and spread it evenly over the tops. Place the 2 remaining sponge layers, 1 on each strip, again pressing lightly to secure them. Spread a thin layer of the reserved buttercream over the top of each strip.

5. Using powdered sugar to keep it from sticking, roll out the marzipan to a rectangle measuring 8 × 16 inches (20 × 40 cm). Cut the marzipan in half lengthwise. Place 1 piece of marzipan on top of each strip. Place a sheet of baking paper on top of the strips followed by an inverted sheet pan. Invert the strips to place them upside down on the sheet pan with the marzipan against the baking paper. Refrigerate until thoroughly chilled.

6. Remove the strips from the refrigerator and turn them right side up. Adjust the viscosity of the opera glaze as needed. Working on 1 strip at a time, pour enough glaze on top of the marzipan to be able to spread the glaze in a thin layer that covers the marzipan; do not glaze the sides. Refrigerate the strips until the glaze is firm.

7. Using a sharp knife dipped in hot water and wiped clean after each cut, and holding the knife at a 90-degree angle, carefully trim the long sides on each strip to make them even and remove the excess marzipan. The strips should now measure approximately 3½ inches (8.7 cm) wide. Using the same procedure to heat and clean the knife, cut each strip into 12 slices.

8. Decorate the top of each pastry with piping chocolate and a small piece of candied flower.

Othellos yield: 25 pastries, 2 inches (5 cm) in diameter (Color Photo 17)

Othellos are a classic pastry whose name comes from the Shakespearean tragedy in which the title character, a Moor, is made mad with jealousy by the evil Iago and subsequently kills his loving and faithful wife, Desdemona. The brown glaze symbolizes the color of Othello's skin; in fact, these pastries are known as *mohrenkopf* ("Moor's head") in most of Europe. While I use plain pastry cream for the filling, a chocolate-flavored pastry cream or custard is traditional.

Although the individual pastry is by far more common, Othello has also lent his name to a rich Danish layer cake that somewhat resembles a large Othello pastry — it consists of pastry cream between two layers of Othello sponge, all iced with chocolate. Desdemona and Iago pastries, named for the other characters in the play, are made with different fillings and icings but also start with Othello shells, as does the pastry known as Rosalinda, which is named for a character in another one of Shakespeare's plays, *As You Like It*.

Othello pastries are often made to resemble peaches, plums, or potatoes. In this case, the shells are filled with flavored pastry cream, then covered with marzipan that is shaped and colored like the appropriate fruit or vegetable. The shells for any and all of these Othello variations can be made in advance and kept, covered, in a dry place until needed. The filling should always be custard or at least contain custard as the base. The shells absorb moisture from the custard, giving them a soft, pleasant consistency. With this in mind, it is important that the custard is not too firm, or the pastries will be dry.

Melted unsalted butter	1 recipe Apricot Glaze (page 774)
Bread flour	1 recipe Chocolate Glaze (page 774)
Othello Sponge Batter (recipe follows)	Dark Piping Chocolate (page 543), melted
1 pound (455 g) Pastry Cream (page 773)	

1. Butter and flour 2 full-size sheet pans. Use a plain cookie cutter, 2 inches (5 cm) in diameter, to mark 25 circles on each pan (see Chef's Tip). Place the Othello batter in a pastry bag with a No. 7 (14-mm) plain tip. Pipe the batter within the circles on the sheet pans, making mounds about ¾ inch (2 cm) high.

Rather than buttering and flouring the sheet
pans and then marking them with the cookie
cutter, draw 2-inch (5-cm) circles on sheets of
baking paper and invert the papers on sheet
pans. Better yet, if you make Othellos regularly,
you can obtain special pans made specifically
for these shells. The pans have shallow round
indentations, about the same diameter as the
shells specified in this recipe, with a protruding
center that creates a pocket in the baked
shells and eliminates the need to hollow them.
Lastly, if you wish to use Silpats rather than
baking paper, you can mark the Silpats by dipping a cookie cutter in flour and firmly tapping
the cutter on the mat to mark the rings.

2. Bake immediately at 450°F (230°C) for approximately 10 minutes or until golden brown. Let cool completely.

3. Use a melon ball cutter to make a hole the size of a cherry in the bottom of each pastry shell. Divide the shells into 2 equal groups as you make the holes, with the better-looking shells (to be used for the tops) in 1 group. Using a knife or a grater, trim the round side of the other group of shells (the bases) just enough to make them stand straight. Arrange both groups of shells with the holes facing up.

4. Place the pastry cream in a pastry bag with a No. 6 (12-mm) plain tip. Pipe the cream into all of the shells. Sandwich the shells together in twos, enclosing the cream. Place right-side up and brush apricot glaze over the tops of the pastries. Once filled, the Othellos should be glazed right away, as the pastry cream begins to soften the shells rather quickly, which makes them hard to work with.

5. Place the Othellos on an aspic rack or cake cooler with a sheet pan underneath. Cover the tops and sides of the pastries with chocolate glaze, following the instructions on pages 678 to 679 for glazing or icing with fondant (see Figures 13-6 and 13-7, with the instructions).

6. Place light or dark piping chocolate in a piping bag and cut a small opening. Starting in the center, pipe a spiral design on the top of each pastry.

7. Store the finished Othellos in the refrigerator, placed in a box to protect the chocolate glaze from the moist air.

OTHELLO SPONGE BATTER yield: approximately 50 pastry shells, ¾ × 2 inches (2 × 5 cm)

3 ounces (85 g) granulated sugar	6 egg yolks (½ cup/120 ml)
3 ounces (85 g) cornstarch	8 egg whites (1 cup/240 ml)
3 ounces (85 g) bread flour	½ teaspoon (1 g) cream of tartar

1. Combine half of the sugar with half of the cornstarch. Set aside.

2. Sift the remaining cornstarch with the flour. Set aside.

3. Whip the egg yolks with the remaining sugar until the consistency is light and fluffy.

4. Whip the egg whites and cream of tartar for a few minutes, until they quadruple in volume. Lower the mixer speed and gradually add the sugar and cornstarch mixture. Increase the speed and whip to stiff but not dry peaks. Carefully fold half of the egg whites into the whipped egg yolks. Fold in the flour mixture, then fold in the remaining whites. Use immediately.

Petite Chocolate and Brandied Cherry Pastries yield: 24 pastries (Color Photo 16)

If you use the premade transfer sheets that are now readily available (instead of making your own, as instructed), these elegant, tasty little pastries turn out looking quite modern. Better yet, use the transfer strips specifically designed for this type of application or for wrapping around the side of a cake. These come 2 inches (5 cm) wide, so all you have to do is cut them into the proper length and spread the dark chocolate on top. Even though cutting the larger transfer sheets into the proper width and length works just fine and still saves time (versus the scratch method), the strips are easier to handle because they are slightly thicker. Color Photo 16 shows the pastries made using both methods. The photograph also shows the white chocolate lines from Step 1 piped in crosshatch design rather than a diagonal pattern. You may want to make an assortment of pastries using these variations to create more diversity on your pastry tray. These pastries can also be served as a plated dessert; see Brandied Cherry Ganache Towers with Pink Champagne Aspic (page 384; Color Photo 81).

Melted white chocolate

Melted dark chocolate

1 layer Chocolate Sponge Cake (page 795), ⅛ inch (3 mm) thick

Brandied Cherry Ganache (recipe follows)

Brandied Cherry Mousse (recipe follows)

Chocolate Mirror Glaze (page 775)

½ cup (120 ml) heavy cream, whipped to stiff peaks

Candied flower petals and/or Chocolate Figurines (page 545)

1. Have ready 16 tubes, 2 inches tall and 1¾ inches (4.5 cm) in diameter across the inside. Cut out 16 strips of acetate, 2 inches wide and 5½ inches long (5 × 13.7 cm). Working with 1 or 2 strips at a time, place them on top of a sheet of baking paper and pipe thin parallel lines of white chocolate diagonally over the top. Transfer the strips to another (clean) area of the paper (Procedure 3-1a) and repeat until you have piped lines on all 16 strips. Let the chocolate lines harden before proceeding.

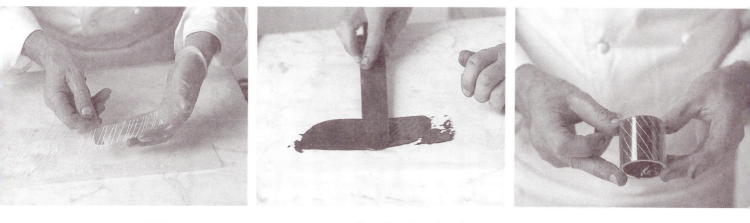

PROCEDURE 3-1a White chocolate lines piped over a strip of acetate set on a sheet of baking paper

PROCEDURE 3-1b Spreading dark chocolate over the white chocolate lines after the white chocolate has hardened

PROCEDURE 3-1c The chocolate-covered acetate strip in a plastic tube

2. Again, working with 1 or 2 strips at a time, spread a thin layer of dark chocolate over the white chocolate lines, completely covering each acetate strip (Procedure 3-1b). Immediately pick up 1 strip at a time and place it, chocolate-side in, inside 1 of the plastic tubes (Procedure 3-1c). The strip should be level inside the form, and the ends should just meet but not overlap. Use the tip of a paring knife to adjust the strip as needed. Repeat to line the remaining forms. Set aside, but do not refrigerate.

3. Cut out 16 rounds of sponge, 1¾ inches (4.5 cm) in diameter. Make certain the chocolate inside the tubes has hardened, then push a sponge round into the bottom of each form.

CHEF'S TIP

You may omit the glaze and simply pipe a large rosette of cream on each pastry so the top is completely covered.

CHEF'S TIP

If you do not have tubes that are 2 inches (5 cm) tall, tubes 1 inch (2.5 cm) high will still hold the plastic in place. Alternatively, you can make a form to hold the plastic in place by drilling holes, 1¾ inches (4.5 cm) in diameter, into fine-grain particleboard that is 1 inch (2.5 cm) thick. This is the same idea as the form used for Chocolate Ganache Towers (see Figure 4-13, page 157), but it is simpler to complete.

4. Place the brandied cherry ganache in a pastry bag with a No. 5 (10-mm) plain tip. Pipe the ganache into the molds, dividing it evenly; they will be filled approximately halfway.

5. Place the brandied cherry mousse in a pastry bag with a No. 7 (14-mm) plain tip. Pipe the mousse into the molds on top of the ganache, filling them to the top. Spread the tops level with a spatula. Freeze for at least 2 hours to set the mousse.

6. Glaze the tops of the pastries with chocolate mirror glaze. Place the pastries in the refrigerator for a few minutes to set the glaze, if needed.

7. Remove the pastries from the molds and peel off the plastic strips. Place the whipped cream in a pastry bag with a No. 4 (8-mm) star tip. Pipe a small rosette of cream in the center on top of each pastry. Decorate each rosette with a small candied flower petal and/or a chocolate figurine.

BRANDIED CHERRY GANACHE yield: 3 cups (720 ml)

14 ounces (400 g) brandied Guinettes cherries (see Note)

9 ounces (255 g) sweet dark chocolate, melted

2 ounces (55 g) glucose *or* light corn syrup

2 ounces (55 g) unsalted butter, at room temperature

2 tablespoons (30 ml) kirschwasser

1. Puree the cherries with any juice clinging to them in a food processor.

2. Set aside 2 ounces of the puree to use in making the mousse. Combine the remainder with the melted chocolate. Incorporate the glucose or corn syrup, butter, and kirschwasser and mix until smooth.

NOTE: Remove the cherries from the jar using a slotted spoon so you include that amount of juice that clings to them naturally; do not drain them in a strainer to make them completely dry. (For further information, see "About Guinettes Cherries," page 388.)

BRANDIED CHERRY MOUSSE yield: 4 cups (960 ml)

Do not make this filling until you are ready to pipe it into the forms.

¹⁄₂ cup (120 ml) liquid from the brandied cherries	4 ounces (115 g) drained brandied Guinettes cherries
¹⁄₄ cup (60 ml) cold water	1¹⁄₂ cups (360 ml) heavy cream
1 tablespoon (9 g) unflavored gelatin powder	2 ounces (55 g) brandied cherry puree, reserved from making the ganache

I. Combine the cherry liquid and water. Sprinkle the gelatin powder over the top and set aside to soften.

2. Chop the brandied cherries coarsely.

3. Whip the cream to a soft consistency.

4. Heat the cherry liquid mixture to dissolve the gelatin. Stir in the reserved cherry puree. Quickly stir the mixture into one-third of the whipped cream. Still working quickly, incorporate the remaining cream, then stir in the chopped cherries. Use immediately.

Petits Fours Glacés yield: about 80 pieces, 1¹⁄₄ to 1¹⁄₂ inches (3.1 to 3.7 cm) each

Should you not need the full yield of petits fours from this recipe, make the full recipe through Step 2, then wrap and freeze what you do not need. Although it is easy enough to divide the recipe in half, making the full amount is more sensible because it is no more work, and the quality of the pastries will not suffer from being frozen. The layered petits fours sheet can also be made into French pastries by cutting the pieces larger — portion-size rather than bite-size.

About Petits Fours Glacés and Petits Fours

Petit four literally translates to "small oven." The name is said to have originated from the practice of cooking small pastries *à petit four* — that is to say, in a low-temperature oven. The designation *petits fours* is applied to myriad small sweets, including chocolate-covered and plain candied fruits and elegant bite-sized cakes. The latter are produced in many shapes containing various layered cake mixtures and fillings. Although petits fours glacé are generally either glazed with fondant or dipped in chocolate before the final decoration is added, the term *glacé* is also used to indicate any iced pastry — such as a small tartlet or one made from pâte à choux or meringue — provided it is small enough to be consumed in one or two bites. Small almond cakes may also be wrapped in marzipan or modeling chocolate and served as petits fours. Individual pastries, such as Opera Slices or Orange Truffle Cuts, can be prepared as for the normal size and simply cut into small shapes, leaving the sides uncovered to expose the layer structure. This category of small, fancy treats also includes the more elaborately finished Viennese petits fours.

Petits fours are typically served at the end of a meal with coffee or tea as a separate dessert course, or they may be used to garnish or accompany another dessert — a parfait or ice cream bombe, for example. The French terms *friandise* and *mignardise* are also used for all of these items; however, friandise and mignardise can also include chocolate candies, nougats, fruit jellies, and more. For a more detailed description see page 116.

1 Petits Fours Sponge (recipe follows)

1 pound 4 ounces (570 g) Ganache (page 770)

1½ ounces (40 g) Vanilla Buttercream (Swiss Method; page 753)

Powdered sugar

8 ounces (225 g) marzipan, untinted

1 recipe Fondant (page 578; see Chef's Tip)

Simple syrup

Piping Chocolate (page 543), melted

1. Unmold the sponge sheet and cut it across into 3 equal pieces, leaving the baking paper attached (see Note). Each sheet should measure approximately 16 × 8 inches (40 × 20 cm).

2. Place 1 sheet, paper-side down, on an inverted sheet pan or a cake cardboard. Top with half of the ganache (softened first if needed), and spread it evenly. Invert a second sponge sheet onto the ganache and peel the paper from the back. Spread the remaining ganache on the second sheet. Top with the third sheet and press the top with a baking pan to make sure the ganache and sheets are firmly attached. Peel away the baking paper. Spread the buttercream in a thin film over the top sheet.

3. Using powdered sugar to prevent it from sticking, roll out the marzipan to a rectangle just slightly larger than the stacked sponge sheets and ⅛ inch (3 mm) thick. Roll the marzipan up on a dowel, then unroll it over the buttercream. Invert the cake onto a clean sheet pan or cardboard and peel the paper off the top. Trim away any marzipan that protrudes outside the cake. Refrigerate, upside down, until the ganache is firm, about 1 hour.

4. Leave the cake upside down and cut out shapes as desired (Figure 3-16). Keep all of the shapes around 1¼ inches (3.1 cm) in size; in other words, make the rectangles longer than the squares but not quite as wide, and so on, so that all the pieces will look uniform. Keep in mind that cutting squares, rectangles, and diamond shapes will yield more petits fours and less waste than cutting circles, hearts, or any other shape that does not have straight sides.

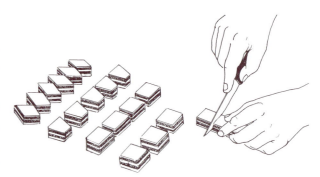

FIGURE 3-16 **Cutting the layered sponge cake and ganache into small shapes for Petits Fours Glacés**

5. Place the petits fours, marzipan-side up, on an aspic or cooling rack set over a clean sheet pan. Space them at least 1 inch (2.5 cm) apart.

6. Warm the fondant over simmering water, stirring constantly, to around 100°F (38°C). Do not get it too hot or it will lose its shine when it dries. Thin to the proper consistency with simple syrup. Test the thickness by coating 1 or 2 pastries; the layers on the sides should be clearly visible through the fondant.

7. Coat the petits fours with fondant by either piping it on using a pastry bag with a No. 3 (6-mm) plain tip or by pouring it from a saucer (see Figures 13-6 and 13-7, page 679; for a third method of applying fondant, see Step 5, page 114). Always start with the pastry farthest away from you so you will not drip over the pastries once you have coated them. Continue to warm the fondant as needed throughout the coating process so it is always at the correct temperature. If a skin forms on top of the fondant supply while you are working with it, pour hot water on top to cover, wait a few seconds, then pour the water off, stir, and continue. The fondant that drips onto the sheet pan under the pastries can, of course, be warmed and used again. If you wish to tint the fondant, see Steps 4 and 5, page 679. When all of the petits fours are coated, let the fondant set completely before moving them.

CHEF'S TIP

If you are making fondant for this recipe of petits fours glacés only and have no other use for it, you can probably get away with making just three-quarters of the fondant recipe, provided you keep it free of crumbs and mix the colors carefully. However, as fondant will keep for many months if stored properly, it usually makes sense to make the full batch.

8. Decorate the tops of the petits fours with piping chocolate, using the designs shown on pages 546 and 547. You can enhance the decoration by piping a small buttercream rosebud on top, adding a small piece of candied violet or pistachio nut, or filling in part of your design with strained strawberry jam or preserves or milk chocolate. The finished petits fours glacés can be stored at room temperature for 1 to 2 days. They will keep fresh and shiny for up to 5 days if refrigerated in a covered box.

NOTE: If the petits fours sponge has been stored for a day or more, the skin on top will probably be loose. If this is the case, remove as much of it as will come away easily before using the sheet.

PETITS FOURS SPONGE yield: 1 sheet, 16 × 24 inches (40 × 60 cm)

14 ounces (400 g) almond paste, at room temperature

12 egg yolks (1 cup/240 ml), at room temperature

7 ounces (200 g) granulated sugar

4 whole eggs, at room temperature

1 teaspoon (5 ml) vanilla extract

1 teaspoon (5 g) salt

Grated zest of 1 lemon

5 ounces (140 g) cake flour

1. Using the paddle attachment on the mixer, soften the almond paste by adding the egg yolks 1 at a time to avoid lumps. Incorporate the sugar, then the whole eggs, 1 at a time. Mix in the vanilla, salt, and lemon zest. Beat the batter until it is light and fluffy, approximately 5 minutes. Stir in the cake flour.

2. Spread the batter evenly over a sheet of baking paper, 16 × 24 inches (40 × 60 cm). Drag the paper onto a sheet pan (see Figure 9-22, page 481).

3. Bake at 400°F (205°C) for approximately 20 minutes or until baked through.

Petits Fours Glacés with Frangipane and Apricot Filling

yield: approximately 70 petits fours, 1¼ inches (3.1 cm) square

Although, at first glance, this recipe and the recipe for Petits Fours Glacés (page 111) may seem similar, the textures and flavors are quite different. The almond and apricot combination is light and refreshing and also less costly to produce than the pastries filled with ganache. The two varieties could be served together to allow your guests to enjoy the contrasting flavors and to provide an option for those who do not eat chocolate.

1 Frangipane Sheet (recipe follows)

14 ounces (400 g) strained apricot jam

2 ounces (55 g) Vanilla Buttercream (Swiss Method; page 753) (see Note)

Powdered sugar

10 ounces (285 g) marzipan, untinted

1 recipe or approximately 5 pounds (2 kg 275 g) Fondant (page 578)

Simple syrup

Piping Chocolate (page 543), melted

Candied violets or rose petals

1. Unmold the frangipane sheet and use a knife with a straight edge to scrape off the skin on top of the sheet (a tapered knife, such as a chef's knife, does not work as well). Cut the sheet across into 3 equal pieces, each approximately 8 inches (20 cm) wide, leaving the baking paper attached.

2. Place 1 piece of frangipane sheet, baking paper–side down, on a corrugated cardboard cake sheet or an inverted sheet pan. Spread half of the jam evenly over the top. Invert a second piece of frangipane sheet on top of the jam and peel away the baking paper. Spread the remaining jam evenly over the top. Invert the last frangipane sheet on top of the jam and peel away the baking paper. Spread the buttercream on top in a thin layer.

3. Using powdered sugar to prevent it from sticking, roll out the marzipan to ⅛ inch (3 mm) thick and into a rectangle just slightly larger than the assembled cake. Roll up the marzipan on a dowel and unroll it over the cake. Invert the cake onto a sheet pan lined with baking paper or onto a cardboard cake sheet. Trim the marzipan to make it even with the sides of the cake. Place a sheet of baking paper on top of the assembled cake, top with a flat, even sheet pan, and then top the sheet pan with evenly spaced weights. Refrigerate for 1 hour. If you must leave the cake in the refrigerator longer than 1 hour, wrap it well before adding the sheet pan and the weights.

4. Remove the weights, sheet pan, and baking paper. Leaving the cake upside down, trim 1 long side to make it even; then, starting from that side, measure and cut 6 strips lengthwise, each 1¼ inches (3.1 cm) wide. Cut each strip into 12 squares, each side measuring 1¼ inches (3.1 cm). Be sure to hold your knife at a 90-degree angle so the sides will be straight.

CHEF'S TIP
When you warm the fondant and adjust the viscosity, adding a small amount of light corn syrup (in addition to the simple syrup) will help make the shine last longer. It is still important not to overheat the fondant or the shine will be lost.

5. Warm the fondant to 100°F (38°C) over a bain-marie (see Chef's Tip). Adjust the viscosity as needed with simple syrup (see Step 6, page 112). Coat the petits fours with fondant in the following way: Use a 2- or 3-pronged dipping fork to push 1 petit four at a time into the fondant, marzipan-side down. Use the fork to remove the petit four from the fondant. Inverting it, set the petit four, marzipan-side up, on an icing rack set over a sheet pan lined with a Silpat. The fondant should be thin enough that the dipping fork does not leave any marks in the finish.

6. Pipe a design on each petit four using piping chocolate (see pages 546 and 547). Decorate with a small piece of candied violet or rose petal, if desired.

NOTE: If you have no buttercream on hand and no other use for it, spread a thin layer of apricot jam on top of the final cake layer instead to hold the marzipan in place. This works just as well if you will be completing the pastries the same day. If not, use the smallest possible amount of jam, as the marzipan can become sticky from the moisture in the jam.

FRANGIPANE SHEET yield: I sheet, 16 × 24 inches (40 × 60 cm)

14 ounces (400 g) almond paste

14 ounces (400 g) granulated sugar

14 ounces (400 g) unsalted butter, at room temperature

3½ cups (840 ml) eggs, at room temperature

7 ounces (200 g) cake flour

1. Place the almond paste and sugar in a mixer bowl. Using the paddle attachment, gradually incorporate the soft butter while mixing at low speed. Scrape down the sides of the bowl frequently to produce a smooth mixture.

2. Add the eggs a few at a time, still mixing at low speed. Add the flour and mix to incorporate thoroughly.

3. Line a full sheet pan (16 × 24 inches/40 × 60 cm) with baking paper or a Silpat. Spread the batter evenly over the pan.

4. Bake at 350°F (175°C) for approximately 30 minutes or until the center springs back when pressed lightly. Let cool completely before using. Preferably, cover and refrigerate overnight.

Petits Fours yield: about 50 petits fours, approximately I¼ inches (3.I cm) in diameter

10 ounces (285 g) Short Dough (page 791)

2 ounces (55 g) smooth strawberry jam

2 pounds 5 ounces (1 kg 50 g) Frangipane Filling (page 769)

Powdered sugar

2 pounds (910 g) marzipan, untinted

Vanilla Buttercream (Swiss Method; page 753)

2 pounds 4 ounces (1 kg 25 g) Ganache (page 770)

1 small stalk candied angelica

1. Line the bottom of a quarter-sheet pan (12 × 8 inches/30 × 20 cm) with baking paper (see Chef's Tip). Roll out the short dough to ⅛ inch (3 mm) thick and slightly larger than the base of the pan and place it in the pan. Trim the edges so the dough covers just the bottom of the pan and not the sides. Reserve the dough scraps for another use. Spread the jam in a thin layer over the dough in the pan. Spread the frangipane filling evenly over the top.

2. Bake at 375°F (190°C) until baked through, about 25 minutes. Let cool to room temperature.

3. When the frangipane sheet has cooled completely (preferably, the day after baking), cut off the skin and level the top. Use a plain cookie cutter, approximately 1 inch (2.5 cm) in diameter, to cut out rounds.

4. Using powdered sugar to prevent it from sticking, roll out the marzipan to ⅛ inch (3 mm) thick and into a rectangle approximately 4½ inches wide (11.2 cm). Brush any powdered sugar off the top. Texture the marzipan by rolling a waffle-pattern marzipan rolling pin (see "About Marzipan Rolling Pins," page 97) down the length of the strip (do not roll it across the width, or the strip will become too wide). Invert the marzipan sheet so the plain side faces up.

5. Measure and trim the long edges so the width of the marzipan strip is precisely the same as the circumference of the cutouts. Next, measure the height of the cutouts, then cut across the marzipan strip, making the pieces ¼ inch (6 mm) wider than your measurement (if the cutouts are 1¼ inches/3.1 cm high, cut the marzipan strips 1½ inches/3.7 cm wide).

6. One at a time, pick up a frangipane sheet cutout, spread a thin film of buttercream on the sides, and roll the cutout along a marzipan strip so that the marzipan wraps around it. Start by having the short dough side even with 1 edge of the marzipan so the opposite side of the marzipan extends ¼ inch (6 mm) above the frangipane side. Stand the pastries on their short dough ends.

7. Soften the ganache to a pipeable consistency. Place in a pastry bag with a No. 7 (14-mm) star tip. Pipe a rosette of ganache on top of each cutout.

8. Decorate each petit four with a diamond-shaped piece of candied angelica.

PETITS FOURS SECS

The following ten recipes are classified as *petits fours secs*. The French word *sec* translates to "dry" in English, which doesn't sound appealing and might lead you to believe that these bite-sized pastries are unfilled or unadorned. In fact, they are delicious, elegant, miniature creations — far from dry. A small amount of ganache, buttercream, or jam is used to either sandwich the pastries together or to decorate the tops, and they are often dipped in chocolate. These decorated cookies look beautiful lined up on silver trays to be served with afternoon tea. They are also frequently served as an accompaniment to after-dinner digestives such as grappa or cognac, and, of course, with coffee. When served in this way they are typically made even smaller and may then be referred to as *mignardise* (see box, page 111). Petits fours secs can also be used to garnish ice cream coupes or any dessert where the serving dish is placed on a plate with a doily. Many cookie recipes can be converted to petits fours secs simply by making them smaller and, in some cases, enhancing the decoration, just as many of the following recipes can be made into traditional cookies by cutting or making them larger.

Almond Doubles yield: approximately 95 cookies, 1¾ inches (4.5 cm) in diameter (Color Photo 18)

Of all the miniature creations in this section, Almond Doubles are probably the most frequently found as a larger pastry — usually about 3 inches (7.5 cm) in diameter — in European pastry shops. They are something of a cross between a fancy cookie and a simple pastry.

2 pounds (910 g) Short Dough (page 791)

½ recipe or 1 pound 12 ounces (795 g) Macaroon Decorating Paste (page 779)

10 ounces (285 g) smooth raspberry jam

10 ounces (285 g) smooth apricot jam

Simple syrup

Dark coating chocolate, melted (optional)

1. Roll out the short dough to ⅛ inch (3 mm) thick. Using a fluted cookie cutter, 1¾ inches (4.5 cm) in diameter, cut out round cookies. Place the rounds on a sheet pan lined with baking paper. Continue rerolling the scraps and cutting cookies until you have used all of the dough.

2. Place the macaroon paste in a pastry bag with a No. 3 (6-mm) plain tip. Pipe the paste onto the cookies by first piping a line all the way around the edge, then continuing straight across the middle in an unbroken line.

3. Make 2 pastry bags from baking paper. Put the raspberry jam in one and the apricot jam in the other. Pipe the jam within the macaroon frames, filling 1 side with each flavor.

4. Bake the cookies at 400°F (205°C) for about 12 minutes or until golden brown.

5. As soon as the cookies come out of the oven, brush simple syrup on the macaroon borders without disturbing the jam.

6. For a fancier look (and taste), dip the base of each cookie into melted coating chocolate: Hold a dipping fork under the cookie and press lightly into the melted chocolate, coating the bottom and the sides up to the macaroon border. Drag off the excess chocolate on the rim of the bowl and place the cookies on sheet pans lined with baking paper (see Figures 3-1 to 3-5, page 94).

Brandy Pretzels yield: 72 cookies, 2½ inches (6.2 cm) wide (Color Photo 18)

For an easy variation of this recipe, make Sugared Brandy Pretzels by forming the pretzels as directed in Step 2 below, but before placing them on the baking sheet, invert them in granulated sugar to coat the tops. Place, sugar-side up, on sheet pans and bake as directed. Omit dipping in chocolate in Step 4.

6 ounces (170 g) granulated sugar

10 ounces (285 g) unsalted butter, at room temperature

¼ cup (60 ml) brandy

1 teaspoon (5 ml) vanilla extract

1 pound 2 ounces (510 g) bread flour

Tempered sweet dark chocolate or dark coating chocolate, melted

Soybean oil or a commercial thinning agent if using coating chocolate; cocoa butter if using tempered chocolate

1. Combine the sugar and butter. Add the brandy and vanilla. Incorporate the flour and mix to form a smooth dough. If the dough is too soft to work with, refrigerate it until it becomes firm.

2. Divide the dough into 4 pieces, 9 ounces (255 g) each. Roll the pieces into ropes and cut each rope into 18 small pieces. Roll each small piece into a string 8 inches (20 cm) long and slightly tapered at the ends, using little or no flour. Form the strings into pretzels (Figure 3-17). Place on sheet pans lined with baking paper.

3. Bake at 375°F (190°C) for about 8 minutes or until light golden brown and baked through. Let cool completely.

4. Dip the baked pretzels into dark coating chocolate thinned with soybean oil or a commercial thinning agent. (Use approximately 2 parts chocolate to 1 part oil by volume.) Thin tempered chocolate by adding cocoa butter. Add 2 or 3 cookies at a time to the bowl of melted chocolate, then use a dipping fork to remove them one by one.

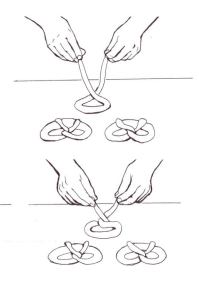

FIGURE 3-17 Forming pretzels

Scrape each cookie against the side of the bowl as you remove it to eliminate as much excess chocolate as possible. Place on sheet pans lined with baking paper.

Chocolate-Filled Macadamia Morsels

yield: 50 filled cookies 1½ inches (3.7 cm) in diameter (Color Photo 18)

Use a plain round cookie cutter, 1 inch (2.5 cm) in diameter, to mark rings in the flour on the prepared sheet pan. This is a convenient way to gauge size as you pipe and ensures that the cookies will be uniform. Do not use baking paper or Silpats or the cookies will spread and become too flat. If you do not have macadamia nuts on hand, make these cookies with pine nuts instead; they are equally delicious. For variation, instead of streaking chocolate over the cookies, you can dip the entire top cookie into melted chocolate before sandwiching the two cookies together.

Melted unsalted butter	4 egg whites (½ cup/120 ml)
Bread flour	6 ounces (170 g) bread flour
10 ounces (285 g) unsalted macadamia nuts	6 ounces (170 g) Ganache (page 770)
8 ounces (225 g) granulated sugar	Dark coating chocolate, melted
6 ounces (170 g) unsalted butter, at room temperature	

1. Lightly grease 2 full-size sheet pans with melted butter. Place a band of bread flour at the edge on 1 long side, then tilt the pan to cover it with flour. Tap the sheet pan against the table to remove any excess. Repeat with the second pan.

2. Grind the macadamia nuts and sugar together in a food processor to a very fine consistency.

3. Beat the butter until light and creamy. Add the ground nut mixture. Mix in the egg whites, 1 at a time, and beat until smooth. Mix in the flour.

4. Place the batter in a pastry bag with a No. 6 (12-mm) plain tip. Pipe out 100 mounds, 1 inch (2.5 cm) wide and about ½ inch (1.2 cm) high, onto the prepared pans.

5. Bake at 325°F (163°C) until deep golden brown around the edges, approximately 12 minutes. Let the cookies cool completely.

6. Turn half of the cookies upside down. Warm the ganache to a soft, pastelike consistency and place it in a pastry bag with a No. 5 (10-mm) plain tip. Pipe a small amount of ganache on the inverted cookies. Place the remaining cookies on top, pressing lightly to sandwich the flat sides together and squeeze the ganache to the edge of the cookies.

7. Place the melted dark coating chocolate in a piping bag and pipe straight lines close to each other across the cookies. Store in airtight containers to keep the cookies crisp.

Hazelnut Cuts yield: about 80 cookies, 2 inches (5 cm) long (Color Photo 18)

As a less time-consuming alternative, you can simply pipe the ropes of meringue in pairs with the long sides touching. Omit joining the pieces together and dip the cut pieces a little further into the melted chocolate.

8 egg whites (1 cup/240 ml)	2 ounces (55 g) cornstarch
12 ounces (340 g) granulated sugar	Tempered sweet dark chocolate or dark coating chocolate, melted
14 ounces (400 g) hazelnuts, finely ground	

1. Combine the egg whites and sugar in a mixer bowl, place over a bain-marie, and heat to 110°F (43°C) while whipping constantly. Remove the bowl from the heat and continue whipping until the mixture has cooled and stiff peaks have formed.

2. Combine the hazelnuts with the cornstarch and fold into the meringue by hand.

3. Place the meringue in a pastry bag with a No. 5 (10-mm) plain tip. Pipe ropes of meringue, 1 inch (2.5 cm) apart, onto full-size sheet pans lined with baking paper, making the ropes the full length of the sheet.

4. Bake at 300°F (149°C) for approximately 25 minutes or until just light golden. Do not dry the meringue completely or it will break when you cut the cookies.

5. Before the meringue is completely cold and while it is still soft, cut the ropes into pieces, 2 inches (5 cm) long. Let cool completely.

6. Sandwich the flat sides of the pieces together with coating or tempered chocolate by dipping only the surface of 1 piece into the chocolate, then placing a plain piece on top. After joining all of the pieces, dip the ends of each pastry into chocolate to coat about ⅛ inch (3 mm) at each end. On a sheet pan lined with baking paper, place the pastries on their sides so the chocolate in the center is visible on top.

About Hazelnuts
Hazelnuts, also known as *filberts* and, less commonly, as *cobnuts*, are grown throughout Europe; Turkey and Italy are the largest producers. Their distinctive flavor is much improved by toasting, which is also the easiest way to remove most of the nut's rough, dark brown skin. Hazelnuts are used in cakes, cookies, candies, and pastries; finely ground hazelnuts are used in Linzer dough and in place of flour in some tortes. They are also used to make hazelnut paste, an important flavoring agent.

Hazelnut Flowers yield: 75 cookies, 2 inches (5 cm) in diameter

If you don't want to use hazelnuts for decoration, dip your index finger in water to keep it from sticking, then make an indentation in the center of each cookie after piping the macaroon paste. Pipe a little apricot jam into the hollows before baking.

2 pounds (910 g) Hazelnut Short Dough (page 792)

⅓ recipe or 1 pound 5 ounces (595 g) Macaroon Decorating Paste (page 779)

75 whole hazelnuts, lightly toasted, skins removed

Simple syrup

1. Roll out a portion of the short dough ⅛ inch (3 mm) thick. Using a cutter, approximately 2 inches (5 cm) in diameter, cut out star-shaped cookies. Place them on sheet pans lined with baking paper or Silpats. Repeat with the remaining dough and scraps until you have used all of it to make 75 cookies.

2. Place the macaroon decorating paste in a pastry bag with a No. 2 (4-mm) plain tip. Pipe the paste onto the cookies in a series of small teardrop shapes, starting at the end of each point of the star and ending in the center to form a flower pattern (see Procedure 3-2a and Chef's Tip, page 123). Place 1 hazelnut, pointed end up, in the center of each cookie (Procedure 3-2b).

3. Bake at 400°F (205°C) for about 12 minutes. Brush simple syrup lightly over the cookies as soon as they come out of the oven.

PROCEDURE 3-2a **Piping macaroon paste in a flower petal design onto short dough cookies that have been cut out in the shape of stars**

PROCEDURE 3-2b **Placing a hazelnut in the center of each cookie after the macaroon paste has been piped**

Macaroon Candies yield: about 70 cookies, I to 2 inches (2.5 to 5 cm) each

This type of cookie is popular in Europe, and even though it is not really a petit four sec, the color can really enliven the cookie tray. Macaroon Candies are often referred to as *almond paste petits fours*. Leave out more egg white than usual when you make the macaroon decorating paste. The paste will be too firm to pipe but, if you use the warming method to soften it rather than add egg whites, the cookies will spread less while they bake.

3 pounds 8 ounces (1 kg 590 g) or 1 recipe Macaroon Decorating Paste (page 779)	Raisins or currants
Food coloring	Candied orange peel
Almonds, blanched, skins removed	Granulated sugar
Pistachios	Simple syrup
	Dark coating chocolate, melted

1. Warm the macaroon paste in a saucepan over low heat, stirring constantly, until it is soft enough to pipe out without effort. Color the paste, if desired, creating pale shades.

2. Pipe the paste in various shapes onto sheet pans lined with baking paper or Silpats, using a pastry bag with a No. 4 to No. 6 (8- to 10-mm) plain or star tip, separately or in combination. Use your imagination and creativity, but keep all of the shapes to 1½ to 2 inches (3.7 to 5 cm) in size.

3. Decorate the cookies with whole or slivered almonds, pistachios, raisins, and candied orange peel. Granulated sugar may be sprinkled over the tops, but this should be done immediately after the cookies are piped and decorated, before a skin has formed on the top. Set the cookies aside at room temperature overnight to allow them to dry slightly before baking.

4. Bake the cookies, double-panned, at 425°F (219°C) for about 8 minutes or until they just start to show color. Brush simple syrup over the cookies as soon as they come out of the oven. Let cool completely before attempting to remove them from the paper or Silpats. If the cookies stick to the baking paper, turn the paper (with the cookies attached) upside down and peel the paper away from the cookies rather than trying to lift the cookies off the paper.

5. Dip some of the cookies partially into melted coating chocolate for a nice contrast. Store in airtight containers. Macaroon candies may be frozen but, if so, should not be dipped in chocolate.

VARIATION
MACAROON FIGURES

This paste can be used to make animal forms such as chickens, ducks, and rabbits, as shown in Figure 3-18. The chicken's tail is candied orange peel, the duck's beak is a pine nut, and the rabbit's ears are made of sliced almonds.

FIGURE 3-18 **Bird and animal shapes made from macaroon decorating paste for Macaroon Figures**

Miniature Palm Leaves

yield: about 45 cookies, 2 inches (5 cm) wide × 2 inches (5 cm) high (Color Photo 18)

It is of the utmost importance that the puff pastry be rolled out as thin as is specified when making Miniature Palm Leaves. If the folded layers are too thick, the cut cookies will be too wide, and the layers will tear apart as they expand in the oven. An easy way around this, but one that produces a less intricate cookie, is to omit folding the strip in half crosswise, which gives you just a double turn instead. You should still make the indentation before folding the strip in half lengthwise.

Cut and bake only as many palm leaves as you will be serving within one or two days. The unsliced folded dough can be refrigerated for one day or frozen to use later.

12 ounces (340 g) Puff Pastry (page 784)	Dark coating chocolate, melted
4 ounces (115 g) granulated sugar	

1. Roll out the puff pastry in the granulated sugar to make a strip measuring 20 × 8 inches (50 × 20 cm) and about ¹⁄₁₆ inch (2 mm) thick. Keep turning and moving the dough as you roll it out, spreading the sugar evenly under and on top of the puff pastry at the same time to keep the dough from sticking to the table. If the dough is uneven or too large on any side, trim it to the proper dimensions.

2. Fold the long sides in to meet in the center. Fold the strip in half crosswise to make it 10 inches (25 cm) long. Use a thin dowel to make a light indentation lengthwise down the center of the strip. Fold in half on this mark. Refrigerate until firm.

3. Cut the folded strip into slices, ⅛ inch (3 mm) thick (Figure 3-19). Place the slices, on sheet pans lined with baking paper or Silpats. Keep in mind as you place them on the pans that their width will spread about 3 times while baking.

4. Bake at 425°F (219°C) until the sugar starts to caramelize and turn golden on the bottoms, about 6 minutes.

5. Remove the pan from the oven and, using a spatula or metal scraper, quickly turn each cookie over on the pan. Return the cookies to the oven and bake for a few minutes longer or until as much sugar as possible has caramelized on the tops; watch them closely at this point, as they can burn quickly. Let the cookies cool completely.

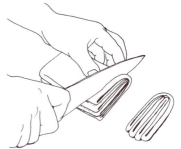

FIGURE 3-19 Slicing Miniature Palm Leaves

6. Dip the wider end of each cookie into melted coating chocolate.

NOTE: The cookies can also be served without chocolate, or sandwiched together with buttercream, depending on the other petits fours secs you are serving.

Strawberry Hearts yield: 90 cookies, 1³⁄₄ inches (4.5 cm) wide (Color Photo 18)

I often make these using a slightly larger cutter to create a quick and colorful addition to a buffet table. They are especially appropriate for a Mother's Day celebration or as a complimentary treat at the end of the meal on Valentine's Day.

2 pounds (910 g) Short Dough (page 791)

½ recipe or 1 pound 12 ounces (795 g) Macaroon Decorating Paste (page 779)

12 ounces (340 g) smooth oven-stable strawberry jam

Simple syrup

Dark coating chocolate, melted

I. Roll out half of the short dough to ⅛ inch (3 mm) thick. Using a cutter that measures approximately 1¾ inches (4.5 cm) across the widest point, cut out heart-shaped cookies. Place the cookies on sheet pans lined with baking paper or Silpats. Repeat with the remaining dough and scraps until you have cut 90 hearts. Cover and save any leftover dough for another use.

2. Place the macaroon decorating paste in a pastry bag with a No. 3 (6-mm) plain tip. Pipe a border of paste around each heart. The paste should be just soft enough to stick to the dough; if it is too soft, it will run when it bakes (see Chef's Tip).

3. Place the jam in a disposable pastry bag made from baking paper. Pipe just enough jam inside the macaroon border to cover the short dough.

4. Bake the cookies at 400°F (205°C) until golden brown, about 12 minutes. Brush simple syrup on the macaroon border as soon as the cookies come out of the oven, taking care not to smear the jam. Let the cookies cool completely.

5. Place the melted coating chocolate in a piping bag and cut a very small opening. Streak the chocolate diagonally over the cookies.

CHEF'S TIP

If the cookies slide as you pipe the paste, place the pan in a warm oven for about 30 seconds, which will make the cookies stick to the paper or Silpat. Ideally, do this far enough in advance to allow the short dough to become firm again before piping the macaroon paste on top. If the short dough becomes very soft, the paste can distort the shape of the dough.

Three Sisters yield: about 90 cookies, 1¾ inches (4.5 cm) in diameter (Color Photo 18)

You can obtain a special cutter for these cookies that will cut out the three holes at the same time that you cut out the cookie itself, which is helpful if you are making a large quantity. To make the variation known as *Bull's Eyes,* cut out one large hole in the center of half of the cookies instead of three small ones. This will produce a cookie that looks something like a flat, raspberry-filled bouchée. If you have short dough (made with butter) on hand, you can use that in place of the dough used here. The cookies will not be quite as tender but will certainly be acceptable.

1 pound 5 ounces (595 g) unsalted butter, at room temperature

10 ounces (285 g) powdered sugar

3 egg yolks (¼ cup/60 ml)

1 teaspoon (5 ml) vanilla extract

1 pound 13 ounces (825 g) bread flour

12 ounces (340 g) smooth raspberry jam

Powdered sugar

I. Beat the butter and sugar for a few minutes with the paddle at medium speed. Mix in the egg yolks and vanilla. Add the flour and mix until you have a smooth, pliable dough. Refrigerate the dough if it is too soft to work with.

2. Roll out a piece of dough to ⅛ inch (3 mm) thick. Using a fluted cutter, 1¾ inches (4.5 cm) in diameter, cut out round cookies. Place the cookies on sheet pans lined with baking paper or Silpats. Repeat with the remaining dough and scraps until all the dough is used. Using a

No. 4 (8-mm) plain piping tip, cut 3 small holes, evenly spaced, in the center of half of the cookies.

3. Bake the cookies at 400°F (205°C) until they are golden, about 10 minutes. Let the cookies cool completely.

4. Place the jam in a disposable pastry bag made from baking paper. Pipe a dot of jam on top of the plain cookies. Do not use too much jam or it will ooze out the sides. Place the cut cookies on the jam and press down lightly. Sift powdered sugar lightly over the tops.

Viennese Petits Fours yield: about 85 pieces, 1¼ to 1½ inches (3.1 to 3.7 cm) each

Nothing is more elegant to serve with afternoon tea or with cordials at the end of dinner than a tray of Viennese Petits Fours, arranged perhaps with some Macaroon Candies (page 121). To produce the best look and most variety in this type of petit four, you need an assortment of individual small molds, approximately 1¼ to 1½ inches (3.1 to 3.7 cm) in diameter or length and ½ inch (1.2 cm) high. The molds can be purchased in sets containing six or eight different shapes. To effect a precise and professional-looking finish, line only half of the molds (of each shape) at one time. Use the back of a knife to trim the dough even with the edge of the molds instead of using your palm or thumb. Place the remaining empty molds on top and press them lightly into the dough. Bake the shells this way until they are almost done. Quickly remove the empty molds on top and continue to bake a few minutes longer until the shells are light brown inside.

1 pound 6 ounces (625 g) Short Dough (page 791) *or* 1 pound 6 ounces (625 g) Hazelnut Short Dough (page 792) *or* 1 pound 6 ounces (625 g) Linzer Dough (page 778)

6 ounces (170 g) almond paste

4 ounces (115 g) unsalted butter, at room temperature

2 tablespoons (30 ml) dark rum

2 tablespoons (30 ml) orange liqueur

8 ounces (225 g) Ganache (page 770)

6 ounces (170 g) Vanilla Buttercream (Swiss Method; page 753)

1 tablespoon (15 ml) cherry or mint liqueur

Tempered chocolate or dark or light coating chocolate, melted

Apricot Glaze (page 774) or Red Currant Glaze (page 777)

Slivered almonds

Pistachios

Hazelnuts

Candied orange peel

Candied violets

Small Chocolate Figurines (page 545)

1. Line the molds with short dough, hazelnut short dough, or Linzer dough (or use some of each) rolled ¹⁄₁₆ inch (2 mm) thick. Cover and reserve the dough scraps for another use. Prick the shells, then bake at 375°F (190°C) for about 8 minutes. Let the shells cool, then carefully remove them from the molds.

2. Fill the shells, using your imagination as well as your good taste. You might, for example, soften the almond paste to a pipeable consistency with butter, then flavor it with rum; add orange liqueur to the ganache; or flavor vanilla buttercream with cherry or mint liqueur. The quantities given in the ingredient list are based on using 3 different fillings. If you wish to use just 1 or 2 fillings, adjust the quantities accordingly. Pipe the fillings into the shells in the shape of a mound or rosette.

3. Dip the tops of the pastries in chocolate, or brush apricot or currant glaze on top.

4. Decorate with slivered almonds, pistachios, hazelnuts, candied orange peel, candied violets, or chocolate figurines.

Princess Pastries yield: 45 pastries, approximately 2¼ inches (5.6 cm) in diameter (Color Photo 17)

These pretty, petite pink pastries are a staple in many pastry shops across Europe. They can vary in filling, in name, and in the texture of the marzipan; both basketweave and ruffled designs look great. The marzipan rings can be made ahead and used to frame other pastries as well. Follow the procedure in Step 5, cutting the marzipan strips to fit the circumference of the item you are going to make. Once the strips are cut, brush a little water on one short end; then, using an appropriately sized plain cookie cutter as a guide, roll the strip around the cutter and press the ends together. Carefully stand the marzipan frames upright on a sheet pan lined with baking paper. Allow the rings to dry overnight at room temperature before using.

The marzipan rings can be used to create many quick pastries. For example, cut out circles of sponge cake to fit within the rings (they need to fit snugly so they don't fall out), then fill with pastry or Bavarian cream, arrange fresh fruit on top, and brush apricot glaze over the fruit. The many other possibilities depend on the ingredients you have on hand.

1 recipe Chiffon Sponge Cake I batter (page 797)	1 pound 8 ounces (680 g) Pastry Cream (page 773)
8 ounces (225 g) smooth strawberry jam	1 quart (960 ml) heavy cream
Powdered sugar	2 tablespoons (30 g) granulated sugar
2 pounds (910 g) marzipan, tinted light pink	Fresh cherries or strawberries
10 ounces (285 g) Vanilla Buttercream (Swiss Method; page 753)	45 Chocolate Figurines (page 545)

1. Line the bottom of a half-sheet pan (16 × 12 inches/40 × 30 cm) with baking paper or a Silpat. Fill the pan with the sponge cake batter, spreading it out evenly. Bake immediately at 400°F (205°C) for about 15 minutes or until the cake springs back when pressed lightly in the center. Let cool completely.

2. Cut around the sides of the pan and invert to remove the sponge. Peel the paper or Silpat from the back and turn right-side up. Cut the skin from the top and level the top at the same time. Cut horizontally into 2 layers.

3. Spread the strawberry jam over the bottom layer, then place the top layer on the jam.

4. Using a plain cookie cutter, cut out 45 rounds, 2 inches (5 cm) in diameter. To get the full number, you will need to keep the cuts close together and stagger the rows. Save the scraps for a trifle or for rum ball filling.

5. Using powdered sugar to prevent it from sticking, roll out half of the marzipan to ⅛ inch (3 mm) thick and into a rectangle measuring approximately 7½ × 16 inches (18.7 × 40 cm). Roll a waffle-pattern marzipan rolling pin lengthwise over the strip to texture the top. The marzipan should increase in size as you do this. Invert the strip and trim it to 7¼ inches (18.1 cm) wide. Cut across the strip to make pieces 1½ inches (3.7 cm) wide. Repeat with the remaining marzipan to make a total of 45 strips. Cover the leftover marzipan and save for another use.

6. Place the buttercream in a disposable pastry bag made from baking paper. Pipe a rope of buttercream lengthwise in the center of each marzipan strip. Fasten a strip around the side of

You can pick up each strip of marzipan and press it in place with your hand. Alternatively, simply leave the strips in place on the table and pick up the cake rounds, one at a time, and roll the side of the cake along the marzipan strip so the buttercream flattens and glues the marzipan to the cake.

each cake round so the buttercream sticks to the sponge and the bottom long edge of the marzipan is even with the bottom of the sponge cake (see Chef's Tip). The strips should overlap slightly so you can press them together.

7. Place the pastry cream in a pastry bag with a No. 4 (8-mm) plain tip. Pipe the cream over the tops of the cakes in a spiral pattern, completely covering the sponge.

8. Whip the heavy cream and granulated sugar to stiff peaks. Place in a pastry bag with a No. 3 (6-mm) star tip. Pipe the whipped cream decoratively on top of the pastry cream, within the marzipan border, making loops left to right and right to left (Figure 3-20).

9. Pit the cherries and cut them in half, or cut the strawberries into small wedges. Stand a chocolate figurine in the whipped cream in the center of each pastry. Place a cherry half or strawberry wedge next to the figurine. Princess pastries should be served the same day they are finished. If they must be kept overnight, they should be boxed and refrigerated.

FIGURE 3-20 The progression in piping the whipped cream on top of Princess Pastries

Walnut-Orange Tartlets yield: 30 pastries, 2½ inches (6.2 cm) in diameter

Most of us are more accustomed to using royal icing for piping decorative patterns on showpieces or wedding cakes and for decorating cookies and holiday specialties than the way it is used in this recipe. Spreading royal icing over a pastry prior to baking, however, is an old trick. Other recipes that utilize this method are Cinnamon Stars (page 460) and Conversations.

Here is a simple cookie featuring baked royal icing that you might want to try: Roll out 6 ounces (170 g) puff pastry into a rectangle measuring 8 × 12 inches (20 × 30 cm); it should be a little thinner than ⅛ inch (3 mm). Refrigerate until firm, then spread a thin film of royal icing on top. The icing should be thin enough to spread easily, but should not be runny. Freeze partially. Cut in half lengthwise, then cut each piece across into 10 rectangles, using a knife dipped in water to keep it from sticking. Allow the icing to dry until a skin forms. Bake at 400°F (205°C) until baked through, approximately 15 minutes. The sweet, crisp icing complements the unsweetened flaky puff pastry beautifully.

1 pound 6 ounces (625 g) Short Dough (page 791)	Grated zest of 1 lemon
6 ounces (170 g) almond paste	2 ounces (55 g) candied orange peel, finely chopped
2 ounces (55 g) granulated sugar	4 ounces (115 g) walnuts, finely chopped
4 ounces (115 g) unsalted butter, at room temperature	¼ recipe or 1¼ cups (300 ml) Royal Icing (page 680; see Chef's Tip)
3 eggs, at room temperature	30 small walnut halves (or large quarters) for decorating
1 ounce (30 g) bread flour	

1. Roll out the short dough ⅛ inch (3 mm) thick and use it to line 30 plain (not fluted) round tartlet pans, 1¼ inches (3.1 cm) high and 2½ inches (6.2 cm) across the top. Combine the short

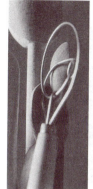

About Walnuts

California produces about 90 percent of the world's supply of the most common commercial walnut, the English variety. Walnuts are second only to almonds in the number of ways they are used in baking. Walnuts enhance the flavor of many types of breakfast pastries and muffins, cookies, breads, brownies, ice creams, and tortes. They are always purchased shelled for use in commercial production; you can buy halves for decorating and broken pieces at a lower price. Because of their high oil content, it is difficult to grind walnuts without them turning into a paste. Grinding them with some of the granulated sugar in a recipe helps alleviate this problem. Also because of their high oil content, it is preferable not to chop the nuts in a food processor; chop them by hand with a sharp knife instead. Be sure to store shelled walnuts in the refrigerator or freezer.

dough scraps and roll the dough again to ⅛ inch (3 mm) thick. Chill both the lined forms and the rolled sheet.

2. Place the almond paste and the sugar in a mixing bowl. Using the paddle, add the butter gradually while mixing at low speed. Mix just until the ingredients are combined and smooth. Add the eggs, 1 at a time. Combine the flour, lemon zest, orange peel, and chopped walnuts. Add the flour mixture to the almond paste mixture.

3. Place the filling in a pastry bag with a No. 7 (14-mm) plain tip. Pipe the filling into the lined forms, filling them almost to the top. Use the rounded end of a small spatula to spread the filling evenly to the edge all around the forms, making the surface slightly concave in the center. Put the filled shells back in the refrigerator long enough for the filling to become firm.

4. Spread a thin layer of royal icing on top of the filling. If the icing is too thick to spread easily, thin it with a little egg white. Place a walnut half in the center of each pastry on top of the icing.

5. Using a fluted pastry wheel, cut the reserved short dough sheet into strips, ¼ inch (6 mm) wide. Center 1 small strip on each side of, and parallel to, the walnut on each pastry. Use your thumbs and press the ends of the strips against the sides of the forms, removing the excess dough and securing the strips to the sides. Cover the scrap dough and save for another use. Set the forms aside until the icing forms a crust on top, about 30 minutes.

6. Bake the tartlets at 400°F (205°C) for about 15 minutes or until baked through. Let cool before unmolding.

7. Stored in a cool, dry place, the tartlets will stay fresh for up to 3 days. The pastries may also be stored in the refrigerator or freezer for up to 1 week before baking. Let them sit at room temperature until the icing forms a crust before putting them in the oven.

CHEF'S TIP

Omit the cream of tartar and add 1 teaspoon (2.5 g) cornstarch to the quarter-recipe of royal icing. Do not overwhip. It is important not to use any acid, such as tartaric acid, cream of tartar, or lemon juice, when making the royal icing; use a small amount of cornstarch instead. This will prevent the icing from browning excessively during baking.

Baked Vanilla-Infused Pineapple with   130
Mango-Avocado Ice Cream and Mango
Fruit Wafer

Baklava with Mascarpone Bavarian and   134
Cherry Sauce

Blueberry Pirouettes   137

Caramel Boxes with Caramel–Macadamia   140
Nut Mousse

Caramelized Apple Galette in Phyllo   143
Dough with Kumquat Sauce

Cherry Baskets with Cherry Compote and   146
Black Pepper Frozen Yogurt

Chèvre Cheesecake in a Cocoa-Nib   150
Florentina Cup with Port-Poached Pears

Chocolate-Banana Tart with Almond Ice   151
Cream and Spun Sugar

Chocolate Bread Pudding with Cookie   152
Citrus Rind

Chocolate Ganache Towers   154

Date-Stuffed Saffron-Poached Pears with   158
Chardonnay Wine Sauce

Dessert Sampling Platter   162

Forbidden Peach   164

Honey Truffle Symphony   167

Hot Chocolate Truffle Cake   169

Individual Croquembouche   173

Marjolaine   174

Mascarpone Cheesecake with Lemon   177
Verbena Panna Cotta

Orange-Chocolate Towers with Orange   179
Syrup and Caramel Screens

Red Banana Truffles in Phyllo Dough   181

Strawberries Romanoff   183

Strawberry Pyramids   185

Trio of Chocolates with Marzipan Parfait   187

Triple Treat   191

Tropical Mousse Cake   195
    ROUND TROPICAL MOUSSE CAKE   197
    KIWI MOUSSE CAKE   197

Valentine's Day Hearts   197

Wild Strawberries Romanoff in Caramel   201
Boxes

Plated Desserts

A beautifully arranged dessert plate is just about everyone's favorite way to end a meal. Whether a humble warm apple tart served with creamy Calvados custard or an architecturally stunning tower composed of multiple layered fillings covered with decorated sponge, garnished with elaborate chocolate and caramel decorations, and served with two or three sauces, a plated dessert is designed to delight. The creation of plated desserts is one of the most important jobs for a pastry chef working in a restaurant.

Throughout history, the dessert course has traditionally been served after the last course of a meal and can include such diverse sweets as cakes, pies, tarts, custards, ice creams and sorbets, puddings, Bavarian creams, pastries, soufflés, cookies, and fresh or cooked fruit. These may be served hot or cold, and it is common to find a combination of both hot and cold on the same plate — for example, warm cake with ice cream or baked fruit with cold custard.

The word *dessert* comes from the French *desservir,* which

means "to clear the table" or "to remove the dishes." The term found favor in its now common usage in the United States earlier than it did in Britain, where it wasn't widely accepted until the twentieth century. When dessert first became fashionable, it was meant not only to provide a sweet nibble at the end of a meal, but also to impress one's guests. In her famous *Book of Household Management,* Mrs. Beeton had much to say about proper dessert choices and their presentation. She felt delicately flavored cakes and biscuits, candied fruits, and morsels of chocolate (in the French fashion) should always be accompanied by equally tasteful wines. She thoroughly discussed the presentation and garnishing of desserts using the finest china, silver, and glassware, upon which great amounts of money were often spent.

As was the custom during the late 1800s, dessert showpieces were often composed of massive impressive displays of fruit and sweetmeats in the rococo style, often surrounded by tall candelabra and pastry replicas of historic buildings. Although formal dessert courses such as these have all but disappeared, the French do carry on the tradition of *gros souper* on Christmas Eve, which ends with the presentation of *Les Treize Desserts,* "the thirteen desserts." These are made with local ingredients or baked goods and are said to symbolize Jesus and the twelve apostles.

With the contemporary pastry chef being elevated to higher and higher status — often with her or his name on a separate dessert menu — ornate plated desserts, frequently composed of several elements, are more common than ever.

Baked Vanilla-Infused Pineapple with Mango-Avocado Ice Cream and Mango Fruit Wafer yield: 12 servings

For a special occasion or an important party, this is a great dessert to present tableside using a *guéridon* — a small serving cart on casters that is used in restaurants for cooking tableside and for flambé work — at which each serving can be sliced and assembled to order. The whole baked pineapples can also be set up as an attention-grabbing carving station on a dessert buffet, in which case slice to order, top with a small scoop of ice cream, and garnish with a tuile cookie. The à la carte presentation described here can easily be simplified by choosing either the dragonfly or the mango wafer as a crunchy garnish.

2 medium-size whole ripe pineapples, approximately 8 pounds (3 kg 640 g) total	Cornstarch, as needed
8 ounces (225 g) unsalted butter	3 vanilla beans
8 ounces (225 g) brown sugar	¼ recipe or 8 ounces (225 g) Vanilla Tuile Decorating Paste (page 695)
½ cup (120 ml) pineapple juice	Mango Wafer Puree (page 725)
1 tablespoon (15 ml) vanilla extract	½ recipe Avocado-Mango Ice Cream (page 379)
Pineapple juice, as needed	

I. Cut the tops and bottoms off each pineapple and cut away the skin. Be sure to remove all of the eyes.

2. Place the whole pineapples in a deep roasting pan just large enough to hold them without crowding. Add the butter, brown sugar, pineapple juice, and vanilla extract to the pan. Bake at 375°F (190°C), basting the pineapples with the syrup in the pan every 10 minutes, for about 40 minutes or until the pineapples are cooked through, soft, and golden brown.

About Vanilla

Vanilla is the most widely used flavoring agent in the pastry kitchen. Its uses are endless because its taste complements just about every other flavor and improves many of them. Vanilla also has the distinction of being more expensive than any other flavoring or spice, with the exception of saffron. The expense is due, in large part, to the length of time — up to a year — required to process vanilla from blossom to high-quality cured bean.

Vanilla is the fruit of a tropical vine that is part of the orchid family and is, in fact, sometimes called "the orchid of flavor." The plant requires a humid tropical climate and thrives around the equator from sea level to approximately 2,000 feet (610 m). The vine grows wild, climbing to the top of the tallest trees in the jungle, but as long as the vines can continue to grow upward they will not flower. For this reason, the vines of *Vanilla planifolia*, the species most widely used for commercial cultivation, are pruned regularly and bent into loops to keep the beans within easy reach of the workers.

Clusters of buds are produced on the vines, taking many weeks to develop into orchids, which then bloom from early morning to late afternoon. If the flowers are not pollinated, they drop from the plant by the early evening. Although a healthy vine produces up to 1,000 flowers, only about 10 percent are pollinated naturally. When grown commercially, the flowers are therefore always hand-pollinated and, in the process, thinned to guarantee a good-quality bean. After pollination, the flowers develop into long, thin, cylindrical green beans, which can reach a length of 12 inches (30 cm), although the more common size is around 8 inches (20 cm). The beans are ready for harvest after approximately eight months.

After harvest, the bean may be cured in several ways. The most common and ideal way is to use the sun to finish the ripening process. After a few days of storage, the beans are spread on blankets and left in the sun for several hours. The blankets are folded over to cover the beans for the rest of the day, then wrapped around them and stored in airtight containers so the beans sweat all night. This procedure is repeated for about two weeks until the beans turn from green to dark brown. In the final step, the beans are spread on mats to dry every day for about two months. They are then stored indoors until they are dry enough to be packed and shipped.

According to history, the Spanish stole vanilla cuttings from Mexico and planted them on the island of Madagascar. Madagascar had a monopoly on the crop for hundreds of years; Mexico and Madagascar are still the world's major producers of vanilla. The same species (sometimes referred to as *bourbon vanilla* from the name of one of the Madagascar islands) is grown in both countries. Tahiti is also an important growing area, producing a sweeter and more flowery-tasting bean.

3. Transfer the cooked pineapples to a half-sheet pan lined with baking paper. Cover tightly with foil and reserve in a warm location, such as the top of the stove or in a very low oven.

4. Strain the cooking liquid; you should have approximately 1 cup (240 ml). If necessary, add pineapple juice to make this amount. The sauce should be thick enough to hold its shape on the serving plate. Thicken the liquid with cornstarch, if needed. Split the vanilla beans lengthwise, scrape out the seeds, and stir into the pineapple sauce. Cut the pod halves across and place in a small container. Pour the sauce over the pods, cover, and reserve.

5. Make the dragonfly template (Figure 4-1). The template as shown is the correct size for use in this recipe; however, due to the size of the template, only half of it fits on the page. Trace the template, turn your paper over and match the dotted lines in the center, and trace the other half so the template looks like the small example shown. Cut the template out of 1/16-inch (2-mm) cardboard of the type used for cake boxes. Cut a piece of corrugated cardboard 5 × 16 inches (12.5 × 40 cm). Score a line lengthwise in the center of the cardboard, cutting halfway

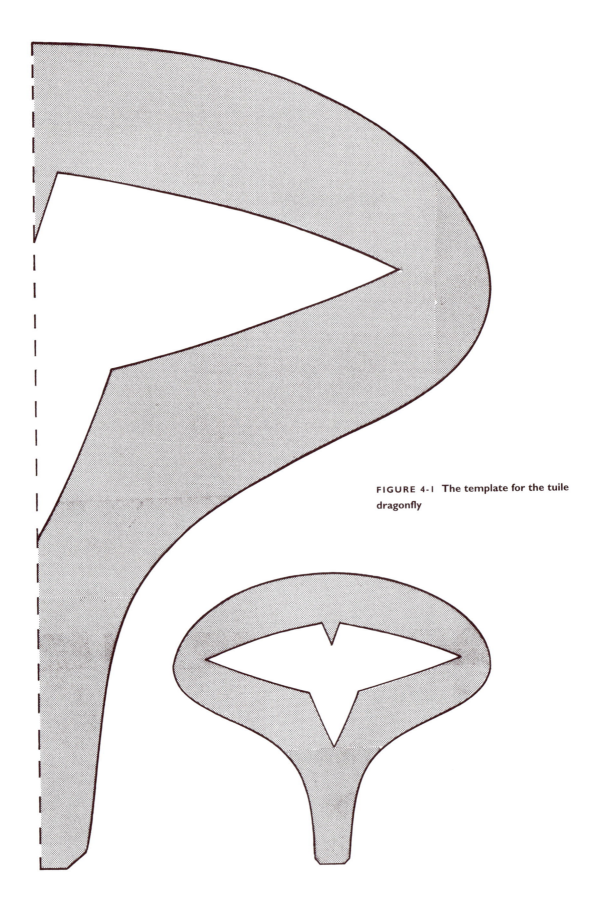

FIGURE 4-1 The template for the tuile dragonfly

PROCEDURE 4-1a Spreading tuile paste on a Silpat within the template to make a dragonfly decoration

PROCEDURE 4-1b Removing a baked decoration after pressing it inside a V-shaped molding strip that is set on an inverted Flexipan

through the thickness. Turn the cardboard over and bend the long edges up to form a *V* with an opening that measures 3 inches (7.5 cm) across. Tape across the top of the opening at the ends to hold the shape. Place the cardboard on top of an inverted muffin tin or Flexipan to hold it steady.

6. Place the template on a Silpat. Spread a portion of the tuile paste thinly and evenly inside the template (see Procedure 4-1a). Do not form more than 4 dragonflies per mat. Repeat until you have made a few more dragonflies than you will need to allow for breakage. Bake 1 pan at a time at 400°F (205°C) for approximately 6 minutes or until the cookies start to show a few spots of light brown color. Remove from the oven and quickly place the cookies inside the *V*-shaped molding strip shaping the 2 wings of the dragonfly at an angle (see Procedure 4-1b).

7. Spread the mango wafer puree into thin ovals, approximately 6 × 4 inches (15 × 10 cm), on Silpats. As with the dragonflies, it is a good idea to make a few extra in case some break. Bake as directed on page 725. As the wafers come out of the oven, quickly bend them into a curved shape on top of a rolling pin or with your hands (they will become crisp very quickly).

8. Presentation: Cut a slice 1½ inches (3.7 cm) wide from a warm pineapple. Using a cookie cutter of an appropriate size, cut out the core. Place the pineapple ring in the center of a dessert plate. Spoon some of the reserved sauce over the slice and into puddles on the plate around it. Form a quenelle-shaped scoop of avocado-mango ice cream and place it in the center of the pineapple ring. Garnish with a cookie dragonfly and one of the vanilla bean pod quarters reserved in the sauce. Place a mango fruit wafer on the side of the plate and serve immediately.

Baklava with Mascarpone Bavarian and Cherry Sauce

yield: 12 servings (Color Photo 20)

Baklava is a phyllo-dough pastry most commonly associated with Greece, although *baklava* is actually a Turkish word, and the confection is popular throughout the eastern part of the Mediterranean and the Near East. Any combination of nuts may be used, but traditionally, nuts indigenous to the Middle East, such as walnuts, almonds, hazelnuts, or pistachios, are included. My version of baklava is paired with a mascarpone Bavarian and cherry sauce. Orange sauce or any other slightly acidic fruit sauce would make a nice accompaniment as well. If you do not have time to make the caramel fences, stand a fresh cherry with the stem attached on a whipped cream rosette; cut the cherry to expose or remove the pit. Baklava can alternatively be offered as an individual pastry instead of a plated dessert. Well covered in the refrigerator, baklava will stay fresh for up to one week.

18 stemmed fresh cherries, cut in half and pitted

Cherry Sauce (page 230)

Mascarpone Bavarian (recipe follows)

Baklava (recipe follows)

Powdered sugar

12 Caramel Fences (page 621)

1. Coat the cherry halves with some of the cherry sauce so they do not become dry. Place the remaining cherry sauce in a piping bottle with a small opening.

2. Presentation: Place a mascarpone Bavarian in the center of a dessert plate. Evenly space 3 pieces of baklava around the Bavarian, with a flat side of each triangle parallel to the sides of the Bavarian. Sift powdered sugar lightly over the baklava and the plate. Pipe 3 large dots of cherry sauce on the plate between the pieces of baklava. Pipe a zigzag design of sauce on top of the Bavarian. Place a cherry half, cut-side up, on each dot of sauce. Stand a caramel fence upright on the Bavarian. Serve immediately.

MASCARPONE BAVARIAN yield: 5½ cups (1 L 320 ml), or 12 servings

This is a variation of the White Chocolate Bavarian Filling (page 41), and the same cautions apply: Do not overwhip the cream or overheat the white chocolate. The chocolate should be warm to aid in incorporating the gelatin, but it must never be left unattended while melting. If the chocolate gets too hot, the filling will break and become gritty. Unfortunately, if that happens, there is nothing to do but start over. To avoid having the filling set prematurely, do not make it until you are ready to use it.

1⅓ cups (320 ml) heavy cream

12 ounces (340 g) mascarpone cheese

1 tablespoon (9 g) unflavored gelatin powder

⅓ cup (80 ml) cold water

2 tablespoons (18 g) pectin powder (see Note)

5 ounces (140 g) granulated sugar

6 egg whites (¾ cup/180 ml)

4 ounces (115 g) white chocolate, melted

1. Place twelve 6-sided or round rings, 3¼ inches in diameter by 1¼ inches high (8.1 × 3.1 cm), on a sheet pan lined with baking paper. If you do not have rings, you can make them easily (see "Making Rings from Acetate," at right), or you may simply divide the filling among 12 ramekins, 3¼ inches (8.1 cm) in diameter, instead. To form the filling in Flexipans, use No. 1269, freeze the filling in the molds, push the frozen servings out of the pans, and let them thaw before serving.

Making Rings from Acetate

Cut strips of acetate or polyurethane to 9½ inches long × 1¼ inches wide (23.7 × 3.1 cm). Overlap the ends ¼ inch (6 mm) and tape together. Use an appropriately sized cookie cutter as a guide as you tape the strips: Wrap the strips around the outside of the cutter to make certain that all of the rings are the same size. At the same time, place the plastic flush with the edge of the cutter to ensure that the rings will stand straight and even.

2. Whip the heavy cream to soft peaks; do not overwhip. Soften the mascarpone, if necessary. Gradually fold the cream into the mascarpone cheese. Reserve in the refrigerator.

3. Sprinkle the gelatin over the cold water and set aside to soften.

4. Combine the pectin powder and granulated sugar in a mixing bowl. Stir in the egg whites. Place the bowl over simmering water and heat, stirring constantly with a whisk, to 140°F (60°C). Remove from the heat and immediately whip the mixture until it has cooled completely and has formed stiff peaks.

5. Place the gelatin mixture over a bain-marie and heat until dissolved. Do not overheat.

6. Quickly stir the gelatin into the melted white chocolate, then quickly stir the chocolate mixture into one-third of the meringue mixture to temper it. Still working quickly, add this to the remaining meringue. Stir in the reserved whipped cream and cheese mixture.

7. Immediately divide the filling among the prepared rings or forms. Spread the tops even and refrigerate for at least 2 hours to set. The Bavarian may be kept in the refrigerator, tightly covered, for 3 to 4 days. Unmold as needed.

NOTE: Use regular canning pectin; pure USP-grade pectin is too strong. If pectin is unavailable, increase the gelatin powder by 1 teaspoon (3 g) for a total of 4 teaspoons (12 g).

About Phyllo Dough

Phyllo dough (also called *filo* or *fillo* — which, appropriately enough, is the Greek word for "leaf") has been used in the Mediterranean since ancient times for both savory and sweet recipes. Phyllo dough originated in Greece and is similar to strudel dough, but it is much thinner and even more delicate. Phyllo dough is not a dough at all in the traditional sense. It is prepared and purchased as paper-thin, leafy sheets made of flour and water. These sheets dry out quickly once exposed to air, so it is important to keep a damp cloth over them to keep them somewhat moist as you are working.

When brushed with melted butter and stacked together, the multiple leaves provide a layer structure similar to that of puff pastry, but phyllo sheets are virtually fat-free, making the dough suitable for the preparation of low-fat and low-cholesterol desserts. Naturally, you must take into consideration the butter that is brushed onto the leaves of dough, but this can be cut down if desired, and vegetable oil can be used if cholesterol is a concern. One option is to spray the melted butter or oil onto the dough instead of using a brush. Some people spray the sheets with a pan coating instead of butter to reduce the fat.

Phyllo sheets vary in size from 12 × 14 inches (30 × 35 cm) to 16 × 18 inches (40 × 45 cm), depending on the brand. Each 1-pound (455-g) package typically contains about twenty-four sheets. Frozen phyllo dough must be allowed to defrost slowly in the refrigerator overnight before it is used. If it is thawed too quickly, the thin sheets tend to break. See page 159 for information about *kadaif* phyllo dough.

BAKLAVA yield: 40 triangular pieces

6 ounces (170 g) pistachios

6 ounces (170 g) pecans

6 ounces (170 g) walnuts

4 ounces (115 g) light brown sugar

1 teaspoon (1.5 g) ground cinnamon

½ teaspoon (1 g) ground cloves

Grated zest of 2 small oranges

½ cup (120 ml) water

¼ cup (60 ml) or 3 ounces (85 g) honey

¼ cup (60 ml) orange juice

7 ounces (200 g) granulated sugar

12 sheets phyllo dough, approximately 8 ounces (225 g)

8 ounces (225 g) unsalted butter, melted

1. Blanch the pistachios in water with a pinch of salt to make the green color more vivid. Remove the skins and dry the nuts.

2. Place the pistachios, pecans, walnuts, and brown sugar in a food processor and grind finely. Mix in the ground cinnamon, ground cloves, and half of the orange zest.

3. Place the water, honey, orange juice, remaining orange zest, and granulated sugar in a heavy saucepan. Bring to a boil over medium heat and boil until the mixture becomes syrupy, about 5 minutes. Add about one-third of the syrup to the nut mixture (just enough to bind it) and mix thoroughly. Reserve the remaining syrup and the nut mixture separately.

4. Unroll the phyllo sheets and keep them covered with a damp towel as you work. Place a sheet of baking paper larger than the phyllo sheets on your work surface. Layer the phyllo sheets on top of the paper, brushing each lightly with melted butter before topping it with the next layer. Brush the top sheet with butter as well.

5. Trim 1 long edge of the phyllo stack, then cut the stack in half crosswise, cutting through the baking paper at the same time. Lift up 1 stack of phyllo and slide it off the paper into a half-sheet pan. Place the phyllo sheets in the corner of the pan so that 2 cut (even) edges touch 2 sides of the pan (see Note).

6. Spread the nut mixture evenly over the phyllo layer in the pan and press it down lightly. Slide the second stack of phyllo sheets on top of the nut mixture, aligning the trimmed edges with those underneath. Trim the 2 remaining sides, cutting through both layers.

7. Cutting through the top layer only, cut the phyllo dough lengthwise into 5 strips, then cut crosswise into 4 strips to make 20 small rectangles. Cut diagonally across each rectangle from corner to corner to make 40 triangles. Do not cut through the nut filling and the bottom layer of dough. It will be easier to make precise cuts if you chill the baklava first.

8. Cut strips of cardboard about 1 inch (2.5 cm) wide and long enough to cover the exposed sides of the baklava. Place the strips against the exposed sides and place weights against the cardboard to hold it in place (Figure 4-2).

9. Bake at 325°F (163°C) for approximately 45 minutes or until dark golden brown. Reheat the remaining syrup

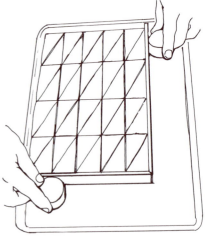

FIGURE 4-2 Placing weights against two cardboard strips to create a frame for Baklava

and pour it slowly and evenly over the baklava immediately after removing it from the oven.

10. After the baklava has cooled completely, cut again following the previous cuts, but this time go all the way through the bottom layer of phyllo dough. Cover the baklava carefully to avoid crushing the phyllo dough and store it in the refrigerator. Baklava tastes best 1 or 2 days after it is baked, after the nuts have absorbed moisture. While baklava should be stored in the refrigerator, the flavor is improved by letting it come to room temperature prior to serving.

NOTE: The instructions are based on using a standard industry half-sheet pan with 1-inch (2.5-cm) sides. If you have a quarter-sheet pan (12 × 8 inches/30 × 20 cm), use that instead to avoid having to make the cardboard support frame; you will probably need to trim the phyllo dough.

Blueberry Pirouettes yield: 16 servings (Color Photo 23)

Like lingonberries, blueberries grow wild on sunny hillsides and in sunny patches of the forest all over Scandinavia and in the northern United States and Canada. When I was a child, my mom and dad kept a close eye on their secret blueberry patches in the early fall, as the berries had to be picked as soon as they turned from a reddish shade to that beautiful blue color. The trouble was that their secret place was often someone else's secret place as well. Whoever didn't get there first was out of luck! The blueberries were harvested in the same way as lingonberries, using a small, handheld screened box with a device on the front that strained out the leaves and twigs, letting the berries fall into the box. You pushed the box through the top of the blueberry bushes in a scooping motion. We kids always had to pick our share before we were allowed to go and play. At first there was much more eating than picking, which was evidenced by our blue-stained teeth. The small wild blueberry that grows in Scandinavia is blue throughout, unlike the cultivated variety, and would temporarily give ample proof of where the majority of the picked berries were being stored.

Blueberries contain a large amount of pectin, which gives the sauce in this recipe a lustrous shine and an easily controllable consistency. Fresh blueberries should be stored in a single layer, if possible. In this manner, they will keep for a week or more in the refrigerator. During the off-season I have, on occasion, used frozen blueberries instead, which works better than you might think given that the colorful (and tasty) sauce really makes this presentation stand out.

1 recipe Vanilla Tuile Decorating Paste (page 695)	2 cups (480 ml) heavy cream
1 teaspoon (2.5 g) unsweetened cocoa powder	8 ounces (225 g) Pastry Cream (page 773)
Dark coating chocolate, melted	Blueberry Sauce (recipe follows)
6 ounces (170 g) shelled pistachios	Caramel Corkscrews (page 620)

1. If you do not have Silpats, grease and flour the back of clean, even sheet pans. Make the template shown in Figure 4-3. The template as shown is the correct size for use in this recipe. Copy or trace the drawing, then cut the template out of cardboard, $\frac{1}{16}$ inch (2 mm) thick. Cake boxes are a good choice for this.

2. Place 2 tablespoons (30 ml) of the tuile paste in a small cup. Stir in the cocoa powder, mixing until it is thoroughly incorporated. Spread the plain tuile paste within the template on the Silpats or sheet pans (see Figures 13-29 and 13-30, page 694). You need 32 cookies for this recipe, but you should make a few extra, as some may break or become too dark in the oven.

FIGURE 4-3 The template for the tuile paste cookies in Blueberry Pirouettes and Crème Caramel Nouvelle

3. Place the cocoa-colored tuile paste in a piping bag and cut a very small opening. Pipe 3 diagonal lines on each cookie, close together, in the center.

4. Bake at 400°F (205°C) until the cookies just start to turn light brown in spots. Immediately wrap each cookie lengthwise around a 1-inch (2.5-cm) dowel so the finished pirouette will be about 4 inches (10 cm) tall; press the seam against the table to weld the edges together. Set the cookies aside to cool. When cool, dip each end of each pirouette ⅛ inch (3 mm) into melted dark chocolate.

5. Blanch the pistachios and remove the skins. Chop the nuts into small pieces and reserve.

6. Whip the heavy cream until stiff peaks form. Fold in the pastry cream and half of the pistachio nuts. Place the mixture in a pastry bag with a No. 6 (12-mm) plain tip. Fill both ends of the tubes with the cream mixture, reserving about ⅓ cup (80 ml). Dip each end into the remaining chopped pistachio nuts. Ideally, the tubes should be filled to order — certainly no longer than 30 minutes before serving.

7. Presentation: Pipe or spoon a raspberry-sized dollop of the reserved cream in the center of a dessert plate (the cream is to prevent the pirouettes from rolling on the plate; it should not show in the final presentation). Place 2 filled pirouettes on top of the cream, leaning one against the other at an angle. Spoon blueberry sauce across the center, using enough to form a small pool on each side of the plate. Decorate with 3 caramel corkscrews.

BLUEBERRY SAUCE   yield: approximately 3 cups (720 ml)

Due to the large amount of pectin in blueberries, the sauce may set up too much. Reheat, stirring, until liquid and smooth again, then adjust with water or simple syrup, depending on the level of sweetness. If cranberry juice is not available, apple juice makes a good substitute; add a very small amount of red food color or Beet Juice (page 750) to enhance the color.

7 ounces (200 g) granulated sugar

1½ cups (360 ml) cranberry juice or apple juice

1 tablespoon (15 ml) lime juice

3 tablespoons (45 ml) rum

2 tablespoons (16 g) cornstarch

1 pint (480 ml) or 12 ounces (340 g) blueberries

Red food coloring or Beet Juice (page 750; optional)

1. Place the sugar and the cranberry or apple juice in a saucepan.

2. Combine the lime juice and rum. Add the cornstarch and stir to dissolve. Mix the solution into the juice mixture in the saucepan. Bring to a boil and cook for a few minutes.

3. Remove from the heat and stir in the blueberries as well as the coloring, if using apple juice. Let cool. Store, covered, in the refrigerator.

Caramel Boxes with Caramel–Macadamia Nut Mousse

yield: 16 servings (Color Photo 21)

Caramel, chocolate, and nuts — if you love this combination, and who doesn't? — this is the dessert for you. Making the boxes and decorations may appear intimidating at first, but as you will find out, the caramel glass paste is actually quite easy to work with. Also, unfilled boxes can be stored for up to ten days in an airtight container, so you can start well ahead. To simplify, you can omit one of the caramel decorations (use either the corkscrews or the caramelized nuts instead of both) without sacrificing the elegance of the presentation. Please do not leave off both decorations, however; they are really so easy, well worth the time and effort, and guests always love fancy sugar decorations — especially these, standing tall and glorious. I have intentionally excluded fruit, mint sprigs, and edible flowers from the presentation to accentuate the subtle gold and brown shades of the caramel, chocolate, and macadamia nuts. For a more colorful presentation featuring caramel boxes, see Wild Strawberries Romanoff in Caramel Boxes (page 201).

Dark coating chocolate, melted

16 Caramel Boxes and Squares (recipe follows)

1 chocolate cake layer, 9 inches (22.5 cm) in diameter and ¾ inch (2 cm) thick (see Note)

Caramel–Macadamia Nut Mousse (recipe follows)

Caramel Corkscrews (page 620)

Caramel-Dipped Macadamia Nuts (page 625)

Milk chocolate curls

¼ recipe Fortified Caramel Sauce (page 19)

1. Place a small amount of melted coating chocolate in a piping bag. Cut a very small opening and pipe 7 or 8 straight lines across the center of the base of 16 dessert plates.

2. Dip the top edge of as many caramel boxes as you will be serving ¼ inch (6 mm) into the same chocolate. Dip the same number of small squares halfway into the coating chocolate diagonally. Set aside for the chocolate to harden.

3. Cut the cake into 1¾-inch (4.5-cm) squares. Place a square of cake in the bottom of as many caramel boxes as you expect to serve by picking up the square with the tip of a paring knife, then lowering it into the box. Place the caramel-nut mousse filling in a pastry bag with a No. 6 (12-mm) plain tip. Pipe the mousse into the boxes, filling them to just below the rim. Reserve in the refrigerator (see Chef's Tip).

4. Presentation: Decorate the top of a filled box with a chocolate-dipped caramel square, caramelized macadamia nuts, and caramel corkscrews. Push the corkscrews into the filling slightly to make them stand at the angle desired, but be careful not to break them. Use the tip of a paring knife to press the bottom of the corkscrew into the filling instead of pushing it down from the top. Spoon chocolate curls on top of the box around the other decorations. Pipe a small dot of filling in the center of one of the decorated plates. Place the filled and decorated box on top, placing it at an angle to the piped chocolate lines. Pipe caramel sauce on the plate around the box in large teardrop shapes. Decorate the plate in front of the box with 2 caramelized macadamia nuts attached with a little chocolate.

NOTE: Any type of moist chocolate cake may be used, including brownies.

CHEF'S TIP

This dessert tastes best when the boxes are crisp. While it is possible to fill the boxes with mousse and hold them in the refrigerator for up to 2 hours before serving, ideally, each box should be filled and decorated to order. This also allows you to keep unfilled boxes for later use.

Making Molding Blocks

You can make the molding blocks used for shaping the glass paste out of Styrofoam and wrap them with aluminum foil or, for sturdier forms that will last forever, cut the shapes out of hard wood (or have them made). Smooth the long edges with sandpaper. Screw a small round-headed screw partway into the center of one short end. The screw can be used as a handle to facilitate lifting the block out of the caramel box, as shown in Figure 4-4.

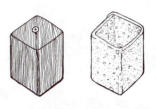

FIGURE 4-4 **The wooden molding block and a caramel box**

CARAMEL BOXES AND SQUARES yield: 16 boxes and square decorations

1 recipe Caramel Glass Paste (page 666)

1. Cut a sturdy cardboard template measuring 4¼ inches × 8½ inches (10.6 × 21.2 cm).

2. Make 2 rectangular molding blocks, 2 inches square and 3½ inches long (5 cm × 8.7 cm; see "Making Molding Blocks").

3. Place 8 ounces (225 g) or one-quarter of the caramel glass paste on a sheet of baking paper. Spread it out to a strip, 9 × 20 inches (22.5 × 50 cm). Transfer the paper to a perfectly flat sheet pan. Repeat 3 times with the remaining paste, placing each strip on its own pan.

4. Bake 1 sheet at a time at 350°F (175°C) for approximately 12 minutes or until light brown. Remove the sheet from the oven carefully; a jarring movement will ripple the soft, thin surface. Let the sheet cool for a few seconds. Then, still working carefully, transfer it to the tabletop or, better yet, to a full sheet–sized cardboard set on the table. Using the template as a guide, cut the sheet into 4 pieces with a chef's knife. Set the cut sheet aside to cool while you bake and cut the remaining sheets in the same manner.

5. Break away the scrap pieces around the edges of all 16 rectangles. Place the larger scrap pieces (slightly apart so they do not touch) on a sheet pan lined with baking paper (see Chef's Tip). Return to the oven until soft. Remove from the oven and cut about 20 squares, 1¾ inches (4.5 cm), out of the softened scraps. Reserve the squares to use in serving. The remaining scrap pieces can be used in rum ball or Danish pastry fillings (or eaten).

6. Reheat the large rectangular pieces, 4 at a time, until they are soft enough to bend yet still firm enough to pick up from the pan. Working at a table close to the oven, invert 1 rectangle onto the table and place the molding block in the corner of one short end. Quickly wrap the glass sheet around the block, pressing down firmly at the end to weld the edges together. Still working quickly, fold the protruding edges against the end of the block as if you were wrapping a package (Figure 4-5). Stand the box upright and press down hard again to weld the bottom together (Figure 4-6). Leave the block inside the box and form the next one. (You may need to warm the pieces again to keep them from breaking.) Carefully pull out the first block; if it sticks, insert a small paring knife between the block and the box

CHEF'S TIP
If necessary, you can weld together a number of smaller pieces if you don't have scraps large enough to make the decorations. Overlap the edges and heat until the pieces melt together.

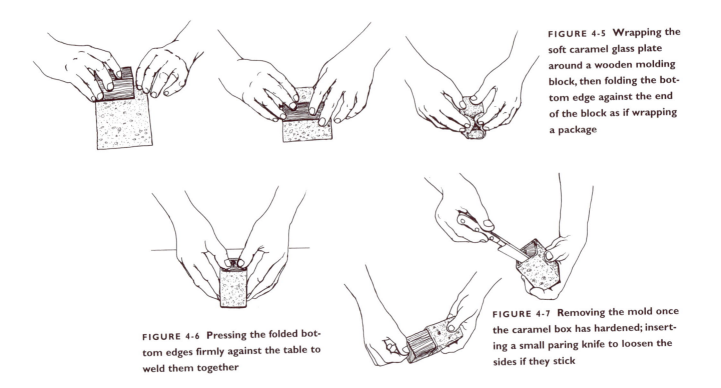

FIGURE 4-5 Wrapping the soft caramel glass plate around a wooden molding block, then folding the bottom edge against the end of the block as if wrapping a package

FIGURE 4-6 Pressing the folded bottom edges firmly against the table to weld them together

FIGURE 4-7 Removing the mold once the caramel box has hardened; inserting a small paring knife to loosen the sides if they stick

(Figure 4-7). Form the remaining boxes (leaving 1 block in place while you use the other) in the same way. You can expedite the molding process by keeping the paring knife chilled in ice water; the cold knife in contact with the sides of the box will make it harden more quickly, and you will be able to pull the molding block out sooner.

7. If you will not be serving the boxes right away, store them in an airtight container (together with the square decorations) until needed. They can be kept this way for up to 10 days.

CARAMEL–MACADAMIA NUT MOUSSE yield: 6 cups (1 L 440 ml)

2 cups (480 ml) heavy cream

2 teaspoons (6 g) unflavored gelatin powder

¼ cup (60 ml) cold water

10 ounces (285 g) granulated sugar

¾ cup (180 ml) hot water

4 eggs

4 ounces (115 g) unsalted macadamia nuts, toasted and coarsely crushed

1. Whip the cream to soft peaks. Set aside in the refrigerator.

2. Sprinkle the gelatin over the cold water and set aside to soften.

3. Caramelize the sugar to a light brown color. It is important to caramelize the sugar dark enough not only to color the filling but also to give it a caramel flavor (see Chef's Tip, page 18). Add the hot water and cook out any lumps. Set aside off the heat.

4. Whip the eggs for about 3 minutes at high speed. Lower the speed and pour the hot caramel into the eggs in a steady stream. Turn back to high speed and continue whipping until the mixture is cold and forms soft peaks. Fold in the reserved whipped cream.

5. Place the gelatin mixture over a bain-marie and heat until dissolved. Do not overheat. Rapidly mix the gelatin into a small portion of the cream, then quickly add that mixture to the remainder of the cream. Fold in the macadamia nuts.

Caramelized Apple Galette in Phyllo Dough with Kumquat Sauce

yield: 16 servings (Color Photo 22)

Given today's rather loose interpretation of the term *galette* (see "About Galettes"), I do not feel the name is out of place here, even though a true galette, in addition to being round, should be rather flat. In this dessert, I have shaped the crust into a basket to give height to the presentation and make it more appealing, and I have placed the fruit on top of phyllo dough instead of the more traditional puff pastry. To make a classic galette, see the variation on the following page.

This pastry is quick and easy to produce. If necessary, the apples can be prepared one or two days ahead, as can the phyllo shells. It is then quite simple to assemble and bake the galettes. Orange sauce can be used as a substitute for the kumquat sauce, if kumquats are unavailable. Don't give up too easily, however, as the wonderful, distinctive flavor of this small citrus fruit is well worth the effort to find, and the peel gives the sauce a deep, vibrant color that adds greatly to the visual appeal of the dish.

24 sheets phyllo dough (1 pound/455 g)	6 ounces (170 g) granulated sugar
2 ounces (55 g) unsalted butter, melted	⅓ cup (80 ml) heavy cream
1 pound (455 g) Pastry Cream (page 773)	½ recipe Chantilly Cream (page 765)
2 ounces (55 g) sweet dark chocolate	Kumquat Sauce (recipe follows)
2 ounces (55 g) hazelnuts, toasted and skins removed	8 whole kumquats, cut in half
5 pounds (2 kg 275 g) Red Delicious apples (approximately 12 medium)	Small mint leaves
	Lavender blossoms
4 ounces (115 g) unsalted butter	

1. Cut a round template, 5½ inches (13.7 cm) in diameter, from cardboard, or have a lid or plate of the same size handy. Unwrap and unroll the phyllo dough; cut the stacked phyllo sheets in half lengthwise. Cut across in thirds, dividing each sheet of dough into 6 pieces. Place the pieces in 2 stacks and cover 1 with a lightly dampened cloth. Place 1 piece from the remaining stack on the table in front of you. Brush some of the melted butter in a circle, 4 inches (10 cm) in diameter, in the center of the dough. Place a second piece of dough on top and brush butter

About Galettes

Galettes are possibly the oldest of all pastries; they can be traced back to the Neolithic period. Generally speaking, a galette is a round cake made of flaky pastry dough. The most celebrated version is the *Galette des Rois*, a pastry served during the Twelfth Night celebration in France. Galette des Rois is actually the same cake as Pithiviers; it is simply given the other name when it is served for this celebration. Twelfth Night is the eve of Epiphany (6 January), the close of the Christmas festivities. Traditionally, the cake contains a small porcelain doll or a single bean, and the person who finds the doll or bean in his serving proclaims himself king for the night and names his queen. The word *galette* is also used for many savory tarts topped with meat and cheese and for items such as fried potato cakes and certain pancakes.

To Make a Classic Galette

Follow the main recipe with the following changes: Omit making the phyllo dough baskets. Instead, roll out 3 pounds 12 ounces (1 kg 705 g) puff pastry (in two portions) to ⅛ inch (3 mm) thick. Refrigerate the dough until it is firm. Using a sharp knife, cut out 16 circles, 6 inches (15 cm) in diameter. Divide the pastry cream, chopped chocolate, and chopped nuts among the circles, leaving an uncovered border of dough, ½ inch (1.2 cm) wide, around the edge of each. Arrange the apples on top. Do not spoon the sugar sauce over the apples. Bake as directed. Brush the sugar sauce on top of the desserts as soon as they are removed from the oven.

on it in the same way. Continue layering and brushing with butter until you have used 8 pieces of phyllo. Do not butter the top of the stack.

2. Place the template on top of the stack. Cut around the template with a paring knife and remove the scraps. Brush butter over the top layer of the circle. Carefully press the stack of dough into a small individual pie form (Figure 4-8; see Note). If the circle does not form an evenly fluted edge, shape the edge with your hands. Repeat to form 15 additional phyllo dough shells. Place the lined forms on 2 sheet pans. Discard any leftover phyllo dough.

3. Place the pastry cream in a disposable pastry bag made from a half-sheet of baking paper. Pipe the cream into the shells, dividing it evenly.

4. Chop the chocolate and the nuts into raspberry-sized pieces. Sprinkle the chocolate and nuts evenly over the pastry cream.

5. Peel and core the apples. Cut them lengthwise into quarters, then cut again in the same direction to get 8 wedges from each apple.

6. Place 4 ounces (115 g) butter in a skillet at least 10 inches (25 cm) in diameter. Melt the butter over medium heat. Sprinkle the sugar evenly over the melted butter. Add the apple wedges and cook over medium heat, shaking the skillet gently to ensure that the apples do not stick and that they cook evenly. Continue cooking the apples in this manner until enough of the apple liquid has evaporated to allow the sugar to turn dark golden brown and caramelize, 30 to 45 minutes. Remove the skillet from the heat and let the apples cool for a few minutes.

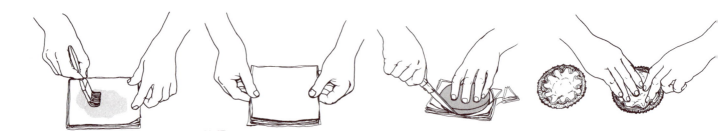

FIGURE 4-8 Brushing butter over a phyllo sheet before placing the next sheet on top; using a template as a guide to cut the layered sheets into a circle; placing the stacked sheets inside an individual pie form so the phyllo dough forms a fluted edge

7. Place the apples on a sheet pan lined with baking paper; reserve the syrup in the skillet. Place 6 pieces of apple on top of the pastry cream in each phyllo shell, arranging the wedges so the rounded sides face up.

8. Add the heavy cream to the sugar syrup remaining in the skillet. Bring to a boil while stirring constantly. Strain the sauce, then spoon it over the apples in each form.

9. Bake the galettes at 400°F (205°C) for approximately 15 minutes. Cool slightly, then remove the desserts from the forms.

10. Whip the Chantilly cream until stiff peaks form. Place in a pastry bag with a No. 6 (12-mm) star tip and reserve in the refrigerator.

11. Presentation: Using a piping bottle, pipe a fluted circle of kumquat sauce, covering most of the base of a dessert plate (see Chef's Tip). Place an apple galette in the center of the sauce. Pipe a rosette of Chantilly cream on top. Decorate the top with a kumquat half and a mint leaf. Sprinkle lavender blossoms around the galette in the sauce.

NOTE: Use individual pie forms that are 7 ounces (210 ml) in capacity. The forms should have slanted sides and measure 4½ inches (11.2 cm) in diameter across the top, 2¾ inches (6.8 cm) in diameter across the bottom, and 1½ inches (3.7 cm) in height. If this size is not available, it is preferable to use slightly smaller forms rather than larger ones.

CHEF'S TIP

To pipe a fluted circle of sauce without first piping a frame (the frame method is described in the Honey Truffle Symphony recipe, page 167), begin by piping a circle that is slightly smaller than the desired finished size. Then, use the tip of the piping bottle to push the edge of the sauce out toward the edge of the plate to create the fluted pattern.

KUMQUAT SAUCE yield: approximately 4 cups (960 ml)

The kumquat peel produces an intense and vibrant orange color; regular orange sauce looks quite pale by comparison. Adjust the amount of sugar to taste depending on the sweetness of the citrus.

1 pound (455 g) kumquats

1½ cups (360 ml) water

2 tablespoons (16 g) cornstarch

2 cups (480 ml) fresh orange juice (from about 6 oranges), strained

8 ounces (225 g) granulated sugar

1. Slice the kumquats without peeling them. Place the fruit and the water in a saucepan and bring to a boil. Cook until the kumquat slices have softened, about 5 minutes. Remove from the heat.

2. Dissolve the cornstarch in a small amount of the orange juice. Mix the solution into the remaining orange juice. Pour the mixture into a noncorrosive saucepan.

3. Puree the kumquat mixture and strain it into the orange juice, pressing as much of the liquid as possible through the strainer. Discard the contents of the strainer. Add the granulated sugar. Bring the sauce to a boil, lower the heat, and cook for 30 seconds, stirring constantly. Remove from the heat and let the sauce cool completely before using. If the sauce is too thick, thin it with water. Store, covered, in the refrigerator.

Cherry Baskets with Cherry Compote and Black Pepper

Frozen Yogurt yield: 16 servings (Color Photo 29)

These impressive-looking baskets are made even more so by their towering handles. They are a lighter version of an Easter basket dessert typically made in Sweden many years ago. Instead of cherries, the baskets were filled with small handmade marzipan Easter eggs. For most Europeans, marzipan is a must at Easter in the form of rabbits, chickens, and, of course, the aforementioned Easter eggs. Try using these templates and instructions to create basket-shaped desserts at Easter, filling them with chocolate or marzipan eggs on top of the cream. If calories are not a concern, you may want to fill the baskets with sweetened whipped cream rather than the lighter Italian cream called for here.

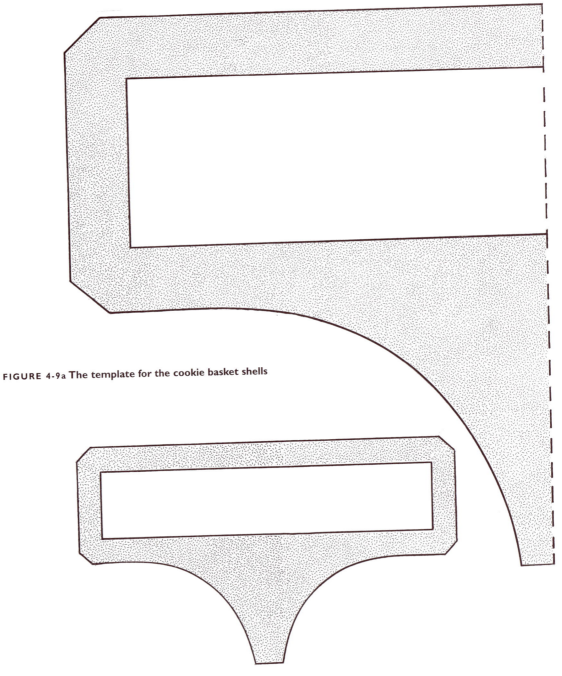

FIGURE 4-9a The template for the cookie basket shells

1 recipe Vanilla Tuile Decorating Paste
(page 695)

2 teaspoons (5 g) cocoa powder

½ recipe Angel Food Cake (page 796; see Note)

2 pounds 4 ounces (1 kg 25 g) Bing cherries

½ recipe Italian Cream (page 771)

Cherry Compote (recipe follows)

1 recipe Black Pepper Frozen Yogurt
(page 403)

1. Make the templates for the cherry baskets and basket handles (Figures 4-9a and 4-9b). The templates are shown at the correct size for the recipe; however, only half fits on the page. Trace as shown, invert your paper, match the dotted line in the center, and trace the other half of each template so they look like the small examples shown. Cut both templates out of cardboard that is ¹⁄₁₆ inch (2 mm) thick (cake boxes work fine for this). Save the solid rectangle cut from the center of the basket template. Overlap the short edges of this piece ³⁄₈ inch (9 mm) and tape together to form a round tube. Compress the tube slightly to make it oval instead of round (see Chef's Tip). Have a small dowel available.

2. If you do not have Silpats, lightly grease the back of 8 even sheet pans, coat with flour, then shake off as much flour as possible.

3. Remove 3 tablespoons (45 ml) of the tuile paste and stir the cocoa powder into it. Put a portion of the cocoa-colored paste into a piping bag, cut a small opening, and reserve.

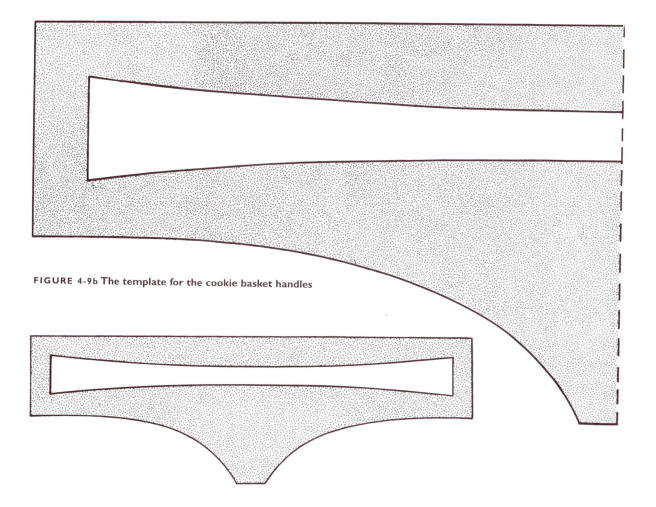

FIGURE 4-9b The template for the cookie basket handles

4. Place the basket template on a Silpat or a prepared sheet pan. Spread some of the plain tuile paste smoothly and evenly inside the template (see Figures 13-29 and 13-30, page 694). Make 4 rectangles on each of 4 pans. Pipe 2 straight lines of cocoa tuile paste the length of each basket rectangle, evenly spaced across the width.

5. Bake 1 pan at a time at 400°F (205°C) for approximately 6 minutes or until the first strip begins to show light brown spots. Leave the pan in the oven with the door open. Working quickly, pick up the strip that has the most brown color and wrap it, top-side out, around the cardboard mold, overlapping the ends. Place the small dowel inside and use it to press down hard on the overlapped edges, pressing them against the work surface to weld them together. Remove the dowel, slide the basket off the mold, and set it aside, standing on end. Quickly repeat with the next most browned strip; continue baking and forming the ovals until you have made 16 baskets. Set the baskets aside.

6. Place the handle template on a Silpat or on a remaining prepared sheet pan. Spread plain tuile paste evenly inside, forming 5 handles per sheet pan. This will give you a few extra — useful, as they break easily. Pipe a line of cocoa tuile paste the full length of the strip, in the center of each handle.

7. Place a rolling pin, 4 inches (10 cm) in diameter, on a sheet pan or on your worktable. Raise both ends of the rolling pin off the table and anchor the pin so it will not roll; a little short dough or a similar material can be used for this purpose. Bake the handle strips, 1 pan at a time, about 4 minutes. As they begin to color, remove the handles and drape them over the raised rolling pin (see Procedure 4-2a). Hold each one against the pin for a few seconds until firm. Lift the rolling pin and carefully pull off the handles (see Procedure 4-2b). Repeat baking and forming the remaining handles.

8. Cut out 16 oval pieces of angel food cake that will fit snugly inside the baskets. Cover and reserve.

9. Wash, stem, and pit the cherries, then cut them in half. Try to do this as close as possible to serving time to avoid oxidation. If you must prepare the cherry halves in advance, toss them in a little lemon juice.

10. Place the Italian cream in a pastry bag with a No. 6 (12-mm) plain tip. Reserve in the refrigerator.

11. Presentation: Place a cake oval in the bottom of a cookie basket. Pipe Italian cream on top, filling the basket to ¼ inch (6 mm) from the rim. Transfer the basket to the

PROCEDURE 4-2a Placing a baked tuile paste basket handle over a rolling pin that has been raised and supported off the table

PROCEDURE 4-2b Removing one of the formed handles after lifting the rolling pin off the raised stand

center of a dessert plate. Place a handle on the basket, carefully pushing the ends into the cream to secure. Top the cream with cherry halves. Spoon cherry compote in an irregular pattern around the basket on the base of the plate. Evenly space 4 small scoops of peppered frozen yogurt around the dessert on the base of the plate. Serve immediately.

NOTE: You can make the full recipe of angel food cake in a tube pan as directed, slice the baked cake in half horizontally, and reserve half for another use. In this case, you may have to utilize some scrap pieces for the last 1 or 2 baskets. Alternatively, make ½ recipe of batter and pour it into a paper-lined cake pan or a cake ring, 12 inches (30 cm) in diameter. The round cake will bake in slightly less time than directed in the recipe.

CHEF'S TIPS

If you will be making a fair number of baskets, use the cardboard mold as a guide to make two oval forming molds out of wood. You also can make a less permanent but quick and easy mold by cutting the same shape from Styrofoam and covering it with foil.

Both the basket shells and the handles can be made several weeks ahead of time, as long as they are stored in an airtight container set in a warm location. Although the baskets should be filled and assembled to order, it is possible to add the cake, cream filling, and cherries up to 30 minutes in advance, if necessary. The cookie shells will get a little soft but will still be fully acceptable. When you have no choice but to put the desserts together ahead of time, you might want to consider Vineyard Barrels (page 314) instead. The barrels are a variation of this dessert but are a little quicker to assemble because the handles are built in, and they're also easier to move after they have been sitting because they are made with a bottom.

CHERRY COMPOTE yield: about 3 cups (720 ml), including the juice

2 pounds (910 g) Bing cherries	⅛ teaspoon (.25 g) fresh coarsely ground black pepper
½ cup (120 ml) water	
¾ cup (180 ml) port wine	1 teaspoon (3 g) pectin powder
1 tablespoon (15 ml) lemon juice	6 ounces (170 g) granulated sugar

1. Wash, stem, and pit the cherries.

2. Combine the water, port, lemon juice, and black pepper in a saucepan. Thoroughly mix the pectin powder and granulated sugar, then add to the mixture in the saucepan. Bring to a boil, add the cherries, and simmer, stirring frequently, for 10 to 12 minutes or until the cherries are very soft but have not fallen apart.

3. Remove from the heat and let cool to room temperature. If the compote seems too thin, strain the cherries and reduce the liquid further. The compote thickens if refrigerated.

Chèvre Cheesecake in a Cocoa-Nib Florentina Cup with Port-Poached Pears yield: 16 servings (Color Photo 1)

The garnishes on this dessert — the port-poached pears drizzled with port wine reduction and topped with a gratinéed sabayon — could actually be served alone as a light dessert, perhaps accompanied by a crisp Florentina or tuile paste decoration. But the flavors are even better when combined with the slightly tangy and creamy goat's milk–mascarpone cheesecake. If you need to simplify, you could choose either the Florentina cup or the tuile decoration.

6 small to medium d'Anjou or Comice pears

6 cups (1 L 440 ml) ruby port wine

6 ounces (170 g) granulated sugar

½ teaspoon (1 g) fresh coarsely ground black pepper

Unsalted butter, melted

Granulated sugar

Cheesecake Mixture (recipe follows)

1 recipe Sabayon made with Champagne (page 311)

16 Cocoa-Nib Florentina Cups (page 689)

16 Spanish Caramel-Flavored Tuile Decorations (page 727)

Powdered sugar

1. Peel the pears, core, and cut in half. Slice each half lengthwise into 6 wedges. Place the wedges in a saucepan with the wine, 6 ounces (170 g) sugar, and pepper. Poach the pear wedges until they are soft to the touch. Remove from the heat and reserve in the liquid.

2. Brush melted butter over the insides of 16 timbale molds, ½ cup (120 ml) in capacity. Cut rounds of baking paper to fit in the bottom of the molds. Place the paper rounds in the molds and brush butter on the papers as well. Coat the molds (including the papers) with granulated sugar.

3. Divide the cheesecake filling evenly among the molds. Place in a hotel pan or other baking pan with high sides. Pour hot water into the pan to reach halfway up the sides of the molds.

4. Bake the cheesecakes at 325°F (163°C) for approximately 40 minutes or until they are set. Remove from the bain-marie and set aside to cool.

5. Drain approximately half of the poaching liquid from the pear wedges, leaving the pears in the remaining liquid. Reduce the removed poaching liquid by one-third. Let cool, then place in a piping bottle.

6. Presentation: Arrange 4 pear wedges in a pinwheel pattern on a dessert plate, leaving room in the center for a cheesecake. Pipe some reduced poaching liquid on top of the pears and around the perimeter of the plate. Drizzle sabayon over the pears, then use a propane torch to lightly brown the sabayon. Unmold a cheesecake by sliding a thin knife around the inside of the timbale mold. Place the cheesecake in a Florentina cup and set it in the center of the plate. Carefully push a tuile decoration into the center of the cheesecake. Sift powdered sugar lightly over the dessert.

CHEESECAKE MIXTURE yield: 6 cups (1 L 440 ml) or 16 servings, 4 ounces (120 ml) each

1 pound 8 ounces (680 g) fresh mild goat's milk cheese, softened

8 ounces (225 g) mascarpone cheese

8 ounces (225 g) granulated sugar

½ cup (120 ml) heavy cream

6 eggs, at room temperature

1. Cream together the goat cheese, mascarpone, and sugar.

2. Combine the heavy cream and the eggs, beating for a few seconds to incorporate. Gradually add the egg mixture to the cheese mixture, blending until smooth. Scrape down the sides of the bowl to make sure there are no lumps.

Chocolate-Banana Tart with Almond Ice Cream and Spun Sugar

yield: 12 servings (Color Photo 25)

Soft chocolate ganache, caramelized bananas, and almond ice cream combined with crunchy phyllo dough rounds — how can you resist? This stacked dessert looks humble before it receives its topping of ice cream and a loose net of spun sugar — the two elements that give it its enticing modern appearance and stop all the jokes in the kitchen about it looking like a hamburger. If you need to downsize you can, of course, skip the spun sugar; often, one has no choice, as spun sugar can be finicky or impossible when the weather is humid. It is just there for show, and the flavors and textures are still wonderful without it.

24 sheeets phyllo dough (1 pound/455 g)

4 ounces (115 g) unsalted butter, melted

½ recipe Kiwi Sauce (page 309)

6 medium-size firm, ripe bananas

Castor sugar or fine granulated sugar

12 Ganache Rounds (recipe follows)

Almond Ice Cream (page 257)

Spun Sugar (page 593), tinted pale pink

Fresh almonds in the husk (optional)

1. Unwrap and unroll the phyllo dough. Place the sheets in a stack with the edges aligned evenly. Cut across into 3 equal rectangles. Stack 2 groups and set aside, covering the sheets with a damp towel. Place 1 sheet from the remaining stack on the work surface in front of you. Brush melted butter lightly over the dough and top with a second sheet of phyllo. Repeat buttering and layering the sheets until you have a stack of 8 sheets. Do not butter the top piece.

2. Using a plain cookie cutter approximately 4¼ inches (10.6 cm) in diameter as a guide, use a small sharp knife to cut out 3 rounds from the layered phyllo sheets. Discard the scraps. Brush butter over the top of the rounds and place them on a sheet pan lined with baking paper or a Silpat. Repeat layering the phyllo dough and cutting the rounds until you have made 24 rounds; you need 2 per serving. Place the rounds on a paper-lined sheet pan and bake at 375°F (190°C) until golden brown; cool.

3. Place a portion of the kiwi sauce in a piping bottle.

4. Presentation: Thinly slice ½ banana. Arrange overlapping banana slices in a circle to cover the top of 1 phyllo dough round. Sprinkle sugar over the bananas and use a blowtorch to melt it. Be careful not to let the edges of the banana slices get too dark or to burn them, which can happen quickly. Place a second phyllo dough round on a sheet pan lined with baking paper or a Silpat. Place a ganache round on top and warm in a 375°F (190°C) oven for 2 to 3 minutes or until the ganache just starts to melt around the edges. Remove from the oven and top with the banana-covered phyllo round. Place the warm dessert in the center of a dessert plate. Place a scoop of ice cream in the center of the banana ring; decorate it with spun sugar. Pipe a band of kiwi sauce around the perimeter of the base of the plate. Cut a fresh almond in half, if using, and place on the left side of the dessert. Serve immediately.

NOTE: You will have 8 extra partial sheets of phyllo so you can afford to discard some if they tear, which is almost inevitable.

GANACHE ROUNDS yield: 12 pieces

6 ounces (170 g) milk chocolate

1 pound (455 g) sweet dark chocolate

4 ounces (115 g) unsweetened chocolate

1 cup (240 ml) heavy cream

8 ounces (225 g) unsalted butter, cut into chunks and at room temperature

1. Chop all 3 chocolates into fine pieces. Place in a bowl set over hot water and melt together, stirring from time to time. Remove from the heat.

2. Bring the cream to a boil. Pour the cream into the melted chocolate and stir to combine. Add the butter chunks and stir until fully incorporated.

3. Cover the bottom of a half-sheet pan (12 × 16 inches /30 × 40 cm) with baking paper. Pour the ganache into the pan and spread evenly. Place a sheet of plastic wrap directly against the top of the ganache and refrigerate to set.

4. Remove the plastic wrap. Using a plain, round cookie cutter, approximately 3¾ inches (9.5 cm) in diameter, cut 12 rounds from the ganache, dipping the cutter into hot water before cutting each round. Place the rounds on a sheet pan lined with baking paper, cover, and refrigerate until needed. Reserve the ganache scraps for another use.

Chocolate Bread Pudding with Cookie Citrus Rind yield: 12 servings (Color Photo 24)

The only old-fashioned part of this bread pudding is the taste, which, although lighter and less sweet than more traditional renditions of bread pudding, has a wonderfully rich chocolate flavor that is amplified by the bitter chocolate. Instead of the familiar method whereby sliced bread is soaked in a custard mixture in its baking dish to make multiple servings, here the bread is cut into small cubes and, after absorbing the custard, is divided among individual cake rings. If the rings are not convenient, bake the pudding in a hotel pan measuring 11 × 9 × 2 inches (27.5 × 22.5 × 5 cm) instead and slice into 12 servings.

The art deco cookie citrus rind used in the presentation is sure to raise a few eyebrows in pleasant surprise. Of course, if you do not feel like going wild with your presentation, you may replace the cookie rind with strips of real orange rind (removed with a zester), sprinkled on top of the powdered sugar. The beautiful, and to many people uncommon, blood oranges are paired with the mousseline sauce not only for color but to add a distinctive flavor. When blood oranges are unavailable (which is, unfortunately, the majority of the year), use perfectly ripe ruby red grapefruit instead.

1 pound 8 ounces (680 g) French bread or other dense white bread, at least 1 day old

6 cups (1 L 440 ml) whole milk

8 ounces (225 g) sweet dark chocolate

6 ounces (170 g) unsweetened chocolate

12 blood oranges

10 eggs

8 ounces (225 g) granulated sugar

2 tablespoons (30 ml) vanilla extract

4 ounces (115 g) Streusel Topping (recipe follows)

2 tablespoons (30 ml) orange liqueur

1 recipe Mousseline Sauce (page 338)

1 recipe Cookie Citrus Rinds and Cookie Figurines (page 698)

Powdered sugar

1. Cut 12 pieces of aluminum foil measuring 6½ inches (16.2 cm) square; if you are using a thin grade of foil, double the thickness. Set a cake ring, 3 inches (7.5 cm) in diameter by 2 inches (5 cm) in height, in the center of each square. Fold and pleat the edges of the foil up against the rings to form a tight seal. Be sure the foil reaches at least three-quarters of the way up the sides of the rings because the puddings will be placed in a water bath. Place the rings in a hotel pan and set aside.

2. Remove the crust from the bread. If you are using baguette loaves, do not remove all of the crust or you will not have enough bread left. Cut the bread into ½-inch (1.2-cm) cubes. Place in a bowl and reserve.

3. Heat the milk to scalding. Chop both chocolates into small pieces and add to the milk. Remove from the heat and stir until the chocolate is completely melted. Finely grate the zest of 6 blood oranges into the chocolate mixture. Reserve the zested oranges with the others.

4. Whisk together the eggs, sugar, and vanilla until well combined, then whisk this mixture into the chocolate mixture. Pour the custard over the bread cubes and stir gently to ensure all of the bread is moistened. Set aside to soak for 30 minutes.

5. Divide the bread filling evenly among the prepared rings. Press down gently to compact the filling and make the tops even. Sprinkle the streusel over the puddings.

6. Place the hotel pan in a 350°F (175°C) oven. Add enough hot water to the pan to reach about ½ inch (1.2 cm) up the sides of the rings. Bake for approximately 40 minutes or until the custard is set. Remove the puddings from the water bath and let cool to room temperature.

7. Remove the rind and all of the white pith from the oranges, then cut out the segments. Place the segments in a single layer on a sheet pan lined with baking paper. Cover and refrigerate.

8. Stir the orange liqueur into the mousseline sauce. Place a portion of the sauce in a piping bottle. Cover the remaining sauce and reserve all of the sauce in the refrigerator until needed.

9. Presentation: Peel the foil from the sides and bottom of a bread pudding. Slide off the cake ring. Place the pudding in the center of a dessert plate. Pipe mousseline sauce on the base of the plate all around the pudding. Arrange 10 to 12 orange segments in a spoke pattern around the dessert on top of the sauce. Use the tip of a paring knife to make 3 small cuts, evenly spaced, on top of the pudding. Gently insert cookie figurines into 2 of the cuts. Push the tip of a cookie citrus rind into the other and arrange the spiraling end of the cookie around the dessert, supporting it on top of the figurines. Sift powdered sugar over the top.

STREUSEL TOPPING yield: 14 ounces (400 g)

This recipe makes more than you need for the bread pudding, but streusel is convenient to have on hand, as it has so many applications. You might actually want to double or triple the recipe and keep the streusel in stock as a regular mise en place item. Chopped nuts may be added for variation.

2 ounces (55 g) light brown sugar

2 ounces (55 g) granulated sugar

4 ounces (115 g) unsalted butter

1 teaspoon (1.5 g) ground cinnamon

¾ teaspoon (3 g) salt

½ teaspoon (2.5 ml) vanilla extract

6 ounces (170 g) bread flour

I. Mix the brown sugar, granulated sugar, butter, cinnamon, salt, and vanilla.

2. Stir in the flour. The mixture should be crumbly and should not come together like a dough; you may need to add extra flour.

3. Store, covered, in the refrigerator to prevent the topping from drying out.

Chocolate Ganache Towers yield: 16 servings (Color Photo 26)

Even with the help of polyurethane or acetate strips and the support frame, this elegant and showy dessert is time-consuming. To speed the process, you can make the towers up to one week ahead, and certainly the presentation can be simplified. The elaborate chocolate butterfly can be replaced with one made from tuile paste, as in Chocolate Ganache Cake (page 27), or a simple chocolate figurine. If you have forms or rings that are 2 inches (5 cm) in diameter or if you have made the support frame (directions follow), it is not necessary to tape the plastic strips together. Just overlap the ends and set them inside the forms or box frame; they will not unroll.

⅓ recipe Baked Chocolate Sheet batter (page 355)

Dark Chocolate Tower Filling (recipe follows)

Light Chocolate Filling (recipe follows)

Unsweetened cocoa powder

Powdered sugar

1½ cups (360 ml) heavy cream

2 teaspoons (10 g) granulated sugar

16 Chocolate Monarch Butterfly Ornaments (page 550)

16 edible flowers

I. Spread the chocolate sheet batter onto a Silpat or sheet of baking paper, forming a strip measuring 6 × 23 inches (15 × 57.5 cm); it will be just short of the full length of a sheet pan. Place on a pan and bake immediately at 375°F (190°C) for about 12 minutes or until baked through. Set aside to cool.

2. Cut 16 strips, 2½ × 7¼ inches (6.2 × 18.1 cm), from a sheet of polyurethane or acetate. Overlap the ends and tape them together to make tubes that are 2 inches (5 cm) in diameter and 2½ inches (6.2 cm) high. Stand the tubes on end on a paper-lined sheet pan or in the support frame (directions for making the frame follow). If you want the filling to set up diagonally, as shown in Color Photo 26, you must use the frame and set it on the angled base (Figure 4-10).

3. Invert the cooled chocolate sheet and peel the Silpat or baking paper from the back. Cut out 16 rounds, 2 inches (5 cm) in diameter. Place a round in the bottom of each tube and set the tubes aside while you make the dark chocolate filling.

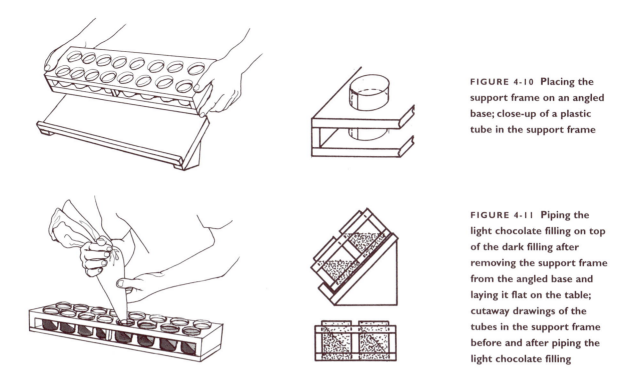

FIGURE 4-10 Placing the support frame on an angled base; close-up of a plastic tube in the support frame

FIGURE 4-11 Piping the light chocolate filling on top of the dark filling after removing the support frame from the angled base and laying it flat on the table; cutaway drawings of the tubes in the support frame before and after piping the light chocolate filling

4. Pipe the dark chocolate tower filling into the plastic tubes on top of the sponge rounds. Be careful not to get any filling on the inside of the tubes above the filling. If you do, remove it carefully or it will detract from the finished appearance. Place the tubes in the refrigerator (leaving them at an angle on the stand, if using).

5. If you are making horizontal layers, you can add the light chocolate filling as soon as you have made it. If you are making diagonal layers, wait until the dark chocolate layer is set enough not to move, then remove the support frame from the angled base and set the frame flat on the table before adding the light chocolate layer. Pipe the light chocolate filling into the tubes on top of the dark filling (Figure 4-11). Place the desserts in the refrigerator until set, about 4 hours.

6. Make the templates shown in Figure 4-12. The templates, as shown, are the correct size for use in this recipe. Trace the drawings, then cut the templates out of cardboard $1/16$ inch (2 mm) thick (cake boxes work well for this). You will need all of the pieces — A, B, and C. You will also need an aluminum pie tin with the bottom removed (see Figures 13-24 to 13-28, page 693). Be sure the pie tin sits flat against the base of your serving plates and that it is large enough to cover most of the rim of the plates. Place template A, with C taped in place, on the base of the inverted pie tin and secure with tape. (Check to be sure the pie tin is not covering any of the template.) Place the pie tin, right-side up, on top of a dessert plate. Using a fine mesh strainer or sifter, sift cocoa powder lightly over the top. Remove the template carefully. Repeat on as many plates as you will be needing for service. Dust off the pie tin and remove template C. Loosely tape template B in place, creating a smaller circle slightly offset to the first one. Tape 3 toothpicks to the bottom of the pie tin at the edge of the cardboard. Carefully place the pie tin on top of one of the plates with cocoa powder. The toothpicks will keep the tin from damaging the cocoa powder design. Lightly sift powdered sugar over the new opening. Remove the template carefully and repeat on the other plates. Set the plates aside where they will not be disturbed.

7. Whip the heavy cream and granulated sugar to stiff peaks. Place in a pastry bag with a No. 8 (16-mm) star tip. Reserve in the refrigerator.

8. Remove the polyurethane or acetate strip from as many desserts as you have decorated plates. The remaining desserts can be kept in the refrigerator for several days with the plastic attached; they should be covered tightly. If the plastic strips do not peel away easily, place the desserts in the freezer for 30 minutes before attempting to remove them.

9. Presentation: Pipe a large rosette of whipped cream on the top of a tower, covering the surface completely. Set the dessert in the center of the cocoa powder circle on a prepared dessert plate. Carefully but firmly place a chocolate butterfly at an angle on the whipped cream. Set an edible flower on the side.

NOTE: After the plastic strips are peeled off, this dessert can be held at room temperature for up to 30 minutes prior to serving. The flavor is actually improved; however, you may need to adjust the consistency of the fillings (see Note at the end of the following recipe).

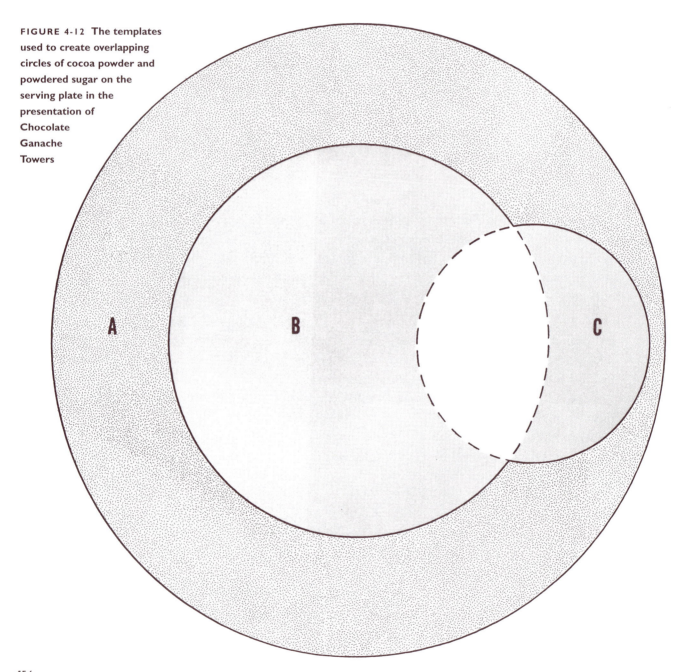

FIGURE 4-12 The templates used to create overlapping circles of cocoa powder and powdered sugar on the serving plate in the presentation of Chocolate Ganache Towers

Making a Support Frame for Acetate Strips

1. Refer to Figure 4-13 in constructing the frame. Cut 2 pieces of plywood, good on both sides and ¹/₂ inch (1.2 cm) thick, to 5¹/₂ × 21¹/₂ inches (13.7 × 53.7 cm). Align the pieces precisely, one on top of the other, and clamp them together. Draw a line on each short end of the top piece 1 inch (2.5 cm) away from the edges, leaving a 19¹/₂-inch (48.7-cm) space between the lines.

2. Starting next to the line on a short end and ¹/₂ inch (1.2 cm) from a long edge, drill 8 holes, 2 inches (5 cm) in diameter and ¹/₂ inch (1.2 cm) apart. Drill a second row of 8 holes, 2 inches (5 cm) in diameter and ¹/₂ inch (1.2 cm) away from the opposite long edge, leaving a ¹/₂-inch (1.2-cm) space in the center between the rows. Remove the clamps.

3. Cut 2 pieces of ¹/₂-inch (1.2-cm) thick wood (plywood or pine) to 1¹/₄ inches wide × 5¹/₂ inches long (3.1 × 13.7 cm). These pieces will be used on the ends of the frame.

4. Cut 2 pieces of ¹/₂-inch (1.2-cm) wooden dowel to 1¹/₄ inches (3.1 cm) long.

5. Using 150-grade sandpaper, sand all of the wooden pieces smooth (including the pieces with the drilled holes). Pay special attention to the cut edges.

6. Align the 2 large pieces with holes, lining up the holes exactly even. Clamp the 2 end pieces in place between them. Drill, countersink, and, using small brass screws, screw the end pieces in place. Remove the clamps.

7. Using screws the same way you attached the ends, attach the dowel pieces opposite each other in the center of the box.

The frame is now ready to use. Place a piece of cardboard covered with baking paper under the frame before placing the acetate strips inside. If you are using the frame to support the acetate tubes at an angle, you will probably need to tape the bottom in place, depending on how you are supporting the frame.

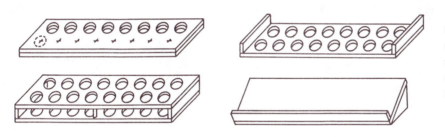

FIGURE 4-13 The sequence in making the support frame and the optional angled base

DARK CHOCOLATE TOWER FILLING yield: 4 cups (960 ml)

Do not make this filling until you are ready to pipe it into the tubes.

8 ounces (225 g) sweet dark chocolate	2 egg yolks
3 ounces (85 g) unsweetened chocolate (see Note)	1 ounce (30 g) granulated sugar
2 cups (480 ml) heavy cream	¹/₄ cup (60 ml) or 3 ounces (85 g) honey

1. Cut the dark and unsweetened chocolates into small pieces. Melt together in a bowl set over simmering water. Set aside but keep warm.

2. Whip the heavy cream to soft peaks. Reserve in the refrigerator.

3. Whip the egg yolks and sugar until light and fluffy, approximately 3 minutes. In the meantime, bring the honey to a boil. Gradually pour the honey into the egg yolks. Continue to whip until the mixture has cooled completely.

4. Working quickly, incorporate the reserved melted chocolate by hand. Rapidly stir in the reserved whipped cream.

NOTE: Depending on the percentages of cocoa solids and sugar in the brand of sweet chocolate you use, you may need to adjust the amount of unsweetened chocolate slightly (up or down) to achieve the desired consistency or flavor in the filling.

LIGHT CHOCOLATE FILLING yield: 4¹⁄₂ cups (1 L 80 ml)

Do not make this filling until you are ready to use it.

2 teaspoons (6 g) unflavored gelatin powder
¹⁄₄ cup (60 ml) cold water
1³⁄₄ cups (420 ml) heavy cream
8 ounces (225 g) milk chocolate

1 ounce (30 g) unsweetened chocolate
2 egg whites (¹⁄₄ cup/60 ml)
¹⁄₄ cup (60 ml) simple syrup

1. Sprinkle the gelatin over the cold water and set aside to soften.

2. Whip the heavy cream to a very soft consistency. The cream should collapse when dropped from the whip. If overwhipped, it is likely to break when the remaining ingredients are added. Cover and reserve in the refrigerator.

3. Melt both chocolates together over simmering water. Set aside but keep warm.

4. Combine the egg whites and simple syrup. Heat to 140°F (60°C) over simmering water while stirring constantly. Remove from the heat and whip until stiff peaks form. Fold into the reserved whipped cream.

5. Heat the softened gelatin mixture to dissolve. Take care not to overheat.

6. Quickly stir the gelatin mixture into the melted chocolate. Still working rapidly, add a small portion of the cream mixture to temper the chocolate, then quickly add this to the remaining cream. If the filling is too thin to hold its shape, mix a little longer.

Date-Stuffed Saffron-Poached Pears with Chardonnay Wine Sauce

yield: 12 servings (Color Photo 28)

When most people think of pears poached in wine, they picture the classic rendition that utilizes red wine, often port, flavored with cinnamon and vanilla as the poaching medium. After cooking the pears, the delicious fruit- and spice-infused wine is usually reduced to a syrupy consistency and served as a sauce. Ruby Pears with Verbena Bavarois and Port Wine Reduction (page 349) is an example of this traditional technique. The same application is also popular for whole figs (see Sherry-Poached Black Mission Figs with Crème Catalan, page 353).

This recipe evolved from Saffron-Poached Pears with Almond Ice Cream and Kadaif Phyllo Nests on page 254. In this presentation, the pears are left whole, the cores are removed, and the cavity is filled with a soft, fresh date. In both recipes the stately Bosc pear, with its distinctive long, elegant curved neck and stem, is the pear of choice.

Pears, and other types of fruit, may be poached to change the texture of the fruit — to cook it so it becomes more tender — to add flavor, and to enhance color, as when fruit is poached in red wine. In many cases, including this recipe, the poaching step accomplishes all three objectives.

Two things that make this recipe a bit different are the use of white wine and the inclusion of saffron, but the component that really stands out is the unusual and eye-catching strands of crisp kadaif phyllo dough draped over and around the top of the pear. The word *kadaif*, also spelled *kataifi*, is actually the name of a Middle Eastern dessert that includes these long, thin strands of crisp dough. However, both terms are also used to describe the dough itself, which is a form of phyllo dough. Like phyllo dough sheets, kadaif phyllo is usually sold frozen, and care must be taken to keep it from drying out as you work with it. Packaged in bulk form, kadaif looks very much like dried Chinese rice noodles or coils of very thin dried pasta.

12 small Bosc pears, stems on	Almond Filling (recipe follows)
Saffron Poaching Liquid (recipe follows)	2 ounces (55 g) kadaif phyllo dough
16 sheets phyllo dough	Chardonnay Wine Sauce (recipe follows)
4 ounces (115 g) unsalted butter, melted	Powdered sugar
12 whole fresh dates	Fresh almonds in the husk or small clusters of grapes for decorating (optional)

1. Peel the pears, keeping the stems intact and placing the fruit in acidulated water as you work to prevent oxidation. Transfer the pears to the saucepan with the saffron poaching liquid and bring to a simmer. Set a lid or plate that fits down inside the pan on top of the fruit to keep it submerged; place a cloth towel or several layers of paper toweling between the lid and the fruit. Poach the pears until they are just cooked through and tender to the touch. Be careful not to overcook the fruit, as it will be baked and served standing on end; overcooking will cause it to lose shape — or, worse, fall apart. Remove the pan from the heat and set aside for a minimum of 6 hours or, preferably, refrigerate overnight to allow the pears to absorb the maximum amount of flavor and color from the liquid.

2. Cut a round template, approximately 5 inches (12.5 cm) in diameter (depending on the size of the phyllo sheets), from cardboard, or have a lid or plate of the same size handy. Unwrap and unroll the phyllo dough and cut the stacked phyllo sheets in half lengthwise. Cut across in thirds, dividing each sheet into 6 pieces. Place the pieces in 2 stacks and cover 1 stack with a lightly dampened cloth. Place a piece from the remaining stack on the table in front of you. Brush some of the melted butter in a circle, 4 inches (10 cm) in diameter, in the center of the dough. Place a second piece of dough on top and brush butter on it in the same way. Continue layering and brushing with butter until you have used 8 pieces of phyllo. Do not butter the top of the stack.

3. Place the template on top of the stack. Cut around the template with a paring knife and remove the scraps. Brush butter over the top layer of the circle. Carefully press the stack of dough into a small individual pie form, 7 ounces (210 ml) in capacity and 4½ inches (11.2 cm) in diameter across the top, 2¾ inches (7 cm) in diameter across the bottom, and 1½ inches (3.7 cm) in height. If the circle does not form an evenly fluted edge, shape it with your hands. Repeat to form the remaining 11 phyllo dough shells. Place the lined forms on 2 sheet pans. Discard any leftover phyllo scraps.

4. Remove the pears from the poaching liquid and pat them dry with paper towels. Using the tip of a paring knife, make a horizontal cut beginning no more than ½ inch (1.2 cm) below the stem, cutting three-quarters of the way through each pear and leaving the stems attached. Cut just enough from the bottom of each pear to allow it to stand straight up. Push an apple corer up through the bottom of each pear to the horizontal cut and remove the cores. If you do not have a corer, this step can be completed with a melon ball cutter. In this case, omit the horizontal cut and proceed with care.

5. Make a cut lengthwise in each date and remove the pit. Push a date into each pear from the bottom. Stand the pears straight up. Using a paring knife, score vertical lines, about ⅜ inch (9 mm) apart, from the bottom to the top of the pears, making softly curved incisions without cutting all the way through to the date. Wrap aluminum foil around the pear stems to keep them from becoming too dark as they bake.

6. Place the almond filling in a pastry bag and pipe it into the phyllo shells, dividing it evenly. Place a pear in each shell and press it down firmly.

7. Bake the pears at 400°F (205°) until the phyllo shells and the almond filling are both light golden brown, about 12 minutes. Remove from the oven and lightly drape strands of kadaif phyllo dough over and around the pears as shown in Color Photo 28; do not cover the pear stems. Return the pears to the oven until the kadaif is golden brown, 3 to 4 minutes longer.

8. Let the pastries cool. Unmold from the forms, then remove the foil covering the pear stems, being careful not to damage the crisp, lacy kadaif strands.

9. Presentation: Place a pastry in the center of a dessert plate. Spoon chardonnay sauce, including and evenly spacing some of the whole grapes in the sauce, in an irregularly shaped ring around the dessert. The sauce should not touch the phyllo shell or the shell will become soggy. Sift powdered sugar over the dessert as well as the surface of the plate. Garnish with fresh almonds or grape clusters, if desired.

SAFFRON POACHING LIQUID yield: 10 cups (1 L 440 ml)

2 quarts (1 L 920 ml) dry white wine

⅓ cup (80 ml) lemon juice

8 whole cloves

2 small cinnamon sticks

1 teaspoon (5 ml) loosely packed saffron threads, crushed (see Note)

1 pound 8 ounces (680 g) granulated sugar

1. Combine all of the ingredients in a nonreactive saucepan large enough to accommodate the pears. Bring to a boil.

2. Use as directed in the main recipe.

NOTE: You can vary the amount of saffron to produce the desired intensity of both the color and flavor that it adds to the pears. Although the age of the saffron affects its potency, saffron has a strong flavor and you should be careful not to use too much.

ALMOND FILLING yield: approximately 1 pound 2 ounces (510 g)

6 ounces (170 g) almond paste

8 ounces (225 g) granulated sugar

4 egg whites (½ cup/120 ml)

1. Using the paddle attachment of the mixer or a spoon, combine the almond paste, granulated sugar, and 1 egg white.

2. When completely smooth, add the remaining egg whites, 1 at a time, again mixing until smooth after each addition to avoid lumps. The mixture should be fairly thin, almost runny. It is not possible to specify the exact number of egg whites needed, as this varies depending on the texture of the almond paste.

CHARDONNAY WINE SAUCE yield: approximately 2 cups (480 ml)

This sauce can also be made with champagne in place of the chardonnay. To improve both flavor and appearance, split a vanilla bean lengthwise, scrape out the seeds, and add them to the finished sauce.

2 cups (480 ml) Chardonnay wine

4 teaspoons (10 g) cornstarch

6 ounces (170 g) small green grapes, stemmed
  (see Note)

6 ounces (170 g) granulated sugar

¼ cup (60 ml) orange liqueur

1. Make a slurry by mixing ¼ cup (60 ml) wine with the cornstarch.

2. Rinse the grapes. Reserve half of them, choosing the smaller ones, depending on the variety. Place the remaining wine, the remaining grapes, the sugar, and the orange liqueur in a nonreactive saucepan. Bring to a boil and cook over medium heat until the grapes split, about 5 minutes.

About Saffron

Saffron is by far the most expensive of all spices. The saffron threads used for flavoring are the bright orange three-pronged stigmata, as well as a portion of the style, of a small variety of purple crocus. That saffron can be harvested by hand only, and that it takes around 75,000 flowers to produce 1 pound (455 g) of threads, explains the high price. Several varieties of this spice grow wild in the Mediterranean area of Europe; however, true cultivated saffron can best be distinguished by its large, loosely hanging stigmata.

Saffron has been used since ancient times; the Romans introduced it to Northern Europe. Later, in the eighth century, the Muslims brought it west to Spain, which today is the largest producer. Saffron is indispensable in making Spanish paella, French bouillabaisse, and Milanese risotto, and it is used to a great extent in Middle Eastern cuisine, as well as in a number of European baked specialties, such as traditional saffron buns and breads.

Saffron should always be purchased as threads, as the ground form can be easily adulterated with other yellow to orange food colorings, such as safflower and marigold petals and ground turmeric. Ground saffron also loses its aroma more quickly than threads do. Store saffron in an airtight container protected from light. Stored in this manner, saffron threads can be kept for years.

3. Strain the mixture through a fine mesh strainer, using a spoon to force as much juice as possible out of the grapes. Discard the solids in the strainer.

4. Stir the reserved cornstarch slurry into the grape juice–wine mixture. Return to the heat and bring to a quick boil. You can, if you wish, test the viscosity at this point by placing a teaspoon of sauce in the refrigerator to chill, then bringing it back to room temperature; the puddle should hold its shape at room temperature. Adjust the consistency, if necessary, by cooking the sauce further to reduce it or by adding more liquid — wine or simple syrup — if it is too thick.

5. Stir in the reserved whole or sliced grapes (see Chef's Tip). Let cool, then store in the refrigerator.

NOTE: Try to use Chardonnay grapes, which are smaller than the more readily available table grapes. If you must use large grapes, slice the reserved grapes before adding them to the syrup.

Dessert Sampling Platter yield: 16 servings (Color Photo 27)

Assorted dessert platters are generally created from items already on the menu, either made into smaller portions by dividing a single portion in half or simply by making a miniature version along with the standard-sized servings. In this presentation each tasting plate is a single serving — although, depending on the number of preceding courses, it could easily be stretched to serve two guests by adding fresh fruit and/or by using the extra Marquise and portioning two triangles per plate. Another option is to include or substitute a Miniature Triple-Chocolate Terrine from the Triple Treat dessert (page 191).

The inspiration for this particular combination was born of leftover Tiramisù and Florentina cones (unfilled) from a Triple Treat dessert that had been served at a graduation gala a few days earlier. I mention this to demonstrate that such an elegant array of shapes and flavors can be prepped up to a point even more than a week ahead to finish as needed. This not only utilizes downtime in the kitchen but also limits waste, as it is difficult to predict exactly how many orders will be required, and once finished — sliced, filled, or garnished — the pieces must be used right away.

16 Chocolate Fans (page 521)

16 Tuile Cookie Wedges (page 709)

½ recipe Fortified Caramel Sauce (page 709)

Unsweetened cocoa powder

16 Miniature White Chocolate Marquises (recipe follows)

16 Miniature Marco Polos (recipe follows)

16 Miniature Florentina Cones (page 193)

16 Miniature Tiramisù (page 194)

Piping Chocolate (page 543), melted

16 mint leaves

16 Chocolate Figurines (page 545)

1. Just before serving, refrigerate as many chocolate fans and tuile wedges as you expect to need for service. Place the caramel sauce in a piping bottle.

2. Presentation: Using a fine mesh sifter, lightly sift cocoa powder over the base of a dessert plate. Pipe dots of caramel sauce, approximately ½ inch (1.2 cm) in diameter and spaced about

1 inch (2.5 cm) apart, around the perimeter of the plate on top of the cocoa powder. Arrange 1 each of the 4 miniature desserts, evenly spaced, in the center of the plate.

3. Place a small amount of piping chocolate in a piping bag and cut a small opening. Pipe a small dot of chocolate behind the white chocolate Marquise and stand a chocolate fan straight up in the piping chocolate. Using the same technique, attach a tuile wedge to the Marco Polo. Decorate the Florentina cone with a mint leaf and place a chocolate figurine on top of the tiramisù. Serve immediately.

MINIATURE WHITE CHOCOLATE MARQUISE

yield: 2 triangular cakes, 16 × 2½ inches (40 × 6.2 cm)

This recipe makes twice as much Marquise as you need for the main recipe, but making less is impractical because the larger quantity does not take much longer, and the leftovers keep for weeks in the freezer.

¼ recipe Ribbon-Pattern Decorated Sponge Sheet (page 672; see Note)

½ recipe White Chocolate and Pistachio Pâté (page 471)

1. You will need 2 triangular forms, 16 inches long × 2½ inches across the top (40 × 6.2 cm). If you do not have forms close to this size, you can make them quickly and easily by following the instructions in the recipe for Strawberry Pyramids (page 185). Alter the instructions to make the forms in the size given here.

2. Cut 2 pieces from the ribbon sponge sheet, 4½ × 16 inches (11.2 × 40 cm), with the ribbons running lengthwise. Arrange the sponge sheets in the forms so the striped sides are against the forms. Divide the pâté filling between the forms and spread it evenly. Cover and place in the freezer for at least 4 hours or, preferably, overnight.

3. Unmold 1 Marquise and cut into 16 slices while still frozen. Reserve the other Marquise for another use. Place the slices in the refrigerator until time of service. Make sure the filling has thawed before serving.

NOTE: When making the quarter-recipe of ribbon sponge, you will need a half-size (16 × 12 inches/40 × 30 cm) Silpat to follow the directions as given. If you have only the full-size Silpat (16 × 24 inches/40 × 60 cm), use only half of the mat and make the chocolate lines run crosswise instead of lengthwise, as directed in the recipe, or, if your freezer space allows it, make a half-recipe (1 sheet) and save half of the sheet for another use.

MINIATURE MARCO POLO yield: 16 pieces, approximately 2¼ inches (5.6 cm) in diameter

¼ recipe Devil's Food Cake Layers batter
    (page 393)
⅓ recipe Spiced Ganache Filling (page 412)

White coating chocolate, melted
Dark coating chocolate, melted

1. Pour the cake batter into a square or round cake pan lined with baking paper, 10 inches (25 cm) square or 12 inches (30 cm) in diameter. Bake at 375°F (190°C) for approximately 20 minutes or until baked through. Let cool completely.

2. Measure the outside circumference of a plain cookie cutter, approximately 2¼ inches (5.6 cm) in diameter. Cut 16 strips of acetate or polyurethane, 1 inch (2.5 cm) wide and ¼ inch (6 mm) longer than the circumference measurement (about 7½ inches/18.7 cm). Form the strips into rings, using the cookie cutter as a guide (see "Making Rings From Acetate," page 135), or just overlap the ends ¼ inch (6 mm) and tape the rings together. Place the rings on a sheet pan lined with baking paper (see Chef's Tip).

3. Using the same cookie cutter, cut 16 rounds from the baked devil's food cake. Cut each cake round into 2 layers. Place 1 cake layer in each of the plastic rings. Divide the spiced ganache filling between the rings. Place the remaining cake layers on top of the filling. Press lightly to make the tops even. Refrigerate for 2 hours to set the filling.

CHEF'S TIP
You can also use ABS or PVC pipe that measures 2¼ inches (5.6 cm) across the inside of the opening, cut to the same height as the plastic strips, to hold the filling. It is unlikely that you will find the pipe in the exact diameter specified, but as long as it is fairly close it is okay. Line the inside of the pipe rings with the plastic strips; the ends do not need to be taped together but should overlap slightly.

4. Remove the plastic strips and return the desserts to the refrigerator. Wash and dry the plastic strips. Place melted white coating chocolate in a piping bag. Place a plastic strip on a piece of baking paper and pipe chocolate across the plastic strip at an angle, first in one direction and then in the opposite direction. Pick up the plastic strip and place it on a sheet pan lined with baking paper. Repeat with the remaining strips. Place in the refrigerator for a few minutes to set the white chocolate.

5. Spread melted dark coating chocolate over the plastic strips and attach the strips to the cake rounds following the directions in Step 8 of the Marco Polo recipe (page 110).

Forbidden Peach yield: 12 servings (Color Photo 31)

This dessert is a refreshing summer treat with lots of visual appeal, and it is simplicity itself — that is, once you have mastered the caramel cages. I have had many students accuse me of withholding some secret when it comes to making these fragile decorations. It looks easy enough when they watch my demonstration, but they have all kinds of problems when they first try to make the cages themselves. Well, as a colleague of mine writes in his book, "It is a little difficult to master at first, but you can have lots of fun practicing." Which is true, provided you have the time and patience. Probably the most common mistake, and one I see all too often, involves cooking the sugar. Typically, the first time students make the caramel they burn it, either as a result of not getting it into the water bath quickly enough when it reaches the correct color or because they don't realize how fast sugar can go from caramelized to burned. Then the next time, because they are understandably afraid of burning it again, they make the mistake of not cooking the sugar long enough. This makes the caramel too soft and causes the cages to either stick to the ladle or collapse soon after they are removed. Properly cooked caramel for this application appears quite dark in the pan when compared to the thin threads of sugar in the finished cage. You may find it helpful to pour a small amount of caramel onto a piece of baking paper to check the color, especially if you are using a copper pan, as the dark color of the pan makes it even more difficult to judge the color of the caramel.

Because the caramel cages are what make this dessert so decorative, you can't really leave them out altogether. However, you can save time by making only half as many cages and create an interesting and different presentation by serving one half cage per dessert. Use a hot knife to melt through the finished cages, creating two quarter-spheres. Present the dessert with the open side of the cage facing the guest. As a third option, make Simplified Caramel Cages (page 619). This is the version shown in Color Photo 31.

5 ounces (140 g) or ⅙ recipe Caramel Glass Paste (page 666)

12 dry Small Almond Macaroons (page 57) *or* purchased amaretti cookies

6 large perfectly ripe freestone peaches, such as Fay Alberta or Hale Haven

¼ cup (60 ml) amaretto liqueur

¼ recipe Italian Meringue (page 780)

1 recipe Clear Caramel Sauce (page 328)

Edible flower petals, such as Johnny-jump-up or pansy

12 Caramel Cages (page 618), approximately 6 inches (15 cm) in diameter and at least 2 ½ inches (6.2 cm) tall

Cashew Ice Cream (recipe follows)

1. Soften the caramel glass paste over a bain-marie then remove from the heat. Chop the macaroons into pea-sized pieces and mix into the paste.

2. Remove the stems from the peaches and cut each fruit in half along the natural crease. Remove the stones. Use a melon ball cutter to make the hollow left by the stones a little larger. If necessary, cut a small slice from the round side of each half so the peach halves will stand straight. Divide the caramel glass paste mixture among the peach halves, placing it loosely in the hollows left by the stones.

3. Brush the amaretto liqueur over the cut surface of the peaches, dabbing some on the filling as well. Place the peaches on a sheet pan lined with baking paper or a Silpat.

4. Bake at 400°F (205°C) for approximately 15 minutes; the filling should be a rich brown color. Remove from the oven and brush additional amaretto over the tops.

5. Presentation: Place a large spoonful of Italian meringue on a peach half. Spread to the edges, covering the entire top of the peach in a rustic-looking dome shape. Use a broiler, salamander, or torch to brown the meringue (this can be done up to 1 hour ahead of serving, if necessary). Cover the base of a dessert plate with caramel sauce (do not use too much or it will interfere with the garnish). Place the peach in the center of the sauce. Arrange flower petals around the peach on top of the sauce. Carefully position a caramel cage over the peach. Serve immediately with cashew ice cream in a side dish.

About Cashews

The cashew tree is native to Brazil. The Portuguese introduced the tree to Africa and India. It belongs to the same family as the mango and the pistachio. The tree produces fleshy applelike fruits, each with a single seed — the cashew nut — growing from the bottom as a hard protuberance. The nut is protected by a double shell — actually three shells, if you count the skin on the nut itself. The space between the inner and outer shells is filled with a toxic oily brown liquid called, appropriately enough, *cashew nut shell oil*. This oil is used to make resins and alkali-resistant flexible materials. Because small amounts of the oil are found on the inner shell and the kernel itself, the nuts are always heated before shelling to destroy the toxicity and avoid burns on the skin of the workers.

Cashew nuts contain almost 50 percent fat and should therefore be stored, covered, in the refrigerator or freezer to prevent them from becoming rancid. As with all nuts, toasting greatly enhances their flavor. Although the pear-shaped cashew apple itself is consumed in the areas where the trees grow, it is not favored as a fruit to eat out of hand, for the most part. Instead, the rather tart, almost astringent apples are used to make vinegar and a liqueur called *Kajü*. This name comes from the word *caju*, which is the Brazilian name for the cashew. The old Brazilian name *acaju* was changed to caju by the Portuguese.

Raw unsalted cashew nuts (whole or in pieces) are not only quite expensive, they can be difficult to find in the retail market. Often, health and natural foods stores are a good place to look. If you must settle for roasted and salted nuts in a recipe calling for toasted cashews, blanch and dry them to rid them of the salt, and omit toasting them. The distinctive buttery-rich flavor of cashews is delightful in combination with fresh ripe fruits such as peaches, nectarines, and, especially, mangoes.

CASHEW ICE CREAM yield: approximately 5 cups (1 L 200 ml)

1 pound (455 g) unsalted cashews, whole or
   in pieces

3 cups (720 ml) whole milk

1 vanilla bean, split lengthwise, *or* 1 teaspoon
   (5 ml) vanilla extract

12 egg yolks (1 cup/240 ml)

10 ounces (280 g) granulated sugar

2 cups (480 ml) heavy cream

1. Toast the cashews, let cool, then crush coarsely. Reserve 2 ounces (55 g) or about ½ cup (120 ml) nuts.

2. Place the remaining nuts in a food processor with ½ cup (120 ml) milk and process to a pastelike consistency. Set the nut paste aside.

3. Pour the remaining milk into a heavy saucepan and add the vanilla bean, if using. Bring to a boil, then remove from the heat and stir in the nut paste. Cover the pan and set the mixture aside to steep for a minimum of 30 minutes.

4. Whip the egg yolks and sugar together until light in color. Return the milk mixture to boiling, then strain through a fine mesh strainer or a cheesecloth (see Note). Remove the vanilla bean and discard. Gradually stir the hot milk into the yolk mixture.

5. Set the bowl over simmering water and, stirring constantly with a whisk or wooden spoon, heat the custard until it is thick enough to coat the spoon. Remove from the heat. Stir in the heavy cream, the vanilla extract, if using, and the reserved crushed cashews. Let cool to room temperature, then cover and refrigerate the custard until it is completely cold.

6. Process in an ice cream freezer according to the manufacturer's instructions. Transfer the finished ice cream to a chilled container. Cover and store in the freezer.

NOTE: Rather than discarding these expensive nuts, try to find a use for them in cookies, a torte, or a filling. Rinse the cashews to remove the milk, then spread on a sheet pan to dry. Use within a few days.

Honey Truffle Symphony yield: 16 servings (Color Photo 33)

You may have already spotted the similarity between this dessert and Chocolate Ganache Towers (page 154). The garnishes and presentations are easily interchangeable. If wild honey is not available for the truffle cream, you may use regular honey; while it does not have the same bite, it still combines nicely with the gianduja to produce a distinctive flavor. Honey Truffle Symphony is as practical as it is elegant, as any servings that are not needed the day they are made can be kept in the refrigerator for several days or may be frozen for weeks, provided they are still wrapped in plastic and are well covered.

1 Ribbon-Pattern Decorated Sponge Sheet (page 672; see Note 1), 23 × 15 inches (57.5 × 37.5 cm)

Wild Honey Truffle Cream (recipe follows)

5 ounces (140 g) strained strawberry preserves

1½ cups (360 ml) heavy cream

2 teaspoons (10 g) granulated sugar

1 recipe Raspberry Sauce (page 173)

Sour Cream Mixture for Piping (page 727)

48 Chocolate Cigarettes (page 516; see Note 2)

16 edible fresh flowers

1. Make 16 acetate tubes, 2 inches (5 cm) in diameter and 2½ inches (6.2 cm) tall (see instructions in the recipe for Chocolate Ganache Towers, page 154).

2. Measure and cut 16 strips from the ribbon sponge sheet, 2½ × 6¼ inches (6.2 × 15.6 cm), as shown in Figure 4-14. You can actually get 18 strips by cutting 3 rows lengthwise and 6 across — plus a narrow end piece — so you have a little extra to work with during assembly. Save any leftovers for other uses. Line the plastic forms with the strips, placing the striped ribbon side against the forms. For the best-looking finished product, the short ends of the sponge sheets should line up against each other (Figure 4-15).

3. Check the consistency of the wild honey truffle cream. If it is too firm to pipe, soften it carefully over a bain-marie. Pipe the cream into the forms, filling them completely. Smooth the tops to make them flat. Cover and refrigerate for at least 4 hours or, preferably, overnight.

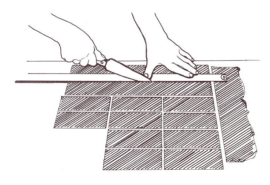

FIGURE 4-14 Cutting pieces of ribbon sponge for Honey Truffle Symphony

FIGURE 4-15 The pieces of ribbon sponge placed in plastic tubes so the edges and the ribbon stripes line up evenly

When preparing Honey Truffle Symphony in large quantities for banquets, I would omit the ribbon sponge and simply pour the Wild Honey Truffle Cream filling straight into a pan 2 inches (5 cm) deep (such as a sheet pan with a frame set on top). The next day I would cut out rounds, decorate them with cocoa powder, a chocolate fan, and a tuile butterfly, and there it was — a tasty, elegant dessert, mass-produced. However, I had leftover filling to deal with (the part left after cutting out the rounds). By warming the filling until it had a thick, mousselike consistency, I was able to put it to good use as the filling for Chocolate Ganache Cake (page 27) — dressing it up, of course, with the ribbon sponge and cookie butterflies.

4. Make the tulip template shown in Figure 13-45, page 715. Place the strawberry preserves in a pastry bag with a No. 1 (2-mm) plain tip. Place the template in the center of a dessert plate. Pipe a thin string of jam on the plate, following the inside edge of the template. Remove the template. Repeat on as many plates as you expect to need for service and set them aside.

5. Whip the heavy cream and sugar to stiff peaks. Place in a pastry bag with a No. 8 (16-mm) star tip and reserve in the refrigerator. Place a portion of the raspberry sauce in a piping bottle. Remove the plastic strips from as many desserts as you plan to serve.

6. Presentation: Fill the center of a prepared dessert plate with raspberry sauce, carefully pushing the sauce out to, but not over, the jam border. Decorate the edge of the sauce with dots of sour cream mixture swirled into hearts (see Figure 13-9 page 682). Pipe a large rosette of whipped cream to cover the entire top of 1 dessert. Gently press 3 chocolate cigarettes, 1 of each size, straight into the cream (wear a food-handling glove on the hand that touches the chocolate to avoid fingerprints). Place a small edible flower next to the cigarettes. Set the decorated dessert in the center of the sauce. Serve immediately.

NOTE 1: When you make the ribbon sponge sheet, make the chocolate lines run diagonally rather than lengthwise, as directed in the recipe. If you already have regular ribbon sponges on hand, you may cut diagonally to get the same effect (Figure 4-16a); however, this method will not produce as many pieces. To get the full number of pieces from regular ribbon sponge sheets, cut so the ribbons run horizontally (Figure 4-16b).

NOTE 2: Make the cigarettes in three distinctively different lengths — 2, 3, and 4 inches (5, 7.5, and 10 cm). Start by making the taller cigarettes; if some do not measure up, you may be able to use them for a smaller size.

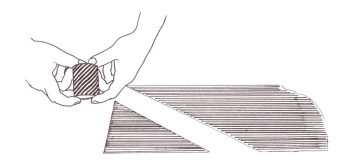

FIGURE 4-16a **Cutting diagonal pieces from a ribbon sponge made with horizontal stripes so the stripes run diagonally on the desserts**

FIGURE 4-16b **Cutting the pieces so the stripes run horizontally to get more usable pieces from the sheet**

WILD HONEY TRUFFLE CREAM yield: 6 cups (1 L 440 ml)

10 ounces (285 g) sweet dark chocolate

3 ounces (85 g) unsweetened chocolate

3 ounces (85 g) gianduja chocolate

2½ cups (600 ml) heavy cream

6 egg yolks (½ cup/120 ml)

2 ounces (55 g) granulated sugar

⅓ cup (80 ml) or 4 ounces (115 g) wild honey

2 tablespoons (30 ml) Frangelico liqueur

1. Chop all 3 chocolates into small pieces. Combine in a bowl and melt over simmering water. Set aside, but keep warm.

2. Whip the heavy cream to soft peaks.

3. Whip the egg yolks and granulated sugar by hand until they are light and fluffy, about 3 minutes.

4. Bring the honey to a boil. Gradually pour the honey into the yolk mixture and continue whipping the mixture until it has cooled.

5. Quickly stir in the reserved melted chocolate and the Frangelico liqueur. Still working quickly, fold in the reserved whipped cream.

Hot Chocolate Truffle Cake yield: 16 servings (Color Photo 40)

This luxurious dessert has become a must for inclusion on many dessert menus, and there are as many versions and titles as there are pastry chefs. They all have one thing in common: a liquid center held in place by a crust baked just enough that the center oozes onto the plate the moment the customer inserts a fork. The molten interior doubles as a thick, delicious sauce.

When I first introduced this recipe at school, I was afraid we were going to have some desserts sent back to the kitchen for not being thoroughly cooked; because the wait staff are also students, they sometimes forget to describe the item properly. Well, it turned out I was only partially right. One young student, rather embarrassed, came to me and said that one of the customers at her table had brought to her attention that the truffle cake was not cooked all the way through — but "it was so good" that his friend wanted to order one as well and had asked if his could be "undercooked" in the same way.

Making the batter is easy. The only difficult part of this recipe is judging the precise baking time. You will get it down after a few practice attempts. If part of the batter seeps from under the rings at the start of baking, roll out short dough (cocoa or plain; you will need about 6 ounces/170 g for 16 servings) to ⅛ inch (3 mm) thick, using flour to prevent it from sticking. Using one of the cake rings that will be used to bake the desserts as a cutter, cut out 16 cookies. Place the short dough cookies inside the cake rings after they have been lined with baking paper, then pour or scoop the cake batter on top. The baked short dough bottom adds a nice contrasting texture to the dessert.

Hot Chocolate Truffle Cake is meant to be served in a simple, unpretentious way, accompanied only by ice cream and/or fresh berries. I have dressed up the plates a bit in this presentation, but you can very well leave out spraying the plates, piping the heart, and using the cookie flower petal. Instead, pipe the raspberry sauce in a zigzag pattern over the base of the plate. Place the ice cream scoops on very thin sponge rounds, 1 inch (2.5 cm) in diameter, to prevent them from sliding on the plates.

Butter and Flour Mixture (page 750)

Chocolate Solution for Spraying (page 557; see Note)

Piping Chocolate (page 543), melted

Vanilla Ice Cream (recipe follows)

Chocolate Truffle Cake Batter (recipe follows)

Raspberry Sauce (recipe follows)

16 Tuile Flower Petals (see "To Make Tuile Flower Petals," at right)

Powdered sugar

1 pint raspberries

16 small mint sprigs

1. Cut 16 strips of baking paper, 9½ × 3 inches (23.7 × 7.5 cm). Brush both sides of each strip with butter and flour mixture and use the strips to line the insides of 16 cake rings, 3 inches in diameter × 2 inches high (7.5 × 5 cm).

2. Make the free-form heart template (Figure 4-17). The template as shown is the correct size to use in this recipe. Trace the drawing, then cut it out of ¹⁄₁₆-inch (2-mm) cardboard, such as the type used for cake boxes. Attach a loop of tape to the top to facilitate lifting the template from the plate. Place the template off-center and to the right on the base of a dessert plate. Weigh it down with a small, heavy object (I use a couple of large bolts wrapped in aluminum foil). Spray the entire plate with the chocolate solution (see "Spraying with Chocolate," page 556, if you need further instructions). Carefully remove the template and repeat with as many plates as you expect to need. Handle the plates carefully to avoid leaving fingerprints and set the plates aside to dry.

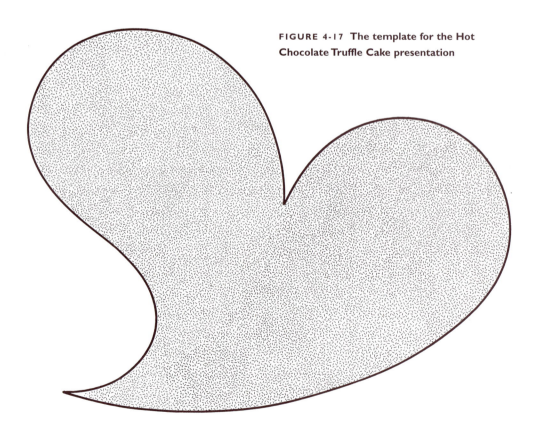

FIGURE 4-17 The template for the Hot Chocolate Truffle Cake presentation

Baking Tips for Hot Chocolate Truffle Cake

To prevent the bottom from becoming too dark, you may need to place a second pan underneath during baking. This will not be necessary if you use ramekins instead of cake rings. You will have to adjust the baking temperature and time to suit your oven and the thickness of the cake rings. If the dessert falls apart when you pull off the ring, it was not baked long enough. Conversely, if a portion of the center is not liquid enough to run out as soon as a spoon or fork is inserted into the dessert, it is overbaked. This will also happen if the dessert cools too long before it is served.

3. Place piping chocolate in a piping bag. Pipe chocolate around the perimeter of the heart design on each of the sprayed plates.

4. Using a 2-ounce (60-ml) ice cream scoop, place as many scoops of vanilla ice cream as you anticipate needing on a half-sheet pan lined with baking paper. Reserve in the freezer.

5. Approximately 20 minutes before serving, place as many prepared rings as needed on a perfectly even inverted sheet pan lined with baking paper or a Silpat. (If you are firing just a few servings at a time, an inverted pie tin or cake pan works fine.) Pipe or scoop the chocolate truffle cake batter into the rings, filling them two-thirds full. Bake at 375°F (190°C) for approximately 15 minutes, as described in "Baking Tips for Hot Chocolate Truffle Cake" above.

6. Presentation: Place the raspberry sauce in a piping bottle and pipe sauce to fill in the heart outline on as many of the reserved plates as you have desserts in the oven. Stand a tuile flower petal on end to the right of the heart at the bottom of each plate. After removing the dessert from the oven, sift powdered sugar lightly over the top. Wait about 30 seconds, then grasp a cake ring with a pair of tongs. Slide a palette knife underneath, lift the dessert using both tools, and set off-center on a prepared plate. Gently slide the knife out, then use the tongs to lift off the ring. Peel the paper away from the dessert, if necessary. Place a prepared ice cream scoop on the base of the cookie. Arrange raspberries and a mint sprig below the cake and serve immediately.

NOTE: If you do not have access to a power sprayer and therefore cannot use the chocolate solution to decorate the plates, you can still make a marbleized pattern using a manual spray bottle and the alternate cocoa solution (recipe follows). It is not possible to use a template with this technique, however.

CHEF'S TIP
If this size cake ring is not available, any size that is close will do; adjust the paper strips accordingly. If all else fails, you can use ramekins, 3¼ inches (8.1 cm) in diameter. Omit the paper; just grease the ramekins and serve the dessert in its baking dish.

To Make Tuile Flower Petals

Follow the instructions for making the petals in Rainbow of Summer Sorbets in a Cookie Flower (page 304), Steps 1, 2, and 3. You will need ½ recipe Vanilla Tuile Decorating Paste and 1 teaspoon (2.5 g) unsweetened cocoa powder. Make about 20 petals to allow for breakage.

COCOA SOLUTION FOR MANUAL SPRAY BOTTLE yield: approximately 3½ cups (840 ml)

This will make a medium-dark spray. Add more cocoa powder if a darker color is desired.

¼ cup (60 ml) light corn syrup
3 cups (720 ml) warm water

2 ounces (55 g) unsweetened cocoa powder

1. Stir the corn syrup into the water.

2. Place the cocoa powder in a bowl. Add just enough of the water mixture to make a smooth paste. Gradually mix in the remaining water. Store in the refrigerator.

VANILLA ICE CREAM yield: approximately 5 cups (1 L 200 ml)

1 quart (960 ml) half-and-half
1 vanilla bean, split lengthwise
10 egg yolks (⅞ cup/210 ml)

10 ounces (285 g) granulated sugar
2 teaspoons (10 ml) vanilla extract

1. Heat the half-and-half with the vanilla bean to scalding.

2. Beat the egg yolks and sugar until light and fluffy. Remove the vanilla bean halves and use the back of a paring knife to scrape out the seeds. Stir the seeds into the half-and-half. Discard the vanilla bean pods.

3. Gradually pour the hot half-and-half into the whipped egg yolk mixture while whisking rapidly. Heat the mixture over simmering water, stirring constantly with a whisk or wooden spoon, until the custard thickens enough to coat the spoon. Be careful not to overheat and break the custard.

4. Remove from the heat and continue to stir for a few seconds to keep the mixture from overcooking where it touches the hot bowl. Stir in the vanilla extract. Let cool to room temperature, then refrigerate, covered, until completely cold, for several hours or, preferably, overnight.

5. Process the chilled vanilla ice cream custard in an ice cream freezer, following the manufacturer's instructions.

6. Transfer to a chilled container and store, covered, in the freezer.

CHOCOLATE TRUFFLE CAKE BATTER yield: 2 quarts (1 L 920 ml)

12 ounces (340 g) sweet dark chocolate
4 ounces (115 g) unsweetened chocolate
12 ounces (340 g) unsalted butter
2 ounces (55 g) cornstarch

1 pound 4 ounces (570 g) granulated sugar
8 whole eggs
8 egg yolks (⅔ cup/160 ml)
1 tablespoon (15 ml) orange liqueur

1. Chop the chocolates into small pieces. Place in a bowl with the butter and set over simmering water to melt. Do not overheat.

2. Use a whisk to mix the cornstarch into the granulated sugar in an oversize bowl. Stir in the melted chocolate and butter. Add the whole eggs, egg yolks, and orange liqueur, stirring just until the mixture develops a smooth consistency, about 2 minutes.

3. Cover and refrigerate for at least 8 hours or, preferably, overnight.

RASPBERRY SAUCE yield: approximately 4 cups (960 ml)

2 pounds (910 g) fresh ripe raspberries or thawed IQF raspberries

3 tablespoons (24 g) cornstarch

2 ounces (55 g) granulated sugar

1. Puree the berries. Using a fine mesh strainer, strain out the seeds. Measure and add water, if necessary, to make 4 cups (960 ml) juice.

2. Place the cornstarch in a saucepan. Mix enough of the juice into the cornstarch to liquefy it, then stir in the remaining juice.

3. Heat the sauce to simmering. Stir in granulated sugar, adjusting the amount as needed, depending on the sweetness of the berries.

4. Cook the sauce for 1 minute while stirring. Cool, strain, and thin with water, if necessary. Store, covered, in the refrigerator.

Individual Croquembouche yield: 16 servings

There is no parallel English word for *croquembouche*, but the literal meaning is "crunch in the mouth," from the words *croquer* ("to crunch") and *bouche* ("mouth"). This ancient, elaborate French specialty consists of small custard-filled cream puffs, or *profiteroles*, glazed with caramelized sugar.

In this recipe, the cream puffs are assembled into individual servings, but in the classic version, they are formed into a large cone-shaped confection typically comprising about 200 small profiteroles dipped in caramel and stacked around a metal cone. Once the caramel hardens, the croquembouche is lifted off the form, placed on a base made of nougatine, and decorated with spun sugar, candied violets, and marzipan or pulled sugar flowers. The classic croquembouche is traditionally featured as a centerpiece *(pièce monté)* at French weddings, First Communion celebrations, and opulent Christmas buffets. This smaller version allows you to create individual servings for plated service.

½ recipe Pâte à Choux (page 783)

1 recipe or 2 pounds (910 g) Quick Bavarian Cream (page 774)

1 recipe Caramelized Sugar with Water (page 613)

1 cup (240 ml) heavy cream

1 teaspoon (5 g) granulated sugar

1 recipe Strawberry Sauce (page 186)

Sour Cream Mixture for Piping (page 727)

Candied violets and/or edible fresh flowers

1. Place the pâte à choux in a pastry bag with a No. 5 (10-mm) plain tip. Pipe out mounds the size of large cherries on sheet pans lined with baking paper or Silpats. You need 128 for this recipe, but you should get about 140. Bake at 400°F (205°C) for about 20 minutes. Be sure the profiteroles bake long enough to hold their shape. Let cool completely.

2. Make a small hole in the bottom of each profiterole. Using a pastry bag with a No. 2 (4-mm) plain tip, fill each with Bavarian cream.

3. Using 2 forks, dip the top and sides of the profiteroles in the caramelized sugar. Place them on sheet pans lined with baking paper, caramel-side up. Reserve in the refrigerator until serving time, but no longer than 2 hours.

4. Whip the heavy cream and granulated sugar to stiff peaks. Place in a pastry bag with a No. 4 (8-mm) star tip. Reserve in the refrigerator. Place a portion of the strawberry sauce in a piping bottle.

5. Presentation: Arrange 4 profiteroles in a square in the center of a dessert plate. Pipe a large dot of whipped cream in the middle to hold them together. Place 3 profiteroles on top, centered on the bottom layer. Pipe a second dot of cream in the middle of these and top with a single profiterole to make a pyramid. Cover the base of the plate around the croquembouche with strawberry sauce. Decorate the strawberry sauce with the sour cream mixture (see decorating instructions on pages 681 to 685). Decorate the dessert with candied violets and/or fresh edible flowers.

Marjolaine yield: 12 servings (Color Photo 19)

Marjolaine, one of the great modern classic desserts, is the best-known dish invented by the late French chef Fernand Point, owner of the three-star restaurant La Pyramide outside of Lyons. It is an unctuously rich creation that alternates moist chocolate sponge cake, crisp nut meringue *(dacquoise)*, praline-flavored buttercream, chocolate whipped cream, and rich chocolate ganache. Many versions have evolved over the years; this is mine.

The Marjolaine requires advance planning. After assembly, it must be refrigerated for at least eight hours or, better yet, overnight to ensure that the meringue softens sufficiently for you to cut cleanly through the layers. The uncut layered sheet will keep fresh in the refrigerator for up to one week, or up to one month in the freezer, if well wrapped. (If it has been frozen, it is best to thaw the sheet before icing the top.) With this in mind, you may want to consider doubling the recipe to make a half-sheet rather than a quarter so you can freeze part of it for later use. Because this cake is so rich, you can stretch the yield by cutting the pieces slightly smaller.

¼ recipe **Chocolate Chiffon Sponge Cake II batter** (page 798)	1½ teaspoons (4.5 g) **unflavored gelatin powder**
Nut Meringue (recipe follows)	1 recipe **Chantilly Cream** (page 765; see Step 3)
Praline Buttercream (recipe follows)	**Unsweetened cocoa powder**
½ recipe **Crème Parisienne** (page 768)	1 recipe **Raspberry Sauce** (page 173)
½ cup (120 ml) **Plain Cake Syrup** (page 789)	**Sour Cream Mixture for Piping** (page 727)
12 ounces (340 g) **Ganache** (page 770)	36 **raspberries**
	12 small **mint leaves**

1. Line the bottom of a half-sheet pan (16 × 12 inches/40 × 30 cm) with baking paper. Spread the sponge batter evenly over the pan. Bake immediately at 400°F (205°C) for about 15 minutes or until the sponge springs back when pressed lightly in the middle. Set aside to cool.

2. Make the nut meringue and the praline buttercream.

3. Whip the crème Parisienne to stiff peaks and reserve in the refrigerator. (Do not whip the Chantilly cream until you are ready to use it.)

4. Cut the meringue sheets in half crosswise to make 4 meringue layers, 8 × 12 inches (20 × 30 cm) each. Do not separate the meringue from the baking paper at this time.

5. Cut around the edge of the sponge sheet and remove it from the pan. Cut it in half crosswise and reserve one half for another use. Cut the skin from the top of the remaining piece, remove the baking paper from the back, and place on a sheet pan or sheet of cake cardboard lined with baking paper. Brush half of the cake syrup over the sponge.

6. To assemble: Reserve one-third of the ganache. Soften the remainder and spread it evenly on top of the sponge sheet. Pick up a meringue layer by the baking paper, invert on top of the ganache, and peel off the paper.

7. Spread the crème Parisienne on top of the meringue. Using the same method as before, add a second meringue sheet; top this one with the praline buttercream. Add the third meringue sheet.

8. Sprinkle the gelatin over the remaining cake syrup and set aside to soften. Whip the Chantilly cream to soft peaks. Place the gelatin mixture over a bain-marie and heat to dissolve. Do not overheat. Rapidly mix the gelatin into a small portion of the cream to temper. Still working quickly, add this to the remaining cream. If the Chantilly cream is too soft to hold its shape, give it a few more turns with the whip. Spread the cream evenly on top of the third meringue sheet. Place the last meringue sheet on top of the cream. If necessary, press the top of the pastry lightly with the bottom of a sheet pan to level the top.

9. Warm the reserved ganache until it is liquid. Spread a thin layer over the top of the Marjolaine. Once the ganache has started to set but before it sets up completely, use the back of a chef's knife to mark diagonal lines, ½ inch (1.2 cm) apart, in both directions, making a diamond pattern in the ganache. Drag the knife across without putting much pressure on it. Refrigerate until firm.

10. Dust cocoa powder lightly over the top of the dessert. Using a thin sharp knife dipped in hot water, trim about ½ inch (1.2 cm) from 1 long side to make a clean edge. Starting from that edge, mark or cut the sheet lengthwise into 3 equal strips, each approximately 2¼ inches (5.6 cm) wide. Trim 1 short end on each, then cut each strip into 4 square pieces (the same length as the width of the strip). Be sure to hold the knife at a 90-degree angle so the sides of the pastries are straight. This cake will keep for several days in the refrigerator if left whole, so it is best not to cut more servings than you expect to need.

11. Place a portion of the raspberry sauce in a piping bottle.

12. Presentation: Pipe a circle of raspberry sauce, 3 inches (7.5 cm) in diameter, centered on the lower half of the base of a dessert plate. Use the tip of the piping bottle or a wooden skewer to form the circle into a heart shape approximately 4½ inches (11.2 cm) long and 4½ inches (11.2 cm) wide at the top, by elongating the bottom of the circle into a point and then widening the top. It is not necessary to make 2 rounded edges on top of the heart. Instead, place a Marjolaine square diagonally on the plate so the bottom corner of the pastry rests in the top of the sauce and creates the heart shape shown in Color Photo 19. Use a piping bag to pipe 2 thin lines of sour cream mixture along the inside perimeter of the heart. Swirl the lines into the sauce with a wooden skewer (see Figure 13-13, page 683). Place 3 raspberries and a small mint leaf on the plate.

NUT MERINGUE yield: 2 sheets, 12 × 16 inches (30 × 40 cm)

6 ounces (170 g) almonds

4 ounces (115 g) hazelnuts

1 ounce (30 g) bread flour

8 egg whites (1 cup/240 ml)

8 ounces (225 g) granulated sugar

1. Grind the almonds and hazelnuts to a fine consistency. Mix in the flour.

2. Whip the egg whites until they are foamy and doubled in volume. Gradually add the sugar and whip to stiff peaks. Carefully fold in the ground nut mixture by hand.

3. Divide the batter equally between 2 half-sheets of baking paper (12 × 16 inches/30 × 40 cm). Using a spatula, spread the batter evenly over the papers to cover them completely. Drag the papers onto half-sheet pans (see Figure 9-22, page 481).

4. Bake immediately at 350°F (175°C) for about 15 minutes or until golden brown and dry.

CHEF'S TIP

If you keep finely ground nuts on hand, purchased from a bakery supplier, use those instead, using all almonds (almond meal) or all hazelnuts, depending on availability.

PRALINE BUTTERCREAM yield: approximately 8 ounces (225 g)

Buttercream tends to break when liquid is added, especially when the buttercream is cold. Should this happen, stir the mixture over a bain-marie until it is smooth.

8 ounces (225 g) Vanilla Buttercream (Swiss Method; page 753)

1 tablespoon (15 ml) Hazelnut Paste (page 778)

¼ teaspoon (1 g) mocha paste *or* 2 teaspoons (10 ml) Coffee Reduction (page 754)

1. Mix a small amount of buttercream into the hazelnut paste to soften it.

2. Mix the tempered hazelnut paste into the remaining buttercream and add the coffee flavoring. Continue to mix until smooth.

Mascarpone Cheesecake with Lemon Verbena Panna Cotta

yield: 12 servings (Color Photo 32)

In this presentation, a lattice-style puff pastry decoration hovers over the cheesecake, taking the place of the graham cracker crust that lines the bottom of conventional cheesecake preparations. There is nothing traditional about this variation, with its lemon verbena–infused panna cotta topping and rich mascarpone-flavored cheesecake. However, if you prefer your cheesecakes to start with a graham cracker crust, combine 8 ounces (225 g) graham cracker crumbs with 3 ounces (85 g) melted unsalted butter. Divide among the rings after they have been lined with aluminum foil and press the crumbs into the bottoms.

Mascarpone Cheesecake Batter (recipe follows)

Lemon Verbena Panna Cotta (recipe follows)

¾ cup (180 ml) heavy cream

1 teaspoon (5 g) granulated sugar

Guinettes Cherry Sauce (page 388)

12 Lattice Puff Pastry Decorations (recipe follows)

12 small sprigs lemon verbena

12 fresh cherries or other small berries

Powdered sugar

1. Cut 12 squares of aluminum foil, 6½ inches (16.2 cm) each. Set a metal cake ring, 3 inches (7.5 cm) in diameter and 2 inches (5 cm) high, in the center of each square. Pleat and fold the edges of the foil tightly against the rings all around to form a tight seal. Be sure the seal reaches at least three-quarters of the way up the sides of the rings because the cakes will be baked in a water bath. Place the rings in a hotel pan and set aside.

2. Divide the batter evenly among the prepared rings; they will be filled about halfway. Take care not to get any batter on the sides of the rings above the filling level. Pour water into the hotel pan halfway up the sides of the rings. Bake in a 300°F (149°C) oven for approximately 40 minutes or until the filling has set to a jellylike consistency. Remove the cakes from the water bath and set aside on a sheet pan to cool slightly.

3. While the cheesecakes are still warm, pour the panna cotta on top, dividing it evenly. Place the forms in the refrigerator for at least 4 hours or, preferably, overnight.

4. Peel away the aluminum foil from as many desserts as you plan to serve. Run a small knife around the inside perimeter and remove the rings. Whip the cream and sugar to stiff peaks and place in a pastry bag with a No. 7 (14-mm) star tip.

5. Presentation: Place a cheesecake in the center of a serving plate. Spoon cherry sauce in an irregular band around it. Carefully push a puff pastry decoration into the top in the center of the panna cotta. Pipe a rosette of whipped cream in front and decorate with a sprig of lemon verbena and a cherry or small berry. Sift powdered sugar over the dessert and serve immediately.

MASCARPONE CHEESECAKE BATTER yield: approximately 5 cups (1 L 200 ml)

12 ounces (340 g) mascarpone cheese, at room temperature

8 ounces (225 g) cream cheese, at room temperature

6 ounces (170 g) powdered sugar, sifted

1 vanilla bean

2 teaspoons (10 ml) vanilla extract

3 eggs, at room temperature

½ cup (120 ml) sweetened condensed milk

½ cup (120 ml) sour cream

½ cup (120 ml) heavy cream

1. Using the paddle attachment on the mixer, blend the mascarpone cheese, cream cheese, and powdered sugar until fully combined, scraping down the sides of the bowl several times to prevent any lumps from forming.

2. Split the vanilla bean lengthwise and scrape out the seeds. Mix the seeds into a small amount of batter at the side of the bowl and mix this combination into the rest of the batter. Add the vanilla extract, then incorporate the eggs, 1 at a time. Add the condensed milk, sour cream, and heavy cream, scraping down the bowl from time to time.

LEMON VERBENA PANNA COTTA yield: approximately 4 cups (960 ml)

½ ounce (15 g) fresh lemon verbena leaves (see Chef's Tip)

3 cups (750 ml) heavy cream

1 cup (240 ml) milk

1½ tablespoons (14 g) unflavored gelatin powder

6 ounces (170 g) granulated sugar

CHEF'S TIP

If lemon verbena is not available, use ¼ cup (60 ml) crème de cassis instead. Omit Step 1. Add the crème de cassis to the milk before sprinkling the gelatin on top in Step 2. It is not necessary to strain the mixture in Step 3. Also in Step 3, reduce the sugar to 3 ounces (85 g).

1. Finely chop the verbena leaves. Pour the cream into a saucepan, add the lemon verbena, and bring to scalding. Remove from the heat, cover, and set aside to infuse for 1 hour.

2. Pour the milk into a bowl and sprinkle the gelatin powder over the surface. Let stand until softened, 10 to 15 minutes.

3. Add the sugar to the lemon verbena cream and heat, just until the sugar has dissolved. Strain through a fine mesh strainer and discard the verbena.

4. Heat the milk to dissolve the gelatin. Stir the milk into the cream mixture. Let cool slightly before pouring the panna cotta on top of the cheesecakes, but do not wait too long or the gelatin will set up.

LATTICE PUFF PASTRY DECORATIONS yield: 3 lattice sheets, 8 × 8 inches (20 × 20 cm) each

12 ounces (340 g) Puff Pastry (page 784)

Egg wash

Granulated sugar

1. Using flour to prevent the dough from sticking, roll out the puff pastry to a rectangle measuring 10 × 16 inches (25 × 40 cm); it should be approximately ⅛ inch (3 mm) thick. Place the puff pastry in the refrigerator to allow the gluten to relax and the dough to firm.

PROCEDURE 4-3a Rolling a lattice cutter over a strip of puff pastry

PROCEDURE 4-3b Stretching one strip to make the lattice pattern (the other has already been stretched)

PROCEDURE 4-3c After the sheets have been baked, using a serrated knife to cut one sheet into decorations

2. Cut the sheet crosswise into 3 narrow strips. Roll a lattice cutter lengthwise over each strip, pressing firmly (see Procedure 4-3a and "About Lattice Cutters," page 485).

3. Place the strips wide apart on 2 half-sheet sheet pans lined with baking paper or Silpats (or use a full sheet pan). Stretch the dough evenly crosswise to produce the lattice pattern (see Procedure 4-3b).

4. Brush egg wash lightly over the top; do not let it drip into the small openings of the pattern. Sprinkle granulated sugar over the dough strips (see Note).

5. Bake at 400°F (205°C) until the pieces are golden brown and the sugar has caramelized on top, about 12 minutes. After the dough sheets have cooled, use a serrated knife with a sawing motion to cut decorations of the desired size (see Procedure 4-3c).

6. Store, covered, in an airtight container.

NOTE: If you are using the baked lattice sheet as a savory decoration, omit the sugar. Allow the first coat of egg wash to dry, then brush on a second coat before baking.

Orange-Chocolate Towers with Orange Syrup and Caramel Screens

yield: 16 servings (Color Photo 34)

This is another version of chocolate Marquise. Both this presentation and the recipe on page 394 utilize unconventional methods to make the desserts. Here, the chocolate filling is formed inside long pipes. Once it has become firm, it is unmolded, wrapped in a decorated sponge sheet, and cut into individual servings. The more common approach is to line individual molds with a thin layer of sponge and pipe the filling into each mold. The technique used here is not only faster but also gives you the option of cutting the servings a bit smaller, should you need a higher yield. You can also cut the pieces at an angle to produce a slanted top edge, as shown in Chocolate Marquise with Passion Fruit Parfait and Lace Cookie Bouquet (Color Photo 82).

Orange-Chocolate Filling (recipe follows)

1 Ribbon-Pattern Decorated Sponge Sheet
   (page 672; see Note)

1½ cups (360 ml) heavy cream

2 teaspoons (10 g) granulated sugar

Orange-Vanilla Decorating Syrup (page 760)

Piping Chocolate (page 543)

16 Caramel Glass Paste Screens (page 666)

Cape gooseberries or other small berries

Powdered sugar

1. Have ready 2 plastic tubes, 22 inches (55 cm) long and with an inside diameter of 1¼ inches (3.1 cm). Cut 2 strips of acetate measuring 22 × 5½ inches (55 × 13.7 cm). Line the tubes with the plastic strips (see Chef's Tip). Cap 1 end of each tube.

2. Position the pipes, capped end down, so they are supported vertically and set low enough that you can see into the interior.

3. Place a portion of the chocolate filling in a pastry bag with a No. 6 (12-mm) plain tip. Pipe the filling into the tubes, piping straight down and filling them to the top. You will need to refill the pastry bag several times. Tap the tubes sharply to remove air pockets as you work your way to the top. Cover the tops of the tubes and refrigerate for a minimum of 2 hours to set the filling. Cover the leftover filling and reserve in the refrigerator.

4. Cut 2 pieces from the ribbon sponge, 22 × approximately 5½ inches (55 × approximately 13.7 cm), or wide enough to wrap around the tubes of filling.

5. Unmold the logs of chocolate filling. If the tubes were lined with plastic, the filling will slide right out; if the tubes were lined with baking paper, gently shake the filling out of the tube until you can reach the baking paper, then use the paper to pull the filling out of the tube.

6. Invert the 2 sponge sheets so the plain sides face up. Spread a thin layer of the reserved filling over each sheet. If the filling is too firm, warm it over a bain-marie to make it sticky. Peel the plastic or baking paper away from the chocolate logs. Place a log of chocolate on each sponge sheet and roll 1 complete turn to enclose the filling. Trim the long edges of the sponge sheets, if needed; the edges should meet with no gap but should not overlap.

7. Heat a thin, sharp knife on the stove or by dipping it into hot water. Trim the short ends of 1 log, then cut it across into 8 equal pieces. Be sure to hold your knife at a 90-degree angle so the deserts will stand straight and be level on top. Repeat with the second log.

8. Whip the heavy cream and sugar together until stiff peaks form. Place in a pastry bag with a No. 8 (16-mm) star tip; reserve in the refrigerator. Place a portion of the orange syrup in a piping bottle.

9. Pipe a design of piping chocolate across the center of as many dessert plates as you anticipate needing for service (see Color Photo 34).

10. Presentation: Place a tower on the top area of a decorated plate, just behind the chocolate decoration. Pipe a rosette of whipped cream on top of the tower and decorate with a cape gooseberry. Position a caramel screen behind the dessert. Pipe an irregular band of orange syrup in front of the dessert. Sift powdered sugar over the dessert and the plate and serve immediately.

NOTE: When you prepare the ribbon sponge sheet, you can, alternatively, create a pattern using a template or screen. Place the template on top of the Silpat and spread the cocoa paste over it. Carefully lift off the template without disturbing the pattern and proceed.

ORANGE-CHOCOLATE FILLING yield: 2 quarts (1 L 920 ml)

Do not make this filling until you are ready to fill the tubes.

14 ounces (400 g) sweet dark chocolate	2 tablespoons (30 g) granulated sugar
2 ounces (55 g) unsweetened chocolate	¼ cup (60 ml) or 3 ounces (85 g) honey
2½ cups (600 ml) heavy cream	¼ cup (60 ml) orange liqueur
4 egg yolks (⅓ cup/80 ml)	

1. Chop both chocolates into small chunks. Place in a bowl over a bain-marie and melt together. Remove from the heat, but keep warm.

2. Whip the heavy cream to soft peaks.

3. Whip the egg yolks and sugar for about 2 minutes; the mixture should be light and fluffy.

4. Bring the honey to a boil and gradually pour it into the egg yolks while whipping. Continue to whip until the mixture has cooled completely.

5. Fold in the warm chocolate, then the liqueur. Quickly stir in the whipped cream.

Red Banana Truffles in Phyllo Dough yield: 16 servings (Color Photo 36)

This is the epitome of a tasty, good-looking dessert that can be prepped ahead, requiring a minimum of time for last-minute assembly. If you are really pressed for time when serving, eliminate piping the chocolate on the plate and pour the sauce into a pool in the center of the plate instead, making sure that it is thick enough not to run. Arrange the cut banana truffle pieces on top of the sauce. Sift powdered sugar over the entire plate, then arrange the fruit in a circle around the sauce on top of the powdered sugar (do not move it once you set it down). Sprinkle pistachio nuts sparingly on top of the sauce. Another nice accompaniment is raspberry sauce as shown in the color photo. If red bananas are not available, use eight medium-size yellow bananas instead. Cut them in half lengthwise and then, keeping the halves together, cut each banana in half again across to make thirty-two pieces.

16 medium-size ripe red bananas	Piping Chocolate (page 543), melted
6 ounces (170 g) Ganache (page 770)	Bourbon Sauce (recipe follows)
5 ounces (140 g) pistachio nuts (see "Preparing the Pistachio Nuts")	Powdered sugar
32 sheets phyllo dough (about 1 pound 6 ounces/625 g)	1 pound (455 g) prepared fresh fruit, approximately (see Note)
4 ounces (115 g) unsalted butter, melted	¼ cup (60 ml) orange liqueur

Preparing the Pistachio Nuts

Blanch the nuts, remove the skins, and dry the nuts. Crush the pistachios into medium pieces. This process yields pieces of various sizes. Reserve the larger pieces (about one-third of the total) for the presentation and use the remaining smaller pieces when assembling the bananas.

1. Peel the bananas. Cut the pointed tip off each end, then cut the bananas in half lengthwise. Turn each piece so the cut side faces up.

2. Place the ganache in a pastry bag with a No. 5 (10-mm) plain tip. Pipe a rope of ganache on the flat side of half of the banana pieces. Working with the remaining banana pieces (those without ganache), pick up 1 at a time and dip the cut side into the crushed pistachio nuts, pressing firmly so they adhere. Then sandwich together with a ganache-topped banana piece.

3. Unwrap and unroll the phyllo dough. Keep the stack of dough covered with a slightly damp — not wet — towel as much as possible while you are working. Place 1 sheet in front of you and brush it lightly with butter; fold it in half lengthwise and brush lightly with butter again. Repeat buttering and folding with a second sheet and place this on top of the first so the stack has 4 layers of phyllo. Place a prepared banana at the short end of the phyllo stack. Bring the sides in on top of the banana, then roll up lengthwise. Place, seam-side down, on a sheet pan lined with buttered baking paper. Repeat with the remaining pieces.

4. Bake at 375°F (190°C) for approximately 25 minutes or until golden brown and baked through. Let cool to room temperature.

5. Place the piping chocolate in a piping bag and cut a small opening. Pipe a narrow, elongated ✕ in the center over an entire dessert plate; repeat on as many plates as you anticipate needing. Set the plates aside. Place a portion of the bourbon sauce in a piping bottle. Reserve it and the remainder of the sauce at room temperature until time of service.

6. Presentation: Pipe bourbon sauce inside both sides of the chocolate ✕ on a prepared plate, covering only the inside portions of the ✕ that are on the base of the plate (see Color Photo 36). Using a serrated knife, carefully cut a banana package in half diagonally and arrange the pieces in the center of the plate. Sift powdered sugar lightly over the whole plate, including the rim. Place 7 or 8 pieces of prepared fruit on each side of the banana pieces, on top of the powdered sugar. After you set the fruit on the plate, do not move it or you will disturb the powdered sugar. Sprinkle some of the reserved pistachio nuts on top of the sauce.

NOTE: Cut 4 types of fruit into distinct pieces; do not chop or slice the fruit haphazardly. Place each variety in a separate bowl. Pour a little orange liqueur into each bowl and toss gently to coat the fruit.

BOURBON SAUCE yield: approximately 4 cups (960 ml)

6 egg yolks (½ cup/120 ml)	1 tablespoon (15 ml) vanilla extract
4 ounces (115 g) granulated sugar	1½ cups (360 ml) heavy cream
¾ cup (180 ml) bourbon whiskey	

1. Whip the egg yolks and sugar together just to combine. Whisk in the bourbon. Place over simmering water and whisk constantly until the mixture thickens to the ribbon stage. Remove from the heat and whip until cold. Add the vanilla.

2. Whip the heavy cream until it thickens to a very soft consistency. Stir into the yolk mixture. Adjust the consistency as desired by adding unwhipped heavy cream to thin it or more whipped cream to thicken it. Serve cold or at room temperature. Bourbon sauce may be stored, covered, in the refrigerator for 3 or 4 days. If the sauce separates, whisk it to bring it back together.

Strawberries Romanoff yield: 16 servings (Color Photo 35)

Strawberries with cream is a delectable combination found in numerous dessert preparations — strawberry ice cream; fresh ripe berries served with crème fraîche; assembled pastries, such as Strawberry Pyramids (page 185) — and in many cake fillings. Strawberries Romanoff takes its name from a Russian family prominent in the history of that country for more than 300 years. The berries are traditionally macerated in liqueur; however, the bona fide version is not served in a chocolate goblet or with orange custard, as in this rendition, and the strawberries and cream are mixed together — tasty, but not an appealing presentation. If you do not have time to make the chocolate goblets, serve this refreshing dessert in silver goblets or saucer-type champagne glasses and omit the orange custard.

4 pounds (1 kg 820 g) small, ripe strawberries

½ cup (120 ml) simple syrup

½ cup (120 ml) plus 2 tablespoons (30 ml) Grand Marnier liqueur

Powdered sugar

Unsweetened cocoa powder

1 cup (240 ml) heavy cream

Orange Custard (recipe follows)

16 Chocolate Goblets (page 522)

16 mint sprigs

16 Tuile Cookie Spoons (page 708)

1. Rinse the strawberries and remove the hulls using a small melon ball cutter. Cut the berries into halves or quarters, depending on their size (see Note). Toss the strawberries gently with the simple syrup and ½ cup (120 ml) of the Grand Marnier. Adjust the amount of syrup in accordance with the ripeness of the fruit and strength of the liqueur flavor desired. Let the strawberries macerate in the liquid at room temperature for at least 30 minutes. Do not let them macerate too long, and definitely not overnight, because the strawberries will become too soft and their color will fade.

2. Make the presentation template (Figure 4-18). The template as shown is the correct size for use in this recipe. Trace the drawing, then cut the template out of ¹/₁₆-inch (2-mm) cardboard. Tape the template to a bottomless pie tin as described on page 692. The pie pan is used to protect the rim of the plate when sifting cocoa powder on top; it also serves as a handle, making it easier to remove the template from the plate. Sift powdered sugar over the base of as many plates as you need. Tape 3 toothpicks to the bottom of the template to elevate it just enough to prevent it from disturbing the powdered sugar design. Place the pie pan on a dessert plate and sift cocoa powder over the top. Repeat this procedure with the rest of the plates. Set the decorated plates aside.

3. Whip the heavy cream with the remaining Grand Marnier until stiff peaks form. Place the cream in a pastry bag with a No. 7 (14-mm) star tip. Reserve in the refrigerator. Using a plain round cookie cutter, 3 inches (7.5 cm) in diameter, cut 8 rounds from each pan of orange custard. Reserve in the refrigerator.

4. Presentation: Place a portion of orange custard in the bottom of a goblet. Top with approximately ¾ cup (180 ml) of the strawberry mixture, including some of the liquid. Be careful not to get fingerprints on the goblets when you handle them. The easiest way to prevent this is to wear food-handling gloves. Set the goblet in the center of a prepared dessert plate. Pipe a rosette of whipped cream on top of the strawberries. Top the cream with a mint sprig. Place a cookie spoon to the right of the cocoa spoon on the plate.

NOTE: If you are unable to find small strawberries, cut larger berries in half lengthwise, then cut each half into 3 or 4 pieces. Ideally, all of the pieces should be about the same size and shape; this makes for the nicest presentation.

FIGURE 4-18 The template for the Strawberries Romanoff presentation

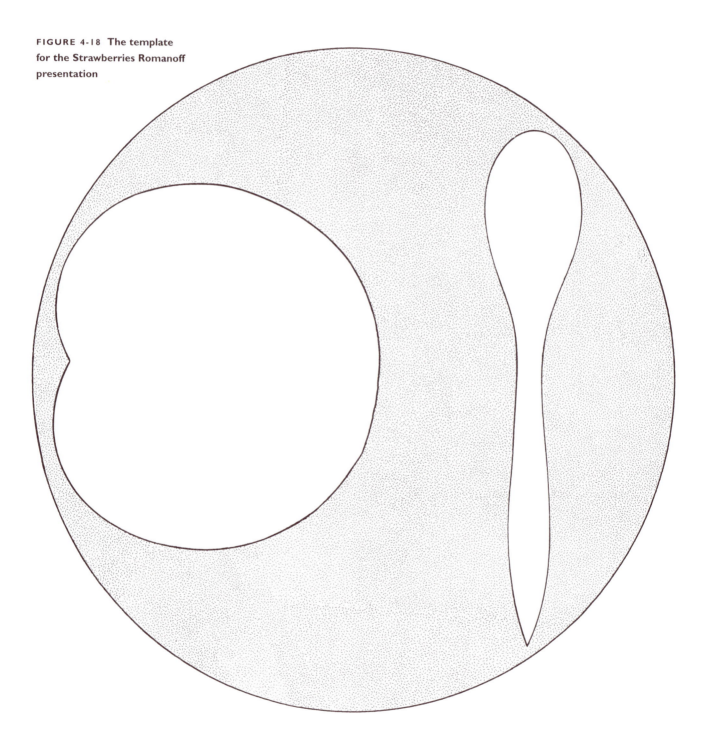

ORANGE CUSTARD yield: 2 pans, 10 inches (25 cm) in diameter

2 quarts (1 L 920 ml) half-and-half

Finely grated zest of 2 oranges

3¹/₂ cups (840 ml) whole eggs (approximately 14)

1 pound (455 g) granulated sugar

1. Bring the half-and-half and the orange zest to the scalding point in a heavy saucepan.

2. Whisk the eggs and sugar together just to combine. Whisk the hot half-and-half mixture into the egg mixture while whisking constantly.

3. Divide the custard between 2 cake pans, each 10 inches (25 cm) in diameter. Place the pans on an even full-size sheet pan and place in a 350°F (175°C) oven. Add enough hot water to the sheet pan to reach halfway up the sides of the sheet pans. Bake for approximately 40 minutes or until the custard is set. Let cool completely. Cover and refrigerate until needed.

Strawberry Pyramids yield: 16 servings (Color Photo 37)

This version of the popular Strawberry Kirsch Cake (page 61) requires advance planning, as you must make a triangular form before you can prepare the pyramids. If the garde manger department (the pantry or cold kitchen) has a triangular form approximately 24 inches (60 cm) long, 3¹/₂ inches (8.7 cm) deep, and 3¹/₂ inches (8.7 cm) across the top and is willing to part with it, you are in luck. If not, you can quickly make one out of cardboard with the directions in the box. The form is similar to, but a little larger than, the one used to make the Chocolate Chalet (page 475).

Granulated sugar

1 Almond Sponge (page 795), 14 × 24 inches (35 × 60 cm)

25 to 30 medium-size strawberries

¹/₂ recipe Kirsch Whipped Cream (page 63)

Strawberry Sauce (recipe follows)

Sour Cream Mixture for Piping (page 727)

16 fanned strawberry halves

16 mint sprigs

1. Sprinkle sugar lightly on top of the almond sponge. Pick up the sponge by the paper and invert it on top of a second sheet of baking paper. Carefully peel the paper from the back of the sponge and trim the cake to 12 inches (30 cm) wide. Again, picking up the sponge by the paper, place it inside the triangular mold with the paper against the mold and 1 long edge even with 1 long edge of the form. Support the top one-third of the sponge that is outside the form with a rolling pin or some cans.

2. Clean the strawberries and cut off both the stem ends and approximately ¹/₄ inch (6 mm) of the tips; save the tips for the sauce. Line the strawberries end to end on their sides next to the form to determine how many you need and to make the assembly go more quickly.

3. Pour enough of the kirsch whipped cream into the sponge-lined form to fill it halfway. Quickly place the strawberries on the cream end to end, cut sides touching. Top with the remaining cream. Depending on the thickness of the sponge and the size of the strawberries, you may have a small amount of the cream left over; do not overfill the form. Fold the supported sponge over the top and trim off any excess. Refrigerate for at least 2 hours.

4. Cut the ends loose from the mold, unmold the pyramid onto a cardboard cake sheet or

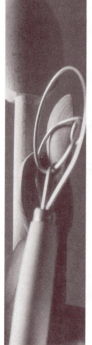

To Make a Triangular Cardboard Form

1. As shown in Figure 4-19, cut a sturdy piece of cardboard to 24 × 7 inches (60 × 17.5 cm). Score (cut halfway through the thickness of the cardboard) a line lengthwise down the center to make it easier to bend the cardboard. Turn the cardboard sheet upside down so the cut is on the bottom, then bend the cardboard along the line and tape across the top at each end so the opening measures 3½ inches (8.7 cm) wide.

2. Cut out 2 triangles of cardboard measuring 3½ inches (8.7 cm) on all sides. Tape the triangles to the ends of the form, then remove the tape on the top.

3. Cut out 2 pieces of cardboard measuring 12 × 4 inches (30 × 10 cm). Score the center of each piece lengthwise; turn upside down and fold. Tape the folded pieces to the sides of the form for support.

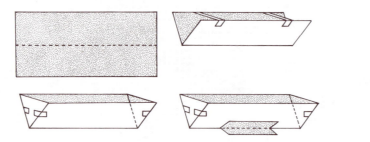

FIGURE 4-19 Making a triangular cardboard form

CHEF'S TIP

If the sponge sheet has been refrigerated overnight, place it in the oven for a minute or so to dry the top. The moist air in the refrigerator tends to make the sponge sticky, which can cause the skin to adhere to the form and possibly pull off when you remove the pastries.

an inverted sheet pan, and remove the paper. Using a thin, sharp knife dipped into hot water and wiped clean between each cut, slice into 16 servings. Arrange the pastries standing on end, seam-side down.

5. Heat a metal skewer by holding it against an electric burner or in a gas flame. Quickly use the skewer to mark 4 horizontal lines on both sides of each pastry by caramelizing the sugar. Place a portion of the strawberry sauce in a piping bottle.

6. Presentation: Stand a pastry off-center in the upper half of a dessert plate. Pipe a circle of strawberry sauce in front of the dessert on the larger uncovered space. Decorate the sauce with the sour cream mixture (see pages 682 to 685). Place a fanned strawberry half and a mint sprig behind the dessert.

STRAWBERRY SAUCE   yield: approximately 4½ cups (1 L 80 ml)

If you have no choice but to use fruit that is not perfectly ripe, add a small amount of raspberry juice or Beet Juice (page 750) — or, as a last resort, 1 or 2 drops of red food coloring — to make the sauce more appealing.

3 pounds (1 kg 365 g) fresh ripe strawberries   4 ounces (115 g) granulated sugar

2 tablespoons (16 g) cornstarch

1. Puree the strawberries. Strain through a fine mesh strainer. Measure and add water, if necessary, to make 4 cups (960 ml) juice.

2. Place the cornstarch in a saucepan. Mix enough of the juice into the cornstarch to liquefy it, then stir in the remaining juice.

3. Heat the sauce to simmering. Add the sugar, adjusting the amount as needed, depending on the sweetness of the strawberries.

4. Simmer the sauce for a few minutes. Let cool, then thin with water, if necessary. Store, covered, in the refrigerator.

Trio of Chocolates with Marzipan Parfait yield: 16 servings (Color Photo 39)

Your initial reaction will probably be that this pretty little box is too labor-intensive for a menu application, but this is not so. True, you must work carefully and deliberately when cutting and assembling the boxes. But considering that you can assemble, fill, and reserve the boxes in the freezer — days ahead, if you cover them well — and you can purchase the truffles instead of making them yourself, it is really not difficult to produce this dessert. The average guest does not know about these shortcuts, and this item always makes customers happy. Not only do they get an unusual and tasty dessert, they also feel they've gotten their money's worth. When wild strawberries are available, fill the box with Wild Strawberry Parfait (page 264), omit the truffles, and decorate with fresh strawberries.

Roux Batter (recipe follows)

2 tablespoons (30 ml) Chocolate Tuile Decorating Paste (page 695)

Piping Chocolate (page 543), melted

1 Sponge Cake (page 794), 10 inches (25 cm) in diameter

½ cup (120 ml) amaretto liqueur

Marzipan Parfait (recipe follows)

Unsweetened cocoa powder

Ganache (page 770) or Piping Chocolate (page 543)

16 Dark Chocolate Espresso Truffles (recipe follows)

16 White Chocolate Truffles with Praline (recipe follows)

32 Milk Chocolate Truffles (recipe follows)

16 edible flowers

I. Copy the templates in Figure 4-20. The templates, as shown, are the correct size to use in this recipe. Using the templates as guides, cut out the following from corrugated cardboard: 2 long side pieces (A), 2 short side pieces (B), and 2 pieces to use for the bottoms and the tops (C). Set aside 1 "C" piece to use in cutting the lids. Tape the remaining pieces together to make a rectangular form (see Note).

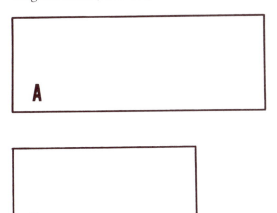

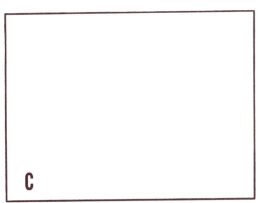

FIGURE 4-20 **The templates for making the container in Trio of Chocolates with Marzipan Parfait**

FIGURE 4-21 The template for the presentation of Trio of Chocolates with Marzipan Parfait

2. Spread the roux batter (it must still be warm) evenly into a 16-inch (40-cm) square on a sheet of baking paper. Work quickly as you do this because the batter becomes difficult to work with as it cools. Place a portion of the chocolate tuile paste in a piping bag and cut a small opening. Pipe parallel lines every ½ inch (1.2 cm), first across and then lengthwise, covering the sheet. Bake at 350°F (175°C) for approximately 12 minutes or until light brown. Let cool.

3. Invert the sheet and remove the baking paper. Turn right side up. Using a serrated knife and the reserved template C, cut 16 pieces to be used as lids. Cut the remaining sheet into strips 1 inch (2.5 cm) wide. Cut the strips into 32 long side pieces, 2¾ inches (7 cm) each, then cut 32

short side pieces that will fit inside the boxes after the longer side pieces are in place. It is a good idea to cut 1 set, place the pieces inside the form, and adjust the length of the pieces, if necessary, before cutting the remainder.

4. Place the 4 side pieces for 1 box inside the cardboard form with the chocolate lines against the form. Weld the pieces together by piping chocolate along the seams. Place in the freezer for a few seconds to set the chocolate. Remove the frame and repeat the process to make the remaining frames.

5. Cut the sponge cake to ¼ inch (6 mm) thick and into pieces that will fit snugly inside the frames. Brush amaretto liqueur over the sponge pieces and place them inside the frames.

6. Stir the marzipan parfait to make it smooth. Spoon the parfait into the boxes, filling them almost completely. Use a small spatula to smooth the tops and make them level. Reserve in the freezer.

7. Make the template shown in Figure 4-21. The template, as shown, is the correct size for this recipe. Trace the drawing, then cut the template out of cardboard that is ¹⁄₁₆ inch (2 mm) thick (cake boxes work fine). Tape the template to the outside of a disposable pie tin with the bottom removed (see page 692). Place the pie tin template on the base of a dessert plate. Sift cocoa powder on top. Remove the template carefully. Repeat to decorate as many plates as you expect to need.

8. Presentation: Pipe a dot of ganache or piping chocolate in the center of a decorated plate. Place a parfait-filled box on top at an angle perpendicular to the cocoa powder lines. Place 1 each of the 3 types of truffles on top of the parfait in the box. Attach 1 milk chocolate truffle on the plate in front of the box with a little ganache or piping chocolate. Place the lid on top of the box at an angle and slightly ajar. Decorate with an edible flower. Serve immediately.

NOTE: Corrugated cardboard varies in thickness. Try to use the double-lined variety that is ¼ inch (6 mm) thick. After taping the longer side pieces against the sides of the bottom piece (do not tape them on top of the bottom piece), adjust the shorter side pieces to fit according to the thickness of the cardboard used. The important thing is that the inside of the box measures 2 × 2¾ inches (5 × 7 cm).

ROUX BATTER yield: 3 cups (720 ml)

6 ounces (170 g) clarified unsalted butter

6 ounces (170 g) cake flour

1 pound (455 g) granulated sugar

3 ounces (85 g) bread flour

6 egg whites (¾ cup/180 ml)

1. Melt the butter in a saucepan. Stir in the cake flour and cook over low heat, stirring constantly, for about 5 minutes. Do not allow the mixture to brown. Remove from the heat.

2. Stir in the sugar, bread flour, and egg whites. Use immediately.

MARZIPAN PARFAIT yield: 6 cups (1 L 440 ml)

8 ounces (225 g) marzipan, untinted

2 tablespoons (30 ml) kirschwasser

3 ounces (85 g) granulated sugar

4 egg yolks (⅓ cup/80 ml)

2½ cups (600 ml) heavy cream

1. Soften the marzipan by mixing in the kirschwasser. Add the sugar and egg yolks and place over simmering water. Whip until the mixture is light and fluffy. Remove from the heat, then continue whipping until cool.

2. Whip the cream to soft peaks. Fold the cream into the marzipan mixture.

3. Place in the freezer for at least 2 hours or, preferably, overnight.

DARK CHOCOLATE ESPRESSO TRUFFLES yield: approximately 60 candies

1 cup (240 ml) heavy cream

1 pound 2 ounces (510 g) sweet dark chocolate, chopped

1 teaspoon (5 ml) vanilla extract

3 ounces (85 g) unsalted butter, melted

1 teaspoon (5 ml) mocha paste

Powdered sugar

Sweet dark chocolate, tempered

1. Heat the cream to the boiling point. Remove from the heat and add the chopped chocolate, stirring until it is completely melted. Cool the mixture to body temperature, approximately 98°F (36°C), then stir in the vanilla, butter, and mocha paste.

2. Wait until the filling starts to thicken, then transfer it to a pastry bag with a No. 6 (12-mm) plain tip. Pipe out in small mounds the size of cherries, or a little less than ½ ounce (15 g) each, on sheet pans lined with baking paper. Refrigerate for a few minutes to set.

3. Using powdered sugar to keep them from sticking, roll the mounds into round balls between your hands. Let them firm up again, then roll on a thin coat of tempered chocolate with your hands. When the coating has hardened and the interiors have reached room temperature, use a round dipping fork to dip the truffles into tempered chocolate. As they are dipped, transfer to a fine wire rack and roll to produce the typical uneven (spiked) surface.

WHITE CHOCOLATE TRUFFLES WITH PRALINE yield: approximately 75 candies

1 cup (240 ml) heavy cream

1 pound 2 ounces (510 g) white chocolate, chopped

3 ounces (85 g) Praline Paste (page 804)

3 ounces (85 g) unsalted butter, at room temperature

3 ounces (85 g) cocoa butter, melted

Powdered sugar

White chocolate, tempered

1. Heat the cream to the boiling point. Remove from the heat and stir in the chopped chocolate. Keep stirring until the chocolate is completely melted. Set aside to cool to approximately room temperature.

2. Combine the praline paste and butter and beat to a creamy consistency. Stir into the chocolate mixture. Mix in the cocoa butter. Wait until the filling starts to thicken, then transfer it to a pastry bag with a No. 6 (12-mm) plain tip. Pipe out in small mounds the size of cherries, or a little less than ½ ounce (15 g) each, on sheet pans lined with baking paper. Refrigerate for a few minutes to set.

3. Using powdered sugar to keep them from sticking, roll the mounds into round balls between your hands. Let them firm up again, then roll on a thin coat of tempered white chocolate with your hands. When the coating has hardened and the interiors have reached room temperature, use a round dipping fork to dip them into tempered white chocolate. As they are dipped, transfer to a fine wire rack and roll to produce the typical uneven (spiked) surface.

MILK CHOCOLATE TRUFFLES yield: approximately 65 candies

1 cup (240 ml) heavy cream

1 pound 5 ounces (595 g) milk chocolate, chopped

1 teaspoon (5 ml) vanilla extract

3 ounces (85 g) unsalted butter, melted

Powdered sugar

Milk chocolate, tempered

I. Heat the cream to the boiling point. Remove from the heat and add the chopped chocolate and vanilla, stirring until the chocolate is completely melted. Cool the mixture to body temperature, approximately 98°F (36°C), then stir in the butter.

2. Wait until the filling starts to thicken, then transfer it to a pastry bag with a No. 6 (12-mm) plain tip. Pipe out in small mounds the size of cherries, or a little less than ½ ounce (15 g) each, on sheet pans lined with baking paper. Refrigerate for a few minutes to set.

3. Using powdered sugar to keep them from sticking, roll the mounds into round balls between your hands. Let them firm up again, then roll on a thin coat of tempered chocolate with your hands. When the coating has hardened and the interiors have reached room temperature, use a round dipping fork to dip them into tempered chocolate. As they are dipped, transfer to a fine wire rack and roll to produce the typical uneven (spiked) surface.

Triple Treat yield: 16 servings

This is a dessert I created especially for one of the graduation luncheons at the California Culinary Academy. Because the junior pastry class was responsible for the dessert preparation on these momentous occasions, they rightfully expected that when they were graduating seniors, the dessert selected by their class would be presented in a way that gave full credit to their special day. In this instance, the graduating seniors voted for a trio of desserts to be served to about 325 guests at their celebration. Making miniature versions of tiramisù, triple chocolate terrine, and Florentina cones provided three distinctive shapes on the plate and the compatible flavor assortment of coffee, chocolate, and nuts. Paired with caramel sauce, the plated desserts were a vision. This was also an easy dessert to prepare and plate, as most of the work could be completed the day before the event. The chocolate terrines were finished and left in the freezer, ready to be sliced. The refrigerated tiramisù needed only to be cut and topped with mascarpone cream. We filled the Florentina cones first thing in the morning, which allowed the cream to begin to soften the shell just a little. (If you fill only the number of cones you will need within a few hours, this dessert can actually be utilized over several days.) Plating the three items with whipped cream rosettes, cookie butterflies, and chocolate figurines was quickly and efficiently executed in assembly-line fashion.

1 cup (240 ml) heavy cream

Fortified Caramel Sauce (page 19)

Unsweetened cocoa powder

16 Miniature Triple-Chocolate Terrine
(recipe follows)

16 Cookie Butterflies (page 695), made using
the smaller template

16 Miniature Florentina Cones (recipe
follows)

16 Miniature Tiramisù (recipe follows)

16 Chocolate Figurines (page 545)

1. Whip the heavy cream to stiff peaks. Place in a pastry bag with a No. 6 (12-mm) star tip and reserve in the refrigerator. Place the caramel sauce in a piping bottle.

2. Presentation: Sift cocoa powder very lightly over the base of a dessert plate; clean the rim of the plate. Pipe dots of caramel sauce, approximately ½ inch (1.2 cm) in diameter and 1 inch (2.5 cm) apart, around the perimeter of the base of the plate. Place a slice of terrine off-center on the plate. Pipe a rosette of whipped cream on a corner of the slice and a pipe a second rosette of cream on the plate a few inches away. Place a cookie butterfly on the rosette on the corner of the terrine. Place a Florentina cone on the second rosette. Place a miniature tiramisù in the remaining open space on the plate. Top the tiramisù with a chocolate figurine. At this point, you can set aside the dessert at room temperature for up to 30 minutes before serving .

MINIATURE TRIPLE-CHOCOLATE TERRINE yield: 2 terrines, 12 × 2¼ inches (30 × 5.6 cm)

This recipe yields twice as much terrine as is needed for sixteen servings. However, because the procedure is rather time-consuming and the extra will keep, well wrapped, in the freezer for up to a month, it does not seem practical to make a smaller quantity.

⅓ recipe Baked Chocolate Sheet batter
(page 355; see Note 1)

2 tablespoons (16 g) bread flour

⅔ recipe Triple-Chocolate Filling (page 356)

1. You will need two forms, 2¼ inches wide × 2¼ inches tall × 12 inches long (5.6 × 5.6 × 30 cm). If you do not have forms this size, you can spread the chocolate sheet batter into a rectangle that corresponds to the forms you have, or you can make a form from corrugated cardboard by following the directions on page 475 (see Note 2). Line the long sides of the forms with strips of acetate or baking paper.

2. Spread the chocolate sheet batter into a rectangle measuring 10 × 12 inches (25 × 30 cm) on a sheet pan lined with baking paper. Bake at 375°F (190°C) for about 12 minutes or until the sponge feels firm on the top. Let cool completely.

3. Invert the sponge sheet and peel the baking paper from the back. Cut the sheet into 4 strips, 12 × 2¼ inches (30 × 5.6 cm). Place 1 sponge strip in the bottom of each reserved form.

4. Layer the chocolate fillings as directed in the main recipe for Triple Chocolate Terrine (page 354). However, because this miniature version does not have sponge layers between the filling layers, it is necessary to quickly place the terrines in the freezer to partially set each layer before adding the next, or the layers may run together. After adding the final dark chocolate layer, place a sponge strip on top of each. Cover the terrines and place them in the freezer.

5. When the terrines are firm, preferably the following day, remove 1 from the freezer, leaving the other for another use. Remove the form and the baking paper or acetate strips. Place the terrine so that the layers run vertically. Using a thin chef's knife dipped in hot water, cut the terrine into 16 slices, ¾ inch (2 cm) thick. If you do not expect to need all 16 servings the same day, cut only the number you need. Place the slices, cut-side down, on a sheet pan lined with baking paper. Reserve in the refrigerator until time of service.

NOTE 1: Follow the instructions given for making the chocolate sheet batter, sifting the extra 2 tablespoons (16 g) bread flour on top as you fold in the egg whites.

NOTE 2: To obtain the proper size when making the cardboard forms, start with 2 pieces of corrugated cardboard, 12 × 7 inches (30 × 17.5 cm). Score (cut halfway through) 2 lines lengthwise to divide the width into 3 sections: one section 2¼ inches (5.6 cm) wide in the center and two sections, each 2⅜ inches (5.9 cm) wide, on the sides. Fold up the outside sections and continue as directed on page 475.

MINIATURE FLORENTINA CONES yield: 16 pieces

2 ounces (55 g) toasted hazelnuts

16 Florentina Cones (page 689)

Dark coating chocolate, melted

1½ cups (360 ml) heavy cream

⅓ recipe Hazelnut Paste (page 778) or commercial hazelnut paste to taste

1. Remove as much of the skin as possible from the hazelnuts. Crush the nuts coarsely and reserve.

2. Dip the top of as many cones as you expect to serve ¼ inch (6 mm) into melted coating chocolate.

3. No more than 3 to 4 hours prior to service, whip the heavy cream to soft peaks. Add a small amount of the cream to the hazelnut paste and mix to soften the paste. Add back to the remaining cream. Place the crushed hazelnuts in a sifter and sift the small pieces into the cream mixture. Continue whipping the hazelnut cream until stiff peaks form. Place in a pastry bag with a No. 6 (12-mm) star tip. Pipe the cream into the Florentina cones, filling them to the top. Sprinkle the crushed hazelnuts on the exposed cream at the ends. Reserve the cones in the refrigerator until time of service.

MINIATURE TIRAMISU yield: 16 pieces

½ recipe Ladyfingers batter (page 801)

3 cups (720 ml) strong coffee

Mascarpone Filling (recipe follows)

Unsweetened cocoa powder

1. Spread the ladyfinger batter into a rectangle measuring 16 × 14 inches (40 × 35 cm) on a sheet pan lined with baking paper. Bake at 400°F (205°C) for approximately 20 minutes or until baked through and light brown on top. Let cool.

2. Invert the sheet, peel the baking paper from the back, and cut the sheet lengthwise into 3 strips, each approximately 4½ inches (11.2 cm) wide. Brush 1 sheet generously with coffee. Top with one-third of the mascarpone filling. Sift cocoa powder over the filling. Generously brush a second ladyfinger sheet with coffee, place coffee-side down on the cocoa powder, and brush coffee on the other side. Top with half of the remaining filling and sift additional cocoa powder on top. Brush the last sponge sheet with coffee and place coffee-side down on top. Brush coffee generously on the other side. Place the remaining filling in a pastry bag with a No. 2 (4-mm) plain tip and reserve in the refrigerator. Cover and place the assembled sheet in the refrigerator for at least 4 hours or, preferably, overnight.

3. Using a plain round cookie cutter, 2 inches (5 cm) in diameter and dipped in hot water, cut 16 portions from the assembled sheet. Dip the cutter in water between each cut. Pipe a spiral of mascarpone filling over the top of each portion of tiramisù. Sift cocoa powder over the mascarpone filling. Reserve in the refrigerator until time of service.

Mascarpone Filling yield: 1 quart (960 ml)

1 teaspoon (3 g) unflavored gelatin powder

¾ cup (180 ml) sweet marsala

3 egg yolks (¼ cup/60 ml)

3 ounces (85 g) granulated sugar

1 cup (240 ml) heavy cream

8 ounces (225 g) mascarpone cheese, at room temperature

1. Sprinkle the gelatin powder on top of ¼ cup (60 ml) of the marsala; reserve.

2. Combine the egg yolks, sugar, and remaining wine in a mixer bowl. Set over a bain-marie and, whisking constantly by hand, heat the mixture until it has thickened to the consistency of sabayon. Remove from the heat and place on the mixer with the whip attachment. Whip the egg mixture at medium speed until cool to the touch. Refrigerate.

3. Whip the heavy cream to stiff peaks; reserve. Gradually stir the egg mixture into the soft mascarpone cheese, followed by the whipped cream. Heat the gelatin mixture to dissolve. Quickly stir the gelatin into a small portion of the cream mixture to temper it. Still working rapidly, add this to the remaining mixture.

Tropical Mousse Cake yield: 16 servings, 2¼ inches (5.6 cm) square (Color Photo 41)

The small black seeds in passion fruit are completely edible, although they are a little harder than those of other fruits such as raspberries, strawberries, and the one I use in the variation of this recipe, kiwi. You may be tempted to strain them out of the passion fruit jelly, as is done when making the filling. This is up to you; they are left in as a purely decorative measure, so the only impact will be to give the final product a less interesting appearance.

Passion Fruit Jelly (recipe follows)

⅓ recipe Cocoa-Almond Sponge batter (page 796)

Passion Fruit Mousse Filling (recipe follows)

2 tablespoons (30 ml) light rum

¼ cup (60 ml) papaya juice or other tropical fruit juice

Cocoa Nib–Macadamia Decorations (instructions follow)

½ recipe Plum Sauce (page 263)

Piping Chocolate (page 543), melted

1. Stretch a sheet of plastic wrap tightly over a sheet of corrugated cardboard just over 10 inches (25 cm) square (see Chef's Tip). Make a frame by cutting 2 strips of corrugated cardboard to 2 × 20 inches (5 × 50 cm). Then cut a straight line halfway through the cardboard in the center across the width of each strip, bend the strips from the uncut side at a 90-degree angle, and tape the corners together to form a 10-inch (25-cm) square. Place the frame on top of the plastic-covered cardboard sheet. Tape the outside of the frame tightly against the plastic (it must sit tightly or the jelly will run out). Set the frame aside.

2. Make the passion fruit jelly and pour it over the bottom of the frame. Chill in the refrigerator until set, about 30 minutes.

3. Make the sponge batter. Immediately spread the batter into a rectangle, approximately 11 × 22 inches (27.5 × 55 cm). Bake at 400°F (205°C) for about 10 minutes or until just done. Let the sponge sheet cool. Cut the sheet in half crosswise and trim the pieces to fit inside the frame.

4. Spread half of the mousse filling evenly on top of the jelly. Top with a sponge sheet. Combine the rum and fruit juice and brush half of the mixture over the sponge. Spread the remaining mousse filling on top of the sponge, then set the second sponge sheet on the filling. Brush the remaining fruit juice mixture over the sponge. Refrigerate for at least 3 hours to set the filling.

5. Cut through the tape around the base of the frame. Place a sheet pan or a sheet of cardboard on top of the frame, then invert the cake. Remove the cardboard and the plastic wrap. Using a thin, sharp knife dipped in hot water, cut around the inside of the frame, then remove it. Trim the sides of the cake, if necessary, then cut it into 4 equal strips, approximately 2¼ inches (5.6 cm) wide. Cut each strip into 4 squares (see Note).

6. Place as many cocoa nib decorations as you anticipate using in the refrigerator for 15 to 30 minutes (see Chef's Tip, page 396). Place the plum sauce in a piping bottle.

7. Presentation: Place a cake square in the center of a dessert plate. Place piping chocolate in a piping bag and pipe a short line of chocolate on the plate behind the cake. Stand a cocoa nib decoration straight up on the chocolate line and hold it until set. Pipe plum sauce in an uneven half circle in front of the cake.

NOTE: At the end of Step 5, the cakes can, alternatively, be cut into 4 equal squares, 5 inches (12.5 cm) each. Cover the sides of these small cakes with chocolate strips decorated with transfer sheets. Cut the transfer sheet or transfer strips to the same width as the height of the cakes and slightly longer than the circumference. Follow the directions in the Chocolate Truffle Cake with Raspberries recipe (page 31) for spreading chocolate over the strips and applying them to the cakes. These 5-inch (12.5-cm) cakes are appropriate to display whole in a pastry case. Each serves 4 to 6 people.

PASSION FRUIT JELLY yield: I cup (240 ml)

1½ teaspoons (5 g) unflavored gelatin powder

½ cup (120 ml) papaya juice or other tropical fruit juice

⅓ cup (80 ml) passion fruit pulp

1½ ounces (40 g) granulated sugar

1. Sprinkle the gelatin over ¼ cup (60 ml) of the fruit juice and set aside to soften.

2. Place the passion fruit pulp in a nonreactive saucepan. Stir in the remaining fruit juice. Add the sugar and bring to a full boil.

3. Remove from the heat, add the softened gelatin, and stir until the gelatin is dissolved. Skim any foam from the surface. Cool until the mixture just begins to thicken before using.

NOTE: If you do not want the seeds in the jelly, strain the mixture before adding the gelatin.

PASSION FRUIT MOUSSE FILLING yield: 10 cups (2 L 400 ml)

2½ tablespoons (23 g) unflavored gelatin powder

2 cups (480 ml) papaya juice or other tropical fruit juice

1 pound (455 g) passion fruit (about 18 medium-sized)

¼ recipe Swiss Meringue (page 782)

2½ cups (600 ml) heavy cream

1 cup (240 ml) unflavored yogurt

1. Sprinkle the gelatin over ½ cup (120 ml) fruit juice and set aside to soften.

2. Cut the passion fruits in half and scoop out the pulp and seeds to make ¾ cup (180 ml). Place the pulp in a noncorrosive saucepan. Stir in the remaining 1½ cups (360 ml) fruit juice and bring to a full boil. Remove from the heat and strain to remove the seeds.

3. Add the softened gelatin to the hot liquid and stir until dissolved.

4. Make the meringue and set aside.

5. Whip the cream to soft peaks. Fold into the yogurt. Fold the yogurt and cream into the reserved meringue. Make sure the gelatin is not too warm or the cream will break. Quickly add the gelatin mixture to a small amount of the cream mixture. Add this back to the remainder, still mixing rapidly. If necessary, let the mousse cool until it starts to thicken before you use it, but do not make the mousse until you are ready to use it in the cake.

COCOA NIB–MACADAMIA DECORATIONS yield: approximately 20 decorations

> 1 recipe Cocoa-Nib Wafer Paste (page 720), made by replacing 2 ounces (55 g) cocoa nibs
> with 2 ounces (55 g) crushed macadamia nuts

I. Have ready 2 No. 10 cans or other round containers approximately 6 inches (15 cm) in diameter.

2. Spread the wafer paste into thin ovals, approximately 5 × 3 inches (12.5 × 7.5 cm), on Silpats. Bake as directed in the wafer paste recipe.

3. Let the wafers cool for 10 to 20 seconds, then cut a small piece from each short end to make a straight edge. Carefully pick up the decoration and invert it over the can or other mold, placing it lengthwise. Form the remaining decorations the same way. Store the wafers in airtight containers.

VARIATIONS

ROUND TROPICAL MOUSSE CAKE yield: 2 cakes, 8 inches (20 cm) in diameter

This recipe can be made into 2 round cakes, 8 inches (20 cm) in diameter. Line the round cake pans with baking paper and divide the sponge batter between them. Bake a little longer than directed for the sponge sheet. Cut the skin from the top of the sponges, leveling the tops at the same time. Slice each sponge into 2 layers. For the jelly, stretch heavy plastic wrap tightly around 2 cardboard cake rounds, 10 inches (25 cm) in diameter (see Chef's Tip, page 196). Place stainless steel cake rings, 8 inches (20 cm) in diameter by 2 inches (5 cm) in height, on top. Seal by applying masking tape around the outside edge. Assemble the cakes as described in the main recipe. Let the cakes set and unmold. Whip 1 cup (240 ml) heavy cream with 1 teaspoon (5 g) granulated sugar. Finish the cakes by piping the whipped cream on the sides, using either a ³⁄₄-inch (2-cm) flat tip or a No. 4 (8-mm) plain tip.

KIWI MOUSSE CAKE yield: 16 servings

Although passion fruit is certainly more tropical and unusual, its season is rather short. By substituting kiwis when passion fruit is not in season, you can make this delicious cake any time of the year. You will need 1 regular-sized kiwi to make the jelly and 4 kiwis for the filling (you should have 1 cup/240 ml of kiwi pulp for the mousse filling). Use only fully ripe kiwis. Remove the skin, puree or mash the fruit, and use as directed in the recipes. Substituting blood orange juice for the papaya or tropical fruit juice produces an attractive color when used with kiwi or passion fruit in both the jelly and the mousse filling.

Valentine's Day Hearts yield: 16 servings (Color Photo 38)

As Valentine's Day draws close, one may imagine Cupid aiming his arrow at unsuspecting suitors, red roses, heart-shaped boxes filled with chocolate candies, and, of course, the all-important Valentine's Day card. Most people are unaware of how this holiday, celebrated on 14 February in many countries, came to be. Several stories are told. The first is a fable of a priest named Valentine who was imprisoned by the Roman Emperor Claudius II. The priest had disobeyed the emperor's order that forbade young men to marry (the theory being that unmarried men made better warriors) and had secretly performed many wedding ceremonies. While he was in jail, he blessed and restored sight to the jailkeeper's blind daughter (with whom he had fallen in love); in the wake of all of this, scores of people were supposedly converted to the Christian faith. Enraged, Claudius II ordered Valentine executed on the sixteenth day before March — 14 February, A.D. 269. As the story goes, the priest wrote a letter to his new love just before he was beheaded and signed it "your Valentine."

Another story associates the holiday with the Feast of St. Valentine of Terni, an old and established celebration of choosing a mate that apparently came about based on a belief that birds choose their mates in the spring, specifically on 14 February. Much controversy surrounds this theory. Many people argue that while not really springtime in most of the world, 14 February represents a feeling of spring in one's heart, inspired by the romancing birds. Others say that 14 February differs little or not at all from winter, and it is simply too early and too cold for either human or bird to develop spring fever.

Even if we can't agree on a connection between the mating of birds and St. Valentine's Day, most people enjoy the mythological idea of a mischievous, naked, winged boy named Cupid, the Greek Eros, son of Venus. The legend of Cupid says that anyone shot with Cupid's arrow will fall in love with the next person they see.

The current practice of sending Valentine's Day cards to friends and loved ones is attributed to the Duke of Orleans who, when imprisoned in the Tower of London, is said to have sent his wife letters filled with love poems. This custom was commercially popular by the seventeenth century in Europe and was brought to the United States by European immigrants.

Whatever its true origin, this holiday unquestionably has a big impact on our business. Other than Christmas, Valentine's Day is usually the busiest time of the year for pastry chefs and candy makers.

½ recipe Baked Chocolate Sheet batter (page 355; see Step 1)	Powdered sugar
1 ounce (30 g) bread flour	8 ounces (225 g) marzipan, tinted red
Red Currant Bavarian Cream (recipe follows)	Red Currant Sauce (recipe follows)
Piping Chocolate (page 543), melted	Fresh red currants
	Sour Cream Mixture for Piping (page 727)

1. Prepare the batter for the baked chocolate sheet, adding the bread flour to the whipped egg yolk and sugar mixture. Spread the batter to a rectangle measuring 12 × 15 inches (30 × 37.5 cm) on a sheet of baking paper. Bake as directed in the recipe and set aside to cool.

2. Line an adjustable frame or a cake pan, 12 × 15 inches (30 × 37.5 cm), with baking paper (see Note). Pour the red currant Bavarian cream into the frame and spread it evenly. Invert the chocolate sheet on top of the Bavarian, leaving the baking paper attached. Cover and refrigerate for at least 2 hours or, preferably, overnight.

3. Place a small portion of piping chocolate in a piping bag and cut a small opening. Using Figure 4-22 as a guide, pipe out figurines to use in decorating (see page 545 for more instructions). Make a few more than you will need to allow for breakage.

4. Remove the baking paper from the baked chocolate sheet. Run a knife around the edge of the pan to loosen the Bavarian. Place a sheet of baking paper and a cardboard sheet (or an even sheet pan) on top and invert. Remove the pan or frame from around the Bavarian and peel off the baking paper from the sides. Using a heart-shaped cookie cutter measuring 3½ inches (8.7 cm) across the widest point, cut out 16 hearts (or as many as you expect to serve) from the Bavarian sheet and place them, cake-side down, on a sheet pan lined with baking paper. Dip the cutter in hot water as you work.

5. Using powdered sugar to prevent it from sticking, roll out the red marzipan to ⅛ inch (3 mm) thick. Mark the top of the marzipan with a waffle or tread pattern rolling pin (see "About Marzipan Rolling Pins," page 97). Using the cutter used to cut the Bavarian hearts, cut out the same number of marzipan hearts. It is necessary to knead the scraps together and roll out again

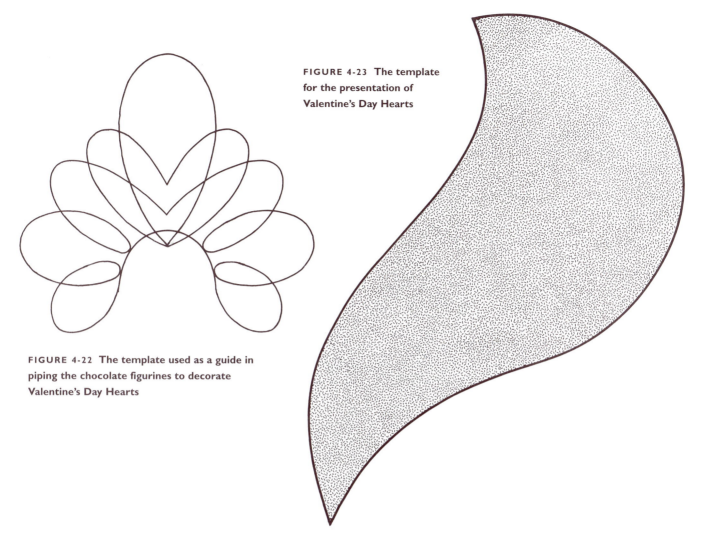

FIGURE 4-23 The template for the presentation of Valentine's Day Hearts

FIGURE 4-22 The template used as a guide in piping the chocolate figurines to decorate Valentine's Day Hearts

to get 16 hearts. Mask 1 side (lengthwise) of a marzipan heart. Sift powdered sugar over the exposed side. Place the marzipan heart on top of a Bavarian heart. Repeat with the remaining hearts. Reserve in the refrigerator for no longer than 4 hours.

6. Make the template shown in Figure 4-23. The template, as shown, is the correct size for use in this recipe. Trace the drawing, then cut the template out of cardboard that is $^1/_{16}$ inch (2 mm) thick. Place the template off-center, to the right, on a dessert plate, with the more tapered end closest to you. Put piping chocolate in a piping bag and, using the template as a guide, pipe the outline of the shape on the same number of dessert plates as you have finished desserts. Refrigerate the figurines. Place a portion of the red currant sauce in a piping bottle.

7. Presentation: Place a Bavarian heart on the left side of a prepared plate so the right side of the heart fits just inside the top left side of the chocolate piping. Fill the inside of the piped design with red currant sauce. Place a row of fresh currants along the straight edge of the heart on the left side. Place a portion the sour cream mixture in a piping bag. Pipe small dots on top of the sauce along the right side of the heart. Run the tip of a wooden skewer through the dots to create hearts (see Figure 13-10, page 682). Using the tip of a paring knife, make 2 small horizontal cuts in the round part of the heart, spacing them the width of the base of the figurines. Pipe a drop of piping chocolate in each cut. Quickly and carefully place a chilled figurine in the cut. Tilt the figurine back slightly and hold for a few seconds until the chocolate is set (this happens quickly because the figurine has been chilled). Serve immediately.

NOTE: If you do not have a pan this size, you can make a frame from corrugated cardboard, or you can shorten a half-sheet pan in the following manner. Cut a strip of corrugated cardboard to 12 × 2 inches (30 × 5 cm). Cut halfway through (score) the cardboard lengthwise down the center. Bend the strip along the score at a 90-degree angle. Place this piece against a short end of the half-sheet pan. Line the pan with a sheet of lightly oiled baking paper, placing the end of the paper against the cardboard brace.

RED CURRANT BAVARIAN CREAM yield: 2½ quarts (2 L 400 ml)

If you use fresh currants in this recipe, remove the stems before weighing the berries. If you use frozen berries, they should be the IQF type (without sugar). Do not use sweetened red currants in this recipe. Do not make the filling until you are ready to use it.

1 pound 6 ounces (625 g) fresh or frozen red currants	3 tablespoons plus 1 teaspoon (30 g) unflavored gelatin powder
2¼ cups (540 ml) dry champagne	6 egg yolks (½ cup/120 ml)
2 cups (480 ml) heavy cream	2 ounces (55 g) granulated sugar
	¼ recipe Swiss Meringue (page 782)

1. Place the red currants and 1½ cups (360 ml) of the champagne in a saucepan. Heat to scalding; do not boil. Puree the currants and pass through a fine mesh strainer. Discard the solids in the strainer. Set the liquid aside to cool.

2. Whip the heavy cream to soft peaks. Reserve in the refrigerator.

3. Sprinkle the gelatin over ½ cup (120 ml) champagne and set aside to soften.

4. Whip the egg yolks and sugar to combine. Add the remaining ¼ cup (60 ml) champagne. Heat the mixture over simmering water, whipping constantly, until it reaches 140°F (60°C) and thickens. Remove from the heat and continue whipping until it is completely cooled. Stir in the reserved red currant puree, the meringue, and the whipped cream.

5. Heat the gelatin mixture to dissolve. Temper by adding the gelatin to about one-quarter of the currant mixture; quickly incorporate this into the remainder. Use immediately.

RED CURRANT SAUCE yield: 4 cups (960 ml)

If you use fresh red currants in this sauce, remove the stems before weighing the berries. If fresh are not available, use IQF berries, which are stemless and do not contain sugar; do not thaw before weighing. Once thawed, the juice separates from the berries and collects at the bottom of the container.

2 pounds (910 g) fresh or frozen red currants	¾ cup (180 ml) dry white wine
1 tablespoon (8 g) cornstarch	10 ounces (285 g) granulated sugar

1. Puree the currants, strain through a fine mesh strainer, and discard the solids. You should have close to 2¼ cups (540 ml) juice; adjust as necessary by adding water if you need more juice or by not using all of the juice if you produce more than the amount specified.

2. Dissolve the cornstarch in the wine. Place the currant juice and the cornstarch mixture in a nonreactive saucepan, add the sugar, bring to a boil, then remove from the heat.

3. Let the sauce cool, then adjust the consistency as needed. Store, covered, in the refrigerator.

Wild Strawberries Romanoff in Caramel Boxes yield: 16 servings (Color Photo 42)

This contemporary adaptation of the classic Strawberries Romanoff is served in an elegant caramel box garnished with golden sugar corkscrews. This presentation was served at a graduation celebration that included over 300 friends, family members, and faculty. The desserts were produced by a class that had had only one month of experience in hands-on pastry production. The point I am trying to make here is that while the large number of steps (when you include making the boxes) and the elegant presentation may suggest that this is a time-consuming and difficult dessert, it is not. For this particular occasion, which happened to be held close to the Fourth of July, we replaced the wild strawberries with a mixture of fresh raspberries and blueberries that, combined with the whipped cream on top, gave the plates a patriotic and colorful appearance. For another version of Strawberries Romanoff, see page 183.

¼ recipe Chiffon Sponge Cake I batter (page 797)

Dark coating chocolate, melted

16 Caramel Boxes and Squares (page 141)

½ cup (120 ml) curaçao liqueur

¼ cup (60 ml) Plain Cake Syrup (page 789)

3 cups (720 ml) heavy cream

1 tablespoon (15 g) granulated sugar

1 teaspoon (5 ml) vanilla extract

¼ recipe Strawberry Sauce (page 186)

1 pound 8 ounces (680 g) wild strawberries (red or a mixture of red and white), stemmed and hulled

16 Caramel Corkscrews (page 620)

16 mint sprigs

1. Bake the cake batter in a greased and floured cake pan, 9 inches (22.5 cm) in diameter. Let the sponge cool.

2. Place a small amount of melted coating chocolate in a piping bag. Cut a very small opening and pipe 2 parallel lines, about ¾ inch (2 cm) apart, across the center of a dessert plate. Turn the plate 90 degrees and repeat. Decorate 16 plates (or as many as you plan to serve) and set them aside so the chocolate can cool and harden. (Set the plates on baking paper to eliminate any mess.)

3. Dip the top edge of the same number of caramel boxes ¼ inch (6 mm) into the chocolate. Set aside to harden.

4. Combine the curaçao liqueur and the cake syrup. Brush the syrup mixture generously over both sides of the sponge. Cut the sponge into 1¾-inch (4.5-cm) squares. Cover and reserve.

5. Whip the heavy cream with the sugar and vanilla until stiff peaks form. Place in a pastry bag with a No. 5 (10-mm) star tip. Reserve in the refrigerator until time of service. Place the strawberry sauce in a piping bottle.

6. Presentation: Place a square of sponge cake in the bottom of a caramel box (insert the tip of a paring knife into the top of the sponge square and guide it into the box). Pipe a layer of whipped cream, ½ inch (1.2 cm) thick, on top of the sponge. Fill the box with wild strawberries. Pipe a dot of whipped cream slightly off-center on one of the decorated plates just behind the spot where the chocolate lines intersect. Pipe a rosette of cream on top of the berries in the box. Pipe a second rosette of cream on the plate, to the right side, between 2 of the parallel lines and near the edge. Using the tip of a paring knife, gently push the bottom of a caramel corkscrew into the rosette. Place a mint sprig next to the corkscrew and arrange a few berries around the rosette. Place the box on the dot of whipped cream near the center of the plate. Stand a caramel square in the rosette on the plate. Pipe strawberry sauce around the plate in small teardrop shapes. Serve immediately.

IN THIS CHAPTER

BOMBES

Basic Bombe Mixture   206

Bombe Aboukir   207

Bombe Bourdaloue   208

Bombe Ceylon   209

Bombe Monarch   211

COUPES

Coupe Bavaria   213

Coupe Belle Hélène   213

Coupe Hawaii   213

Coupe Melba   215

Coupe Niçoise   215

Coupe Sweden   216

COMPOSED FROZEN DESSERTS

Apricot and Fig Tart with Prickly Pear Sorbet   218

Baked Alaska   220

Bénédictine Soufflé Glacé   224

    GINGER SOUFFLÉ GLACÉ   226

Caramel Ice Cream in a Caramel Cage   227

Cassata Parfait with Meringue   228

Cherries Jubilee   232

Cinnamon Semifreddo Venezia with Coffee   233
Bean Crisps

Frozen Hazelnut Coffee Mousse   234

Frozen Raspberry Mousse with Meringues   237

Ice Cream Cake Jamaica   239

Lingonberry Parfait   241

Macadamia Nut Ice Cream in a Chocolate   243
Tulip with Mango Coulis

Mango Ice Cream with Chiffonade of Lemon   245
Mint and a Chocolate Twirl

Meringue Glacé Leda   247

Oven-Braised Black Mission Figs with   250
Honey-Vanilla Frozen Yogurt

Poached Pears with Ginger Ice Cream   251

Profiteroles with Vanilla Ice Cream and   253
Hot Fudge Sauce

Saffron-Poached Pears with Almond Ice   254
Cream and Kadaif Phyllo Nests

Tropical Surprise Packages   258

Vacherin with Plum Ice Cream   261

    MERINGUE GLACÉ CHANTILLY   264

Wild Strawberry Parfait   264

Frozen Desserts

The desserts in this chapter run the gamut from classics like bombes, parfaits, cassata, semifreddo, and Cherries Jubilee to ice cream cakes, meringue glacé, soufflé glacé, frozen mousses, and special presentations for many recipes of delicious and unusual ice creams.

BOMBES

A bombe is a type of frozen dessert made by lining a chilled mold, typically a half-sphere, with ice cream, sorbet, or sherbet, then filling it with a rich cream mixture. Most recipes call for multiple layers of ice cream in different flavors and/or contrasting colors. It is important, in such cases, to freeze each layer until it is firm before attempting to add the next. The bombe mixture that fills the lined mold is made from egg yolks, sugar, and cream in the style of a parfait. The bombe mixture is flavored according to the individual recipe, of which there are dozens upon dozens of classic variations. *Le Répertoire de La Cuisine* — a basic reference to the cuisine of Escoffier — lists 126 bombe preparations, while *Hering's*

Dictionary of Classical and Modern Cookery provides 147 bombe recipes. Five of the classics follow, but you can easily invent your own creations following the guidelines provided here and choosing ice cream recipes from elsewhere in the book. Try combining tropical flavors, such as coconut ice cream and mango and kiwi sorbets; decorate with macadamia nuts or plantain chips. Or layer maple-pecan ice cream with cinnamon ice cream and apple cider–Calvados sorbet, flavor the bombe filling with apple or pear, and garnish with dried apple or pear chips.

When fruit other than candied fruit is added to the bombe mixture, it must first be macerated in liqueur and/or sugar syrup to prevent it from freezing too hard. Once filled, the mold is covered with a lid, and the bombe is frozen. After it is unmolded, the bombe remains inverted to reveal the dome shape. The original bombe dessert was nearly round, and the name, which in the original French is *bombe glacé,* refers to the shape of cannonball-type bombs.

Bombes lend themselves to opulent decorations, so the pastry chef can really express his or her style and fantasy. If the bombe is presented to the guests before being sliced and served, the accompanying sauce should be served separately in a sauceboat. The most common size of bombe mold has a capacity of approximately 5 cups (1 L 200 ml) and serves six to ten people, making this dessert a great timesaver for the chef, especially as the bombe can be prepared well in advance, then unmolded and decorated just before it is needed.

Coupes

These popular and practical individual ice cream servings can be made to look quite elegant by serving them in suitable dishes and decorating them attractively. In the United States, the all-American hot fudge sundae and banana split have been teenage favorites for years. Many people think of this type of dessert — a combination of ice creams or sorbets decorated with sauces, fruits, nuts, and/or whipped cream — as an American invention, however, it originated in France and is extremely popular throughout Europe. In ice cream parlors and *konditorei* (pastry shops) all over Europe, you will find a separate menu (usually illustrated) describing the coupes served. They are typically named for a country or a historical figure or place, according to their composition. Many of the combinations are based on recipes and formulas established many years ago by masters such as Carême and Escoffier. Some coupes are elaborately decorated with cookies and marzipan or chocolate figures, while others are simply presented. Coupes must always be assembled and decorated to order. This chapter includes recipes for some of the most popular of the hundreds of classic coupe variations, along with a few of my own creations.

Composed Frozen Desserts

These selections include classic parfaits, frozen soufflés (soufflé glacé), and frozen mousses. Some of these desserts are not actually frozen per se but include ice cream or ice as an accompaniment. All of the recipes share one instruction: They must be served immediately once they are plated. Unfortunately, this is not always practical, especially when serving a large number at once, but on the positive side, in most cases, all of the prep work can be done far in advance.

Many frozen desserts created years ago, such as Cherries Jubilee, Pears Belle Hélène, Baked Alaska, and Peach Melba, are now classics, but the field still allows plenty of room for your taste and imagination.

PARFAITS

Parfait means something different in Europe than in the United States. In the New World, we use the word *parfait* to describe a dessert of alternating layers of ice cream, fruit, and liqueur, served in a tall glass and topped with whipped cream. By classic definition, this actually constitutes a coupe. The American parfait most likely got its name because the tall serving glasses are similar in shape to the original parfait molds.

The European parfait, which is what I refer to here, is a delicate frozen dessert, usually lighter and less sweet than ice cream, made from a mixture of egg yolks and sugar syrup whipped to the ribbon stage, with the addition of whipped cream and flavoring. To achieve this distinctive, light texture, it is important to combine the ingredients carefully, preserving the air that has been whipped in. The parfait mixture is poured into tall, slender molds and still-frozen (without churning). The dessert is unmolded before serving.

A parfait mixture, which is essentially a bombe mixture, can also be combined with ice cream in elegant ice bombes, or it can be used as, or as part of, a filling in frozen cakes.

SOUFFLE GLACE

Soufflés glacés, or frozen soufflés, are a type of smooth and light-textured dessert in which Italian meringue is added to a parfait or bombe mixture to give the dish a hint of the lightness found in a hot soufflé. The base is flavored with liquor, liqueur, or a fruit mixture in the same way that a parfait is. The filling is then piled high above the rim of a soufflé ramekin (typically a single-serving mold) lined with a supportive collar. The desserts are still-frozen and served in the form with the collar removed.

FROZEN MOUSSES

Frozen mousses are yet another variety of frozen dessert and are closely related to both parfaits and soufflés glacés. Although each of these three desserts is traditionally made with a different formula, in actual practice, the bases are interchangeable. All of them achieve lightness and volume from the air that is whipped into cream, eggs, or meringue. All are still-frozen and, because the freezing process serves to solidify and stabilize the content, they require little or no stabilizer, such as gelatin or pectin. A frozen mousse is distinguished from a parfait by the inclusion of whipped egg whites, which are never used in a true parfait mixture.

Basic Bombe Mixture   yield: enough for 2 bombes, 5 cups (1 L 200 ml) each

8 ounces (225 g) granulated sugar

½ cup (120 ml) water

10 egg yolks (⅞ cup/210 ml)

3 cups (720 ml) heavy cream

1. In a heavy saucepan, dissolve two-thirds of the sugar in the water; cook the mixture until it reaches 240°F (115°C).

2. While the syrup is cooking, whip the egg yolks with the remaining sugar until light and fluffy. With the mixer on slow speed, gradually add the hot syrup to the egg yolks, pouring it in a thin, steady stream between the whip and the side of the bowl. Whip at medium speed until cool.

3. Cover the mixture and place in the refrigerator until needed; at this point, it can be kept for up to 1 week.

4. When you are ready to fill a bombe, whip the heavy cream to soft peaks, then carefully fold the yolk mixture and the desired flavoring into the cream. Pour the filling into the prepared bombe mold, cover, and place in the freezer.

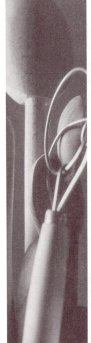

Basic Bombe Assembly

Follow these basic steps in each bombe recipe:

1. Lightly oil the inside of the molds and place in the freezer until thoroughly frozen.

2. Using a spoon dipped in hot water, line the chilled molds with a ¾-inch (2-cm) layer of softened ice cream. If the ice cream becomes too soft, refreeze until you can work with it again. Freeze the ice cream layer in the molds.

3. Pour the bombe mixture into the ice cream shell, cover, and freeze until hard, at least 4 hours.

4. To unmold the bombe, remove the lid and place a thin (⅛-inch/3-mm) sheet of sponge cake (the same size as the base of the mold) on the surface of the filling to prevent the bombe from sliding on the serving platter. Dip the sides of the mold into hot water just long enough to loosen the frozen bombe. Place one hand flat on the base and your other hand on the round side of the mold. In a single motion, push the base down and to one side and place the inverted bombe on a chilled silver tray or other serving platter. The bombe can be decorated at this point or returned to the freezer for a short period of time (see Note). The decorated bombe is traditionally presented to guests before it is sliced. A bombe should not be held in the freezer for more than a short time after it is decorated.

Note: Bombes can also be unmolded, wrapped well, and stored in the freezer for several days — should you need to reuse the molds, for example.

Bombe Aboukir yield: 2 bombes, 5 cups (1 L 200 ml) each

This dessert shares its name with Aboukir Bay, the delta in the northern part of Egypt where the Nile River empties into the Mediterranean; pistachios are indigenous to that region and are an important element of this recipe. History seems to suggest that Bombe Aboukir was named not for the muddy bay but for the Battle of Aboukir, which was fought in 1798 and ended with the English navy, led by Admiral Nelson, defeating the French fleet, isolating Napoleon and his army in Egypt, and restoring British power in the Mediterranean. There is also a cake named Aboukir; it consists of sponge cake baked in a charlotte mold, layered with chestnut cream, and iced with coffee-flavored fondant.

1 quart (960 ml) Pistachio Ice Cream (recipe follows)

1 recipe Basic Bombe Mixture (page 206)

½ recipe Hazelnut Paste (page 778) or 1½ ounces (40 g) commercial hazelnut paste

1 ounce (30 g) pistachios, blanched, skins removed

2 rounds Sponge Cake (page 794), cut ⅛ inch (3 mm) thick and the same diameter as the base of your molds

Whipped cream

Chocolate Cutouts (page 520) or Chocolate Figurines (page 545)

Hazelnuts, toasted, skins removed

Fresh fruit

Chocolate Sauce (page 413)

1. Line the chilled bombe molds with pistachio ice cream. Reserve in the freezer.

2. Add a little of the bombe mixture to the hazelnut paste to soften it, then blend this into the remaining mixture.

3. Chop the pistachios and add them to the filling. Pour the filling into the reserved shells. Freeze and unmold as described on page 206, adding the sponge layers to the bombes.

4. Decorate the bombes with whipped cream rosettes, chocolate cutouts or figurines, hazelnuts, and fruit. Serve with chocolate sauce.

PISTACHIO ICE CREAM yield: approximately 2 quarts (1 L 920 ml)

Contrary to the impression you might get from many commercial pistachio ice creams, pistachios have a mild flavor and are not nearly green enough to color the ice cream to the bright shade commonly seen. This recipe makes an ice cream with a delicious, subtle taste and just a hint of green color, which comes naturally from the nuts.

10 ounces (285 g) pistachios

3 cups (720 ml) whole milk

1 quart (960 ml) half-and-half

1 vanilla bean, split lengthwise

10 egg yolks (⅞ cup/210 ml)

5 ounces (140 g) granulated sugar

2 teaspoons (10 ml) vanilla extract

1. Boil the pistachios in lightly salted water for 1 minute. Drain, cool, and remove the skin by rubbing the nuts between your fingers. Dry the nuts at 325°F (163°C) without toasting. Reserve 2 ounces (55 g) nuts and grind the remainder finely.

2. Combine the ground pistachios with the milk in a saucepan. Heat to scalding, then remove from the heat, cover, and allow to steep for 30 minutes. Strain through a fine mesh strainer or cheesecloth, forcing all of the liquid from the nuts. (Because they are fairly expensive, try to use the nuts for another project, such as a torte or pastry filling, instead of discarding them at this point.)

3. Heat the half-and-half with the vanilla bean halves to scalding.

4. Beat the egg yolks and sugar until light and fluffy. Remove the vanilla bean halves and use the back of a paring knife to scrape out the seeds. Stir the seeds into the half-and-half. Discard the vanilla bean pods. Gradually pour the half-and-half into the whipped egg yolk mixture while whisking rapidly.

5. Heat the mixture over simmering water, stirring constantly with a whisk or wooden spoon, until it thickens enough to coat the spoon. Be careful not to overheat and break the custard. Remove from the heat and continue to stir for a few seconds to keep the mixture from overcooking where it touches the hot bowl.

6. Stir the vanilla extract and the strained pistachio liquid into the custard. Crush the reserved pistachios coarsely and add. Let cool to room temperature, then cover and refrigerate until completely cold.

7. Process in an ice cream freezer following the manufacturer's directions. Store, covered, in the freezer.

Bombe Bourdaloue yield: 2 bombes, 5 cups (1 L 200 ml) each

This is another classic bombe creation. While pretty, the components of Bombe Bourdaloue were chosen for their distinct and complementary flavors rather than to create a visual showpiece, as is done in some other varieties. This bombe is named for a street in Paris, Rue Bourdaloue, where the shop of the pastry chef who invented the recipe, during the Belle Epoque, was located.

5 cups (1 L 200 ml) Vanilla Ice Cream (page 172)	Whipped cream
1 recipe Basic Bombe Mixture (page 206)	Candied violets
3 tablespoons (45 ml) anisette liqueur	Strawberry Sauce (page 186)
2 rounds Sponge Cake (page 794), cut ⅛ inch (3 mm) thick and the same diameter as the base of your molds	

1. Line the chilled bombe molds with the vanilla ice cream. Reserve in the freezer.

2. Flavor the bombe mixture with anisette. Pour into the reserved shells. Freeze and unmold as described on page 206, adding the sponge layers to the bombes.

3. Decorate the bombes with whipped cream rosettes and candied violets. Serve with strawberry sauce.

Bombe Ceylon yield: 2 bombes, 5 cups (I L 200 ml) each

Ceylon is the former name of Sri Lanka, an island nation in the Indian Ocean at the southern tip of India. Despite its relatively small size, the island has a large climatic and geographic diversity. Half of the population relies on agriculture for its livelihood. While rice is the largest crop, the island is most famous for fine tea. The subtle flavor of the jasmine tea ice cream blends beautifully with the chocolate and orange components of this refreshing dessert.

5 cups (1 L 200 ml) Sun-Brewed Jasmine Tea Ice Cream (recipe follows)

1 recipe Basic Bombe Mixture (page 206)

½ cup (120 ml) Cointreau

2 rounds Sponge Cake (page 794), cut ⅛ inch (3 mm) thick and the same diameter as the base of your molds

Mousseline Sauce (page 338)

Whipped cream

Orange segments

Chocolate Cutouts (page 520) or Chocolate Figurines (page 545)

1. Line the chilled bombe molds with the jasmine tea ice cream. Reserve in the freezer.

2. Flavor the bombe mixture with ¼ cup (60 ml) cup Cointreau. Pour into the reserved shells. Freeze and unmold as described on page 206, adding the sponge rounds to the bombes.

3. Add the remaining ¼ cup (60 ml) Cointreau to the mousseline sauce.

4. Decorate the bombes with whipped cream, orange segments, and chocolate cutouts or figurines. Serve with mousseline sauce.

SUN-BREWED JASMINE TEA ICE CREAM yield: approximately 5 cups (I L 200 ml)

To extract the maximum flavor from the tea leaves, leave the mixture to infuse overnight (in the kitchen, not left outside). If this is not an option, the length of time specified in the recipe will still produce a nice flavor.

1 ounce (30 g) jasmine tea leaves

½ cup (120 ml) cold water

1 vanilla bean, split lengthwise

1 quart (960 ml) heavy cream

10 egg yolks (⅞ cup/210 ml)

10 ounces (285 g) granulated sugar

2 teaspoons (10 ml) vanilla extract

1. Combine the tea leaves and water in a glass jar. Cover the jar with cheesecloth and leave to brew outside in the sun or in a warm place in the kitchen for 2 to 3 hours.

2. Use the back of a paring knife to scrape the seeds out of the vanilla bean halves and stir the seeds into the cream. Save the pod halves for another use. Heat the cream and vanilla bean seeds to scalding.

3. Beat the egg yolks and sugar until light and fluffy. Gradually pour the cream into the whipped egg yolk mixture while whisking rapidly.

4. Heat the mixture over simmering water, stirring constantly with a whisk or wooden spoon, until it thickens enough to coat the spoon. Be careful not to overheat and break the cus-

About Tea

Although second to coffee in commercial importance, tea is the most popular beverage in the world. The origin of tea and the infusion of dried tea leaves is a bit uncertain. Experts believe the plant hails from a region in western China. An ancient legend has it that Shen-nung, a famous scholar and philosopher, in making a fire from the branches of the tea plant, accidentally spilled some leaves into the boiling water he was preparing. The flavor proved so exhilarating that in a short time the preparation was common throughout the empire. The first European to write about tea was Marco Polo, who described the stimulating beverage and the many teahouses in China.

Tea was introduced to Europe in the sixteenth century by the Dutch East India Company, and subsequently the drink grew popular in England. The English implemented new growing areas in the Darjeeling and Assam valleys in northeastern India, which became the world's premier tea-growing regions, and also on Ceylon (now Sri Lanka), an island that became well known for its Lipton Tea, produced by the famous tea baron Sir Thomas Lipton. Another Thomas, with the surname of Twining, also made his fortune in the tea business, having the foresight to realize just how popular tea was to become. Tea was (and still is) so enjoyed by the English that they developed an elaborate ritual of afternoon tea, which is served at four o'clock, accompanied by biscuits (cookies), tea cakes, and finger sandwiches.

Green and black tea are made from the same plant. The difference is that black teas are oxidized or fermented. In producing black tea, harvested leaves go through four processes: withering, rolling, fermentation, and firing. Withering is accomplished by spreading the leaves on bamboo or wire racks to dry. The purpose is to make the leaves soft and pliable for the rolling process, during which the cell walls are broken down and the enzyme is released that gives the tea its flavor. The "roll" or, more accurately speaking, the mashed lumps, are passed through a roll-breaker before the young leaves and stems are sifted through a wire mesh. The tea leaves are then spread out in a fermentation room where they oxidize, turning a copper color, and are allowed to ferment.

Next comes the firing: The tea is spread in a thin layer on broad, perforated metal bands that move slowly while a current of hot air passes through them. This stops the fermentation and turns the leaves black. The dried and brittle tea leaves are then sifted through a series of sieves to determine the various grades. Tea grades refer to the size of the tea leaf. Orange pekoe has a fairly large leaf; if it includes the leaf bud as well, it is called flowery orange pekoe. Pekoe leaves are smaller; souchong leaves are round. Broken teas — tea leaves that have broken during processing — are graded as broken orange pekoe; these make up the largest segment. Broken teas are further graded in descending size as broken pekoe; pekoe fannings; and dust, the last being the smallest leaf particles. Fannings are used to fill tea bags.

Oolong tea begins in the same way as black tea. Its fragrance, however, develops more quickly, and when the leaf is dried, it turns a coppery color around the edges while the center remains green. Oolong teas are fruity and pungent.

Green tea is produced like the others, except the leaf is heated before rolling and the leaves are not fermented or made to oxidize. It remains green throughout processing, and the fragrance associated with black tea does not develop. Green teas are graded by age and style.

Although modern methods and equipment have taken over many tea-producing tasks, tea leaves today are still handpicked and, to a great extent, produced in much the same way as they were hundreds of years ago.

tard. Remove from the heat and continue to stir for a few seconds to keep the mixture from overcooking where it touches the hot bowl. Stir in the vanilla extract.

5. Strain the tea mixture and add it to the custard. Cover and place the mixture in the refrigerator overnight or for at least 8 hours to mature.

6. Process in an ice cream freezer following the manufacturer's directions. Remove the ice cream from the ice cream freezer just before it is fully churned and thickened. Transfer to a chilled container and store, covered, in the freezer. The ice cream will become firmer once frozen.

CHEF'S TIP
This ice cream is removed from the ice cream freezer just before it is fully churned. Because the recipe is made with a high proportion of fat — with heavy cream rather than half-and-half — overchurning will result in the formation of tiny lumps of butter in the ice cream.

Bombe Monarch yield: 2 bombes, 5 cups (1 L 200 ml) each

Butterflies are a popular pastry motif; pastry chefs make impressive and elegant decorations from tuile paste, chocolate, and sugar. The shape of butterflies — flat wings that are easy to decorate and then position in a three-dimensional form — along with their graceful, lighter-than-air appearance, makes them a natural for this purpose.

3½ cups (840 ml) Peach Ice Cream (recipe follows)

1 recipe Basic Bombe Mixture (page 206)

3 tablespoons (45 ml) Bénédictine liqueur

2 rounds Sponge Cake (page 794), cut ⅛ inch (3 mm) thick and the same diameter as the base of your molds

Whipped cream

Small Chocolate Monarch Butterfly Ornaments (page 550)

Fresh fruit

Cherry Sauce (page 230)

1. Line the chilled bombe molds with the peach ice cream. Reserve in the freezer.

2. Flavor the bombe mixture with Bénédictine liqueur. Pour into the reserved shells. Freeze and unmold as described on page 206, adding the sponge cake rounds to the bombes.

3. Decorate the bombes with whipped cream rosettes, chocolate monarch butterflies, and fresh fruit. Serve with cherry sauce.

CHEF'S TIP
If you are pressed for time, replace the chocolate butterfly ornaments with Cookie Butterflies (page 695).

PEACH ICE CREAM yield: approximately 6 cups (1 L 440 ml)

If this ice cream will be eaten the same day it is made, skip the macerating step. If the peaches are tree-ripened or perfectly ripe, you can omit pureeing them as well. But do include the amaretto. Peaches and almonds are made for each other. Peach ice cream is great for topping many pies and tarts à la mode, especially those that contain nuts.

2 pounds (910 g) ripe but firm fresh peaches

⅓ cup (80 ml) amaretto liqueur

5 ounces (140 g) granulated sugar

10 egg yolks (⅞ cup/210 ml)

1 quart (960 ml) half-and-half

2½ cups (600 ml) Plain Poaching Syrup (page 789)

1. Pick out 2 of the firmest peaches, wash, remove any fuzz but do not peel, cut in half, and discard the pits. Cut the peaches into pea-sized chunks and macerate them in the amaretto for 4 to 5 hours or, preferably, overnight.

2. Whip the sugar and egg yolks to the ribbon stage. Scald the half-and-half and gradually pour it into the egg yolk mixture while whisking rapidly. Set over simmering water, stirring constantly with a whisk or wooden spoon, and thicken the custard until it coats the spoon. Be careful not to overheat, or the yolks will coagulate. Remove the custard from the heat and let it cool to room temperature. Cover and refrigerate until completely cold, preferably overnight.

3. Wash the remaining peaches, cut in half, discard the pits, and remove the skin. Blanch, then refresh in cold water and the skin will slip right off. If the skin does not come away easily, the peaches are not ripe. Place the peaches in a saucepan with the poaching syrup. Simmer until the fruit starts to fall apart. Remove the fruit from the syrup. Puree the peaches and set the mixture aside to cool. (If you use fruit that is not fully ripe, it may not puree smoothly, in which case pass the pulp through a fine mesh strainer before proceeding.) Discard the poaching syrup.

4. Add the macerated peach chunks and peach puree to the custard. Process the mixture in an ice cream freezer. Place in a chilled container and store, covered, in the freezer.

CHEF'S TIP

For the best result, prepare the macerated peaches and the custard and refrigerate them separately one day before freezing the ice cream. The custard will have a smoother texture if allowed to mature, and the fruit will have a better chance to absorb as much sugar as possible so it will not freeze rock-hard in the ice cream. Do not prepare the peach puree until you are ready to process the ice cream.

Coupe Bavaria

Coffee-Scented Chocolate Ice Cream
   (page 223)

Fresh sweet dark cherries, stemmed and
   pitted

Maraschino liqueur

Whipped cream

Strawberry wedges

Chocolate Cigarettes (page 516)

Miniature Palm Leaves (page 122) or other
   small cookies

I. Presentation for each serving: Place 1 or more scoops, depending on size, of the ice cream in a goblet, coupe glass, or dessert bowl. Top with cherries. Lightly sprinkle maraschino liqueur over the cherries and ice cream. Decorate with whipped cream rosettes, strawberry wedges, and 2 chocolate cigarettes. Place the serving dish on a plate lined with a doily or napkin. Set 1 or 2 cookies on the plate and serve immediately.

Coupe Belle Hélène

Poached pear halves (see Step 1, page 252)

Vanilla Ice Cream (page 172)

Hot Fudge Sauce (page 254)

Pistachios, blanched, skins removed, and
   coarsely chopped

Strawberry Hearts (page 122) or other small
   cookies

I. Fan 1 pear half per serving and reserve.

2. Presentation for each serving: Place 1 or more scoops, depending on size, of vanilla ice cream in a goblet, coupe glass, or dessert bowl. Place a fanned pear half on top of the ice cream. Pour hot fudge sauce over the bottom part of the pear. Sprinkle pistachios on the sauce. Set the serving dish on a dessert plate lined with a doily or napkin. Place a cookie on the plate and serve immediately.

Coupe Hawaii

Fresh Coconut Ice Cream (recipe follows)

Whipped cream

Fresh pineapple slices, cut in half

Miniature Palm Trees (page 255)

Chocolate-Filled Macadamia Morsels
   (page 118)

I. Presentation for each serving: Place 1 or more scoops, depending on size, of coconut ice cream in a goblet, coupe glass, or dessert bowl. Decorate the ice cream with whipped cream rosettes and a half slice of fresh pineapple. Stand a palm tree in the center, pushing the tree down far enough into the ice cream so that it stands straight. Place the serving dish on a plate lined with a doily or napkin. Place a macadamia morsel on the plate and serve immediately.

FRESH COCONUT ICE CREAM yield: approximately 6 cups (1 L 440 ml)

2 fresh coconuts, about 2 pounds (910 g) each

Whole milk, as needed

1 vanilla bean, split lengthwise

About 2 cups (480 ml) heavy cream

10 egg yolks (⅞ cup/210 ml)

3 ounces (85 g) granulated sugar

1. Puncture the 3 eyes on each coconut with an ice pick and drain out the coconut milk, reserving 3 cups (720 ml). If the coconuts do not contain that much liquid, add enough regular whole milk to make the amount needed.

2. Tap the coconuts all around with a hammer or heavy cleaver to help loosen the meat from the shell. Using the same tool, crack the coconuts open. Remove the meat from the shell, then use a vegetable peeler to remove the brown skin from the meat. (If some pieces do not separate from the shell, loosen them by placing them on a sheet pan and baking at 350°F (175°C) for about 30 minutes.) Chop the coconut meat finely in a food processor.

3. Combine the chopped coconut meat and coconut milk in a nonreactive saucepan. Using the back of a paring knife, scrape the seeds out of the vanilla bean halves and add the seeds to the coconut mixture. Save the pods for another use. Heat to scalding, remove from the heat, cover, and let infuse for at least 30 minutes.

4. Strain the mixture, pressing with a spoon to remove as much liquid as possible from the coconut. Discard the coconut meat. Add enough heavy cream to the strained coconut milk to make 5 cups (1 L 200 ml) liquid. Return the mixture to the saucepan and heat to scalding.

5. Beat the egg yolks and sugar together for a few minutes. Gradually pour the hot liquid into the yolk mixture, whisking continuously. Heat the mixture over simmering water, stirring constantly with a whisk or wooden spoon until it thickens enough to coat the back of the spoon. Remove from the heat and continue to stir for 1 minute to prevent overcooking on the bottom or sides. Let cool to room temperature, then cover and refrigerate until completely cold.

6. Process in an ice cream freezer according to the manufacturer's directions. Store, covered, in the freezer.

VARIATION
QUICK COCONUT ICE CREAM yield: approximately 5 cups (1 L 200 ml)

If you just can't live with yourself if you use anything but fresh coconut to make your coconut ice cream — and I agree there is a difference — prepare the preceding recipe. However, if you are short on time, this is a good quick compromise. Prepare the recipe for Vanilla Ice Cream (page 172), replacing 2 cups (480 ml) half-and-half with unsweetened canned coconut milk and using only 4 ounces (115 g) sugar.

Coupe Melba

Poached peach halves (see Step 2, page 165)

Vanilla Ice Cream (page 172)

Melba Sauce (recipe follows)

Whipped cream

Raspberries

Three Sisters (page 123) or other small cookies

1. Fan 1 peach half per serving and reserve.

2. Presentation for each serving: Place 1 or more scoops, depending on size, of vanilla ice cream in a goblet, coupe glass, or dessert bowl. Place a reserved peach half on top of the ice cream. Pour Melba sauce over the peach. Pipe a rosette of whipped cream on top and decorate with a few raspberries. Set the serving dish on a dessert plate lined with a doily or napkin. Place a cookie on the plate and serve immediately.

MELBA SAUCE yield: approximately 4 cups (960 ml)

1 pound 12 ounces (795 g) fresh, ripe red raspberries or thawed IQF frozen raspberries

4 ounces (115 g) red currant jelly

3 tablespoons (24 g) cornstarch

Granulated sugar, as needed

2 tablespoons (30 ml) kirschwasser

1. Puree the raspberries with the red currant jelly. Strain through a fine mesh strainer and discard the seeds. Measure and add water, if necessary, to make 4 cups (960 ml) juice.

2. Place the cornstarch in a saucepan. Add enough of the raspberry juice to liquefy the cornstarch. Stir in the remaining raspberry juice. Bring the sauce to a boil and sweeten with sugar, if necessary. Remove from the heat and stir in the kirschwasser. Let cool, then thin with water if the sauce is too thick. The sauce should be thick enough to coat a piece of fruit, for example, but should be pourable. Store, covered, in the refrigerator.

Coupe Niçoise

Mixed fresh fruit salad (see page 285, Step 1, for suggestions)

Honey Mandarin Sorbet (recipe follows)

Curaçao

Whipped cream

Raspberries or strawberry wedges

Almond Doubles (page 117) or other small cookies

1. Presentation for each serving: Place a portion of fruit salad in the bottom of a goblet, coupe glass, or dessert bowl. Place 1 or more scoops, depending on size, of honey mandarin sorbet on top. Sprinkle curaçao over the sorbet. Decorate with whipped cream rosettes and raspberries (or use strawberry wedges, if raspberries are not available). Place the serving dish on a plate lined with a doily or napkin. Place a cookie on the plate and serve immediately.

HONEY MANDARIN SORBET yield: approximately 6 cups (1 L 440 ml)

Honey mandarins are wonderfully sweet but they contain a lot of seeds, which makes them better suited for juicing than for eating out of hand. To make other citrus sorbets, such as orange, tangerine, or tangelo, simply substitute the desired juice for the mandarin juice in the recipe.

3 pounds 8 ounces (1 kg 590 g) honey
    mandarins (approximately 8 medium)

2 cups (480 ml) simple syrup, at room
    temperature

About 2½ cups (600 ml) water

Few drops Tartaric Acid Solution (page 629)
    or lemon juice

1. Juice the mandarins. Strain the juice and discard the seeds and solids. You should have approximately 2 cups (480 ml) juice. Proceed as long as you have reasonably close to this amount; the measurement need not be exact.

2. Combine the mandarin juice and simple syrup. Add enough water to bring the mixture to between 16° and 20° Baumé (see page 825). Add the tartaric acid or lemon juice.

3. Process in an ice cream freezer following the manufacturer's instructions. Transfer to a chilled bowl, cover, and store in the freezer.

Coupe Sweden

Chunky Apple Filling (recipe follows)

White Chocolate Ice Cream (recipe follows)

Calvados

Whipped cream

Shaved dark chocolate

Florentina Twists (page 690)

1. Presentation for each serving: Cover the bottom of a goblet, coupe glass, or dessert bowl with chunky apple filling. Place 1 or more scoops, depending on size, of the ice cream on top. Sprinkle Calvados over the ice cream. Decorate with whipped cream rosettes, chocolate shavings, and a Florentina Twist. Place the serving dish on a dessert plate lined with a doily or napkin and serve immediately.

CHUNKY APPLE FILLING yield: 2 pounds 12 ounces (1 kg 250 g) or 5 cups (1 L 200 ml)

3 pounds (1 kg 365 g) Granny Smith or
    Pippin apples (about 7; see Chef's Tip)

10 ounces (285 g) granulated sugar

¼ cup (60 ml) water

4 teaspoons (20 ml) lemon juice

1. Peel and core the apples. Chop approximately two-thirds of the apples into ½-inch (1.2-cm) pieces.

2. Place the chopped apples in a saucepan with the sugar, water, and lemon juice. Adjust the amount of sugar according to the tartness of the apples and your own taste. Stir to combine and cook over medium heat, stirring from time to time, until the apples break down and the mixture starts to thicken.

3. Chop the remaining apples into ¼-inch (6-mm) chunks and add to the mixture on the stove.

4. Continue cooking the filling until the apple chunks are soft and the filling has a jamlike consistency, adding a bit more water if it seems necessary. Let cool to room temperature, then store, covered, in the refrigerator.

WHITE CHOCOLATE ICE CREAM yield: approximately 6 cups (1 L 440 ml)

This ice cream is incredibly rich, dense, and luxurious — there is basically zero overrun — but you do have to baby it a little. By adding the white chocolate to the hot custard and stirring until it is melted, you avoid overheating this sensitive ingredient, as can happen so easily when it is melted over heat. Also, be careful not to overchurn the ice cream. The fat from the cocoa butter in the chocolate can quickly make the ice cream gritty.

3 cups (720 ml) half-and-half

2 cups (480 ml) heavy cream

8 egg yolks (⅔ cup/160 ml)

3 ounces (85 g) granulated sugar

10 ounces (285 g) white chocolate, chopped into small chunks

1. Combine the half-and-half and cream in a saucepan. Heat to scalding.

2. Beat the egg yolks with the sugar until light and fluffy. Gradually whisk the hot cream into the egg yolk mixture.

3. Place over simmering water and heat, stirring constantly with a whisk or wooden spoon (do not whip), until the custard is thick enough to coat the spoon.

4. Remove from the heat and add the white chocolate, continuing to stir until all of the chunks are melted. Let cool to room temperature, then refrigerate until completely cold.

5. Process in an ice cream freezer according to the manufacturer's directions. Remove the ice cream from the ice cream freezer just before it is fully churned and thickened (it should be too soft to scoop out). Transfer to a chilled container, cover, and place in the freezer. The ice cream will become firmer once frozen. If the ice cream is allowed to freeze completely while churning, its texture will be compromised, as explained above.

VARIATION
GINGERED WHITE CHOCOLATE ICE CREAM

- Add 1 ounce (30 g) sliced fresh ginger in Step 1 and allow the mixture to steep for 30 minutes off the heat after scalding.

- Strain the mixture at the end of Step 2 to remove the ginger.

- Add ½ ounce (15 g) finely chopped candied ginger in Step 4, after the white chocolate has melted.

Apricot and Fig Tart with Prickly Pear Sorbet yield: 16 servings

This tart features a potpourri of tastes: slightly tart apricots, sweet figs, almond frangipane filling, and lemon cream. You will be pleasantly surprised at how well they all come together with the prickly pear sorbet. If you cannot obtain prickly pears, also known as *cactus pears*, try serving Passion Fruit Parfait (recipe follows) in a passion fruit shell.

1 pound 8 ounces (680 g) Short Dough (page 791)

1 pound 6 ounces (625 g) Frangipane Filling (page 769)

1 pound 4 ounces (570 g) Lemon Cream (page 771; approximately ⅓ recipe)

16 fresh apricots

14 fresh Brown Turkey or large Black Mission figs

Granulated sugar

Powdered sugar

8 prickly pears (see Chef's Tip)

Dark coating chocolate, melted

16 mint sprigs

Prickly Pear Sorbet (recipe follows)

1. Roll out the short dough to ⅛ inch (3 mm) thick and use it to line 8 tartlet pans, 4½ inches (11.2 cm) in diameter × ¾ inch (2 cm) high.

2. Place the frangipane filling in a pastry bag with a No. 5 (10-mm) plain tip. Pipe the filling into the shells, dividing it evenly; they should be about two-thirds full. Top with a ⅛-inch (3-mm) layer of lemon cream. Reserve the remaining lemon cream.

3. Reserve 8 good-looking apricots and 6 figs. Cut the remaining apricots in half, remove the pits, then cut each half again to make quarters. Cut the remaining 8 figs lengthwise into quarters.

4. Alternate 4 wedges of fig and 4 wedges of apricot on the top of each tart, placing the fruit skin-side down, with the pointed ends of each fig wedge directed alternately toward the center and then to the outside, like a fan. Press the fruit lightly into the filling. Sprinkle just enough granulated sugar over the tarts to cover (about 1 teaspoon/5 g per tart).

5. Bake at 375°F (190°C) for 20 minutes. Sift powdered sugar lightly over the tarts, then continue baking until they are dark golden brown and baked through, about 20 minutes longer. Let cool completely, then unmold.

6. Cut the prickly pears in half crosswise. Use a small spoon to scoop out the flesh (reserve to make the sorbet). Cut a small sliver from the bottom of the shells so they stand upright.

7. Cut the tarts in half so that each piece contains 2 apricot wedges and 2 fig wedges. Set aside.

8. Place melted coating chocolate in a piping bag and cut a small opening. Decorate 16 dessert plates (or as many as you will need) by piping the chocolate in a free-form design.

9. Cut the reserved apricots in half, remove the pits, and cut in half again to make quarters. Cut 3 round slices from the sides of each fig, making pieces that are rounded on the skin side and flat on the flesh side. Ideally, cut just as many apricot and fig pieces as you will need right away so the pieces of fruit do not dry.

10. Presentation: Place a tart half on a decorated plate, arranging it so the cut side is in the center of the plate. Pour a small pool of lemon cream on the right corner of the tart and onto the plate. Arrange 1 fig slice and 2 apricot pieces in the sauce. Set a mint sprig next to the fruit. Place a scoop of prickly pear sorbet in a prepared shell (see Note) and set on the left side of the tart. Sift powdered sugar over the plate in back of the dessert. Serve immediately.

NOTE: To prevent the sorbet from melting prematurely, place the prickly pear shells in the freezer for a few minutes before you fill them, but do not freeze them solid, which would detract from the presentation.

CHEF'S TIP

Prickly pear skin can vary from greenish-yellow to dark mahogany red and is found in many other shades as well. The flesh is either yellow or red; the latter is most common in fruit found in the United States. Unless the fruit is firm, it is not practical to serve the sorbet in the prickly pear shell, as directed in Step 6. Obviously, this is also not possible if you make the sorbet from frozen prickly pear juice instead of fresh fruit. An alternative in either case is to serve a scoop of sorbet on a small round of sponge cake, which will prevent the sorbet from sliding on the plate.

PRICKLY PEAR SORBET yield: approximately 3 cups (720 ml)

2 pounds 8 ounces (1 kg 135 g) prickly pears (about 8; see Chef's Tip)

½ cup (120 ml) simple syrup, at room temperature

⅓ cup (80 ml) water

¼ cup (60 ml) kirschwasser

Juice of 1 lime

1. Cut the prickly pears in half crosswise and, using a small spoon, scoop out the pulp. Save the shells to use in serving or discard them. Place the fruit pulp in a food processor and process to a smooth consistency (see Note).

2. Strain the mixture and discard the solids; you should have about 3 cups (720 ml) juice. Add the simple syrup, water, kirschwasser, and lime juice to the fruit juice. Let cool to room temperature.

3. Adjust the Baumé level of the liquid to between 16° and 20° by adding water if it is too high or simple syrup if it is too low.

4. Process in an ice cream freezer following the manufacturer's instructions. Transfer to a chilled container, cover, and store in the freezer.

NOTE: If the prickly pears are not fully ripe, place the fruit pulp, simple syrup, and water in a nonreactive saucepan and heat, stirring, until the fruit falls apart. Do not boil. Process the cooked mixture and continue.

CHEF'S TIP

A quick and perfectly acceptable substitute for the fresh prickly pears in this recipe is frozen prickly pear juice, which is readily available through commercial distributors. Most juices are sold unsweetened or with a minimal amount of sugar added. Check the label and adjust the amount of sugar you add accordingly. You will need 3 cups (720 ml) juice for this recipe.

PASSION FRUIT PARFAIT yield: 2 quarts (1 L 920 ml)

Passion fruit pulp gives this fluffy parfait a refreshingly perfumed taste and enticing aroma that are indisputably tropical. Fortunately, neither the scent nor the flavor dissipates through storage or freezing. The small black seeds of the passion fruit are fully edible, although not everyone enjoys their crunchiness. I prefer to leave them in for texture and character. If you prefer to remove the seeds, warm the pulp (do not boil) until the seeds loosen. Pass through a strainer and discard the seeds. You can also try frozen passion fruit puree, as the frozen product is always sold with the seeds removed.

You can utilize this versatile recipe in several ways. You can pour the mixture into a loaf pan and slice it after freezing. Cutting a slice in half diagonally and leaning one against the other on the serving plate looks pretty. Decorate with fruit or a chocolate ornament, as desired. The mixture can be frozen in Flexipan forms — half-spheres or pyramids, for example — unmolded, and again decorated as you choose. Or you can simply freeze the parfait in a storage container and scoop it out as you would ice cream, serving it in a Florentina Cup (page 687), a Tulip Shell (pages 716 and 717), or in hollowed-out passion fruit shell halves (three per serving).

10 eggs, separated	2 cups (480 ml) heavy cream
⅓ cup (80 ml) or 4 ounces (115 g) light corn syrup	1 cup (240 ml) passion fruit pulp (from about 12 passion fruit)
4 ounces (115 g) granulated sugar	¼ cup (60 ml) curaçao

I. Beat the egg yolks until they are light and fluffy, about 5 minutes. Bring the corn syrup to a boil. Add the corn syrup to the egg yolks while whipping at medium speed. Increase to maximum speed and whip until the mixture has cooled completely.

2. Combine the egg whites and sugar in a mixing bowl. Set the bowl over simmering water and heat, whipping constantly, to 140°F (60°C). Remove from the heat and whip until the mixture has cooled and formed stiff peaks.

3. Whip the heavy cream until soft peaks form. Fold the cream into the yolk mixture together with the passion fruit pulp and the liqueur. Gently incorporate the meringue. Pour the mixture into a suitable container or forms, as described in the recipe introduction, and place in the freezer until firm, at least 4 hours or, preferably, overnight.

Baked Alaska yield: 12 servings

Baked Alaska, though perhaps considered a bit old-fashioned today, is nevertheless a dessert classic. The dish combines cold frozen ice cream wrapped in a thin sheet of soft sponge cake topped with caramelized billowy sweet meringue, to produce an intriguing and pleasing result. The assembled creation was originally placed in a hot oven not so much to "bake" the dessert as the title implies, but to brown the meringue. Today, the meringue is typically browned using a salamander or blowtorch in a professional kitchen, or the dish is flambéed at the table by the server. Regardless of the method used to caramelize the meringue, Baked Alaska demonstrates, especially when an oven is used, the insulating strength of air — both the air in the sponge cake and that in the meringue — which protect the ice cream from the heat and keep it from melting.

2½ cups (600 ml) Vanilla Ice Cream (page 172)

2½ cups (600 ml) Strawberry Ice Cream (recipe follows)

2½ cups (600 ml) Coffee-Scented Chocolate Ice Cream (recipe follows)

1 Almond Sponge sheet (page 795), 14 × 24 inches (35 × 60 cm)

¼ cup (60 ml) Plain Cake Syrup (page 789)

¼ cup (60 ml) orange liqueur

¼ recipe Italian Meringue (page 780)

Powdered sugar

Candied red cherries

2 empty, clean eggshell halves

1 recipe Strawberry Sauce (page 186)

151-proof rum (see Chef's Tip)

1. Layer the 3 ice creams in a chilled bread pan lined with baking paper (or use any other rectangular pan measuring approximately 11 × 4 × 4 inches [27.5 × 10 × 10 cm]. You will need to soften the ice cream a bit first to create smooth, even layers. Let each layer harden in the freezer before adding the next. Reserve in the freezer until firm.

2. Cut a strip from the sponge sheet that is as wide as the pan is long and long enough to wrap all the way around the ice cream block. Unmold the ice cream, remove the paper, and place the ice cream on the sponge sheet. Roll to completely cover all 4 long sides. Use scrap pieces of sponge to cover the ends. Place on a chilled ovenproof serving tray.

3. Combine the cake syrup and orange liqueur and brush lightly over the top and sides of the rectangle.

4. Using a metal spatula to achieve a smooth and even finish, spread a layer of meringue ½ inch (1.2 cm) thick over the top and all 4 sides, sealing the meringue to the serving tray around the bottom edge. Place the remaining meringue in a pastry bag with a No. 4 (8-mm) star tip. Decoratively pipe the meringue onto the iced rectangle, designing 2 nests on top, one near each end, for an eggshell half to hold the rum. Return the assembled dessert to the freezer until serving time.

5. Lightly sift powdered sugar over the meringue. Decorate with cherries. Push the eggshells into the meringue far enough to make them inconspicuous.

6. Place the tray in a hot oven or use a blowtorch or salamander to brown the meringue.

7. Pour strawberry sauce over the base of the tray around the dessert.

8. Turn down the lights in the dining room, pour a little rum into the eggshells, ignite it, and present immediately. Remove and discard the eggshell halves as the portions are sliced.

CHEF'S TIP

Any liqueur or spirit with an alcohol level of 80 percent can be used to flambé, although 151-proof rum is convenient and foolproof, as it will ignite cold. If you use alcohol with a lower proof, you must warm it before igniting. Before using 151-proof rum for all flambé work, however, consider whether or not its flavor will interfere with that of the dessert if it is spooned over the top or used as part of the sauce (as in persimmon pudding, for example).

About Baked Alaska

The forerunner of this dish — minus the meringue — is said to have originated in China. The idea was introduced to France in 1866 when a master cook from a visiting Chinese delegation taught the French chef Balzaac of the Grand Hotel in Paris how to prepare a dessert of vanilla and ginger ice creams baked in a pastry crust. The French took hold of the concept, naming their dish *Surprise Omelette*. The American-born physicist Benjamin Thompson, later titled Count Rumford, is credited with the invention, or realization, that whipped egg whites are both an excellent insulator and a poor conductor of heat and thus can prevent ice cream from melting as meringue browns in the oven. Using this information at the turn of the century, the pastry chef at the Hotel de Paris in Monte Carlo, Jean Giroix, popularized the modern form of the dessert, calling it *Omelette Norwégienne*, presumably because of its resemblance to arctic ice and its frozen interior. Soon afterward, the creation made its way to Delmonico's Restaurant in New York City, where it became known as "Alaska and Florida," representing the temperature differences of these two geographic areas and the two components of the dish. It is said that Fannie Farmer was involved in changing the name to Baked Alaska in celebration of Alaska's 1868 purchase by the United States, although admittedly a bit after the fact. The first recorded use of the term *Baked Alaska* is in the 1909 edition of her cookbook.

STRAWBERRY ICE CREAM yield: approximately 7 cups (1 L 680 ml)

1 quart (960 ml) half-and-half

1 vanilla bean, split lengthwise

10 egg yolks (⅞ cup/210 ml)

9 ounces (255 g) granulated sugar

2 teaspoons (10 ml) vanilla extract

1 pound (455 g) fresh ripe strawberries

½ cup (120 ml) strained raspberry puree (see Note)

1. Heat to scalding the half-and-half with the vanilla bean halves.

2. Beat the egg yolks and 5 ounces (140 g) of the sugar until light and fluffy. Remove the vanilla bean halves and use the back of a paring knife to scrape out the seeds. Stir the seeds into the half-and-half. Discard the vanilla bean pods. Gradually pour the half-and-half into the whipped egg yolk mixture while whisking rapidly.

3. Heat the mixture over simmering water, stirring constantly with a whisk or wooden spoon, until it thickens enough to coat the spoon. Be careful not to overheat and break the custard. Remove from the heat and continue to stir for a few seconds to keep the mixture from overcooking where it touches the hot bowl. Stir in the vanilla extract. Let cool to room temperature.

4. Clean and stem the strawberries. Chop into small pieces. Place in a saucepan with the remaining 4 ounces (115 g) sugar and cook over medium heat, stirring from time to time, until the mixture starts to thicken, about 10 minutes.

5. Add the strawberry mixture to the ice cream custard together with the raspberry puree. Let cool to room temperature, then cover and refrigerate until completely cold.

6. Process in an ice cream freezer according to the manufacturer's instructions. Transfer the ice cream to a chilled container and store, covered, in the freezer.

NOTE: Because this recipe does not use any artificial ingredients, the color may not be as bright as you are used to seeing in commercial strawberry ice creams. The raspberry juice is added to intensify the hue. Adjust the amounts of sugar and raspberry juice according to the ripeness (and sweetness) of the strawberries.

CHEF'S TIP
The strawberries must be prepared with sugar before they are added to the ice cream, unless the ice cream is to be eaten the same day it is made. This is necessary because strawberries contain a large amount of juice, which is not always as sweet as is needed to create a soft rather than an icy texture once frozen overnight.

COFFEE-SCENTED CHOCOLATE ICE CREAM yield: approximately 6 cups (1 L 440 ml)

1 quart (960 ml) half-and-half

4 ounces (115 g) unsweetened cocoa powder

½ cup (120 ml) strongly brewed espresso coffee

1 vanilla bean, split lengthwise, *or* 1 teaspoon (5 ml) vanilla extract

4 ounces (115 g) sweet dark chocolate

8 egg yolks (⅔ cup/160 ml)

6 ounces (170 g) granulated sugar

1. Gradually mix enough half-and-half into the cocoa powder to dissolve it and make a smooth paste. Stir in the remaining half-and-half and the espresso. Bring to the scalding point with the vanilla bean halves, if using.

2. Chop the chocolate into small pieces. Remove the cream mixture from the heat, add the chopped chocolate, and stir until completely melted.

3. Whip the egg yolks with the sugar until light and fluffy. Remove the vanilla bean halves from the half-and-half and use the back of a paring knife to scrape out the seeds. Stir the seeds back into the half-and-half for a more intense flavor. Discard the vanilla bean pods. If using vanilla extract, add it at this point. Gradually pour the hot half-and-half into the yolk mixture while stirring rapidly. Place over simmering water and heat, stirring constantly with a whisk or wooden spoon, until the mixture is thick enough to coat the spoon. Set aside to cool. Cover and refrigerate until thoroughly chilled, preferably overnight.

4. Process in an ice cream freezer according to the manufacturer's directions. Store, covered, in the freezer.

Bénédictine Soufflé Glacé yield: 12 servings

Soufflé Glacé, or frozen soufflé, is much less capricious than its better-known big brother, the hot soufflé, which has a somewhat undeserved reputation for being unpredictable and difficult. The mousselike filling in a soufflé glacé should extend about 2 inches (5 cm) above the rim of the ramekin to resemble a hot soufflé rising from its baking dish. This is achieved by using a collar for support while the dessert freezes. As is true of many frozen desserts, soufflé glacé is an excellent choice when you have no time for numerous last-minute steps.

Although the soufflés are light, using standard soufflé ramekins (3¼ inches/8.1 cm in diameter), as directed, yields a fairly generous serving, especially if you wrap the collars around the outside of the forms. Using smaller forms, 2½ to 3 inches (6.2 to 7.5 cm) in diameter and 3½ ounces (105 ml) in capacity, not only makes the soufflés higher and more attractive but produces 16 servings instead of 12.

If you are serving just a few desserts at a time à la minute, you may omit the gelatin, pectin, and water if you wish (Steps 4 and 6).

4 cups (960 ml) heavy cream	⅓ cup (80 ml) cold water
¼ cup (60 ml) Bénédictine liqueur	½ recipe Italian Meringue (page 780)
2 teaspoons (10 ml) vanilla extract	Cocoa powder
8 egg yolks (⅔ cup/160 ml)	12 Hazelnut Flowers (page 120) or other small cookies
2 teaspoons (6 g) unflavored gelatin powder	
2 teaspoons (6 g) canning pectin powder	

1. Prepare 12 soufflé ramekins, 3¼ inches (8.1 cm) in diameter, as directed on page 226. Reserve in the freezer.

2. Whip the heavy cream to soft peaks. Cover and refrigerate.

3. Add the Bénédictine and vanilla to the egg yolks. Place over simmering water and heat, whisking constantly, until the mixture has thickened to the consistency of a sabayon. Remove from the heat and whip until cold.

4. Sprinkle the gelatin and pectin powders over the cold water and let stand until softened.

5. Fold the whipped cream into the egg yolk mixture. Gradually stir this into the Italian meringue.

6. Place the gelatin mixture over simmering water and heat to dissolve. Do not overheat. Quickly stir the gelatin into a small portion of the filling. Then, still working fast, stir this into the remaining filling.

7. Promptly place the filling in a pastry bag with a No. 7 (14-mm) plain tip and pipe into the prepared molds. It should extend about 2 inches (5 cm) above the rim of the molds for an authentic soufflé look. Place the soufflés in the freezer for at least 4 hours or, preferably, overnight.

8. Trace the drawing in Figure 5-1, then cut the template out of thin cardboard. Cake boxes made of cardboard that is ¹⁄₁₆ inch (2 mm) thick work fine.

CHEF'S TIP

You can make any type of liqueur soufflé glacé by substituting other liqueurs for the Bénédictine. Depending on the strength of the liqueur you choose, you may wish to increase or decrease the amount. Keep in mind, however, that too much alcohol (like too much sugar) will prevent the filling from freezing properly.

9. Presentation: Remove the collar from a soufflé. Place the template on top and sift cocoa powder lightly over the template, taking great care not to get any on the rim of the form. Remove the template carefully without disturbing the pattern. Place the soufflé glacé on a plate lined with a doily or napkin. Place a cookie on the plate and serve immediately.

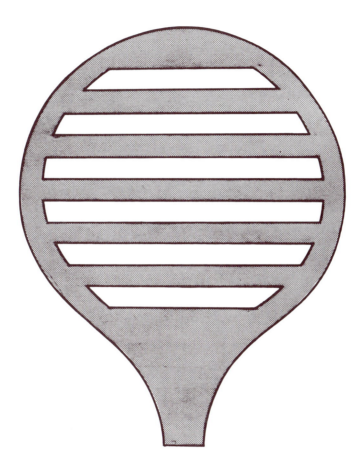

FIGURE 5-1 The template for the presentation of Bénédictine Soufflé Glacé

About Bénédictine

Bénédictine is a sweet liqueur that was first made in the sixteenth century by the Benedictine monks of the Abbey of Fecamp in the Normandy region of France. Dom Bernardo Vincelli is the monk credited with creating the original recipe. Commercial production began in 1863 when Alexandre Le Grand found the recipe in some old family papers. He made a few changes and began selling the product, with immediate success. He named the liqueur Bénédictine in honor of the monks who created it. The labels on the bottles are printed with the initials *D.O.M.* for the Latin phrase *Deo Optimo Maximo*, which translated means "To God, most good, most great." Bénédictine is based on Cognac and is said to be flavored with 27 spices and plants; however, the exact recipe is a highly guarded secret. Bénédictine is traditionally served after coffee, straight or on the rocks, as a digestive. B&B, or Bénédictine and Brandy, is also produced and bottled in Fecamp. It is drier than Bénédictine and is served in the same way.

VARIATION

GINGER SOUFFLÉ GLACÉ

Follow the recipe and directions for Bénédictine Soufflé Glacé (page 224), making the following changes:

- Replace the Bénédictine with an equal amount of muscat or other sweet wine.

- Julienne 1½ ounces (40 g) crystallized ginger. Set aside the 24 best-looking pieces to use for decoration and finely chop the remainder. Add the chopped ginger to the wine (be sure the small pieces are not stuck together) as you add it to the filling in Step 3.

- Place 2 pieces of julienned crystallized ginger on top of the soufflé when serving.

To Prepare Ramekins for Soufflé Glacé

1. Cut 12 polyurethane or acetate strips, 1½ inches (3.7 cm) wide and slightly longer than the inside circumference of the ramekins measured under the recessed lip; this will be approximately 10 inches (25 cm) for 3¼-inch (8.1-cm) ramekins. Make a collar of each strip by taping the ends together, adjusting so it fits snugly around the inside lip of the ramekin. Brush soft butter in a fairly thick layer on the inside of the recessed edge of a ramekin.

2. Place the collar in the butter to make it adhere and adjust to make the top level (Figure 5-2). Repeat with the remaining ramekins. Alternatively, use strips approximately 3 inches (7.5 cm) wide. Adjust them to fit tight against the inside and simply stand them on the bottom of the mold. This eliminates the need to butter the sides and level the tops but makes the strips a bit more difficult to remove later.

   Gluing the collars to the recessed rim of the ramekins gives you the most authentic soufflé rising-from-the-mold look. This is practical, however, only if time is no object. A much more commonly used technique is to use a rubber band to fasten the collars around the outside of the molds so they extend 2 inches (5 cm) above the rim (shown on the right side of the illustration). This yields only 8 servings, as the soufflés will be slightly wider on top.

FIGURE 5-2 Securing a collar inside the recessed edge of a soufflé ramekin; a collar secured around the outside of a ramekin using a rubber band

Caramel Ice Cream in a Caramel Cage yield: 16 servings

In the following presentation, an elegant caramel cage, resting on whipped cream and encircled by a band of decorated chocolate sauce, is all it takes to create a spectacular dessert for a formal occasion. Keep in mind, when you make the cages, that the sugar lines should be very thin, not just for the sake of appearance but, more importantly, so your guests can actually consume them without risk of cutting their mouth on thick, sharp caramel. For this recipe, the caramel cages should be made 4 inches (10 cm) in diameter and 2 inches (5 cm) high.

If you do not have time to prepare caramel cages, you can certainly enjoy the caramel ice cream without them. Top the ice cream with the Chocolate Sauce (page 413) or Hot Fudge Sauce (page 254) and Chantilly Cream (page 765), sprinkle chopped nuts on top, serve the dessert with a cookie, and you will have a delightful coupe or sundae.

1 layer light sponge cake (any variety), 10 inches (25 cm) in diameter and approximately ⅛ inch (3 mm) thick
1 recipe Chocolate Sauce (page 413)
1 recipe Chantilly Cream (page 765)

Caramel Ice Cream (recipe follows)
Shaved chocolate
16 Caramel Cages (page 618)
Sour Cream Mixture for Piping (page 727)

1. Use a plain, round cookie cutter, 2 inches (5 cm) in diameter, to cut 16 rounds from the sponge layer. Cover and reserve.

2. Place a portion of the chocolate sauce in a piping bottle.

3. Place the Chantilly cream in a pastry bag with a No. 6 (12-mm) plain tip. Reserve in the refrigerator.

4. Presentation: Using a No. 10 (4-ounce/120-ml) scoop, place a scoop of caramel ice cream on top of a sponge round. Place the sponge and ice cream in the center of a dessert plate. Pipe small mounds of Chantilly cream, tall enough to elevate the caramel cage above the ice cream, on the plate, forming a ring around the base of the ice cream scoop. The whipped cream ring should be the same size as the bottom of the caramel cages. Place chocolate shavings on top of the ice cream. Set a caramel cage over the ice cream, resting it on the whipped cream mounds. Pipe just enough chocolate sauce on the plate around the dessert to cover the base of the plate. Decorate the sauce with the sour cream mixture (see pages 681 to 685). Serve immediately.

CARAMEL ICE CREAM yield: approximately 5 cups (1 L 200 ml)

½ recipe Clear Caramel Sauce (page 328)
1 quart (960 ml) half-and-half
10 egg yolks (⅞ cup/210 ml)

2 cups (480 ml) heavy cream
½ recipe Nougatine Crunch (page 586)

1. Reserve ⅓ cup (80 ml) of the caramel sauce. Place the remaining caramel sauce and the half-and-half in a saucepan and heat the mixture to the scalding point.

2. Whip the egg yolks and the reserved caramel sauce until fluffy. Gradually add the scalded half-and-half mixture to the egg yolks while whipping rapidly. Heat the mixture over simmering water, stirring constantly with a whisk or wooden spoon, until it is thick enough to coat the spoon. Remove from the heat and blend in the heavy cream. Let the custard cool slightly at room temperature, then cover and refrigerate until thoroughly chilled.

3. Process in an ice cream freezer according to the manufacturer's directions. Stir in the nougatine crunch and store the finished ice cream, covered, in the freezer.

Cassata Parfait with Meringue yield: 16 servings (Color Photo 44)

This variation of the traditional Italian dessert *cassata Neapolitan* is a good choice to make ahead. All of the components can be prepared in advance and held in their proper place for quick last-minute assembly. Although advance preparation is possible with most frozen desserts, this one has quite an elegant appearance. If you must leave out the pâte à choux ornaments to save time, the dessert will still look and taste great; it will simply be a bit more ordinary in appearance.

Because the whole cherries used for garnish are unpitted, I always cut 1 in half to expose the pit, just before putting it on the plate. I think it looks good and it also alerts the customer to the pits.

1 recipe French Meringue (page 780)

Dark coating chocolate, melted

$\frac{1}{2}$ cup (120 ml) heavy cream

Cassata Parfait (recipe follows)

$\frac{1}{2}$ recipe Cherry Sauce (recipe follows)

16 Lace Pâte à Choux Decorations (recipe follows)

Approximately 75 fresh cherries, stems on

Powdered sugar

1. Cut out a cardboard rectangle measuring $3\frac{1}{2} \times 2\frac{1}{2}$ inches (8.7×6.2 cm). Using the cardboard as a guide and a heavy marking pen, trace 20 rectangles, evenly spaced, on a sheet of baking paper. Place a second sheet of baking paper on top.

2. Place the meringue in a pastry bag with a No. 3 (6-mm) plain tip. Pipe out rows of meringue within each rectangle in a back-and-forth pattern. Drag the paper with the meringue onto a sheet pan. Place a new sheet of paper over your template and pipe 20 additional rectangles in the same manner. (You need only 32 for this recipe, but some will inevitably break.) Drag the second sheet of meringue rectangles to a second sheet pan.

3. Bake the meringue rectangles at 210° to 220°F (99° to 104°C) until dry, approximately 2 hours. Let cool completely.

4. Dip the short ends of the rectangles into melted coating chocolate, covering $\frac{1}{2}$ inch (1.2 cm). Set aside. If you do not plan to serve all of the meringues the same day, dip only as many as you expect to need (2 per serving). Before they are dipped in chocolate, the meringue rectangles can be kept for several weeks, stored in a warm, dry place. If they soften, they can be dried again in a low oven.

5. Whip the heavy cream to stiff peaks. Place in a pastry bag with a No. 4 (8-mm) plain tip. Reserve in the refrigerator.

6. Unmold the frozen cassata parfait and, using a knife dipped in hot water, cut it into slices, ³/₄ inch (2 cm) thick. Do not cut more slices than you will need. Place each slice on top of an inverted meringue rectangle (you will have meringue rectangles left over). Reserve the assembled cassatas (and any uncut cassata) in the freezer. Place the cherry sauce in a piping bottle.

7. Presentation: Pipe a small dot of whipped cream on the base of a dessert plate toward the back. Place a prepared cassata on top. Pipe a rosette of whipped cream on top of the cassata on the left side. Position a meringue rectangle in back of and partially on top of the cassata to expose the parfait. Place a pâte à choux decoration against the front of the cassata. Place 4 or 5 cherries on the left in front of the dessert. Following the curve of the plate, pipe dots of cherry sauce in decreasing size between the fresh cherries and the dessert. Sift powdered sugar lightly over the entire plate and serve immediately.

CASSATA PARFAIT yield: 8 cups (1 L 920 ml)

The traditional candied fruit mixture includes cherries as well as orange or other citrus peel. If you are unable to find candied cherries, you may substitute maraschino cherries. Cut them in half, then stem, rinse, and dry thoroughly. The green color of angelica adds a nice contrast if you can find it. Please do not substitute artificially colored green cherries.

2¹/₂ cups (600 ml) heavy cream	2 tablespoons (30 ml) water
2 whole eggs	4 ounces (115 g) mixed candied fruit
6 egg yolks (¹/₂ cup/120 ml)	4 ounces (115 g) Small Almond Macaroons (page 57)
2 ounces (55 g) granulated sugar	
3 tablespoons (45 ml) honey	¹/₄ cup (60 ml) maraschino liqueur

1. If you do not have a rectangular form measuring 12 × 3¹/₂ × 2¹/₂ inches (30 × 8.7 × 6.2 cm), use the instructions given in the recipe for White Chocolate and Pistachio Pâté (page 472) to make a form of this size from corrugated cardboard. You can use any form close to the specified size. Adjust the size of the meringue rectangles accordingly. Line the inside of the form with baking paper and set aside.

2. Whip the heavy cream to stiff peaks. Cover and reserve in the refrigerator.

3. Whip the whole eggs and egg yolks at high speed for 3 minutes. While the eggs are whipping, combine the sugar, honey, and water in a saucepan. Bring to a boil, lower the speed on the mixer, and add the hot syrup to the whipped eggs. Whip at high speed until the mixture is light and fluffy and has cooled completely.

4. Cut the candied fruit into raisin-sized pieces. Cut the macaroons into ¹/₂-inch (1.2-cm) pieces. Put the cookie pieces in a bowl. Add the maraschino liqueur and toss to coat the cookies with the liqueur. Add the chopped fruit and combine.

5. Fold the reserved whipped cream into the whipped egg mixture. Fold in the fruit and cookie mixture. Spoon into the prepared form and spread the filling smooth on top. Place in the freezer for at least 4 hours or, preferably, overnight.

CHERRY SAUCE yield: 2 cups (480 ml)

I like to use Bing cherries here when I can get them, because their dark skin gives the sauce a rich color. If you use canned cherries, strain out the syrup and reserve for another use or discard. You may want to adjust the amount of sugar, depending on the type of cherries and wine used.

1 pound (455 g) fresh cherries *or* canned sweet cherries

1½ cups (360 ml) red wine

8 ounces (225 g) granulated sugar

Grated zest of 1 lemon

2 tablespoons (16 g) cornstarch

1 teaspoon (5 ml) vanilla extract

1. Wash the cherries, pit them, and place in a saucepan.

2. Reserve ¼ cup (60 ml) wine. Add the remaining 1¼ cups (300 ml) to the cherries in the pan. Stir in the sugar and lemon zest. Bring to a boil and cook over medium heat until the cherries are soft; cook canned cherries only about 5 minutes. Puree the mixture, then strain. Discard the solids in the strainer. Return the juice to the cleaned saucepan.

3. Dissolve the cornstarch in the reserved wine. Stir into the strained cherry liquid. Bring to a boil and cook for a few seconds. Remove from the heat and add the vanilla. Serve hot or cold.

LACE PATE A CHOUX DECORATIONS yield: variable

Unlike tuile paste, Florentina batter, caramel glass paste, and some other materials used to create decorations, pâte à choux cannot be formed into a three-dimensional shape after baking. It must be baked in the precise shape desired — curved, in this case — which makes these ornaments that much more interesting and unusual to anyone who realizes the technique required.

¼ cup (60 ml) whole milk

½ ounce (15 g) unsalted butter

3 tablespoons (22.5 g) bread flour

¼ teaspoon (1 g) salt

2 egg yolks

Whole milk, as needed

1. Prepare the ingredients listed as you would pâte à choux (see page 783). Force the finished paste through a fine strainer and cover tightly.

2. Using a dark marking pen, trace the design shown in Figure 5-3 onto a sheet of baking paper. The figure, as shown, is the correct size for use in this recipe.

3. Cut out at least 20 rectangles of baking paper measuring 6½ × 3½ inches (16.2 × 8.7 cm). Place 1 or 2 heatproof circular molds, 6 to 8 inches (15 to 20 cm) in diameter, on a sheet pan and secure them so they do not roll. Round stainless steel bain-marie inserts are ideal.

4. Make a piping bag slightly larger than usual and fill with a portion of the pâte à choux. Cut a very small opening in the bag. Place a baking paper rectangle on top of the template and pipe the pâte à choux on top, tracing the design. Drape the baking paper over the mold with the design going across the mold so the pattern is curved end to end. Tape the baking paper in place. Repeat to make as many decorations as will fit on your molds.

5. Bake at 375°F (190°C) for approximately 6 minutes or until light golden brown. Remove the ornaments carefully; they slide off the baking paper easily once they are baked. Repeat piping and baking until you have made as many decorations as you need, allowing a few extra for breakage. The ornaments can be stored for up to 2 weeks in an airtight container.

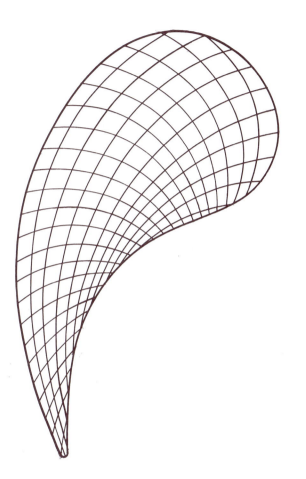

FIGURE 5-3 **The template used to create Lace Pâte à Choux Decorations**

Cherries Jubilee yield: 8 servings

There was a time when Cherries Jubilee was *the* dessert to end an elegant dinner. Not much can be done to change or improve this classic flambéed dessert, except, possibly, in the manner of the presentation. One way to dress up the plate is to serve the ice cream in a container made from meringue, tuile paste, or cocoa-nib wafer paste. (For a meringue shell, follow the directions in the recipe for Vacherin with Plum Ice Cream, page 261.) Place a scoop of white chocolate ice cream in the meringue shell, set it on the plate, and spoon the flaming cherries on top. In the United States, vanilla ice cream is traditional, but I suggest white chocolate ice cream instead because its rich texture is a perfect complement to the cherries.

It is always a good idea to keep macerated cherries in the refrigerator so you can pamper an unexpected guest or friend. This dessert is simple to prepare, and people always enjoy the theatrics of flambéed dishes.

1 pound 6 ounces (625 g) pitted fresh cherries (preferably Bing or Rainier) *or* 1 pound 8 ounces (680 g) drained Guinettes cherries

1 cup (240 ml) kirschwasser

1½ cups (360 ml) Plain Poaching Syrup (page 789) *or* ¾ cup (180 ml) syrup from Guinettes cherries

2½ cups (600 ml) White Chocolate Ice Cream (page 217)

1 tablespoon (8 g) cornstarch

1. If using fresh cherries, poach them as directed for Cherry Sauce (page 230). Reserve ¾ cup (180 ml) poaching liquid and discard the remainder or save for another use. Add the cherries and ¾ cup (180 ml) kirschwasser to the poaching syrup or juice. Macerate the cherries in the liquid for at least 1 hour. If using Guinettes cherries, simply combine the cherries and the syrup they were packed in and proceed; they are already macerated.

2. Scoop ice cream into individual servings; place on a serving platter and reserve in the freezer.

3. About 15 minutes before serving, dissolve the cornstarch in a small portion of the macerating liquid, then stir this back into the remaining liquid and cherries. Transfer to a chafing dish or copper sauté pan. Bring to a boil over medium heat, stirring constantly. Reduce the heat and let simmer for about 1 minute to eliminate the cornstarch flavor.

4. Presentation: Transfer the chafing dish or sauté pan filled with cherries to the stand of the guéridon in the dining room. Put the prepared ice cream and appropriate serving dishes or dessert plates nearby. Continue simmering the cherries, stirring from time to time, for a few minutes. Spoon the ice cream onto the serving dishes. Pour the remaining ¼ cup (60 ml) kirschwasser over the cherries in the pan, raise the flame, and let the liqueur heat a few seconds. Do not stir the liqueur into the sauce. Tilt the pan to ignite the liqueur (this looks a little showier than using a match or lighter) and spoon the flaming cherries over the ice cream. Serve immediately.

Cinnamon Semifreddo Venezia with Coffee Bean Crisps

yield: 12 servings, 4 ounces (120 ml) each

If you do not have individual forms, or are pressed for time, you can use a small loaf pan, 6 cups (1L 440 ml) in capacity, instead. Line the bottom and sides with baking paper, letting the paper extend over the top of the pan on all sides. Fill with the semifreddo mixture and cover the top with the flaps of paper. Freeze, unmold, remove the paper, and slice into individual servings.

½ recipe Joconde Sponge Base II (page 671; see Note)

2½ cups (600 ml) heavy cream

9 egg yolks (¾ cup/180 ml)

6 ounces (170 g) plus 1 teaspoon (5 g) granulated sugar

½ cup (120 ml) dry marsala

1 tablespoon (15 ml) lemon juice

1½ teaspoons (2 g) ground cinnamon

Finely grated zest of 1 orange

1½ ounces (40 g) candied orange peel, finely chopped

2 ounces (55 g) roasted coffee beans, coarsely crushed to the size of cocoa nibs

½ recipe Cocoa-Nib Wafer Paste (page 720), made without cocoa nibs

½ recipe Orange-Vanilla Decorating Syrup (page 760)

Zested orange peel

Powdered sugar

1. Make the Joconde sponge batter. Spread it out evenly to cover a full-size Silpat (or a sheet pan lined with baking paper). Bake at 400°F (205°C) for approximately 5 minutes or until baked through. Invert onto a sheet of baking paper dusted lightly with bread flour. Let the sponge cool.

2. Peel the Silpat or baking paper off the sponge sheet. Use a plain cookie cutter, 2¼ inches (5.6 cm) in diameter, to cut out 12 rounds. Cover and set aside. Cover the remaining Joconde sheet and reserve for another use. Prepare 12 timbale forms that measure 2¼ inches (5.6 cm) in diameter across the opening and are approximately 2¼ inches (5.6 cm) in height by covering the bottoms of the forms with rounds of baking paper. Set the forms aside.

3. Whip 1½ cups (360 ml) of the heavy cream to soft peaks. Reserve in the refrigerator.

4. Beat the egg yolks and 6 ounces (170 g) of the granulated sugar in a stainless steel bowl until light and fluffy. Beat in the marsala and lemon juice. Place the bowl over simmering water and continue to whip constantly until the mixture reaches 160° to 180°F (71° to 82°C). Be careful not to overheat, or the eggs will curdle. The mixture should be light in color and thick enough to coat a spoon.

5. Remove the bowl from the heat and set it over ice water. Continue whipping until it is cold. Stir in the cinnamon, grated orange zest, and candied orange peel. Fold this mixture into the reserved whipped cream.

6. Divide the mixture among the prepared timbales. Cover the top of each with a sponge round. Cover and place in the freezer for a minimum of 4 hours.

7. Stir the crushed coffee beans into the wafer paste. Spread half of the paste into a very thin strip, 6 inches (15 cm) wide, on a Silpat. Bake at 375°F (190°C) until done, approximately 8 minutes. Let cool. Break the strip into irregularly shaped pieces the width of the strip. Continue with the remaining batter until you have made a few more garnishes than needed.

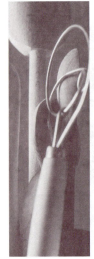

About Semifreddo

Semifreddo is an Italian word denoting a cold dessert, literally half frozen. A semifreddo is indeed put in the freezer, but because the base contains a large proportion of sugar and/or alcohol, it does not become completely hard.

The basic semifreddo mixture is made from whipped eggs or egg yolks, sugar, and various flavorings, usually including a spirit or liqueur. Whipped cream and/or meringue are folded into this mixture and the base is still frozen. The semifreddo base could be described as a combination of a sabayon and a parfait. In one version of semifreddo, the base is poured into individual forms before freezing and the frozen desserts are unmolded for service. Semifreddos are also made by layering the base with cake, custard, fruit ice or macerated fresh fruit, ice cream, crushed cookies, chopped chocolate, or nuts. These are typically made in sizes for multiple servings, molded in a loaf or half-sphere, and sliced to create servings. Further, the term *semifreddo* is used generically in some cases to refer to any dessert that is served chilled or partially thawed. In Spain, where the dessert is also popular, it is known as *semifrío*.

8. Adjust the consistency of the orange syrup so it will flow into a smooth, even puddle. Pour the syrup into a piping bottle. Add a small amount of syrup to the zested orange peel and mix to coat the zest with the sauce. This is done to make the zest shine; do not use so much syrup that the pieces of zest stick together.

9. Whip the remaining 1 cup (240 ml) heavy cream and 1 teaspoon (5 g) sugar to stiff peaks. Place in a pastry bag fitted with a large star tip. Reserve in the refrigerator.

10. Presentation: Using a blowtorch, warm the side of a timbale, or quickly dip the mold into hot water. Unmold and place, sponge-side down, in the center of a serving plate; if necessary, peel the paper away from the top. Pipe orange syrup into irregular puddles around the dessert. Decorate the syrup randomly with zested orange peel. Pipe a rosette of whipped cream on top of the dessert and place a coffee-bean crisp at an angle on top of the cream. Sift powdered sugar lightly over the crisp and serve immediately.

NOTE: One Joconde sheet will yield about 50 sponge rounds of the size needed here but it makes sense to prepare the extra, as it is not practical to make a smaller portion, the remaining sheet can be refrigerated and/or frozen for weeks, and Joconde is always useful to have in reserve. If you have chocolate sponge cake on hand, you can use that instead. Slice it very thin, then cut out rounds.

Frozen Hazelnut Coffee Mousse yield: 16 servings (Color Photo 43)

Austria's capital, Vienna, plays a significant role in the history of baking and pastry making. Some of the many famous creations said to have originated in or been inspired by this noble city are croissants, pretzels, Gugelhupf, and Sacher Torte. Vienna is also known for its numerous special blends of coffee, the most famous of which is called Viennese roast. While the city is full of *kaffehauses* (coffee houses) that display tempting pastries to accompany cups of coffee, smaller shops, all over town and throughout Austria, sell nothing but coffee in every imaginable combination of roast, flavor, and strength. These shops generally have no chairs; instead, everyone stands at a long counter sipping and savoring that perfect cup of fresh coffee.

Frozen hazelnut coffee mousse is an adapted version of a dessert I had years ago at the Palais Schwarzenberg restaurant in Vienna. Although the combination of coffee and hazelnuts is a classic, I think you will find they come together particularly well here. When you serve this with an excellent cup of coffee, the meal will certainly end on a happy note.

Hazelnut-Coffee Mousse Filling (recipe follows)

½ recipe Orange Sauce (page 278)

½ recipe Raspberry Sauce (page 173)

Piping Chocolate (page 543), melted

16 Cocoa-Nib Florentina Cups (page 689)

2 cups (480 ml) raspberries

1½ cups (360 ml) blueberries

16 Black-Tie Strawberries (procedure follows)

1. Divide the hazelnut coffee mousse filling evenly among 16 tubes 2½ inches (6.2 cm) tall × 2 inches (5 cm) wide lined with strips of acetate. Alternatively, use any round molds that are close to the same size and capacity — such as, appropriately enough, espresso coffee cups with straight sides. Level the tops, then place the molds in the freezer for at least 4 hours or, preferably, overnight.

2. Unmold as many mousses as you plan to serve by pushing them out of the tubes and removing the plastic or by dipping each mold into hot water for about 10 seconds, just long enough to loosen the filling. Insert a small fork into the mousse, invert, and twist the fork to unmold. Place on a sheet pan lined with baking paper and reserve in the freezer.

3. Place the orange sauce and the raspberry sauce in separate piping bottles.

4. Presentation: Pipe orange sauce and raspberry sauce in irregular bands around the perimeter of the base of a dessert plate. Pipe a large dot of piping chocolate in the center of the plate. Place a serving of mousse in a Florentina shell and set the shell on the chocolate. Arrange a few raspberries and blueberries around the mousse in the shell. Top the mousse with a black-tie strawberry. Serve immediately.

HAZELNUT-COFFEE MOUSSE FILLING yield: 10 cups (2 L 400 ml)

3 ounces (85 g) lightly toasted hazelnuts (see Chef's Tip)

2 teaspoons (6 g) pectin powder (see Note)

10 ounces (280 g) granulated sugar

3 cups (720 ml) heavy cream

1 teaspoon (3 g) unflavored gelatin powder

¼ cup (60 ml) cold water

¼ cup (60 ml) coffee liqueur

¼ cup (60 ml) strong brewed coffee

7 eggs, separated

1. Remove as much skin as possible from the toasted hazelnuts by rubbing them between your palms or in a towel. Thoroughly combine the pectin powder and 2 ounces (55 g) of the sugar. Add the toasted nuts and use a food processor to grind the mixture to a very fine consistency.

2. Whip the heavy cream to soft peaks. Cover and reserve in the refrigerator.

3. Sprinkle the gelatin powder over the cold water and set aside to soften.

4. Add the coffee liqueur and brewed coffee to the egg yolks. Heat, whipping constantly, over

About Hazelnuts

Hazelnuts, also known as *filberts,* are the acorn-shaped fruit of the hazel tree. Generally, in Europe the two names are used interchangeably, but in the United States the word *hazelnut* denotes the wild variety and *filbert* denotes either of the two species of cultivated nuts: the cob and the filbert. Both cob nuts and filberts are larger than the wild hazelnut.

Hazelnuts (and filberts) are harvested in the early fall and are sold in many forms: in the shell, shelled, whole, skin-on, blanched, chopped, and ground. After almonds, hazelnuts are the most widely used nut in the bakeshop; their flavor complements many of the ingredients we use every day, especially chocolate and many varieties of fruit.

The skin on hazelnuts does not have to be removed, but as the flavor of the nuts is intensified by toasting and as toasting, in turn, loosens the skin, it is usually removed. The easiest way to remove the skin is to rub the toasted nuts in a dry towel. This will remove the majority of the skin from the majority of the nuts. If you want to remove all of the skin, begin by blanching the raw nuts in water to which a bit of baking soda has been added. Let the nuts stand in the water for about 5 minutes, drain, and then rub the skin off in a towel. The blanched nuts can then be toasted, if desired.

CHEF'S TIP

If you have ground hazelnuts on hand, toast and use them in this recipe; skip Step 1 and add all the sugar and the pectin powder to the egg whites.

simmering water until the mixture reaches 140°F (60°C). Do not overheat. Remove from the bain-marie and whip to a light and fluffy consistency.

5. Add the remaining 8 ounces (225 g) sugar to the egg whites. Heat over simmering water, stirring constantly, until the mixture reaches 140°F (60°C). Remove from the heat and continue whipping until stiff peaks form and the meringue is cooled. Fold the yolk mixture into the reserved whipped cream together with the nut mixture. Mix into the meringue.

6. Heat the gelatin over a bain-marie to dissolve. Do not overheat. Quickly stir the gelatin mixture into a small portion of the filling. Working rapidly, add this to the remaining filling.

NOTE: This measurement is for regular canning pectin sold in grocery stores. If you have the stronger commercial pectin, use only half the amount.

BLACK-TIE STRAWBERRIES yield: variable

These cute dressed-up berries should not be restricted to plated dessert decorations. They make a great addition to a buffet or to a cookie or pastry tray, and they can be made a day ahead if kept, well covered, in the refrigerator. Use large berries or, better, long-stemmed strawberries to make them even more elegant.

When making the black-tie strawberries, be sure enough melted white chocolate is in the bowl for the berries to be dipped straight down without touching the bottom. It is a good idea not to dip the berries straight from the refrigerator but to allow them to come to room temperature first. If the strawberries are cold, condensation may form on the skin, which would ruin the chocolate coating.

Fresh, well-shaped large strawberries, stems on

Tempered white chocolate or white coating chocolate, melted

Tempered sweet dark chocolate or dark coating chocolate, melted

1. Wash and thoroughly dry the strawberries.

2. Holding the hull, dip 1 berry at a time into the melted white chocolate, coating three-quarters of the berry. Move the berry up and down over the bowl of chocolate a few times to allow excess chocolate to drip off, then scrape the bottom against the side of the bowl to remove more chocolate. Set the strawberry on a sheet pan lined with baking paper. Repeat with the remaining berries. If the chocolate spreads out around the berry on the pan, forming a foot, drag the berry to a clean spot on the baking paper before the chocolate hardens.

3. To put tuxedo jackets on the strawberries, pick up a white chocolate–coated berry by the hull and dip the lower two-thirds into melted dark chocolate, first at a 45-degree angle to the left side and then at the same angle to the right (see Color Photo 43). Return the berry to the sheet pan lined with baking paper, setting it on a clean section of the pan. Repeat with the remaining berries, moving them on the paper as before if they begin to form feet.

4. Place a small amount of melted dark chocolate in a piping bag and cut a very small opening. Pipe 3 small buttons and a bow tie on the white shirt portion of each strawberry.

5. Chill a sheet pan lined with baking paper. A few at a time, pipe dots of dark chocolate, ¾ inch (2 cm) in diameter, on the pan and stand a strawberry in the chocolate, holding it for a few seconds until the chocolate hardens.

CHEF'S TIP

To make the black-tie strawberries easier to handle and more pastrylike, place them on top of a small cookie made from short dough. Roll out short dough to ⅛ inch (3 mm) thick. Use a plain or fluted cutter, 1½ inches (3.7 cm) in diameter, to cut out cookies. Bake, let cool to room temperature, and place in the refrigerator until the cookies are chilled. Pipe a large dot of dark chocolate on each cookie and top with a strawberry standing on end.

Frozen Raspberry Mousse with Meringues yield: 16 servings, 5 ounces (150 ml) each

Mousse is a hard-to-define French word for a dish made in so many ways it is impossible to generalize. Savory mousses, usually offered as an appetizer, can be made from seafood, poultry, meat, vegetables, or liver. These may be served hot or cold, but never frozen. In the pastry kitchen, the term *mousse* typically refers to a sweet dessert, flavored with fruit or liqueur, served either cold or frozen. The classic sweet mousses, of course, are flavored with chocolate or coffee and are made in innumerable variations. Frozen dessert mousses, sometimes called *ice mousses,* are similar in composition to parfaits, except that a parfait contains beaten egg yolks rather than whipped egg whites. A dessert mousse sometimes has both.

Frozen mousses do not need to be fortified with gelatin, as do most cold mousses — chocolate mousse being the exception, as chocolate is itself a thickening agent. In the recipe for raspberry mousse that follows, a small amount of pectin is used to help prevent the filling from losing its shape when the desserts begin to thaw as they are prepared for service.

Raspberry Mousse Filling (recipe follows)

½ recipe Meringue Noisette batter (page 781), made with 5 egg whites

1 cup (240 ml) heavy cream

1 teaspoon (5 g) granulated sugar

1 recipe Mousseline Sauce (page 338)

¼ cup (60 ml) Riesling wine

Small fresh raspberries

Chocolate Sauce for Piping (page 681)

I. Place 16 cake rings, 3 inches (7.5 cm) in diameter and 2 inches (5 cm) in height, on a sheet pan lined with baking paper (see Note). Line the inside of the rings with strips of acetate or polyurethane. Divide the raspberry mousse filling evenly among the rings, filling them three-quarters full so the mousses are 1½ inches (3.7 cm) tall. Tap the pan firmly against the table to level the tops of the mousses. Cover and place in the freezer for at least 4 hours or, preferably, overnight.

2. Place the meringue noisette batter in a pastry bag with a No. 3 (6-mm) plain tip. Pipe out 3-inch (7.5-cm) circles following the instructions given in the recipe for Meringue Noisette (see Figure 14-2, page 782). You need 32 for this recipe, but you should get about 35. Bake at 250°F (122°C) for about 40 minutes or until dry. Set aside the 16 best-looking shells to use for the tops.

3. Remove the cake rings from as many servings of frozen mousse as you are planning to serve and peel away the strips of plastic. If you used plastic strips alone instead of cake rings, simply cut the strips. Place an unmolded mousse on each of the bottom meringues and set the reserved meringues on top. Press lightly to be sure they adhere. Return the servings to the freezer.

4. Whip the cream and sugar to stiff peaks. Place in a pastry bag with a No. 3 (6-mm) star tip. Reserve in the refrigerator until time of service. Flavor the mousseline sauce with the Riesling and place a portion of the sauce in a piping bottle.

5. Presentation: Pipe mousseline sauce in a circle on the base of a dessert plate, leaving a small area exposed in the center of the plate. Pipe a dot of whipped cream on the uncovered spot and place a frozen raspberry mousse on top. Pipe a border of small dots or kisses of whipped cream on the top meringue. Place 5 raspberries, standing on end, within the cream border. Decorate the mousseline sauce with the chocolate sauce for piping (see pages 681 to 685). Serve immediately.

NOTE: If you do not have the correct size of cake rings available, you can easily make your own. Cut 16 strips of polyurethane or acetate to 9½ × 1½ inches (23.7 × 3.7 cm). Tape the ends together, overlapping them ½ inch (1.2 cm), to create rings measuring 3 inches (7.5 cm) in diameter. As a second alternative, use soufflé ramekins, 3¼ inches (8.1 cm) in diameter and 5 ounces (150 ml) in capacity. Unmold each frozen mousse from its ramekin by dipping the bottom and sides of the mold briefly into hot water, just long enough to loosen the mousse, then gently use a fork to help remove it. Take care not to get any water on the mousse itself.

RASPBERRY MOUSSE FILLING yield: about 2¾ quarts (2 L 640 ml)

3 cups (720 ml) heavy cream

2 tablespoons (18 g) pectin powder (see Note)

8 ounces (225 g) granulated sugar

5 egg whites (⅝ cup/150 ml)

3 ounces (90 ml) Chambord

1 pound (455 g) fresh raspberries, pureed and strained (see Chef's Tip)

1. Whip the cream to stiff peaks. Cover and reserve in the refrigerator.

2. Combine the pectin powder and sugar. Add the egg whites. Heat the mixture over simmering water, whipping constantly, until it reaches 140°F (60°C). Be careful not to let the egg whites get too hot, or they will coagulate. Remove from the heat and whip until the mixture has cooled and formed stiff peaks.

3. Add the liqueur to the raspberry puree. Gradually (to prevent lumps) fold the puree into the reserved whipped cream. Fold this mixture into the whipped egg whites.

NOTE: Use regular pectin for canning fruit. Pure pectin is too strong for this purpose.

> **CHEF'S TIP**
> A quick alternative is to use frozen unsweetened raspberry juice, which is now readily available.

Ice Cream Cake Jamaica yield: 2 cakes, 10 inches (25 cm) in diameter

Ice cream cakes, like all cakes, are a faster and more efficient way of preparing a number of servings instead of making individual portions. They are also a bit unusual today and can remind us of ice cream sandwiches we enjoyed as children, which consisted of a rectangular slab of ice cream between two cake-like chocolate cookies, a treat that has been around since the early 1900s. Here, dark rum — both in the ice cream and in the mousseline sauce — give this dessert its Caribbean nametag.

1 ounce (30 g) unsweetened cocoa powder

2 ounces (55 g) plus 2 tablespoons (30 g) granulated sugar

½ recipe French Meringue (page 780; see Step 2)

Dark coating chocolate, melted

Rum Parfait (recipe follows)

2½ cups (600 ml) Vanilla Ice Cream (page 172)

1 quart (960 ml) heavy cream

Macadamia nuts, toasted and coarsely crushed

½ recipe Mango Coulis (page 244)

Rum Decorating Syrup (page 762)

Plantain Chips (page 722)

1. Draw 4 circles, 10 inches (25 cm) in diameter, on baking papers. Invert the papers, place them on sheet pans, and set aside.

2. Combine the cocoa powder and 2 ounces (55 g) of the granulated sugar and add to the French meringue on low speed as it is finished whipping.

3. Place the meringue in a pastry bag with a No. 3 (6-mm) plain tip. Pipe the meringue inside the circles on the reserved papers, starting in the center and making a spiral to the outside (see Figure 14-2, page 782).

4. Bake at 210° to 220°F (99° to 104°C) for approximately 1 hour or until dry. Let the

About Jamaican Rum

Rum production began in the Caribbean in the early 1600s, years after Christopher Columbus brought sugarcane to the area from the Azores. The rum industry developed in step with the growth of sugar plantations on the islands. Rum is distilled from byproducts of the sugar-making process; molasses is typically used as the base. The darker and heavier rums, known as *Jamaican-style rums*, are produced mostly in (not surprisingly) Jamaica, Barbados, and Guyana, which is on Central America's east coast, along the Demerara River. These are made from a combination of molasses and the skimmings from sugar boiling vats. The mixture is allowed to ferment to improve the rum's aroma and flavor. After distilling, the rum is darkened with caramel and is aged (in oak barrels for the finer varieties) up to seven years.

meringues cool completely, then brush a thin layer of melted coating chocolate on the top of all 4 meringue circles.

5. Place 2 of the meringues, chocolate-side up, on cardboard cake rounds, 12 inches (30 cm) in diameter, for support. Place cake rings, 10 inches (25 cm) in diameter, on top of the meringues and trim the meringues to fit the rings. If the rings are not made of stainless steel, line the insides with polyurethane or acetate strips to prevent the metal from staining the filling. (If you do not have cake rings, using the plastic strips alone works fine. Wrap them around the trimmed meringues and tape the ends together.) Place in the freezer until chilled.

6. Gradually add the rum parfait to the vanilla ice cream; the ice cream must be soft but should not be liquid. Divide the mixture between the prepared forms. Place the remaining meringue shells, chocolate-side down, on top of the filling. Trim the meringues, if necessary, to fit them inside the rings. Cover and place in the freezer for at least 4 hours or, preferably, overnight.

FIGURE 5-4 Placing a pastry tip outside the bag over a tip already in place

7. Whip the heavy cream with the remaining 2 tablespoons (30 g) sugar until stiff peaks form. Remove the cake rings and plastic strips from the cakes. Return 1 cake to the freezer. Spread just enough whipped cream on the top and sides of the other cake to cover.

8. Cut the cake into serving pieces. Sprinkle macadamia nuts over the center 6 inches (15 cm) of the cake. Return the cake to the freezer. Repeat with the second cake.

9. Place the remaining whipped cream in a pastry bag with a No. 7 (14-mm) star tip. Reserve in the refrigerator until time of service. Place a portion of the mango coulis in a piping bottle. Place the rum syrup in a second piping bottle.

10. Presentation: Pipe a small dot of whipped cream slightly off-center on a chilled dessert plate. Place a slice of cake on top. Place a No. 4 (8-mm) plain tip on the outside of

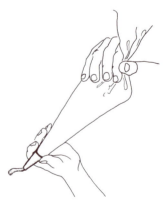

FIGURE 5-5 Holding the new tip in place as the contents are piped out

the pastry bag with the whipped cream and hold it in place as you pipe (Figures 5-4 and 5-5). Pipe whipped cream onto the iced side of the slice in a vertical zigzag pattern. Remove the plain tip and pipe a rosette on top of the slice near the end. Place a small piece of plantain chip on the rosette. Pipe mango coulis and rum syrup decoratively on the plate.

RUM PARFAIT yield: 8 cups (1 L 920 ml)

5 ounces (140 g) golden raisins

¾ cup (180 ml) dark rum

⅓ cup (80 ml) or 4 ounces (115 g) light corn syrup

8 egg yolks (⅔ cup/160 ml)

1 tablespoon (9 g) unflavored gelatin powder

¼ cup (60 ml) cold water

4½ cups (1 L 80 ml) heavy cream

1. Combine the raisins and rum in a nonreactive saucepan and heat to about 175°F (80°C). Remove from the heat and let the raisins macerate in the rum overnight.

2. Place the corn syrup in a small saucepan and bring to a boil. Whip the egg yolks for 1 minute. Gradually pour the hot corn syrup into the egg yolks while whipping constantly and continue to whip until the mixture is cool and fluffy.

3. Sprinkle the gelatin over the cold water and set aside to soften.

4. Whip the heavy cream to soft peaks.

5. Place the gelatin mixture over a bain-marie and heat until dissolved. Do not overheat. Rapidly mix the gelatin into a small part of the whipped cream, then stir this into the remaining cream. Gradually fold the rum, raisins, and the egg mixture into the cream. Although the filling must be used soon after it is made, it should start to thicken slightly before it is used to fill the cakes. If it is too liquid, it may leak out.

CHEF'S TIP
If you do not have time to macerate the raisins overnight, it is better to omit them. If the raisins do not absorb enough rum, they will be hard and unpleasant to eat when frozen.

Lingonberry Parfait yield: 16 servings

Lingonberry parfait is a simple and spectacular choice to cool and refresh your guests on a hot day. The pretty, pale pink, slightly tart parfait is a perfect companion to the sweeter, vibrant red cranberry coulis. The recipe assumes you are using lingonberries from a can or jar, to which sugar is invariably added. Depending on the sweetness of your brand, you may need to adjust the amount of sugar in the recipe. Not only should the flavor of the parfait be on the tart side but, in addition, too much sugar will inhibit freezing.

In the event you are lucky enough to find fresh or frozen berries, you must first cook them to a jam-like consistency, adding sugar to taste (reserve a few fresh berries for decoration). Cranberries, fresh or frozen, may be substituted for the lingonberries with excellent results, although the parfait will not have quite the same exotic taste or appeal as when made with the "red gold" of the Scandinavian forest.

For simplicity, the chocolate cake rounds may be left out, in which case you may have to freeze the batter to thicken it slightly before filling the rings to avoid leakage. It is also a good idea to pipe a dot of whipped cream in the center of the dessert plates before putting the parfaits on top to keep the desserts from sliding.

Dark Chocolate Cake Rounds (recipe follows)

Parfait Filling (recipe follows)

¾ cup (180 ml) heavy cream

1 teaspoon (5 g) granulated sugar

Cranberry Coulis (recipe follows)

Sour Cream Mixture for Piping (page 727)

16 Chocolate Figurines (page 545) *or* 16 Chocolate Cutouts (page 520)

1. Place 16 cake rings, 3 inches (7.5 cm) in diameter and 2 inches (5 cm) in height, on a sheet pan lined with baking paper. Line the rings with strips of acetate, other thin plastic, or baking paper. If you do not have cake rings this size or slightly smaller, you can make them easily from polyurethane or acetate. To make plastic rings, cut 16 strips, 9½ × 1½ inches (23.7 × 3.7 cm) each. Bend the strips around the outside of a plain 3-inch (7.5-cm) cookie cutter to form them, tape the ends together, and remove from the cutter. These forms do not need to be lined.

2. Place the cake rounds inside the rings. Divide the parfait filling equally among the rings. Cover and place in the freezer for at least 4 hours or, preferably, overnight.

3. Whip the heavy cream and sugar to stiff peaks. Place in a pastry bag with a No. 8 (16-mm) star tip. Reserve in the refrigerator.

4. Remove the rings and peel away the paper or plastic from as many parfaits as you plan to serve; parfaits left in the rings can be stored in the freezer for up to 2 weeks if well covered. Return the parfaits to the freezer. Place a portion of the cranberry coulis in a piping bottle (if necessary, first adjust the consistency of the coulis so that it just levels out when piped).

5. Presentation: Pipe just enough cranberry coulis over the base of a dessert plate to cover. Using a piping bag, pipe 2 concentric circles of sour cream mixture, about ½ inch (1.2 cm) apart, close to the perimeter of the coulis. Drag a wooden skewer through the lines toward the outside of the plate, every 1 inch (2.5 cm) or so, all around the sauce. Place a parfait in the center of the plate. Pipe a rosette of whipped cream on top. Decorate the cream with a chocolate figurine or chocolate cutout and serve at once.

DARK CHOCOLATE CAKE ROUNDS

yield: I sheet, 12 × 16 inches (30 × 40 cm), or 16 rounds, 3 inches (7.5 cm) in diameter

8 eggs, separated

5 ounces (140 g) granulated sugar

7 ounces (200 g) sweet dark chocolate, melted

1½ ounces (40 g) bread flour, sifted

1. Beat the egg yolks with half of the sugar until light and fluffy. Set aside.

2. Whip the egg whites to a foam. Gradually add the remaining sugar and whip to soft peaks.

3. Combine the melted chocolate with the egg yolk mixture. Carefully fold in the egg whites and the flour. Spread the batter to a rectangle measuring 12 × 16 inches (30 × 40 cm) on a sheet of baking paper. Drag the paper onto a sheet pan (see Figure 9-22, page 481).

4. Bake immediately at 375°F (190°C) for about 15 minutes or until the top feels firm and springy. Let cool completely.

5. Unmold and remove the baking paper from the baked sheet. Use a 3-inch (7.5-cm) plain cookie cutter to cut out 16 rounds. If you are using cake rings of a different size in Step 1 of the main recipe, adjust the size of the cake rounds accordingly.

PARFAIT FILLING yield: approximately 9 cups (2 L 160 ml)

14 ounces (400 g) sweetened lingonberries
(to use fresh lingonberries, see introduction to main recipe)

⅓ cup (80 ml) lime juice (from 2 limes)

3 cups (720 ml) heavy cream

5 whole eggs

6 egg yolks (½ cup/120 ml)

4 ounces (115 g) granulated sugar

1. Puree the lingonberries just until smooth. Do not overpuree, or you will add too much air and the mixture will lose color. Stir in the lime juice and set aside.

2. Whip the heavy cream to soft peaks. Cover and reserve in the refrigerator.

3. Whip the whole eggs, egg yolks, and sugar over simmering water until the mixture reaches 140°F (60°C). Remove from the heat and continue whipping until the mixture has cooled completely; it should be light and fluffy. Gently fold the reserved whipped cream into the egg mixture, being careful not to deflate it. Fold in the lingonberry puree.

CRANBERRY COULIS yield: 3 cups (720 ml)

12 ounces (340 g) fresh or frozen cranberries

8 ounces (225 g) granulated sugar

2 cups (480 ml) water

1. Combine the cranberries, sugar, and water in a saucepan. Bring to a boil, then reduce the heat and simmer for 10 minutes. The cranberries should be soft and have popped open.

2. Remove from the heat. Puree immediately and strain. Return to a quick boil, then let cool.

3. Skim off any foam that forms on the surface. Store the cranberry coulis, covered, in the refrigerator, but serve it at room temperature. If the coulis is too thick after it cools, thin it with water.

Macadamia Nut Ice Cream in a Chocolate Tulip with Mango Coulis

yield: 16 servings

Pairing macadamia ice cream with vibrant mango coulis in a starkly contrasting chocolate tuile shell makes for a beautiful tropical presentation. Papayas, one of Hawaii's treasures, were grown there long before macadamia nuts were introduced. The Hawaiian chocolate industry, however, is still getting started. It currently markets a good-quality chocolate made from cocoa beans grown at plantations in Kona and Keaau on the big island of Hawaii.

2 kiwis

1 papaya

Mango Coulis (recipe follows)

½ cup (120 ml) Chocolate Sauce (page 413)

Macadamia Nut Ice Cream (recipe follows)

16 Chocolate Tulip Shells (see Note)

2 ounces (55 g) unsalted macadamia nuts,
toasted and crushed

Powdered sugar

About Macadamia Nuts

The macadamia, the king of nuts, is indigenous to Australia and was named for a chemist from that country, Dr. John Macadam, who first discovered the nuts in a Queensland rain forest in 1857. In the late 1800s, the nuts were brought to Hawaii and planted at Kukuihaele on the big island. Soon the macadamia industry was in full bloom. Today, macadamias are the island's third most important agricultural commodity, exceeded only by sugar and pineapple, and Hawaii accounts for approximately 90 percent of the world's macadamia production.

1. Remove the skin from the kiwis as shown in Figure 5-10, page 259. Cut them in half lengthwise, then slice thinly. Remove the skin from the papaya, cut it in half, and scrape out the seeds. Cut the fruit into 16 pieces. Cover and reserve.

2. Place a portion of the mango coulis in a piping bottle.

3. Presentation: Pipe a large, round pool of mango coulis in the center of a dessert plate. Using a piping bag, decorate the perimeter of the coulis with the chocolate sauce (see pages 681 to 685). Use 2 soupspoons to portion a large oval (quenelle-shaped) scoop of ice cream into a chocolate tulip. Set the tulip in the center of the coulis. Garnish the ice cream with the prepared fruit and a sprinkling of macadamia nuts. Sift powdered sugar lightly over the top and serve immediately.

NOTE: Follow the instructions for making the tulip shells on page 715, substituting Chocolate Tuile Decorating Paste (page 695) for the vanilla paste.

MANGO COULIS yield: 4 cups (960 ml)

Use only perfectly ripe mangoes for this sauce. They should yield easily to light pressure and have a pleasant, sweet smell. Unfortunately, the ripe fruits are extremely difficult to peel. I have found the best way is to slice off the two broader sides as close to the large, flat seed as possible, then scoop the flesh from these halves and discard the skin. Cut and scrape the remaining flesh away from the seed.

3 pounds 8 ounces (1 kg 590 g) ripe mangoes (5 or 6) (see note)	¼ cup (60 ml) orange juice
¼ cup (60 ml) lime juice	

1. Peel the mangoes and cut the flesh away from the skin and seed.

2. Place the mango pulp in a food processor with the lime and orange juices. Puree, then use a fine mesh strainer to remove the stringy fibers. Bring the strained puree to a quick boil. Adjust the flavor and consistency with additional lime or orange juice, as desired. Store, covered, in the refrigerator.

NOTE: You may skip both steps 1 and 2, and instead use 3½ cups (840 ml) thawed, frozen mango puree. However, most brands need to be thickened by adding 1 tablespoon (8g) cornstarch and bringing the mixure to a boil. If you add the thickener your will create a sauce rather than a coulis.

MACADAMIA NUT ICE CREAM yield: approximately 2 quarts (1 L 920 ml)

1 pound (455 g) unsalted macadamia nuts

1 quart (960 ml) whole milk

1 vanilla bean

12 egg yolks (1 cup/240 ml)

14 ounces (400 g) granulated sugar

2 cups (480 ml) heavy cream

1 teaspoon (5 ml) vanilla extract

1. Toast the macadamia nuts and set aside to cool. Grind or crush the nuts coarsely, combine with ½ cup (120 ml) of the milk, and grind to a paste in a food processor.

2. Add the vanilla bean to the remaining 3½ cups (840 ml) milk and bring to a boil. Mix in the nut paste. Remove from the heat, cover, and set aside to steep for at least 30 minutes.

3. Whip the egg yolks and sugar until they are light and fluffy and form a slowly dissolving ribbon. Reheat the milk mixture to boiling, then strain through a fine mesh strainer or cheesecloth (see Note). Remove the vanilla bean, cut it in half lengthwise, and, using the back of a paring knife, scrape out the seeds. Stir the seeds into the strained mixture. Discard the vanilla bean pod. Gradually add the hot milk to the beaten yolks while stirring constantly.

4. Cook the custard over hot water, stirring with a whisk or wooden spoon, until it thickens enough to coat the spoon. Stir in the heavy cream and the vanilla extract. Let cool to room temperature, then cover and chill the mixture until it is completely cold.

5. Process in an ice cream freezer according to the manufacturer's directions. Transfer to a chilled container and store, covered, in the freezer.

NOTE: Do not discard these costly nuts. Dry the fine pieces and use them in cookies or in a nut torte. The nuts will not keep long, however, after being soaked in milk.

Mango Ice Cream with Chiffonade of Lemon Mint and a Chocolate Twirl yield: 16 servings (Color Photo 49)

The spectacular chocolate twirls featured in the presentation can be utilized to decorate many desserts. They are especially appropriate with chocolate offerings, and I use them frequently to top a slice of chocolate decadence cake or to decorate Chocolate Ganache Cake (page 27) instead of using a cookie butterfly. Although the twirls are a bit time-consuming to prepare, they can be made up many days in advance (as can the tuile shells and the ice cream) if stored in their protective plastic tubes in a cool, dry place. When preparing the twirls, it is inevitable that some will break. The broken pieces can be used as you would Chocolate Noodles (page 529) — either to decorate another dessert or to be placed on top of the mango ice cream here for a different and almost-as-impressive finish.

½ recipe Cherry Sauce (page 230)

Powdered sugar

16 Magnolia Cookie Shells (see "To Make Magnolia Cookie Shells")

Mango Ice Cream (recipe follows)

Approximately 24 lemon mint leaves, cut in chiffonade

16 Chocolate Twirls (page 533; see Chef's Tip)

To Make Magnolia Cookie Shells

Follow Steps 1 through 4 in the recipe for Red Currant Sorbet in Magnolia Cookie Shells (page 307), using Figure 6-11, page 308, to make only the smaller-size shell, marked B in the template. You will need ½ recipe Vanilla Tuile Decorating Paste (page 695). Before spreading the paste within the template, remove 2 tablespoons (30 ml) paste and color it by thoroughly mixing in 1 teaspoon (2.5 g) sifted cocoa. Before baking the cookie shells, pipe a vertical line of cocoa-colored paste on each flower petal.

CHEF'S TIP

To stabilize the chocolate twirls for this presentation (and keep them from bending or rolling on top of the round ice cream scoop), pipe a thin line of melted coating chocolate, the same length as a finished twirl, on a sheet of baking paper. Set a twirl on top before the chocolate line hardens and hold it in place a few seconds until set. The chocolate will set up faster if you chill the twirls briefly first. Place the twirl so the chocolate line is on the bottom when you put it on the dessert.

1. Place the cherry sauce in a piping bottle and reserve in the refrigerator.

2. Presentation: Sift powdered sugar lightly over the base of a dessert plate. Place a magnolia cookie shell in the center of the plate and fill with a large scoop of mango ice cream. Pipe dots of cherry sauce, 1 inch (2.5 cm) in diameter, on the base of the plate, evenly spaced around the dessert. Sprinkle mint over the sauce dots. Carefully set a chocolate twirl on top of the ice cream by inserting the handle of a wooden spoon in the twirl and using this to lift and position it. Serve immediately.

Mango Ice Cream yield: approximately 6 cups (1 L 440 ml)

3 cups (720 ml) whole milk

1 cup (240 ml) heavy cream

2 eggs

10 ounces (285 g) granulated sugar

2 pounds (910 g) fresh whole ripe mangoes (approximately 3 medium)

⅓ cup (80 ml) lime juice

1. Combine the milk and cream in a saucepan and heat to scalding. Whip the eggs and sugar in a mixing bowl until well combined. Gradually whisk the hot milk mixture into the eggs. Place the bowl over a bain-marie and cook, stirring with a whisk or a wooden spoon, until the custard has thickened slightly (nappe stage). Set aside to cool.

CHEF'S TIP

If you must use fruit that is not fully ripe, it is better to first peel the mangoes and then cut the flesh away from the stones.

2. Slice each mango into halves by cutting through vertically on both sides of the large flat stone. Use a spoon to scrape the flesh away from the skin and the stones. Puree the mango and pass through a strainer. Stir the mango puree and the lime juice into the cooled custard. Cover and place in the refrigerator until completely cold, preferably overnight.

3. Transfer the custard to an ice cream freezer and process following the manufacturer's direction. Store, covered, in the freezer.

Meringue Glacé Leda yield: 16 servings

Meringue Glacé Leda — a reference to the Greek myth — is composed of crisp meringue, smooth ice cream, and lightly cinnamon-flavored cookies in the shape of the swan's wings, all surrounded by ethereal spun sugar. The presentation is quite special and certainly befits a romantic occasion. However, the dessert is relatively easy both to prep and to assemble; other than the spun sugar, all of the components may be prepared well in advance.

¼ recipe French Meringue (page 780)

¾ recipe Hippen Decorating Paste (page 722)

½ teaspoon (1.25 g) unsweetened cocoa powder

Spun Sugar (page 593), tinted pale pink

1 cup (240 ml) heavy cream

2 teaspoons (10 g) granulated sugar

Rum-Raisin Ice Cream (recipe follows)

1. Place the meringue in a pastry bag with No. 8 (16-mm) star tip. Pipe into 16 cone-shaped shells, 3 inches (7.5 cm) long, on a sheet pan lined with baking paper (Figures 5-6 and 5-7). Bake at 210° to 220°F (99° to 104°C) approximately 3 hours or until dry.

2. Color 1 tablespoon (15 ml) Hippen paste with cocoa powder. Cover and reserve.

3. Make the templates for the swan wings and neck (Figure 5-8). The templates, as shown, are the correct size for this recipe. Trace the drawings, then cut them out of cardboard that is ¹⁄₁₆ inch (2 mm) thick; cake boxes work fine.

4. If you do not have Silpats, lightly grease the back of even sheet pans, coat with flour, and shake off as much flour as possible. Adjust the consistency of the Hippen paste, if necessary; it should spread easily but should hold its shape. Spread the paste flat and even within the templates on the prepared pans (see Figures 13-29 and 13-30, page 694). Make a few extra head-neck pieces to allow for breakage. Make 16 wings, then turn the template over and make 16 more so you will have a left and right wing for each swan.

5. Place the reserved cocoa-colored paste in a piping bag and pipe 1 small dot on each head for an eye. Do not make the eyes too large; a tiny eye looks elegant, whereas a large eye looks cartoonish.

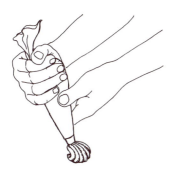

FIGURE 5-6 **Starting to pipe the bodies for the swans, using an up-and-over motion to make the wide end of the meringue**

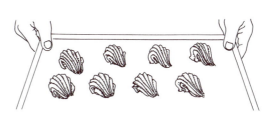

FIGURE 5-7 **The piped meringue swan bodies**

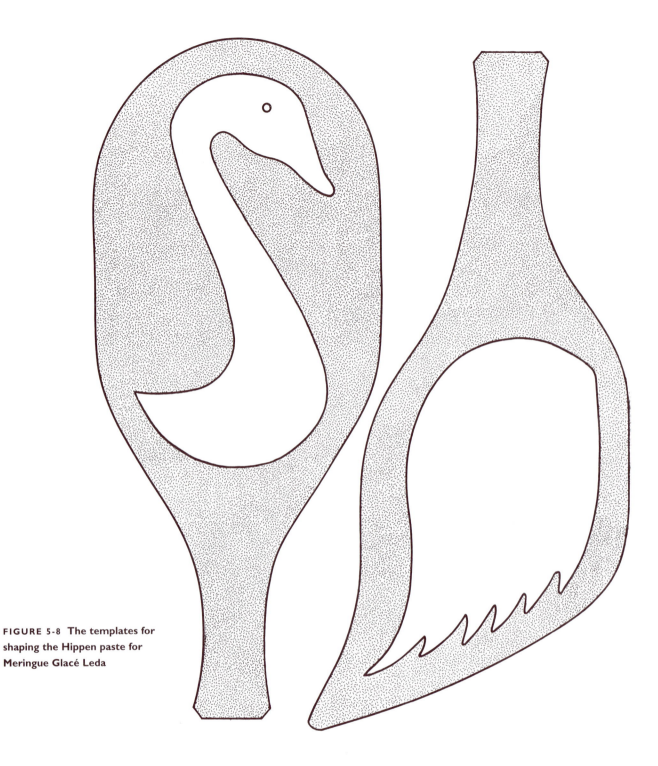

FIGURE 5-8 The templates for shaping the Hippen paste for Meringue Glacé Leda

6. Bake at 375°F (190°C) until the pieces start to color slightly, about 10 minutes. Let cool completely before removing from the sheet pans. Reserve in an airtight container. At this point, the baked pieces can be stored for up to 1 week.

7. Make the spun sugar as close to serving time as possible. Reserve in an airtight container. It is a good idea to place a small amount of dehumidifying agent—for example, silica gel or limestone—in the container to protect the sugar against moisture, even if it is made only a few minutes before serving time, and this is essential if the sugar will be kept any longer.

8. Whip the heavy cream and sugar to stiff peaks. Place in a pastry bag with a No. 8 (16-mm) star tip. Reserve in the refrigerator.

9. Presentation: Pipe a small dot of whipped cream in the center of a chilled dessert plate. Place a meringue shell on the cream. Use an ice cream scoop to portion a scoop of rum-raisin ice cream on top of the meringue. The scoop must be large enough to slightly protrude beyond the sides of the meringue. Attach 1 left and 1 right wing to the ice cream, with the top sides facing out and the flat sides against the ice cream. Place a head-neck piece between the meringue and ice cream, angled back over the body. Pipe a small amount of whipped cream at the back for a tail. Arrange spun sugar on the plate around the swan. Serve immediately.

> **CHEF'S TIP**
>
> If the weather is humid or rainy, attractive spun sugar is difficult to produce. In this situation, you may want to substitute Chocolate Sauce (page 413) decorated with Sour Cream Mixture for Piping (page 727). The decoration shown in Figure 13-13, page 683, would be appropriate to suggest waves.

RUM-RAISIN ICE CREAM yield: approximately 5 cups (1 L 200 ml)

1 cup (240 ml) light rum	1 vanilla bean, split lengthwise
¼ cup (60 ml) dark rum	10 egg yolks (⅞ cup/210 ml)
8 ounces (225 g) raisins	5 ounces (140 g) granulated sugar
1 quart (960 ml) half-and-half	2 teaspoons (10 ml) vanilla extract

1. Heat the light and dark rum to around 150°F (65°C), then add the raisins. Cover and let macerate at room temperature overnight.

2. Heat the half-and-half with the vanilla bean to scalding.

3. Beat the egg yolks and sugar until light and fluffy. Remove the vanilla bean halves and use the back of a paring knife to scrape out the seeds. Stir the seeds into the half-and-half. Discard the vanilla bean pods. Gradually pour the half-and-half into the whipped egg yolk mixture while whisking rapidly.

4. Heat the mixture over simmering water, stirring constantly with a whisk or wooden spoon, until it thickens enough to coat the spoon. Be careful not to overheat, as the custard will break. Remove from the heat and continue to stir for a few seconds to keep the mixture from overcooking where it touches the hot bowl. Stir in the vanilla extract. Cool to room temperature, then refrigerate, covered, for several hours or, preferably, overnight, until completely cold.

5. Pour the custard into an ice cream freezer and process following the manufacturer's directions until the ice cream begins to thicken. Add the raisins and any rum that has not been absorbed. Finish churning. Transfer the ice cream to a chilled container. If necessary, stir gently to distribute the raisins. Cover and store in the freezer.

> **CHEF'S TIP**
>
> Don't skip macerating the raisins in the rum. The step is necessary not only to prevent them from freezing into little rocks but also because it gives the raisins a wonderful rum flavor that comes across the instant you bite into them. The alcohol keeps the ice cream soft and pliable, even when stored overnight.

About Figs

The fig tree is an ancient type of ficus that has been growing on the earth virtually since the beginning of time. (You'll recall that Adam and Eve covered themselves with fig leaves in the Garden of Eden.) Like the grapevine, fig trees were held in high regard by the ancient Greeks and Romans. The Greeks, believing the tree was a gift to Athens from Ceres, the goddess of grain and agriculture, planted a grove of fig trees in their main public square. The Romans also honored the fig, recalling that their founding princes, Romulus and Remus, were born under its sheltering branches. They offered a sacrifice each year in the fig grove planted in the forum. Since these classical beginnings, figs have been a predominant fruit along the Mediterranean seaboard. Today, they are also widely cultivated in California.

Figs are botanically classified as a *fruit receptacle,* which means an inside-out flower. Although considered a fruit, the fig is actually a flower that is inverted into itself. The seeds are drupes, or the real fruit. The fruit grows right where the leaves are attached to the branches without any visible flowering having taken place. Figs are also unusual in that they provide two crops annually.

The several hundred fig varieties grow in a wide range of colors and shapes, from small, squat, and round to large and pear-shaped, and from almost white to dark purple or black. One of the most common commercial figs is the Brown Turkey variety, also referred to as *Black Spanish.* These are quite large, with mahogany purple skin and juicy red flesh; they are the first figs on the market each year. Mission or Black Mission figs, which have a dark pink interior, are the most readily available and are the best overall for cooking. Kadota figs, the principal variety used for canning, are quite large, with yellow-green skin and white to purple flesh.

Smyrna figs, from Turkey (known as *Calimyrna* when grown in California), are large, greenish, squat, extremely sweet figs that are available fresh but are mostly used for drying; these are the only figs that are not self-pollinating. Smyrna figs instead rely on a unique pollination method provided by a tiny wasp known as *blastophaga,* which lives inside the inedible figs that grow on the Capri fig tree. When the wasp larvae mature, they leave the Capri fig tree and look for another tree to serve as a nest in which to reproduce. Growers of Smyrna figs intervene just before this happens, placing baskets of Capri figs throughout their orchards. The female wasps work their way through the bottom of the Smyrna figs, carrying pollen on their wings and bodies. Once they discover that the inside of the Smyrna fig is not suitable for laying their eggs they retreat, leaving pollen behind.

Unripe figs can be ripened at room temperature; they should be placed away from direct sunlight and turned from time to time. Ripe figs may be stored in the refrigerator for up to three days. They bruise easily and should be arranged in a single layer, covered with plastic.

Oven-Braised Black Mission Figs with Honey-Vanilla Frozen Yogurt

yield: 12 servings

Because fig season is rather short, approximately June to September, and fresh figs are not good keepers, you may sometimes want to consider trying canned figs in this recipe. The Kadota fig, with its greenish-yellow skin, is readily available in cans, typically packed in heavy syrup. When using canned figs, reduce the braising time by half and replace the water and granulated sugar with 2 cups (480 ml) syrup from the can, poured over the figs while braising.

36 medium-size fresh Black Mission figs

½ cup (120 ml) water

8 ounces (225 g) granulated sugar

8 ounces (225 g) toasted pine nuts

2 tablespoons (30 ml) honey

⅓ cup (80 ml) Armagnac

3 ounces (85 g) unsalted butter

36 Sponge Cake rounds (see Note)

½ recipe Honey-Vanilla Frozen Yogurt
(page 276)

Edible flower petals

1. Place the whole figs, standing on end, in a buttered ovenproof dish just large enough to hold them in 1 layer.

2. Heat the water and sugar in a saucepan until the mixture is simmering and the sugar is dissolved. Pour the syrup over the figs. Bake at 375°F (190°C) for 15 minutes, basting the figs with the cooking liquid from time to time. Add the pine nuts and continue cooking for approximately 10 minutes longer or until the figs are soft.

3. Transfer the figs to another dish (leaving the pine nuts in the liquid) and let them cool at room temperature.

4. Pour the cooking liquid and the nuts into a skillet and boil until the mixture is syrupy. Add the honey and Armagnac and cook the sauce, stirring constantly, until the ingredients are completely incorporated. Swirl in the butter. Let the sauce cool to room temperature.

5. Presentation: Place 3 figs close together in the center of a dessert plate. Spoon a portion of the sauce over the figs and more in 3 uneven pools, evenly spaced, on the base of the plate around the figs; make sure you include some of the pine nuts in the sauce. Place a sponge round between each of the sauce pools. Top each sponge with a small oval scoop of yogurt (use an oval ice cream scoop or use 2 soupspoons to make quenelles). Decorate with edible flowers and serve immediately.

NOTE: Use any type of light sponge cake you have on hand. Slice it thin, then cut out 36 rounds with a plain cookie cutter, ½ to ¾ inch (1.2 to 2 cm) in diameter. Cover until needed.

Poached Pears with Ginger Ice Cream yield: 16 servings

This recipe features the always-popular combination of poached pears and ice cream, presented colorfully with two very different sauces: raspberry and cream. While the directions that follow are for à la carte service, I have successfully served this dessert at large banquets; the task simply requires proper planning and, for very large groups, a few modifications. Because assembling each serving involves several steps (though each step is quite easy in itself), the pear halves and the dessert plates must be thoroughly chilled. The sponge round is used to keep the ice cream from sliding on the plate, and a chilled plate will help even more. The pear halves must be not only well chilled but also blotted dry, or they will start to melt the ice cream and/or slip off the ice cream scoop. Even with all of the components well chilled and the desserts put together quickly, you may have a window of no more than 2 to 3 minutes between assembly and pickup, depending on the temperature in your workstation. So, as is true of many desserts, hot and cold, getting this one to the table in perfect condition requires the cooperation of the waitstaff.

If you are serving this to a very large group, consider these two options in order to preserve both your reputation and the dessert. Either omit the ice cream altogether — the dessert will still be attractive, refreshing, and flavorful — or serve the ice cream on the side of the plate, on the sponge round, as directed, or in a small tuile shell. This allows you to scoop the ice cream ahead of time, reserve the scoops in the freezer, then quickly add the ice cream and its holder to each plate after the pears have been decorated with the sauces.

8 Bartlett pears, stems attached

7½ cups (1 L 800 ml) Spiced Poaching Syrup (page 790)

4 thin slices fresh ginger

2 ounces (55 g) pistachios

16 sponge cake rounds (see Note)

1 recipe Gingered White Chocolate Ice Cream (page 217)

Romanoff Sauce (recipe follows)

1 recipe Raspberry Sauce (page 173)

16 Marzipan Leaves (page 644)

1. Peel the pears and cut in half lengthwise, cutting through the stems as well. Prevent oxidation of the cut fruit as you work by placing it directly in a large saucepan containing the poaching syrup. Add the fresh ginger and poach the pears until they are tender. Remove from the heat and let cool in the syrup.

2. Blanch the pistachios, adding a pinch of salt to the blanching water to amplify their green color. Remove the skins and dry the nuts. Crush to a fine consistency. (If you dry the nuts in an oven, do not toast them, or you will lose the color.)

3. Remove the pear halves from the poaching liquid, core, and pat dry with towels. Chill the pear halves and dessert plates in the refrigerator. If necessary, soften the ice cream.

4. Presentation: Place a sponge round in the center of a dessert plate. Put a small scoop of ice cream on top and lightly flatten the ice cream with the back of the scoop. Arrange a pear half, flat side down, on top of the ice cream, pressing it down to secure. Cover the stem half of the pear with Romanoff sauce, spooning it straight across the center and letting it run onto the plate next to the pear. Spoon raspberry sauce over the bottom half of the pear in the same manner. Make sure that the sauces are thick enough to cover the pear but fluid enough to run onto the plate. Do not use so much sauce that the entire base of the plate is covered. Sprinkle a thin line of pistachios across the center where the two sauces meet. Place a marzipan leaf next to the stem of the pear and serve immediately.

NOTE: Use any type of light sponge cake you have on hand. Slice it thin; then, using a 1½-inch (3.7-cm) plain cookie cutter, cut out 16 rounds. Cover and reserve.

About Pears

Because of the pear's distinctive form — spherical on the bottom, with a tapered top — the adjective *pear-shaped* is widely used and readily understood. Pears are grown in temperate regions worldwide in thousands of varieties. Their name stems from the Latin *pirum*; the pear is called *poire* in French, *birne* in German, and *päron* in Swedish.

The most popular pear in the United States is the Bartlett, which is used in this recipe. Known as *Williams* in Europe, this variety was developed in eighteenth-century England and brought to the colonies by early settlers. Here, it was named for Enoch Bartlett, a Massachusetts resident who promoted and popularized the variety. Bartlett pears turn from dark green to light golden yellow when they are perfectly ripe (great for eating fresh, but for poaching a less than completely ripe pear is preferable). A pretty red-skinned strain of Bartlett has also been developed. These pears are great in fruit displays and fruit baskets, or served fresh with cheese. Red Bartletts are of no significance for peeling and cooking, as the flavor is no different from the original. Pears not only rival the apple in popularity, but the two are actually closely related. Both are members of the rose family and are classified as pome fruits, meaning they have a distinct seeded core.

ROMANOFF SAUCE yield: approximately 4 cups (960 ml)

3 cups (720 ml) heavy cream   1 cup (240 ml) sour cream

1. Mix the heavy cream with the sour cream and whip them together until the mixture has thickened to the consistency of molasses.

2. If the sauce is not to be used immediately, adjust the consistency at serving time by whipping the sauce to thicken it or adding heavy cream to thin it. Store the sauce, covered, in the refrigerator.

Profiteroles with Vanilla Ice Cream and Hot Fudge Sauce yield: 16 servings

Profiteroles are found in classic desserts such as croquembouche and gâteau Saint-Honoré and are also offered individually with a variety of sweet and savory fillings. One old-fashioned dessert enjoying a renaissance on contemporary dessert menus is profiteroles filled with ice cream. The dish is simple to make and serve and never seems to lose its appeal. Make certain that the profiteroles are thoroughly baked so they are dry and crisp. The contrast in texture is an important element of the dessert.

½ recipe Pâte à Choux (page 783)   1 recipe Vanilla Ice Cream (page 172)
Hot Fudge Sauce (recipe follows)   Powdered sugar
8 whole strawberries   16 Caramelized Sugar Spheres (page 299)

1. Place the pâte à choux in a pastry bag with a No. 6 (12-mm) plain tip. Pipe out approximately 50 mounds, about 1¾ inches (4.5 cm) in diameter, onto sheet pans lined with baking paper or Silpats.

2. Bake at 400°F (205°C) until puffed, about 15 minutes. Reduce the heat to 350°F (175°C) and bake until the pastries are lightly browned, well dried and crisp on the exterior, and will hold their shape, about 10 minutes longer. Remove from the oven and let cool completely.

3. Cut the top off each profiterole. If the profiteroles have become soft, place the top portions in a hot oven for a few minutes to make them crisp (make sure they are cool before using). Place the fudge sauce in a piping bottle with a large opening and set aside in a warm water bath. Rinse the strawberries, cut them in half, and fan the halves.

4. Presentation: Place a small scoop of ice cream on each of 3 profiterole bases. Sift powdered sugar lightly over 3 profiterole tops. Arrange the filled profiteroles on a dessert plate. Pipe fudge sauce over the ice cream, then replace the profiterole tops (be careful not to get fingerprints on the sugar). Set a sugar sphere in the center of the profiteroles. Decorate with a fanned strawberry half and serve immediately.

HOT FUDGE SAUCE yield: 4 cups (960 ml)

5 ounces (140 g) unsweetened cocoa powder, sifted

6 ounces (170 g) light brown sugar

6 ounces (170 g) granulated sugar

1¼ cups (300 ml) heavy cream

8 ounces (225 g) unsalted butter

½ teaspoon (3 g) salt

1. Thoroughly combine the cocoa powder, brown sugar, and granulated sugar.

2. Place the cream, butter, and salt in a saucepan over low heat. Bring the mixture to the scalding point, stirring to melt the butter.

3. Whisk in the sugar and cocoa mixture gradually to avoid lumps. Cook over low heat, stirring constantly with the whisk, until the sugar dissolves and the mixture is smooth. Serve immediately, or keep warm over a bain-marie.

Saffron-Poached Pears with Almond Ice Cream and Kadaif Phyllo Nests yield: 12 servings (Color Photo 45)

Saffron has long been associated with savory dishes, especially those from the Mediterranean, such as risotto Milanese, bouillabaisse, and paella. However, I first created this presentation for a banquet at a conference for food professionals on the topic of Asian cooking and the flavors of the Pacific Rim.

You may have trouble finding the kadaif phyllo called for here, as these thin strands are not as readily available as the more familiar thin sheets. If you can find it, the crispy threads add even more interest to an already exciting dish that contains unusual colors, flavors, textures, and an eye-catching cookie palm tree. Even if you must omit the phyllo dough strands, the palm tree will still provide a nice crunchy textural contrast. See "About Saffron" (page 161) and page 159 for more information about kadaif phyllo.

12 small Bosc pears, stems on

Saffron Poaching Liquid (page 160)

1 sheet Joconde Sponge II (page 671)

Saffron-Vanilla Syrup Reduction (recipe follows)

½ recipe Almond Ice Cream (recipe follows)

1 teaspoon (5 ml) saffron threads, lightly packed

2 ounces pistachios, blanched and coarsely chopped

12 Miniature Palm Trees (recipe follows)

12 Kadaif Phyllo Nests (recipe follows)

Powdered sugar

1. Peel the pears, keeping the stems intact and placing them in acidulated water as you work to prevent oxidation. Transfer the pears to a saucepan with the saffron poaching liquid. Bring the liquid to a simmer. Place a lid or plate that will fit inside the pan on top of the pears to keep them submerged. Poach the fruit until it is tender, but be careful not to overcook it because the pears are presented standing on end in the finished dish, which will not be possible if they become too soft or begin to fall apart.

2. Place several sheets of paper towels or a clean kitchen towel in the pan between the lid or plate and the pears; this will ensure that the pears are not exposed to the air, which would keep them from coloring evenly. Set the pears aside in the liquid for at least 6 hours or, preferably, overnight.

3. Remove the pears from the liquid and pat them dry. Save the liquid for the reduction. Cut each pear in half, cutting through the stem as well. Use a melon ball cutter to remove the core and, at the same time, make a round hollow in the center of each pear half. Set the pears aside, keeping the halves of each pear together.

4. Cut 12 rounds, 1½ inches (3.7 cm) in diameter, from the sponge sheet. Wrap the remaining sponge and reserve for another use.

5. Pour the saffron-vanilla syrup into a piping bottle.

6. Presentation: Place a sponge round in the center of a dessert plate. Place a medium-size scoop of almond ice cream on top. Pipe some of the syrup reduction over the flat sides of 2 pear halves and use a small brush to brush the syrup over the pears, making sure the vanilla bean seeds are evenly distributed and visible. Arrange the pears against the ice cream, with the top of each half pointing in an opposite direction (see Color Photo 45). Drizzle syrup on the base of the plate around the dessert. Sprinkle a few saffron threads and a few pistachios on the syrup. Attach a palm tree to the ice cream behind the pears. Place a phyllo nest to the right of the pears. Sift powdered sugar lightly over the dessert and the plate; serve immediately.

SAFFRON-VANILLA SYRUP REDUCTION yield: approximately 1 cup (240 ml)

2 cups (480 ml) reserved saffron poaching liquid	1 vanilla bean, split lengthwise

1. Strain the poaching liquid into a saucepan. Using the back of a paring knife, scrape the seeds from the vanilla bean halves and add them to the poaching liquid. Save the vanilla bean pod halves for another use.

2. Bring the syrup to a boil and reduce to approximately 1 cup (240 ml). Test the viscosity of the reduction by removing about 1 teaspoon (5 ml) syrup and chilling it on a plate. When the puddle is at room temperature, it should be thin enough to pipe and flow out a bit but thick enough not to run. If too thin, cook the syrup in the pan a bit longer. If too thick, add water.

MINIATURE PALM TREES yield: approximately 24 decorations

½ recipe Vanilla Tuile Decorating Paste (page 695)	½ teaspoon (1 g) unsweetened cocoa powder

1. Make the palm tree template in Figure 5-9. The template, as shown, is the correct size for use in this recipe. Trace the drawing, then cut the template out of cardboard that is ¹⁄₁₆ inch (2 mm) thick; cake boxes work fine.

2. Place 1 tablespoon (15 ml) of the tuile paste in a small bowl and stir in the cocoa powder, mixing until it is thoroughly incorporated. Place in a piping bag and set aside.

3. If you do not have Silpats, grease and flour the back of flat, even sheet pans.

4. Spread the plain tuile paste flat and even within the template on a Silpat or prepared sheet pan (see Figures 13-29 and 13-30, page 694). Repeat until you have formed a few more palm trees than you expect to need. Cut a small opening in the piping bag with the cocoa tuile paste. Pipe 5 or 6 angled lines across the trunk on each tree.

5. Bake at 400°F (205°C) for approximately 4 minutes or until the trees become brown in a few spots. Remove from the oven, let cool, and store in an airtight container until needed.

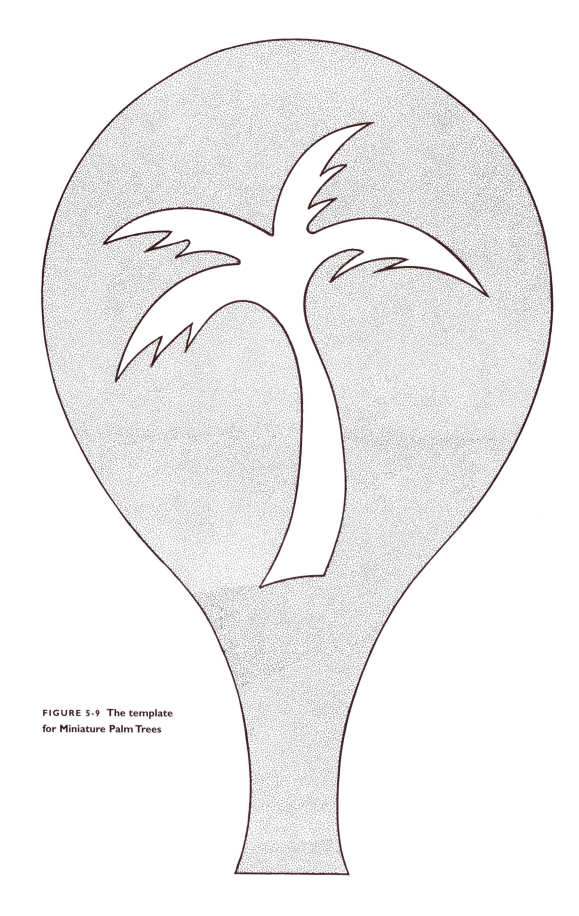

FIGURE 5-9 The template
for Miniature Palm Trees

KADAIF PHYLLO NESTS yield: 12 decorations

4 ounces (115 g) kadaif phyllo dough, thawed if frozen

Powdered sugar

Pan spray or unsalted butter, melted

I. Form the phyllo strands in 12 tight rounds, approximately 2½ inches (6.2 cm) in diameter. Place them on a sheet pan lined with baking paper or a Silpat, spacing them evenly. Spray pan spray lightly over each round or brush with melted butter. Sift powdered sugar lightly over the tops.

2. Bake the phyllo nests at 375°F (190°C) for approximately 6 minutes or until golden brown. Let cool. Store in an airtight container, unless the decorations will be used within a few hours of baking.

ALMOND ICE CREAM yield: 5 cups (1 L 200 ml)

If you like, you can substitute almond meal for the blanched almonds called for in this recipe. Use a few ounces less because the almond meal will absorb more moisture than the finely ground nuts. Add the almond meal and the sugar directly to the milk; there is no need to grind them together.

1 pound (455 g) blanched almonds (see Chef's Tip)

12 ounces (340 g) granulated sugar

3 cups (720 ml) whole milk

8 egg yolks (⅔ cup/160 ml)

½ cup (120 ml) amaretto liqueur

2 cups (480 ml) heavy cream

I. Place the almonds and sugar in a food processor and process until the mixture has a very fine, even consistency, but do not grind the mixture so fine that it begins to cake. Place in a saucepan and add the milk. Bring to scalding, remove from the heat, and set aside at room temperature to infuse until the almond milk has cooled completely.

2. Strain the almond milk through a piece of cheesecloth, squeezing the cloth to remove as much liquid as possible. You should have close to 3 cups (720 ml) almond-flavored milk. Discard the ground almonds.

3. Place the egg yolks and amaretto in a bowl. Set the bowl over simmering water and heat, whipping constantly, until the mixture is thick enough to coat a spoon. Add the heavy cream and heat until close to scalding, stirring with a wooden spoon or heatproof spatula; do not let the mixture boil. Remove from the heat and stir the cream mixture into the almond milk. Let cool to room temperature, then cover and refrigerate until thoroughly chilled or, preferably, overnight.

4. Process in an ice cream freezer following the manufacturer's directions. Store the finished ice cream, covered, in the freezer.

CHEF'S TIP
Use any variety of blanched almonds here — sliced, slivered, or whole. If you blanch the nuts yourself and they become stained from the brown skin, soak them in cold water for 1 hour after you remove the skins to whiten the nuts. Allow the almonds to dry at room temperature, preferably until the next day, before you grind them. If you do not have time to wait, dry the almonds in a low oven, but be careful not to brown them.

Tropical Surprise Packages yield: 16 servings (Color Photo 55)

If you follow the directions carefully, wrapping a frozen filling inside a hot cookie is not as far-fetched as you might think. However, it does take its toll on your fingers, especially if you are not (as I strongly recommend) using Silpats, because with sheet pans you have to deal with hot fat as well as hot cookies. I got the idea for this rather daring and unusual combination from the presentation of a dessert served in Raymond Blanc's Le Manoir aux Quat' Saisons restaurant not far from London. There, it was prepared with a lemon mousse filling and served with strawberry sauce. When I had my version on the menu a few years ago, a server came to me and said that one of his guests, a Londoner in San Francisco for a holiday, "would just die" for the recipe. Like most chefs, I am not in the habit of giving out recipes to guests, but as he had come so far (and for something so near, had he but known), I did not have the heart to say no.

The content of the package is easy to vary; the only requirement is to keep the size the same so it will fit the wrapper. For a chocolate version, make ¹/₂ recipe Chocolate Ganache Filling (page 28). For a lighter option, use 1¹/₃ recipes Lemon Chiffon Filling (page 43). Change the sauce in the presentation to suit the filling and, of course, change the name of the dessert accordingly.

Tamarind Parfait (recipe follows)
1 recipe Vanilla Tuile Decorating Paste
  (page 695)
1 teaspoon (2.5 g) unsweetened cocoa powder

16 medium kiwis, ripe but firm
¹/₂ recipe Mango Coulis (page 244)
Pomegranate seeds
Powdered sugar

1. Make a frame measuring 9 inches (22.5 cm) square from cardboard cut into strips, 1¹/₂ inches (3.7 cm) wide. Tape the strips together at the corners. Place the frame on a sheet pan or a sheet of cardboard and line the bottom and sides with plastic wrap.

2. Pour the tamarind parfait into the frame and place it in the freezer to harden.

3. Make the template (Figure 5-11) from cardboard that is ¹/₁₆ inch (2 mm) thick; cake boxes are ideal. The template, as shown, is the correct size for this recipe. However, it is possible to show only half of it on the page. Trace the template, then turn the paper over, match the dotted lines in the center, and trace the other half to make the shape shown in the illustration. If you do not have Silpats, lightly grease and flour the back of even sheet pans.

4. Color 2 tablespoons (30 ml) of the tuile paste with the cocoa powder. Set aside.

5. Using the template as a guide, spread the remaining paste on Silpats, or on the reserved sheet pans, spreading it thin, flat, and even within the template (see Figures 13-29 and 13-30, page 694). Do not place more than 3 per sheet pan. Place the cocoa-colored paste in a piping bag. Pipe a design, which will look like ribbons tying the package closed, on each tuile paste shape by piping a bow in the center (see Procedure 5-1a). Reserve in the refrigerator. If desired, you can prepare the wrappers up to this point several hours ahead of time.

6. Once the tamarind parfait has frozen firm, use a knife dipped in hot water to cut it into pieces 2¹/₄ inches (5.6 cm) square. Place the squares in the freezer and remove them 1 at a time as you wrap the packages.

7. Bake 1 pan of prepared tuile paste at 400°F (205°C) until the wrappers start to turn golden brown at the edges, approximately 5 minutes. Do not overbake (see Chef's Tip). Remove from the oven and quickly turn each wrapper upside down onto the table. Place a frozen parfait

PROCEDURE 5-1a Piping the cocoa-colored tuile paste ribbons and bows on top of tuile paste that has been spread within the template

PROCEDURE 5-1b Wrapping the 3 short sides around the square

PROCEDURE 5-1c The finished package

square in the center of a cookie. Quickly wrap the 3 short sides around the square (Procedure 5-1b), then invert the wrapped portion on top of the long side. Place the wrapped package (Procedure 5-1c) in the freezer and continue to assemble the remainder in the same way. Ideally the desserts should be served the same day as they are assembled; however, if kept well covered, the wrapped packages will stay crisp in the freezer for a few days.

8. Using a spoon to retain the natural shape of the fruit, peel 1 kiwi for each dessert you anticipate serving (Figure 5-10). Place the peeled kiwis on their sides, cut off the narrow ends, then cut each fruit into thin round slices; you should get 7 to 8 slices from each. Keep the slices and end pieces from each fruit together, cover, and reserve. Place the mango coulis in a piping bottle and reserve.

9. Presentation: Arrange a ring of slightly overlapping kiwi slices from 1 kiwi in the center of a dessert plate. Place the end pieces in the center of the ring and flatten them slightly so they are level; be sure to remove the small, hard portion from the stem end first if it is present. Place a tropical surprise package on top of the kiwi end pieces, centering it on the ring of kiwi slices. Pipe large teardrops of mango coulis on the base of the plate around the kiwi slices. Place a pomegranate seed on each teardrop of sauce. Sift powdered sugar lightly over the seeds. Serve immediately.

CHEF'S TIP

If the wrappers are left in the oven too long, because you either overbaked them or baked them at too low a temperature, they will crumble and fall apart before you have a chance to cover the parfait. The best method is to bake just 2 or 3 wrappers at a time so you can form them quickly while they are still warm. If properly baked, the wrappers may be returned to the oven to soften if they should cool off before you can form them.

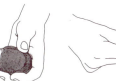

FIGURE 5-10 Inserting a spoon between the skin and the flesh of a kiwi; gradually pushing the spoon to the bottom of the kiwi while turning the kiwi at the same time; after twisting the spoon all the way around inside the skin, pulling the spoon out to remove the peeled kiwi

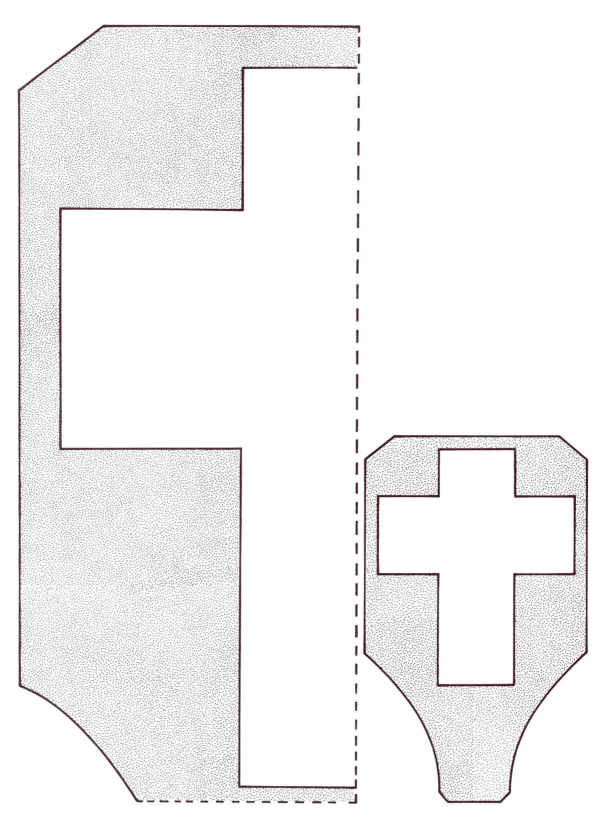

FIGURE 5-11 The template for the wrappers for Tropical Surprise Packages

About Tamarind

Tamarinds, originally from the Asian and African rain forests, are cultivated today in the tropics and subtropics all over the world. They are also known as *sour dates* and *Indian dates*. Tamarind pods, which have a hard, reddish-brown shell, can grow up to 8 inches (20 cm) long; the pods hang in clusters from the tall evergreen trees. The white flesh surrounding the black seeds turns light brown and dries up when the fruit is ripe. Tamarinds have a distinctive sweet-sour taste. They can be obtained fresh beginning in the late fall and into the winter. They are also available, dried or as a sticky paste, year-round in grocery stores specializing in Asian food. In addition to their use in frozen desserts, tamarinds and tamarind paste appear in Asian cooking and in the preparation of curries. Store tamarind pods in a plastic bag in the refrigerator.

TAMARIND PARFAIT yield: 5½ cups (1 L 320 ml)

14 ounces (400 g) fresh tamarind pods *or* 5 ounces (140 g) tamarind paste (see Note)

1¼ cups (300 ml) hot water

8 egg yolks (⅔ cup/160 ml)

4 ounces (115 g) granulated sugar

½ cup (120 ml) or 6 ounces (170 g) light corn syrup

2 cups (480 ml) heavy cream

1. Peel the tamarind pods; remove the seeds and stringy membranes from the flesh and discard. Cut the flesh into chunks and place in a bowl. Cover with the hot water and leave to soak for a few hours or, if possible, overnight.

2. Transfer the mixture to a saucepan and cook over low heat until it reaches a fairly thick consistency, approximately 10 minutes. Press as much as possible through a fine sieve and set it aside to cool. Discard the contents of the sieve.

3. Whip the egg yolks and sugar until light and fluffy. Bring the corn syrup to a boil in a heavy saucepan. Lower the mixer speed and gradually pour the hot corn syrup into the yolk mixture. Whip at medium speed until the mixture has cooled completely.

4. Whip the heavy cream to soft peaks. Add the cooled tamarind puree to the yolk mixture. Gradually fold this combination into the whipped cream.

NOTE: If you use the more convenient tamarind paste, which saves you the tedious labor of peeling the tamarind pods, follow the recipe and directions as given but reduce the sugar by about half, as the paste is usually prepared with sugar. The sugar content varies by brand.

Vacherin with Plum Ice Cream yield: 16 servings (Color Photo 53)

Like many popular dessert creations, Vacherin has many variations, all of which combine meringue with ice cream, whipped cream, or both. One simple but delicious example is Meringue Glacé Chantilly (recipe follows). The classic rendition of Vacherin consists of two or three crisp meringue rings (or rings made from almond macaroon paste) stacked on top of one another and placed on a meringue base to make a decorative edible bowl. The shell is then filled with fruit and/or Chantilly cream. A glacé or frozen Vacherin is filled with ice cream, decorated with whipped cream, and garnished with fresh or crystallized fruit. Vacherin may be made in large sizes for multiple servings or in individual portions, as follows.

A nice variation can be produced by substituting Peach Ice Cream (page 212) for the plum ice cream and Fortified Caramel Sauce (page 19) for the plum sauce.

½ recipe French Meringue (page 780)

Melted dark coating chocolate

½ recipe Plum Ice Cream (recipe follows)

1 cup (240 ml) heavy cream

1½ teaspoons (8 g) granulated sugar

4 small plums

1 recipe Plum Sauce (recipe follows)

1. Draw 32 circles, 3 inches (7.5 cm) in diameter, on sheets of baking paper. Invert the papers on sheet pans. Place the meringue in a pastry bag with a No. 4 (8-mm) plain tip. Using the circles as a guide, pipe the meringue onto the prepared baking papers (see Figure 14-2, page 782). To make the cases, as you come to the outside of each of 16 circles, pipe 2 additional rows of meringue on top of the outside ring to form the sides of the case. Use the remaining 16 circles as guides when piping out the lids: Using a No. 2 (4-mm) plain tip held in place over the bag as you pipe, pipe 5 equally spaced parallel lines of meringue across 1 circle, then pipe 5 lines at a 45-degree angle to the first set to make a diamond pattern. Repeat to make the remaining 16 lids.

2. Bake the meringues immediately at 210° to 220°F (99° to 104°C) until dry. The lids will take about 2 hours and the cases about 4 hours. Made up to this point, the meringue shells will keep for several weeks in a warm, dry place. Therefore, finish only the amount you expect to serve right away.

3. Holding the cases upside down, dip the rims in melted dark coating chocolate. To prevent drips, carefully shake off excess chocolate before setting them right-side up.

4. Fill each Vacherin with plum ice cream. Place the filled meringue shells in the freezer.

5. Whip the cream and sugar to stiff peaks. Place in a pastry bag with a No. 3 (6-mm) plain tip. Reserve in the refrigerator. Cut the plums into quarters. Fan the pieces and reserve in the refrigerator. Place a portion of the plum sauce in a piping bottle and reserve.

6. Presentation: Pipe the whipped cream in a spiral on top of a Vacherin, starting in the center and continuing to the chocolate-covered rim, in the same way that you piped the base of the shells. Place a lid on top. Top with a fanned plum garnish. Pipe a small dot of whipped cream off-center on a dessert plate and place the finished Vacherin on top to prevent it from sliding. Pipe a small pool of plum sauce in front of the Vacherin. Serve immediately.

PLUM ICE CREAM yield: approximately 6 cups (1 L 440 ml)

While I generally try to get the Laroda or Casselman variety of plum for cooking, the skin of the Santa Rosa plum gives this ice cream a wonderful color and a tart, puckery taste. It is a wonderful companion to many sweet desserts, particularly those based on meringue.

2 pounds (910 g) tart plums (see Chef's Tip)

¼ cup (60 ml) simple syrup

¼ cup (60 ml) plum brandy *or* liqueur

1 recipe Spiced Poaching Syrup (page 790)

5 ounces (140 g) granulated sugar

10 egg yolks (⅞ cup/210 ml)

1 quart (960 ml) half-and-half

1. Wash the plums, cut them in half, and discard the pits. Cut one-third of the fruit into pea-sized chunks. Combine the chunks with the simple syrup and brandy or liqueur. Set aside to macerate for a few hours or, preferably, overnight.

2. Place the remaining plum halves in a saucepan with the poaching syrup. Cook until the plums are soft and beginning to fall apart. Remove from the heat and strain off the poaching liquid, reserving 1 quart (960 ml) to use as a sauce for the ice cream, if desired, or discard. (To use the poaching liquid as a sauce, reduce it by approximately half or until it has thickened to a nappe consistency.)

3. Whip the sugar and egg yolks to the ribbon stage. Heat the half-and-half to scalding. Gradually pour the hot half-and-half into the egg yolk mixture while whisking rapidly. Place over simmering water and heat, stirring constantly with a whisk or wooden spoon, until the custard is thick enough to coat the spoon. Remove from the heat and stir in the reserved poached plums and the macerated plum chunks. Let cool at room temperature, then cover and refrigerate until completely cold.

4. Process in an ice cream freezer following the manufacturer's directions. Place the finished ice cream in a chilled container and store, covered, in the freezer.

CHEF'S TIP

When the season for fresh local plums is over, canned tart plums may be a better choice than the sometimes tasteless imported varieties. Drain; use the liquid as part of the poaching syrup, adjusting the sweetness and quantity as needed. Canned plums require only about 5 minutes of poaching.

PLUM SAUCE yield: 4 cups (960 ml)

Santa Rosa and Casselman plums are good choices when in season, but in any case, use a red or purple variety to give the sauce a pleasant pastel red color.

2 pounds 8 ounces (1 kg 135 g) pitted fresh plums *or* **2 pounds (910 g) drained canned pitted plums**

3 cups (720 ml) water or liquid from canned plums

6 ounces (170 g) granulated sugar

3 tablespoons (24 g) cornstarch

1. If using fresh plums, cut them into quarters.

2. Reserve ¼ cup (60 ml) water or canning liquid and place the plums in a saucepan with the remaining liquid and the sugar; if you are using canned plums packed in syrup, omit the sugar. Bring to a boil and cook over medium heat until the fruit is soft enough to fall apart, approximately 15 minutes for fresh plums, 1 minute for canned.

3. Remove from the heat. Strain, using the back of a spoon or ladle to force as much of the pulp as possible through the strainer. Discard the contents of the strainer.

4. Dissolve the cornstarch in the reserved liquid. Add to the sauce. Return the mixture to the saucepan and bring to a boil. Cook for 1 minute to remove the taste of the cornstarch. Serve hot or cold. When served cold, the sauce may need to be thinned with water. Store, covered, in the refrigerator.

MERINGUE GLACE CHANTILLY yield: 16 servings

Vacherin glacé is actually meringue glacé Chantilly in a fancy shape. You can make this classic by following the same procedure and using the same ingredients, plus chocolate shavings.

1. Place the French meringue in a pastry bag with a No. 6 (12-mm) star tip. Pipe the meringue into 16 corkscrews (telephone cords), 2½ inches (6.2 cm) long, or other pretty shapes.

2. Bake, cool, and dip the pieces halfway into melted dark coating chocolate.

3. Place the whipped cream in a pastry bag with a No. 9 (18-mm) star tip. Pipe a large rosette of cream on the serving plate. Sprinkle chocolate shavings on top.

4. Arrange the ice cream, meringue, plum sauce, and a fanned plum in an attractive presentation around the rosette. Be sure to put a little whipped cream under the ice cream to keep it from sliding.

Wild Strawberry Parfait yield: 12 servings

Wild strawberries are also known as *fraises des bois* and *Alpine strawberries*. These tiny wild strawberries grow in the open patches and meadows of woodlands all over Europe, from Italy in the south to Lapland in Sweden in the north, and in the United States as well. These intensely sweet strawberries are, for good reason, considered the queen of their species. They produce a bounty of fruit from early June until the first frost appears. As children, we picked wild strawberries and threaded them on the tall, thin stalks of a weed to make beautiful, edible necklaces — that is, any that did not go straight into our mouths.

Commercially, wild strawberries are fairly expensive, mainly because they are time-consuming to pick and the fruit is susceptible to hot spells in the weather. The two varieties are known as *red* and *white*, but white wild strawberries are actually a pale yellow color. Unlike their larger counterparts, red wild strawberries are still pale white inside even when they are fully ripe.

When I was starting out as an apprentice in Sweden, Wild Strawberry Parfait was considered *the* dessert to order when money was no object and only the best would do. If you have not yet been exposed to wild strawberries, you are in for a treat.

3 pounds 8 ounces (1 kg 590 g) fresh wild strawberries (see Chef's Tip)	3½ cups (840 ml) heavy cream
3 whole eggs	Orange-Vanilla Decorating Syrup (page 760)
2 egg yolks	12 Miniature Tuile Crowns (page 717)
2 ounces (55 g) granulated sugar	12 Florentina Twists (page 690)
½ cup (120 ml) or 6 ounces (170 g) honey	

1. Line the inside of a bread pan, 4 × 3½ × 8 inches (10 × 8.7 × 20 cm) or any size close to this, with baking paper. Set the form aside.

2. Select approximately 80 of the nicest-looking strawberries and set them aside, stems attached, to use in serving. Remove the stems from the remaining berries. Reserve about one-quarter of the stemmed berries; puree the remainder. Set the puree and the 2 groups of berries aside separately.

3. Whip the whole eggs, egg yolks, and sugar until light and fluffy, about 3 minutes. Bring the honey to a boil and gradually pour it into the egg mixture while whipping constantly. Continue to whip until the mixture is cold.

4. Whip 2½ cups (600 ml) of the heavy cream until soft peaks form. Gently incorporate the whipped egg mixture into the cream. Fold in the reserved strawberry puree, then the whole stemmed strawberries. Pour the mixture into the prepared form and place in the freezer for at least 4 hours or, preferably, overnight.

5. Whip the remaining heavy cream until stiff peaks form. Place in a pastry bag with a No. 5 (10-mm) star tip and reserve in the refrigerator. Place the orange syrup in a piping bottle.

6. Remove the frozen parfait from the form. Using a sharp thin knife dipped in hot water, cut it into 12 slices, each slightly less than ¾ inch (2 cm) thick. Place the slices on a chilled sheet pan lined with baking paper as you work. Cover and reserve in the freezer.

7. Presentation: Place 5 reserved wild strawberries with stems attached in a tuile crown. Pipe a small dot of whipped cream in the center of a prepared dessert plate. Working quickly, place a slice of parfait on top of the cream. Pipe a rosette of cream on top of the slice and set a reserved strawberry on the rosette. Drizzle an uneven band of orange syrup around the parfait. Lean a Florentina twist against 1 side of the parfait slice and set the filled tuile crown on the plate on the other side of the slice. Serve immediately.

CHEF'S TIP

It is best to use a mix of red and white berries, or all red. Using exclusively white wild strawberries will not produce as appetizing a color; however, the flavor will be just as good. If you have to use all white berries, add a few tablespoons of raspberry puree or Beet Juice (page 750) to improve the color.

Apricot Gratin with Sabayon of Muscat Wine — 269

Asian Pear Tart with Honey-Scented Pear Frozen Yogurt — 270

Baked Bananas with Banana-Tofu Frozen Yogurt — 273

Blood Orange Gratin — 275

Caramelized Pineapple Barbados — 276
   CARAMELIZED PINEAPPLE WITH COCONUT ICE CREAM — 278

Crepes Vienna — 279
   CREPES EMPIRE — 280
   CREPES JACQUES — 280

Dacquoise Baskets with Fresh Raspberries, Raspberry Sauce, and Mango Coulis — 280

Fresh Strawberries with Champagne Sabayon — 283

Frosted Minneola Tangelo Givré with Toasted Meringue and Cookie Citrus Rind — 283

Fruit Salad — 285

Fruit Valentines — 287

Global Fresh Fruit Baskets with Feijoa Sorbet — 289

Kardinals with Sambuca-Scented Italian Cream and Fresh Fruit — 291

Lemon Chiffon Pouches — 292

Low-Cholesterol Sponge Cake — 293
   LOW-CHOLESTEROL CHOCOLATE SPONGE CAKE — 294

Lychee Charlotte Royal — 294
   STRIPED LYCHEE CHARLOTTE — 296

Marbled Cheesecake with Quark Cheese — 297

Oeufs à la Neige with Caramelized Sugar Spheres — 298

Omelet Pancake with Sautéed Star Fruit, Pomegranate Sauce, and Mango Coulis — 300

Pears California with Cointreau-Flavored Almond Filling — 302

Rainbow of Summer Sorbets in a Cookie Flower — 304

Red Currant Sorbet in Magnolia Cookie Shells — 307

Sabayon — 311
   ZABAGLIONE — 311
   COLD SABAYON — 312

Salzburger Soufflé — 312

Strawberry-Peach Yogurt Creams — 313

Vineyard Barrels — 314

Winter Fruit Compote in Late-Harvest Wine Syrup — 316

Zinfandel-Poached Pears with Honey-Scented Pear Frozen Yogurt — 318
   FANNED ZINFANDEL PEARS — 319

Light and Low-Calorie Desserts

We live in an era of heightened health awareness and food consciousness; beyond this, the United States is obsessed with weight loss. Thin is definitely in, and people realize they cannot eat whatever and whenever they want and still remain healthy. Everyone seems to be trying to reduce fat and sodium intake, lower blood pressure and blood cholesterol levels, and increase consumption of low-fat foods. Exercise, too, plays a big role in the current fitness frenzy, and I have always felt fortunate that my love of exercise has prevented any weight gain associated with my love of food. (Of course, there are those who say you should never trust a skinny chef.)

The desserts in this chapter should not be confused with dietetic desserts, which, in my experience, usually taste as if something is missing. I have been preparing many of these recipes for years, long before today's emphasis on lighter food.

In addition to the recipes in this chapter, others found throughout the book can be served as light desserts, in some cases with only small modifications, which are noted when applicable. Also, the sorbet recipes and most of the frozen yogurt recipes given throughout the text make excellent light choices. A selection of sorbets or fresh fruit ices, attractively presented, is always good to have on your menu as an alternative for guests looking for a low-fat, nonchocolate, or nondairy option.

Many restaurants today offer reduced-calorie and reduced-fat alternatives to their regular menu selections. But a tasty and attractive dessert variation is not always as easy to produce as, for example, grilled rather than fried fish, or chicken breasts poached in reduced stock rather than sautéed in butter. The principal ingredients used in the pastry kitchen are virtually bursting with calories. Per cup, butter has an amazing 1,600 calories (184 grams of fat); granulated sugar, 770 calories (0 grams of fat); whole eggs, 360 calories (25 grams of fat); egg yolks, 870 calories (75 grams of fat); all-purpose flour, 455 calories (1.5 grams of fat); and heavy cream, 820 calories (88 grams of fat).

In some cases, it is possible to achieve fairly good results simply by replacing a high-fat or calorie-rich ingredient with a low-calorie or low-fat one. Meringue can be substituted for whipped cream, nonfat sour cream for regular sour cream, nonfat milk for whole milk, egg whites for whole eggs. Yogurt or tofu can be used as a base for ice cream instead of egg yolks and heavy cream. Unfortunately, these changes can yield a less satisfying dessert, because without further modifications, the alternative ingredients usually change the texture, moisture content, cooking time, and/or appearance of the final product. While ingredient substitutions may be appropriate for the home chef, a professional, to save time, will find it more reliable to use a recipe that starts out lower in calories or fat or, like those in this chapter, was created from the outset as a light dessert and thoroughly tested.

Pastry chefs are often blamed for tempting the hapless consumer to devour excess calories and fat. Yes, you can certainly gain weight — and plenty of it — by indulging in sweets if you do not limit yourself to occasional or small portions. However, I do feel dessert, in moderation, can be part of a balanced diet and a healthy lifestyle.

The recipes here are all sweet and satisfying; yet none contains over 400 calories per serving, and more than half contain under 300. None uses artificial ingredients, and only a few exceed the recommendation for no more than 30 percent total calories from fat. These recipes simply use ingredients naturally low in fat and calories and sometimes are served in a small portion. Happily, these desserts can be enjoyed not only for what they are not but also for what they are: delicious.

Note: The calorie and fat counts given with each recipe are calculated with the assumption that when yogurt is listed as an ingredient (in the main recipe or a subrecipe), nonfat yogurt is used.

About Apricots

Apricots, a stone fruit (drupe), are part of the rose family, which includes, not surprisingly, peaches, plums, and nectarines. But it *is* surprising to note that this family also includes cherries, almonds, and coconuts. All have one seed (the kernel), which is enclosed in a stony endocarp called a *pit*. As is true of the other well-known drupes (plums, nectarines, and peaches in particular), apricots come in cling-free and clingstone varieties. They are thought to have originated in China, where they have been cultivated since at least 2000 B.C. From China, the apricot made its way to Iran and then to Rome and Greece in the first century A.D. The Greeks gave the apricot its botanical name, *prunus armeniaca;* however, this was due to their mistaken belief that the fruit had originated in Armenia. The Romans named the fruit *praecocium,* meaning precocious (advanced), because apricots ripen earlier than other stone fruits. This is the origin of the name *apricot.*

Apricot trees were taken to England and Italy in the mid-1500s, but they did not prosper in those climates. The fruit made its way to Virginia in the early eighteenth century, where again the climate was too cool. Finally, apricots arrived in California, via Mexico and the Spanish, where they flourished and continue to do so today.

Nearly all apricots sold in the United States are grown in California. In most areas, and certainly in California, apricots are available fresh from May through September. Unfortunately, apricots are picked and shipped before they are ripe, as are peaches and plums, to protect them during transport. Ripe, plump, juicy apricots simply would not travel far without being bruised and damaged. Ripe apricots are not good keepers. They should be stored in the refrigerator but will last no longer than one week, depending on how carefully they have been handled.

Apricots are used in cakes, mousses, and fruit salads as well as in savory dishes. Both apricot jam and apricot glaze are used extensively in the pastry shop. Dried apricots are often found in fruitcakes and tea breads. Apricot seeds are made into a kernel paste similar to almond paste, but with a bitter aftertaste.

Apricot Gratin with Sabayon of Muscat Wine

yield: 8 servings, approximately 365 calories and 6.5 grams of fat per serving

This simple and refreshing dessert can easily be prepared in less than an hour. If the apricots are nice and ripe, that time can be cut in half by skipping the maceration part of Step 3. On the other hand, if there is no hurry and you want to dress up the plate a little, make Miniature Tulips (page 716) and fill them with a small scoop of Honey-Vanilla Frozen Yogurt (page 276). Place the filled shell on top of the sauce in the center of the plate just before serving. The crisp cookie shell and cold yogurt each add another dimension and pleasant contrast to the dessert.

20 large, fresh ripe apricots (approximately 3 pounds/1 kg 365 g)

10 ounces (285 g) granulated sugar

4 cups (960 ml) muscat wine or another sweet white wine, such as a late harvest Riesling

10 egg yolks (⅞ cup/210 ml)

Small edible whole fresh flowers, such as borage, or edible flower petals

1. Cut the apricots in half. Remove the pits and discard them.

2. Add approximately one-third of the granulated sugar to the wine. Heat the mixture to about 150°F (65°C), stirring to dissolve the sugar completely. Remove from the heat.

3. Add the apricot halves to the sweetened wine and set aside to infuse until they have cooled completely. Once the wine and apricots have cooled, remove the apricots carefully with

I do not remove the apricot skins in this dish, but if you wish to do so, blanch the whole apricots in boiling water for just a few seconds, transfer to cold water, and peel off the skins. Be careful, as ripe apricots can fall apart quickly. Conversely, if you are unable to find perfectly ripe apricots, you can soften them easily by heating the muscat wine to the boiling point and leaving the apricots in the wine off the heat until they are soft. Watch them closely, because they will soften fairly quickly. Lastly, if the apricots are overripe, they can still be used, but omit macerating them altogether.

a slotted spoon. Measure and reserve 2½ cups (600 ml) muscat wine mixture. Save the remainder for cake syrup or another use.

4. Cut 32 of the best-looking apricot halves in half again to make 64 quarters. Place these and the 8 remaining apricot halves on a sheet pan lined with baking paper. Cover and set aside.

5. Place the remaining sugar in a bowl with the egg yolks. Set the bowl over simmering water and whisk for 1 minute to thoroughly combine. Add the reserved muscat wine and heat, whisking constantly, until the mixture is thick and fluffy. Remove from the heat. The sauce should be used within 30 minutes. If you are unable to use the sabayon within that time, whisk it over an ice bath until completely cold as soon as you remove it from the heat.

6. Presentation: Place an apricot half, flat-side down, in the center of an ovenproof dessert plate. Arrange 8 apricot quarters in a spoke pattern around the apricot half. Spoon or pipe approximately 1 cup (240 ml) sabayon over the fruit. The sauce should coat the apricots, but the outline of the fruit should still be visible. If the sauce is too thick, thin it with a little of the left-over muscat wine mixture. Place the plate under a broiler or salamander to gratinée. Sprinkle edible flowers or flower petals over the top and serve immediately.

Asian Pear Tart with Honey-Scented Pear Frozen Yogurt

yield: 12 servings, approximately 390 calories and 10 grams of fat per serving (Color Photo 64)

This tart features poached Asian pears surrounded by layer upon layer of crisp phyllo dough. Unfortunately, Asian pears are not available throughout the year, as so many other pear varieties are. If you can't obtain Asian pears, try using Bosc pears instead, as they have the same attractive long stems (and, like Asian pears, require a longer poaching time than most other varieties). Peel the Bosc pears and poach them whole with the stems attached. After poaching, cut off the stem, including 1 inch (2.5 cm) of the top of the pear, to use in the presentation.

4 pounds (1 kg 820 g) Asian pears
   (approximately 10; see Note)

1 recipe Spiced Poaching Syrup (page 790)

24 sheets phyllo dough (approximately 1 pound/455 g)

½ cup (120 ml) clarified unsalted butter, melted

1 pound (455 g) Pastry Cream (page 773), made with low-fat milk

Cinnamon sugar

Raspberry Sauce (page 173)

½ recipe Honey-Scented Pear Frozen Yogurt (recipe follows)

Isomalt Bubble Sugar (page 617)

Powdered sugar

1. Peel the pears and cut in half lengthwise. Poach in the poaching syrup until soft to the touch. Asian pears take longer to poach than European varieties — up to 45 minutes, even if they are ripe. Let the pears cool in the liquid.

2. Use a melon ball cutter to remove the cores. Slice the pear halves lengthwise into ¹/₂-inch (1.2-cm) wedges, approximately the size of an orange section. Place the pear wedges on a sheet pan lined with baking paper.

3. Cut a round template, 6 inches (15 cm) in diameter, from cardboard, or have a lid or plate of about the same size handy.

4. Carefully unroll the stacked phyllo sheets. Cut into 4 sections, each large enough to have circles cut from it using the template. Place the template on top to determine where to make the cuts. Depending on the size of the phyllo dough sheets, you will probably have to stagger the cuts to fit. Do not cut around the template at this point. Place the cut pieces in 2 stacks. Cover 1 stack loosely with plastic wrap, then with a lightly dampened towel.

5. Place a sheet from the remaining stack on the table in front of you. Brush melted butter very lightly on top. Place a second sheet of dough on top and brush butter lightly over this piece. Continue until you have 8 sheets stacked with butter between them. Do not brush butter on the top sheet. Cover the remaining phyllo sheets.

6. Working quickly, place the round template on top of the stacked sheets and cut around it with a paring knife. Remove the scrap pieces and discard or save for another use. Brush melt-

About Asian Pears

Asian pears are rapidly growing in popularity. Most varieties have a roundish shape, similar to that of an apple, which has led to the frequent but mistaken use of the name *apple-pear*. These are true pears, also known as *Oriental pears, Chinese pears,* and *sand pears.*

This delicious, juicy fruit was brought to the United States by Chinese gold miners during the gold rush. The trees are exceptionally attractive. In spring, their bright white flowers contrast with leathery green leaves; in fall, the leaves offer a cascade of colors.

The cultivation of Asian pears is much the same as for European pear varieties, except that Asian pears should be allowed to ripen on the tree. When ripe, the fruit is still quite firm to the touch and does not yield to slight pressure. The best indicator of ripeness is a sweet aroma.

Asian pears are available from late summer through the holiday season. They can be stored at room temperature for up to two weeks and in the refrigerator for much longer. They are excellent for cooking and poaching; however, they take much longer to cook than the common European pear. Asian pear trees are commonly used as rootstock in commercial pear orchards.

Hosui — Medium-sized fruit with a golden russet skin. They have a crisp, refreshing apple flavor and keep exceptionally well. Hosui ripen in early August.

Nijisseiki — These Japanese pears are the most common commercial Asian pear variety; they are also called Twentieth Century. The fruit is roundish but squat and often lopsided, with a tender, smooth greenish-yellow skin. The flesh is pure white and slightly tart. These ripen in early September.

Shinseiki — Also known as New Century, these are similar to the Nijisseiki, with the same flattened, roundish shape; however, these are more uniform. The skin is yellow and slightly tough. The flesh is white, crisp, and sweet. Shinseiki pears ripen in mid-August.

Yali — This hardy variety is exceptional among Asian pears in that the fruit is *pyriform,* meaning "shaped like a pear." The pears look like overripe Bartletts, with their white to yellow skin. The flesh is aromatic with a mild, sweet taste. These ripen in early October.

Holiday Presentation

I like to feature this tart on the menu around November and December, served with Pomegranate Sauce (page 302). Both pears and pomegranates have a holiday feel, and both are at their prime during the season. As a variation, try this festive presentation: Follow the directions given in Step 10 of the main recipe, replacing the raspberry sauce with pomegranate sauce and sprinkling a few pomegranate seeds around the tart.

ed butter over the top layer of the round stack. Immediately and carefully press the dough into an individual tart pan or flan ring, 4 inches (10 cm) in diameter (see Figure 4-8, page 144).

7. Pipe approximately one-twelfth of the pastry cream into the form on top of the dough. Arrange 8 pear wedges on top of the pastry cream in a spoke pattern. Fold the sides of the phyllo dough in toward the center all around, using gentle pressure, but enough so the dough stays in place. Lightly brush butter over the exposed phyllo dough edges.

8. Repeat Steps 5, 6, and 7 to make a total of 12 tarts. Place the forms on a sheet pan. Sprinkle cinnamon sugar over the tops of the tarts.

9. Bake at 400°F (205°C) for approximately 20 minutes or until the phyllo dough is golden brown. Let cool before removing the desserts from the forms.

10. Presentation: Spin raspberry sauce on a serving plate (see page 686). Place a tart in the center of the plate. Top with a scoop of frozen yogurt. Using the tip of a paring knife, make a cut on top of the yogurt. Carefully stand a bubble sugar decoration straight up in the cut. Sift lightly with powdered sugar and serve at once.

NOTE: Both Asian and Bosc pears vary tremendously in size. Try to get small or medium-sized fruit for this recipe; it is difficult to arrange wedges from larger pears attractively.

HONEY-SCENTED PEAR FROZEN YOGURT yield: approximately 6 cups (1 L 440 ml)

2 pounds (910 g) Bosc pears (about 5 medium)

1 recipe Plain Poaching Syrup (page 790)

¼ cup (60 ml) or 3 ounces (85 g) honey

2 eggs

4 ounces (115 g) granulated sugar

4 cups (960 ml) unflavored nonfat yogurt

1. Peel and core the pears. Cut them in half, placing them in acidulated water as you work to prevent oxidation. Remove the pear halves from the water and place them in a saucepan with the poaching syrup. Poach until soft; drain. Puree the pears until smooth. Set aside to cool. Discard the syrup or save for another use.

2. Bring the honey to a boil in a small saucepan. At the same time, whisk the eggs and sugar together until frothy, about 1 minute. Add the honey to the egg and sugar mixture, whipping constantly. Continue to whip until the mixture has cooled to room temperature.

3. Stir the egg mixture into the yogurt together with the cool pear puree.

4. Process in an ice cream freezer following the manufacturer's directions. Store, covered, in the freezer.

Baked Bananas with Banana-Tofu Frozen Yogurt

yield: 16 servings, approximately 250 calories and 11 grams of fat per serving

Only about 5 percent of the bananas sold in the United States are cooked before they are eaten, which is a shame, because cooked bananas have a rich and exotic flavor. While the bananas for this recipe should be ripe, if overripe they will turn to mush when they bake. The bananas in a retail produce market are typically sold in one of the last three stages of ripeness: yellow with green tips (in this stage, they are firmest to the touch), completely yellow, or yellow with brown spots. In the third stage, all of the starch has dissolved and become sugar. While such bananas are at their sweetest, they should not be used for cooking except as a puree in banana bread, for example, because they are likely to melt into a syrupy pulp. Bananas at the all-yellow stage are perfect for cooking. To keep them from ripening any further, place them in the refrigerator; the flavor will not suffer, although the skin will eventually turn brown and then black. Raw bananas taste best at room temperature.

As a variation, try grilling the bananas instead of baking them. Sprinkle evenly with granulated sugar and cook the banana halves on a hot grill, turning once, until they are heated through and have distinctive grill stripes or markings. Present as directed in the main recipe.

3 oranges	2 ounces (55 g) unsalted butter, at room temperature
¼ cup (60 ml) or 3 ounces (85 g) honey	6 cups (1 L 440 ml) Banana-Tofu Frozen Yogurt (recipe follows)
1 tablespoon (15 ml) vanilla extract	Mint sprigs
8 medium-sized ripe bananas	
Lemon juice	

1. Using a zester, remove the zest from the oranges in long threads. Extract the juice from the oranges and combine with the zest, honey, and vanilla. Set aside.

2. Peel the bananas and cut in half lengthwise. Rub a little lemon juice on the bananas to keep them from getting brown. Place, cut-side up, in a hotel pan or other ovenproof dish (see Chef's Tip). Place a piece of butter on top of each, dividing the total amount evenly. Cover the dish with aluminum foil, crimping the foil against the edge of the dish to seal it tightly.

3. Bake the bananas at 375°F (190°C) for approximately 6 minutes or until they are soft; the time will vary with the ripeness of the fruit.

4. Presentation: Cut a banana half in 5 or 6 places along the outside (longer) edge, cutting at a 45-degree angle and going almost to the opposite side. Place it, flat-side up, on a dessert plate and bend into a half-circle to fan the cut pieces. Omitting the zest, spoon some of the orange juice mixture over the banana. Place a scoop of banana-tofu frozen yogurt inside the circle and place some of the orange zest on the yogurt. Garnish with a mint sprig and serve immediately.

CHEF'S TIP

If you wish to cook the bananas à la carte, or if you are making only a few servings, cut pieces of aluminum foil to the appropriate size, place a banana half on one side of each piece of foil, and top with butter as above. Fold the foil over and crimp the edges to seal. Place the individual packets on a sheet pan to bake.

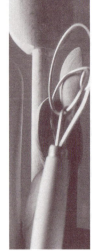

About Bananas

The yellow banana was one of the first plants to be cultivated, and one could easily argue that the banana is an ideal food in many ways. Bananas are plentiful and inexpensive all year long. They are easy to transport, as they are shipped before they are ripe while still hard. Bananas are easy to peel and they can be digested by people of just about all ages. It is easy to understand why so many bananas never make it into the kitchen.

Nutritionally bananas contain more carbohydrate (a great energy source) than any other fruit except the avocado, but, unlike avocados, which are very high in fat and calories, bananas have only a trace amount of fat and are low in calories. A medium-sized ripe banana, 6 to 7 inches (15 to 17.5 cm) long, is not only a delicious and sweet snack, it has only about 80 calories (and like all fruits and vegetables, no cholesterol), is almost fat-free, and is both high in carbohydrates and an excellent source of potassium. Bananas are composed of about 75 percent water and 20 percent sugar; the remaining 5 percent is a combination of starch, fiber, protein, and ash.

BANANA-TOFU FROZEN YOGURT yield: approximately 6 cups (1 L 440 ml)

The first reaction my students always have to this recipe title is a frown, but that changes when they taste the finished product. The flavor is great—slightly tart and very refreshing—and it has a smooth texture that normally requires a considerable quantity of cream and eggs to achieve.

12 ounces (340 g) soft tofu packed in water

2 pounds (910 g) ripe bananas (about 4 medium)

4 teaspoons (20 ml) lime juice

½ cup (120 ml) vegetable oil

1½ cups (360 ml) unflavored nonfat yogurt

¾ cup (180 ml) or 9 ounces (255 g) honey

2 teaspoons (10 ml) vanilla extract

1. In a food processor, puree the tofu, peeled bananas, and lime juice until smooth. Transfer to a bowl. Stir in the oil, yogurt, honey, and vanilla.

2. Process in an ice cream freezer following the manufacturer's instructions. Transfer to a chilled bowl and store, covered, in the freezer.

**30. Pink Lady Apple and Pear Cream
with Orange Syrup and an Apple Chip**

(clockwise from top left) **31. Forbidden Peach**
32. Mascarpone Cheesecake with Lemon
Verbena Panna Cotta 33. Honey Truffle
Symphony   34. Orange-Chocolate Tower
with Orange Syrup and Caramel Screen

(clockwise from top left) **35. Strawberries Romanoff   36. Red Banana Truffles in Phyllo Dough   37. Strawberry Pyramids**
38. Valentine's Day Hearts   39. Trio of Chocolates with Marzipan Parfait   40. Hot Chocolate Truffle Cake

(clockwise from top left) **41. Tropical Mousse Cake 42. Wild Strawberries Romanoff in Caramel Boxes 43. Frozen Hazelnut Coffee Mousse 44. Cassata Parfait with Meringue 45. Saffron-Poached Pears with Almond Ice Cream and Kadaif Phyllo Nests**

46. Opera Cakes (optional decorations)

47. Opera Cake

(clockwise from top left) **48. Rainbow of Summer Sorbets in a Cookie Flower 49. Mango Ice Cream with Chiffonade of Lemon Mint and a Chocolate Twirl 50. Caramelized Pineapple Barbados 51. Omelet Pancake with Sautéed Star Fruit, Pomegranate Sauce, and Mango Coulis 52. Kardinals with Sambuca-Scented Italian Cream and Fresh Fruit 53. Vacherin with Plum Ice Cream**

(clockwise from left) **54. Dacquoise Baskets with Fresh Raspberries, Raspberry Sauce, and Mango Coulis 55. Tropical Surprise Packages 56. Global Fresh Fruit Baskets wth Feijoa Sorbet 57. Lemon**

(clockwise from top left) **58. Red Currant Sorbet in Magnolia Cookie Shells 59. Red Currant Sorbet in Magnolia Cookie Shells (optional presentation) 60. Apple Crème Brûlée 61. Chocolate Mousse in Ribbon Teardrops 62. Cappuccino Mousse with Sambuca Cream in a Chocolate Coffee Cup 63. Zinfandel-Poached Pears with Honey-**

Blood Orange Gratin yield: 16 servings, approximately 300 calories and 12 grams of fat per serving

Gratin is the term applied to a dish placed briefly under a broiler or salamander to form a golden brown crust or skin on the surface.

Even though the orange gratin is not baked per se, be certain that the dessert plates or dishes are heatproof, as browning the surface of the sabayon takes quite a bit longer than, for example, browning a meringue-topped dessert.

This dessert should be started a day in advance of serving, or at least 4 hours before service (see Step 3).

16 large blood oranges	**4 egg yolks (⅓ cup/80 ml)**
1 ounce (30 g) fresh ginger	**¾ cup (180 ml) unflavored nonfat yogurt**
⅓ cup (80 ml) or 4 ounces (115 g) honey	**1¼ cups (300 ml) heavy cream**
¾ cup (180 ml) water	**2½ cups (600 ml) Honey-Vanilla Frozen Yogurt (recipe follows)**
2 tablespoons (30 ml) orange liqueur	**Dark coating chocolate, melted**
½ cup (120 ml) grenadine	**16 Miniature Tulips (page 716)**
½ teaspoon (1 g) ground allspice	

1. Peel the blood oranges and cut out the segments, holding the oranges over a bowl to catch the juice. Place the segments in rows in a hotel pan as you remove them. Squeeze all of the juice from the orange membranes into the juice bowl. Reserve the segments and juice separately.

2. Peel the ginger and cut it into 2 or 3 slices. Place the honey and water in a saucepan. Heat to simmering, then add the ginger. Reduce the syrup by half. Add the reserved orange juice and the orange liqueur. Mix in the grenadine and the allspice.

3. Cool the mixture slightly, then pour it over the reserved orange segments; avoid stirring to prevent breaking the segments. Remove and discard the slices of ginger. Cover the orange segments and refrigerate for at least 4 hours or, preferably, overnight to develop the flavors.

4. Beat the egg yolks for a few seconds just to combine, then mix in the unflavored yogurt. Whip the cream to soft peaks and fold the yogurt mixture into the cream.

5. Tilt the pan and pour off the liquid from the orange segments. Measure ¾ cup (180 ml) liquid and stir it into the cream mixture. Discard the remainder or save for another use.

6. Line up the orange segments on paper towels and pat somewhat dry to ensure that the sauce will adhere properly.

7. Scoop 16 small scoops of honey-vanilla frozen yogurt, taking care to keep them neat and uniform. Place them on a chilled sheet pan lined with baking paper. Place the chocolate in a piping bag. Streak the chocolate across the frozen yogurt scoops in 2 directions. Reserve in the freezer.

8. Presentation: Arrange 10 to 12 orange segments in a spoke pattern on the base of an ovenproof serving plate. Check the consistency of the cream and yogurt mixture; if too thin, it will run off the segments without coating them. If necessary, whip the mixture to thicken it, then place in a piping bottle with a large opening. Pipe just enough of the mixture on top of the orange segments to coat them and the base of the plate. Avoid piping any more than necessary on the plate surface. Place under a hot broiler or salamander until light brown. Place a tulip in the center of the dessert. Using 2 spoons to transfer it, place 1 reserved yogurt scoop in the tulip. Serve immediately, or the yogurt will melt on the warm plate.

HONEY-VANILLA FROZEN YOGURT yield: approximately 5 cups (I L 200 ml)

6 ounces (170 g) granulated sugar

⅓ cup (80 ml) or 4 ounces (115 g) honey

1 tablespoon (15 ml) lemon juice

1 tablespoon (15 ml) vanilla extract

2 eggs, separated

4 cups (960 ml) unflavored nonfat yogurt

I. Place half of the sugar, the honey, and the lemon juice in a saucepan. Bring to a boil, stirring to dissolve the sugar. Boil for 1 minute, then remove from the heat and add the vanilla.

2. Beat the egg yolks lightly. Stir in some of the sugar syrup to temper them, then add the remaining syrup. Let cool to room temperature.

3. Whip the egg whites until foamy. Gradually add the remaining sugar and whip to stiff peaks.

4. Place the yogurt in a bowl; stir smooth with a whisk. Fold in the syrup and egg yolk mixture, then the whipped egg whites.

5. Process in an ice cream freezer according to the manufacturer's directions. Store, covered, in the freezer.

Caramelized Pineapple Barbados

yield: 12 servings, approximately 260 calories and 2 grams of fat per serving (Color Photo 50)

The name of Barbados, the colorful easternmost island of the West Indies, is given to this dessert not so much for the pineapple, which is certainly grown there, as for the rum-flavored sauce. Sugarcane and refined sugar, together with their byproducts — molasses and rum — were the core of the island's commerce for many years, and Barbados rum has long been considered among the world's finest dark rums (see "About Jamaican Rum," page 240).

Choosing a ripe pineapple can be difficult, as color is not necessarily an indication of ripeness. You can get some idea by pulling on the small leaves in the center of the crown; they come away fairly easily if the pineapple is ripe. Don't get too carried away with this, however, as you need those leaves for the presentation, and there are usually not quite enough as it is. To supplement, cut some of the larger leaves at an angle that mimics the look of small pineapple leaves. Another good way to assess a whole pineapple is by the fragrance; a ripe pineapple has a sweet smell.

A simple way of trimming the pineapple slices into the octagonal shapes called for in this recipe is to use a template as a guide. This way, you get not only precise shapes but also servings that are all the same size.

2 fresh pineapples, about 4 pounds (1 kg 820 g) each

4 ounces (115 g) granulated sugar

2 cups (480 ml) Orange Sauce (recipe follows)

¼ cup (60 ml) or 3 ounces (85 g) honey

½ cup (120 ml) dark rum

2 tablespoons (30 ml) brined green peppercorns, chopped

2½ cups (600 ml) Honey-Vanilla Frozen Yogurt (recipe above)

Fresh pineapple leaves

I. Twist off the pineapple crowns and reserve them to use in the presentation. Cut the top and bottom off each pineapple, stand the fruit upright, and cut away the rind. It is not necessary

About Pineapples

This handsome tropical fruit got its English name from its vague resemblance to a pine cone. In most European languages, pineapples are called *ananas,* derived from the Paraguayan word *nana,* meaning "excellent fruit." Pineapples are native to Central and South America. They did not reach Hawaii until 1790, when Captain James Cook brought them there. Hawaii is now the world's biggest producer of pineapples.

Pineapple is among the most widely eaten tropical fruits, probably second only to the banana — and, like bananas, they are available all year. Pineapples generally grow one to a plant, growing out of the crown (the leafy part attached to the top when the fruits are marketed). The fruit develops from a bunch of small, lavender-colored flowers on a short stalk that grows from the center of the leaves; the stalk becomes the core of the mature pineapple. A pineapple is actually composed of many small hexagonal fruits merged together, which is reflected in the pattern on the tough skin. The skin must be removed before the fruit is eaten.

Distinguishing a sweet, ripe pineapple ready for harvest can be difficult, as color is not a reliable indication, but doing so is important; the starch in the fruit will no longer convert to sugar after the pineapple is removed from the plant. Some sources say a good test is to see if a leaf will pull easily from the crown, but a sweet fragrance is probably the best indicator, just as it is in choosing a pineapple in the market.

Pineapples, like many other tropical fruits, contain an enzyme (bromelain) that is beneficial to digestion but not to protein-based gelatin, in which it inhibits or prevents coagulation. The way around this is to use agar-agar or cornstarch for thickening, or simply to bring the fruit to a quick boil (which destroys the enzyme) before adding it to gelatin.

To remove the rind from a pineapple, begin by rinsing the fruit and twisting off the crown, which may be discarded or used for decorating. Cut off the base of the pineapple to make it level. Stand the fruit on end and remove the rind by cutting from the top to the bottom, following the curve of the fruit. Once the peel is removed, you can see that the eyes follow a spiral pattern. Remove them by cutting spiral grooves that wind around the pineapple from the top to the bottom. This extra effort not only enhances the fruit's appearance but saves a great deal of flesh that would be lost if you cut away enough of the entire surface to remove the eyes.

Cut the pineapple crosswise into slices of the desired thickness and, using a cookie cutter, remove the core from each slice. Alternatively, cut the pineapple lengthwise into quarters after removing the eyes, then use a knife to slice the core off each quarter. A large part of the core can be eaten; it makes a chewy treat. Pineapples become softer and juicier (but not sweeter) if left at room temperature for a few days. Ripe pineapples should not be stored in the refrigerator longer than four to five days, as cold can damage the fruit.

to cut deep enough to remove all of the eyes, as the edges will be trimmed. Cut the pineapples into slices approximately ¾ inch (2 cm) thick. Using a plain ¾-inch (2-cm) cookie cutter, cut the core out of each slice, then trim the sides to make the slices octagonal. Make 12 slices.

2. Place the pineapple slices on sheet pans lined with baking paper. Sprinkle half of the granulated sugar evenly over the top. Turn the slices over and sprinkle the remaining sugar on the other side. Rub some of the sugar that collects on the pan over the cut sides.

3. Combine the orange sauce, honey, and rum in a saucepan. Bring to a boil over high heat and reduce to a saucelike consistency. Pour into a container and reserve at room temperature.

4. Place the pineapple slices under a hot salamander and cook until the sugar is caramelized. Quickly turn the slices and caramelize the other side (see Note).

5. Presentation: Pour a round pool of sauce in the center of a dessert plate. Place a slice of caramelized pineapple on top. Sprinkle some of the chopped peppercorns over the pineapple. Place a small scoop of honey-vanilla frozen yogurt in the center of the slice and decorate with a few small, fresh-looking pineapple leaves from the reserved crowns. Serve immediately.

NOTE: While it would be ideal to cook the pineapple slices to order, this is often not practical. However, the slices should not be cooked more than 1 hour in advance, and they should be held at room temperature. If you do not have a salamander, cook the pineapple in a very hot skillet to caramelize the topping.

ORANGE SAUCE yield: approximately 4 cups (960 ml)

When refrigerated overnight, this sauce sets to a jellylike consistency, the result of the large amount of natural pectin present in oranges. Forcing the sauce through a fine mesh strainer is usually all that is needed to make it smooth again but, if necessary, reheat to thin it.

4 cups (960 ml) strained fresh orange juice (from 10 to 12 oranges)

5 tablespoons (40 g) cornstarch

2 tablespoons (30 ml) lemon juice

About 6 ounces (170 g) granulated sugar

1. Add enough orange juice to the cornstarch to make it liquid. Stir this into the remaining orange juice. Add the lemon juice and sugar, adjusting the taste by adding more or less sugar as needed, depending on the sweetness of the orange juice.

2. Heat to boiling in a stainless steel or other noncorrosive pan. Lower the heat and cook for 1 minute, stirring constantly. Let cool completely. If the sauce is too thick, thin with water. Store, covered, in the refrigerator.

VARIATION

Bitter Orange Sauce

Follow the recipe for Orange Sauce, making the following changes:

- Cut the peel of half of the oranges into about 6 pieces each and add these to the juice. It is not necessary to strain the juice. Follow the procedure for making orange sauce, including the peels with the juice.

- Set the sauce aside to allow the peels to macerate for 30 minutes. Strain to remove the orange peel as well as any pits or sediment.

VARIATION

CARAMELIZED PINEAPPLE WITH COCONUT ICE CREAM

If you do not need to watch calories, caramelized pineapple is wonderful served with Fresh Coconut Ice Cream (page 214). Spoon Fortified Caramel Sauce (page 19) on the base of the plate and set the pineapple slice on top. Decorate the edge of the caramel sauce with Chocolate Sauce for Piping (page 681). Place a scoop of coconut ice cream on the pineapple, then sprinkle a few Candied Lime Peels (page 756) or toasted macadamia nuts on the ice cream. Garnish with fresh pineapple leaves.

Crepes Vienna yield: 16 servings, approximately 250 calories and 8 grams of fat per serving

The humble pancake, called *pfannkuchen* in German and *crepe* in French, is made from ingredients so basic they can be found on any farm that raises chickens for eggs, has cows for milk and butter, and grows wheat for flour. However, this once-unassuming breakfast food has come to play a part in elegant dessert offerings on restaurant menus all over the world, generally using the French name. These dressed-up versions are often drenched in fruit syrups or liqueurs, filled with creams, wrapped around or folded over fruit fillings, or flambéed at the table. A number of these desserts, such as Crepes Suzette, Crepes Empire, Crepes Jacques, and Crepe Soufflé, have become classics.

The recipe for Crepes Vienna that follows could be prepared with the fruit filling of your choice. The perfect accompaniment is a scoop of frozen yogurt or ice cream served on the side.

¼ cup (60 ml) orange liqueur

1 ounce (30 g) dark raisins

1 ounce (30 g) golden raisins

½ recipe Crepe batter (page 755)

4 oranges

1 dry pint (480 ml) raspberries

⅓ cup (80 ml) heavy cream

½ teaspoon (3 g) granulated sugar

1 recipe or 4 cups (960 ml) Orange Sauce (page 278)

Fresh raspberries

1. Warm the orange liqueur. Add the dark and golden raisins and set aside to plump.

2. Make 16 crepes. If you will not be serving all 16 portions the same day, do not cook any more crepes than you expect to use (see Chef's Tip).

3. Cut the peel from the oranges and cut out the segments, holding the oranges over a bowl as you do so to catch the juice for the orange sauce. Cut the orange segments in half crosswise.

4. Place the crepes in front of you with the golden brown side down. Place 4 or 5 pieces of orange and an equal amount of raspberries in a line down the center of each crepe. Roll the crepes tightly around the fruit and place them, seam-side down, in a single layer on paper-lined sheet pans.

5. Whip the heavy cream and sugar until soft peaks form. Cover and reserve in the refrigerator.

6. Gently stir the plumped raisins and the orange liqueur into the orange sauce.

7. Presentation: Place a filled crepe, seam-side down, in the center of a dessert plate. Spoon orange sauce, including some of the raisins, across the crepe in the center, forming a small pool of sauce on either side. Place a small dollop of softly whipped cream on top of the crepe in the center. Place a raspberry on the cream.

CHEF'S TIP
The crepe batter can be stored for up to 3 days in the refrigerator. While leftover crepes (cooked the previous day) are suitable for many hot dishes (crepe soufflé, for example), day-old crepes should not be used in this recipe, as they tend to be rubbery when cold.

NOTE: If you are serving this as part of your regular menu and the calorie count is not crucial, use 2 crepes per serving.

CREPES EMPIRE

Fill the crepes with diced pineapple macerated in kirsch. Serve with Cherry Compote (page 149).

CREPES JACQUES

Fill the crepes with sliced bananas sautéed in a small amount of butter. Serve with Apricot Sauce (page 303) and orange liqueur.

Dacquoise Baskets with Fresh Raspberries, Raspberry Sauce, and Mango Coulis yield: 16 servings, approximately 375 calories and 12 grams of fat per serving (Color Photo 54)

The people who live in the town of Dax, located in the southwestern part of France, are known as *Dacquoise*, just as the inhabitants of Boston are known as Bostonians. The Dacquoise cake is traditional in that region, especially so in that town, and came to share the name. A classic dacquoise contains layers of Japonaise meringue sandwiched with flavored whipped cream or buttercream, fresh fruit, and/or nuts. In my version, the meringue is formed into pretty individual baskets instead of cake layers. I use fewer ground nuts in the meringue than is typical to keep the color light; more nuts would turn the meringue golden brown when baked.

The dacquoise baskets may be prepared several hours ahead of service and refrigerated if you are using them as part of a buffet display. In that case, to prevent the meringue from softening, fill them with buttercream flavored with orange liqueur instead of the Italian cream and raspberry filling. The buttercream filling complements not only raspberries but many other types of fruit as well. Fill the baskets about two-thirds full of flavored buttercream, then place a scrap piece of meringue on top (for this purpose, you may want to pipe out some thin disks of any meringue left after piping the baskets). Pipe a small amount of additional buttercream on top of the meringue before mounding the raspberries on top. Of course, with buttercream filling, the pastries no longer qualify as a light dessert.

16 to 20 paper cones, such as the type used for shaved ice	$\frac{1}{3}$ cup (80 ml) raspberry juice *or* Raspberry Sauce (page 173)
$\frac{1}{2}$ recipe French Meringue (page 780; see Note)	$\frac{1}{2}$ recipe Italian Cream (page 771; see Chef's Tip)
4 ounces (115 g) finely ground blanched almonds (almond meal)	Raspberry Sauce (page 173)
Dark coating chocolate, melted	Mango Coulis (page 244)
Simple syrup	1 pound (455 g) fresh raspberries

1. Trim the open end of the paper cones to make the cones 2½ inches (6.2 cm) tall. Be sure to make straight cuts so the baskets will stand straight up and not lean. You need only 16 cones for this recipe, but it is a good idea to make a few extra to allow for breakage. Wrap the outside of the cones with plastic wrap. Use only as much plastic as is needed to cover the paper, pull it tight, then secure the end inside the cone at the bottom. Place the wrapped cones, spaced well apart, on a sheet pan lined with baking paper.

2. Place the French meringue in a pastry bag with a No. 4 (8-mm) plain tip. Pipe the meringue around the cones in concentric circles, one on top of the other, starting the first circle on the baking paper at the base of the cone (Figure 6-1).

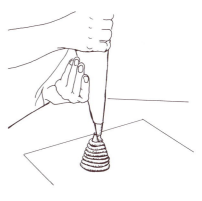

3. Bake the cones at 200°F (94°C) for about 2 hours or until completely dry. Let cool completely.

4. Carefully remove the paper cones from the inside of the meringue baskets by pulling the plastic wrap away from the meringue all around the bottom, then pulling it out. Use a small, thin knife to trim the narrow end of the cones to make them flat and to make the cones stand straight once they are inverted to become baskets.

5. Brush melted coating chocolate on the inside of the cones to cover the bottom 1 inch (2.5 cm) of the narrow ends. This reinforces the bottom so the cones will be sturdier when filled. Dip the top rim of the cones into melted coating chocolate, moving them up and down a few times over the bowl to remove excess, so the chocolate will not drip on the sides as the baskets are placed right-side up. Stand the cones on their narrow ends and let the chocolate set up.

6. Pipe 16 rounds of chocolate, 1½ inches (3.7 cm) in diameter, on a sheet of baking paper, spacing them at least 2 inches (5 cm) apart. Stand 1 cone in the center of each circle before the chocolate sets up.

7. Using a heavy pen, trace the template in Figure 6-2 onto a piece of paper. The template,

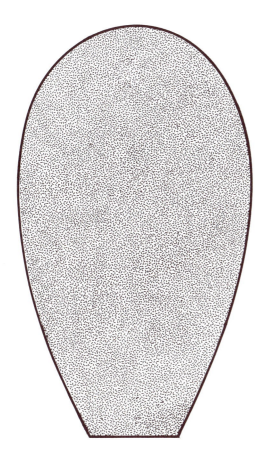

FIGURE 6-2 The template used as a guide to pipe the chocolate handles for the baskets

CHEF'S TIP

One-half recipe of Italian cream requires one-eighth recipe of Italian meringue. This tiny quantity is not practical to make; therefore, it makes sense to prepare one-quarter recipe Italian meringue and either discard half, use half for another project, or use the meringue to make a full recipe of Italian cream and use the other half of the filling somewhere else.

CHEF'S TIP

Because the dacquoise should be served crisp, it is best to fill the baskets to order; however, if necessary, they can be filled and refrigerated for up to 2 hours. The meringue baskets and handles may be stored in an airtight container for a few days at room temperature. If at all possible, however, store the baskets with the paper cones removed and without any chocolate, so they can be returned to the oven to dry if necessary.

as shown, is the correct size for use in this recipe. Place a sheet of baking paper on top of your drawing. Thicken ¾ cup (180 ml) melted coating chocolate with about 5 drops simple syrup, or enough to make the chocolate thick enough to hold its shape when piped. Place the thickened chocolate in a small pastry bag with a No. 0 (1-mm) plain tip. Pipe out a solid line following the curved edge of the template, followed by an intersecting wavy line on top, as shown in Color Photo 54. Slide the baking paper to the side so an unused portion of baking paper is over the template. Continue in the same manner until you have made 20 handles, which allows for breakage.

8. Refrigerate the handles and the baskets for a few minutes before removing them from the paper (see Chef's Tip).

9. Stir the raspberry juice or ⅓ cup (80 ml) raspberry sauce into the Italian cream. Place in a pastry bag with a No. 6 (12-mm) plain tip and reserve in the refrigerator. Adjust the consistency of the raspberry sauce and mango coulis, if needed, so each has the viscosity of a thick syrup. (To thin either sauce, add simple syrup or water; to thicken, boil gently until reduced, then cool before using.) Place the sauces in piping bottles.

10. Presentation: Pipe the cream filling into a basket, filling it to about ½ inch (1.2 cm) from the top (see Chef's Tip). Carefully push a handle into the cream. Top with raspberries. Pipe a ring of mango coulis, 2 inches (5 cm) wide, around the perimeter of a dessert plate. Fill the center with raspberry sauce, keeping the border where the 2 sauces meet circular. Use the blunt side of a wooden skewer to feather the sauces together (see Figure 13-8, page 682). Place a filled basket in the center of the plate. Serve immediately.

NOTE: Follow the recipe and instructions for French meringue, making this change: Stir a small handful of the granulated sugar into 4 ounces (115 g) finely ground blanched almonds (almond meal). Fold this into the finished meringue.

Fresh Strawberries with Champagne Sabayon

yield: 16 servings, approximately 200 calories and 4 grams of fat per serving

This classic and refreshing dessert is both simple and fast — it can be made from start to finish in less than 30 minutes — and it is definitely the one to choose when you have access to perfect, fully ripe, red, sweet berries. Although strawberries are the most traditional choice for topping with hot sabayon (many of us have seen the dish prepared in a few minutes while sitting at the counter of an exhibition kitchen), most other soft fresh fruits can also be paired successfully — raspberries, figs, and apricots, for example. A popular variation of this dessert is made by arranging the fresh fruit on a plate, topping it with sabayon, and placing the dish under a salamander to gratinée the top (see Apricot Gratin with Sabayon of Muscat Wine, page 269, and Blood Orange Gratin, page 275).

3 pounds 12 ounces (1 kg 705 g) strawberries, perfectly ripe	2 recipes Sabayon (page 311), made with champagne
2 tablespoons (30 ml) curaçao	Candied Lime Peels (page 756)

1. Clean the strawberries and reserve 16 of the largest and most attractive berries. Cut the remaining strawberries into ½-inch (1.2-cm) chunks. Macerate the cut strawberries in the curaçao for at least 1 hour but no longer than 2 hours, tossing gently from time to time. Cut the reserved berries into thin slices lengthwise.

2. Presentation: Line the sides of 16 saucer-type champagne glasses, 6 ounces (180 ml) in capacity, with the sliced strawberries, placing the cut sides against the glass. Divide the macerated berries evenly among the glasses. Pour hot sabayon on top. Decorate with the candied lime peels and serve immediately. If you do not need all 16 servings at once, the sabayon may be kept warm over a bain-marie for about 30 minutes. Assemble each serving as ordered.

Frosted Minneola Tangelo Givré with Toasted Meringue and Cookie Citrus Rind
yield: 12 servings, approximately 290 calories and 5 grams of fat per serving

If you are able to obtain tangelos or mandarins with the stems on and a few leaves attached, try this pretty variation: Fill the fruit shells with sorbet to within ⅛ inch (3 mm) of the top and return to the freezer; place the lids in the refrigerator to keep the leaves fresh looking. Remove the rind from one or two additional tangelos or mandarins and cut ⅛-inch (3-mm) round slices, about the same diameter as the tops of the filled givrés. To serve, place a slice of fruit on top of the filled givré; the idea is to give it the appearance of the natural fruit when the top is just cut off. Pipe a small rosette of whipped cream to one side on the fruit slice and set the lid on the cream at an angle to reveal the top. Serve immediately.

12 Minneola tangelos

Simple syrup

Water

½ recipe Italian Meringue (page 780)

Powdered sugar

12 Cookie Figurines (page 698)

12 Cookie Citrus Rinds (page 756), made slightly smaller than directed in the recipe

1 pint (480 ml) fresh raspberries

1. Wash the tangelos. Cut off approximately one-quarter of the top end on each fruit. If necessary, cut just enough from the opposite end so each tangelo will stand straight and level. Working over a bowl, use a melon ball cutter to carefully remove the flesh from the inside of the shells and from the pieces removed from the tops. Be sure to keep the shells intact for use in the presentation. Discard the tops. Cover the shells and place in the freezer.

2. Squeeze as much juice as possible from the tangelo flesh. Strain through a fine mesh strainer. Discard the seeds and the pulp. Measure the juice. Add an equal amount of simple syrup. Add enough water to bring the mixture to between 16° and 20° Baumé.

3. Process in an ice-cream freezer following the manufacturer's directions. Transfer to a chilled container.

4. Fill the reserved tangelo shells with the tangelo sorbet, spreading it level on the tops. Cover the filled shells and place in the freezer for at least 1 hour.

5. Place the Italian meringue in a pastry bag with a No. 8 (16-mm) plain tip. Pipe a large mound of meringue on top of the sorbet in each tangelo shell. Use a small spoon to create a rough surface with peaks and swirls. Make sure that all the sorbet is covered by meringue and the meringue is sealed to the edges of the fruit. Return the shells to the freezer until time of service.

6. Presentation: Remove a tangelo givré from the freezer. Sift powdered sugar lightly over the meringue. Brown the meringue by placing the tangelo shell under a salamander or broiler

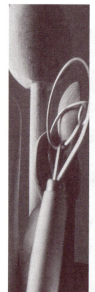

About Givré

The terms *givré* and *frosted* are both used to describe a frozen fruit shell filled with a sorbet or ice made from the removed fruit pulp — for example, lemon givré and frosted tangerines. Citrus fruits, including lemons, grapefruits, oranges, mandarins, and, as in this recipe, tangelos, are most commonly used for these presentations, but melon is a good choice for multiple servings. Because the whole fruit is used in the presentation of a givré, it is important to select the fruit carefully, avoiding bruises or other imperfections in the shell, and choosing fruit that is evenly shaped.

To make a givré, slice the top off the whole fruit and reserve it to use later as a lid. Using a spoon or melon ball cutter, hollow the shell. Be careful not to damage the skin or rind of the fruit shell; also, take care not to scrape any of the bitter white pith into the flesh to be used for the filling. Freeze the hollow shells while you prepare the filling. In the classic version, the filling is always a sorbet, but ice cream can also be used. Fill the frozen shells with the mixture either by scooping it into the shells and flattening the surface, if it is to be topped with meringue, as in this version, or by using a plain or star tip on a pastry bag to pipe the filling into the shells decoratively, finishing with a design on top. If meringue is used, pipe or spread it over the filling, then quickly brown it with a salamander or blowtorch. Set the reserved lids on the tops at an angle to reveal the filling.

or by using a blowtorch in a sweeping motion. Place the tangelo shell in the center of a dessert plate. Push a cookie figurine into the meringue on top of the dessert. Push the tail end of a cookie citrus rind into the meringue next to the figurine, then arrange the rest of the rind carefully so it sits on top of the meringue and trails down to the plate. Sift powdered sugar over the dessert and the plate. Sprinkle 6 to 8 raspberries around the base of the plate and serve immediately.

Fruit Salad yield: 16 servings, approximately 200 calories and 0 grams of fat per serving

Serving a fruit salad is one of the least time-consuming dessert options, surpassed in this respect only by serving whole fresh fruit in a basket. Fresh fruit, in addition to its familiar use in dessert salads, these days is incorporated into appetizer salad course offerings — for example, citrus segments, pears, or fresh cherries with greens, and fruit and vegetable slaws. These combinations are especially welcome on lighter menus. As simple as it is, a fresh fruit salad made with top-quality, ripe seasonal ingredients can be visually appealing, delicious, and a healthy alternative to more traditional desserts.

12 cups (2 L 880 ml) prepared fresh fruit (see Step 1)

½ recipe or 2 cups (240 ml) Orange Sauce (page 278)

¼ cup (60 ml) orange liqueur

6 ounces (170 g) strawberry preserves

Powdered sugar

Small edible whole fresh Flowers, such as Johnny-jumpups, or edible flower petals

1. Choose seasonal ripe fruit for the filling, such as apricots, peaches, orange and grapefruit segments, bananas, kiwis, and melons. Cut the fruit into chunks, approximately ¾ inch (2 cm) in size. Do not cut thin slices or roughly chop the fruit, but try instead to make the pieces uniform and attractive. Use a melon ball cutter for the melons. Coat banana pieces lightly with lime or lemon juice to prevent oxidation. Use blueberries, raspberries, or cut strawberries in the presentation, but do not include them in the mixture because they will stain the other fruit.

2. If the orange sauce was made ahead, warm it, then add the orange liqueur; if the sauce is freshly prepared and still warm, skip reheating. Gently fold the prepared fruit into the sauce while it is still warm. Place in the refrigerator and allow the fruit to chill in the sauce. Do not leave it any longer than 2 to 3 hours, or the fruit will begin to fall apart.

3. Force the strawberry preserves through a fine sieve. Cover and set aside.

4. Make the template shown in Figure 6-3. The template is the correct size for this recipe, but it can be altered to fit a particular plate. It should lie flat on the base of your dessert plate, leaving some room between the template and the perimeter of the base (not the rim). Trace the drawing, then cut the template out of cardboard that is ¹⁄₁₆ inch (2 mm) thick; cake boxes work fine. Attach a small loop of tape in the center to help lift the template off the plate.

5. Place a portion of the strawberry preserves in a piping bag and cut a small opening.

6. Presentation: Place the template in the center of a dessert plate. Lightly sift powdered sugar over the exposed part of the plate, including the rim. Carefully remove the template. Following the outline left by the template, pipe a thin string of strawberry preserves next to the

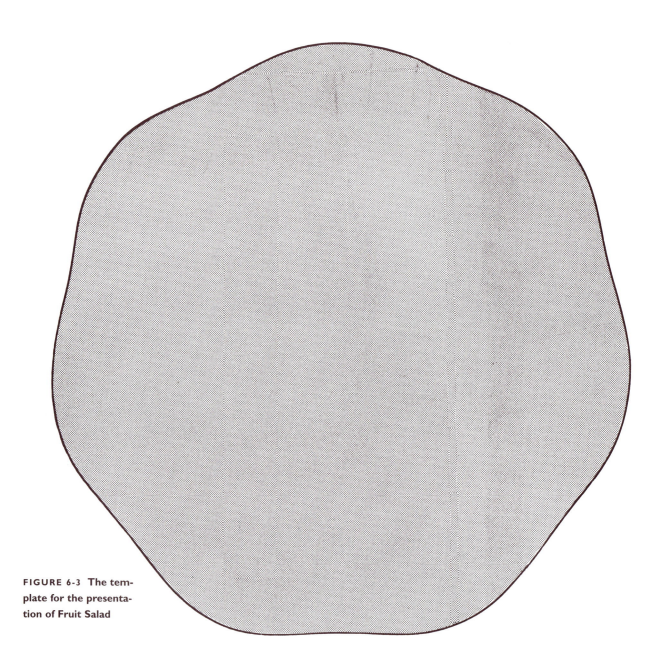

FIGURE 6-3 The template for the presentation of Fruit Salad

powdered sugar. Arrange approximately ¾ cup (180 ml) well-chilled fruit and sauce mixture attractively within the border of jam, letting the sauce flow to the edge of the jam but not over it. Decorate the top of the fruit salad with a few fresh raspberries, blueberries, or cut strawberries and several edible flowers. Be careful not to get fingerprints on the powdered sugar border when serving.

Fruit Valentines yield: 16 servings, approximately 300 calories and 2 grams of fat per serving

Think of this tempting light dessert not only for Valentine's Day or Mother's Day but any time you need a simple yet elegant presentation for low-calorie fresh fruit. Use a colorful mixture featuring at least three types of fruit or berries. One nice combination is blueberries or blackberries with raspberries, strawberries, and either kiwis or honeydew melon. Leave berries, other than strawberries, whole. Cut the fruit into small pieces about the size of the berries. To prevent the fruits from staining one another, which detracts from the presentation, keep each covered separately in the refrigerator until you are ready to assemble a dessert.

If you can afford a few more calories, fill the shells with frozen yogurt before adding the fruit mixture. The frozen yogurt may be placed in the shells ahead of time and the filled shells reserved in the freezer to top with fruit to order.

½ recipe French Meringue (page 780)

Dark coating chocolate, melted

2 tablespoons (30 ml) orange liqueur

¼ cup (60 ml) simple syrup

3 pounds (1 kg 365 g) well-chilled fresh fruit, prepared as described in the introduction

Sour Cream Mixture for Piping (page 727)

Raspberry Sauce (page 173)

1. Make the fruit valentine template (Figure 6-5). The template, as shown, is the correct size for use in this recipe. Trace the drawing, then cut the template out of cardboard that is ¼ inch (6 mm) thick, such as corrugated cardboard used for cake rounds. Draw 16 hearts on 2 sheets of baking paper (8 on each), tracing around the inside of the template.

2. Invert 2 sheet pans and cover the back of the pans with additional baking paper (not the paper with the tracing) or with Silpats. Fasten the papers to the pans with a little meringue to keep them from slipping. (Silpats do not need to be fastened.) Form 8 meringue hearts on each pan, spreading the meringue flat and even within the template (see Figures 13-29 and 13-30, page 694).

3. Place the remaining meringue in a pastry bag with a No. 3 (6-mm) plain tip. Pipe 2 ropes of meringue, one on top of the other, around the edge of the hearts.

4. Invert 2 more sheet pans and attach the reserved baking papers as before, inverting the papers so the tracing is on the bottom. Place a No 2. (4-mm) plain tip on the outside of the pastry bag and hold it in place as you pipe (see Figures 5-4 and 5-5, page 240). Pipe a border of meringue around the traced hearts, then 4 diagonal lines across the inside of each, attaching the lines to the frame on both ends.

5. Bake all of the meringues at 200°F (94°C) for approximately 2 hours or until dried through. Remove the thinner hearts (the lids) sooner if they begin to color. Let the meringues cool completely.

6. Place a small amount of melted coating chocolate in a piping bag and cut a small opening. Streak the chocolate on the thinner hearts in diagonal lines at right angles to the lines of meringue (Figure 6-4).

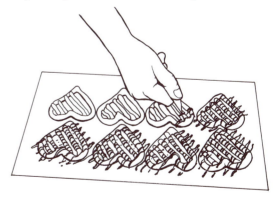

FIGURE 6-4 Streaking the chocolate over the baked meringue lids

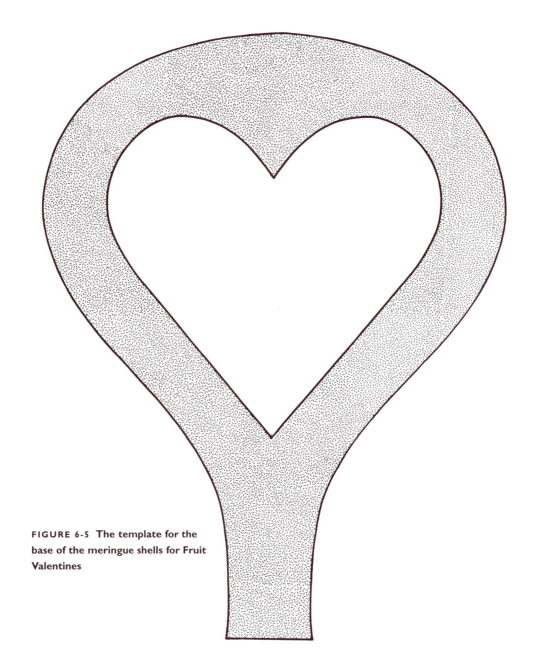

FIGURE 6-5 The template for the base of the meringue shells for Fruit Valentines

7. Combine the orange liqueur and the simple syrup.

8. Presentation: Place ¾ cup (180 ml) mixed prepared fruit in a small bowl. Add a little of the orange syrup and toss gently to coat. Pipe a small dot of sour cream mixture in the center of the upper half of a dessert plate. Place a meringue case on top. Fill the case with the fruit filling, mounding it on top and letting it spill out onto the plate on one side. Place a lid leaning against the other side of the filled heart. Pour a small pool of raspberry sauce in front of the dessert and decorate the sauce with sour cream mixture for piping (see pages 681 to 685). Serve immediately.

Global Fresh Fruit Baskets with Feijoa Sorbet

yield: 8 servings, approximately 400 calories and 10 grams of fat per serving (Color Photo 56)

This dessert was inspired by the recent upside-down seasonal availability of some types of fresh fruit. The wonderful fruits and berries that reach their peak in California around July and August are now, thanks to the affordability of air freight, available in the winter from Down Under producers, such as New Zealand and Australia, and South American countries, especially Chile. This means we in the United States now have the opportunity to enjoy summer fruits twice a year. (The quality of the imported fruit suffers little or not at all from its long journey because most commercially grown stone fruits, such as peaches, nectarines, apricots, and, in some cases, even plums, are picked and shipped before they are fully ripe to avoid bruising.) Going the opposite direction, subtropical fruits, such as feijoas, star fruit, and the annonas, which include cherimoyas and their close relative, the sweetsop or sugar apple — previously shipped from Down Under in late summer — are now grown commercially in California and Florida and are not only readily available during our early winter months but also affordable.

The idea in this dessert is that not only can you put together an unusual mix of fresh fruit that years ago would have been impossible to combine, but also you can offer it twice a year, either combining fresh local summer fruit with imported winter varieties or fresh local winter fruits with imported summer varieties. In any case, use a mixture of both berries and soft fruit and include four to six types with contrasting colors for the best effect.

You may find it difficult to handle and form the large cookie bowls at first, but with practice, you will soon get the hang of it. If they harden too quickly, or if you form them off-center, just reheat to soften, then start over. Keep in mind that if the cookies are not baked long enough — they should be brown on the edges and have random brown spots all over — they will not harden into delicious, crisp shells.

½ recipe Vanilla Tuile Decorating Paste (page 695)

1½ teaspoons (4 g) unsweetened cocoa powder, sifted

2 pounds (910 g) assorted fresh fruit, as described in the introduction

Piping Chocolate (page 543), melted

¼ cup (60 ml) orange liqueur

¼ cup (60 ml) orange juice

½ recipe Feijoa Sorbet (recipe follows)

I. Make a stencil with a round opening, 9 inches (22.5 cm) in diameter, from cardboard that is ¹⁄₁₆ inch (2 mm) thick; a cake box works fine.

2. If you do not have Silpats, grease and flour the back of 4 perfectly even sheet pans.

3. Work the tuile paste to make it smooth, if necessary. Remove 3 tablespoons (45 ml) of the paste and stir the cocoa powder into it. Cover and reserve this portion. Spread the plain paste flat and even within the stencil, making 2 circles on each Silpat or prepared sheet pan (see Figures 13-29 and 13-30, page 694).

4. Place a portion of the cocoa-colored paste in a piping bag. Cut a small opening and pipe a repeating design of horizontal S-shapes around the edge of each circle.

5. Have ready 4 shallow soup plates or bowls, approximately the same size as the tuile circles, to form the cookies as they come out of the oven. Ideally, 2 should be slightly smaller so they will fit inside the others. Bake the cookies, 1 sheet at a time, at 400°F (205°C) for approximately 8 minutes or until light brown spots appear in a few places.

6. Keep the sheet pan in the oven and leave the oven door open. Turn the 2 smaller bowls upside down. Using a small palette knife, pick up a baked circle and quickly invert it on top of an upside-down bowl. Still working quickly, adjust the circle so it is centered over the bowl, then place a larger bowl on top. Press down firmly to mold the cookie into a bowl shape. Form the second cookie in the same manner. Wait 30 seconds or so to ensure the cookies will hold their shape. Repeat baking and forming the cookies until you have made 8 shells.

7. Prepare the fruit by cutting it into pieces, approximately ½ inch (1.2 cm) in size. Do not chop the fruit; cut each variety according to its shape. Cut cubes or wedges rather than slices, with the exception of star fruit, which should be sliced. Keep each fruit separate. Cover and reserve in the refrigerator until time of service.

8. Place a small amount of piping chocolate in a piping bag and cut a small opening. Pipe out 8 chocolate figurines, about 2 inches (5 cm) long, on baking paper, making horizontal S-shapes to match the design on the cookie shells.

9. Presentation: Mix the orange liqueur and orange juice. In a separate bowl, combine 1 cup (240 ml) assorted prepared fruit. Place the mixed fruit in the center of a cookie bowl and place the bowl on a dessert plate. Pour 1 tablespoon (15 ml) orange juice mixture on top. Place a medium scoop of feijoa sorbet in the center. Place a chocolate figurine on the sorbet. Serve immediately.

FEIJOA SORBET yield: approximately 5 cups (1 L 200 ml)

It has been a long time since a dessert was as enthusiastically received by my students as this feijoa sorbet. We experimented with several batches in order to achieve the correct balance between the lime and pineapple juices, and the word quickly spread around campus that something brand-new and rather unusual was being created. I introduced this recipe in mid-January, when the domestic feijoa crop is available and relatively inexpensive. The imported fruit, from Australia as well as Chile and other South American countries, can be enjoyed later in the year, but the price is a bit higher.

Feijoas, or *pineapple guavas*, as they are commonly known, have a distinctive flavor — roundly complex and unquestionably tropical. Just picking up the fruit and smelling its perfume tells you it is out of the ordinary. The petals of the feijoa flower measure up to 1½ inches (3.7 cm) across. They are somewhat fleshy, pinkish white on the outside and deep pink within, and have an incredibly sweet tropical flavor all their own. They can be used as a garnish or added to the sorbet. To use the petals in the sorbet, heat the pineapple juice to scalding in a noncorrosive saucepan. Stir in ¼ cup (60 ml) flower petals and set aside to cool to room temperature. Combine with the remaining ingredients in Step 3 of the sorbet recipe.

If properly covered, feijoa sorbet can be stored in the freezer for several weeks. However, based on my experience, long-term storage is an unlikely concern. The strainer and other utensils used here must be made of a noncorrosive material, or the acid will discolor the fruit.

3 pounds (1 kg 365 g) feijoas	2 cups (480 ml) simple syrup, at room temperature
½ cup (120 ml) lime juice	½ cup (120 ml) water
1½ cups (360 ml) unsweetened pineapple juice	

1. Use a vegetable peeler to remove the skin from the feijoas. You should have approximately 2 pounds (910 g) fruit left. Cut the fruit into small pieces.

2. Place the fruit pieces in a food processor with the lime juice. Process to a smooth puree. Force the mixture through a fine mesh strainer; discard the seeds and solids.

3. Add the pineapple juice and simple syrup to the puree. Add enough of the water (or additional simple syrup, depending on the ripeness of the fruit) to bring the mixture to between 16° and 20° Baumé.

4. Process in an ice cream freezer according to the manufacturer's instructions. Transfer the finished sorbet to a chilled container and store, covered, in the freezer.

Kardinals with Sambuca-Scented Italian Cream and Fresh Fruit

yield: 16 servings, approximately 350 calories and 10 grams of fat per serving (Color Photo 52)

In this recipe, meringue and sponge batter are piped out together, baked until feather-light, dry, and crumbly, then filled with sambuca cream. The Italian meringue in the filling makes it light, palatable, and merciful to the waistline, while the anise-flavored liqueur makes a nice bridge between the cream and the slightly acidic fresh fruit. I like this dessert just as well when it is a day old; the sponge and meringue sheets absorb moisture from the filling and become a bit chewy.

¼ recipe French Meringue (page 780)

½ recipe Ladyfingers batter (page 801)

2 teaspoons (6 g) unflavored gelatin powder

¼ cup (60 ml) cold water

1 recipe Italian Cream (page 771; see Note 1)

¼ cup (60 ml) sambuca liqueur

Unsweetened cocoa powder

2 pounds (910 g) prepared fresh fruit, approximately (see Note 2)

1. Draw 4 strips, 3¾ inches (9.5 cm) wide, evenly spaced crosswise on a sheet of baking paper. Invert the paper on a sheet pan. Place the meringue in a pastry bag with a No. 8 (16-mm) plain tip. Pipe 3 ropes of meringue within each of the marked strips, piping 2 along the outside edges and the third down the center, with equal space on each side (Figure 6-6).

2. Squeeze any remaining meringue out of the bag and discard. Place the ladyfinger batter in the same pastry bag. Pipe 2 ropes of batter per section, piping them between the meringue ropes.

3. Bake at 210° to 220°F (99° to 104°C) until both batters are dry and the ladyfinger batter has turned golden brown, approximately 2 hours. Let the strips cool.

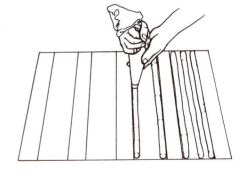

FIGURE 6-6 Piping 3 evenly spaced rows of meringue in each section between the lines drawn as a guide on a sheet of baking paper

4. Sprinkle the gelatin over the cold water and set aside to soften.

5. When the meringue and ladyfinger strips have cooled, invert and peel the paper from the back. Place the strips, right-side up, on a sheet of cardboard or an inverted sheet pan.

6. Heat the gelatin mixture to dissolve. Quickly mix the gelatin into one-quarter of the Italian cream. Then, still working quickly, mix this into the remaining cream. Select the 2 best-looking meringue and ladyfinger strips to use for the tops. Place the Italian cream mixture in a pastry bag with a No. 8 (16-mm) plain tip and pipe the entire amount over the other two strips.

Set the top strips on the cream and press down lightly to be sure they adhere. Cover and refrigerate for at least 2 hours or, preferably, overnight.

7. Make a stencil with a round opening, 6 inches (15 cm) in diameter. Attach the stencil to an appropriately sized bottomless pie tin (see page 692 for more information).

8. Cut the chilled dessert strips into 8 pieces each; the pieces will be approximately 1¾ inches (4.5 cm) wide.

9. Presentation: Place the stencil against the base of a dessert plate. Sift cocoa powder lightly over the stencil and over a dessert slice. Carefully remove the template and place the slice in the center of the cocoa round. Arrange fresh fruit around the cocoa on the base of the plate.

NOTE 1: Make the Italian Cream as directed, adding ¼ cup (60 ml) sambuca liqueur to the heavy cream before whipping.

NOTE 2: Use 4 or 5 varieties of fruit, cut into distinct pieces (not chopped or sliced thinly). Reserve each type of fruit separately in a covered bowl until serving time.

Lemon Chiffon Pouches

yield: 16 servings, approximately 225 calories and 11 grams of fat per serving (Color Photo 57)

The technique of filling crepes and shaping them into appealing little pouches can be applied to other desserts with other wrappers. For example, pair phyllo dough with a filling that can be baked. When using phyllo dough, make several layers of dough and melted butter, place the filling in the center, gather the edges of the dough together, then twist and pinch closed above the filling but below the edges of the dough. Be certain the pouches are securely closed, especially if the filling will expand in the oven; you may need to use a little egg wash on the inside or tie the pouches closed. Brush butter over the outside of the dough before baking. A nice stuffing for phyllo dough pouches is Chunky Apple Filling (page 767). Serve these hot in a pool of Crème Anglaise (page 754), topped with a sprinkling of cinnamon and powdered sugar.

As a variation on the following recipe, try filling the crepe pouches with berries instead of, or in addition to, the lemon chiffon filling. Insert one or two small berries in the center of the filling before tying the pouches closed, or use all berries for a dessert even lower in calories.

½ recipe Crepe batter (page 755)	Lemon Chiffon Filling (recipe follows)
Oranges	1 recipe Strawberry Sauce (page 186)

1. Make 16 crepes, 7 inches (17.5 cm) in diameter. Make sure the crepes are thin and uniform in size and shape. If they are not round, place a plate or other round object of the correct size on top and trim the edges. Cover and reserve.

2. Using a citrus stripper, cut 16 strips of orange rind, 8 inches (20 cm) in length, to use as strings to tie the pouches closed.

3. Center each crepe on top of a soufflé ramekin or other form, 3 inches (7.5 cm) in diameter, with the nicer side on the bottom. Push the center of each crepe into the form.

4. When the lemon filling has started to set slightly, place it in a pastry bag with a No. 6 (12-

mm) plain tip. Pipe the filling on top of the crepes, dividing it equally among the forms. Bring up the sides of a filled crepe, lift it out of the form, and tie it closed with a strip of orange rind (Figure 6-7). Place on a sheet pan lined with baking paper. Repeat this procedure with the remaining crepes. Cover and refrigerate until serving time, but no longer than a few hours.

5. Place a portion of the strawberry sauce in a piping bottle.

6. Presentation: Pipe a 5-inch (12.5-cm) circle of strawberry sauce in the center of a dessert plate. Do not cover the entire base of the plate. Place a pouch in the center of the sauce. Serve immediately.

NOTE: Should calories not be an issue, include 2 pouches in each serving.

FIGURE 6-7 Using a strip of orange zest to secure a Lemon Chiffon Pouch

LEMON CHIFFON FILLING yield: approximately 4 cups (960 ml)

½ cup (120 ml) lemon juice

2 teaspoons (12 g) finely grated lemon zest

3 eggs

⅓ cup (80 ml) water plus ¼ cup (60 ml) cold water

3½ ounces (100 g) granulated sugar

1 tablespoon (9 g) unflavored gelatin powder

¾ cup (180 ml) heavy cream

1. Combine the lemon juice and grated lemon zest. Set aside.

2. Whip the eggs until they are thick and light in color. Combine ⅓ cup (80 ml) of water with the sugar and boil until the syrup reaches 230°F (110°C). Gradually whisk the hot syrup into the whipped eggs in a steady stream. Continue whipping until the mixture is cold.

3. Sprinkle the gelatin over the ¼ cup (60 ml) of cold water and set aside to soften.

4. Whip the heavy cream to soft peaks. Combine the egg mixture, whipped cream, and lemon juice with zest.

5. Place the gelatin mixture over a bain-marie and heat until dissolved. Do not overheat. Place about one-fourth of the cream mixture in a separate bowl and rapidly mix in the dissolved gelatin; quickly mix this into the remaining cream.

Low-Cholesterol Sponge Cake

yield: 1 cake, 10 inches (25 cm) in diameter, or 12 servings, approximately 195 calories and 3.5 grams of fat per serving

This cake bears a close resemblance to angel food cake. Although not quite as feather-light, it is much easier to make. Using this cake as a base, you can create many light dessert variations. For a delightful light cream cake, fill and ice this sponge with Italian Cream (page 771); decorate the top with seasonal fruit.

5 ounces (140 g) cake flour

1½ ounces (40 g) arrowroot

16 egg whites (2 cups/480 ml)

Few drops of lemon juice

10 ounces (285 g) granulated sugar

1 teaspoon (5 ml) vanilla extract

2 ounces (55 g) unsalted butter, melted

1. Line the bottom of a cake pan, 10 inches (25 cm) in diameter, with baking paper.

2. Sift the cake flour and the arrowroot together twice.

3. Whip the egg whites until they triple in volume. Continuing to whip at high speed, add the lemon juice, then gradually incorporate the sugar. Whip until the meringue holds stiff peaks. Carefully fold in the flour mixture, then gently incorporate the vanilla and the melted butter. Pour the batter into the prepared pan.

4. Bake at 350°F (175°C) for approximately 20 minutes or until the center of the cake springs back when pressed lightly. Dust flour over the top and invert onto a paper-lined sheet pan to cool.

VARIATION
LOW-CHOLESTEROL CHOCOLATE SPONGE CAKE

Make the Low-Cholesterol Sponge Cake as directed above, replacing 1½ ounces (40 g) cake flour with unsweetened cocoa powder.

Lychee Charlotte Royal yield: 16 servings, approximately 350 calories and 10 grams of fat per serving

Lychees are not only the most famous but also the most popular of Chinese fruits. In the mid-1980s, when I traveled to China with two other chefs, Jacques Pépin and Cindy Pawlcyn, to teach Western-style cooking, it seemed that lychees and either mandarins or oranges were just about the extent of what we were served for dessert — although after the incredible banquets featuring twenty or even thirty courses, that was plenty.

The wide-spreading lychee tree has dense green foliage and loose clusters of fruit growing on long stems. Fresh lychees have a scarlet-colored knobby shell enclosing a firm, translucent, white or pinkish juicy pulp, which, in turn, surrounds a large brown inedible seed. Lychees are at their peak in June and July; to enjoy one fresh, peel from the stem down to keep the fruit in one piece. Lychees are also known as *litchis* and, in their dried form, are called *lychee nuts*. Fresh lychees can be difficult to find, but the fruit is commonly available canned in syrup.

This recipe was obviously inspired by an old classic — Charlotte Royal. To make the original version, follow the instructions for lining the forms as directed here, then fill with Classic Bavarian Cream (page 767). For the presentation, pipe a rosette of whipped cream on top of the charlotte and decorate the cream with a raspberry or slice of strawberry. This presentation can also be used for the lychee charlotte if you are not offering it as a light dessert.

½ recipe **Almond Sponge** batter (page 795)	**Red Currant Glaze** (page 777)
8 ounces (225 g) smooth raspberry jam	½ recipe **Raspberry Sauce** (page 173)
Lychee Bavarois (recipe follows)	

1. Spread the sponge batter evenly to ¼ inch (6 mm) from the edge on all sides of a perfectly even full sheet pan, 16 × 24 inches (40 × 60 cm), lined with a Silpat or baking paper. Bake immediately at 425°F (219°C) for about 8 minutes or until just done. To prevent the thin sponge from drying out, slide it onto a cool sheet pan or the table. Let cool.

2. Invert the sponge sheet onto a second sheet of baking paper, then peel the Silpat or paper off the back. (If the sponge is made ahead and refrigerated, the skin will become loose; remove it from the top before inverting the sponge.) Trim ½ inch (1.2 cm) from each long side of the sponge. Spread just enough raspberry jam on top to cover the sponge and make it sticky. Starting from the top long edge and rolling toward you, roll the sheet lengthwise into a tight rope (see Figure 9-9, page 454). Pull the paper toward you as you work to help tighten the roll. Leaving the paper around the roll, hold the bottom of the paper in place with your left hand and, with your right, push a dowel or ruler against the roll on top of the paper; the paper will wrap around the roll and make it tight (see Figure 9-10, page 454). Place the sponge roll in the freezer to firm up and make it easier to slice while you are making the lychee bavarois.

3. Cut the firm sponge roll into slices, ⅛ inch (3 mm) thick. Use the slices to line the bottom and sides of deep, round bavarois molds, Flexipan No. 1268 (see Note), or other suitable molds (appropriately shaped coffee cups work great) with an approximate capacity of ½ cup (120 ml), placing 1 slice in the bottom of each mold and 4 slices around the sides (Figure 6-8). Fill the molds with lychee bavarois as soon as it shows signs of thickening. Refrigerate for at least 2 hours to set.

FIGURE 6-8 Lining the mold with jelly roll slices to make Lychee Charlotte Royal

4. Unmold as many charlottes as you anticipate serving the same day by gently pressing the back of a spoon around the edge on top of each to loosen the filling, then inverting onto a sheet pan lined with baking paper. You may need to dip the forms in hot water briefly, but be careful not to melt the bavarois. Brush red currant glaze over the jelly roll slices. Reserve in the refrigerator until needed.

5. Place a portion of the raspberry sauce in a piping bottle.

6. Presentation: Place a charlotte in the center of a dessert plate. Pipe raspberry sauce around the dessert.

NOTE: If you use a Flexipan, place the assembled desserts in the freezer at the end of Step 3. When they have frozen solid, invert the pan and push the desserts out of the form by turning each indentation inside out. Place the desserts right side up on a sheet pan lined with baking paper and thaw before brushing with glaze and serving.

LYCHEE BAVAROIS yield: 7 cups (1 L 680 ml)

8 egg yolks (⅔ cup/160 ml)

2 ounces (55 g) granulated sugar

2 tablespoons (18 g) unflavored gelatin powder

½ cup (120 ml) cold water

1 vanilla bean, split lengthwise

2 cups (480 ml) strained lychee juice (see Chef's Tip)

1 cup (240 ml) heavy cream

¼ recipe Swiss Meringue (page 782; see Note, page 781)

1. Whip the egg yolks and sugar until light and fluffy.

2. Sprinkle the gelatin over the cold water and set aside to soften.

3. Scrape the seeds out of the vanilla bean halves and add them to the lychee juice. Discard the pods or save for another use.

Your chance of finding fresh lychees is limited by where you live and the time of year. If you are lucky enough to find them fresh, it would be a shame to puree this exceptional and fragrant fruit, especially as the canned variety works just fine in this recipe. You need approximately 3 pounds (1 kg 365 g) canned lychees to get 2 cups (480 ml) strained juice. Strain the canned lychees and reserve the liquid. Puree the fruit and pass it through a fine sieve. Add the reserved liquid, if needed, to make 2 cups (480 ml) juice. The recipe assumes you are using lychees canned in sugar syrup.

4. Bring the lychee juice to the scalding point. Gradually pour the hot liquid into the yolk mixture, whipping rapidly. Return the mixture to the heat and bring back to the scalding point, stirring constantly. Do not boil. Remove from the heat, stir in the reserved gelatin, and set aside to cool, stirring from time to time.

5. Whip the cream to soft peaks. Gradually stir the whipped cream into the Swiss meringue. When the custard has cooled, slowly stir it into the cream and meringue mixture.

VARIATION
STRIPED LYCHEE CHARLOTTE yield: 16 servings

This method shows horizontal stripes of sponge and jam on the sides of the charlottes.

1. Make a full recipe of almond sponge batter and make a second sponge sheet, the same size as the first. Make 1 sheet into a jelly roll, as directed above. Weigh out an additional 8 ounces (225 g) jam. Use soufflé ramekins, 3¼ inches (8.1 cm) in diameter and 5 ounces (150 ml) in capacity, instead of the bavarois molds.

2. Invert and remove the paper from the second sponge sheet. Cut a rectangle measuring approximately 8 inches (21.2 cm) wide and the length of the sheet. Adjust the width, if necessary, so it matches the circumference of the inside of the ramekins you are using. Reserve the remaining piece of sponge.

3. Cut the rectangle across into 4 equal pieces, each approximately 8½ × 5¾ inches (21.2 × 14.5 cm). Cut 2 more pieces the same size from the reserved piece of sponge. Save the remainder for another use.

4. Stack the pieces, layering raspberry jam between them. Place in the freezer to make the sponge firm and easier to slice.

5. Use thin, ⅛-inch (3-mm) slices of the roulade (the rolled sponge sheet) to line the bottom of the ramekins. (You will have some roulade left; wrap and reserve in the freezer for another use.) Using a serrated knife dipped in hot water, cut ⅛-inch (3-mm) slices lengthwise from the layered sponge strip. Use these pieces to line the sides of the ramekins (Figure 6-9).

6. Fill the lined ramekins and follow the instructions in the main recipe.

FIGURE 6-9 Lining soufflé ramekins with a jelly roll slice in the bottom and layered sponge strips on the side for Striped Lychee Charlotte

Marbled Cheesecake with Quark Cheese

yield: 1 cake, 10 inches (25 cm) in diameter, or 16 servings, approximately 350 calories and 11 grams of fat per serving

Quark is a continental-style fresh cheese, similar to the cottage cheese found in the United States. This curd cheese is slightly more acidic than cottage cheese and low in fat and calories, typically containing about 1 gram of fat and 85 calories per 3½-ounce (100-g) serving. Quark is immensely popular in Germany, accounting for almost half of the cheese consumption there, the majority used in cooking.

In addition to its obvious application in cheesecake, quark is used in a number of German cakes, including the delicious *quarksahnetorte* (quark and cream cake); it is also an ingredient in dishes such as quark *apfelkuchen* (quark apple pie) and quark *pfannkuchen* (quark pancakes).

When some of the fat skimmed off during processing is added back to the lean curd at the end, the cheese is called *speisequark*. This enriched quark is sold plain or mixed with fruit and fruit pulp, much as yogurt is packaged in the United States. Quark is often available in ethnic markets, but if you are unable to find it, low-fat cottage cheese can be substituted in this recipe with good results. You can replace up to half of the cream cheese in this recipe with Yogurt Cheese (see page 804) to lower the calorie and fat counts further.

¼ cup (60 ml) vegetable oil	1 tablespoon (15 ml) vanilla extract
8 ounces (225 g) Graham Cracker Crumbs (page 777)	6 eggs
1 pound 5 ounces (595 g) quark cheese	1½ ounces (40 g) unsweetened cocoa powder, sifted
12 ounces (340 g) low-fat cream cheese, at room temperature	1 ounce (30 g) powdered sugar, sifted
14 ounces (400 g) granulated sugar	¼ cup (60 ml) water

1. Combine the vegetable oil and graham cracker crumbs and pat the mixture evenly over the bottom of a cake pan, 10 inches (25 cm) in diameter and 2 inches (5 cm) in height.

2. Place the quark in a food processor and process until completely smooth, scraping down the sides and bottom of the processor bowl once or twice. Using the paddle attachment in an electric mixer, beat the cream cheese for a few seconds, just until smooth. Add the quark to the cream cheese and mix until they are combined. Add the granulated sugar and vanilla, then gradually incorporate the eggs at medium speed, scraping down the bowl several times to eliminate lumps. Be careful not to overmix.

3. Combine the cocoa powder and powdered sugar in a small bowl. Add the water and stir to make a smooth paste. Incorporate the paste into 2 cups (480 ml) cheesecake batter and reserve.

4. Set aside 1 cup (240 ml) plain batter. Pour the remaining plain batter into the prepared pan. Pour the chocolate batter in the center, making a circle, 6 inches (15 cm) in diameter, on top of the plain batter. Pour the remaining plain batter in the center on top of the chocolate batter; you should see 3 rings of batter. Use a spoon to swirl the batters together into a marble pattern; do not overmix. Place the pan in a hotel pan or other suitable baking dish and add hot water to come halfway up the sides.

5. Bake at 350°F (175°C) for about 45 minutes or until the cake is set and golden on the top (see Note). Carefully remove the cake pan from the bain-marie and set it aside to cool at room temperature. Once the cake has cooled, cover it and place in the refrigerator for at least 4 hours or, preferably, overnight. At this point, the cake can be kept refrigerated for up to 3 days.

6. To unmold the cake, stretch a sheet of plastic film over the top of the cake pan, place a cardboard cake circle on top of the plastic, then invert the cake. Remove the pan. Place a second cake cardboard on top of the inverted cake (on the bottom) and invert again to place the cake, right-side up, on the cardboard. Carefully peel away the plastic film without damaging the top of the cake. Using a thin, sharp knife dipped in hot water, cut the cake into 16 servings; wipe the knife clean between each cut.

NOTE: If the cake is not baked long enough for the plain filling to turn golden on top, the top of the cake will stick to the plastic when the cheesecake is inverted.

Oeufs à la Neige with Caramelized Sugar Spheres

yield: 12 servings, approximately 380 calories and 3 grams of fat per serving

Oeufs à la Neige, which translates to "snow eggs" in English, is close to — and more often than not confused with — Floating Island (Île Flottante). One can easily see why: In both desserts, fluffy, soft meringue floats on a light custard sauce. The main difference is that Floating Island consists of one large round island baked before it is set on the sea of custard; this can be an individual portion or a meringue round large enough to serve four guests. In Oeufs à la Neige, the beaten egg whites are formed into small, egg-shaped pieces and poached rather than baked; three or four "eggs" are offered per serving. (The old-fashioned French version of Floating Islands did not use meringue at all; instead, rounds of sponge cake were moistened with liqueur or covered with jam, then topped with a layer of whipped cream and served in a pool of custard sauce.) Do not be too generous when shaping the snow eggs; they increase in size considerably as they poach. Snow eggs can be poached in advance and reserved in the refrigerator in a single layer, preferably on top of the custard or in about 1 inch (2.5 cm) milk in a shallow pan. The snow eggs may also be poached using a microwave oven. Place the quenelles, well spaced, on a Silpat and microwave on high for about 20 seconds. Be certain to place the caramel sphere so it rests on the meringue. If the thin strings of spun sugar are placed in the sauce or come into contact with it, the caramel will melt into the custard within a few minutes.

14 egg whites (1¾ cups/420 ml)	Light Vanilla Custard Sauce (recipe follows)
1 pound (455 g) granulated sugar	12 Caramelized Sugar Spheres (directions follow)
2 teaspoons (10 ml) vanilla extract	Edible fresh flower petals
6 cups (1 L 440 ml) low-fat milk	

1. Following the usual procedure for making meringue, whip the egg whites until they triple in volume. Gradually add the sugar, then the vanilla, and continue whipping until the meringue holds stiff peaks; be careful not to overwhip.

2. Pour the milk into a sauté pan, 10 inches (25 cm) in diameter, and bring to a simmer.

3. Using 2 soupspoons dipped in cold water to prevent the meringue from sticking, shape 2-inch (5-cm) ovals (quenelles) of meringue, dropping each carefully into the milk as it is formed. Do not crowd; poach only as many as will fit without touching. Poach the ovals for 3 to 4 minutes, turn carefully, and cook for approximately the same length of time.

4. Remove the meringues with a slotted spoon and drain on a towel. Remove any skin that forms on the surface of the milk. Continue shaping and poaching the remaining meringue in the same manner. Measure 4½ cups (1 L 80 ml) poaching milk to use in making the sauce. Discard the remainder. Set the meringues aside until serving time. If this will be longer than 1 hour, place in the refrigerator, as described in the introduction.

5. Presentation: Pour ⅓ cup (80 ml) light vanilla custard sauce on the base of a deep dessert plate. Space 3 meringue ovals evenly on top of the sauce, forming a circle in the center of the plate. Place a sugar sphere on the meringues in the center of the plate. Sprinkle flower petals over the meringue.

CARAMELIZED SUGAR SPHERES yield: 12 decorations

When humidity is high, making spun sugar is virtually impossible. If this is the case, increase the glucose or corn syrup a little and prepare the sugar just before it will be served or use a sugar substitute such as Isomalt (see page 615). Under dry conditions, spun sugar can be prepared well in advance, provided it is placed in an airtight container and stored in a warm place with a dehumidifying agent.

1 recipe Caramelized Spun Sugar (page 594)

1. Follow the directions in the carmelized spun sugar recipe, spinning the sugar across a dowel held in one hand (see Procedure 6-1a). You may want to cover the dowel tightly with plastic wrap to prevent the sugar from sticking.

2. As you spin the sugar, form it into loose balls, each about the size of a large orange (see Procedure 6-1b).

3. As you form each sugar sphere, set it aside on top of an egg carton that has been covered with plastic wrap (see Procedure 6-1c).

4. Store the spheres in an airtight container with a desiccant until needed.

PROCEDURE 6-1a **Spinning the sugar across a dowel**

PROCEDURE 6-1b **The spun sugar formed into a loose ball**

PROCEDURE 6-1c **Sugar spheres resting on an egg carton**

LIGHT VANILLA CUSTARD SAUCE yield: 5½ cups (I L 320 ml)

4½ cups (1 L 80 ml) low-fat milk, reserved
from poaching the meringues (Step 4,
page 299)

1 vanilla bean, split lengthwise

4 eggs

4 ounces (115 g) granulated sugar

I. Pour the milk into a heavy saucepan. Using the back of a paring knife, scrape the seeds from the vanilla bean and add them to the milk. Discard the pods or save them for another use. Bring the milk to scalding. Remove from the heat and let steep for 30 minutes.

2. Place the saucepan back on the stove and reheat the milk to simmering.

3. In an oversized bowl, whisk the eggs and sugar until well combined. Gradually whisk in about one-third of the hot milk to temper the eggs. Then, still whisking constantly, add the remaining milk. Place the bowl over a bain-marie and heat, continuing to stir, until the sauce has thickened enough to coat the back of a spoon. Do not heat to simmering, or the eggs may curdle.

4. Let the sauce cool, then store in the refrigerator.

Omelet Pancake with Sautéed Star Fruit, Pomegranate Sauce, and Mango Coulis yield: 16 servings, approximately 320 calories and 12.5 grams of fat per serving (Color Photo 51)

I originally created this sweet omelet for a special event where the host had requested a dessert that was unusual, light, and seasonal, and which did not contain chocolate. As this was in the late fall, when both star fruit and pomegranate are available, I decided to use them. If these fruits are not in season when you want to make this dessert, you can substitute any fruit that looks attractive sliced, such as strawberries, kiwis, figs, or papaya. None of these need to be sautéed or poached. Actually, poaching is not essential for the star fruit either, but it is done to add flavor, because they tend to be rather bland without it. This is probably why star fruit are used primarily for garnish rather than for eating. Use either raspberry or strawberry sauce with these other fruit fillings. Because pomegranate sauce is time-consuming to produce, you may want to make the substitution to save time even when pomegranates are available.

If it is not possible to cook both the star fruit and the pancakes to order, you can cook all of the star fruit in advance in the following manner: Bring the sugar and water to a boil (or use 1⅓ cups/320 ml simple syrup). Reduce to a simmer, add the star fruit slices, and poach for 2 minutes. Remove the slices, place in a shallow pan, and pour the cooking syrup on top. Set aside until needed. Do not do this too far ahead, as the fruit starts to lose its juice once combined with the sugar, and the slices begin to look a little ragged. Each dessert should be made to order, as soufflé type pancakes fall quickly. Although they taste the same, the pancakes look much more attractive when a bit puffy.

2 pounds (910 g) star fruit, about 8 medium
(see Chef's Tip)

1 cup (240 ml) water

8 ounces (225 g) granulated sugar

1 recipe Mango Coulis (page 244)

1 recipe Pomegranate Sauce (recipe follows)

Vegetable oil

Omelet Pancake Batter (recipe follows)

Sour Cream Mixture for Piping (page 727)

Powdered sugar

1. Using a vegetable peeler, remove the hard skin from the top of the 5 ridges on each star fruit. Slice the fruit across, ¼ inch (6 mm) thick. Re-form each fruit to keep the slices from drying out, placing the cut sides together and including the end pieces. Cover and set aside.

2. Combine the water and granulated sugar in a saucepan. Bring to a boil and boil for 2 minutes. Remove from the heat and set aside.

3. Place a portion of the mango coulis and a portion of the pomegranate sauce into separate piping bottles.

4. Place 5 to 7 slices of star fruit (depending on size), including 1 end piece, in a skillet with 2 tablespoons (30 ml) sugar syrup. Bring to a boil, shaking the pan and stirring the fruit, and cook for 1 minute. Remove from the heat.

5. Brush a thin film of vegetable oil over a standard crepe pan. Heat the pan, then pour just over 1 cup (240 ml) batter into the center. The batter is rather thick, so you will need to tilt the pan to make the batter cover the entire surface. Cook over medium heat for about 2 minutes. Turn the pancake and cook the other side 1 minute longer. Slide the pancake out of the pan.

6. Presentation: Following the perimeter of the base, pipe the mango coulis in a band, 1½ inches (3.7 cm) wide, on the bottom half of a dessert plate. Pipe pomegranate sauce on the lower half of the base of the plate, leaving room for the pancake above. Pipe a line of sour cream mixture along the border where the sauces meet. Using a wooden skewer, feather the sauces together with a circular motion (see Figure 13-18, page 685). Arrange the cooked star fruit slices (reserving the end piece) along the lower edge of the pancake. Fold the top of the pancake over, covering the top half of the star fruit slices and leaving the bottom half of each slice visible. Dust powdered sugar over the top of the dessert, then carefully set it on the plate, partially on top of the pomegranate sauce, so the fruit is in the sauce and a band of both pomegranate sauce and mango coulis are visible. Decorate the top of the omelet with the reserved end piece of star fruit. Serve immediately.

> **CHEF'S TIP**
> Star fruit vary considerably in size, and often you do not have much choice. If you cannot obtain medium-sized fruit (about 4 inches/10 cm long), smaller fruit will work fine. For aesthetic reasons, avoid large mango-sized star fruit in this recipe.

OMELET PANCAKE BATTER yield: about 16 pancakes, 6 inches (15 cm) in diameter

Do not whip and fold in the egg whites until you are ready to cook the pancakes. Prior to whipping the whites, the batter can be held, covered and refrigerated, for several hours or even overnight.

4 ounces (115 g) unsalted butter

2 ounces (55 g) bread flour

2 ounces (55 g) cornstarch

½ teaspoon (2.5 g) salt

1¼ cups (300 ml) whole milk, at room temperature

8 eggs, separated

Grated zest of 3 lemons

6 ounces (170 g) granulated sugar

1. Melt the butter in a heavy saucepan. Mix in the flour, cornstarch, and salt to form a paste. Cook the roux for 1 minute without browning. Stir in the milk and bring the mixture to a boil, stirring constantly. Remove from the heat and stir until smooth.

2. Whisk in the egg yolks, a few at a time, followed by the lemon zest.

3. Whip the egg whites and sugar to soft peaks. Fold the egg whites into the batter. Use immediately.

POMEGRANATE SAUCE yield: approximately 4 cups (960 ml)

3 pounds (1 kg 365 g) pomegranate seeds *or* 3 cups (720 ml) pomegranate juice (see Note)

3 tablespoons (24 g) cornstarch

6 ounces (170 g) granulated sugar

¾ cup (180 ml) grenadine

1. Place the pomegranate seeds in a food processor and process for just a few seconds to break open the seeds and release the juice; do not crack or pulverize the tiny white pits inside each seed. Force the mixture through a fine mesh strainer, pressing hard on the solids to extract as much juice as possible. Discard the solids. You should have close to 3 cups (720 ml) juice; add water if needed to make this amount.

2. Add enough of the juice to the cornstarch to dissolve the starch. Place the remaining juice, the cornstarch mixture, sugar, and grenadine in a nonreactive saucepan. Bring to a boil while stirring. Let cool to room temperature, then store, covered, in the refrigerator.

NOTE: You will need approximately 10 pomegranates, 8 to 10 ounces (225 to 285 g) each. For a more rustic-looking sauce, reserve ½ cup (120 ml) of the seeds before processing and add these seeds to the finished sauce.

Pears California with Cointreau-Flavored Almond Filling

yield: 16 servings, approximately 320 calories and 7.5 grams of fat per serving

This dessert derives its name from its combination of pears, apricots, and almonds, each of which plays a large part in California's agricultural industry. The majority of the state's pear crop is made up of Bartlett or Bartlett-style fruit, such as Comice or Anjou, but I prefer to use the Bosc variety here. They stand tall and majestic, and the long, thin Bosc stems seem to stay on better than the stems from some of the other types.

For this presentation, try to find nicely shaped, medium pears that all have the same degree of ripeness. A pear that is too large will look clumsy, although it can be trimmed down, to some extent, as you remove the peel. Peel the pears with a vegetable peeler, working from top to bottom and removing the skin in long strips to retain the natural pear shape. Keep the fruit as smooth as possible (it should not look like a peeled potato when you have finished), as any imperfection on the surface will show in the presentation. To make the surface of the pears completely smooth, see Step 3 in Tarte Tatin Moderne, page 417.

16 medium Bosc pears, stems attached	Apricot Sauce (recipe follows)
Spiced Poaching Syrup (page 790)	Sour Cream Mixture for Piping (page 727)
About ¼ cup (60 ml) Cointreau	Chocolate Sauce for Piping (page 681)
10 ounces (285 g) almond paste	16 Chocolate Leaves (page 527)

1. Peel the pears, leaving the stems attached. Place the pears in acidulated water as you work to prevent browning. Poach the fruit in poaching syrup until soft and tender; this can take up to 45 minutes, depending on the stage of ripeness. Let the pears cool in the syrup to fully absorb the flavor of the spices.

2. Mix just enough Cointreau into the almond paste to make it pipeable. Place in a pastry bag with a No. 6 (12-mm) plain tip and reserve.

3. Remove the pears from the poaching syrup and pat them dry. Make a horizontal cut ½ inch (1.2 cm) below the stem on each pear, going only three-quarters of the way through to keep the stem attached. Push a corer through the bottom of the pears up to the cut and remove the cores. Pipe the almond paste mixture into the cavities. Reserve the pears in the refrigerator until ready to serve.

4. Presentation: Pour just enough apricot sauce on a dessert plate to cover the surface. Decorate a 2-inch-wide (5-cm) band at the outer edge of the sauce with sour cream mixture for piping and chocolate sauce for piping. On a separate plate, pour apricot sauce over one of the filled pears so it is completely covered. Carefully, without disturbing the sauce coating, transfer the pear to the center of the sauce on the plate. Cut a small slit ¼ inch (6 mm) below the stem at a downward angle and attach a chocolate leaf inside. Serve immediately.

APRICOT SAUCE yield: approximately 4 cups (960 ml)

2 pounds 8 ounces (1 kg 135 g) pitted fresh apricots	3 ounces (85 g) granulated sugar
	2 tablespoons (16 g) cornstarch
3 cups (720 ml) plus 2 tablespoons (30 ml) water	

1. Cut the apricots into quarters. Place in a saucepan with 3 cups (720 ml) water and the sugar. Bring to a boil, then cook over medium heat until the fruit is soft. This will take approximately 10 minutes, depending on the ripeness of the fruit.

2. Strain the mixture, forcing as much of the fruit as possible through the strainer with the back of a spoon or ladle. Pour the sauce back into the saucepan.

3. Dissolve the cornstarch in the remaining 2 tablespoons (30 ml) water. Stir into the sauce. Return the sauce to a boil and cook for about 1 minute to remove the flavor of the cornstarch. Store the sauce, covered, in the refrigerator. If the sauce is too thick, thin it with water .

Rainbow of Summer Sorbets in a Cookie Flower

yield: 16 servings, approximately 360 calories and 11 grams of fat per serving (Color Photo 48)

If you have traveled in the eastern Mediterranean, you are probably familiar with street vendors peddling snowlike cracked or shaved ice in paper cones. These frozen refreshments are offered with a choice of syrup toppings made from colorful fruits and other flavorings. This custom is also widespread in the Caribbean, where the ices are known as *frío frío,* and in South America. Flavored shaved ice is popular because of the method's venerability and simplicity. In Persia, fruit ice is known as *sharbat,* the source of our word *sherbet.* In France, it is known as *sorbet* or *granité,* and in Italy it is called *granità.* These names are a trifle confusing, however, because sorbets are distinguished from sherbets not by language but by the fact that sorbets never contain dairy products.

The sorbets used in this recipe give the presentation a bright and colorful appearance; keep color contrast in mind if you decide to substitute other flavors. Unless you are using overripe or very soft fruit, save the best-looking pieces to use for decorating. Garnishing the plate with the same kind of fruit used in the preparation helps guests identify the flavor of the ice and is also a subtle indication that the sorbets were made from fresh fruit rather than purchased fruit juice. The sorbet can be scooped onto the flower petals and reserved in the freezer for up to 2 hours before serving. (Before they are filled, the tuile cookie petals may be stored in an airtight container for up to 1 week.) Avoid the temptation to chill the dessert plates, even if you eliminate the powdered sugar on them. The chilled plates will fog up and look unattractive when they are exposed to room temperature.

1 recipe Vanilla Tuile Decorating Paste (page 695)

1¼ teaspoons (4 g) cocoa powder, sifted

Powdered sugar

Gooseberry Sorbet (recipe follows)

Double Cherry Sorbet (recipe follows)

White Nectarine Sorbet (recipe follows)

About 2 pounds (910 g) fresh fruit (see Chef's Tip)

1. Make the template shown in Figure 6-10. The template, as shown, is the correct size to use in this recipe. Trace the drawing and cut the template out of cardboard that is ¹⁄₁₆ inch (2 mm) thick; cake boxes work fine. If you do not have Silpats, grease and flour the back of flat, even sheet pans, and shake off as much flour as possible.

2. Color 3 tablespoons (45 ml) tuile paste with the cocoa powder, mixing to form a smooth paste. Cover and reserve. Spread the plain tuile paste on top of Silpats or the prepared sheet pans, spreading it flat and even within the template (see Figures 13-29 and 13-30, page 694). Make 8 to 10 cookie petals per pan or mat.

3. Place some of the reserved cocoa-colored tuile paste in a piping bag. Pipe 3 thin lines the length of each petal, starting evenly spaced at the wide end and ending together at the tip. Bake the cookies, 1 pan at a time, at 400°F (205°C) until they begin to turn light brown in a few places. Leave the pan in the oven with the door open. Quickly pick up a petal and drape it, striped-side up, across a rolling pin approximately 4 inches (10 cm) in diameter. Gently press both ends of the cookie against the pin so the cookie follows the curved shape. Form the other cookies on the pan in the same way. Repeat spreading the paste and baking and forming the cookies until you have made 55 to 60 cookie petals. You need a total of 48 for this recipe, 3 per serving, but making a few extra allows for breakage.

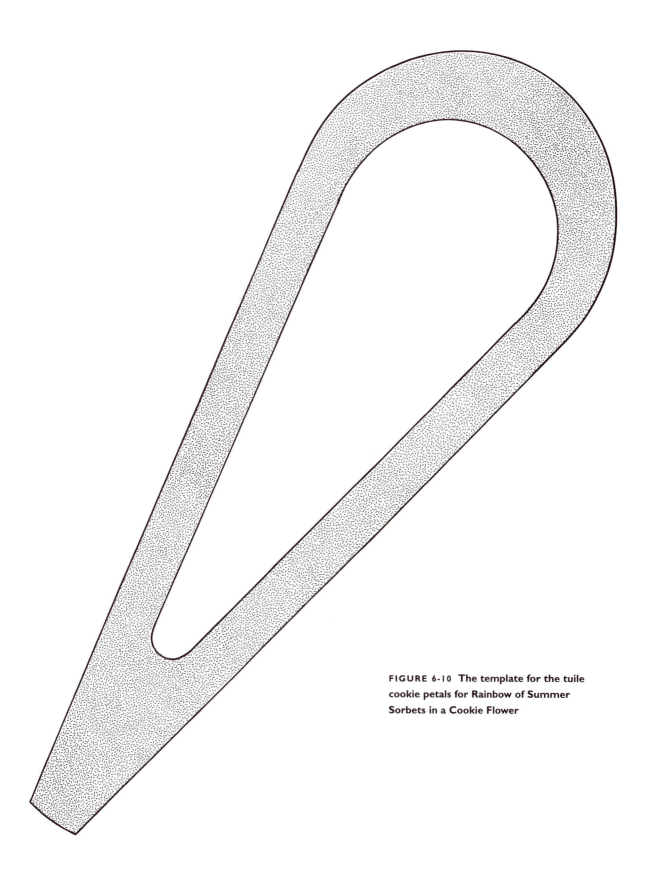

FIGURE 6-10 The template for the tuile
cookie petals for Rainbow of Summer
Sorbets in a Cookie Flower

CHEF'S TIP
Ideally, use the same type of fruit for decorating as was used to make the sorbets, reserving a portion as you prepare the sorbet mixture. Cut gooseberries in half, cut cherries in half and remove the pits, and cut white nectarines into uniform pieces about the size of cherries; do not chop the fruit. Reserve each type of fruit separately so the colors do not bleed together.

4. Presentation: Sift powdered sugar over the base of a dessert plate. Using a 1½-ounce (45-ml) ice cream scoop, place a different flavor of sorbet on the wide section of each of 3 cookie petals; be careful not to break the curved tips of the petals in the process. Quickly and carefully, use a palette knife to lift the filled cookie petals and arrange them, evenly spaced, in the center of the plate with the tips pointing toward the center. Decorate the plate with fresh fruit. Serve immediately.

GOOSEBERRY SORBET yield: approximately 6 cups (1 L 440 ml)

If you cannot obtain fresh gooseberries, prepare this sorbet with canned, which require only about 5 minutes of cooking. Because canned gooseberries are usually sold in sugar syrup, adjust the amount of granulated sugar accordingly or leave it out altogether. The flavor of canned gooseberries is usually a bit bland, so it is a good idea to add a few drops of Tartaric Acid Solution (page 629) or lemon juice to enhance the taste.

3 pounds 8 ounces (1 kg 590 g) fresh gooseberries	½ cup (120 ml) water
12 ounces (340 g) granulated sugar	1½ cups (360 ml) simple syrup, at room temperature

1. Rinse the gooseberries. Place in a saucepan with the sugar and water and stir to combine. Cook over medium heat, stirring from time to time, until the gooseberries burst, about 10 minutes. Force the mixture through a fine mesh strainer; discard the seeds and solids.

2. Add most of the simple syrup to the gooseberry juice. Test the sugar content with a saccharometer (Baumé thermometer) and add enough additional simple syrup to bring the mixture to between 16° and 20° Baumé.

3. Process in an ice cream freezer following the manufacturer's directions. Transfer to a chilled container and store, covered, in the freezer.

DOUBLE CHERRY SORBET yield: approximately 6 cups (1 L 440 ml)

2 pounds (910 g) fresh Bing cherries	1½ cups (360 ml) simple syrup, at room temperature
2 pounds (910 g) fresh Royal Anne cherries	
4 ounces (115 g) granulated sugar	Few drops of Tartaric Acid Solution (page 629) or lemon juice
1 cup (240 ml) water	

1. Rinse, stem, and pit the cherries. Place in a saucepan with the sugar and water. Stir to combine and bring to a boil. Cook over medium heat, stirring from time to time, until the cherries start to soften, about 10 minutes. Puree the mixture in a food processor. Force through a fine mesh strainer and discard the solids.

2. Combine the cherry juice with most of the simple syrup. Using a saccharometer, test the Baumé level and, if needed, add more simple syrup to bring the mixture to between 16° and 20° Baumé. Add the tartaric acid or lemon juice.

3. Process in an ice cream freezer following the manufacturer's instructions. Transfer to a chilled container and store, covered, in the freezer.

WHITE NECTARINE SORBET yield: approximately 6 cups (1 L 440 ml)

2 pounds 8 ounces (1 kg 135 g) ripe white nectarines (see Variation)

2 cups (480 ml) water

2 cups (480 ml) simple syrup, at room temperature

Few drops of Tartaric Acid Solution (page 629) or lemon juice

1. Wash and stone the nectarines; cut into small pieces. Place in a saucepan with the water and half of the simple syrup. Bring to a boil and cook, stirring occasionally, until the fruit falls apart, about 10 minutes. Remove from the heat and force through a fine mesh strainer.

2. Let cool to room temperature. Add enough of the remaining simple syrup to bring the mixture to between 16° and 20° Baumé. Add the tartaric acid or lemon juice.

3. Process in an ice cream freezer according to the manufacturer's directions. Transfer the finished sorbet to a chilled container, cover, and store in the freezer.

VARIATION
Nectarine or Peach Sorbet

If you cannot obtain white nectarines, you can easily substitute regular nectarines or peaches. The color of the sorbet will be golden rather than ivory — unless, of course, you use white peaches.

Red Currant Sorbet in Magnolia Cookie Shells

yield: 16 servings, approximately 320 calories and 11 grams of fat per serving (Color Photos 58 and 59)

The dramatic cookie shells, modeled after the magnificent cup-shaped blossoms of the magnolia tree, make an impressive holder for any sorbet (or ice cream) — which, or course, could be scooped into the shells instead of piped. If red currants are unavailable, try another red sorbet, such as blood orange or raspberry; either would go well with the kiwi sauce.

1 recipe Vanilla Tuile Decorating Paste (page 695)

Kiwi Sauce (recipe follows)

Red Currant Sorbet (recipe follows)

16 clusters of fresh red currants

1. Make the 2 magnolia templates (A and B) shown in Figure 6-11. The templates, as shown, are the correct size for use in this recipe; however, it is possible to show only half on the page. Trace the drawings, then match the broken lines in the center to draw the other half so they look like the small example shown. Cut the templates out of cardboard that is $^1/_{16}$ inch (2 mm) thick; cake boxes work fine. If you do not have Silpats, grease and flour the backs of clean, even sheet pans.

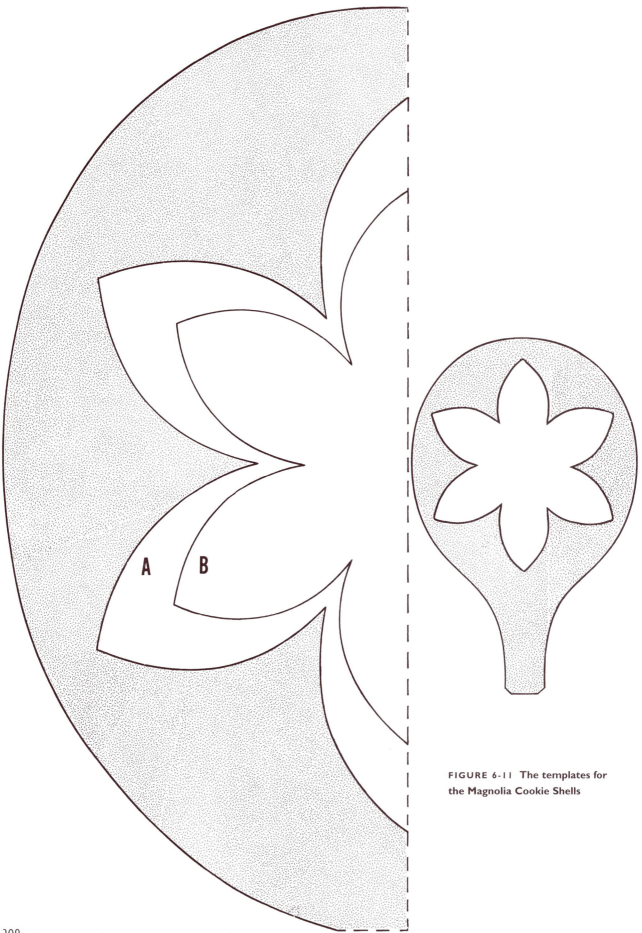

FIGURE 6-11 The templates for
the Magnolia Cookie Shells

2. Spread the tuile paste flat and even within the templates on the prepared sheet pans or Silpats mats (see Figures 13-29 and 13-30, page 694). Place 4 large or 8 small flowers per pan or mat and make sure you have enough bowls and cups available to form them.

3. Bake 1 pan at a time at 400°F (205°C) for approximately 8 minutes or until a few light brown spots show on the cookies. Leave the sheet pan in the oven with the door open.

4. Quickly place a cookie, top-side up, in a cup or bowl of the appropriate size and shape and gently press it against the sides of the form. Let each cookie sit in the form until it is crisp, about 30 seconds, less for the smaller size. Repeat baking and forming the cookies until you have at least 16 each of the small and large size; it doesn't hurt to have a few spares.

5. Place a portion of the kiwi sauce in a piping bottle and reserve. As close as possible to serving time, place a portion of the sorbet in a pastry bag with a No. 8 (16-mm) star tip. Pipe a large, pointed rosette of sorbet inside as many of the small cookie shells as you anticipate serving (see Chef's Tip). Return the filled shells and the remaining sorbet to the freezer.

6. Presentation: Cover the base of a dessert plate with a thin layer of kiwi sauce. Place a large cookie shell in the center of the sauce. Using 2 spoons, 1 on each side, carefully set a filled small cookie shell inside the larger one. Decorate with fresh red currants and serve immediately.

> **CHEF'S TIP**
> Any sorbet stored in a pastry bag will become too hard to pipe, so it is not practical to fill the shells to order. However, filled shells should not be stored in the freezer for more than a few hours, while unfilled shells will stay fresh for up to 1 week, covered, in a dry place, so it is important to fill only as many shells as you can use within 2 to 3 hours.

KIWI SAUCE yield: approximately 4 cups (960 ml)

Like most subtropical fruits, kiwis contain an enzyme that inhibits gelatin from setting up. In this recipe, because the fruit juice needs to set up just to the consistency of a pourable sauce, the problem is not as great as it is when preparing a molded dessert, for example. Cooking the fruit or puree kills the enzyme, but the brilliant green color is compromised; kiwi goes from bright green to yellowish at about 140°F (60°C). That the color is damaged at a high temperature is the reason this sauce is not thickened with cornstarch, as many other fruit sauces are, as cornstarch must be brought to a boil. This is also the reason you need to be careful not to overheat the sauce in Step 4.

If you do not mind using a bit of green food coloring and want more control over the thickness of the sauce, omit the gelatin and water and use 2 tablespoons (16 g) cornstarch instead. Add enough kiwi juice to the cornstarch to dissolve, stir in the remaining juice and the sugar, and bring to a boil. Add the food coloring to the finished sauce.

4 tablespoons (36 g) unflavored gelatin powder	1 pound 12 ounces (795 g) ripe kiwis (approximately 12) *or* 3 cups (720 ml) kiwi juice (see Note 1)
½ cup (120 ml) cold water	6 ounces (170 g) granulated sugar

1. Sprinkle the gelatin over the cold water and set aside to soften (see Chef's Tip).

2. Peel the kiwis. Process in a food processor just to puree. If the fruit is processed for too long, many of the black seeds will break and give the sauce a muddy appearance (see Note 2).

Strain the puree through a fine mesh strainer and discard the solids; you should have about 3 cups (720 ml) juice. Adjust as necessary by adding water, provided the missing amount is not too great.

3. Heat the gelatin mixture over a water bath to dissolve.

4. Add the sugar and dissolved gelatin mixture to the kiwi juice. Heat the mixture to approximately 110°F (43°C), stirring constantly. Be careful not to overheat. Remove from the heat and, if necessary, continue stirring until all of the gelatin is dissolved. Store, covered, in the refrigerator. If the sauce sets or becomes too thick during storage, carefully warm it, stirring constantly, until it reaches the desired consistency.

NOTE 1: Frozen kiwi juice is now readily available from food supply companies. In most cases it is unsweetened, but should you need to use sweetened juice adjust the amount of sugar in the recipe. To use the prepared juice, omit Step 2 in the procedure.

NOTE 2: If you would like to include some of the distinctive black seeds in the sauce, strain the puree through a coarse strainer. Some of the pulp will come through as well, making the sauce less smooth. You can get around this, to some extent, by first straining all of the seeds through a piece of cheesecloth, then adding a few back in without adding any pulp. The cheesecloth works well because the pulp tends to stick to the fabric.

RED CURRANT SORBET yield: approximately 4 cups (960 ml)

2 pounds (910 g) fresh red currants (see Chef's Tip)

¾ cup (180 ml) water

1¼ cups (300 ml) ruby port wine

5 ounces (140 g) granulated sugar

Few drops of Tartaric Acid Solution (page 629) or lemon juice

Water or simple syrup, at room temperature, as needed

1. Wash the currants and remove the berries from the stems. Place the currants in a saucepan with the water, port wine, and sugar. Stir to combine and bring the mixture to a boil.

2. Puree the mixture and strain through a fine mesh strainer; discard the solids. Add the tartaric acid or lemon juice to the liquid. Let cool to room temperature.

3. Add additional water or simple syrup as needed so the sugar content measures between 16° and 20° Baumé.

4. Process in an ice cream freezer following the manufacturer's instructions. Place the finished sorbet in a chilled container, cover, and store in the freezer.

Sabayon
yield: about 4 cups (960 ml), or 8 servings, approximately 155 calories and 4 grams of fat per serving

Used as a sauce, sabayon is the classic companion to many hot soufflés, especially liqueur-flavored soufflés. Sabayon is also poured over fresh strawberries or other fruits and served as is or gratinéed. It can be a light dessert by itself without the fruit, served plain or garnished with a light sprinkling of nutmeg. Try to make the sabayon as close to serving time as possible; it tends to lose some of its fluffiness and will separate if it stands too long. Should this happen, return it to the stove and repeat the thickening process.

6 egg yolks (½ cup/120 ml)	1½ cups (360 ml) dry white wine or champagne
6 ounces (170 g) granulated sugar	

1. Beat the egg yolks and sugar in a stainless steel bowl until light and fluffy. Add the wine or champagne.

2. Place over simmering water and continue to whip constantly until the mixture is hot and thick enough to coat a spoon. Serve hot as soon as possible.

VARIATIONS
ZABAGLIONE

To make Italian zabaglione, substitute sweet marsala for the wine and use only 4 ounces (115 g) sugar.

About Sabayon

Sabayon is the French version of the great Italian dessert zabaglione. The only difference is that marsala is used to make zabaglione and sabayon is made using white wine or champagne. This popular dessert sauce has many versions (including several in this text); this one is my favorite. It uses a minimum amount of egg yolks, so it does not have the unpleasant eggy flavor that some recipes produce, and the formula is easy to remember: 6 (yolks) + 6 (ounces of sugar) = 12 (ounces of wine). The procedure used to cook the sauce should be familiar to everyone who works in a professional kitchen. The egg yolks, sugar, and wine are whipped together over a bain-marie, or in a saucepan over direct heat, until the mixture is thick and fluffy.

Sabayon is included in the category of stirred custards, meaning custards that are thickened on top of the stove rather than in the oven. Sabayon is whipped constantly during cooking both to incorporate air and to prevent it from curdling. The addition of alcohol aids in this by lowering the boiling point of the mixture. Other stirred custards used in the pastry kitchen are vanilla custard sauce, lemon curd, and — the most common of all — pastry cream. Lemon curd and pastry cream are stirred not so much to prevent curdling — as pastry cream contains a starch and lemon curd doesn't have any milk or cream — but to keep them from burning.

COLD SABAYON

1. Soften ½ teaspoon (1.5 g) unflavored gelatin powder in 1 tablespoon (15 ml) of the wine or champagne. Stir into the remaining liquid.

2. Continue as for hot sabayon.

3. Once the mixture has thickened, remove from the heat and place over ice water, then whip slowly until cold. Stir in additional wine or champagne as needed, depending on how you are serving the sabayon.

Salzburger Soufflé yield: 4 servings, approximately 250 calories and 8 grams of fat per serving

Anyone who has traveled in Austria and dined in Salzburg has certainly encountered this wonderful dessert specialty, in one form or another, under the name *Salzburger Nockerl*. Salzburger soufflé is basically a meringue, lightly baked and browned in the oven. It requires a delicate touch when folding in the egg yolks, and the dish must be presented immediately after baking, before the meringue begins to collapse. Like a hot soufflé, the *nockerl* (which means "little mountain" in reference to the three distinctive ridges of the Alps near Salzburg; the word is also used for dumplings) is always made to order for two or more persons. Nockerl is nice accompanied by Chocolate Sauce (page 413) or Crème Anglaise (page 754) and fresh raspberries or strawberries.

6 egg whites (¾ cup/180 ml)	1 teaspoon (6 g) grated lemon zest
4 ounces (115 g) powdered sugar, sifted, plus more for the presentation	3½ tablespoons (20 g) bread flour
3 egg yolks (¼ cup/60 ml)	2 tablespoons (30 g) unsalted butter
1 tablespoon (15 g) Vanilla Sugar (page 803)	2 tablespoons (30 ml) half-and-half
	1 teaspoon (5 ml) vanilla extract

1. Taking the usual precautions for whipping meringue, whip the egg whites at full speed until they triple in volume. Lower the speed and gradually add the 4 ounces (115 g) sifted powdered sugar. Continue whipping at high speed until stiff peaks form, but do not overwhip.

2. Beat the egg yolks with the vanilla sugar for a few seconds, just to combine. Stir in the lemon zest and flour. Carefully fold the egg yolk mixture into the egg whites, mixing them only halfway; you should still be able to see swirls of yolk in the whites.

3. Place the butter in a shallow, oval ovenproof dish. Warm the dish in the oven until the butter melts. Add the half-and-half and vanilla to the pan. Using a rubber spatula, place the egg mixture in the baking dish, forming 3 large, triangular ridges *(nockerln)* (Figure 6-12).

4. Bake at 450°F (230°C) for about 8 minutes or until the top is dark brown. The inside should remain creamy. Sift powdered sugar lightly over the top and serve immediately.

NOTE: You will need an oval dish approximately 12 inches (30 cm) long if, as is traditional, you are baking and presenting the dessert in the same dish.

FIGURE 6-12 Making triangular ridges in the meringue in the baking pan for Salzburger Soufflé

Strawberry-Peach Yogurt Creams

yield: 16 servings, approximately 240 calories and 9.5 grams of fat per serving

Don't miss out on serving Strawberry-Peach Yogurt Creams at least once every summer, when local peaches and strawberries are ripe, plentiful, and inexpensive. The desserts are simple to put together, and they can be ready in less than 4 hours. The majority of that time they spend setting up in the refrigerator while you work on other projects. Because they are fast to make, there is no reason to prep them a day ahead, and it's not a good idea anyway because the decorative strawberries on top may bleed slightly. If you must leave them overnight, this problem can be nearly eliminated by using strawberries that are firm and ripe, but not overripe, for the decoration. If you have no choice but to use peaches that are not fully ripe, be sure to poach them properly, or the filling will oxidize and turn light brown. The accompanying strawberry sauce balances the slightly tangy yogurt-based cream perfectly.

Citrus Aspic (recipe follows)

14 medium strawberries, round rather than cone-shaped

Peach Cream Filling (recipe follows)

1 recipe Strawberry Sauce (page 186)

Sour Cream Mixture for Piping (page 727)

I. Cover the bottom of 16 baba molds or other molds of about the same shape and size, such as timbale forms, with the citrus aspic, dividing it evenly. Place the molds in the refrigerator to set the aspic.

2. Cut 3 strawberries across to make 16 thin, round slices; do not use the pointed ends. Place 1 strawberry slice on the firm aspic in each form.

3. Divide the peach cream filling among the molds. Return the molds to the refrigerator and chill for about 3 hours to set.

4. Unmold as many servings as you anticipate needing by dipping the forms briefly into hot water and inverting onto a sheet pan lined with baking paper (don't place them in the water too long, or the filling will melt and the presentation will look sloppy). Reserve the unmolded servings in the refrigerator.

5. Rinse the remaining strawberries and remove the hulls. Place a portion of the strawberry sauce and the sour cream mixture into piping bottles.

6. Presentation: Place a yogurt cream in the center of a dessert plate. Pipe strawberry sauce around the dessert to cover the base of the plate. Pipe 5 dots of sour cream mixture, ¾ inch (2 cm) in diameter, in the strawberry sauce around the dessert. Pull a wooden skewer through the dots to make large hearts with a small curved tail at each end (see Figure 13-17, page 685). Cut a strawberry into 8 wedges and place 5 of them, cut-side up, between the sour cream hearts, with the pointed ends toward the edge of the plate.

CITRUS ASPIC yield: approximately ¼ cup (60 ml)

2 tablespoons (30 ml) cold water

1 teaspoon (5 ml) lime juice

2 tablespoons (30 ml) orange liqueur

1 teaspoon (3 g) unflavored gelatin powder

1. Combine the cold water, lime juice, and orange liqueur. Sprinkle the gelatin over the mixture and set aside to soften.

2. Place the mixture over a bain-marie and heat to dissolve. Remove from the heat and use immediately.

PEACH CREAM FILLING yield: approximately 8 cups (1 L 920 ml)

3 pounds (1 kg 365 g) ripe peaches (approximately 6 medium)

Plain Poaching Syrup (page 789)

½ cup (120 ml) lime juice

½ cup (120 ml) orange juice

2 tablespoons plus 1 teaspoon (21 g) unflavored gelatin powder

1½ cups (360 ml) heavy cream

3 ounces (85 g) granulated sugar

1 pound (455 g) unflavored nonfat yogurt

1. Poach the peaches in the poaching syrup until they are soft but not falling apart. If they are fully ripe, 5 minutes is probably enough. Plunge into ice water, then remove the skin. Cut the peaches in half, remove the pits, and place the fruit in a food processor. Add half of the lime juice and puree until smooth. Force through a fine mesh strainer and place in the refrigerator to chill.

2. Combine the remaining lime juice and the orange juice. Sprinkle the gelatin on top and set aside to soften.

3. Whip the cream and sugar until soft peaks form. Stir in the yogurt and the reserved peach puree. Place the gelatin mixture over a bain-marie and heat until dissolved. Be careful not to overheat. Rapidly stir the gelatin into a small portion of the cream. Still working quickly, add this to the remaining cream.

NOTE: The filling can be prepped ahead of time up to the point of adding the gelatin. Do not add the gelatin until you are ready to use the filling.

Vineyard Barrels yield: 16 servings, approximately 280 calories and 10.5 grams of fat per serving

This simplified version of the cherry basket dessert on page 146 is a better choice if you are making quite a few servings, or if you are serving it as a pastry rather than a plated dessert. In addition to the time saved in not having to make and connect the fragile separate handles on the cherry baskets (the built-in handles here are virtually unbreakable), the barrels are easier to move and work with because they have an attached bottom.

If they are stored, covered, in a warm place, the barrel shells can be made several days in advance. Fill the barrels and top with grapes as close as possible to serving time. They will become a bit soft but are still acceptable 30 minutes after filling; however, they should not be held any longer than that. Vineyard Barrels make an impressive addition to a pastry display or buffet table, because not only are they eye-catching, but it is easy to see that the three-dimensional barrels are formed from a single piece of cookie. Arranging the barrels on fresh grape leaves makes a particularly nice display.

½ recipe Vanilla Tuile Decorating Paste (page 695)

1 teaspoon (2.5 g) unsweetened cocoa powder, sifted

½ recipe Angel Food Cake (page 796)

½ recipe Italian Cream (page 771)

2 pounds (910 g) Champagne grapes or other small seedless grapes or berries

1. Make the Vineyard Barrels Template (Figure 6-13). The template, as shown, is the correct

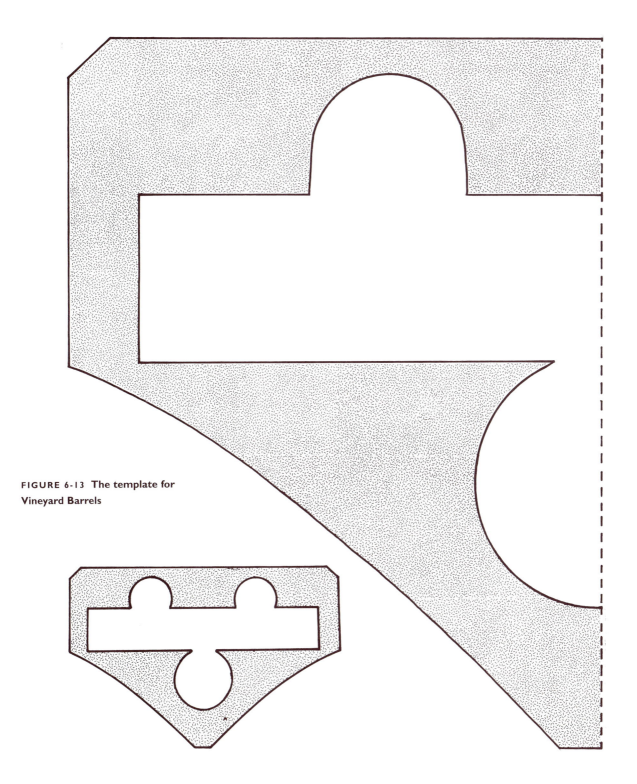

FIGURE 6-13 The template for Vineyard Barrels

size for use in this recipe; however, due to its size, only half of it can be shown on the page. Trace the drawing, invert your paper, match the broken line in the center, then trace the other half so the template looks like the small example. To form the barrels, you will need 2 or more cake rings, approximately 2½ inches (6.2 cm) in diameter, or a few pieces of PVC or other plastic tubing of the same diameter. If you use plastic tubes, cut them to about 4 inches (10 cm) in length.

2. If you do not have Silpats, lightly grease the backs of 4 even sheet pans, coat with flour, and shake off as much flour as possible.

3. Stir the cocoa powder into 2 tablespoons (30 ml) of the tuile paste. Place a portion of the cocoa-colored paste in a piping bag and reserve.

4. Spread the plain tuile paste flat and even within the template on Silpats or the prepared pans (see Figures 13-29 and 13-30, page 694). Make 4 barrels on each pan for a total of 16. Pipe 2 lines of cocoa-colored tuile paste the length of each barrel, evenly spaced across the width. Pipe 1 small dot in the center of each handle.

5. Bake 1 pan at a time at 425°F (219°C) for approximately 6 minutes or until the first cookie begins to show a few brown spots. Leave the pan in the oven with the door open.

6. Working quickly, pick up the cookie that has the most brown spots and place it flat on the table, upside-down, with the large circle (the part that will become the bottom of the barrel) closest to you. Place a cake ring or piece of pipe on top of the circle and quickly pull the remainder of the strip up and around the ring. Lay the barrel on its side with the seam underneath to prevent it from unfolding. Remove the next cookie with the most brown color and form it in the same way. Continue baking and forming the cookies until you have made 16 barrels.

7. Use a cookie cutter to cut round pieces of angel food cake that will fit inside the barrels. Cover and reserve.

8. Place the Italian cream in a pastry bag with a No. 6 (12-mm) plain tip. Refrigerate.

9. To assemble, place a cake round in the bottom of a cookie barrel. Pipe Italian cream inside the barrel to within ¼ inch (6 mm) of the rim. Arrange grapes on top of the cream in a mound so the barrel appears to be full of grapes. If the barrels are served as a plated dessert, accompany with a fruit sauce or sabayon.

NOTE: Champagne grapes are small grapes also called Zante currants and Black Corinth grapes. If you are not able to find these or another petite variety, other types of fresh fruit can be substituted; berries work especially well. Cut larger fruits into pieces about the size of a raspberry; leave raspberries, blackberries, and blueberries whole.

Winter Fruit Compote in Late-Harvest Wine Syrup

yield: 12 servings, approximately 215 calories and 3.5 grams of fat per serving

Compote is a Latin word meaning "to bring together" or "to unite." The term is usually applied to a mixture of fresh and dried fruit cooked slowly in a sugar syrup with spices or flavorings. Compotes are most often served chilled, but they can also be offered warm or at room temperature. These simple dishes are found all over the world, influenced by local cuisine and the availability of ingredients. Be sure to cook the fruit gently so the pieces retain their natural shape. You can substitute Gewürztraminer or muscat for the Riesling or, in a real pinch, use a dry wine and add extra sugar. This compote, with its slightly spicy syrup, tastes great paired with a slice of pound cake.

12 whole prunes, pitted

24 dried apricot halves

24 dried peach halves

1 orange

3 cups (720 ml) late-harvest Riesling wine

1 cinnamon stick

1 vanilla bean, split lengthwise

1 bay leaf

2 ounces (55 g) granulated sugar

1 teaspoon (5 ml) whole cloves

8 whole dried green peppercorns

4 whole dried black peppercorns

3 medium-size, firm Bartlett or Anjou pears

6 tablespoons (90 ml) Crème Fraîche (page 755)

12 Caramelized Walnuts (recipe follows)

Mint sprigs

1. Soak the prunes, apricots, and peaches in hot water for 10 minutes.

2. Slice the orange into quarters and put the pieces in a saucepan together with the wine, cinnamon stick, vanilla bean, bay leaf, and sugar. Tie the cloves and peppercorns in a piece of cheesecloth and add to the wine mixture. Bring to a boil and let simmer for 10 minutes.

3. Peel, core, and quarter the pears. Add to the wine mixture.

4. Drain the dried fruits, pat dry, and add to the wine mixture. Simmer until the pears are lightly poached but not falling apart. Remove from the heat and let the fruit cool in the liquid.

5. Remove and discard the vanilla bean, cinnamon stick, bay leaf, orange pieces, and the spices in the cheesecloth bag. Reserve the poached fruit, in the poaching liquid, at room temperature until ready to serve.

6. Presentation: Spoon 1 prune, 2 apricot halves, 2 peach halves, and 1 pear quarter into a glass serving bowl or onto a dessert plate. Top with some of the poaching liquid. Spoon approximately ½ tablespoon (8 ml) crème fraîche on top of the fruit. Place a caramelized walnut half on the crème fraîche and garnish with a sprig of mint.

CARAMELIZED WALNUTS yield: 14 ounces (400 g)

7 ounces (200 g) walnut halves

Vegetable oil

6 ounces (170 g) granulated sugar

½ teaspoon (2.5 ml) lemon juice

2 tablespoons (30 ml) water

½ ounce (15 g) unsalted butter

1. Very lightly toast the walnut halves and keep them warm.

2. If you do not have a Silpat, lightly oil a marble slab or a sheet pan.

3. Place the sugar, lemon juice, and water in a copper or heavy-bottomed saucepan. Cook over medium heat until the temperature reaches 240°F (115°C) on a sugar thermometer; brush down the sides of the pan with water a few times during the cooking process.

4. Remove the pan from the heat and immediately add the warm nuts. Stir gently with a wooden spoon or spatula.

5. Return the mixture to medium heat and reheat, continuing to stir gently. The mixture will appear crystallized at this point but will start to melt as it is heated. Keep stirring until the sugar starts to caramelize and turn golden brown, at 320°F (160°C).

6. Remove the pan from the heat, add the butter, and stir until it is completely incorporated.

7. Pour the mixture onto the Silpat or oiled marble slab or sheet pan. Using 2 forks, quickly turn the walnut halves over, making sure the sugar coats all of the nuts, and separate the nuts so none of the sides touch. As the caramel starts to cool, you can do this more effectively with your fingertips. Store the caramelized walnuts in an airtight container.

Zinfandel-Poached Pears with Honey-Scented Pear Frozen Yogurt

yield: 12 servings, approximately 355 calories and 5.5 grams of fat per serving (Color Photo 63)

In any dessert featuring a whole poached pear or pear halves, I prefer to serve the fruit standing on end. Pears have such a graceful contour, and it's an easy way to give the presentation some height. One exception is the fanned variation of this dessert, which allows you to show off the pretty two-tone color of the wine-poached pears. If Zinfandel wine is not available, Merlot will work just fine; however, if you must use a lighter red wine, the pears should be left in the poaching liquid a bit longer to allow the color to penetrate. The time (and therefore color) can be adjusted to suit your taste, but the pears look best if they are left in the syrup long enough for the wine to color the pears about $1/2$ inch (1.2 cm) deep, giving the fruit just the right color contrast. In addition to showing off the color contrast a bit more, the fanned presentation offers a lower calorie alternative and a smaller portion size.

12 medium-size Bosc pears

7 cups (1 L 680 ml) Zinfandel wine

1 cup (240 ml) grenadine

1 pound 4 ounces (570 g) granulated sugar

4 or 5 whole cloves

1 cinnamon stick

$1/2$ recipe Cointreau Pear Sauce (recipe follows)

Piping Chocolate (page 543), melted

12 Miniature Tuile Crowns (page 717)

$1/2$ recipe Honey-Scented Pear Frozen Yogurt (page 272)

12 Tuile Leaves (page 709; see Chef's Tip)

Edible fresh flowers or flower petals

1. Peel the pears, keeping the stems intact. Place the pears in acidulated water as you work to keep them from oxidizing.

2. Combine the Zinfandel, grenadine, sugar, cloves, and cinnamon stick in a large nonreactive saucepan. Add the pears and poach over medium heat until the pears are soft to the touch. To avoid light spots on the cooked pears, keep the pears submerged in the poaching liquid at all times by placing one or two plates on top of them to weight them down. Place a layer of paper towels between the pears and the plates. Light spots and uneven coloring can also occur if the pears are too crowded in the pan. Remove the pan from the heat and set the pears aside at room temperature until they are cool, then place in the refrigerator (still covered and submerged) to macerate in the liquid for at least 24 hours.

3. Remove the pears from the poaching syrup. Carefully cut a vertical wedge out of each, removing approximately one-sixth of the pear, cutting into and removing the core but keeping the stem intact. Using a melon ball cutter, remove the core from the cut-out wedges and any remaining seeds or core from the inside of the pears. Do not overdo it; the hole should not be large. Cut the wedges lengthwise into thin slices, keeping them attached at the top.

4. Place a portion of the Cointreau pear sauce into a piping bottle and reserve. Place a small portion of melted piping chocolate in a piping bag. Pipe a zigzag pattern of chocolate on the left side of the base of as many dessert plates as you anticipate using.

5. Presentation: Stand a poached pear on end in the upper right side of the base of a prepared dessert plate, with the open cut-out portion visible. Place a fanned wedge to the left of the pear on top of the chocolate lines. Fill a tulip crown with a small scoop of frozen yogurt and place on the plate below the fanned wedge. Carefully slide a cookie leaf underneath so it points toward the fanned wedge. Pipe a small pool of Cointreau pear sauce in front of the pear and decorate with edible flowers or flower petals. Serve immediately.

COINTREAU PEAR SAUCE yield: approximately 4 cups (960 ml)

5 pounds (2 kg 275 g) ripe flavorful pears, preferably Bartlett or Anjou (approximately 9 medium-size)

2 recipes Spiced Poaching Syrup (page 790)

2 tablespoons (30 ml) lemon juice

½ cup (120 ml) water

1 ounce (30 g) cornstarch

¼ cup (60 ml) Cointreau liqueur

Granulated sugar, as needed

1. Peel the pears, cut in half, and poach in the poaching syrup until very soft but not falling apart. Drain, reserving 1 cup (240 ml) syrup. Save the remaining syrup for another use or discard.

2. Remove the pear cores and stems. Place the pears in a food processor together with the reserved syrup and puree until smooth. Strain the puree, then discard the contents of the strainer. Add the lemon juice to the puree.

3. Stir enough of the water into the cornstarch to dissolve it. Add the cornstarch mixture and the remaining water to the pear puree. Bring to a boil. Remove from the heat and stir in the Cointreau. Let cool. Add sugar to sweeten as needed. Thin with water if the sauce is too thick.

VARIATION

FANNED ZINFANDEL PEARS

1. Cut a wedge out of each poached pear; remove the core and seeds as directed for the upright version. Save the cut-out wedges for another use.

2. Place the pear on its cut side and push down carefully to flatten it. Starting ½ inch (1.2 cm) from the stem, cut the pear into thin slices vertically, leaving the top intact.

3. Pipe a zigzag pattern of melted dark chocolate over the left side of the base of a dessert plate. Allow the chocolate to harden. Place the sliced pear half, flat-side down, on the right side of the plate so part of the pear rests on the chocolate lines. Fan the pear slices decoratively. Serve with either Honey-Scented Pear Frozen Yogurt or Cointreau Pear Sauce, but not both.

Apple Crème Brûlée — 325

Cappuccino Mousse with Sambuca Cream in a Chocolate Coffee Cup — 328

Charlotte Charente — 332

    CHARLOTTE RUSSE — 333

Chocolate Mousse in Ribbon Teardrops — 334

Chocolate Rum Pudding with Chocolate May Beetles — 336

Citrus Cream with Pink Grapefruit and Orange — 338

Crème Brûlée Catalan — 340

Crème Brûlée on a Caramel Spider with a Sugar Shard — 341

Crème Caramel Nouvelle — 342

Cupid's Treasure Chest — 345

Pink Lady Apple and Pear Cream with Orange Syrup and an Apple Chip — 348

Ruby Pears with Verbena Bavarois and Port Wine Reduction — 349

Sherry-Poached Black Mission Figs with Crème Catalan — 353

Triple Chocolate Terrine — 354

White Chocolate and Pistachio Mousse with Chocolate Lace — 357

White Chocolate Neapolitan Bavarian — 360

Wine Foam and Blackberry Bavarian Greystone — 363

    BLACKBERRY BAVARIAN PASTRIES — 366

SOUFFLES

Liqueur Soufflé — 367

    CHOCOLATE SOUFFLÉ — 368

    HARLEQUIN SOUFFLÉ — 369

Blueberry Soufflé — 369

    FRUIT SOUFFLÉS — 370

Pecan-Raisin Soufflé — 370

Soufflé Rothschild — 370

Charlottes, Custards, Bavarian Creams, Mousses, and Soufflés

The desserts in this chapter have a smooth, creamy texture and, with the exceptions of custards and hot charlottes (as opposed to cold charlottes, which are filled with Bavarian cream), they also share a light, fluffy texture that comes from the inclusion of beaten egg whites and/or whipped cream.

Charlottes

The term *charlotte* is used for two significantly different desserts: hot charlottes, which are baked with a fruit filling, and cold charlottes, which have a Bavarian cream or custard filling. The two types of charlotte share two characteristics: the bottom and sides of the charlotte molds are always lined before the filling is added and, once the filling has set, the desserts are unmolded before they are served. In the case of the well-known Charlotte Royal and Charlotte Russe, the molds are lined with jellyrolls and ladyfingers, respectively. In other recipes, the molds are lined with sponge cake, meringue products, buttered bread, or thinly sliced fruit. Charlottes are made in individual servings or in forms that serve up to ten people. The first recognized chilled charlotte was Charlotte Russe, which was invented by Antonin Carême at the beginning of the nineteenth century and was derived from the original classic, warm apple charlotte.

Custards

Simply stated, custard is a liquid — milk, cream, or a combination of the two — that is thickened with eggs and heat. The coagulation of the egg protein sets the custard. Custards are easy to prepare, can be made one to two days in advance, and need little or no finishing touch. The most basic custard formula contains simply eggs and sugar plus milk or cream. The consistency of the finished product is determined by the fat content of the milk or cream used and the ratio of whole eggs and/or egg yolks to that liquid.

Custards can be baked in the oven or stirred on top of the stove. The three best-known baked custards are crème caramel, pots de crème, and crème brûlée. All are baked in a bain-marie to protect the custard from high heat. Heating custard above 185°F (85°C) causes it to curdle and become watery, because the moisture separates from the toughened protein. Baked custards are generally prepared in individual earthenware cups, but they can be made in larger ovenproof dishes to serve on a buffet.

- Crème Caramel uses the least rich mixture of the three custards: 1¾ whole eggs to 1 cup (240 ml) whole milk. This custard is firm enough to unmold after baking and chilling.

- Each Pot de Crème contains ¾ whole egg plus 1 egg yolk per 1 cup (240 ml) half-and-half. This custard is softer than crème caramel because of the additional fat in the half-and-half and because less egg white is present. It is too soft to unmold and is served in its baking dish.

- Crème Brûlée is the softest and richest of the three custards. Its formula contains 2 egg yolks per 1 cup (240 ml) heavy cream, with 1 whole egg added for stability for every 7 cups (1 L 680 ml) cream. Like pots de crème, crème brûlée is served in its baking form.

Custards that are cooked and thickened on top of the stove are called *stirred custards*. Pastry cream and vanilla custard sauce, also known as *crème anglaise,* are examples of stirred custards. Some stirred custards are cooked over direct heat; others must be cooked over a water bath.

Bavarian Creams

Bavarians, or Bavarian creams, are chilled desserts made by adding whipped cream and gelatin to a custard sauce made with whole eggs. The mixture is then flavored with fruit puree, liqueur, chocolate, or nuts and poured into molds, in which case it is unmolded before it is served, or it is used as a filling in cakes, pastries, or cold charlottes. Many modified versions of Bavarians are created by using egg yolks alone in the custard base, by adding whipped egg whites instead of, or in addition to, the whipped cream, or simply by adding whipped cream and flavoring to a prepared vanilla custard sauce.

Because Bavarian creams are set by chilling the gelatin-strengthened mixture, the chef does not have the same control as when making a cooked product, where the cooking time can be adjusted to achieve the desired texture. Therefore, precise measurement and proper incorporation of the gelatin are essential. If too little gelatin is used, or if the gelatin is added improperly so part of it starts to set up (forms lumps) before it can be fully incorporated, the dessert will not hold its shape and will be impossible to unmold. On the other hand, if too much gelatin is used, the Bavarian cream will be tough and rubbery. It is also important to remember that many tropical fruits inhibit the gelatinization of protein (animal-based) gelatin unless they are first cooked or heated to a temperature above 175°F (80°C) to destroy the enzyme bromelain, or, in the case of papaya, papain. Like other gelatin-based desserts, Bavarian creams can be made up and used over two to three days if they are kept properly covered and refrigerated in their original molds.

To unmold a Bavarian from a metal or ceramic form, dip the outside of the form into hot water for a few seconds, wipe the bottom, and invert onto a serving plate or a paper-lined sheet pan. Repeat the dipping procedure if the dessert does not unmold easily. With experience, you will learn how long to hold the form in the water. Take care not to immerse the form too long, or you will melt the filling. A Bavarian can also be helped out of its mold by using the back of a spoon to gently push the filling away from the side of the mold, thereby breaking the suction. If you are using Flexipans or other silicone molds, freeze the deserts in the Flexipans (fully or partially) to ensure they will come out cleanly and have a shiny surface. After unmolding, thaw the desserts before serving, in the refrigerator or at room temperature, depending on your timeline for serving the item.

Although the name *Bavarian* obviously connects this dessert to Bavaria, a region of Germany, no one seems to know just how. *Bavarois* is the French word for Bavarian or Bavarian cream; the term is also used for the filling in a cold charlotte.

Mousses

The word *mousse* means "foam" or "lather" in French. In the culinary world, a mousse is a fluffy mixture, either sweet or savory, that acquires this texture from the incorporation of air. Dessert mousses generally fall into one of two categories, fruit and chocolate, although many variations exist. Dessert mousses are served chilled or frozen. The basic ingredients are whipped egg whites, sugar, whipped cream, and the desired flavoring agent, such as fruit puree or chocolate; some recipes use egg yolks as well. Mousses are simple to produce and can be made well in advance.

A chocolate mousse should not require any thickener other than the chocolate itself. A fruit or liqueur mousse usually is fortified with pectin or gelatin. When using either thickener, take care not to get it too hot, or you may melt and deflate the cream. In some recipes, the egg whites are incorporated ahead of the cream; the goal is to prevent overmixing the cream as the egg whites are added, which can result in a loss of volume. However, by whipping the cream to soft peaks only, it can be added before the egg whites with no ill effect.

Frozen dessert mousses, sometimes called *ice mousses,* are similar in composition to parfaits (see page 205), except that a parfait never contains whipped egg whites but instead uses beaten egg yolks, whereas a dessert mousse can contain both.

Soufflés

The French word *soufflé* literally means "to puff" or "to expand." Unfortunately, soufflès have a somewhat undeserved reputation as being not only delicate and airy but also a rather frustrating test of the chef's skill, as they may fail to rise at all or, having done so, may collapse at the wrong time. The phrase "timing is everything" certainly applies here.

Probably no dessert causes more fear and insecurity in cooks than the soufflé — at least until they realize how easy it actually is — and apparently we are not alone. Mrs. Beeton proclaimed in her 1861 classic cookbook: "Soufflés demand, for their successful manufacture, an experienced cook." She also advised that "The most essential thing to insure success of these, the prettiest but most difficult of all entremets, is to secure the best ingredients from an honest tradesman." Louis Eustache Ude's *The French Cook* (1813) had this to say about soufflés: "If sent up in proper time they are very good eating, if not, they are no better than other puddings." The soufflé even took its toll on the great Augustus Escoffier, who at one important dinner party was so worried about the timing of his soufflés that he fired batches every three minutes to ensure that some would be ready at exactly the right moment. (I must confess that this is a trick I have employed myself at times, although no one ever told me about it. I guess if you are thrown in the water, you learn to swim.)

I vividly remember, from the time I was just starting out in the pastry kitchen of a large hotel, being told by the head chef, "Bo, starting tomorrow, you are in charge of the soufflés." I knew he expected the best. His standard joke, which he played on every unsuspecting new cook, was to peek into the oven about the time the soufflés he had made himself were finished and say, "Quick, hand me a knife. I need to cut my soufflé away from the top of the oven!" This was his way of letting us know he was proud of the height of his soufflés.

I think what really worries people about making soufflés is that, should they make a mistake, no quick recovery is possible, as it takes at least 15 minutes to produce a replacement. However, no mistake need occur. Once the daunting soufflé myths are overcome and your self-confidence returns, making soufflés is just another part of the day's work. This is exactly what I tell my students when I do my soufflé lecture and demonstration. As for the tales that caution you to whisper and tiptoe around the kitchen while the soufflés are in the oven, only one has any foundation — not to open the oven door during baking. I nevertheless do just that about halfway through, but only for a second, and I close the door very gently. When I remove the soufflés from the oven, puffed twice as high as the ramekins, to the amazement of my students, I tell them I think I just proved my point.

Soufflés fall into two categories: sweet and savory. Cheese soufflé is probably the best known of the savory variety; recipes are also made with spinach, other vegetables, and seafood. Among sweet dessert soufflés, the classic liqueur soufflé cannot be beat; this category includes the famous and tremendously popular Soufflé Grand Marnier and the Harlequin Soufflé, which, with its two types of batter baked together, offers the ultimate proof that the chef has mastered the soufflé technique.

A liqueur soufflé always rises higher than a fruit soufflé because the evaporating alcohol fumes contribute to the rising process. Essentially, the air trapped in the whipped egg whites becomes lighter and expands as it is heated. Soon after the soufflé is removed from the oven, the trapped air begins to escape, and the soufflé deflates like a punctured balloon. While you don't want this to happen before the guest has seen the dessert, it is actually desirable and a good test of a perfectly prepared soufflé. If a soufflé just sits there high and mighty and never deflates, it is either overbaked and dried out from below, so you are looking at an empty shell, or it is much too heavy and probably tastes more like pudding than a soufflé.

To aid the soufflé batter in rising straight up, it should always be baked in a traditional round soufflé ramekin with straight sides. The two most common sizes for individual servings are 3¼ inches (8.1 cm) in diameter with a capacity of approximately 5 ounces (150 ml), and 4½ inches (11.2 cm) in diameter, which holds about 1 cup (240 ml). The largest size used has a 2-quart (1L 920 ml) capacity and serves eight to ten people.

Fruit soufflés can get a little bit tricky and, depending on the variety, you may have to use trial and error when reducing the fruit pulp. Enough moisture must be removed to concentrate the flavor and keep the mixture from being too thin, but if the pulp is too dense, the egg whites will not support it. Fruit soufflés are sometimes baked in a fruit shell, often an orange. These soufflés are really more show than substance, however, as the batter must be little more than flavored whipped egg whites in order to puff up and out of the fruit.

Crepe soufflés, as their name indicates, are made by baking soufflé batter inside a crepe. This is generally done by spreading the batter on a cooked crepe, folding it in half, and baking it à la minute, as any other soufflé. My complaint about this method is that the desserts turn out flat, and the identifying characteristic of a soufflé should be its height. Therefore, I place the crepe inside a ramekin so it lines the bottom and sides, fill it with soufflé batter, bake, and then carefully remove the crepe from the ramekin and transfer to a serving plate. The crepe becomes an edible shell that holds the soufflé in something closer to the familiar shape. Even with the ramekin for support, this type of soufflé does not rise as high as a conventional soufflé, as the batter sticks to the crepe on the sides.

Other desserts influenced by soufflés are the soufflé omelette and soufflé pancakes. Both include whipped egg whites folded into a batter, which cause it to expand rapidly in a hot oven.

Apple Crème Brûlée yield: 12 servings (Color Photo 60)

This unusual adaptation of the classic and delicious — but let's face it, rather boring in the visual department — crème brûlée offers an opportunity for creative pastry work as well as the always welcome combination of custard and fruit. As with many of the recipes in this text, the presentation can be simplified without losing the entire effect. By omitting the caramelized apple wedge, you can cut the preparation time and reduce the skill level needed to complete the dessert. Another option is to bake the custard directly in the hollowed-out apples. In this case, do not poach the apples first. The only disadvantage to baking the fruit and custard together is that the skin on the apples becomes wrinkled and discolored, which detracts from the appearance of the finished dish.

If you need a substitute for the macadamia nuts, hazelnuts are a good choice; blanch and toast them before dipping in the caramel. Although the crunchy nuts are used primarily for decoration, they also provide a nice textural contrast to the soft custard and the apple shell.

Vanilla-Bean Crème Brûlée Custard (recipe follows)

12 medium-size green apples, such as Pippin, Greening, or Granny Smith

2 recipes Spiced Poaching Syrup (page 790)

3 ounces (85 g) unsalted macadamia nuts, lightly toasted

Clear Caramel Sauce (recipe follows; see Chef's Tip)

Granulated sugar

Ground cinnamon

12 raspberries or other fruit for decoration

12 small mint leaves

12 Caramel-Dipped Apple Wedges (page 625)

I. Pour the custard into a ceramic baking form. The form can be any shape but should be close to the size of a cake pan that is 10 inches (25 cm) in diameter. Place the form inside a larger pan and add cold water to reach approximately the same level as the custard.

2. Bake at 350°F (175°C) for 25 to 30 minutes or until the custard is set. Set aside to cool.

3. Slice the top and bottom off of each apple, cutting the bottoms even so the apples will stand straight. Use a melon ball cutter to scoop out the insides, leaving a ³/₈-inch (9-mm) shell all around the inside, including the bottom. Place the apple shells in acidulated water as you work to prevent oxidation; the apple flesh is not used in this recipe.

4. Bring the poaching syrup to a simmer. Add the apple shells and cook for about 5 minutes, making sure the shells are completely submerged in the liquid. The apples are done when they just start to soften. Overcooking the apples causes the peel to wrinkle. Remove the apples from the poaching syrup and let them cool, upside-down, to drain.

5. Using 2 spoons, portion the baked custard into the apple shells, keeping the skin on the top of the custard upright as much as possible so it becomes the top of the filling. Depending on the size of the apples, you may have a little custard left over. Wipe off any custard on the sides of the apples. Place the apples in the refrigerator until needed.

6. Chop (do not crush) the macadamia nuts into raisin-sized pieces. Place a portion of the caramel sauce in a piping bottle and reserve.

CHEF'S TIP

To make the caramel sauce thick enough so it does not run on the plate, hold back some of the water at the end. If you do not have a piping bottle handy, pour ¹/₃ cup (80 ml) sauce in the center of the plate and use the back of a small spoon to spread and shape it into a circle.

7. Presentation: Sprinkle just enough granulated sugar over the custard in a filled apple to cover the custard. Caramelize the sugar by placing the apple under a broiler or salamander or by using a blowtorch. Pipe a 5-inch (12.5-cm) circle of caramel sauce in the center of a dessert plate. Using a fine mesh strainer, sift ground cinnamon lightly over the rim of the plate. Place the apple in the center of the sauce. Sprinkle chopped macadamia nuts around the apple. Decorate the top of the apple with a raspberry and a mint leaf. Lean a caramelized apple wedge against the side of the apple crème brûlée. Serve immediately.

About Apples

The native home of the apple is not known for certain, but the fruit was enjoyed by the ancient Greeks and Romans. Apples came to the New World with European settlers and were carried west by travelers. One famous historical figure is John Chapman, known as Johnny Appleseed, who planted a multitude of apple trees throughout the American Midwest from the time of American independence in 1776 up to his death in 1845. He is said to have been an eccentric but smart businessman (and a student of the Swedenborgian Religious Philosophy, no less).

It is generally accepted that modern apple varieties are the result of natural cross-pollination involving many ancestors, as modern varieties are *heterozygous,* meaning they do not always reproduce authentically to type. For example, when growers set out to create hybrids, each seedling is selected to contribute half of the heritage. There is still an unknown element, however, because characteristics may eventually emerge in the new tree that were totally hidden in the parent trees. So the result — either improvement, as hoped for, or the cultivation of an inferior variety — is not known until the tree bears fruit.

Apple trees are propagated by grafting; a bud from the desired varietal, called a *scion,* is inserted into the base of the seedling tree, known as the *rootstock.* The stock itself may be from a propagated (hybrid) tree but, in most cases, buds are developed on seedling trees. For home gardeners as well as large commercial operations, rootstocks are selected not only in an attempt to generate a certain improvement or change in the fruit but also to control the size of the tree. Uniform tree height is important for commercial orchards, and dwarf rootstocks are popular where space is an issue.

Certain apple varieties are heads of large groups, or families. The descendants of these families are "born" in one of two ways: either as a direct result of planned breeding and cultivation or as a natural genetic change or mutation. Unplanned genetic alterations can occur at any time and without obvious reason. Suddenly, one tree branch is different from the others and produces a variation in bud and fruit; these surprises are referred to in the fruit growing industry as *sports.* In most cases, sports have no value, but just as many inventions are the result of an accident, once in a while a sport develops into a significant new strain.

The Three Fundamental Apple Varieties

McIntosh, the oldest of the three, was discovered by John McIntosh at his Canadian nursery around 1810. The strain did not become available until 1835, however, when the grafting technique was fully developed. McIntosh apples were widely known by the beginning of the 1900s. McIntosh trees produce the best spurs for grafting; they are known as Macspurs. Popular in breeding, some of the better-known descendants of McIntosh are Macoun, Empire, Cortland, Summer Red, and Spartan.

Delicious is the best-known modern apple. It was first grown in an Iowa orchard in 1870. The original tree was thought to be a seedling from a nearby bellflower tree. The owner, Jessie Hiatt, cut down the tree not once but twice, yet it continued to sprout anew, and finally he let it be. Ten years later, when the tree reached maturity, it produced some of the best apples Mr. Hiatt had ever tasted. Naturally occurring sports produced redder apples, including Red Queen, Richard, Royal Red, and Hi Early. Grafting spurs from the Delicious include Oregon Spur, Wellspur, and Starkrimson. Delicious is also a parent of the Melrose.

Jonathon was first grown in Kingston, New York, from seeds from a Spitzenberg variety. The story goes that a judge in Albany, New York, liked the apple well enough to introduce it to the local horticultural society, and he named the variety after the person who had given him the apple. Jonathon was the most popular apple variety in the United States until it was surpassed by Delicious. Sports of Jonathon are Jon-a-Red and Jonnee (also a red variety). Hybrids include Jonagold, Idared, Melrose, and Monroe.

VANILLA-BEAN CREME BRULEE CUSTARD
yield: 12 servings, 6 ounces (180 ml) each, made in traditional crème brûlée ramekins, or in 1 pan, 10 inches (25 cm) in diameter

1 whole vanilla bean	7 cups (1 L 680 ml) heavy cream
12 ounces (340 g) granulated sugar	1½ teaspoons (7.5 g) salt
14 egg yolks (1¼ cups/300 ml)	1 teaspoon (5 ml) vanilla extract
1 whole egg	

1. Cut the vanilla bean lengthwise in half and, using the back of a paring knife, scrape out the seeds (save the pod halves for another use). Combine the seeds with the sugar by rubbing the mixture lightly with your fingertips.

2. Mix (do not whip) the egg yolks, whole egg, and vanilla-flavored sugar until well combined. Heat the cream to the scalding point, then gradually pour it into the egg mixture while stirring constantly. Add the salt and vanilla.

3. Use as directed in the apple crème brûlée recipe, or bake in individual ramekins in a bain-marie.

CLEAR CARAMEL SAUCE
yield: approximately 4 cups (960 ml)

2 pounds (910 g) granulated sugar	1½ cups (360 ml) hot water
1 teaspoon (5 ml) lemon juice	

1. Place the sugar and lemon juice in a small, heavy-bottomed saucepan. Cook over medium heat, stirring constantly with a wooden spoon, until all of the sugar is melted. Continue to cook and stir the sugar until it reaches a light to medium golden color.

2. Immediately remove the pan from the heat and carefully pour in the hot water. Stand back a little as you do this, because the syrup may splatter.

3. Return to the heat and cook, stirring constantly, to melt any lumps.

4. Let the sauce cool completely, then add water as needed to thin it to the proper consistency. You must wait until the sauce has cooled before judging its thickness, which varies with the degree to which you caramelized the sugar.

Cappuccino Mousse with Sambuca Cream in a Chocolate Coffee Cup

yield: 16 servings (Color Photo 62)

Of the many ways to present a mousse, this is probably about as fancy as you can get (or as fancy as you would want to get). There is, of course, a price to pay in the many steps it takes to complete this whimsical dessert. But if you compare this presentation to the typical mousse — piped into a champagne glass with a rosette of whipped cream on top — the effort is worthwhile; besides the aesthetic difference, the whole presentation is edible. Luckily, all of the components can be prepared ahead of time.

I mention in the procedure not to fill any more chocolate coffee cups than you will be serving right away. This is to prevent wasting any of the labor-intensive cups, because while the mousse must be kept cold, the cups should not be chilled for more than a few hours, or they will discolor from condensation when they are removed from the refrigerator. The mousse can be made ahead and refrigerated. It is easy to soften it to a pipeable consistency as required.

If you want to give the dessert more color, use Raspberry Sauce (page 173) as a border for the mousseline sauce. For a different presentation, pipe a small round of sauce in the center of the plate, make a spoon-shaped cocoa powder silhouette as shown in Color Photo 16, and set the tuile spoon next to the silhouette.

Cappuccino Mousse (recipe follows)	1 cup (240 ml) heavy cream
16 Chocolate Coffee Cups (recipe follows)	Finely ground coffee
1 recipe Mousseline Sauce (page 338)	16 Tuile Cookie Spoons (page 708)
½ cup (120 ml) sambuca liqueur	Edible flowers

1. If necessary, soften the cappuccino mousse to a pipeable consistency by stirring it briefly over hot water. Place the mousse in a pastry bag with a No. 7 (14-mm) plain tip. Pipe the mousse into the chocolate cups, forming a smooth mound on the top of each. Do not fill more chocolate cups than you plan to serve within 2 to 3 hours. Reserve in the refrigerator. (The filled cups can be refrigerated for that length of time without damage.)

2. Flavor the mousseline sauce with half of the sambuca liqueur. Place a portion of the sauce in a piping bottle and reserve in the refrigerator with the remaining sauce.

3. Add the remaining liqueur to the cream and whip to soft peaks. Cover and refrigerate.

4. Presentation: Cover the base of a dessert plate with mousseline sauce. Hold the plate in one hand and tap the rim with the palm of your other hand to make the surface of the sauce flat and even. Lightly sift coffee over the sauce. Use a spoon to place a large dollop of sambuca cream on top of the mousse in a prepared cup. Hold a cookie spoon by the handle and gently push the tip partway into the cream. Do not hide the entire bowl of the spoon, or the effect will be wasted. Place an edible flower next to the spoon. Place the cup in the center of the plate, giving it a careful twist to ensure that it will not slide in the sauce. To avoid leaving fingerprints, wear food handling gloves when handling the chocolate cups.

CHEF'S TIP
If you are preparing several of these desserts and must start the assembly ahead of time, always add the spoon at the very last moment, or it may soften and fall over.

CAPPUCCINO MOUSSE yield: 8 cups (1 L 920 ml)

3 cups (720 ml) heavy cream	¼ cup (60 ml) coffee liqueur
6 egg yolks (½ cup/120 ml)	10 ounces (285 g) sweet dark chocolate
⅓ cup (80 ml) or 4 ounces (115 g) honey	4 ounces (115 g) unsweetened chocolate

1. Whip the heavy cream to soft peaks. Cover and refrigerate.

2. Whip the egg yolks to the ribbon stage.

3. Heat the honey just until it starts to boil, then immediately whip it into the egg yolks. Because the amount is so small, be sure to scrape all of the honey out of the pot. Continue whipping until the mixture has cooled. Stir in the liqueur.

4. Melt the dark chocolate and unsweetened chocolate together. Rapidly incorporate the melted chocolates into the egg mixture. Fold in the whipped cream.

CHOCOLATE COFFEE CUPS

Tempered sweet dark chocolate or dark
  coating chocolate

16 small balloons (see Note)

Vegetable oil

Simple syrup

1. Bring the chocolate to the appropriate temperature for the variety you are using (see pages 511 to 514).

2. Inflate the balloons to the size that will make the finished chocolate cups 3½ inches (8.7 cm) wide when measured across the top. Make a few test cups if you are unsure of the size (see Step 4).

3. After tying the balloons, wash your hands and use them to squeeze the middle section of the balloon to force air into the bottom (round) end to make sure the rubber is stretched evenly. This is necessary because the balloons are not fully inflated, which leaves a small area of thicker rubber at the round end. If not properly stretched, this area absorbs part of the oil and sticks to the chocolate. Lightly coat the portion of the balloons that will be dipped into the chocolate with the vegetable oil by rubbing it on with your hand. Do not use too much oil, which can prevent the chocolate from adhering; it can also ruin the remaining chocolate supply if the oil becomes incorporated.

4. Push the oiled round end of a balloon into the chocolate, holding it straight and covering the bottom 2 inches (5 cm) with chocolate. Let excess chocolate drip back into the bowl (Figure 7-1). Scrape the bottom of the balloon against the side of the bowl to remove more excess chocolate (Figure 7-2). Blot the bottom on baking paper (Figure 7-3), then carefully set the dipped balloon on a sheet pan lined with baking paper. Repeat to make 16 cups.

5. Place the cups in the refrigerator for 2 minutes to set the chocolate. Wearing food handling gloves to avoid leaving fingerprints, gently twist and pull the balloons away from the chocolate cups (Figure 7-4). This method makes it possible to reuse the balloons. If you find you are breaking the cups, or if you do not need to reuse the balloons, a much easier and foolproof method is to deflate the balloons. Puncture them with a toothpick at the very top, next to where

FIGURE 7-1 **Dipping the round end of a balloon into melted chocolate and letting excess chocolate drip back into the bowl**

FIGURE 7-2 **Removing more excess chocolate by scraping the bottom of the balloon against the side of the bowl**

FIGURE 7-3 **Blotting the bottom of the balloon on baking paper before setting the balloon aside**

FIGURE 7-4 Removing the balloon from the hardened chocolate cup, wearing a glove on the hand that touches the chocolate to prevent fingerprints

FIGURE 7-5 Using a heated metal spatula to smooth the top of the chocolate cup

they are tied closed, then set them aside to release the air slowly. Do not pop the balloon, or the chocolate will shatter.

6. If necessary, warm a metal spatula and use it to smooth the top edge of each cup (Figure 7-5).

7. Copy the template shown in Figure 7-6. Secure a piece of baking paper over the template. Make piping chocolate by adding a few drops of simple syrup to approximately ⅓ cup (80 ml) melted chocolate. Place in a piping bag, cut a small opening, and pipe out handles, using the drawing as a guide (Figures 7-7 and 7-8). Make about 20 handles to allow for breakage. Place

FIGURE 7-6 The template used as a guide to pipe out handles for the chocolate cups

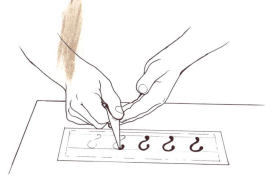

FIGURE 7-7 Piping the chocolate handles on a sheet of baking paper with the template drawing under the paper

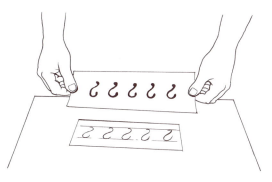

FIGURE 7-8 Lifting the sheet of baking paper with the finished chocolate handles

Charlottes, Custards, Bavarian Creams, Mousses, and Soufflés 331

- An easy way to attach the handles to the cups, and one that works particularly well if you are making a large number, is to invert the cups so the open side rests on the table. With the cups in this position, the handles will be supported by the table and you will not have to hold each one until it is set. Two other advantages of this method are that it ensures that all the handles are placed at the same level and that they are not placed too low on the sides of the cups, which can cause the handles to break when the cups are placed on the plates.

- The handles on the chocolate cups will be flat on one side. You can make fully formed handles by doing the following: As you remove the handles from the paper at the end of Step 7, invert each one so the flat side faces up. Pipe chocolate over the flat side, following the shape of the handle. Let the chocolate set in the refrigerator for 1 minute before attaching the handles to the cups.

- The same chocolate shells, made without handles, can be used to hold other mousses or desserts. You can alter the shape and size of the finished cups by using different sizes and shapes of balloons and by varying the height to which you dip them. The cups can be made 4 or 5 days ahead of time, provided they are stored in a cool place.

the handles in the refrigerator for 1 minute to harden the chocolate. Remove them from the paper, quickly dip the ends in chocolate, and attach the handles to the cups (Figure 7-9).

NOTE: Use the smallest round or tear-shaped balloons you can find. You may need to buy a package of assorted sizes and pick out the smaller balloons.

FIGURE 7-9 Attaching a handle to the side of a chocolate coffee cup, wearing gloves on both hands to prevent fingerprints

Charlotte Charente yield: 16 servings

Charlotte Charente hails from the wonderful, gastronomically rich Bordeaux region of northwestern France, which includes the provinces of Charente, Dordogne, and Gironde. The region is famous for its red wine, Cognac, and the highly touted species of black truffle from the Périgord. This is my version of a local specialty called *Plessis Charente*. I discovered this dessert in a small restaurant in Sainte, just a few miles from the better-known town of Cognac.

If time does not permit you to make the ladyfingers, don't let that stop you from enjoying the unusual flavor combination of Cognac, port wine, and dried currants. Simply pipe the Charente Bavarois into small individual molds, unmold when set, decorate with a whipped cream rosette, and serve with fresh fruit. Although it is convenient to use ramekins when assembling the desserts with the ladyfingers, small cake rings, 3 inches (7.5 cm) in diameter, placed on a lined sheet pan work as well. You can also make your own rings from polyurethane or acetate; cut strips measuring 9 ½ × 1 ½ inches (23.7 × 3.7 cm), overlap the ends ½ inch (1.2 cm), and tape together.

1½ recipes Chocolate Ladyfingers batter (page 801)

Charente Bavarois (recipe follows)

3 cups (720 ml) heavy cream

2 tablespoons (30 g) granulated sugar

1 recipe Mousseline Sauce (page 338)

2 tablespoons (30 ml) Cognac or brandy

Chocolate Sauce for Piping (page 681)

Shaved dark chocolate

16 small strawberry wedges

I. On baking paper, draw 6 sections, each 2 inches (5 cm) wide and the length of a full sheet pan, spacing them ½ inch (1.2 cm) apart. Invert the paper on a sheet pan. Place the ladyfinger batter in a pastry bag with a No. 3 (6-mm) plain tip. Pipe the batter onto the pan crosswise between the lines over the length of the pan. Pipe left to right and right to left, continuing within the 2-inch (5-cm) sections, so that when the ladyfingers are baked, each section will form a solid, wavy strip.

2. Bake at 425°F (219°C) for about 10 minutes or until dark golden brown. Immediately transfer the strips, still attached to the paper, to cold sheet pans or the tabletop to prevent the ladyfingers from drying out as they cool.

3. Line the sides of 16 soufflé ramekins, 3¼ inches (8.1 cm) in diameter, with strips of polyurethane or acetate to prevent the ladyfingers from sticking.

4. Trim enough from 1 long side of each ladyfinger strip to make a straight edge on that side and to make the strip 1¾ inches (4.5 cm) wide. Cut each strip into 3 pieces; each will be a little less than 8 inches (20 cm) long. Fit 1 strip inside each prepared ramekin, arranging the strip so the trimmed, even edge is in the bottom of the mold and the flat (bottom) side faces the inside of the mold (Figure 7-10). If you have trouble bending the strips, follow the directions for softening a roulade sheet in the Note on page 795.

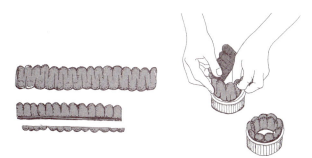

FIGURE 7-10 The baked ladyfinger strip with the bottom edge trimmed; using the trimmed piece to line a ramekin

5. Divide the bavarois among the lined forms. Refrigerate until set, at least 2 hours.

6. Whip the heavy cream with sugar to stiff peaks. Place in a pastry bag with a No. 4 (8-mm) plain tip. Reserve in the refrigerator.

7. Make the mousseline sauce and stir in the Cognac or brandy. Place a portion of the sauce in a piping bottle.

8. Presentation: Unmold a charlotte from the soufflé ramekin by dipping the bottom briefly into hot water and inverting the dessert into the palm of your hand. If you are using rings, simply remove them. Place the charlotte, flat-side down, in the center of a dessert plate. Pipe mousseline sauce around the dessert to cover the base of the plate. Use a piping bag to decorate the mousseline sauce with the chocolate sauce for piping (see pages 681 to 685). Pipe dots of whipped cream the size of hazelnuts on top of the charlotte, covering the entire surface. Decorate the whipped cream with shaved chocolate and a strawberry wedge.

VARIATION

CHARLOTTE RUSSE

Follow the instructions for lining the forms with ladyfingers as described. Fill the molds with Classic Chocolate Bavarian Cream (page 768). Follow the same presentation instructions given with Charlotte Charente.

CHARENTE BAVAROIS yield: 6 cups (I L 440 ml)

D o not make this filling until you are ready to use it. Allow it to thicken slightly before filling the prepared forms to prevent the currants from sinking to the bottom.

2½ ounces (70 g) dried currants

½ cup (120 ml) port wine

¼ cup (60 ml) Cognac

1 tablespoon (9 g) unflavored gelatin powder

6 egg yolks (½ cup/120 ml)

¼ cup (60 ml) simple syrup

1 pint (480 ml) heavy cream

3 egg whites

4 ounces (115 g) granulated sugar

1. Macerate the currants in half of the port wine, preferably the day before and at least several hours before proceeding with the recipe.

2. Add the Cognac to the remaining port. Sprinkle the gelatin over the mixture and set aside to soften.

3. Whip the egg yolks for 1 minute. Bring the simple syrup to a boil and gradually incorporate into the yolks while whipping rapidly. Continue whipping until the mixture has a light, fluffy consistency.

4. Whip the cream to soft peaks. Set aside in the refrigerator.

5. Combine the egg whites and sugar in a bowl. Set over simmering water and heat to 140°F (60°C), whipping constantly. Remove from the heat while continuing to whip, then whip until the meringue is cold and holds soft peaks.

6. Combine the yolk mixture and whipped cream. Fold in the meringue. Heat the gelatin and wine mixture to dissolve the gelatin. Quickly add all of the gelatin to about one-quarter of the cream mixture to temper it. Still working quickly, add this to the remaining cream. Fold in the macerated currants, including the port.

Chocolate Mousse in Ribbon Teardrops

yield: 16 servings, 4 ounces (115 g) each (Color Photo 61)

W hile this presentation is elegant, it is admittedly time-consuming as well. However, the teardrop shells can be made up well in advance during a slow time and, stored properly, will keep for weeks. When the shells are made ahead, it is best to leave the plastic strips attached until serving time. Even the mousse fillings can be prepared up to three days before serving if they are kept, well covered, in the refrigerator. Other ways to save time are to make only one flavor of mousse and use it to fill all three shells, and to omit the chocolate noodles, instead piping a rosette of whipped cream on top with the fruit garnish.

The procedure for making the chocolate teardrops can be used to form many shapes and paired with a variety of fillings. If desired, you can also make a bottom on the shells by following the instructions in the Chef's Tip with the recipe for Cupid's Treasure Chest (page 347).

Dark Chocolate Mousse Filling (recipe follows)

White Chocolate Mousse Filling for Teardrops (recipe follows)

Tempered dark chocolate or dark coating chocolate, melted

Tempered white chocolate or white coating chocolate, melted

Unsweetened cocoa powder

48 Chocolate Figurines (page 545)

16 Cape gooseberries or other berries

White Chocolate Noodles (page 529)

Dark Chocolate Noodles (page 529)

1. Make the dark and white chocolate mousse fillings, cover, and refrigerate separately while making the chocolate ribbon teardrops.

2. Cut 48 strips of polyurethane or acetate measuring 9 × 1¼ inches (22.5 × 3.1 cm). Spread the dark and white chocolate on the strips following the instructions for making Chocolate Ribbons (page 530). To shape the ribbons into teardrops, bend the plastic strips with the chocolate on the inside to make the short ends meet. Hold the ends together with a paper clip. Stand the teardrops on a sheet pan lined with baking paper. They can be stored this way until needed; however, to ensure a glossy surface, they should always be placed briefly in the refrigerator just before removing the plastic.

3. Wearing food handling gloves to avoid leaving fingerprints on the chocolate, remove the paper clips and gently pull the plastic strips away from the hardened chocolate.

4. Presentation: Sift cocoa powder lightly over the base of a dessert plate avoiding the rim. Wipe the rim of the plate clean as needed. Stir the fillings to make them smooth and place them in 2 pastry bags, each with a No. 6 (12-mm) plain tip. Place 3 chocolate teardrops as far off-center on the plate as possible, with the pointed ends angled toward one another (again, at this point you should be wearing food handling gloves to prevent fingerprints). Pipe white chocolate mousse into the center shell. Pipe dark chocolate mousse into the outer shells. Place a chocolate figurine on top of each teardrop. Place a Cape gooseberry where the tips of the teardrops meet. Arrange dark and white chocolate noodles on the plate in front of the teardrops.

DARK CHOCOLATE MOUSSE FILLING yield: 8 cups (1 L 920 ml)

¼ recipe Swiss Meringue (page 782)

2½ cups (600 ml) heavy cream

4 ounces (115 g) unsweetened cocoa powder

¾ cup (180 ml) warm water

¼ cup (60 ml) dark rum

8 ounces (225 g) sweet dark chocolate

6 egg yolks (½ cup/120 ml)

¼ cup (60 ml) or 3 ounces (85 g) light corn syrup

1. Make the Swiss meringue and set it aside.

2. Whip the heavy cream to stiff peaks and set it aside in the refrigerator.

3. Mix the cocoa powder into the warm water. Add the rum. Melt the sweet dark chocolate and add it to the cocoa powder mixture. Set aside and keep warm.

4. Whip the egg yolks for a few moments, just until broken up. Bring the corn syrup to a boil; gradually pour the hot syrup into the yolks while continuing to whip constantly. Whip until the mixture is thick and fluffy. Fold the warm chocolate mixture into the egg yolks. Fold into the reserved whipped cream, then gradually stir this mixture into the reserved Swiss meringue. Cover and place in the refrigerator.

WHITE CHOCOLATE MOUSSE FILLING FOR TEARDROPS yield: 4½ cups (1 L 80 ml)

1½ cups (360 ml) heavy cream

2 teaspoons (6 g) unflavored gelatin powder

¼ cup (60 ml) cold water

1 tablespoon (9 g) pectin powder (see Note)

3 ounces (85 g) granulated sugar

4 egg whites (½ cup/120 ml)

8 ounces (225 g) white chocolate, melted

1. Whip the heavy cream to soft peaks; do not overwhip. Cover and refrigerate.

2. Sprinkle the gelatin over the cold water and set aside to soften.

3. Combine the pectin powder and sugar in a mixing bowl. Stir in the egg whites. Place the bowl over simmering water and heat, stirring constantly with a whisk, until the mixture reaches 140°F (60°C). Remove from the heat and immediately whip until the meringue has cooled completely and has formed stiff peaks.

4. Place the gelatin mixture over simmering water and heat to dissolve. Working quickly, first stir the gelatin into the melted white chocolate, then stir the chocolate mixture into one-third of the meringue to temper it. Add this to the remaining meringue. Stir in the reserved whipped cream. Cover and refrigerate.

NOTE: Use regular canning pectin. If pectin is not available, increase the gelatin by 1 teaspoon (3 g) for a total of 1 tablespoon (9 g).

Chocolate Rum Pudding with Chocolate May Beetles

yield: 16 servings (Color Photo 65)

This dressed-up pudding presentation features a whimsical chocolate beetle perched on an edible leaf also made of chocolate. To simplify, you can replace both the beetle and the leaf with a whipped cream rosette topped with a chocolate figurine. The delicious flavor will still be there, but the originality rating will suffer a bit. When I last featured this recipe on the menu, my students told me that the small glazed pudding cakes looked just like Ding-Dongs — before they were decorated — a nickname that did not sit well with me. During one lunch service, after hearing "ordering, one Ding-Dong" and "ordering, two Ding-Dongs" dozens of times, I firmly stated that from now on I did not want that name used in my kitchen and that the dessert was to be fired using its proper name. When I told my wife (who was born and raised in the United States) that I wanted to change the shape of the dessert so it would not look like a mass-produced grocery-store snack cake, I was told that yes, they do look like Ding-Dongs, but I was overreacting. The shape remains.

16 Chocolate Rum Puddings (recipe follows)

1 recipe Chocolate Glaze (page 774)

Mousseline Sauce (recipe follows)

¼ cup (60 ml) dark rum

Unsweetened cocoa powder

Chocolate Sauce for Piping (page 681)

16 Chocolate Leaves (page 527)

Candied violets

16 Chocolate May Beetles (page 527)

1. Unmold the puddings and place them, crust-side down, on an aspic rack or cake cooling rack, allowing plenty of room between them. Set the rack on a sheet pan and pour or pipe the chocolate glaze over the puddings (see directions and Figures 13-6 and 13-7, page 679). The glaze should run down the sides and cover the puddings completely. Adjust the consistency of the glaze as needed to ensure proper coverage.

2. Once the glaze has formed a skin, use a palette knife to remove the puddings from the rack. Refrigerate until serving time or, for a short period, reserve at room temperature.

3. Combine the mousseline sauce with the rum. Place a portion of the sauce in a piping bottle. Reserve it and the remainder of the sauce in the refrigerator.

4. Presentation: Sift cocoa powder lightly over the rim of a dessert plate. Cover the base of the plate with mousseline sauce. Pipe a ring of chocolate sauce just inside the perimeter of the mousseline sauce. Drag a wooden skewer through the ring of sauce, toward the center of the plate, at 1-inch (2.5-cm) intervals. Place a pudding in the center of the sauce and decorate it with a chocolate leaf, a small piece of candied violet, and a chocolate beetle.

CHOCOLATE RUM PUDDING yield: 16 servings, 5 ounces (150 ml) each

6 ounces (170 g) white bread crumbs, toasted

3 cups (720 ml) heavy cream

2 teaspoons (10 ml) vanilla extract

Melted unsalted butter

Granulated sugar to coat the forms

8 ounces (225 g) sweet dark chocolate

8 ounces (225 g) unsalted butter, at room temperature

8 ounces (225 g) granulated sugar

8 eggs, separated

6 ounces (170 g) almonds, finely ground

¼ cup (60 ml) dark rum

1. Combine the bread crumbs, cream, and vanilla. Set aside for 15 minutes.

2. Brush melted butter over the inside of 16 ramekins, 3¼ inches (8.1 cm) in diameter, or use coffee cups or other ovenproof molds with straight sides and approximately the same diameter. Coat the forms with sugar.

3. Melt the dark chocolate; set aside, but keep warm.

4. Beat the butter with 4 ounces (115 g) of the sugar to a light and creamy consistency. Add the egg yolks, a few at a time, then quickly incorporate the melted chocolate. Add the ground almonds, rum, and bread crumb mixture.

5. Whip the egg whites and remaining 4 ounces (115 g) sugar to soft peaks. Gradually fold the chocolate mixture into the egg whites.

6. Fill the prepared molds with the batter. Set the forms in a larger pan and add hot water around the forms to come halfway up the sides.

7. Bake at 350°F (175°C) for about 35 minutes; the puddings should spring back when pressed lightly. Set aside to cool.

About Rum

Rum is a spirit distilled from fermented sugarcane juice and/or molasses. The islands of the Caribbean produce most of the world's rum supply. The lighter rums — white rum and the amber or golden-colored rums — are produced, for the most part, in Puerto Rico, Cuba, and the Virgin Islands, while the heavier and darker varieties come primarily from the islands of Jamaica and Barbados. Sugarcane grown along the banks of the Demerara River in Guyana is used to make the strongest and darkest rum. Rum, by law, must be at least 60-proof (30 percent alcohol), but most brands are 80-proof; the extreme is 151-proof rum, which is convenient for flambé work because it will ignite without being heated. Rum is used extensively in the pastry shop as a flavoring for ice cream, candies, and pastries such as baba au rum, and for flambé work.

MOUSSELINE SAUCE yield: approximately 4 cups (960 ml)

In the recipes in this book, creamy mousseline sauce is usually flavored with a spirit or liqueur that complements a particular dessert. If you are serving this sauce with a dessert that does not specify a flavoring, you may want to add ¼ cup (60 ml) of the liqueur or spirit of your choice.

3 ounces (85 g) granulated sugar

6 egg yolks (½ cup/120 ml)

⅓ cup (80 ml) boiling water

1 teaspoon (5 ml) vanilla extract

1½ cups (360 ml) heavy cream

1. Whip the sugar and egg yolks together just to combine. Whisk in the boiling water. Place the bowl over simmering water and whisk constantly until the mixture thickens to the ribbon stage. Remove from the heat and whip until cool. Add the vanilla.

2. Whip the heavy cream until it thickens to a saucelike consistency. Fold into the yolk mixture. If needed, thin the sauce with a little heavy cream. If the sauce is too thin for your particular use, thicken it by mixing in additional softly whipped cream. Store the mousseline sauce, covered, in the refrigerator for 3 to 4 days. If the sauce separates, whisking will bring it back together.

Citrus Cream with Pink Grapefruit and Orange

yield: 16 servings, 4 ounces (120 ml) each (Color Photo 66)

This dessert evolved from one of the most popular cakes I make: Lemon Chiffon Cake (page 42). Although the filling does contain cream, Citrus Cream with Pink Grapefruit and Orange is decorated with fresh fruit rather than all of the whipped cream used in icing the chiffon cake. While that is not quite enough to qualify it for the Light Dessert chapter, it's at least a step in the direction of the public's growing health consciousness.

Because this dessert requires quite a few steps to complete, if necessary, some alterations can be made to speed the process without taking too much away from the appearance. For example, I have made the citrus cream without the sponge in the bottom; to do this, start at Step 3. Another way to save time is to simply pour a pool of sauce in front of or all around the dessert instead of piping a chocolate teardrop to hold the sauce.

½ recipe Chiffon Sponge I batter (page 797)

½ cup (120 ml) Plain Cake Syrup (page 789)

Citrus Cream (recipe follows)

Piping Chocolate (page 543), melted

Segments cut from approximately 8 peeled grapefruit

½ recipe Raspberry Sauce (page 173)

Sour Cream Mixture for Piping (page 727)

Segments cut from approximately 5 peeled oranges

Small mint leaves

1. Spread the sponge batter into a rectangle, 15 × 22 inches (37.5 x 55 cm), on a Silpat. Bake at 425°F (219°C) until the sponge is baked through and begins to color, about 6 minutes. Invert the sponge onto a sheet of baking paper lightly dusted with flour. Peel the Silpat from the back of the sponge. If you do not have a Silpat, spread the batter over a sheet of baking paper and drag the paper onto a sheet pan. After removing from the oven, transfer the sponge to a second (cool) sheet pan.

2. Place 16 cake rings, 3½ inches (8.7 cm) in diameter by 1 inch (2.5 cm) in height, on a sheet pan lined with baking paper (see Note). Line the rings with strips of acetate or polyurethane. Using a plain cookie cutter, 3½ inches (8.7 cm) in diameter, cut 16 circles from the sponge sheet. Brush or spray the cake syrup over the sponge circles. Place a sponge circle in the bottom of each cake ring.

3. Divide the citrus cream among the rings, filling them to the top. Spread the surface smooth and even. Cover with baking paper, pressing the paper gently so it adheres to the filling. Refrigerate for at least 2 hours or, preferably, overnight.

4. Remove the cake rings and peel away the plastic strips, or simply cut the tape and peel away the polyurethane or acetate, if using that instead of metal rings.

5. Cut baking paper strips to the exact circumference and height of the unmolded citrus creams. Place 2 strips at a time on a full sheet of baking paper. Place piping chocolate in a piping bag and cut a small opening. Pipe the chocolate in parallel lines at a 45-degree angle to the paper strips across and outside the strips (onto the paper), first in one direction and then in the other (see Figure 7-11, page 358, as an example). Pick up the first strip and wrap it, chocolate-side-in, around one of the citrus creams so the chocolate sticks to the filling as shown in Figure 7-13, page 358, but leave the cream in place on the work surface. You will achieve a better finish if you wait until the chocolate is just beginning to set up before you wrap it. If done immediately, the chocolate lines will flatten, to some degree, when pressed against the side. Continue making chocolate strips and wrapping them around the desserts until all of the creams are covered. Place the desserts back on the sheet pan and cover the tops with grapefruit segments in a circular pattern. Refrigerate until ready to serve.

6. Place the raspberry sauce in a piping bottle.

7. Presentation: Place a small amount of piping chocolate in a piping bag and cut a small opening. Pipe a curved teardrop of chocolate on 1 side of a dessert plate. Wait for the chocolate to set up, then fill the teardrop with raspberry sauce. Pipe a line of sour cream mixture in the center of the sauce the length of the teardrop. Swirl it into the sauce using a wooden skewer. Carefully pull the paper strip away from a citrus cream, leaving the chocolate lines on the side of the dessert, and transfer it to the center of the plate. Place 3 orange segments and a mint leaf to the right of the dessert.

NOTE: You can easily make the cake rings from polyurethane or acetate. Use the same cookie cutter you used to cut the sponge as a guide, wrapping the strips around the cutter and taping the short ends.

CITRUS CREAM yield: 8 cups (1 L 920 ml)

Do not make this filling until you are ready to use it. You may substitute orange juice for the lemon juice, if desired. If you do so, add 1 tablespoon (45 ml) orange flower water to the juice.

2 tablespoons (18 g) unflavored gelatin powder

⅓ cup (80 ml) light rum

10 eggs, separated

12 ounces (340 g) granulated sugar

¾ cup (180 ml) lemon juice

3 cups (720 ml) heavy cream

1. Sprinkle the gelatin over the rum to soften.

2. Beat the egg yolks with approximately one-quarter of the sugar to the ribbon stage. Add the lemon juice and whip over a bain-marie until the mixture reaches 140°F (60°C) and is light and foamy. Remove from the heat.

3. Place the gelatin mixture over the bain-marie and heat until just dissolved. Whisk the softened gelatin and rum into the egg yolk mixture. Set aside, but keep warm.

4. Whip the heavy cream to soft peaks and set aside.

5. Combine the egg whites with the remaining sugar. Set the bowl over the bain-marie and heat to 140°F (60°C), whipping constantly. Remove from the heat and whip until the mixture has cooled completely and stiff peaks have formed.

6. Fold the lemon mixture into the egg whites. Fold in the whipped cream.

Crème Brûlée Catalan yield: 12 servings

You would be hard pressed to find a restaurant in Barcelona that does not feature this Catalonian favorite on their menu. There it is known as *crema Catalan* or *crema de San Jose*, the latter in reference to the custom of serving this dessert on St. Joseph's Day. Unlike a traditional baked French crème brûlée, this custard is thickened on the stovetop. Catalan custard is also less rich, as it uses a combination of milk and half-and-half rather than the heavy cream of the classic crème brûlée formula, and it contains a hint of cinnamon.

Catalan Custard (recipe follows)

Granulated sugar

12 blood orange or navel orange segments

Fresh berries

12 mint sprigs

Powdered sugar

Small cookies or petits fours secs

1. Divide the custard among 12 crème brûlée forms, 4½ inches (11.2 cm) in diameter × ¾ inch (2 cm) in height, or other suitable forms of approximately the same size. Cover and refrigerate for a minimum of 2 hours or, preferably, overnight.

2. Presentation: Sprinkle enough granulated sugar on top of a custard to cover the surface. Caramelize the sugar using a salamander or blowtorch. Arrange an orange segment, a few berries, and a mint sprig on 1 side of the top. Lightly sift powdered sugar over the fruit. Place the custard on a dessert plate covered with a folded napkin or a doily. Place a cookie next to the ramekin and serve.

CATALAN CUSTARD yield: approximately 6 cups (1 L 440 ml)

1 cup (240 ml) cream sherry	3 cups (720 ml) whole milk
1 ounce (30 g) cornstarch	2 cups (480 ml) half-and-half
Zest of 2 oranges	12 egg yolks (1 cup/240 ml)
1 large or 2 small cinnamon sticks	10 ounces (285 g) granulated sugar

1. Combine the sherry and cornstarch, stirring until smooth.

2. Place the orange zest, cinnamon sticks, milk, and half-and-half in a heavy saucepan. Bring to a boil and remove from the heat.

3. Whisk the egg yolks and sugar together until well combined. Gradually beat the hot milk mixture into the egg mixture, followed by the cornstarch slurry.

4. Return the custard to the saucepan and cook over medium heat, stirring constantly, just to the boiling point; stop cooking as soon as the first bubble appears. Immediately remove from the heat and strain the custard into a bowl. Discard the cinnamon sticks.

Crème Brûlée on a Caramel Spider with a Sugar Shard

yield: 12 servings using Flexipan No. 1897 (Color Photo 68)

If you were asked to prepare a fancy crème brûlée with an unusual presentation for a special event or a party, this would be the recipe to choose. My personal frustration with crème brûlée is that no matter how good the flavor is or how smooth the texture, the classic presentation is plain and simple. At the same time, you are almost forced to include crème brûlée on your menu because so many people love it.

For this presentation, you need to use a Flexipan, although not necessarily the size specified here. If you do not have time to make the spiders, make the sugar shards and/or the bubble sugar, both of which are simple to produce; either, combined with the unmolded custard, fruit, and orange syrup, will create an impressive, if less spectacular, presentation.

Keep in mind that the spiders, sugar shards, and bubble sugar can all be made in advance. Be sure to alert the wait staff that the spiders are not connected to the plate so they will be careful not to let them slide around as they are carried into the dining room. Alternatively, you can fasten two or three of the legs to the plate by carefully warming the base of each leg until it becomes sticky (see Step 6, page 353, for more information).

1 recipe Vanilla-Bean Crème Brûlée Custard (page 328)	Coarse or granulated sugar
Assorted seasonal fruit and/or berries	12 Caramel Spiders (page 622)
½ recipe Orange-Vanilla Decorating Syrup (page 760)	12 small pieces Bubble Sugar (page 615) *or* Sugar Shards (page 628)

1. Place a No. 1897 Flexipan on a perfectly even full-size sheet pan. Divide most of the custard among 12 indentations. Transfer the pan to the oven and top off with the remaining custard; the indentations should be filled to the top. Pour enough hot water into the sheet pan so it reaches three-quarters of the way up the side of the Flexipan.

2. Bake at 325°F (163°C) for about 30 minutes or until the custard is just set; take care not to overcook. Carefully remove the sheet pan from the oven. Set aside to allow the water to cool and the custard to stabilize.

3. Carefully, so as not to damage the custard, pull up a corner of the Flexipan and tilt the sheet pan slightly to pour out as much of the water as possible. Keep an eye on the custard and hold on to the Flexipan as you increase the angle of the sheet pan. A small amount of water remaining is okay. Place the pan in the freezer for a minimum of 4 hours or, preferably, overnight. The custard must be frozen solid.

4. To free the Flexipan from the sheet pan, allow the custard to stand at room temperature for no more than 5 minutes, or set the sheet pan on top of a hot second sheet pan for a few seconds instead. Invert the Flexipan and unmold the frozen custards by pushing them out of the indentations from the back of the pan. Place them, inverted, on a sheet pan lined with a Silpat or baking paper. Thaw in the refrigerator or at room temperature, depending on your time frame.

5. Prepare the fruit and/or berries for garnish. Place the orange decorating syrup into a piping bottle.

6. Presentation: Dip the end of an offset spatula (preferably one with a wide blade, such as the type more frequently used in the hot kitchen) in water and use it to pick up a serving of custard. Sprinkle coarse or granulated sugar on top of the custard and caramelize with a blowtorch. (Avoid using a high flame or excessive heat at the edge of the custard.) Transfer the custard to the top of a caramel spider, carefully sliding it off the spatula with the help of another spatula. Pick up the spider from underneath and place it in the middle of a serving plate. Randomly pipe orange syrup in small puddles around the dessert and sprinkle 8 to 10 pieces of prepared fruit on top. Heat the tip of a small knife and quickly melt through a small part of the caramelized sugar in the center of the brûlée. Push a sugar decoration into the melted opening so it stands up straight. Serve immediately.

Crème Caramel Nouvelle **yield: 16 servings (Color Photo 69)**

Traditional crème caramel is a custard baked in a mold with caramelized sugar coating the bottom. This dessert is known as *crème renversée* in French, literally translated as "upside-down cream"; in Spanish, the name is *flan*. The caramel coating colors and flavors the bottom of the custard during baking, and this portion becomes the top when the dessert is inverted. When the chilled custard is placed upside-down on a serving plate, the liquefied portion of the caramel runs over and around the dessert, doubling as a sauce.

Not much is left of the old classic in this contemporary interpretation. The original dessert, although good if made correctly and served nice and cold, is a little plain; we used to call crème caramel *general custard,* as a pun on General Custer that referred to the dessert's "general" and bland look. This nouvelle presentation demonstrates that it is easy, with a little attention and imagination, to make a ho-hum dessert exciting.

For the best visual effect, suspend the caramel spirals high enough to make five or six loops before the bottom loop comes to rest on top of the fruit. The spiral will then bounce gently as the dessert is presented to the guest. To be certain of this, pipe the sugar thin and keep the loops of the spiral fairly close together.

¼ recipe Vanilla Tuile Decorating Paste (page 695)

1½ teaspoons (4 g) unsweetened cocoa powder

16 Gingered Caramel Custards (recipe follows)

1 recipe Clear Caramel Sauce (page 328)

2 pounds (910 g) assorted fresh seasonal fruit (preparation instructions follow)

Caramel Spirals (page 622)

1. Place 3 tablespoons (45 ml) of the tuile paste in a small cup. Add the cocoa powder and stir until smooth. Set aside. Spread the remaining tuile paste into 20 rectangles; follow the instructions and use the template for Blueberry Pirouettes (page 137). You need only 16 rectangles, but some will inevitably break as you form them.

2. Place a portion of the cocoa-colored tuile paste in a piping bag and cut a very small opening. Pipe 3 diagonal lines in the center of each rectangle. Bake and form the cookies following the directions in the Blueberry Pirouettes recipe.

3. Unmold as many custards as you plan to serve and place them in the refrigerator until serving time (see Chef's Tip). The remainder can be stored, refrigerated, in their baking forms, for several days. Store extra cookies in an airtight container. Place a portion of the caramel sauce in a piping bottle and reserve.

4. Presentation: Place a custard in the center of a dessert plate. Pipe just enough caramel sauce around

CHEF'S TIP
Unmold the custards on a separate plate, then transfer to the serving plate using a small spatula or palette knife (or you may reserve the custards on a sheet pan lined with baking paper). To unmold, run a thin knife around the inside of the form without cutting into the custard; you need only loosen the top skin from the sides of the form. Invert the form on top of the plate and, holding the form and plate together, shake vigorously up and down a few times until the custard falls onto the plate. Another option is to use a spoon to gently press the skin away from the sides of the custard on top and then, holding the custard about 1 inch (2.5 cm) above the plate, use the back of the spoon to lightly push part of the custard away from the side of the form to release the suction; the custard should drop right out.

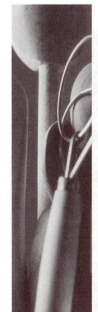

Baking Custard

It is of the utmost importance that the temperature on the sides of the baking forms never exceed 212°F (100°C). A baked custard — as opposed to pastry cream, for example — does not contain any starch (which acts as a barrier preventing the egg proteins from binding together), and overheating will cause the custard to separate or curdle (see page 322). For this reason, crème caramel is always baked in a water bath. The first sign of curdling is the appearance of small brown dots on the sides of the custard.

If you are unfamiliar with the oven you are using, it is a good idea to start out with a slightly lower temperature than called for. You can always bake the custard a little longer. If you are not certain your oven temperature is accurate, test it with an oven thermometer. If you do not have a removable thermometer, start cooking the custards at a setting of 325°F (163°C). After 30 minutes, if the custard is still as liquid as when you started, your thermostat is incorrect and you should increase the temperature. Wasting 30 minutes is better than overcooking the custard because of a poorly calibrated oven.

I have heard and read about various ways to prevent curdling, from starting with cold water in the bain-marie to placing newspaper in the bottom of the same. I suppose that if your oven tends to be hot on the bottom, the paper will help insulate the custards, but so would double-panning (placing a sheet pan underneath), which would be less messy. Starting with cold water, however, does seem to work well.

To Prepare Fresh Fruit

Although you are, of course, limited to whatever fresh fruit is in season in your area, try to use at least four varieties with contrasting colors. To preserve brightness of color and texture, cut the fruit into pieces as close to serving time as possible, making each piece about the size of a raspberry. Keep each variety separate. Stone fruits, such as peaches, nectarines, apricots, and plums, which tend to look dry a short time after they are cut, should be refreshed with a little orange liqueur before being placed on the serving plate.

the custard to cover the plate. Arrange prepared fruit on top of the sauce, including 3 or 4 pieces of each variety. Gently push a baked cookie tube halfway into the center of the custard; make sure it is standing straight. Place a caramel spiral on top of the tube. Serve immediately.

GINGERED CARAMEL CUSTARDS yield: 16 servings

2 tablespoons (30 ml) finely chopped fresh ginger

2 quarts (1 L 920 ml) whole milk

2 pounds 8 ounces (1 kg 135 g) granulated sugar

¼ teaspoon (1.25 ml) lemon juice

3½ cups (840 ml) eggs (approximately 14)

1. Combine the ginger and milk in a saucepan. Bring to the scalding point, then remove from the heat and set aside to infuse while preparing the caramel.

2. Place 1 pound 8 ounces (680 g) of the sugar and the lemon juice in a heavy saucepan. Set over medium heat and stir constantly with a wooden spoon until the sugar melts and caramelizes to a rich brown color. Immediately plunge the bottom of the pan into cold water to stop the cooking and keep the caramel from getting any darker.

3. Pour a ⅛-inch (3-mm) layer of caramel on the bottom of 16 soufflé ramekins, 3¼ inches (8.1 cm) in diameter, or coffee cups of approximately the same size with straight sides. Set the forms aside.

4. Reheat the milk to the scalding point. Whisk together the remaining sugar and the eggs. Gradually add the hot milk to the sugar mixture, whisking constantly. Strain the custard; discard the ginger.

5. Place the forms in a hotel pan or other suitable pan. Fill the forms almost to the top with custard. Add cold water to the larger pan to reach about three-quarters up the sides of the forms. Transfer to the oven. Fill each form to the top with custard.

6. Bake at 350°F (175°C) for approximately 45 minutes or until the custard is just set (it will be soft and should move as a single mass within the form). Let cool completely, then refrigerate for a minimum of 4 hours.

7. Unmold and serve as directed in the main recipe.

Cupid's Treasure Chest   yield: 16 servings (Color Photo 72)

This dessert was originally created for a Valentine's Day dinner. Cupid's Treasure Chest also makes a beautiful presentation on many other occasions when a romantic dessert is called for, such as an anniversary dinner or engagement celebration. For an engagement dinner, you can place two interlocking marzipan rings on the chocolate shavings under the lid.

Both the chocolate cases and the lids can be made in advance. The treasure chest lid can be used alone to garnish a slice of cake, a serving of mousse, or an individual pastry whenever you want to create a romantic look. If you do not have a free-form heart template from making these desserts previously, just trace around a heart-shaped cookie cutter of the appropriate size.

For an even more elegant look, try piping white chocolate onto the acetate strips before spreading the dark chocolate on top (see Miniature Marco Polo, page 164, Color Photo 27).

Dark coating chocolate, melted	1 recipe Raspberry Sauce (page 173)
Piping Chocolate (page 543), melted	Shaved dark chocolate
1 Sponge Cake (page 794), 10 inches (25 cm) in diameter	16 Marzipan Rosebuds (page 651)
	16 Marzipan Leaves (page 644)
Orange liqueur	Sour Cream Mixture for Piping (page 727)
Raspberry–White Chocolate Mousse (recipe follows)	

1. Cut 16 strips of thin polyurethane or acetate, 1¼ inches (3.1 cm) wide and slightly shorter than the inside circumference of a heart-shaped cookie cutter approximately 4 inches (10 cm) across at its widest point; the length will be approximately 12¾ inches (32 cm). The strips will not follow the heart shape precisely, but don't worry — if anything, the freeform shape adds to the appearance.

2. Place 1 strip on a sheet of baking paper in front of you. Spread a thin layer of melted coating chocolate over the strip, covering it completely; it will be necessary to spread a little chocolate onto the baking paper all around. Slide the tip of a knife underneath 1 short end of the strip then lift it off the table (see Procedure 7-1a). Hold the plastic strip vertically and run your thumb

PROCEDURE 7-1a
Picking up an acetate strip after spreading a thin layer of chocolate on top
PROCEDURE 7-1b
While holding the strip in one hand, running the thumb and index finger of the other hand along the edges

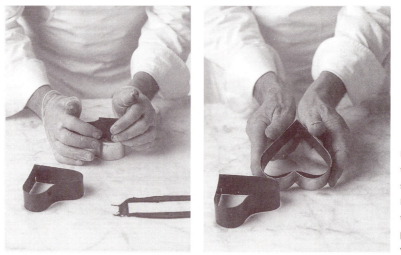

PROCEDURE 7-1c **Placing the strip inside a heart-shaped cookie cutter**
PROCEDURE 7-1d **Aligning the bottom edge of the plastic strip so the heart will stand straight**

and index finger along both sides of the long edges for a cleaner look (see Procedure 7-1b). Position the strip inside the heart cutter with the plastic side against the cutter starting with the ends meeting at the point of the heart (see Procedure 7-1c). Press lightly to make sure the bottom edge lines up evenly so the chocolate frame will stand straight on the plate (see Procedure 7-1d). Refrigerate for a few minutes to set. (Making the frames will obviously go faster if you have more than one cutter, but if you don't, you can work on the lids as you wait.)

3. When the chocolate has set, brush additional chocolate at the tip where the ends join. Because the heart is cold, this chocolate will set immediately. Carefully remove the heart from the mold — run a thin knife around the inside perimeter if it is stuck — leaving the plastic strip attached. Place on a sheet pan. Repeat to make a total of 16 hearts. Place the hearts in the refrigerator for 1 minute to ensure a glossy finish. Do not leave them too long, or they could become brittle and break. Remove from the refrigerator and, wearing food handling gloves, carefully peel off the plastic strips.

4. To make the lids for the heart boxes, place 1 chocolate heart on a piece of cardboard, such as a cake box. Trace and cut out the shape. Use this template to draw 20 hearts on a sheet of baking paper; you need to make a few extra lids to allow for breakage. Invert the baking paper.

5. Place piping chocolate in a piping bag and cut a small opening. Pipe the chocolate onto the paper, first tracing the outline of one heart, then filling in the center by piping back and forth on the diagonal in both directions, spacing the lines about ½ inch (1.2 cm) apart. Make sure you connect with the outline on each side. Pipe chocolate over the remaining hearts. Set aside to harden.

6. Cut the skin from the top of the sponge cake, leveling it at the same time. Slice the sponge into 3 thin layers. Using the same template used to trace the lids, cut out 16 hearts, or use a smaller heart-shaped cutter, if you have one. Using the template is preferable because cake cut with a cutter will not fit precisely within the shell, and the filling may run out at the bottom. Brush orange liqueur over the cake pieces. Cover and reserve in the refrigerator.

7. Place the raspberry–white chocolate mousse in a pastry bag with a No. 7 (14-mm) plain tip. Reserve in the refrigerator until time of service. Place a portion of the raspberry sauce in a piping bottle.

8. Presentation: Place a heart-shaped sponge in the bottom of a chocolate heart. Wearing food handling gloves to protect the chocolate, center the heart on the top half of a dessert plate. Pipe the mousse into the shell, filling it to the top. Use a spoon to carefully sprinkle chocolate shavings over the mousse without getting any on the plate. Place a marzipan rosebud and leaf in the upper right side of the heart, pressing the bud lightly into the filling. Run a thin knife under one of the piped lids to loosen it. Place the lid on top of the heart, inserting it partially into the filling on the left side to hold it in a half-open position. Pipe a large pool of raspberry sauce in front of the dessert and decorate the sauce with the sour cream mixture, making a series of hearts (see Figure 13-10, page 682). Serve immediately.

RASPBERRY-WHITE CHOCOLATE MOUSSE yield: 1 quart (960 ml)

1 cup (240 ml) heavy cream

5 teaspoons (15 g) powdered pectin for canning *or* 2 teaspoons (6 g) pure pectin powder

3 ounces (85 g) granulated sugar

½ cup (120 ml) egg whites

1½ teaspoons (5 g) unflavored gelatin powder

¼ cup (60 ml) cold water

4 ounces (115 g) white chocolate, melted

1¼ cups (300 ml) strained raspberry juice, at room temperature (see Note)

3 tablespoons (45 ml) lemon juice

1. Whip the heavy cream to soft peaks. Cover and reserve in the refrigerator.

2. Combine the pectin powder and granulated sugar. Add the egg whites. Heat the mixture over simmering water until it reaches 140°F (60°C), whisking constantly to make sure the egg whites on the bottom do not get too hot and cook. Remove from the heat and whip at high speed until the mixture is cold and has formed stiff peaks.

3. Sprinkle the gelatin over the cold water and set aside to soften.

4. Stir the melted white chocolate into the raspberry juice. Add the lemon juice.

5. Place the gelatin mixture over a bain-marie and heat until dissolved. Do not overheat. Quickly add the gelatin to the raspberry mixture. Gradually (to avoid lumps) fold this mixture into the reserved meringue. Fold into the reserved whipped cream. Use as directed in the main recipe or pipe into dessert glasses or cups and refrigerate for about 2 hours to set.

NOTE: You will need approximately 1 pound (455 g) fresh or frozen raspberries to make the juice. If fresh raspberries are out of season or too expensive, substitute frozen berries. If the berries are frozen in sugar or sugar syrup, use only half the amount of sugar called for in the recipe.

Pink Lady Apple and Pear Cream with Orange Syrup and an Apple Chip yield: 12 servings, 4 ounces (120 ml) each (Color Photo 30)

Many apple varieties make good apple chips. The Lady apples used in this recipe happen to be my favorite for this purpose because of their interesting shape and unusual blush-pink flesh. Unfortunately, some of the pretty color will dissipate when the chips are dried but, by paying close attention when they are in the oven, you can retain most of the tint. In Color Photo 30, the apple chip includes a thin slice of the apple stem. Although this looks elegant, it is not practical when making more than a small quantity of chips, as you can produce only 1 or 2 chips per apple that have a perfect cut through the stem. As long as you make the chips very thin and dry them properly so they are perfectly flat, a plain chip without the stem will do just fine.

Apples, pears, and pomegranates are all fall fruits, and the optional pomegranate seeds add a nice splash of color and crunch. Sprinkle a few seeds on the bottom of the molds before piping the filling inside, and use a few more on the plate as part of the presentation.

Pink Lady Apple and Pear Cream (recipe follows)
½ cup (120 ml) heavy cream
1 teaspoon (5 g) granulated sugar
½ teaspoon (25 ml) vanilla extract
1 recipe Orange-Vanilla Decorating Syrup (page 760)

12 Caramel Spider Decorations (page 622)
Raspberry Sauce (page 173)
Pomegranate seeds (optional)
12 Apple Chips (page 721)
Powdered sugar

1. Using a pastry bag with a medium plain tip, pipe the apple and pear cream into 12 forms, each approximately 4 ounces (120 ml) in capacity, or into the indentations of Flexipan No. 1269. Cover the forms and place in the refrigerator for a minimum of 2 hours or, preferably, overnight to set the filling. If using a Flexipan, place the pan in the freezer instead.

2. Whip the heavy cream with the sugar and vanilla to stiff peaks. Place in a pastry bag with a No. 8 (16-mm) star tip and reserve in the refrigerator.

3. Place a portion of the orange syrup in a piping bottle; reserve.

4. Unmold as many desserts as you anticipate needing for service by warming the outside of the forms. Depending on the type of forms used, you may do this with a blowtorch or by dipping the forms briefly into hot water. If you used a Flexipan and the desserts are frozen, push them out of the pan by turning each indentation inside out; set the desserts aside to thaw before serving. If you need them fairly soon, let them thaw at room temperature; otherwise, refrigerate them.

5. Presentation: Place an inverted dessert on top of a caramel spider. Carefully lift the spider from the bottom of its base (not by grasping the legs) and place in the center of a dessert plate. Pipe orange syrup in an uneven band between the dessert and the perimeter of the plate, covering half the area in a semicircle. Pipe evenly spaced dots of raspberry sauce along the center of the syrup band. Drag a skewer through the dots to form hearts (see Figure 13-9, page 682). Sprinkle a few pomegranate seeds on the uncovered portion of the plate, if desired. Pipe a rosette of whipped cream on the top of the dessert and stand an apple chip in the cream. Sift powdered sugar lightly over the front portion of the plate and serve immediately.

PINK LADY APPLE AND PEAR CREAM yield: 3 quarts (2 L 880 ml)

Do not make this filling until you are ready to use it.

1 pound (455 g) Pink Lady apples (about 4)

12 ounces (340 g) Bartlett or Anjou pears (about 3)

1 recipe Plain Poaching Syrup (page 789)

¼ cup (60 ml) lime juice

¼ cup (60 ml) orange liqueur

5 teaspoons (15 g) unflavored gelatin powder

1 cup (240 ml) apple juice

1½ cups (360 ml) heavy cream

I. Peel the apples and pears, placing the fruit in acidulated water as you work. Remove the cores and cut the fruit in half. Poach the fruit in the syrup until soft. The apples are ready when they just begin to fall apart. In most cases, you will need to remove the apples and continue to poach the pears a little longer.

2. Strain the apples and pears; reserve the poaching liquid for another use. Puree the fruit in a food processor. Strain the puree through a fine sieve and discard the solids. Measure the puree; you should have approximately 3 cups (720 ml). Proceed as long as the quantity is reasonably close; if necessary, adjust by adding poaching syrup. Stir the lime juice and orange liqueur into the fruit puree.

3. Sprinkle the gelatin over the apple juice and set aside to soften.

4. Whip the heavy cream to soft peaks.

5. Place the apple juice and gelatin over a bain-marie and warm just until the gelatin dissolves; do not overheat. Fold the fruit puree into the whipped cream. Quickly whisk the dissolved gelatin into a small portion of the fruit cream. Still working quickly, stir this back into the remainder of the filling.

Ruby Pears with Verbena Bavarois and Port Wine Reduction

yield: 16 servings, 4½ ounces (135 ml) each (Color Photo 92)

A free-form heart filled with deep red syrup combined with graceful tuile circles make this dessert a natural for Valentine's Day. To make the tuile circles even more dramatic, cut out the center of the largest bottom circle as well. Keep in mind, however, that this makes the decoration more fragile and so probably not a realistic option if you are making a large number. Because both the presentation and the preparation of the tuile circles are fairly complicated, you'll find it helpful to refer to Color Photo 92 for clarification.

Using a Flexipan for this recipe, as opposed to conventional metal or plastic half-sphere molds, is a great advantage. Because the frozen servings of bavarois are easily popped out of the flexible indentations, there is no risk of melting the filling and staining the pears. With other types of molds, which must be dipped into hot water to loosen the filling, it is impossible to produce this type of perfectly clean finish.

Note that both the poached pears and the verbena cream for the bavarois need to stand overnight, so you must plan to make this dessert a day ahead.

6 medium-sized pears, preferably Bosc

2 quarts (1 L 920 ml) ruby port

8 ounces (225 g) plus 1 teaspoon (5 g) granulated sugar

½ recipe Joconde Sponge Base I (page 670)

Verbena Bavarois (recipe follows)

Dark Piping Chocolate (page 543), melted

Port Wine Reduction (recipe follows)

1 cup (240 ml) heavy cream

16 Tuile Symphony of Circles (page 712)

16 edible flowers

Powdered sugar

1. Peel and core the pears, then cut them in half. Place the pears in a nonreactive saucepan with the port and 8 ounces (225 g) of the granulated sugar. Poach the pear halves until soft to the touch. Remove from the heat and set aside to cool. Refrigerate until the following day.

2. Spread the Joconde batter evenly over a Silpat or a sheet pan lined with baking paper, forming a rectangle measuring approximately 15 × 23 inches (37.5 × 57.5 cm). Bake at 425°F (219°C) for 8 to 10 minutes or until baked through. Let cool.

3. Place Flexipan No. 1593 on an even sheet pan or have ready 16 half-sphere molds, approximately 4½ ounces (135 ml) in capacity. Using a plain cookie cutter the same size as the openings of the molds, cut out 16 rounds from the Joconde sheet; if using the Flexipan specified, this will be 3 inches (7.5 cm). Cover the cake rounds and set aside. Cover and reserve leftover Joconde sheet for another use.

4. Remove the pear halves from the poaching liquid; reserve 2 cups (480 ml) of the liquid to make the port wine reduction; save the remainder for another use. Pat the pears dry. Slice each pear half crosswise into 8 to 10 thin slices. Using only the pear slices that show a defined indentation where the core was removed, arrange 5 pear slices, evenly spaced, around the inside of each mold. Place the pear slices so the ends overlap in the bottom of the molds (see Procedure 7-2a).

5. Using a plain cookie cutter, 1 inch (2.5 cm) in diameter, cut away and remove the overlapping ends of the pear slices in the center (bottom) of each mold, leaving the slices on the sides of the forms only (see Procedure 7-2b). If you are using a Flexipan, do this carefully so you do not damage the pan. Discard the cut pieces. Set the molds aside while preparing the bavarois.

PROCEDURE 7-2a
Placing the pear slices in the mold
PROCEDURE 7-2b
Using a cookie cutter to remove the center of the slices

6. If necessary, wait until the bavarois starts to thicken, then place it in a pastry bag with a No. 6 (12-mm) plain tip. Pipe the bavarois into the molds, filling them to just below the rim. Place a reserved sponge round on top of each mold and press lightly to secure. Cover and place in the refrigerator for at least 4 hours or, preferably, overnight. If using a Flexipan, place the pan in the freezer.

7. Place a small portion of piping chocolate in a piping bag and cut a small opening. Pipe a stylized heart outline on the right side of the base of a dessert plate. Pipe decorative curved chocolate lines from the tip of the heart toward the bottom of the plate as shown in Color Photo 92. Repeat to decorate as many plates as needed; set the plates aside.

8. Put the port wine reduction in a piping bottle and reserve. Whip the heavy cream with 1 teaspoon (5 g) sugar to just short of stiff peaks and place in a pastry bag with a No. 7 (14-mm) star tip. Reserve in the refrigerator.

9. If you made the bavarois in Flexipans, unmold as many servings as you anticipate needing by pushing the frozen desserts out of the molds from the reverse side, turning the molds inside out (see Procedure 7-2c). Set the bavarois on a sheet pan lined with baking paper, cover, and let thaw at room temperature or in the refrigerator. The desserts should be thawed all the way through but still cold when they are served. If they were made in conventional forms, unmold as many desserts as needed by quickly dipping the outside of each mold into hot water to loosen the filling, then inverting. Set the unmolded desserts aside, covered, in the refrigerator.

PROCEDURE 7-2c Unmolding a frozen dessert from a Flexipan

10. Presentation: Place a bavarois on the left side of a prepared dessert plate at the tip of the chocolate heart. Pipe port syrup into the chocolate heart outline. Pipe a rosette of whipped cream on top of the bavarois. Carefully push a tuile decoration through the center of the rosette and into the bavarois. The tuile circles should curve toward the front of the plate. Decorate the dessert with an edible flower. Sift powdered sugar lightly over the plate in front of the dessert and serve immediately.

About Lemon Verbena

Lemon verbena, as we usually refer to this fragrant herb in the United States, is also known as *lemon vervain* and, more simply, as *verbena*. It is native to Chile and is common throughout South and Central America, where it can reach heights of up to 25 feet (8 m 25 cm), though it rarely grows higher than 6 feet (1 m 80 cm) in temperate climates. Like many herbs and spices, verbena was originally brought to Europe by early explorers returning from sea voyages. This graceful perennial, deciduous shrub has long, pale, pointed leaves and light lilac to purple flowers that grow in clusters. The sweet, lemon-scented leaves can be used at any time but are most fragrant when the plant is in bloom.

Verbena has many uses in the pastry kitchen, where it gives ices, pound cakes, and creams a wonderful, distinctive flavor. Tea made from verbena is said to have a soothing, sedative effect and to help bronchial and nasal congestion.

VERBENA BAVAROIS yield: 10 cups (2 L 400 ml)

2 cups (480 ml) whole milk

1 ounce (30 g) fresh lemon verbena leaves

2 tablespoons (18 g) unflavored gelatin powder

½ cup (120 ml) cold water

4 egg yolks (⅓ cup/80 ml)

8 ounces (225 g) granulated sugar

2 cups (480 ml) heavy cream

4 egg whites (½ cup/120 ml)

1. Bring the milk to scalding; remove from the heat. Finely chop the verbena leaves and add them to the hot milk. Cover and let steep for 2 to 4 hours or, preferably, refrigerate overnight.

2. Sprinkle the gelatin over the water and set aside to soften.

3. Strain the infused milk; discard the lemon verbena. Place the milk in a heavy saucepan and again heat to scalding.

4. Combine the egg yolks and a few tablespoons of the sugar in a mixing bowl and whip to combine. Gradually pour the milk into the egg mixture, beating rapidly.

5. Heat the gelatin until it dissolves and stir into the milk. Set aside until the mixture cools to just over body temperature, stirring occasionally. To speed the cooling process, place the mixture over ice water and stir. Should it get too firm or become lumpy, reheat to melt the gelatin and cool again.

6. Whip the heavy cream to soft peaks. Cover and reserve in the refrigerator.

7. Place the egg whites and the remaining sugar in a mixer bowl and set over a bain-marie. Heat to 140°F (60°C), stirring constantly. Remove from heat and whip at high speed until the meringue is stiff and has cooled to room temperature (see Chef's Tip). Gradually stir the milk mixture into the reserved heavy cream. Fold into the meringue. Portion into the forms as the bavarois begins to thicken.

PORT WINE REDUCTION yield: approximately 1 cup (240 ml)

2 cups (480 ml) pear poaching liquid, reserved in Step 4 of the main recipe

1. Strain the poaching liquid into a saucepan. Bring to a boil and cook until the liquid is reduced to approximately 1 cup (240 ml) or thickens to a syrupy consistency.

2. To test the viscosity, remove the pan from the heat and place a small puddle of syrup (1 teaspoon/5 ml) on a plate; let it cool to room temperature (place in the refrigerator to speed the process if desired). If the syrup is too thin, boil it longer; if it is too thick, add water. Use the syrup cold or at room temperature, as desired.

Sherry-Poached Black Mission Figs with Crème Catalan

yield: 12 servings (Color Photo 71)

The Catalan region of Spain takes great pride in this custard. Traditionally, the cream is served simply. In this modern presentation, the figs are the main component, and the small portion of creamy custard is used to add a complementary texture and flavor. To serve a larger portion of custard, double the recipe and divide the mixture among 12 indentations in Flexipan No. 1269. For a more conventional presentation, see Crème Brûlée Catalan (page 340).

1 quart (960 ml) dry sherry	3 ounces (85 g) macadamia nuts, chopped and toasted
12 ounces (340 g) granulated sugar	
36 Black Mission figs	12 Red Pepper Sails (page 726)
12 Caramel Spider Decorations (page 622)	Powdered sugar
Small Catalan Custards (recipe follows)	

1. Place the sherry and sugar in a saucepan, stir, and heat to dissolve the granulated sugar. Add the figs and poach for just a few minutes until tender (see Chef's Tip). Place a small lid or saucer directly on top of the fruit to keep it submerged and set aside until cooled completely.

2. Remove the figs from the liquid and carefully place them on a pan lined with baking paper.

3. Strain the poaching liquid and return it to the stove. Bring to a boil and cook until reduced to a syrupy consistency. You should have approximately 1½ cups (360 ml) left. Test the viscosity by quickly chilling a small puddle of syrup in the refrigerator to see how thick the syrup will be once it has cooled. The syrup should be pourable but not runny, about the same consistency as maple syrup.

4. Cut in half as many figs as you will need for service (3 halves per serving), cutting through the stems as well.

5. Place the sherry reduction in a piping bottle.

6. Presentation: Wearing food handling gloves to avoid fingerprints on the caramel, pick up a caramel spider and heat the underside of 2 opposite legs until they become sticky; be careful not to melt or break the legs. Ideally, use a hand torch, or set a very low flame if your only choice is a regular blowtorch. Quickly attach the spider to the center of a dessert plate. Place a serving of custard on top of the spider. Pipe sherry syrup in an irregular pattern between the dessert and the perimeter of the plate. Place 3 fig halves in the syrup around the dessert. Sprinkle macadamia nuts on top of the syrup between the figs. Carefully insert a red pepper sail in the center of the custard. Sift powdered sugar lightly over the dessert and the plate and serve immediately.

CHEF'S TIP

Depending on their size and that of the saucepan on hand, it might be preferable to poach the figs in two batches to ensure that the fruit will not be too crowded; they are easily crushed. Of course, you can also use a larger saucepan and simply increase the volume of the sherry and sugar mixture. In that case, you will not need to reduce all of the liquid in Step 3.

SMALL CATALAN CUSTARDS

yield: approximately 1¾ cups (420 ml) custard or 12 small servings made in Flexipan No. 1560

1½ teaspoons (5 g) gelatin powder	1 small cinnamon stick
½ cup (120 ml) cream sherry	Zest of 1 orange
1 cup (240 ml) whole milk	2 egg yolks
1½ teaspoons (6 g) cornstarch	2 ounces (55 g) granulated sugar

1. Sprinkle the gelatin over the sherry and set aside to soften. Stir enough of the milk into the cornstarch to make a slurry; reserve.

2. Combine the remaining milk, the cinnamon stick, and the orange zest in a heavy saucepan. Bring to a boil. Remove from the heat and let the mixture infuse for 30 minutes.

3. Thoroughly whip the egg yolks and sugar together. Gradually whisk the infused milk into the yolk mixture.

4. Heat the gelatin to dissolve and incorporate into the milk-egg mixture. Gradually but quickly whisk in the reserved cornstarch slurry. Return the mixture to the saucepan and cook the custard over medium heat, stirring constantly, just until the first bubbles appear. Immediately remove from the heat and strain.

5. Divide the custard among 12 indentations in Flexipan No. 1560 or pour into 12 small forms, approximately 1½ ounces (45 ml) in capacity (see Note). Refrigerate for a minimum of 2 hours or, preferably, overnight.

6. Using the appropriate method for the forms, unmold the custards. If a Flexipan was used, place the pan in the freezer until the custards are firm enough to be popped out, then let the custards thaw completely before serving. For ceramic molds, dip the bottom and sides of the forms in hot water for a few seconds. If the molds or rings are metal, use a blowtorch to warm the outside instead.

NOTE: If you do not have small forms, use timbale molds and fill each only part way.

Triple Chocolate Terrine yield: 16 servings (Color Photo 70)

Because this dessert is popular and keeps well in the freezer, it makes a lot of sense to prepare more than you need while you are at it. The time required does not expand relative to the yield and, if wrapped properly, the terrines will keep in the freezer for up to one month with no loss in quality. In other words, if you don't need sixteen servings, it is silly to scale the recipe down; in fact, most of the time I double it. The base is very rich — a chocoholic's dream — and the presentation quite appealing, so I guarantee the terrines won't be taking up your freezer space for long.

Another plus here is that plating and finishing the servings are quite simple, which makes this dessert a favorite of mine when I need an elegant offering that can be served by someone with limited experience. All that is required is to remove the terrines from the freezer, slice the pieces, and set them on the plates. While the slices are softening, there is plenty of time to add the sauce and garnish.

Baked Chocolate Sheet (recipe follows)

Triple Chocolate Fillings (recipes follow)

1 recipe Raspberry Sauce (page 173)

Sour Cream Mixture for Piping (page 727)

Raspberries

16 small mint sprigs

1. Line the bottom and 2 long sides of a terrine mold, approximately 12 × 3½ × 3½ inches (30 × 8.7 × 8.7 cm), with baking paper. Cut the chocolate sheet into 4 pieces, each the size of the bottom of the mold. Place 1 piece in the bottom of the mold.

2. Add the milk chocolate filling. Place a second sheet of cake on top. Add the white chocolate filling and place another cake layer on top. Add the dark chocolate filling and top with the remaining cake sheet. Cover and place in the freezer for at least 3 hours or, preferably, overnight.

3. Remove the terrine from the freezer. Remove the form and peel away the baking paper. Position the terrine so the layers run vertically. Using a thin knife dipped in hot water, cut the terrine into 16 slices, each ¾ inch (2 cm) thick. As you cut them, place the slices on a sheet pan lined with baking paper. Reserve in the refrigerator until serving time (see Chef's Tip). Make sure each slice has thawed before serving.

4. Presentation: Carefully center a thawed slice of terrine in the rear portion of a dessert plate. Pour a pool of raspberry sauce in front of the slice and decorate the sauce with the sour cream mixture (see Figure 13-10, page 682). Place 3 raspberries and a mint sprig behind the dessert. Serve immediately.

NOTE: If the bakers are using all of their bread forms and the garde manger department will not part with their pâté molds, you can make a form out of corrugated cardboard by following the directions given in the White Chocolate and Pistachio Pâté recipe (page 472).

CHEF'S TIP

The terrine should be sliced while it is frozen, but the slices must be allowed to thaw before serving. If you know you will use all 16 servings within a short period, place the frozen slices directly on dessert plates instead of the sheet pan to avoid moving them twice.

BAKED CHOCOLATE SHEET yield: 1 sheet, 12 × 14 inches (30 × 35 cm)

6 eggs, separated

4 ounces (115 g) granulated sugar

6 ounces (170 g) sweet dark chocolate, melted

1. Beat the egg yolks with half of the sugar until light and fluffy. Set aside.

2. Whip the egg whites to a foam. Gradually add the remaining sugar and whip to soft peaks.

3. Combine the melted chocolate with the egg yolk mixture. Carefully fold in the egg whites. Spread the batter to a rectangle measuring 12 × 14 inches (30 × 35 cm) on a sheet of baking paper. Drag the paper onto a sheet pan. Bake immediately at 375°F (190°C) for about 15 minutes.

TRIPLE CHOCOLATE FILLING BASE

3 ounces (85 g) granulated sugar

6 egg yolks (½ cup/120 ml)

2 whole eggs

1 cup (240 ml) heavy cream

1. Prep the base and the ingredients for the 3 filling recipes simultaneously, but assemble and add the completed fillings to the terrine individually as you are ready to use them.

2. Combine the sugar, egg yolks, and whole eggs in a mixing bowl. Set the bowl over simmering water and heat the mixture, stirring constantly, to 140°F (60°C). Remove from the heat and whip at high speed until the mixture has cooled completely.

3. Whip the heavy cream to soft peaks, then carefully fold the egg mixture into the cream. Divide into 3 equal portions, approximately 1¼ cups (300 ml) each, and proceed with the following recipes.

Milk Chocolate Filling

½ teaspoon (1.5 g) unflavored gelatin powder

1 tablespoon (15 ml) cold water

6 ounces (170 g) milk chocolate, melted

⅓ recipe Triple Chocolate Filling Base

CHEF'S TIP
Because such a small amount of gelatin is used, it is impractical to soften and heat it in a separate container and then add it to the chocolate. By softening and dissolving the gelatin in the mixing bowl, you will not lose any of it.

1. In an oversized mixing bowl, sprinkle the gelatin over the cold water and set aside to soften.

2. Make sure the melted chocolate is warm but not hot. Quickly stir the chocolate into a small portion of the filling base to temper it and prevent lumps. Then, still working quickly, add this mixture to the remainder of the filling base.

3. Place the gelatin mixture (still in the mixing bowl) over a bain-marie and heat to dissolve the gelatin. Do not overheat. Quickly add a small part of the chocolate mixture to the gelatin in the bowl, then stir in the remaining chocolate mixture.

White Chocolate Filling

½ teaspoon (1.5 g) unflavored gelatin powder

1 tablespoon (15 ml) cold water

6 ounces (170 g) white chocolate, melted

⅓ recipe Triple Chocolate Filling Base

1. Follow the directions for Milk Chocolate Filling. Take care not to overheat the white chocolate, or it will become grainy.

Dark Chocolate Filling

½ teaspoon (1.5 g) unflavored gelatin powder

1 tablespoon (15 ml) cold water

5 ounces (140 g) sweet dark chocolate, melted

⅓ recipe Triple Chocolate Filling Base

1. Follow the directions for Milk Chocolate Filling.

White Chocolate and Pistachio Mousse with Chocolate Lace

yield: 16 servings (Color Photos 15 and 67)

Although some of the steps are rather delicate, the final assembly — wrapping the chilled mousse in the chocolate lace — is actually much easier than it appears, providing you are properly organized, possess a light touch, and have some experience in piping chocolate.

It is important that you pipe the chocolate lines for the lace as close together as specified and that the tubes of mousse are well chilled, or even still partially frozen, when you attach the lace. The chocolate lace is not only decorative but also helps support the mousse after it thaws and softens. One could, of course, add extra gelatin for support, but the texture would suffer. If it is not possible, or practical, for you to assemble the plates to order, you can decorate them with the sauces up to 30 minutes ahead of time and keep the desserts in the refrigerator, filled with raspberries, ready to be set on the plates as needed. Wear food handling gloves when moving the desserts. If it is available, use the thicker grade of baking paper for both lining the tubes and piping the chocolate lace. The thinner grade will wrinkle slightly from the moisture in the filling, and the wrinkles will be visible on the side of the mousse.

To create the presentation shown in Color Photo 15, make a solid spoon template by tracing the spoon in Figure 13-39 (page 708). Use the template to create a cocoa-powder silhouette as shown. Follow the presentation instructions in Step 7, but remove the paper from the dessert before setting it on the plate, and decorate the left side of the plate rather than the front.

White Chocolate Mousse Filling (recipe follows)	Bitter Chocolate Sauce (page 413)
Piping Chocolate, melted (page 543)	Small raspberries
½ recipe White Chocolate Sauce (page 803)	Pistachios reserved from the filling

1. Line 16 tubes that have an inside diameter of 1¾ inches (4.5 cm) and are 3 inches (7.5 cm) in height with baking paper cut to 3 × 6 inches (7.5 × 15 cm). The paper will overlap inside the tubes about ½ inch (1.2 cm); see Chef's Tip. Stand the tubes on end on a sheet pan.

2. Cut 20 additional rectangles of baking paper that measure 4 × 5½ inches (10 × 13.7 cm). You need only 16, but it rarely hurts to have a few extra.

3. Place the white chocolate mousse filling in a pastry bag with a No. 6 (12-mm) plain tip. Pipe the filling into the tubes. Place the tubes on the sheet pan in the refrigerator overnight or in the freezer for at least 2 hours to set.

4. Place 2 reserved baking paper rectangles on a full sheet of baking paper. Place the piping chocolate in a larger-than-normal piping bag; use a large enough bag and enough chocolate so you can complete 2 desserts without refilling. Cut a small opening in the bag. Pipe a straight line along the top long edge of 1 sheet. Next, pipe a zigzag pattern diagonally over the paper, first in 1 direction and then the opposite way, spacing the lines about ¼ inch (6 mm) apart (Figure 7-11). Be sure the diagonal lines extend onto the larger sheet of paper on all sides. Repeat on the second sheet of paper.

5. As soon as you finish piping on the second sheet of paper, pick up the first without disturbing the chocolate and place it in front of you (Figure 7-12). Place a cold serving of mousse at the edge of the paper, even with the bottom, so there is 1 inch (2.5 cm) of piping above the mousse, including the straight chocolate line. Roll the paper around the mousse so the piped chocolate and the paper stick to it (Figure 7-13). Do not overlap the ends; they should line up evenly. Stand the

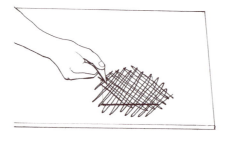

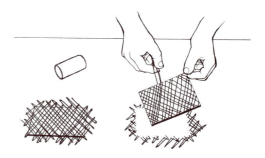

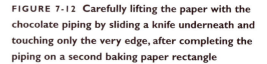

FIGURE 7-11 **Piping diagonal lines of chocolate in both directions after first piping a solid chocolate line along the top edge of the baking paper rectangle**

FIGURE 7-12 **Carefully lifting the paper with the chocolate piping by sliding a knife underneath and touching only the very edge, after completing the piping on a second baking paper rectangle**

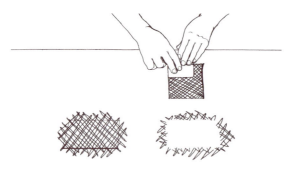

FIGURE 7-13 **Wrapping the chocolate lace around a serving of frozen mousse; the bottom edge of the mousse is even with the edge of the baking paper so a portion of the chocolate lace and the solid chocolate line extend above the mousse at the opposite end**

mousse on end. Repeat with the second sheet of paper. Cover the remaining servings with chocolate lace in the same way. Reserve in the refrigerator with the papers attached (see Note).

6. Adjust the consistency of the white chocolate sauce so it is thick enough to hold its shape. Place a portion of the sauce in a piping bottle and reserve.

7. Presentation: Stand a serving of mousse on end, centered in the top half of the base of a dessert plate. Carefully peel away the paper. Pipe dots of white chocolate sauce, ¾ inch (2 cm) in diameter, very slightly apart, in a half-circle in front of the dessert at the very edge of the base of the plate. Using a piping bag, pipe a much smaller dot of bitter chocolate sauce in the center of each white dot. Drag a wooden skewer through the chocolate dots in a wavy pattern to create a series of hearts (see Figure 13-16, page 684). Place approximately 12 small raspberries on top of the dessert inside the chocolate basket. Sprinkle a few raspberries between the dessert and the sauce. Sprinkle some of the reserved pistachio nuts around the raspberries.

CHEF'S TIP

I use plastic tubing that has an opening 1¾ inches (4.5 cm) in diameter and cut it into 3-inch (7.5-cm) lengths. The tubing can be purchased at a plastic or hobby supply store. Alternatively, you can make your own tubes by cutting pieces of polyurethane or acetate into rectangles, 3 × 6¼ inches (7.5 × 15.6 cm), overlapping the short ends, and taping them together. This will give you a finished tube that is 1¾ inches (4.5 cm) in diameter. Be certain that the tubes stand up straight and, if they do not, adjust as necessary before lining them with baking paper.

It is not as important that the tubes measure 1¾ inches (4.5 cm) in diameter as it is that the width of the paper on which the chocolate lace is piped is cut to the same size as the inside circumference of the tubes. The long edges can either miter together precisely or be slightly apart, but they must not overlap, or the lace will break when the paper is removed.

About Pistachios

Pistachios are popular for their distinctive green color. They are often used as a garnish on petits fours and candies and, of course, to make pistachio ice cream. Pistachios need hot, dry summers and cold winters. The largest share of the nuts is grown in the Middle East, although the United States, which began producing a commercial crop in 1976, is now one of the largest producers in the world.

The nuts have two shells: a red outer shell that is removed before packing and a thin inner shell, beneath which a thin skin surrounds the nut itself.

The practice of dyeing the inner shell red is said to have been started by a New York street vendor, and the red color became so expected and associated with the nuts that at one time most pistachios were sold this way. Dyeing the shells is no longer as popular; less than 20 percent of the nuts sold today are dyed. When pistachios are purchased in the shell (the thin inner shell), the shells should be partially opened. If they are completely closed, it means the nuts were harvested before they were fully mature. To show off the green color to its fullest, remove the skins by blanching the nuts in boiling water, then pinching them between your fingers or rubbing them in a towel. Adding salt to the water heightens the color.

NOTE: If frozen, the mousse will take about 3 hours to thaw in the refrigerator. If you need to serve the desserts sooner than that, leave them at room temperature for 30 minutes before applying the chocolate or, better yet, do not freeze them after filling the tubes; let the mousse set up in the refrigerator instead. If you use this method, you will have to be especially careful when you attach the chocolate lace because the mousse will not be as firm. In any case, do not remove the paper from the desserts until you are ready to serve. The paper protects the chocolate, and the desserts can be refrigerated overnight this way with no ill effects.

WHITE CHOCOLATE MOUSSE FILLING yield: 6 cups (1 L 440 ml)

Be sure not to whip the cream any further than soft peaks. Also, be careful not to overheat the white chocolate. Not paying attention here will cause the filling to separate and become grainy. If this happens, there is nothing to do but start over. Don't make the filling until you are ready to use it, because it will start to set fairly quickly.

6 ounces (170 g) pistachio nuts	2 tablespoons (18 g) pectin powder (see Note)
2 cups (480 ml) heavy cream	4 ounces (115 g) granulated sugar
4 teaspoons (12 g) unflavored gelatin powder	4 egg whites (½ cup/120 ml)
½ cup (120 ml) cold water	12 ounces (340 g) white chocolate, melted

1. Blanch the pistachio nuts. Remove the skins and chop the nuts coarsely. Reserve half of the nuts to decorate the desserts, choosing the more brightly colored pieces.

2. Whip the heavy cream to soft peaks; do not overwhip. Cover and refrigerate.

3. Sprinkle the gelatin over the cold water and set aside to soften.

4. Combine the pectin powder and the granulated sugar in a mixing bowl. Stir in the egg whites. Place the bowl over simmering water and heat, stirring constantly with a whisk, until the mixture reaches 140°F (60°C). Remove from the heat and immediately whip until the meringue has cooled completely and has formed stiff peaks.

5. Place the softened gelatin over simmering water and heat until dissolved. Working quickly, stir the gelatin into the melted white chocolate, then stir the chocolate mixture into one-third of the meringue to temper it. Add this to the remaining meringue. Stir in the reserved whipped cream and nuts.

NOTE: Use regular canning pectin; pure pectin is too strong here. If pectin is not available, increase the gelatin by 1 teaspoon (3 g) for a total of 5 teaspoons (15 g).

White Chocolate Neapolitan Bavarian yield: 16 servings (Color Photo 77)

This rather exotic presentation requires a few extra but worthwhile steps. If you don't mind just one more, try serving the Bavarian with a Curved Caramel Glass Paste Wedge (page 669). It adds a crunchy texture and gives the plate a contemporary look. Attach the wedge behind and partially under the Bavarian so the top of the caramel triangle curves over the top of the Bavarian. This dessert looks best if served the day it is made. While the dessert is acceptable if kept for more than one day, the raspberry juice layer tends to bleed slightly and stain the orange filling.

You will need a triangular form to make this recipe — ideally, one made from stainless steel and measuring approximately 16 inches (40 cm) long, 3¾ inches (9.3 cm) deep, and 3¾ inches (9.3 cm) wide at the top. If you do not have a stainless steel form, you can use either the form from the Strawberry Pyramids recipe (page 185), sectioned off at 16 inches (40 cm), or the Chalet Support Box (page 476). Line either of these with plastic strips or baking paper. Use a heavier grade of paper, as the thinner standard-grade will wrinkle slightly from moisture as the filling sets. If you are making a cardboard form specifically for this recipe, use the measurements above and follow the instructions for the Chalet Support Box.

½ cup (120 ml) strained raspberry juice

1 teaspoon (5 ml) Beet Juice (page 750)

⅓ cup (80 ml) orange juice

Grated zest of 1 orange

6½ teaspoons (20 g) gelatin powder

⅓ cup (80 ml) dark rum

6 ounces (170 g) granulated sugar

6 egg whites (¾ cup/180 ml)

2½ cups (600 ml) heavy cream

6 ounces (170 g) white chocolate, melted

3 ounces (85 g) sweet dark chocolate, melted

1 ounce (30 g) unsweetened chocolate, melted

Unsweetened cocoa powder

¼ recipe Chocolate Sauce (page 413; see Note)

¼ recipe Romanoff Sauce (page 253)

1. Boil the raspberry juice until it is reduced to ⅓ cup (80 ml). Stir in the beet juice and set aside to cool.

2. Combine the orange juice and zest. Sprinkle 2 teaspoons (6 g) of the gelatin on top.

3. Sprinkle 2 teaspoons (6 g) of the gelatin on top of the cooled raspberry juice.

4. Sprinkle the remaining 2½ teaspoons (8 g) gelatin on top of the rum.

5. Combine the sugar and egg whites in a mixer bowl. Place the bowl over a bain-marie and heat, whipping constantly to prevent the egg whites from cooking, to 140°F (60°C). Remove from the heat while continuing to stir. Place the bowl on the mixer and whip at high speed until soft peaks form. Reserve the meringue.

6. Whip the heavy cream to soft peaks. Cover and reserve in the refrigerator.

7. Quickly add the melted white chocolate to about one-third of the reserved meringue to temper it; the chocolate can be warm but must not be hot. Add this, still stirring rapidly, to the remaining meringue. Divide the Bavarian base into 3 equal portions.

8. Heat the orange juice mixture to dissolve the gelatin. Quickly incorporate the juice into 1 portion of the Bavarian base. Fold in one-third of the reserved whipped cream. Spoon into the bottom of the triangular form described in the introduction. Spread the surface level, taking great care not to get any filling on the long sides of the form above the layer. Place the form in the refrigerator.

9. Heat the raspberry juice to dissolve the gelatin. Rapidly add this to 1 portion of the Bavarian base. Fold in half of the remaining whipped cream. Spoon this filling on top of the orange layer and spread level in the same manner. Replace the form in the refrigerator.

10. Heat the rum to dissolve the gelatin. Stir into the melted dark and unsweetened chocolates. Quickly mix in about one-quarter of the remaining Bavarian base to temper the mixture. Still working quickly, add this combination to the remainder of the base. Fold in the remaining whipped cream. Spread the chocolate filling on top of the raspberry filling in the form.

11. Place the finished dessert in the refrigerator for at least 2 hours to set the filling.

12. To remove the Bavarian from a stainless steel form, quickly dip the bottom 1 inch (2.5 cm) into a hot water bath or use a blowtorch to warm the sides, then run a knife dipped in hot water around all four sides, at the same time gently pushing the Bavarian away from the sides to let in air and release the suction. Invert onto a sheet of cardboard covered tightly with plastic wrap. Use a palette knife to smooth the long edges as necessary to remove any melted Bavarian and create a clean look. If you are using a form lined with baking paper, as directed in the intro-

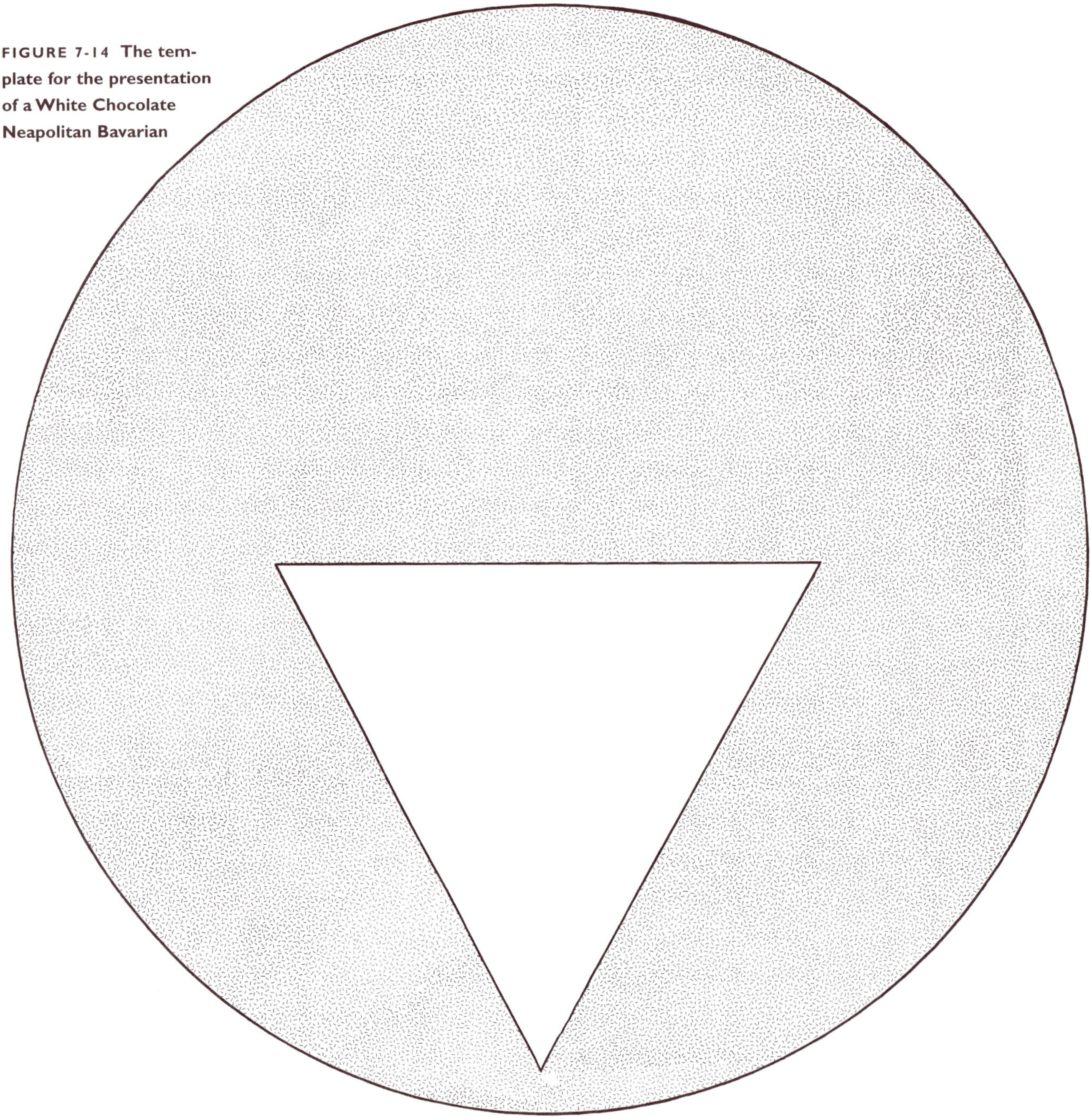

FIGURE 7-14 The template for the presentation of a White Chocolate Neapolitan Bavarian

duction, cut the Bavarian free from the form at the short ends, invert, and leave the baking paper attached. Refrigerate until time of service.

13. Presentation: Copy the template in Figure 7-14 and cut it out of cardboard that is $^1/_{16}$ inch (2 mm) thick; cake boxes work well. The template, as shown, is the correct size to use in this recipe. Attach the template to a pie tin frame (see page 692). Place the template on a dessert plate with the point of the triangle that touches the rim of the template toward you. Lightly sift cocoa powder over the template, then remove it carefully. Repeat on as many dessert plates as you expect to need. Check the consistency of the chocolate sauce and the Romanoff sauce. They must be fairly thick so they will not run on the plate, and both must have the same consistency. Adjust if necessary. Place each sauce in a piping bottle and reserve.

14. Peel the baking paper away from the Bavarian if applicable. Using a thin, sharp knife dipped into hot water, trim 1 short end of the Bavarian, if needed, to make a clean edge, then cut a slice just slightly less than 1 inch (2.5 cm) wide. (Be sure to dip the knife into hot water and wipe it clean between each cut when slicing the remaining servings.) Stand the slice on end just behind the cocoa-powder triangle on a prepared dessert plate, so the cocoa powder appears as a shadow. Pipe ½-inch (1.2-cm) dots of chocolate sauce, evenly spaced approximately ¾ inch (2 cm) apart, around the perimeter of the base of the plate. Pipe a dot of Romanoff sauce the same size between each of the chocolate sauce dots. Run a skewer through the center of the dots in a single long, sweeping motion around the plate. Serve immediately.

NOTE: Prepare the chocolate sauce using ½ cup (120 ml) less water than specified in the recipe. If you are using sauce that was previously prepared, add melted chocolate to thicken it to the proper (not too runny) consistency.

Wine Foam and Blackberry Bavarian Greystone yield: 16 servings (Color Photo 74)

This was one of the sweets offered at the grand opening of Greystone, The Culinary Institute of America's Napa Valley campus. The theme was "A Harvest of the Valley," so with the melon, blackberries, and wine grapes grown right there, this seemed a natural. I got the idea for the presentation from the CIA's Hyde Park master pastry chef, Joe McKenna. To make my template for the cookie grape leaf, I simply strolled over to the school's vineyard and selected a leaf, but I have included a template for those who do not have that option. A Joconde sheet with another pattern could be substituted for the ribbon-pattern sheet.

1 Ribbon-Pattern Decorated Sponge sheet (page 672)	16 Cape gooseberries
Blackberry Bavarian (recipe follows)	2 small honeydew melons, about 4 pounds (1 kg 820 g) total
4 ounces (115 g) Short Dough (page 791)	1 recipe Orange-Vanilla Decorating Syrup (page 760)
1 teaspoon (2.5 g) unsweetened cocoa powder	½ recipe Raspberry Sauce (page 173)
½ recipe Vanilla Tuile Decorating Paste (page 695)	Marzipan, tinted brown

1. Line the insides of 16 cake rings or plastic tubes, 2 inches (5 cm) in diameter and 2 inches (5 cm) in height, with plastic strips.

2. Cut strips, crosswise, from the sponge sheet, making them 1 inch (2.5 cm) wide and long enough to fit snugly inside the rings. Place the sponge strips inside the rings with the decorated side against the plastic. Place the rings on an even sheet pan lined with baking paper.

3. Use a plain cookie cutter, approximately 1¾ inches (4.5 cm) in diameter, to cut out 16 rounds from the sponge sheet. Place these in the bottom of the rings. Cover the remaining sponge and freeze for another use. Divide the blackberry filling among the prepared forms. Refrigerate for at least 2 hours to set.

4. Roll out the short dough to ⅛ inch (3 mm) thick. Using a 1¾-inch (4.5-cm) fluted cutter, cut out 16 rounds. Place the rounds in plain tartlet forms of about the same diameter. Use a

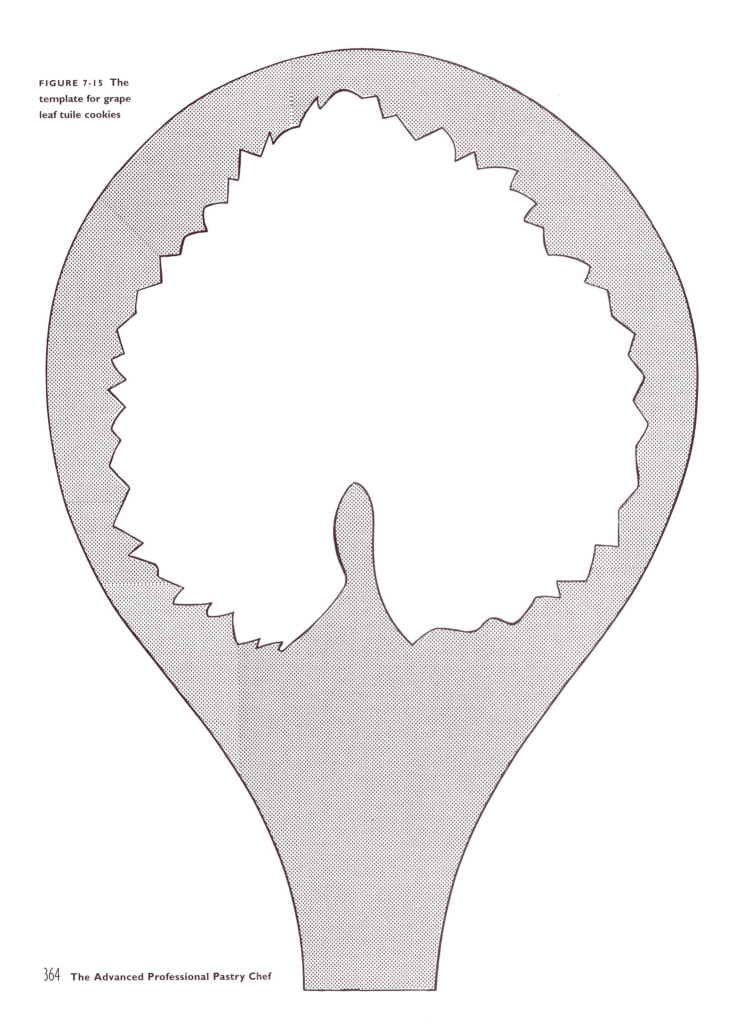

FIGURE 7-15 The
template for grape
leaf tuile cookies

plain cookie cutter, 1 inch (5 cm) in diameter, to cut the center out of each. Bake the cookie rings at 375°F (190°C) for about 10 minutes.

5. To make the tuile grape leaves, begin by tracing the drawing in Figure 7-15. The template, as shown, is the correct size required for this recipe. Cut the template out of cardboard that is ¹⁄₁₆ inch (2 mm) thick; cake boxes work fine. Stir the cocoa powder into 2 tablespoons (30 ml) of the tuile paste. Place the cocoa-colored paste in 1 or 2 piping bags and set aside. If you do not have Silpats, grease and flour the back of flat, even sheet pans. Spread the plain tuile paste on the Silpat, spreading it flat and even within the template (see Figures 13-29 and 13-30, page 694); form 6 to 8 leaves on each Silpat. Cut a small opening in the reserved piping bags and pipe veins on each leaf. Bake at 400°F (205°C) for approximately 6 minutes or until the decorations start to turn golden brown at the edges. Remove the pan from the oven and quickly place the grape leaves, inverted and crosswise, on a rolling pin or a similar object. Repeat until you have made a few more decorations than needed.

6. Using small, pointed scissors, cut between the ridges on the husk of the Cape gooseberries. Open each berry so the husk resembles flower petals and the fruit inside is exposed.

7. Using a very small melon ball cutter, cut out as many honeydew melon balls as you will need for service right away (allow 12 to 14 per serving). Place the melon balls in a bowl and toss them with a small amount of the orange syrup. Place the remaining orange syrup and the raspberry sauce in separate piping bottles.

8. Using the brown marzipan, form 16 grape stems.

9. Unmold as many dessert servings as you anticipate needing for service.

10. Presentation: Place a Bavarian pastry on the bottom of a grape-leaf cookie. Set the leaf on the upper part of the base of a dessert plate. Place a cookie ring on top of the pastry. Top with one of the prepared Cape gooseberries. Pipe an oval pool of orange syrup on the right side of the plate and arrange 12 to 14 melon balls to look like cluster of grapes. Attach a reserved grape stem. Pipe a zigzag of raspberry sauce on the left side of the dessert and serve.

About Cape Gooseberries

These rather unusual-looking fruits, also called *physalis*, are each surrounded by a loose, beige, ballooning, parchmentlike husk called a *calyx*. When ripe, the seedy yellow berry inside is about the size of a cherry and has a sweet orange flavor with a touch of acidity. The Cape gooseberry grows in two main varieties: the edible one discussed here *(physalis pruinosa)*, also known as *ground cherry* and *strawberry-tomato*, and the ornamental variety *(physalis franchetii)*, known as *Chinese lanterns* because of the bright orange-red lantern-shaped calyx that forms around the ripened berries. The ornamental physalis are often used in late fall floral arrangements.

With their papery husks removed, Cape gooseberries are great for pies and preserves, but their price is usually prohibitive for this type of application. A better way to utilize these eye-catching berries is decoratively, with the attractive husk left on. Begin by snipping the husk open from the tip with a small pair of scissors. Loosely spread the petals of the husk like a flower about to bloom, or spread the petals of the husk all the way back to the stem and dip the fruit into chocolate or fondant flavored with Cointreau or kirsch to serve as a candy or unusual mignardise (another name for an assortment of petits fours). Stored in the refrigerator, Cape gooseberries keep fresh for many weeks. If stored too long, however, the berry begins to dry up, and eventually just the empty husk is left.

NOTE: If you do not have metal cake rings or clear plastic tubes of the proper size, or simply do not have enough, PVC pipe works great when cut to the proper height and lined with plastic strips. If you have neither, make rings by taping strips of acetate or polyurethane together to make rounds (see Note 2, page 412).

VARIATION
BLACKBERRY BAVARIAN PASTRIES
yield: 12 pastries, 2 inches (5 cm) in diameter and 3 inches (7.5 cm) in height

To make a great-looking, stylish pastry instead of a plated dessert, follow the directions for preparing the molds through Step 3, lining 12 rings rather than 16. The molds should be 2½ inches (6.2 cm) tall rather than 2 inches (5 cm). Fill the molds with the Bavarian cream and let set as directed. Whip ½ cup (120 ml) heavy cream with ½ teaspoon (2.5 ml) granulated sugar to stiff peaks. Place in a pastry bag with a No. 7 (14-mm) star tip. Pipe a rosette of whipped cream on top of each Bavarian. Cut open the husks of the Cape gooseberries, pull them all the way back, and press them together at the stem above the exposed fruit. Place 1 berry on each whipped cream rosette. If you don't have Cape gooseberries, small blackberries make a good substitute and should also be left whole.

BLACKBERRY BAVARIAN   yield: approximately 5 cups (1 L 200 ml)

Do not make this recipe until you are ready to use it. The filling is quite thin when made correctly, so do not be alarmed at its consistency.

1¼ cups (300 ml) Riesling wine

8 ounces (225 g) blackberries

5 teaspoons (15 g) unflavored gelatin powder

4 egg yolks (⅓ cup/80 ml)

¾ cup (180 ml) heavy cream

¼ recipe Swiss Meringue (page 782)

1. Add ¼ cup (60 ml) of the wine to the blackberries. Puree, strain, and set aside.

2. Sprinkle the gelatin over half of the remaining wine and set aside to soften.

3. Add the remaining wine to the egg yolks. Place over a bain-marie and whip to the consistency of sabayon. Remove from the heat and continue whipping until cold.

4. Whip the heavy cream to soft peaks. Combine the whipped cream with the meringue. Fold in the sabayon and the blackberry juice mixture. Heat the softened gelatin to dissolve. Quickly incorporate the dissolved gelatin into about one-quarter of the mixture, then rapidly mix this into the remainder.

Liqueur Soufflé

yield: 12 soufflés, 3¼ inches (8.1 cm) in diameter, or 8 soufflés, 4½ inches (11.2 cm) in diameter

This recipe can be used to make any type of liqueur soufflé. Simply use the desired liqueur in the soufflé base and to flavor the sauce. Some liqueurs will not give the soufflé enough flavor; intensify the flavor by soaking ladyfingers in additional liqueur and placing two in the middle of the soufflé batter as you fill the forms.

Melted unsalted butter

5 ounces (140 g) granulated sugar, plus more to coat the forms

1½ ounces (40 g) cornstarch

2 ounces (55 g) bread flour

2 ounces (55 g) unsalted butter, at room temperature

2 cups (480 ml) whole milk

10 egg yolks (⅞ cup/210 ml)

1 teaspoon (5 ml) vanilla extract

½ cup (120 ml) liqueur

10 egg whites (1¼ cups/300 ml), at room temperature

1 recipe Sabayon (page 311; see Chef's Tip)

Powdered sugar

Small Batch Liqueur Soufflé

yield: 4 soufflés, 3¼ inches (8.1 cm) in diameter, or 2 soufflés, 4½ inches (11.2 cm) in diameter

Melted unsalted butter

2 ounces (55 g) granulated sugar, plus more to coat the forms

2 tablespoons (16 g) cornstarch

1 ounce or 4 tablespoons (30 g) bread flour

1 ounce or 2 tablespoons (30 g) unsalted butter, at room temperature

¾ cup (180 ml) milk

3 egg yolks (¼ cup/60 ml)

¼ teaspoon (1.25 ml) vanilla extract

3 tablespoons (45 ml) liqueur

3 egg whites, at room temperature

⅓ recipe Sabayon (page 311; see Chef's Tip)

Powdered sugar

---

1. Use the melted butter to thoroughly coat the insides of the appropriate number of soufflé ramekins, depending on the size of ramekins used. Fill 1 of the forms halfway with granulated sugar. Twist the form so the sugar coats the entire inside, then pour the sugar into the next form. Repeat until all the forms are coated, adding more sugar as necessary. Set the forms aside.

2. Combine about one-third of the measured sugar with the cornstarch. Reserve this mixture and the remaining sugar separately.

3. Mix the flour and butter to form a paste. Heat the milk to the scalding point in a heavy saucepan. Add the butter and flour mixture and stir with a whisk; it will melt into the milk. Quickly mix in one-third of the egg yolks. Bring to a boil over low heat, stirring constantly. Cook the mixture until it thickens, about 1 minute. Remove from the heat but continue to stir for 10 to 15 seconds to ensure a smooth cream.

4. Add the remaining egg yolks, vanilla, liqueur, and the sugar and cornstarch mixture. Cover the mixture and reserve. It will keep for up to 2 days if refrigerated.

1. About 35 minutes before serving, whip the egg whites until they quadruple in volume and have a thick, foamy consistency. Gradually whip in the reserved two-thirds of the granulated sugar, then whip a few seconds longer until the egg whites are stiff but not dry. Gradually fold the reserved custard mixture into the egg whites.

2. Immediately place the soufflé batter in a pastry bag with a No. 8 (16-mm) plain tip. Pipe into the prepared soufflé ramekins, making a smooth mound slightly above the rim of each ramekin. Be sure the batter does not stick to the rim itself.

3. Bake immediately at 400°F (205°C) for about 25 minutes or until done. The sides and top should be light brown. While the soufflés are baking, make the sabayon and pour into sauce pitchers.

4. Presentation: Quickly remove the soufflés from the oven and sift powdered sugar lightly over the tops. Place the ramekins on dessert plates lined with doilies. Serve immediately with the accompanying sauce.

CHEF'S TIP

Traditionally, a liqueur soufflé is served with sabayon. However, you may want to substitute Crème Anglaise (page 754), which is much more convenient, as it can be made ahead of time and therefore allows you to concentrate on the soufflé at the last moment. If you wish, flavor the custard sauce with a little of the liqueur used in the soufflé.

FOR A LA CARTE SERVICE

1. Whip the egg whites and sugar as needed for each order as it comes in. Until you have enough experience to divide those ingredients into single portions by eye, whip extra whites to ensure that you will have enough (in which case you will also need more sugar than was set aside).

2. Combine approximately 2 parts whipped egg whites with 1 part custard base and spoon into the form. Unless you have another order immediately, do not use any leftover whipped egg whites. If you suspect that you will need all of the soufflés, but not all at the same time, you can assemble them all together and hold them (unbaked) in a hot bain-marie (about 160°F/71°C). You can hold them for up to 30 minutes before baking without compromising the quality. When you are ready to proceed, remove them from the bain-marie and bake as directed above, reducing the baking time by a few minutes.

VARIATIONS

CHOCOLATE SOUFFLE

yield: 12 soufflés, 3¼ inches (8.1 cm) in diameter, or 8 soufflés, 4½ inches (11.2 cm) in diameter

Prepare the full recipe for Liqueur Soufflé as directed, with the following changes:

- Substitute an equal amount of crème de cacao for the liqueur in the batter.
- Mix 1½ ounces (40 g) unsweetened cocoa powder with the cornstarch.
- Add 1 ounce (30 g) melted sweet dark chocolate to the warm custard.
- Add 2 additional egg whites. Bake and serve as directed for either banquet or à la carte service.
- Substitute crème anglaise flavored with crème de cacao for the sabayon.

For the small batch, add 5 teaspoons (12.5 g) unsweetened cocoa powder, ½ ounce (15 g) melted sweet dark chocolate, and 1 extra egg white.

HARLEQUIN SOUFFLE yield: 12 soufflés, 3¼ inches (8.1 cm) in diameter

After coating the soufflé ramekins with butter and sugar, stand a piece of cardboard in the center of each form (Figure 7-16). Prepare the full Liqueur Soufflé recipe as directed, making the following changes:

FIGURE 7-16 **The cardboard separator in the center of a ramekin for making a Harlequin Soufflé**

- Divide the custard, reserved sugar, and egg whites in half separately.

- Add 1 ounce (30 g) unsweetened cocoa powder and 1 tablespoon (15 ml) melted sweet dark chocolate to 1 portion of the custard.

- Add 1 additional egg white to 1 portion of the egg whites. Set next to the chocolate-flavored custard to distinguish it.

- Combine the custard with sugar and egg whites as directed, making 2 separate batters and using the larger group of egg whites in the chocolate batter to compensate for the addition of the chocolate.

- Using pastry bags with No. 6 (12-mm) plain tips, fill 1 side of each of the prepared forms with the plain and chocolate batters. Pull the cardboard straight up and out. Bake and serve as directed for either banquet or à la carte service.

Blueberry Soufflé yield: 12 soufflés, 3¼ inches (8.1 cm) in diameter

1 recipe Liqueur Soufflé batter (page 367)
1 pound 6 ounces (625 g) fresh or thawed frozen blueberries

3 ounces (85 g) granulated sugar
Powdered sugar
1 recipe Raspberry Sauce (page 173)

1. Prepare the full recipe of soufflé batter and the ramekins through Step 4, omitting the liqueur.

2. Puree the blueberries with the granulated sugar. Place in a heavy saucepan and reduce by half over low heat, forming a thick pulp. Stir frequently, especially when the blueberries start to thicken, to prevent the mixture from burning. Remove from the heat and let cool completely.

3. Add the blueberry pulp to the soufflé batter base.

4. About 30 minutes before the soufflés are to be served, whip the egg whites and sugar to stiff peaks, using 8 egg whites rather than 10, and fold the soufflé base into the egg whites. For à la carte service, follow the directions for the liqueur soufflé, but use 1½ parts base to 2 parts egg white. Pipe the batter into the prepared ramekins, filling them to the top.

5. Bake immediately at 400°F (205°C) for approximately 20 minutes or until done. The sides should be light brown.

6. Sift powdered sugar lightly over the tops. Serve immediately with individual pitchers of raspberry sauce.

FRUIT SOUFFLES

The recipe for blueberry soufflé can be prepared with other fruits and berries as well. Depending on the natural sweetness of the fruit you choose, you might need to adjust the amount of sugar added when you puree it. Fruits such as apricots or plums in season are excellent choices. Use the same amount of fruit called for in the blueberry soufflé recipe (weigh the fruit after you remove the stones). If using plums, leave the skin on; it adds a nice color to the pulp. Puree and reduce as directed for the blueberry soufflé.

Black currant soufflé is another distinctive variation. Follow the directions for blueberry soufflé, substituting black currants for the blueberries. Serve with Apricot Sauce (page 303). If using canned black currants in heavy syrup, drain and discard the syrup before weighing the fruit (or use it for sorbet after adjusting the Baumé level); omit the sugar called for in the recipe.

Pecan-Raisin Soufflé yield: 12 soufflés, 3¼ inches (8.1 cm) in diameter

1 recipe Liqueur Soufflé batter (page 367)
½ cup (120 ml) whiskey
½ recipe Crème Anglaise (page 754)
¼ recipe Caramelized Pecans (page 626)

1 tablespoon (12 g) Hazelnut Paste (page 778)
2 ounces (55 g) dark raisins
Powdered sugar

1. Prepare the full recipe of soufflé batter and the ramekins through Step 4, substituting ¼ cup (60 ml) of the whiskey for the liqueur.

2. Add the remaining ¼ cup (60 ml) whiskey to the crème anglaise and reserve. If refrigerated, bring the sauce to room temperature before serving.

3. Coarsely crush the caramelized pecans. Mix the pecans, hazelnut paste, and raisins into the soufflé batter before combining it with the whipped egg whites. Fill the soufflé ramekins and bake as directed in the liqueur soufflé recipe for either banquet or à la carte service.

4. Sift powdered sugar over the tops and serve immediately with individual pitchers of the whiskey-flavored sauce.

Soufflé Rothschild yield: 12 soufflés, 3¼ inches (8.1 cm) in diameter

6 ounces (170 g) mixed candied fruit (see Note)
¾ cup (180 ml) Danzinger Goldwasser liqueur
½ recipe Mousseline Sauce (page 338)

1 recipe Liqueur Soufflé batter (page 367)
Powdered sugar

1. Chop the candied fruit into small pieces, approximately the size of dried currants. Add a little more than ½ cup (120 ml) of the Danzinger Goldwasser liqueur; save the remainder to flavor the sauce. Set the fruit aside to macerate for at least 1 hour.

2. Flavor the mousseline sauce with the remaining liqueur and reserve. If refrigerated, bring the sauce to room temperature before serving.

About Goldwasser

Goldwasser is German for "gold water." This full-bodied liqueur is pale yellow, flavored with herbs, caraway seed, orange peel, and spices, and has flecks of edible gold leaf suspended throughout that are harmless to drink. The best-known brand is Danziger Goldwasser. Goldwasser is used to add flavor to a variety of desserts, pastries, and confections.

3. Prepare the ramekins and the full recipe of liqueur soufflé batter, substituting the fruit-liqueur mixture for the liqueur.

4. Fill the prepared soufflé forms and bake as directed in the liqueur soufflé recipe for either banquet or à la carte service.

5. Sift powdered sugar lightly over the tops and serve immediately with individual pitchers of the mousseline sauce.

NOTE: The candied fruit mixture should include candied cherries. If candied cherries are not available, use maraschino cherries. Rinse the cherries and dry thoroughly before chopping them.

Anise-Scented Lemon Parfait with Lemon Cookie Tumbleweeds   375

Baked Plantains in Gingered Meyer Lemon Syrup with Avocado-Mango Ice Cream   377

Blueberry Financier with Toasted Lemon Verbena Sabayon and Mascarpone Sherbet   380

Brandied Cherry Ganache Towers with Pink Champagne Aspic and Curvy Tuile Strips   384

Buried Ruby Treasure   385

Caramel-Centered Milk Chocolate Mousse with Black Currant Sauce   389

Chocolate Dome Cake with Cherry Sauce and Chocolate Lace   391

Chocolate Marquise with Passion Fruit Parfait and a Lace Cookie Bouquet   394

Cocoa Nib–White Chocolate Ice Cream with a Chocolate Lace Igloo and Tuile Polar Bear   396

Coconut Ice Cream in a Red Pepper Tuile with Strawberry Salsa and Tomatillo Lace   399

Espresso Chocolate Cake with Coffee-Bean Crisps   401

Frozen Lemon Mousse with Orange Syrup and a Tuile Spiral   405

Lemongrass Parfait with Green Tea Syrup, Mango Wafer Orbs, and Macadamia Nuts   406

Milk Chocolate Marquise with Finger Banana Center and Red Currant Sauce   408

Spiced Ganache and Tea Ice Cream Marco Polo   410

Snowbird in a Chocolate Cage   413

Striped Chocolate Cups with Tuile Steam Decorations   415

Tarte Tatin Moderne   416

Modernist Desserts

Fanciful garnishes, towering presentations, abstract designs, desserts so spectacular that customers are sometimes afraid to take a bite — we have seen all of this and more coming out of the pastry kitchen in the last decade or so. Certainly a change from when I started in this business.

Almost forty years ago, before we had traveled to the moon; before the invention of home computers, telephone answering machines, fax machines, pagers, and cell phones; before home kitchens had food processors, electric ice cream machines, and electric pasta makers; before VCRs, CDs, and DVDs, so you had to go to an actual movie theater to see a movie — *and* it was considered a big event — way back then, I had already finished my five-year apprenticeship, worked for three establishments, and completed my masters exam in culinary school. That was the spring of 1965, and I was still living in Sweden. At that time, it was common practice for a chef to sign on one or two apprentices to help in the business in exchange for training. Not only did this provide extra hands in the shop, it was in the interest of the chef to train them well because, if they passed their apprenticeship test after their five-year ordeal, he or she received a substantial bonus from the government.

Over the years, this method of learning and progressing slowly has just about ended, as few chefs can devote the time required to properly train a real beginner, nor can most shops afford to pay for the mistakes bound to occur in the process. Perhaps just as significant, fewer would-be chefs have the time, patience, or funds to support themselves during years of training — they are anxious to start earning a living.

Thirty or forty years ago, almost everything was made from scratch. Convenience products like those we use today were quite limited, and freezers were not only expensive but, to many chefs and most consumers, were associated with inferior quality. On the other hand, as discussed already, plenty of inexpensive labor was available.

Naturally, we have seen immense changes in our industry over the last decades with respect to equipment. As an apprentice, my first duty in the morning was to light the stove that produced steam for the proof box. Today, I would not dream of opening a shop without a state-of-the-art rack oven and a computer-controlled combination freezer, refrigerator, and proof box. With these tools, the chef can, for example, place a rack of croissants in the freezer at 1:00 P.M., set the controls, and take on other tasks knowing that the freezer will, at the proper time, slowly turn into a refrigerator and then a proof box complete with controlled humidity. When the baker arrives at 5:00 the next morning, the croissants are ready to be sprayed with egg wash, and the whole rack can be rolled into the preheated rack oven.

Small equipment, too, is mind-boggling in its advances. First, silicone had not even been invented in the early 1960s, so there was no such thing as lining sheet pans with Silpats — or, for that matter, with baking paper. Instead, the sticky pans had to be scraped and cleaned by you-know-who — the apprentice. And heaven help that apprentice if the chef turned his baked cookies upside down and found them gray on the bottom from a dirty metal pan. Those sheet pans were made out of heavy-duty sheet metal (and I do mean heavy), not the lightweight aluminum pans we are used to today.

It seemed as if the poor apprentices could never win — in the summer, they risked being stung by the yellow jackets that swarmed around the outdoor cleaning table and, in the winter, they had to place the pans in the oven to melt the coating of cold fat before the pans could be washed. They could quite easily burn their hands on the hot pans.

Today, we not only have silicone-coated baking paper, but we have Flexipans, silk screens, intricate stencils, disposable pastry bags, acetate strips, cake decorating combs, chocolate and fondant funnels, transfer sheets, aerosol chocolate and sugar coolant, digital scales with memory, dough sheeters, machines that make ice cream in seconds, immersion blenders, food handling gloves, silicone spatulas, all manner of thermometers with digital readouts and computer technology — the list is endless. Utilizing this modern technology wisely can result in a high-quality finished product with an extended shelf life and plenty of eye appeal. Some chefs, however, take matters a bit too far.

Today's painstaking, elaborate, now-how-did-they-do-that presentations are just about required in top establishments. Unfortunately, all too often, the dessert's presentation is given more importance than its flavor. These designs do, no doubt, impress consumers and make them feel special — as they should — but overambition too often leads to a dessert with more flair than flavor. In many cases, there actually isn't any flavor at all, because everything on the plate is a decoration. I have seen "desserts," for example, consisting of a cast-sugar plate topped with brittle pulled-sugar ornaments and a riot of fruit sauces; it looks impressive, but what is there to eat?

I believe every dessert should strike a balance between appearance, flavor, and practicality of production. The latter varies with the number of desserts to be produced and the food and labor costs that can be justified. A good question to ask yourself is this: "Will the design I am using enhance the dessert or take away from its overall quality?" For example, if you want to serve a towering cylinder of mousse 6 inches (15 cm) tall but to do so you have to use so much gelatin that the texture will be rubbery, or if your presentation is so complicated that you must prep the components hours ahead of service and sacrifice freshness, the effort simply isn't worth it. Remember, in the end, someone is going to eat your creation, and there *is* a difference between a dessert and a showpiece. Moderation in our line of work, as in most aspects of life, is often the key to success.

Anise-Scented Lemon Parfait with Lemon Cookie Tumbleweeds

yield: 12 servings, 4 ounces (120 ml) each

The technique of covering the sides of a dessert or pastry with a thin decorative strip of chocolate has been utilized for many years, since well before the availability of clear plastic strips and transfer sheets. In the old days, we used waxed paper; the process was a bit more difficult, so this type of decoration was not as common as it is today. You will find recipes throughout this book in which acetate strips are used to create what are, essentially, customized transfer sheets. A chocolate design is piped onto the plastic, a thin, solid layer of contrasting chocolate is spread on top, and the strip is wrapped around the dessert (see Petite Chocolate and Brandied Cherry Pastries, page 109). In other cases, the chocolate band is made from solid chocolate without a design. Last are recipes in which the chocolate is piped onto the plastic in a fishnet design through which the dessert is visible (this is done in Citrus Cream with Pink Grapefruit and Orange, page 338, and White Chocolate and Pistachio Mousse with Chocolate Lace, page 357).

The method used here is a variation on this last theme; it also employs the same technique used in making chocolate noodles. A solid layer of chocolate is applied to the plastic, then half of it is removed with a trowel to create evenly spaced parallel chocolate stripes. The result is an unusual and eye-catching finished pastry.

Licorice Decorating Syrup (page 760)

12 Joconde sponge rounds, 2 inches (5 cm) in diameter (see Steps 1 and 2, page 405)

8 ounces (225 g) granulated sugar

½ cup (120 ml) egg whites

4 lemons

2 cups (480 ml) heavy cream

1 cup (240 ml) unflavored yogurt

3 tablespoons (45 ml) sambuca liqueur

Dark coating chocolate, melted

½ recipe Kiwi Sauce (page 309)

12 Cookie Tumbleweeds (page 699; see Note)

1. Line the inside of 12 cake rings or plastic tubes, 2 inches (5 cm) in diameter and 2½ inches (6.2 cm) in height, with strips of acetate (see Chef's Tip).

2. Brush the licorice syrup on top of the sponge rounds. Place the rounds in the bottom of the lined forms.

3. Combine the sugar and egg whites in a mixing bowl. Place over a bain-marie and heat to 140°F (60°C), whisking constantly. Immediately transfer to a mixer bowl and whip at high speed until the meringue has cooled and formed stiff peaks.

4. While the meringue is being whipped, wash the lemons, finely grate the zest, extract the juice, strain, and combine the juice with approximately three-quarters of the lemon zest. Reserve the remaining zest to use in making the tumbleweed decorations.

5. Whip the heavy cream to soft peaks. Fold the yogurt, sambuca, and lemon juice with zest into the cream. Fold in the meringue in 3 additions.

6. Using a pastry bag with a large plain tip, divide the parfait among the prepared forms, filling them to the top. Use a spatula to smooth and level the tops, cover, and freeze for a minimum of 4 hours or, preferably, overnight.

7. Remove the rings or tubes and the acetate strips from the desserts you plan to serve. Return the desserts to the freezer. Wash, dry, and trim the length of the acetate strips so the ends just meet when placed inside the forms (the length should equal the circumference of the parfait, and the ends should not overlap).

8. Place a trimmed plastic strip on a sheet of baking paper. Spread a thin layer of melted coating chocolate on top of the plastic, then use the tip of a small knife to move the strip to a clean spot on the paper (see Procedure 3-1a and 3-1b, page 109). Immediately drag a square notched trowel across the strip crosswise. Wait until the chocolate starts to set, then quickly wrap the plastic around a parfait. Repeat to cover the sides of the remaining desserts on which you have removed the rings. Return them to the freezer.

9. Place the kiwi sauce in a piping bottle.

10. Presentation: Carefully peel the plastic away from a dessert and set it in the center of a serving plate. Drizzle kiwi sauce around the parfait. Decorate the top with a cookie tumbleweed. Serve immediately.

NOTE: Before making the cookie tumbleweeds, thoroughly stir the reserved grated lemon zest from Step 4 into the batter.

CHEF'S TIP

If you do not have suitable metal cake rings or clear plastic tubes, PVC pipe works great if cut to the proper size and lined with strips of plastic. Alternatively, make rings by taping strips of acetate or polyurethane together to make rounds. See the introduction to Frozen Lemon Mousse with Orange Syrup and a Tuile Spiral (page 405). The acetate used to line the rings can be either the standard thinner variety or the less common heavyweight plastic. However, to reuse the strips to create the chocolate decorations, as directed in Steps 7 and 8, you must start with the thinner grade of plastic.

Cooking Meringue Base

In this recipe, the hot sugar and egg white mixture is transferred to a second bowl before whipping to quickly stop the cooking process and eliminate the risk of the eggs overcooking from continued contact with the hot bowl. When making a larger quantity, it is usually fine to skip this step and warm the egg whites and sugar in the same bowl used for whipping. To avoid hot spots, however, it is always a good idea to keep whisking for a minute or two after taking the bowl off the bain-marie and before placing it on the mixer.

Baked Plantains in Gingered Meyer Lemon Syrup with Avocado-Mango Ice Cream yield: 8 servings (Color Photo 78)

The plantain is a starchy variety of banana with an unusual distinction: It must be cooked before being consumed. Eating a raw plantain is no more pleasant than eating a raw potato. Plantains are used mostly in savory dishes, but they also appear in dessert preparations, generally roasted, fried, or baked, as in this recipe.

I first encountered plantains on a dessert menu at the La Curva restaurant when I was teaching in Mexico City. This is also where I first tasted avocado-mango ice cream, although the plantains and the ice cream were not part of the same presentation, as they are in this recipe. As I recall, the plantains were simply presented, but I enjoyed their flavor and was intrigued by the originality of the idea. Plain mango ice cream (without the avocado) is equally nice with this dish, if the idea of using both plantains and avocados for dessert is a bit much for you or your guests.

Small piece of fresh ginger, approximately 1 × 2 inches (2.5 × 5 cm)

¼ cup (60 ml) Meyer lemon juice

¾ cup (180 ml) water

6 ounces (170 g) granulated sugar, plus more for sprinkling

4 medium-size, fully ripe plantains

6 ounces (170 g) kadaif phyllo dough

1 cup (240 ml) clarified butter, hot (see Note 1)

Powdered sugar

4 whole vanilla beans

Ginger Cake (recipe follows)

½ recipe Avocado-Mango Ice Cream (recipe follows)

8 Plantain Chips (page 722; see Note 2)

1. Peel the ginger and slice it thinly. Place in a saucepan with the lemon juice and water. Stir in 6 ounces (170 g) of the granulated sugar. Bring the mixture to a boil and boil for 1 minute to dissolve the sugar. Remove from the heat and set aside to steep.

2. Cut both ends off the plantains, leaving the peel intact. Place the plantains on a rack set on a sheet pan. Bake at 375°F (190°C) until the fruit feels tender and is fragrant. Depending on the degree of ripeness, this can take from 30 to 45 minutes. Set the plantains aside to cool with the peel on.

3. Divide and shape the phyllo dough, making 8 somewhat flat yet airy rounds about 4 inches (10 cm) in diameter and 1 inch (2.5 cm) high; they will weigh approximately ¾ ounce (22 g) each. Place the nests on a sheet pan lined with baking paper as you form them. Spray the clarified butter over the phyllo dough. If you use a brush, be careful not to damage the fragile strands. Sift powdered sugar lightly on top of the nests. Bake at 400°F (205°C) until golden brown, approximately 8 minutes. Let cool to room temperature.

4. Strain the reserved syrup and discard the ginger. Cut the vanilla beans in half lengthwise and scrape out the seeds. Thoroughly mix the seeds into the syrup (see Chef's Tip). Reserve the pod halves. Return the syrup to the stove and boil until reduced by one-third. The finished syrup should have the consistency of simple syrup. To test the consistency, place a teaspoon or so in the refrigerator until the syrup cools to room temperature. Place the syrup in a piping bottle and reserve.

CHEF'S TIP
To prevent the vanilla bean seeds from clumping or caking, scrape them directly into 2 tablespoons (30 g) granulated sugar. Rub the mixture to separate the seeds before adding it to the syrup.

5. Cut 8 rounds, 3 inches (7.5 cm) in diameter, from the ginger cake. You will need only half of the cake; reserve the remainder for another use. Pipe a small amount of the reserved syrup on top of the rounds; cover and reserve.

6. Peel the plantains and cut on an angle into thin slices.

7. Presentation: Place a round of ginger cake in the center of a dessert plate. Top with a kadaif phyllo nest. Using ½ plantain per serving, arrange the slices on a flat, heatproof surface, separating them slightly. Sprinkle granulated sugar lightly over the slices and use a blowtorch to caramelize the sugar. Pipe a band of ginger syrup on the base of the plate around the cake. Arrange the caramelized plantain slices, evenly spaced, on top of the syrup. Place an oval scoop of ice cream on top of the phyllo nest. Push a plantain chip into the ice cream so it stands straight up. Coat a reserved vanilla bean pod half with a little ginger syrup to make it shiny. Lean the pod against the ice cream. Sift powdered sugar lightly over the dessert. Serve immediately.

NOTE 1: The clarified butter must be hot to be applied with a spray bottle. You must also work with a larger quantity of butter than you will actually use on the nests. If you do not have clarified butter on hand, you may substitute pan spray.

NOTE 2: To create the twisted plantain chip shown in Color Photo 78, hold the plantain at each end after removing from the oven, twist, and hold for a few seconds until crisp (see Figure 13-23, page 690, as an example).

About Plantains

Plantains are closely related to the yellow banana, but this "ugly relation" is considerably larger, averaging about 12 inches (30 cm) in length and weighing as much as 1 pound (455 g). Though they are indeed a fruit, plantains are starchy and are sometimes referred to as the *vegetable banana* or *cooking banana* because they are cooked like a vegetable rather than eaten raw; their ripening process, like that of the potato, does not convert all of the starch to sugar. Plantains are used in Latin American countries similar to the way that potatoes are used in the United States. The way they are cooked depends on their degree of ripeness.

Plantains that are not grown commercially are left to ripen on the tree. The fruit changes color from all green to all black and becomes slightly wrinkled when fully ripe. We usually see both green and fully ripe plantains in the market. Try to purchase them at a stage somewhere in between, when their thick, slightly blemished skin has started to turn reddish brown.

Removing the peel from a raw plantain is quite a bit harder than removing the skin from a banana. If the plantains are to be boiled or baked, leave the skin on; it will slip right off after cooking. Otherwise, use a sharp knife to cut off both ends so part of the fruit is exposed, then cut lengthwise along the edge of one of the ridges without cutting into the pulp. Repeat with the adjacent ridge and use the edge of the knife to lift up the cut section of peel and pull it away in one piece. Repeat this procedure with each remaining segment of peel or until the remaining skin can be removed in one piece.

Plantains should be refrigerated only if overripe. The exposure to cold interrupts their ripening cycle, never to resume, even if the fruit is returned to room temperature. A rock-hard green plantain can take up to two weeks to ripen. If the fruit is stored improperly during shipping, it may never ripen and instead may just dry up.

Several varieties of plantains are available in most grocery stores today; it is no longer necessary to go to Latin or Asian markets to find them, at least in large coastal cities. The two sorts most commonly found are the giant plantain, also known as the *Puerto Rican plantain*, and the horse plantain.

GINGER CAKE yield: 1 sheet, 12 × 16 × ¾ inches (30 × 40 × 2 cm)

8 ounces (225 g) cake flour

8 ounces (225 g) bread flour

2 teaspoons (8 g) baking soda

2 tablespoons (12 g) ground ginger

½ teaspoon (1 g) ground cloves

½ teaspoon (2.5 g) salt

8 ounces (225 g) unsalted butter, at room temperature

7 ounces (200 g) brown sugar

2 eggs, at room temperature

1 pound (445 g) dark molasses

8 ounces (225 g) honey

1½ ounces (40 g) crystallized ginger, minced

1 cup (240 g) boiling water

1. Sift together the cake flour, bread flour, baking soda, ground ginger, cloves, and salt.

2. Using the paddle attachment on the mixer, cream the butter until it is light and fluffy. Add the brown sugar and beat until the mixture is smooth. Beat in the eggs, 1 at a time, scraping down the bowl after each addition. Add the molasses and the honey, beating until the ingredients are thoroughly combined, and scraping down the bowl again as needed.

3. Add the flour mixture and blend until just incorporated. Remove the bowl from the mixer; stir in the minced ginger and boiling water by hand.

4. Pour the batter into a half-sheet pan (12 × 16 inches/30 × 40 cm) lined with baking paper or a Silpat.

5. Bake at 375°F (190°C) approximately 30 minutes or until baked through.

AVOCADO-MANGO ICE CREAM yield: 2 quarts (1 L 820 ml)

This recipe uses a combination of mangoes and avocados, but you can be a purist and make it with either all avocados or all mangoes. (If you use all avocados, you will probably need additional simple syrup.) Combining the two fruits produces a wonderful flavor and texture; the color is a delicate pale green. Because the sweet mangoes are high in fiber and avocados can contain up to 30 percent oil, it is possible to achieve a soft, smooth creamy texture without adding egg yolks or a lot of dairy fat in the form of heavy cream, as is typical in most ice creams.

1 pound 6 ounces (625 g) perfectly ripe avocados (about 3 small)

1 pound 8 ounces (680 g) perfectly ripe mangoes (about 2 medium)

⅓ cup (80 ml) lime juice (3 to 4 limes)

1½ cups (360 ml) simple syrup, approximately

1 cup (240 ml) half-and-half

2 cups (480 ml) whole milk

1. Peel and pit the avocados and mangoes. Discard the pits and place the pulp in a food processor or blender. Process to a smooth consistency.

2. Stir in the lime juice and about two-thirds of the simple syrup. Strain the mixture to remove stringy mango fibers. Stir in the half-and-half and the milk.

3. Adjust the sweetness by adding simple syrup as needed.

4. Process in an ice cream freezer following the manufacturer's instructions. Store, covered, in the freezer.

Blueberry Financier with Toasted Lemon Verbena Sabayon and Mascarpone Sherbet yield: 16 servings (Color Photo 79)

A few years ago, I was asked to contribute two recipes to *Chocolatier* magazine's book, *A Modernist View of Plated Desserts;* this is one of them. As the title suggests, the idea was for contributing chefs to create desserts with spectacular modern presentations. Naturally, a dessert must be appealing, but I have always believed it more important that a dessert taste good and that the recipe be producible in a normal commercial operation. Too often, one sees photographs of desserts obviously produced for the photo studio only; they could never be part of a restaurant menu, due to cost and/or a presentation that simply cannot be moved from the kitchen to the dining room. Creating a dessert that tastes great, looks impressive, and is practical can be like walking a tightrope. The trick, of course, is to make it to the other side — or, to put it another way, to create a dessert that is impressive and appears complicated to execute but that is nevertheless doable — with a few tricks up your sleeve.

Financiers have become popular on dessert menus in many restaurants today, enjoyed alone or as a small accompaniment that provides a complementary taste and texture, as in this recipe. Financiers are traditionally made in small rectangular molds (just as their close relatives, madeleines, are made in shell-shaped molds). Try using this fancy batter for muffins; they are irresistible. Not only are they are moist and tender inside and chewy and crunchy outside but, due to the moisture of the blueberries, they stay fresh for days.

The presentation can easily be simplified by using only one crescent and omitting the sugar stick, in which case there is no need to cut holes in the crescent decoration. If lemon verbena is not available, try flavoring the sabayon with lemongrass instead, using twice the amount; omit the verbena in the financier.

1 pound (455 g) unsalted butter	2 cups (480 ml) fresh blueberries, cleaned
1 pound 2 ounces (510 g) powdered sugar	Lemon Verbena Sabayon (recipe follows)
5 ounces (140 g) bread flour	Crescent Decorations (instructions follow)
5 ounces (140 g) almond meal	Mascarpone Sherbet (recipe follows)
14 egg whites (1¾ cups/420 ml), at room temperature	Sugar Sticks (page 595)
2 tablespoons (30 ml) finely grated lemon zest	½ recipe Blueberry Sauce (page 139)
2 ounces (55 g) lemon verbena leaves, minced finely, plus sprigs for garnish	

I. Grease the insides of 16 metal cake rings, 3 inches (7.5 cm) in diameter and 2 inches (5 cm) in height. Place on a sheet pan lined with a Silpat or sheet of baking paper and set aside.

2. Place the butter in a skillet and cook over low heat until golden brown (the result is called *beurre noisette*); this will take about 5 minutes.

3. Sift together the powdered sugar and bread flour. Blend in the almond meal. Place in a mixer bowl with the paddle attachment. Add the egg whites while mixing at low speed, continuing to blend until the ingredients are thoroughly incorporated. Scrape down the bowl and gradually add the beurre noisette. Beat at high speed until well combined. Add the lemon zest and minced verbena. Remove the bowl from the mixer and gently fold in the blueberries by hand, being careful not to crush them.

4. Divide the batter evenly among the prepared cake rings. Bake at 325°F (163°C) for approximately 25 minutes or until the tops feel firm. Let cool slightly before removing the cake rings. Invert the baked cakes, cover, and set aside until needed (see Note).

5. Presentation: Refer to Color Photo 79. Cover the base of a serving plate with lemon verbena sabayon, using approximately ½ cup (120 ml). Using a salamander or a blowtorch, brown the surface of the sauce (gratiné). Cut a slit, approximately ½ inch (1.2 cm) deep, across the center of a blueberry financier and place it, cut-side up, in the center of the plate. Carefully insert a flat crescent cookie, points down, in the cut. Using a No. 30 (1½-ounce/45-ml) ice cream scoop, place a scoop of mascarpone sherbet on top of the financier toward the right. Carefully push 1 point of a curved crescent cookie underneath the left side of the standing cookie, leaning it against the sherbet with the other end in front, slightly curved upward above the straight crescent cookie. Quickly warm a sugar stick and thread it through 1 hole in each cookie at the right side. Bend the sugar into a soft curve above the cookies and then into the holes on the left side. Spoon 3 pools of blueberry sauce on top of the sabayon around the dessert. Place a sprig of lemon verbena on top of the sherbet and serve immediately.

NOTE: Blueberry financier should be served at room temperature, but it may be prepared through Step 4 up to 2 days in advance and stored in the refrigerator.

LEMON VERBENA SABAYON yield: approximately 10 cups (2 L 400 ml)

3 cups (720 ml) champagne or dry white wine

2 ounces (55 g) lemon verbena leaves, minced finely

12 egg yolks (1 cup/240 ml)

12 ounces (340 g) granulated sugar

1. Combine the champagne or wine with the lemon verbena and heat to about 180°F (82°C); do not boil. Remove from the heat and set aside to infuse for a minimum of 30 minutes, preferably 1 hour.

2. Beat the egg yolks and sugar together in a stainless steel bowl until the mixture is light and fluffy. Strain the wine mixture, then whisk it into the egg yolk mixture.

3. Place the bowl over simmering water and continue to whip constantly until the sabayon is hot and thick, at approximately 160°F (71°C).

NOTE: If the sabayon must be prepared more than 1 hour before service, cook it a bit further, to 180°F (82°C), to create a more stable mixture. Remove from the heat, transfer to the mixer, and whip at high speed until the sauce no longer feels warm to the touch.

CRESCENT DECORATIONS yield: approximately 40 decorations

You will need a softly curved mold to shape half of the baked cookies. A tube or bain-marie insert measuring 4 to 4½ inches (10 to 11.2 cm) in diameter works fine. If you do not have a form, you can make one easily by bending a thin strip of aluminum into a curved shape.

1 recipe Vanilla Tuile Decorating Paste (page 695)

1 teaspoon (5 ml) unsweetened cocoa powder

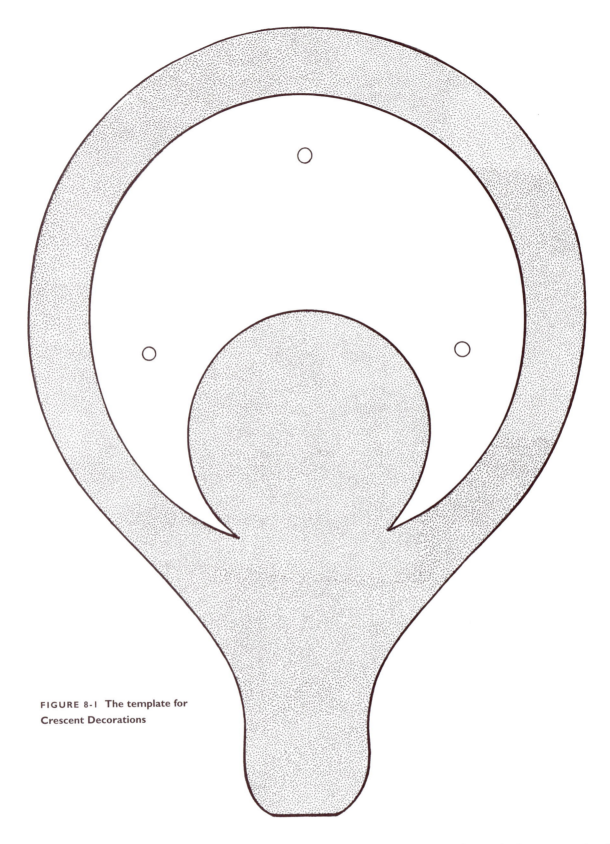

FIGURE 8-1 **The template for Crescent Decorations**

I. Copy the template shown in Figure 8-1. The template, as shown, is the correct size for use in this recipe. Trace the drawing, then cut the template out of cardboard that is $\frac{1}{16}$ inch (2 mm) thick; cake boxes work well.

2. Place 2 tablespoons (30 ml) of the tuile paste in a small container. Add the cocoa powder and stir until completely smooth. Cover and set aside.

3. Place the template on top of a Silpat (see Note). Spread a thin layer of the plain paste within the template, then lift off the template (see Figures 13-29 and 13-30, page 694). Repeat until you have made approximately 40 cookies (2 are used for each serving, and some will inevitably break).

4. Place the reserved cocoa-colored paste in 1 or 2 piping bags and cut very small openings. Pipe a curved design on top of the cookies, as shown in Color Photo 79.

5. Bake 1 sheet at a time at 400°F (205°C) until baked halfway, about 3 minutes. Remove from the oven and, using a No. 2 plain piping tip, cut 2 or 3 holes from each cookie as shown in Figure 8-1. Return to the oven and continue baking until the first cookie turns golden brown in a few spots.

6. Working quickly, remove the cookies 1 at a time and place on the curved form, top-side up. Depending on how many cookies are on the pan, you may have to remove the sheet pan from the oven while working to prevent the last cookies from getting too dark. Continue baking and forming until you have made 20 curved cookies. Once a pan of cookies has been removed from the oven, you may not be able to curve all of them before they become too brittle. In this case, leave them flat and continue with the next pan, as you need an equal amount of curved and flat cookies for the presentation. Bake the remaining cookies in the same manner, but do not curve them.

7. Store the finished cookies in an airtight container at room temperature. They can be kept this way for up to 1 week.

NOTE: If Silpats are not available, use the back side of flat, even sheet pans, coating them lightly with melted butter and flour.

MASCARPONE SHERBET yield: approximately 7 cups (1 L 680 ml)

Mascarpone produces a smooth, rich sherbet. If you are not making your own mascarpone, be certain to use a high-quality product, or the cheese may separate in Step 2 or during churning.

3 cups (720 ml) water

½ cup (120 ml) or 6 ounces (170 g) honey

8 ounces (225 g) granulated sugar

⅓ cup (80 ml) lemon juice

12 ounces (340 g) Mascarpone Cheese (page 779)

1½ cups (360 ml) Crème Fraîche (page 775)

1. Place the water, honey, sugar, and lemon juice in a saucepan. Heat, stirring, until the sugar is dissolved. Let cool at room temperature.

2. Beat the mascarpone cheese for 1 or 2 minutes or until smooth. Add the crème fraîche and mix to combine. Gradually incorporate the syrup into the cheese mixture.

3. Process in an ice cream freezer following the manufacturer's directions. Store, covered, in the freezer.

Brandied Cherry Ganache Towers with Pink Champagne Aspic and Curvy Tuile Strips yield: 16 servings (Color Photo 81)

I tell my students that a plated dessert must feature a minimum of three components: the dessert itself, a sauce or syrup, and a garnish, which, in addition to being decorative, provides a complementary yet contrasting texture. The curvy tuile strips used here accomplish just that by adding a nice crunch; they also add height to the plate, which is popular in today's presentations. The unusual touch here is the pretty little pink aspic cubes used instead of a sauce or syrup. If you prefer to serve a sauce, both Guinettes Cherry Sauce (page 388) and Orange-Vanilla Decorating Syrup (page 760) are wonderful paired with the chocolate ganache.

½ cup (120 ml) heavy cream	16 brandied cherries
2 teaspoons (10 g) granulated sugar	Pink Champagne Aspic (recipe follows)
16 Petite Chocolate and Brandied Cherry Pastries (page 109), glazed but not decorated	16 Curvy Tuile Strips (page 704)
	Powdered sugar

1. Whip the heavy cream with the sugar until stiff peaks form. Place in a pastry bag with a No. 5 (10-mm) star tip and reserve in the refrigerator.

2. Peel the plastic strips away from as many pastries as you anticipate needing for service.

3. Place a dessert in the center of a dessert plate. Pipe a rosette of cream on top and place a brandied cherry on the cream. Sprinkle champagne aspic on the base of the plate all around the dessert. Lean a curvy tuile strip against the dessert. Sift powdered sugar lightly over the plate and serve.

PINK CHAMPAGNE ASPIC yield: 10 ounces (285 g), or enough to decorate 16 dessert servings

This unique method of celebrating with champagne makes for an attractive presentation. The aspic adds visual interest, as it catches the light. It also represents a nice change of pace from the more typical fruit sauce. If you have leftover brandied cherry syrup from making the pastries, add ¼ cup (60 ml) and decrease the simple syrup to ¾ cup (180 ml). If you do not have extra cherry syrup but still want to add a hint of cherry flavor, do the same using cherry liqueur instead. In addition to the complementary flavor, the cherry syrup or liqueur gives the aspic a deeper pink hue.

1 tablespoon (9 g) unflavored gelatin powder	1 cup (240 ml) simple syrup
¼ cup (60 ml) cold water	¾ cup (180 ml) dry pink champagne

1. Cover a round of corrugated cardboard, 10 inches (25 cm) in diameter, with a sheet of plastic wrap. Hold the cardboard inside a hot oven for a few seconds to shrink the plastic tightly around the cardboard. Set a stainless steel cake ring, 8 inches (20 cm) in diameter, on top of the cardboard. Tape around the base of the ring on the outside to seal it to the cardboard.

2. Sprinkle the gelatin over the water and set aside to soften.

3. Place the simple syrup in a saucepan, add the gelatin mixture, and heat, stirring constantly to dissolve the gelatin; do not let the liquid boil. Remove from the heat and stir in the champagne.

4. Pour the aspic into the prepared frame. Refrigerate until firm.

5. When the aspic is firmly set, remove it from the mold (it will pop right out) and cut it into ¼-inch (6-mm) cubes. Cover and refrigerate until needed.

NOTE: If you do not have a cake ring of the size specified, use any noncorrosive form of approximately the same size that will yield a layer of aspic ¼ inch (6 mm) thick.

Buried Ruby Treasure   yield: 16 servings (Color Photo 80)

I created this dessert for a gala charity dinner for more than 200 guests. I knew the dessert had to be showy and unusual, as the event was elegant and the price per person quite high. I am pleased to say these Buried Ruby Treasures were a big hit. Not only does the unusual pyramid shape catch the eye but the soft, creamy white chocolate filling with its entertaining hidden cherry-flavored jelly center contrasts beautifully — both in taste and appearance — with the crisp dark chocolate shell. The brandied cherry sauce, too, contributes a lively red color and pleasing flavor.

Although certainly not necessary, cutting the dessert to expose the red center before presenting it to the guest makes it even more appealing. This is shown in Color Photo 80. To save time, substitute Wavy Tuile Strips (page 718) for the tuile spoons. For a whimsical presentation, decorate the pyramids with Tuile Camels instead of the spoons, attaching a camel to the plate with melted chocolate to the right and in front of the pyramid. If you are making a large number of servings or just need to make them ahead of time, prepare the desserts through spraying the outside with chocolate in Step 8; store them, well covered, in the freezer for one to two weeks.

½ recipe Joconde Sponge Base II (page 671)

White Chocolate Treasure Filling (recipe follows)

Ruby Fruit Jelly Centers (recipe follows)

Chocolate Solution for Spraying (page 557)

Guinettes Cherry Sauce (recipe follows)

Cherry Tuile Spoons (recipe follows) or Tuile Camels (instructions follow)

Mint sprigs

1. Have ready Flexipan No. 1585 or 16 pyramid-shaped molds, ½ cup (120 ml) in capacity.

2. Spread the Joconde sponge batter evenly over a sheet pan lined with baking paper or a Silpat, to make a rectangle approximately 23 × 15 inches (57.5 × 37.5 cm). Bake at 425°F (219°C) for 8 to 10 minutes or until baked through. Let cool.

3. Invert the cooled sponge sheet and peel away the baking paper or Silpat. Cut out 16 squares of sponge that are slightly smaller than the openings of the molds you are using; the sponge will become the base of the finished pastry. If using the Flexipan, cut the pieces into 2½-inch (6.2-cm) squares. In either case, some sponge will be left over; you can cut 45 squares of the size needed for the Flexipan from 1 full sheet of Joconde sponge. Cover the extra sponge and reserve for another use.

4. Pipe the white chocolate treasure filling into the forms, filling them to just below the top; do not fill them completely. If the filling seems very soft, to prevent the ruby jellies from sinking to the bottom of the molds, allow it to set for few minutes at room temperature before proceeding; do not refrigerate.

5. Working quickly, push a ruby jelly into the center of the filling in each mold. Use a spat-

CHEF'S TIP

If you are making a small number of servings and/or you have room to store the desserts on the serving plates — in the refrigerator or at room temperature — transfer them to the prepared serving plates as soon as you finish spraying them with chocolate, while they are still firm and easy to handle. You will, of course, have to spray the plates ahead of time. If you are making a large batch, you will probably need to leave the desserts on the sheet pans. In either case, it is a good idea to test one serving to see how much time is needed for the filling to thaw to the correct consistency.

If, after thawing, the desserts become too soft to transfer to a dessert plate without cracking or breaking the chocolate shell, set the tray of desserts in the freezer for 10 minutes. The chocolate shell will firm up, allowing you to handle the desserts easily, but the interior will remain soft.

ula to spread the tops of the filling even. If you have any filling left over, and/or if necessary, pipe it into the cavities made by the ruby jelly so each jelly is completely covered.

6. Still working quickly, place the sponge squares on top of the molds and press down to secure. Press hard enough so the filling rises up all around the edges of the mold. Use a spatula to remove excess filling. Cover and place in the freezer for at least 6 hours or, preferably, overnight.

7. Unmold the desserts onto sheet pans lined with baking paper (see Note). Cover and reserve in the freezer.

8. Spray the desserts with the chocolate solution following the instructions on pages 556 to 557. The desserts must be frozen solid when you apply the chocolate spray for the coating to attain the proper texture.

9. Let the desserts thaw for 1 to 2 hours to allow the mousse filling and the ruby jelly to soften. Depending on how soon you will be serving and how much space you have, several options for thawing and storage are available; see Chef's Tip.

10. Spray 16 dessert plates with chocolate solution.

11. Presentation: Center a dessert in the upper portion of a prepared dessert plate. Using a lightly heated thin knife to melt through the chocolate crust, cut the pyramid in half to expose the ruby center. Carefully separate the halves at the front, leaving them connected at the back. Place a spoonful of cherry sauce in front of the dessert and partially between the halves, using the spoon to cover up any imperfections in the chocolate spray made when the dessert halves were separated. Stand a tuile spoon at the back of the dessert, wedged between the halves. Decorate with a sprig of mint in front.

NOTE: To unmold the desserts from a Flexipan, pull the sides of the indentations away from the frozen dessert servings, invert, and place on a sheet pan lined with baking paper. To unmold desserts made in metal forms, heat the outside of the forms with a blowtorch or by briefly immersing them in hot water. To unmold desserts made in plastic forms, immerse the base in hot water just long enough to loosen the filling; invert.

WHITE CHOCOLATE TREASURE FILLING yield: enough for 16 molds, $\frac{1}{2}$ cup (120 ml) in capacity

4 teaspoons (12 g) unflavored gelatin powder

1¼ cups (300 ml) whole milk

4 egg yolks (⅓ cup/80 ml)

4 ounces (115 g) granulated sugar

Seeds from 1 whole vanilla bean

6 ounces (170 g) white chocolate, finely chopped

1¼ cups (300 ml) heavy cream

4 egg whites (½ cup/120 ml)

1. Sprinkle the gelatin over approximately one-third of the milk and set aside to soften.

2. Whip the egg yolks and approximately one-fourth of the sugar to the ribbon stage.

3. Heat the remaining milk together with the vanilla bean seeds to the scalding point. All at once, pour the hot milk into the egg yolk mixture while whisking rapidly. Stir in the chopped white chocolate and continue to mix until the chocolate is completely melted.

4. Whip the heavy cream to soft peaks. Cover and reserve in the refrigerator.

5. Heat the softened gelatin and milk to dissolve the gelatin. Stir into the warm white chocolate mixture. Set aside at room temperature.

6. Place the egg whites and remaining sugar in a mixing bowl and set over a bain-marie. Heat to 140°F (60°C), stirring constantly. Remove from the heat and whip until the meringue is stiff and has cooled to body temperature (see Note).

7. Quickly stir the whipped cream into the white chocolate mixture (warm the chocolate mixture slightly first, if it has become too thick). Stir this into the meringue. Use immediately.

NOTE: Try to avoid making the meringue before you need it. If it is left even for a few minutes, it may cake or stiffen. If this should happen, stir it smooth before adding the egg yolk and chocolate mixture, or you will end up with small lumps of meringue.

RUBY FRUIT JELLY CENTERS yield: 1½ cups (360 ml), or enough for approximately 30 dessert centers

This recipe will produce more centers than are needed for the main recipe, but making a smaller batch is not practical.

2 tablespoons (30 ml) cold water

2 tablespoons (30 ml) cherry liqueur

1½ teaspoons (5 g) unflavored gelatin powder

¾ cup (180 ml) lightly sweetened or unsweetened cherry juice, strained (see Note)

2 ounces (55 g) glucose *or* light corn syrup

2 ounces (55 g) white chocolate, finely chopped

1. Have ready small half-sphere molds, approximately 1 tablespoon (15 ml) in capacity. If you have no choice, you may use molds that are taller, provided the diameter is no greater than 1½ inches (3.7 cm). Flexipan No. 2265 is ideal; foil candy cups are another option.

2. Combine the water and cherry liqueur. Sprinkle the gelatin over the top and set aside to soften.

3. In a saucepan, combine the cherry juice and glucose or corn syrup. Bring to a boil, remove from the heat, and add the gelatin mixture, stirring until the gelatin dissolves. Stir in the white chocolate, continuing to stir until it is melted and fully incorporated.

4. Pour slightly less than 1 tablespoon (15 ml) of the mixture into each of the molds.

5. Place in the freezer for a minimum of 6 hours or, preferably, overnight.

6. Unmold onto a sheet pan lined with baking paper. Cover tightly and reserve in the freezer until you are ready to assemble the desserts.

NOTE: Canned or frozen fruit juice works fine here. However, do not use sweetened juice containing more than 10 percent sugar (or measuring more than 8° to 10° Baumé), or the centers may not freeze. If the juice contains more sugar, reduce the amount of corn syrup to compensate.

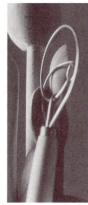

About Guinettes Cherries

Guinettes are a special type of brandied cherry imported from France. They are labeled "semi-confit," meaning they are partially cooked or preserved. The pitted cherries are packed in bottles with sugar and brandy and, sometimes, kirsch (cherry liqueur). Both the cherries themselves and the liquid in the bottle are wonderfully delicious. Simply serving them over vanilla ice cream makes an excellent, easy treat. Of course, because they are packed in alcohol, they are perfect for flambéed dishes, such as Cherries Jubilee.

The word *guinettes* is actually the name of a small red cherry varietal grown in France. However, guinettes has come to refer to the finished brandied cherry product in the same way, for example, that most people use the word *cabernet* to refer to the wine rather than the Cabernet grape from which it is made. Another popular label is *Griottines*.

GUINETTES CHERRY SAUCE yield: 2 cups (240 ml)

1 pound 2 ounces (510 g) Guinettes cherries, including syrup

Simple syrup

2 tablespoons (16 g) cornstarch

¼ cup (60 ml) cold water

1. Reserving the syrup, strain the cherries, using the back of a spoon to gently press out as much liquid as possible. Measure the syrup and add simple syrup to make a total of 1 cup (240 ml). Reserve the cherries separately.

2. Dissolve the cornstarch in the cold water. Place in a saucepan along with the 1 cup (240 ml) syrup. Stir together and bring to a boil. Boil for 30 seconds. Remove from the heat.

3. Add the reserved cherries. Store, covered, in the refrigerator.

CHERRY TUILE SPOONS yield: approximately 20 decorations

¼ recipe Vanilla Tuile Decorating Paste (page 695)

White coating chocolate, melted

20 Guinettes cherries, patted dry

1. Make the spoon template on page 708. The drawing, as shown, is the correct size for this recipe. Trace the drawing, then cut the template out of cardboard that is ¹/₁₆ inch (2 mm) thick; cake boxes work fine. If you do not have Silpats, grease and flour the backs of even sheet pans.

2. Place a Silpat on top of a perfectly even sheet pan. Spread the tuile paste on the mat (or 1 of the prepared sheet pans) within the spoon template, forming 4 to 6 spoons per pan.

3. Bake at 400°F (205°C) for approximately 4 minutes or until the spoons are light golden brown around the edges. Shape the soft cookies by pressing them between 2 soupspoons or teaspoons that are as close to the size of the tuile spoons as possible. Repeat until you have formed at least 20 spoons, which allows for breakage.

4. Place a small amount of white chocolate in a piping bag and cut a small opening. Pipe a pea-sized dot in the bowl of each spoon and place a cherry on each chocolate dot. Allow the chocolate to set. The spoons can be stored overnight in an airtight container, if necessary.

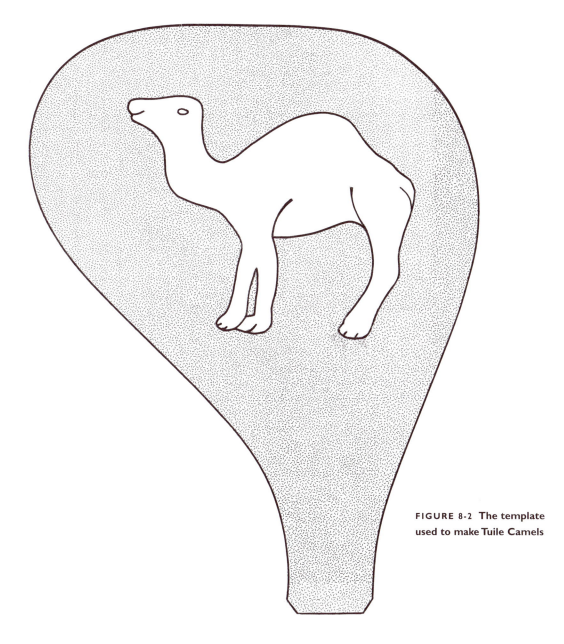

FIGURE 8-2 The template
used to make Tuile Camels

TUILE CAMELS

Follow the recipe for Tuile Polar Bears, page 398, using the camel template (Figure 8-2) instead.

Caramel-Centered Milk Chocolate Mousse with Black Currant Sauce

yield: 16 servings, 4 ounces (120 ml) each (Color Photo 76)

This is an interesting and unusual dessert, due to its shape and its secret caramel filling. If you cannot obtain fresh currants for garnish, you should still make the sauce — frozen black currants and black currant juice are both readily available — as the rich mousse and sweet caramel filling need the acidity the sauce provides, and the color is lovely.

This recipe is made in small oval molds, 1½ inches (3.7 cm) in height. Lining the insides of the molds with strips of acetate cut 2½ inches (6.2 cm) wide makes them the proper height to hold 4 ounces (120 ml) filling. This is a good trick to keep in mind should you want to increase the volume or height of a molded pastry or dessert, especially one in which the top must be perfectly flat. Any mold of approximately the same size and volume can be substituted here as long as the forms can be filled all the way to the top so the surface can be spread level.

1 Ribbon-Pattern Decorated Sponge Sheet (page 672)

½ recipe Fortified Caramel Sauce (page 19)

Orange–Milk Chocolate Mousse (page 410)

Red Currant Glaze (page 777)

Black Currant Sauce (recipe follows)

16 Miniature Tulips (page 716)

16 small clusters fresh red, black, and/or white currants

16 Chocolate Corkscrews (page 518)

16 small mint leaves

Fresh black currants

Powdered sugar

1. Line 16 oval molds, 2½ inches (6.2 cm) long × 1¾ inches (4.5 cm) wide, and 1½ inches (3.7 cm) in height, with acetate strips cut to 7¼ × 2½ inches (18.1 × 6.2 cm).

2. Cut 16 strips from the ribbon sponge, 1¼ inches (3.1 cm) wide and long enough to fit snugly inside the molds. Place the sponge strips in the molds with the decorative side against the plastic and the ends meeting in the center on 1 long side.

3. Use a plain oval cookie cutter the same size as the molds (if unavailable, you can easily make one from a round cutter by bending it to size) to cut out 16 pieces from the remainder of the sponge sheet. Place a sponge piece in the bottom of each lined mold. Cover and refrigerate.

4. Place a portion of the caramel sauce in a piping bottle with a large opening. Reserve in the refrigerator.

5. Make the chocolate mousse filling and place it in a pastry bag with a No. 6 (12-mm) plain tip. Pipe the filling into the prepared molds, filling them three-quarters full. Working quickly with a melon ball cutter dipped in water to keep it from sticking, make a small indentation, about the size of a Bing cherry, in the center on the surface of the filling in each mold. If the filling is too soft to hold its shape, wait a few minutes before scooping out the hollows.

6. Pipe caramel sauce into each indentation. Pipe the remaining chocolate filling on top to fill the molds. Spread the tops level with a palette knife or scraper, pressing hard enough against the filling to eliminate air bubbles, which would be visible on the exposed portion of the sides above the sponge in the finished pastries. Cover and place in the freezer for at least 2 hours or, preferably, overnight.

7. Remove as many desserts from the freezer as you anticipate needing for service. Spread a thin layer of red currant glaze on each. Return the desserts to the freezer for a few minutes to set the glaze. Remove the forms and peel away the plastic strips. Place the desserts in the refrigerator; they need a minimum of 30 minutes there to thaw to the proper texture.

8. Presentation: Place a dessert on the upper left side of the base on a dessert plate. Spoon black currant sauce in front of the mousse. Place a miniature tulip to the right of the dessert and arrange clusters of fresh currants inside. Lean a chocolate corkscrew against the left side of the mousse. Decorate the right side of the dessert with a mint leaf and 1 or 2 black currants. Lightly sift powdered sugar over the front part of the plate. Serve immediately.

BLACK CURRANT SAUCE yield: 4 cups (960 ml)

If you use fresh currants, remove the stems before weighing the berries. If fresh berries are unavailable, use IQF frozen berries, which are stemless and do not contain sugar. Do not thaw the berries before weighing; once thawed, the juice separates and collects at the bottom of the container.

2 pounds (910 g) fresh or frozen black currants

About ¾ cup (180 ml) dry white wine

1 tablespoon (8 g) cornstarch

10 ounces (285 g) granulated sugar

1. Puree the currants, strain through a fine mesh strainer, and discard the solids. You should have close to 2¼ cups (540 ml) juice; add wine if needed to make this amount.

2. Dissolve the cornstarch in ¾ cup (180 ml) wine. Place the currant juice and the cornstarch mixture in a nonreactive saucepan, add the sugar, and bring to a boil, stirring to dissolve the sugar. Remove from the heat.

3. Let the sauce cool, then adjust the consistency as needed by adding wine. The sauce should be thick enough to form a puddle but should not run out around the berries. Store the sauce, covered, in the refrigerator.

Chocolate Dome Cake with Cherry Sauce and Chocolate Lace

yield: 16 servings (Color Photo 73 and back jacket)

For several years, I have had the honor of participating in an event called Chefs' Holidays, held each year at the beautiful Ahwahnee Hotel in Yosemite National Park. A few years ago, I was partnered with Master Chef Roland Henin — the corporate chef for the company responsible for the kitchens at the Ahwahnee and other national park hotels — and Hubert Keller, chef and co-owner of San Francisco's celebrated Fleur de Lys restaurant. Given such illustrious colleagues, I knew I had to come up with something extra-special, even though the guest count at these five-course dinners is usually around 200, which can be limiting.

I decided on the chocolate dome cake not only because it has a wonderful hazelnut chocolate flavor and can be prepped ahead of time, but because the dome shape is both trendy and a practical choice for a cake to be covered with chocolate glaze. For the event, however, I changed the presentation slightly. Instead of glazing the domes, I sprayed them with chocolate (see page 556) immediately after removing them from the Flexipans rather than letting them sit at room temperature, as directed in Step 5 here. When chocolate spray is applied to a frozen dessert, it crystallizes, creating an interesting velvet finish. I removed the desserts from the refrigerator long enough before they were served so the filling inside the crispy chocolate shell had time to soften, creating a wonderful contrast in textures. I presented the plates with half of each dome covered with chocolate sauce and a spoonful of cherry sauce placed in front. I called the dessert *Chocolate Half Dome* on the menu in honor of the famous cliff in the park.

Devil's Food Cake batter, prepared through Step 2 (recipe follows)

½ cup (120 ml) syrup from Guinettes cherries

Gianduja Cream Filling (recipe follows)

48 Guinettes cherries

Dark Chocolate Glaze (recipe follows)

Guinettes Cherry Sauce (page 388)

Chocolate Fans (page 521)

Edible gold leaf

Chocolate Lace Decorations (page 525)

1. Line the bottom of a half-sheet pan (12 × 16 inches/30 × 40 cm) with a Silpat or a sheet of baking paper. Spread slightly less than half of the cake batter evenly into the pan; it should be approximately ⅛ inch (3 mm) thick. Pour the remaining batter into a round cake pan, 10 inches (25 cm) in diameter, lined on the bottom with a round of baking paper. Bake the sheet at 425°F (219°C) for approximately 6 minutes and the round cake at 375° (190°C) for approximately 15 minutes, or until both cakes are baked through. Let cool.

2. Invert the cake sheet, peel the Silpat or baking paper from the back, and cut out 16 rounds, 2¾ inches (7 cm) in diameter. Unmold the round cake, peel away the baking paper, and invert again. Trim enough from the top of the cake to make the remaining layer ¾ inch (2 cm) thick. Cut sixteen 1½-inch (3.7-cm) squares from the round cake layer. Reserve the scrap pieces of cake for another use, if desired.

3. Brush the Guinettes cherry syrup lightly over each of the cake pieces. Cover and set aside.

4. Pipe the gianduja filling into Flexipan No. 1268 (see Note), filling 16 indentations halfway. Working quickly, place 3 brandied cherries on top of the filling in each mold. Set a cake square on top of the cherries and press into the filling firmly enough so the filling is forced up all around the cake square and the top of the cake is well below the top of the mold. Pipe the remaining filling into the molds, dividing it evenly. Level the tops of the filling. Place a cake circle on top of the filling in each mold, moistened side down. Place the pan in the freezer for at least 1 hour to allow the filling to set.

5. Push the frozen desserts out of the Flexipan and place them, flat-side down, on an icing rack set over a sheet pan lined with baking paper. Let the desserts stand at room temperature for approximately 30 minutes before proceeding with Step 6, or refrigerate them if you will not be glazing the desserts within that time. The desserts can be refrigerated overnight with no loss of quality. While the dome cakes are easiest to remove from the molds when frozen solid, if you attempt to apply the glaze immediately after unmolding them, the glaze will freeze before it can flow down and coat the desserts evenly.

6. Warm the chocolate glaze as needed to bring it to a thin consistency. Spoon the glaze over the desserts, shaking the rack gently from time to time, to produce a thin, even coating and to ensure the desserts are completely covered. Allow the glaze to set partially, then remove the desserts and place them on paper-lined sheet pans until needed.

7. Presentation: Spoon cherry sauce in a random pattern around the circumference of a dessert plate, leaving a small empty space in the center. Using a palette knife, place a dome cake in the center of the plate. Carefully push a chocolate fan into the back of the dome. Attach a small piece of gold leaf in front of the fan. Lean a chocolate lace decoration against the side of the dessert.

NOTE: Flexipan No. 1268 has dome-shaped indentations that are 4 ounces (120 ml) in capacity and measure approximately 2¾ inches (7 cm) across the opening. If these molds are not available, use any other mold or form of a similar size and volume. Adjust the size of the cake circles used to cover the tops of the molds after they are filled. If you use nonflexible molds, you will need to dip the outside of the forms briefly in hot water to release the desserts.

DEVIL'S FOOD CAKE yield: I layer, 10 inches (25 cm) in diameter

10 ounces (280 g) granulated sugar

2 ounces (55 g) unsweetened cocoa powder

4 ounces (115 g) bread flour

4 ounces (115 g) cake flour

1 teaspoon (4 g) baking soda

1 teaspoon (4 g) baking powder

3 eggs

1 cup (240 ml) buttermilk

1 cup (240 ml) sour cream

6 ounces (170 g) unsalted butter, melted

4 ounces (115 g) finely grated raw purple beets

I. Sift together the sugar, cocoa powder, bread flour, cake flour, baking soda, and baking powder. Set aside.

2. Beat the eggs for 1 minute. Stir in the buttermilk and sour cream. Add the reserved dry ingredients, mixing until well combined and smooth. Mix in the melted butter and the beets.

3. Pour the batter into a round cake pan, 10 inches (25 cm) in diameter, lined with a round of baking paper. Level the top of the batter. Bake at 350°F (175°C) for approximately 40 minutes or until the cake springs back when pressed lightly in the center. Allow the cake to cool completely before unmolding. Frost with chocolate frosting or whipped cream.

GIANDUJA CREAM FILLING yield: approximately 6 cups (I L 440 ml)

3 ounces (85 g) sweet dark chocolate

1 ounce (30 g) unsweetened chocolate

8 ounces (225 g) gianduja chocolate

2 cups (480 ml) heavy cream

3 ounces (85 g) toasted macadamia nuts, coarsely chopped

I. Cut all 3 types of chocolate into small pieces, place in a bowl over a bain-marie, and stir constantly until melted. Be careful not to overheat.

2. Whip the heavy cream until it is thick enough to drop in a stream from the whisk but will hold a peak. It should be as thick as eggs whipped to the ribbon stage.

3. Place approximately half of the cream in a separate bowl and, stirring vigorously (not whisking) with a whisk, add all of the melted chocolate to the cream to temper it. Still working quickly, stir in the remaining cream, followed by the macadamia nuts. Continue to stir with the whisk as needed until the filling is thick enough to hold its shape.

DARK CHOCOLATE GLAZE yield: 4 cups (960 ml)

1 pound (455 g) sweet dark chocolate, chopped

10 ounces (225 g) unsalted butter, at room temperature

½ cup (120 ml) or 6 ounces (170 g) light corn syrup

2 tablespoons (30 ml) orange liqueur

I. Melt the chocolate over a bain-marie. Remove from the heat, add the butter, and stir until fully incorporated.

2. Stir in the corn syrup and the liqueur. Cool, stirring occasionally, until the glaze has a spreadable consistency.

Chocolate Marquise with Passion Fruit Parfait and a Lace Cookie Bouquet yield: 12 servings (Color Photo 82)

Like the Blueberry Financier (page 380), this dessert was created for *A Modernist View of Plated Desserts*. Chocolate Marquise is a classic that few consumers can resist. Here, I have dressed up the original components for a more modern look. I have advocated this idea for many years: Isolate the essential elements of a time-honored favorite and build on them to create a presentation with the grandeur demanded in today's competitive fine dining restaurants. You will see many examples of this premise in this chapter and throughout this book. Two illustrations are Crème Caramel Nouvelle (page 342) and Cappuccino Mousse with Sambuca Cream in a Chocolate Coffee Cup (page 328). Both recipes start with traditional desserts — crème caramel and chocolate mousse are about as basic as you can get, and neither is exciting to look at in its conventional presentation — and transform them into dessert spectaculars.

As important as appearance is, a dessert's practicality of production is equally important. This depends on the particular kitchen, the skill level of the chef, the price that can be charged, the client base, and, to some degree, the number of servings to be made. It is one thing to produce a relatively time-consuming dessert (as this one no doubt is) for a party of twelve or as part of a menu offering several items for the guest to choose from, but it is a different matter to make it in large quantity for a banquet. For a large party, you will most likely have to scale down somewhat, using only one chocolate cigarette (or eliminating the cigarettes altogether), and a simplified tuile decoration instead of the cookie bouquets.

Chocolate Marquise Filling (recipe follows)	**Passion Fruit Coulis (recipe follows)**
Ribbon-Pattern Decorated Sponge Sheet (page 672; see Chef's Tip)	**Passion Fruit Parfait (page 220)**
12 Lace Cookie Bouquets (page 723)	**Chocolate Cigarettes (page 516)**
Powdered sugar	

1. Cut 2 rectangles, 22 × 5½ inches (55 × 13.7 cm), from acetate or polyurethane. Use the sheets to line the insides of 2 plastic pipes, 22 inches (55 cm) long and with openings 1¼ inches (3.1 cm) in diameter (see Note 1). Cap 1 end of each pipe.

2. Arrange the pipes standing vertically, with the capped ends on the bottom, and support them so they stand straight on their own. The pipes should be set low enough to allow you to see into the interior. Place a portion of the Marquise filling in a pastry bag with a No. 6 (12-mm) plain tip and pipe the filling straight down into the bottom of one tube; try to avoid hitting the side of the tube with the filling. Tap lightly to remove air pockets and continue to add more filling to the pastry bag and to the tubes until both tubes are filled to the top. Cover the open ends and refrigerate until the filling is set, at least 2 hours. Reserve the remaining filling.

3. Cut the decorated sponge into 2 pieces, each 22 inches (55 cm) long and approximately 5½ inches (13.7 cm) wide, or wide enough to wrap around the chocolate tubes. Soften the reserved filling to a sticky consistency, if necessary, then invert the sponge pieces and spread a thin layer of filling over the sheets; you will have filling left over.

4. Remove the chocolate tubes from the pipes. If the pipes were lined with baking paper rather than plastic, shake them gently until you can pull out the chocolate by the baking paper (see Note 2). Peel off the plastic or baking paper. Place each chocolate tube on top of a prepared sponge sheet. Roll 1 complete turn to cover each chocolate tube with sponge. Trim 1 long edge of the sponge sheets, if necessary; the long edges should meet with no gap but should not overlap.

5. Using a sharp, thin knife dipped in hot water, trim the end of 1 tube, then cut it into 6 equal pieces; alternate between a 45-degree cut and a 90-degree cut each time so the finished pieces have 1 flat side and 1 angled side. Repeat with the second tube. Stand the servings on their flat ends on a sheet pan lined with baking paper; cover and refrigerate until needed. If you do not anticipate needing all 12 servings at once, cut only the number of servings required.

6. Presentation: Place a Marquise in the center of a serving plate. Spread a small amount of reserved filling underneath the chocolate base of a lace cookie bouquet and carefully attach to the angled top of the Marquise. Sift powdered sugar over the dessert and the base of the serving plate. Spoon passion fruit coulis into 3 pools around the Marquise. Place a small scoop of passion fruit parfait to the right of the Marquise. Decorate the top of the Marquise and the parfait scoop with 4 chocolate cigarettes. Serve immediately.

NOTE 1: If plastic is not available, use baking paper to line the tubes, preferably the thicker grade. Cut the paper about 1 inch (2.5 cm) longer and attach the protruding end to the outside of the pipe to secure it. To avoid catching the filling on the paper, which will wrinkle the paper and pull it out of place, pay attention when piping the filling into the tubes.

NOTE 2: If the chocolate tubes stick and are difficult to remove, place them in the freezer. They will shrink slightly as they harden and become easier to remove.

CHOCOLATE MARQUISE FILLING yield: 6 cups (1 L 440 ml)

Do not make this filling until you are ready to use it.

10 ounces (285 g) sweet dark chocolate

2 ounces (55 g) unsweetened chocolate

1¾ cups (420 ml) heavy cream

3 egg yolks (¼ cup/60 ml)

2 ounces (55 g) granulated sugar

¼ cup (60 ml) or 3 ounces (85 g) honey

2 tablespoons (30 ml) Frangelico liqueur

1. Chop the sweet and unsweetened chocolates into small chunks. Place in a bowl set over simmering water and melt together. Set aside; keep warm.

2. Whip the heavy cream until soft peaks form.

3. Whip the egg yolks with the sugar for about 2 minutes; the mixture should be light and fluffy. Bring the honey to a boil and gradually whip it into the egg yolks. Continue whipping until cooled completely.

4. Fold in the reserved chocolate and the Frangelico liqueur. Quickly stir in the whipped cream.

PASSION FRUIT COULIS yield: approximately ¾ cup (180 ml)

12 ripe passion fruit	About ¼ cup simple syrup

1. Cut the passion fruit in half and scoop out the pulp and seeds, taking care not to include any of the reddish-white pith.

2. Add enough simple syrup to sweeten to taste. Cover and refrigerate until needed.

Cocoa Nib–White Chocolate Ice Cream with a Chocolate Lace Igloo and Tuile Polar Bear yield: 16 servings (Color Photo 83)

This whimsical dessert is sure to bring a smile to anyone who sees it. Color Photo 83 shows a variation in which the polar bear was handmade from marzipan rather than shaped from tuile paste. This is not practical for most operations, but if you have experience in working with marzipan, you might want to try it for a special occasion. Another option is to press the bears out of marzipan using a mold, which does not require modeling skill. To simplify the presentation, you can eliminate the polar bear and instead center the chocolate igloo on the plate on top of the ice cream. You will still have an interesting and unusual dessert.

Cocoa Nib–White Chocolate Ice Cream (recipe follows)	Kumquat Compote (recipe follows)
Cocoa Nib Wafer Paste (page 720)	16 small mint sprigs
Sponge cake	16 Chocolate Lace Igloos (page 526)
16 Tuile Polar Bears (recipe follows)	½ recipe Kumquat Sauce (page 145)
Dark coating chocolate, melted	Powdered sugar

1. Spread the ice cream on a sheet pan lined with baking paper to make a 14-inch (35-cm) square; the ice cream should be approximately ½ inch (1.2 cm) thick. Cover and place in the freezer for at least 2 hours.

2. Dip a plain cookie cutter, 3½ inches (8.7 cm) in diameter, into hot water and cut out 16 rounds of ice cream from the frozen sheet. Cover the rounds and return them to the freezer until needed. Combine the ice cream scraps; cover them and place in the freezer for another use.

3. Divide the cocoa-nib wafer paste evenly between 2 sheet pans lined with baking paper. Spread the paste into rectangles, 14 × 18 inches (35 × 45 cm). The paste will be very thin and pieces of cocoa nib will make a few holes, but these will fill in during baking.

4. Bake 1 sheet at a time at 350°F (175°C) until caramelized. Remove from the oven, wait a few seconds to cool very slightly, then carefully slide the baking paper off the sheet pan and onto a sheet of corrugated cardboard. Working quickly and using the same 3½-inch (8.7-cm) cutter, cut out 18 to 20 rounds. Bake the second sheet and transfer to a cardboard sheet in the same manner. Cut out approximately 20 wedges, 5 to 6 inches (12.5 to 15

CHEF'S TIP
Several products on the market will, with the press of a button, deliver a spray of frozen air to immediately set and harden melted chocolate (or sugar). This eliminates the need to chill dessert plates and decorations and cuts way down on the time needed to hold the decorations in place until the chocolate (or sugar) hardens.

cm) in height, plus approximately 35 additional wedges a few inches smaller. This will give you extra in case of breakage. If the baked cocoa sheets become too firm to cut without breaking, reheat them as needed while you are working. Remove the scrap pieces from both sheets and reserve for another use. Store the wedges and rounds in an airtight container until needed.

5. Cut 16 paper-thin slices of sponge cake that will fit under the ice cream disks without showing. Cover and set aside.

6. Chill as many dessert plates, tuile polar bears, and cocoa-nib wafer wedges as you will need: 1 large and 2 small wedges per serving. Do not refrigerate the wedges or cookies for more than 30 minutes, or they will soften (see Chef's Tip, page 396).

CHEF'S TIP

Another way to make the cocoa-nib wedges stand on end is to start by placing them in the freezer for a few minutes. While they are chilling, pipe out small ovals of tempered dark chocolate on a sheet of baking paper. Wait until the ovals begin to set, then place the wide end of a cocoa-nib wedge in the chocolate, holding it vertical for a few seconds until it can stand on its own. Repeat with the remaining wedges. Attach the wedges to the dessert plate with a drop of melted chocolate or a bit of ganache.

7. Presentation: Place melted coating chocolate in a piping bag and pipe 3 short, thick lines over the upper right side on the base of a dessert plate. Place 1 large and 2 smaller cocoa-nib wedges on the chocolate lines and hold them straight up (so they suggest giant ice blocks or glaciers) until the chocolate hardens. Place a sponge round on the left side of the plate. Set an ice cream round on the sponge. Top the ice cream with a round cocoa-nib wafer. Spoon a small portion of kumquat compote on top of the wafer and decorate with a sprig of mint. Using the tip of a paring knife, carefully lift a chocolate igloo and place it over the wafer on the ice cream. Pipe 2 dots of chocolate between the igloo and the upright wedges. Attach a tuile polar bear to the plate on the chocolate dots and hold for a few seconds until it can stand on its own. Pipe dots of kumquat sauce in a curved line, starting with large dots next to the igloo and gradually making them smaller as you continue. Sift powdered sugar over the entire plate and serve immediately.

COCOA NIB–WHITE CHOCOLATE ICE CREAM yield: 9 cups (2 L 160 ml)

Cocoa nibs are produced in one of the first stages of chocolate manufacturing. After whole cocoa beans are roasted, they are crushed and the shells or husks are removed; the small roasted kernels of cocoa bean that remain are called *nibs*. Many more steps must be completed to transform these into finished chocolate, but added as is to ice cream, cake batter, or decorating paste, cocoa nibs contribute an intense roasted chocolate flavor and a pleasant crunchy texture. Cocoa nibs can be purchased from most large chocolate purveyors.

Because of the white chocolate in the recipe, it is important not to overchurn the ice cream, or the texture can become gritty and the ice cream unusable.

4½ cups (1 L 80 ml) half-and-half

3 cups (720 ml) heavy cream

12 egg yolks (1 cup/240 ml)

4 ounces (115 g) granulated sugar

12 ounces (340 g) white chocolate, cut into small chunks

4 ounces (115 g) cocoa nibs

1. Combine the half-and-half and cream and heat to scalding.

2. Beat the egg yolks with the sugar until light and fluffy. Gradually whisk in the hot cream.

3. Place over simmering water and heat, stirring constantly with a whisk or wooden spoon (do not whip), until the custard is thick enough to coat the spoon.

4. Remove from the heat and add the white chocolate, continuing to stir until all of the chunks are melted. Let cool to room temperature, then refrigerate until completely cold.

5. Process in an ice cream freezer according to the manufacturer's directions. Remove the ice cream from the ice cream freezer just before it is fully churned and thickened; it should be too soft to scoop out. Transfer to a chilled bowl, stir in the cocoa nibs, cover, and place in the freezer. The ice cream will become firmer once frozen. If allowed to freeze completely while churning, the texture could be compromised.

KUMQUAT COMPOTE yield: approximately 1 cup (240 ml)

6 ounces (170 g) fresh kumquats	⅓ cup (80 ml) water
3 ounces (85 g) granulated sugar	¼ cup (60 ml) Kumquat Sauce (page 145)

1. Wash the kumquats and slice thinly. Remove the seeds and place the slices in a saucepan with the sugar and water. Cook over low heat until the slices are soft, about 10 minutes.

2. Strain off and discard the syrup. Stir the kumquat sauce into the cooked kumquat slices.

N O T E : If kumquats are unavailable, substitute another fruit, such as cherries or oranges, using the same fruit for the sauce as well.

TUILE POLAR BEARS yield: 24 decorations

¼ recipe Vanilla Tuile Decorating Paste (page 695)	½ teaspoon (2.5 ml) unsweetened cocoa powder

1. Trace the polar bear template shown in Figure 8-3, then cut it out of cardboard that is ¹⁄₁₆ inch (2 mm) thick; cake boxes work fine. The template, as shown, is the correct size for use in this recipe.

2. If you do not have Silpats, grease and flour the backs of 2 flat, even sheet pans.

3. Place 1 tablespoon (15 ml) of the tuile paste in a small container. Thoroughly mix in the cocoa powder and place in a piping bag.

4. Spread the plain tuile paste on Silpats or prepared sheet pans, spreading it flat and even within the template (see Figures 13-29 and 13-30, page 694).

5. Cut a small opening in the piping bag; pipe the eyes, ears, tail, mouth, and lines to indicate the legs on each bear, as shown in the drawing.

6. Bake at 400°F (205°C) for approximately 6 minutes or until the cookies just begin to turn light brown in a few spots. Let cool on the pans and become crisp. Remove and store in airtight containers.

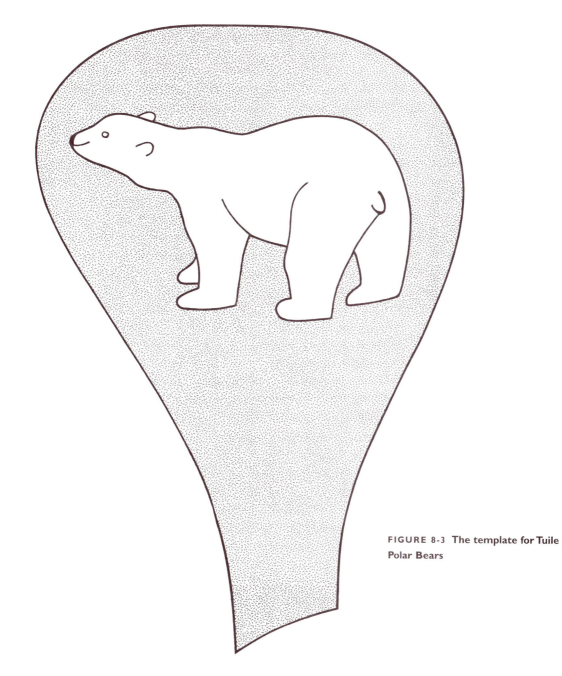

FIGURE 8-3 The template for Tuile Polar Bears

Coconut Ice Cream in a Red Pepper Tuile with Strawberry Salsa and Tomatillo Lace yield: 12 servings (Color Photo 75)

This contemporary dessert features an entertaining presentation — few people have seen the lace tomatillo decorations before — and it combines compatible flavors with a southwestern twist. The red bell pepper shells are unusual and can be served with other accompaniments, such as tropical ice creams or sorbets, to add interest to your menu. The red pepper batter also can be used to make decorations in a similar way to tuile paste; one such variation follows the recipe below and another, Red Pepper Sails, is on page 726. The batter is too thin, however, to use with a template as you would tuile paste.

½ recipe Kiwi Sauce (page 309)

Piping chocolate (page 543), melted

12 Red Pepper Shells (recipe follows)

Strawberry Salsa (recipe follows)

Fresh Coconut Ice Cream (page 214)

12 Tomatillo Lace Decorations (page 728)

Powdered sugar

1. Place the kiwi sauce in a piping bottle. Place as many dessert plates as you anticipate needing in the refrigerator.

2. Presentation: Pipe a large pool of piping chocolate in the center of a chilled dessert plate. Place a red pepper shell on top and hold it, tilted at a slight angle toward the front of the plate, until the chocolate hardens (see Chef's Tip on page 396). Spoon 3 or 4 pools of salsa on the base of the plate around the shell. Pipe kiwi sauce in a random pattern between the salsa pools. Carefully, so as not to damage the fragile shell, place a scoop of coconut ice cream inside it. Place a tomatillo decoration on top of the ice cream. Sift powdered sugar on the plate in front of the dessert and serve immediately.

RED PEPPER SHELLS yield: variable

2 medium-sized red bell peppers

Vegetable oil

2 ounces (55 g) powdered sugar, sifted

2 teaspoons (5 g) bread flour

1. Coat the peppers with vegetable oil and place them on a sheet pan. Use a blowtorch to blacken the skin, turning the peppers to cook all sides. If you are making more than a single recipe, roast the peppers at 450°F (230°C) until blackened, turning them once or twice.

2. Wrap the peppers in a moist towel or place in a plastic bag; set aside to cool to room temperature.

3. Peel the peppers and remove the seeds and stems. Puree the roasted pepper flesh in a food processor, then force the puree through a strainer (you want both pulp and juice so do not use a very fine strainer). Stir the powdered sugar and flour into the puree.

4. Have ready 1 or, preferably, 2 ladles, each 6 to 8 ounces (180 to 240 ml) in capacity. Also have 1 or 2 small oranges or grapefruit that fit loosely inside the ladles (chilling the fruit makes the shells harden more quickly) and a container close to the same height as the length of the ladle handles (a round bain-marie insert usually works). Hook the ladles over the top of the container so their bowls are resting on the table as level as possible (see Figure 13-20, page 688, as an example).

5. Spread the batter on Silpats in thin, even rounds, approximately 7 inches (17.5 cm) in diameter. Bake at 200° to 250°F (94° to 108°C) until the batter is dry and light brown in a few spots. Using a wide caulking spatula, pick up the pieces 1 at a time and place inside a prepared ladle. Use the chilled fruit to carefully press the baked batter into the ladle, creating a free-form shell. Repeat until you have made a few more shells than you need. Store the finished shells in an airtight container.

Red Pepper Decorations

1. Make the batter as directed above.

2. Spread the batter onto Silpats in a thin, even layer, making free-form shapes of approximately 2 × 3 inches (5 × 7.5 cm). Bake as directed above.

3. As soon as they come out of the oven, use a spatula to transfer the decorations to a flat surface to cool; be careful, as they are quite fragile. If desired, the warm decorations may be molded in the same way as tuile paste. Store as directed above.

STRAWBERRY SALSA yield: approximately 3 cups (720 ml)

2 pounds 8 ounces (1 kg 135 g) or approximately 3 pints (1 L 440 ml) strawberries

½ cup (120 ml) orange liqueur

½ cup (120 ml) simple syrup

¼ cup (60 ml) water

2 teaspoons (8 g) cornstarch

1. Wash and hull the strawberries. Cut them into small, even-sized wedges or cubes.

2. Place the strawberries in a bowl and add the liqueur, simple syrup, and water. Toss to combine and to coat the fruit pieces with the liquid. Set aside to macerate for 1 to 2 hours (see Chef's Tip).

3. Remove a small amount of syrup from the strawberries and mix it into the cornstarch to make a slurry.

4. Place the remaining strawberry mixture in a saucepan, bring to a boil, lower the heat, and simmer for 1 to 2 minutes, stirring constantly. Strain, return the syrup to the pan, and set the strawberries aside. Add the cornstarch slurry to the syrup and bring to a boil while stirring. Remove from the heat and add the strawberries. Serve warm.

CHEF'S TIP

The strawberries should be prepped and macerated the same day they will be served; letting them sit longer than 2 hours can adversely affect their appearance and texture. At the same time, they do need at least 1 hour to absorb the flavor of the liqueur and to impart their flavor and color to the syrup.

Espresso Chocolate Cake with Coffee-Bean Crisps

yield: 16 servings (Color Photo 87)

Espresso Chocolate Cake may be simplified easily and without sacrificing overall appeal by using a single coffee-bean crescent made in a size between the large and small sizes specified here. Place the cookie with the points inserted into the cake as directed, or place it upside down for a different look. Eliminating the sugar stick as well means you will not have to make holes in the crescents. Raspberry sauce can take the place of the cherry compote, and many flavors of ice cream will complement the dish if the black pepper frozen yogurt does not appeal to you; vanilla, almond, and cinnamon are all good choices. Espresso Chocolate Cake can be baked in Flexipan No. 1897, in which case you should not use a bain-marie. Chill or freeze the cakes and then simply push them out of the Flexipan forms, turning each indentation inside out. If the cakes are frozen, thaw before serving.

Melted unsalted butter

1 pound 2 ounces (510 g) sweet dark chocolate

¾ cup (180 ml) brewed espresso coffee

12 ounces (340 g) granulated sugar

12 ounces (340 g) unsalted butter, melted

8 eggs

10 ounces (285 g) blanched almonds, finely ground

Coffee-Bean Crisps (recipe follows)

Powdered sugar

Sugar Sticks (page 595)

Cherry Compote (page 149)

Black Pepper Frozen Yogurt (recipe follows)

Mint sprigs

I. Cut out 8 squares of aluminum foil measuring 6½ inches (15.2 cm). Set a cake ring, 3 inches (7.5 cm) in diameter and 2 inches (5 cm) in height, in the center of each square. Fold and pleat the edges of the foil up around the rings to make a tight seal. Be certain that the foil reaches at least three-quarters of the way up the sides of the rings because the cakes will be baked in a water bath. Place the rings in a shallow pan. Brush melted butter inside the rings and over the bottom of the foil inside. Set the pan aside. The cakes can also be baked using Flexipan No. 1897, in which case, skip this step and simply place the Flexipan on a flat, even sheet pan.

2. Cut the chocolate into small pieces. Bring the espresso coffee and 8 ounces (225 g) of the granulated sugar to a boil. Remove from the heat and stir in the chocolate, continuing to stir until the chocolate is completely melted and thoroughly incorporated. Gradually add the butter and stir until blended. Set aside at room temperature.

3. Whip the eggs and the remaining 4 ounces (115 g) granulated sugar at high speed until light and fluffy, about 3 minutes. Take care not to incorporate too much air, as this will make the finished cakes crumbly and difficult to work with. Gently fold the melted chocolate mixture into the egg mixture. Fold in the ground almonds. Pour the batter into the prepared cake rings, dividing it equally among them. Pour enough hot water into the pan around the rings to reach about ½ inch (1.2 cm) up the sides.

4. Bake immediately at 350°F (175°C) for approximately 30 minutes or until the tops of the cakes feel firm. Remove from the water bath, allow to cool slightly, then refrigerate for a least 1 hour or, preferably, overnight.

5. Presentation: Unmold as many desserts as you anticipate serving. Using a thin, sharp knife, cut a cross on top of 1 cake, slicing down about one-third of the height. Stand a small round coffee-bean crisp in the center with the slit facing straight up. Place a small crescent at a 90-degree angle, securing it in the slit. Place a large crescent at a 90-degree angle on top; gently push it down and secure it in the slit of the small crescent. Place the cake in the center of a dessert plate, making sure the decoration stands straight. Sift powdered sugar over the cake and the base of the plate; wipe off any sugar that gets on the rim. Warm a sugar stick and thread through the holes in the larger coffee bean crescent so it curves above it. Spoon cherry compote into 3 pools evenly spaced around the cake. Place a small scoop of frozen yogurt in each pool. Garnish with small mint sprigs. Serve immediately.

BLACK PEPPER FROZEN YOGURT yield: 5 cups (1 L 200 ml)

Don't expect a sharp bite here. The pepper adds just a hint of spiciness that contrasts nicely with the sweet coolness of the frozen yogurt. This yogurt pairs especially well with cherry sauce and cherry desserts.

6 ounces (170 g) granulated sugar	2 eggs, separated
4 ounces (115 g) honey	4 cups (960 ml) unflavored yogurt
2 teaspoons (10 ml) lemon juice	1 teaspoon (5 ml) coarsely ground black pepper
2 teaspoons (10 ml) vanilla extract	

1. Place half of the sugar, the honey, and the lemon juice in a saucepan. Bring to a boil and cook for 1 minute. Remove the syrup from the heat and add the vanilla.

2. Beat the egg yolks, stir in some of the hot sugar syrup to temper them, then stir in the remaining syrup. Let cool to room temperature.

3. Whip the egg whites until foamy. Gradually add the remaining sugar and whip to stiff peaks.

4. Place the yogurt in a bowl and stir with a whisk until smooth. Stir in the pepper. Fold in the syrup and the egg yolk mixture. Fold in the whipped egg whites.

5. Process in an ice cream freezer following the manufacturer's directions. Store, covered, in the freezer.

COFFEE-BEAN CRISPS yield: variable

1 ounce (30 g) whole roasted coffee beans	6 ounces (170 g) granulated sugar
8 ounces (225 g) sliced blanched almonds	3 tablespoons (45 ml) light corn syrup
7 ounces (200 g) unsalted butter	¼ cup (60 ml) heavy cream

1. Use a rolling pin to finely crush the coffee beans. Separately crush the sliced almonds.

2. Combine the butter, sugar, corn syrup, and cream in a saucepan. Bring to a boil, then stir in the crushed coffee beans and almonds. Cook over medium heat for 3 minutes, stirring constantly. Remove the batter from the heat.

3. Bake a spoonful of the batter on a sheet pan lined with baking paper or on a Silpat at 375°F (190°) to test it. If the batter spreads too thin, return the saucepan to the heat and boil a little longer. If the batter does not spread enough, add 1 to 2 tablespoons (15 to 30 ml) heavy cream and heat, stirring to combine. Test again and correct as needed.

4. While the batter is still warm, use 2 spoons to divide it into 18 equal portions between 2 sheet pans lined with baking paper, flattening and spreading the batter into rounds approximately 4 inches (10 cm) in diameter. Wet the spoons as necessary to keep the batter from sticking.

5. Bake at 375°F (190°C) for approximately 10 minutes or until light brown, baking 1 pan at a time so you have time to cut out the shapes before the cookies harden.

6. Have ready 3 plain cookie cutters, approximately 4½ inches (11.2 cm), 2½ inches (6.2 cm), and 1¼ inches (3.1 cm) in diameter. Also have on hand a small plain piping tip, such as No. 2 (4-mm). Refer to Figure 8-4 in cutting the shapes.

7. Carefully slide the baking paper off the sheet pan and onto a sheet of corrugated cardboard. If you are using a Silpat, you can leave it on the sheet pan. Wait a few seconds after removing the first pan from the oven, then use the largest cutter to cut out a cookie (shown as the solid outline in the drawing). Using the medium cutter, cut out a cookie centered at the bottom of the large cookie, transforming the large cookie into a crescent (shown as the larger round broken line in the drawing). Center the smallest cutter at the bottom of the medium cookie and cut out a round cookie, (shown as the smaller round broken line in the drawing) making the medium cookie a crescent. Quickly repeat to cut the remaining cookies, warming the whole cookies as needed to keep them from breaking as they are cut. Repeat with the second pan.

8. Once the cut cookies have cooled and become hard and crisp, separate them; save the outside scraps for another use. Warm all of the cut pieces. Using a paring knife, cut a small wedge out of the rounds and at the top center of the smaller crescents, as shown in the drawing. Using the piping tip, cut a small hole on each side of the large crescents. Trim the edges on both sides of the large crescents (shown as the shaded area at the base of the drawing.) Store the cookie decorations in an airtight container. They will keep for up to 2 weeks.

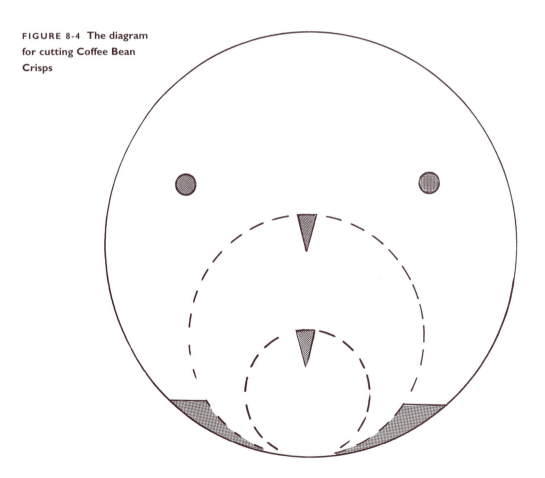

FIGURE 8-4 The diagram for cutting Coffee Bean Crisps

Frozen Lemon Mousse with Orange Syrup and a Tuile Spiral

yield: 12 servings, 4 ounces (120 ml) each (Color Photo 85)

As with many other desserts in this book, if you do not have the proper size cake rings or you do not have enough of them, it is quite simple to make forms yourself by taping together the ends of acetate strips cut to the proper length and width. To ensure the acetate rings will stand straight when placed on end, it is best to wrap the acetate around a ring or tube of the proper diameter set on an even surface. Be sure the long side of the acetate strip that will become the bottom of the mold is pressed tightly against the work surface all around before securing with tape. When using this method, keep in mind that the size of your new molds will increase by the thickness of the ring or tube used to form them. In other words, if you use a tube with a 2-inch (5-cm) opening, but the material of the tube is ¼ inch (6 mm) thick, the opening in your finished molds will actually be 2½ inches (6.2 cm) wide — 2 inches (5 cm) for the opening plus ¼ inch (6 mm) times 2 for both sides of the tube.

The addition of gelatin to this frozen mousse not only makes the dessert hold up well for large banquets (or small ones where flexibility is needed) but also gives you the option of serving the dessert merely chilled and not frozen (if you do so, don't forget to change its name). If you opt for simply chilling the mousse, you can serve these desserts as part of a pastry tray. Eliminate the sauce and garnish; instead, decorate the tops with a small rosette of whipped cream and a small slice or wedge of lemon.

In any case, it is important that the sponge rounds fit snugly inside the forms to prevent the filling from leaking out before it has set. Adjust the size of the cake rounds to match your forms.

½ recipe Joconde Sponge Base II (page 671)	1¾ cups (420 ml) heavy cream
Bread flour	Piping Chocolate (page 543)
1 tablespoon (9 g) unflavored gelatin powder	Orange-Vanilla Decorating Syrup (page 760)
½ cup (120 ml) light rum	12 Triangular Tuile Spirals (page 706)
5 lemons	Small slices of fruit and small berries
6 eggs, separated	12 small sprigs lemon verbena
8 ounces (225 g) granulated sugar	Powdered sugar
⅓ cup (80 ml) water	

1. Immediately after making the Joconde sponge base, spread it evenly over a full-sheet-sized Silpat. Bake at 400°F (205°C) for about 10 minutes or until baked through. Invert the sponge onto a sheet of baking paper dusted lightly with bread flour. Peel away the Silpat and let the sponge cool. (If you do not have a Silpat and are baking the sponge on baking paper, let the sponge cool before removing the paper.)

2. Using a cutter 2 inches (5 cm) in diameter, cut out 12 rounds of sponge (see Note). Cover the rounds. Reserve the remainder of the sponge sheet in the refrigerator or freezer for another use.

3. Line the inside of 12 plastic tubes or metal rings, 2 inches (5 cm) in diameter and 2½ inches (6.2 cm) in height, with strips of acetate. Place a sponge round in the bottom of each ring, cover, and set aside.

4. Sprinkle the gelatin over the rum. Set aside to soften.

5. Wash and finely grate the zest from 3 of the lemons. Juice all of the lemons, strain, and measure the juice. You should have approximately ¾ cup (180 ml); adjust if necessary. Add the grated zest to the juice. Reserve.

6. Beat the egg yolks with 4 ounces (115 g) of the granulated sugar to the ribbon stage. Add the lemon juice and zest. Place over a bain-marie and whip until the mixture thickens. Add the rum and softened gelatin. Cool to body temperature.

7. Combine the remaining 4 ounces (115 g) granulated sugar with the water in a saucepan. Bring to a boil and cook to 230°F (110°C; see Chef's Tip). Beat the egg whites until soft peaks form. Gradually add the sugar syrup and whip until the mixture has cooled.

8. Whip the heavy cream to soft peaks. Fold the beaten egg whites into the cooled yolk mixture, then fold in the whipped cream.

9. Quickly pipe the mousse into the prepared cake rings. Place in the freezer for at least 4 hours.

10. Using piping chocolate, pipe a wavy border on the base of as many dessert plates as you anticipate needing, making a simplified flower shape with the tips of the petals 1 inch (2.5 cm) from the perimeter of the base of the plates (see Color Photo 85). Set aside.

11. Adjust the consistency of the orange syrup as necessary so it is thick enough to hold its shape on the plate. Place the syrup in a piping bottle.

12. Presentation: Peel the acetate away from a frozen mousse serving and stand it in the center of a prepared plate. Pipe orange syrup in a thin band all around the outside of the chocolate piping. Place a tuile spiral on top of the mousse, gently pressing it into place, and garnish with fruit, berries, and a small sprig of lemon verbena. Sift powdered sugar lightly over the dessert. Serve immediately.

NOTE: If you are making your own molds from acetate, as described in the introduction, you can use them instead of a cookie cutter to cut out the sponge rounds. Simply push each plastic ring into the soft sponge; you thus cut the round and secure it in the bottom of the ring in a single step.

Lemongrass Parfait with Green Tea Syrup, Mango Wafer Orbs, and Macadamia Nuts yield: 16 servings, 4 ounces (115 g) each (Color Photo 84)

Lemongrass, known botanically as *citronella,* is a perennial grass, native to tropical parts of Asia, that grows abundantly in warm, humid climates. It has a delicate lemon flavor you may have encountered in savory Asian cooking, especially in recipes from Thailand. Because the lemongrass is used only to impart flavor here and is not an element in the final dish, it is important not to skimp on the time it infuses with the milk. For the same reason, don't be afraid of adding one or two more stalks if you have extra. For best flavor, this recipe should be started the day before it is to be served.

If you do not have ripe mangoes for the decorations, make Mango Chips (page 721) instead, as that recipe calls for firm rather than ripe mangoes.

16 thin rounds Joconde sponge (see Steps 1 and 2, page 405), a generous 2 inches (5 cm) in diameter

Lemongrass Parfait (recipe follows)

5 ounces (140 g) whole unsalted macadamia nuts

Simple syrup

16 stalks lemongrass

Green Tea Decorating Syrup (page 759)

16 Curved Tuile Wedges (page 702)

16 Mango Wafer Orbs (recipe follows)

I. Prepare 16 tubes, 2 inches (5 cm) in diameter and 2½ inches (6.2 cm) in height, by lining them with strips of acetate or, if acetate is not available, baking paper (see Note). Press the Joconde rounds inside the prepared tubes. Ideally, the cake rounds should be just slightly larger than the tubes to create a tight seal that will prevent the parfait from seeping out at the bottom before it is frozen. Place the tubes on a flat sheet pan lined with baking paper. Divide the lemongrass parfait evenly among the tubes. Cover and place in the freezer for at least 4 hours.

2. Set aside 16 whole macadamia nuts. Cut the remaining nuts into halves or quarters. Coat all of the nuts with simple syrup and strain off the excess. Spread the nut pieces on a sheet pan lined with baking paper or a Silpat. Place the whole nuts in a single layer on another prepared pan. Toast at 400°F (205°C) until golden brown.

3. Trim the lemongrass stalks to make 16 pieces appropriate for decorating. Place the green tea syrup in a piping bottle.

4. Presentation: Remove a parfait from the freezer, gently push it out of the tube, and peel away the plastic strip. Place the parfait in the center of a dessert plate. Carefully lower a tuile decoration over and around the parfait. Pipe small puddles of green tea syrup all around the base of the plate. Place a mango orb and 1 whole macadamia nut on top of the parfait. Sprinkle a few chopped nuts around the parfait and lean a lemongrass stalk against the parfait. Serve immediately.

NOTE: If you do not have tubes in the size specified here, you can use shorter tubes, as long as the acetate liners are cut to 2½ inches (6.2 cm) in height. Alternatively, you can make the tubes from acetate, as described in the recipe introduction on page 405.

LEMONGRASS PARFAIT yield: 9 cups (2 L 160 ml)

1 pound (455 g) fresh lemongrass

1½ cups (360 ml) whole milk

8 egg yolks (⅔ cup/160 ml)

1 whole egg

6 ounces (170 g) granulated sugar

1½ cups (360 ml) heavy cream

I. Cut off the narrow leafy tops as well as the root end of each stalk of lemongrass. Remove any dry, tough, or brown outer leaves. Split the stalks lengthwise and slice thinly (see Note).

2. Add the lemongrass to the milk and heat to the scalding point. Remove from the heat and pour into a bowl. Refrigerate for at least 12 hours or, preferably, overnight to infuse the milk with the flavor of the lemongrass.

3. Whip the egg yolks, whole egg, and sugar together until the mixture is pale and thick. At the same time, heat the reserved milk mixture to scalding. Strain the milk, pressing as much liquid out of the lemongrass as possible; discard the lemongrass pieces. Slightly less than 1½ cups (360 ml) milk should be left.

4. Gradually whisk the hot milk into the egg mixture. Place the bowl over a bain-marie and heat, stirring constantly, until the mixture is thick enough to coat a spoon. Do not allow to boil. Remove from the heat and whip until the custard is cool to the touch.

5. Whip the heavy cream until stiff. Stir the custard gradually into the cream.

N O T E : If you find it difficult to slice through the lemongrass, trim off more of the outer leaves. Use only the tender middle section of the stalks.

MANGO WAFER ORBS yield: about 20 decorations

1 recipe Mango Wafer Decorations (page 725)

1. Cover a large empty (30-count) cardboard egg carton with a sheet of plastic wrap, pushing the wrap partially inside each indentation.

2. Follow the directions for forming and baking the fruit puree in Mango Wafer Decorations (page 725), making the rounds approximately 5 inches (12.5 cm) in diameter, with a natural-looking uneven edge.

3. As soon as you can remove the baked rounds from the Silpat, form each into a loose ball with the edges of the round tucked underneath so they do not show. Place the formed rounds in the prepared egg carton.

Milk Chocolate Marquise with Finger Banana Center and Red Currant Sauce yield: 16 servings, 4 ounces (120 ml) each (Color Photo 88)

This recipe uses curved, teardrop-shaped molds, 1½ inches (3.7 cm) in height. The molds are lined with a strip of acetate, 2 inches (5 cm) in height and 9 inches (22.5 cm) in length. The acetate is used both to make it easier to remove the desserts from the molds and to increase their height. Due to the curve at the narrow end of each mold, it is necessary to tape the ends of the acetate strips together and place the joined section at the tip of the teardrop.

Should you not have or not wish to use the mold specified, any molds of approximately the same size and capacity will do as long as they can be filled to the top and the filling can be made level. In other words, if the molds are too large, you will not be able to fill them all the way to the rim, which is necessary here. Regardless of the forms used, it is a good idea to line them with strips of plastic to make it easier to remove the pastries. If none of these options work for you, or if you need to produce a fair amount of these desserts, the forms can be made entirely of acetate strips left freestanding. In that case, your options for shapes will be limited to rounds (see Frozen Lemon Mousse with Orange Syrup and a Tuile Spiral, page 405) or plain rather than curved teardrops (see Chocolate Mousse in Ribbon Teardrops, page 334). The sponge pieces used to line the bottom of the molds can be made from any thin plain or chocolate sponge cake, should you have extra on hand or not want to use the decorated Joconde sponge called for.

1 Wood-Grain–Pattern Decorated Sponge Sheet (page 675)

Orange–Milk Chocolate Mousse (recipe follows)

4 small finger bananas (see Note 1)

Red Currant Glaze (page 777)

16 Striped Chocolate Cornets (page 535)

Powdered sugar

Coating chocolate, meted

16 small clusters fresh red currants

16 mint sprigs

Red Currant Sauce (page 200)

1. Line 16 curved teardrop molds with acetate, as described in the introduction to this recipe.

2. Cut 16 strips from the decorated sponge, 2 inches (5 cm) wide and long enough to fit snugly inside the molds. Place the strips in the molds with the decorated side against the plastic and the ends meeting at the tip.

3. Use a curved teardrop cutter to cut out 16 pieces from the remainder of the decorated sponge sheet (see Chef's Tip). Place the sponge pieces on the bottom of the lined molds. Cover and reserve in the refrigerator while making the orange-milk chocolate filling.

4. Peel the finger bananas and cut them crosswise into 4 pieces each.

5. Place the milk chocolate filling in a pastry bag with a medium plain tip. Pipe the filling into the molds, filling them to the top of the sponge sheet on the sides. Working quickly, push a banana piece into the center of the filling in each mold. Pipe the remaining filling into the molds, filling them to the top of the acetate strips (you are likely to have leftover filling, as it is impossible to gauge the exact amount needed, given that the size of the banana pieces will vary). Use a spatula to smooth the tops, making them perfectly level. Cover and place in the refrigerator for at least 4 hours or, preferably, overnight.

6. Remove as many desserts from the refrigerator as you anticipate needing for service. Spread a thin layer of red currant glaze on top of each. Place the desserts in the freezer to set the glaze; do not leave them in the freezer longer than necessary.

7. Remove the desserts from the forms and peel off the acetate strips. If the chocolate filling on the side of the first dessert looks rough after peeling the plastic off, place the remaining desserts in the freezer until firm enough for the plastic to come away cleanly, or use a warm knife or spatula to smooth the sides after unmolding all of them. Place the desserts in the refrigerator. Chill as many chocolate cornets as you anticipate needing for service (see Note 2); do not leave them in the refrigerator longer than 30 minutes.

8. Presentation: Sift powdered sugar lightly over the base of a dessert plate. Center a teardrop pastry on the right side of the plate. Place a small amount of melted chocolate in a piping bag and pipe a dot of chocolate on the back of the plate to the left of the pastry. Stand a chocolate cornet upright on the chocolate dot. Fill the cornet with a cluster of currants and a mint sprig. Spoon red currant sauce on the front portion of the base of the plate and serve.

NOTE 1: If finger bananas are unavailable, use either red or yellow bananas (in that order of preference). You will need 3 small red bananas cut into 6 pieces each, or 2 small yellow bananas sliced ¼ inch (6 mm) thick.

NOTE 2: If you have aerosol chocolate coolant and use it to quickly set and harden the coating chocolate as you attach the chocolate cornets, you can skip chilling the decorations.

CHEF'S TIP

If you do not have a curved teardrop cutter, use a plain round cookie cutter of approximately the same size to cut circles that will fill the larger round portion of the molds; then add a small wedge-shaped piece of sponge at the tip to fill the remaining space.

ORANGE-MILK CHOCOLATE MOUSSE yield: approximately 2 quarts (1 L 920 ml)

12 ounces (340 g) milk chocolate

3 tablespoons (45 ml) orange liqueur

1 tablespoon (15 ml) water

1 teaspoon (3 g) unflavored gelatin powder

3 cups (720 ml) heavy cream

4 eggs, separated

4 ounces (115 g) granulated sugar

I. Cut the chocolate into small pieces. Place in a bowl and melt over a bain-marie. Set aside; keep warm.

2. Combine the liqueur and water. Sprinkle the gelatin over the top and set aside to soften.

3. Heat 1 cup (240 ml) heavy cream to scalding.

4. Whip the egg yolks with 2 tablespoons (30 ml) of the sugar to a light and creamy consistency. Gradually whisk the hot cream into the egg yolk mixture to temper it. Place the mixture over a bain-marie and, whipping constantly, heat until it has thickened to the ribbon stage. Set aside to cool.

5. Whip the remaining 2 cups (480 ml) heavy cream to soft peaks. Cover and reserve in the refrigerator.

6. Combine the egg whites with the remaining sugar. Heat over a bain-marie, whipping constantly, until the mixture reaches 145°F (63°C). Remove from the heat and continue to whip until the meringue has cooled and formed stiff peaks.

7. Warm the chocolate, if necessary, and quickly fold it into the reserved whipped cream. Still working rapidly, incorporate the egg yolk mixture. Stir in the meringue.

8. Heat the gelatin solution to dissolve. Temper by quickly incorporating it into one-quarter of the chocolate mixture before mixing it into the remainder.

Spiced Ganache and Tea Ice Cream Marco Polo yield: 16 servings (Color Photo 86)

This dessert is named for Marco Polo in honor of his association with the spices, green tea, and ice cream used in the recipe. For a mint-flavored variation of this dessert, in the Spiced Ganache Filling substitute mint liqueur for the orange liqueur; use twice the quantity and omit the ginger and cloves. Use mint ice cream rather than the tea-flavored ice cream called for here, and decorate the desserts with a mint sprig. I went one step further for a St. Patrick's Day special and colored the stripes of the ribbon sponge pale green.

1 recipe Devil's Food Cake batter (page 393)

1 Ribbon-Pattern Decorated Sponge Sheet (page 672; see Note 1)

Spiced Ganache Filling (recipe follows)

Sweet dark chocolate, tempered, or dark coating chocolate, melted

Florentina Cookies for Marco Polo (page 690)

½ recipe Chocolate Sauce (recipe follows)

½ recipe Fortified Caramel Sauce (page 19)

Unsweetened cocoa powder

Powdered sugar

Piping Chocolate (page 543), melted

1 recipe Sun-Brewed Jasmine Tea Ice Cream (page 209)

32 Curly Cues (page 700)

1. Spread the devil's food cake batter out over a half-sheet pan (12 × 16 inches/40 × 60 cm) lined with baking paper or a Silpat. Bake at 375°F (190°C) for approximately 15 minutes or until baked through. Let the cake cool completely.

2. Measure the outside circumference of a plain cookie cutter approximately 3½ inches (8.7 cm) in diameter. Cut 16 strips of acetate or polyurethane 1¼ inches wide (3.1 cm) and ¼ inch (6 mm) longer than the circumference measurement, about 11¾ inches (29.5 cm). Using the cookie cutter as a guide (see Note 2), join and tape the ends together to form rings, or just overlap the end ¼ inch (6 mm) and tape together. Place the rings on a sheet pan lined with baking paper.

3. Using the same cookie cutter, cut 8 rounds from the cake sheet. Cut each round in half horizontally. Place these inside the plastic rings.

4. Using the same cookie cutter, cut 16 rounds from the ribbon sponge sheet. Approximately one-third of the sheet will be left for another use.

5. Reserve about ½ cup (120 ml) of the ganache filling to use in the presentation. Place the remainder in a pastry bag with a No. 6 (12-mm) plain tip. Pipe the filling into the rings on top of the sponge circles, dividing it evenly. The top of the filling should be slightly below the top of the rings.

6. Place the ribbon sponge rounds on top of the filling, striped-side up, and press down lightly to make the tops level. Refrigerate for at least 2 hours to set the filling.

7. Remove the tape and peel the plastic strips away from the pastries. Return the pastries to the refrigerator. Wash and dry the plastic strips.

8. Place a plastic strip on a piece of baking paper. Spread a thin layer of melted coating chocolate or tempered dark chocolate on top; to cover the strip completely, it is necessary to spread a little chocolate onto the baking paper all around the plastic. Carefully lift up 1 end of the strip by sliding the tip of a paring knife underneath. Holding the strip by 1 short end, run the thumb and index finger of your other hand down the long edges to remove excess choco-

About Marco Polo

Marco Polo was an Italian merchant and explorer from Venice who, along with his father and uncle, is given much of the credit for opening the European trade route to China, especially the all-important spice trade. The Polos ventured to China for the first time in the mid-thirteenth century. When Marco returned to Italy in 1295 after spending twenty years roaming through China in service to the Mongolian emperor, who had taken a liking to him, he dictated an account of his experience. His report was not given much credit at the time but rather was received in disbelief. Not until the seventeenth century did Jesuit missionaries verify his astonishing stories.

Among Marco Polo's fascinating tales was the news that pasta, in various forms, was eaten in China long before it became so closely associated with Italy. He also spoke of tea — a drink not encountered in the West until the beginning of the seventeenth century — and the great teahouses in China. But most interestingly for us, Marco Polo's journal tells of a device used to fabricate ice creams and sorbets. As we know, just as salt raises the boiling point of water, it also lowers the freezing point. Having observed the Chinese pouring snow and saltpeter over containers filled with syrup, he brought the secret back to Italy, a country that much later became known as much for its wonderful ices as for its pasta.

late and give the strip a cleaner look. Position the strip with the chocolate against the side of a pastry and gently push it against the pastry all around. The strip will be just a little too long. Do not overlap the ends and press together; rather, allow the extra piece to stick out. Cover the sides of the remaining pastries with chocolate in the same fashion. Before removing the plastic strips, place the pastries in the refrigerator for a few minutes or until time of service.

9. Place as many Florentina cookies as you expect to need in the refrigerator, allowing 1 large and 1 small cookie per serving. Place the chocolate sauce in a piping bottle. Place the caramel sauce in a second piping bottle.

10. Presentation: Sift cocoa powder lightly over the rim of a dessert plate. Pipe a zigzag design of chocolate sauce over the base of the plate. Pipe random dots of caramel sauce, making various sizes, around the chocolate piping. Pipe a dot of the reserved ganache filling off-center on the plate. Place a Marco Polo standing on its side, seam-side down, on top of the ganache. Sift powdered sugar lightly over the top of the pastry. Pipe a dot of piping chocolate directly to the right of the Marco Polo. Pipe a second dot a few inches in front of the first one. Quickly secure a large Florentina cookie on the back dot, arranging it so that the Florentina curls over the pastry. Place a small cookie on the other dot. Hold both cookies in place for a few seconds until the chocolate hardens (this happens quickly because the cookies are cold from the refrigerator). Place a small scoop of tea ice cream on the base of the small cookie. Lean 2 curly cues on the ice cream. Serve immediately.

NOTE 1: Follow the directions for making the ribbon sponge sheet, but do not make straight lines in the chocolate tuile paste. Instead, move the trowel side to side in a zigzag pattern to create a softly curved design. The back-and-forth motion tends to create small air bubbles in the baked sheet, which is undesirable but unavoidable. If you are using a small trowel, which requires that you make several passes over the sheet, hold the trowel at an angle rather than perpendicular to the edges of the sheet, which will avoid creating a buildup of batter along the edge of each pass.

NOTE 2: This is necessary if you are making a large quantity but also helpful for just 16 rings. If you use the cutter as a guide, each of the rings will be the same size, and they will sit flat and level. To make the rings, first cut the plastic strips and have small pieces of tape ready. Place the cookie cutter against the work surface, top (thicker) edge down. Attach a small piece of tape to 1 end of a plastic strip. Place the opposite end of the strip against the outside of the cutter. Holding that end in place, wind the plastic around the cutter, pushing the bottom of the plastic flush against the edge of the cutter. The ends must overlap about 1/4 inch (6 mm). Tape in place and pull the ring off of the cutter.

SPICED GANACHE FILLING yield: 7½ cups (1 L 800 ml)

15 ounces (430 g) milk chocolate	¼ cup (60 ml) or 3 ounces (85 g) honey
3 ounces (85 g) sweet dark chocolate	2 tablespoons (30 ml) orange liqueur
2¾ cups (660 ml) heavy cream	1 teaspoon (2 g) ground ginger
3 egg yolks (¼ cup/60 ml)	½ teaspoon (1 g) ground cloves
1½ ounces (40 g) granulated sugar	

1. Chop the milk chocolate and sweet dark chocolate into small chunks. Place in a bowl set over simmering water and melt together. Set aside; keep warm.

2. Whip the heavy cream until soft peaks form. Set aside.

3. Whip the egg yolks with the sugar for about 2 minutes; the mixture should be light and fluffy. Bring the honey to a boil and gradually whisk it into the yolks. Continue whipping until the mixture has cooled completely.

4. Fold in the melted chocolate, orange liqueur, ground ginger, ground cloves, and whipped cream.

CHOCOLATE SAUCE yield: approximately 4½ cups (1 L 80 ml)

This versatile sauce can be kept on hand and is good either hot or cold. It is best suited to garnishing a dessert — a slice of cake, a pastry, or poached fruit, for example. If you want a chocolate sauce to serve as a main components of a dessert, especially ice cream, use Hot Fudge Sauce (page 254) instead.

2 cups (480 ml) water

10 ounces (285 g) granulated sugar

½ cup (120 ml) glucose *or* light corn syrup

4 ounces (115 g) unsweetened cocoa powder, sifted

1 pound (455 g) sweet dark chocolate, melted

1. Combine the water, sugar, and glucose or corn syrup in a saucepan. Bring to a boil, then remove from the heat.

2. Add enough of the syrup to the cocoa powder to make a soft paste, stirring until the mixture is completely smooth. Gradually add the remaining syrup to the paste.

3. Remove from the heat, add the melted chocolate, and stir until combined. If necessary, strain the sauce before serving.

NOTE: Chocolate sauce, like Clear Caramel Sauce and Fortified Caramel Sauce, is much thinner when it is hot. If you plan to serve the chocolate sauce cold, let it cool to room temperature first; if it is too thick, add a little water. If the sauce has been refrigerated, warm it to room temperature before adjusting. The recipe as is makes a fairly thick sauce when cold — ideal for covering a pear, for example — but it is too thick to mask a plate without adding water. On the other hand, if you want the sauce to be thicker, incorporate more melted chocolate after warming the sauce.

VARIATION

Bitter Chocolate Sauce

Replace 3 ounces (85 g) melted sweet dark chocolate with an equal amount of melted unsweetened chocolate. Increase the water by ½ cup (120 ml).

Snowbird in a Chocolate Cage yield: 16 servings (Color Photo 89)

While an intricate dessert such as this one is not really suitable for a large banquet or mass production — although it is technically feasible if the labor cost can be justified — it can be scaled down without losing its appeal. The following presentation can be greatly simplified by eliminating the cage and serving the snowbirds "free-range," resting in their nests of spun sugar. Not only will you save yourself some work but you will save your guests some calories as well. Moreover, if the uncaged birds are filled with the lighter Italian Cream (page 771) instead of whipped cream, the result is a dessert that is very low in fat. These appealing little birds can also be used alone (without the cage and sugar) to enhance a simple dessert such as Bavarian cream or a serving of ice cream. Another alternative is to create spectacular individual French pastries by filling the birds with flavored buttercream instead of whipped cream.

2 cups (480 ml) heavy cream

2 teaspoons (10 g) granulated sugar

16 Chocolate Cages (page 543)

1 recipe Kiwi Sauce (page 309)

16 Snowbirds (recipe follows)

Spun Sugar (page 593; see Chef's Tip)

1. Whip the heavy cream and sugar to stiff peaks. Place in a pastry bag with a No. 5 (10-mm) plain tip. Reserve in the refrigerator.

2. No more than 30 minutes before serving, refrigerate as many chocolate cages as you anticipate needing. Place a portion of the kiwi sauce in a piping bottle.

CHEF'S TIP
Make the spun sugar as close to serving time as possible and reserve in an airtight container. Place a dehumidifying agent in the container to protect the sugar against moisture. This is a good idea even if you make the spun sugar just before serving, and it is essential if it will be stored longer.

3. Presentation: Pipe a pearl pattern of whipped cream in a ring the same size as the bottom of a chocolate cage, centered on the base of a dessert plate. Pipe whipped cream between the halves of the body on an assembled bird, completely filling the open space and mounding the filling slightly above the sides. Attach the neck and head to the front. Arrange a little spun sugar inside the whipped cream ring on the plate, then a set a snowbird on top of the nest. Carefully place a chocolate cage on top of the whipped cream ring. Pipe kiwi sauce around the dessert to cover the base of the plate. Serve immediately.

FIGURE 8-5 The marzipan beak and meringue head-and-neck piece for the snowbird; after attaching the marzipan beak and piping the chocolate eye on the head

FIGURE 8-6 The grouped pieces ready to assemble one snowbird, with chocolate piped on the body pieces to attach the wings; after attaching the wings to the body pieces

FIGURE 8-7 Attaching the assembled body and wing pieces to the short dough base with lines of chocolate; the assembled snowbird

SNOWBIRDS yield: 20 birds

4 ounces (115 g) Short Dough (page 791)

¼ recipe French Meringue (page 780)

Finely ground almonds or hazelnuts

½ ounce (15 g) marzipan, tinted red

Dark coating chocolate, melted

1. Using flour to prevent it from sticking, roll out the short dough to ⅛ inch (3 mm) thick. Using a plain cookie cutter, cut out 20 cookies, 1½ inches (3.7 cm) in diameter. Reserve the dough scraps for another use. Bake the cookies at 375°F (190°C) until golden brown. Set aside to cool.

2. Place the meringue in a pastry bag with a No. 6 (12-mm) plain tip. Pipe out approximately 50 teardrop shapes, 2½ inches (6.2 cm) long, for the bodies of the birds (each body requires 2 pieces) on a sheet pan lined with baking paper or a Silpat. Hold a No. 4 (8-mm) plain tip in place over the other tip (see Figures 5-4 and 5-5, page 240) and pipe out approximately 50 teardrops, 1½ inches (3.7 cm) long, on a second pan lined with baking paper or a Silpat, for the wings. Sprinkle ground nuts over the wings. Replace the No. 4 tip with a No. 3 (6-mm) tip. Pipe out 25 neck and head shapes, 1½ inches (3.7 cm) long, on the pan with the wings (see Color Photo 89).

3. Bake all of the meringue shapes at 210°F (99°C) for 1 to 2 hours or until dried all the way through. The necks will be done quite a bit sooner than the bodies.

4. To assemble the birds, select the 20 most attractive head-neck pieces. Trim just a little from the front of the head to create a flat edge. Roll the red marzipan into a string, 6 inches (15 cm) long. Cut the string into 20 equal pieces. Roll the pieces into tiny cones, pressing the bottom of each cone against the table so it becomes flat. Place the cones and the head-neck pieces of meringue together on a plate or cardboard and refrigerate for a few minutes until cold.

5. Place melted chocolate in a piping bag. Cut a small opening and pipe a tiny drop of chocolate on the flat side of a marzipan cone, then press it gently against the flat side of a snow-bird head. Hold in place for a just a few seconds; the chilled surfaces will cause the chocolate to set quickly. Repeat with the remaining pieces. Pipe an eye on each head (Figure 8-5).

6. Arrange the bodies, wings, and short dough bases as shown in Figure 8-6. Refrigerate just long enough to chill the pieces. It is best to do this in small groups so none of the pieces loses its chill as you work on the others. Working with 1 group of parts at a time, pipe chocolate on the body pieces as illustrated and attach the wings. When the wings are set, pipe 2 lines of chocolate on the short dough base and quickly attach the 2 body-wing pieces perpendicular to the base, angling the pieces so the tails touch in back and there is an opening about ¾ inch (2 cm) wide in front (Figure 8-7). Hold a few seconds until set. Pipe a little chocolate inside the tail to hold the side pieces more securely until the birds are filled. Assemble the remaining birds in the same manner.

CHEF'S TIP
Although the unfilled birds can be stored in a dry place for several days, it is best not to assemble more birds than you can use right away, as the individual meringue pieces (before assembly) can easily be dried in the oven should they soften during storage.

Striped Chocolate Cups with Tuile Steam Decorations

yield: 12 servings (Color Photo 91 and jacket spine)

12 Striped Chocolate Cups (page 536)	½ recipe Raspberry Sauce (page 173)
Milk Chocolate Filling (recipe follows)	Dark Piping Chocolate (page 543)
½ cup (120 ml) heavy cream	12 orange segments
1 teaspoon (5 ml) granulated sugar	12 mint sprigs
½ recipe Orange-Vanilla Decorating Syrup (page 760)	12 sets Tuile Steam Decorations (page 712)
	Powdered sugar

1. Wearing food handling gloves, arrange 12 striped chocolate cups set at a 45-degree angle on top of appropriately sized rings or drinking glasses set on a sheet pan.

2. Place a portion of the milk chocolate filling in a pastry bag with a No. 8 (16-mm) plain tip. Pipe the filling into the prepared chocolate cups, filling them to the rim of the front edge (see Color Photo 91). Add more filling to the bag as needed until you have filled all of the cups. Place the filled cups in the refrigerator until the filling is set, approximately 1 hour. If they will be left longer than 1 hour, they must be well wrapped.

3. Whip the heavy cream with the sugar to stiff peaks. Place in a pastry bag with a Saint-Honoré tip; reserve in the refrigerator. Place the orange decorating syrup and raspberry sauce into piping bottles.

4. Presentation: Pipe orange syrup in a zigzag pattern on the base of a serving plate. Pipe dots of raspberry sauce in varying sizes between the orange lines. Pipe a large dot of piping chocolate in the center of the plate. Wearing food handling gloves to protect the chocolate from fingerprints, set a chilled chocolate cup at a 45-degree angle on top on the dot of piping chocolate. Hold the cup in place for a few seconds until the piping chocolate is set. Pipe a wedge of whipped cream in the center of the cup. Garnish with an orange segment and a mint sprig. Stand a set of tuile steam decorations straight up around the whipped cream. Lightly sift powdered sugar over the dessert and the front of the plate.

MILK CHOCOLATE FILLING yield: approximately 7 cups (1 L 680 ml)

Do not make this filling until you are ready to use it.

14 ounces (400 g) milk chocolate	½ cup (120 ml) whole milk, at room
2½ cups (600 ml) heavy cream	temperature

1. Chop the chocolate into small pieces and melt over a bain-marie, stirring frequently. Set aside; keep warm.

2. Whip the heavy cream just until it has thickened to a very soft consistency.

3. Stir the milk into the warm chocolate, continuing to stir until it is fully incorporated and the mixture is smooth. Working quickly, stir half of the whipped cream into the chocolate mixture, then stir in the remainder. Use immediately.

Tarte Tatin Moderne yield: 16 servings (Color Photo 90)

When I worked for The Culinary Institute of America at Greystone in the Napa Valley, I once had the pleasure of working with Chef Ferdinand Metz, then the school's president, and a fellow instructor in the pastry kitchen at the school preparing a version of this tarte Tatin for a banquet in honor of Paul Bocuse. Each dessert was presented to the guest under a sugar dome approximately 5 inches (12.5 cm) in diameter. The domes were designed to resemble the classic silver half-spheres used in restaurants to keep food warm and to allow a dramatic flourish as the waiter lifts it to reveal the dish. Unusually enough, after a bit of experimenting, we made our sugar domes using a shot put as the mold. The shot put had the right circumference to make the size domes we needed and, because it was a heavy, solid iron ball, it stayed cold, which caused the sugar to set up quickly and made it easier to remove the domes.

A bolt was screwed into the ball to act as a handle, and we then dipped the chilled ball halfway into pale pink sugar syrup to create beautiful translucent semi-spheres. Each sugar shell was topped with a marzipan lion's head to symbolize Lyons, France, the hometown of Mr. Bocuse. The lion heads were used as handles whereby the waiters lifted the domes from the dessert plates when they were presented to the guests.

We prepared all of this for seventy guests, which was quite labor intensive, but at least the three of us doing the work were all rather experienced, if I do say so. Instead of the cinnamon-flavored cookie stick used here, we served a chocolate cigarette dusted with cinnamon to look like a cinnamon stick. The dessert received high praise from the guests, which was especially meaningful, as they were all in our profession.

To simplify this presentation, the chocolate paper decorations may either be left flat or eliminated altogether, as the dessert will still have both the short dough base and the cinnamon cookie for contrasting texture.

Unsalted butter, melted	1 tablespoon (15 ml) Calvados
16 large apples, Granny Smith or Golden Delicious	Translucent Chocolate Teardrops (recipe follows)
Apple Cider–Caramel Sauce (recipe follows)	Piping Chocolate (page 543), melted
1 ounce (30 g) cinnamon sugar	16 Cookie Cinnamon Sticks (recipe follows)
1 pound (455 g) Short Dough (page 791)	16 small strawberry halves, stems attached
1 cup (240 ml) heavy cream	Powdered sugar
1 teaspoon (5 g) granulated sugar	

1. Brush melted butter over the insides of 16 ramekins, 3¼ inches (8.1 cm) in diameter and at least 1¾ inches (4.5 cm) in height; see Chef's Tip.

2. Cut a small slice from both the top and bottom of each apple so that the apples stand straight and level and are about 2 inches (5 cm) tall. Using a vegetable peeler, peel the apples.

3. Trim the circumference of 1 apple by pressing a round cookie cutter, 3 inches (7.5 cm) in diameter, straight down over the top from the stem end. Round the cut edges of the apple with the vegetable peeler. Using a clean dish-scouring pad (see Note) as if it were sandpaper, sand the edges of the apple to make them perfectly smooth. Center a round cookie cutter, 1½ inches (3.7 cm) in diameter, on top of the stem end of the apple and cut straight down, pushing the cutter halfway into the apple. Remove the cookie cutter and use a melon ball cutter to carefully scoop out the seeds and core inside the cut. Repeat with the remaining apples.

4. Pour 2 tablespoons (30 ml) cider-caramel sauce into each of the prepared ramekins; reserve the remaining sauce. Sprinkle ½ teaspoon (2.5 ml) cinnamon sugar over the sauce in each ramekin. Place the apples in the ramekins, hollow-side down. Gently press the apples into the forms to ensure that they touch the sauce. Arrange the ramekins on a sheet pan without crowding. Cover each ramekin with aluminum foil.

5. Bake at 375°F (190°C) for approximately 30 minutes or until the apples feel soft and the

CHEF'S TIP

Soufflé ramekins can vary from 1½ inches to 2½ inches (3.7 to 6.2 cm) in height. To prevent the caramel sauce from boiling over in the oven, the ramekins used here must be at least 1¾ inches (4.5 cm) tall. If you do not have ramekins of the proper size or do not have enough of them, use ovenproof coffee cups or even disposable aluminum forms of approximately the size specified.

caramel has penetrated the bottom of the fruit. Set aside to cool. If the apples will not be served the same day, refrigerate once they are cool, then reheat them for service.

6. Roll out the short dough to ⅛ inch (3 mm) thick. Place the dough in the refrigerator to firm up. Use the teardrop-shaped template (Figure 8-8) to cut 16 cookies from the chilled dough. Refrigerate the dough again as needed during the process; attempting to cut soft dough will result in misshapen teardrops.

7. Place the cookies on a sheet pan lined with baking paper and prick lightly. Bake at 375°F (190°C) for approximately 12 minutes or until light golden brown. Set aside to cool.

8. Whip the cream, sugar, and Calvados to soft peaks. Reserve, covered, in the refrigerator. Chill as many chocolate teardrops as you anticipate needing for service. Place the remaining caramel sauce in a piping bottle and reserve. If the apples were baked ahead, warm as many servings as needed.

9. Presentation: Place a cookie teardrop on a dessert plate, positioning it slightly off-center and with the pointed end facing you. Invert a ramekin over a second plate to unmold an apple, keeping the sauce in the hollow. Carefully transfer the apple to the wide end of the cookie, with

FIGURE 8-8 The template used to cut out short dough cookies for Tarte Tatin Moderne

the hollow facing up. Add apple cider–caramel sauce and any spilled sauce from the unmolding plate to fill the hollow of the apple. Using 2 spoons, form whipped cream into a quenelle shape and place the cream on the point of the teardrop next to the apple. Drizzle caramel sauce in front of the teardrop. Pipe a small amount of piping chocolate on the plate behind the apple. Stand a chilled chocolate teardrop straight up on top against the apple; hold it in place until the chocolate hardens (see Chef's Tip, page 396). Lean a cookie cinnamon stick against the right side of the apple. Place a strawberry half in front of the whipped cream. Sift powdered sugar lightly over the top of the dessert. Serve immediately.

NOTE: Start with a new scouring pad; be certain it is not the type that comes coated with soap and chemicals. Reserve the pad for this use only. Sterilize the scouring pad by placing it in boiling water for 1 minute before using it the first time and again after each use.

APPLE CIDER–CARAMEL SAUCE yield: approximately 3½ cups (840 ml)

1 vanilla bean	6 ounces (170 g) unsalted butter
1 pound 13 ounces (825 g) granulated sugar	1½ cups (360 ml) apple cider, heated to scalding
¾ cup 180 ml) water	3 tablespoons (45 ml) Calvados
1 teaspoon (5 ml) lemon juice	
⅓ cup (80 ml) glucose *or* light corn syrup	

1. Split the vanilla bean lengthwise. Scrape the seeds into 3 ounces (85 g) of the sugar on a sheet of baking paper. Rub the mixture between your hands until the seeds are thoroughly mixed into the sugar. Set the vanilla sugar aside and save the pod halves for another use.

2. Cook the remaining 1 pound 10 ounces (740 g) granulated sugar with the water and lemon juice, stirring until the mixture comes to boil. Add the glucose or corn syrup, return to a boil, and cook without stirring until the syrup is a light brown caramel color; wash down the sides of the pan frequently with a clean pastry brush dipped in water.

3. Remove the pan from the heat and stir in the reserved vanilla sugar and half of the butter. Stir in the apple cider carefully, as it will create steam (having the cider hot will minimize this). Stir in the remaining butter and the Calvados. Allow the sauce to cool before using.

CHEF'S TIP
It is sometimes difficult to judge the color of caramelized sugar, especially if you are using a copper pan. One option is to pour a small puddle of syrup onto a sheet of baking paper to get a better look. Or, as I do, roll up a small piece of baking paper very tightly (I use triangles precut for piping bags as they are always around), then use it as a dipstick to test the color.

TRANSLUCENT CHOCOLATE TEARDROPS yield: 16 decorations

1 recipe Chocolate Paper Paste (page 719)

1. Using approximately 1½ ounces (40 g) paste for each, form 2 teardrops with curved tips on a full-size Silpat, making them about 6½ inches (16.2 cm) at the widest point and 11 inches (27.5) long; the paste should be thin and even. Form the teardrops on the pan vertically with the round base at the bottom and the curved tip at the top. Use your palette knife to remove 1 inch (2.5 cm) of paste from the bottom of the rounded side (opposite the tip) to make a straight edge as shown in Figure 8-9.

2. Bake at 375°F (190°C) for approximately 6 minutes (see Note). Have ready 2 very cold aluminum soft drink cans wrapped in aluminum foil.

3. Remove the sheet pan from the oven. Wait for a few seconds until the teardrops can be handled. Align the bottom (straight edge) of 1 teardrop with the bottom of a soft drink can. Carefully fold the bottom portion of 1 long side of the teardrop halfway around the can, leaving the remainder of the cookie, including the pointed tip, flat on the sheet pan (see Color Photo 90). The tip of the cookie should point to the left and resemble a wave about to crest. Repeat with the second teardrop. Because the decorations are thin and the cans are cold, the paste will firm up almost immediately.

4. Place the finished decorations on their sides on a sheet pan lined with baking paper; do not attempt to store them standing upright. Repeat, making 2 decorations at a time, until you have 16.

NOTE: Because the chocolate paste is quite dark, it may be difficult to judge when the decorations are finished baking, especially when you are inexperienced with the recipe. If the paste does not bake long enough, the decorations will not become crisp and will not hold their shape. If baked too long, the teardrops will be difficult to form, and the flavor may be bitter. For a reference point, place a few sliced almonds next to the teardrops on the Silpat; when the almonds begin to turn golden brown, the decorations are done as well.

COOKIE CINNAMON STICKS yield: approximately 24

6 ounces (170 g) Puff Pastry (page 784) *or* Quick Puff Pastry (page 788)	Egg wash
6 ounces (170 g) Short Dough (page 791)	Cinnamon sugar

1. Using flour to prevent the dough from sticking, roll out the puff pastry to an 8-inch (20-cm) square, approximately ⅛ inch (3 mm) thick.

2. Roll out the short dough to the same thickness as the puff pastry.

3. Brush egg wash over the top of the puff pastry. Sprinkle cinnamon sugar over the egg wash. Place the short dough on top. Lightly, without increasing the size of the dough sheets, roll a rolling pin over the top to glue the dough pieces together. Place the dough in the refrigerator to chill and firm up.

4. Using a ruler or dowel as a guide and a plain pastry wheel or sharp knife, cut strips ⅜ inch (9 mm) wide.

5. Twist each strip into a tight corkscrew shape by rolling the ends in opposite directions against the table.

6. Brush or spray water on an unlined sheet pan (see Chef's Tip). Place

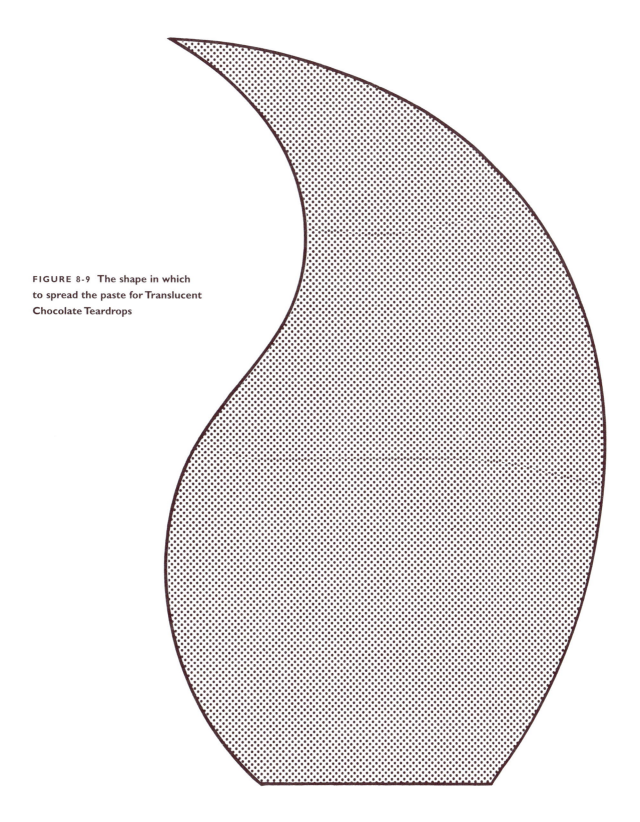

FIGURE 8-9 **The shape in which to spread the paste for Translucent Chocolate Teardrops**

the cinnamon sticks on the pan; keep them straight, stretch them slightly as you place them on the pan, and press the ends of the sticks firmly to attach them to the pan.

7. Bake, double-panned, at 350°F (175°C) for approximately 12 minutes or until golden brown. After the cookies have cooled, trim the ends even and store in a covered container. The cookies will stay fresh up to 3 days.

IN THIS CHAPTER

BREADS

Bread Basket   425

Braided Stollen   430

Chestnut Bread   432

Dresdener Stollen   434

Lucia Buns   436

Panettone   437

Sweet Pigs' Heads   438

    PIG'S HEAD DINNER ROLLS   439

    WHOLE LARGE PIG PASTRIES   440

Swedish Spice Bread (*Vörtbröd*)   440

Triestine Bread   441

CAKES, TARTS, AND TORTES

Brandied Gingerbread Cake   443

Soft Gingerbread Cake   443

    GINGERBREAD MUFFINS   444

Chestnut Rum Torte   444

    CHESTNUT CAKE   446

Florentine Torte   447

Lemon Verbena–Scented Fruitcake   449

Traditional Fruitcake   450

Panforte   451

    DARK PANFORTE (*PANFORTE SCURO*)   453

Yule Logs (*Bûches de Noël*)   453

COOKIES AND PASTRIES

Chocolate Snow Hearts   456

Christmas Cookie Ornaments   457

Christmas Tree Pastries   458

Cinnamon Stars   460

Gingerbread Cookies   461

Holiday Candle Pastries   462

Lebkuchen Bars   463

Lebkuchen Hearts   464

Springerle   466

Yule Log Pastries   468

PLATED HOLIDAY DESSERTS

Bûche de Noël Slices with Pomegranate   469
Sauce and Star Fruit

Chocolate Chalet with White Chocolate and   470
Pistachio Pâté and Bitter Chocolate Sauce

Mont Blanc with Pomegranate Seeds and   477
Vanilla Curly Cues

Persimmon Charlotte   478

Persimmon Cream Slices with Cookie   480
Christmas Trees and Cranberry Coulis

Persimmon Dome Cake with Gingerbread   484
Lattice

    BANANA RUM PUDDING WITH BRANDIED WHIPPED   486
    CREAM AND GINGERBREAD LATTICE

Persimmon Pudding   486

Pumpkin Crème Brûlée   488

GINGERBREAD HOUSES

Traditional Gingerbread House   490

Santa's Gingerbread Chalet   499

Holiday Classics and Favorites

The Christmas season is hectic for many people, especially those of us in the foodservice industry. Like me, you probably find yourself wishing for more hours in the day to enable you to take advantage of all the business and still leave a little time to celebrate your own traditions. Although it is a lot of fun getting into the Christmas spirit and preparing all the special treats we haven't seen since last year, come Christmas Eve, we are usually glad it's over. Unfortunately, most retailers simply start too early; Christmas decorations go up in the stores before Thanksgiving, and Santa often arrives in the malls before December 1st. I am afraid the day will come soon when parents and children will make a single trip to the lot to choose the Halloween pumpkin and the Christmas tree.

Having grown up on a farm in Sweden, with all of the traditional customs, I am saddened to see Christmas so commercialized. At home, the holiday season started early, but in a much more subtle way. Four weeks before Christmas, Advent began with the lighting of the first of four candles; one more was lit each week until Christmas, when all four were burning. We children had our Advent calendar with a window to open each day of December; each window showed a different picture, the last being a picture of *Jultomten* (Santa Claus) on Christmas Eve. My father saved a few wheat husks from the harvest, which we attached to a broomstick and put out for the birds as soon as the first snow covered the ground.

Early in December, my father and a neighbor slaughtered a pig. The two families shared it, and my mother made delicious dishes from it for our Christmas table. There was also baking to be done, from the *Vörtbröd* to the gingerbread figures my sister and I helped decorate for the Christmas tree. And there could not be Christmas without marzipan candies, one of which was always a pig. In addition, we arranged an abundance of nuts, bunches of large dried raisins on the stem, dates, and citrus fruits from California. In the midst of all of these preparations, Saint Lucia's Day, the darkest day of the year, was celebrated with its own special ceremony and traditional breakfast pastries, including Lucia Buns.

The week before Christmas, my father and I walked into the snow-covered forest to cut down a tree. We put it in a special stand with water to keep it from getting dry. This was especially important because we used real candles as well as other ornaments to decorate the branches. The tree remained in place until 13 January, twenty days after Christmas.

On Christmas Eve, the culmination of all of this preparation and anticipation, we shared the most lavish meal of the year with our friends and relatives. It was customary to save the broth from cooking the ham, and the feast officially started with the ceremony known as *doppa i grytan,* or "dip in the pot," where everyone dipped a piece of *Vörtbröd* into the broth. The traditional rice pudding was served for dessert, with one bitter almond hidden inside; the story was that whoever found the almond would marry in the next year.

The Christmas Eve buffet was always eaten early so my father could "go to the neighbor's house to lend a helping hand," and every year, by coincidence, this was when Santa arrived at our house, dressed in his red suit and carrying our presents. After Santa left, we moved the furniture (Dad was always back by then to help) and brought the Christmas tree to the center of the room. Everyone then joined hands around the tree and sang Christmas songs.

On Christmas Day, we ate the inevitable *lutfisk* (sun-dried and lime-cured ling cod; not too popular with children) for dinner, accompanied by a white sauce and homemade mustard. For dessert, the custom called for *Riz à la Malta* served with cherry sauce, a light, fluffy rice dessert made by adding whipped cream and chopped almonds to the leftover rice pudding that had been served on Christmas Eve.

Today, a large part of these traditional food preparations is just a memory. Only the most dedicated farmers continue to slaughter their own pigs and few people make all of the sweets at home. Instead, most Christmas food is purchased ready-made.

In the pastry shops, preparations of all the candies, chocolates, and marzipan items started in late November. The first Sunday of Advent was also the big "window display Sunday" all over Sweden. The shops tried to outdo one another, as well as their own displays from the previous year, and people crowded outside the windows to view the fantasy worlds inside. At the end of my five-year apprenticeship, I was proud to be given the responsibility of decorating the shop window. I made an entire landscape of gingerbread houses and marzipan figures. Though I have certainly created more elaborate work since then, this project remains special to me as one of my first accomplishments.

Although many items are made only at Christmastime — either because of the availability of the ingredients or just simply for tradition — many of the recipes in this chapter can be made in any season, and many are suited to other holidays as well: Chocolate Snow Hearts for Valentine's Day, Cinnamon Stars for the Fourth of July, and Pumpkin Crème Brûlée for Halloween or Thanksgiving. Gingerbread cookies and cakes can be adapted to serve year-round, and in the recipes that use persimmon, try substituting another fruit with approximately the same texture — apricots, bananas, or peaches, for example.

Conversely, you can dress up many standard pastries and desserts for the holidays by placing a Christmas decoration on top. For example, rum balls can be made in a log shape, lightly dusted with powdered sugar, and topped with a tiny gingerbread heart with a red dot piped in the center. Princess cake, with its green marzipan cover, lends itself easily to a Christmas presentation: Decorate each slice as directed for Christmas Tree Pastries (page 458), dot here and there with red piping gel for ornaments, and sift powdered sugar lightly over the top for snow.

BREADS

Bread Basket yield: 1 basket, 15 × 12 × 15 inches (37.5 × 30 × 37.5 cm)

This decorative woven bread basket is ideal for displaying freshly baked rolls or bread on a buffet table, in a shop window, or for a special holiday occasion. This is a big project, but you can be proud of the result. Be sure to read through all of the instructions before you begin.

Before you can make the basket, you must make the guide used when weaving the dough. While constructing the form takes a little work and requires special equipment, it will last forever. (Note, however, that if carpentry is not your favorite hobby (as it is mine) or you simply don't have the time or tools to make the form, bread basket forms are available from bakery suppliers.)These instructions are for a medium-sized oval basket with slanted sides. If you wish to make another design, keep in mind that it must maintain an even number of dowels spaced approximately 1½ inches (3.7 cm) apart. If you want to keep the oval shape but would like to make a smaller or larger basket, modify the template to the size desired and increase or decrease the weight and thickness of the dough strings.

Weaver's Dough (recipe follows)

Egg wash

½ recipe Caramelized Sugar for Decorations (page 613)

1. To start the form for the basket, cut a rectangle, 14½ × 9½ inches (36.2 × 23.7 cm), from ¾-inch (2-cm) particleboard.

2. Copy and enlarge the template (Figure 9-1) to make an oval measuring 12 × 8½ inches (30 × 21.2 cm). Center the drawing on top of the particleboard and mark the position of the holes. Remove the paper.

3. Using a small drill bit, make pilot holes, then using a ⁵⁄₁₆-inch (8-mm) drill bit, drill the holes at a slight outward angle. If you do not have a drill guide to ensure the same angle for all the holes, cut a piece of wood to the proper angle and hold this in front of the drill bit. If you try to approximate the angle freehand, you are sure to end up with an uneven circumference in your finished basket.

4. Cut 20 wooden dowels, ⁵⁄₁₆ inch (8 mm) in diameter, to 6 inches (15 cm) in length.

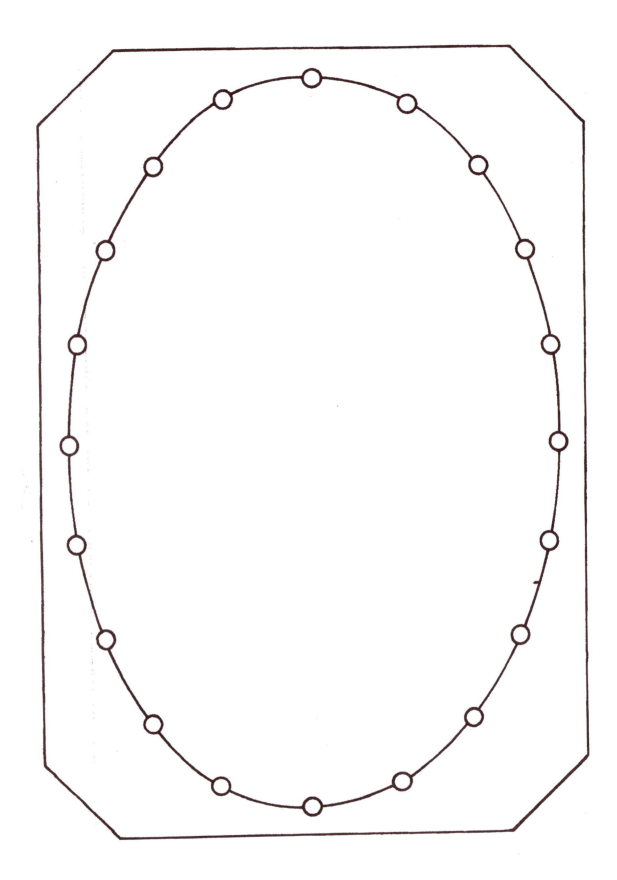

FIGURE 9-1 Template for the woven Bread Basket form

Divide the weaver's dough as follows:

- 8 pieces weighing 7 ounces (200 g) each for the sides of the basket
- 1 piece weighing 12 ounces (340 g) for the bottom (form into an oval shape before refrigerating)
- 2 pieces weighing 1 pound (455 g) each for the handle
- 2 pieces weighing 10 ounces (285 g) each for the border (see Note)
- 4 pieces weighing 1 ounce (30 g) each for the dowels

Leave out the 8 pieces weighing 7 ounces (200 g) each to work with. Cover and refrigerate the remaining pieces.

5. Using the same technique as for forming baguettes, pound and roll each of the 7-ounce (200-g) pieces into strings; do not use any flour as you are rolling. Because the dough must be firm and rubbery (glutenous), the strings must be rolled out only a little at a time, left to relax for a few minutes, then rolled and stretched a bit farther. Set a plate with a small amount of water nearby. Work on the strings alternately, moistening the palm of your hand with the water as needed to prevent the strings from sliding instead of rolling. Keep the strings uniform in thickness and continue rolling until they are 3 feet (90 cm) long. Keep the strings covered with a damp towel during this process.

6. While you are waiting for the strings to relax, cover the particleboard base with aluminum foil. Press the foil on top of the holes so you can see their location, then push the wooden dowels through the foil and into the holes. Cover the dowels with aluminum foil. Set the form aside.

7. Using flour to prevent the dough from sticking, roll out the 12-ounce (340-g) piece of dough into an oval slightly larger than the base of the basket. Reserve, covered, in the refrigerator.

8. Weave the first string of dough in and out around the dowels on the foil (Figure 9-2). Weave a second string on top of the first, alternating the sequence in front of and behind the dowels and stretching the strings slightly as you weave (see Chef's Tip). Add the remaining strings in the same manner, starting and finishing each of the strings staggered along one long side. Cut the strings to fit where the ends meet and, using a little egg wash as glue, press them together. Because the sides of the basket are slanted, you will have extra dough left from the lower strings. However, making all of the strings the same length to begin with is the simplest way of ensuring they all have the same thickness and the ones for the wider part of the basket will be long enough. Adjust the strings as you weave to be sure the height of the basket is even all around.

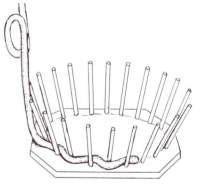

FIGURE 9-2 Weaving the first dough string around the dowels on the form

9. Brush egg wash over the bottom ½ inch (1.2 cm) of the strings inside the basket. Place the reserved oval piece of dough inside the basket, stretching it slightly and pressing it against the egg wash. Prick the bottom of the basket thoroughly. Brush egg wash on the inside base and on both the inside and outside of the basket. Place the particleboard on a sheet pan.

10. Bake the basket at 350°F (175°C) until golden brown, approximately 1½ hours. Let cool completely, then remove the wooden dowels by twisting as you pull them out.

11. Cover the outside of the basket with aluminum foil. Remove it from the particleboard and place the basket, upside down, on a sheet pan. Return the basket to the oven and bake until the bottom is golden brown, approximately 30 minutes.

12. While the basket is baking, make the handle (see "How to Make a Three-Dimensional Handle"). Using the same method used to roll the strings for the sides, roll each of the 1-pound (455-g) pieces of dough to 7 feet (2 m 10 cm) long. If you do not have a table long enough to allow for the full length, loosely curl one end of the string as you are working on the other.

13. Braid the strings into a two-string braid (see instructions on page 430). Because it would take a great deal of room to braid the strings at their full length, curl the ends loosely as needed as you place one on top of the other to form the *X*. The finished braid should be 3 feet (90 cm) long; stretch if necessary.

14. Place the braid on a sheet pan lined with baking paper and form it into a softly curved semicircle measuring 14 inches (35 cm) across the bottom. Bend the lower 5 inches (12.5 cm) of each side inward slightly to conform to the angle of the slanted sides of the basket (Figure 9-3).

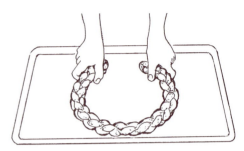

FIGURE 9-3 **Bending the lower edges of the handle before baking to make the angle conform to the slanted sides of the Bread Basket**

15. Brush the handle with egg wash. Bake at 350°F (175°C) until golden brown, approximately 1 hour. It is important to bake the handle and the basket to the same color, or the handle will not look attractive on the finished basket. Let the handle cool.

16. To make the border: Using the same method as you did to braid the handle, roll out the 10-ounce (285-g) pieces of dough to 8 feet (2 m 40 cm) each. Braid the pieces together in a two-string braid. Allowing the dough to relax as needed, stretch the finished braid to 38 inches (95 cm) long. Carefully transfer the braid to a sheet pan lined with baking paper and shape into an oval the same size as the top of the baked basket. Using a little egg wash to make them stick, press the ends together.

17. Brush the braided oval with egg wash. Bake at 350°F (175°C) until golden brown, approximately 35 minutes. Again, it is important to bake this piece to the same color as the handle and the basket.

CHEF'S TIP

Although the weaver's dough is very firm, the weight of the top strings tends to flatten and compress the bottom 2 or 3 strings as you weave the sides of the basket. To avoid this, after weaving the first 2 strings, place the basket in the freezer long enough for them to firm. Repeat after weaving 2 more, and so on. The strings are intentionally rolled out too short. By stretching them and making them stick to the dowels as you weave, you ensure they will remain in place. After baking, the dowels are easy to pull out because of the aluminum foil.

18. Roll each of the remaining 1-ounce (30-g) pieces of dough to 25 inches (62.5 cm) long. These pieces must be perfectly even in diameter. Let the dough relax, then cut each rope into 5 pieces, each 5 inches (12.5 cm) long. Place the pieces on a sheet pan lined with baking paper, keeping them perfectly straight.

19. Brush the dough with egg wash. Bake at 350°F (175°C) until golden brown, approximately 15 minutes. Let cool.

20. Using a serrated knife, trim both ends of the basket handle flat so they can stand against the bottom of the basket. The dough is hard, so this will take some patience. Trim the sides of the lower part of the handle as needed so they will fit snugly inside. If the handle does not fit correctly, warm it in the oven, then bend it to the proper angle. Plan to place the handle so the flat side (the side that was against the sheet pan) is facing the side of the basket where the strings were joined.

21. Insert the bread dough dowels into the holes around the rim of the basket; you may need to trim them a bit with a file or coarse sandpaper.

22. Using a serrated knife or file, trim the top of the basket as necessary so the border lies flat and even on top. Trim the inside of the border, if needed, where the handle will be placed inside.

23. Follow the recipe for Caramelized Sugar for Decorations (page 613), cooking the syrup until it just starts to show a hint of golden-brown color. Immediately place the pan in a bowl of cold water and hold it there for a few moments to stop the cooking process. Take the pan out of the water and let the syrup cool until it is thick enough to be applied with a metal spatula.

24. When the sugar has reached the proper consistency, spread a thin layer in 4 or 5 places on the bottom of the border. Immediately press the border in place, placing the seam on the side of the basket where the strings meet.

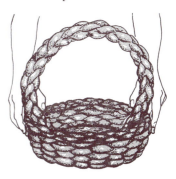

25. Quickly and carefully apply sugar to the inside of the basket where the handle will sit and to the outside of the handle where it will touch the inside of the basket. Position the handle in the basket and press it into place (Figure 9-4). Hold the handle straight for a few minutes until the sugar is hard.

All that is required now is to bake rolls and bread knots to fill up the basket. Tying a satin ribbon to the top of the basket handle adds a nice touch.

FIGURE 9-4 Holding the handle in place at the proper angle until the sugar hardens

NOTE: If you do not have time to make a border, use the extra dough for 2 additional strings. Your basket will look just fine.

How to Make a Three-Dimensional Handle

Unfortunately, it is impossible to bake the basket handle standing up. Therefore, the side that is against the sheet pan is flat after baking and not very attractive. This is fine if the basket is to be displayed in a corner or against a wall, but it doesn't look good if visible from all sides. If this is the case, it is best to make two thinner handles and glue them together with sugar after baking to achieve a more three-dimensional effect. In Steps 12 and 13, divide the 1-pound (455-g) pieces of dough into 4 pieces each. Roll out the pieces evenly to the length given, but braid the 8 pieces into 2 braids following the instructions for Four-String Braid I instead (page 430). Bake as directed, cool, then glue the flat sides of the handles together with boiled sugar or Royal Icing (page 680). Attach the handle to the basket.

Preserving the Bread Basket

While the bread dough portion of the basket will last almost indefinitely, the sugar glue, if untreated, will absorb moisture from the air and soften and fall apart fairly quickly. To prevent this, spray or brush the basket with food lacquer and store in an airtight plastic bag. Alternatively, the handle and border can be attached with Royal Icing (page 680). This will last forever, like the bread dough, but will take approximately 24 hours to harden completely. If time permits, this is the practical way of assembling the basket. Hold the handle in place while the icing dries by wrapping plastic wrap over the handle and securing it underneath the basket.

WEAVER'S DOUGH yield: 8 pounds 2 ounces (3 kg 695 g) dough

Weaver's dough is used to make ornaments and decorations. Because of its elasticity, it is well suited to long pieces — strings for a bread basket, for example. Because the dough does not contain yeast, pieces made of it look exactly as you shaped them. For the same reason, the results are quite hard and not very appetizing. They are intended for purely decorative purposes.

¼ cup (60 ml) vegetable oil

2 eggs

2 ounces (55 g) salt

2 ounces (55 g) granulated sugar

4½ cups (1 L 80 ml) water

5 pounds 12 ounces (2 kg 615 g) bread flour

Egg wash

1. Add the oil, eggs, salt, and sugar to the water in a mixer bowl.

2. Incorporate all but a handful of the flour. Using the dough hook, knead for approximately 10 minutes to make a smooth and elastic dough. Adjust with additional flour as needed.

3. Cover the dough and let it rest for about 1 hour before using. Weaver's dough can be stored, covered, in the refrigerator for up to 4 days without deteriorating and, frozen, will keep for months.

4. Shape as desired.

5. Before baking the dough pieces, brush them with egg wash. For the maximum amount of shine on the finished pieces, let the first layer of egg wash dry, then apply a second coat.

6. Bake at 350°F (175°C) until the pieces have a nice deep golden color.

INSTRUCTIONS FOR MAKING A TWO-STRING BRAID

1. Form the strings as directed.

2. Place the strings in a wide × shape in front of you.

3. Pick up the two ends of the bottom string and move them straight across the other string so they change sides but do not cross over each other.

4. Repeat the procedure with the other string. Repeat until the braid is finished.

INSTRUCTIONS FOR MAKING A FOUR-STRING BRAID I

1. Form the strings as directed.

2. Braid 2 over 3.

3. Braid 4 over 3 and 2.

4. Braid 1 over 2 and 3.

5. Repeat braiding sequence.

Braided Stollen yield: 4 loaves, 1 pound 2 ounces (510 g) each

This is a simplified version of the usual richer stollen, which is studded with the familiar candied and dried fruits. Although it lacks most of those goodies, braided stollen has a delightful flavor of its own supplied by orange zest, orange flower water, and golden raisins (known in Europe as *sultana raisins*). While the *Dresdener* and *Weihnacht* varieties of stollen are made for Christmas only (see "About Stollen," page 435), many other types of stollen are enjoyed throughout the year in Germany and Switzerland. Some of these — with almond, quark or cottage cheese, or poppy seed filling — resemble Danish-style coffee cakes more than anything else and are made to be enjoyed with a cup of coffee or tea.

Braided stollen can be baked directly on sheet pans lined with baking paper if suitable loaf pans are not available. It is delicious toasted and topped with sweet butter as soon as the hot slices pop out of the toaster, so the butter melts into the bread.

2 ounces (55 g) fresh compressed yeast	½ teaspoon (2.5 ml) vanilla extract
1½ cups (360 ml) warm water (105° to 115°F/40° to 46°C)	2 eggs
1 ounce (30 g) granulated malt extract *or* 3 tablespoons (45 ml) or 2 ounces (55 g) honey	3 ounces (85 g) blanched almonds, finely ground
	4 ounces (115 g) unsalted butter, at room temperature
3 ounces (85 g) granulated sugar	7 ounces (200 g) golden raisins
1 tablespoon (15 g) salt	About 2 pounds (910 g) bread flour
Grated zest from 1 orange	Egg wash
½ teaspoon (2.5 ml) orange flower water	Cinnamon sugar

1. Dissolve the yeast in the warm water. Add the malt extract or honey, granulated sugar, and salt. Combine the orange zest, orange flower water, vanilla, and eggs. Add this mixture to the yeast mixture, together with the almonds, butter, and raisins.

2. Reserve a handful of the bread flour and incorporate the remaining flour into the mixture, kneading for a few minutes. Adjust the consistency of the dough by adding the reserved flour, if necessary, to make a soft and elastic dough. Cover the dough and let it rise in a warm place until it has doubled in volume.

3. Punch down the dough and divide it into 4 equal pieces, approximately 1 pound 2 ounces (510 g) each. Divide each of these pieces into 4 pieces again. Pound and roll each of the 16 small pieces into a rope 12 inches (30 cm) long. Braid each group of 4 ropes following the instructions for Four-String Braid II (instructions follow).

4. Place the braided loaves in greased bread pans measuring 8 × 4 × 4 inches (20 × 10 × 10 cm). Brush with egg wash, then sprinkle cinnamon sugar over the tops. Let the loaves rise until 1½ times the original size.

5. Bake at 400°F (205°C) for approximately 30 minutes or until baked through. Immediately remove from the pans and transfer to racks to cool.

INSTRUCTIONS FOR MAKING A FOUR-STRING BRAID II

1. Form the dough strings as instructed in Step 3.

2. Line the strings up next to one another and start braiding in the center, working toward you.

3. Braid 4 over 3.

4. Braid 2 over 3.

5. Braid 1 under 2.

6. Repeat braiding sequence.

7. Squeeze the ends pieces together and tuck underneath. Turn the braid around on its axis (keeping it right-side up) and repeat the braiding sequence to braid the other half.

Chestnut Bread yield: 4 loaves, 1 pound 10 ounces (740 g) each

I nearly gave up on this recipe in the beginning because while the flavor was great, it seemed that no matter what I did or how carefully I treated the dough, I simply could not get a healthy, attractive oven-spring in the baked bread. I singled out the chestnuts as the culprit, but it took a few tries before I realized exactly how they were adversely affecting the loaves: Because of their high starch content, the chestnuts reduced the gluten strength of the bread flour I was using to approximately that of ordinary cake flour. Switching to high-gluten flour made all the difference.

You can enjoy chestnut bread any time of the year by making it with canned chestnut puree and packaged whole roasted chestnuts. (The best-quality whole chestnuts seem to be the French imports packed in glass jars.) This bread also makes an excellent poultry stuffing for Thanksgiving — the chestnuts are already included. If you do not have bannetons to form the bread, make regular round or oval free-form loaves; these will be just as good, with the same rich chestnut flavor.

SPONGE

1 ounce (30 g) fresh compressed yeast

1 cup (240 ml) warm water (105° to 115°F/40° to 46°C)

¼ cup (60 ml) or 3 ounces (85 g) honey

8 ounces (225 g) high-gluten bread flour

DOUGH

1 pound 12 ounces (795 g) chestnuts in the shell *or* 1 pound 8 ounces (680 g) shelled chestnuts

2 ounces (55 g) unsalted butter

1½ ounces (40 g) fresh compressed yeast

2 cups (480 ml) warm milk (105° to 115°F/40° to 46°C)

12 ounces (340 g) unsweetened chestnut puree

4½ teaspoons (23 g) salt

8 ounces (225 g) whole wheat flour

About 1 pound 10 ounces (740 g) high-gluten bread flour

1. To make the sponge, dissolve the yeast in the warm water, then add the honey and the bread flour and stir until the mixture is smooth. Cover and let the sponge proof in a warm place until it has doubled in volume and starts to fall.

2. If using chestnuts in the shell, remove the shells (see Chef's Tip), then proceed. Chop the shelled chestnuts into ½-inch (1.2-cm) pieces. Place in a skillet with the butter and sauté gently over medium heat until they feel soft to the touch.

3. To start the dough, dissolve the yeast in the warm milk in a mixer bowl (make certain the milk is no hotter than specified or you risk damaging the yeast). Add the chestnut puree, salt, the sponge, and the whole wheat flour, mixing until combined.

4. Reserve a handful of the bread flour and incorporate the remainder into the dough. Using the dough hook at low speed, knead for 8 to 10 minutes. Adjust the consistency by adding the reserved flour (or more) if necessary to make a smooth and elastic dough. Add the prepared chestnuts and mix only until they are incorporated.

5. Cover and allow the dough to rest in a warm place until it has doubled in volume.

CHEF'S TIP

To remove the shells from fresh chestnuts: Cut a small × on the flat side of each shell or cut through the shell all around the center of each nut. Roast in a 375°F (190°C) oven for 10 to 15 minutes or cook in boiling water for 5 to 15 minutes, depending on whether or not the chestnuts will be cooked further. Chestnuts are easiest to peel while they are still warm. Cutting the × goes faster and works fine if you do not need the chestnuts to remain whole. Cutting through the shell all around takes more time, but the two halves of the shell pull apart during cooking, making it easy to remove each chestnut whole.

About Chestnuts

Botanically, chestnuts are classified as a fruit rather than a nut, as they contain a greater amount of starch than oil. The chestnuts (typically, two or three of them) develop inside a prickly green husk and ripen about the time of the first frost in October. Each golden nut is enclosed in a thin brown membrane, then covered by a smooth, mahogany-colored, leathery shell. The nuts are found fresh in the markets during the late fall and winter months and must be cooked and peeled before they are eaten. Just as they are in Europe today, chestnuts were once plentiful in the United States until a blight, transferred from a newly planted Far East variety, destroyed most of the trees early in the twentieth century. Though slowly on their way back, the chestnuts produced by the variety of chestnut tree found in the United States are much smaller, although sweeter, than the better-known Spanish variety. Consequently, most fresh chestnuts are imported from Europe — for the most part, from Italy.

In addition to fresh in the shell or fresh vacuum-packed, chestnuts can be purchased dried, either whole or ground into flour; canned in brine; frozen; dehydrated; as a puree, either sweetened or unsweetened; and last, but certainly not least when it comes to flavor, are the wonderful and luxurious *marrons glacés* (candied chestnuts), which are outrageously expensive but sensationally delicious. Fresh or cooked chestnuts should be kept in the refrigerator. The unsweetened puree should not be stored longer than a week, but marrons glacés will keep just about indefinitely.

Because fresh chestnuts are available in winter, they play a big role in holiday creations, both savory and sweet. The most simple of all chestnut preparations is whole nuts roasted over an open fire, made famous by a popular Christmas song and sold by street vendors in some cities in the winter. These are prepared using a special skillet-type of roasting pan with a long handle and a perforated bottom. For all other uses, there is no way to avoid the tedious task of removing the shell and skin.

Sweetened chestnut puree is used alone as a filling and to flavor buttercream; whole candied chestnuts can be used to decorate cakes; chopped candied chestnuts can be added to candies and ice creams.

6. Divide the dough into 4 equal pieces, approximately 1 pound 10 ounces (740 g) each. Dust 4 round bannetons with bread flour. Form each piece of dough into a round loaf and place, seam-side up, in the prepared forms. Let proof until 1½ times their original size.

7. Gently invert the loaves onto sheet pans lined with baking paper. Bake at 400°F (205°C) for approximately 35 minutes or until the loaves feel light when handled and sound hollow when tapped sharply on the bottom.

About Bannetons

Bannetons are coiled reed or willow baskets available in round, oval, or rectangular shapes. The baskets are used to imprint a rustic-looking beehive pattern on loaves of bread as the dough rises and expands. The baskets are dusted with flour before the formed bread loaves are left to proof inside. The flour is used not only to keep the bread from sticking to the basket but so the flour itself will form a distinct spiral pattern on the dough where the flour was pressed into the crevices of the basket. The risen loaves are carefully turned out onto a paper-lined sheet pan or onto a baker's peel to be transferred to the oven. As an alternative, you can use any type of woven basket approximately 8 inches (20 cm) in diameter and 3 to 4 inches (7.5 to 10 cm) deep. If you use a basket not specifically made for this purpose, be certain it has not been coated with lacquer or paint, and cover the interior with cheesecloth before dusting with flour.

Dresdener Stollen yield: 3 loaves, 1 pound 5 ounces (595 g) each (Color Photo 112)

This recipe is a combination of the traditional recipes for Dresdener stollen and German Christmas stollen: I reduced the amount of butter in the classic Dresdener style and added a few eggs instead, which makes the yeast easier to manage; the dough is still plenty rich. A nice variation is to replace about 2 ounces (55 g) of the raisins with candied angelica chopped to the same size. The angelica adds an attractive contrasting color, but if you can't get it, please do not substitute glacéed green cherries.

Well wrapped, a properly baked stollen will keep fresh for many weeks in the refrigerator, or for months in the freezer. This Christmas treat is a must for anyone of German heritage and for some Swedes as well. I often bring it as a house gift at the holidays, and every time, someone who is unsure will ask "Is this stollen?" And I can never resist answering, "Of course not, I baked it myself."

FRUIT AND NUT MIXTURE

2 ounces (55 g) glacéed red cherries

4 ounces (115 g) candied orange peel

4 ounces (115 g) pecans

4 ounces (115 g) golden raisins

4 ounces (115 g) dark raisins

¼ cup (60 ml) dark rum

DOUGH

1½ ounces (40 g) fresh compressed yeast

¾ cup (180 ml) warm whole milk (105° to 115°F/40° to 46°C)

1½ teaspoons (8 g) salt

1½ teaspoons (5 g) granulated malt extract *or* 1 tablespoon (15 ml) honey

1½ ounces (40 g) granulated sugar

2 eggs

1½ teaspoons (3 g) ground cardamom

1 teaspoon (1.5 g) ground cinnamon

½ teaspoon (1 g) ground cloves

½ teaspoon (1 g) ground allspice

1 pound 6 ounces (625 g) bread flour

10 ounces (285 g) unsalted butter, at room temperature

OPTIONAL ALMOND FILLING

8 ounces (225) almond paste

2 to 4 egg whites (¼ cup/60 ml to ½ cup/ 120 ml)

Unsalted butter, melted

Quick Vanilla Sugar (recipe follows)

1. For the fruit and nut mixture: Chop the cherries, candied orange peel, and pecans into raisin-size pieces. Add the golden raisins, dark raisins, and rum. Let macerate for at least 24 hours, stirring from time to time, if possible.

2. To make the dough: Dissolve the yeast in the warm milk (make certain the milk is no hotter than specified or you risk damaging the yeast). Add the salt, malt extract or honey, granulated sugar, eggs, cardamom, cinnamon, cloves, and allspice. Mix in about half of the flour. Add the soft butter and the remaining flour.

3. Knead until the dough is soft and elastic, about 10 minutes. Cover and let proof in a warm place until doubled in volume.

4. Flatten the dough and spread the fruit and nut mixture over the surface, pressing the mixture into the dough with your hands so it sticks. Fold the dough in half to enclose the fruit and nuts. Cover and let rise in a warm location until doubled in volume.

5. To make the almond filling: Add enough egg white to the almond paste to make it just soft enough to pipe through a pastry bag. Place it in a pastry bag with a No. 9 (18-mm) plain tip and set aside.

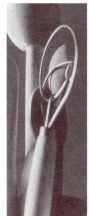

About Stollen

Stollen is the name of rich German yeast bread laden with fruit and nuts and topped with sugar. The shape of the loaves resembles a giant, curved Parkerhouse roll but was originally intended to symbolize Jesus Christ as he was found wrapped in swaddling clothes—the German word *stollen* means "support." The most popular types of stollen are Christmas stollen, also known as *Weihnacht* stollen and the better-known Dresdener stollen, named for the German city of Dresden. Although they look very much the same, their formulas and flavors differ in that Dresdener stollen contains nearly three times more butter than Christmas stollen and it does not contain eggs. Dresdener stollen traditionally features a core of almond paste filling. The filling may be formed into a rope and simply placed on top of the dough before folding, or it can be piped over the dough as is done here. The Christmas stollen, confusingly enough, generally lacks the spices we associate with Christmas treats, such as cloves, cardamom, and cinnamon.

6. Punch down the dough, stretching and shaping it into a flat rectangle at the same time. Divide the dough into 3 equal pieces, approximately 1 pound 5 ounces (595 g) each. Shape the pieces into oval loaves, keeping the fruit and nut mixture inside. If any of the fruit or nuts fall out as you work, tuck them back inside the dough. The idea is to keep the fruit and nuts covered with dough rather than exposed on the surface; that way, they will not dry out or burn during baking. Roll the loaves against the table to make them slightly tapered at the ends, then leave them, seam-side down, on the table.

7. Using a dowel, roll the loaves flat, keeping the same general shape. Press the dowel lengthwise in the center of each loaf to make a slight indentation, but do not press too hard. To add the almond center, pipe a thick rope of almond filling into each indentation, dividing it evenly among the 3 loaves. Fold the flattened pieces almost in half lengthwise, making the bottom part about ½ inch (1.2 cm) wider than the top half. Bend the loaves into a slightly curved shape, with the fold on the inside of the curve (Figure 9-5). Place the loaves on sheet pans lined with baking paper. Let rise until the loaves are 1½ times their original size.

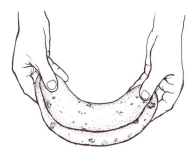

FIGURE 9-5 Bending a folded Dresdener Stollen into a slightly curved shape, with the folded side on the inside of the curve

8. Bake, double-panned, at 375°F (190°C) for about 1 hour or until baked through. Brush the loaves with melted butter immediately after removing them from the oven. As soon as they are cool enough to handle, invert the loaves into quick vanilla sugar.

QUICK VANILLA SUGAR yield: 12 ounces (340 g)

2 teaspoons (10 ml) vanilla extract   4 ounces (115 g) powdered sugar

8 ounces (225 g) granulated sugar

1. Using your hands, rub the vanilla into the granulated sugar.

2. Mix in the powdered sugar until thoroughly blended.

Lucia Buns yield: 30 rolls, approximately 2½ ounces (70 g) each

Lucia Buns (also called *Lucia Cats* because some of the shapes resemble a cat) are traditionally made in Sweden for Saint Lucia's Day, 13 December. This is the darkest, shortest day of the year, and we celebrate that the days grow lighter and longer from that point.

Every city or village crowns a *Lucia* or *Ljusets Drottning*, which means "Queen of Light." Bearing on her head a wreath made of pine boughs studded with candles and wearing a simple, long white dress, she brings light to the darkest day. Lucia appears in the morning, singing and offering coffee, Lucia buns, and gingerbread hearts.

Lucia buns are made from cardamom dough flavored with saffron, but it is a good idea to make some without, as not everyone cares for the flavor. Saffron wreaths and breads are also traditionally made for Christmas in Sweden. They are always left undecorated except for the raisins, either in the dough or on top, and the sugar and almonds sprinkled over them.

Rich Cardamom Yeast Dough (recipe follows)	Egg wash
About 1 teaspoon (1g) saffron, firmly packed	2 ounces (55 g) crystal sugar (optional)
1 tablespoon (15 ml) hot water	2 ounces (55 g) sliced almonds (optional)
2 ounces (55 g) dark raisins	

I. If desired, set aside a portion of the dough to prepare without saffron, decreasing the amount of saffron used accordingly. Soak the saffron in the hot water for a few minutes. Add the saffron to the remainder of the dough and knead the saffron into the dough until it is thoroughly incorporated and no yellow streaks are visible. Cover the dough and let it rest for 10 minutes. At this stage, the dough can be placed in the freezer, well wrapped, for later use.

2. Divide the dough into 3 equal pieces, approximately 1 pound 10 ounces (740 g) each. Roll each piece into a rope and cut each rope into 10 equal pieces, about 2½ ounces (70 g) each. Keep the pieces well covered.

3. When you are ready to form the buns, divide each piece in half. Roll the small pieces into ropes about 5 inches (12.5 cm) long and taper the ends. Using 2 ropes per roll, form the desired shape or shapes, as shown in the top row of Figure 9-6. Alternatively, leave some or all of the pieces whole and use a single rope for each bun, as shown in the bottom row of the illustration. You will probably need to roll these pieces a bit longer than 5 inches (12.5 cm), depending on the shape(s) you create.

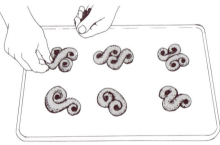

FIGURE 9-6 Decorating Lucia Buns with raisins before baking

4. Place the formed buns on sheet pans and decorate with raisins, as shown. Be sure to press the raisins in firmly, all the way to the bottom of the dough, or they will fall off in the oven. Let the buns rise until they are 1½ times their original size.

5. Brush the buns with egg wash. Combine the crystal sugar and sliced almonds and sprinkle over the tops of the buns, if desired. Bake at 400°F (205°C) for about 15 minutes or until golden and baked through.

CHEF'S TIP

This dough can be formed into braided loaves (see pages 430 and 431) and wreaths. Sprinkle these with a combination of equal parts crystal sugar and sliced almonds. Bake at a slightly lower temperature for a little longer.

RICH CARDAMOM YEAST DOUGH yield: 5 pounds (2 kg 275 g)

2 ounces (55 g) fresh compressed yeast

1 pint (480 ml) warm whole milk (105° to 115°F/40° to 46°C)

6 ounces (170 g) granulated sugar

2 tablespoons (12 g) ground cardamom

1 tablespoon (15 g) salt

4 eggs

About 2 pounds 10 ounces (1 kg 195 g) bread flour

7 ounces (200 g) unsalted butter, melted

1. In a mixer bowl, dissolve the yeast in the warm milk (be certain the milk is no hotter than specified or you risk damaging the yeast). Add the sugar, cardamom, salt, and eggs. Reserve a few ounces of the flour and mix in the remainder. Mix in the butter.

2. Using the dough hook, knead the dough for a few minutes, then adjust by adding the reserved flour, if required, to make the dough firm enough to roll out. Continue to knead until the dough is smooth and elastic, approximately 6 minutes. Cover and let rest 10 minutes before using.

Panettone yield: 4 loaves, 1 pound 6 ounces (625 g) each

Panettone molds can be the reusable type made of metal, or paper ones that stay around the bread when it is sold. If panettone molds are not available, use empty cans, 4 inches (10 cm) in diameter × 4¹/₂ inches (11.2 cm) in height, lined with baking paper, 6-inch (15-cm) cheesecake forms, or even trimmed paper bags. (If you use cans, do not remove the bottoms to form rings, or the dough will proof and bake out from both ends.)

This recipe uses the straight dough method, meaning it does not start with a sponge. It contains slightly smaller quantities of butter and egg yolks than the very rich old-fashioned recipes that called for proofing and punching the dough down many times. Given that some of these older recipes took most of the day to complete, they are not practical by today's standards.

2 ounces (55 g) fresh compressed yeast

2 cups (480 ml) warm water (105° to 115°F/40° to 46°C)

6 ounces (170 g) powdered sugar

6 egg yolks (¹/₂ cup/120 ml)

1 tablespoon (15 g) salt

Grated zest of 2 lemons

1 tablespoon (15 ml) orange flower water

About 2 pounds 11 ounces (1 kg 220 g) bread flour

8 ounces (225 g) unsalted butter, at room temperature

6 ounces (170 g) golden raisins

4 ounces (115 g) Candied Orange Peel (page 756), diced

Egg wash

1. Dissolve the yeast in the warm water.

2. In a separate bowl, combine the powdered sugar with the egg yolks and beat for a few seconds. Add to the yeast mixture. Incorporate the salt, lemon zest, orange flower water, and all but a handful of the flour. Add the soft butter and, using the dough hook, knead for 5 minutes. Adjust by adding the remaining flour, if necessary, to make a smooth, elastic dough. Cover and let rise in a warm place until the dough has doubled in volume.

3. Knead the raisins and candied orange peel into the dough by hand.

4. Line the inside of panettone molds with baking paper. Scale the dough into 4 equal pieces, approximately 1 pound 6 ounces (625 g) each. Form each piece into a round ball, then roll the balls against the table to make cylinders that fit inside the forms. Place the loaves in the forms with the seams hidden, taking care not to wrinkle the baking paper. Let rise in a warm place until the dough just crests above the rim of the forms. Brush egg wash over the tops.

5. Bake at 375°F (190°C) for approximately 35 minutes or until baked through. To be certain they are done, check 1 loaf by removing it from the form — it should have a light brown crust all over. As soon as you take the breads out of the oven, unmold and let cool on a rack, lying on their sides. If they are left in the baking forms, the loaves will become soggy from condensation.

Sweet Pigs' Heads yield: 9 breakfast pastries

As discussed elsewhere in this chapter, the domestic pig earns celebrity status at Christmastime in both Scandinavia and the German-speaking countries of Europe. In Sweden, many of the items on the Christmas *smörgåsbord* are made from pork; edible pigs are created out of marzipan, chocolate, cookie dough, and many yeast doughs; and pig-shaped decorations are formed from weaver's and salt doughs as well.

These adorable pig's-head pastries never fail to bring a smile, and they are quick and easy to produce. The only equipment necessary is a saucer or a bread and butter plate, a few cookie cutters, and a plain piping tip. An amusing variation (in addition to the individual dinner rolls that follow) is to make a whole pig pastry instead of just the head; the pig is admittedly a little abstract but clearly well-fed; see the illustration with the dinner roll variation.

1 recipe Rich Cardamom Yeast Dough
  (page 437)

Egg wash

1 pound 8 ounces (680 g) Pastry Cream
  (page 773)

Whole wheat flour

Royal Icing (page 680)

Dark coating chocolate

I. Divide the dough into 2 equal pieces and form each into a ball. Cover the dough rounds and refrigerate for 30 minutes.

2. Cut an × on top of each ball of dough, cutting down to the center of the ball. Push the corners out on each round to form 2 squares. Roll out each piece of dough to a rectangle measuring 16 × 24 inches (40 × 60 cm); the dough should be approximately ⅛ inch (3 mm) thick. Return the dough sheets to the refrigerator (or place briefly in the freezer) to relax and firm.

3. Using the tip of a knife and a 6-inch (15-cm) plate as a guide, cut out 18 circles. Using a plain cookie cutter, 2½ inches (6.2 cm) in diameter, cut out 9 circles. With a No. 4 (8-mm) plain pastry tip, cut 2 holes across the middle of the small circles to form snouts.

4. Roll some of the larger dough scraps to ¹⁄₁₆ inch (2 mm) thick. Using a plain cookie cutter, 3 inches (7.5 cm) in diameter, cut out 9 circles. Using the same cutter, cut 2 ears out of each circle by making 2 cuts that meet in the center to create 2 pointed ovals. Place these ears in the refrigerator. Cover and refrigerate the remaining dough; save for another use.

5. Brush egg wash over 9 of the larger circles.

6. Insert the same pastry tip used to cut the snout holes in a pastry bag and add the pastry cream. Pipe the cream, dividing it evenly, over the 9 egg-washed rounds, starting at the center and making concentric circles toward the outside. Leave a ½-inch (1.2-cm) border uncovered.

7. Place the 9 remaining large circles on top of the filling and press down firmly all around the outside of the circles to make sure the edges stick, or the filling will ooze out as it bakes. Brush the top of the filled heads with egg wash. Place the snouts on the lower half of the heads. Attach the ears to the top of the heads, curving them forward. Brush egg wash over the snouts and ears.

8. Using a medium mesh sifter, sift whole wheat flour over the heads, covering them completely. These pastries do not require much proofing and will probably be ready to bake after assembly.

9. Bake at 375°F (190°C) until golden brown and baked through, about 25 minutes. Let cool.

10. When the pastries have cooled, scrape away the whole wheat flour at 2 spots fairly close together between the ears and the snout where the eyes should be. Pipe a pea-sized dot of royal icing on each mark. Pipe a small dot of melted coating chocolate on the royal icing to mark the pupils. You can have some fun here by making the pig look left, right, or cross-eyed.

VARIATIONS

PIG'S HEAD DINNER ROLLS yield: 18 rolls (Color Photo 113)

The pigs' heads can also be made into whimsical dinner rolls. Alternatively, use the white bread dough to make bread loaves shaped like whole pigs following the instructions for Whole Large Pig Pastries. The loaves are shown in Color Photo 113 along with the rolls.

White Bread Dough (recipe follows)	Royal Icing (page 680)
Egg wash	Dark coating chocolate
Whole wheat flour	

1. Roll out the dough to make a rectangle measuring 23 × 16 inches (57.5 × 40 cm) and about ¼ inch (6 mm) thick. Cut out 18 circles, 4 inches (10 cm) in diameter, and 18 circles, 1½ inches (3.7 cm) in diameter. Use a No. 2 (4-mm) plain tip to cut the holes in the smaller circles to make snouts. Press the dough scraps together (do not knead them) and refrigerate.

2. Brush egg wash over the larger circles and the snouts. Sift whole wheat flour over the snouts, then attach them close to the lower edge on each head.

3. Roll the scrap dough to ⅛ inch (3 mm) thick. Using a 2-inch (5-cm) cutter, cut the ears as in Step 4 of the main recipe. Attach the ears at the top of the heads and curve them forward. Brush egg wash over the ears. Let the rolls rise until 1½ times the original size.

4. Bake at 400°F (205°C) for about 15 minutes. Decorate as directed in the main recipe (Figure 9-7).

NOTE: For a different look, assemble and egg-wash the pigs' heads first, then sift whole wheat flour over the entire pastry, as in the filled version.

FIGURE 9-7 Piping the eyes on Pig's Head Dinner Rolls; a Whole Large Pig Pastry before and after baking (whole wheat flour was sifted over the rolls and the loaf before baking)

WHOLE LARGE PIG PASTRIES yield: 2 pigs (Color Photo 113)

To make two large pigs, omit the pastry cream filling and make only ½ recipe cardamom yeast dough. Roll out the dough to a rectangle measuring 11 × 25 inches (27.5 × 62.5 cm) and ¼ inch (6 mm) thick. Chill the dough briefly so it is relaxed and firm. Cut out 2 rounds, 10 inches (25 cm) in diameter, for the bodies of the pigs; 2 rounds, 5 inches (12.5 cm) in diameter, for the heads; and 2 rounds, 2 inches (5 cm) in diameter, for the snouts. Using a No. 4 (8-mm) plain pastry tip, cut 2 holes across the center of the snouts. Roll some of the remaining dough to ⅛ inch (3 mm) thick and cut out 2 circles, 2½ inches (6.2 cm) in diameter. Using the same cutter, cut 2 oval ears out of each. Pound and roll 2 small pieces of the leftover dough into thin 7-inch (17.5-cm) strings, tapered at the ends, for the tails.

To assemble the pigs, brush egg wash on the bodies and place the heads at the bottom of the circles. Brush egg wash over the heads and place the snouts at the base of the heads. Attach the ears to the top of the heads, then attach the tails in a curled position at the top of the bodies. Brush egg wash over the snouts, ears, and tails. Sift whole wheat flour over the pigs, covering them completely. Do not let the pigs proof much, if at all. Bake, cool, and form the eyes as instructed in the main recipe.

White Bread Dough yield: 18 rolls, about 3 ounces (85 g) each

2 ounces (55 g) fresh compressed yeast

1 pint (480 ml) cold whole milk

1 pound (455 g) bread flour

1 pound (455 g) cake flour

2 ounces (55 g) granulated sugar

1½ tablespoons (22 g) salt

4 ounces (115 g) unsalted butter, at room temperature

1. Dissolve the yeast in the milk. Add the bread flour, cake flour, sugar, and salt. Using the dough hook, mix until the dough forms a ball. Incorporate the butter.

2. Knead at medium speed until a fine gluten structure develops, 8 to 10 minutes. Test by pulling off a small piece of dough and stretching it lightly; if it forms an almost translucent membrane, the dough has been kneaded enough. Do not overknead, or the gluten structure will be permanently damaged, resulting in a loose and hard-to-work dough that will not rise properly, if at all, because the damaged gluten cannot trap enough air.

3. Place the dough in an oiled bowl, turn to coat both sides, cover, and let rise until doubled in volume.

Swedish Spice Bread (Vörtbröd) yield: 4 loaves, 1 pound 2 ounces (510 g) each

Vört is the Swedish word for "wort," the sweet brown liquid that forms after the first three basic steps in beermaking are completed. The barley is first soaked to facilitate germination. The partially germinated kernels are then dried to stop the enzymes in the process of digesting the starch and to develop the proper color and flavor. Finally, the barley is mashed in warm water, reconstituting the enzymes and producing the wort, or vört. In the old days, this liquid could be purchased from breweries and through bakery suppliers during November and December.

To provide the strong flavor necessary for a good vörtbröd, the vört is boiled until reduced by two-thirds. Porter or dark beer can be substituted but these are relatively expensive for large commercial

½ cup (120 ml) brandy

8 ounces (225 g) golden raisins

8 ounces (225 g) currants

8 ounces (225 g) pecan quarters

6 ounces (170 g) Candied Citron Peel (page 756), chopped to raisin-size pieces

6 ounces (170 g) dried apricots, coarsely chopped

6 ounces (170 g) dried sweet cherries, coarsely chopped

Unsalted butter, melted

10 ounces (285 g) unsalted butter, at room temperature

10 ounces (285 g) granulated sugar

5 eggs, at room temperature

2 tablespoons (30 ml) golden syrup

About 4 cups (960 ml) brandy

Grated zest of 1 orange

Grated zest of 1 lemon

6 ounces (170 g) bread flour

6 ounces (170 g) cake flour

1. Combine all the ingredients for the fruit mixture and let macerate for 24 hours, stirring occasionally.

2. Brush the melted butter over the inside of 2 loaf pans, 8 × 4 inches (20 × 10 cm). Line the pans with baking paper and brush the paper with melted butter.

3. Cream the soft butter with the sugar until light and fluffy. One at a time, incorporate the eggs. Combine the golden syrup, 2 tablespoons (30 ml) of the brandy, the orange zest, and the lemon zest. Add to the butter and sugar mixture.

4. Sift the bread flour and cake flour together. Remove a handful of flour and toss with the macerated fruit mixture. Mix the remaining flour into the batter. Fold in the fruit mixture. Divide the batter between the loaf pans.

5. Bake at 300°F (149°C) for 1 hour. Lower the heat to 275°F (135°C) and continue to bake approximately 30 minutes longer or until a wooden skewer inserted in the middle of the cake comes out dry. Unmold onto a cake rack and let cool.

6. Pierce the bottom of the cakes all over with a skewer. Brush ½ cup (120 ml) brandy over the bottom and sides of the cakes. Wrap the cakes tightly. Each day for 7 days, unwrap the cakes and brush with additional brandy, otherwise keeping the cakes tightly covered. Don't be a miser; use ⅓ to ½ cup (80 to120 ml) brandy every time you brush the cakes.

Panforte yield: 42 pieces, 1 × 2 inches (2.5 × 5 cm) each

Panforte, a dense Italian fruit and nut cake, is traditionally served with a coating of powdered sugar sifted over the top, especially when a whole cake is displayed for sale, in which case the sugar coating is usually quite heavy. I find the sugar can be messy and think the top of the cake looks more appetizing left unadorned because of the profusion of goodies in the filling. However, if you are displaying the small rectangles from this recipe on a platter, an attractive presentation can be achieved by alternating sugar-dusted pieces with plain pieces. In this case, sift powdered sugar lightly over half of the pieces after cutting; be careful not to touch the tops as you are arranging the rectangles on the serving platter.

Unsalted butter, melted

5 ounces (140 g) blanched almonds

5 ounces (140 g) hazelnuts

4 ounces (115 g) walnuts

4 ounces (115 g) Candied Orange Peel (page 756)

4 ounces (115 g) Candied Lemon Peel (page 756) or other citrus peel

4 ounces (115 g) dried apricots

2 ounces (55 g) dried figs

Finely grated zest of 1 lemon

Finely grated zest of 1 orange

¾ cup (180 ml) or 9 ounces (255 g) honey

⅓ cup (80 ml) golden syrup *or* light corn syrup

6 ounces (170 g) light brown sugar

2 ounces (55 g) bread flour

2 ounces (55 g) cake flour

2 teaspoons (3 g) ground cinnamon

½ teaspoon (1 g) ground nutmeg

¼ teaspoon (.5 g) ground white pepper

Powdered sugar (optional)

I. Butter the bottom of a quarter-size sheet pan (12 × 8 inches/30 × 20 cm; see Note) and line with baking paper. Brush melted butter over the paper and the sides of the pan.

2. Chop the almonds, hazelnuts, and walnuts into small pieces about the size of pine nuts. Chop the orange peel, lemon or other citrus peel, apricots, and figs into pieces approximately the same size as the nuts. Thoroughly combine the chopped fruit, chopped nuts, and the grated citrus zests, mixing with your hands and making certain the pieces of fruit do not stick together.

3. Place the honey, golden syrup or corn syrup, and brown sugar in a saucepan. Stir to combine, then bring to a boil, washing down the sides of the pan with a brush and clean water. Continue to boil until the syrup reaches the soft-ball stage (240° to 245°F/115° to 118°C; see Chef's Tip). Remove from the heat.

4. Sift the bread flour, cake flour, cinnamon, nutmeg, and white pepper together into an oversize bowl. Mix in the chopped fruit and nut mixture. Pour the sugar syrup on top and stir until completely incorporated.

5. Transfer the mixture to the prepared sheet pan and press it into the pan using your hands or a spatula to make it flat and even. You must work quickly because it will thicken rapidly as it cools.

6. Bake at 375°F (190°C) for approximately 20 minutes or until baked through. Let cool completely. It is preferable to wrap and refrigerate the cooled cake overnight before proceeding.

About Panforte

Panforte, also known as *Siena cake* and as *Panforte di Siena,* originated in the city of Siena in northern Italy. This flat, unleavened cake can be described as being denser than a sweet cake such as gingerbread, but not quite as rich as a candy. It could also be likened to a chewy distant relative of fruitcake.

Panforte is classically baked in pans lined with oblaten (*ostia* in Italian), an edible paper best known to most people as the little wafer given at holy communion in the Catholic church. The paper serves to keep the cakes from sticking to the pan. Rice paper can also be used with a good result although neither product is necessary. Today, panforte is most often found at Christmastime but, just as you can't visit Vienna without experiencing a taste of Sacher Torte, the thing to do on a trip to Siena is to enjoy panforte, which is made there year-round.

7. Cut around the inside perimeter of the baked sheet, then invert to remove it from the pan. If the cake sticks, warm the pan slightly (warming melts the butter used to grease the pan and releases the cake). Peel the paper from the bottom of the sheet. If the paper is difficult to remove, brush water over the paper, wait a few minutes, and try again. Trim the 2 long edges and cut the panforte lengthwise into 4 strips approximately 2 inches (5 cm) wide. Cut each strip crosswise into 10 pieces approximately 1 inch (2.5 cm) wide.

NOTE: If you do not have a quarter-size sheet pan, see page 97 for directions on modifying a half-sheet pan to the correct size. Using a quarter-size pan will yield a panforte approximately ¾ inch (2 cm) thick. If you use a larger or smaller pan, adjust the baking time accordingly. You can also divide the batter between 2 round cake pans, 8 inches (20 cm) in diameter (prepared as directed in Step 1), and cut each baked cake into 16 narrow wedges. A heavy cake batter like this does not increase much in size during baking.

VARIATION

DARK PANFORTE (Panforte Scuro)

Replace 1 ounce (30 g) cake flour with 1 ounce (30 g) unsweetened cocoa powder. Replace 2 ounces (55 g) of either the candied lemon peel or candied orange peel with an additional 2 ounces (55 g) dried figs.

Yule Logs (Bûches de Noël) yield: 2 logs, 11 inches (27.5 cm) each (Color Photo 116)

It seems as if every pastry chef has his or her own version of *Bûche de Noël* (the French translation of Yule, or Christmas, log). It is customary to cover the logs with a rough coat of chocolate buttercream to simulate tree bark. My rendition is not only iced with chocolate buttercream but also covered with layers of marzipan and dark chocolate. This combination both looks and tastes good and prevents the sponge cake from drying out.

Use your imagination in decorating the logs. It might not make sense to make up a batch of meringue just to produce four or five mushrooms unless you can use the remainder. If you have small gingerbread cookies, such as deer, stars, or hearts, from another project, use them instead to decorate the logs. You can create a stunning showpiece by placing a seated marzipan Santa on the log (see instructions with the Marzipan Pig with Two Santas, page 657), guiding a gingerbread sleigh filled with marzipan packages and led by gingerbread deer. (I always put a tiny drop of red royal icing or red piping gel on the nose of the lead deer.) If you do not have rum ball filling on hand, use the reserved sponge scraps mixed with enough buttercream to make a doughlike mixture, or you can also use marzipan — but this is a rather expensive option, as this portion of the log often is not served.

1 recipe Cocoa Almond Sponge batter (page 795)

Powdered sugar

3 ounces (85 g) marzipan, tinted green

½ ounce (15 g) marzipan, tinted red

1 pound 12 ounces (795 g) Chocolate Buttercream (page 752)

8 ounces (225 g) Rum Ball Filling (page 790)

14 ounces (400 g) marzipan, untinted

Sweet dark chocolate, tempered, or dark coating chocolate, melted

Piping Chocolate (page 543), melted

Meringue Mushrooms (recipe follows)

1. Spread the sponge batter evenly over a sheet of baking paper or a Silpat 24 × 16 inches (60 × 40 cm). Drag the paper onto a sheet pan (or use an offset spatula to spread the batter onto a paper- or Silpat-lined sheet pan). Bake at 425°F (219°C) for about 10 minutes or until just done.

2. Dust a sheet of baking paper with flour and invert the sponge on top to prevent it from becoming dry from sitting on the hot pan. Let cool. If the sponge is needed immediately but seems too dry to roll into a log, follow the procedure in the Note on page 795 to soften it. If made for later use, store the sponge sheet, covered, in the refrigerator (see Note).

3. Using powdered sugar to prevent sticking, roll out the green marzipan to ¹⁄₁₆ inch (2 mm) thick. Using a plain cookie cutter, 2½ inches (6.2 cm) in diameter, cut out circles. Using the same cutter, make 2 cuts that meet in the center to create 2 pointed ovals to be used as leaves. Make about 12 leaves for the 2 logs. Use the back of a small knife to mark veins on the leaves. Use a No. 3 (6-mm) plain piping tip to cut a scalloped edge around the leaves so they look like holly. Set the leaves on a dowel and leave them to dry in a curved shape. Roll the scraps to the same thickness as before and cut out 2 strips, 5 × 1 inch (10 × 2.5 cm); set these aside.

4. Roll the red marzipan into pea-size balls for holly berries. Make 3 balls for every 2 leaves made in Step 3.

5. Peel the Silpat or baking paper from the back of the inverted sponge sheet, leaving the other paper underneath, and trim the sponge to 22 × 15 inches (55 × 37.5 cm). Reserve the scraps for use in Step 8, if desired.

6. Spread approximately four-fifths of the chocolate buttercream evenly over the sponge sheet; use less buttercream on the bottom 1 inch/2.5 cm of the long edge, or it will ooze out as the log is rolled.

7. Starting from the top long edge and rolling toward you, roll up the cake (Figure 9-9). Pull the paper toward you as you roll to help make the log tight. Leaving the paper around the log, hold the bottom of the paper in place with your left hand and push a dowel or ruler against the log on top of the paper; the paper will wrap around the log and make it tighter (Figure 9-10). Refrigerate the roulade, covered and seam-side down, until the buttercream is firm.

FIGURE 9-9 Using the baking paper underneath to facilitate rolling the sponge sheet and buttercream into a roulade for the Yule Log

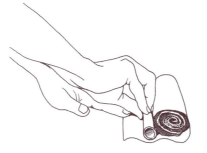

FIGURE 9-10 Pushing a dowel against a Yule Log with a sheet of baking paper between the Yule Log and the dowel while holding the opposite end of the baking paper steady to force the paper to wrap tightly around the Yule Log and compact it slightly

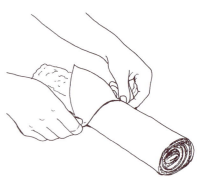

FIGURE 9-11 Pulling a folded piece of baking paper with a straight edge along the length of the Yule Log to make the buttercream smooth and even

8. Roll the rum ball filling into a rope 5 inches (12.5 cm) long and approximately 1½ inches (3.7 cm) in diameter. Roll out 2 ounces (55 g) of the untinted marzipan to ¹⁄₁₆ inch (2 mm) thick. Spread a thin film of buttercream on top and wrap the rum ball rope in the marzipan sheet without overlapping the edges. Refrigerate until cold and firm. Cut the rope in half, then cut each piece in half again at a 45-degree angle to make the pieces straight on 1 end and slanted on the other. Dip these branch stumps into melted chocolate to cover completely. Set aside to let the chocolate harden.

9. Place the chilled roulade on an inverted sheet pan covered with baking paper. Spread a thin layer of the reserved buttercream over the log, spreading it to where the log meets the sheet pan. Smooth the surface of the buttercream by pulling a folded sheet of baking paper around the log (Figure 9-11). Add the buttercream that was scraped off to the remainder.

10. Using powdered sugar to prevent sticking, roll out the remaining 12 ounces (340 g) of untinted marzipan to ¹⁄₁₆ inch (2 mm) thick, rolling it wide and long enough to cover the log to where it meets the pan. Like the buttercream, the marzipan does not go underneath or on the ends. Using your hands to press it in place and smooth it, cover the log with the marzipan. Trim excess marzipan to even the ends. Remove the buttercream from the trimmings; save the marzipan for another use.

11. Spread melted dark chocolate over the marzipan, spreading it back and forth rapidly until the chocolate starts to set up. It should not look completely smooth but rather show long marks from the palette knife, like bark.

12. Using a knife dipped in hot water, trim both ends of the log, then cut the log into 2 equal pieces, each approximately 11 inches (27.5 cm) long. Cover the exposed ends of each log with part of the remaining chocolate buttercream.

13. Dip the slanted ends of the reserved branches into melted dark chocolate and fasten them to the top of the logs, 1 on each side, close to the ends. This is much easier to do if you chill either the logs or the stumps, so the chocolate will harden immediately. Using piping chocolate as glue, decorate the logs with meringue mushrooms and the marzipan holly leaves and berries, placing 2 leaves and 3 berries next to the branch stumps.

14. Make a larger-than-normal piping bag and cut a larger-than-normal opening. Place piping chocolate in the bag and pipe a spiral on the ends of the branch stumps and on the ends of the logs. Sift powdered sugar over the logs for a snow effect.

15. Using piping chocolate in a piping bag with a small opening, write "Merry Christmas" or "Happy Holidays" on each reserved strip of green marzipan. Using piping chocolate as glue, fasten 1 strip in the center of each log.

NOTE: If the sponge sheet is refrigerated overnight, the skin on the top tends to separate from the sponge. Scrape it free from the top before peeling the paper from the back in Step 5.

MERINGUE MUSHROOMS yield: about 90 decorations

¼ recipe French Meringue (page 780)   Piping Chocolate (page 543; see Chef's Tip)
Unsweetened cocoa powder

1. Place the meringue in a pastry bag with a No. 5 (10-mm) plain tip. To make the mushroom caps, pipe out mounds, approximately 1 inch (2.5 cm) in diameter, on a sheet pan lined with baking paper or a Silpat. Use approximately two-thirds of the meringue.

2. To make the stems from the remaining meringue, hold a No. 3 (6-mm) plain tip in place on the outside of the other tip (see Figures 5-4 and 5-5, page 240) and pipe 1-inch (2.5-cm) lengths.

3. Bake at 215°F (102°C) until dry, approximately 2 hours. Let cool.

4. Using the tip of a paring knife, drill a small hole in the back of the mushroom caps.

5. Using a medium mesh strainer, sift cocoa powder lightly over the caps to create large dots of cocoa powder.

6. Place melted piping chocolate in a piping bag. One at a time, pick up a mushroom cap by the edges so as not to disturb the cocoa powder, pipe chocolate into the hole, and push a meringue stem into the chocolate.

COOKIES AND PASTRIES

Chocolate Snow Hearts yield: 120 cookies, 2 inches (5 cm) wide (Color Photo 115)

This delightful, chewy holiday cookie is made in both Switzerland and Germany, where they are actually made all through the year, but in different shapes — the Swiss make them in the shape of a flower and call them *Brunsli*. Although they do not become hard or unpleasant if slightly overbaked, just crunchy, I like the snow hearts best when they are moist and chewy. You can soften dry cookies by placing them in airtight containers with a few slices of apple or, better yet, pineapple quince, if you have it. You will notice a difference in texture after just a few hours, but leaving them overnight will soften the cookies all the way through. Like Cinnamon Stars (page 460), Chocolate Snow Hearts are a variety of macaroon.

1 pound 6 ounces (625 g) finely ground blanched almonds (almond meal)	14 ounces (400 g) sweet dark chocolate, melted
1 pound (455 g) powdered sugar	Granulated sugar
4 egg whites (¹⁄₂ cup/120 ml)	

1. Process the ground almonds, half of the powdered sugar, and the egg whites in a food processor to make a fine paste. Transfer to a mixing bowl and stir in the remaining powdered sugar and the chocolate. Cover and refrigerate until firm.

2. Work the dough smooth with your hands; then, using granulated sugar to prevent sticking, roll it out to ¹⁄₄ inch (6 mm) thick. Use a heart-shaped cutter measuring 2 inches (5 cm) across the widest point to cut out cookies, placing the cuts to yield a minimum of scrap dough. Place the cookies on sheet pans lined with baking paper or Silpats. Knead the scrap dough together, then roll out and cut the remainder of the cookies in the same manner.

3. Bake the cookies at 425°F (219°C) for about 8 minutes or until slightly puffed. Be careful: They are easy to overbake because of the high heat, and the color of the dough can make it difficult to judge when they are done. Do not try to remove the cookies from the baking paper before they are completely cold. If they stick, invert the cookies and peel the paper away from the cookies instead of pulling the cookies off the paper. If this does not help, brush water lightly over the back of the paper, wait a few minutes, and try again. Store the cookies in airtight containers.

Christmas Cookie Ornaments

yield: approximately 65 cookies, 2 inches (5 cm) in diameter (Color Photo 115)

It is traditional in Sweden to decorate the Christmas tree in part with edible ornaments, such as chocolate figures, marzipan Santas, and decorated gingerbread cookies. The cookies were not to be touched by eager little hands when I was growing up, only looked at with wide eyes. We each had our favorites picked out and spoken for long before Christmas Day, when we were finally allowed to eat them. The recipe can be made into regular Christmas cookies instead of ornaments; just omit the hole for the string.

8 ounces (225 g) Gingerbread Cookies dough (page 461)

Lemon-Butter Cookie Dough (recipe follows)

Egg Wash (page 763)

Whole blanched almonds

Piping Chocolate (page 543)

Royal Icing (page 680)

Powdered sugar

Dark coating chocolate

1. Make the gingerbread dough the day before you plan to use it; cover and refrigerate.

2. Roll out the lemon-butter cookie dough to $^3/_8$ inch (9 mm) thick. Mark the top with a tread-pattern marzipan rolling pin (see page 97) or drag a fork across the dough to mark it. Transfer the dough to a sheet pan or a cardboard cake sheet. Lightly brush egg-yolk wash over the dough, brushing in the same direction as the tread, and place it in the refrigerator or freezer for a few minutes to dry the wash a little.

3. While the lemon dough is in the refrigerator, roll out the gingerbread dough to $^1/_{16}$ inch (2 mm) thick. Transfer to a sheet pan or a cardboard cake sheet and reserve in the refrigerator.

4. Remove the lemon dough from the refrigerator and cut out stars, hearts, and round shapes, about 2 inches (5 cm) in diameter. Place on sheet pans lined with baking paper or Silpats. Knead the scrap dough together well, roll it out, brush with yolk wash, chill, and cut more cookies. Repeat until all of the dough has been used. Set the cookies aside.

5. Remove the gingerbread dough from the refrigerator. Cut out small shapes that will contrast with and fit on top of the lemon cookies. Smaller heart and star shapes look good placed in the center of a lemon cookie of the same shape, as does a small gingerbread heart in the center of a round lemon cookie, surrounded by 4 or 5 blanched almonds. If you have holiday cutters that are small enough, use these to cut out the shapes.

6. Decorate the lemon cookies with the gingerbread shapes and blanched almonds. If you plan to hang the

CHEF'S TIP

You can reverse the decorations and place the lemon dough on top of the gingerbread dough. In that case, of course, you will need more gingerbread dough and, as it is useful to have on hand, I suggest you make the full recipe. Roll both doughs to $^1/_8$ inch (3 mm) thick. Mark the lemon dough with the tread roller in the same way, but do not attempt to mark the gingerbread dough, as it is too thin to do so without tearing.

cookies on the tree, use a No. 3 (6-mm) plain piping tip to cut a hole in each for a string or ribbon.

7. Bake at 375°F (190°C) for about 15 minutes or until golden brown. When the cookies have cooled, decorate with piping chocolate, royal icing, and/or sifted powdered sugar. Alternatively, dip whole cookies without contrasting dough on top into coating chocolate thinned with soybean oil and decorate with royal icing or piping chocolate, writing "Merry Christmas" or a person's name. When the chocolate and icing are dry, tie ribbons or gold thread through the holes.

LEMON-BUTTER COOKIE DOUGH yield: 3 pounds 12 ounces (1 kg 750 g)

14 ounces (400 g) powdered sugar

14 ounces (400 g) unsalted butter, at room temperature

3 eggs

Grated zest of 1 lemon

1 teaspoon (5 ml) vanilla extract

1 pound 12 ounces (795 g) bread flour

1. Mix the powdered sugar and butter well, but do not cream. Add the eggs, lemon zest, and vanilla.

2. Incorporate the flour and mix just until combined. It is important not to overmix this dough because the additional air would make the cookies puff and change shape during baking. Refrigerate the dough, if necessary, to make it easier to handle.

Christmas Tree Pastries yield: 52 pastries (Color Photo 117)

These are year-round pastries that are decorated at Christmastime, just like we do with real trees. They are a variation of the recipe for Angelica Points which appears in *The Professional Pastry Chef: Fundamentals of Baking and Pastry*. These, however, are cut into a more elongated triangle and covered with green marzipan rather than untinted. The decoration used here can be applied to other pastries and to larger cakes as well to give them an instant holiday air. Just as the triangular shape of these pastries lends itself to simulating a tree, the ring shape of Paris-Brest or Spritz cookies, for example, makes those easy to turn into wreaths by adding a bow at the top made from marzipan or piped chocolate. However, I strongly recommend against tinting either dough green. A brioche can become a plump, squat Santa by decorating the smaller ball as his head, piping the features with royal icing or piping chocolate, and adding a red marzipan hat on top and a white marzipan beard below. A triangle shape, such as this pastry or a slice of cake, can also be made into a Santa; the top point makes a natural hat, and the wider bottom is easy to decorate as his coat.

1 pound 5 ounces (595 g) Short Dough (page 791)

5 ounces (140 g) smooth strawberry jam plus 3 tablespoons (45 ml) strained

4 pounds 10 ounces (2 kg 105 g) Frangipane Filling (page 769)

2 ounces (55 g) Vanilla Buttercream (Swiss Method; page 753)

1 pound (455 g) marzipan, tinted light green

Sweet dark chocolate, tempered, or dark coating chocolate, melted

Piping Chocolate (page 543)

Powdered sugar

1. Line the bottom of a half-sheet pan (16 × 12 inches/40 × 30 cm) with baking paper. Roll out the short dough to ⅛ inch (3 mm) thick and line the bottom of the pan. Cover the dough scraps and reserve for another use.

2. Spread 5 ounces (140 g) strawberry jam over the dough. Top with the frangipane and spread it evenly.

3. Bake the sheet at 375°F (190°C) until baked through, about 40 minutes. Let cool to room temperature, then refrigerate.

4. When the frangipane sheet is cold (preferably the day after baking), cut off the skin, leveling the top at the same time. To do this, leave the frangipane sheet in the pan and, using the edge of the pan as a guide, cut with a serrated knife held parallel to the top of the cake. Run the tip of a chef's knife around the inside edge of the pan, then invert the sheet to unmold. If the bottom of the sheet sticks to the pan, do not force it. Instead, place a hot sheet pan on the outside for a few seconds to soften the fat in the short dough (or use a blowtorch), then try again. Remove the sheet pan and the baking paper and turn the sheet right-side up. Spread a thin film of buttercream on top of the frangipane.

5. Roll out the marzipan to ¹⁄₁₆ inch (2 mm) thick; it should be slightly larger than the frangipane sheet. Roll up the marzipan on a dowel and unroll on top of the buttercream. Place a clean cardboard cake sheet on top and invert. With the pastry upside down, trim away the excess marzipan. Remove any crumbs or buttercream and save the marzipan trimmings for another use. Refrigerate until the buttercream is firm — but no longer than a few hours, or the marzipan will become damp and sticky from the moist air in the refrigerator.

6. Still working with the pastry upside down and holding the knife at a 90-degree angle so the edges are straight, trim both long sides, then cut the sheet lengthwise into 4 strips; a serrated knife or the very tip of a sharp chef's knife works best.

7. Cut each strip into 13 triangles, with 2 longer sides and a narrower base. Place the pieces, marzipan-side up, on a sheet pan lined with baking paper.

8. Dip each triangle into melted dark chocolate, coating the bottom and sides up to the marzipan (as shown in Figures 3-1 to 3-5, page 94).

9. Place the piping chocolate in a piping bag and cut a small opening. Pipe an abstract tree outline on each pastry, starting at the top and piping back and forth, left to right, as shown in Color Photo 117; end the design about ⅜ inch (9 mm) from the bottom. Pipe 2 vertical lines in the center at the base of the pastry to mark the tree trunk.

10. Place the strained strawberry jam in 2 piping bags and cut small openings. Pipe a dot of jam at the top point on each pastry plus 6 or 7 among the branches below. Sift powdered sugar lightly over the pastries.

NOTE: You can use red piping gel or another flavor of strained red jam or jelly for decorating, as long as it is thick enough to hold its shape when piped.

Cinnamon Stars yield: approximately 75 cookies, 2¼ inches (5.6 cm) wide (Color Photo 115)

Cinnamon Stars are a typical Swiss-German holiday cookie. They are not only easy to make but their cinnamon flavor, chewy texture, and crisp topping make them an unusual addition and a welcome alternative to the traditional assortment of chocolate and butter cookies. They will keep for many weeks, provided the dough is not made too dry by incorporating more ground almonds than necessary.

When you make the dough, take into consideration that the ground almonds will continue to absorb moisture as the dough rests, making it firmer; the finer the almonds are ground, the more moisture they absorb. Do not make the dough too loose, however, just to play it safe; if the dough is too soft, the cookies will not hold their shape during baking, which detracts greatly from their appearance.

1 pound (455 g) granulated sugar

2 tablespoons (30 ml) light corn syrup

4 egg whites (½ cup/120 ml)

3 tablespoons (15 g) ground cinnamon

About 1 pound 5 ounces (595 g) finely ground blanched almonds

1 cup (240 ml) Royal Icing (page 680; see Chef's Tip)

Powdered sugar, as needed

Egg whites, as needed

1. Combine the sugar, corn syrup, egg whites, and cinnamon. Hold back a small amount of the ground almonds; using the paddle attachment in a mixer or working by hand with a spoon, incorporate the remainder. Adjust the consistency, if necessary, by adding more almond to form a smooth, workable paste. Place on a sheet pan lined with baking paper, cover, and refrigerate for at least 1 hour or, preferably, until the next day.

2. Using flour to prevent sticking, roll out the dough to ⅜ inch (9 mm) thick. Place on a cardboard cake sheet or an inverted sheet pan.

3. Adjust the royal icing to a spreadable but not runny consistency by adding powdered sugar or egg whites as needed. Spread just enough on top of the dough to cover the surface. Refrigerate for about 30 minutes, or place in the freezer for a few minutes to firm the dough and icing.

4. Use a 2¼-inch (5.6-cm) star cutter to cut out cookies, placing the cuts so you have a minimum of scrap dough (see Note). Place the cookies, icing-side up, on sheet pans lined with baking paper. Work the scrap dough to completely incorporate the royal icing, then roll out and spread with more icing, as you did the first time. Continue to cut the cookies and reroll the dough until all the dough has been used.

CHEF'S TIP
Do not use any lemon juice when making the royal icing. Instead, add a small amount of cornstarch. Omitting the lemon juice will help prevent the icing from becoming too brown in the oven.

5. Bake at 425°F (219°C) for about 6 minutes or until the icing just starts to turn light brown at the edges. Watch the cookies carefully; they can become overbaked quickly. Let the cookies cool completely before removing them from the paper. Store in airtight containers.

NOTE: If you have difficulty removing the cookies from the cutter without damaging the icing, either the icing contains too much powdered sugar or the dough and icing were not chilled long enough.

Gingerbread Cookies yield: about 90 cookies, 3 inches (7.5 cm) in diameter

It is interesting to note that the Swedish name for this type of gingerbread cookie, *pepparkakor*, suggests that pepper is one of the ingredients. But this is not so. Although black pepper was used in lebkuchen when it was first made many centuries ago, in gingerbread cookies the word *peppar* is simply a reference to the overall spicy flavor.

It is important to plan ahead with this recipe, as the dough must be refrigerated overnight to develop a workable consistency. Because the dough will keep fresh stored, covered, in the refrigerator for several months and even longer in the freezer, there is really no reason to make just the amount required for one project or to try to make the dough just before it is needed. Keeping a ready supply comes in handy during the holidays, not only to provide freshly baked cookies for the cookie tray, but also for gingerbread figures and ornaments and small decorations on Yule logs, gingerbread houses, and plated desserts.

These cookies are brittle and crisp, which is part of their charm, but the proper texture is achieved only if the dough is rolled out extremely thin, as instructed. Failing to do so will result in hard, unpleasant cookies. Because the dough quickly becomes soft when rolled out so thinly, it is important to work with only a small portion at a time, keeping the remainder chilled.

In Sweden, this type of gingerbread cookie is made throughout the year using round or fluted cutters. Heart-shaped ones are generally reserved for Christmas. To make larger cookies or traditional Christmas figures, like gingerbread people, angels, and Santas, roll out the dough a bit thicker ($^1/_8$ inch/3 mm).

For gingerbread houses, make a firmer and less expensive dough by replacing the butter with margarine and increasing the flour by 6 ounces (170 g). You do not necessarily need the butter flavor in a gingerbread house, as by the time it is eaten (if it is) it will most likely be stale, and butter can cause the dough to shrink when used in combination with the additional flour, which means longer kneading. Baked gingerbread cookies will remain fresh for many weeks if stored in airtight containers in a dry place.

15 ounces (430 g) unsalted butter	2 pounds 10 ounces (1 kg 195 g) bread flour
15 ounces (430 g) granulated sugar	1 tablespoon (12 g) baking soda
1$^1/_2$ cups (360 ml) or 1 pound 2 ounces (510 g) light corn syrup	4 tablespoons (20 g) ground cinnamon
$^3/_4$ cup (180 ml) whole milk	2 tablespoons (12 g) ground cloves
	2 tablespoons (12 g) ground ginger

1. Place the butter, sugar, corn syrup, and milk in a saucepan. Heat, stirring the mixture constantly, just until the butter and sugar have melted and the mixture is smooth; do not overheat.

2. Sift the flour, baking soda, cinnamon, cloves, and ginger together. Place the butter mixture in a mixer bowl. Using the paddle attachment, incorporate the dry ingredients and mix well.

3. Line the bottom of a sheet pan with baking paper. Dust the paper with flour and place the dough on top. Flatten the dough, then refrigerate, covered, overnight.

4. Roll out a small portion of dough at a time to $^1/_{16}$ inch (2 mm) thick. Keep the dough you are not working with in the refrigerator. The dough will feel sticky, but do not be tempted to mix in additional flour. The flour used in rolling the dough will be enough, and too much flour will make the baked cookies hard and unpleasant-tasting.

5. Use a 3-inch (7.5-cm) heart- or star-shaped cookie cutter to cut out cookies. Place them, staggered, on sheet pans lined with baking paper. Add the dough scraps to the fresh dough as you roll out the next batch.

6. Bake the cookies at 400°F (205°C) for 10 minutes, or until they have a rich brown color.

Holiday Candle Pastries yield: 40 pastries, 2¼ inches (5.6 cm) in diameter (Color Photo 117)

These are really cute and quite easy to produce — they are nothing more than a mazarin pastry dressed up for the holidays. When combined with Christmas Tree Pastries (page 458) and the petite Yule Log Pastries (page 468), they impart an elegant seasonal appearance to your pastry selection. To simplify, make plain mazarins (omitting the marzipan rings and dipping the top of the pastries in chocolate), top with apricot glaze and fondant, push the marzipan candles gently into the glaze on top of the pastries, and place the small cookies around the edges before the glaze starts to dry. This quicker version has a shorter shelf life than the chocolate-dipped holiday pastries, which stay fresh up to 1 week.

1 pound (455 g) Short Dough (page 791)

4 ounces (115 g) smooth raspberry jam

1 pound 6 ounces (625 g) Frangipane Filling (page 769)

Bread flour

Powdered sugar

12 ounces (340 g) marzipan, untinted

4 ounces (115 g) Gingerbread Cookies dough (page 461) or Short Dough (page 791)

Dark coating chocolate, melted

Marzipan Candles (directions follow)

1. Using just enough flour to prevent sticking, roll out the short dough to ⅛ inch (3 mm) thick. Line 40 mazarin forms with the dough (see Note). Place the forms, staggered, on a sheet pan. Cover the scrap dough and reserve for another use.

2. Place the jam in a piping bag and pipe a small dot of jam, about ¼ teaspoon (1.25 ml), on the bottom of each form. Place the frangipane filling in a pastry bag with a No. 5 (10-mm) plain tip. Pipe the filling into the forms, filling them to just below the rim.

3. Bake at 400°F (205°C) for approximately 12 minutes or until light brown around the edges. Remove from the oven, dust bread flour lightly over the tops, and invert. Set aside to cool upside down. Remove the forms before the pastries have cooled completely.

4. Using powdered sugar sparingly so it will not be visible on the marzipan, roll out the marzipan to slightly thicker than ⅛ inch (3 mm). Texture the surface with a waffle roller (see page 97). Using a plain cookie cutter, 2¼ inches (5.6 cm) in diameter, cut out 40 circles. Using a plain cutter, ¾ inch (2 cm) in diameter, cut out the centers, leaving rings. (If you are working with the precise amount of marzipan called for, you will have to roll out and cut about half of the circles, cut out the centers, and reroll the centers to make the second half.) Set the marzipan rings aside.

5. Roll out the gingerbread dough or short dough to ¹⁄₁₆ inch (2 mm) thick. Cut out 120 small hearts or stars, about ¾ inch (2 cm) in diameter. Bake at 400°F (205°C) until brown (light brown for short dough), about 4 minutes. Set the cookies aside.

6. Hold the pastries upside down and dip the top surface into melted coating chocolate. Set right-side up on a sheet pan lined with baking paper. Place a marzipan ring on top and insert a marzipan candle in the center of each ring before the chocolate hardens. After a while, you will be able to determine how many pastries you can dip before stopping to place the marzipan pieces on top. Be careful not to get chocolate on the marzipan or the sides of the pastries.

7. Place a small amount of melted chocolate in a piping bag. Pipe 3 very small, evenly spaced dots around the candle on the marzipan ring. Set a small cookie on top of each dot.

NOTE: The quantities of short dough and frangipane filling specified are based on using small mazarin forms, 2¼ inches (5.6 cm) in diameter across the top, 1¾ inches (4.5 cm) across the bottom, and ¾ inch (2 cm) in height. Any type of form, fluted or plain, that is close to this size can be substituted, but the amounts of filling and dough may need to be increased or decreased. The size of the marzipan rings should be adjusted as well if a different size form is used.

MARZIPAN CANDLES yield: 40 decorations, 1 inch (2.5 cm) each

10 ounces (285 g) marzipan, untinted
Red food coloring

Few drops of egg white

1. Divide the marzipan into 2 equal pieces and roll each into a rope 20 inches (50 cm) long. Place the ropes side by side and cut them into pieces 1 inch (2.5 cm) long. If the marzipan has become soft from rolling the ropes, refrigerate the ropes for a short time before cutting to produce clean cuts without flattening the ends.

2. Use a small melon ball cutter to scoop out a half-sphere at an angle on 1 end of each piece. Work the cut-out pieces together and reserve. Using your thumb and forefinger, smooth and shape the cut end of each candle; place them in straight rows on a sheet pan or cardboard cake sheet lined with baking paper as you finish each.

3. Color about ¾ ounce (22 g) of the reserved marzipan (a piece about the size of an unshelled pecan) with red food coloring. Reserve the remaining marzipan for another use. Roll the red marzipan into a rope 20 inches (50 cm) long. Cut the rope into 40 equal pieces. Roll the pieces into round balls, then into ½-inch (1.2-cm) ovals, pointed at both ends.

4. Using a pointed marzipan tool or a No. 1 (2-mm) plain pastry tip, make a small hole in the scooped-out end of each candle. Use a little egg white to glue the candle flames in place.

CHEF'S TIP
To give the candles an authentic burning look, roll tiny pieces of the leftover untinted marzipan into teardrop shapes to simulate drops of melted wax. Using egg white, attach a drop to the front of each candle, hanging from the lower, rounded edge.

Lebkuchen Bars yield: 1 pan, 16 × 12 inches (40 × 30 cm), or 24 pieces

This recipe is a simplified filled version of lebkuchen in which the filling is mixed with the dough, then the mixture is spread into a baking pan and cut into bars after baking. The recipe for Lebkuchen Hearts (page 464) makes a more traditional cookie.

Covered and refrigerated, Lebkuchen Bars will keep fresh for up to five days. It is best, however, to slice the pieces as needed if the cookies are to be stored for that length of time.

1 teaspoon (2 g) ground nutmeg

1 teaspoon (1.5 g) ground cinnamon

1 teaspoon (2 g) ground cloves

1 teaspoon (5 g) salt

½ teaspoon (2 g) baking powder

½ teaspoon (2 g) baking soda

10 ounces (285 g) bread flour

4 ounces (115 g) mixed Candied Citrus Peel (page 756), finely chopped

2 ounces (55 g) candied angelica *or* candied red cherries, finely chopped

3 ounces (85 g) blanched almonds, finely chopped

3 eggs

4 ounces (115 g) brown sugar

Grated zest and juice of ½ lemon

1 cup (240 ml) or 12 ounces (340 g) honey

½ cup (120 ml) Fondant (page 578)

Simple syrup

1. Add the nutmeg, cinnamon, cloves, salt, baking powder, and baking soda to the flour. Sift together and reserve.

2. Combine the candied citrus peel, candied angelica or cherries, and the almonds.

3. Whip the eggs and brown sugar together until the mixture is light and fluffy. Add the lemon zest and juice, honey, and half of the flour mixture. Blend until smooth. Incorporate the remaining flour mixture. Stir in the candied fruit and almonds.

4. Line a half-sheet pan (12 × 16 inches/30 × 40 cm) with baking paper. Spread the batter evenly over the pan. Bake at 375°F (190°C) for approximately 25 minutes or until baked through. Let the sheet cool just long enough for you to be able to handle it comfortably.

5. Adjust the consistency of the fondant by adding simple syrup or water as needed to make it easy to spread. Spread the glaze evenly over the warm lebkuchen. Set aside until completely cool.

6. Run a knife around the perimeter of the pan, invert, peel the paper from the back, and turn right-side up. Use a sharp knife to trim all 4 sides, then cut the sheet into 24 bars. Store, well wrapped, in the refrigerator.

Lebkuchen Hearts yield: about 80 cookies, 3 inches (7.5 cm) wide

These cookies require advance planning, as the starter dough must rest for at least two days in the refrigerator.

1 pound 8 ounces (680 g) or 2 cups (480 ml) honey

4 ounces (115 g) or ⅓ cup (80 ml) molasses

6 ounces (170 g) granulated sugar

⅓ cup (80 ml) water

1 pound 4 ounces (570 g) rye flour

1 pound 2 ounces (510 g) bread flour

3 tablespoons (15 g) ground cinnamon

2 teaspoons (4 g) ground cloves

2 teaspoons (4 g) ground cardamom

2 teaspoons (4 g) ground nutmeg

1 teaspoon (5 g) salt

4 egg yolks (⅓ cup/80 ml)

4 teaspoons (14 g) ammonium carbonate

⅓ cup (80 ml) whole milk

2 teaspoons (7 g) potash *or* 1 tablespoon (12 g) baking soda

Egg white

1. Heat the honey and molasses to about 120°F (49°C); set aside and keep warm.

2. Place the sugar and water in a saucepan, bring to a boil, then stir into the honey and molasses mixture. Set aside to cool to approximately 85°F (29°C).

3. Incorporate the rye flour and 7 ounces (200 g) of the bread flour, mixing just until you have a smooth dough. Cover tightly and let rest in the refrigerator for a minimum of 2 days or, preferably, 1 week.

4. Remove the dough from the refrigerator and let stand at room temperature until slightly softened. Add the cinnamon, cloves, cardamom, nutmeg, and salt to the egg yolks and stir to make a smooth paste.

5. Dissolve the ammonium carbonate in half of the milk, and the potash or baking soda in the other half. Add the egg yolk and spice mixture, both leavening mixtures, and the remaining 11 ounces (310 g) bread flour to the dough, mixing until smooth.

6. Place the dough on a sheet pan lined with baking paper and dusted with flour. Cover and refrigerate until the dough is firm enough to work with, preferably overnight.

7. Using the minimum amount of flour necessary to prevent sticking, roll out the dough in portions to ¼ inch (6 mm) thick. Using a heart-shaped cookie cutter, 3 inches (7.5 cm) across the widest part, or another shape of approximately the same size, cut out cookies. Place on sheet pans lined with baking paper or Silpats and brush egg white lightly over the tops.

8. Bake double-panned at 425°F (219°C) for approximately 12 minutes or until dark brown. As soon as you remove the cookies from the oven, lightly brush egg white over the tops again. If you don't manage to do this immediately, just skip this step.

About Lebkuchen

German *lebkuchen* have a flavor similar to gingerbread cookies, but they are softer, chewier, and much thicker, due to the addition of honey and the use of leavening agents. There are many well-known lebkuchen variations, such as *honig kuchen, pfefferkuchen,* and the Swiss *Basler Leckerli.*

Lebkuchen was originally made using yeast for leavening, but yeast was found to be too strong as it caused the dough to expand in all directions, making it impossible to create the precise shapes desired. Experiments with ammonium carbonate and potash eventually proved that using a combination of these leaveners was the best solution. Further trial and error developed the technique of preparing a starter lebkuchen dough without leavening. This was left to rest for two or three days before incorporating the leavening and the remaining ingredients and forming the cookies. In some old-fashioned recipes the initial dough was left to rest for months, as the resting period favorably changed the taste and lightened the texture of the finished product. The use of two leavening agents, combined with the resting period, resulted in a more even rise to the dough, allowing for more exact designs. The art of making lebkuchen was further refined as molds carved from wood, made from earthenware, and cut from metal, came to be used to shape the cookies.

Decoration has always been important in making lebkuchen. Tinted icings were piped on the cookies in artistic designs that reflected the style of the times. During the Romantic period, small colored pictures depicting angels, Santas, and other seasonal motifs were glued to the top of the shiny dark brown cookies. Lebkuchen cookies are also made with fillings of almond paste, nuts, and candied fruit.

Springerle yield: variable, depending on the size of the molds used

If you do not share the old-country love of anise flavoring, substitute lemon oil or finely grated lemon zest. The baked cookies can be left plain to enjoy with coffee or tea (sometimes they get so hard they need a little dunking first), or they can be painted and used as ornaments. For ornaments, use a small, plain pastry tip to make a hole for a ribbon before baking; thread ribbon through the hole after decorating.

Springerle molds can be used to press designs into rolled marzipan in much the same way as they are used to shape the cookies (of course, the marzipan is not baked as the cookies are). The marzipan pieces may be used as ornaments or placed on top of a cake or pastry, left plain, painted, or coated with a thin film of melted cocoa butter. Use firm marzipan so it holds the image from the mold.

½ teaspoon (1.75 g) ammonium carbonate	4 ounces (115 g) unsalted butter, at room temperature
¼ cup (60 ml) whole milk, at room temperature	1 teaspoon (5 g) salt
6 eggs, at room temperature	1 teaspoon (5 ml) anise oil
1 pound 9 ounces (710 g) powdered sugar, sifted	2 pounds 4 ounces (1 kg 25 g) cake flour

1. Stir the ammonium carbonate into the milk to dissolve. Set aside.

2. Using the paddle attachment, beat the eggs with a handful of the sugar until light and fluffy, about 5 minutes. Slowly add the remaining sugar and continue beating several minutes longer until creamy and smooth. Beat in the soft butter, followed by the ammonium carbonate mixture, the salt, and the anise oil.

3. Gradually incorporate the flour. Place the dough on a sheet pan lined with baking paper, cover, and place in the refrigerator until well chilled.

4. Remove a portion of the dough from the refrigerator and work it smooth. Keep the dough you are not working with covered and chilled to prevent its surface from drying. Using just enough additional sifted powdered sugar to prevent sticking, roll the dough to ¼ inch (6 mm) thick; deep molds require thicker dough. Rub the surface of the dough with powdered sugar; it should not show. Firmly press the springerle mold straight down into the dough without moving it from side to side. Remove the mold and cut the image out of the dough, leaving a frame of dough around the design or not, as desired. Transfer the cookies to sheet pans lined with baking paper.

5. After forming all of the cookies, cover them lightly with a cloth or towel and set aside at room temperature to dry overnight.

6. Bake the cookies at 250°F (122°C) for approximately 20 minutes (see "Making Perfect Springerle"); large cookies will take up to twice as long. Store in airtight containers at room temperature. The flavor and texture of the cookies will improve after several days of storage; they can be kept for many weeks. Decorated cookie ornaments that will not be eaten should be left in the open to dry thoroughly; they can be sprayed with lacquer.

64. Asian Pear Tart with Honey-Scented Pear Frozen Yogurt (holiday presentation)

(clockwise from top left) **65. Chocolate Rum Pudding with Chocolate May Beetles   66. Citrus Cream with Pink Grapefruit and Orange   67. White Chocolate and Pistachio Mousse with Chocolate Lace   68. Crème Brûlée on a Caramel Spider with a Sugar Shard**

(clockwise from top) **69. Crème Caramel Nouvelle 70. Triple Chocolate Terrine 71. Sherry-Poached Black Mission Figs with Crème Catalan**

(clockwise from top left) **72. Cupid's Treasure Chest 73. Chocolate Dome Cake (alternate presentation) 74. Wine Foam and Blackberry Bavarian Greystone 75. Coconut Ice Cream in a Red Pepper Tuile with Strawberry Salsa and Tomatillo Lace
76. Caramel-Centered Milk Chocolate Mousse with Black Currant Sauce 77. White Chocolate Neapolitan**

(clockwise from top left) **78. Baked Plantains in Gingered Meyer Lemon Syrup with Avocado-Mango Ice Cream 79. Blueberry Financier with Toasted Lemon Verbena Sabayon and Mascarpone Sherbet 80. Buried Ruby Treasure 81. Brandied Cherry Ganache Tower with Pink Champagne Aspic and a Curvy Tuile Strip**

(clockwise from top left) **82. Chocolate Marquise with Passion Fruit Parfait and a Lace Cookie Bouquet 83. Cocoa Nib–White Chocolate Ice Cream with a Chocolate Lace Igloo and Marzipan Polar Bear (variation) 84. Lemongrass Parfait with Green Tea Syrup, Mango Wafer Orbs, and Macadamia Nuts 85. Frozen Lemon Mousse with Orange**

(clockwise from top) **86. Spiced Ganache and Tea Ice Cream Marco Polo   87. Espresso Chocolate Cake with Coffee-Bean Crisps   88. Milk Chocolate Marquise with Finger Banana Center and Red Currant Sauce**

(clockwise from top) **89. Snowbird in a Chocolate Cage 90. Tarte Tatin Moderne 91. Striped Chocolate Cups with Tuile Steam Decorations (optional presentation)**

About Springerle

Springerle are traditional German Christmas cookies, possibly so named because they were originally shaped in the form of animals. In the pre-Christian era it was customary for German tribes to celebrate the winter solstice by sacrificing live animals or token animals shaped from dough. These beautifully molded, anise-flavored cookies have been closely associated with Christmas festivities for centuries. Bakers in German villages inspired the early intricately carved molds by holding annual competitions in time for Christmas baking, with each shop hoping its carver would produce the most elaborate molds.

Making Perfect Springerle

It takes experience to get a feel for working with springerle dough and molds. Keep the following points in mind:

- The dough must be firm enough — that is, contain enough flour — to keep it from sticking to the mold and also so it retains the imprint from the mold precisely. However, too much flour will give the cookies a floury taste and can make the dough too firm to pick up intricate or small designs. The dough becomes firmer as it chills; work with it cold and firm from the refrigerator.

- Work in a well-lit area so you can see if the print is clear. If it is not, gather the dough, reroll, and try again. A light source directed from the side is best to help you see complex patterns.

- Be sure the mold is clean before making each impression; use a brush to remove excess flour, powdered sugar, or tiny bits of dough stuck in the design. Do not use a sharp object, such as a knife tip, to remove bits of dough, or you may damage the mold.

- When using deep molds, it is sometimes easier to get a clear impression by pressing the dough into the mold rather than the other way around. To use this method, place the mold on the table, design-side up, and cover it with a piece of dough just slightly larger than the mold. Use your fingertips to gently press the dough into the mold, being careful not to move the dough from side to side and paying special attention to the deepest areas of the mold. Roll a rolling pin over the top of the dough, then place a sheet of cardboard on top and carefully invert; be extremely careful not to move the mold or the dough, even a fraction, or you can blur the image. Remove the mold, then slide the cookie off of the cardboard and onto the sheet pan.

- If you have cutters of the same dimension as your molds (cutters and molds that match exactly can sometimes be ordered together), use these to cut the images out of the dough. The cutters must match exactly unless you want to have a frame of dough around the image, which sometimes looks nice. In the case of molds with multiple images, cut the cookies apart with a pastry wheel. If the edges look ragged, trim again after the cookies have dried overnight.

- Using a gentle hand and a soft brush, remove excess powdered sugar from the cookies before baking. If there is only a light dusting, it is best to remove it after the cookies have dried overnight, as you are less likely to disturb the image, but large specks should be brushed away prior to drying because they can create a tiny dent in the surface. So much sugar on the cookies probably means you are using too much or the dough is too soft, indicating a lack of flour, not being cold, or both.

- Before you risk ruining a large, intricate design, bake as many small test cookies (1 at a time) as needed until the oven temperature is adjusted correctly. If it is too hot, the cookies will puff too much, and the carefully created image will disappear. Double- or even triple-panning may be necessary. Watch the cookies closely as they bake; they should become light golden brown on the bottom but should not change color on top and should not change shape at all, except for puffing up slightly.

Yule Log Pastries yield: 40 pastries, 2¼ inches (5.6 cm) each (Color Photo 117)

Some classic ethnic holiday specialties are almost never made except at Christmas — springerle, lebkuchen, fruitcake, gingerbread figures, and dozens of others. Conversely, many year-round pastries can be modified slightly to sport a seasonal facade. Three of the individual pastries from the companion volume to this book, *The Professional Pastry Chef: Fundamentals of Baking and Pastry,* are turned into Christmas pastries in this chapter. Angelica Points become Christmas Tree Pastries (page 458), Mazarins are transformed into Holiday Candle Pastries (page 462), and Rum Chocolate Spools are a natural source for these miniature Yule logs.

Chocolate and marzipan are always a delicious combination. The small decorative tree branches, which at first glance appear tedious and time-consuming, are actually pretty easy if you plan appropriately. If the chilled rum ball ropes have gotten close to room temperature, chill the branch stumps quickly in the freezer (or simply put them in the refrigerator before you begin to cut the ropes). Before attaching the branches to the logs, one or the other must be cold so the chocolate sets up immediately. In addition to the opportunity to use dry or leftover cake and cookie scraps in the rum ball filling, here is also a chance to use leftover cocoa-colored marzipan or marzipan that got crumbs mixed into it. Leftover marzipan tinted red and green for other projects can be combined to produce a light brown tint and used here as well.

½ recipe or 2 pounds 12 ounces (1 kg 250 g) Rum Ball Filling (page 790)

1 pound 2 ounces (510 g) marzipan, untinted

2 ounces (55 g) Vanilla Buttercream (Swiss Method; page 753)

3 ounces (85 g) Gingerbread Cookies dough (page 461) or Short Dough (page 791)

Dark coating chocolate, melted

Strained strawberry jam or strawberry preserves

Powdered sugar

1. Divide the rum ball filling into 5 equal pieces, approximately 9 ounces (255 g) each. Cover and set aside.

2. Using powdered sugar to prevent sticking, roll the marzipan into a rectangle, 16 × 20 inches (40 × 50 cm). It should be very thin, about ¹⁄₁₆ inch (2 mm).

3. Using powdered sugar to prevent sticking, roll each piece of rum ball dough into a rope the same length as the width of the marzipan (16 inches/40 cm).

4. Trim the short side of the marzipan closest to you to make it straight and even. Spread a thin film of vanilla buttercream on top of the marzipan. Place a rum ball rope on top of the marzipan next to the straight edge. Roll the marzipan around the rum ball rope to enclose it, then cut away the excess marzipan (Figure 9-12). The edges of the marzipan should line up evenly on the enclosed rope, not overlap. Cover the remaining ropes in the same way. To reroll the marzipan sheet during the covering process, scrape the buttercream off the top, knead the marzipan back together, and roll out again.

5. Roll each rope against the table to stretch it to 18

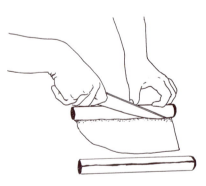

FIGURE 9-12 **Cutting away the excess marzipan sheet after rolling the marzipan around a rope of Rum Ball Filling for Yule Log Pastries. The edges of the marzipan just meet but do not overlap.**

inches (45 cm). Transfer the ropes to a sheet pan; if they do not fit, cut them in half first. Place in the refrigerator until firm, about 1 hour.

6. While the ropes are chilling, scrape all of the buttercream from the leftover marzipan scraps, weigh out a 2-ounce (55-g) piece of marzipan, and roll it into a thin rope 20 inches (50 cm) long and about ³⁄₈ inch (9 mm) in diameter. Cover the remaining scraps and use for another project. Cut the rope into 40 pieces, each ½ inch (1.2 cm) long. Cut these pieces in half at a 45-degree angle to make 2 branch stump decorations for each log. Set the decorations aside.

7. Roll out gingerbread cookie dough or short dough to ¹⁄₁₆ inch (2 mm) thick. Using a heart-shaped cutter ½ inch (1.2 cm) wide, cut out 40 cookies. Bake the cookies at 375°F (190°C) for approximately 6 minutes or until baked through.

8. Cut each chilled rum ball rope into 8 pieces, each 2¼ inches (5.6 cm) long. Immediately, while the logs are still cold, attach 2 branch stumps to each log by dipping the angle-cut side of the stumps into the melted chocolate and attaching them to the top of each log, slightly off-center at opposite ends, so they grow in the same direction.

9. One at a time, set the logs on a dipping fork and dip into the coating chocolate. As you remove each log, move it up and down over the bowl to drain off as much chocolate as possible. Finish this process by scraping the bottom of the pastry against the rim of the bowl. Place the dipped logs on a sheet pan lined with baking paper (see Figures 3-1 to 3-5, page 94, but do not insert the fork into the pastries, as in the illustration). Place a cookie heart flat on top of each log, centered between the branch stumps, before the chocolate hardens. Pipe a small drop of strawberry jam or preserves in the center of each cookie. Sift powdered sugar lightly over the pastries.

Bûche de Noël Slices with Pomegranate Sauce and Star Fruit

yield: 16 servings (Color Photo 114)

Some form of bûche de Noël is always featured on a holiday menu in my kitchen — certainly not for its practicality, for the logs can be time-consuming, but because tradition and the public demand it. However, the complexity of the logs can be offset by the relative simplicity of some of the other desserts offered. For example, a nicely balanced selection of plated holiday desserts is Persimmon Pudding (page 486), Frosted Minneola Tangelo Givré (page 283), Princess Cake (with a Christmas decoration), and Bûche de Noël Slices with Pomegranate Sauce and Star Fruit, all but this one being rather easy.

Because the Yule Log slices should be presented standing upright and considering their journey to the dining room via wait staff, it is important that the sponge batter not be spread too thick. Also, although the slices are cut at an angle to the log, they must be cut straight down so they do not lean over. Both slices with thick sponge (which makes them taller) and slices that lean are prone to falling over in the sauce. If your slices seem so "inclined," it is better to arrange the plate presentation with the slice flat on the plate. If you suspect a problem even before the log is sliced, cut it into wedges instead (as if you were cutting croissants from a single strip). Creating a wider end will prevent accidents, and you will still achieve the desired height.

1 recipe Yule Logs (page 453; see Step 1 below for specifics)

8 to 10 medium-sized star fruit

Sweet dark chocolate, tempered, or dark coating chocolate, melted

1 recipe Pomegranate Sauce (page 302)

Seeds from 1 pomegranate

Powdered sugar

1. Skipping Step 8 and omitting the rum ball filling and the meringue mushrooms, follow the recipe for Yule Logs through Step 11, making 16 holly leaves and 48 holly berries; you will need approximately 1 ounce (30 g) red marzipan and 4 ounces (115 g) green marzipan. Place the iced log in the refrigerator until the buttercream is set, 30 to 60 minutes. Place the holly leaves and berries in the refrigerator as well, but do not leave them for more than 1 hour, or they will start to get sticky from the moist air.

2. Using a vegetable peeler, remove the skin from the ridges of the star fruit. Thinly slice the fruit, reshape with the cut sides together, cover, and reserve in the refrigerator.

3. Using a knife dipped in very hot water, slice the log crosswise at an angle into 16 pieces.

4. Using melted chocolate as glue, attach 1 chilled holly leaf decoration and 3 berries to the top of each slice.

5. Presentation: Stand a decorated Yule log slice at the center rear of a dessert plate. Arrange 5 to 6 slices of star fruit in front of the dessert on the left side of the plate. Pour a pool of pomegranate sauce to the right of the fruit slices. Sprinkle a few pomegranate seeds on top of the sauce and over the base of the plate. Sift powdered sugar lightly over the Yule Log slice and the plate; powdered sugar should be visible on the pomegranate seeds in the sauce.

Chocolate Chalet with White Chocolate and Pistachio Pâté and Bitter Chocolate Sauce yield: 16 servings (Color Photo 108)

Here he goes again," you are probably saying, "with one of these labor-intensive, complicated desserts that no one could realistically produce outside of a cooking school, where there are an unlimited number of students available." Wrong. First of all, at times, more is not necessarily better and, in general, I would rather have one trained worker than six trainees. But that aside, this dessert is much easier than it appears at first. One year, when I was teaching at the California Culinary Academy in San Francisco, a graduation ceremony was scheduled a few days before the Christmas holiday break. However, due to all of the other work connected with the holidays, we had only one full day to prepare all of the components for 320 guests. The desserts came out beautifully, although we did cut corners by using gingerbread hearts instead of marbleized chocolate hearts. You can speed the process further by eliminating the chimney on the chalet. If you still think the presentation is too complex, consider that both the chocolate chalets (assembled or in pieces) and the white chocolate pâté can be prepared weeks in advance. I guarantee your efforts will pay off when you serve this creation — it looks spectacular, and the flavors marry wonderfully well.

White Chocolate and Pistachio Pâté (recipe follows)

2 ounces (55 g) Gingerbread Cookies dough (page 461)

Royal Icing (page 680)

Dark coating chocolate, melted

Powdered sugar

Bitter Chocolate Sauce (page 413)

Seeds from 1 medium pomegranate

Chocolate Chalets (directions follow)

Chocolate Fences (page 476)

1. Line a pâté mold or other suitable form approximately $3\frac{1}{2} \times 3\frac{1}{2} \times 12$ inches long (8.7 × 8.7 × 30 cm) with baking paper. If making a cardboard form — directions follow — line this as well. Pour the white chocolate pâté into the form. Cover and place in the freezer until firm, at least 4 hours or, preferably, overnight.

2. Roll out the gingerbread dough to $\frac{1}{16}$ inch (2 mm) thick. Using a deer-shaped cookie cutter, cut out 16 small deer (plus a few extra in case of breakage). Place them on a sheet pan lined with baking paper and bake at 400°F (205°C) for about 5 minutes or until baked through. Set aside to cool.

3. Work the royal icing smooth and adjust by adding more egg white, if necessary, for a soft but not runny consistency. Place a small amount of icing in a piping bag and pipe tiny dots on the deer cookies to mark the eyes. Place a small amount of melted coating chocolate in a piping bag and pipe an even tinier dot on the icing dots to mark the pupils. Lightly sift powdered sugar over the deer. Do not shake the sifter; instead, tap it with the back of a knife to create clearly defined spots on the deer. Set the deer aside.

4. Remove the frozen pâté from the form. Using a thin chef's knife and dipping it into hot water after each slice, cut the pâté across into 16 slices, each $\frac{3}{4}$ inch (2 cm) thick. For you to cut cleanly through the pistachio nuts in the filling, the pâté must be sliced while still firm; however, it should not be served for at least 30 minutes so it has time to thaw. Try not to cut and thaw more slices than you will be serving right away. Store the thawed slices, covered, in the refrigerator until needed.

5. Place a portion of the bitter chocolate sauce in a piping bottle, adjusting the consistency first as needed so the sauce holds its shape without running.

6. Presentation: Pipe large, irregular teardrop shapes of chocolate sauce over the base of a dessert plate. Set a slice of pâté in the center of the plate. Sprinkle pomegranate seeds around the pâté on the base of the plate. Wearing food handling gloves so you do not leave fingerprints on the chocolate, place a chocolate chalet in a corner of the pâté slice, pushing it all the way down to the plate. If you hit a pistachio in the pâté, do not force the chalet, or it will break; instead, lift it up and shift the position a little. Place a chocolate fence in front of the chalet and to the left, positioning it so the fence is parallel to the left edge of the pâté slice. Place a deer between the fence and the chalet toward the right side of the pâté slice. Sift powdered sugar lightly over the chalet and the plate and serve.

How to Make a Box Form for the White Chocolate and Pistachio Pâté

Necessity, they say, is the mother of invention, and this handy, easy-to-make box came about in the same way as many of the other forms in this book. Having enough molds and forms to go around in a busy kitchen is impossible, and sometimes one just gives up and makes his or her own. If you measure and cut precisely, you will create a straight and uniform mold that, if completely lined, can be used over and over. However, if the filling should leak and stain the cardboard, the box must be discarded. To make the form you need a utility knife, a sheet of corrugated cardboard, and a glue gun or masking tape.

1. Using a utility knife with a sharp blade, cut a full-sized flat sheet of corrugated cardboard that is lined on both sides into a rectangle measuring 18½ × 9 inches (46.2 × 22.5 cm).

2. Measure and draw 2 lines, 3 inches (7.5 cm) apart, lengthwise; keep in mind that the side of the cardboard you draw on and cut will become the outside of the box. Measure and draw a line 3 inches (7.5 cm) in from each short end (Figure 9-13). You now have 3 equal squares at each short end. Draw dotted lines just outside each center square, as indicated by the dotted lines in Figure 9-14. Cut on the dotted lines and across the line of the corner squares bordering the left and right long rectangles; remove the corners (Figure 9-15).

3. Cut halfway through the remaining solid lines. Invert the cardboard. Bend all 4 sides up to make a rectangular box. Use a glue gun to glue the short ends onto the center, or tape the box together around the outside at the corners.

Block-style cream cheese is often packaged in sturdy rectangular cardboard boxes, and I have used these not only to hold this pâté but also to mold ganache and parfaits until set. Those I use measure 9¼ × 3¼ × 3 inches (23.1 × 8.1 × 7.5 cm). Place a divider in the center of one box and set a weight against it; you will need 1½ boxes of this size to mold the pâté recipe.

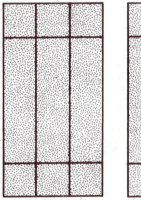
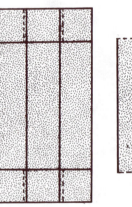

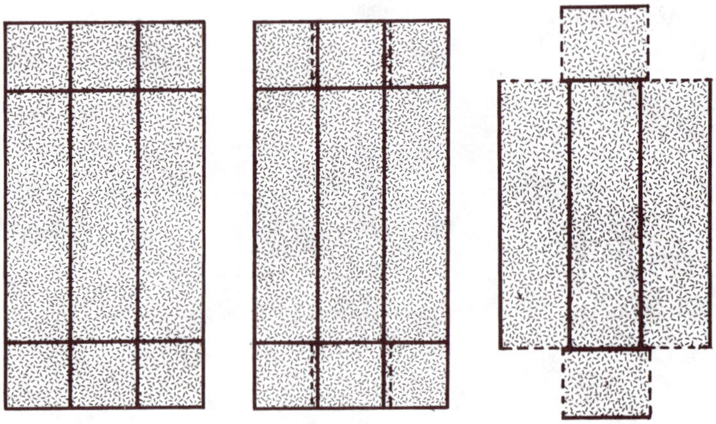

FIGURE 9-13 (LEFT)
The lines drawn on the cardboard rectangle after measuring
FIGURE 9-14 (MIDDLE)
The dotted lines drawn as instructed
FIGURE 9-15 (RIGHT)
The dotted lines showing where the cuts were made to remove the corners

WHITE CHOCOLATE AND PISTACHIO PATE yield: 8 cups (1 L 920 ml)

4 ounces (115 g) pistachio nuts	10 ounces (285 g) white chocolate
2½ cups (600 ml) heavy cream	3 tablespoons (27 g) pectin powder (see Note)
4 teaspoons (12 g) unflavored gelatin powder	8 ounces (225 g) granulated sugar
½ cup (120 ml) cold water	1 cup (240 ml) egg whites

1. Add a pinch of salt to a small pan of boiling water; blanch the pistachio nuts, drain, and remove the skins. Set aside.

2. Whip the heavy cream to soft peaks; do not overwhip. Reserve in the refrigerator.

3. Sprinkle the gelatin over the cold water and set aside to soften.

4. Chop the white chocolate into small pieces and melt over a bain-marie set over low heat; stir frequently to prevent overheating. Set aside; keep warm.

5. Combine the pectin powder and sugar in a mixing bowl. Stir in the egg whites. Place over a bain-marie and heat, stirring constantly with a whisk, until the mixture reaches 140°F (60°C). Remove from the heat and immediately whip to stiff peaks.

6. Quickly stir the melted white chocolate into one-third of the meringue to temper. Then, still working quickly, add this to the remaining meringue.

7. Heat the gelatin mixture to dissolve. Rapidly mix the gelatin into the meringue mixture. Fold in the pistachio nuts, then the reserved whipped cream.

NOTE: Use regular fruit canning pectin; pure pectin would be too strong here. If pectin is unavailable, increase the gelatin to a total of 2 tablespoons (18 g).

CHOCOLATE CHALETS yield: 16 chalets

The technique of spreading chocolate into a thin sheet, letting it set, then using a warm knife to cut the sheet into precise pieces (with or without a template) is quite common; it is often used to create small, elegant chocolate boxes to hold truffles and other candies. When made from plain chocolate, the lid of the box (and sometimes the sides) is usually decorated by piping intricate chocolate designs on top. When making boxes from marbleized chocolate, this is not necessary — in fact, if it is done at all, it should be kept to a minimum, or the combination will look busy. Using the method described for these chalets, you can build an elegant bonbon box, as it is commonly referred to in the industry, or practically anything else.

If you need to simplify the chalet construction, replace the chocolate heart with a gingerbread heart, or use hearts made of plain or cocoa short dough. If you are making this dessert around the holidays (as intended), gingerbread makes an appropriate substitute, especially if you are using gingerbread deer as part of the presentation. If you substitute gingerbread, you will have about one-third of the marbleized chocolate sheet left over and you will need about 6 ounces (170 g) Gingerbread Cookies dough (page 461).

> 1 full sheet Marbleized Chocolate (page 539)   Piping Chocolate (page 543)
> Chalet Support Box (directions follow)

1. Trace the chalet templates A and B in Figure 9-16 and cut them out of sturdy cardboard, such as the type used for matting pictures. Have ready a heart-shaped cookie cutter approximately 3 inches (7.5 cm) wide and 3 inches (7.5 cm) tall. If you do not have such a cutter, cut template C out of cardboard as well.

2. Set up your workstation next to the stove, with the marbleized chocolate, still attached to its baking paper, on a wooden surface. Place a pan containing ½ inch (1.2 cm) water on the stove and keep it at the scalding point.

3. Wearing food handling gloves to protect the chocolate, place the heart cutter in the water for a few seconds to heat the metal; if you are making a large number of chalets, it is best to work with 2 cutters. Shake the water off the cutter against a towel; then, starting from a long edge so the other long edge is left intact to cut the roof strips, cut a heart out of the marbleized chocolate sheet by letting the hot cutter melt through the chocolate. Reheat the cutter as needed and repeat to cut a total of 16 hearts, alternating the cuts up and down to minimize scrap pieces. If the chocolate breaks, either you are pushing too hard or the cutter is not hot enough. As you cut the hearts, slide a palette knife underneath and transfer them to a sheet pan lined with bak-

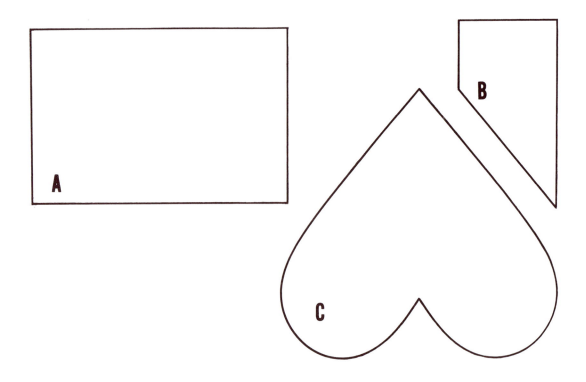

FIGURE 9-16 The templates for cutting the marbleized chocolate sheet for the Chocolate Chalet

ing paper before the chocolate hardens and causes them to stick together. If you are using template C as a guide instead of a metal cutter, place it on top of the chocolate and, with the tip of a hot knife, cut around the outside.

4. Heat a thin chef's knife over a gas burner or use a blowtorch. Use the roof template (A) to gauge and measure the width, then cut out 3 strips the full length of the chocolate sheet, wiping the knife clean and reheating it as needed. Slide a palette knife (not the warm chef's knife) under each strip as it is cut and transfer it to a cardboard cake sheet or an inverted sheet pan. Using the roof template as a guide, cut across the strips to make 32 roof pieces.

5. Using the same technique of heating the knife, follow template B to cut 16 chimney pieces from the strips and from any scrap pieces large enough. Be sure you are cutting each chimney with the template right-side up, or you will have to attach them on different sides of the roofs later. Save the remaining scraps; they can be used as part of a filling, for example. Place the hearts and chimneys in the refrigerator.

6. Still wearing gloves, arrange 8 pairs of roof pieces in the support box, marbleized side down, with their short ends touching, as shown in Figure 9-17. Place melted piping chocolate in a piping bag and cut a small opening. Weld the roof pieces together by piping chocolate where they meet, covering about ½ inch (1.2 cm) of the seam on each end but without covering the center of the seam.

7. Use the tip of a paring knife to lightly mark the center of the roof pieces vertically. Remove 8 hearts from the refrigerator. Holding a heart upside down by the rounded edge, pipe choco-

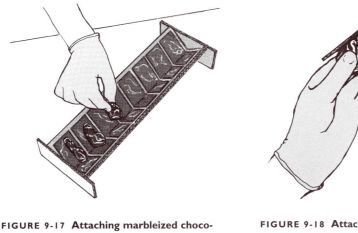

FIGURE 9-17 **Attaching marbleized chocolate hearts between pairs of marbleized
chocolate roof pieces set in the support box**

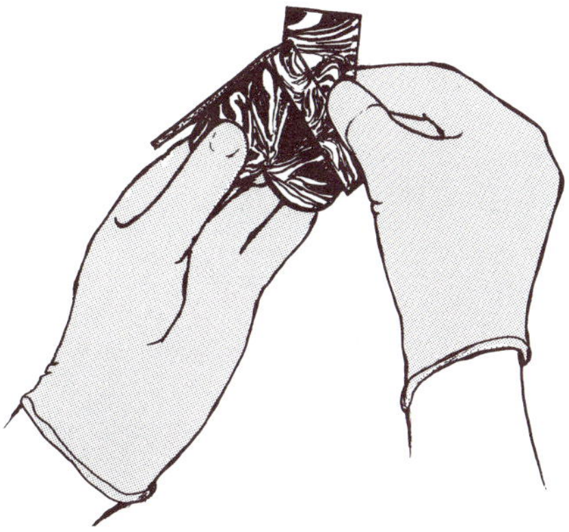

FIGURE 9-18 **Attaching a chimney to
the roof of a Chocolate Chalet**

late along the straight edges up to the curve. Immediately position the heart between 2 roof
pieces, using your marks to find the center (Figure 9-17). Be certain the heart is standing
straight. Repeat with the remaining 7 hearts. Let the chocolate harden.

8. Remove the chalets from the support box and place them on a sheet pan lined with baking paper with the marbleized side of the hearts facing up.

9. Repeat Steps 6, 7, and 8 to form the remaining 8 chalets.

10. Remove 8 chimney pieces from the refrigerator. Attach the chimneys to the right sides
of the roofs by piping chocolate on the bottom edge of a chimney and holding it in place on the
roof a few seconds until set; be sure the chimney is straight and that the left short side extends
fully above the crest of the roof (Figure 9-18). Repeat until all 16 chimneys have been attached.
Cover the chalets and reserve in a cool, dry area until needed; do not refrigerate.

Chalet Support Box

This box is also useful for shaping Cookie Butterflies (page 695), Chocolate Monarch Butterfly
Ornaments (page 550), and dragonfly decorations (page 131).

1. Use a sharp utility knife to cut a rectangle 6 × 21 inches (15 × 52.5 cm) from corrugated cardboard, such as a cardboard cake sheet. Measure and cut 2 pieces, 2³/₈ inches (5.9 cm)
wide, from 1 end of the strip, as shown in Figure 9-19.

2. Measure and cut a line lengthwise in the center of the large piece, cutting only halfway
through. Invert the piece and bend the sides up into a *V* shape. Place the heart cookie cutter (or
template) used to cut the chocolate chalet hearts in the *V*, adjust the sides so they are snug against
the cutter, and tape across the top of the box to hold the sides at this angle (Figure 9-19).

3. Hold a small cardboard piece centered against 1 short side of the *V*, making sure it is level.
Trace the *V* onto the end piece where it touches, marking on the top side of the *V*. Repeat with
the other end piece on the opposite side.

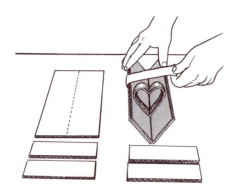

FIGURE 9-19 Taping across the top of the support box with the cutter in place to hold the sides of the box at the proper angle

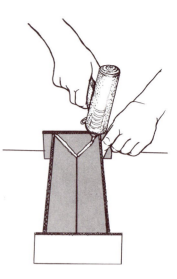

FIGURE 9-20 Applying glue to the inside of the box after gluing the end pieces in place and removing the tape

CHEF'S TIP
To simplify, skip Steps 3 and 4 and place the V-shaped mold on top of an inverted muffin tin for support. When you are finished, remove the tape to flatten the mold for storage.

4. Using a hot glue gun, apply lines of glue just below your marks on the end pieces and secure them to each end of the support box. Remove the tape across the top. Apply a little additional glue around the inside edge as needed (Figure 9-20).

NOTE: Although, if properly handled, this box will last through many uses, making a support box from wood is the ideal long-term solution. In that case, it makes sense to build a box as long as a full sheet pan.

CHOCOLATE FENCES yield: 16 to 20 decorations

Unless you are making a large number of fences, it is not necessary to copy multiple rows of the template. The following procedure works fine to produce fences for one Chocolate Chalet recipe.

Piping Chocolate (page 543)

1. Using a heavy black pen, trace the pattern shown in Figure 9-21 onto a small piece of baking paper or use a copy machine to copy it onto regular paper. Place a sheet of baking paper over the template with the tracing positioned under the top left edge of the larger paper.

2. Place piping chocolate in a piping bag and cut a larger-than-normal opening. Following the tracing, pipe out 1 fence, piping the vertical lines (the fence posts) first. Slide the drawing to the right underneath the larg-

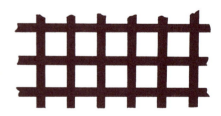

FIGURE 9-21 The template used as a guide to pipe out the Chocolate Fences

er paper and pipe out the second fence in the same way. Continue around the perimeter of the paper until you have made about 20 fences. You need only 16, but some breakage is likely.

3. Store the chocolate fences, attached to the baking paper, in a cool, dry place until need-ed. Refrigerate the fences briefly, if necessary, to make them easier to handle before removing them from the paper.

Mont Blanc with Pomegranate Seeds and Vanilla Curly Cues yield: 12 servings

Mont Blanc is a picturesque mountain in the French Alps, near Italy. Because of its high elevation, the top of the mountain is capped with snow all year. Mont Blanc has lent its name to this specialty, consisting of vermicelli-like strands of vanilla-scented chestnut puree formed into a fragile mountain topped with chantilly cream. According to an old-world tradition, Mont Blanc is eaten slowly with a small silver spoon.

Mont Blanc is a classic chestnut dessert, and one of the most elaborate. If you are making a fair num-ber, piping the chestnut puree into shapely little mountains can be a bit time-consuming. Many chefs rec-ommend forcing the puree through a ricer or even a colander, but I find that a small hand-cranked meat grinder, clamped onto the edge of the table — which gives you one free hand to turn the plate as the chestnut puree is extruded — works much better, although you do not have the precise control that comes with piping by hand.

¼ recipe French Meringue (page 780)	¼ recipe Vanilla Tuile Decorating Paste (page 695)
1 recipe Chestnut Puree (page 445; see Step 3 below and Chef's Tip)	½ recipe Chantilly Cream (page 765)
2 cups (480 ml) whole milk	½ cup (120 ml) pomegranate seeds
1 vanilla bean	Powdered sugar

1. Draw 12 circles, 3 inches (7.5 cm) in diameter and evenly spaced, on a sheet of baking paper. Invert the paper and place on a sheet pan. Place the French meringue in a pastry bag with a No. 1 (2-mm) plain tip. Pipe the meringue into spirals within the circles, starting in the center (see Figure 14-2, page 782).

2. Bake immediately at 210° to 220°F (99° to 104°C) for approximately 1 hour or until the meringue is dry. Let cool.

3. Follow the recipe for the chestnut puree, but do not puree the chestnuts after peeling. Instead, chop the peeled chestnuts coarsely and place in a saucepan with the milk and vanilla bean. Cover and simmer over low heat, stirring from time to time, for 20 minutes. Drain, reserv-ing the milk and vanilla bean.

4. Add ¼ cup (60 ml) of the reserved milk to the chestnuts. Puree the mixture until com-pletely smooth, adding more of the reserved milk, if necessary. The puree should have the con-sistency of firm mashed potatoes. Do not overprocess, or it will become gummy. Discard any leftover milk. Place the puree in a bowl and reserve at room temperature if serving within 1 hour; cover and refrigerate for longer storage.

5. Split the vanilla bean lengthwise and scrape out the seeds. Stir the seeds into the tuile paste. Use the paste to make at least 24 Curly Cues, following the directions on page 700; omit the chocolate tuile paste line in the center.

6. Place the chestnut puree, a portion at a time, in a pastry bag with a No. 1 (2-mm) plain tip. If the puree has been refrigerated, you may need to stir it smooth first. Pipe the puree on top

As removing the shell and skin from fresh chestnuts is time-consuming, cooked or dried chestnuts can be a blessing. These are available vacuum-packed, frozen, or packed in water. The chestnuts in water tend to be soggy and lacking in flavor; they are not recommended for this recipe. Canned unsweetened chestnut puree, usually imported from France, can be used in this recipe and will cut the preparation time just about in half; unfortunately the flavor will suffer a bit. If you substitute canned chestnut puree, sweeten with simple syrup and flavor with vanilla extract as needed.

of the meringue disks in a somewhat random pattern — for example, a series of figure eights at different angles — letting the puree fall so it forms pointed mounds 2 inches (5 cm) wide.

7. Presentation: Place a small dollop of chantilly cream in the center of a dessert plate. Place a Mont Blanc on the cream. Use two soupspoons to form a large quenelle-shaped scoop of cream and place on top of the mound. Sprinkle pomegranate seeds around the dessert on the base of the plate. Lean 2 curly cues against the dessert from opposite sides. Dust powdered sugar lightly over the plate.

Persimmon Charlotte yield: 12 servings, 5 ounces (150 ml) each

This dessert just barely earns the title "charlotte," as the forms aren't actually lined with persimmon slices. The fruit circles are just a decoration; a true charlotte is always made in a lined form (see page 321). Slicing the Fuyu persimmons crosswise reveals the decorative spoke pattern produced by the eight soft, flat seeds inside. Although persimmons are most bountiful around Christmas, don't limit their use to holiday desserts; they can usually be obtained from November through the end of February. Persimmons often hit the market in October, but these early arrivals often don't belong there; in some cases, they are so unripe that the fruit has not yet turned orange. The persimmons available in January and February, on the other hand, which for the most part are the Fuyu, are ripe, sweet, and juicy.

Persimmon puree can be purchased; it is usually packaged with sugar added. If you use prepared sweetened puree in this recipe, reduce the amount of sugar in the bavarois filling.

Because this is a good recipe to use several months out of the year, a rather neutral presentation is specified here. When presenting persimmon charlotte around the holidays, you might want to add a few seasonal touches, such as the Cookie Christmas Trees and/or the persimmon stars used for Persimmon Cream Slices (page 480).

3 medium-sized Fuyu persimmons	Simple syrup or orange liqueur, as needed
Persimmon Bavarois (recipe follows)	Mint leaves, cut into julienne (see Note)
½ recipe Cranberry Coulis (page 243)	Powdered sugar

1. The Fuyu persimmons should be firm to the touch so they can be sliced easily. Place the persimmons on their sides and, using a sharp knife, slice them crosswise to ⅛ inch (3 mm) thick. Using a plain round cookie cutter, 2 inches (5 cm) in diameter, cut rounds from the slices. Place 1 slice in the bottom of each of 12 soufflé ramekins, 3¼ inches (8.1 cm) in diameter, and 5 ounces (150 ml) in capacity, or other smooth-sided forms of approximately the same size. If you use other forms, choose an appropriate cutter to produce persimmon slices slightly smaller than the bottom of the forms. Save the leftover persimmon pieces to use in the bavarois.

2. Divide the persimmon bavarois evenly among the prepared forms. Refrigerate until set, about 2 hours.

3. Place the cranberry coulis in a piping bottle.

4. Presentation: Unmold a charlotte by dipping the bottom of the mold briefly into hot water, inverting, and unmolding in the center of a dessert plate. If the persimmon slice appears dry on top, brush simple syrup or orange liqueur over it. Pipe cranberry coulis around the dessert on the base of the plate in an uneven circular pattern; do not cover the plate entirely. Sprinkle julienned mint leaves over the coulis. Sift powdered sugar lightly over the entire plate. Serve immediately.

NOTE: To cut the mint leaves, stack 3 or 4 together and use a chef's knife to slice the stack crosswise into ⅛-inch (3-mm) pieces. Discard the pieces from the tip and stem ends.

PERSIMMON BAVAROIS yield: approximately 9 cups (2 L 160 ml)

Do not make this filling until you are ready to use it.

1 pound 8 ounces (680 g) perfectly ripe Fuyu or Hachiya persimmons	⅓ cup (80 ml) cold water
1 tablespoon (15 ml) lime juice	⅓ cup (80 ml) or 4 ounces (115 g) light corn syrup
3 cups (720 ml) heavy cream	4 eggs, separated
4½ teaspoons (14 g) unflavored gelatin powder	4 ounces (115 g) granulated sugar

1. Cut the persimmons in half. Using a melon ball cutter or a small spoon, scoop out the flesh, scraping the inside of the skin well to remove all of the pulp. Puree the pulp and force through a fine mesh strainer. You should have approximately 2 cups (480 ml) puree. Stir in the lime juice and reserve.

2. Whip the heavy cream to soft peaks. Cover and reserve in the refrigerator.

3. Sprinkle the gelatin powder over the cold water and set aside to soften.

4. Place the corn syrup in a small saucepan and bring to a boil. At the same time, start whipping the egg yolks. Gradually beat the corn syrup into the yolks. Continue whipping until the mixture is light and fluffy.

5. Place the egg whites and sugar in a bowl set over simmering water and heat, stirring constantly, until the mixture reaches 140°F (60°C). Remove from the heat and whip until stiff peaks have formed and the meringue has cooled completely.

6. Fold the whipped cream into the meringue together with the egg yolk mixture and the persimmon pulp. Heat the gelatin to dissolve. Working quickly, add the gelatin to a small portion of the bavarois to temper; then, still working fast, stir this into the remainder. Use immediately.

Persimmon Cream Slices with Cookie Christmas Trees and Cranberry Coulis yield: 16 servings (Color Photo 110)

As is true of many desserts and pastries in this chapter, this recipe is versatile and should not be categorized as a holiday-only dessert. The small triangular pieces can be offered as part of a buffet assortment in any season; the only decoration needed is a little powdered sugar sifted over the top. When persimmons are not in season, I make this recipe with mangoes or papayas instead. Using either of those fruits, you must bring the strained puree to a quick boil to neutralize the enzyme they contain, as the raw fruit will inhibit the gelatin from setting. Also replace the ginger and nutmeg in the sponge with 1 teaspoon (1.5 g) ground cinnamon and use honey in place of the molasses.

For a different plate presentation, keep the pieces square instead of cutting each one diagonally to form triangles and serve with Orange Sauce (page 278). Alternatively, roll out marzipan, cut out tiny ribbons, and place them on top of the squares to transform the cream slices into wrapped presents. Follow the presentation instructions in Tropical Surprise Packages (page 258), including the sliced kiwi garnish and sauce. Regardless of the filling or presentation you use, try not to cut more pieces than you will use within a few hours. The uncut sheet will keep fresh for several days, covered, in the refrigerator.

Gingerbread Sponge (recipe follows)	3 firm Fuyu persimmons
Persimmon Filling (recipe follows)	½ recipe Cranberry Coulis (page 243)
2 tablespoons (30 ml) cold water	Simple syrup or orange liqueur
2 tablespoons (30 ml) brandy	16 Cookie Christmas Trees (directions follow)
1 teaspoon (3 g) unflavored gelatin powder	Powdered sugar
1 recipe Chantilly Cream (page 765; see Step 3 below)	16 whole cranberries

1. To make this recipe, you need a pan or frame that is 10 inches (25 cm) square and approximately 2 inches (5 cm) in height. If necessary, make a frame by cutting 2 strips of corrugated cardboard to 2 × 20 inches (5 × 50 cm). Cut halfway through the cardboard across the width of both strips. Bend the strips from the uncut side at a 90-degree angle and tape the corners together to form a 10-inch (25-cm) square. Set the frame on an inverted sheet pan lined with baking paper.

2. Peel the paper from the back of the gingerbread sponge sheet. Invert and scrape the skin from the top of the sponge, removing it entirely if it is loose or just the pieces that come off easily if not. Cut two 10-inch (25-cm) squares from the sponge sheet. Place 1 square, skin-side up, in the pan or frame. Pour the persimmon filling on top and spread it evenly. Place in the refrigerator until partially set; to accelerate the process, place in the freezer.

3. Combine the cold water and brandy. Sprinkle the gelatin powder over the top and set aside to soften. Whip the chantilly cream to soft peaks. Heat the gelatin to dissolve. Quickly add the gelatin to a small portion of the cream to temper, then quickly add this to the remaining cream. Immediately spread the chantilly cream on top of the persimmon filling.

4. Place the remaining sponge sheet on top with the skin side against the cream. Press the sponge lightly so it adheres and is level. Cover and place in the refrigerator for at least 2 hours to set completely; preferably, chill overnight.

5. Stand the persimmons on their sides, trim away the ends, and cut 6 slices, ⅛ inch (3 mm) thick, from each. Use a star-shaped cookie cutter measuring 2¼ inches (5.6 cm) across to cut a star out of each slice (use a smaller cutter, if needed, to stay within the persimmon slice). Place the stars on a sheet pan lined with baking paper. Cover and reserve.

6. Remove the assembled cake from the refrigerator. If the cake was assembled in a pan, cut around the inside perimeter, invert the cake onto a sheet of cardboard, then invert again to turn right-side up. If you used a frame, simply remove it. Using a thin sharp knife dipped in hot water, trim the sides, if necessary, then cut the cake into 4 strips, approximately 2¼ inches (5.6 cm) wide. Cut each strip into 4 squares. Be sure to hold the knife at a 90-degree angle so the sides of the cake will be straight.

7. Place the cranberry coulis in a piping bottle. Brush simple syrup or orange liqueur over the persimmon star garnishes.

8. Presentation: Pipe cranberry coulis in a zigzag pattern across the base of a dessert plate. Cut a persimmon square diagonally in half to make 2 triangles. Arrange the pieces, 1 on its sponge side and 1 on a shorter filling side, slightly off-center on top of the coulis. Place a cookie Christmas tree next to the taller triangle. Sift powdered sugar over the dessert and the plate. Place a cranberry or a small piece of persimmon on top of the triangle that is resting on its sponge side. Lean a persimmon star against the cranberry. Serve immediately.

GINGERBREAD SPONGE yield: I sponge sheet, 12 × 22 inches (30 × 55 cm)

4 ounces (115 g) unsalted butter, at room
    temperature

1 ounce (30 g) light brown sugar

8 ounces (225 g) cake flour

1 tablespoon (6 g) ground ginger

½ teaspoon (1 g) ground nutmeg

1 teaspoon (4 g) baking soda

3 eggs, separated, and at room temperature

½ cup (120 ml) warm water

¼ cup (60 ml) or 3 ounces (85 g) molasses

2 ounces (55 g) granulated sugar

Bread flour

1. Beat the butter and brown sugar together until light and fluffy. Sift together the flour, ginger, nutmeg, and baking soda.

2. Beat the egg yolks for a few seconds just to combine. Slowly mix in the water and molasses.

3. Add the dry ingredients to the butter and brown sugar mixture in 2 portions, alternating with the egg yolk mixture. Set aside.

4. Whip the egg whites to a thick foam. Gradually add the granulated sugar and continue to whip to stiff peaks. Slowly mix the reserved batter into the whipped egg whites.

5. Spread the batter evenly to 12 × 22 inches (30 × 55 cm) on a sheet of baking paper. Drag the paper onto a sheet pan (Figure 9-22).

6. Bake immediately at 375°F (190°C) for about 12 minutes or until just baked through.

7. Dust bread flour lightly on top of a sheet of baking paper. As

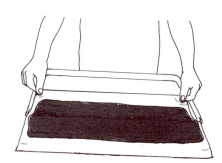

FIGURE 9-22 **Dragging a sheet of baking paper onto a sheet pan after spreading the cake batter over the paper. This technique is used instead of spreading the batter over the paper while it is in place on the pan to prevent the sides of the pan getting in the way. Alternatively, the batter can be spread directly over the lined pan usng an offset spatula.**

soon as possible after the sponge has come out of the oven, pick it up by the 2 corners on 1 long side of the baking paper and invert it onto the floured baking paper. Let cool completely. If the sponge will not be used within a short time, cover and refrigerate.

PERSIMMON FILLING yield: 5 cups (I L 200 ml)

Do not make this filling until you are ready to assemble the dessert. If it sets prematurely, softening the filling will ruin its texture.

1 pound 12 ounces (795 g) perfectly ripe Hachiya persimmons	½ cup (120 ml) cold water
Finely grated zest and juice of 2 limes	1½ cups (360 ml) heavy cream
½ cup (120 ml) orange liqueur	2 ounces (55 g) granulated sugar
5 teaspoons (15 g) unflavored gelatin powder	2 tablespoons (30 ml) vanilla extract

1. Cut the persimmons in half. Using a small spoon, scoop out the flesh and scrape the inside of the skin thoroughly. Do not be concerned if some nonblemished skin is added to the flesh; discard the remaining skin.

2. Puree the persimmon pulp, strain through a fine sieve, and measure. You should have approximately 2 cups (480 ml) pulp; proceed as long as the quantity is reasonably close. Stir in the lime zest and juice and the orange liqueur. Set aside.

3. Sprinkle the gelatin over the cold water and set aside to soften.

4. Whip the heavy cream to soft peaks with the sugar and vanilla.

5. Place the gelatin mixture over a bain-marie and heat to dissolve. Do not overheat.

6. Gradually fold the persimmon mixture into the whipped cream. Quickly mix the dissolved gelatin into a small portion of the mixture; then, still working fast, mix this back into the remainder of the filling.

COOKIE CHRISTMAS TREES yield: about 30 decorations

¼ recipe Vanilla Tuile Decorating Paste (page 695)	Green food coloring
1 teaspoon (2.5 g) cocoa powder	Sweet dark chocolate, tempered, or dark coating chocolate, melted

1. Make the Christmas tree template shown in Figure 9-23; it is the correct size to use in this recipe. Trace the drawing, then cut the stencil out of cardboard that is ¹⁄₁₆ inch (2 mm) thick; cake boxes work fine. If you do not have Silpats, butter and flour the back of even sheet pans.

FIGURE 9-23 The template for Cookie Christmas Trees

2. Place 2 tablespoons (30 ml) tuile paste in a cup or small bowl and mix in the cocoa powder, stirring until completely smooth. Cover and set aside. Color the remaining paste pale green.

3. Spread the green tuile paste onto the Silpats or prepared pans, spreading it flat and even within the template (see Figures 13-29 and 13-30, page 694). Do not place more than 8 trees on one pan.

4. Place a portion of the cocoa-colored paste in a piping bag and cut a small opening. Without overdoing it, pipe a few lines to indicate branches and a tree trunk on each tree; the trees should be mostly green.

5. Bake 1 pan at a time at 400°F (205°C) for approximately 5 minutes or until the trees begin to turn light brown around the edges. Leave the pan in the oven with the door open. Quickly remove the cookies 1 at a time and drape them, upside-down and lengthwise, over a rolling pin so they are slightly curved left to right (not top to bottom) and are concave rather than convex. Once the trees are firm, place them in the refrigerator just long enough to make them cold; do not leave them too long, or they will soften and lose the curl (see Chef's Tip).

6. Pipe out 1 dot of melted chocolate, approximately 1 inch (2.5 cm) in diameter, per tree on a sheet of baking paper. Space the dots far enough apart that the trees can stand up in them without touching. Watch closely; as soon as the first dot of chocolate shows signs of setting up, stand a tree straight up in its center. Repeat with the remainder. Store the trees in an airtight container in a cool, dry place.

Persimmon Dome Cake with Gingerbread Lattice

yield: 12 servings, 4 ounces (120 ml) each (Color Photo 111)

This elegant contemporary version of persimmon pudding can be enjoyed all year long by replacing the persimmons with bananas (see the variation following the main recipe), producing what you might call a Pacific Rim–influenced version of the traditional banana bread. With either version, try replacing the spicy gingerbread lattice decoration with Plantain Chips (page 722).

½ recipe Persimmon Pudding batter (page 486)	Orange segments
	Powdered sugar
⅓ recipe Kiwi Sauce (page 309)	Gingerbread Lattice Decorations (recipe follows)
½ recipe Brandied Whipped Cream (page 488)	
Zested orange peel	Ground nutmeg

1. Place Flexipan No. 1268 on an even sheet pan or use 12 ramekins, 3¼ inches (8.1 cm) in diameter (if using ramekins, brush melted butter inside and line each with a round of baking paper). Divide the persimmon pudding batter evenly among 12 indentations in the Flexipan or among the ramekins.

2. Bake at 350°F (175°C) for approximately 45 minutes or until baked through. Let the puddings cool in the molds.

3. If you are using a Flexipan, place it in the freezer for at least 1 hour so the puddings become hard. Unmold the puddings by inverting the pan and pushing the indentations inside out. To unmold from ramekins, cut around the inside edge, if needed, invert, and peel the paper from the bottom.

4. Place the kiwi sauce in a piping bottle.

5. Presentation: Place a pudding in the center of a serving plate. Evenly space 3 quenelle-shaped ovals of brandied whipped cream on the plate around the pudding. Place a small strip of orange zest on top of each quenelle. Place 1 orange segment between each whipped cream oval, setting them at the rim of the base of the plate. Pipe a small oval puddle of kiwi sauce between each orange segment and the pudding. Lightly sift powdered sugar on top of a lattice decoration. Make a slit in the center on top of the pudding and carefully push a lattice decoration straight into the cut so it stands upright. Sprinkle ground nutmeg lightly over the plate.

GINGERBREAD LATTICE DECORATIONS yield: 3 lattice sheets, 8 × 10 inches (20 × 40 cm) each

Refer to Procedure 4-3a, 4-3b, and 4-3c on page 179.

> 8 ounces (225 g) Gingerbread Cookies dough
> (page 461)

1. Divide the gingerbread dough into 3 equal pieces. Using bread flour to prevent sticking, roll out each piece to a rectangle measuring 4 × 16 inches (10 × 40 cm) and approximately ¹/₁₆ inch (2 mm) thick.

2. Roll a lattice dough roller lengthwise over 1 strip, pressing firmly. Place the strip on a sheet pan lined with baking paper and evenly stretch the dough crosswise to produce the lattice pattern. Repeat with the remaining strips.

3. Bake at 400°F (205°C) for about 10 minutes or until the dough develops a rich brown color. Let the gingerbread strips cool.

4. Use a serrated knife with a sawing motion to cut 4 unevenly shaped decorations from each sheet. Store, covered, in an airtight container.

About Lattice Cutters

Two tools are available to cut lattice patterns in dough. They are most often used for lattice crust on pies but, as with this recipe, they have other uses as well. For the gingerbread decorations, use a *lattice dough roller*. This tool is made entirely from plastic or from stainless steel with a wooden handle. It is a rolling cutter, 5 inches (12.5 cm) wide, with seventeen blades. As the tool is rolled over a sheet of dough, it cuts a precise pattern of slits. When the dough is lifted and stretched, the slits open into the diamond-shaped openings of a lattice pattern.

The second tool is called a *lattice dough cutter*. This is a flat, round two-piece tool, 12 inches (30 cm) in diameter. Both pieces have diamond-shaped cutouts. A rolled sheet of dough is placed over the bottom cutter and the top round is pushed down on top, cutting through and making the diamond-shaped holes.

A one-piece version of the lattice dough cutter is also available. This is a raised circular metal grill imprinted with the lattice design. The sheet of dough is placed on top and a rolling pin is rolled over the dough to cut out the diamond shapes.

BANANA RUM PUDDING WITH BRANDIED WHIPPED CREAM AND GINGERBREAD LATTICE yield: 12 servings

Banana Rum Pudding (recipe follows)

⅓ recipe Kiwi Sauce (page 309)

½ recipe Brandied Whipped Cream (page 488; see directions below)

Zested orange peel

Orange segments

Powdered sugar

Gingerbread Lattice Decorations (page 485)

Ground cinnamon

1. Follow the directions and presentation instructions for Persimmon Dome Cake with Gingerbread Lattice, substituting dark rum for the brandy in the brandied whipped cream and decorating the plates with cinnamon instead of nutmeg.

Banana Rum Pudding yield: approximately 5 cups (1 L 200 ml)

8 ounces (225 g) dates, chopped into raisin-size pieces

¾ cup (180 ml) dark rum

1 pound 2 ounces (510 g) bananas

1 tablespoon (15 ml) lime juice

14 ounces (400 g) granulated sugar

2 teaspoons (10 ml) vanilla extract

7 ounces (200 g) bread flour

1½ teaspoons (6 g) baking soda

1 teaspoon (1 g) ground cinnamon

5 ounces (140 g) macadamia nuts, chopped into raisin-size pieces

¾ cup (180 ml) unsweetened coconut milk

1. Combine the dates and rum and set aside to macerate.

2. Peel and puree the bananas. Mix in the lime juice, sugar, and vanilla.

3. Sift together the flour, baking soda, and cinnamon. Mix the dry ingredients into the banana mixture. Stir in the macadamia nuts, coconut milk, and the date mixture, including all of the rum. Bake and unmold as directed in the main recipe.

Persimmon Pudding yield: 2 puddings, 2 quarts (1 L 920 ml) each, or 24 servings

Early settlers in the mid- and southeastern portion of what was to become the United States had quite a culinary experience when they first encountered native persimmons. For as delicious, creamy, and sweet as the perfectly ripe fruit can be — they should be so ripe, in fact, that they are just about falling apart — taking a bite of an unripe persimmon will make you pucker and reach desperately for a glass of water to wash away the unpleasant sour and bitter taste and the peculiar dry feeling it leaves in your mouth. But through trial and error and from seeing that the Native Americans used persimmons extensively (to make puddings and breads, among other dishes), the settlers were soon supplementing their diet with the bountiful wild persimmons. These have a different flavor and are much smaller than the Asian variety, usually known as *Japanese persimmons*, which are found in the markets in the fall.

I first made this recipe many years ago for a lavish banquet at which each of the fifty states was represented by a regional specialty; this pudding was the pride of Indiana. If you have never tried persimmons, or had a bad experience eating a raw unripe one, or think you do not like persimmon pudding, my guess is you will be pleasantly surprised by this dessert. Many people have told me they never liked persimmon pudding until they tried this recipe.

8 ounces (225 g) dark raisins

8 ounces (225 g) golden raisins

1½ cups (360 ml) brandy

Butter and Flour Mixture (page 750)

2 pounds 8 ounces (1 kg 135 g) ripe Hachiya
persimmons

1 pound 12 ounces (795 g) granulated sugar

2 tablespoons (30 ml) vegetable oil

1 tablespoon (15 ml) vanilla extract

14 ounces (400 g) bread flour

1 tablespoon (12 g) baking soda

2 teaspoons (10 g) salt

1 teaspoon (2 g) ground cloves

1 teaspoon (2 g) ground nutmeg

10 ounces (285 g) coarsely chopped walnuts

1½ cups (360 ml) whole milk

Brandied Whipped Cream (recipe follows)

Ground nutmeg

Cranberries

Mint sprigs

1. Combine the raisins and brandy and set aside to macerate.

2. Cut 2 rings of baking paper to fit the bottom of 2 angel food cake pans, 2 quarts (1 L 920 ml) in capacity, or other flat-bottomed tube pans of about the same size. Place the paper in the pans, then brush the entire inside of the pans, including the paper, with butter and flour mixture.

3. Slice the persimmons in half and use a melon ball cutter or small spoon to scoop out the flesh, scraping the skin thoroughly. Discard the skin. Puree the pulp and measure: You should have close to 4 cups (960 ml). Mix the persimmon puree with the sugar, oil, and vanilla.

4. Sift together the flour, baking soda, salt, cloves, and nutmeg. Mix the dry ingredients into the puree mixture. Stir in the walnuts, milk, and the raisin mixture, including all of the brandy. Divide the batter evenly between the reserved pans.

5. Bake at 325°F (163°C) for about 1 hour and 15 minutes or until baked through. Let the puddings cool in the pans completely. Unmold, remove the baking paper rings, and cut the puddings into 12 slices each.

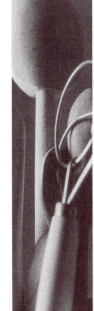

About Persimmons

The Hachiya persimmon is the variety most commonly found in stores. It has a slightly oblong shape and is pointed at the bottom. The Hachiya is high in tannin and can be eaten raw only when fully ripe (the fruit should be almost jellylike throughout); otherwise, it has an unpleasant, astringent, almost rough taste. The smaller Fuyu persimmon is shaped like a tomato. It has very little tannin and can therefore be eaten raw before it is completely ripe and soft. This persimmon is easy to peel with a vegetable peeler.

The unpleasant, dry taste of the unripe Hachiya disappears when the fruit is cooked, so it is acceptable to use unripe fruit in the persimmon pudding, if necessary. Unripe Hachiyas must first be frozen solid and then thawed to make them soft enough to puree. (After freezing and thawing, the fruit will be as soft as when perfectly ripe but will still have the tannic taste.) If you can plan far enough ahead, place the fruit in a plastic bag with a ripe apple for a few days; this will speed the ripening process and eliminate the dry taste.

When either variety is ripe and soft to the point of falling apart, just remove the stems, puree with the skin on, then force through a fine strainer. Prepared persimmon puree freezes well. Add 1 tablespoon (15 ml) lemon juice for every 2 cups (480 ml) puree. As persimmons are not available year round, it is a good idea to prepare persimmon pulp to store in the freezer. Pack in freezer containers, cover, and freeze. If you use the puree in a recipe that also calls for lemon or lime juice, leave it out, as it is already in the puree.

6. Presentation: Place a slice of persimmon pudding on its side in the center of a dessert plate. Spoon brandied whipped cream over the narrow end of the slice, letting some fall onto the plate in front of the dessert. Sprinkle nutmeg lightly over the cream. Place 3 cranberries (in a triangle, to look like holly berries) in the cream on the plate. Set a mint sprig next to the berries.

7. Holiday Table Presentation: Place a whole pudding on a serving platter. Heat ⅓ cup (80 ml) brandy to the scalding point, but do not boil. Pour the brandy into a small flameproof cup and place it in the middle of the pudding ring. Turn down the room lights, ignite the hot brandy, and spoon it, flaming, on top of the pudding. Serve brandied whipped cream on the side.

BRANDIED WHIPPED CREAM yield: 6 cups (1 L 440 ml)

3 cups (720 ml) heavy cream	1 teaspoon (2 g) grated nutmeg
2 tablespoons (30 g) granulated sugar	1 teaspoon (5 ml) vanilla extract
⅓ cup (80 ml) brandy	

1. Whip the cream and sugar until the mixture is quite thick but still pourable. Stir in the brandy, nutmeg, and vanilla.

2. Cover and reserve in the refrigerator. Adjust the consistency of the sauce at serving time; it should be thick enough to not run on the plate. To thin the sauce add heavy cream; to thicken it whip further.

Pumpkin Crème Brûlée yield: 12 servings

This is a great alternative to the more mundane pumpkin pie. If you want to dress up the presentation, serve the custard inside hollow miniature pumpkin shells, such as those of the Jack Be Little variety, which are about the size of an apple. Follow the directions for cooking the pumpkin shells, preparing the custard, and assembling and serving the dessert as described in Apple Crème Brûlée (page 325). Instead of decorating the dessert with a caramelized apple wedge, save the pumpkin tops (try to choose pumpkins with attractive stems intact) and use them as part of the presentation. You may want to bake the lids separately so their color better matches the pumpkin shells. Any fruit puree with approximately the same consistency and moisture content as pumpkin puree may be substituted, so you can make various flavors all year round.

1 whole vanilla bean	1½ teaspoons (7.5 g) salt
12 ounces (340 g) granulated sugar, plus additional for sprinkling	1 teaspoon (5 ml) vanilla extract
14 egg yolks (1¼ cups/300 ml)	Seasonal fruit, such as cranberries, sliced citrus, or sliced persimmon
1 whole egg	Bubble Sugar (page 615) or Sugar Shards (page 628)
6½ cups (1 L 560 ml) heavy cream	
1 cup (240 ml) pumpkin puree	

1. Cut the vanilla bean in half lengthwise and scrape out the seeds (save the pod halves for another use). Mix the vanilla bean seeds with 12 ounces (340 g) sugar. Rub the mixture lightly with your fingertips to combine.

2. Mix — but do not whip — the egg yolks, whole egg, and vanilla-flavored sugar until well combined. Heat the cream to the scalding point, then gradually pour into the egg mixture, stirring constantly. Mix in the pumpkin puree, followed by the salt and vanilla.

3. Place crème brûlée forms (see Note) or other ovenproof forms, such as soufflé ramekins, 3¼ inches (8.1 cm) diameter, in hotel pans or other suitable pans and fill them close to the top with the custard. Add hot water around the forms to reach about three-quarters of the way up the sides. Move the pan to the oven, then top off each form with the remaining custard. Be sure to fill the forms all the way to the top because crème brûlée, like all custards, settles slightly while cooking.

4. Bake at 350°F (175°C) for about 25 minutes or until the custards are set; if using soufflé ramekins, add a few minutes to the baking time. Do not overcook, or the custard may break and have an unpleasant texture (see Chef's Tip). Remove the custards from the water bath and let them cool slightly at room temperature, then refrigerate until thoroughly chilled. Covered tightly in their baking forms, the custards can be stored in the refrigerator for 4 to 5 days.

5. Presentation: Sprinkle just enough granulated sugar on top of a custard to cover the surface. Clean off any sugar from the edge or the outside of the form. Caramelize the sugar using a salamander or a blowtorch or by placing the dish under a broiler. Decorate the top of the crème brûlée with fruit and a sugar garnish. Place the custard dish on a plate lined with a napkin.

NOTE: Traditional crème brûlée dishes are made of ceramic and are 4½ inches (11.2 cm) in diameter and ¾ inch (2 cm) deep.

CHEF'S TIP

If you are not certain your oven temperature is accurate, test it with an oven thermometer. If you do not have a removable thermometer, start cooking the custards at 325°F (163°C). If after 30 minutes the custard is still as liquid as when you started, your thermostat is incorrect and you should increase the temperature. Wasting 30 minutes is better than overcooking the custard due to a poorly calibrated oven.

GINGERBREAD HOUSES

Exactly when the custom of building gingerbread houses at Christmastime began is not clear, but we do know it was after the Grimm brothers retold the tale of Hansel and Gretel in the nineteenth century. Building and displaying a small gingerbread house is a traditional part of Christmas for many families in Sweden. It can be a project for the whole family; the children not only love to help assemble the house but also to tear it apart after Christmas. A gingerbread house is also a typical part of the pastry shop's seasonal decor. These showpieces are usually large, elaborate creations that light up at night and are displayed in the shop windows. Smaller, simpler houses are made for sale, such as the Santa's Gingerbread Chalet (page 499) or a smaller version of the traditional gingerbread house. If the houses are made in an assembly-line fashion, they can be a profitable line for your business, and they fill the shop with old-fashioned Christmas spirit.

Using a dough sheeter is the ideal way to roll out the dough for a gingerbread house. It not only saves time, but perhaps more importantly, ensures an even thickness throughout, giving the house a more professional appearance.

Traditional Gingerbread House

yield: 1 house, approximately 8 inches (20 cm) wide, 10 inches (25 cm) long, and 11 inches (27.5 cm) tall, excluding the chimney (Color Photos 102, 103, and 105)

I realize that this thirty-three-step-plus project may appear overwhelming to a novice at gingerbread house construction, but I assure you that for many years, dozens of nonprofessional students constructed this same house during a one-day gingerbread house workshop I conducted each Christmas. After two hours of lecture and demonstration covering assembly and decorating, each student was given the baked pieces for one house, as well as icing, candies, other decorating materials, and a marzipan Santa. After three hours of fun (and help when needed), each student took his or her beautiful creation home. If you don't feel you are up to the job without that kind of head start, try Santa's Gingerbread Chalet (page 499). The chalet can be finished in about two hours, even without a teacher in your kitchen.

The decorating instructions in this recipe are for making a fairly ornate house, which can be changed and simplified according to your own imagination. You can enlarge the templates accordingly to make this size, or reduce or enlarge them to any size you like to create a smaller or larger house (if you are making a larger house, see the information on page 498). Of course, you must enlarge or reduce all of the templates equally so the pieces will fit together. The roof pieces should always be large enough for a 1-inch (2.5-cm) overhang on all four sides. Smaller houses limit the decorating possibilities quite a bit, which makes them suitable for decorating identically in an assembly-line fashion.

1 recipe Gingerbread Cookies dough (page 461; see Step 1)	1 cotton ball
Red cellophane	Marzipan Santa (page 660)
2 recipes Royal Icing (page 680)	Marzipan Children (page 656)
¼ cup (60 ml) egg whites	Powdered sugar
½ recipe Boiled Sugar Basic Recipe (page 575; see Step 14)	

1. Make the gingerbread cookie dough through Step 3, replacing the butter with margarine and increasing the flour by 6 ounces (170 g). Cover and place in the refrigerator overnight.

2. Make a platform base measuring 12 × 16 inches (30 × 40 cm) from 2 sheets of corrugated cardboard, each ¼ inch (6 mm) thick, glued together, or make a reusable base from plywood (see page 498).

3. Enlarge the gingerbread house templates in Figures 9-24 to 9-29 to the size specified in the yield (or as desired), then trace and copy onto sturdy cardboard, such as the type used to mat framed artwork. Use a utility knife to cut out the templates.

4. Work the gingerbread dough smooth with your hands. Using as little flour as possible, roll out one portion at a time to ¼ inch (6 mm) thick (or slightly thinner, for a small house). Place the pieces on sheet pans lined with baking paper and reserve in the refrigerator.

5. When the dough is firm, place the templates on top and cut out the pieces; use a paring knife or utility knife to cut the windows and door:

- Cut out 2 pieces of identical dimensions for the front and back; cut 1 window and 1 door from the front piece and 2 windows from the back piece (Figure 9-24). When you cut out the piece for the door, save it to attach later.

- Cut out 2 identical long pieces for the sides (Figure 9-25).

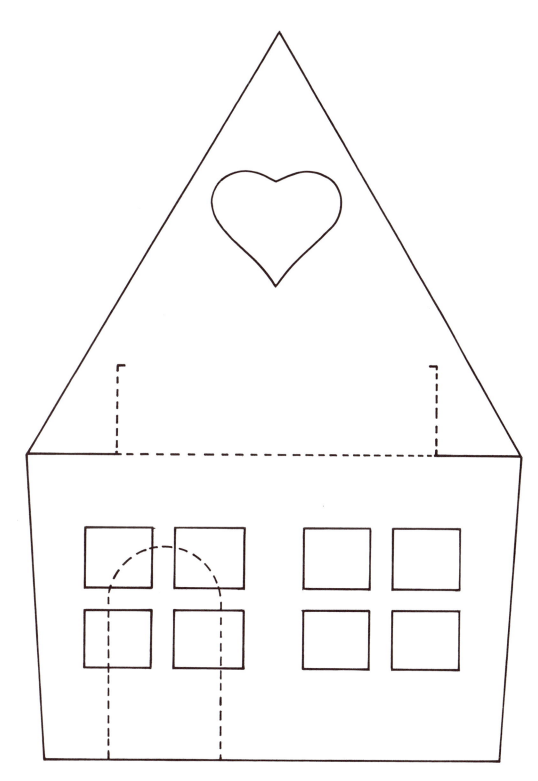

FIGURE 9-24 The template used as a guide to cut out the front and back of the Gingerbread House; make one piece with two windows and the other with one window and a door (indicated by the curved dotted line); the dotted lines on the second story indicate the placement of the balcony

FIGURE 9-25 The template used as a guide to cut the sides of the Gingerbread House; cut two identical pieces

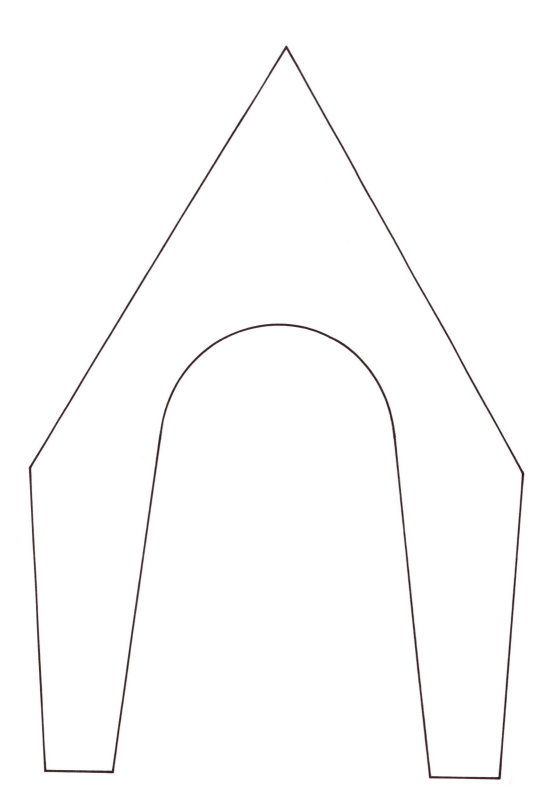

FIGURE 9-26 The template used as a guide in cutting a center support piece for large houses

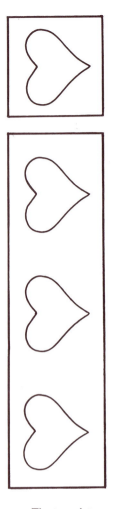

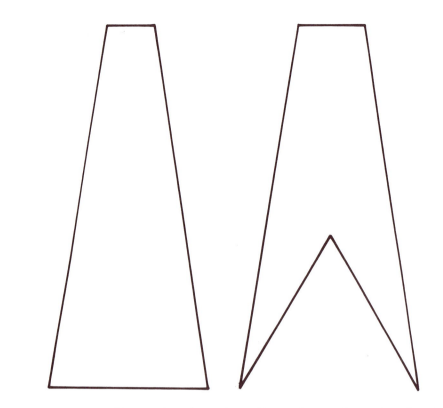

FIGURE 9-28 The templates for cutting a chimney that attaches to the point of the roof; cut two of each

FIGURE 9-27 The templates used as guides when cutting the balcony pieces; cut two of each, but cut hearts out of only one of the longer pieces

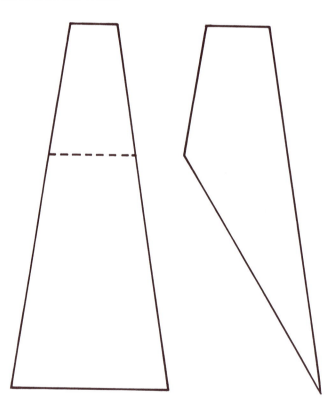

FIGURE 9-29 The templates for cutting a chimney that attaches to the slope of the roof; cut two of each, making one of the pieces shown on the left side of the drawing only as large as the part of the drawing above the dotted line

- If making a large house (see page 498), cut out the center support piece (Figure 9-26).

- Make a balcony (Figure 9-27) to attach to the front of the house later. Cut 2 of each piece; the 2 long pieces will be the front side panel and the floor, and the short pieces will be the sides. Decorate 1 long balcony piece by pressing horizontal lines into the dough with the back of a knife, then cut out small hearts as shown. Leave the other long piece solid for the floor.

- Choose a chimney design. The chimney that attaches to the point of the roof (Figure 9-28) will make a small house look bigger; the other chimney design (Figure 9-29) goes on the slope of the roof. Cut out 2 sets of either design (4 pieces total per chimney).

If you like, make a brick design in the dough for the chimney before you cut the pieces. Roll out a piece of the scrap dough left from cutting the sides that is large enough for all 4 chimney pieces and ⅛ inch (3 mm) thick. Use a straight piece of the cardboard used to make the templates or a ruler with an edge ¹⁄₁₆ (2 mm) thick to press parallel lines into the dough every ¼ inch (6 mm). Cut a strip of cardboard ¼ inch (6 mm) wide and use the end to press lines at a 90-degree angle to the parallel lines, staggering the rows to simulate bricks. If the dough becomes soft as you are imprinting the brick pattern, place it in the refrigerator to firm, then cut out the chimney pieces.

- If you are using the templates at the size specified in the yield, make an additional template that measures 8 inches (20 cm) on each left and right side, 13 inches (32.5 cm) across the top, and 11½ inches (28.7 cm) across the bottom. Increase or decrease the size of the template proportionally if using another size for the other pieces. Make either the left or right side straight (at a 90-degree angle to the top and bottom) and the other side slanted. Use the template to cut out 2 pieces for the roof; remember to invert the template when you cut the second piece so the point of the overhang will match later. Save all of the scrap dough.

- Choose a fence design: either a ranch style fence or the picket fence shown in the Color Photos. For the ranch-style fence, use scrap pieces and/or reroll scrap dough and cut out fence posts and planks. Make the plank pieces slightly bent and uneven for a rustic look. For the picket fence, make 2 fence sections 12 inches (30 cm) long and 2 fence sections 18 inches (45 cm) long, following the directions in Steps 6 and 7 on page 500 in Santa's Chalet.

- Use your imagination in cutting out the other scrap pieces to create your own personalized house. For example, you can make shutters and windowsills for the windows and turn extra fence posts into a stack of fireplace logs.

- To decorate the roof, roll out a piece of gingerbread dough to ⅛ inch (3 mm) thick and cut out 12 strips, ½ inch (1.2 cm) wide and as long as the roof. You actually only need 8 to 10 (4 or 5 on each side, depending on the size of the house), but it is always a good idea to make a few extra. Like the ranch-style fence planks, the strips for the roof should be bent so they are slightly uneven and resemble pieces cut from a tree that was not perfectly straight.

- Cut out 4 pieces of dough, 7 × 1 inch (17.5 × 2.5 cm), to trim the edges of the roof overhang. Place them on a sheet pan and use a small heart cutter to cut out hearts vertically along the length of each piece (the design is cut with the dough on the sheet pan because it is difficult to move the dough without disturbing the pattern after the hearts are cut). You may want to make extras of these because they break easily.

- Roll out additional dough slightly thinner ($^1/_{16}$ inch/2 mm) and cut out hearts with a heart-shaped cutter measuring 1 to 1$^3/_4$ inches (2.5 to 4.5 cm) across. The number of hearts required depends on how you plan to decorate the roof. If you place hearts between the roof planks and on the sides of the chimney, as shown in the Color Photos, you will need about 40. Alternatively, you can omit the roof planks and use the smaller hearts as shingles in Step 22, covering the entire roof.

- You can create a miniature tree by tying small pieces of pine to a dowel. Later, drill a hole in the iced cardboard or plywood platform to secure the tree trunk. Alternatively, you can cut out large and small trees from scrap gingerbread dough using the templates from Santa's Gingerbread Chalet (Figure 9-30, page 500) or the template for the Cookie Christmas Trees (Figure 9-23, page 483), enlarging as desired.

6. Bake the pieces at 375°F (190°C) until they are dark brown and done. Make sure the larger pieces are baked all the way through. Avoid placing large and small pieces on the same pan so you will not have to move them before they are cool. Set the pieces aside to cool completely.

7. When the gingerbread has cooled, trim the edges of the side and roof pieces so they fit together as well as possible. Treat the edges of the chimney and balcony pieces in the same way. Woodworking files and No. 50 to No. 80 grade sandpaper work well for this, but a serrated paring knife or utility knife can also be used. As you trim the pieces, be careful not to press too hard, or they might break. Turn the pieces upside down.

8. Cut pieces of red cellophane slightly larger than each of the windows; set aside.

9. Soften 2 cups (480 ml) royal icing by adding $^1/_4$ cup (60 ml) egg whites. Using the side of a paring knife to force the icing into the pores of the gingerbread, spread a thin film of icing over the back of the trimmed pieces to protect them from moisture. This is absolutely essential if you are not using a light inside the house and a good idea even if you do. Any gingerbread figures or trees to be placed on the platform must be treated in the same way to prevent them from collapsing. One at a time, ice the back of the side house pieces and immediately press the cellophane squares over the windows while the icing is wet. Once you have installed all of the windows, place a portion of the icing in a piping bag and pipe additional icing at the edge of the cellophane squares. Use your fingertip to smooth that icing out to the icing on the gingerbread so the cellophane pieces are secure. Leave all of the pieces upside down until dry to the touch.

10. Turn the front, side, and back pieces right-side up. Using a piping bag with a small opening, pipe royal icing (not the thinned portion) on the pieces, making any design you wish around the outline of the door and windows and around the edges. Set aside with the roof pieces.

11. To assemble the chimney, pipe a thin line of royal icing next to the edge of the long sides on the 2 wider chimney pieces. Fit the other 2 pieces between them, adjusting so the edges line up properly. Set aside to dry.

12. To assemble the balcony, pipe a thin line of royal icing at the front top edge of the bottom balcony piece (without hearts) and attach the long front piece to the bottom. Repeat to attach the 2 short sides. Set the balcony aside to dry with the other pieces for at least 2 hours or, preferably, overnight before continuing.

13. Draw lines on the platform to show exactly where the house will be attached.

14. Boil the sugar to the hard-crack stage (310°F/155°C).

15. Use a knife to spread a little of the sugar on the edges of 1 side piece and the front piece. Quickly attach these to the platform and to each other. I suggest you recruit an extra pair of hands for this part. Attach the remaining side and the back of the house in the same way. Be careful as you complete these steps not to get any boiled sugar on the windows or on the front of the pieces. Place a portion of the royal icing in a pastry bag with a No. 3 (6-mm) plain tip. Pipe a string of icing along all 4 inside seams, floor to ceiling, for extra support.

16. Test the roof pieces to make certain they fit. If not, trim the edges of the frame on the platform as needed. Carefully but quickly spread sugar on the underside of the roof pieces in a 1-inch (2.5-cm) band where the roof will connect with the sides of the house. One at a time, attach the pieces, holding each until secure.

17. Check that the angle of the chimney will fit with the angle of the roof so the chimney will stand straight. Using sugar to secure it, attach the chimney to the roof. Take a good look at the chimney from all sides to be certain it is standing straight.

18. Attach the balcony with boiled sugar. Pipe strings of royal icing over the 3 seams where the balcony meets the house.

19. Adjust the consistency of the remaining royal icing, if necessary, until it is spreadable but not runny. To thin the icing, mix in egg white; to thicken it, incorporate sifted powdered sugar.

20. Spread enough icing on the roof to completely cover the gingerbread, including the sides of the chimney, unless you have made a brick pattern on the chimney. Smooth over and fill in any cracks where the chimney is attached to the roof, but do not make the icing completely smooth; it should look a little rustic. Alternatively, leave the chimney plain, without icing on the sides, and decorate it with piped icing later as you would the brick-style chimney. Try to make the icing hang over the bottom edge of the roof, then make icicles by immediately pulling the icing down randomly across the sides. If the icing falls off in chunks instead of forming icicles, it is too thick. Thin the icing or use a little less to compensate.

21. Attach the roof planks on each side of the roof, pressing them lightly into the icing. Skip this step if you want to make a shingled roof.

22. Using the royal icing in the pastry bag as glue, attach rows of gingerbread hearts between the roof planks. Alternatively, use small hearts as shingles to cover the roof. If you do this, begin placing them at the bottom edge of the roof and work your way toward the roofline, overlapping each heart partway (most people start at the top, then realize too late the overlapping is turning out backwards).

23. Use your imagination to decorate the base platform. Make 1 or 2 small hills on the platform by gluing baked scrap pieces together with royal icing. Spread a covering of icing over the hills. Spread a thick covering of icing over the entire platform around the house. Stack firewood pieces in a pile. Use a palette knife to clear a path through the snow to the front door.

24. To build the ranch-style fence, use a melon ball cutter to scrape away small spots of royal icing ½ inch (1.2 cm) from the edge of the platform and approximately 4 inches (10 cm) apart around its perimeter. Do not forget to make an opening for a gate. Rewarm the boiled sugar, if

Adding a Light to Your Gingerbread House

It is not necessary to light smaller houses, where electricity is a purely decorative option, but large houses should always be illuminated — not only for decorative value but also to keep the house warm and prevent the gingerbread from softening and eventually collapsing as it absorbs moisture from the air. Turn on the light for a few hours at least once each day.

Building a Plywood Platform and Connecting a Light Inside the House

These instructions are for making a platform for a larger house measuring 11 × 15 × 15 inches (27.5 × 27.5 × 37.5) without the chimney. If you are constructing the regular-size house from the main recipe but want to set it on a plywood platform, cut the wood to 12 × 16 inches (30 × 40 cm) instead.

1. Cut a rectangle measuring 16 × 24 inches (40 × 60 cm) out of ½-inch (1.2-cm) plywood. Cut out a square opening approximately 3 × 3 inches (7.5 × 7.5 cm) or large enough to insert a small light bulb (and your fingers), should you need to replace it. To use the space on the platform in the most efficient way, I recommend that you place the house in one corner, with the long sides of the house parallel to the long sides of the platform and the front door facing the open garden area. For the best lighting effect, cut the opening so the bulb is just about in the center of the assembled house. Keep the location of the house in mind when cutting the opening.

2. Cut out 4 small pieces of plywood from your scraps and glue or nail 1 under each corner to raise the platform and allow space for the electrical cord.

3. Screw a light-bulb holder to the plywood next to the opening and attach a cord that will just reach to 1 side of the platform. Attach a male plug to the end of the cord. (It is more practical to use a short cord like this attached to the house itself and combine it with whatever length extension cord is necessary so you will not have a long cord in your way; also, you can relocate the platform easily by changing the extension cord.)

4. Draw lines on the platform exactly where you want to attach the house (remember that, ideally, the light attachment is in the center). Screw a 15- to 25-watt bulb into the holder; plug it in, and test to make sure it works before you build the house. Place a piece of foil over the bulb while you are working.

Special Instructions for Larger Houses

If you are making a larger house, such as one with the dimensions given in the platform instructions, cut out a piece of gingerbread dough to make a center supporting wall (it should fit across the width of the house) when you cut the other gingerbread pieces (Figure 9-26, page 494). For the larger house, you will need 2 recipes gingerbread cookie dough and 3 recipes royal icing. Increase the size of the fence, trees, and other decorations proportionally.

necessary, dip the bottom of the fence posts in it, and attach them to the platform at the markings made in the icing. Make sure the posts are straight. Glue the fence planks to the posts with royal icing, attaching 1 end of each plank at the top of the posts and another halfway down.

25. To attach the picket fence, use a fine saw or a serrated knife to carefully trim the pieces to the proper length for your design. Place them ½ inch (1.2 cm) away from the edge of the platform, pushing them into the soft icing. Using the icing in the pastry bag as glue, pipe icing to connect the fence pieces at the corners.

26. Apply icing trim by piping from top to bottom at each corner of the house. Pipe icing on the short sides of the roof, covering the exposed gingerbread. Attach a heart (or a pretzel, as shown in the Color Photos) at the very top of the house on each side. Carefully push the 4 roof trim pieces with the heart cutouts in place in the icing.

27. Pipe a line of icing along the bottom of the balcony and use the tip of the pastry bag to pull the icing down into icicles, as you did on the long sides of the roof.

28. If you are using trees made of pine, drill holes the same diameter as the dowels in the platform where you want the trees to stand, then secure them with royal icing. Alternatively, place gingerbread trees here and there, and maybe a few gingerbread deer among them.

29. Attach the door in an open position. If you have made a marzipan figure to stand in the doorway, put it in place first.

30. Pipe around the fence posts to cover any exposed sugar. Apply snow by piping icing on top of the fence posts and planks. Be certain the planks of the ranch-style fence are dry, or the weight of the snow will cause them to fall off. Pipe icing around the top of the chimney, around the top edge of the balcony, on top of the firewood, and on the gingerbread trees. Dot icing on the branches of the pine trees, if using, and on any other exposed landscape element.

31. Fasten a thin stream of cotton inside the chimney to simulate smoke. Place the marzipan Santa in the garden and the marzipan children on the balcony.

32. Dust the whole house and garden with powdered sugar, blowing at the same time to make some windblown snow adhere to the sides of the house.

33. Stand back and enjoy your masterpiece. If your house is equipped with electricity, plug in the light inside first. A time-consuming and elaborate house like this does not have to be thrown away after the holidays. Cover it with a plastic bag, store it in a dry area, and use it again next year, perhaps with some renovation or repair.

CHEF'S TIP
You can use fairly stiff royal icing rather than boiled sugar to assemble the gingerbread house, but you must do so in stages, supporting the sides at the beginning and letting them set for several hours before adding the roof, chimney, and balcony, which must also be supported until dry. At that point, allow the house to dry overnight before decorating. It is much more practical to use sugar, which makes it possible for you to decorate and finish the house immediately after assembling it.

Santa's Gingerbread Chalet

yield: 1 house, approximately 4 × 7 × 8 inches (10 × 17.5 × 20 cm) (Color Photo 104)

Of all of the holiday pastries and other goodies, gingerbread, and especially gingerbread figures, are probably the most loved. They are certainly among the sweets most closely associated with the holiday season — a decorated gingerbread man or woman immediately makes you think of Christmas — and a large part of their popularity hinges on three factors: they are inexpensive, they are easy to make, and everyone in the family can participate in making them. Even if you are not a great artist, gingerbread figures are pretty hard to ruin; it simply takes a sensitive nose to tell when the dough is done.

This cute little chalet was originally made using a thicker German lebkuchen type of gingerbread dough. It also had four sides, as do most houses. But after a few Scandinavian remodeling touches, it became the slightly whimsical version that follows. The chalet is perfect if you do not have time to make a larger, more traditional house; once you have made the dough and cut out the templates, it will take only a few hours to complete. The only time-consuming step is making Santa's head out of marzipan, and this really should not be left out, as Santa has lent his name to this creation.

1 ounce (30 g) bread flour

¼ recipe or 1 pound 2 ounces (510 g) Gingerbread Cookies dough (page 461)

½ recipe Royal Icing (page 680)

1 teaspoon (5 ml) egg white

¼ recipe Boiled Sugar Basic Recipe (page 575; see Step 12)

1 Marzipan Santa's Head (instructions follow)

Coating chocolate, melted

Powdered sugar

I. Work the extra bread flour into the gingerbread dough. Continue to work the dough until it is smooth, then roll it out to a rectangle measuring 10 × 18 inches (25 × 45 cm) and approximately ¼ inch (6 mm) thick. Place the dough on an inverted sheet pan lined with baking paper and refrigerate until firm.

2. Trace the chalet templates (Figure 9-30) and copy onto sturdy cardboard, such as the type used to mat artwork. If you have heart-shaped or tree-shaped cookie cutters approximately the size of the templates, use them instead. Using a utility knife, cut out the templates.

3. Place a cardboard cake round, 9 inches (22.5 cm) in diameter, on top of the firm gingerbread dough, leaving the dough in place on the inverted pan. Cut around the cardboard to make the base for the chalet (see Chef's Tip). Using the tip of a paring knife, cut 2 heart-shaped pieces (A) from the dough sheet. Using a plain round cookie cutter, 2 inches (5 cm) in diameter, cut a hole two-thirds of the way from the point on 1 heart piece, as in the drawing.

4. From the scrap pieces, cut out the chimney (B) and 6 fence posts. Make the fence posts 1¾ inches (4.5 cm) tall and ¼ inch (6 mm) wide. Also cut out 1 tree (C) and 1 tree support (D). Leave all of the cut pieces in place on the inverted pan.

5. Work the remaining scrap pieces together and roll out to a rectangle just slightly larger than 7 × 8 inches (17.5 × 20 cm); the dough should be the same thickness as before (¼ inch/ 6 mm). Cut out 2 identical pieces for the roof (E).

6. Combine and roll the scrap pieces again, rolling the dough ⅛ inch (3 mm) thick and at least 6 inches (15 cm) long. Cut 2 strips, 6 × ¼ inch (15 cm × 6 mm), to use for the fence planks. Cut deer from the leftover dough, if desired. Place all of the pieces cut from the scrap dough on a second sheet pan lined with baking paper.

7. To make the fence, line up the first and last fence post pieces with 5 inches (12.5 cm) between them. Evenly space the remaining 4 posts between the end pieces. Use a chef's knife or ruler to align the tops of the posts so they are all at the same height. Place the 2 fence planks horizontally on top of the posts, approximately ⅜ inch (9 mm) from both the top and the bottom so they are ¾ inch (2 cm) apart; they will overlap the posts on both sides.

8. Bake all of the pieces at 400°F (205°C) until dark brown, approximately 12 minutes. You may need to remove the smaller pieces a little earlier. Let the pieces cool completely.

9. Place the 2 heart pieces back to back and use a file or No. 50 grade sandpaper to trim the straight sides on both pieces so they are even; if they are not, the roof will not fit flat against them. Trim the side of the chimney that attaches to the roof so it is flat. Trim the tree support piece to the proper angle so the tree will stand straight.

10. Combine ½ cup (120 ml) royal icing with the egg white. Place some of the mixture in a piping bag and cut a larger-than-normal opening. Holding the bag close to the pieces, pipe flat lines of icing on the back side of the fence, tree, and the deer, if used. Use a small spatula to

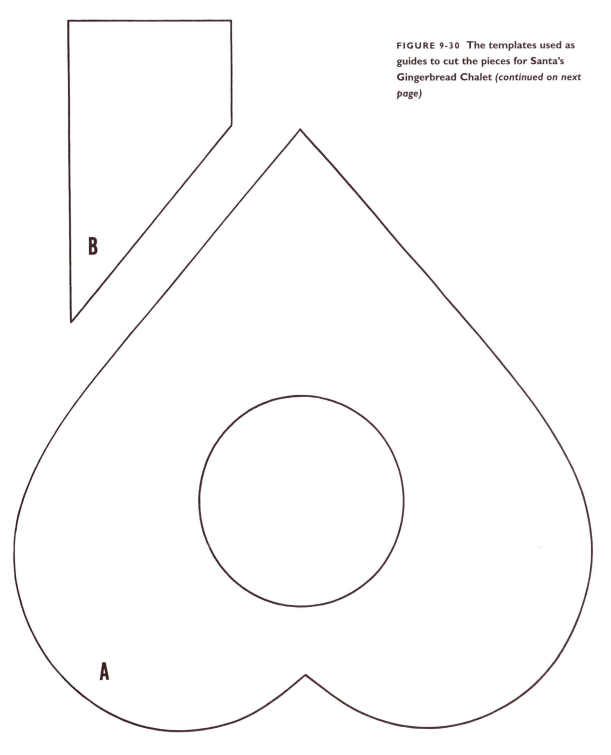

FIGURE 9-30 The templates used as guides to cut the pieces for Santa's Gingerbread Chalet (continued on next page)

spread a thin film of icing on the back of each remaining piece. Leave the iced pieces, icing-side up, until dry to the touch, about 30 minutes. It is important not to skip this step: The icing will protect the gingerbread from moisture and the subsequent collapse of your chalet.

11. Work the remaining royal icing smooth and adjust the consistency with egg white or powdered sugar as needed to make it easily spreadable but not runny. Spread a generous amount of icing in an uneven pattern on top of the circular base; give it small peaks to resemble snow drifts. Hold a heart upside down and stand it 1½ inches (3.7 cm) from the far edge of

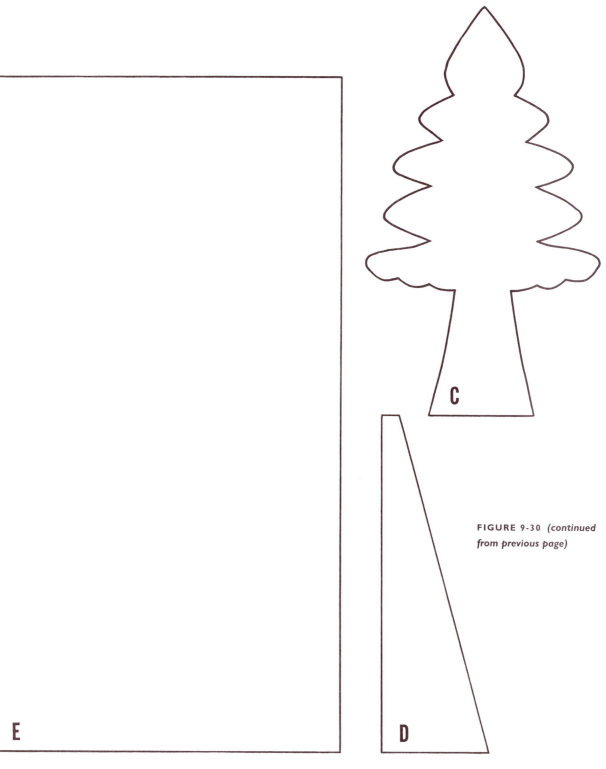

FIGURE 9-30 *(continued from previous page)*

the base, centering it left to right. Lift it up and move the heart 2 inches (5 cm) straight toward you, then set it down to make a second set of marks. Set the heart aside. Using a melon ball cutter, scrape away the icing on the base at the 4 marks made by the heart.

12. Cook the boiled sugar to the hard-crack stage (310°F/155°C). Let the syrup cool until it has thickened considerably and can be spread.

13. Spread a little syrup on the rounded edges of the solid heart. Quickly stand the heart at the first set of marks (closest to the edge of the base) with the iced side facing the center. Hold the heart straight for 30 seconds or so until set. Attach the heart with the hole in the same manner at the second set of marks, placing it so the icing side faces the other heart. The 2 hearts must line up perfectly, or the roof will be crooked.

14. Spread a small amount of syrup on the iced edge of the roof pieces where they attach to the sides. Set them in place and hold a few seconds until secure. Use syrup to attach the chimney to the roof, placing the chimney so the icing side faces the back of the chalet.

15. Working on 1 side at a time, spread enough icing on the roof to completely cover the gingerbread. Before the icing forms a skin, create icicles by pulling the icing down randomly across the sides and front with a paring knife.

16. Chill the marzipan Santa's head in the freezer for 1 minute. Place a small amount of royal icing in a piping bag. Place a small amount of melted coating chocolate in a second piping bag. Pipe a dot of chocolate on the bottom of the hole in the heart. Immediately position Santa's head on the chocolate and pipe a second dot to attach his hat to the top of the door. Hold until secure. Pipe royal icing around the spots where the head is attached, piping so it shows as little as possible. The icing will hold the head more securely than the chocolate in the event the chocolate becomes warm.

17. Pipe royal icing on the front of the tree to decorate it and use icing to attach the tree support to the back. Set the tree aside.

18. Place royal icing in a pastry bag with a No. 2 (4-mm) plain tip. Pipe a string of icing along each side where the roof connects with the sides.

19. Attach the fence to the left side of the base in front of the chalet, pushing it into the icing on the base. Using a small amount of icing, attach the tree to the right side of the base. Put the deer in place, if using. Pipe icing on top of the chimney, fence, and tree to simulate a heavy snowfall. Dust powdered sugar over the entire house.

CHEF'S TIP

Instead of cutting the base from gingerbread dough, you can use 2 corrugated cardboard cake circles, 9 inches (22.5 cm) in diameter, glued together. Spread the icing directly on the cardboard; do not forget to ice the edge so it doesn't show. You will not need as much gingerbread dough, and you can cut all of the thicker pieces from the first roll-out of dough.

TO MAKE THE MARZIPAN SANTA'S HEAD

To create the Santa shown in the chalet in Color Photo 104, use the beard variation described in the introduction on page 660.

½ ounce (15 g) untinted marzipan for the head and beard

¼ ounce (7 g) light pink marzipan for the face

⅓ ounce (10 g) red marzipan for the hat

Egg white

Royal Icing (page 680)

Dark coating chocolate, melted

1. Follow the procedure in Steps 5 through 16 on pages 662 and 663.

IN THIS CHAPTER

CHOCOLATE TEMPERING   511

CHOCOLATE DECORATIONS

Making Chocolate Decorations Using the
Instant-Set Method   515

Chocolate Cigarettes   516

Two-Tone Chocolate Cigarettes   518

Chocolate Corkscrews   519

Chocolate Cutouts: Squares, Rectangles,   520
Circles, Hearts, and Triangles

   CHOCOLATE CUTOUTS USING TRANSFER SHEETS   521

Chocolate Fans   521

Chocolate Goblets   522

Marbled or Multicolored Goblets   524

Chocolate Lace Decorations   525

Chocolate Lace Igloos   526

Chocolate Leaves   527

Chocolate May Beetles   527

Chocolate Noodles   529

Chocolate Ribbons   530

Chocolate Shavings and Small Curled   531
Shavings

Chocolate Shingles   532

Chocolate Twirls   533

Honeycomb Chocolate Decor   534

Striped Chocolate Cornets   535

Striped Chocolate Cups   536

PATTERNED CHOCOLATE SHEETS

Chocolate with Wood Grain   537

Marbleized Chocolate   539

MODELING CHOCOLATE

Dark Modeling Chocolate   541

   MILK CHOCOLATE MODELING CHOCOLATE   541

White Modeling Chocolate   542

Chocolate Roses   542

**PIPING CHOCOLATE AND PIPED
CHOCOLATE DECORATIONS**

Piping Chocolate   543

Chocolate Cages   543

Chocolate Figurines   545

Chocolate Monarch Butterfly Ornaments 550

Decorating Plates with Piped Chocolate 552

Streaking   553

Chocolate Casting   553

Cocoa Painting   555

Hollow Chocolate Figures Using Molds   555

SPRAYING WITH CHOCOLATE

Chocolate Solution for Spraying   557

Cocoa Solution for Manual Spray Bottle 558

CHOCOLATE CANDIES

Branchli (Branches)   558

Fig Logs   559

Finlander Praline   560

Gianduja   560

Gianduja Bites   561

Hazelnut Cinnamon Ganache   561

Chocolate-Covered Orange Creams   562

Marzipan Pralines   563

Mimosa   564

Pistachio Slices   564

Chocolate Candy Box   565

Chocolate Artistry

Many describe chocolate as the world's most perfect food; some even consider it to have mystical properties. Around the world, with the exception of Asia, it is probably the best-loved flavor. Certainly, life would be very different for anyone in our profession without this most wondrous ingredient. The transformation of the bitter cocoa bean into a delicious, smooth, creamy chocolate candy or an elegant chocolate dessert is a lengthy and complex process, as was the evolution of the production technique itself, which covered hundreds of years and much of the globe.

Chocolate is derived from the fruit of the cocoa tree, which the Swedish botanist Carl von Linné designated *Theobroma* (Greek for "food of the gods") *cacao* in 1728. But long before that time, chocolate was enjoyed as a beverage by ancient civilizations, including the Mayans, Aztecs, and Toltecs. The cocoa tree originated in South America and was brought north to Mexico by the Mayans prior to the seventh century

A.D. It seems the Aztecs would have appreciated von Linné's name for chocolate as they too subscribed to the theory that chocolate was indeed heaven sent, believing it to be a gift from their god Quetzalcoatl.

The word *chocolate* came into English by way of Spanish from the Aztec word *xocolatl,* meaning "bitter water" or "cocoa water," referring to the beverage made by the Aztecs from ground cocoa beans. The Aztecs valued cocoa beans so highly they used them as a form of currency. They flavored their chocolate drink with spices, even chiles, but did not add any sweetener; I'm sure anyone who has tasted unsweetened baking chocolate can understand the "bitter" designation. Columbus brought cocoa beans to Spain when he returned from his fourth and final voyage (1502–1504), but it is the explorer Hernán Cortés who is given credit for popularizing and making the importance and great potential of cocoa understood by introducing the drink known as *chocolate* to Spain after his 1519 Mexican expedition. Cortés first tasted chocolate at a ceremony with the Aztec emperor Montezuma. One of Cortés's lieutenants, Bernal Díaz del Castillo, in writing about their journey, said that Montezuma believed the chocolate to have powers as an aphrodisiac. His report noted that though Montezuma "ate very little," he drank more than fifty golden cups a day that were "filled with foaming chocolate."

The Spanish added sugar to the beverage, resulting in something vaguely similar to today's hot chocolate, although it was prepared with water rather than milk, and its popularity spread through Europe. Chocolate became a fashionable drink, and chocolate houses, like coffeehouses, were important social meeting places in the seventeenth and eighteenth centuries. In the 1600s the Dutch sent cocoa beans to New Amsterdam (known today as New York City) and, by the early 1700s, chocolate, in beverage form, was being offered by pharmacists in Boston, who touted it as a cure-all. Dr. James Baker founded America's first chocolate company in 1765.

At that time, there was still no "hard" form of chocolate comparable to the candy we know today. That development did not occur until 1828, when the Dutchman Conrad J. Van Houten, whose family had a chocolate business in Amsterdam, produced chocolate powder with the invention of a screw press that removed the majority of the cocoa butter from the finely ground cocoa beans. His intention was to use the chocolate powder to make the chocolate drink less rich and oily. However, the extracted pure cocoa butter proved the key ingredient that led to hardened eating chocolate. By adding extra cocoa butter to the chocolate powder, a paste was developed that was smoother, more malleable, and more easily combined with sugar. Though it was still a far less refined product than that we are familiar with, this forerunner of modern chocolate caught on in a big way. Cocoa butter, because it melts at a temperature just under body temperature, is the ingredient that gives chocolate and especially chocolate candy its melt-in-the-mouth consistency.

To further improve the chocolate beverage, Van Houten also invented the process known as *Dutching.* This involves treating either the chocolate nibs (the crushed cocoa beans) or the chocolate liquor (the paste produced during the initial step in chocolate production) with an alkaline solution to raise its pH level. This produces cocoa powder that is darker in color, sometimes reddish, and milder in taste. The terms *Dutch process* and *Dutch cocoa* are still used for unsweetened cocoa powder that has been treated with an alkali, usually potassium carbonate.

With the process of making chocolate candy using additional cocoa butter established, two English firms, the Cadbury Company and Fry and Sons, were selling the product by the mid-1800s. The next significant development occurred in 1875, when the Swiss manufacturer Daniel Peter added to chocolate the newly discovered product condensed milk, producing the first milk chocolate. The person responsible for the invention of condensed milk in Europe was none other than Henri Nestlé of Switzerland, who was at that time manufacturing baby foods. (To this day, Nestlé Brands is one of the world's largest producers of food products. In 1939, it created the first chocolate chip made for cookies.) In 1879, Rodolphe Lindt, also of Switzerland, invented the technique known as *conching*. This process, named for the shell-shaped trough Lindt used to hold the mixture, consists of slowly kneading the chocolate to develop a smooth texture and incorporate still a greater ratio of cocoa butter. Conching elevated chocolate standards considerably. Jules Suchard created the first molded and filled chocolate shells in 1913.

None of these European companies set up shop to mass-produce milk chocolate in the United States, however. That distinction belongs to American-born Milton Snaveley Hershey (1857–1945), whose candy career began in 1894. In 1903, after a few years of attempting to manufacture several candies, Hershey decided to specialize in chocolate and started a factory in a town known at that time as Derry Church. What started as housing for the Hershey factory employees ultimately became the city of Hershey, Pennsylvania. The Hershey Bar was a phenomenal success, and the Hershey factory eventually became the world's largest chocolate manufacturing plant. Today, Hershey Park is located at the site of the original factory. It attracts millions of visitors every year and includes a 23-acre rose garden, amusement park rides, and the Hotel Hershey (which features a circular dining room, because Mr. Hershey is said to have disliked restaurants where "they put you in a corner"). Hershey was the first manufacturer of powdered hot chocolate or hot cocoa mix, and invented the ever-popular foil-wrapped candy, the Hershey Kiss.

Two other chocolate companies, Ghirardelli and Guittard, were started in California after the gold rush, and both are still major U.S. producers. Italian immigrant Domingo Ghirardelli founded his eponymous company in 1852. The site of the original Ghirardelli chocolate plant in San Francisco is now a popular tourist spot called Ghirardelli Square and features restaurants, art galleries, and specialty shops. In the late 1990s, the Lindt chocolate company purchased Ghirardelli, but the factory continues to produce under the Ghirardelli name. The Guittard Chocolate Company is located just south of San Francisco.

During World War II, chocolate bars were included in the rations issued to U.S. soldiers, resulting in a shortage of chocolate in the stores back home. The Nestlé Company capitalized on this in their marketing efforts, proclaiming that "chocolate is a fighting food; it supplies the greatest amount of nourishment in the smallest possible bulk." Scientist Alexander Von Humbolt (1769–1859) had expressed an almost identical sentiment when he stated, "Nature has nowhere else concentrated such an abundance of the most valuable foods in such a limited space as in the cocoa bean." Although some nutritionists today may not endorse this assessment, the popularity of chocolate is more widespread than ever. Besides being a pleasure to the palate, chocolate is still a favorite source of quick energy, used by some athletes to prevent fatigue and maintain stamina during sporting events.

Over the years, the public's devotion to chocolate has generated thousands of books and magazines devoted to the subject. It has inspired competition among chefs to create the richest, most intensely chocolate, most decadent desserts. Large numbers of people go so far as to say they are addicted to chocolate, referring to themselves as *chocoholics*.

Modern scientific research has been conducted to study the possibility of medicinal properties in chocolate, which has long had a place in folk medicine, and many people strongly believe in chocolate's mood-lifting ability. There is some scientific basis for this theory:

Chocolate is rich in phenylethylamine, a naturally occurring substance that acts similarly to amphetamines. Two American psychiatrists have introduced a hypothesis that people who go on chocolate-eating binges as a result of depression are actually trying (perhaps unknowingly) to stabilize their body chemistry by ingesting phenylethylamine. An article in the *San Francisco Examiner* newspaper that appeared in February 2000 reports on a Washington State research project that found compounds in chocolate to have cardiovascular benefits. Responding to this study and describing his own research, Carl Keen, chairman of the nutrition department at the University of California at Davis, stated, "Our data would suggest that chocolate can be part of a healthy diet." Keen conducted a study in which healthy adults ingested water mixed with cocoa powder and sugar, then had their blood levels tested over the following six hours. He found their blood platelets became less active and less likely to clump, meaning the blood was less likely to clot, when compared to test subjects who drank a mixture of water, caffeine, and sugar. This test was a follow-up to laboratory research that showed that compounds in chocolate known as *flavonoids* have a positive effect on the formation of nitric oxide, a chemical that relaxes the blood vessels. Flavonoids are also found in vegetables, fruits, tea, and red wine. They act as antioxidants, destroying free radicals associated with disease and aging. Chocolate also contains caffeine, although a significant amount is not consumed unless one eats a large quantity of straight chocolate liquor or unsweetened baking chocolate — which is unlikely. Commercial chocolate products contain about 0.1 percent caffeine, and an average serving of chocolate candy contains far less caffeine than a cup of coffee.

Taste or flavor is the most subjective element and can be a matter of individual opinion. In judging the chocolate, look for:

- Temper: The temper, or structure, of chocolate is largely based on the crystallization of cocoa butter particles. The grain structure should be tight and even throughout. The chocolate should break sharply rather than bend or crumble (naturally, the chocolate must be at the appropriate temperature — 64° to 68°F/18° to 20°C — to judge this accurately).

- Texture: The texture of the chocolate when it is eaten should be smooth, with no gritty or sandy feel. Chocolate should melt readily as soon as it is in your mouth.

- Color: Chocolate should have an even color throughout, with no streaking.

- Aroma: Chocolate easily picks up foreign odors. It should smell only of chocolate and deliberately added flavorings, such as nut paste.

Chocolate Production

The cocoa or cacao tree is an evergreen found all through the equatorial belt (within 20 degrees north or south) where the average temperature is 80°F (26°C) and humidity is high, in areas including Costa Rica, Guatemala, Nicaragua, Nigeria, Panama, Trinidad, and the Ivory Coast. The trees can grow taller but in most plantations are kept to about 25 feet (7 m 50 cm). Like the trees of the citrus family, cocoa trees bear buds, blossoms, and fruit all at the same time. Each tree produces about 30 oblong fruits, or pods, which, unlike other types of fruit, grow directly on the trunk and branches. Each pod is 6 to 10 inches (15 to 25 cm) long, 3 to 4 inches (7.5 to 10 cm) in diameter, and contains anywhere from 20 to 50 beans, 1 inch (2.5 cm) in length, embedded in the fleshy interior. The majority of the world crop of cocoa beans (which averages 2 million tons annually) comes from Africa. The largest African producer by far is the Ivory Coast, where the Forastero bean is cultivated; Ghana is a distant second.

The cocoa fruits are harvested year round, although the first few months are generally a slower time, and the main harvests take place twice a year following the rainy seasons. The seeds, along with the white flesh, or pulp, are scraped out of the pods by hand and placed in heaps covered with banana leaves or left in boxes with slatted bottoms to allow the liquid to drain. The beans are then left to ferment, a process crucial to developing flavor. This takes from as little as a few days to three weeks, depending on the climate. During the fermentation process, the pulp breaks down and the temperature rises, biochemical changes take place, the cell walls in the beans are broken down, and some of the bitterness is eliminated.

The fermented beans are spread on mats and dried in the sun to remove most of the water content. The beans develop a more pronounced cocoa aroma after drying. Next, they are packed into jute sacks and shipped to chocolate factories, where they are thoroughly cleaned. Generally, several types of beans are blended at this point to create the desired flavor and to ensure a consistent finished product. The beans are then roasted at a fairly low temperature (250°F/122°C) to develop a richer flavor and aroma. After cooling, the whole beans are crushed. Then the shells or husks are separated, using an air current to blow the lighter husk away; this process is known as *winnowing*. The husks are used as both fertilizer and animal feed. The roasted, crushed kernels of cocoa bean are called *cocoa nibs*.

The nibs are milled very fine, producing a thick liquid known as *cocoa mass, cocoa paste,* or *chocolate liquor,* which contains 53 to 55 percent cocoa butter (the term *chocolate liquor* has no reference to alcohol and should not be confused with spirits known as *chocolate liqueurs*). This is the main ingredient for a variety of chocolate products. All processing, after this point, is additional refinement to create specific products. Part of the cocoa mass is placed under high hydraulic pressure to extract the cocoa butter, a valuable aromatic fat that is an essential part of every chocolate recipe and the ingredient that gives chocolate a fine texture and attractive glaze. The cocoa cakes left after the fat is removed are crushed, ground into a fine powder, and sifted to produce pure unsweetened cocoa powder.

Cocoa butter, sugar, and milk powder, in the case of milk chocolate, are added to the cocoa mass to make chocolate. The combination is kneaded together in large mixers with S-shaped blades until a smooth, homogeneous mixture has developed. This can now be called *chocolate,* but it is not yet the smooth confection we think of when we use the word.

To remove the gritty texture still present at this stage, the chocolate is conveyed to large refiners, heavy machines with rollers 40 to 60 inches (1 to 1.5 m) long and 12 to 16 inches (30 to 40 cm) in diameter. The mixture is passed through the rollers, each set of rollers becoming progressively more narrow (like rolling out pasta dough with a manual machine), until the particles are so fine as to be undetectable on the palate.

The chocolate is now ready for the final refining process, called *conching*. Chemical changes take place during conching that further develop chocolate's characteristic flavor. The chocolate is placed in machines that knead and roll it on rotary bases continuously for two to three days; the microscopic sugar and fat particles do not become any smaller, but the sharp edges become rounded. During this process, the mixture is typically warmed to between 70° and 160°F (21° and 71°C) — although the temperature can be as high as 200°F (90°C) for some dark chocolate varieties. At the same time, the chocolate is exposed to blasts of fresh air, which allows excess

Chocolate Production

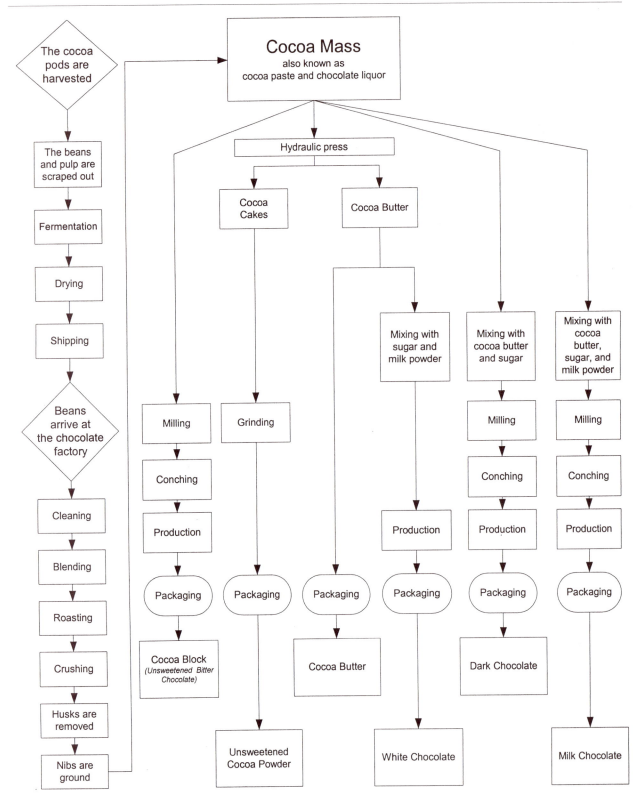

FIGURE 10-1 The chocolate production process

Tips for Melting Chocolate

Using a serrated knife and keeping the size of the pieces as uniform as possible, chop the chocolate into small pieces. If you are using purchased ready-to-melt chocolate pellets, skip this step.

Place the chocolate pieces in a bowl and set the bowl over a water bath with hot — not boiling — water. If the bowl sits above boiling water, the chocolate will be heated by steam, which is much hotter than boiling water. However, here the water is ideally no higher than 140°F (60°C), which is below the boiling point of 212°F (100°C). The important thing is that the water not be so hot that it creates steam. Steam is a problem not only because of the heat factor but also because the chocolate will seize if steam or water gets into it.

Place a spoon in the chocolate. Stir dark chocolate from time to time until it is completely melted. Stir milk or white chocolate constantly until it is completely melted. The temperature of the chocolate itself should not exceed 120°F (49°C). Coating chocolate should generally be between 100° and 110°F (38° and 43°C). Viscosity is crucial when using either tempered or coating chocolate for dipping pastries. If the chocolate is too cold and therefore too thick, the result will be a clumsy-looking, heavy coating that will not drape and conform to the shape of the pastry as it should, and your cost will be higher because you will use more product. Conversely, coating chocolate that is too hot will lose its satin shine and set up with a dull, lackluster finish instead. If the chocolate is too hot when you dip a pastry topped with buttercream in it, part of the buttercream will melt, ruining both the shape of the pastry and the supply of chocolate.

Overheating to 140°F (60°C) and above can damage dark chocolate to some extent and will make milk and white chocolate unusable for both decorative chocolate work and use in dessert mixtures. Of course, the chocolate will still be technically edible; however, its texture will be compromised. This occurs because the dry ingredients in the chocolate absorb the moisture. The cocoa butter, like any fat, will not absorb or combine with moisture, which is why the chocolate would separate if a large amount of water were to be added.

moisture to evaporate. For the highest-quality chocolate, additional cocoa butter is added. Liquid flavorings, such as vanilla, and emulsifiers, such as lecithin, are added at this time as well, if they are part of the formula. Lecithin, a soybean derivative, is less expensive than cocoa butter, brings out the chocolate flavor (which might otherwise be overpowered by excess cocoa butter), and is used to establish the viscosity necessary for smooth flow in coating and molding. The result is a velvety-smooth chocolate product. The chocolate is poured and formed into blocks, wrapped, and stored in a cool, well-ventilated room. Dark chocolate will keep this way (if unopened) for up to one year, milk and white chocolates for slightly less time. Figure 10-1 illustrates the process of chocolate production.

CHOCOLATE TEMPERING

To achieve the high gloss and hard, brittle texture that is desirable in chocolate, and to make it more resistant to warm temperatures, the chocolate must be tempered. The cocoa butter in chocolate consists of many fat groups with melting points that vary from just under 60° to 110°F (16° to 43°C). The fats that melt at the higher temperature are also the first to solidify as the melted chocolate cools. These fats, when distributed throughout, give chocolate its gloss and solidity (a properly tempered chocolate should break with a crisp snap). One might say that these high-melting-point fats act as the starting point around which the remaining chocolate solidifies.

Various methods are used to temper chocolate by hand. They all consist of three basic steps: melting, cooling, and rewarming. The most commonly used methods are *tabliering* and *seeding*. Many busy chefs today prefer to speed the process by cooling the chocolate over ice water, referred to in the following instructions as the *cold water method*.

TABLIERING METHOD

1. Cut the chocolate into small pieces (a serrated knife works best) and place it in a bowl over hot water to melt. Stir it constantly to avoid overheating or burning; this is especially important if you are working with milk chocolate, which tends to get lumpy if overheated. Stirring is essential when melting white chocolate, which can become grainy and useless very quickly. To completely melt all of the fats, heat dark chocolate to 115° to 120°F (46° to 49°C) and milk or white chocolate to 110° to 115°F (43° to 46°C).

2. Remove the chocolate from the heat and dry the bottom of the bowl. Cool the melted chocolate to approximately 95°F (34°C), stirring constantly. Pour approximately one-third (or up to two-thirds, if you are more experienced) of the cooled chocolate onto a marble slab. Using a metal spatula in combination with a metal scraper, spread the chocolate and scrape it back together until it cools further and shows signs of thickening, indicating the high-melting-point fats are starting to crystallize. Before the chocolate sets completely, stir it back into the remaining melted chocolate; continue to stir until it forms a homogeneous mass. Check the temperature: If it is near 80° to 82°F (26° to 28°C), just continue stirring until it reaches that temperature. If it is quite a bit warmer, pour a portion of the chocolate off and repeat the scraping together and cooling process, then add this back and test again. When the chocolate is smooth and homogeneous and the temperature of dark chocolate registers 80° to 82°F (26° to 28°C) and milk or white chocolate 78° to 80°F (25° to 26°C), proceed to the next step.

3. The chocolate is now too thick to use and must be warmed. However, there is no point in warming it to the working temperature before you test the temper. To test, dip the corner of

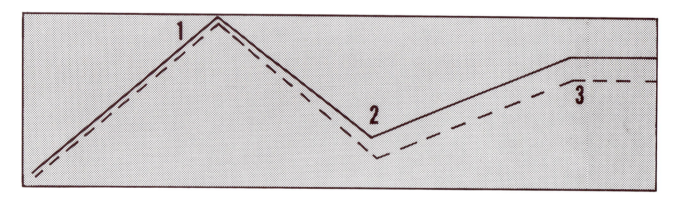

FIGURE 10-2 The three steps in tempering chocolate

Dark Chocolate (solid line)
1. Melt and heat to 115°–120°F (46°–49°C).
2. Cool to 80°–82°F (26°–28°C).
3. Warm slowly to 87°–90°F (30°–32°C).

Milk or White Chocolate (broken line)
1. Melt and heat to 110°–115°F (43°–46°C).
2. Cool to 78°–80°F (25°–26°C).
3. Warm slowly to 85°–87°F (29°–30°C).

a small piece of baking paper into the chocolate. Fold the dipped part of the paper back onto the clean area of the paper and let the chocolate cool at a room temperature of 64° to 68°F (18° to 20°C). Within 5 minutes, the chocolate should have set to the point that it is not sticky when you pull the folded paper apart, and if scraped with a knife, it should roll up like a Chocolate Cigarette (see page 516). You can expedite the test by placing the paper with chocolate in the refrigerator; the chocolate should break in half with a clean snap after 1 or 2 minutes. If the chocolate passes this test, proceed to warm it as follows. If not, repeat steps 1 and 2.

4. Warm the tempered chocolate slowly over hot water to the correct working temperature: 87° to 90°F (30° to 32°C) for dark chocolate and 85° to 87°F (29° to 30°C) for milk or white chocolate. If the chocolate is still too thick to use for a particular purpose at this temperature, thin it with a small amount of cocoa butter. Great care must be taken in the final warming step. If the chocolate gets just a few degrees above the recommended temperature, too much fat will melt, and the chocolate will require a longer time to set. It also will be less attractive, because part of the fat will separate and show on the surface in the whitish pattern known as *bloom*.

SEEDING

1. Cut the chocolate into pieces and melt over a water bath as for the tabliering method. Remove the bowl from the heat source and cool to 95°F (34°C), stirring frequently.

2. Gradually stir in grated, shaved, or finely chopped chocolate at a rate of 5 to 10 percent of the weight of the melted chocolate, waiting until each addition is completely incorporated before adding the next. Example of the seeding chocolate ratio: For 2 pounds 8 ounces or 40 ounces (1 kg 135 g) melted chocolate, use 2 to 4 ounces (55 to 115 g) seeding chocolate.

3. When the chocolate is perfectly smooth and the temperature of dark chocolate has dropped to 88° to 90°F (30° to 32°C) and temperature of milk or white chocolate has dropped to 85° to 87°F (29° to 30°C), hold the chocolate at this temperature, stirring constantly, for at least 2 minutes. Test the temper as described in Step 3 of the tabliering method. Properly tempered chocolate is ready to use. When using this method, it is important that the seeding chocolate itself be tempered chocolate.

Block Method

This shortcut variation is appropriate for small batches. In Step 2 of the seeding method add one solid piece of tempered chocolate to the melted chocolate and stir until the melted chocolate reaches the working temperature. Remove the unmelted portion of the piece. Test the temper as described above. The chocolate is ready to use if it passes the test. Like the seeding method, the block method does not produce the same long-lasting temper as tabliering.

COLD WATER METHOD

Cooling the chocolate by placing the bowl of melted chocolate over ice water is the quickest and most efficient method for tempering. You will find, however, that chocolate manufacturers do not recommend it because the quality of the temper is not high enough and water can easily get in the chocolate and ruin it. Still, this is a good method to keep in mind for emergencies.

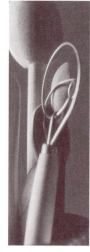

Tempering Tips

Testing the Tempered Chocolate: Before starting to work with the product, it is always a good idea to check whether or not the chocolate has been tempered correctly, regardless of the method used. See Step 3 of the tabliering method (page 512).

Warming Tempered Chocolate: If you are working with tempered chocolate and it starts to cool and set up, use a hair dryer or heat gun to gently heat the outside of the bowl, or add warm melted and tempered chocolate to restabilize the cocoa butter and make the chocolate more fluid. Estimate the amount needed, add the warm chocolate all at once, then stir the two together. One's natural inclination is to stir in a slow stream of chocolate until the desired consistency is reached, as this is the way one usually creates an emulsion, but the slow approach will actually destabilize the temper. Alternatively, provided the chocolate has not set completely, you can warm it to the correct working temperature using a microwave oven on a low setting or by placing it over a bain-marie.

1. Chop the chocolate into pieces, place in an oversize bowl, and melt over a water bath, as for tabliering.

2. Place the bowl over ice water and stir from time to time during the first few minutes. When the chocolate begins to set up on the sides and bottom of the bowl, remove the bowl from the ice water, scrape down the sides and stir constantly until the chocolate is thick and pasty, around 82°F (28°C). Test the temper as described in Step 2 of the tabliering method.

3. Place the bowl over a bain-marie and warm the chocolate to 85° to 90°F (29° to 32°C), depending on the type of chocolate.

USING PRETEMPERED CHOCOLATE (Direct Method)

Because all commercial chocolate is tempered at the factory before packaging and shipping, it can be used without undertaking any of the tempering procedures described here, provided you are able to warm dark chocolate to the correct working temperature without allowing any part of it to exceed 90°F (32°C); milk or white chocolate should not exceed 85° to 87°F (29° to 30°C). To achieve this, the water in the bain-marie must not exceed 140°F (60°C). You must stir the chocolate constantly because the part closest to the heat source will always be hotter than the remainder, and you must monitor the temperature closely.

If you have a special thermostatically controlled bain-marie and no need to hurry, it is also possible to melt pretempered chocolate very slowly, provided the temperature never exceeds the guidelines. This can take up to 12 hours.

When melting pretempered chocolate in a microwave, use chocolate produced by the manufacturer in small pellets or buttons (also known as *pistoles* or *rondos*). Stir the chocolate frequently and use a low setting. It is impossible to chop chocolate into perfectly even pieces by hand, and the smaller pieces will overheat before the larger pieces are melted.

Making Chocolate Decorations Using the Instant-Set Method

This quick tempering method is a good one to pull out of your bag of tricks in an emergency, but it is also fine for producing many decorations even if you are not short on time. Because it is so fast, you can even use this technique to make the decorations à la minute. Chocolate decorations produced by this method should be used the same day. If necessary, however, the decorations may be stored under perfect conditions for up to 2 days.

You will need a marble slab approximately 12 inches (30 cm) square. If you keep the marble stored in the freezer you will be ready to make decorations at any time. If not, chill the marble slab in the freezer for at least 1 hour before you begin. You will also need a metal trowel or putty knife, depending on what you plan to make, a metal spatula, and a knife.

This technique can be used only with untempered chocolate (see Step 1). Both coating chocolate and tempered chocolate will set up too quickly. Milk chocolate and white chocolate will work, but dark chocolate, which is thinner when melted, is easiest. After the chocolate is spread over the frozen marble, it can be lifted off easily and quickly shaped in your hands as desired.

1. Melt the chocolate, heating it to approximately 120°F (49°C); heating to this temperature will take it out of temper.

2. Pour the melted chocolate on top of the frozen marble slab and quickly spread it as thinly as possible before it sets up. Cut the chocolate sheet into the appropriate size and shape for the decorations you are making. For example, to make chocolate fans, cut the sheet into strips measuring approximately 3 × 7 inches (7.5 × 17.5 cm). Wearing food handling gloves, use the trowel to quickly lift the chocolate off the marble, then form it in your hands into a pleated fan (see Procedure 10-1a). Continue until you have used as much of the chocolate sheet as possible.

PROCEDURE 10-1a Holding up the chocolate and forming a pleated fan

PROCEDURE 10-1b Piping strands of chocolate

PROCEDURE 10-1c Hanging chocolate strands from the edge of a tube

3. Remove all of the excess chocolate from the marble and save the scrap pieces. Wipe off any condensation on the marble and repeat the process.

This method may also be used for piped decorations. One attractive design can be made by piping out a series of straight lines, piping back and forth, left to right, across the marble in one continuous line (see Procedure 10-1b). Cut across both ends where the lines are connected to separate them. Pick up the group of strands from both ends and quickly twist them together. Hang the group of strands from a tall plastic tube until you are ready to use them (see Procedure 10-1c). To use the decoration, place it so it hangs off the edge of a tall serving dish or glass. Whenever it becomes difficult to remove the chocolate from the marble, it is time to refreeze the slab. Do not forget to wear food handling gloves whenever you touch the chocolate.

Chocolate Cigarettes (Color Photos 33 and 82)

These elegant cylinders are longer and thinner than real cigarettes, but the name is classic and used all over the world. Chocolate Cigarettes take a bit of practice to master. One helpful point to remember is that the ideal room temperature for chocolate work is approximately 68°F (20°C). The more the temperature varies from this figure in either direction, the harder it will be to work with the chocolate. Getting the chocolate just the right consistency to curl is the key. If it is too soft, it will just smear and stick to the knife instead of curling. If this happens, wait a few seconds until it has set further. If that does not help (if the room and/or the surface is too warm), place a chilled sheet pan on top. If, on the other hand, the chocolate has set too hard, it will break when you try to curl it. If you are using coating chocolate, use a hair dryer to soften it. With tempered chocolate, provided you have spread the chocolate thin enough, you can warm it by rubbing your hand over the top as you work your way down the strip. If you must use a knife rather than a caulking spatula, a long slicing knife is preferable to a chef's knife because its width is uniform throughout a greater portion of its length; the blade of a chef's knife is more tapered, giving you a smaller area to work with.

CHOCOLATE CIGARETTES USING COATING CHOCOLATE

1. Pour a strip of melted coating chocolate on a marble or perfectly smooth hardwood surface (see Note). Using a palette knife, spread it as close to the edge as possible in a strip about $^{1}/_{16}$ inch (2 mm) thick, or as thin as possible without being able to see the surface through the chocolate. Make the strip a bit wider than the length you want the finished cigarettes (Figure 10-3).

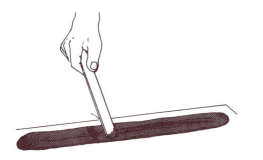

FIGURE 10-3 Spreading the thin strip of chocolate for Chocolate Cigarettes. The strip is made a bit wider than the desired length of the finished cigarettes.

FIGURE 10-4 Cutting lengthwise next to each edge to make the center section of the chocolate strip as wide as the desired length of the finished cigarettes

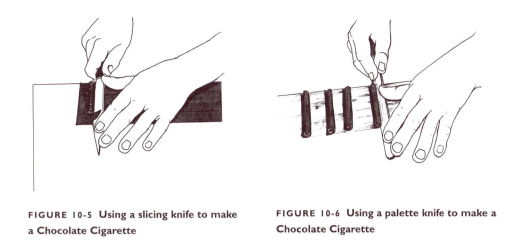

FIGURE 10-5 **Using a slicing knife to make a Chocolate Cigarette**

FIGURE 10-6 **Using a palette knife to make a Chocolate Cigarette**

2. As soon as the chocolate has set up, make a cut lengthwise next to each edge to even the sides and to make the strip as wide as the desired length of the finished cigarettes (Figure 10-4).

3. Hold a long slicing knife, palette knife, or caulking spatula at a 45-degree angle to the surface and push the knife away from you to cut off and curl about 1 inch (2.5 cm) of the strip (Figures 10-5 and 10-6).

NOTE: Working in a kitchen without temperature control during hot weather makes it just about impossible to produce chocolate cigarettes without a marble slab or table (and still not easy even with one). Conversely, when the room temperature is cold, working on marble may be too much of a good thing, and a wooden surface may be preferable. Do not use a wooden cutting board or a wooden workbench or table, or bits of wood will be scraped up into the curls. The wooden surface must be made of smooth hardwood with few or no cuts on it.

CHOCOLATE CIGARETTES USING TEMPERED CHOCOLATE

1. Cut the chocolate into small pieces. Melt over a bain-marie and temper using the cold water method (page 513). Have ready 1 or 2 clean and perfectly even sheet pans.

2. Place a sheet pan in the oven for just a few seconds so it is just slightly warmer than body temperature (you should be able to remove the pan comfortably with your bare hands, but it should not feel cool to the touch). Invert the sheet pan.

3. On the back of the sheet pan, spread the tempered chocolate in a strip approximately $^1/_{16}$ inch (2 mm) thick, or as thin as possible without being able to see the pan underneath. Let the chocolate set up. To speed the process, you can place the pan in the refrigerator, but only for the amount of time it takes for the chocolate to become firm.

4. When the chocolate has set, immediately brace the pan between your body and the back of the table so it is held steady. Push the blade of a knife or caulking spatula against the chocolate to make a cigarette of the desired shape and size. By manipulating the angle and pressure of the blade together with the length of the strip curled, it is possible to make either loose curls or tight and compact curls. Wearing food handling gloves so as not to leave fingerprints, transfer the curls to a sheet pan lined with baking paper.

NOTE: If you need chocolate cigarettes that are all precisely the same length, follow Step 2 in Chocolate Cigarettes Using Coating Chocolate, but be careful not to cut into the metal pan.

Chocolate Artistry 517

Two-Tone Chocolate Cigarettes (Color Photos 47 and 73)

Two-tone, or striped, chocolate cigarettes are formed using the same technique as the solid-color variety, but they require a few extra steps at the start. The timing of when to apply the contrasting color chocolate as well as its temperature are both important factors in achieving the desired outcome. Using coating chocolate, as directed here, is quickest and most convenient, unless you have at least one type of chocolate already tempered and/or you have a tempering machine. Read through the more detailed instructions for chocolate cigarettes on pages 516 to 517 if you are not familiar with making them.

White or light coating chocolate, melted   **Dark coating chocolate, melted**

1. Have ready a trowel with square notches measuring ¹⁄₁₆ inch (2 mm) each, a bench scraper or caulking spatula, and a hair dryer.

2. Pour a strip of white or light coating chocolate on a marble table or slab. Use a palette knife to spread it to 1 inch (2.5 cm) from the table edge, making the strip a bit wider than the desired length of the finished cigarettes and approximately ¹⁄₁₆ inch (2 mm) thick. Drag the trowel along the length of the strip, moving in a straight line and pressing hard to ensure the lines made by the notches are completely free of chocolate (see Procedure 10-2a, page 534, as an example). Use a plastic scraper to remove smeared chocolate on both long sides and to adjust the width of the strip. Let the chocolate set until firm.

3. Pour a layer of warm — not hot — dark coating chocolate on top of the chocolate lines and quickly spread it into a thin layer that just covers the stripes. As soon as the top layer of chocolate begins to set, cut both long sides of the strip to make them even and to make the strip as wide as the desired length of the cigarettes.

CHEF'S TIP
Although light (milk-chocolate-colored) coating chocolate can be purchased, I simply combine dark and white coating chocolates to create the desired shade.

4. Push the blade of a bench scraper or caulking spatula along the strip at the angle appropriate for the desired thickness of the finished cigarettes; a 10-degree angle is the norm. As the chocolate becomes firm and breaks instead of curls, use the hair dryer to warm and soften it.

5. Store the cigarettes covered in a cool, dry location.

Chocolate Corkscrews Yield: 16 decorations (Color Photo 76)

Sweet dark chocolate, tempered, or dark
coating chocolate, melted (see Note)

Transfer sheets

1. Wrap 2 dowels, ⅝ inch (1.5 cm) in diameter, with plastic wrap (spoon handles are often the correct thickness and can be used as well). The plastic must be tight and free of wrinkles. Hold the wrapped dowels inside a hot oven for a few seconds to melt the plastic slightly so it shrinks tight around the dowels. Set aside.

2. Cut 16 strips, 11 inches × ½ inch (27.5 × 1.2 cm), from a transfer sheet. Color Photo 76 shows these decorations made using a transfer sheet with a gold fleck pattern, but you may use any pattern you like.

3. Place a transfer strip, pattern-side up, on a sheet of baking paper, positioning it horizontally near the top of the paper. Spread a thin layer of chocolate over the strip. To cover the strip completely in an even layer, you must spread the chocolate onto the paper around the edges. Use the tip of a paring knife to pick up the strip and move it to the clean area of the paper.

4. Wait until the chocolate begins to set but is still tacky. Holding the prepared dowel in 1 hand, pick up the strip with the other and place it at a 45-degree angle to the dowel with the chocolate side of the strip next to the dowel (see Chef's Tip). Quickly turn the dowel and allow the strip to wind loosely around the dowel and form a spiral (see Figure 13-36, page 702, as an example). Do not wrap the strip too tightly, or you will not be able to remove the corkscrew. Place the dowel in the refrigerator.

CHEF'S TIP
You can vary the length and shape of the corkscrew by adjusting the angle at which the strip winds around the dowel. For example, placing the strip at close to a 90-degree angle to the dowel will produce a short, tightly wound decoration resembling a telephone cord.

5. Repeat Steps 3 and 4 to make a second corkscrew. Remove the first dowel from the refrigerator. Peel the plastic transfer sheet away from the chocolate, then carefully slide the corkscrew off the dowel. Repeat to make the remaining decorations.

NOTE: If you use coating chocolate, be sure it is not too warm, or it may melt the design on the transfer sheet.

Chocolate Cutouts: Squares, Rectangles, Circles, Hearts, and Triangles

This is a quick method for creating decorations that can be made up in advance. Use the assorted chocolate shapes to decorate the sides of a cake, or place them at an angle on top. Enhance finished chocolate cutouts with the streaking technique described on page 553, applying the same or a different color chocolate for contrast. Chocolate cutouts are smart to have on hand to use as a finishing touch; they can be placed on virtually any dessert to give it a special finesse.

1. Place a sheet of baking paper on the table and pour coating or tempered chocolate on top. Using a palette knife, spread it thin (¹⁄₁₆ inch/2 mm) and even (Figure 10-7). Make sure the table around the paper is clean so you do not have to worry about spreading the chocolate beyond the paper onto the table.

2. Immediately pick up the paper by 2 diagonal corners (Figure 10-8) and place it on a cardboard or inverted sheet pan. Allow the chocolate to set partially. Do not refrigerate.

3. Using a sharp knife (Figure 10-9) or a multiple pastry wheel (Figure 10-10), cut squares or rectangles. Avoid cutting through the paper. Use cookie cutters to cut out circles, hearts, or other shapes. If necessary, heat the cutter by dipping it in hot water; quickly shake off the water and dry the cutter on a towel before using. You can probably cut 4 or 5 pieces before reheating the cutter. When just a few triangles are needed, use a knife to cut them out from strips.

4. Store the chocolate cutouts, still attached to the paper, in a dark, cool place. Do not store them in the refrigerator. To use, place one hand underneath and push up gently to separate the decorations from the paper as you lift them off with your other hand (Figure 10-11). This technique is especially helpful when working with large, extra-thin, or unusual shapes.

FIGURE 10-7 **Spreading a thin coating of melted chocolate over a sheet of baking paper**

FIGURE 10-8 **Lifting the chocolate-covered paper by two diagonal corners**

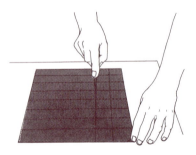

FIGURE 10-9 **Using a chef's knife to cut out chocolate squares**

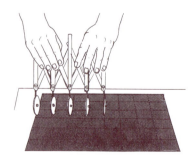

FIGURE 10-10 **Using a multiple pastry wheel to cut out chocolate squares**

FIGURE 10-11 **Pressing gently underneath the paper to facilitate removing the hardened Chocolate Cutouts**

CHOCOLATE CUTOUTS USING TRANSFER SHEETS

Follow the directions above, but instead of pouring the chocolate over a sheet of baking paper in Step 1, pour it over a transfer sheet, design-side up; spread and continue as directed.

Chocolate Fans yield: variable (back jacket)

Unless you are a chocolatier by profession, producing perfect and consistent chocolate fans, or *ruffles*, as they are also called, requires practice and patience — and, regardless of your skill level, the right weather. The latter, of course, is not a concern if you have a temperature-controlled work area (keep it around 68°F/20°C), but if not, try to make these on a cool day. Working with chocolate when the temperature is over 90°F (32°C) or in high humidity is not only time-consuming but frustrating. If you have no choice but to try to produce these decorations under adverse temperature conditions, add 2 tablespoons (30 ml) vegetable shortening (do not substitute butter or another fat) to every 1 pound (455 g) chocolate as it melts. This will make the chocolate a bit more malleable. Alternatively, you can make the fans using the instant-set method on page 515. It is also helpful to keep a few new sheet pans reserved for this use only, as once they have been used for baking, they not only become stained and scratched, they are also susceptible to warping.

Make the fans using fresh (new) chocolate that has not been previously melted. To create longer ruffles — for covering the top of a cake in four or five concentric rings, for example — use the same technique as for fans, making the half-circles much longer and wider (using a greater area on the pan) to form the size needed. Place the ruffles directly on the cake, shaping to fit as necessary. Instead of combining sweet and unsweetened chocolates, you may substitute 1 pound (455 g) bittersweet chocolate.

10 ounces (285) sweet dark chocolate	6 ounces (170 g) unsweetened chocolate

1. Cut the chocolates into small pieces and melt over hot water, stirring frequently and taking care not to overheat. Have ready 2 perfectly even, clean full-size sheet pans (16 × 24 inches/40 × 60 cm) or 4 half-sheet pans (12 × 16 inches/30 × 40 cm).

2. Place a sheet pan in the oven for a few seconds to warm it; you should be able to remove it comfortably with your bare hands. If it becomes too hot, wait until it has cooled down a bit before proceeding.

3. Invert the warm pan on the table. Immediately spread half (or one-quarter, if using the smaller pans) of the melted chocolate evenly over the back of the pan.

4. To set the chocolate, place the pan in the freezer for about 10 minutes or the refrigerator for at least 30 minutes.

5. Repeat the pan warming, chocolate spreading, and chilling sequence with the remaining pan(s) and chocolate.

6. Remove the first pan from the freezer or refrigerator and let it stand at room temperature until the consistency is just right. To determine this, try to curl some chocolate on one edge of the pan. If the chocolate is too hard, it will shatter as you try to curl it; if too soft, it will cake up on the tool. When the texture is right, brace the sheet pan between your body and the back of the table (or other suitable object) to hold it steady. Grasp the blade of an offset palette knife next to the handle with your right hand and hold the end of the blade with your left hand (switch this if you are left-handed). Position the blade at a 10-degree angle to the chocolate and move the blade in a sweeping motion, making a half-circle clockwise (from the 9 o'clock position to the 3 o'clock position) with your right hand, keeping the end of the blade almost still with your left hand (Figure 10-12). The left hand acts as a pivot as the chocolate is gathered tight at the base of the fan (see Note). Work from left to right and top to bottom on the pan.

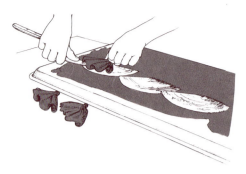

FIGURE 10-12 **Making chocolate fans**

7. After forming the first fan, check the bottom. If the chocolate has picked up metal shards from the sheet pan, you are pressing too hard, or your palette knife has a rough or nicked edge; if this happens, discard the fan. As you form each fan, transfer it to a sheet pan lined with baking paper. Adjust the angle of the ruffle as needed and/or trim the fans while they are still slightly soft and flexible. Wear food handling gloves so as not to leave fingerprints when adjusting or transferring the fans. One at a time, remove the remaining sheet(s) of chocolate from the refrigerator or freezer. Continue until you have made the desired number of fans.

8. Store the finished chocolate fans in a cool, dry location. If you are unable to do so because of the weather or if the chocolate is particularly soft, store them in the refrigerator. While this is not generally recommended for chocolate or chocolate decorations because the change in temperature will cause moisture to collect on the surface when they are removed, it is preferable to losing the fans. If the fans are placed on the dessert at the last possible moment before serving, the condensation will not have time to form.

NOTE: If you prefer, you can use a caulking spatula with a blade 3 to 4 inches (7.5 to 10 cm) wide to form the fans. Use the same technique described in Step 6 but instead move the tool counterclockwise, from the 3 o'clock position to the 9 o'clock position.

Chocolate Goblets (Color Photo 35)

Dipping inflated balloons into dark or white chocolate to produce tulip-shaped goblets is not much more difficult than creating the chocolate containers used for Cappuccino Mousse with Sambuca Cream in a Chocolate Coffee Cup (page 328). You just need a little practice in creating the rounded sides in an even height all around.

Small balloons (see Chef's Tip)
Vegetable oil

Sweet dark chocolate, tempered, or dark coating chocolate, melted

I. Blow up to the size of large oranges as many balloons as you are making goblets and tie knots at the ends (see Note). After tying the balloons, wash your hands, then use your hands to squeeze the middle section of the balloons to force air into the round end to make sure the rubber is evenly stretched. This is necessary because the balloons are not fully inflated, which leaves a small area of thick rubber at the round end. If not properly stretched, this area will absorb oil and stick to the chocolate.

2. Using the palm of your hand, rub oil on the portion of each balloon that you will be dipping to lightly coat it. Avoid using too much oil, which will prevent the chocolate adhering in a thin, even edge at the top and can also ruin the remaining chocolate supply should too much oil become incorporated into the bowl of chocolate. Set the balloons aside.

3. Warm or melt the chocolate to the appropriate temperature for the variety you are using. Based on the amount of chocolate, select a bowl that permits ample room to move the balloon around inside it, with the melted chocolate deep enough to allow you to execute the design.

4. Push the round end of a balloon into the chocolate, then tilt it slightly from side to side to create a roundish leaf shape on 2 opposite sides. Repeat, this time tilting the balloon front to back, so the the base of the balloon is coated with chocolate and 4 even, round edges form at the top of the chocolate coating in a scallop pattern (see Color Photo 35). Let the excess chocolate drip into the bowl. Scrape the bottom of the balloon against the edge of the bowl to remove more chocolate, blot the bottom of the balloon on a piece of baking paper, then set it on a sheet pan lined with baking paper (see Figures 7-1 to 7-3, page 330, as an example). The top edge of the chocolate coating will not be straight and level, as in the illustrations.

5. After dipping as many balloons as desired, place the goblets in the refrigerator for 2 minutes to harden the chocolate.

6. Puncture the balloons with a small wooden skewer at the very top where they are tied closed and set them aside to allow the air to release slowly. If punctured where the rubber is tightly stretched, the balloons will pop and the chocolate could shatter. You can speed the process by moving the skewer within the hole to widen the opening while carefully holding the balloon with your other hand.

7. Wearing food handling gloves to prevent fingerprints on the chocolate, pull the deflated balloons away from the chocolate goblets. As mentioned above, the balloons have a tendency to stick at the bottom. Occasionally, you have no choice but to pull the balloon out with a bit of chocolate attached, creating a hole. If the hole is small and does not show on the sides, it can be repaired; place the goblet on the sheet pan and plug the hole by piping chocolate inside using a piping bag.

8. Store the goblets, covered, in a cool, dry location.

NOTE: You can purchase a convenient and inexpensive hand pump made specifically for this purpose. Not only is it faster and easier, it is also preferable from a sanitation standpoint, as the balloons do not come in contact with your mouth.

Marbled or Multicolored Goblets

Although the principles for making marbled or multicolored goblets are the same as for dark chocolate goblets, these take a little more experience and a lot more chocolate. Marbled and multicolored goblets can be made with either dark or white chocolate as the base, although multicolored goblets usually look best when the base is made of white chocolate or white coating chocolate. Because you will probably have more use for the leftover chocolate if you start with a dark base, however, this may be a more practical alternative. The following instructions can be used to make dark chocolate goblets with a white or milk chocolate design or white chocolate goblets with a dark or milk chocolate design. See also Striped Chocolate Cups, page 536.

Sweet dark chocolate, tempered, or dark coating chocolate, melted

White chocolate, tempered, or white coating chocolate, melted

Milk chocolate, tempered, or light coating chocolate, melted (see Chef's Tip, page 518)

Fat-soluble food coloring

1. Blow up the balloons and coat with oil as directed for Chocolate Goblets, page 522.

2. If needed, warm or melt the chocolates to the appropriate temperature. Pour a 2-inch (5-cm) layer of the base chocolate — dark or white — in a shallow, wide pan, such as a hotel pan.

3. Place some of the contrasting-color chocolate for the design — dark, white, or milk — in a piping bag and cut a small opening. Pipe or streak this chocolate over the base chocolate in the pan, creating the desired design. The design you make on the surface of the base chocolate will appear on both sides of the goblets.

4. Place a balloon on top of the chocolate in a position that allows you to tilt the balloon in all 4 directions to complete the goblet without using more of the piped chocolate design than necessary. Do not push the balloon into the chocolate, as is done when making the solid-color goblets, and avoid dragging it. Instead, gently rock it back and forth clockwise, creating 5 or 6 roundish leaves of equal height, skimming the surface only to pick up the piped chocolate lines. If you dip the balloon too deep and pick up the base chocolate underneath the lines, the design will be visible only on the inside of the goblet. Let the excess chocolate drip into the pan, blot the bottom against a sheet of baking paper, and set the balloon on a sheet pan lined with baking paper. Repeat with additional balloons until all the lines on the surface have been picked up.

5. Skim the surface of the base chocolate to one side in the pan or remove it to another container. Pipe more contrasting chocolate lines on the cleaned base chocolate surface; continue until you have made the desired number of goblets or until the chocolate in the pan becomes too marbled to use. If you use dark chocolate as the base, the leftover marbled chocolate can be used to replace part of the chocolate called for in recipes such as brownies, decadence cake, or other chocolate-rich baked goods.

TO MAKE MULTICOLORED GOBLETS

Proceed as above, using white or dark chocolate as the base layer in the pan and coloring white chocolate with fat-soluble coloring to create the desired shade or shades for piping the design on top.

Chocolate Lace Decorations (back jacket)

These elegant, lacy chocolate tubes appear to be complex and difficult to produce but actually the opposite is true. The procedure is simple and they can be prepared far in advance, in which case the decorations should be stored still rolled up in their plastic sheets until needed. The PVC or polyurethane sheets used must be thin — just slightly thicker than baking paper — or the decorations will break when you unroll the plastic. The thin plastic needed here is also sold in rolls from which you can cut the size piece required, but the precut sheets are preferable. You can make the decorations in any length or width you choose, but there must always be a minimum of 8 inches (20 cm) of uncovered plastic above the piped chocolate lines to roll around the portion of plastic covered with chocolate.

> **Sweet dark chocolate, tempered, or Piping**
> **Chocolate (page 543), melted**

1. Cut sheets of plastic (as described in the introduction) to 15 × 11 inches (37.5 × 27.5 cm); each sheet of this size will produce 2 decorations 5½ inches (13.7 cm) long. Place a larger piece of baking paper on your work surface and set a plastic sheet on top with the long edges on the left and right sides and the bottom edge of the plastic approximately 4 inches (10 cm) from the bottom edge of the baking paper. Place a second sheet of baking paper on top of the plastic so that it covers all but a strip 2½ inches (6.2 cm) wide along the bottom edge of the plastic.

2. Place a portion of chocolate in a piping bag and cut a small opening. Quickly pipe a zigzag pattern of chocolate lines back and forth at a 45-degree angle the length of the exposed plastic strip, moving left to right, then repeat right to left at the opposite 45-degree, angle making sure that the ends of the lines extend onto the baking paper (see Figure 7-11, page 358, as an example). Carefully remove the protective baking paper.

3. Pipe a solid line of chocolate along the top edge of the piped chocolate lines; this will hold the lace together when the lines are rolled into a tube.

4. Wait until the chocolate just begins to crystallize, then roll up the sheet of plastic from the bottom, making sure that the bottom edge of the plastic aligns precisely with the solid line of piped chocolate, and continue rolling all the way to the top. The extra plastic wrapped around the chocolate-covered portion several times ensures that the tube will be perfectly round and that the plastic will not unroll; secure the plastic with masking tape if needed.

5. Repeat to make as many decorations as desired. Store the rolled-up tubes in a cool location (not the refrigerator) until needed.

6. To unmold, place a tube in the refrigerator for a few minutes. Carefully unroll the plastic, leaving the lace tube on the work surface. Use a hot knife to cut the tube in half to make 2 decorations. To move the decorations, insert a spoon handle and use this to lift the tube. Avoid touching the chocolate with your hands, but if you must, wear food handling gloves.

Chocolate Lace Igloos

yield: 16 to 20 decorations, 3¼ inches (8.1 cm) in diameter at the base (Color Photo 83)

20 small ballons	Sweet dark chocolate, tempered, or dark coating chocolate, melted

1. Blow up the balloons so that the widest part is approximately 3¼ inches (8.1 cm) in diameter (see Note, page 523).

2. Secure a small weight to the end of 3 or 4 balloons so they can stand on their own (see Note). Place a weighted balloon on a sheet of baking paper. Place melted chocolate in a piping bag and cut a small opening. Streak lines of chocolate over the balloon across the top and about halfway down the sides, first in one direction and then at a 90-degree angle. Pick up the balloon and turn it sideways to pipe a base around its circumference at the bottom of the lines; this should be in the center of the balloon. Set aside to harden. Continue with the remaining weighted balloons.

3. To separate the chocolate igloos from the balloons, place them in the refrigerator for a few minutes to chill. Wearing food handling gloves, rest an igloo in the palm of one hand, remove the weight, then carefully and slowly insert the point of a wooden skewer next to the knot in the balloon to let the air escape very slowly. If the air escapes too fast, the igloo will shatter. Remove the deflated balloon, leaving the igloo, upside down, in your palm. Trim the base of the igloo as needed to allow it to stand straight. This may be done with scissors or a hot knife. Carefully turn the igloo right-side up and set aside. Repeat, reusing the weights, to make a minimum of 16 igloos.

NOTE: To weight the balloons, I use bolts that are 1 inch (2.5 cm) long and ½ inch (1.2 cm) in diameter and have 2 nuts on each bolt, and I tighten the end of the balloon between the nuts (it is not necessary with this method to tie a knot in the balloon). This should make the balloon stand straight enough to pipe on it, but if you have trouble, place the balloon on top of a 1-cup (240-ml) measuring cup or, better yet, on top of an empty portion-size yogurt container, with the weight hanging inside.

CHEF'S TIP

Igloos that are just a little too wide for use in the presentation of Cocoa-Nib White Chocolate Ice Cream with a Chocolate Lace Igloo and Tuile Polar Bear (page 396) can be corrected in the following way: Using a 3½-inch (8.7-cm) cookie cutter as a guide, draw circles on a sheet of baking paper. Invert the paper and pipe a border of dark chocolate, ⅛ inch (3 mm) wide, inside (not on top of) a drawn circle. Immediately pick up an igloo by inserting the tip of a small knife through the top (do not use your hands); place the igloo on top of the chocolate border. Allow the chocolate to harden before removing from the paper.

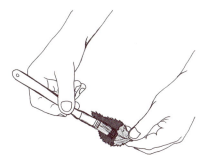

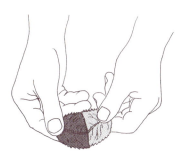

FIGURE 10-13 **Brushing melted chocolate over the back of a real leaf to create a chocolate leaf**

FIGURE 10-14 **Peeling the real leaf away from the chocolate leaf after the chocolate leaf has hardened**

Chocolate Leaves

METHOD I

1. Spread tempered chocolate or melted coating chocolate over a sheet of baking paper, as described in the directions for Chocolate Cutouts (page 520).

2. When the chocolate has set partially, use the tip of a small knife to cut out leaves of the appropriate size and shape (short and wide for rose leaves, long and narrow for pear leaves).

3. Carefully, without cutting all the way through, score the top to show the veins of the leaf. Let set, store, and remove as directed in Chocolate Cutouts, page 520.

METHOD II

1. A more eye-catching but also more time-consuming way to make chocolate leaves is to paint a thin layer of tempered chocolate or melted coating chocolate on the back of a real leaf, typically a rose leaf (Figure 10-13). Naturally, you want to make sure the leaves you use are non-toxic; roses and citrus trees are safe, and small citrus leaves produce a good result.

2. Let the chocolate set, then carefully peel the real leaf away from the chocolate leaf (Figure 10-14). You should be able to use the same leaf 3 or 4 times before the chocolate begins to stick.

3. Any type of leaf can be produced in this manner as long as the leaf itself is thin enough to be bent and peeled from the chocolate leaf without the chocolate breaking.

Chocolate May Beetles yield: 16 decorations (Color Photo 65)

Animals and insects have long been a source of inspiration and a favorite form of creative expression for bakers and pastry chefs, especially in Europe. Chocolate and sugar are used to make elegant decorations as varied as butterflies, ladybugs, and cute, shy porcupines. These are reproduced in cakes, breads, and pastries — and what could be more appropriate on a small child's birthday cake than an edible teddy bear? Holiday seasons are marked by rabbits and chickens at Easter, cats at Halloween, and at Christmastime, the domestic pig is everywhere in Sweden — in some European countries, it is as popular as reindeer.

Spring, which is always welcome after the harsh winters in central and northern Europe, brings the friendly little May beetle, which is celebrated seasonally in the pastry shops. There they are produced in large quantities as a candy, or as a decoration for cakes and pastries. For large-scale production, the beetle legs are available ready made, which makes it practical to produce and sell the candies competitively.

5 ounces (140 g) Dark Modeling Chocolate (page 541; see Note)

16 whole almonds, skin on

Piping Chocolate (page 543), melted

I. Work the modeling chocolate smooth with your hands, then roll it against the table to make a rope 16 inches (40 cm) long.

2. Cut the rope into 16 equal pieces. Leaving the pieces lined up, make a cut through each one to divide it into 2 pieces, one ¼ inch (6 mm) long and one ¾ inch (2 cm) long.

3. One at a time, roll each of the larger pieces into a round ball and then into a pointed teardrop shape, as shown in Figure 10-15. The teardrops must be the same length as in the drawing to ensure the assembled bodies will fit on top of the legs. Set the pieces on a cardboard cake sheet lined with baking paper. Using a paring knife, carefully and without deforming the shape press the wide end of each body vertically to create a flattened spot where you will attach the head later.

4. Roll each of the small pieces of chocolate into a round ball; these will be the heads of the beetles. Place the pieces in front of the pointed bodies, but do not attach them yet. Set aside in the refrigerator.

5. Stand the almonds on their narrow sides and use a serrated knife with a back and forth motion to separate each nut into 2 halves for the wings. Line them up, cut-side down, on a cardboard cake sheet, keeping the halves from each nut together. Refrigerate the almond halves.

6. Attach the heads to the bodies by dipping the flat spot on each head (the bottom of the ball where it was sitting on the paper) into piping chocolate and quickly pressing it against the flat spot on the body. Set the beetles aside.

7. Place a small amount of piping chocolate in a piping bag and cut a larger-than-normal opening. Using the template (Figure 10-16) as a guide, pipe out about 20 sets of beetle legs on

CHEF'S TIP

Unless you are making a large number of beetles, it is not worth the time it takes to copy multiple rows of the template onto baking paper. To produce one recipe's worth of legs, use a heavy black pen to trace the template from the book onto a small piece of baking paper. Place the copy under a sheet of baking paper, setting it at the edge. Pipe 1 set of legs, slide the drawing underneath to one side, and pipe the next, continuing around the perimeter of the paper.

You can produce a more realistic beetle by placing the legs on top of a thick dowel or other cylindrical object about 2 inches (5 cm) in diameter, such as a piece of PVC pipe. This method causes the legs to set up in a walking position rather than flat on the paper. Cut rectangles that measure 2 × 2½ inches (5 × 6.2 cm) from baking paper, cutting a few more sheets than you need in case of breakage. Center a paper rectangle over the template and pipe out the legs. Drape the paper lengthwise over the dowel or pipe. Attach the bodies as soon as the legs begin to set up, or remove and store the legs, attached to the papers, to assemble later. When you are ready to assemble the beetles, return the legs to the dowel, pipe a little chocolate on top, and attach the bodies. This is obviously more complicated than the squashed version, but the effect of the walking bug is adorable.

FIGURE 10-15 The shapes for the beetle heads and bodies

FIGURE 10-16 The template used as a guide to pipe out the beetle legs

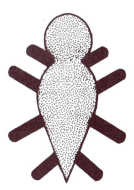

FIGURE 10-17 The chocolate beetle head and body positioned over the legs

a sheet of paper (see Chef's Tip). You need only 16, but breakage is likely. Before the chocolate sets up, position the beetles on top of the legs (Figure 10-17). For the best result, do not do this immediately, as the weight of the bodies will displace the chocolate piping. If you wait too long, however, and the legs have set up completely, pipe a thin line of chocolate down the center to make the body adhere.

8. To finish the beetles, pipe a tiny dot of piping chocolate on both sides of each body in back of the head, then attach an almond half to each side, placing the almonds flat-side down with the wider part of the almond next to the head of the beetle. The cold almonds will set the chocolate quickly, but you will need to hold them in position for a few seconds (or spray them with chocolate coolant, if you have it, in which case you do not need to chill the almonds). Depending on the temperature of your kitchen, you may need to keep the beetles in the refrigerator during service. The legs have a tendency to break if the chocolate becomes soft. For longer storage, keep them as you would anything made from chocolate — in a cool, dry place. To remove the beetles from the baking paper, carefully slide a thin knife underneath.

NOTE: If you do not have modeling chocolate on hand and do not have time for it to set up overnight, substitute marzipan that has been colored and flavored with cocoa powder.

Chocolate Noodles yield: variable (Color Photo 61)

Chocolate noodles are an eye-catching garnish — they look very much like curled dried fettuccini. The noodles can be used individually — a single noodle can be placed on top of a cake slice — or formed into a little pile on the base of a plate next to a serving of dessert (see Color Photo 61). Mixing dark, light, and white chocolate noodles produces a particularly good effect. Broken Chocolate Twirls (page 533) can be used just like chocolate noodles.

> Sweet dark, milk, or white chocolate,
>   tempered, or dark, light, or white coating
>   chocolate, melted

1. Have ready at least 4 clear plastic or PVC tubes, 6 inches (15 cm) long and 2¼ inches (5.6 cm) across the inside diameter. If you are making quite a few noodles it is helpful to have more tubes. Cut a strip of acetate or polyurethane 8 × 3 inches (20 × 7.5 cm) for each decoration you are making. Place a strip of acetate or polyurethane horizontally on top of a sheet of baking paper. Spread a thin layer of tempered dark, light, or white chocolate on top.

2. Use the tip of a paring knife to pick up the strip and place it in front of you, keeping it in the same position. Place a metal bar used for candy making, or a small ruler, next to 1 long edge and on top of about ⅛ inch (3 mm) of the chocolate-covered plastic strip. Cover only the smallest portion of chocolate required to be able to use the metal bar or ruler as a guide and to hold the plastic steady. Quickly, before the chocolate sets up, drag a trowel with ⅛- or ¼-inch (3- or 6-mm) square notches that are ¹⁄₁₆ inch (2 mm) deep along the strip to remove half of the chocolate in a ribbonlike pattern (see Procedure 10-2a, page 534, as an example). To avoid moving the plastic, be sure to press down firmly as you drag the trowel.

3. With the chocolate on the inside, push the plastic diagonally into 1 of the plastic tubes, forming a loose spiral; the plastic edges must not overlap. Repeat until you have made as many chocolate noodles as desired.

4. Refrigerate for a few minutes to set the chocolate.

5. Hold a tube close over a small bowl or a sheet pan. Carefully remove the plastic strip and unroll it. The noodles will fall off the plastic into the container. Some noodles might break, but they are still usable for most applications. Store, covered, in a cool, dry location.

Chocolate Ribbons (Color Photo 61)

Chocolate ribbons are formed by the same technique as ribbon sponge sheets, using dark and white chocolate instead of tuile paste and sponge cake. When the chocolate pattern is formed on narrow plastic strips as directed, the ribbons can be used to produce containers of any shape, as described in "Molded Chocolate Strips" on page 540. The striped chocolate strips may also be used to wrap the outside of a cake or pastry. Whole sheets of ribbon chocolate may also be created using this method, starting with polyurethane or acetate sheets approximately the size of a full sheet pan; these may need to be secured in the corners with straight pins. Use a warm knife to cut out pieces for constructed forms like Chocolate Chalets (page 470) and the boxes in Trio of Chocolates with Marzipan Parfait (page 187), or for Chocolate Cutout Decorations (page 521).

Sweet dark chocolate, tempered, or dark coating chocolate, melted	White chocolate, tempered or white coating chocolate, melted

1. Cut the number of polyurethane or acetate strips you need into the desired length and width for the containers you are creating. Place 1 strip at a time in front of you, horizontally, in the top left corner (if you are right-handed) on top of a sheet of baking paper. Spread a thin layer of dark chocolate over the strip, covering it completely. You will have to spread a little chocolate onto the baking paper all around it. Use the tip of a paring knife to find the edge of the plastic strip at 2 corners. Pick up the plastic and move it to the lower area of the paper.

2. Working quickly, place a metal bar for candy making, or a small ruler, along the lower, long side of the strip. Using the metal bar as a guide to keep the lines straight, drag a trowel with $\frac{1}{16}$-inch-deep (2-mm) square notches over the chocolate (see Procedure 10-2a, page 534, as an example). Press down hard as you drag the trowel to make sure the lines are completely free of chocolate and the plastic strip does not move. Set the strip aside and repeat until you have prepared the desired number of strips. If your work area is a bit cool for chocolate work or if you are using coating chocolate (which sets more quickly than tempered chocolate), prepare only 2 strips up to this point and finish them before making more. Otherwise, the strips will start to curl, and it will be impossible to apply the white chocolate in an even layer.

3. Place 1 chocolate-coated strip at a time in front of you on a clean sheet of baking paper. Quickly spread a thin layer of white chocolate on top, filling in the empty lines left by the trowel. Be sure the white chocolate is not so warm that it melts the dark chocolate lines. Pick up the strip the same way as before and, holding the plastic by the edges at 1 short end, run your thumb and index finger along both long edges to smooth them. Before the chocolate sets up, bend the strip into the desired shape inside a mold, such as a cookie cutter, or by securing the short ends with a paper clip for a free-form design — in either case, the chocolate side faces the interior, not the mold. Once you have a sense of how fast the chocolate sets up, you can speed the production process by coating several strips with chocolate before picking 1 up to shape it. To ensure the chocolate will have a glossy surface, always place the shaped strips in the refrigerator for a few minutes before removing the plastic.

Chocolate Shavings and Small Curled Shavings

Chocolate shavings are made by holding a small knife at a 90-degree angle to a piece of chocolate and scraping away from you, letting the shavings fall onto a paper-lined sheet pan (Figure 10-18).

Use a melon ball cutter with a sharp edge in the same way to create small, elegant 180-degree curls. Move the melon ball cutter away from you in short strokes (Figure 10-19).

FIGURE 10-18 Making chocolate shavings by scraping the surface of the chocolate with a small, sharp knife

FIGURE 10-19 Using a melon ball cutter to make curled chocolate shavings

As described in the instructions for many chocolate decorations, the chocolate must have the correct consistency to produce a good result with any of the three methods. If it is too warm, chocolate will cake up on the tool; if too cold, it will break into small, unattractive specks and pieces. Using milk or light chocolate, which by nature is softer than dark chocolate, will make it much easier to create thin shavings or pretty curled shavings. Store the shavings or curls, covered, in a cool, dry place to use as needed. Do not store in the refrigerator. You can refrigerate the shavings for just a few minutes immediately before using them if necessary to keep them from melting and sticking to your hand — if you are placing them on the side of a cake, for example. In most instances, where the shavings are to be sprinkled on top of the dessert, it is best to use a spoon to avoid contact with the heat of your hands.

A third method, and one that is handy if you need to produce a fair amount of shavings, is to use the same technique as for chocolate cigarettes. Have a hair dryer ready to warm the chocolate, if necessary. Spread a thin layer of tempered chocolate or melted coating chocolate over a marble slab. Wait until the chocolate just starts to set up, then make parallel cuts over the sheet, first in one direction and then again at a 90-degree angle to the first set to create small squares. Use the tip of a knife and work quickly. The size of the squares will determine the size of the curls. Hold a putty knife at an angle, press down firmly, and push the blade down the length of the sheet to scrape away the curls. Place the blade next to where you started and repeat until you have removed all of the chocolate. Use the hair dryer to warm the chocolate if it becomes too firm to curl.

Chocolate Shingles yield: approximately 150 decorations

8 ounces (225 g) sweet dark chocolate   4 ounces (115 g) unsweetened chocolate

1. Chop both chocolates into small pieces. Melt them together and temper (using any of the methods described on pages 511 to 514).

2. Using a medium palette knife, dab thin shingles, about 1 × 1½ inches (2.5 × 3.7 cm), onto a sheet of baking paper, starting at the top of the paper and making straight rows from left to right as you work toward the bottom. If you space them evenly, making 8 rows of 18 each (144 in all), you can fit all of the shingles on 1 sheet of paper. You will need approximately 130 for the Dark Chocolate Shingle Cakes (page 32), but this amount allows for breakage.

3. Place the baking paper, with the shingles attached, on a sheet pan and refrigerate for a few minutes to allow the chocolate to harden.

4. To remove the decorations from the paper, push from the bottom of the paper with 1 hand as you lift them off with the other (see Figure 10-11, page 520). Wear food handling gloves so you do not mar the chocolate.

NOTE: A total of 12 ounces (340 g) semisweet or bittersweet chocolate may be substituted for the sweet and unsweetened chocolate.

Chocolate Twirls (Color Photo 49)

Your guests will be amazed when they see these elaborate decorations delicately balanced on top of their desserts. Chocolate twirls are specified in the presentation instructions for the plated version of mango ice cream, but they can be used to crown many other items in this book as well. Although narrow highball glasses can be used in a pinch to create a larger twirl, if you will be making a large number of twirls, it is a good idea to buy clear plastic pipe from a plastic supply store or PVC pipe from the hardware store (the clear pipe is more expensive but easier to use because you can see the decoration inside). Ideally the inside diameter of the pipe should be 1³/₄ inches (4.5 cm), and the pipe should be cut into pieces 3 inches (7.5 cm) long. The size of the tubes specified here is one that is used elsewhere in this book, so it would be convenient to have them on hand. Although it is not practical to make smaller twirls, larger sizes can be very showy. Whenever you use a different size tube, adjust the size of the plastic strip—it must always be ¹/₈ to ¹/₄ inch (3 to 6 mm) wider than the diameter of the tube or the strip will not curl.

Sweet dark chocolate, tempered, or dark
    coating chocolate, melted

1. Cut strips of acetate or polyurethane, 2 inches (5 cm) wide and 7 inches (17.5 cm) long.

2. Make a piping bag, fill it with a small amount of chocolate, and reserve it in a warm spot where the chocolate will not set up and the bag will be at hand when you need it. (I heat a cake pan in the oven, then set the bag on the hot inverted pan next to where I am working.)

3. Position a plastic strip horizontally near the top of a sheet of baking paper. Spread a thin layer of melted dark coating chocolate or tempered dark chocolate over the plastic. To cover the plastic quickly and completely, you will have to spread chocolate onto the paper around the edges as well.

4. Use the tip of a paring knife to pick up the strip and move it to the lower (clean) area of the paper, keeping it in the same position. Place a metal bar used for candy making, or a small ruler, at the bottom long edge so it covers about ¹/₈ inch (3 mm) of the chocolate-covered plastic strip. Cover the smallest possible portion of the strip that will still allow you to use the metal bar or ruler as a guide and to hold the plastic steady.

5. Quickly, before the chocolate sets up, use the metal bar or ruler as a guide and drag a small trowel with notches that are ¹/₈ inch or ¹/₄ inch (3 or 6 mm) wide and ¹/₁₆ inch (2 mm) deep along the strip to remove half of the chocolate in a ribbon pattern (see Procedure 10-2a). To avoid moving the plastic, press down firmly as you drag the trowel. Remove the metal bar or ruler.

6. Cut a small opening in the prepared piping bag and pipe a line of chocolate across each short end so the strips of chocolate will be attached when the plastic is removed.

7. Still working quickly before the chocolate sets up, lift up the plastic strip and curl it diagonally, with the chocolate on the inside of the plastic, by pushing the strip into a plastic tube or PVC pipe at an angle (see Procedure 10-2b). The strip will protrude slightly on both ends; the plastic must not overlap at any point, or the curls will be impossible to remove without breaking. If the plastic starts to overlap as you push the strip into the tube (in other words, if the front end does not slide into the tube at the same rate as you push the opposite end), help the front end along with the tip of a paring knife. Repeat the procedure until you have made as many

PROCEDURE 10-2a Using a trowel to form lines of chocolate on an acetate strip

PROCEDURE 10-2b Inserting the acetate strip into one end of a plastic tube while covering the opposite end of the tube with the other hand, forcing the plastic to curl within the tube

PROCEDURE 10-2c Lifting a chocolate twirl by inserting a spoon handle inside and peeling away the acetate strip with the other hand

PROCEDURE 10-2d The finished twirls

twirls as needed or until you run out of tubes. Place the tubes in the refrigerator for 1 or 2 minutes. Carefully remove the plastic strips from the tubes. The plastic will shrink in the refrigerator, and the plastic will fall right out of the tubes if you are not careful. Insert the handle of a wooden spoon or a small wooden dowel in the twirl. Lift it off the table and peel the plastic away from the chocolate (see Procedure 10-2c); do not touch the decorations with your hands. Store the finished chocolate twirls in a cool, dry place.

Honeycomb Chocolate Decor (Color Photos 46 and 97)

This fast and easy yet impressive decoration is made using the bubble wrap material designed for packaging. The wrapping can be purchased from a office supply store or your local post office. You should not reuse old wrapping material left from a purchase unless the decoration is for display only and will not be eaten. Bubble wrap is generally available in three sizes that relate to the thickness of the sheets and the size of the bubbles. The wrap with $3/16$-inch (5-mm) bubbles produces the best result.

You can use the finished sheets in two ways: Leave the thin coating of chocolate on the back of the sheet, or punch or melt through some or all of the indentations to create holes.

Sweet dark, milk, or white chocolate,
    tempered, or dark, light, or white coating
    chocolate, melted

I. Have as many pieces of bubble wrap ready as required; sheets measuring 12 inches (30 cm) square are a convenient size to work with. Place the wrap, flat-side down, on a Silpat or a sheet of baking paper. Pour chocolate over the top and spread it out so just a thin layer covers the bubbles; unless you have a design in mind that makes it essential, it is not necessary to cover the entire sheet. Transfer the bubble wrap to a sheet pan and set aside to allow the chocolate to harden. Repeat to make as many sheets as desired. The sheets can be stored at this point in a cool, dry location for 1 or 2 days.

2. To unmold, place the sheet(s) in the refrigerator for a few minutes. Invert a sheet of chocolate and carefully, wearing food handling gloves, pull the plastic away from the chocolate. To melt through the holes, warm the pointed end of a small knife-sharpening steel, or any other tool that will fit the holes, and melt through the thin chocolate backing of as many bubbles as desired. You may also use a small wooden dowel to punch through the holes without melting.

Striped Chocolate Cornets (Color Photo 88)

The procedure for making these decorations combines the techniques used for Two-Tone Chocolate Cigarettes (page 518) and Chocolate Fans (page 521). Just like chocolate cigarette and fan making, mastering cornet making takes practice and a favorable environment. As with many decorations made from chocolate, not only your skill level determines the outcome; you are also at the mercy of the climate and temperature of your kitchen.

The cornets can be made in dark or white chocolate alone as well as the two-tone striped pattern.

I. Have ready a hair dryer and a caulking spatula or putty knife with a blade 3 to 4 inches (7.5 to 10 cm) wide. Follow the instructions for making Two-Tone Chocolate Cigarettes (page 518) through Step 3, making the strip approximately 4 inches (10 cm) wide. The width of the chocolate strip will determine the height of the finished cornets. The angle at which you hold the tool as you form the cornets determines the circumference of their opening.

2. In Step 4 of the cigarette recipe, instead of pushing the metal blade in a straight line as directed, move it counterclockwise in a quarter-circle, from 3 o'clock to 12 o'clock (or 11 o'clock, if you want the cornet a bit wider). Continue until you have made the desired number.

3. To make a base for the cornets, begin by moving the bottom of each cone back and forth over a lightly warmed cake pan, continuing until the base is flat and approximately ½ inch (1.2 cm) wide. Be sure to wear food handling gloves to prevent fingerprints on the decorations. Place the cornets in the refrigerator until they are cold. (If you have chocolate coolant you may skip this step.)

4. Pipe out dots of dark chocolate, 1 inch (2.5 cm) in diameter, on a Silpat or sheet of baking paper. Stand a cornet on each chocolate round before the dots set up; make sure the cornets stand straight. Store, covered, in a cool, dry location.

Striped Chocolate Cups yield: 12 to 14 cups (Color Photo 91, back jacket, and spine)

12 to 14 small balloons

1 pound (455 g) sweet dark chocolate, tempered, or dark coating chocolate, melted

6 ounces (170 g) white chocolate, tempered, or white coating chocolate, melted

1. Have ready a container with straight sides, 4 inches (10 cm) in diameter and approximately 3½ inches (8.7 cm) deep. Pint-size (480 ml) plastic storage containers work great.

2. Blow up the balloons to the size that will make the finished chocolate cups 2½ to 3 inches (6.2 cm to 7.5 cm) wide, measured across the top (see Chef's Tip and Note on page 523). Put the inflated balloons in a bucket or another large container so they do not roll about.

3. Have piping bags folded and ready to use. Keep the chocolates warm while you work by placing each over a bain-marie at 100° to 110°F (38° to 43°C).

4. Transfer approximately half of the white chocolate to a separate container. Add enough dark chocolate (1 to 2 tablespoons/5 to 10 ml) to the white chocolate in the container to make it the color of milk chocolate. Pour 1½ cups (360 ml) of the remaining dark chocolate into the reserved straight-sided container, filling it to about 1 inch (2.5 cm) from the top. Place a portion of the white and light chocolates in separate piping bags. Pipe rounds of white chocolate, slightly less than 1 inch (2.5 cm) in diameter, around the perimeter in 4 to 6 evenly spaced pools on top of the dark chocolate in the container (see Procedure 10-3a). Pipe smaller rounds of light chocolate between each white chocolate pool. Each pool should be about ¼ inch (6 mm) deep.

5. Push a prepared balloon straight down into the chocolate to a depth of 2 inches (5 cm), then pull it straight up (see Procedure 10-3b). The 3 colors of chocolate will be transferred to the balloon in a striped pattern. Blot the bottom of the balloon and set it straight up on a sheet pan lined with baking paper.

6. Using a soupspoon, skim off the majority of the remaining milk and white chocolate pools from the dipping container, but try to remove as little of the dark chocolate as possible. Save the skimmed-off chocolate for another use. Stir the remaining dark chocolate to eliminate

PROCEDURE 10-3a **Piping small pools of white chocolate on top of the dark chocolate in the container**

PROCEDURE 10-3b **After dipping a balloon into the chocolate, pulling it straight up to create the striped pattern**

any streaks and repeat the process, piping the white and milk chocolate pools and dipping the remaining balloons. Add more dark chocolate from your supply as needed.

7. Place the balloons in the refrigerator for approximately 2 minutes to harden the chocolate.

8. Puncture the balloons with a small wooden skewer at the very top where they are tied and set them aside to allow the air to release slowly. If punctured where the rubber is tightly stretched, the balloons will pop and the chocolate could shatter. You can speed the process by moving the skewer within the hole to widen the opening while carefully holding the balloon with your other hand.

9. Wearing food handling gloves to prevent fingerprints on the chocolate, pull the deflated balloons away from the chocolate cups. The balloons have a tendency to stick at the base. If you have no choice but to pull the balloon out with a bit of chocolate attached, creating a hole, the hole can be repaired, provided it is small and does not show on the sides. Place the cup back on a lined sheet pan and fill in the hole by piping chocolate inside the cup.

10. Store the cups, covered, in a cool, dry location.

Chocolate with Wood Grain

Making this unusual wood-grain design in chocolate takes time to master fully. In addition to practice and patience, you will need one or two wood-graining tools. These are small, inexpensive plastic tools that were formerly available only at hardware or art supply stores, made for texturing paint on furniture. Using them to make a pattern in chocolate has become popular enough that the tools are now specially made for our industry — generally in sizes 4 to 6 inches (10 to 15 cm) long — and are available from companies that sell pastry supplies. It is helpful to work with two tools so you can switch quickly and continue working before the chocolate sets up if one tool becomes clogged. You will also need a hair dryer, sheets or strips of acetate or polyurethane, depending on the size of the decoration you are making (the sheets must be thick enough to lie flat), a sheet pan or corrugated cardboard, and, of course, melted chocolate. Chocolate decorated with a wood-grain pattern can be used to form the Chocolate Candy Box on page 565, for other containers, and for larger Chocolate Cutouts (page 520). This technique is also suitable for use in making a chocolate strip to wrap around the side of a cake or a pastry, or for making small forms from chocolate strips (see "Molded Chocolate Strips," page 540). In addition, the wood-grain pattern can be produced on Joconde sponge sheets (see page 670).

As with any chocolate work, the room temperature should be around 68°F (20°C) for the best result. Hot or humid weather, unless your work area is temperature-controlled, makes it much harder and, after a point, impossible to achieve the desired effect.

Sweet dark chocolate, tempered, or dark coating chocolate, melted	White chocolate, tempered, or white coating chocolate, melted

1. If you are using white coating chocolate, take care not to overheat it. Not only will it become gritty, it will also melt and smudge the dark chocolate pattern when it is spread on top.

2. Check that both of your graining tools are clean. Just before starting, use the hair dryer to warm the tools slightly.

TO MAKE SHEETS

3. Place the acetate or polyurethane sheet on top of an inverted sheet pan or sheet of double-layered corrugated cardboard, positioning it so that a short side is closest to you. Secure the plastic so it will not move as you work. Spread a very thin layer of dark chocolate over the plastic sheet. Use the hair dryer, as needed, in smooth sweeping motions to prevent the chocolate from starting to set up as you cover the sheet.

4. Starting at the top left (long) side of the sheet, working in a straight line toward yourself, press the graining tool hard against the chocolate, lightly pivoting the surface of the tool up and down in smooth motions covering ½ inch (1.2 cm) of chocolate each time; at the same time, drag the tool in a straight line to the bottom of the sheet (if longer wood grains are desired, drag the tool a little farther between each rocking motion). Use the hair dryer in your other hand as needed throughout the process to keep the chocolate from starting to set. If it does, it will clog the grooves of the tool, which will then not leave an impression in the chocolate. If this happens, switch to the other tool.

5. When you finish making the first row, start again at the top to make the design in a parallel row. Continue until the whole sheet is covered by the wood-grain design (see Procedure 10-4). Warm the chocolate as necessary; however, do not direct the hair dryer toward areas of the sheet where the design has already been formed. Place the sheet in the refrigerator for a few minutes to set the chocolate.

PROCEDURE 10-4 After spreading a thin layer of chocolate over a sheet of acetate, forming the wood pattern using the graining tool

6. Spread white chocolate over the entire sheet, just thick enough to cover the dark chocolate if the sheet is to be used to decorate desserts and pastries, or to ⅛ inch (3 mm) thick if it will be used for constructing bonbon boxes or other containers. Place the sheet in the refrigerator until the chocolate is set. Avoid leaving it too long when making the thinner sheets, as they tend to curl (see Chef's Tip).

CHEF'S TIP

Unless the layer of white chocolate spread on top of the wood-grain pattern is at least ⅛ inch (3 mm) thick — the sheet is to be used to construct a bonbon box, for example — the sheet will curl as the chocolate hardens. To prevent this, place a sheet of baking paper on top of the white chocolate as soon as it is no longer sticky. Top with 1 or 2 cutting boards to keep the sheet flat as the chocolate sets.

7. Invert the hardened sheet, peel off the plastic, and use as desired. If possible, leave the chocolate attached to the plastic during storage.

TO MAKE STRIPS TO COVER THE SIDES OF A CAKE

1. Cut polyurethane or acetate strips to the exact width and length needed to cover the side the cake. Conveniently, acetate strips are available in widths from 1 to 4 inches (2.5 to 10 cm) both cut into various lengths and in a continuous roll.

2. Place 1 strip on the upper part of an inverted sheet pan or sheet of corrugated cardboard lined with baking paper. Secure the strip so it will not move as you work.

3. Spread the dark chocolate as directed for the sheet; you will have to spread the chocolate onto the baking paper around the strip in order to cover it completely. Make 1 pass lengthwise with the graining tool, keeping the distance between pivoting and dragging the tool short for the best effect and following the same instructions for warming the chocolate as needed to keep it from setting up as you work.

4. Use a paring knife to pick up the strip at 2 corners and move it to a clean area of the paper. Refrigerate briefly to set the dark chocolate; the strips will curl if left longer than a few seconds.

5. Spread white chocolate over the strip just thick enough to cover it completely. Immediately pick up the strip and wrap it around the cake; do not let the ends overlap, or you will not be able to remove the plastic without breaking part of the chocolate band. Chill briefly to set the chocolate, then peel away the plastic.

Marbleized Chocolate yield: 1 full sheet, 16 × 24 inches (40 × 60 cm) (Color Photo 108)

Marbleized chocolate can be used to make Chocolate Cutouts (page 520) and to construct containers or forms using the method described in Chocolate Chalet (page 473). You can also form the marbleized pattern on strips of polyurethane or acetate, and wrap the strips around a cake or pastry or use them to form containers, as described in Chocolate Mousse in Ribbon Teardrops (page 334) and Cupid's Treasure Chest (page 345). Because, in these applications, you use the back of the chocolate (the side against the plastic strip), reverse the order in the instructions, piping the white chocolate lines first and spacing them well apart so they do not blend together completely later. Using an offset palette knife or the even side of a plastic scraper to gently flatten and swirl the piped lines into irregular shapes, spread the dark chocolate on top. Make thinner layers of chocolate on strips that will be bent.

1 pound (455 g) sweet dark chocolate, tempered, or dark coating chocolate, melted	6 ounces (170 g) white chocolate, tempered, or white coating chocolate, melted

1. If you are using coating chocolates, be careful not to overheat them. Use low heat and stir frequently, or the chocolate will become gritty. Keep the chocolates warm (about 110°F/43°C for the coating chocolate) over their bain-maries in your workstation.

2. Invert a clean, perfectly even full-sized sheet pan and place a full sheet of baking paper on the back; the thicker reusable grade is best because it does not curl much after the chocolate hardens. If even sheet pans are scarce or unavailable, place the paper on a full sheet of corrugated cardboard. Have ready a wooden skewer, a paper pastry bag, and a hair dryer.

3. Quickly spread the dark chocolate over the paper into a rectangle measuring 15 × 23 inches (37.5 × 57.5 cm), or 11 × 15 inches (27.5 × 37.5 cm) for a half recipe; the chocolate will be approximately $^{1}/_{16}$ inch (2 mm) thick (see Note).

4. Immediately place the white chocolate in the prepared pastry bag and cut a small opening. Pipe a continuous line of white chocolate back and forth lengthwise over the entire sheet of dark chocolate, then repeat crosswise; use all of the white chocolate (Figure 10-20).

5. Still working quickly, use the tip of the wooden skewer to feather the chocolates togeth-

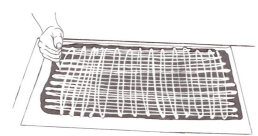

FIGURE 10-20 Piping lines of white chocolate lengthwise and crosswise over the dark chocolate for Marbleized Chocolate

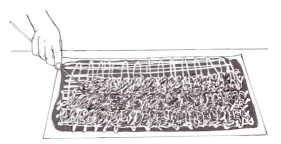

FIGURE 10-21 Using the tip of a wooden skewer to swirl the dark and white chocolate together, creating the marble design

er. Move the skewer in a circular pattern lengthwise over the sheet, left to right and then right to left, without picking it up; make 4 passes over the sheet (Figure 10-21). Do not push the skewer all the way through to the paper, which can create small holes in the finished sheet and cause the chocolate to break at those points. Let the chocolate sheet harden.

NOTE: Because, compared to tempered chocolate, coating chocolate at the proper temperature sets rather quickly, if you are using coating chocolate you may need to warm the sheet pan by placing it in the oven briefly or warm the chocolate with a hair dryer in order to have time to properly marbleize the chocolate before it sets up, especially if you are working in a cold room. If you are using tempered chocolate, this problem is unlikely to occur. Another technique is to warm the back of the sheet pan by holding it about 8 inches (20 cm) above a gas burner, moving it back and forth until it is evenly warm all over.

Molded Chocolate Strips

With this method, it is possible to make round, oval, teardrop, or heart-shaped containers to hold mousses, Bavarians, or other dessert items; see Chocolate Mousse in Ribbon Teardrops (page 334; Color Photo 61) and Cupid's Treasure Chest (page 345; Color Photo 72) for examples. In addition to use with plain chocolate, as described here, this technique can be used with Chocolate Ribbons (page 530).

Sweet dark chocolate, tempered, or dark coating chocolate, melted

1. Cut strips of polyurethane or acetate as wide as the height of the projected container and to the precise length of its circumference. Place 1 plastic strip on a sheet of baking paper and spread a thin layer of tempered chocolate or coating chocolate on top, covering the strip completely by spreading the chocolate onto the baking paper all around.

2. Before the chocolate sets, carefully pick up the strip and, with the chocolate on the inside, bend it into the desired shape. Place inside a cookie cutter or mold as needed. To make a teardrop, join the ends and secure with a paper clip.

3. Once the chocolate has hardened, peel away the plastic while wearing food handling gloves. You may need to refrigerate the item briefly first.

4. If the container needs a base, thinly spread tempered chocolate or coating chocolate on a sheet of baking paper and set the container on top. Pipe a string of chocolate around the inside bottom perimeter. Let the chocolate set partially. Cut around the outside with a thin knife and let it set completely.

   A chocolate strip can also be wrapped around the side of a cake, as described in Chocolate Truffle Cake with Raspberries (page 31).

Dark Modeling Chocolate yield: 1 pound 8 ounces (680 g)

Also known as *plastic chocolate,* this pliable and edible paste can be used to create figurines and flowers or to drape around a cake, much as you would marzipan. It should be said, however, that it is a bit more difficult to work with than marzipan, because modeling chocolate, like all chocolate, sets up rather quickly when left alone. Therefore, you must shape your design in a quick and precise manner to achieve a satisfactory result. Do not substitute coating chocolate in this recipe, as it is the large amount of cocoa butter in conjunction with the cocoa mass in chocolate that gives modeling chocolate both the pliability necessary for shaping it and stability after the shape is formed. These qualities will vary to some degree with the chocolate used and its ratio of cocoa butter to cocoa mass.

14 ounces (400 g) sweet dark chocolate

2 ounces (55 g) unsweetened chocolate

⅔ cup (160 ml) or 8 ounces (225 g) light corn syrup

1. Chop the chocolates into small pieces. Place in a bowl and melt over simmering water, stirring constantly; do not heat above approximately 110°F (43°C). Remove from the heat.

2. Heat the corn syrup to the same temperature. Pour the syrup into the melted chocolate and stir until thoroughly combined. Allow the modeling chocolate to cool completely. Cover and let stand at room temperature for at least 24 hours.

3. Work the mixture into a smooth paste by forcing it against the table with the back of a knife and/or by using the warmth of your hands. If you are working with a substantial amount, a manual pasta machine can accelerate this tedious and sometimes difficult step.

NOTE: You may have to adjust the recipe to the brand of chocolate you are working with, increasing or decreasing the amount of corn syrup accordingly.

VARIATION

MILK CHOCOLATE MODELING CHOCOLATE

yield: 1 pound 8 ounces (680 g)

Follow the recipe for Dark Modeling Chocolate, substituting milk chocolate for both the sweet dark and unsweetened chocolates in the recipe.

CHEF'S TIP

If you need only a small amount of milk chocolate modeling chocolate and have white and dark modeling chocolates on hand, simply combine them to create the desired milk chocolate shade.

White Modeling Chocolate yield: 1 pound 14 ounces (855 g)

This versatile white chocolate paste can be used for many applications. It can replace marzipan or rolled fondant for covering cakes or pastries or for making ribbons, and it can be formed, much like marzipan, into fruit, flower, or animal decorations. To make thin sheets, roll it out with a rolling pin or use a dough sheeter. Use powdered sugar to keep the chocolate paste from sticking. White modeling chocolate doesn't color well, as white chocolate is actually an ivory or pale yellow color from the cocoa butter. The chocolate paste will soften as you work with it but will firm rather quickly after it is shaped and set aside. As with all chocolate products, modeling chocolate should not be stored in the refrigerator, but it can be chilled for short periods, if necessary, with no ill effects. Ideally, make the modeling chocolate two or three days before you will need it in case it requires more time to set. With some brands of chocolate, the cocoa butter may separate from the paste, making the mixture look broken. Ignore this, set it aside as directed, then use the back of a knife to work the cocoa butter back into the mixture.

You may need to adjust the recipe to the brand of chocolate you are using. If the paste is too hard, increase the glucose or corn syrup. If too soft, increase the amount of chocolate.

1 ½ ounces (40 g) cocoa butter	5 ounces (140 g) glucose *or* light corn syrup
1 pound 5 ounces (595 g) white chocolate	½ cup (120 ml) simple syrup

1. Cut the cocoa butter and white chocolate into small pieces. Place in a bowl and set over hot water. Heat, stirring constantly, just until melted. Do not overheat.

2. Remove the bowl from the heat and stir in the glucose or corn syrup and simple syrup. Continue mixing until smooth. Cover and let the mixture rest overnight to set up.

3. To use, work the mixture into a smooth paste by forcing it against the table with the back of a knife and/or by using the warmth of your hands. A small manual pasta machine is a big help. If the chocolate is too soft to work with after resting overnight, leave it to set further (dry) until the next day. This is usually all it takes. If you must use the chocolate right away, add more melted chocolate to correct the consistency.

4. Store the chocolate paste, tightly covered, in a cool place. It will keep for several weeks, but as it becomes older it will harden and require a little extra effort to soften.

Chocolate Roses yield: about 10 medium-sized production roses

Successful chocolate roses can be created from a properly made, firm, modeling chocolate only — one that may require a few extra minutes to work into a malleable paste. Very warm working conditions make it hard, if not impossible, to make chocolate roses.

½ recipe Dark, Milk, or White Modeling
     Chocolate (preceding recipes)

1. Work the chocolate to make it soft and pliable.

2. Following the directions for Marzipan Roses (pages 651 to 653), form the chocolate.

Piping Chocolate yield: 1 cup (240 ml)

Piping chocolate can be purchased ready-made from chocolate manufacturers, but the quality of the product is not commensurate with the price, considering that you can make the same thing for about one-eighth of the cost. For practical reasons, I prefer to use coating chocolate for piping chocolate decorations that will be moved after they have hardened, as I can be certain the coating chocolate will set up firm. If you do not have or do not want to use coating chocolate, real chocolate must be perfectly tempered to be used in the same way. In cases where the decoration is not moved — when it is piped directly onto a pastry or is used for decorating a dessert plate, for example — untempered chocolate can be used, as the addition of a liquid will aid in setting the chocolate sufficiently. Piping chocolate made from real chocolate should be a bit thicker than piping chocolate made from coating chocolate.

| 12 ounces (340 g) dark coating chocolate | ¼ to ½ teaspoon (1.25 to 2.5 ml) simple syrup or liqueur |

1. Chop the chocolate into small pieces, place in a small bowl, and set over simmering water, stirring until melted. Do not overheat.

2. Using a drop bottle, gradually add the simple syrup or liqueur while stirring constantly. The amount of syrup or liqueur required will vary with the brand of chocolate. Add enough so the chocolate forms soft peaks.

3. Piping chocolate will keep as long as any dark chocolate if stored, covered, in a cool place. Melt over hot water to use.

Chocolate Cages (Color Photo 89)

Making chocolate cages is a delicate procedure and should not be attempted on a hot day without the proper facility for working with chocolate. Because the piped chocolate mesh must be open enough — that is, the lines must be spaced far enough apart — to display the item the finished cage encloses, the cages are very fragile.

| Small balloons | Piping Chocolate (above) |
| Vegetable oil | |

1. Have ready small, wide glasses, such as on-the-rocks glasses or other suitable containers, on which to rest the balloons after piping the chocolate; you will need 1 for each cage you are making. Have an equal number of binder clips or paper clips available (see Chef's Tip). Blow up as many balloons as needed to the size of grapefruit (see Note, page 523). Secure the ends either by tying a knot, then attaching a binder clip to the knot (the weight of the clip helps keep the balloon steady on top of the glass), or by twisting the end, then attaching the clip. If using the straw method (see Chef's Tip), fold the end of the straw in half, then secure with a clip.

2. Wash your hands. Using the palm of one hand, generously oil as much of each balloon

There are several methods of securing the inflated balloons, the obvious being simply tying a knot, but this means the balloons must be punctured in order to deflate them and remove the cages, and therefore they cannot be reused. This is of little consequence if you are making just a few cages but could make a difference if you need to produce a large number — not so much because of the cost of the balloons but it can be difficult to find a large quantity of balloons that work well (see Chef's Tip, page 523). If, instead, you twist the end of the balloon shut, then clamp a binder clip on top, you can deflate the balloon without puncturing it and reinflate it to use again.

Another method is to use short straws with the same diameter as the necks of the balloons. Coat the outside end of the straws with silicone caulking to form a tight seal between the straw and the balloon and insert the silicone-coated end into the neck of the balloon. Once the silicone has dried, blow up the balloons through the straws. Fold the end of the straw in half and secure it with a binder clip or paper clip. Be careful to apply silicone to the outside of the straw only; if the silicone gets inside, it will plug the hole, and you will not be able to inflate the balloon. With this method, the balloons can be reused many times; it is especially efficient for making a fair amount of cages. If your cages tend to shatter when you deflate the balloons (this is usually caused by not greasing the top of the balloon sufficiently or letting the air out too fast), use the knot method so the air leaks out naturally and slowly.

as you plan to pipe on, then set each balloon on top of a glass. If the top of any of the balloons seems dry when you are ready to pipe the chocolate, re-oil that portion.

3. Place piping chocolate in a piping bag and cut a small opening. Pick up a balloon, hold it steady with your free hand, and pipe the chocolate over the top in smooth overlapping circles (see Figure 11-13, page 619, as an example). Turn the balloon to the side and continue the same pattern down to the widest point, creating an even base all around at the same time. Carefully return the piped cage to the top of the glass. Prepare the remaining cages in the same way. Place the cages in the refrigerator for a few minutes to set the chocolate.

4. Wearing food handling gloves, remove the set cages from the balloons in one of the following ways. If you tied a knot, use the tip of a wooden skewer to make a hole as close to the knot as possible on each balloon. Return the balloons to their resting places and replace in the refrigerator. The air will slowly leak out and the balloon will fall to the bottom of the container, leaving the cage perched on top. If you used a binder clip method, remove the clips and ever so slowly untwist or unfold to release the air gradually, depositing the cage in the palm of your hand. Be patient in doing this; if the air escapes too fast, the delicate cage is likely to break.

5. Handling them carefully, place the cages on a pan and store in a cool, dry place. Refrigerate the cages for a few minutes to strengthen the chocolate before attempting to pick them up.

Chocolate Figurines

In addition to its obvious value in covering pastries, cookies, and cakes, coating chocolate is practical for piping decorative ornaments freehand, directly onto a cake or petit four or onto baking paper (freehand or with a template) for later placement on a dessert. (Tempered chocolate may also be used in these ways, but not every kitchen has someone available and/or a temperature-controlled work area.) Piping decorations on baking paper is an efficient way of making figurines when you are not too busy, because they can be made up far in advance and stored in a dark, cool place (not the refrigerator). If you want the chocolate to flow out slightly, use it as is, but if it is important to the design that the chocolate stay in precise lines, use piping chocolate.

Some figurines look especially nice with a combination of dark, milk, and white chocolate in the same design. To create these, make the frame with piping chocolate and let it harden. Fill in the design with coating or tempered chocolate in the desired shade or shades. When the chocolate has set, place these two-tone designs on the cake or pastry, flat-side up. Different shades and colors can also be obtained by blending various types of chocolate or by tinting white chocolate with fat-soluble coloring.

Because the tip and the opening of the piping bag are so small, the chocolate will set up very quickly in that spot. When you pause while piping, hold the tip between your pinched fingers to keep it warm. If you forget but only the chocolate at the very tip of the bag has set up, hold the tip against the side of a warm pot on the stove or on the oven door to melt it quickly.

I. Use a copy machine or trace onto a sheet of paper any of the small individual designs you would like to make from the examples shown in Figure 10-22, drawing as many as you need of each design. Figures 10-23 and 10-24 show border and lettering designs, which are piped directly onto a cake, pastry, or rolled sheet of marzipan.

2. Attach the paper securely to a sheet of cardboard. Place a piece of baking or waxed paper on top and attach it securely so it will not shift as you pipe the designs.

3. Make a piping bag and fill it with a small amount of melted coating chocolate, tempered chocolate, or piping chocolate. Cut a small opening in the bag. Pipe the chocolate over the design, tracing it in one unbroken line as much as possible.

4. Let the chocolate harden, then store the figures attached to the paper. To remove them, place one hand under the paper and push up gently to separate the chocolate from the paper as you lift the design off with the other hand. If the designs are fragile, slide the blade of a thin knife between the figurines and the paper instead.

CHEF'S TIP

Although it may seem that only a small amount of chocolate is involved, piping bags with chocolate left inside (partially used bags or bags with chocolate that set up before it could be used) should not be discarded. Put the used bag in the refrigerator to harden, then open it up; the chocolate will fall right out and can be put back into the bowl to melt again.

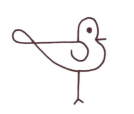

FIGURE 10-22 Piping designs

FIGURE 10-22 (continued)

Chocolate Artistry 547

FIGURE 10-22 (continued)

FIGURE 10-23 Border designs that can be piped out using piping chocolate or royal icing

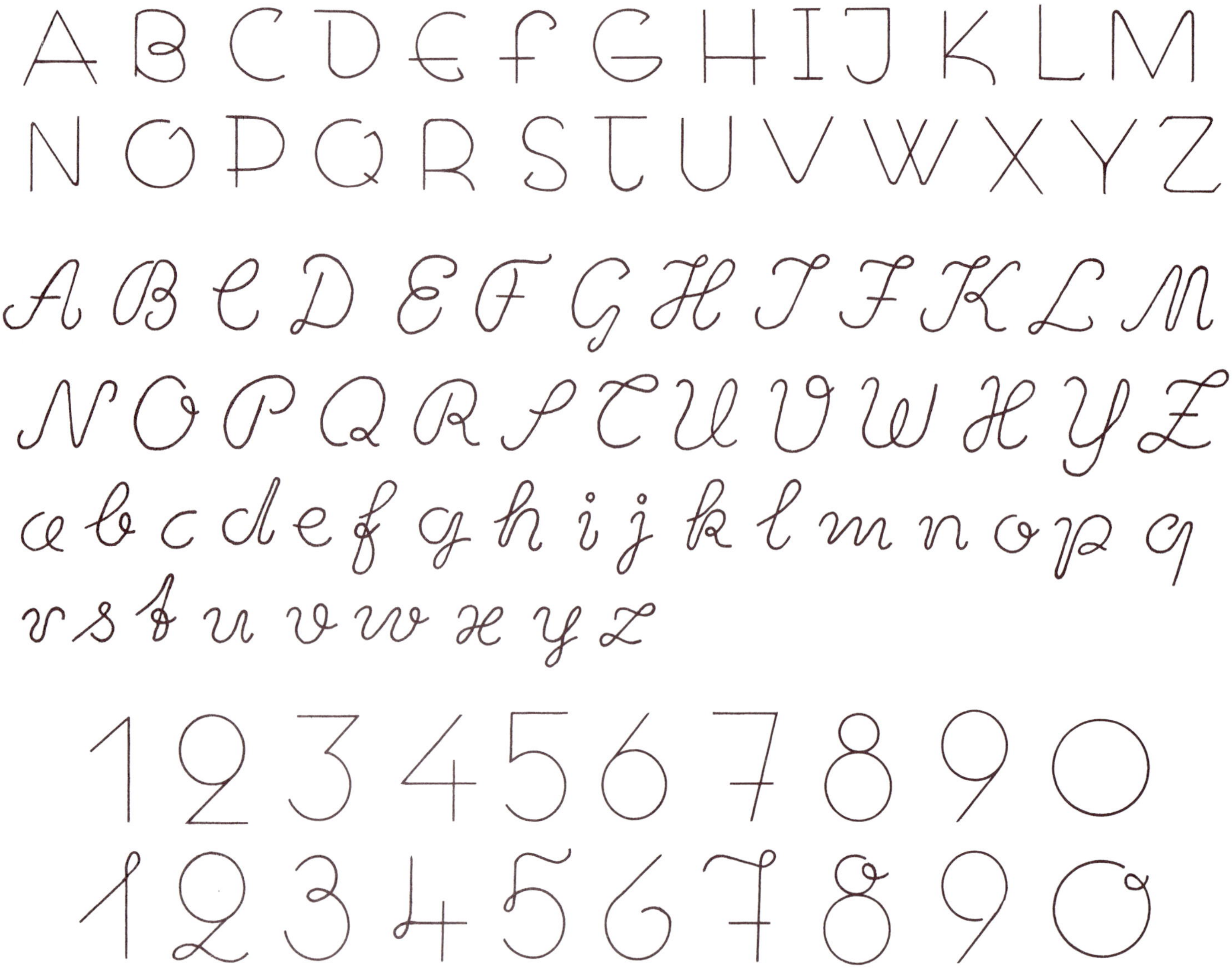

A B C D E F G H I J K L M
N O P Q R S T U V W X Y Z

A B C D E F G H I J K L M
N O P Q R S T U V W X Y Z

a b c d e f g h i j k l m n o p q
r s t u v w x y z

1 2 3 4 5 6 7 8 9 0
1 2 3 4 5 6 7 8 9 0

FIGURE 10-24 Examples of lettering and numeral designs

Chocolate Monarch Butterfly Ornaments (Color Photo 26)

The smaller and sturdier of the two butterfly designs that follow can be assembled simply by placing the wings between two metal bars or wooden dowels to hold them at the proper angle while you attach them to the bodies. To save time, you can omit the antennae without sacrificing too much appeal. The larger, more elegant butterfly design requires a *V*-shaped assembly box. If you do not have one, you can make one following the instructions for the Chalet Support Box (page 475), or you can construct a scaled-down form as follows: Score a cut lengthwise down the center of a strip of corrugated cardboard that is 6 inches (15 cm) wide and 16 inches (40 cm) long. Bend the strip into a *V* and tape across both ends to hold the *V* at the proper angle. To secure the form as you are working, place it between the rows of an inverted muffin tin. The larger butterfly design is shown in Color Photo 26.

Piping Chocolate (page 543)

Fat-soluble orange food coloring

White coating chocolate, melted, or white chocolate, tempered

Light coating chocolate, melted, or milk chocolate, tempered

SMALL BUTTERFLIES

1. Trace the wings only of the butterfly template in Figure 10-22, page 547, onto a sheet of paper (you will pipe the antenna and body freehand). Attach the template to a sheet of cardboard.

2. Cut baking paper into squares slightly larger than the butterfly, cutting 1 square of paper for each butterfly you plan to make. Place a square on top of the template and secure it with paper clips or a small piece of tape.

3. Place a small amount of piping chocolate in a piping bag. Cut a small opening and pipe out the chocolate following the outline and patterns of the wings; do not connect the wings to each other. Remove the square of paper with the wings and set it aside on a sheet pan. Secure another square of paper over the template, pipe the next set of wings, set it aside, and continue until you have piped all of the wings.

4. Use the fat-soluble coloring to tint a portion of the white chocolate orange. After the chocolate wings are set, fill in the interior sections with white, light, and orange coating chocolate or tempered chocolate. Let the chocolate set and reserve the wings.

5. Using dark piping chocolate, pipe out 2 antennae for each butterfly on a sheet of baking paper. Start by piping a small dot about the size of the head of a pin, then attach a slightly curved line approximately 1 inch (2.5 cm) long. Set the antennae aside.

6. Place 2 metal bars (or wooden dowels secured with a piece of dough) about 1½ inches (3.7 cm) apart on a sheet pan covered with baking paper. Place piping chocolate in a piping bag and cut a large opening. Pipe an oval, ¼ inch (6 mm) long, of chocolate between the bars with a tapered body, ¾ inch (2 cm) long, behind it; try to approximate the one in the drawing.

7. Wearing food handling gloves to avoid fingerprints on the chocolate, insert 2 wings, flat-side up, into the chocolate body, leaning them against the bars to get the proper angle. Repeat until all of the wings are attached. Once you can gauge how fast the chocolate sets up, you can pipe out several bodies at once.

8. Place the antennae in the refrigerator for a few minutes. Wearing food handling gloves, dip the plain ends (not the ends with the dots) in dark chocolate and fasten to the front of each butterfly in a *V* shape (Figure 10-25). The chilled antennae will stick immediately, which is essential because holding them very long would cause them to melt between your fingers. Once the chocolate is firmly set, remove the bars and store the butterflies in a cool, dark place (not the refrigerator).

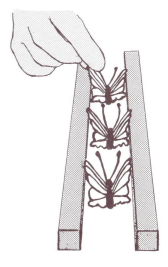

FIGURE 10-25 **Attaching the antennae to the small version of Chocolate Monarch Butterflies**

FIGURE 10-26 The template used as a guide in piping the wings for the larger version of Chocolate Monarch Butterflies. The shaded area indicates where to fill in with white and orange chocolate.

LARGE BUTTERFLIES

1. Follow the instructions for small butterflies through Step 3, tracing the butterfly design in Figure 10-26 instead.

2. Let the frames harden, then partially fill in the interior sections with white and orange coating or tempered chocolate, leaving part of each wing unfilled. Set aside to harden.

3. Line the inside of a *V*-shaped form (see introduction on page 550) with baking paper. Wearing food handling gloves, carefully remove the wings from their papers and line up as many pairs, flat-side up, in the form as will fit.

4. Place piping chocolate in a piping bag and cut a large opening. Pipe a body between each set of wings, tapering it toward the end. Let the chocolate harden, then remove the butterflies carefully. Repeat Steps 3 and 4 until all of the butterflies are assembled.

Decorating Plates with Piped Chocolate

Even if you are proficient at piping and can pipe a perfectly straight line of chocolate — or, even more challenging, a series of parallel straight lines — it is still virtually impossible to do so without leaving a tiny dot of chocolate at the beginning and end of each line. To eliminate these small imperfections, mask the portion of the plate where the lines begin and end. To pipe parallel lines over the base of a serving plate without piping on the rim, as shown in Color Photos 21 and 34,

Caramel Boxes with Caramel Macadamia Nut Mousse, place a piece of masking tape, wide enough to cover the rim of the plate, on the left and right sides of the plate (9 o'clock and 3 o'clock positions). Set the plate in the center of a Silpat or a sheet of baking paper. Pipe dark coating chocolate (piping chocolate is too thick for this application) across the plate, covering the plate and tape and extending the lines out onto the Silpat or baking paper on each side, using the same back-and-forth motion as for streaking (see below). To create a second series of lines so the pattern forms a + or × shape, apply tape at the appropriate positions and repeat. Remove the tape before the chocolate sets. Transfer the plate to a sheet pan and repeat to decorate as many plates as needed.

Streaking

A simple, elegant way to decorate petits fours, pastries, candies, and serving plates is to pipe a series of very thin lines across them. The lines can be piped in just one direction, as in Strawberry Hearts (Color Photo 18), or in opposite directions to form a crisscross pattern (Figure 10-27). To keep the lines thin, it is important to cut a very small opening in the piping bag. Fill the bag with a small amount of tempered chocolate or melted coating chocolate. Pipe the chocolate, moving the bag quickly over the item, alternating left to right and right to left. Extend the lines just beyond the edge of the item and let them fall on a paper to get the desired effect. For some designs piped onto serving plates, this may not be appropriate (see preceding instructions).

FIGURE 10-27 **Streaking chocolate over a tart by quickly moving back and forth in two directions, overlapping the edges**

Chocolate Casting (Color Photo 93)

This procedure builds on the piping technique described for making individual decorations such as Chocolate Figurines (page 545) and the butterfly ornaments on page 550 to create stunning showpieces with chocolate. The only prerequisites are a steady hand and a good eye for composing the shades of chocolate in the design.

1. Use a copy machine, draw, or trace your picture on a sheet of paper. If you are new to this technique, use an uncomplicated design with clean lines; the photo features an advanced chocolate painting requiring a bit of experience. Attach the paper to a solid base, such as an inverted even sheet pan or a sheet of corrugated cardboard. Remember the design will be reversed (mirror image) in the finished piece. If that matters — for example, with lettering — follow the directions in the Chef's Tip with Method II for Tracing onto Marzipan (page 635) to reverse the image.

2. Fasten a piece of Plexiglas or a sheet of acetate or polyurethane (a thicker grade than for lining cake rings) on top of the drawing. As a last resort, stretch a sheet of plastic wrap around it tightly and hold in a hot oven for a few seconds to shrink the plastic. The plastic must be absolutely wrinkle-free because any imperfection will show in the finished piece.

3. Using Piping Chocolate (page 543) in a piping bag with a small opening (see Chef's Tip), trace the drawing. Fill in the interior areas with different shades made by blending dark, light, and white coating chocolate, as desired (because the finished piece is not meant to be eaten, there is no reason to use real chocolate). You can color white coating chocolate with fat-soluble coloring. Think of the plastic or Plexiglas as your canvas, the chocolate as your paint, the piping bag as your brush, and yourself as the artist.

4. When you have finished your artwork, move the painting to a corner or other safe place with the proper temperature, where it can remain for at least a few hours once the background chocolate is poured.

5. Place metal bars around the edges, or use any other straight object that will keep the poured chocolate from leaking out. Corrugated cardboard, cut into strips, will work if oiled on the side that will be next to the chocolate. Seal the base of the frame all around the outside with masking tape. Apply the background by pouring coating chocolate of the desired shade over the design within the frame. Make absolutely sure the temperature of the chocolate you pour is not above 105°F (40°C), or it can partially melt and destroy your piping underneath. On the other hand, if it is too cold (and therefore too thick), it will not flow out and cover the piped lines properly, leaving an uneven and rough finish. To avoid bubbles, pour the chocolate very close to the painting. Gauge the thickness of the background in proportion to the size of the painting. For example, if the painting is 12 × 16 inches (30 × 40 cm), the background should be ½ inch (1.2 cm) thick for the proper strength. Leave your artwork to set for at least several hours.

6. In the meantime, make a base and stand. For the size painting above, pour coating chocolate into a circle about 10 inches (25 cm) in diameter and ½ inch (1.2 cm) thick. For the rear support, pour a triangular piece with 1 long side at a right angle to the short side, about 8 inches (20 cm) across the bottom, 14 inches (35 cm) tall, and the same thickness as the base.

7. Place the painting in the refrigerator for 10 minutes to ensure a glossy finish. Carefully remove the metal bars or cardboard frame from around the painting; cut them free with a thin knife if they do not separate easily. Place an inverted sheet pan or sheet of heavy cardboard on top, hold on securely with both hands, and turn the painting right-side up. Remove the other sheet pan or cardboard, as well as the plastic or Plexiglas, to reveal the painting. You may wish to add a border of piped chocolate or molded marzipan before placing it on the stand.

8. Chill the base of the stand and the rear support (see Note). Dip the bottom of the support in coating chocolate and quickly fasten it to the base. Hold it straight until it has set. Pipe chocolate down the front of the support and carefully attach the painting. Hold until set. Pipe additional chocolate at the bottom behind the painting.

N O T E : If you have aerosol chocolate coolant, it is not necessary to chill the pieces before assembly.

CHEF'S TIP
If the piping chocolate sets up too hard, the thin lines will pull away from the surface (this will also happen if the room you are working in is too cold) and can cause the background chocolate to seep under when it is poured later. You can remedy this by thinning the piping chocolate slightly with soybean oil or a commercial thinning agent.

Cocoa Painting (Color Photo 94)

Although cocoa painting is quite an advanced decorating technique, with some practice and a stencil, even a beginner can create simple designs with attractive results. Naturally, prior experience in drawing or in painting with watercolors is helpful.

The canvas for a cocoa painting is usually untinted marzipan or pastillage. I prefer the off-white color of marzipan, which blends in more subtly with the various cocoa tones, rather than the stark white of pastillage. The marzipan is rolled out in cornstarch rather than powdered sugar, which would leave small grains of sugar on the surface that would absorb the cocoa paint and leave unsightly dots on the finished piece. For the same reason, the marzipan must be rolled completely smooth. Let the marzipan dry slightly after it is rolled out.

If you do not have a natural talent for drawing freehand, the stenciling technique described in Method I or II for Tracing onto Marzipan (page 635) can help frame an outline for your design. With Method II, the stenciling should be done before the marzipan is left to dry.

Cocoa paint is made from unsweetened cocoa powder diluted with water to produce an extensive number of varying shades. To create the lightest tones, add a few drops of clear liquor, such as vodka. Use food coloring sparingly for the most tasteful result. Most cocoa painting is done exclusively in brown tones.

Using a thin artist's brush, start by framing the outer lines of the image using darker tones of cocoa. Next apply the lighter shades to the interior portion and finish with the darker interior tones. Practice blending the shades together so no clear line is visible where the lighter tone ends and the darker one starts. When completed, the painting can be used to decorate the top of a cake, or it can be framed in marzipan and used as a showpiece.

Hollow Chocolate Figures Using Molds

Chocolate figures are most often made at Christmas and Easter. In some cases the larger sizes are intended only for use as showpieces, in which case there is no reason to use anything other than coating chocolate. Even a smaller figure can be embellished to create a miniature showpiece, as illustrated in Color Photo 96. Only metal or plastic chocolate molds in perfect condition should be used to make hollow figures because the smallest scratch can cause the chocolate to stick.

1. Using soap and hot water, clean, rinse, and thoroughly dry the molds. Polish the inside of the molds with cotton balls. If using metal molds, dip the cotton balls in a little powdered chalk, then remove any trace of the chalk with a clean cotton ball. The molds as well as the work area must be around 68°F (20°C).

2. To eliminate small bubbles on the surface, coat the inside of the mold with a thin layer of tempered chocolate before filling, using a good brush .

3. Immediately clip the two halves of the mold together and fill with chocolate. If the thin layer of chocolate is left to set up completely before filling, it can separate from the rest of the mold later. Lightly tap the side of the mold with a dowel to release bubbles.

4. Wait a few minutes to be sure a thick enough layer of chocolate has formed that the mold

When making molds with two or more different chocolates (a white beard on a Santa, for example, or spots of milk chocolate on a dark-chocolate rabbit), brush or pipe on the contrasting color first and allow it to set slightly before continuing. Mix milk, white, and dark chocolates to create shades; tint white chocolate with fat-soluble coloring. Decorate finished figures if desired by spraying them with chocolate solution, as described below.

will not break when handled (large molds need thicker layers), then invert the mold over the bowl of chocolate and allow the chocolate to run back out. Tap the mold lightly with a dowel to help remove the chocolate.

5. Stand the mold upright on a sheet pan lined with baking paper. Once the chocolate starts to set, remove the clips and refrigerate for a few minutes until the chocolate has begun to shrink away from the mold (this is easy to see with a plastic mold; you will just have to take an educated guess with a metal mold). Carefully remove the mold. From this point, to avoid fingerprints, wear food handling gloves whenever you touch the figures.

6. To enclose the bottom of the figure, spread a thin layer of chocolate on a sheet of baking paper, place the hollow chocolate figure on top, twist it gently, and let it set. Use a thin sharp knife, lightly heated, to cut away excess chocolate around the figure. If a seam protrudes where the two halves of the mold were joined, remove it with the same knife.

SPRAYING WITH CHOCOLATE

Although most people associate power sprayers with house paint, they have been used in our industry for quite some time, even as far back as when I was attending culinary school in Sweden. At that time, we were shown how to use power sprayers to apply egg wash to proofed doughs such as croissants, braided bread, and other delicate items. Using a power sprayer for egg wash has three advantages: speed, production of a perfectly even coating, and no risk of deflating the item by using a heavy hand with a brush. Back then, this technique was practical only in a high-volume shop because besides being bulky, the sprayers were also expensive. Today, one can buy a small electric power sprayer for less than the cost of a set of good-quality pastry cutters; be sure your model has an adjustable nozzle and allows you to control the air pressure.

Sprayed chocolate can be utilized in many ways. You can enhance plates used for dessert presentations by spraying chocolate lightly and evenly over the whole surface (this is especially appropriate if the plates are solid white), or a portion of the plate can be highlighted by fanning the chocolate over one side. To decorate plates with chocolate using a template, attach a loop of tape to the template as a handle; place the template on the base of the plate and hold it steady by placing a small heavy object, such as a metal nut or bolt, on top. Using low air pressure, spray the solution over the plate. Remove the template by the handle and let the chocolate set. Fill in the exposed area with a sauce or leave it plain.

For the reverse effect, place a stencil on the plate and spray the chocolate over it to create a chocolate silhouette of the shape (see Procedure 10-5a and b). (See Color Photo 40 for the finished look.) This is a nice way to add a seasonal motif, such as a tree or a star, on one side of the base of a plate. Another option is to use a stencil with a design that will appear over the entire base of the plate, either protecting the rim of the plate to leave it without decoration or covering the rim with chocolate at the same time. If possible, set the spray gun on low whenever you

PROCEDURE 10-5a **Spraying chocolate over a plate using a stencil**

PROCEDURE 10-5b **Removing the stencil after having applied the chocolate spray**

are using a template or stencil to avoid disturbing the pattern as you spray. To alter the look made with any of these techniques, place the plates in the freezer for a few minutes before spraying; the chocolate will set up immediately with a velvet finish. If you do not have a power sprayer, plates can be decorated with a spray bottle using Cocoa Solution for Manual Spray Bottle (page 558) instead.

Molded chocolate figures can also be sprayed for an unusual look. Just like plates, they can be placed in the freezer beforehand to alter the finish. Chocolate designs may also be sprayed onto Chocolate Cutouts (page 520) and chocolate candies.

It may seem obvious, but it is worth stating that under no circumstance should you use the same spraying equipment for food as for paint or other nonfood items. At the minimum, have a complete set consisting of piston, housing pump, spray tip assembly, filter assembly, and, of course, the container, reserved for kitchen use only. The main portion, the gun assembly, can be used for any purpose because liquid does not pass through it. However, the ideal is to dedicate a sprayer to the pastry kitchen alone.

Spraying chocolate solution is really no different from spraying thick paint, so read the instructions from the sprayer manufacturer before starting. Before you spray, be sure to protect the immediate surrounding areas with sheets of baking paper. To learn this technique, practice with inexpensive chocolate thinned with a commercial thinning agent or vegetable shortening, as cocoa butter is expensive.

Chocolate Solution for Spraying   yield: 1 quart (960 ml)

1 pound (455 g) sweet dark chocolate   **1 pound (455 g) cocoa butter**

1. Chop the chocolate and cocoa butter into small pieces, place together in a bowl, and melt over simmering water. Continue to heat the mixture to 130°F (54°C); for the best result, hold the mixture as close to this temperature as possible while spraying.

2. Have ready your plates and the template or stencil, if you are using one. Warm the spray gun to ensure the chocolate does not set up inside. Place the warm solution in the sprayer and spray the design over the serving plates with or without a template or stencil, as desired. Let the plates dry. Unless your work area is adversely warm, this should not take more than 10 minutes. If the area is unduly hot, place the plates in the refrigerator to expedite drying, or use the velvet-finish method discussed on the previous page. The plates can be decorated many hours ahead of service and reserved in a cool, dry place.

3. Disassemble and clean the sprayer after you finish spraying, unless you plan to use it again in the near future. If the chocolate has set up, warm the gun in a very low oven with the door open to melt the chocolate so you can pour it out to use again; then wash the container and the other parts except the body containing the motor. Be careful not to overheat the gun and damage it; the cocoa butter–rich chocolate requires little heat to melt. However, if you use the spray gun more or less daily, just remove the chocolate container and store the rest of the gun intact, covered, on a sheet pan. It is necessary to clean the assembly thoroughly only every two days or so, depending on use. If the spray gun container is made of plastic, which I highly recommend, the solution can be stored there until next time, then melted in a microwave oven or over a bain-marie. Regardless of the storage container, cover the leftover solution; it will keep for up to six months.

NOTE: The neutral 50-50 proportion of this mixture produces a very fine texture. For a coarser and darker finish, use a ratio of up to 2 parts chocolate to 1 part cocoa butter. However, when using that much chocolate, temper it first.

Cocoa Solution for Manual Spray Bottle yield: approximately 3½ cups (360 ml)

This will make a medium-dark spray. Add more cocoa powder if a darker color is desired.

¼ cup (60 ml) light corn syrup

3 cups (720 ml) warm water

2 ounces (55 g) cocoa powder

1. Stir the corn syrup into the water.

2. Place the cocoa powder in a bowl. Add just enough of the water mixture to make a smooth paste. Gradually mix in the remaining liquid. Store in the refrigerator.

CHOCOLATE CANDIES

Branchli (Branches) yield: approximately 75 candies, 1¾ inches (4.5 cm) each

12 ounces (340 g) Gianduja (page 561) *or* purchased gianduja chocolate, softened

6 ounces (170 g) Hazelnut Paste (page 778)

4 ounces (115 g) powdered sugar, sifted

7 ounces (200 g) sweet dark chocolate, melted

⅓ cup (30 ml) coconut oil, melted

Nougat for Branchli (recipe follows)

Sweet dark chocolate, tempered

1. Mix together the gianduja, hazelnut paste, powdered sugar, melted sweet dark chocolate, and coconut oil. Set aside until the mixture becomes firm.

2. Using a palette knife, work one portion of the paste at a time against the table until it has a pipeable consistency. Place in a pastry bag with a No. 4 (8-mm) plain tip and pipe out straight ropes, 16 inches (40 cm) long, on sheet pans lined with baking paper. Cut the ropes into pieces 1¾ inches (4.5 cm) long.

3. Stir enough of the nougat into the tempered dark chocolate for an approximate ratio of 1 part nougat to 3 parts chocolate. Dip the candies into the melted chocolate.

NOUGAT FOR BRANCHLI yield: approximately 1 pound (455 g)

7 ounces (200 g) finely chopped or thinly sliced blanched almonds

10 ounces (285 g) granulated sugar

1 teaspoon (5 ml) lemon juice

1. Have ready a Silpat or oiled marble slab and an oiled rolling pin.

2. Warm the almonds in a low-temperature oven. Set them aside; keep warm.

3. Place the sugar and lemon juice in a heavy saucepan. Cook over low heat, stirring constantly, until all of the sugar is fully melted and turns light golden. Stir in the warm almonds.

4. Place the nougat on the Silpat or marble slab and quickly, before it hardens, roll it out into a thin sheet. Let the nougat cool completely, then chop or crush it fine; the pieces should be about the size of rice grains.

5. Sift the crushed nougat to remove the powder and any very small pieces. Store in an airtight container, preferably with a desiccant.

Fig Logs yield: 72 candies

4 ounces (115 g) dried figs

8 ounces (225 g) blanched almonds, lightly toasted

12 ounces (340 g) powdered sugar

1 tablespoon (15 ml) light rum

1 teaspoon (5 ml) vanilla extract

Sweet dark chocolate, tempered

1. Remove the stems from the figs. Place the figs in a saucepan with enough water to cover. Bring to a boil and cook for 10 minutes, then drain. Puree the figs in a food processor. Set aside.

2. Process the almonds and half of the sugar in a food processor until the mixture is the consistency of granulated sugar. Transfer to a bowl and stir in the remaining sugar, the rum, vanilla, and fig puree. Adjust with additional rum as needed to make a firm paste.

3. Divide the filling into 6 equal pieces approximately 4 ounces (115 g) each. Using powdered sugar to prevent sticking, roll each piece into a rope 18 inches (45 cm) long. Place the ropes next to each other and cut each crosswise into 12 pieces, 1½ inches (3.7 cm) long. Place the pieces slightly apart on a sheet pan lined with baking paper and allow them to dry overnight on a covered rack.

4. Using a 2-pronged dipping fork, dip the candies into tempered dark chocolate. Slide off onto sheet pans lined with baking paper. Before the chocolate sets, mark the top of the candies with the dipping fork, making 2 lines in the center of each log perpendicular to the long sides.

Finlander Praline yield: 96 candies

I don't know how these classic candies came to be named Finlander. The only thing I can think of is that all Scandinavians love almonds, and the people of Finland are no exception. As in any recipe where the cooking time determines the texture of the finished product, you may need to experiment a bit to get the consistency just right. Cooking the sugar too long, even to a light caramel stage, will make the pralines too firm and chewy, yet if you play it safe and don't cook the mixture long enough, the candies will not set properly and will be difficult or impossible to work with. Once the filling is made, you cannot return it to the heat and continue cooking to make it firmer. You can, however, use a too-soft filling in the following way: Stirring constantly over low heat, warm the filling to make it pipeable. If the butter separates, add 2 tablespoons (30 ml) heavy cream to bring it back together. Pipe the filling almost to the top of small foil candy cups measuring approximately 1 inch across the top and ³/₄ inch deep (2.5 × 2 cm). Allow the candies to cool, then seal the tops with chocolate.

12 ounces (340 g) mixed candied fruit

7 ounces (200 g) blanched almonds, toasted and coarsely crushed

4 ounces (115 g) hazelnuts, toasted and finely ground

¹/₃ cup (80 ml) or 4 ounces (115 g) honey

4 ounces (115 g) almond paste

12 ounces (340 g) granulated sugar

¹/₂ cup (120 ml) water

2 tablespoons (30 ml) glucose *or* light corn syrup

5 ounces (140 g) unsalted butter, at room temperature

Sweet dark chocolate, tempered

1. Chop the candied fruit into raisin-size pieces. Combine the fruit, almonds, and hazelnuts.

2. Combine the honey and almond paste.

3. Combine the sugar and water in a heavy saucepan and bring to a full boil. Add the glucose or corn syrup. Taking the usual precautions for sugar boiling, cook to a light amber color, approximately 315°F (157°C). Remove from the heat and stir in the almond paste mixture, followed by the butter and then the reserved fruit and nut mixture.

4. Arrange candy-molding bars, ¹/₂ inch (1.2 cm) thick, to form a rectangle measuring 8 × 12 inches (20 × 30 cm). Mold the praline filling within the bars. Roll a dowel over the top to make the surface even. Allow to cool and become firm.

5. Remove the candy-molding bars. Precoat by brushing dark chocolate over the top of the candy sheet. Allow the chocolate to set, then invert the sheet. Cut into 8 even strips lengthwise, then cut each strip crosswise to make pieces 1 inch (2.5 cm) long.

6. Using a 3-pronged dipping fork, dip the candies into dark chocolate. Mark the top of each candy diagonally with the prongs of the fork after removing it from the chocolate.

Gianduja yield: 3 pounds 12 ounces (1 kg 705 g)

Gianduja is a creamy chocolate confection flavored with toasted nut paste. While actually a candy, gianduja is also used a great deal in the pastry shop as a flavoring and in fillings. It is quite easy to make, but today, most professionals purchase it from a supplier.

10 ounces (285 g) hazelnuts

10 ounces (285 g) blanched almonds, toasted

1 pound (455 g) powdered sugar

4 ounces (115 g) cocoa butter, melted

1 pound 4 ounces (570 g) sweet dark chocolate, melted

1. Lightly toast the hazelnuts and remove the skins. Process the hazelnuts, almonds, and sugar in a high-speed food processor, grinding until the oil begins to separate from the nuts and the mixture forms a thick paste. If the mixture turns into a powder rather than a paste, which can happen if your food processor is not powerful enough, for example, just proceed with the recipe; the gianduja will not be as smooth, but it will still be quite usable.

2. Combine the melted cocoa butter and chocolate. Add the nut mixture and stir until you have a smooth mass. Place in a covered container. Store and melt as you would chocolate. Gianduja will keep fresh for up to 6 months.

Gianduja Bites yield: approximately 100 candies

1 pound (455 g) Gianduja (above) *or* purchased gianduja chocolate, melted

12 ounces (340 g) milk chocolate, melted

6 ounces (170 g) sliced almonds, toasted

100 whole blanched almonds, lightly toasted

Milk chocolate, tempered

1. Combine the gianduja, melted milk chocolate, and sliced almonds. Pour into a ring, 10 inches (25 cm) in diameter, placed on a lined sheet pan. Allow to set.

2. Using a plain candy or cookie cutter 1 inch (2.5 cm) in diameter, cut out rounds. Knead the scraps together, form, cut, and repeat until you have cut the entire amount of filling. Using a small drop of melted chocolate, attach a whole almond to the top of each candy.

3. Using a 3-pronged dipping fork, dip the candies in the tempered chocolate.

Hazelnut Cinnamon Ganache yield: 96 candies, approximately 1½ inches (3.7 cm) square

As is true of most candies in this chapter, these are quick and easy to prepare. What sets them apart from the usual ganache-type candies is that they comprise two layers, which gives them an interesting appearance and great flavor.

GIANDUJA LAYER

4 ounces (115 g) milk chocolate, chopped

7 ounces (200 g) Gianduja (page 561), cut into small pieces

1½ ounces (40 g) unsweetened chocolate, chopped

CINNAMON LAYER

7 ounces (200 g) milk chocolate, chopped

3 ounces (85 g) sweet dark chocolate, chopped

½ cup (120 ml) heavy cream

1 tablespoon (15 ml) glucose *or* light corn syrup

1 teaspoon (1.5 g) ground cinnamon

Milk chocolate, tempered

1. Combine the ingredients for the gianduja layer in a bowl. Melt together over a bain-marie, stirring from time to time. Heat the mixture to 120°F (49°C) and temper to 82°F (28°C).

2. Line a flat, even sheet pan or sheet of corrugated cardboard with baking paper. Arrange

4 candy-molding bars, ¾ inch (2 cm) thick, on the lined sheet to make a rectangle measuring 9 × 8 inches (22.5 × 20 cm).

3. Spread the gianduja filling evenly within the frame. Refrigerate.

4. To make the cinnamon layer, combine the milk chocolate and dark chocolate in a bowl and melt together over a bain-marie, stirring from time to time.

5. Bring the cream and glucose to a quick boil and stir into the melted chocolate. Add the cinnamon and continue to stir until thoroughly combined. Let the mixture cool until it is the consistency of heavy cream, then beat well for a few minutes. Spread evenly over the top of the chilled gianduja layer. Cover and let set overnight, but do not refrigerate.

6. Remove the candy-molding bars. Brush a thin layer of tempered milk chocolate over the top of the sheet. Let set.

7. Invert the sheet; cut it into six 8-inch (20-cm) strips, then cut each into 16 pieces.

8. Using a 3-pronged dipping fork, dip each piece into tempered milk chocolate. To decorate the top, draw the fork over the top of each candy as you set it down.

Chocolate-Covered Orange Creams yield: approximately 65 candies

Grated zest of 2 small oranges	2 tablespoons (30 ml) orange liqueur
6 ounces (170 g) unsalted butter, at room temperature	1 pound (455 g) sweet dark chocolate, tempered
6 ounces (170 g) Fondant (page 578), smooth	Milk chocolate, tempered

1. Mix the orange zest into the butter and fondant and cream the mixture together well. Stir in the orange liqueur. Gradually mix in 1 pound (455 g) tempered dark chocolate (see Chef's Tip). Wait until the filling starts to thicken, then pour into a ring, 9 inches (22.5 cm) in diameter, set on a sheet pan or cardboard lined with baking paper. Allow the filling to set up.

2. Use a plain cookie cutter, 1½ inches (3.7 cm) in diameter, to cut out rounds. Roll the scraps between sheets of baking paper and continue to cut rounds until all of the filling is used. Cut each round in half.

3. Using a 3-pronged dipping fork, dip each candy into tempered milk chocolate. Place on sheet pans lined with baking paper, turning the candies over as you remove them from the fork to mark the tops.

CHEF'S TIP
Generally, chocolate does not need to be tempered when it is added to a filling. In this recipe, tempering helps harden the interior, but it is not absolutely necessary.

Marzipan Pralines yield: 90 candies

This candy can be produced without tempering chocolate, which can be a big timesaver if your kitchen is not equipped with a tempering machine. Marzipan Pralines also have the advantage of adding a touch of color to your candy assortment. Be careful not to use too much buttercream or ganache when attaching the marzipan sheet to the candy — use just enough to act as glue — or the marzipan will slide off as the candies are cut.

10 ounces (285 g) milk chocolate

1 pound 2 ounces (510 g) Gianduja (page 560) or purchased gianduja chocolate

1 pound 2 ounces (510 g) Praline (page 804; see Note)

9 ounces (255 g) hazelnuts, toasted, skins removed, and finely ground

Dark coating chocolate, melted

Powdered sugar

1 pound (455 g) marzipan, tinted pale green

Buttercream or ganache

Cocoa butter, melted

Sweet dark chocolate, tempered (optional)

1. Arrange metal candy-molding bars, ½ inch (1.2 cm) thick, on an even sheet pan lined with baking paper to form a square measuring 10 × 10 inches (25 × 25 cm). If candy-molding bars are not available, make a frame from corrugated cardboard (see "Making Your Own Cake Frames," page 59).

2. Chop the milk chocolate and gianduja into small chunks and melt over hot water, stirring to combine. Remove from the heat. Stir in the praline and the ground hazelnuts.

3. Spread the mixture within the prepared frame in a perfectly even layer and allow it to set.

4. Remove the metal bars or cut the mixture away from the cardboard. Brush a thin layer of melted dark coating chocolate over the top of the candy. When the chocolate has set, invert the sheet.

5. Using powdered sugar to prevent sticking, roll out the marzipan to a 10-inch (25-cm) square. Texture the top of the marzipan with a tread-pattern marzipan rolling pin to make a striped pattern (see "About Marzipan Rolling Pins," page 97). Brush or spread a thin film of soft buttercream or ganache over the top of the candy sheet. Roll up the marzipan sheet on a dowel and unroll it over the candy, textured-side up. Press gently to be certain it adheres.

6. Brush a thin film of hot cocoa butter over the marzipan. Be sure the cocoa butter is hot and therefore thin; if too thick, it will leave an amber hue on the marzipan. Allow to dry.

7. Invert the sheet so the marzipan side is on the bottom. Measure, then cut the sheet lengthwise into 5 equal strips. Cut each strip crosswise into 18 slices. Turn the pieces marzipan-side up. If desired, dip the sides of each piece of candy into tempered dark chocolate.

NOTE: If you are not making your own praline but instead are using a ready-made product, use less than specified because the purchased products are generally more concentrated. However, each brand varies in strength.

Mimosa yield: approximately 60 candies

Tempered chocolate is thick enough that the marks left by the dipping fork will remain when the candy is inverted onto the baking paper. If you substitute coating chocolate, slide the candy off the fork instead and wait until the chocolate starts to thicken (about 30 seconds, if the chocolate is at the proper temperature), then mark two lines crosswise in the center by placing the dipping fork into the chocolate and pulling the fork straight up.

6 ounces (170 g) granulated sugar

Few drops of lemon juice

¾ cup (180 ml) heavy cream, hot

1 pound 4 ounces (570 g) milk chocolate, melted

Milk chocolate, tempered

Semi-sweet chocolate (aproximately 65% cocoa, 35% sugar), tempered

Candied violets

1. Place the sugar and lemon juice in a heavy saucepan. Cook over medium heat, stirring constantly with a wooden spoon, until all of the sugar has melted and the syrup has turned light golden brown. Quickly and carefully, to avoid being splattered, add the hot cream. Stir over the heat until any lumps have cooked out.

2. When the mixture is smooth, remove it from the heat and stir in the melted milk chocolate. If you overcaramelize the sugar, the mixture will separate. To bring it back together, add 1 tablespoon (15 ml) heavy cream. Return to the heat and stir until the cream is mixed in and the mixture is smooth.

3. Pour the mixture into a ring, 9 inches (22.5 cm) in diameter, placed on a sheet pan lined with baking paper. Let set.

4. Use an oval cookie cutter, 1¼ inches (3.1 cm) long, to cut out ovals. Knead the scraps of filling together, form, cut, and repeat until you have cut the entire amount of filling.

5. Brush the top of the candies with a thin layer of tempered milk chocolate to prevent them from sticking to the dipping fork.

6. Place the candies, chocolate-side down, on a 2-pronged dipping fork and dip into tempered dark chocolate. Place them on sheet pans lined with baking paper, turning the candies over as you remove them from the fork to mark the tops. Place a small piece of candied violet about the size of a grain of rice in the center of each candy before the chocolate hardens.

Pistachio Slices yield: 80 candies

10 ounces (285 g) Praline Paste (page 804)

4 ounces (115 g) cocoa butter, melted

4 ounces (115 g) milk chocolate, melted

4 ounces (115 g) sweet dark chocolate, melted

4 ounces (115 g) blanched pistachios, skins removed and chopped fine

Milk chocolate, tempered

Sweet dark chocolate, tempered

1. Arrange metal candy-molding bars, ½ inch (1.2 cm) thick, on an even sheet pan lined with baking paper in a rectangle measuring 8 × 7½ inches (20 × 18.7 cm). If candy-molding bars are unavailable, make a frame from corrugated cardboard (see "Making Your Own Cake Frames," page 59).

2. Combine the praline paste, cocoa butter, melted milk and dark chocolates, and pistachios. Pour the mixture into the frame and allow it to set. You may want to help it along by placing it in the refrigerator briefly.

3. Cut the sheet lengthwise into 5 strips, 1½ × 8 inches (3.7 × 20 cm) each.

4. Brush a thin layer of tempered milk chocolate over the strips and allow to set.

5. Place the strips, chocolate-side down, on a wire rack, positioning them so the wires run at a 90-degree angle to the strips, which will make it easier to remove them later. Using a spatula, spread a thin layer of tempered milk chocolate on the top and sides of each strip. Immediately transfer the strips to a sheet pan or cardboard lined with baking paper. Streak thin lines of tempered dark chocolate across the width of the strips.

6. Cut each strip crosswise into 16 slices, ½ inch (1.2 cm) wide.

Chocolate Candy Box

yield: 1 octagonal box, 6 inches (15 cm) in diameter and 1½ inches (3.7 cm) in height (Color Photo 95)

To make your chocolate box even more special, prepare a small sheet of Honeycomb Chocolate Decor (page 534) as you are working with the chocolate to make the box. Cut a piece of honeycomb chocolate that will just fit inside the finished box (use the lid template but cut each side a little smaller). Place in the bottom of the box before adding the candies. This adds a nice touch and looks something like the cushioned paper that is generally found on the bottom of a box of candy. It also adds height so your candies will be more visible.

1 pound (455 g) dark coating chocolate, melted, or sweet dark chocolate, tempered
Piping Chocolate (page 543)

Chocolate Solution for Spraying (page 557)
Chocolate decorations for the lid, as desired
Chocolate candies

1. Place a sheet of acetate or baking paper on a marble, granite, or other perfectly even surface. Tape the corners of the plastic or paper so the sheet will not move. Arrange metal candy-forming bars, ⅛ inch (3 mm) thick, on top to form a rectangle 7½ × 22 inches (18.7 × 55 cm). Pour the chocolate into the frame and spread the surface level with the top of the bars. You can do this with a palette knife, but dragging a third metal bar across the top is an even better choice to ensure the chocolate layer will have an even thickness. Let the chocolate set.

2. Trace the templates shown in Figure 10-28. The pieces as shown are the correct size. Cut all 3 pieces out of heavy cardboard. Mark both the larger and smaller octagonal templates to indicate which sides are at the top in the drawings.

3. Remove the bars from the set chocolate sheet. Although it is not necessary to wear food handling gloves to protect the chocolate from fingerprints, as the finished box will be sprayed with the chocolate solution, it is still a good idea to wear gloves whenever you handle the chocolate from this point. Place the templates on top of the chocolate. Using a knife that has been lightly heated with a blowtorch, cut out 1 large and 1 small octagonal pieces and 8 of the small side pieces. Mark the chocolate octagonals as you did the templates. Place an inverted pie tin with a perfectly flat base over a pan of hot water. Rub the edges of the 8 side pieces gently over the warm surface to smooth the cut edges and flat sides as needed. At the same time, make cer-

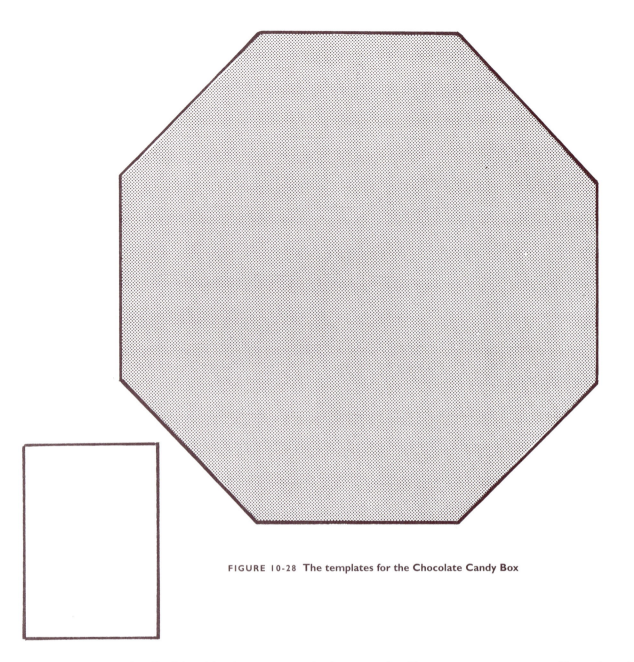

FIGURE 10-28 **The templates for the Chocolate Candy Box**

tain all of the side pieces are exactly the same size. If necessary, use a warm offset palette knife to smooth the tops of the octagonal pieces. If you erase the marks, re-mark the pieces.

4. Center the smaller octagon on top of the larger one, placing it so that the top marked edges are parallel. Use the tip of a paring knife to lightly mark the larger piece of chocolate by tracing around the edges of the smaller piece. These marks will be your guide in attaching the side pieces.

5. Place the side pieces standing on edge on the larger octagon, following the traced lines. If the pieces do not fit together precisely, trim and smooth the edges as needed. When you are ready to assemble the box, pipe a string of piping chocolate over 2 adjacent lines and stand 2 side pieces on top. Hold the pieces straight for a few seconds until the chocolate has set. Repeat to attach the remaining 6 pieces, 2 at a time. Pipe chocolate in the vertical joints where the side pieces meet, filling in the gaps created by the angle of the sides. Once the chocolate has hardened, use a warm spatula to create a smooth finish all over the box, and to level the top. The

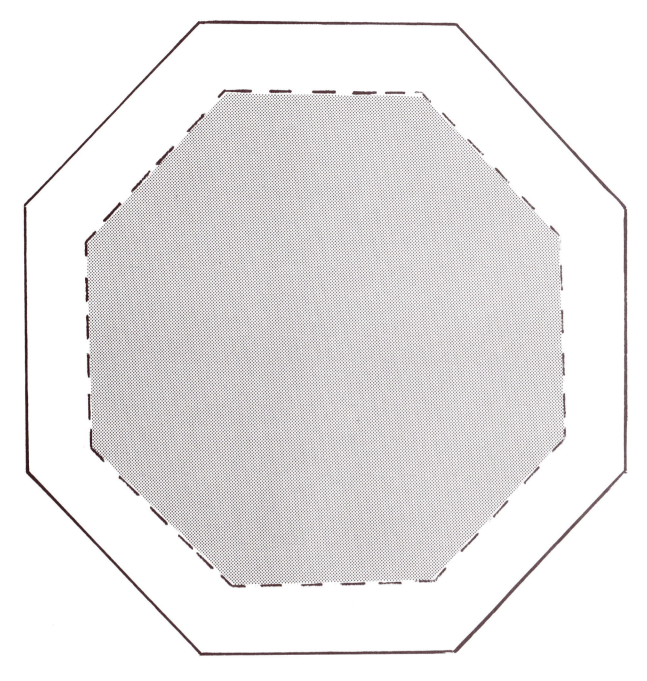

FIGURE 10-28 (*continued*)

chocolate spray will cover any smudges or fingerprints but will not hide drips of chocolate or gaps.

6. Spray the box and the lid with the chocolate solution, following the directions on pages 556 to 558. To create the velvet finish shown on the round chocolate box in Color Photo 95, freeze the chocolate box and lid for about 10 minutes before applying the spray.

7. Wearing food handling gloves, decorate the lid as desired (see examples in Color Photo 95). Fill the box with candies and place the lid on top at an angle so the candies are visible.

IN THIS CHAPTER

BASIC RECIPES AND CANDIES

Boiled Sugar Basic Recipe   575

Boiled Sugar Method I   576

Boiled Sugar Method II   577

Fondant   578

Glacéed Fruit and Nuts   580

Gum Paste with Gum Tragacanth   581

Leaf Croquant   582

Marshmallows   583

Nougatine   584

Nougat Montélimar I   586

Nougat Montélimar II   587

Pastillage   588

Pâte de Fruit: Lemon, Raspberry, and   591
Strawberry Jellies

Rolled Fondant   592

SUGAR DECORATIONS

Spun Sugar   593
CARAMELIZED SPUN SUGAR   594

Sugar Crystals for Decoration   594
SUGAR CRYSTAL SHEETS   595

Sugar Sticks   595

Rock Sugar   596

Cast Sugar   597

PULLED AND BLOWN SUGAR   605

Pulled Sugar Rose   606

Pulled Sugar Bow with Ribbons   608

Sugar Blowing   610

CARAMELIZED SUGAR AND CARAMELIZED SUGAR DECORATIONS

Caramelized Sugar, Dry Method   612

Caramelized Sugar with Water   613

Caramelized Sugar for Decorations   613

Bubble Sugar   615
TWICE-COOKED BUBBLE SUGAR   616
ISOMALT BUBBLE SUGAR   617

Caramel Cages   618
CARAMEL CAGES USING A HALF-SPHERE   619
SIMPLIFIED CARAMEL CAGES   619

Caramel Corkscrews   620

Caramel Fences   621

Caramel Spiders   622

Caramel Spirals   623

Caramel-Dipped Fruit and Nuts   624

Caramelized Nuts   626
SUGAR-COATED NUTS   627

Caramel Fans   627

Sugar Shards   628
NONCARAMELIZED SUGAR SHARDS AND   629
TINTED SUGAR SHARDS

Tartaric Acid Solution   629

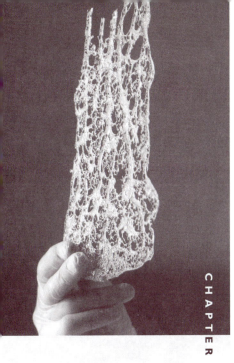

Sugarwork

Sugar is a truly amazing ingredient, and one that is indispensable to the baker. While sugar is the sweetener in almost every recipe in this book, this chapter deals with the artistic side of its use. Sugar can be boiled into a thick syrup and turned into a variety of shapes by casting, blowing, or pulling, or it can be spun into delicate threads to be used as decoration. With the addition of gum tragacanth or gelatin, sugar can be made into a paste to be rolled, formed, or molded in almost any way imaginable. Caramelized sugar is used to coat fruit and nuts for dessert garnishes; it can be made into fragile cages to showcase a simple dessert like ice cream and make it special; or it can be piped out to form ornaments, figurines, and even flexible spirals. Adding nuts to caramelized sugar yields nougatine, which has many decorative uses. Royal icing is made by mixing powdered sugar and egg whites; it too can be used to create decorative ornaments to garnish cakes and pastries, and it can be used for showpieces.

To master all or even a few of the many techniques of decorative sugarwork takes many years of experience, but the good news is that time is the only investment you need to make, as many projects can be completed with little equipment, and sugar itself is inexpensive.

Equipment and Ingredients Required to Work with Sugar

The single most expensive item you need to get started in sugarwork is a professional sugar thermometer; a digital thermometer is best. You can buy a regular home-use candy thermometer for about one-tenth of the price, but these are easily broken and must be checked for accuracy before use; the thermometer must read exactly 212°F/100°C when placed in boiling water at sea level. Also, if using a glass thermometer, make certain it contains alcohol rather than mercury; it is illegal in some states to use mercury-filled thermometers in professional kitchens (see page 630 for more information). The first thing required for sugar boiling is, obviously, a heat source. It need not be a stove; a portable electric burner can be used for this purpose and often makes more sense if you set up an area for sugarwork out of the way of other production. The burner must be powerful enough to bring the syrup to a boil quickly and to keep it boiling rapidly at the specified temperature. The other basic equipment you should have is as follows:

- a copper or stainless steel pan with a capacity of 2 quarts (1 L 920 ml)

- a bain-marie; the bowl should be large enough to hold the pan

- a small bowl with a brush dedicated for use in sugar boiling

- a sugar thermometer, as described above

- a Bunsen burner

- a metal scraper

- a pair of scissors

- a sieve or perforated spoon for skimming

- food handling gloves

- a small drop bottle

- a one-way air pump with a wooden or plastic mouthpiece

- a pint or quart measuring cup

- a fixative syringe or air brush for spraying finished pieces with color or lacquer

- a marble or granite worktable or a small slab of either material

- at least 1 Silpat

- an air blower or hair dryer with warm and cold settings and an adjustable stand so your hands are free

- a sugar warming case with an infrared heat lamp and a frame on which to place the sugar (see page 609)

Basic ingredients needed for sugarwork are:

- clean water measured into the pan according to the individual recipe, in the small bowl with the brush, and in the bain-marie

- crystal sugar or granulated sugar, preferably a newly opened bag to eliminate the risk of contamination

- tartaric acid solution in the drop bottle, prepared 1:1 (tartaric acid powder dissolved in an equal amount of hot water by weight)

- food coloring in liquid, paste, or powdered form (powders and pastes are many times more concentrated; before powders can be used in sugarwork, they must be dissolved in water)

- edible lacquer and a dehumidifying agent to protect the finished pieces (discussed in more detail in the following section)

- glucose or light corn syrup

Storing and Protecting Finished Sugar Pieces

Because sugar is hygroscopic, meaning that it attracts and absorbs moisture, it must be protected both from contact with moisture and against absorption of moisture in the air. This is especially important for finished pieces that are stored, whether a simple pulled-sugar rose or ribbon or an elaborate showpiece, but it also applies to leftover sugar scraps and pulled sugar prepared ahead and ready to reheat and use. Showpieces can be both displayed and preserved

About Sugar

The term *sugar* can be applied to more than 100 naturally occurring organic compounds that by definition form white or clear crystals when purified, are sweet in flavor, and are water soluble. Sugar most commonly refers to granulated table sugar. However, many other types of sugar, with different chemical structures, are used in the pastry shop as well. All forms of sugar are part of the carbohydrate food group. Sugar as we know it in the kitchen — granulated, powdered, confectioners', or brown — is sucrose and is the product of an extensive refining process that begins with sugarcane or sugar beets. Although these two plants are totally different in their botanical composition and are often cultivated on opposite sides of the globe, you cannot identify by taste alone whether the sugar you use to sweeten your coffee came from sugarcane or sugar beets; their chemical composition and their flavor are identical after refining.

Sugars are divided into two basic groups: double sugars, called *disaccharides*, which consist of two simple sugars linked together — these include sucrose (beet and cane sugar), maltose (known as *malt sugar*), and lactose (the sugar found in milk) — and single sugars, or simple sugars, which are called *monosaccharides*. Simple sugars include glucose (also called *dextrose*) and fructose (also called *levulose*). In sugarcane and sugar beets, glucose and fructose combine chemically to form sucrose. Glucose is used as a sweetener in wine and drug production and is added to boiled sugar for many of the techniques in this chapter. Glucose is also the form of sugar into which digested carbohydrates are metabolized in the body. Fructose is used as a food preservative as well as a sweetener. Different types of sugar vary a great deal in their sweetness. Lactose is less sweet than sucrose, and fructose is sweeter than either lactose or sucrose.

Sugar Production

Sugarcane and sugar beets are the primary materials of commercial sugar production, which consists of harvesting these sucrose-rich plants and converting the sucrose into crystallized sugar. Other sources that yield sucrose are maple sap, sorghum cane, some date and palm trees, watermelons, and grapes, but their cultivation for the purpose of sugar production is negligible in comparison. The world's largest producers of cane sugar are Brazil, India, Cuba, Mexico, the United States, and Pakistan. Producers of beet sugar include Ukraine, Russia, Germany, France, and the United States.

All green plants manufacture glucose in their leaves through a process called *photosynthesis,* by which plants transform the sun's energy into food. In the leaves, the glucose is converted to sucrose before being transported to the roots and stems. Most plants convert the sucrose a step further, making it into starch for storage. Sugarcane and sugar beets manufacture sucrose in great quantities, but unlike most other plants, they store it unchanged. Figure 11-1, page 574, illustrates the process for refining sugarcane and sugar beets.

Refining and Processing Sugarcane

Sugarcane is a tropical grass cultivated in warm, moist climates. The canes grow from a little less than a year to close to three years before harvest, each attaining a height of 10 to 20 feet (3 to 6 meters). Raw cane sugar contains 12 to 14 percent sucrose. Sugarcane is produced in the United States in Florida, Louisiana, Hawaii, and Texas. The production process takes place in two locations: sugar mills and sugar refineries. The plants are harvested by cutting the cane off close to the ground with machines — or, in some areas, by hand using a machete. The leaves are stripped from the stalks, which are transported to a sugar mill. The refining process begins with crushing and shredding the stalks. The resulting material is passed through and pressed under a series of heavy rollers to extract the cane juice. The waste product left from this process is called *bagasse* and is most often used as fuel to run the mills; it is also processed into paper. The cane juice is clarified by adding milk of lime (made from quicklime) and carbon dioxide. As the carbon dioxide creates bubbles, the lime forms calcium carbonate, and these chalklike crystals bubble through the mixture, attracting the nonsugar matter, such as wax, fats, and gums, away from the juice. The calcium carbonate and other materials then settle to the bottom, leaving the clarified sugarcane juice.

Next, the juice is concentrated by boiling it in several stages under vacuum, which allows it to boil at a lower temperature, thus protecting it from caramelizing. At this stage, it becomes a thick brown syrup called *massecuite.* The syrup is crystallized by evaporating the last amount of water and is then passed into a centrifuge with a perforated basket at the center. After spinning and drying, the result is golden raw sugar; this is not the same as the product labeled *raw sugar* that is sold commercially. Molasses is a byproduct of the boiling and spinning stages.

in glass or Plexiglas boxes or domes with silica gel or quicklime hidden inside the holder. For storage only, a plastic bag works great (blow up the bag so the plastic does not touch the sugar); you still need the dehumidifying agent inside. Stored in an airtight container with silica gel or quicklime, portioned slabs or pieces of prepared sugar will keep for many months.

Silica gel and quicklime are the most common dehumidifying agents used to protect sugar from moisture. Silica gel is a polymer of silicic acid separated from the whole by water and formed from two hydroxide groups. It changes color depending on its water content. When dry, the crystals are blue; when it has absorbed the maximum amount of moisture possible, the color changes to pink. When this happens, the crystals can be dried out in a 300°F (149°C) oven for a few minutes until they return to the original blue color; silica gel crystals are reusable indefinitely.

Quicklime is a type of sedimentary rock that forms and solidifies over millions of years. It is quarried, crushed, and burned for many hours at an extremely high temperature, during which

The raw sugar is approximately 96 to 98 percent sucrose. The crystals are light brown because they are covered by a thin film of molasses, which contains sugar, water, and impurities, such as plant materials. At this stage, the raw sugar is transported from the sugar mill to the sugar refinery, almost always by ship, which is why many major refineries are located at seaports.

At the refinery, the raw sugar is transformed into granulated sugar, brown sugar, and other products for both consumers and the food industry. The raw sugar is first mixed with a warm syrup made of water and sugar, which essentially washes the raw sugar to loosen the molasses coating. The mixture is spun in large centrifuges again, separating the molasses film from the crystals. The crystals are washed and dissolved into a syrup that is filtered to remove any remaining molasses and impurities. The sugar is now a clear golden liquid. Further filtering removes the remaining color, leaving a naturally transparent white syrup. Some of the water content is removed, and the concentrated syrup is conveyed to a vacuum, where fine sugar crystals are added. As evaporation occurs, larger sugar crystals form around the fine crystal seeds, resulting in crystals of the proper size. The sugar goes to a centrifuge again, where any noncrystallized syrup is spun off and the crystals are washed. The damp crystals then go to dryers; after drying, the sugar granules are sifted through screens to separate the various sized crystals for packaging.

Refining and Processing Sugar Beets

Sugar beets grow in temperate climates and store sugar in their roots. In the United States, sugar beets are raised in California, Colorado, Idaho, Michigan, Ohio, Oregon, Washington, and many of the Great Plains states. The sugar beet crop provides slightly less than half of the total U.S. sugar crop. Sugar beets weigh about 2 pounds (910 g) each and contain 16 to 18 percent sucrose in their raw form. Their growing season lasts about five months. Unlike sugarcane's, the process for refining sugar beets takes place all at one location, generally near the growing area, as the beets do not travel well. Sugar beet factories operate seasonally in response to the harvest; during this time, the facilities may be in production continuously, day and night, seven days a week.

The refining process is basically the same as for sugarcane, although not as many steps are involved. The first step at the factory is to wash and slice the beets, which then go into a tank known as a *diffuser*, where they are agitated as hot water washes over them. The sugar-laden water is drawn off and the remaining beet pulp is processed separately, usually for livestock feed. The watery beet juice is treated with milk of lime (a liquid made from quicklime) and carbon dioxide in carbonation tanks, as is sugarcane juice. After the juice is filtered, it is thin and light brown. This is evaporated under vacuum, resulting in a syrup. The syrup is filtered again and boiled again, and crystals now begin to form. The crystal and syrup combination, as in cane sugar production, is called *massecuite*. The massecuite is sent to a centrifuge; after spinning, it is washed to produce pure white crystals of sugar. These are dried and sifted to separate the crystals by size before they are packaged.

time, through chemical reaction, it becomes CaO, calcium oxide. Three areas in Europe where quicklime is found are the White Cliffs of Dover in Great Britain, White Stone of Ulm in Germany, and Champagne in France . Quicklime is also known as *burnt lime* and simply *lime*. The production of many industrial chemicals requires its use, as does the processing of cane and sugar beet juices. When cold water comes in contact with quicklime, it produces an impressive reaction of steam and heat — up to 212°F (100°C). Quicklime is strongly caustic and can severely irritate skin; it should therefore never be touched, especially with wet hands. As quicklime absorbs humidity, it turns to powder and must be replaced. This can take from a few days to a year, depending on the percentage of humidity and the amount of quicklime used. In most cases, only a few small chunks are needed. The quicklime should be kept apart from the sugar it is protecting in a small container with airholes to prevent any mess as it disintegrates. Both silica gel and quicklime are available as dehumidifying agents under various brand names.

Sugar Production and Refinement

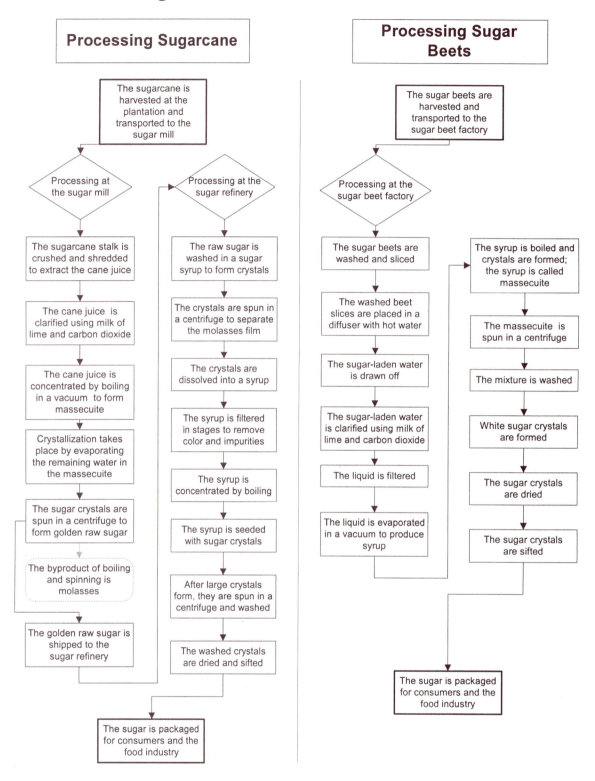

Processing Sugarcane

The sugarcane is harvested at the plantation and transported to the sugar mill

Processing at the sugar mill

Processing at the sugar refinery

The sugarcane stalk is crushed and shredded to extract the cane juice

The cane juice is clarified using milk of lime and carbon dioxide

The cane juice is concentrated by boiling in a vacuum to form massecuite

Crystallization takes place by evaporating the remaining water in the massecuite

The sugar crystals are spun in a centrifuge to form golden raw sugar

The byproduct of boiling and spinning is molasses

The golden raw sugar is shipped to the sugar refinery

The raw sugar is washed in a sugar syrup to form crystals

The crystals are spun in a centrifuge to separate the molasses film

The crystals are dissolved into a syrup

The syrup is filtered in stages to remove color and impurities

The syrup is concentrated by boiling

The syrup is seeded with sugar crystals

After large crystals form, they are spun in a centrifuge and washed

The washed crystals are dried and sifted

The sugar is packaged for consumers and the food industry

Processing Sugar Beets

The sugar beets are harvested and transported to the sugar beet factory

Processing at the sugar beet factory

The sugar beets are washed and sliced

The washed beet slices are placed in a diffuser with hot water

The sugar-laden water is drawn off

The sugar-laden water is clarified using milk of lime and carbon dioxide

The liquid is filtered

The liquid is evaporated in a vacuum to produce syrup

The syrup is boiled and crystals are formed; the syrup is called massecuite

The massecuite is spun in a centrifuge

The mixture is washed

White sugar crystals are formed

The sugar crystals are dried

The sugar crystals are sifted

The sugar is packaged for consumers and the food industry

FIGURE 11-1 The sugar production and refinement process

The Importance of Sugar in the Pastry Kitchen

By looking at the ingredients listed in most pastry recipes, you can clearly see that a pastry chef would find it almost impossible to produce the majority of traditional bakery products, keeping the desired flavor and appearance, without using some type of sugar. In addition to providing a sweet flavor that seems universally popular, sugar acts as an emulsifying (creaming) agent by incorporating air when mixed with fat; it becomes a foaming agent when mixed with eggs; it weakens the gluten structure of flour, contributing to a tender and fine-textured product; it provides food for developing yeast; it enhances the smoothness and mouth feel of frozen ice cream; it caramelizes when heated, lending an appetizing color and crust to just about all baked items; it delays coagulation of egg proteins in custards; it helps prevent jams and preserves from spoiling; and, lastly, by retaining moisture, it increases the shelf life of baked goods.

BASIC RECIPES AND CANDIES

Boiled Sugar Basic Recipe **yield: 3 cups (720 ml) or 1 pound 8 ounces (680 g)**

This recipe is used for spun sugar, cast sugar, and pulled or blown sugar. Make sure both the sugar and your tools are absolutely clean. Scoop the top layer of sugar to one side in the bin before taking out what you need. Use crystal sugar, if possible, and never use the flour scoop to measure sugar.

There are two important reasons for using glucose when boiling sugar: It helps prevent recrystallization, and it gives the finished sugar mass some elasticity. Tartaric acid is used in cooking sugar for its low pH value and because it too delays or prevents recrystallization as it inverts (or splits) part of the sugar into fructose and glucose. It must be added at the proper time with a drop bottle. Be precise when measuring the acid. Too much will make the finished sugar too soft and difficult to work with. There are some recipes that use boiled sugar without tartaric acid because it makes the sugar soft. This is desirable for pulled sugar, for example, but would be a problem for spun sugar. For this reason, I have listed the tartaric acid as optional.

If you work with sugar frequently, make a larger batch of this recipe. Cook the sugar through Step 3, then store and finish cooking in smaller portions as needed.

1 cup (240 ml) water

2 pound 8 ounces (1 kg 135 g) crystal sugar *or* granulated sugar

8 ounces (225 g) glucose *or* light corn syrup

Food coloring (optional)

12 drops of Tartaric Acid Solution (page 629; optional)

1. Fill a bowl large enough to hold the pan used to cook the sugar with enough cold water to reach halfway up the sides of the pan. Set the bowl of water aside.

2. Place the water and sugar in a sugar pan or heavy saucepan. Stir the mixture gently over low heat until all of the sugar has dissolved and the syrup has started to boil. If any scum accumulates on top from impurities in the sugar, remove it with a skimmer or small sieve, or it may cause the sugar to recrystallize later. Add the glucose or corn syrup, stirring until it is thoroughly incorporated. Do not stir any further after this point.

CHEF'S TIP

It is a good idea, especially if you are boiling a large amount of sugar, to remove the pan from the heat a few degrees before it reaches the specified temperature, watch the mercury rise to the required temperature off the heat, then plunge the pan into cold water.

About Sugar Pans

A sugar pan is a heavyweight unlined copper pan made especially for cooking sugar. The thickness of the pan helps the sugar cook evenly without hot spots, and the acidity of the copper produces a chemical reaction in which some of the sugar breaks down into invert sugar, which is more resistant to recrystallization, during the cooking process. The sugar also cooks faster in this type of pan. Sugar pans have a small spout on the rim that makes it easy to pour out the boiled sugar. They are available in sizes from 2 cups to 5 quarts (480 ml to 4 L 800 ml).

Most sugar pans have hollow handles, sometimes made from a different material, such as stainless steel, to make the handle resistant to heat; some have a wide metal ring attached about halfway up the side of the pan that sticks out to catch drips. Another helpful accessory sold with some pans is a lid with a hole in the top designed to accommodate a sugar thermometer. This has two advantages: The chef does not have to hold the thermometer suspended in the sugar solution, and he or she can monitor the temperature of the sugar even when the pan is covered.

3. Raise the heat to medium, place a lid on the pan, and let the sugar boil hard for a few minutes. The steam trapped inside the pan will wash down the sugar crystals that form on the sides of the pan. Or you can wash down the sides with a clean brush dipped in water (the brush should be dedicated to use in sugar boiling).

4. Place a sugar thermometer in the pan. When the temperature reaches 265°F (130°C), add the coloring, if directed in the individual recipe. Stop brushing and boil the sugar to 280°F (138°C); then add the tartaric acid solution, if directed in the individual recipe. Continue to boil, watching the temperature constantly, until the desired temperature is reached according to the specific recipe and use.

5. Remove the pan from the heat and place the bottom of the pan into the bowl of cold water for 10 seconds to stop the temperature from going any higher (see Chef's Tip, page 575).

CHEF'S TIP

Pour the extra sugar into a rectangular shape on the oiled marble or a Silpat. When a skin has formed on the top, use an oiled metal scraper to mark the sugar into pieces of the appropriate size for your project. Let it solidify and cool completely. Break the sugar into sections at the markings, then store the pieces in an airtight container with a dehumidifying agent to absorb moisture. The sugar can be stored this way for many weeks.

To reheat the stored sugar, place it on the working frame of a sugar warming box (or on a Silpat) under the heat lamp of the box. Depending on the amount of sugar and the number of heat lamps, it can take from 5 to 25 minutes for the sugar to become soft enough to work with. Keep turning the sugar every few minutes to assure even heat distribution and to prevent recrystallization from overheating.

Boiled Sugar Method I

These instructions are used for Pulled and Blown Sugar.

1. Following the recipe and directions in the Boiled Sugar Basic Recipe, boil the syrup to 297°F (148°C). Quickly plunge the bottom of the pan into cold water to stop the cooking process. Let stand for about 10 seconds, then remove the pan from the water and wipe off the bottom with a cloth. Set the sugar aside a few seconds longer to allow most of the bubbles to subside. Remove the sugar thermometer and pour the syrup in a steady stream into a round puddle on a lightly oiled marble slab or table or a Silpat (which does not need to be oiled). If you do not plan to use all of the sugar right away, see Chef's Tip.

2. As soon as the sugar has formed a skin, slide

an oiled metal spatula under the edge of the sugar puddle and fold it in toward the center. Repeat, moving evenly around the circle, until the sugar no longer runs and has cooled to the point that it can be pulled in your hands. Start to aerate the sugar as described in the instructions for Pulled and Blown Sugar (page 605).

Boiled Sugar Method II yield: 6 cups (1 L 440 ml) or 3 pounds (1 kg 365 g)

This recipe is also used for Pulled and Blown Sugar. It is especially suitable for preparing ahead because the precooked sugar can be warmed and softened in a microwave. If sugar crystals form on the sides of the pan during the boiling period, they must be washed down as described in Boiled Sugar Basic Recipe.

2 pounds (910 g) crystal sugar *or* granulated sugar

3½ cups (840 ml) or 2 pounds 10 ounces (1 kg 195 g) light corn syrup

10 ounces (285 g) glucose *or* light corn syrup

Food coloring (optional)

12 drops of Tartaric Acid Solution (page 629) *or* ½ teaspoon (1 g) cream of tartar dissolved in 1 teaspoon (5 ml) water (see Note)

1. Fill a bowl large enough to hold the pan used for cooking the sugar with enough cold water to reach halfway up the sides of the pan. Set the bowl aside.

2. Combine the sugar, corn syrup, and glucose in a sugar pan (see "About Sugar Pans") or a heavy stainless steel saucepan. Stir constantly over low heat until the mixture comes to a boil. Brush down the sides of the pan and continue boiling over medium heat. When the temperature reaches 265°F (130°C), add food coloring if directed. It is important to add the color at this temperature to ensure it has sufficient time to blend with the sugar syrup without stirring and to provide ample time for more color to be added if it seems necessary. If the sugar is to be stored, see Step 5.

3. Boil the sugar to 280°F (138°C), then add the tartaric acid solution or cream of tartar solution if directed. Boil to 305°F (152°C). Immediately plunge the bottom of the pan into the cold water in the bowl for about 10 seconds to stop the cooking process. Remove the pan from the water and wipe off the bottom with a towel, wait a few seconds longer, then pour the sugar in a puddle on a lightly oiled marble slab or table or a Silpat (which does not need to be oiled).

4. As soon as the sugar has formed a skin, slide an oiled metal spatula under the edge of the sugar puddle and fold it in toward the center. Repeat, moving evenly around the circle until the sugar no longer runs and has cooled to the point that it can be pulled in your hands. Start to aerate the sugar, as described in the instructions for Pulled and Blown Sugar (page 605).

5. If the sugar is to be stored, pour it directly into 3 or 4 separate microwavable plastic containers at the end of Step 2 (if you are not sure they can stand up to the heat of the sugar, test the containers first). When the sugar is completely cold, cover and store until needed. To use the sugar, reheat it in a microwave just long enough so the sugar can be removed from the container. It does not need to be totally liquid; do not boil it. Pour the sugar onto the oiled marble slab or table or a Silpat. To ensure the sugar cools evenly, use a lightly oiled metal scraper to fold the outside of the puddle in toward the middle continuously until the sugar has cooled to the

Adding Color to Boiled Sugar

If the entire batch of sugar is to be colored (this applies to Spun, Cast, Pulled, and Blown Sugar), add regular water-soluble food coloring (or powdered coloring dissolved in water) when the sugar reaches 265°F (130°C), blending the three primary colors of red, yellow, and blue, as desired, to make various shades. You can make black food coloring, if it is not available, by mixing equal amounts of the primary colors. Milk-white is obtained by adding a liquid whitener (a food coloring containing glycerin and titanium dioxide) at the rate of 1/2 teaspoon (2.5 ml) for the basic sugar recipe or 1 teaspoon (5 ml) for Boiled Sugar Method II. The whitener is added at the same temperature as any other color (265°F/130°C), but for the best milk-white effect, stop boiling the sugar at 295°F (146°C); a drawback, however, is that the sugar will not be as rigid.

You can make your own liquid whitener, if necessary, from calcium carbonate (also known as *precipitated chalk*), which can be ordered from a laboratory supplier. It is made from natural limestone, or chalk, which contains nearly 100 percent calcium carbonate. Stir 8 ounces (225 g) chalk into 2/3 cup (160 ml) water and mix into a smooth paste. Store in a sealed glass jar and use as needed. This paste is not as strong as the commercial whitener; you will need to add 3 times as much solution to obtain a proper milk-white color. The liquid whitener or precipitated chalk can also be added to any other color to make it opaque; this is especially desirable with cast-sugar pieces. When designing your project, keep in mind that adding a whitener will make the shade lighter. If the sugar is to be pulled, whitening it is not necessary. As the sugar is pulled, the air worked into it produces a pleasant, opaque white color.

To color small cast figures, see "Spraying Colors on Sugar Pieces" (page 604).

point where it no longer runs. Start to aerate the sugar, as described in the instructions for Pulled and Blown Sugar (page 605), as soon as you can pick it up.

NOTE: Be precise when measuring the acid. Too much will make the finished sugar too soft and difficult to work with.

Fondant yield: 2 quarts (1 L 920 ml)

Fondant is a sugar syrup recrystallized to a creamy white paste. It is widely used in the pastry shop for glazing and decorating. If properly applied, fondant dries to a silky-smooth icing shell that not only enhances the appearance of a pastry but preserves it as well by sealing it from the air. Glucose and cream of tartar are used to invert part of the sugar to achieve the proper degree of recrystallization. Without these ingredients, the cooked sugar would harden and be impossible to work with. Conversely, if too much glucose or cream of tartar is used, recrystallization will be inadequate, and the fondant will be soft and runny.

Although fondant is inexpensive and relatively easy to make (once you get the hang of it), in a professional kitchen it is almost always purchased, either ready to use or in a dehydrated form to which water is added.

To make fondant, you need a precise sugar thermometer (test in boiling water to determine accuracy), a sugar pan (see page 576) or a heavy saucepan, a wide spatula or bench scraper, a marble slab (2 × 2 feet/60 × 60 cm for this recipe), 4 steel or aluminum bars, and, as in all sugar work, quick reaction time when the sugar has reached the proper temperature.

Vegetable oil for the equipment

1 cup (240 ml) cold water

2 cups (480 ml) water

4 pounds (1 kg 820 g) granulated sugar

⅔ cup (160 ml) glucose *or* light corn syrup, warmed

½ teaspoon (1 g) cream of tartar

1. Clean, dry, and lightly oil the marble slab and metal bars with vegetable oil. Place the bars at the edge of the marble to make a frame to hold the hot syrup when it is poured on the slab. Oil a stainless steel scraper and place 1 cup (240 ml) cold water close by.

2. Combine the remaining 2 cups (480 ml) water and the sugar in a saucepan. Bring to a boil, stirring to dissolve the sugar. Reduce the heat to medium, stop stirring, and brush the sides of the pan with additional water. Be sure to brush down all of the crystals. It takes only a few particles of sugar left on the sides to make the mixture recrystallize before you want it to when the sugar becomes hotter.

3. When the temperature reaches 225°F (108°C), add the warm glucose or corn syrup and the cream of tartar dissolved in a little hot water. Continue boiling until the syrup reaches 238° to 240°F (114° to 115°C). Pay close attention; the syrup will reach this temperature quicker than you might think.

4. Immediately pour the syrup onto the prepared surface and sprinkle about 2 tablespoons (30 ml) of the reserved cold water on top. It is critical that the temperature does not exceed 240°F (115°C), so if your marble is not right next to the stove, place the saucepan in a bowl of cold water for a few seconds first to prevent overcooking. Insert the sugar thermometer into the thickest part of the puddle and let the sugar cool to 110°F (43°C).

5. Remove the metal bars and start to incorporate air into the sugar mixture: Using the oiled stainless steel scraper, work the sugar by sliding the scraper under the edge of the sugar, lifting it, and folding it in toward the center. After a while, the sugar will start to turn white and become firmer. Continue to work the fondant slowly, either by hand or in a mixer bowl (see Chef's Tip), until it has a smooth and creamy consistency.

6. Pack the fondant against the bottom of a plastic container and pour the remaining cold water on top to prevent a crust from forming. Store at room temperature. The fondant must rest about 24 hours to become soft enough to use.

7. Covered properly, fondant will keep for weeks. Pour off the water before using and keep the bowl covered with plastic wrap while you are working. Add a new layer of water, then cover to store until the next use.

CHEF'S TIP

If you are making a large batch of fondant, you can work the sugar in a mixer instead of by hand. Carefully pour the cooled syrup into the mixing bowl by holding the bowl next to the table and scraping the mixture in with the bench scraper. Do not get any syrup on the sides of the bowl. Using the paddle, mix on low speed until the fondant is smooth and creamy. You may need to scrape down the sides of the bowl to ensure all of the fondant is mixed evenly. Scoop the fondant into a container and cover with the cold water, as in Step 6.

Glacéed Fruit and Nuts

Small, fresh stemmed strawberries, glazed with sugar boiled to the hard-crack stage, can be used as a garnish for a strawberry soufflé, as part of a petits fours tray served after a meal, or on top of a Valentine dessert. They are quite elegant and look magnificent. Orange, apple, and pear wedges can be glazed and used to enhance the presentation of desserts made with those fruits, such as pear or apple charlotte or a Grand Marnier soufflé.

Because the juices released when fresh fruits are dipped into hot caramel will eventually penetrate and melt the sugar shell, glazed fruits should be prepared as close as possible to serving time. Glazed dried fruits hold up better and can be kept in an airtight container for a few days if needed, but this is not ideal. They are generally used as a colorful addition to a candy or petits fours tray rather than to garnish a dessert.

Walnut halves sandwiched together with flavored marzipan can be glazed with sugar in the same way; they make a nice addition to a selection of glazed fruit.

Vegetable oil	**Rum**
Fresh or dried fruit	**Simple syrup**
Lemon juice	**Food coloring**
Plain Poaching Syrup (page 789)	**Pistachio extract**
Walnut halves	**Boiled Sugar Basic Recipe (page 575)**
Marzipan, untinted	

1. If you do not have a Silpat on which to place the dipped pieces, lightly oil a baking sheet to hold the glazed fruits.

2. Prepare the fruits or nuts to be dipped in the following ways:

- Small strawberries: Leave whole, stem on if possible.

- Oranges: Peel by hand, not with a knife. Pull the segments apart. Remove as much of the white pith as possible.

- Apples and pears: Leave the skin on for color, cut into thin wedges, and coat with lemon juice to prevent oxidation. Poach the wedges for 1 or 2 minutes in a small amount of plain poaching syrup. Blot dry.

- Filled walnuts: Flavor a small amount of marzipan with rum; roll into olive-shaped pieces; use simple syrup to attach a walnut half to each side of the marzipan pieces.

- Filled dates, dried figs, and prunes: Cut open and remove the pits from medium-sized dates or prunes. Color a small amount of marzipan light pink and fill the fruit so some of the marzipan is visible along the cut. Form the fruit so the pieces are uniform in shape.

- Filled dried apricots: Flavor a small amount of marzipan with pistachio extract. If desired, tint the marzipan pale green. Sandwich the marzipan between 2 apricot halves; shape them like the dates.

3. Insert a wooden skewer into each of the fruit pieces or nut candies (dip stemmed strawberries by holding onto the stem).

4. To glaze about 25 pieces, make half of the boiled sugar basic recipe (you will have some sugar left over, but this cannot be avoided; you need this amount in order to dip the fruit properly into the syrup) and boil the syrup to 310°F (155°C). Immediately place the bottom of the saucepan into cold water for about 10 seconds to stop the cooking process. Remove the pan from the water and wait until most of the bubbles have disappeared before dipping the fruit.

5. Quickly dip each fruit or candy into the syrup, holding it by the skewer, then gently move it up and down over the syrup to remove excess sugar. Lightly scrape the bottom against the side of the pan to remove the last drips and place on the Silpat or oiled sheet pan. Reheat the syrup as it starts to cool and thicken. It is essential that the fruits have only a very thin shell of caramel, or they will be both unattractive and impossible to eat. Let cool completely; then, holding a candy in place with a fork, pull out the skewer. Avoid touching the glazed candies with your fingers.

Gum Paste with Gum Tragacanth yield: 3 pounds (1 kg 365 g)

Using gum tragacanth rather than gelatin in gum paste produces a paste that is more pliable and more convenient to work with, as it does not dry out as quickly. This is also due, in part, to the addition of shortening, which acts as a moistening agent. Gum paste with gum tragacanth is ideal for small, time-consuming projects — for example, sculpting the head or arms of a figure, or when rolling out the paste and marking an intricate design, such as the bricks in a castle wall — as the paste allows you more working time. The time can be extended up to 2 hours by rubbing a thin film of vegetable shortening over the surface as soon as the paste has been rolled out, cut, or formed. This will delay the formation of a crust while you finish your design; the shortening will be absorbed slowly by the paste and will not be visible in the finished piece. The drawback to using shortening in the paste and/or rubbed on the surface is that the finished showpiece will take up to 1 week longer to dry completely than if made with a gelatin-based paste. Gum paste with gum tragacanth is not a practical choice when a large quantity of paste is called for, as gum tragacanth is not as readily available as powdered gelatin and is about 10 times more expensive.

2 pounds 10 ounces (1 kg 195 g) powdered sugar

2 tablespoons (18 g) gum tragacanth powder

½ cup (120 ml) water

2 tablespoons (30 ml) glucose *or* light corn syrup

1 tablespoon (15 ml) lemon juice

About 1 ounce (30 g) white vegetable shortening

Food coloring (optional)

1. Sift the powdered sugar and reserve a few handfuls.

2. Thoroughly mix the gum tragacanth into the remaining sugar. Set aside in a mixer bowl.

3. Combine the water, glucose or corn syrup, and lemon juice. Warm the mixture slightly, stirring until well blended.

4. Using the dough hook attachment, gradually incorporate the liquid into the powdered sugar mixture, adding some of the reserved powdered sugar, if needed, to make a fairly stiff paste. The consistency of the paste should be firm enough that it can be rolled out easily.

5. Mix in the shortening and continue kneading with the dough hook until you have an easily moldable paste. It takes some experience to get the consistency just right. You may need to add more shortening, depending on the amount of powdered sugar used. If so, or if you are adding extra shortening to extend the working time, just rub it onto the top of the paste and

About Gum Tragacanth

This jelling substance comes from the shrub *Astralas gummifier*, native to the Middle East. It is collected and dried to a powder that is then combined with water to form a gooey, gelatinous substance. This is an essential ingredient of gum paste. It is flavorless, colorless, and odorless. Used in the same fashion as gum arabic, this vegetable gum is also used as an emulsifier, thickener, and stabilizer. It helps prevent crystallization in many processed foods, such as ice cream, candy, jams, and commercial sauces.

knead it in by hand. If any portion of the paste is to be tinted, use water-soluble food coloring and mix it in at this point.

6. Cover the gum paste with plastic wrap and store in an airtight container. It will keep at normal room temperature for several weeks. The paste will harden a little, but it can be reworked with a small amount of additional shortening.

Leaf Croquant yield: approximately 84 candies

When layering the nut paste and making the turns, it is important not to allow the caramel to become too warm, or the paste will simply be absorbed into the sugar instead of remaining a separate thin layer. This can be compared to the process of making laminated doughs — for example, puff pastry: If the basic dough is rolled too thin or the butter is too soft, the butter and dough will blend together instead of forming the desired layer structure, and the result will be less than satisfactory.

If you are going to make another type of candy in addition to Leaf Croquant, Branchli (page 558) would be a good choice. Make the leaf croquant first, then use the scrap pieces of croquant in the chocolate used to coat the branchli instead of making the separate branchli nougat.

12 ounces (340 g) blanched almonds	½ teaspoon (2.5 ml) lemon juice
2 ounces (55 g) powdered sugar	2 ounces (55 g) glucose *or* light corn syrup
1 pound (455 g) granulated sugar	Dark sweet chocolate, tempered (optional)

1. Grind the almonds with the powdered sugar until the mixture forms a paste (see Note).

2. Place the granulated sugar on a sheet of baking paper. Using the palms of your hands, rub the lemon juice into the sugar. Use the dry method to caramelize the sugar mixture (see page 612) until it reaches a light caramel color. Stir in the glucose or light corn syrup. Pour the syrup into the center of a Silpat or oiled marble slab in as rectangular a shape as possible. Pick up the edges of the mat and let the syrup run to shape the sugar into a rectangle measuring 12 × 8 inches (30 × 20 cm). If using a marble slab, use a metal scraper to form the sugar.

3. Evenly distribute one-third of the almond mixture crosswise over two-thirds of the sugar rectangle. Fold over the remaining uncovered portion of sugar so it covers half of the almond mixture, then fold the remaining almond-covered side over the top as if you were making a single turn in preparing a laminated dough (see Figures 14-8 and 14-9, page 788).

4. Turn the caramel slab one-quarter turn so the longer sides are on the right and left. Using a heated rolling pin, roll out the slab to 12 × 8 inches (30 × 20 cm). As you roll, warm the

About Leaf Croquant

Croquant is a French adjective that means "crisp" or "crackling." The German spelling, *krokant*, is more commonly used when referring to a type of chewy nut brittle, such as this recipe. The French also call it *edible nougatine* to differentiate it from the classic, harder nougatine used for showpieces and other decorations. Like nougatine, croquant may be eaten as is, dipped into chocolate, or used as an ingredient in recipes. If the candies are completely coated with chocolate, the interior will become soft and chewy after a few days.

Leaf croquant gets its name from its many thin layers or leaves. The technique used to produce the leaves is rather unusual in candy making; it is more commonly associated with the preparation of laminated doughs. Utilizing this layering and turning process is, however, a clever way to produce a tasty candy with a unique fragile texture, starting with nothing more than a slab of plain caramelized sugar. Unlike toffees, which use cream and/or butter to add flavor to the sugar and feature a chewy or crunchy texture depending on how long the sugar is cooked, leaf croquant gets its buttery flavor from the ground almonds and features a delightful, uncommon crumbly texture.

caramel intermittently as needed by setting the Silpat on a baking sheet and placing it in a hot oven to keep it soft and pliable and to prevent cracking. If you do not have a Silpat, move the caramel sheet from the marble slab to a sheet pan lined with baking paper and place this in the oven.

5. Repeat Steps 3 and 4 twice, so you use the entire amount of almond filling and have given the caramel a total of 3 single turns.

6. Roll out the caramel and fold it in thirds one more time, this time without adding filling. Roll out to 12 × 8 inches (30 × 20 cm).

7. While the caramel is still warm (or after warming it, if necessary), trim 1 long side of the rectangle, then cut the sheet lengthwise into 7 strips, each 1 inch (2.5 cm) wide. Cut each strip into 12 pieces to make 1-inch (2.5-cm) squares. Serve the candies plain or use a 3-pronged dipping fork to dip them into tempered dark chocolate, marking the top of each piece crosswise with the fork. If the candies are not dipped in chocolate, they must be stored in an airtight container to prevent them from becoming soft and sticky.

NOTE: If the almonds are not freshly blanched and therefore dry, you may not be able to obtain a pastelike consistency with any tool other than a professional high-speed food processor. You can either use the mixture as a moist powder or add simple syrup to thin it into a paste.

Marshmallows

yield: I sheet, 12 × 8 inches (30 × 20 cm) and approximately ¾ inch (2 cm) thick, or 75 pieces, I½ × ¾ inch (3.7 × 2 cm) each

Cornstarch

3 tablespoons (18 g) unflavored gelatin powder

1 cup (240 ml) cold water

1 pound (455 g) granulated sugar

2 ounces (55 g) glucose *or* light corn syrup

4 egg whites (½ cup/120 ml)

Sweet dark chocolate, tempered (optional)

I. Prepare a quarter-sheet pan (12 × 8 inches/ 30 × 20 cm) or other suitable pan of approximately the same size by lining the bottom with baking paper and dusting lightly with cornstarch.

About Marshmallows

Marshmallows were originally made from the root of the marshmallow plant, *Althaea officinalis*, a perennial herb that earned its nickname because it is related to the common mallow and grows in marshes throughout Europe and Asia. In the United States, the wild plant can still be found today, mainly along the east coast. The leaves and flowers are used both medicinally and for culinary purposes. As early as 1880 there were recipes for cooking the root to make a spongy sweet candy, but this is rarely done nowadays.

Modern marshmallows are made with egg white, sugar, water, and gelatin. A similar substance, called *pâte de guimauve*, is made in France and flavored with rose water or vanilla.

2. Sprinkle the gelatin over ½ cup (120 ml) of the water and set aside to soften; be sure to pour the water into a bowl wide enough to allow all of the gelatin to become moist.

3. Combine the sugar, glucose or corn syrup, and the remaining ½ cup (120 ml) water in a saucepan. Start cooking the mixture over medium heat.

4. Place the egg whites in a mixer bowl with the whip attachment.

5. Heat the gelatin mixture to dissolve; reserve, but keep warm.

6. When the sugar has reached 230°F (110°C), start whipping the egg whites at high speed. Watch the sugar syrup closely; it will reach 245°F (118°C) very quickly. When the syrup reaches this temperature, remove it from the heat. Lower the speed of the mixer and gradually, but in a steady stream, pour the sugar syrup into the egg whites, taking care to pour it between the whip and the side of the bowl. Add the reserved gelatin in the same way, making certain all of it is added; use a small spatula or your thumb to scrape out the last bit. Return the mixer to high speed. As soon as the meringue has a smooth, light, and fluffy consistency, pour it into the prepared sheet pan and spread to even the top. The sheet should be about ¾ inch (2 cm) thick. Lightly sift cornstarch over the top and set aside to cool completely. You can accelerate the cooling process by placing the sheet in the refrigerator.

7. The marshmallow sheet can be stored at room temperature, covered, for 1 week. Use a knife dipped in hot water to cut the marshmallow sheet away from the sheet pan. Invert the sheet and peel off the paper. Brush away the cornstarch. Then, dipping the knife in hot water again, cut the sheet lengthwise into 5 strips, 1½ inches (3.7 cm) wide. Cut each strip crosswise into 15 pieces. Dip the pieces entirely or partially into tempered chocolate, if desired.

Nougatine yield: about 1 pound 10 ounces (740 g)

Nougatine is made of caramelized sugar and sliced or chopped almonds. Popularized in the 1800s, it has many uses in the pastry shop. It can be served as a candy, cut into small bars and left plain or dipped in chocolate; it can be crushed and added to ice creams or fillings; it can be made into shells for individual dessert presentations; and it can be molded and cut into various shapes to create tall, elaborate, spectacular showpieces known as *pièces montées*. These last are used to hold candies or fruit, as cake pedestals for a towering croquembouche, or alone simply for ornamentation. Unlike other decorative materials, such as pastillage, nougatine not only looks great but is also quite tasty.

Although the recipe itself is quite simple, it takes a lot of practice, proper planning, and fast, precise steps to make a nougatine showpiece or even a dessert mold. Except for molds, no special equipment is needed. Because it contains almonds, nougatine is relatively expensive compared to other sugar formulas used in similar ways. Nougatine is also known as *praline* and as *croquant* (see Leaf Croquant, page 582) or *krokant*. Nougatine should not be confused with nougat (see "About Nougat," page 587), a chewy candy made from sugar, honey, roasted nuts, and egg whites.

Before you begin, assemble the tools and equipment you will need to form the nougatine. Cut your pattern out from heavy paper, such as a cake box. If applicable, lightly oil the mold or the object you are planning to form the nougatine in (or over) with vegetable oil. Clean and oil a heavy rolling pin, preferably one made of metal, a metal spatula, and a chef's knife. Clean, dry, and lightly oil a marble slab, or you may use a Silpat, and one or two flat and even inverted sheet pans.

10 ounces (285 g) blanched almonds, finely chopped or thinly sliced	2 ounces (55 g) unsalted butter (optional)
1 teaspoon (5 ml) lemon juice	Royal Icing (page 680)
1 pound (455 g) granulated sugar	

1. Using a large flour sifter to remove any small broken pieces or powder that could cause the sugar to recrystallize, sift the almonds. Warm them in a low oven, set aside, and keep warm.

2. Rub the lemon juice into the sugar using your hands. Place the mixture in a sugar pan or a heavy saucepan, preferably one made of copper. Cook over low heat, stirring constantly until all of the sugar has melted and is light golden.

3. Stir in the almonds and continue stirring until the mixture turns a little darker, about 1 to 2 minutes. Stir in the butter, if using, and continue to stir until the butter is incorporated.

4. Quickly pour the nougatine onto the prepared marble slab or a Silpat. Let it cool for a few seconds, then flip it over with the spatula so it will cool evenly and not become any darker. As soon as you can, roll the nougatine to about ⅛ inch (3 mm) thick; for the best appearance and flexibility, it should never be more than ¼ inch (6 mm) thick.

5. Transfer the nougatine to the sheet pan(s). To keep the sheet warm and malleable, place it in front of a 250°F (122°C) oven with the door open. The work area should be as close to the oven as possible.

6. Place your pattern on top and quickly cut out shapes with the oiled chef's knife. Form the pieces, if required. Let cool, then glue the pieces together with royal icing or sugar cooked to the hard-crack stage, 310°F (155°C).

7. If the nougatine becomes too hard to work with at any time during rolling, cutting, or shaping, place it on the sheet pan inside the oven until it is soft and workable again. Be careful not to overheat the nougatine and darken it, or you might have several different shades in your finished showpiece, which would not look good.

8. To reuse scrap pieces, place them on top of one another and soften in the oven, then roll out the sheet again. Alternatively, store the scraps in airtight containers and use as candy or for Nougatine Crunch (instructions follow).

CHEF'S TIP
Nougatine can be made without butter, but butter gives it extra shine and a better flavor and texture if it is to be eaten.

NOUGATINE CRUNCH

1. Using a heavy dowel or rolling pin, crush cooled nougatine into currant-size pieces.

2. Store in airtight containers. If the stored nougatine crunch becomes soft and sticky, dry it in a low oven for a few minutes, then recrush it to separate the pieces.

Nougat Montélimar

The following two recipes use different cooking techniques but produce a similar result. Nougat Montélimar II has a more predominant honey flavor and a darker color. I prefer Nougat Montélimar I, in which the moisture in the meringue is cooked out on top of the stove. This method produces a more attractive, lighter color in the finished candy, though it does require more labor. Because the texture of the finished candy is determined by the temperature to which you boil the sugar (see "About Nougat"), it is important to be precise in this step. If the sugar is overcooked, the candy will be too hard, making it unpleasant to eat. If not cooked long enough, the nougat will be so soft it cannot be cut into pieces.

Nougat Montélimar I yield: approximately 80 candies

Powdered sugar

5 ounces (140 g) whole blanched almonds, lightly toasted

5 ounces (140 g) whole toasted hazelnuts, skins removed

3 ounces (85 g) pistachios, skins removed, lightly dried

5 ounces (140 g) candied red cherries, coarsely chopped

4 egg whites (½ cup/120 ml)

¾ cup (180 ml) or 9 ounces (255 g) honey

12 ounces (340 g) granulated sugar

12 ounces (340 g) glucose *or* light corn syrup

½ cup (120 ml) water

Cocoa butter, melted

Sweet dark chocolate, tempered

1. Dust a small area of a marble slab or table with powdered sugar.

2. Combine the almonds, hazelnuts, pistachios, and cherries. Cover and set aside in a warm place, such as a very low oven.

3. Whip the egg whites for a few seconds, just until foamy. Bring the honey to a boil; then, with the mixer at low speed, gradually pour it into the egg whites in a steady stream. Increase to high speed and continue whipping until the mixture has cooled and formed stiff peaks. Set aside.

4. Take the usual precautions for sugar boiling (see page 575) and boil the sugar, glucose or corn syrup, and water to 295°F (146°C). Immediately pour the hot syrup into the egg white mixture in a slow steady stream, stirring constantly with a whisk.

5. Return the mixture to the saucepan and continue to cook over medium heat for about 10 minutes longer, stirring rapidly. Test to see if the mixture has cooked long enough by dropping a small piece into cold water. It should be quite firm.

6. Stir in the reserved warm nuts and cherries. Pour the nougat mixture onto the prepared marble surface. Using a rolling pin dusted lightly with powdered sugar, roll and form the mixture into a rectangle approximately 6 × 8 inches (15 × 20 cm) and ¾ inch (2 cm) thick. Let cool.

7. Brush away the excess powdered sugar from the top and bottom of the nougat sheet. Cut lengthwise into 4 strips, 1½ inches (3.7 cm) wide. Cut each strip crosswise into slices ⅜ inch (9 mm) thick; use a serrated knife with a sawing motion if the nougat sticks to a chef's knife.

8. Brush 1 cut side of each piece with a thin film of hot cocoa butter.

9. Use a 3-pronged dipping fork to dip the bottom and sides into melted dark chocolate, leaving the cocoa butter side exposed on the top.

Nougat Montélimar II yield: approximately 150 candies

2 ounces (55 g) cocoa butter, melted, plus more for coating

8 ounces (225 g) whole almonds

4 ounces (115 g) hazelnuts, toasted and skins removed

4 ounces (115 g) pistachios, blanched and skins removed

3 ounces (85 g) Candied Orange Peel (page 756), diced

3 ounces (85 g) candied cherries

1 pound (455 g) granulated sugar

¼ cup (60 ml) or 3 ounces (85 g) glucose *or* light corn syrup

¾ cup (180 ml) water

1 cup (240 ml) or 12 ounces (340 g) honey

3 egg whites (⅓ cup/80 ml)

Powdered sugar

Sweet dark chocolate, tempered

1. Combine 2 ounces (55 g) of the cocoa butter and the almonds, hazelnuts, pistachios, candied orange peel, and candied cherries. Reserve in a warm place, such as a very low oven.

2. Take the usual precautions for boiling sugar (see page 575). Reserve 2 ounces (55 g) of the granulated sugar and start boiling the remaining sugar with the glucose or corn syrup and the water. At the same time, in a separate pan, bring the honey to a quick boil. When the sugar syrup reaches 310°F (155°C), add the boiled honey and continue to cook until the temperature

About Nougat

Nougat is a confection made from honey and/or sugar, plus roasted nuts and, sometimes, candied fruit. The texture is generally chewy, although some versions are hard and the candy hardens as it ages. The firmness of the finished product is also influenced by the degree to which the honey or sugar syrup is cooked; higher temperatures make for harder candies. White nougat, such as Nougat Montélimar, is made with beaten egg whites, which give it a softer texture. Brown nougats contain caramelized sugar. The cooked mixture is poured into shallow pans lined with rice paper; in some old-fashioned recipes, unleavened dough is specified (this was not consumed with the candy). The top of the mixture is weighted to compact the finished candy. In the two recipes given here, the cooked mixtures are heavy enough to roll out as opposed to being poured into a pan and set up under a weight. Nougat is popular in Italy, where it has been made since the Roman Empire, and in southern France. Nougat Montélimar takes its name from the town of that name in Provence. This is the most widely known form of nougat; the word *Montélimar* is sometimes used as a generic term for any nougat. Genuine nougat Montélimar, by French standards, must contain 30 percent nutmeats, of which 28 percent must be almonds and the remaining 2 percent pistachios. The word *nougat* comes from the Old Provençal *noga*, which in turn came from the Latin *nux*, both terms for "nut," most often "walnut." *Torrone* and *turrón* are, respectively, the Italian and Spanish words for nougat.

returns to 307°F (153°C). Immediately plunge the bottom of the pan into cold water for a few seconds to stop the cooking and prevent the temperature from rising further.

3. Whip the egg whites with the reserved 2 ounces (55 g) sugar until foamy. Gradually pour the hot sugar syrup into the egg whites in a slow, steady stream, whipping constantly. Whip at high speed for a few minutes longer. Stir in the reserved warm fruit and nut mixture.

4. Dust a small area of a worktable with powdered sugar. Roll and form the nougat on top of the table, making a rectangle approximately 8 × 12 inches (20 × 30 cm) and ¾ inch (2 cm) thick. Dust with more powdered sugar as needed to prevent sticking. Let cool.

5. Brush off excess sugar. Using a serrated knife in a sawing motion, trim 1 long side to make it even, and cut the nougat lengthwise into 5 strips, 1½ inches (3.7 cm) wide. Cut each strip across into slices ⅜ inch (9 mm) thick. If the nougat is too soft and sticky to make clean cuts, place it in the refrigerator to become firm before you slice it.

6. Brush 1 cut side of each piece with a thin film of hot cocoa butter. Use a 3-pronged dipping fork to dip the bottom and sides into melted dark chocolate, leaving the cocoa butter side exposed on the top.

Pastillage yield: 5 pound 8 ounces (2 kg 500 g)

Pastillage is also known as *gum paste,* from the time when a vegetable gum such as gum tragacanth (see page 582) was used in place of gelatin. This sugar paste is perfectly suited for making show and display pieces and other decorative items. Some artists prefer pastillage over marzipan as a canvas for cocoa paintings. Pastillage can be molded around almost any object and cut or pressed into many shapes, and it is inexpensive to produce.

Theoretically, pastillage is edible, but it is rarely intended to be — nor should it be — eaten when it is dry. It is as hard and brittle as glass, and I really do not recommend you try it even if you have a ravenous appetite, strong teeth, and good insurance.

Pastillage is usually left pure white, but it can be colored before it is rolled out and formed, or it can be painted or sprayed after it is dry. As always when using colors on or in food, take care to keep them to soft pastel shades. The same precautions that must be taken when making marzipan apply to working with pastillage as well to preserve its white color. Use a stainless steel bowl for mixing; never use a bowl made of a corrosive, such as aluminum, which will turn the paste gray. Always wash and dry the rolling pin (see Chef's Tip) and work surface thoroughly — try to use marble, if possible, which will give the rolled paste the smooth, even surface essential for cocoa painting — and make certain your hands are clean before touching the paste.

Pastillage dries and forms a crust almost immediately if left exposed, so assemble everything you will require ahead of time and keep the unused portion of the paste covered with a wet towel while you work. Have your templates cut out and ready, and be sure to use cardboard thick enough to allow you to quickly and precisely cut around the patterns with a thin, pointed, sharp knife. If the pastillage is to be molded, dust the forms or the object you are shaping it around with cornstarch to keep it from sticking. Make a plan for cutting the sheet of pastillage before you roll it out; you will not have time to stop and think once it is rolled. Try to use as much of each rolled sheet as possible, as the scrap pieces can rarely be softened and reused.

Use a very small amount of cornstarch to keep the pastillage from sticking. Too much will cause the surface to dry rapidly and form a crust; the cornstarch draws moisture out of the paste, which will then crack when it is shaped. For attractive, elegant pieces, roll it out to $^1/_8$ inch (3 mm) thick. If rolled too thick, pastillage looks clumsy and amateurish. Cut out the desired shapes, then carefully transfer the cutouts to an even surface or to the mold, if you are using one. As soon as the pieces are partially dry and can be handled, turn them over or remove them from the molds to allow the bottom to dry. Continue to turn them from time to time so they dry evenly (the moisture tends to sink to the bottom). This is especially important in large, flat pieces, which have a tendency to curl if not turned properly. Once dry, the pieces can be filed and sanded to help them fit together better and to smooth any sharp edges.

Pastillage is assembled with royal icing as glue. Take care not to use too much, as none will be absorbed and the excess will squeeze out when the pieces are pressed together, spoiling the final appearance. Because royal icing does not set up quickly after it is applied (as chocolate and boiled sugar do), the pieces must be supported for several hours. Use any object that fits to hold a particular shape or angle. It can take several days to assemble a larger design. Once completely dry, if it is stored, covered, in a dry place, the finished showpiece will keep forever.

This is intentionally a fairly small recipe, but as the paste is so quick and easy to make and does not stay workable very long, you might even consider measuring several half-batches and making each up as you use the previous one.

1 ounce (30 g) unflavored gelatin powder	10 ounces (285 g) cornstarch
1¼ cups (300 ml) cold water	1 teaspoon (2 g) cream of tartar
4 pound 3 ounces (1 kg 905 g) powdered sugar	

1. Sprinkle the gelatin over the cold water and set aside to soften.

2. Sift together the sugar, cornstarch, and cream of tartar and place in a stainless steel mixer bowl. Place the gelatin mixture over a bain-marie and heat until dissolved. Do not overheat. Gradually, while mixing on low speed with the dough hook, add the gelatin mixture to the sugar mixture.

3. Continue mixing, scraping down the sides occasionally, until you have a smooth, elastic paste (it will stick to the bottom of the bowl). Cover the paste with a wet towel immediately.

NOTE: Do not make more pastillage than you can use within 1 hour, and do not make it until you are ready to begin working with it. If the pastillage becomes too firm, you can soften it, to some degree, by kneading it a little longer in the mixer; the friction will warm both the paste and the gelatin.

CHEF'S TIP
A PVC pipe, 16 inches (40 cm) long and 2 to 3 inches (5 to 7.5 cm) in diameter, makes an excellent tool for rolling out pastillage. Stainless steel rolling pins are great as well, but fairly expensive. The advantage of either the pipe or the steel pin over a conventional wooden pin is that the surface is completely smooth, with no nicks or scratches to mar the surface of the pastillage sheet.

PASTILLAGE DISPLAY STAND FOR A COCOA PAINTING SHOWPIECE

yield: 1 stand, 7³/₄ inches (19 cm) tall × 4¹/₂ inches (11.2 cm) wide

¹/₂ recipe Pastillage (page 588)   Royal Icing (page 680)

1. Trace the drawing shown in Figure 11-2 and cut the template out of sturdy cardboard. The template as shown is the correct size to make a stand with the dimensions specified in the

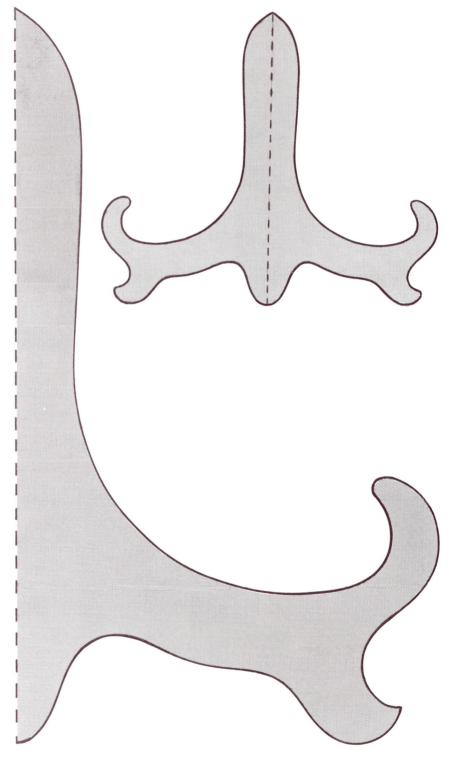

FIGURE 11-2 The template used to make a pastillage display stand

yield; however, the drawing may be enlarged or reduced as desired. The smaller drawing shows how the stand will look when the two sides are joined.

2. Following the directions for working with pastillage, roll out the paste to ⅛ inch (3 mm) thick. Place the template on top of the paste and cut out the shape. Invert the template and cut out a second piece to produce both a left and a right side.

3. Let the pieces dry and then sand the edges smooth.

4. Fit the 2 sides together at the correct angle to hold your showpiece. The angle required will depend on the size of your showpiece. Glue the long edges together by piping royal icing from top to bottom where they meet. Allow the stand to dry overnight. You may need to support the sides of the stand as it dries; if necessary, place a box or another object against each outside edge.

Pâte de Fruit: Lemon, Raspberry, and Strawberry Jellies

yield: 64 pieces, each 1 inch (2.5 cm) square

Pâte de fruit is a French confection with a pleasant, chewy, jellylike consistency. It contains few ingredients, just pureed fruit and/or fruit juice and sugar. The mixture is cooked, poured into a square mold, and left to set and jell. The candy becomes firm due to the natural pectin in the fruit in combination with the cooked sugar. The set mixture is cut into small squares that are throroughly coated with granulated sugar; the coating adds a nice crunch and makes it possible to handle the candy without it being sticky. Pâte de fruit is often offered at the end of a meal together with other small confections. The refreshing fruit flavors and pretty colors provide a nice contrast to the more typical, rich chocolate and cream candies.

9 ounces (255 g) cooked apple puree

9 ounces (255 g) peeled and pitted apricots, fresh or canned

1 pound 2 ounces (510 g) granulated sugar

5 ounces (140 g) fresh raspberries or hulled and sliced strawberries *or* 3 tablespoons (45 ml) lemon juice

Granulated sugar

1. Cover a cardboard cake round, 10 inches (25 cm) in diameter, with plastic wrap. Place the cardboard in the oven for a few seconds to shrink and tighten the plastic. Set a square frame, 8 × 8 inches (20 × 20 cm), on top of the plastic and tape around the base of the frame on the outside to secure the frame and prevent leakage (see Chef's Tip).

2. Place the apple puree, apricots, and sugar in a saucepan. Add the raspberries, strawberries, or lemon juice. Using an immersion blender, process the mixture until smooth. Cook over medium heat until thick, stirring constantly.

3. To test the mixture to see if it is thick enough, dip a whisk in the fruit and hold it horizontally. The fruit mixture will stay on the whisk and form small balls if it is thick enough. If it runs back into the pan, continue cooking.

4. Pour the cooked fruit into the prepared frame. Let the

CHEF'S TIP

If you do not have an 8-inch (20-cm) square frame or another suitable mold, you can prepare a frame in the following way: Cut 2 strips of thick corrugated cardboard, 1 × 16 inches (2.5 × 40 cm). Cut halfway through across each piece in the center. Bend the pieces at a 90-degree angle and place them on the prepared cardboard to make a square, taping the free ends together.

mixture cool and set at room temperature for at least 3 hours. If the mixture is still soft after cooling, cook and cool again.

5. Run a knife around the inside of the frame, then remove it. Invert the fruit square onto a sheet of baking paper heavily coated with sugar. Coat the top heavily with sugar.

6. Using a knife dipped into hot water, cut the fruit into strips 1 inch (2.5 cm) wide, then cut each strip crosswise to make 1-inch (2.5-cm) squares. Coat each piece with granulated sugar, covering all sides. Store at room temperature; if refrigerated, the sugar will melt.

Rolled Fondant

yield: 2 pounds 6 ounces (1 kg 80 g) or enough to cover 3 cakes, 10 inches (25 cm) in diameter, or 1 cake, 12 inches (30 cm) in diameter, plus 1 cake, 4 inches (10 cm) in diameter

Rolled fondant actually has more in common with Pastillage (page 588) than it does with its namesake, Fondant (page 578), which is used as a glaze or icing. Rolled fondant is essentially pastillage made with only one-third of the gelatin and about half as much sugar. It is primarily used to cover wedding cakes — and for the customer who wants a true white wedding cake, nothing is whiter than fondant. Both buttercream that is made with butter (as it should be) and marzipan always have an ivory tint. Most professional chefs purchase rolled fondant ready made; while this makes sense for most operations, you will see here that not much is involved in making it yourself.

Because this recipe produces a very soft paste, rolled fondant must be prepared 1 day ahead of time to allow the gelatin to slowly thicken the mixture. A relatively small amount of gelatin is used so the paste will thicken only to a point rather than setting up completely. The gelatin also develops an elastic consistency.

1 tablespoon (9 g) unflavored gelatin powder	1½ tablespoons (22 ml) glycerin (optional; see Note)
½ cup (120 ml) water	2 pounds (910 g) powdered sugar
4 ounces (115 g) light corn syrup	Vegetable shortening

1. Sprinkle the gelatin over the water, set aside until soft, then heat to dissolve. Remove from the heat and add the corn syrup and glycerin, if used.

2. Add the gelatin mixture to the powdered sugar and knead until fully incorporated; the mixture will be fairly soft.

3. Roll the mixture into a log. Coat the log with vegetable shortening. Wrap the coated log in plastic wrap. Let stand overnight at room temperature; the fondant will become tighter and firmer.

4. Using powdered sugar to prevent sticking, roll out the fondant to ⅛ to ¼ inch (3 to 6 mm) thick. Roll up the sheet on a dowel and unroll over a cake, smoothing it into place with your hands. Trim around the base as needed.

NOTE: The glycerin is used to prevent the fondant from becoming too hard when it has dried. If you do not have glycerin on hand, it may be omitted. Instead, increase the light corn syrup by 2 ounces (55 g) and the powdered sugar by 3 to 4 ounces (85 to 115 g).

Spun Sugar yield: variable (Color Photo 25)

Spun sugar is traditionally used to decorate ice cream desserts, but it can be used to dress up many others as well. It looks showy but is actually easy to make. The mass of thin, hairlike sugar threads is also used to decorate *pièces montées*, such as Croquembouche. Gâteau Saint-Honoré is also decorated with spun sugar on some occasions.

Unless the weather is dry, it is best to make spun sugar immediately before serving. Moisture is gradually absorbed by the thin threads, which become sticky and eventually dissolve. When spun sugar is used as part of a plate presentation, do not allow it to come in contact with a sauce, or it will melt.

As with any sugarwork, you should prepare everything you will need before you begin to boil the sugar. Clean, dry, and lightly oil 2 wooden or metal dowels. Place them, parallel, about 18 inches (45 cm) apart, extending over the edge of the table. Place a heavy cutting board on top at the back to hold them in place. Place a couple of sheet pans on the floor beneath the dowels to catch drips. Cut the end off a metal whisk and spread the wires apart slightly (Figure 11-3; see Chef's Tip). Have an airtight container handy in which to place the sugar as it is ready. If you are adding color, keep in mind that the color will appear much lighter after the sugar is spun into thin threads, so a darker shade than usual is called for here.

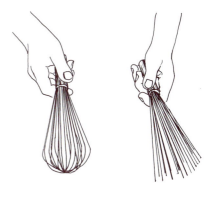

FIGURE 11-3 **A metal whisk before and after removing the round end and spreading the wires apart slightly to use in making spun sugar**

Boiled Sugar Basic Recipe (page 575)   **Food coloring (optional)**

1. Following the boiled sugar basic recipe but omitting the tartaric acid, boil the syrup to 310°F (155°C), the hard-crack stage, adding the coloring at 265°F (130°C), if using. Immediately remove from the heat and plunge the bottom of the pan into cold water for a few seconds to stop the cooking process. Take the pan out of the water, dry the sides and the bottom of the pan, and let the syrup stand until slightly thickened before you start to spin to prevent too many drops falling off the whisk during the spinning process. Do not stir the sugar.

2. Dip the cut whisk about ½ inch (1.2 cm) into the sugar. Gently shake off excess by moving the whisk up and down just above the surface of the sugar syrup. Do not hold the whisk up too high when you do this, or the sugar drops will cool too much as they fall back into the pan, which can cause the sugar to recrystallize.

3. Spin the sugar by flicking the whisk rapidly back and forth between the 2 dowels (Figure 11-4). Continue dipping and spinning the sugar until a reasonable amount has accumulated on the dowels.

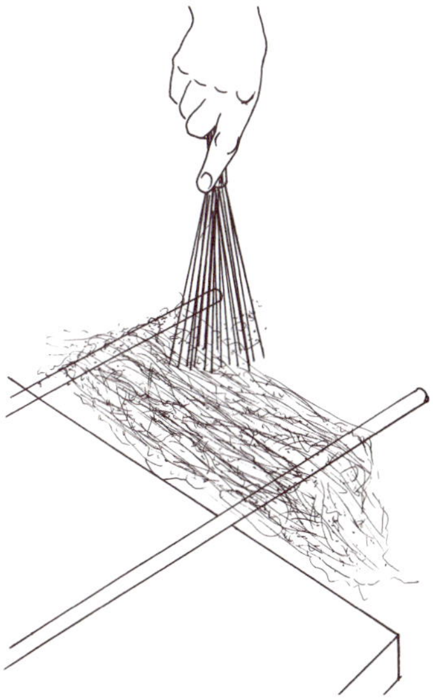

4. Gather the sugar threads off the dowels and place in an airtight

FIGURE 11-4 **Making spun sugar by flicking the hot syrup back and forth between the dowels extended over the edge of a table**

container. Continue spinning the remaining sugar. Sugar will start to accumulate on the whisk and glue the wires together. Remove it by striking the whisk sharply against the inside edge of a sink or use the method in the Chef's Tip. If the syrup cools too much, warm it over low heat, stirring constantly to prevent the sugar from becoming any darker than necessary.

NOTE 1: It is impossible to predict a precise yield when spinning sugar. On a rainy or humid day, you will get a much smaller volume. Also, depending on how many times you have to reheat the sugar, you may not be able to use all of the syrup.

NOTE 2: If you spin the sugar in a dry place, you can store it for up to 2 days in an airtight container lined with a dehumidifying agent and covered with a sheet of foil.

VARIATION

CARAMELIZED SPUN SUGAR

Follow the preceding directions, cooking the sugar until it is golden brown, approximately 320°F (160°C). Remember that the color will appear lighter after the sugar is spun. Do not add food coloring.

Sugar Crystals for Decoration yield: variable

This is a recipe — actually, a procedure — I often use to demonstrate to my students how easy it is for sugar crystals to form whenever a foreign material is introduced to sugar syrup. In most cases, this is the opposite of what we want when boiling sugar; we usually take precautions to *prevent* recrystallization. When it is done intentionally, as in this recipe, it is known as *controlled recrystallization*. Other examples of recipes involving controlled recrystallization are Fondant (page 578), toffees and brittles, and Sugar-Coated Nuts (page 627). In addition to being an amusing experiment, the sugar crystals can be made into interesting cubes for use in decorating.

To produce sugar crystals, you will need clean, sterilized canning jars with clean sterilized lids that have one or more small holes punched through the top, and wooden skewers or thick string. If you use thick string, such as trussing string, soak it in simple syrup one day ahead, then allow it to dry before you proceed. Because we are trying to encourage the formation of crystals, no glucose, corn syrup, or tartaric acid is used. The jars are sterilized so we can assume no impurities are present other than those we deliberately introduce.

| 2 pounds (910 g) granulated sugar | Marzipan or almond paste |
| 1½ cups (360 ml) water | |

1. Place the sugar and water in a heavy saucepan. Stir to combine, bring to a boil, and let boil for 1 minute. Set aside until cooled to just slightly above room temperature.

2. Pour the syrup into 2 small canning jars, filling them at least two-thirds full. Punch at least 1 small hole in the lids, as discussed above.

3. Insert a wooden skewer or heavy string through each hole in the lids. Attach a tiny piece of almond paste or marzipan about the size of a pin head to the bottom end of each skewer or string. Attach the lids to the jars. Use a tiny piece of marzipan or almond paste to secure a skewer or string on top of each lid so it is suspended in the syrup without touching the bottom or sides of the jar. If you use more than 1 skewer or string per jar, they must not touch one another.

4. Set aside overnight. The crystals should be visible on the skewers or strings the next day, and they will continue to grow. The container must not be disturbed or only small crystals will grow. To create larger crystals, use a skewer or string from a previous batch and immerse it in fresh sugar syrup.

5. Once the crystals have reached the desired size, they may be colored with an airbrush.

VARIATION
SUGAR CRYSTAL SHEETS

To make a large, flat bed of sugar crystals — for a landscape as part of a showpiece, for example — pour the syrup into a sterilized hotel pan and, after it cools, lightly sprinkle coarse sugar over the surface to act as seeds.

Another way to form large sugar crystals is to place blown sugar pieces in a bath of sugar syrup; the crystals will form over the piece in a furry growth.

Sugar Sticks yield: variable (Color Photos 79 and 87)

Sugar sticks are spaghetti-thin strings of sugar that can be used to garnish desserts in a number of ways. You can use the decorations as is or warm them and bend them into a graceful, curved shape. Sugar sticks, straight or curved, look great simply placed atop, leaning against, or partially inserted into a dessert, but the most eye-catching result comes from bending the soft sugar and looping it through small holes in a tuile paste or Florentina decoration. To accomplish this you must work quickly, or the fragile, thin sticks will break as you bend them through the holes. This type of ornament is always intriguing to guests who know even a little bit about cooking; they will ponder your creation, wondering how you managed to weave the brittle sugar through the openings.

As you pipe out the sugar lines, make sure they are of uniform thickness throughout. If they are not, if and when you later warm the sticks to soften and bend them, they will not soften evenly and you will be unable to make elegant curves.

Sugar sticks can also be made by pulling cooked sugar. Use a piece of cooked sugar prepared and aerated as for Pulled Sugar (page 605). Soften the sugar to the proper consistency, then pull straight thin sticks away from the main mass. These can be left straight, curved right away while still soft, or softened later to shape as desired.

1 pound (455 g) granulated sugar	3½ ounces (100 g) glucose *or* light corn syrup
¾ cup (180 ml) water	Food coloring (optional)

1. Combine the sugar and water in a heavy saucepan. Heat and allow the syrup to boil for a few seconds to ensure all of the sugar has melted. Add the glucose or corn syrup and cook the syrup until it reaches 260°F (127°C), brushing down the sides of the pan from time to time to prevent sugar crystals from forming.

2. If you are using food coloring, add it at this point, then continue cooking the syrup to 310°F (155°C). For caramelized sugar sticks, continue cooking the syrup to approximately 320°F (160°C) or just until you see the first hint of light brown color.

3. Immediately plunge the bottom of the pan into a bowl of cold water to stop the sugar from cooking. Leave the pan in the water for 10 seconds, remove it, dry the bottom and sides, and set it aside.

4. Have ready a Silpat or lightly oiled sheet of baking paper, a pair of clean scissors, a dry towel, a pastry bag made from a double thickness of baking paper for safety, and a blowtorch.

5. When the sugar has cooled to a fairly thick consistency (approximately as thick as molasses), pour a little more than 1 cup (240 ml) into the prepared paper pastry bag. Close the top securely and cover the top of the bag with a towel to protect your hands from the heat as you work. Cut a small opening in the bag.

6. Pipe the sugar syrup over the Silpat or oiled paper, moving left to right and right to left in one continuous line, forming straight lines crosswise. The lines should be about 15 inches (37.5 cm) long. To separate the sticks, heat a knife and melt through the curved edges that connect the lines. Discard the trimmings.

7. Store the sticks in an airtight container with a desiccant to keep them from softening.

8. To curve the sticks, place a sheet pan topped with a Silpat in the oven until it is fairly hot (you will have to experiment a bit to determine just how hot you need it). Take the pan and mat out of the oven and place as many sugar sticks as you want to bend on top of the hot mat; wait just long enough for them to soften enough to pick up and shape as desired. If the pan is too hot or if the sticks are left too long, they will fall apart in your hands as you try to bend them. On the other hand, if you attempt to shape them before they are warm enough (while the sugar is brittle), the sticks will break rather than bend. This technique requires practice and a bit of trial and error before you get the feel of it.

Rock Sugar   yield: I piece of decorative sugar, approximately 8 × 6 inches (10 × 15 cm)

Rock sugar is named for its porous, rough, rocklike appearance. It adds an unusual decorative touch to showpieces. Once it has hardened, it can be broken into irregular chunks or cut into precise shapes with a serrated knife. It is amazing to see how the white mass of sugar rises up in the pan — resembling milk about to boil over — once the royal icing is incorporated. The eruption (swelling) and recrystallization occur as a reaction to quickly beating in the egg white and sugar in the icing. Rock sugar, unlike other types of sugar, withstands moisture well. It is quite easy to make once you get the timing down.

1 cup (240 ml) water	Food coloring (optional; see Chef's Tip)
2 pounds (910 g) granulated sugar	2 tablespoons (30 ml) firm Royal Icing (page 680; see Note)

1. Preheat the oven to 250°F (122°C). Line the inside of a bowl, about 8 inches (20 cm) in diameter, with aluminum foil. Have a large absolutely clean spoon available.

2. Combine the water and sugar in a large copper or other heavy saucepan; the sugar mixture will swell to double in size, so the pan must be large enough to accommodate it. Stir over high heat until all of the sugar has dissolved and the mixture starts to boil. Take the usual precautions for boiling sugar: Remove any scum that accumulates on the surface, brush the sides of the pan clean of sugar crystals, and partially cover the pan, then turn the heat to medium and boil for a few minutes. Uncover and place a sugar thermometer in the syrup. If using, add food coloring when the sugar reaches 255°F (124°C).

3. Continue boiling to 285°F (141°C). Remove the pan from the heat and quickly stir in the royal icing, mixing it in well. Do not overwork the mixture; you may have to try a few times to get the right feel here, so don't be discouraged if it does not work the first time.

4. Stop stirring. The sugar will rise to almost double its original volume, fall slowly, then start to rise again. If it fails to rise again, you can help it along by stirring rapidly for 1 or 2 seconds. After the second rising, quickly pour the sugar into the prepared bowl. The sugar will continue to increase in size. Immediately place the bowl in the oven for 10 minutes to harden the sugar and prevent it from falling again. Set the sugar aside, still in the bowl, uncovered in a dry place for about 8 hours.

5. Remove the rock sugar from the bowl. Break or cut it with a serrated knife into pieces suitable for your decoration.

NOTE: For a lighter and slightly more crumbly rock sugar, add a bit more royal icing.

CHEF'S TIP
Instead of adding food coloring to rock sugar as it is cooking, you can spray colors on with a syringe or airbrush to achieve special effects. This is best done once the pieces are placed on the showpiece. See "Spraying Color on Sugar Pieces" (page 604).

Cast Sugar (Color Photo 98)

For the average pastry chef, casting is probably the easiest way of making spectacular showpieces from sugar, as it does not demand the years of practice and experience that pulled and to a greater extent blown sugar do. Casting sugar can be a relatively inexpensive occasional recreation, but you do need to have the basics down on how to boil and handle sugar. As for most artwork, you need a good eye for color and proportions, you should be neat and precise, and yes, it does take a steady hand to pour the sugar, especially for small, narrow shapes.

If you do not have much experience, start by casting small, simple figures, such as the rooster, baker, or peasant girl (Figures 11-6, 11-7, and 11-8). These templates can be enlarged to make the figures any size you like. The baker is designed to hold a tray in his hand as part of the display. You might want to make him 12 inches (30 cm) tall to hold a small tray with a few candies on it as a buffet showpiece, or as large as 3 feet (90 cm) tall to place in the shop window holding a large serving platter. Make him a tray by casting a small, thin oval or circle of sugar whose diameter is in proportion to the size of the figure; attach it later as directed, placing it flat on his hand. This can be the actual tray for the small figure, or you can place a real serving tray on top of the sugar circle on the larger figure if you make the circle large enough to support it.

Because you will need so much sugar and must boil it in so many different batches (especially for large, complicated castings), it is a good idea to calculate about how much you will need and then make a large quantity of basic sugar solution. It is better to make too much than not enough; leftover syrup can be stored in a sealed jar for many weeks. To prevent fingerprints, wear food handling gloves whenever you touch the cast pieces.

1. Follow the recipe and instructions for Boiled Sugar Basic Recipe (page 575) but omit the tartaric acid solution (see Note 1). Let the sugar boil gently for a few seconds before adding the glucose or corn syrup to make certain all of the sugar crystals have dissolved. Add the glucose or corn syrup. After the syrup returns to a boil, boil 1 minute, brushing down the sides of the pan. Remove from the heat.

2. As you prepare to cast each section in various colors, measure off the amount of sugar needed and continue boiling the smaller amount to the proper temperature. When casting a small figure, it is best to pour the various parts or sections in one color only, plain or white, then apply the color with a brush or sprayer, as it is difficult to boil a small amount of sugar accurately.

3. Lightly grease a marble slab or table with vegetable oil. Treat the inside of your individual forms or molds in the same way and wipe off excess with a cloth. Arrange the forms on the oiled marble, or use a Silpat, if you have one large enough to hold the forms. If any of the forms do not lie flush, weigh them down, or the sugar will leak out. You can also place aluminum foil on top of any flat surface and arrange the forms, metal or plastilina, on this. Tape the corners down to secure the foil. The obvious advantage to using foil or a Silpat is that you do not need a marble surface, and the cast pieces can be easily moved when cool. The back of the cast sugar will also be free from oil, as it is not necessary to grease the foil or mat. However, when using foil, the back of the sugar will have an uneven surface, so do not use it when casting clear sugar (as opposed to opaque shades). The foil is easily peeled off once the sugar has hardened (see Note 2).

4. Boil the measured amount of sugar to 265°F (130°C) and add food coloring or whitening, if using. Continue boiling until the sugar reaches 305°F (152°C). Immediately remove from the heat and plunge the bottom of the pan into cold water for a few seconds. Wipe the bottom of the pan dry.

5. As soon as bubbles stop appearing on the top, pour the sugar into the molds in a thin, steady stream (Figure 11-5); use a metal scraper to catch any drops as you move from one mold to the next. Vary the thickness of the sugar in proportion to the size of the piece. For a figure 12 inches (30 cm) tall, pour the sugar to ¼ inch (6 mm) thick; for a figure 3 feet high (90 cm), cast the sugar to ¾ inch (2 cm) thick.

6. If you are making a mirror image (such as the chickens in Figure 11-8) and using forms made of metal strips, wait a few seconds after the sugar is poured to allow the sugar closest to the form to harden a little. Tap the metal strip lightly with the back of a knife and remove the form. Invert the form and place it in another area on the marble.

FIGURE 11-5 Pouring boiled sugar into a metal mold for cast sugar

Then cast a second chicken, this one facing in the opposite direction. If the sugar in the pan starts to cool and thicken before you are finished, set it back over medium heat, stirring constantly to heat the sugar evenly. If any of the pieces are to be marked or outlined — for example, marking vertical lines in the baker's hat — do this as soon as a skin has formed on the top.

7. Loosen the cast pieces from the marble by carefully sliding the blade of a metal spatula underneath after they have cooled but before they harden completely. Remember that disturbing them too soon will leave unsightly wrinkles.

FIGURE 11-6 The template for a cast sugar rooster

FIGURE 11-7 The template for a cast sugar baker; the outstretched arm is designed to hold a tray

FIGURE 11-8 The template for a cast sugar peasant girl

8. When joining pieces by casting one next to the other, as in the neck and tail of the rooster, first burn off the connecting edges with a red-hot knife to remove any oil, which would prevent the pieces from adhering. Heat the tip of an old knife over a Bunsen burner until it is red-hot. Quickly wipe the knife on a wet towel to cool it slightly, then move it back and forth over the adhesion points. The larger you make the figures, the more important this procedure is. Make sure the knife is hot enough to melt the sugar but not so hot that it caramelizes, which will cause ugly stains.

9. When casting a small shape inside a large piece, cast the larger piece first so the heat of the larger piece will not soften and disturb the shape of the smaller one.

10. Before assembling the figures, first spray any pieces that are to be colored (see "Spraying Color on Sugar Pieces," page 604). If individual pieces are to be assembled on top of each other, burn off any oil from the back of the pieces to be glued. This can give the baker, for example, a more three-dimensional look. The baker's head, shoes, and sleeve (but not his hand) can be cast separately and pasted on top of the existing figure (you would still cast the entire figure first) to make it look as if his hand is coming out of his jacket.

11. To paste the pieces together, reheat some of the sugar left over from casting. Let it start to thicken slightly before using, do not use too much, and do not use it too hot, or you can soften the pieces you are gluing. Always assemble the pieces flat on the table to ensure the parts stay in the position you want until the sugar is cold.

12. Cast a wedge-shaped back support, as well as a base, for any figure to be displayed vertically. Make these pieces in proportion to the size of the figure and in the same thickness. Shape the back support so 1 long side of the wedge (the side attached to the figure) and the bottom are at right angles to ensure the figure stands straight. Once the base and back support have been cast and allowed to harden, carefully move the figure to the edge of the table and burn the bottom edge, where the base will go.

13. Carefully raise the figure (depending on the size, you may need an assistant to finish the assembly) and burn the back where the back support will attach. Attach the base with the sugarglue, making certain the figure is standing straight. Then glue on the back support with slightly thicker sugar; hold the figure until the back support is set. Coat the whole figure with food lacquer or spray it with a fast-drying clear lacquer as a protection against moisture and fingerprints.

14. Depending on the shape of the figure, you may need to attach a second support horizontally or vertically. The baker's outstretched arm and hand, for example, will slowly collapse if not supported. The second support should angle down to the main vertical support. This is especially necessary because the arm and torso are usually cast in white (the color of a chef's jacket), and white sugar is softer.

15. If you are not using white or another opaque color (see "Adding Color to Boiled Sugar," page 578) and you are not spraying on the colors after casting, the colored sugar will be translucent. This does not look good, especially if you are supporting the figure from the back or if it can be seen from all sides. To remedy this, first cast a thin layer of the whole figure in milk white.

Making Casting Forms

You can make your own forms for casting from metal strips (the kind used to secure crates and boxes) or plastilina, which is a variant of plasteline, a nonhardening modeling clay made from clay mixed with oil or wax, or both in combination. Molds made from metal strips can be used over and over, but the metal strips are difficult and time-consuming to bend into small or intricate shapes, while plastilina can be rolled out to a sheet of the required thickness and cut into any shape with a thin, sharp knife. To use plastilina, make or enlarge a copy of the drawing, glue it to a piece of sturdy paper, such as a cake box, and cut out the shape with a utility knife.

Transfer the rolled plastilina sheet to a piece of cardboard, place the drawing on top, and cut out by tracing around the shape. Slide the cut piece back onto an oiled marble slab or table or onto a Silpat (which does not need to be oiled). Just like the marble surface, any side of the plastilina that will come into contact with the sugar must be lightly greased with vegetable oil. The drawback with this method is that you can use the mold only once. A third option is to use the plastilina cutout instead of the frame that is left to make a silicone rubber casting template (directions follow on page 604).

When making the mold from metal strips, place a piece of baking paper or other translucent paper on top of the drawing to keep it clean. Fasten the drawing to a sheet of cardboard. Form and solder the metal strips according to the directions that follow. Whether using either plastilina or metal strips, be sure you make the forms deep enough.

Soldering Metal Casting Forms

Working with metal strips, also known as *band iron,* takes a little extra effort because they have to be soldered after they are shaped. But they can be used indefinitely, and one form can be used in either direction to make a mirror image. If you are making a butterfly, for example, you have to make only one wing form. Metal strips may be a little hard to find, as plastic strips are used more often today to secure boxes for shipping. If the local hardware store does not have any, you may find used strips at the lumberyard. Choose ¹/₂-inch-wide (1.2-cm) strips, if you find them, as they are the easiest to work with. You also need soldering wire, flux (a paste that acts as a liason in joining the pieces), cold water, a blowtorch, flat- and round-nosed pliers, a metal cutter, and a metal file.

1. Using your hands and the pliers, form the strip until it matches the drawing. Overlap the ends by ¹/₂ inch (1.2 cm).

2. Smear flux at the solder points, or dip them into solder fluid.

3. Cut off a small piece of soldering wire, fold it in half, and place it between the two ends, holding them in place with the pliers. The pieces must line up exactly so the form will lie flat.

4. Heat the ends from both sides with the blowtorch until the solder melts. Dip into cold water and file off any excess solder to even the joint.

Then, using that as the base, section off and cast the various colors on top of the white. The back of the figure will be clean, look good, and be well supported (although it will look a little too thick from the side).

NOTE 1: Because a cast-sugar figure must be solid enough to support itself, to some degree, and as tartaric acid gives sugar flexibility, leave it out when cooking sugar for casting to ensure maximum rigidity in the cast pieces.

NOTE 2: It is sometimes desirable to have the back wrinkled to reflect the light in an interesting way. In this case, crumple the foil, then smooth it out again before using.

Making Silicone Casting Templates

Instead of making a plastilina frame, the plastilina can be used in reverse (using the cutout) by making a silicone template or mold to cast figures in series or to make customized motifs for special occasions. Although the process requires a bit more time and expense, the templates can be used over and over. Silicone and rubber templates are also available for purchase.

1. Roll out plastilina to the desired thickness (as deep as you want the molds). Place the cardboard cutout of your drawing (or a cutter, if using) on top; cut out the design.

2. Place a Silpat on a sheet pan or sheet of corrugated cardboard, or stretch plastic wrap over a sheet of corrugated cardboard. (You can place the Silpat or a sheet of plastic directly on the work surface, if it can be left there undisturbed for 24 hours.) Arrange the cutouts on top, at least 1 inch (2.5 cm) apart. Frame the cutouts with metal bars, such as those used for making candy, or strips of corrugated cardboard wrapped in plastic. Secure them with weights on the outside.

3. Carefully brush vegetable oil over the top and sides of the cutouts and over the inside edges of the frame.

4. Mix the jelling agent into the silicone rubber following the manufacturer's instructions. Avoid stirring in air bubbles. Pour the silicone rubber mixture around your cutouts inside the frame up to the top edge of the cutouts; do not cover them. You usually have a few minutes before the mixture turns viscous, so pour slowly and precisely. Leave the silicone rubber to harden; this usually takes about 24 hours.

5. Remove the frame from around the edges. Pull out the plastilina cutouts, placing one hand underneath to aid in removing them.

6. Use the tip of a sharp utility knife to cut away threads of rubber around the bottom of the rubber molds.

7. Place the template on a sheet of foil, a marble surface, or a Silpat as directed in the casting instructions and proceed.

Spraying Color on Sugar Pieces

Instead of adding color to the boiled sugar syrup, as with pulled and blown sugar, a different method is used when casting small figures because it is not practical to split the sugar into different boils and color them separately. In addition to being time-consuming, it is hard to boil a small amount of sugar syrup to a precise temperature. You often have to remove the sugar thermometer from its protective casing and hold it while you tilt the pan to make the solution deep enough to get a reading, and this is not realistic. It is easy to overheat the sugar, which can caramelize in an instant at temperatures above 310°F (155°C). Therefore, it makes sense to cast the whole figure in one base color (preferably off-white), then spray on the desired shades. The color can be sprayed or blown on using a clever little tool called a *fixative syringe* (see page 607). You submerge one end in the color and put the other in your mouth, then spray by blowing air into the syringe. A more modern and convenient method is to use an airbrush. You can obtain different shades by spraying at an angle to the flat surface because more color will adhere to the area closest to the sprayer. You can also cover part of the surface with paper to achieve a contrasting effect.

Make your own colors for spraying by mixing a small amount of water-soluble food coloring with food lacquer in a small stainless steel cup (see Note here and also "About Food Lacquer," page 611). Try to make up only the amount you need at that time. First spray the color onto a paper to check the effect and strength of the color before applying it to the cast sugar. Naturally, the closer you hold the sprayer to the sugar and the more forcefully you blow into the syringe or the higher the setting on the airbrush, the more concentrated the color will be. When you are finished, clean the container and the syringe or airbrush with denatured alcohol. You can also use this technique to apply color to blown sugar pieces.

NOTE: The food lacquer provides a protective coating along with the color. If that is not necessary, or you do not want to use the expensive lacquer, mix the colors with any clear spirit, such as vodka.

This type of sugarwork requires you to have an artist's hand and many years of practice before you can produce anything close to what you see in the specialty sugar books. Unfortunately, for these reasons, pulling and blowing sugar are becoming more obsolete every day. It is one thing to learn and practice the techniques in school and another to incorporate them in the workplace without going broke. The problem, of course, is that learning to blow and pull sugar takes a large amount of time away from your other chores and regular production work. Therefore, you must be interested enough in these types of sugarwork to make them a hobby. The weather also plays an important role: If you live in a damp climate, you will find it difficult to work with sugar because the humidity accelerates recrystallization. If you are a beginner, making a rose from pulled sugar, or blowing a small piece of fruit or even a vase, is a realistic starting point once you have a basic knowledge of sugarwork. Color Photo 98 shows examples of pulled, blown, and cast sugar arranged together in a showpiece.

Both pulled and blown sugar can be made following the instructions for Boiled Sugar Method I (page 576) or Boiled Sugar Method II (page 577). The procedure for cooking, aerating, and forming the sugar is the same for both. Using Method II may give you an edge because the sugar is less likely to recrystallize, plus it is easier to soften in the microwave as needed while you work. Method II is not suitable, however, for large pulled or blown sugar pieces.

After the sugar is cooked, aerate it by drawing it out evenly with your hands, folding it up, and pulling it out again as many times as necessary until enough air has been mixed in to give the sugar a silky sheen (Figure 11-9; also see jacket photo). Wearing food handling gloves will help protect your hands from the heat if they are not yet callused; however, you should wear gloves at all times to protect the sugar from sweat on your hands as you work with it. The sugar is now ready to use for either pulling or blowing; it can also be stored in an airtight container at this stage for later use. Place a dehumidifying agent in the container to absorb moisture. Be careful not to work the sugar too long; if over-pulled, it will recrystallize and take on a dull matte finish. This will also happen if the sugar is allowed to become too hard or cold while it is being pulled.

Once the sugar has been aerated, leave the part you are not working with under a heat lamp at all times to keep it soft while you are forming your design. Check the sugar and turn it frequently to make sure it is not getting overheated. If a thin part of the surface of the sugar should harden, do not attempt to mix it back into the remaining sugar without softening it first; the hardened part will not melt but break into small pieces, ruining the appearance.

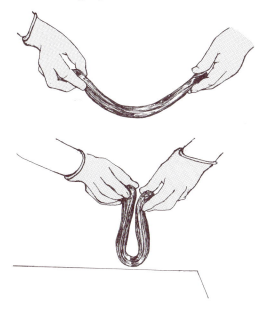

FIGURE 11-9 **Aerating boiled sugar by repeatedly drawing it out, folding it in half, and drawing it out again.**

Before you begin the following two projects, you will need:

- a heat lamp or lamps (see "About Sugar Lamps and Warming Cases," page 609)

- a warming case or sugar workbox with a silicone frame (see page 610)

- a pair of clean scissors

- a Bunsen burner

- a leaf mold to form the larger rose leaves or a ¾-inch (2-cm) oiled dowel for the sugar bow

- a hand sprayer (called a *fixative syringe*) or an airbrush for spraying the finished pieces (see "About Fixative Syringes").

Pulled Sugar Rose

1. Prepare pink and green pulled sugar, as described above. Once the sugar has the proper consistency and shine, form each piece into a tight ball. Draw out a thin strip from the pink ball about 1 inch (2.5 cm) wide and 4 inches (10 cm) long. Cut off this piece with scissors.

2. Coil the strip into a small conical shape, about 1 inch (2.5 cm) long, to make the center of the rose. If the strip sets and is too firm to bend, warm it under a heat lamp until pliable. (You can also form the rose center with the same technique used for Marzipan Roses; see Figures 12-10 to 12-13, pages 651 and 652).

3. Using both thumbs and forefingers, pull up the top part of the pink sugar ball into a thin ridge (Figure 11-10). Grasp the center of the ridge and draw the edge away to make a slightly elongated petal (Figure 11-11). Separate the petal from the sugar ball by pinching it off with your other hand. Quickly curl the top of the petal back as you would for a marzipan rose (see Figure 12-16, page 653), then immediately attach it to the center of the rose. Support the rose on a small cookie cutter as you are working, increasing the size of the cutter as the rose becomes larger. Pull and shape 2 additional elongated petals of the same size and attach them evenly around the center.

4. Make the remaining petals slightly larger and more rounded, folding the tops back a little more and forming them into a rather hollow shape, like a cupped hand. Attach them as you form them (see Chef's Tip).

5. To make a rosebud, use just the 3 elongated petals and the center. Fasten the petals together in a close triangular shape around the base, 1 inside the other.

6. Using the same technique as for the elongated petals, pull small, pointed green leaves to

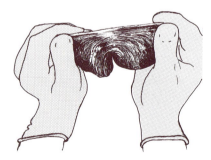

FIGURE 11-10 **Pulling the edge of a soft ball of sugar into a thin ridge for the first step in making a Sugar Rose petal**

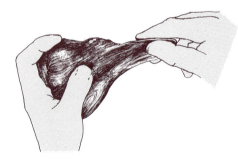

FIGURE 11-11 **Pulling an elongated petal out of the thin ridge**

About Fixative Syringes

This is a hand tool used to apply color to finished pieces in sugarwork; it is also known as a *hand sprayer*. The syringe consists of two tubes connected by a hinge; one tube is slightly longer and thinner than the other and is cut on an angle at the bottom so it can be placed in the liquid without blocking the flow. The tubes are bent at a 90-degree angle when the tool is in use, and they fold flat for storage. The liquid coloring is sprayed (blown) on the sugar by submerging the end of the thin tube in the color and placing the end of the other tube in your mouth. When you blow air into the syringe, the color is sprayed in a fine mist. Although designed for the application of coloring, the tool can be used for spraying a fine mist of other liquids as well.

the desired length from the green sugar ball. Bend the points back and attach the ends to the roses or buds. Make slightly larger and wider leaves to go on the stems of the roses. Quickly and firmly press them into the leaf mold to transfer the leaf pattern to the sugar. Warm the leaves, if necessary, and bend them into a nicely curved shape; reserve a few if desired to place around your rose display.

7. To make a rose stem, cut a ridged wire, such as a coat hanger, to the desired size. Push the wire through the soft, green sugar ball. The faster you push it through, the thinner the coating of sugar will be. If you move too fast, the sugar will simply break; it may take a few tries to get just the right speed. Heat the tip of the wire over a Bunsen burner and push it into the base of the rose. If you prefer not to have the wire inside — for example, if you are laying the rose on a cake or garnishing an individual dessert serving — just pull out a thin rope of green sugar for the stem. However, if you want to display the rose standing up, as in a basket, you must use the wire. Heat the base of the rose leaves made in Step 6 and attach to the stem.

8. Curls or tendrils are easy to make and are a nice complement to your rose display. To make them, lightly oil the round handle of a small wooden spoon, or use a pen about the same shape and diameter. Pull a thin rope out of the green sugar ball and quickly wind it around the spoon or pen like a telephone cord; slide it off once it has hardened (see Figures 11-15 and 11-16, pages 620 and 621).

9. Display your roses with a few buds, leaves, and tendrils on a small base cast in sugar or within a frame made by curling a thick rope of green sugar into a round disk.

10. To prevent the finished sugar pieces from deteriorating due to moisture, keep them in an airtight container with a dehumidifying agent. The pieces can also be sprayed with food lacquer or, if they are to be used for display purposes only, with a thin film of fast-drying, clear shellac.

CHEF'S TIP
Instead of attaching each petal to the center as you make it, you can make up all of the petals individually, then assemble the rose by heating the base of each hardened petal to attach it. The drawback to this method is that you cannot mold or alter the shape of the rose as you can when the petals are attached while they are still soft.

Pulled Sugar Bow with Ribbons

yield : 1 bow, about 4 inches (10 cm) across, with 2 ribbons, each 6 inches (15 cm) long

Making a beautiful sugar bow to decorate a petit four or candy tray, for example, or to use as part of a showpiece, can be done fairly quickly — especially if you have pieces of aerated colored sugar left from previous sugarwork. If so, you will need only to pull the sugar back and forth a few times to bring back its sheen. To make one bow with ribbons, you need three or four pieces of colored sugar (for the best appearance one should be white) weighing about 12 ounces (340 g) each.

If you do not have any scrap sugar, make one recipe Boiled Sugar Method II (page 577). After you add the tartaric acid, continue boiling the sugar approximately 1 minute longer. Divide the syrup into three or four batches, depending on the number of colors you want to use, then boil, color, and aerate each batch individually, following the instructions. You should make at least three colors, ideally one of them white.

1. Keep the colored sugar soft under a heat lamp. Pull out a rope of sugar about 4 inches (10 cm) long from each color. Each rope should be approximately ¼ to ½ inch (6 mm to 1.2 cm) thick, depending on how much of that color you want to use in your bow and ribbons. You can, of course, use the same color twice. Place the ropes next to one another (not stacked) in the desired pattern. The ropes should be warm enough to stick together. If necessary, leave them this way under the heat lamp until they are soft enough to stick, turning them from time to time. Do not get any oil on the sugar ropes, as this can prevent them from sticking together.

2. Once the ropes are attached side by side, take the entire strip out from under the lamp and let it cool for approximately 30 seconds, turning it over a few times; do not place it directly on a marble slab or marble table, or it will cool too much; a Silpat is useful here.

3. Slowly pull out the whole strip of sugar lengthwise until about doubled in length.

4. Using an oiled pair of scissors, cut the strip in half crosswise. Lay the 2 halves side by side under the heat lamp and leave them until they stick together. Pull out the strip lengthwise a second time until doubled in length. Depending on how thin the sugar is at this point, you can stop here or repeat the cutting and pulling procedure once more for a very elaborate ribbon. If the strip is thinner and narrower than you would like, you are probably pulling too fast, working with sugar that is too soft (warm), or both (see Note).

5. To make the ribbons, start by pulling out one end of the striped sugar to make a thin strip approximately 1 inch (2.5 cm) wide and 12 inches (30 cm) long. Don't just hold onto 1 end and pull it out to the final length all at once. To make the strip uniform in width and thickness, you need to pull a few inches, then move your fingers back to where you started, pull a few inches further, start at the base again, and so on.

6. Using oiled scissors, trim the very end of the strip, which will be thick and unattractive. Cut off 2 pieces, each 6 inches (15 cm) long, crosswise at an angle. Pleat the pieces slightly. Attach 2 narrow ends together to make an upside-down V. Set this piece aside.

7. To make the loops of the sugar bow, you need 13 pieces, each 4 inches (10 cm) long (it is a good idea to make a few extra to allow for breakage). Pull out 1 piece at a time from the thick piece of sugar, making the pieces the same width and thickness as the ribbons. Continue to warm the sugar as needed to maintain the correct consistency. Cut off each piece as you pull it

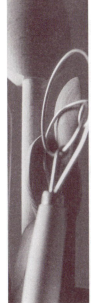

About Sugar Lamps and Warming Cases

A sugar lamp, also commonly referred to as a *warming lamp*, is an essential tool of sugar pulling and sugar blowing. The lamp is used to warm and soften hard portions of cooked and stored sugar and to keep the sugar mass malleable while the chef is forming it. A sugar lamp is generally composed of a large infrared bulb of 250 watts and 125 volts attached either to the top of a warming case (see below) or a flexible gooseneck stem. The opaque top of the bulb drives the light and its corresponding heat down to the round bottom surface and onto the work surface below. The bulb can be moved up and down to adjust the intensity of the heat, still leaving room between the work surface and the lamp where the sugar can be worked on by the chef.

A sugar warming case, sold by pastry equipment suppliers, is a large box with a solid top and bottom and transparent panels on the back, left, and right sides, leaving the front open. The top of the box accommodates a sugar lamp; a removable elevated silicone-covered frame fits inside the base and is used to hold the sugar. The case is large enough that the chef can work on the sugar with his or her hands inside the box, protecting the sugar from air drafts and foreign particles. The cases are expensive and most likely not worth the investment unless you do a fair amount of sugarwork. To make a simplified version, see "Making a Sugar Workbox" (page 610).

out and quickly form it into a smooth, curved loop by bending it in half over an oiled wooden dowel or other round object approximately ¾ inch (2 cm) in diameter; then pinch the flat ends together. Immediately pinch the attached flat edges in the opposite direction so the bottom of the loop comes together in a point and the sides of the loop pleat slightly; this will make it easier to fit the loops together when assembling the bow later. Warm the loops under the heat lamp while you are working so they are soft enough to shape easily, but be sure that the sugar has cooled sufficiently to hold its shape before removing each loop from the dowel and setting it aside.

8. To assemble the bow, start by flattening a small disk of sugar to approximately ¾ inch (2 cm) in diameter. Attach 7 evenly spaced loops around the edge of the disk with the tips pointing in, first softening the tip of each loop until sticky by holding it over a Bunsen burner. You can also make the tip sticky by holding it right next to the heat lamp, but you risk deforming the thin loops. Attach a second layer of 5 loops in the same way, placing these overlapping the first set slightly and attaching them closer to the center of the disk. Finish by attaching a loop to cover the center of the disk.

9. Attach the finished bow to the reserved ribbons by softening the sugar at the tip where the ribbons meet, then carefully setting the bow on top.

10. Using a fixative syringe or airbrush, spray the bow and ribbons with food lacquer; do not forget to spray the bottom. Store in an airtight container with a dehumidifying agent, if desired, for extra protection against moisture. If the sugar is completely sealed, you should be able to use this mini-showpiece many times.

NOTE: Keep in mind that the faster the pulled sugar cools at this point, the better it will retain both its shape and its shine.

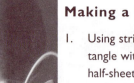

Making a Sugar Workbox

1. Using strips of plywood or cut wood trim, 2½ to 3 inches × 2 inches (6.2 to 7.5 × 5 cm), make a rectangle with the outside dimensions of 11½ × 15½ inches (28.7 × 38.7 cm). This size box will fit on a half-sheet pan, which is convenient.

2. Glue and screw the sides together, then sand the edges smooth. (It is bad enough to get blisters on your fingers from hot sugar; you don't need splinters, too!)

3. Stretch a sheet of silicone, ¹⁄₁₆ to ⅛ inch (2 to 3 mm) thick, over the frame and staple in place. If you cannot obtain silicone, use a piece of nylon window screen instead. The sugar should not actually be worked on the frame; it is just used to support the sugar while it is being softened or warmed under the heat lamps.

If you do not have time to build a frame, a Silpat makes an excellent substitute on which to place the sugar under the heat lamps. However, the ideal arrangement is 1 half-size mat on top of the box and another (half or full-size) next to the workbox, which allows you to move the sugar between the two areas to regulate the heat as needed. If none of these options works for you, or if you need additional space to hold the sugar while working on a large project, shrink-wrap a quadruple layer of plastic wrap on top of a hotel pan, 3 to 4 inches (7.5 to 10 cm) deep.

Sugar Blowing

In addition to the tools needed for sugar pulling, you will need a cooling fan (a hair dryer with a cool air setting placed on a stand can be used), a small brush, and a one-way, hand-operated air pump with a plastic or wooden nozzle (see "About Air Pumps"). If you do not have an air pump, you can blow the sugar by mouth in much the same way that glassblowers produce their magic, using blowpipes with various openings. Sugar blowing was done this way before the hand pump was developed some sixty years ago. Because sugar takes longer to cool than glass and the blowpipes do not have a one-way valve to prevent air from escaping, the hand pump is much easier to use. Cooling time becomes a real issue when you blow larger pieces; using a more powerful fan can help.

1. Prepare the sugar as directed on page 605. Once it has been aerated and has developed the proper shine and temperature, form the amount of sugar needed into a tight ball at one end of the piece, then cut off the remainder with scissors, keeping the ball shape. Place the cut-off portion under the lamp.

2. Make an indentation in the cut surface of the ball with your finger. Attach a separate small piece of sugar around the nozzle of the air pump or one end of the blowpipe, heat both this and the indented surface, and join the 2 together, leaving a small, natural air chamber from the indentation.

3. If using an air pump, pump the air in with one hand to expand the air chamber while shaping the sugar with the other hand. If using a blowpipe, blow the air into the tube; this leaves both hands free to shape the sugar. If the ball of sugar is of uneven thickness or is warmer on one side than the other, the thinner or warmer side will expand faster. To control this, even the temperature; cool the warmer areas by holding them next to the fan or by covering them with your hand while you warm the cooler areas under the lamp.

About Air Pumps

An air pump, also called a *bulb pump*, is a hand tool used in blown sugarwork. The pump consists of a small rubber hose with a wooden or plastic nozzle on one end, which is inserted into a ball of sugar, and a rubber bulb on the opposite end, which is squeezed to force air into the sugar. The higher-end models have a one-way valve to prevent the air from flowing back into the bulb after it has been blown into the sugar. Another version has a foot-operated pump, which leaves both hands free to work on the sugar.

About Food Lacquer

Food-grade lacquer in an aerosol spray is primarily used to protect showpieces made from pulled and blown sugar, nougatine, and marzipan; it also adds shine. Depending on the product it is used on, food lacquer is used either to seal the product and prevent it from absorbing moisture from the air or to keep the product from drying out. For marzipan, use a lacquer with a matte or eggshell finish instead of the glossy product.

4. Begin by making a sphere of the appropriate size. Gradually work the sphere away from the blow tube or nozzle to produce a small neck, which you will use later to separate the finished piece from the tool. For example, to make a Bosc pear, elongate the shape of the sphere, then warm the area close to the mouthpiece while stretching and bending it slightly to produce the curved neck typical of the pear. Start a vase the same way but keep the elongated sphere straight; then warm the opposite end while pumping or blowing in air until it expands to the size you want. Flatten the bottom so the vase will stand straight.

5. Once the pieces are formed, cool them with a fan so they do not change shape. Reheat the neck later over a Bunsen burner and cut the nozzle or blow tube away with scissors while the sugar is warm; smooth the cut edge. Using a red-hot knife, even the top of the vase.

6. Follow the directions in "Spraying Color on Sugar Pieces" (page 604) to decorate the pieces. To make the tiny spots typical of a pear, dip the top of the bristles of a fairly stiff brush in color, then bend them back to make the color fly off.

7. Protect the finished pieces by the same methods described for pulled sugar.

CARAMELIZED SUGAR AND CARAMELIZED SUGAR DECORATIONS

Sugar starts to turn from golden to light brown in color and to caramelize when the temperature reaches 320°F (160°C). There are two ways of bringing the sugar to this temperature: the dry method and the wet method. Caramelizing sugar dry takes about half the time, and you do not have to worry about recrystallization, but it requires more attention, as the sugar must be stirred constantly to prevent it from caramelizing too fast (before all of the sugar granules have melted) or, worse, from burning. If you use the dry method, do not use a skillet or pan any larger than necessary, or you will have too large an area to cover when stirring and may not be able to keep the sugar from getting too dark. In the wet method, by adding a small amount of water to the sugar, the caramel does not need to be stirred throughout the entire cooking process, but it takes longer to caramelize because you must wait for the water to evaporate.

Both ways are much faster and easier if you use a sugar pan — an unlined copper pan made especially for cooking sugar (see "About Sugar Pans," page 576). The acidity of the copper reacts

Removing Sugar from the Cooking Pan

When cooking sugar it is always better to make more than you need than to risk running out, as your time is more valuable than the sugar. Also, many projects require that you work with more sugar than is actually used, and therefore the amount of leftover sugar in the pan can be substantial. You should never pour hot sugar into the sink or garbage can and you should never place a hot sugar pan or a sugar pan filled with hardened sugar in the dishwashing station. If the pan contains ¹/₂ inch (1.2 cm) of cooked sugar or less, simply add enough water to cover, place the pan on the stove, and boil to dissolve the sugar. This syrup can be poured into the sink without danger of clogging the drain. If the pan contains more than ¹/₂ inch (1.2 cm) of sugar and you do not need to use the pan again right away, set it aside in a safe place and let it cool until the sugar has hardened. Remove the hardened sugar in the following way: Set the pan over low heat and warm the sugar just long enough to be able to pull the cake of sugar out of the pan in 1 piece using a fork. Throw the sugar cake into the garbage, add water to the pan, and boil the pan clean as directed above. Note: if you are using an induction burner and working with a thick layer of sugar, be very careful and use a low setting. The induction heat can melt the center of the cake as well as the bottom and the sides, and the hot sugar in the center can erupt through the top like a geyser.

If you need to discard hot sugar immediately — for example, you caramelized sugar and the mixture got too dark and you need to reuse the pan right away — line an oversized mixing bowl with a double thickness of baking paper or aluminum foil, pour the sugar into the bowl, and set aside in a safe place until the sugar has hardened and can be placed in the garbage. If you have a Silpat available and the quantity of sugar will fit, you can also pour the hot sugar onto a Silpat placed on a sheet pan and set this aside to harden. Boil the pan clean as directed above.

with the sugar in such a way that some of the sugar breaks down into invert sugar, which is more resistant to recrystallization. Invert sugar is a mixture of equal parts glucose and fructose. Be careful, though: Because the copper is almost the same color as the caramelized sugar, it is hard to tell the exact moment the pan should be pulled off the heat and placed in cold water to stop the cooking process. It is helpful to pour a few small test puddles on sheet of baking paper, or to dip the tip of a piping bag into the sugar, to determine the color more accurately. If the sugar is heated much above 320°F (160°C) and you are not using it immediately, you cannot stop it right there; the sugar will continue to darken, even as it sits in the water off the stove, from its own residual heat. This problem is intensified by the copper pan. You do not have to use a sugar thermometer when caramelizing sugar because its color will tell you when it is done.

Caramelized Sugar, Dry Method yield: 2¹/₄ cups (540 ml)

The addition of lemon juice or tartaric acid not only makes the sugar softer, it also delays the actual caramelization, allowing more time to properly melt all of the sugar.

2 pounds (910 g) granulated sugar

1 teaspoon (5 ml) lemon juice *or* 12 drops of Tartaric Acid Solution (page 629)

1. Fill a bowl large enough to hold the pan used for cooking the sugar with enough cold water to reach halfway up the sides of the pan. Set the bowl aside.

2. Place the sugar and lemon juice in a copper or stainless steel pan. Cook, stirring constantly over low heat, until the sugar is completely melted. Continue cooking until the sugar has caramelized to just a shade lighter than the desired color.

3. Remove the caramel from the heat and immediately place the bottom of the pan in the bowl of cold water to stop the cooking process. Use as directed in individual recipes. If you need to reheat the caramel, stir it constantly over low heat to prevent it from getting any darker than necessary.

Caramelized Sugar with Water yield: 2¼ cups (540 ml)

1 cup (240 ml) water
2 pounds (910 g) granulated sugar

¼ cup (60 ml) or 3 ounces (85 g) glucose *or* light corn syrup

1. Fill a bowl large enough to hold the pan used for cooking the sugar with enough cold water to reach halfway up the sides of the pan. Set the bowl aside.

2. Place 1 cup water and the sugar in a copper or stainless steel pan. Stir to combine and dissolve the sugar in the water over low heat. Using a brush dedicated to sugar boiling, wash down the sides of the pan with water.

3. Bring the mixture to a rolling boil, add the glucose or corn syrup, then lower the heat to medium to ensure the liquid will not boil too hard. Do not stir once the sugar starts boiling. Instead, brush down the sides of the pan with water as needed until the sugar reaches 280°F (138°C), the crack stage. Keep boiling until the sugar has caramelized to the desired color.

4. Quickly remove the pan from the heat and place the bottom of the pan in cold water to stop the cooking process. Use as directed in individual recipes.

Caramelized Sugar for Decorations yield: 2¾ cups (660 ml)

The old-fashioned dry method for caramelizing sugar is still the fastest and easiest way when only a small amount of caramel is needed — for a few ornaments or a batch of crème caramel, for example. If necessary, you can speed the process in the following recipe in a similar way, by cutting both the water and the glucose or corn syrup in half, provided you are careful. If you use the full amount of water and glucose or corn syrup called for, there will be plenty of liquid to help the sugar dissolve properly.

The most convenient method for caramelizing sugar for decorations is to keep a stock of sugar syrup on hand (as described in Step 3 following). Simply pour off whatever amount is needed and continue cooking it to the desired stage.

2 cups (480 ml) cold water

2 pounds (910 g) granulated sugar

½ cup (120 ml) or 6 ounces (170 g) glucose *or* light corn syrup (see Note)

1. Fill a bowl large enough to hold the cooking pan with enough cold water to reach halfway up the sides of the pan. Set the bowl aside.

2. Place 2 cups water and the sugar in a copper or stainless steel pan. Bring to a boil over high heat, stirring constantly, and remove any scum that accumulates on the surface.

3. Add the glucose or corn syrup. Bring the syrup back to boiling. Using a clean brush dedicated to sugar boiling, wash down the sides of the pan with water. Remove any additional scum from the surface. If you are making sugar syrup for general mise en place, pour it into a clean container at this point (or just pour off the excess) and store until needed.

4. Continue cooking the sugar, washing down the sides of the pan as long as sugar crystals are accumulating; do not stir from this point on. When the sugar begins to change from clear to light amber, watch it closely; it will turn golden brown quickly, as most of the water has evaporated at this point and the temperature is now around 315°F (157°C).

CHEF'S TIP
If the sugar recrystallizes despite all of your precautions, it may be the fault of the tap water in your area. To eliminate this problem, use bottled water or distill your water first, including the water used for washing down the sides of the pan.

5. When the syrup just starts to show a hint of golden brown, remove the pan from the stove and set it in the bowl of cold water. Hold it there for about 10 seconds or until all of the bubbles have subsided. Remove the pan from the water, wipe the bottom of the pan, and let the sugar cool at room temperature as necessary, depending on the use.

NOTE: Because glucose is not readily available in the United States, I use light corn syrup most of the time, and it works fine.

CARAMELIZED SUGAR DECORATIONS

A few words of caution are called for at this point, as working with cooked sugar is potentially dangerous. Most of us have accidentally splashed boiling water on bare skin and know how painful that is. Consider this: Boiling water is only 212°F (100°C). I say "only" because when you heat sugar, boiling more and more moisture out of it to the point of caramelization, it is between 320°F and 330°F (160° and 166°C). And it sticks. Getting this hot syrup on your skin can literally scar you for life. I do not want to discourage anyone doing this for the first time, but I do want to stress the importance of taking precautions and using plain old-fashioned common sense.

First of all, especially if you are new to this type of work, wear food handling gloves to protect your hands (although they will help only to a point; you must still, of course, use a pot holder when taking hold of the pan). Do not move around a crowded kitchen with a pan of hot sugar. If you absolutely must do so, let your colleagues know in no uncertain terms that you are walking past them by saying clearly and firmly, "Hot pan coming through." Be sure to walk slowly, holding the sugar pan in one hand and extending your other hand as a bumper. This is especially important when going around corners; in many professional kitchens, the unwritten law is to say, loud and clear, "Corner!" as one comes around. A much more sensible way is to work with the sugar next to where it is cooked.

Making spun sugar and caramel corkscrews, for example, is by no means as dangerous, nor does it take as much skill and tolerance of heat, as piped sugar decorations. Because using a strong and secure pastry bag, even one made of vinyl, is out of the question for piping hot sugar, I make bags out of baking paper in the usual way, but I use a double thickness to ensure the bag will not break under pressure, which could splash the hot sugar all over my hands.

You can make a bag of a good workable size by folding a full sheet of baking paper (24 × 16 inches/60 × 40 cm) in half crosswise and forming the doubled sheet into a disposable bag in the usual way. Be certain that the tip is pulled tight so it will not leak. You cannot put the sugar syrup into the bag with a spoon or scraper as you would with other fillings, so again, take care when filling the bag with the hot syrup. Look around to be sure no one is going to bump you, then hold the paper pastry bag securely in one hand, carefully pick up the sugar pan with your other hand, and pour the sugar into the bag in a steady stream, filling it with no more than 1½ cups (360 ml) or half of the Caramelized Sugar for Decorations recipe. Close the top securely, wrap a towel around the bag to protect your hands from the heat, and cut a small opening in the tip with scissors. Pipe out the sugar as directed in the individual instructions that follow.

As the sugar cools, it will clog the tip of the bag. It is therefore important that you work quickly so you will not have to stop in the middle of your design. Once the tip is clogged, the only thing you can do is cut a larger opening and squeeze the lump through. If this leaves too large an opening, squeeze all of the sugar out of the bag into the saucepan and start over. If the opening is not too large, you should still be able to create thin, elegant strands by holding the bag a little higher and moving it a little faster as you pipe. Reheat the sugar in the pan as needed, stirring constantly over low heat to protect it from getting any darker than necessary.

You can make clear or colored decorations by following the instructions given for cooking and coloring the sugar in Spun Sugar (page 593). All sugar decorations are susceptible to moisture and should be made as close to serving time as possible. You can increase their resistance and store them for up to 1 week under optimal conditions if you spray the finished shapes on both sides with food lacquer (see page 611) and include a desiccant in the storage container. This should be done immediately after the decorations have cooled and not as a means of trying to save pieces that have already started to get sticky.

Bubble Sugar yield: 16 decorations or 2 full-size sheets (Color Photo 98 and back case cover)

You can use any type of clear spirit — such as vodka, tequila, or gin — to make these edible bubbled decorations. However, if they are to be used only for show and will not be consumed, use denatured alcohol for the best result.

In addition to making large decorations as instructed below, the sugar mixture may also be poured over 2 prepared sheets of baking paper or 2 Silpats. After the sugar sheets have hardened, they can be broken into garnishes of the desired size. Liquid food coloring may be added to the sugar mixture to produce tinted decorations instead of decorations with the natural amber color of the caramelized sugar.

1 recipe Caramelized Sugar for Decorations (page 613)   ½ cup (120 ml) clear liquor

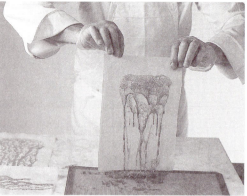

PROCEDURE 11-1a Pouring a line of sugar along one short edge of a sheet of baking paper

PROCEDURE 11-1b Picking up the paper and holding it vertically to force the sugar to run over the sheet

1. Cut 16 pieces of baking paper, 8 × 12 inches (20 × 30 cm) each. Crinkle the sheets, then press them flat. Alternatively, have Silpats ready if making the larger size.

2. Cook the sugar as directed, then briefly place the pan in cold water to stop the cooking process. Do not allow the sugar to thicken; use it immediately.

3. Brush the liquor over a prepared sheet of baking paper. Quickly pour a line of sugar along 1 short edge (see Procedure 11-1a), pick up the paper or Silpat by the 2 corners of the edge with the sugar, hold it vertical, and shake gently to force the sugar to run over the sheet (see Procedure 11-1b). Allow excess sugar to run off onto a Silpat or sheet of paper for easy cleanup. Repeat to make the remaining decorations.

4. Let the sugar cool and harden. To use, peel the decorations away from the paper or Silpats. For storage, leave the sugar attached to the papers and stack the sheets in an airtight container with desiccant. To store decorations made on Silpats, peel them away from the Silpats and layer them, separated by sheets of baking paper, in an airtight container with desiccant.

VARIATIONS

TWICE-COOKED BUBBLE SUGAR yield: approximately 36 decorations

This method has several advantages: You gain greater control over the size and shape of the decorations; it produces more decorations per recipe of sugar; and, because the sugar is cooked twice, you can partially prepare it ahead of time and quickly finish as many decorations as needed at the last minute. The powder can be stored at the end of Step 2 for several weeks if placed in an airtight container with a desiccant. Without a desiccant the powder will form a cake. Crushing it with a rolling pin or processing in a food processor will make it usable.

½ recipe Caramelized Sugar for Decorations
(page 613)

1. Cook the sugar as directed and immediately pour it onto a Silpat; set aside to cool.

2. Break the sugar into pieces and process to a powder in a food processor. Sift using a fine mesh strainer and discard the contents of the strainer.

3. For each decoration place 1½ teaspoons (7.5 ml) of sugar powder on a Silpat. Use a soup-spoon to spread the powder into a thin round approximately 4 inches (10 cm) in diameter. Use the tip of the spoon to create about 6 small holes in the sugar round (it will take some experimentation to determine the number of holes to make and how far apart to place them for the desired appearance; bake a test batch to check before forming all of the decorations). Repeat to form as many decorations as desired; staggered, 12 will fit on a full-size Silpat.

4. Bake at 400°F (205°C) for approximately 8 minutes or until golden brown. Store in an airtight container with a desiccant.

ISOMALT BUBBLE SUGAR yield: I sheet, 12 × 16 inches (30 × 40 cm) (Color Photo 64)

This recipe makes striking decorations that are as perfectly flat and smooth as a thin sheet of glass and, because Isomalt is used rather than real sugar, the decorations may be stored uncovered (at normal room temperature) without a desiccant for 1 or 2 weeks without deteriorating or becoming sticky. To make tinted decorations, lightly sprinkle powdered food coloring over the granulated Isomalt in Step 1.

1½ ounces (40 g) granulated Isomalt

1. Place a half-sheet Silpat (12 × 16 inches/30 × 40 cm) on a flat, even sheet pan of the same size. Sprinkle the Isomalt in an even layer over the mat. Invert a second Silpat on top without disturbing the layer of Isomalt.

2. Transfer to the oven carefully so the grains stay in an even layer. Bake at 400°F (205°C) for 10 minutes; the Isomalt will melt and bubble between the mats. Let cool.

3. Peel the top Silpat away from the baked sheet. Leaving the sheet on the mat, use the tip of a knife to break it into decorations of the desired size.

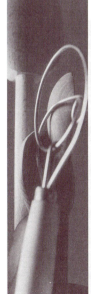

About Isomalt

Isomalt is the trademarked name of a sugar substitute, made from sugar. It is used in the manufacture of numerous foods and pharmaceuticals and is preferred by many pastry chefs for making sugar decorations. Isomalt was discovered in the 1960s and has been used in Europe since the early 1980s. It has been sold in the United States since 1990 in commercial products such as hard candies, lollipops, cough drops, breath mints, and throat lozenges. Isomalt is noncariogenic and low glycemic, meaning products made with it are less likely to cause tooth decay and to affect blood glucose levels than those made with sugar.

For decorative sugarwork, Isomalt has two major advantages over real sugar: It has a low hygroscope level, meaning that pieces made from it are not as susceptible to moisture as those made from real sugar are, and it will not crystallize, eliminating the need to add acid or glucose. Isomalt can be used for spun, pulled, blown, and cast sugar. The downside is that Isomalt must be cooked to a higher temperature than sugar (340°F/171°C) and it must be brought to this point quickly, or the Isomalt will lose some elasticity. Because it must cook quickly the amount of water used in cooking is just 10 percent of the weight of the Isomalt.

Isomalt is made from sucrose and looks much like table sugar. It is white, crystalline, and odorless. It is a mixture of two disaccharide alcohols — gluco-mannitol and gluco-sorbitol. Sucrose, by comparison, is a disaccharide sugar, gluco-fructose.

Caramel Cages yield: variable

This amount of caramel can make about 25 cages if you are experienced and don't break too many. It is virtually impossible not to break any, so do not be discouraged if your first attempts are unsuccessful. With a little practice, you will find it is not difficult to make thin, elegant cages. If you are making a large quantity of cages (for a beginner, that can simply mean more than one), you may want to start with the Simplified Caramel Cages that follow.

1 recipe Caramelized Sugar for Decorations (page 613)   **Vegetable oil**

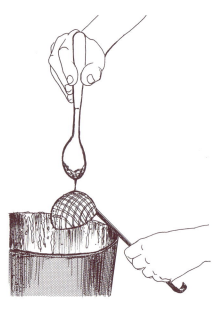

FIGURE 11-12 Streaking lines of caramel across a ladle in two directions for a Caramel Cage

1. Use a ladle or any dome-shaped object, such as a bowl, approximately 2½ inches (6.2 cm) high and 4 inches (10 cm) in diameter. If you are working with 2 ladles, have ready a small tub filled with granulated sugar in which to place the handle of the first ladle as you make the next cage. Chill the ladles or other forms before starting. Hold the ladle or bowl upside down and use the palm of your hand to coat the outside lightly with a thin film of oil. Too much oil will cause the caramel to slide off as you apply it (this can also happen if the caramel is too cool and therefore too thick). You should be able to make several cages before regreasing.

2. Let the caramel cool until it can be picked up with a spoon and drizzled into lines that do not run. Scoop up a small amount of caramel with a soupspoon. Holding the chilled ladle or bowl in your other hand, streak the caramel across the ladle or bowl in straight, thin lines about ½ inch (1.2 cm) apart. Turn the ladle or bowl 45 or 90 degrees to create either diamond- or square-shaped openings and streak a second set of lines in the other direction (Figure 11-12). It is important that the consistency of the sugar is just right. Both the thickness of the lines and the speed at which the caramel falls can be controlled by how high above the surface you hold the spoon. This could be from 2 to 12 inches (5 to 30 cm). The higher the spoon is held, the thinner the line of caramel will be and the easier the sugar will be to control because it falls at a slower pace as it cools on the way down.

3. Use a hot knife to trim the base of the cage as needed.

4. If you are working with 2 ladles or bowls, set the first aside to harden at this point and make the next cage in the same manner. If you are using a single ladle or bowl, wait briefly until the cage is hard (this will take about 10 seconds; placing the ladle or bowl in the refrigerator between cages will speed hardening), then cup your hand around the cage and gently lift it off the ladle or bowl.

CHEF'S TIP

If the cage does not cool and set up right away, either the mold is not cold enough or the lines of sugar are too thick. Thick lines not only take longer to cool but also make for an unattractive, clumsy-looking cage. Thick lines are often the result of the sugar in the pan having cooled too far. Aesthetics aside, caramel that is too cool also tends to slide off the ladle even when applied in thin lines. To reheat the caramel, place the pan over low heat and stir constantly to make sure the caramel at the bottom does not become too dark. You may also find it helpful to chill the ladle or bowl in the refrigerator while warming the sugar.

CARAMEL CAGES USING A HALF-SPHERE

This variation uses the same technique as the main recipe, but it has the advantages of giving you more control as you drizzle the caramel and leaving both of your hands free while you work, as you do not have to hold the ladle or bowl.

1. Lightly oil the outside of 1 or 2 half-sphere molds approximately 6 inches (15 cm) in diameter and 3 inches (7.5 cm) in height. Refrigerate until the molds are cold.

2. Place a Silpat or sheet of baking paper on your work surface to aid in cleanup. Place a can or another object, about 5 inches (12.5 cm) tall and 3 inches (7.5 cm) in diameter, on the mat or paper. Set a chilled mold on top and proceed as directed in Steps 2, 3, and 4 of the main recipe.

SIMPLIFIED CARAMEL CAGES (Color Photo 31)

Simplified caramel cages are easier to produce than regular cages, making them a good choice when a large number is needed or for a beginner. Just as when piping with chocolate, it is easier to make curved lines than it is to make lines that are perfectly straight. For this recipe, use a large ladle, about 2½ inches (6.2 cm) high and 6 inches (15 cm) in diameter.

1. Hold the oiled ladle or bowl over a Silpat or sheet of baking paper to catch stray caramel.

2. Instead of making straight lines, drizzle and swirl the sugar over the ladle or bowl to form intersecting curved lines (Figure 11-13). Each line must connect to the others, following the principles of basic building, so the cage will hold together. Create your own design but don't overdo it; you should be able to see through the cage.

3. Remove the cage from the bowl following the instructions in the main recipe (Figure 11-14).

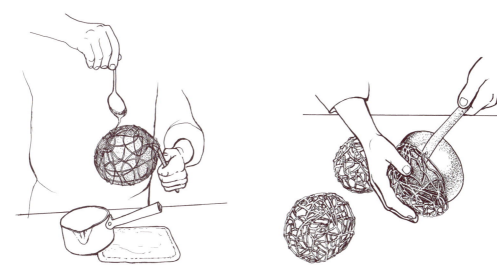

FIGURE 11-13 **Creating intersecting curved lines of sugar over a ladle for a Simplified Caramel Cage**

FIGURE 11-14 **Removing the finished caramel cage by cupping it gently while lifting**

Caramel Corkscrews yield: variable (Color Photos 21 and 23)

This is the easiest of the caramel decorations discussed in this section, and it is also the safest to produce, yet the corkscrews look incredibly showy spiraling high into the air. An added advantage is that they can be made from leftover caramel — for example, caramel left after making piped decorations or dipping fruit or nuts — as the caramel must be very thick but still sticky. Forming the corkscrews on a knife-sharpening steel works well because steels are the right diameter; the fine grooves and the way the tools are made make them nonstick, so it is unnecessary to oil the surface; and the tapered ends allow you to push each corkscrew off easily. The handle helps by giving you something to hold on to. You can, however, use any smooth, glossy object of the appropriate thickness. I use a ballpoint pen for very narrow corkscrews or tendrils, for example. I think you will find the technique for corkscrews easy to learn with just a little practice. The key, besides having the syrup at the correct consistency, is a smooth rhythm when rotating the sugar around the steel.

> 1 recipe Caramelized Sugar for Decorations   Vegetable oil
>   (page 613)

1. Let the caramelized sugar cool until it is very thick. You will find out rather quickly if the sugar is too thin because the strands created by moving the spoon around the steel will not be strong enough to wind and will simply fall to the table.

2. Oil a sheet of baking paper to hold the finished corkscrews; they are extremely fragile and will break if they stick to the surface.

3. Dip a soupspoon into the caramel and swirl it around until a small amount of caramel sticks to the spoon. Pull a thread of sugar out of the mass as you pull the spoon out of the pan. If the caramel just runs off the spoon, it is still too warm. Hold the steel in your other hand and rotate the thread of caramel around the steel, starting about 6 inches (15 cm) from the tip and

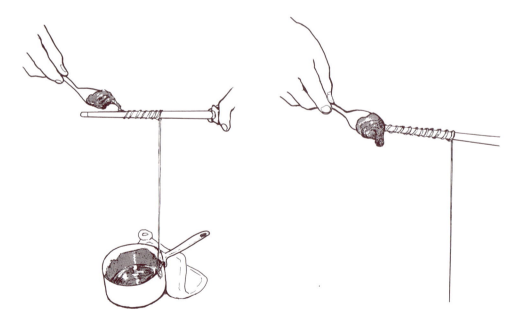

FIGURE 11-15 **Winding a thin strand of caramel around a knife-sharpening steel to make a Caramel Corkscrew**

continuing to the end (Figure 11-15). If necessary, break off any sugar sticking out from the end where you started, then push the finished corkscrew off (Figure 11-16) and place it on the oiled baking paper. If the sugar was cooked to a golden brown caramel and the corkscrews are as thin as they should be, they will set up immediately.

4. Repeat to make as many as desired, plus a few extra to allow for breakage. Reheat the caramel as needed, stirring constantly.

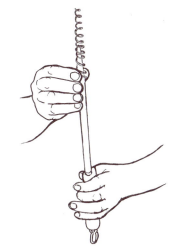

FIGURE 11-16 Pushing the finished corkscrew off the steel

Caramel Fences yield: variable (Color Photo 20)

  1 recipe Caramelized Sugar for Decorations   Vegetable oil
    (page 613)

1. Read the instructions and precautions for Caramelized Sugar Decorations (page 614) and make a disposable pastry bag from a double thickness of baking paper, as described. It is important to use a double thickness to ensure the bag will not break as it is squeezed, which would cause serious burns. The extra paper also helps protect your hands from the heat as you work.

2. Oil a marble slab, or have a Silpat ready. Alternatively, you can use a sheet of silicone-coated baking paper, but unless it is the thicker reusable type, it tends to buckle.

3. Let the sugar cool until it is the consistency of a thick syrup. Ideally, the cooled sugar should be thick enough to start to set immediately as it touches the surface. If the sugar is too thin (too hot), it will bleed together and subsequently break where the lines cross.

4. Carefully pour about 1 cup (240 ml) syrup into the paper bag. Do not attempt to work with a larger amount at once, and be sure the bag is sealed on the other end. Wrap a towel around the bag and cut a small opening.

5. Pipe out the sugar in the fence shape (Figure 11-17). This should be done in a single continuous motion, piping 5 zigzag lines, 4 inches (10 cm) long and about ³⁄₈ inch (9 mm) apart, with smooth, round corners, then another set of 3 lines on top of the first at a 90-degree angle.

FIGURE 11-17 Piping out Caramel Fences

Caramel Spiders yield: variable (Color Photos 30, 68, 71, and 91)

These extraordinary-looking spider decorations are designed to serve as small pedestals on which to place a dessert component. They are a great way of adding height and interest to many presentations. The spiders can be made in just about any size and with varying numbers of legs — they don't need the technically correct eight — by choosing a Flexipan that corresponds to the size of the dessert to be placed on top. Typically, you will use a pan the same size as the one the dessert was baked or molded in. If you have more than 1 pan of the same size, you can make the decorations while the desserts are setting up. If not, another pan that is close in size (it can be slightly larger but not smaller) can be used as long as it has a flat bottom. If you have only 1 appropriate pan, it is best to make the decorations first and set them aside — they can be stored for up to 1 week in an airtight container with desiccant — rather than to wait until the desserts have been unmolded before making the spiders.

**1 recipe Caramelized Sugar for Decorations
        (page 613)**

1. Choose a Flexipan of the appropriate size, as described in the introduction above. If making the spiders for Crème Brûlée on a Caramel Spider with a Sugar Shard (page 341), use Flexipan No. 1897; for Sherry-Poached Black Mission Figs with Crème Catalan (page 353), use Flexipan No. 1269. Invert the pan on a perfectly even sheet pan and set aside.

2. Following the directions with the recipe, cook the sugar to a light caramel color. Quickly remove it from the heat and shock the sugar by placing the bottom of the saucepan in a bowl of cold water. Leave for 10 seconds to stop the cooking process. Set the sugar aside in a safe location until it has cooled to the consistency of a thick syrup.

3. Make 1 or 2 disposable pastry bags with a double thickness of baking paper, as described in Caramelized Sugar Decorations (page 614). Have a dry towel and a pair of clean scissors at hand.

4. Pour approximately 1 cup (240 ml) sugar syrup into a paper pastry bag (see Procedure 11-2a). Cut a small opening and pipe a small puddle of sugar on top of an inverted cup of the

PROCEDURE 11-2a **Pouring the caramel syrup into a double-thick paper pastry bag**

PROCEDURE 11-2b **Piping a spider on the back side of a Flexipan**

PROCEDURE 11-2c **Removing a spider from the Flexipan; a finished spider**

Flexipan, then continue piping to form 3 to 8 evenly spaced legs that run down the sides of the cup, ending each leg with a small dot of caramel (see Procedure 11-2b). Use every other cup on the pan if the spiders stick together. Let cool completely.

5. To remove the spiders, carefully push the Flexipan away from the sugar between each leg (see Procedure 11-2c), then lift the spider straight up and off the pan. Store in airtight containers.

Caramel Spirals yield: variable (Color Photo 69)

It seems that all caramel decorations make a big impression, but this simple space-age spiral has got to be at the top of the list. It never ceases to amaze guests that sugar can be so flexible as they watch it bounce up and down above the plate when it is presented; most of the time they cannot resist trying this for themselves, pulling on the bottom with their fingers or a spoon. I featured Caramel Spirals in the television program "Spectacular Desserts" in the presentation of Crème Caramel Nouvelle. Of all of the techniques I demonstrated, the spirals were by far the item that attracted the most interest from the viewers.

The only real skill required to make spirals successfully is a fairly high tolerance to heat, as it is necessary to put even pressure on the hot pastry bag for a much longer time than it takes to make Caramel Fences, for example.

> **1 recipe Caramelized Sugar for Decorations (page 613)**

1. Read the instructions and precautions for Caramelized Sugar Decorations (page 614) and make a few disposable pastry bags with a double thickness of baking paper, as described. It is important to use a double thickness to ensure the bags will not break as you pipe, which would cause serious burns. The extra paper also helps protect your hands from the heat as you work. To keep the bags from unfolding, fold the bottom 2 inches (5 cm) of the tip back and make a sharp crease down 1 side with your fingers. Have 1 or 2 Silpats ready.

2. Let the sugar cool until it is the consistency of a thick syrup. As the lines of the spirals do not touch each other, if your hands are up to it, you can actually start piping the spirals much sooner in comparison to other decorations. Still, if the sugar is too hot, it will shrink into little droplets when it hits the cooler surface instead of forming a line.

CHEF'S TIP

The thinner the lines and the more concentric circles in each spiral, the more elegant the finished decorations will look. Making them too thin, however, is pointless, as they will break when you lift them off the mat. Piping the caramel too thick, on the other hand, not only looks clumsy but also prevents the sugar from flexing, and the spiral will just sit on top of the dessert instead of falling down around it. This can happen even when the sugar is thin if you do not pipe the circumference of the spiral wide enough so the large outer rings pull the spiral down with their weight.

3. Unfold the bottom of a paper pastry bag and carefully pour about 1½ cups (360 ml) or half of the caramelized sugar recipe into the bag. Do not attempt to work with a larger quantity. Close the top of the bag securely. Wrap a towel around the bag and cut a small opening at the tip.

4. Starting in the center with a small teardrop, pipe out spirals about 7 inches (17.5 cm) in diameter (Figure 11-18). The teardrop will facilitate balancing the spiral on top of a dessert later.

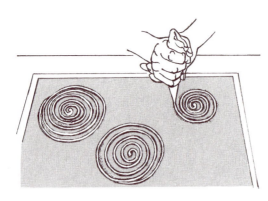

FIGURE 11-18 **Piping out Caramel Spirals**

FIGURE 11-19 **Lifting a finished spiral off a silicone mat**

Close the spiral by piping the very last 1 inch (2.5 cm) or so on top of the previous circle. If you plan ahead and position the spirals correctly, you can fit 6 on each full-size Silpat or sheet of baking paper. Lift the spirals off the mat (Figure 11-19).

Caramel-Dipped Fruit and Nuts

This technique is similar to the one used for Glacéed Fruit and Nuts (page 580), except here the caramel is cooked further — to 320°F (160°C) — to produce a golden brown color. Also, the tartaric acid is omitted, which makes the sugar set up hard and hold its shape after it cools. If desired, you can make these decorations with clear or colored sugar instead, following the instructions in the Glacéed Fruit and Nuts recipe. Although I limit the instructions for fruit to figs and apple wedges, the technique can be applied to other fruits, whole or sliced, as well.

1 recipe Caramelized Sugar for Decorations (page 613)	Fruits or nuts, as specified in individual instructions

CARAMEL-DIPPED FIGS

1. Let the sugar cool until it is very thick but still liquid.

2. Prepare your work area by placing sheets of baking paper on the floor in front of your worktable. Place a ruler or thin strip of wood at the edge of the table and set a heavy can on top at each end to hold it in place (setting a couple of weights from your baking scale at each end also works well). Have ready as many wooden skewers as you will need (1 for each fig).

3. Insert the pointed end of a skewer horizontally through the base of a fig about ¹⁄₃ inch (8 mm) from the bottom without pushing the skewer all the way through. Dip the whole fig into the caramel syrup; lift it out, holding it so the stem end is pointing down, and secure the blunt end of the skewer under the ruler. The fig should extend from the table over the floor above the baking papers in order to catch excess caramel, with the stem end of the fig pointing straight down. Dip the remaining figs in the same manner, working from left to right if the sugar pot is on your right and from right to left if the sugar pot is on your left, so you do not drip across the dipped figs.

4. When the caramel on the figs has hardened, heat the blade of a knife and use it to melt through the caramel tail at the desired length, anywhere from 4 to 8 inches (10 to 20 cm) from the fig (Figure 11-20).

5. Transfer the figs to a sheet pan, holding them up by the wooden skewer; if it is possible, leave them in place until needed (see Chef's Tip). Touching the caramel with your hands will leave fingerprints. When you are ready to remove the skewers, wear a food handling glove on the hand that touches the caramel, hold the fruit securely, and twist out the skewer with the other hand.

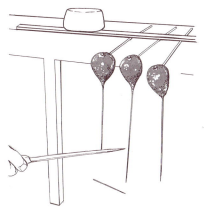

FIGURE 11-20 **Using a hot knife to cut the tail of a Caramel-Dipped Fig to the desired length, in this case approximately 8 inches (20 cm)**

CARAMEL-DIPPED APPLE WEDGES

1. Coat apple wedges with lemon juice to prevent oxidation. If you are making the decorations for the Apple Crème Brûlée presentation (page 325), poach the wedges for 1 or 2 minutes in the liquid left over from poaching the hollowed-out apples; if using them for another recipe, poach in a small amount of Plain Poaching Syrup (page 789). If the apples are not poached before being dipped in caramel, the juice on the cut sides will cause the hot caramel to bubble instead of leaving a smooth surface. Blot the wedges dry.

2. Proceed as for Caramel-Dipped Figs above, inserting the skewers from the side at either end of the wedges and positioning the skewers after dipping so the caramel tails form in a smooth line from the apple wedges, as shown in Color Photo 60.

CARAMEL-DIPPED MACADAMIA NUTS OR HAZELNUTS

1. Follow the instructions for Caramel-Dipped Figs. Dipping nuts is actually a much easier undertaking requiring much less caramel. The only trick to master is inserting the skewers into the sides of the nuts. If you push them in too far or from the wrong side, you will divide the nut into halves; if you do not push them in far enough, the nuts will fall off the skewers into the caramel.

2. Arrange the dipped nuts so the tiny point on the nut faces straight down, creating a tail in a straight line from that point, as shown in Color Photo 21. Be extra careful when you remove the skewers.

CHEF'S TIP

As mentioned in other recipes, it is crucial that the fruit be dipped in caramel as close to serving time as possible. The hot caramel will start to cook the surface of the fruit, softening it and causing the juice to leak out. Leaving the skewer in the fruit until the last moment helps it hold up a little better. Be careful not to tilt the skewers down as you move the figs, because they can slip off.

Caramelized Nuts yield: 14 ounces (400 g)

This recipe works well with almonds, hazelnuts, walnuts, and pecans.

7 ounces (200 g) nuts	½ teaspoon (2.5 ml) lemon juice
Vegetable oil	2 tablespoons (30 ml) water
6 ounces (170 g) granulated sugar	½ ounce (15 g) unsalted butter

1. If using almonds or hazelnuts, remove the skin (see "Removing the Skin from Nuts"). Toast the blanched almonds at 350°F (175°C) until golden brown. Keep the nuts warm.

2. If you do not have a Silpat, lightly oil a marble slab or a sheet pan.

3. Place the sugar, lemon juice, and water in an unlined copper or other heavy saucepan. Cook over medium heat until the temperature reaches 240°F (115°C); brush down the sides of the pan with water a few times during the cooking process.

4. Remove the pan from the heat and immediately add the warm nuts. Stir gently with a wooden spoon or spatula.

5. Return the mixture to medium heat and reheat, continuing to stir gently. The syrup will appear crystallized at this point but will start to melt as it becomes hotter. Keep stirring until the sugar starts to caramelize and turns golden brown; 320°F (160°C).

6. Remove the pan from the heat, add the butter, and stir until the butter is completely incorporated.

7. Pour the mixture onto a Silpat or oiled marble slab or sheet pan. Using 2 forks, turn the nuts over, making sure the sugar coats all of the nuts, and separate the nuts so that they don't touch. As the caramel starts to cool, you can do this more effectively with your fingertips. Store the caramelized nuts in airtight containers.

8. If the nuts are to be crushed after they are caramelized, there is no need to separate them. Instead, let the mixture cool completely on the mat, marble, or sheet pan, then crush it to the desired coarseness. For a denser caramelization, crush the nuts before putting them in the hot syrup.

Removing the Skin from Nuts

To remove the skin from almonds, pour boiling water over them, cover, and let soak for 5 minutes. Drain the water and immediately pinch the nuts between your fingers to remove the skin.

The skin on hazelnuts is easiest to remove by toasting the nuts in a 400°F (205°C) oven for about 10 minutes or until they start to turn golden, provided they are to be toasted anyway. Let cool, then rub the nuts between your hands or in a towel to remove the skin. This method will not remove all of the skin on all of the nuts. For recipes where that is necessary, one option is to toast more nuts than you will need, allowing you to pick out the better-looking ones and use the others where a little remaining skin does not matter. Or, to remove all of the skin, and in cases where you do not want toasted nuts, pour boiling water with a little baking soda added (1 teaspoon/4 g to 1 quart/960 ml) over the nuts, let stand 5 minutes, drain, then remove the skins. For the preceding recipe the nuts would then need to be toasted.

Walnuts and pecans are always caramelized (and otherwise used) with the skin on.

SUGAR-COATED NUTS yield: approximately 10 ounces (285 g)

3½ ounces (100 g) granulated sugar

3 tablespoons (45 ml) water

6 ounces (170 g) almonds, hazelnuts, or macadamia nuts

1 ounce (30 g) unsalted butter

1. Place the sugar and water in a small, heavy saucepan, stir to combine, and cook until the sugar reaches the thread stage, approximately 220°F (104°C).

2. Place the nuts in a bowl and pour the syrup over them. Stir the mixture until the sugar begins to crystallize.

3. Place the nut mixture back in the saucepan and return it to the heat. Cook, stirring constantly, until the sugar melts again and caramelizes on the nuts, toasting them in the process. Stir in the butter, mixing thoroughly.

4. Pour out the mixture onto a cold marble slab or a Silpat. Separate the nuts immediately as described in the main recipe.

Caramel Fans yield: variable

1 recipe Caramelized Sugar for Decorations (page 613)

Vegetable oil or pan spray

1. Read the instructions and precautions on pages 614 and 615 for Caramelized Sugar Decorations. Make a few disposable pastry bags from a double thickness of baking paper, as described.

2. Lightly oil or coat with pan spray the surface of an aluminum cake-decorating turntable, 12 inches (30 cm) in diameter, preferably the type with a heavy cast-iron base. Set the turntable on a sheet pan lined with a Silpat or a sheet of baking paper. Have a pair of scissors and a dry towel ready.

3. Let the caramelized sugar cool until it is the consistency of a thick syrup. Pour the syrup into a prepared pastry bag, close the top securely, wrap the towel around the bag, and cut a small opening at the tip.

4. Pipe 6 fans on the turntable as follows: Start each fan by piping a small dot of sugar near the center of the turntable, then pipe 5 or 6 lines extending from the dot and over the edge of the turntable to make each fan about 4½ inches (11.2 cm) wide at the edge of the turntable and approximately 3½ inches (8.7 cm) tall. Let the sugar strands fall over the edge of the turntable and collect on the Silpat or paper below (see Procedure 11-3a). Spin the turntable as needed. The fans will harden fairly quickly.

5. To remove the caramel fans, gently, but quickly, push them from the center toward the edge of the turntable and off. Place the fans on a sheet pan lined with a Silpat or bak-

PROCEDURE 11-3a **Piping a Caramel Fan on the turntable**

CHEF'S TIP
If desired, you may trim the edges of the caramel fans to make them perfectly even. In some cases you may have no choice but to trim them if the sugar was too cool and therefore too thick. Use a blowtorch to heat the blade of a chef's knife. Trim the edges of the fan where they meet the edge of the turntable or, wearing food handling gloves, hold a fan in your hand while you trim the edge (see Procedure 11-3b).

PROCEDURE 11-3b Using a heated paring knife to trim a finished fan holding it in your hand

ing paper. Continue to pipe out the remaining sugar, making as many decorations as needed, plus a few extra, as the fans are rather fragile. Store as described in the introduction to caramelized sugar decorations.

Sugar Shards yield: variable (Color Photo 68)

Sugar shards are most appropriate for use on desserts that are assembled à la minute because if prepared correctly, the shards will be as thin as spun sugar and will not hold up for any length of time in a humid atmosphere. They cannot be used on anything that will be refrigerated for more than just a few minutes, or they will collapse. If stored in an airtight container with a desiccant, the shards can be made up days in advance.

Sugar shards made from caramelized sugar provide a fitting decoration for the classic custards, such as crème caramel and crème brûlée — the traditional presentations of which are a bit dull by today's standards. By simply pushing a sugar shard into the top of the custard right before it is served, you easily add height, interest, and another texture. For crème brûlée, you may need to make a slit through the caramelized crust before inserting the shard.

If the sugar is inadvertently overcaramelized, just throw it out; do not be tempted to use it. Even though the color will lighten as you pull out the shards, sugar that is cooked too dark tastes bitter and hardens more quickly, making it difficult to work with.

1 pound (455 g) granulated sugar	2 tablespoons (30 ml) glucose *or* light corn syrup
¾ cup (180 ml) water	

1. Taking the usual precautions, follow the directions for Caramelized Sugar for Decorations (page 613), cooking the ingredients listed to a light caramel color. Remove from the heat and watch until the sugar has developed the desired tint. (It will continue to cook and darken off the heat.)

2. Immediately pour the syrup into an oval puddle in the center of a full-size Silpat placed on a flat, even surface. One at a time, pick up each corner of the mat, tilting it to allow the sugar to flow out and form a slightly larger and thinner oval. Let the sugar cool until the edges begin to set up.

3. Pull the edges of the sugar away from the center into thin, irregular shapes. Use scissors to cut them away from the main mass and place the decorations on a second Silpat or a lightly oiled sheet of baking paper. While the decorations should be thin, if they are too thin, they will break when you try to pick them up.

4. Continue pulling and cutting away the decorations. If necessary, you may reheat the sugar, but it will become darker each time you do.

NONCARAMELIZED SUGAR SHARDS AND TINTED SUGAR SHARDS

These instructions are for making clear shards or tinted shards. When adding food coloring to the syrup for the tinted sugar shards, keep in mind that the color will look much lighter in the finished decorations because the sugar is pulled out until very thin. Compensate by coloring the syrup a little darker than you want it to be in the finished product.

1. Fill a bowl large enough to hold the pan used to cook the sugar with enough cold water to reach halfway up the sides of the pan. Set the bowl of water aside.

2. Place ¾ cup water and the sugar in a sugar pan (see page 576) or a heavy saucepan. Stir the mixture gently over low heat until all of the sugar has dissolved and the syrup has started to boil. If scum accumulates on top from impurities in the sugar, remove it with a skimmer or small sieve so it does not cause the sugar to recrystallize later. Add the glucose or corn syrup, stirring until thoroughly mixed in. Do not stir any further after this point.

3. Turn the heat to high, place a lid on the pan, and let the sugar boil hard for a few minutes. The steam trapped inside the pan will wash down the sugar crystals that form on the sides of the pan at this stage. Alternatively, you can wash down the sides with a clean brush dipped in water (the brush should be dedicated to use in sugar boiling).

4. Place a sugar thermometer in the pan. When the temperature reaches 265°F (130°C), add the coloring, if using. Stop brushing and boil the sugar to 310°F (155°C), watching the temperature constantly.

5. Remove the pan from the heat and dip the bottom of the pan into the bowl of cold water for about 10 seconds to stop the temperature from going any higher. Dry the sides and the bottom of the pan.

6. Proceed from Step 2 of the main recipe.

Tartaric Acid Solution yield: approximately ¾ cup (180 ml)

½ cup (120 ml) hot water   4 ounces (115 g) tartaric acid

1. Mix hot water and tartaric acid until all of the granules are dissolved.

2. Pour the liquid into an eyedropper bottle (available in pharmacies and through professional pastry supply stores).

About Thermometers

An accurate thermometer is an invaluable tool in the professional kitchen, and it is especially important for sugarwork. Thermometers are made of many materials in different shapes and sizes for specific uses. One of the most common types of thermometer used for cooking consists of a mercury-filled glass tube with or without a stainless steel casing. Although they are frequently used in residential kitchens and found in most retail kitchen equipment stores, it is important to note it is illegal to use them in professional kitchens in some states (see below).

Thermometers should always be handled carefully. Glass thermometers are fragile and can break easily, and almost all types of thermometers can give inaccurate readings if they are dropped, handled roughly, or jostled in a drawer full of other tools. Mishandling can also cause the mercury to separate in a mercury thermometer. Some thermometers use an alcohol solution to register temperature, and mishandling can cause air bubbles to form in the liquid.

Thermometers used for measuring the temperature of food products must be kept impeccably clean, and you should follow the manufacturer's instructions for doing so. Food residue left on a thermometer poses a risk of bacterial contamination. Furthermore, in working with boiled sugar, any foreign particle can cause the sugar to recrystallize.

Testing and Calibrating Thermometers

One-piece probe thermometers, both digital and manual, as well as glass thermometers can be tested using either the ice-point method or the boil-point method. The probe types can be recalibrated if they give an inaccurate reading. If a glass thermometer fails the test, your only choice is to compensate for the discrepancy when you use it by adding or subtracting the difference in degrees. This assumes it is off by just a few degrees; if the reading is way off, the thermometer should not be used.

- To test using the ice-point method, fill a clean container with ice and water and place the thermometer in the liquid without allowing it to touch the container. It should register 32°F (0°C). If the reading is incorrect, recalibrate a bimetallic stemmed probe thermometer, commonly called an *instant-read thermometer,* in the following way: Keep the stem in the ice water and use a pair of pliers to firmly hold the adjusting nut located under the head. Turn the thermometer head until the pointer reads 32°F (0°C). Some one-piece digital thermometers have a reset button. These can be calibrated by pushing the button while the thermometer tip is submerged in the ice water.

- To test using the boil-point method, bring water to a boil in a clean pan and keep it boiling. Place the thermometer in the water without letting it touch the pan. It should read 212°F (100°C). If needed, recalibrate following the same instructions given for the ice-point method, in this case making the adjustment or pushing the reset button while the stem is submerged in the boiling water.

Regulations Regarding the Use of Mercury-Filled Glass Thermometers in Professional Kitchens

In the state of California, it is illegal to use mercury-filled glass thermometers in a professional kitchen. The California Uniform Retail Food Facility Law governs such practices, and the law is clear that mercury thermometers are not approved for use in commercial or public food preparation facilities. The reason is the potential risk of contaminating food with mercury, which is highly poisonous, should the glass break. Glass thermometers that use alcohol to indicate the temperature may be used; however, the state recommends that restaurant and commercial kitchens use bimetallic stem probe thermometers or digital probe thermometers instead. With these, the risk of broken glass is eliminated as well as the risk of mercury poisoning. In the case of thermocouple digital probe thermometers, because different probes are used for different types of food products, the risk of cross-contamination is less. If you are unsure as to whether a thermometer contains mercury or alcohol, the alcohol solution in thermometers that contain it is generally tinted red or blue, whereas mercury is a dull silver-gray color. For the record, California state law does not prohibit the use of glass mixing bowls, measuring cups, and other glass tools or utensils in commercial kitchens, but these items are impractical and really have no place in a professional setting. Because state rather than federal law governs these practices, you should contact the proper authority to determine the regulations for the state you work in.

Types of Thermometers

Candy Thermometer, Sugar Thermometer, or Confection Thermometer — This glass thermometer is used to determine temperature during the cooking of boiled sugar, fondant, candies, jams, and jellies. A thermometer is essential during the preparation of these items, where miscalculating by a few degrees in either direction can significantly alter the outcome. Candy thermometers register from 100° to 400°F (38° to 205°C) and are marked to indicate the various standard cooked sugar stages such as soft ball, hard ball, soft crack, and so on. It is especially important for a candy thermometer to be marked in at least 2-degree increments so even slight changes in the temperature of the sugar can be detected. Candy thermometers made for professional use are suspended inside a metal cage to protect against breakage and to elevate the glass so it does not rest on the bottom of the pan.

Digital Thermometer — Digital thermometers measure temperature through either a metal probe or a sensing area and display the temperature on a digital readout. They use either a thermocouple sensor or a thermistor sensor to detect temperature. Most allow you to switch between Celsius and Fahrenheit. They are made in a variety of models, from small, one-piece pocket styles to those in which a probe attached to a flexible wire leads to a separate base unit placed on the work surface. The most sophisticated of these are computerized and capable of storing data. The base contains the on/off switch and the digital display; higher-end models also feature other switches and display panels that give further information. These two-piece digital thermometers are available with a single probe attached to the base by the wire or with a connector on the base that allows the user to plug in different kinds of probes.

Thermometer with Detachable Probes — Basic types of probes include surface (used to measure the temperature of flat cooking equipment), immersion (used to measure the temperature of liquids), penetration (used to measure the internal temperature of food products), and air (used to measure the temperature inside an oven or a refrigerator). Almost all digital thermometers that can be used with multiple types of detachable probes use the thermocouple sensor system; however, the term *thermocouple* itself does not refer to the ability to plug in different probes.

Digital Thermocouple Thermometer with Detachable Probes — Although relatively expensive, these are extremely fast and accurate and are the type of thermometer recommended for use in commercial kitchens by the Food and Drug Administration and the U.S. Department of Agriculture. The temperature range varies with the model, but some thermocouple thermometers can measure as wide a range as −112° to 1,999°F (−80° to 1,100°C).

Marzipan   635

MARZIPAN DECORATIONS

Marzipan Apples   636

Marzipan Bear   637

Marzipan Bumblebees   639

Marzipan Carrots   639

Marzipan Coffee Beans   640

Marzipan Easter Bunny   641

   RESTING EASTER BUNNY   642

   SLEEPING EASTER BUNNY   642

Marzipan Easter Chicken   642

Marzipan Forget-Me-Not Flowers   644

Marzipan Rose Leaves   644

Marzipan Oranges   645

Marzipan Pears   645

Marzipan Piglet   646

   WHIMSICAL MARZIPAN PIG   648

Marzipan Polar Bear   649

Marzipan Roses   651

MARZIPAN HOLIDAY DECORATIONS

Marzipan Angel   653

Marzipan Children for the Traditional   656
Gingerbread House

Marzipan Pig with Two Santas   657

Marzipan Santa for the Traditional   660
Gingerbread House

Marzipan Modeling

Marzipan is used extensively in European pastry shops, particularly in Germany, Austria, Switzerland, and Scandinavia. It is made of almond paste and powdered sugar plus a moistening agent, such as glucose or corn syrup. Some recipes substitute egg whites or even fondant, but the purpose is the same.

There was a time when every pastry chef had to make his or her own almond paste by passing blanched almonds and an equal weight of sugar through the rollers of an almond mill until the mixture became a fine paste. Today, almond paste is readily available, making it much more convenient, in turn, to make your own marzipan.

Marzipan must be made in a stainless steel bowl to prevent discoloration. Due to its high sugar content (60 to 70 percent), marzipan dries quickly when exposed to air and should be kept covered at all times. If the marzipan becomes partially dry, you can reconstitute it by kneading in a small amount of water, although this will shorten its shelf life considerably. Keep your tools and workplace scrupulously clean, and always wash your hands immediately prior to rolling or molding marzipan with your hands. The almond oil brought to the surface as you work the marzipan will pick up and absorb even a small trace of dirt on your hands, which not only ruins the off-white color of the marzipan but can lead to spoilage.

Marzipan is rolled out in the same manner as pastry dough, but powdered sugar is used instead of flour to prevent the paste from sticking. The rolled sheet can be left smooth or may be textured in various patterns before being used to cover cakes, petits fours, and pastries. It is an ideal surface to decorate and pipe on, either freehand, using the technique described in Designs Pressed into Marzipan to be Traced over and/or Filled in with Fondant (page 677), or using the tracing method that follows. Marzipan is also used on petits fours and pastries that are to be coated with fondant or chocolate to achieve an even surface and to keep the coating from soaking into the sponge. When melted chocolate or chocolate glaze is used to cover a cake iced in buttercream, a thin layer of marzipan placed on top of the buttercream prevents the chocolate and buttercream from mixing together on top of the cake. Not only does the marzipan make a smooth finish possible, but the combination of chocolate and marzipan also gives the pastry a special and distinctive flavor. With few exceptions, marzipan should not be rolled out thicker than ⅛ inch (3 mm), or it can look clumsy and unattractive and, when used on top of cake or pastry, the flavor can be overwhelming.

Coloring Marzipan

Water-soluble food coloring can be used to tint marzipan, but keep the colors to soft pastel shades as much as possible. A green shade (such as for Princess cake) should usually be toned down with the addition of yellow. When adding color to a small amount of marzipan, or when you need only a hint of color, put a drop of color on a piece of baking paper and use the tip of a knife to add some of it to the marzipan. Knead the marzipan until the color is completely worked in. Use unsweetened cocoa powder to produce various shades of brown, unless for some reason you do not want or need the chocolate flavor; it is obviously a lot less expensive to use food coloring. Work the desired amount of cocoa powder into the marzipan and keep kneading until the marbled look is gone and the marzipan is smooth and evenly colored. If you add a large amount of cocoa powder, you may need to compensate by working in a bit of simple syrup or water to prevent the marzipan from getting too dry. To color marzipan bright white, use 4 to 6 drops of titanium dioxide for every 1 ounce (30 g) untinted marzipan. Note: Titanium dioxide should be used only for figurines or showpieces that will not be eaten.

Storage

Marzipan will keep almost indefinitely if you take proper care in its mixing and handling. Store it in airtight containers in a very cool place or in the refrigerator. It can also be stored in the freezer, should you need to keep it for a long time. If the oil separates from the marzipan after it thaws, making it crumbly and hard to work with, add a small amount of water and some powdered sugar. Knead the marzipan until smooth and elastic.

Marzipan yield: approximately 4 pounds 6 ounces (1 kg 990 g)

2 pounds (910 g) almond paste (see Chef's Tip)

½ cup (120 ml) or 6 ounces (170 g) glucose *or* light corn syrup

2 pounds (910 g) sifted powdered sugar

1. Place the almond paste and the glucose or corn syrup in a stainless steel mixer bowl. Using the hook attachment, mix at low speed until combined.

2. Start adding the sugar, scraping down the sides of the bowl as necessary. Add enough powdered sugar to make a fairly firm yet workable dough.

3. Wrap the marzipan in plastic, place in an airtight container, and store in a cold location.

NOTE: The amount of powdered sugar required will vary with the consistency of the almond paste. Always mix at low speed and take care not to overmix. The friction generated by overmixing will make the marzipan warm and soft, and you will end up adding too much powdered sugar.

CHEF'S TIP
The quality of the marzipan will depend largely on the quality of the almond paste. It must be perfectly smooth — free of tiny pieces of almond or specks of almond skin — as even the most minute pieces will show in finished marzipan products.

Tracing onto Marzipan

The templates and illustrations in this book (and any other drawings) can be traced quite easily onto a sheet of marzipan using either of the following methods.

METHOD I

1. Using the smallest possible amount of powdered sugar, roll out high-quality marzipan a little thinner than ¹⁄₁₆ inch (2 mm). The marzipan will be translucent.

2. Place the marzipan on top of the drawing and cut the edges to the proper size and shape.

3. Using either piping chocolate or piping gel, trace over the design. Transfer to the top of a cake or store to use later.

METHOD II

Tinted marzipan may not be translucent even when rolled out as directed above. This method allows you to transfer the image to the marzipan, but because it involves transferring pencil marks directly onto the marzipan, the technique is not recommended for anything other than show or display cakes. Another option is to use the technique described on page 677.

1. Using a soft pencil, trace the drawing onto baking paper.

2. Using no powdered sugar at all on the top so it stays fairly sticky, roll out the marzipan to ⅛ inch (3 mm) thick.

CHEF'S TIP
Remember this will produce a mirror image. If this makes a difference in the image you are using you can correct it in one of two ways. Turn the baking paper over and trace over the design again with the soft pencil. Use this side when transferring the image. If you are using copy paper (which is not translucent like baking paper), rub a small amount of vegetable oil on the back of the paper to make it transparent, invert the drawing, place another piece of paper on top, then retrace the picture so the image appears as the reverse of the way you want it to appear on the marzipan.

3. Invert your drawing on top of the marzipan and roll a rolling pin gently over the drawing, transferring the image onto the marzipan (see Chef's Tip).

4. Remove the drawing and pipe over the pencil marks as directed above.

Marzipan Apples yield: 24 decorations

These simple little apples can be used to decorate many cakes and pastries in this book. In addition to their appealing diminutive size, they are completely edible and — unlike real apples — seed-free. When placed on a dessert with an apple filling, this garnish gives the customer a clear indication of the flavor inside.

If you make the apples more than a few days ahead of when they will be eaten, keep the outside of the marzipan from drying out by using the tip of a brush to coat the apples lightly with warm melted cocoa butter; do this after applying the red color. You may also place a few apples at a time in the palm of one hand and apply the cocoa butter using the fingertips of your other hand. In general, it is a good idea to apply cocoa butter to marzipan decorations because in addition to sealing them from air it gives them a nice satin shine.

4 ounces (115 g) Marzipan (page 635), tinted pale green	24 whole cloves
Powdered sugar	Beet Juice (page 750) or red food coloring

1. Take the usual precautions for working with marzipan by making certain that your hands and your workspace are perfectly clean. Work the marzipan in your hands until it is soft and pliable. Using powdered sugar, if necessary, to prevent it from sticking to your work surface, roll it into a rope 12 inches (30 cm) long. Cut the rope into 24 pieces, each ½ inch (1.2 cm) long.

2. Roll each piece between your palms first into a round ball, then into a slightly oblong shape. Use a marzipan tool to make a small dimple in each end.

3. Make a hole on top of each apple and carefully, without altering the shape, insert the clove end of a whole clove so only the stem protrudes.

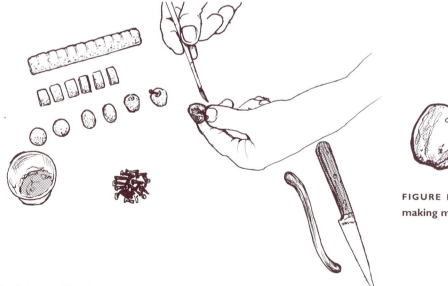

FIGURE 12-1 Sequence of steps in making marzipan apple decorations

4. Put a tiny amount of beet juice or red food coloring (less than a drop) on a piece of paper and apply the color to the very tip of a coarse, flat brush. Holding each apple by the stem, streak the color from top to bottom (Figure 12-1).

Marzipan Bear yield: 1 figure, 3½ ounces (100 g) in weight (Color Photo 101)

3½ ounces (100 g) Marzipan (page 635), untinted

Egg white

Royal Icing (page 680)

Dark coating chocolate, melted

1. Refer to Figure 12-2 as a guide in constructing the bear. Be certain that your hands and work area are absolutely clean. Divide the marzipan as follows:

- 1 piece weighing ⅔ ounce (20 g) for the rear legs
- 1 piece weighing ½ ounce (15 g) for the front legs
- 1 piece weighing ½ ounce (15 g) for the head
- 1 piece weighing ⅙ ounce (5 g) for the tail

Cover these pieces with plastic to prevent them from drying out.

2. Use the remaining marzipan for the body. Roll this large piece between the palms of your hands for a few seconds to make it soft and pliable. Roll it into a smooth, round ball. Position the ball between the lower part of your palms and taper half of the ball almost to a point. Form

FIGURE 12-2 The marzipan shapes for the Marzipan Bear; the assembled bear

the opposite end to narrow it slightly, leaving the center of the ball in a rounded shape that will become the stomach of the bear. Roll and shape the body to make it 2 inches (5 cm) long. Slightly flatten the narrow end on top (the neck). Set the body aside.

3. Divide the piece of marzipan reserved for the rear legs into 2 equal pieces. Roll the pieces separately between your hands to soften them, then roll them into smooth, round balls. Place a ball between the lower part of your palms and roll it to 2 inches (5 cm) in length, tapering 1 end slightly. Bend the front part of the narrow end on the leg to form a paw. Repeat with the other ball. Apply a small amount of egg white to the inside of the legs where they will touch the body. Attach the legs to the wide end of the body, placing the bear in a seated position and pressing to flatten and widen the rear part of the legs at the same time. Position the body in the way you want the bear to pose — leaning forward or sitting back.

4. Repeat Step 3, using the piece reserved for the front legs, but roll the front leg pieces to only 1¾ inches (4.5 cm) long. Attach them to the upper part of the body. Depending on how you arrange the front legs, they may need to be supported until firm.

5. Pinch off a raisin-size piece from the piece reserved for the head to make the ears; cover and set aside. Roll the remainder of the marzipan for the head to make it soft, then roll it into a smooth, round ball. Place the ball between the lower part of your palms and taper 1 side to a small, delicate point; leave the opposite side of the head round, not oblong. Hold the head in the palm of 1 hand. Use the tip of a small knife to make a cut ¼ inch (6 mm) long just below the tip of the nose for the mouth. Twist the knife to open the mouth slightly. Use a marzipan tool or another object with a small rounded end to make 2 shallow indentations for the eyes. Apply a thin film of egg white to both the neck and the bottom of the head; wait until the egg white is almost dry but still sticky. Carefully (so you do not deform the head) place the head on the neck, giving it a slight twist to seal the pieces together. (If the figure is to be used for display only, support the head by pressing part of a toothpick into the body first so just the tip is sticking out from the neck.)

6. Roll the small piece for the ears between your thumb and forefinger to make it soft. Divide in half and roll the pieces, 1 at a time, into smooth, round balls. You may need to adjust the size of the pieces if they look too large; remember, bears have very small ears. Using egg white as glue, press the ears into the top of the head with the same rounded tool you used to make the indentations for the eyes.

7. Roll the remaining piece of marzipan soft and round. Roll it into an oblong shape and fasten it to the back of the bear as the tail.

8. Using a marzipan tool or a blunt-pointed object, such as an instant-read thermometer, make 3 small grooves in the end of each paw to make the bear's claws.

9. Set the figure aside in a warm place for a few hours or overnight to allow the surface to dry slightly.

CHEF'S TIP
If the figure is to be kept for some time, brush a thin film of hot cocoa butter over the marzipan before piping on the royal icing or the chocolate.

10. Place a little royal icing in a piping bag and cut a small opening. Pipe icing into the indentations made for the eyes.

11. Place melted coating chocolate in a second piping bag and cut an even smaller opening. Pipe a small dot of chocolate in each of the marks made for the claws. Pipe a larger dot of chocolate on the tip of the bear's nose. Wake the bear up by piping a small dot of chocolate on top of the icing in the eyes to mark the pupils. Lastly, pipe a thin eyebrow above each eye.

Marzipan Bumblebees yield: 16 decorations

Though it can be a bit tricky to work with tiny pieces of marzipan, as in this recipe, do not be tempted to plump up the bumblebees; they can easily begin to take the shape of hummingbirds. The two may share an interest in flowers, but the larger creatures look quite out of place on a beehive. Following these instructions produces life-size bees, admittedly rather simplified.

4 ounces (115 g) Marzipan (page 635), untinted	Yellow food coloring
Unsweetened cocoa powder	Egg white
	Sliced almonds

1. Be certain both your work area and your hands are absolutely clean. Color ½ ounce (15 g) of the marzipan dark brown by mixing in the cocoa powder. Roll it out to a rope 6 inches (15 cm) long, then cut it into 16 equal pieces. Cover the pieces and set them aside.

2. Color the remaining piece of marzipan pale yellow. Roll this piece out to make a rope 16 inches (40 cm) long and cut it into 16 equal pieces. Roll a yellow piece between the palms of your hands to make it soft and pliable, then roll it into a round ball. Roll the ball against the work surface to make it oblong, about 1 inch (2.5 cm) in length and slightly tapered at each end. Repeat with the remaining pieces of yellow marzipan to form the bodies of the remaining bees.

3. Roll a reserved cocoa-colored piece of marzipan between your thumb and forefinger to make it soft and pliable. Divide the piece in half. Roll each of these 2 small pieces into a smooth round ball.

4. Slightly flatten 1 end of a bee body and, using egg white as glue, attach a cocoa-colored ball. This is the bee's head; it should be slightly larger than the end of the bee to which it is attached. Cut the body of the bee in half crosswise, flatten the second cocoa-colored ball, and use egg white to attach it between the body halves. Secure a dowel, 2 inches (5 cm) in diameter, to a sheet pan lined with baking paper. Place the bee on top of the dowel so it will dry in a slightly curved position. Assemble the remaining marzipan bumblebees in the same way.

5. For the wings, select 32 unbroken almond slices. Pair them so the wings on each bee will be the same size. Use a paring knife to make a small insertion point on each side of each bee just behind the head, then carefully push the narrow end of an almond slice into each cut. If necessary, leave the bees on the dowel until they hold their shape.

Marzipan Carrots yield: 24 decorations (Color Photo 96)

5 ounces (140 g) Marzipan (page 635), untinted	Green, red, and yellow food coloring

1. Color 1 ounce (30 g) of marzipan green. Cover and reserve. Use red and yellow food coloring to tint the remainder orange.

2. Divide the orange marzipan into 2 equal pieces. Roll each one into a 9-inch (22.5-cm) rope. Place the ropes next to each other.

3. Roll the green marzipan into a rope the same length as the orange ropes and place it next to them. Cut through all 3 ropes together, cutting each one into 12 equal pieces. Cut each of the

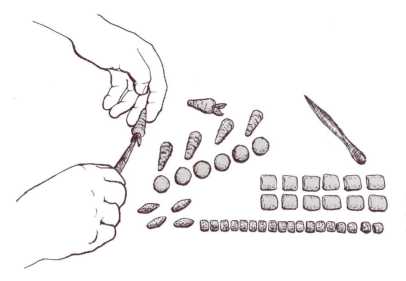

FIGURE 12-3 Sequence of steps in making marzipan carrot decorations

green pieces in half. You should now have 24 orange pieces and 24 smaller green pieces, 1 orange and 1 green for each carrot. Keep the pieces covered with plastic to prevent them from drying out.

4. Roll the orange pieces into round balls between your palms. Roll the balls into cone shapes, about 1 inch (2.5 cm) long, by rolling them back and forth against the table.

5. Mark the cones crosswise with the back of a knife to make them look ringed like a carrot. Starting at the wide end, turn them slowly and make random marks, crosswise, all around. Make a small round hole in the wide end of each carrot, using a marzipan modeling tool or the end of an instant-read thermometer.

6. One at a time, roll each of the small green pieces into a ¹/₂-inch (1.2-cm) string, tapered on both ends. Insert one end of the green stem into the hole in each carrot. Cut and fan the other end of each one to resemble a carrot top (Figure 12-3).

Marzipan Coffee Beans yield: 24 decorations

2 ounces (55 g) Marzipan (page 635), untinted   Unsweetened cocoa powder

1. Color the marzipan dark brown by kneading in a small amount of cocoa powder.

2. Roll the marzipan into a rope 12 inches (30 cm) long. Cut the rope into 24 equal pieces.

3. Roll 1 piece at a time between your palms to make it soft, then roll into a ball. Roll the ball into an oval. Place the oval in the palm of your hand and use a marzipan tool or the back of a chef's knife to make a mark lengthwise in the center, pushing the tool halfway into the bean. Make the remaining decorations the same way.

Marzipan Easter Bunny yield: 1 figure, 3 ounces (85 g) in weight

3 ounces (85 g) Marzipan (page 635), untinted

Egg white

Dark coating chocolate, melted

Royal Icing (page 680)

1. Refer to Figure 12-4 as a guide while constructing the bunny. Weigh out 2⅓ ounces (65 g) marzipan to use for the body. Cover and reserve the remaining ⅔ ounce (20 g) to use for the head. Be sure the work area and your hands are impeccably clean.

2. Roll the larger piece of marzipan between your hands for a few seconds until soft, then form it into a completely smooth, round ball.

3. Place the marzipan on the table in front of you and roll the ball into a cone-shaped body, 4 inches (10 cm) long, with a blunt tip at the tapered end.

4. Use a thin, sharp knife to cut a very small slice off the thick end to flatten it; the cone should stand straight when turned upright. Cover and reserve the piece you cut off for the tail.

5. Stand the cone so the wide cut end is flat on the table. Carefully bend the marzipan so the front one-third is also on the table and the middle is up about 1½ inches (3.7 cm) in the air, like the silhouette of a cat about to pounce.

6. Make a cut lengthwise in the front end and twist the pieces toward the center so the cut sides are against the table. Spread the 2 pieces slightly apart to form the front legs of the bunny. (Remember: These steps must be completed quickly to prevent the softened marzipan from hardening again and cracking or wrinkling as you mold it.)

7. Place the body over a dowel of suitable thickness to hold the curved shape, if necessary; set aside.

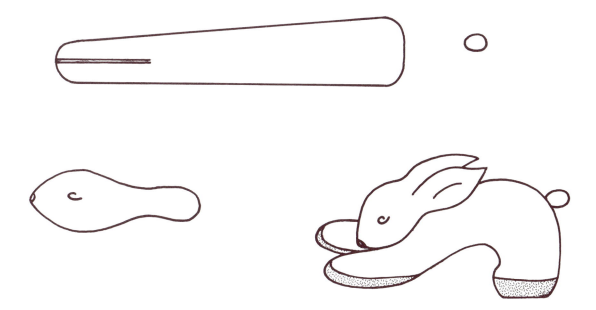

FIGURE 12-4 **The marzipan shapes for the Marzipan Easter Bunny; the assembled bunny with the base dipped in chocolate**

8. Roll the piece of marzipan reserved for the head to make it soft, then roll it into a round ball. Form the ball between the lower part of your palms to make it into a shape resembling a bowling pin, but tapered at the wide end. The piece should be 2¼ inches (5.6 cm) long.

9. Place the head on the table and make a lengthwise cut, 1 inch (2.5 cm) long, starting at the narrow end. Spread the 2 pieces apart and flatten the ends with your fingers a little to form the ears. Make 2 small indentations for the eyes.

10. Using egg white as glue, attach the head to the body, placing the nose between the front legs. Roll the small remaining piece into a ball and glue it in place as the tail. Set the figure aside in a warm place for a few hours or overnight to allow the surface to dry.

11. Dip the bottom ¼ inch (6 mm) of the bunny in melted chocolate. Pipe a small dot of royal icing in each of the indentations made for the eyes. Lastly, make the bunny come alive by piping a smaller dot of melted chocolate on the tip of the nose and on top of the royal icing to make pupils in the eyes.

VARIATIONS
RESTING EASTER BUNNY

To give the bunny a different look, cut the wide end of the cone instead of the narrow end in Step 6. Bend the cut halves so the flat sides face the table and spread them out and forward alongside the body on both ends. Flatten the uncut narrow end slightly and place the head on top.

SLEEPING EASTER BUNNY

As a third alternative, taper both ends of the body when rolling it out, cut both ends, position 1 front leg over the other, and arrange the rear legs in the same way to resemble a rabbit lying on its side.

Marzipan Easter Chicken *yield: 1 figure, 2 ounces (55 g) in weight*

⅓ ounce (10 g) Marzipan (page 635), untinted	1 blanched almond or sliver of almond
1⅔ ounces (45 g) Marzipan (page 635), tinted pale yellow	Dark coating chocolate, melted
Egg white	Royal Icing (page 680)

1. Refer to Figure 12-5 as a guide while constructing the chicken. Make sure your work area and your hands are perfectly clean. Roll the untinted marzipan in your hands until it is soft, then roll into a ball. Place the ball on the table and make a shallow depression on the top with your thumb, pressing hard enough to make the ball slightly flat on the bottom so it will not roll (it should be about 1 inch/2.5 cm in diameter). Set this piece aside for the nest.

2. Cover and reserve a little less than ⅓ ounce (8 g) of the yellow marzipan. Roll the remainder between your palms to soften it, then roll it into a smooth, round ball. Roll the ball between the lower part of your palms to form a cone 2½ inches (6.2 cm) long and rounded on both ends.

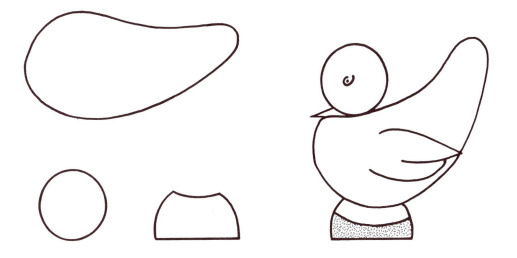

FIGURE 12-5 The marzipan shapes for the **Marzipan Easter Chicken**; the assembled chicken with the base dipped in chocolate

3. Bend the narrow end up slightly and press to flatten it a bit. To form a tail, use a marzipan tool or the back of a paring knife to mark 2 lines on top of the flattened portion.

4. With small scissors, make a thin cut from the rear about midway on both sides of the wide end to form the wings. Bend the cut parts down slightly and mark each wing in 2 places, as for the tail. Using egg white as glue, attach the chicken to the reserved nest.

5. Cut a pointed piece out of the almond to use for the chicken's beak.

6. Roll the reserved piece of yellow marzipan soft, then into a perfectly round ball. Make a small depression in the chicken's body where the head should go; use egg white to attach the head.

7. Push the blunt end of the beak between the head and the body. Use a marzipan tool or another small pointed object to mark a small point on each side of the head (not in the front) for the eyes. Allow the figure to dry in a warm place for a few hours or overnight.

8. Dip the bottom ¼ inch (6 mm) of the nest into melted coating chocolate. Place a small amount of royal icing in a piping bag and pipe a small dot of icing in the impressions made for the eyes. Pipe an even smaller dot of chocolate on top of the icing for pupils. If you plan to keep the figure for some time, follow the instructions in the Chef's Tip on page 647.

Marzipan Forget-Me-Not Flowers yield: 20 flowers, 1 inch (2.5 cm) in diameter

Crystal sugar

Powdered sugar

3 ounces (85 g) Marzipan (page 635), tinted
   light pink

Granulated sugar

½ ounce (15 g) Marzipan (page 635), tinted
   yellow

Piping Chocolate (page 543), melted

1. Fill a cake pan, 10 inches (25 cm) in diameter (or use a similar form), with a layer of crystal sugar 1 inch (2.5 cm) thick. Smooth the top even and set aside.

2. Using powdered sugar to prevent it from sticking, roll the pink marzipan out to slightly thinner than ⅛ inch (3 mm). Using a fluted cookie cutter, 1 inch (2.5 cm) in diameter, cut out circles. Place the circles on top of the crystal sugar in the cake pan.

3. Using your thumb, press down in the center of each circle, pushing it into the sugar and making it concave. Gather the scrap pieces of marzipan, roll them out again to the same thickness, and continue cutting circles and placing them in the sugar in the same manner until you have made 20.

4. Put a small amount of granulated sugar in a saucer or any small form. Roll the yellow marzipan into a rope ¼ inch (6 mm) in diameter. Cut the rope into 20 equal pea-size pieces. Use both hands to roll the pieces into round balls, 2 at a time, between your thumbs and index fingers, then drop them into the granulated sugar on the saucer. Roll the balls in the sugar so the sugar sticks to the marzipan.

5. Place the piping chocolate in a piping bag and cut a small opening. Pipe a small dot of chocolate in the center of each pink marzipan circle. Place a yellow marzipan ball on top of the chocolate before the chocolate sets up. Let the flowers dry for 1 day in a warm place; do not cover them.

6. As you remove the flowers from the crystal sugar, brush off any sugar that sticks to the back of the marzipan. Store, covered, in a dry place.

Marzipan Rose Leaves

A nice thing about producing leaves using the following method, as opposed to using a leaf cutter or leaf stamp, is that each leaf will be slightly different, just as in nature.

Marzipan (page 635), tinted light green

1. Roll out the marzipan to ¹⁄₁₆ inch (2 mm) thick. Using a sharp paring knife, cut out leaves of the appropriate size (Figure 12-6). Keep the tip of the knife clean and free of marzipan, or the cut edges will have a ragged and unattractive appearance.

2. Using the back of the knife, mark veins on the leaves.

3. Place a dowel on a sheet pan and attach a small piece of marzipan under each end to prevent it from rolling. Put

FIGURE 12-6 Cutting marzipan leaves and drying them over a dowel to curve them

the leaves on the dowel so they will dry with a slight curve. Let the leaves dry in a warm place for a few hours or, preferably, overnight.

Marzipan Oranges yield: 60 decorations

5 ounces (140 g) Marzipan (page 635), tinted orange

Melted cocoa butter (optional)

1. Divide the marzipan into 2 equal pieces and roll each piece into a rope 15 inches (37.5 cm) long. Cut each rope into 30 pieces, ½ inch (1.2 cm) long.

2. Roll the small pieces into balls and cover them to keep them from becoming dry.

3. Roll the balls lightly over a fine grater to give them an orange peel texture. Using a small wooden skewer, make a small indentation in 1 end of each orange where the stem would be.

4. The finished oranges can be stored for weeks. To keep them looking fresh, coat them with a thin film of cocoa butter. Place a small amount of cocoa butter in your palm and gently, without altering their shape or texture, roll a few marzipan oranges at a time between your palms.

Marzipan Pears yield: 16 decorations

Do not limit the use of these decorations to pear-flavored desserts, although they certainly are a smart way of indicating their flavor. Marzipan pears can also be served as a candy, included in a selection for a bonbon box or on a pastry tray. They are completely edible, except for the cloves used for the stems. If the pears are made more than a few days ahead of time, keep the outside from becoming dry by coating them lightly with melted cocoa butter after applying the red color. You can apply the cocoa butter with a brush or simply use your fingers as you roll the pears in the palm of your other hand. In addition to protecting the marzipan, the cocoa butter adds a nice satin shine.

4 ounces (115 g) Marzipan (page 635), tinted pale green

Powdered sugar

16 whole cloves

Beet Juice (page 750) or red food coloring

1. Take the usual precautions for working with marzipan by making sure that your hands and work area are perfectly clean. Work the marzipan in your hands until it is soft and pliable. Using powdered sugar, if necessary, to prevent it from sticking, roll it against the work surface to make a rope 12 inches (30 cm) long. Cut the rope into 16 pieces, ¾ inch (2 cm) long.

2. Roll each piece into a round ball, then taper 1 end to form a pear-shaped neck.

3. Using a marzipan tool, make a small dimple in both ends of each pear. Make a hole in the top of the stem end and carefully, without altering the shape, insert the clove end of a whole clove so just the stem is visible.

4. Put a tiny amount of red coloring, less than a drop, on a piece of baking paper. Apply a bit of color to the very tip of a coarse, flat brush. One at a time, hold a pear by the stem and, using a light touch of the brush, streak a few lines of color from top to bottom.

Marzipan Piglet yield: 1 figure, 3½ ounces (100 g) in weight

3 ½ ounces (100 g) Marzipan (page 635), tinted light pink

Red food coloring

Egg white

Royal Icing (page 680)

Dark coating chocolate, melted

1. Refer to Figure 12-7 as you construct the piglet. Starting with clean hands and a clean working surface, work a small portion of the marzipan soft in your hands, then roll it out to ¹/₁₆ inch (2 mm) thick. Cut out 2 triangles measuring 1 inch (2.5 cm) on all sides; these will be the pig's ears. Cover and set aside.

2. Color a small piece of the rolled scraps, about the size of a pea, with red food coloring. Roll it round and set it aside.

3. Combine the remaining rolled scraps with the remaining marzipan. Pinch off a piece about the same size used to make the two ears, cover it, and reserve for the tail.

4. Roll the remaining marzipan in your hands until soft, then roll it into a round ball. Place the ball on the table and roll out to a cone 4 inches (10 cm) long, keeping the wide end nicely rounded.

5. Place your thumb and index finger on either side of the narrow end, press lightly, and at the same time use the flat edge of the blade of a small knife to flatten the narrow end of the cone,

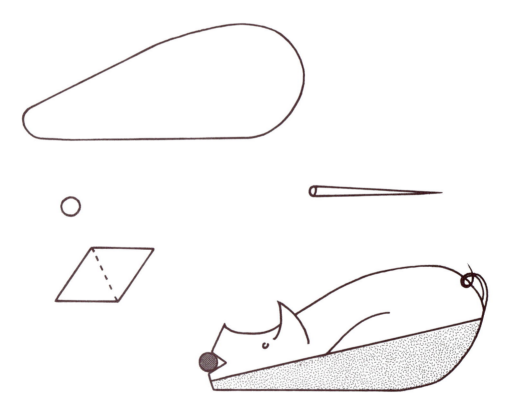

FIGURE 12-7 The marzipan shapes for the Marzipan Piglet; the assembled piglet with the base dipped in chocolate

moving the knife from the bottom to the top, to form the snout of the pig. Make a small cut for the mouth about two-thirds of the way from the top. Open the cut and place the reserved red ball (the apple) in the mouth.

6. Use a cone-shaped marzipan tool or an instant-read thermometer to make 2 deep holes for the ears to sit in, placing them about 1 inch (2.5 cm) from the snout. One at a time. form the reserved triangles around the tip of the cone tool, put a little egg white on the base, then push the ears into the holes. Angle the ears so they point forward slightly.

7. Using the same tool, make 2 small indentations for the pig's eyes, placing them close together between and below the ears. Make 2 identical marks in the upper part of the snout.

8. Place both index fingers on the sides of the pig about ¼ inch (6 mm) behind the head. Angle your fingers 45 degrees toward the back and press hard, making 2 deep indentations, to form the pig's body. Use a marzipan tool or the back of a paring knife to make a vertical indentation in the center of the back end of the pig.

9. Roll the small piece of marzipan reserved for the tail to make it smooth, then roll it into a thin rope, 2 inches (5 cm) long, tapered to a point at 1 end. Use a little egg white to attach the tail to the body, curling the pointed end. Let the pig dry in a warm place for a few hours or, preferably, overnight.

10. Using a piping bag, pipe 2 small dots of royal icing in the indentations made for the eyes, but remember: pigs have small eyes set close together. Using a piping bag with a small opening, pipe 2 smaller dots of chocolate on the royal icing to indicate the pupils. Dip the bottom of the pig into the melted chocolate, holding it at an angle to coat the pig about ¼ inch (6 mm) in the front and halfway up the sides in the back.

CHEF'S TIP

If you plan to keep the figure more than a week or so, to keep it from drying, brush a thin film of cocoa butter on it before piping the eyes and dipping in chocolate.

Using a Silk Screen to Decorate Marzipan

To use a silk screen to decorate marzipan, follow the same procedure in Steps 1 and 2, on pages 674 and 675, but place the screen directly on a sheet of thinly rolled marzipan instead of a Silpat. After printing, allow the cocoa paste to dry (the marzipan is not baked as the sponge cake is). The marzipan can be cut into a round to fit the top of a cake, or it can be cut into strips to wrap around the side of a cake.

WHIMSICAL MARZIPAN PIG yield: 10 decorations

This easy alternative uses marzipan rolled out into a sheet instead of molded in your hands. This allows you to create several decorations at the same time in a quick assembly-line fashion.

Powdered sugar	Dark coating chocolate, melted
14 ounces (400 g) Marzipan (page 635), tinted pale pink	Egg white
	Royal Icing (page 680)

1. Refer to Figure 12-8 as a guide in constructing the whimsical pigs. Using powdered sugar to prevent it from sticking, roll out the marzipan to ³⁄₈ inch (9 mm) thick. Using a plain cookie cutter, 2¼ inches (5.6 cm) in diameter, cut out 10 circles. Using a smaller plain cutter, 1¾ inches (4.5 cm) in diameter, cut out 10 more. Cover the scrap pieces and reserve them.

2. Using the back of a paring knife or a marzipan tool, mark the large circles with a slightly curved line to suggest the rear leg on each pig, as shown in the drawing.

3. One at a time, set each marzipan circle (both sizes) on a dipping fork and dip the bottom and the sides into melted coating chocolate, leaving the top exposed. Scrape the bottom against the side of the bowl, then blot on a sheet of baking paper to remove the excess chocolate (see Figures 3-1 to 3-5, page 94, but do not insert the dipping fork as shown in the illustrations). Set the circles aside.

4. Spread a portion of melted chocolate on a sheet of baking paper to make a 6½-inch (16.2-cm) square, slightly more than ⅛ inch (3 mm) thick. Let the chocolate harden, then use a warm knife to cut out 10 rectangles, 3 inches long × 1¼ inches wide (7.5 × 3.1 cm). Line up the rec-

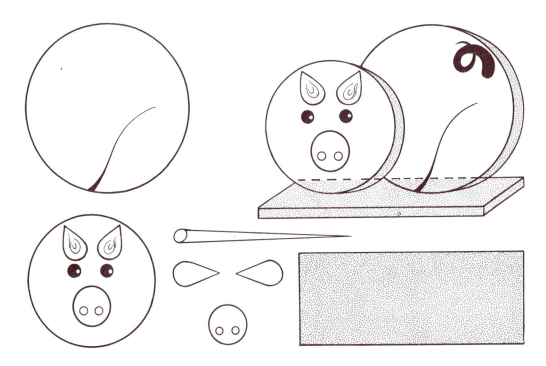

FIGURE 12-8 The marzipan shapes for the Whimsical Pig variation; the finished pig on its chocolate stand

tangles on a sheet pan lined with baking paper or on a cardboard cake sheet and place in the refrigerator.

5. Roll out a small piece from the reserved scraps of marzipan to ⅛ inch (3 mm) thick. Using a No. 7 (14-mm) plain pastry tip, cut out 10 circles for the pigs' snouts. Using a pointed marzipan tool, mark 2 small holes across the center of each snout.

6. Using egg white as glue, attach the snouts to the lower half of the 1¾-inch (4.5-cm) marzipan circles. Using a blunt marzipan tool or other suitable instrument, make 2 indentations above each nose to mark the pigs' eyes. Make 2 more indentations at the top of each head where the ears will be attached.

7. Roll the remaining marzipan scraps into a rope, 15 inches (37.5 cm) long. Cut the rope into 30 pieces, each ½ inch (1.2 cm) long — 20 will be used as ears and 10 as tails. One at a time, roll 10 pieces against the table into tapered strings, 1 inch (2.5 cm) long, then curl them for the tails. Reserve the tails in the refrigerator.

8. Roll the remaining small pieces of marzipan into cones, ½ inch (1.2 cm) long, for the ears. Using egg white as glue, attach the ears to the heads, using a blunt marzipan tool to create a round indentation at the base of each ear as you press it into place. At the same time use your other hand to bend the tips of the ears so they point forward.

9. Remove the chocolate rectangles and pigs' tails from the refrigerator. Attach the pig heads and bodies to the rectangles by piping dots of chocolate on the base before standing the circles upright on top. Using chocolate, fasten the tails to the bodies.

10. Place a small amount of royal icing in a piping bag and pipe dots of icing in the indentations made for the eyes. Decorate the bodies with dots of icing, if desired. Pipe a small dot of chocolate on top of the icing in the eyes to mark the pupils.

Marzipan Polar Bear   yield: I figure, 3 ounces (85 g) in weight (Color Photo 83)

3 ounces (85 g) Marzipan (page 635), untinted	Royal Icing (page 680)
Egg white	Dark coating chocolate, melted

1. Before working with marzipan, be sure that your hands, tools, and work surface are all impeccably clean. Have scissors and a few simple marzipan modeling tools at hand. Refer to Figure 12-9 as a guide in constructing the polar bear. Cut off a small piece of marzipan, about the size of a small pea, and set it aside. Roll the remaining marzipan into a ball between the palms of your hands. Use a light dusting of cornstarch on your hands if the marzipan seems sticky. Place the ball between the lower part of your palms and mold it by making the upper half narrower to create a shape like a bowling pin that is round on the bottom. Pinch the sides of the smaller end (the head) to create a slightly pointed snout.

FIGURE 12-9 The marzipan shapes for the Marzipan Polar Bear; the assembled bear

2. Use the scissors to make a cut ³⁄₈ inch (8 mm) deep into the stomach underneath the neck, extending the cut half the length of the body. Cut the piece that is now standing away from the larger piece in half lengthwise to form the 2 front legs of the bear (the legs are still attached to the larger piece of marzipan at the top). Use the marzipan tools or a paring knife to shape the body, spreading the legs apart, to form a sitting polar bear. Mark the toes on the paws, mark the bear's jaw, and make 2 small indentations to indicate the eyes.

3. Use the small reserved piece of marzipan to make 2 ears and a tail. Use egg white to attach these pieces.

4. To finish the bear, pipe a very small dot of royal icing in the indentations made for the eyes. Pipe smaller dots of dark chocolate on top to indicate the pupils of the eyes. Pipe tiny dots of chocolate to mark the toes and the nose as well.

Marzipan Roses **yield: 8 medium roses, ²/₃ ounce (20 g) each**

A marzipan rose may not be as elegant as a pulled sugar rose, but it certainly is more practical, as it can be made in minutes and, in addition, is much more pleasant to eat. A marzipan rose made for a special occasion should have 12 or more petals, depending on its shape and size, but a nice-looking production rose can be made using just 3 petals attached to the center. The three-petal rose is, naturally, quicker and easier to make, and it actually looks very much like a rosebud about to bloom.

Work on either a marble table or slab or a hardwood board or table. Do not use a wooden surface that has been cut on a great deal because the uneven surface will make it difficult to produce an optimum result. Take the usual precautions for working with marzipan by making sure your hands and work surface are clean and dry. Also, make sure the marzipan has a firm, smooth consistency. If it is too dry or hard, the marzipan will crack when you shape the petals; if it is too soft, it cannot be worked thin enough without it sticking to the knife and falling apart. Adjust the consistency by incorporating a small amount of water or powdered sugar as needed.

Although you need to start with 10 ounces (285 g) marzipan, you will have quite a bit left over when you finish the roses and cut off the bottoms.

> **10 ounces (285 g) Marzipan (page 635), tinted
> light pink or yellow, if desired**

1. Begin by working one-fourth of the marzipan in your hands until it is smooth and pliable, keeping the remainder covered with plastic. Roll the marzipan out to a rope 16 inches (40 cm) long.

2. Place the rope approximately 1 inch (2.5 cm) away from the edge of the table in front of you. Use your palm to flatten the rope into a wedge shape, with the narrow side facing the edge of the table (Figure 12-10). Keep the rope in a straight line and make sure it sticks to the table; use powdered sugar to prevent the marzipan from sticking to your hand.

3. Lightly coat a palette knife or a chef's knife with vegetable oil. Holding the palette knife at an angle to keep the wedge shape, work the knife over the rope, making long, even strokes and using enough pressure to flatten the rope to a strip 1 inch (2.5 cm) wide (Figure 12-11). The strip should be paper-thin in the front.

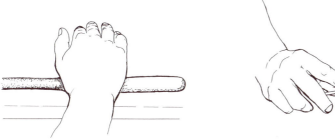

FIGURE 12-10 Using the palm to flatten a marzipan strip into a wedge with the narrow side closer to the edge of the table

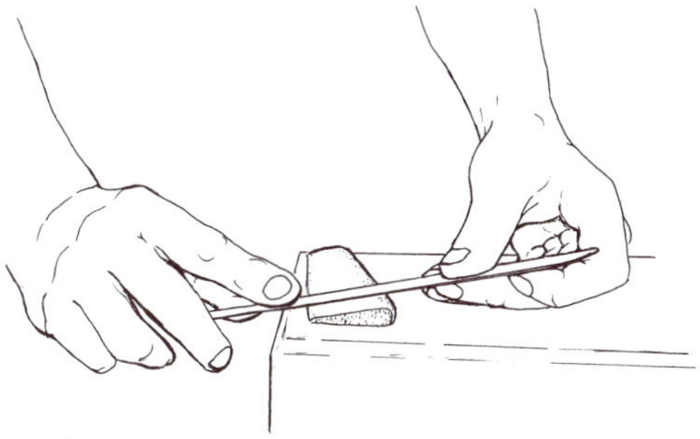

FIGURE 12-11 Using a palette knife with long even strokes to flatten the wedge further, making it paper-thin in front

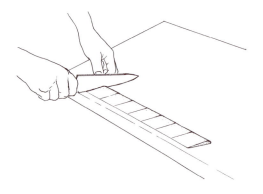

FIGURE 12-12 Cutting the flattened strip diagonally into 2-inch (5-cm) pieces

FIGURE 12-13 The center cone for a marzipan rose as it is formed from one of the cut pieces into the shape of a bud

4. Cut the flattened strip away from the table by sliding a thin knife underneath, moving under the length of the strip in one smooth motion. Cut the strip diagonally into 8 pieces, each 2 inches (5 cm) long (Figure 12-12).

5. Roll each piece around itself to form a cone, with the narrow part of the piece at the top. Fold 1 end back slightly so it looks like a bud about to open.

6. Squeeze the bottom of the bud to secure the shape and set it on the table in front of you (Figure 12-13). Repeat with the remaining 7 pieces. When you have finished making the centers, clean the work surface by scraping away any marzipan residue.

7. Work the remaining marzipan to make it soft. Roll it into a rope 18 inches (45 cm) long. Cut the rope into 24 pieces, ³⁄₄ inch (2 cm) long. Roll each piece into a round ball. Place 3 to 6 balls (depending on how much workspace you have) spaced 8 inches (20 cm) apart in a row in front of you at the edge of the table or marble slab. Keep the remaining pieces covered with plastic.

8. Flatten 1 side of each ball, as you did with the rope, to make a wedge shape; the flattened part should be on the left or right rather than the back or front. Make sure the pieces stick to the table.

9. Use an oiled chef's knife or palette knife held parallel to the table to enlarge the pieces, keeping the round shape and working them out paper-thin on the flat side (Figure 12-14). This can also be done using the top of a light bulb or a plastic scraper.

10. Cut the pieces away from the table by sliding a knife underneath, but leave them in place. Use the tip of your index finger to make an indentation on the thicker side of each piece (Figure 12-15); this will make it easier to bend the petals into the proper shape.

11. Pick up 1 piece and curl the thin edge back slightly to form a petal (Figure 12-16). Repeat with the remaining pieces

12. Attach 3 petals around one of the rose centers made earlier. Squeeze just above the base of the rose to secure the petals and make them open out slightly.

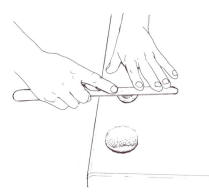

FIGURE 12-14 **Using a palette knife to extend and flatten a marzipan circle for a rose petal, making it paper-thin on one side**

FIGURE 12-15 **Using the index finger to create an indentation on the thicker side of each petal**

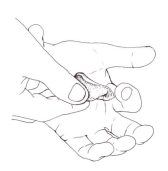

FIGURE 12-16 **Curling the edge of the petal back slightly**

13. Cut away the excess marzipan from the bottom and save it for another use. Repeat to make the remaining roses. Take care not to flatten too many petals at once, as they dry quickly and become difficult to form. The completed roses, however, can be made up days in advance without looking wilted. The thin edges will dry and become lighter in color, but that actually makes them look more realistic.

NOTE: For a rose stem, roll light green marzipan into a thin string. Make the thorns by making small angled cuts in the stems here and there with scissors. As on a real rose stem, the thorns should point upward. Instructions for making Marzipan Rose Leaves are on page 644.

MARZIPAN HOLIDAY DECORATIONS

Marzipan Angel yield: 1 figure, 3½ ounces (100 g) in weight

Biblically, angels are said to be messengers of God, belonging to the lowest class in the celestial hierarchy (in culinary jargon, this is probably the equivalent of an apprentice). The word is used to signify something or someone good or good for you, a person with a high standard of morality or virtue, or someone who watches over you, such as a guardian angel. *Angel* is employed in the food world in such names as angel hair pasta, angels on horseback, angel food cake, and angel or angelica parfait.

Using a mold to press out marzipan figures — which is becoming more common every year due to the time it takes to mold marzipan by hand — is the quickest method, but this angel is one of the easiest handmade figures to produce. It does require a bit of advance planning because several pieces, particularly the wings, must dry overnight before the figure can be finished.

4½ ounces (130 g) Marzipan (page 635),
   untinted

Yellow food coloring

Powdered sugar

Red food coloring

Egg white

Royal Icing (page 680)

Dark coating chocolate, melted

1 small candle (such as a birthday cake
   candle)

I. Refer to Figure 12-17 as a guide when constructing the angel. As always when working with marzipan, be sure your hands and working area are spotlessly clean. Divide the marzipan into 2 pieces weighing ⅓ ounce (10 g) each, 1 piece weighing 2½ ounces (70 g), leaving another piece weighing a bit more than 1 ounce (40 g).

2. Color the 1-ounce (40-g) piece pale yellow. Using powdered sugar to prevent it from sticking, roll it out a little thinner than ⅛ inch (3 mm).

3. Using a heart-shaped cutter, 2½ inches (6.2 cm) wide, cut out a heart. Place the heart on a sheet of cardboard. To make the wings, make a cut starting at the pointed tip of the heart and going three-quarters of the way toward the top. Spread the cut apart at the tip so it is open ½ inch (1.2 cm). Set the wings aside in a warm area.

4. To make the hair, color a scrap piece left from the wings with cocoa powder to a dark brown, or leave it yellow. Roll it out even thinner and, using a fluted cutter, ½ inch (1.2 cm) in diameter, cut out a fluted circle. Cover and reserve this piece. (You will have some yellow marzipan left over; cover and save for another use.)

5. Use a very small amount of red food coloring to color 1 of the ⅓-ounce (10-g) pieces pale pink. Pinch off a tiny piece the size of a pinhead and color this piece red to use for the mouth (see Note). Set aside. Roll the rest of the piece (the head) into a perfectly round ball. Holding it carefully in one of your palms (so it will remain perfectly round), use a marzipan tool or another small, blunt object to mark 2 small indentations for the eyes.

6. Keeping the head in your palm, roll the small red piece for the mouth round between the thumb and index finger of your free hand; using egg white for glue, attach it to the head. Using a pointed marzipan tool or an instant-read thermometer, press in the center of the mouth to make a small round hole; the mouth should appear as if the angel is singing.

7. Using egg white, fasten the reserved round fluted piece (the hair) to the top of the head. Set the head aside.

8. Take out the large reserved piece and roll it between your hands until soft and pliable, then roll it into a ball. Place the ball on the table and roll it into a cone, 3 inches (7.5 cm) long, with a blunt tip at the narrow end. Pick up the cone and firmly tap the wide end against the table a few times to flatten it so the angel will stand upright.

9. Brush egg white down the center of the reserved wings above the cut. Lay the cone on top of the wings, placing the narrow end level with the top in the center.

10. Roll the final reserved piece of marzipan into a rope 4 inches (10 cm) long and very tapered at each end. Fasten the rope (arms) to the body with egg white, draping it from the shoulders to the waist. Leave the body flat for 24 hours in a warm place to allow the wings to dry.

II. Cut the bottom flat, if necessary, and stand the angel up. Use egg white to attach the head to the body.

FIGURE 12-17 The marzipan shapes for the Marzipan Angel; the finished angel

12. Using a piping bag with a small opening, pipe dots of royal icing in the indentations for the eyes. Place melted chocolate in a second piping bag and pipe 2 very small dots of chocolate on the icing for pupils. Pipe a very fine line above each eye for eyebrows. Gently place the candle in the arms.

NOTE: When coloring such small pieces of marzipan, it is impossible not to add too much color if you add it directly. Instead put a drop of color on a piece of baking paper or on a saucer and use the very tip of a paring knife to add just a speck of color to the marzipan.

CHEF'S TIP

If you wish to decorate the body with royal icing — buttons above the arms or a pattern to mark the skirt — do this while the figure is lying down. If you are planning to keep the figure for any length of time, brush a thin film of hot cocoa butter over the figure before piping.

Marzipan Children for the Traditional Gingerbread House

yield: 4 partial figures (Color Photo 105)

If you work regularly with marzipan, you probably have a supply of tinted portions on hand, in which case you can ignore the instructions here for tinting the small pieces. If you do not, my recommendation is to tint a base supply, using food coloring to make red, yellow, and green shades and cocoa powder for a brown shade. Keep these on hand for future projects, adjusting and mixing the colors as needed. Although red and green can be combined to make brown, cocoa powder gives the marzipan a nice chocolate flavor, so I prefer to use that instead. Leftover pieces of marzipan can be stored for a year or more if they are kept tightly wrapped in an airtight container, so it is impractical to tint small pieces for each new project.

However, if I have failed to convince you, and you prefer to tint only enough marzipan for these figures, use the directions that follow and read the Note on page 655. Be sure to clean your hands thoroughly after working with each color, so specks are not transferred from one piece to another. Refer to Color Photo 105 as you make the children. If you want to add ears and noses to the faces, as shown in the photograph, start with a bit more marzipan and reserve slightly larger pieces of pink and brown in Steps 3 and 5.

3½ ounces (100 g) Marzipan (page 635), untinted	Egg white
Red and yellow food coloring	Royal Icing (page 680)
Cocoa powder	Dark coating chocolate, melted

1. As always when working with marzipan, be sure your hands and work area are spotlessly clean before you start. Weigh out 2 ounces (55 g) marzipan and roll it into a rope 4 inches (10 cm) long. Cut the rope into 4 pieces; they do not need to be exactly equal in length, but they should all be roughly as long as the height of the balcony for the Traditional Gingerbread House because the heads of the figures will be placed on these pieces for support. If the pieces are much shorter, the heads will not be visible; if they are too tall, the bases will show. Stand these pieces (the bodies) on end and reserve.

2. Roll out the remaining marzipan to the same length as before and mark the rope into 5 equal sections. Cut off one-fifth; wrap this piece in plastic and reserve.

3. Cut the remaining four-fifths in half and tint 1 piece pale pink. Pinch off a pea-size piece of pink and reserve with the first untinted one-fifth of the rope.

4. Divide the remaining pink piece in half and roll both halves into round balls; set aside.

5. Divide the remaining larger untinted piece in half and tint 1 piece pale yellow and the other light brown. Pinch off a pea-size piece of each, set the small pieces aside, roll the larger pieces into round balls, and place them with the pink balls.

6. Use a marzipan tool or other suitable tool to make indentations in all 4 heads to mark the eyes. Using tiny balls of pink marzipan made from the pea-sized piece (do not use all of it), make 4 mouths. Using a pointed tool to push them into place, attach the mouths to the faces; at the same time, make them look round and open.

7. Use the reserved piece of yellow to make hair and, using egg white as glue, attach to 1 of the pink heads. Divide the reserved brown marzipan in half and use half for hair on the remaining pink head and the remainder, tinted slightly darker with cocoa powder, to make hair on the brown head. Using egg white, attach the hair to the heads.

8. Make and attach ears and noses, if desired (see introduction).

9. Roll a small piece of untinted marzipan into a flattened string. Use this to add a hood to the yellow face by wrapping it around the top of the head and securing it with egg white.

10. Pipe a small dot of royal icing in the indentations made for the eyes. Pipe a smaller dot of melted chocolate on top to mark the pupils.

11. Place the bodies (Step 1) on the gingerbread house balcony, securing them with a little royal icing.

12. Roll the remaining untinted marzipan into 4 small balls. Using egg white as glue and pressing to flatten them slightly, place them on top of the bodies to suggest necks. Brush a little egg white on top of the necks and carefully set the heads in place.

Marzipan Pig with Two Santas

yield: 1 showpiece, 10 pounds (4 kg 550 g) in weight (Color Photos 106 and 107)

As discussed in the introduction to the Holiday Favorites chapter, many Scandinavian holiday meals are based on pork — the Christmas ham being the most traditional — and that is why the pig is featured in many decorations and ornaments at that time of the year. This marzipan pig, transporting not one but two Santas, makes a whimsical showpiece sure to delight and bring a festive old-world touch to your display. All of the components are edible, but if you do not have the heart to cut into your artistry, wrap it carefully and store it in a cool, dry place until next year. The marzipan will be very hard and no longer fit for consumption, but the pig and Santas can be used again for display with just a few small cosmetic repairs to restore them to their original glory. Refer to Color Photos 106 and 107 as you create the pig and the Santas.

Marzipan (page 635), portioned and tinted as follows:

FOR THE PIG

- body: 9 pounds 6 ounces (4 kg 265 g) untinted marzipan
- tongue: $^1/_{10}$ ounce (3 g) light pink marzipan
- eye ridges: $^1/_6$ ounce (5 g) untinted marzipan
- ears: 3 ounces (85 g) untinted marzipan
- tail: $^2/_3$ ounce (20 g) untinted marzipan

FOR THE SANTAS' BODIES AND ACCESSORIES

- legs: 2 pieces green marzipan, $^5/_6$ ounce (25 g) each
- bodies: 2 pieces red marzipan, $^5/_6$ ounce (25 g) each
- arms: 2 pieces red marzipan, $^2/_3$ ounce (20 g) each

- sack: $^5/_6$ ounce (25 g) brown marzipan
- mittens: $^1/_3$ ounce (10 g) yellow marzipan
- boots and cuffs: $^1/_2$ ounce (15 g) brown marzipan
- gifts and jacket decorations: 2 pieces scrap marzipan in any color, $^1/_3$ ounce (10 g) each

FOR THE SANTAS' HEADS

- heads and beards: 2 pieces untinted marzipan, $^1/_2$ ounce (15 g) each
- faces: 2 pieces light pink marzipan, $^1/_4$ ounce (7 g) each
- hats: 2 pieces red marzipan, $^1/_3$ ounce (10 g) each

Egg white

Hot cocoa butter

Royal Icing (page 680)

Dark coating chocolate, melted

Because such a large piece of marzipan is used for the pig's body, it can take some time to work it smooth and soft enough to form. If the marzipan is very firm, either because of its quality or a low room temperature, you can speed the softening process by placing it in a microwave oven for 5-second intervals. This is preferable to using an electric mixer to soften the marzipan, which can cause some of the oil to separate.

I. Make sure your work surface and your hands are impeccably clean. Cover all the pieces for the Santas and set them aside.

TO FORM THE PIG

2. To form the pig's body, work that piece of marzipan smooth and soft with your hands (see Chef's Tip). Roll it into a cylinder 15 inches (37.5 cm) long, well rounded on 1 end and tapered on the other. Bend the body to make it curve slightly left to right. Flatten the tapered end by pressing against the marzipan with the blade of a chef's knife, moving the knife straight up at the same time until you have a slightly oval flat area in the front, about 1½ inches (3.7 cm) in diameter, for the pig's snout.

3. Starting at about the center of the pig, make a cut on the inside curve at a 45-degree angle. Pull this piece out and form the rear leg. Starting about 3 inches (7.5 cm) from the snout, make a second cut at the same angle, pull it out, and form the front leg. Form and shape the body and legs while the marzipan is still soft and pliable.

4. Make a small vertical indentation on the front at the base of each leg to form the feet.

5. Carefully bend the front 4 inches (10 cm) of the pig upward. Support the head with a piece of scrap marzipan until it holds the desired angle. Make a small cut in the lower part of the pig's snout for the mouth and open it slightly. Use a pointed tool to make 2 holes in the front of the snout.

6. Form the pink marzipan into a small, flat tongue (just the tip as shown in the Color Photos); attach it inside the pig's mouth.

7. Use a round marzipan tool or another suitable object to mark fat folds in the bend behind the snout.

8. Mark the spots for the eyes. Roll the marzipan reserved for the eye ridges into round pieces and, using a little egg white for glue, attach them, pushing them in place with a rounded tool to create a curved crescent above each eye.

9. One at a time, roll the ear pieces between your hands to make them smooth. Form each ear into a triangle with 2 long sides, 3 inches (7.5 cm) each, and a base that is 2 inches (5 cm) wide. Use egg white to attach the ears to the head, placing them 1 inch (2.5 cm) behind the eye ridges. Shape the ears so they first curve backward, then fold over in front. Support the ears with scrap marzipan until they are firm enough to hold their shape.

10. Roll the piece reserved for the tail between your hands until round and smooth, then roll it into a tapered rope 4 inches (10 cm) long. Use a marzipan tool or the back of a chef's knife to mark a vertical line at the back of the pig where the rear leg meets the body. Using egg white, attach the tail at the top in a curled shape. Let the marzipan harden sufficiently for the ears and head to support themselves before moving the pig.

MAKING THE SANTAS

II. Roll a green marzipan leg piece until smooth, then roll it round between your palms. Place on the table and roll into a rope 5 inches (12.5 cm) long and slightly tapered at the ends. Bend the rope in half to make 2 legs. Using egg white, attach the legs straddling the pig's back

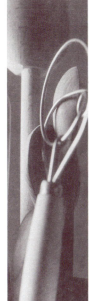

About Pigs

In general, the domestic pig has gotten a bad rap, for contrary to its reputation, it is a clean creature. Pigs roll in mud to protect themselves from heat and to get rid of parasites — as, in fact, do many other mammals. Pigs are among the most intelligent of all domestic animals. They are easily trained, and some species are kept as household pets, notably the Vietnamese potbellied pig. Pigs also have a highly developed sense of smell that enables them to sniff out the renowned and extremely expensive truffles found in the French Périgord region. Unfortunately, we humans have a bad habit of using the word *pig* to describe someone who is greedy, dirty, selfish, chauvinistic, or otherwise undesirable, to say nothing of someone with bad table manners or a generous appetite.

The domesticated pig was introduced to North America by Columbus in 1493, and pig farming has been an important agricultural industry in the United States since the late 1800s. Pigs have always been a popular farm animal, one reason certainly being the pig's ability to eat and gain weight from just about any food source, thus converting scraps into meat quickly and efficiently with a minimum of expense for feed. Just about every part of the pig carcass is used and marketed, from the flesh, which is turned into roasts, chops, sausage, bacon, headcheese, and ham, to the stomach, which is eaten as tripe, and the feet, which some consider a delicacy. The fat is sold as lard, and the hide is tanned to make leather.

and slightly behind the ears so the feet are right next to the eyes. Form the second pair of legs in the same way; attach these sitting on top of the pig at the back by the rear leg, with both legs hanging over the front side of the pig (the side of the pig with legs).

12. Roll a red body piece to make it smooth and round. Place the ball between the lower part of your palms and shape it into a slightly pear-shaped oval, 1½ inches (3.7 cm) tall. Use your thumb to make a smooth indentation in the center at the top of the front pair of legs. Using egg white, attach the oval body on top, placing the wider end on the legs. Repeat to form and attach the body of the back Santa.

13. Roll out a red marzipan arm piece in the same way as for the legs, making it 4 inches (10 cm) long. Cutting from shoulder to shoulder, make a slit ½ inch (1.2 cm) deep across the top of the body of the front Santa. Open the edges of the cut, flatten the marzipan in the center of the arms, and push the arms into the opening; attach with egg white. Use your forefinger and thumb to press the edges of the cut together; at the same time form a flat surface, sharply angled down toward the front of the body, on which to place the head. Form and attach the arms on the back Santa in the same way.

14. Roll the brown marzipan for the sack, shaping it into an oval as for the bodies. Open the top (narrow end) of the sack by carefully pushing a rounded marzipan tool or similar object into the top and rotating it gently. Using a marzipan tool or the back of a knife, make a windowpane design on the sides of the sack. Use egg white to attach the sack to the rear Santa's left side.

15. Cut the yellow marzipan for the mittens into 4 equal pieces. One at a time, roll the pieces into cones, ¾ inch (2 cm) long. Bend the pointed third of the cone against the remainder to form a thumb. Bend the mitten into a slightly curved position, as if starting to close the hand, taking into account which side the thumb should be on. Repeat with the remaining 3 pieces so you have 2 left and 2 right hands. Using egg white, attach all 4 mittens to the ends of the arms, placing the front Santa's mittens so he is holding onto the ears of the pig and the rear Santa's mittens so he is holding onto his sack.

16. Divide the brown marzipan for the boots into 6 equal pieces. Roll 4 of the pieces into balls and, using egg white as glue, press a boot onto the bottom of each leg. Divide the 2 remaining brown pieces in half to form 4 small pieces. One at a time, roll these between your fingers into very thin ropes, then flatten them. Wrap 1 piece around the end of each arm above the mitten to hide the seam where the arm and mitten meet. Attach with egg white, trimming any excess, and, using a pointed marzipan tool, decorate the cuffs.

17. Use the 2 scrap marzipan pieces to decorate the Santas' jackets, as shown in the photographs, and to form 2 or 3 presents for the sack. Secure these pieces with egg white.

18. Using the marzipan specified for the heads, follow the instructions on pages 662 to 663, Steps 5 through 14. Using just enough egg white to make the surface sticky, attach the heads to the bodies; too much egg white will allow the heads to slide off.

19. To protect the marzipan, use a brush or spray bottle to apply a light coat of hot melted cocoa butter to the Santas and the pig.

20. Place a small amount of royal icing in a piping bag and cut a very small opening. Pipe eyes on the Santas and the pig.

21. Place a small amount of melted chocolate in a piping bag and cut a very small opening. Pipe the pupils on the eyes of the Santas and the pig. The pig and the front Santa can look at one another. Pipe a thin line of chocolate above the Santas' eyes for eyebrows, on the top of the pig's eye ridges, and in the indentations on the pig's feet.

Marzipan Santa for the Traditional Gingerbread House

yield: I figure, 3½ ounces (100 g) in weight (Color Photo 103)

This standing Santa is the most complex marzipan figure featured in this text. Although it can be made without them, marzipan modeling tools make the project much easier. It is not necessary to own a bona fide set imported from Europe. The simple sets of wooden sculpture tools sold at art supply stores make a good substitute and are generally available for about one-tenth the cost of a twelve-piece marzipan set.

The following directions are for a fully equipped Santa, but you may simplify without offending him too much. By deleting the sack, you can also omit the mittens and the gifts. Add the 15 g marzipan for the sack (without tinting it green) to the weight for the body instead. For a different look, shown in Photo 104, form the beard by rolling a small piece of marzipan to ⅛ inch (3 mm) thick, then use a ruffled rolling pin, a marzipan tool, or the back of a knife to press vertical lines on top. Using a fluted cutter, 1¼ inches (3.1 cm) in diameter, cut out a round. Using just the bottom half of a fluted cutter, ¾ inch (2 cm) in diameter, cut away about one-quarter of the top to create a crescent-shaped beard with a scalloped edge. Before adding the mustache, use egg white to attach the beard to the head just under the face.

3½ ounces (100 g) Marzipan (page 635), untinted	Egg white
Green and red food coloring	Royal Icing (page 680)
Cornstarch	Dark coating chocolate, melted

I. Before you begin work, make certain your hands and work area are perfectly clean. Refer to Figure 12-18 in forming the Santa. Divide the marzipan as follows, using a gram scale:

FIGURE 12-18 **The marzipan shapes for the Marzipan Santa; the finished Santa**

- 50 g for the body
- 10 g for the head
- 15 g for the sack; color this piece green

Color the remainder (25 g) red. Divide this into one 10-g piece for the boots and mittens and one 15-g piece for the cape.

TO MAKE THE BODY

2. Cover and reserve all of the pieces other than the piece for the cape. Using cornstarch to prevent it from sticking, roll out this piece to a circle $\frac{1}{16}$ inch (2 mm) thick. Using a plain round cookie cutter, approximately $2\frac{3}{4}$ inches (6.7 cm) in diameter, cut out the cape. Cover and reserve the cape and the scrap pieces separately. The scrap pieces will be used to make the hat and to tint the face.

3. Roll the large piece of untinted marzipan for the body between your palms for a few seconds to make it soft and pliable. Roll it into a smooth round ball, then position the ball between the lower part of your palms and roll the lower half of the ball into a thick rope (Figure 12-19) to form the rounded stomach and upper torso of the Santa; the piece should be $2\frac{1}{2}$ inches (6.2 cm) long overall.

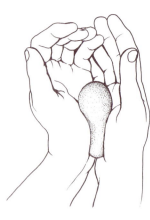

FIGURE 12-19 Forming the body for the Marzipan Santa

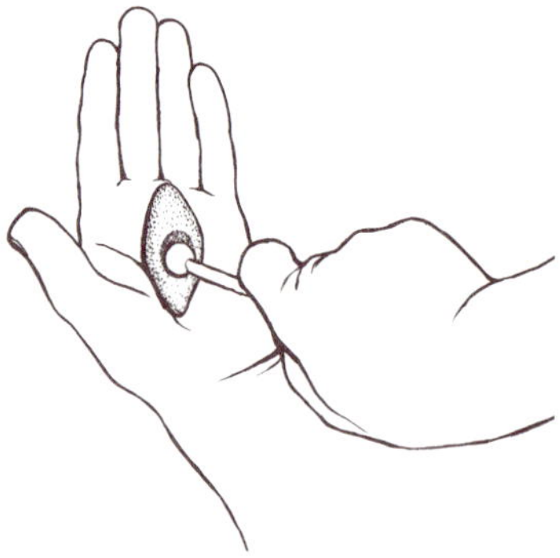

FIGURE 12-20 Using a round marzipan tool to press a shallow indentation in the marzipan for Santa's face

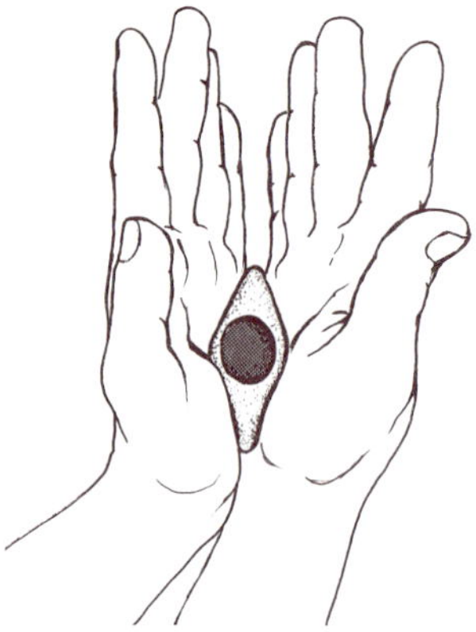

FIGURE 12-21 Using the lower part of the palms to taper the ends of the marzipan piece

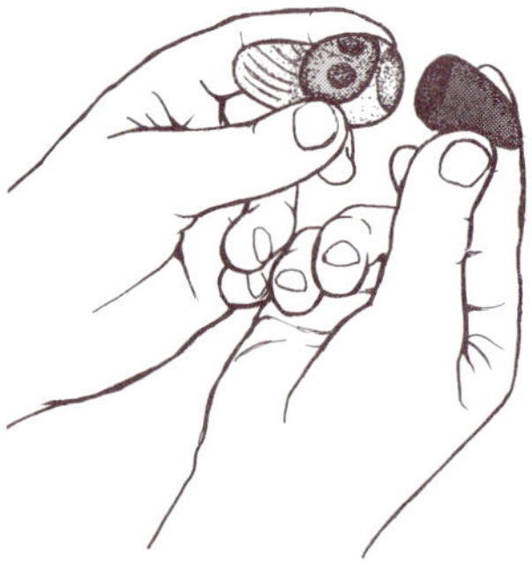

FIGURE 12-22 Attaching the hat to the top of the Santa's head

4. Lay the body down and flatten the side against the table slightly. Cut off a small piece at the narrow end, cutting at a 45-degree angle to create a flat, slanted surface for the neck. Reserve the body piece, uncovered.

TO MAKE THE HEAD

5. Add just enough of the red scrap piece left from the cape to the untinted piece cut off the neck to color it pale pink. Work the pieces together well; reserve for the face.

6. Roll the untinted marzipan for the head smooth, then into a round ball. Position your hands as you did to form the body and roll the ball between the lower part of your palms so it is 1 inch (2.5 cm) long and tapered at each end. Using a round marzipan tool or the back of a ½-inch (1.2-cm) or smaller melon ball cutter, press a shallow hole in the center (Figure 12-20).

7. Cover and set aside 2 tiny pieces of pink marzipan, about the size of peppercorns, for the ears, and 1 slightly smaller piece for the nose. Roll the remainder into a smooth, round ball. Put a little egg white in the indentation in the head and attach the round piece for the face.

8. Position the head piece between your palms as before and finish shaping it by rolling it to 1½ inches (3.7 cm) long and pointed at both ends (Figure 12-21).

9. Use a marzipan modeling tool or any tool with a smooth round end about ¼ inch (6 mm) in diameter to mark 2 indentations for the eyes.

10. Using a spade-shaped tool, lightly flatten the untinted marzipan on 1 side of the face, then make vertical indentations to create the beard. If you do not have a spade-shaped marzipan tool, use the back of a paring knife to make the vertical marks. Cut off the pointed portion of untinted marzipan on the other end of the head; cover and reserve.

11. Roll the remaining scraps of red marzipan smooth and round, then taper 1 end only to form the hat. Cut a small slice off the wide end to make it flat. Bend the opposite end into a gentle curve. Using egg white as glue, attach the hat to the top of the head (Figure 12-22).

12. Roll a very small piece of the reserved untinted marzipan into a rope 2 inches (5 cm) long and flatten it. Using egg white as glue, wrap the band around the bottom of the hat, hiding the seam where the hat meets the head.

13. Roll the tiny reserved ear pieces into round balls between your thumb and forefinger. Attach to the head with egg white. Roll the nose piece round, then flatten it slightly and attach in the same way.

14. Roll a tiny piece of the reserved untinted marzipan, about the same size used for the ears, between your fingers to make it ¾ inch (2 cm) long and pointed on both ends. Attach as a mustache at the point on the head slightly above where the white beard begins. Bend the edge of the beard so it curves gently toward Santa's face.

15. Roll another untinted piece about the same size into a ball; attach at the top of the hat.

16. Place a small amount of royal icing in a piping bag and cut a small opening. Pipe icing into the indentations made for the eyes.

17. Place melted coating chocolate in a piping bag and cut a very small opening. Pipe small dots of chocolate on top of the royal icing to mark the pupils in the eyes. Pipe a tiny line of chocolate above each eye for an eyebrow. Set the head aside.

TO FINISH THE BODY

18. Divide the 10-g piece of red marzipan for the boots and mittens into 4 equal pieces. Roll 2 of the pieces between your palms to make round balls, then make them slightly oval. Press to flatten half of each piece across the width. Stand Santa's body up and place these 2 pieces so their rounded edge protrudes in front as boots (it is not necessary to use egg white here). Press the body forward so it stands securely; at the same time, the boot pieces will flatten against the table.

19. Make the mittens by rolling the 2 other pieces into round balls as before, then tapering 1 end on each to make cones 1 inch (2.5 cm) long. Bend one-third of the narrow end around against the wider end to make the thumb portion of the mitten. Bend the thumb on 1 mitten to the left and the other to the right so you have both a left and a right hand. Curl the mittens slightly as if the hands are holding something. Set aside.

20. Roll the green marzipan for the sack into a smooth, round ball, then taper 1 end, as for the body, to make a sack 1¼ inches (3.1 cm) long. Use the same round tool with which you made the face indentation to make an opening in the top of the sack. Using the same tool you used to make the beard, press vertical and horizontal lines into the sides of the sack. Set aside.

TO ASSEMBLE THE SANTA

21. Use your finger to spread just enough egg white on the cut part of the Santa on top of the body to make the surface sticky (too much will allow the head to slide off). Carefully, using light pressure, attach the head. Spread a little egg white on the back side of the round cape piece and drape it around the shoulders to form a collar as well as a support for the head. Using a little egg white and the round tool used to make the indentation in the top, press the sack into place under the beard. Using a little egg white and a light touch, attach 1 mitten so it protrudes from under the coat and the other mitten holding onto the sack; a marzipan tool will be helpful here.

22. Use scraps to make a small rectangular package; attach in the sack opening.

23. If the Santa is to be kept for a long time, use a small artist's brush to brush a thin film of hot melted cocoa butter over the surface, except for the eyes, eyebrows, and mustache. In addition to protecting the marzipan from drying out, the cocoa butter gives the surface an attractive satin shine.

IN THIS CHAPTER

CARAMEL GLASS PASTE DECORATIONS

Caramel Glass Paste 666

Caramel Glass Paste Screens 666

FLUTED CARAMEL WEDGES 668

SIMPLE CARAMEL GLASS PASTE WEDGES 669

Curved Caramel Glass Paste Wedges 669

DECORATED SPONGE SHEETS

Joconde Sponge Base I 670

Joconde Sponge Base II 671

Ribbon-Pattern Decorated Sponge Sheets 672

Decorated Sponge Sheets Using a Silk Screen 674

Wood-Grain–Pattern Decorated Sponge Sheet 675

DECORATING WITH FONDANT 676

DECORATING WITH ROYAL ICING

Royal Icing 680

DECORATING WITH SAUCES

Chocolate Sauce for Piping 681

Corkscrew Pattern 682

String of Hearts Pattern 682

Curved String of Hearts Pattern 682

Weave Pattern 683

Spiderweb Pattern 683

Ripple Pattern 683

Hearts with Weave Pattern 683

Spiral Spiderweb Pattern 684

Two-Tone String of Hearts Pattern 684

Hearts with Stems Pattern 684

Feathered Two-Tone Pool Pattern 685

Swirled Zigzag Pattern 685

Sauce Designs Using a Turntable 686

FLORENTINA DECORATIONS

Florentina Cups 687

COCOA-NIB FLORENTINA CUPS 689

Florentina Cones 689

Florentina Cookies for Marco Polo 690

Florentina Twists 690

Hartmund Florentina Garnish 691

HAZELNUT COOKIE WAFERS 691

PIE TIN TEMPLATES AND TEMPLATE HOLDERS 692

TUILE PASTE DECORATIONS

Vanilla Tuile Decorating Paste 695

Chocolate Tuile Decorating Paste 695

Cookie Butterflies 695

Cookie Citrus Rinds and Cookie Figurines 698

Cookie Tumbleweeds 699

Curly Cues 700

Curved Tuile Wedges 702

Curvy Tuile Strips 704

Triangular Tuile Spirals 707

Tuile Cookie Spoons 708

Tuile Leaves and Cookie Wedges 709

TUILE MAPLE LEAVES 711

Tuile Steam Decorations 712

Tuile Symphony of Circles 712

Tulips 715

Miniature Tulips 716

MINIATURE TULIP CROWNS 717

Wavy Tuile Strips 718

OTHER DECORATIONS

Chocolate Paper Paste 719

Cocoa-Nib Wafer Paste 720

Mango Chips 721

Apple or Pear Chips 721

Plantain Chips 722

Hippen Decorating Paste 722

HIPPEN MASSE 722

Lace Cookie Bouquets 723

Mango or Strawberry Wafer Decorations 725

Red Pepper Sails 726

Seaweed Wafer Decorations 726

Sour Cream Mixture for Piping 727

Spanish Caramel-Flavored Tuile Decorations 727

Tomatillo Lace Decorations 728

PIPING DESIGNS FOR SPECIAL-OCCASION CAKES 730

Advanced Decorations

The key to decorating — besides having a steady hand and an awareness of neatness and symmetry — is to make the finished product look tasteful and elegant rather than busy or cluttered. This chapter offers methods and techniques, as well as a few tricks of the trade, for using basic materials to create decorations quickly and economically. The decorating formulas covered here include caramel glass paste decorations, decorated sponge sheets, decorating with fondant and royal icing, decorating with sauces (or sauce painting), the production of Florentina decorations and containers, tuile paste decorations and containers, unusual and tasty decorating pastes made from fruit and vegetable purees that can be shaped into fanciful forms, and piping design templates for special-occasion cakes.

Many of these techniques are much easier to produce today, thanks to the now readily accessible tools, such as Silpats, Flexipans, acetate sheets, and decorating combs, that make labor-intensive handmade decorative ornaments and elaborate design work practical even in a competitive marketplace.

Unfortunately, more and more shops now use decorations manufactured in factories. While in some instances it makes good sense to use prefabricated designs — for marzipan and chocolate ornaments, for example — I believe that everything placed on a cake or pastry should be edible. Plastic cars and animals on a child's birthday cake, especially when combined with too many bright artificial colors, can be frightful. One exception to this rule is the use of fresh flowers. In addition to using one or two edible fresh flowers to decorate an individual dessert serving, cascades of flowers (not meant to be consumed) can be artistically arranged on a wedding cake for a popular, easy, and refreshing alternative to traditional white buttercream alone; these are removed by the person slicing the cake before it is served. If the cut stems are inserted into the top of the cake layers, they should be covered in plastic wrap unless edible. Naturally, even though the flowers are not served, you should use nontoxic varieties.

Caramel Glass Paste yield: approximately 2 pounds (910 g)

This versatile paste can be used to make a great number of interesting and trendy decorations, including containers to hold ice cream, sorbets, or sherbets. Unlike tuile decorating paste, however, this batter will not stay in a precise shape but instead will flow out slightly as it bakes.

If you use baking paper, spread the caramel glass paste as soon as you portion it onto the paper. Portioning all of the paste and then going back to spread it into the desired shape will cause the paper to become wet and wrinkled, and the paste will be difficult to shape. The paste should be soft enough to spread easily. If it has been stored, even at room temperature, you may need to warm it gently over a bain-marie to soften the butter and make it workable.

11 ounces (310 g) unsalted butter, at room temperature	¼ cup (60 ml) or 3 ounces (85 g) glucose *or* light corn syrup
11 ounces (310 g) powdered sugar, sifted	6 ounces (170 g) bread flour, sifted

1. Cream the soft butter with the sugar. Add the glucose or corn syrup and mix to combine, scraping the sides of the bowl. Incorporate the flour.

2. Use as directed in individual recipes. The paste can be stored at room temperature for 2 or 3 days. Refrigerate for longer storage.

Caramel Glass Paste Screens yield: 16 decorations (Color Photo 34)

1 recipe Caramel Glass Paste (above)	Dark coating chocolate, melted

1. Trace templates B and C in Figure 13-1; as shown, they are the correct size for use in this recipe. Cut the templates out of cardboard that is ¹⁄₁₆ inch (2 mm) thick; cake boxes work fine. Label each of the templates with *top* or *this side up* on the side that faces up as you cut out the pieces. Be sure this side faces up when you later use the templates to cut the paste. If either of the pieces is inverted by accident when you cut, the screens will not fit together. The center area

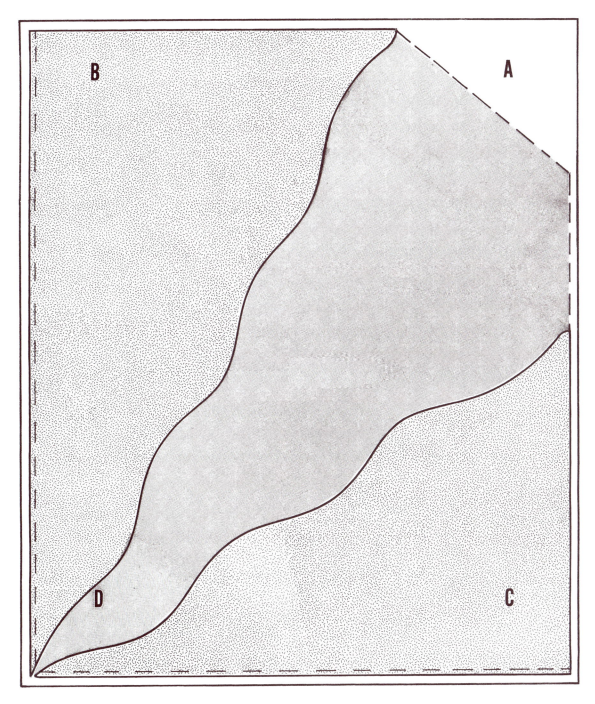

FIGURE 13-1 The template for Caramel Glass Paste Screens

marked D is used to make another decoration (see page 668). Lastly, cut out template A, a cardboard rectangle measuring 6 × 7 inches (15 × 17.5 cm).

2. Place one-quarter (8 ounces/225 g) of the caramel paste in the center of a sheet of baking paper and spread it to make a rectangle, 8 × 24 inches (20 × 50cm). Transfer the paper to a perfectly flat, even sheet pan. Repeat 3 times to spread the remaining paste on 3 additional sheets of paper, placing each on a separate flat sheet pan.

3. Bake 1 sheet at a time at 350°F (175°C) for approximately 12 minutes or until the paste turns a golden caramel color. Remove the pan from the oven carefully; any jarring movement will cause ripples in the soft surface of the caramel. Let the caramel cool for a few seconds, then transfer the baking paper with the caramel attached to the tabletop or to a sheet of heavy corrugated cardboard.

4. With the rectangular template as a guide, use a chef's knife to cut out 4 rectangles from the caramel sheet. Lift the baking paper to transfer the cut caramel sheet back to the baking pan. Bake and cut the remaining 3 pans of caramel in the same way.

5. Once the caramel sheets have cooled and hardened, carefully separate the rectangles and break away the scrap pieces as gently as possible to avoid chipping the corners. Discard the scraps, or save for another use.

6. Place 3 rectangles on a sheet pan lined with baking paper, leaving some space around them. Return to the oven just until they are soft enough to cut through; do not overheat the caramel, or you will alter the shape. Remove from the oven and transfer the baking paper back to the tabletop or sheet of corrugated cardboard. Place the wedge templates B and C on top of a rectangle, aligning the corner edges with the corners of the caramel so the sides are straight. One at a time, while holding the template in place against the caramel with your other hand, use a paring knife to cut along the scalloped edge of each template. Repeat with the remaining 2 caramel rectangles on the paper.

7. Reheat and cut the remaining 13 rectangles, 3 at a time (1 in the last batch).

8. Carefully separate the 3 sections of each cut rectangle. Group them by placing all of the longer wedges together and all of the shorter wedges together, keeping them separate. The center pieces (scalloped on both sides) can be reserved at this point in an airtight container for Fluted Caramel Wedges (instructions follow).

9. To assemble the screens, place 4 sets of longer and shorter wedges in the refrigerator to chill for just a few minutes. Dip only the very edge of the longest side of 1 shorter and 1 longer wedge into dark chocolate. Stand them up, top sides facing forward, and attach the 2 chocolate sides together at a 90-degree angle, at the same time making sure the shorter sides are level on the table so the screens stand straight. Because the pieces are cold, the chocolate will set up quickly. Assemble the remaining screens in the same way.

VARIATIONS
FLUTED CARAMEL WEDGES yield: approximately 16 decorations

The center fluted piece of caramel left over from making caramel screens can be used as a decoration by itself. Alternatively, rather than waiting to accumulate leftover wedges, you can cut out only the center template, D, to make fluted caramel wedges alone. If you already have the fluted wedges left from making caramel screens, simply begin at Step 8 here to shape them.

½ **recipe Caramel Glass Paste (page 666)**

1. Trace the template marked D in Figure 13-1. Cut the shape out of cardboard that is ¹⁄₁₆ inch (2 mm) thick; cake boxes work fine.

2. Place half of the caramel glass paste (8 ounces/225 g) in the center of a full sheet of baking paper and spread it to form a rectangle measuring 8½ × 20 inches (21.2 × 50 cm). Transfer the paper and the paste to a perfectly flat sheet pan. Repeat with the remaining paste.

3. Bake 1 sheet at a time at 350°F (175°C) for approximately 12 minutes or until the paste turns a light caramel color. Carefully remove the sheet pan from the oven without shaking or jarring it, which would cause the soft surface to ripple.

4. Let the sheet cool for just a few seconds, then transfer the baking paper and paste to the tabletop or a full-size sheet of heavy corrugated cardboard set on the table.

5. Place the fluted template on top of the paste at the left edge; hold it in place with one hand and use the other to cut around the template with a paring knife. Work your way across the sheet, cutting around the template and warming the caramel if it becomes too firm to cut. Do not overheat, however, or the paste will change shape, and the cut lines will melt back together. Position your template to the best advantage for the fewest scraps by inverting it with every other cut; you should get 8 to 10 decorations from the sheet. Set aside to cool.

6. Repeat Steps 3, 4, and 5 to bake and cut the second sheet of decorations.

7. When the cut caramel sheets have cooled and hardened, carefully separate the decorations from the scrap pieces. Discard the scraps or save them for another use, if desired. The decorations can be stored at this point, or you may curve them (instructions follow).

8. To curve the fluted wedges, reheat a few at a time just until they become soft; do not heat them to the point where they change shape. Invert the soft caramel wedges, top-side down, over a round of some type, such as a bain-marie insert, bucket, or cake ring, 8 to 10 inches (20 to 25 cm) in diameter; they will harden and hold the curve almost immediately. Store the decorations, covered, at room temperature; they do not require an airtight container.

SIMPLE CARAMEL GLASS PASTE WEDGES

If you need to produce a large number of wedge-shaped decorations or simply want to speed things up a bit, don't use the template; instead, cut the baked sheet into straight-sided wedges. At Step 5, trim both long sides to create a strip 8 inches (20 cm) wide. Cut the strip into 3-inch (7.5-cm) wedges.

Curved Caramel Glass Paste Wedges yield: approximately 16 decorations

½ recipe Caramel Glass Paste (page 666)

1. Place half of the paste in the center of a full sheet of baking paper. Spread the paste to form a rectangle measuring 8½ × 20 inches (21.2 × 50 cm). Transfer the paper to a flat sheet pan. Repeat with the remaining paste.

2. Bake 1 sheet at a time at 350°F (175°C) until the paste turns a light caramel color. Remove the pan carefully without jarring. Let the caramel cool for a few seconds, then transfer the baking paper and the paste to the tabletop or to a full-size sheet of heavy corrugated cardboard set on the table.

3. Trim both long sides of the rectangle to create a strip 8 inches (20 cm) wide. Cut the strip into wedges measuring 2½ inches (6.2 cm) at the base. Bake and cut the second sheet of caramel paste in the same way.

4. Starting with the strip that was baked and cut first, separate the wedges and discard the scrap pieces.

5. Have ready a round object, 8 inches (20 cm) in diameter, such as a bain-marie insert or a cake ring. Warm the wedges, a few at a time, just until they become soft; do not heat them to the point where they change shape. Quickly drape each wedge over the round mold; they will harden quickly. Remove and continue to form the remaining wedges. Store the decorations at room temperature; they do not require an airtight container.

DECORATED SPONGE SHEETS

Joconde Sponge Base I yield: 2 sheets, 23 × 15 × ⅛ inch (57.5 × 37.5 cm × 3 mm)

This version of Joconde yields two quite thin but elegant-looking sheets, which means you have little leverage in spreading the batter. Care must also be taken when baking the sheets because a hot oven is essential and, as thin as they are, they can overbake quickly. Watch them carefully while they are in the oven. If you do not mind slightly thicker sheets, use Joconde Base II, which is a bit easier to work with.

5 whole eggs	2 ounces (55 g) bread flour, sifted
4 egg yolks (⅓ cup/80 ml)	4 egg whites (½ cup/120 ml)
7 ounces (200 g) granulated sugar	2 ounces (55 g) unsalted butter, melted
7 ounces (200 g) blanched almonds, finely ground (or almond meal; see Note)	

1. Place the whole eggs, egg yolks, and half of the sugar in a bowl. Set the bowl over simmering water. Heat the mixture to 120°F (49°C), stirring constantly. Remove from the heat and whip at high speed for 1 minute.

2. Thoroughly combine the ground almonds and flour.

3. Whip the egg whites with the remaining sugar until they have the appearance of snow; the egg whites should be thick and foamy but should not hold a peak.

4. Carefully fold the reserved almond mixture into the whipped whole egg mixture. Stir in the melted butter. Gradually fold in the beaten egg whites.

5. Spread and bake at 425°F (219°C) or as directed in individual recipes.

NOTE: The almonds should be ground to a consistency as fine as granulated sugar to compensate for the reduced flour in the sponge. You can purchase this product, known as *almond flour* or *almond meal,* from bakery suppliers. If it is unavailable and you must use a food processor to grind the nuts, add most of the sugar used in Step 1 (saving a few tablespoons to whip with the whole eggs and egg yolks) to the almonds when you grind them. The sugar will absorb oil and prevent the mixture from caking. Use the remaining half of the sugar measurement when whipping the egg whites as directed.

Joconde Sponge Base II

yield: I full sheet, 16 × 24 × ¼ inch (40 × 60 cm × 6 mm), and I half-sheet, 16 × 12 × ¼ inch (40 × 30 cm × 6 mm), or 2 full sheets if made slightly thinner

As mentioned in the introduction to Joconde Sponge Base I, this recipe yields a thicker finished product that is easier to manipulate and can be used for purposes other than decorated sponge sheets, such as Opera Cake and Opera Slices. Joconde Sponge Base II is also a good choice if you need to prepare the sheets ahead of time. The sheets can be kept, well wrapped, in the refrigerator for several days or in the freezer for up to I month.

9 ounces (255 g) blanched almonds, finely ground (or almond meal; see Note)

6 ounces (170 g) powdered sugar

3 ounces (85 g) bread flour

9 whole eggs

3 egg yolks (¼ cup/60 ml)

6 egg whites (¾ cup/180 ml)

3 ounces (85 g) granulated sugar

3 ounces (85 g) unsalted butter, melted

Small-Batch Joconde Sponge Base II
yield: I half-sheet, 16 × 12 inches (40 × 30 cm)

3 ounces (85 g) blanched almonds, finely ground (or almond meal; see Note)

2 ounces (55 g) powdered sugar

1 ounce (30 g) bread flour

3 whole eggs

1 egg yolk

2 egg whites (¼ cup/60 ml)

1 ounce (30 g) granulated sugar

1 ounce (30 g) unsalted butter, melted

I. Place the ground almonds, powdered sugar, and bread flour in a mixer bowl and gradually incorporate the whole eggs. Beat with the paddle attachment for 5 minutes at high speed, scraping down the sides of the bowl once or twice (if making the smaller recipe, this can be done by hand with a whisk).

2. Incorporate the egg yolks, mixing at medium speed until well combined. Set aside.

3. Whip the egg whites with the granulated sugar until they just barely hold a soft shape. Fold half of the meringue into the egg mixture. Stir in the melted butter, followed by the remaining meringue.

4. Spread and bake at 425°F (219°C) or as directed in individual recipes.

NOTE: If almond meal is unavailable and you must grind the almonds in a food processor, add 3 ounces (85 g) granulated sugar to the nuts when you grind them and decrease the amount of powdered sugar in the recipe by 3 ounces (85 g). The granulated sugar will absorb the oil released by the almonds during processing and prevent the mixture from caking. The almonds should be ground to the consistency of granulated sugar.

Ribbon-Pattern Decorated Sponge Sheets

yield: 2 sheets, 23 × 15 inches (57.5 × 37.5 cm) (Color Photos 2 and 4)

Thin, ornate sponge sheets with striped patterns in various configurations can be made easily using Silpats and a special scraper made to fit them. This tool, called a *decorating comb*, consists of a frame and interchangeable blades, typically made of rubber, that have notched edges. The blades are available in various sizes and patterns. A similar but less expensive tool is a molded plastic comb with two patterns, one on each side. This comb is intended for chocolate work but can be used for sponge sheets as well. Because the plastic combs are smaller, it is necessary to make two passes over a full sheet instead of one. For more information, see "About Decorating Combs with Frames" (page 674).

The two recipes for Joconde Sponge Base are fairly similar and can be used interchangeably. Sponge Base II takes a bit longer to make, but it is a better choice if you plan to add food coloring to the base portion. With either recipe, be sure to keep the whipped egg whites and sugar very soft because a thinner batter will flow out and fill in much more tightly between the tuile paste lines. Being careful not to overwhip the egg whites will also help prevent air bubbles in the finished sponge sheets, which can detract from their appearance.

14 ounces (400 g) Chocolate Tuile Decorating Paste (page 695)

1 recipe Joconde Sponge Base I (page 670) *or* 1 recipe Joconde Sponge Base II (page 671)

4 ounces (115 g) cocoa butter, melted (see Note)

1. Spread the chocolate tuile paste evenly over 2 full-size Silpats, covering them completely; the paste should be approximately ¹⁄₁₆ inch (2 mm) thick. Use a decorating comb to remove half of the paste in straight lines lengthwise, crosswise, or diagonally on each sheet (Figure 13-2).

2. Lift the Silpats by the edges (Figure 13-3) and set them on top of inverted sheet pans. Place in the freezer to firm the tuile paste while you make the Joconde sponge base. If you are not proceeding to the next step immediately, the prepped Silpats can be left at room temperature for several hours. When you are ready to resume, place them in the freezer for a few minutes to firm the paste.

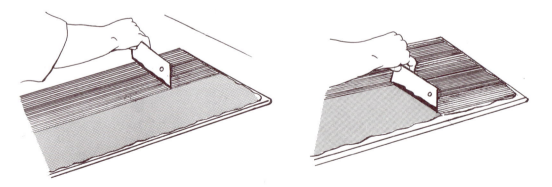

FIGURE 13-2 Using a decorating comb to remove tuile paste in straight lines for Ribbon-Pattern Sponge Sheets

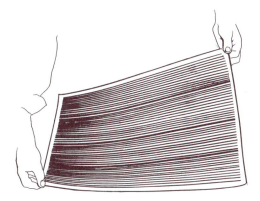

FIGURE 13-3 **Lifting the Silpat by the edges**

FIGURE 13-4 **Peeling the Silpat away from the baked ribbon-pattern sponge sheet**

3. Leave the mats in place on the inverted pans. Divide the Joconde sponge base between the 2 mats, spreading it evenly on top of the chocolate lines. Tap the pans quite firmly against the table to set the batter and remove air bubbles.

4. Bake immediately at 450° to 500°F (230° to 260°C) for approximately 4 minutes or until the sponge begins to color slightly.

5. Dust flour lightly over the top of the sponge sheets. Invert them onto sheets of baking paper and let cool for 2 minutes. Carefully peel away the Silpats (Figure 13-4). Spray or brush melted cocoa butter over the patterned side of the sheets. The cocoa butter will help keep the sheets flexible and prevent them from sticking to the forms or rings when the sheets are used in assembling cakes or other desserts. Cover the decorated sponge sheets with plastic wrap and store in the refrigerator for up to 1 week or in the freezer for up to 1 month.

NOTE: The amount of cocoa butter specified in the ingredient list is far more than you will need if you use a brush to apply it. However, if you use a spray bottle, the additional liquid is required for the sprayer to work well.

CHEF'S TIP

Both Silpats and plastic decorating combs are readily available and relatively inexpensive, and both are tools that no professional — or serious amateur — should be without. In addition to making straight lines lengthwise, crosswise, and diagonally, try using the decorating comb to make curved or wavy lines. To create a colorful decorated sponge, substitute vanilla tuile decorating paste for the chocolate paste and color it as desired to create special effects. Or color the Joconde sponge base to contrast with either plain or chocolate lines. There are many possible combinations and the results can be stunning, but use restraint; colors that are too bright or combinations involving too many colors can be garish.

You do not have to limit these impressive sponge sheet designs to ribbons. A wide variety of decorative stainless steel templates made to fit the Silpats is available from Europe (although they are not cheap) in patterns such as diamond, herringbone, and polka dot, to name just a few. Plastic versions are available at a lower cost but they are not as practical, as they break easily. Other options are to use a silk screen (see page 674) or photo transfer sheets (see page 675) to decorate the sponge sheet.

About Decorating Combs with Frames

These two-piece tools are used in combination with Silpats to produce decorated sponge sheets. The tool consists of a stainless steel frame sold with a set of several interchangeable rubber blades called *combs* or *trowels*. The combs have square notches on the edges in assorted designs. The width, depth, and spacing of the notches determine the pattern they produce. Each comb has two patterns, one on each long edge. To use, the comb is attached to the frame. Tuile decorating paste is spread over a silicone mat in a very thin, even layer. The comb is pulled across the mat, through the paste, and the notches remove rows of decorating paste, leaving a pattern of parallel lines on the mat. The combs are 27 to 28 inches (67.5 to 70 cm) long, so they can cover a full-size mat in a single pass. Straight lines can be formed lengthwise, crosswise, or at an angle, or the comb can be moved in a wavy motion to produce a pattern of curved lines. After the lines are formed, sponge batter is spread on top and the sheet is baked. When the baked sheet is inverted, the tuile paste pattern appears on the sponge.

Plastic decorating combs are used in the same way and for the same purpose as the rubber combs described above, but they are made of rigid plastic with rubber notches and do not need to be attached to a separate frame. The plastic combs come in 14-inch (35-cm) lengths (these require you to make more than one pass over the mat) and 28-inch (70-cm) lengths.

A square notched plastic trowel designed for applying glue can be purchased at a hardware store and used as a substitute for the professional square-notched tool, but it is not practical for use in mass production.

Decorated Sponge Sheets Using a Silk Screen

yield: 2 sheets, 23 × 15 inches (57.5 × 37.5 cm)

Silk screens can be used to create incredibly detailed images on thin sheets of sponge cake. These are most often cut into strips and used to decorate the sides of cakes or pastries. A silk screen can also be used to print a design on a thin sheet of rolled marzipan (directions follow), in which case the marzipan is usually placed on the top of a cake. Silk screens come in many patterns. Some are abstract, such as marbled or swirled designs; others depict musical notes, fruits, or flowers; and some even portray hobbies, such as boating, golfing, or fishing. In addition, virtually any design can be custom made.

Each screen is made up of material tightly stretched within a permanent frame. The pattern you will see on your finished product is imprinted on the material as a negative image, just as with other printing processes. In addition to the screen, you need a special long rubber trowel that is used to push the cocoa paste through the fabric evenly and without damaging the thin material. The screens come in sizes to fit standard full- and half-sheet Silpats and sheet pans. Silk screens must be handled and cleaned carefully, as even the smallest tear in the fabric can make the screen unusable.

¾ cup (180 ml) water

2 ounces (55 g) sifted unsweetened cocoa powder

1 recipe Joconde Sponge Base I (page 670) *or* 1 recipe Joconde Sponge Base II (page 671)

4 ounces (115 g) cocoa butter, melted (see Note, page 673)

I. Gradually stir the water into the cocoa powder, mixing until you have a smooth, thin paste; it should be pourable but not runny. If necessary, pass the paste through a fine-mesh strainer. Let stand at room temperature for 30 minutes. Check the consistency of the paste and add more water, if necessary.

2. Place a silk screen on top of a Silpat (a new or little-used Silpat is best). Pour a ribbon of cocoa paste along the top short edge. Pull the rubber trowel evenly along the length of the screen, pushing the cocoa paste through the silk and transferring the pattern onto the Silpat. (Baking paper can be used instead of a Silpat, but the paper tends to wrinkle.) Repeat to make a design on a second Silpat using the same silk screen or one with a different pattern. (If you reuse the silk screen, you must wash it and pat it dry before using it a second time.) Transfer the Silpats to the backs of 2 inverted sheet pans and allow the designs to dry.

3. Follow Steps 3, 4, and 5 on page 673 for Ribbon-Pattern Decorated Sponge Sheets.

Decorated Sponge Sheets Using Photo Transfer Sheets

Photo transfer sheets are used to produce elaborate patterns on Joconde sponge sheets in the same way that chocolate transfer sheets are used to create decorated chocolate strips and sheets. Unlike chocolate transfer sheets, which are made from plastic and cannot be placed in the oven, photo transfer sheets consist of a sheet of baking paper imprinted with a pattern of cocoa, oven-stable edible dye, or both. To use, spread Joconde batter in a thin, even layer over the imprinted side of the sheet (see Procedure 13-1a). Drag the paper to a sheet pan and bake as usual. After baking, peel away the paper to reveal the pattern on the sponge sheet (see Procedure 13-1b).

Photo transfer sheets can also be used in combination with tuile paste (see the musical note pattern on the right side of Color Photo 46). For tuile paste decorations, spread a thin layer of tuile paste over the imprinted side of a photo transfer sheet, bake as directed, invert quickly and peel away the transfer paper, then mold the tuile paste as desired. Alternatively, bake the sheet partially, cut it into strips or other shapes, finish baking, then remove the paper and shape as desired. With this method, you can create strips to wrap around a cake, for example.

PROCEDURE 13-1a Spreading sponge batter over a photo transfer sheet

PROCEDURE 13-1b After baking, peeling away the transfer paper to reveal the pattern on the sponge sheet

Wood-Grain–Pattern Decorated Sponge Sheet yield: 1 full sheet (Color Photo 88)

This decorated sponge sheet uses the technique applied in making Chocolate with Wood Grain (page 537). Instead of dark chocolate on a white chocolate background, here the pattern is created using cocoa paste and Joconde sponge base. You will need one or two wood-graining tools; see page 537.

¾ cup (180 ml) water

2 ounces (55 g) sifted unsweetened cocoa powder

½ recipe Joconde Sponge Base I (page 670) *or* ½ recipe Joconde Sponge Base II (page 671)

4 ounces (115 g) cocoa butter, melted (see Note, page 673)

I. Gradually stir the water into the cocoa powder, mixing until you have a smooth, thin paste; it should be pourable but not runny. If necessary, pass the paste through a fine mesh strainer. Let stand at room temperature for 30 minutes. Check the consistency of the paste and add more water if necessary.

2. Place a full size Silpat on top of an inverted sheet pan or sheet of corrugated cardboard, positioning it so a short side is closest to you. Secure the Silpat so it will not move as you work. Spread a very thin layer of cocoa paste over the Silpat.

3. Starting at the top left (long) side of the sheet and working in a straight line toward the bottom, press the graining tool hard against the cocoa paste, lightly pivoting the surface of the tool up and down in smooth motions covering ½ inch (1.2 cm) cocoa paste each time. At the same time, drag the tool in a straight line to the bottom of the sheet. If you want longer wood grains, drag the tool a little farther between each rocking motion.

4. When you come to the bottom of the sheet after making the first row, start again at the top to make the design in a parallel row, spacing the rows slightly apart. Continue until the whole sheet is covered by the wood-grain design. Allow the cocoa paste to dry at room temperature.

5. Follow Steps 3, 4, and 5 on page 673 to add the Joconde batter and bake the sheet.

DECORATING WITH FONDANT

Fondant is an excellent decorating material for use in making designs with a piping bag. For this application it must be cooler than the usual working temperature when piping the outline (85° to 95°F/29° to 34°C) and quite firm. After bringing the fondant to temperature, add just enough simple syrup to make it pipeable, if needed; it should still hold its shape, however, after it is piped out. For filling in the piped designs, you need to warm the fondant just a little (not over 100°F/38°C), then thin it, as needed, with simple syrup so it will flow out slightly within the outline. To test its consistency, drag the tip of a paring knife along the top of the fondant; the line should remain visible for just a second and then disappear, leaving a smooth surface. Be sure to keep the fondant covered at all times to prevent a skin from forming. Place a wet towel on top of the bowl for shorter periods; pour a small amount of water on top for longer storage.

FONDANT ORNAMENTS

I. To make small, individual ornaments, place a perfectly flat sheet of acetate or polyurethane about ¹⁄₁₆ inch (2 mm) thick on top of your drawing (you may want to use the designs shown on pages 546 and 547 or your own creations). Secure the plastic with tape so it will not shift as you pipe. Depending on the type of plastic used, you may need to rub a thin film of vegetable oil over the top to keep the ornaments from sticking.

2. Put a small amount of fondant in a piping bag and pipe a thin frame of fondant around the figures. Unlike chocolate ornaments made with a similar method, fondant ornaments are placed right-side up on the cake or pastry.

3. Fill in the outline with warmer fondant, moving the piping bag back and forth to create a smooth surface and building up your design to create height. Be careful not to disturb the frame. The fondant can be tinted with water-soluble food coloring or chocolate if desired; see Steps 4 and 5 in "Glazing or Icing with Fondant" (page 679) for information on mixing colors.

4. Let the designs dry overnight in a warm place. Loosen the ornaments by moving the plastic over a sharp edge, while bending the plastic down lightly. Place the finished decorations on top of your cake or pastry. If you are not using the decorations right away, leave them attached to the plastic until needed.

FONDANT DESIGNS PIPED DIRECTLY ONTO A CAKE OR PASTRY

Fondant can be piped directly on top of a cake or pastry in the same way as the fondant ornaments above, if you have the skill to pipe a design freehand. Even if you are not a great artist (and most of us are not), you can use the following tracing method to create almost any design you like on a sheet of marzipan, which can then be placed on top of a cake.

DESIGNS PRESSED INTO MARZIPAN TO BE TRACED OVER AND/OR FILLED IN WITH FONDANT

1. Trace the design onto a sheet of baking paper or use a copy machine to copy onto standard paper. To make the figure face in the same direction as the drawing after stamping it on the marzipan, simply invert baking paper or rub vegetable oil onto copy paper to make it transparent, then invert the paper so the design appears backward. If a mirror image will not matter on the cake, you can omit this step. In other words, in the illustration, it does not matter which direction the bear is walking — except maybe to the bear — but lettering would be backward without this step.

2. Tape the drawing to a sheet of cardboard. Place a small piece of plastic at least $1/4$ inch (6 mm) thick — or at least thick enough that it will not bend — on top of the drawing. (For a glass option here, see Chef's Tip.)

3. Make a small amount of royal icing. Put the icing in a piping bag, cut a small opening, and trace over your design. Let the royal icing harden overnight.

4. Roll out marzipan to $1/8$ inch (3 mm) thick. Cut out a round or oval shape slightly larger than the design. Hold the plastic upside down and press the royal icing design into the marzipan. Remove the plastic and, using a piping bag with an opening just large enough to cover the lines, trace the design with fondant, royal icing, or chocolate (Figure 13-5). The design can be

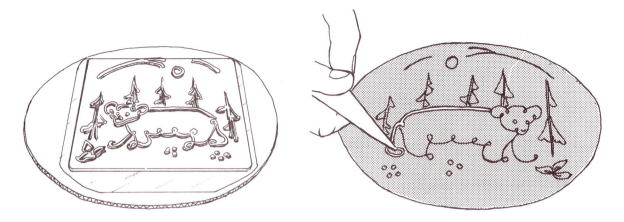

FIGURE 13-5 **A design piped in royal icing on a small piece of glass following the lines of a drawing set under the glass; filling in the design with piped royal icing after pressing the hardened royal icing lines into a thin sheet of rolled marzipan (the finished design appears as a mirror image of the original drawing)**

left as is, with just the outline, or filled in partially or completely with additional fondant, as in Method I. Let set until the fondant is firm, then place the plaque on the cake.

This is a good way to make up a supply of cake decorations on a slow day to have ready for a busy time like Easter, Mother's Day, or Christmas. You can keep the marzipan looking fresh by coating it with a thin layer of cocoa butter before you stamp out the pattern. To use this method on a cake that is entirely covered with marzipan (Princess cake, for example), press the design into the marzipan just before you place it on the cake, then pipe over it once it is in place. A decoration made this way is certainly handmade, and no one will know you had a little help from a friend.

GLAZING OR ICING WITH FONDANT

I. Warm fondant over simmering water, stirring constantly, until it reaches approximately body temperature, 98°F (37°C). When fondant is heated over 100°F (38°C), it begins to lose its shine and, at the extreme, becomes hard and unpleasant to eat as well. Should you overheat the fondant, wait until it has cooled to the correct temperature before you apply it (unless it has melted into a syrup, in which case you should discard it). To prevent a skin from forming, either cover the fondant or stir it while it cools. On the other hand, if you try to play it safe and the fondant is not hot enough when you apply it, it will take too long to form a skin and will not have a nice satin shine. Furthermore, the pastries will be sticky and hard to work with and can collect dust while they are drying.

CHEF'S TIP
Some chefs use egg whites or heavy cream alone (without simple syrup) to thin fondant to ensure a good shine. If you use egg whites, make sure they are pasteurized. A small amount of corn syrup may be added along with either egg white or cream to further increase the shine.

2. Thin the warm fondant to the proper consistency with simple syrup (adding egg white along with the simple syrup will add an extra shine; see Chef's Tip). Test the thickness by coating a few pastries. The contours and separate layers of a petit four should be clearly visible through the icing.

3. Either pipe or pour fondant on top of petits fours or Othellos. Never coat these pastries by dipping the pastry into the fondant, or you will get crumbs in the fondant. If you are coating only a few dozen pastries, the most practical method is to pipe the fondant on

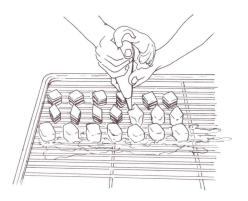

FIGURE 13-6 Using a pastry bag to apply fondant to petits fours

FIGURE 13-7 Using a saucer to apply fondant to petits fours

top (Figure 13-6) or to use a fondant funnel (see "About Fondant Funnels"). When covering a large number of pastries, a much faster way is to pour the fondant from a saucer. Line up the pastries or petits fours to be covered on an aspic rack or cake cooling rack as you would if you were piping the fondant on top. Hold the bowl of fondant in one hand and the saucer in the other. Scoop up fondant in the saucer and pour it slowly and evenly over the pastries from just above them (Figure 13-7). Always start with the pastry farthest away from you so you will not drip on the pastries once they are coated. Have enough fondant in the saucer so you can cover each row in one stroke. The drawback with this method is that you need to work with a large amount of fondant; however, the fondant that drips onto the pan can be reused or saved for later use.

4. If you plan to tint a portion of the fondant, start by coating as many petits fours as desired in white, then tint part of the white fondant yellow. Use the leftover yellow to make green, and reserve any leftover green. Next, make and apply pink fondant, made by tinting the remaining white fondant. If any of that is left, you can combine it with the green to make a mocha color.

5. To make chocolate fondant, quickly add melted unsweetened chocolate to the warm fondant. The chocolate will thicken the fondant, so you will need to add additional simple syrup.

About Fondant Funnels

This tool is also known as a *chocolate funnel*, a *portion funnel*, and a *sauce gun*. It is cone-shaped, with a hinged, spring-loaded attachment on the handle, which controls a cover that slides open and closed at the bottom. The tool allows you to stop and start the flow of liquid from the funnel using only one hand. Different-sized tips can be attached to the opening to produce a thin or more generous flow of liquid. Fondant funnels are used to apply fondant or other icings and glazes onto petits fours and pastries and to fill chocolate truffle shells; they can also be used to portion sauce onto a serving plate. Stands that hold a filled funnel in an upright position between uses are available. A less expensive and sophisticated model is also available that does not have the spring trigger mechanism to open and close the aperture. Instead, a long cone-shaped wooden stick is moved up and down by hand to open and close the hole at the bottom.

Royal Icing yield: 6 cups (1 L 440 ml) or 3 pounds 7 ounces (1 kg 565 g)

Royal icing is also called *decorating icing*, because that is its principal use. It is one of the best materials with which to practice piping. It is inexpensive and easy to make, and it can be piped and formed into almost any shape. Royal icing is used a great deal around Christmastime to decorate gingerbread and Christmas cookies, and it is essential for making gingerbread houses. Royal icing can also be used to pipe on plastic or glass templates for decorations on marzipan, as described in "Designs Pressed into Marzipan to Be Traced Over and/or Filled In with Fondant" (page 677). Because it becomes hard and brittle when dry, royal icing is used more for decoration than for eating. However, it is traditional in some countries to use it on special-occasion cakes, such as wedding cakes. Personally, I limit its use to showpieces or to a small amount piped on a cake, cookies, or pastries.

Be careful to keep royal icing covered at all times and to clean off any icing from the side of your cup or bowl. The icing dries quickly, and the small lumps will interfere with your piping. A wet towel on top functions well while you are working, but you should pour a layer of water on the icing and wrap the container in plastic for longer storage (pour the water off before using the icing).

1 cup (240 ml) egg whites (see Note)	½ teaspoon (1 g) cream of tartar
2 pounds 8 ounces (1 kg 135 g) sifted powdered sugar	

1. Pour the egg whites into a mixer bowl. Using the paddle attachment with the machine set at low speed, gradually add all but a few handfuls of the powdered sugar, and the cream of tartar. Mix until a smooth paste forms, adding the remaining powdered sugar if necessary.

2. If you are using the royal icing for piping, beat at high speed for just a few seconds. If you will be spreading the icing — on the top of a gingerbread house, for example — beat the icing a bit longer to make it light and fluffy.

3. Immediately transfer to a clean container and cover to prevent a skin from forming. If you are going to use the icing within a few minutes, place a damp towel on top instead. Stored, covered, in the refrigerator, royal icing will keep for up to 1 week.

NOTE: As mentioned above, royal icing is used mostly for decorating showpieces and, as such, is rarely intended for consumption. If it is used as a major component of an item that will be eaten (more than just a decorative touch on a pastry, for example), make it with pasteurized egg whites for safety.

CHEF'S TIP

This recipe makes a large amount of royal icing. If you need only a small amount — to pipe a design on a few petits fours, for example — simply add powdered sugar to 1 egg white until the icing reaches the proper consistency; stir rapidly until the mixture is light and fluffy. Add a small pinch of cream of tartar or a drop of lemon juice to prevent the icing from yellowing. This will make approximately ¾ cup (180 ml) icing.

ROYAL ICING ORNAMENTS AND SHOWPIECES

Fancy royal icing ornaments and showpieces, typically composed in elaborate lace patterns, are easy to make in the following manner.

1. Place a thin sheet of acetate or polyurethane on top of a drawing of the design you want to make. Fasten the plastic and the paper together with paper clips so they will not move as you pipe. For small ornaments, you may want to use some of the designs shown on pages 546 to 548; only those designs in which all of the lines connect to the outline will work.

2. Using a piping bag, trace over your design with royal icing. Before the icing hardens, you can curve the sheet in the degree desired, either draping it over a mold and taping the ends to secure or joining the edges of the plastic and securing with paper clips.

3. Let the design dry overnight, then carefully peel away the plastic. Join the shapes with additional royal icing as needed. Frequently, to make a showpiece more durable, part of it is made from pastillage rather than royal icing.

DECORATING WITH SAUCES

SAUCE PAINTING

These are general decorating ideas for sauces. They can, of course, be combined or changed to suit a particular taste or occasion. The designs shown in a small pool of sauce can be made over the entire surface of the plate, and vice versa. Keep in mind that the more complicated the design, the less suitable it is for serving a large number of guests. Even though, in some cases, the sauce can be poured on the plates in advance, the decoration must be piped on just before the desserts are served, or it will start to deteriorate.

It is essential that the piping mixture or contrasting sauce and the sauce on the plate be the same consistency, or you will not get a good result. In most cases, the base sauce should be applied with a piping bottle with a fairly large opening, the exception being when the base sauce is piped as a frame (such as a hollow teardrop design) to be filled in with the contrasting sauce. The piping mixture or contrasting sauce should be applied with a piping bottle with a small opening or with a piping bag. The exception is when the contrasting sauce is piped directly onto the plate next to the other sauce, as in the Feathered Two-Tone Pool Pattern (page 685). I use small plastic squeeze bottles with a capacity of approximately 2 cups (480 ml). If you store left-over sauce in the bottles, be sure to check the consistency before using again and shake, strain, thin, thicken, etc., as necessary, as the consistency often changes during storage.

CHOCOLATE SAUCE FOR PIPING

Make Chocolate Sauce (page 413) and adjust the consistency to make it the same as the other sauce you are using. Add water to make the chocolate sauce thinner or melted chocolate to make it thicker (warm the sauce first to prevent lumps).

WEAVE PATTERN

1. Place the dessert in the center of the upper half of the plate. Using a piping bottle, pipe a small oval pool of sauce in front (the side that will be facing the customer).

2. Pipe 3 or 4 horizontal lines of the contrasting sauce across the pool.

3. Drag a small wooden skewer through the lines toward the edge of the plate. You can also alternate directions to make a herringbone pattern (Figure 13-11), or drag the lines through on the diagonal.

FIGURE 13-11 Making a herringbone-style weave pattern

SPIDERWEB PATTERN

1. Place the dessert in the center of the upper half of the plate. Using a piping bottle, pipe a small oval or round pool of sauce in front (the side that will be facing the customer).

2. Pipe a thin spiral of the contrasting sauce on top, making it oval or round to correspond with the pool.

3. Drag a small wooden skewer from the center to the outside in evenly spaced lines (Figure 13-12), or from the outside toward the center, or in alternating directions.

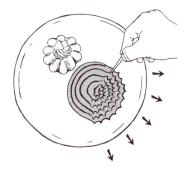

FIGURE 13-12 Making a spiderweb pattern

RIPPLE PATTERN

This design is quick to make and especially useful when there is little space on the plate.

1. Place a slice of cake in the center of the dessert plate. Using a piping bottle, pipe a small oval pool of sauce at the tip of the slice, letting the sauce flow out on both sides of the slice.

2. Pipe 2 lines of the contrasting sauce close together at the edge of the pool.

3. Drag a small wooden skewer through the lines, making connected circles, as for the Corkscrew Pattern (Figure 13-13).

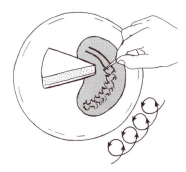

FIGURE 13-13 Making a ripple pattern

HEARTS WITH WEAVE PATTERN

This design creates both hearts and a herringbone pattern.

1. Place the dessert in the center of the upper half of the plate. Using a piping bottle, pipe a teardrop-shaped pool of sauce on the plate so the narrow end of the pool wraps halfway around the dessert.

2. Using the contrasting sauce, pipe a line of small dots, spaced about ½ inch (1.2 cm) apart, then 2 parallel solid lines under the dots, centered across the width of the pool.

FIGURE 13-14 Making a hearts with weave pattern

3. Drag a small wooden skewer up and down through the pattern without picking it up, dragging through both the dots and the solid lines when moving toward the edge of the plate and through the solid lines between each dot when moving toward the dessert (Figure 13-14).

SPIRAL SPIDERWEB PATTERN

This spiderweb pattern is formed using the reverse of the technique for the plain spiderweb pattern. Instead of piping the sauce in a spiral and dragging the skewer in radiating lines, the sauce is piped in a spoke pattern, then the skewer is dragged through in a spiral.

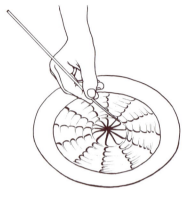

FIGURE 13-15 **Making a spiral spiderweb pattern**

1. Cover the base of the plate with a thin layer of sauce. Pipe the contrasting sauce on top in a spoke pattern.

2. Starting at the edge of the sauce pool, drag a small wooden skewer through the sauces in a spiral, ending in the center of the plate (Figure 13-15). Place the dessert in the center of the sauce.

TWO-TONE STRING OF HEARTS PATTERN

This is another variation on the string of hearts pattern. You can use just two sauces or use a third type (and color) for the center dots (hearts).

FIGURE 13-16 **Making a two-tone string of hearts pattern**

1. Cover the base of a plate with a thin layer of sauce. Pipe dots of the contrasting sauce fairly close together around the perimeter of the sauce, making them about 1 inch (2.5 cm) in diameter. Pipe smaller dots of the first sauce in the center of each 1-inch (2.5-cm) dot.

2. Drag a small wooden skewer in a curved side-to-side pattern through the center of the small dots, moving all the way around the plate in one continuous line (Figure 13-16). Place the dessert in the center of the plate.

HEARTS WITH STEMS PATTERN

This design makes a more elaborate heart shape than the other heart patterns.

1. Cover the base of the plate with a thin layer of sauce. Pipe five 1-inch (2.5-cm) dots of the contrasting sauce, evenly spaced and centered in the area that will be left between the dessert serving and the edge of the base sauce.

2. Dip the tip of a small wooden skewer into one of the dots of contrasting sauce to pick up

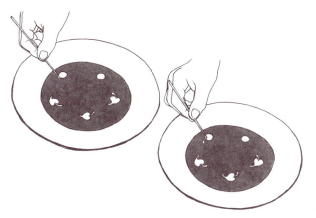

FIGURE 13-17 **Making a hearts with stems pattern**

a little bit on the skewer. Place the tip of the skewer in the sauce on the plate about ½ inch (1.2 cm) away from the dot, then drag it through the dot and out the other side in a slightly curved motion, creating a heart with a stem (Figure 13-17). Repeat with the remaining dots. Place the dessert in the center of the plate.

FEATHERED TWO-TONE POOL PATTERN

1. Using a piping bottle, pipe a pool of sauce in the center of a plate large enough to accommodate the dessert serving and leave a border of sauce visible. Using a second piping bottle, cover the base of the plate around the pool with a layer of the contrasting sauce.

2. Drag a wooden skewer in a series of connecting circles through both sauces where they meet (Figure 13-18). Place the dessert in the center of the plate.

FIGURE 13-18 **Making a feathered two-tone pool pattern**

N O T E : Depending on the sauces used and the amount of contrast desired, use either the pointed or the blunt end of the skewer. This pattern can also be used by piping the sauces in two half-circles that cover the base of the plate side by side, meeting in the center.

SWIRLED ZIGZAG PATTERN

This looks best with a round dessert.

1. Place the dessert in the center of the plate and use a piping bottle to pipe sauce all around to cover the base of the plate. Pipe a continuous, curved zigzag line of the contrasting sauce between the dessert and the edge of the sauce on the plate.

2. Drag a small wooden skewer through the center of the line all the way around the plate in one continuous motion (Figure 13-19).

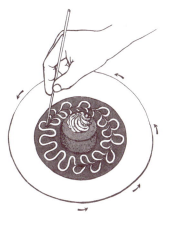

FIGURE 13-19 **Making a swirled zigzag pattern**

SAUCE DESIGNS USING A TURNTABLE

Of the many ways to apply sauce or decorating syrup to a serving plate, this method produces what is perhaps the most dramatic finish (see Color Photo 64). The base of the plates used should measure at least 7 inches (17.5 cm) across, and should be white with a plain white rim or with a simple design. An elaborate pattern on the china will clash with the flashy sauce design. The sauce or syrup should have the consistency of molasses; make a few trial spins and adjust as needed. The sauce or syrup may be spun so that it remains within the base of the plate, or it can be made to spray out onto the rim, but it should never go over the rim, which would look sloppy and would also make the plates difficult to pick up for serving. You will need a cake decorating turntable with a heavy cast iron base, a cake pan 12 inches (30 cm) in diameter and 2 inches (5 cm) in height, wide masking tape, and heavy string such as that used for trussing.

1. Make 4 large loops of masking tape sticky side out and place them evenly spaced around the edge of the turntable. Place the cake pan on top and press down firmly. Use masking tape to secure 1 end of a string approximately 48 inches (1 m 20 cm) long to the top of the rod underneath. Wind the string tightly around the top of the rod; it must not cover the portion of the rod that fits inside the base, or the table will not spin. Place the turntable in the base. Make 4 more loops of tape in the same way as before and place these evenly spaced inside the cake pan. Center a serving plate inside the cake pan and press down to secure.

2. Pour or pipe a pool of sauce or syrup approximately 3 inches (7.5 cm) in diameter in the center of the plate (see Procedure 13-2a). Grasp the string a few inches from the end and pull hard to spin the turntable — this is a bit like the action of firmly pulling a cord to start a lawnmower (see Procedure 13-2b). Use your other hand to hold onto the base of the turntable, then use this hand to stop the turntable when the sauce reaches the desired size on the plate. The length of the string and the degree of effort you use when you pull it — both of which determine the speed at which the turntable rotates — as well as the viscosity of the sauce, all influence the pattern created. If the sauce does not spin out as far as you would like the first time, spin it a second time.

3. Remove the plate and repeat to decorate as many plates as needed.

NOTE: If your serving plates do not fit inside the cake pan specified, use a larger pan or set the plate directly on the tape loops of the turntable. The second option does not offer as much protection should the sauce fly off the plate.

PROCEDURE 13-2a Piping a pool of sauce in the center of plate placed inside the cake pan on top of the assembled turntable

PROCEDURE 13-2b Pulling the string to spin the turntable

Florentina Cups yield: 20 cups

This batter can also be used to make traditional (flat) Florentina cookies. One recipe will make 36 cookies, 3¼ inches (8.1 cm) in diameter.

7 ounces (200 g) unsalted butter	**¼ cup (60 ml) heavy cream**
7 ounces (200 g) granulated sugar	**7 ounces (200 g) sliced almonds, lightly crushed**
3 tablespoons (45 ml) or 2 ounces (55 g) glucose *or* corn syrup	

1. Combine the butter, sugar, glucose or corn syrup, and cream in a saucepan; bring to a boil. Add the almonds and cook over medium heat for 2 to 3 minutes. Remove from the heat.

2. Try baking a small piece of batter as a test. If the batter spreads too thin, cook the batter in the saucepan a little longer. Conversely, if the batter does not spread enough, add a little more cream and test again; you will need to warm the batter to mix in the cream. Pour the batter into a bowl and refrigerate.

3. Have ready 1 or, preferably, 2 ladles, 6 to 8 ounces (180 to 240 ml) each; 1 or 2 oranges or small grapefruit that fit loosely inside the ladles (chilling the fruit will make the shells harden more quickly); and a container that is close to the same height as the length of the ladle handles (a round bain-marie insert usually works well). Hook the ladles to the top of the container so the bowls of the ladles are resting on the table as level as possible. Set aside.

4. Make a template by drawing 10 circles, 5½ inches (13.7 cm) in diameter, on a full sheet of baking paper with a black marking pen (see Note). Space the circles evenly and arrange them in a staggered pattern to make 3 rows, placing 3 rounds in both the top and bottom rows and 4 rounds in the center row. This template can be reused many times.

5. Place a second sheet of baking paper on top of your template; tape the edges to the table, if necessary, to keep the papers from sliding.

6. Divide the chilled and thickened Florentina mixture into 2 equal pieces. Using a small amount of flour, if necessary, to keep the dough from sticking to your hands and the table, roll out each piece into a rope 10 inches (25 cm) long, then cut each rope into 10 equal pieces.

7. Place 10 of the small slices centered inside the circles on the baking paper set over the template. Press each piece with your fingers to flatten it and bring it to ½ inch (1.2 cm) from the edge of the drawn circle. Remove the paper from the template and place the paper with the cookies attached on a perfectly flat sheet pan.

8. Place a new sheet of baking paper over your template and repeat Step 7 with the remaining 10 slices of Florentina dough.

9. Bake 1 sheet pan of Florentinas at a time at 350°F (175°C) for approximately 10 minutes or until golden brown. Remove the pan from the oven and let the cookies cool for just a few minutes or until they are firm enough to be lifted off the pan with a spatula (see Note).

10. Working quickly, transfer a cookie, right-side up, to the bowl of one of the ladles and

FIGURE 13-20 **Using an orange to press a soft Florentina cookie into the bowl of a ladle to form a Florentina cup. Left to right: 2 finished Florentina cups; a bain-marie supporting 2 ladles in an upright position; a baked cookie waiting to be formed**

press it into the ladle with an orange to form the cup shape (Figure 13-20). If you are using 2 ladles, as suggested, leave the first cup in place, form a second cup in the other ladle, then go back and remove the first one. Repeat until you have formed all 10 cups (see Note). If the cookies on the pan become too firm to shape, return the pan to the oven for 1 or 2 minutes to soften them. Repeat Steps 9 and 10 to form the remaining 10 cups.

NOTE: If you want the top edge of the cups to be perfectly even, you can bake the cookies in Flexipans (use pan No. 2452) or trim them after baking but before forming the cups as follows. If the baked cookies are just a little uneven, place a cookie cutter that is slightly larger than the baked cookie around a cookie (not on top) as soon as the pan of cookies comes out of the oven. Using a circular motion, push the soft cookie into a nice, even round shape. If the cookies are very uneven, or have spread too far beyond the lines, transfer the baking paper with the baked cookies on it to a full sheet of corrugated cardboard or an even tabletop. Use a cookie cutter 5½

CHEF'S TIP

If you do not have the proper size ladles or prefer not to use that method to shape the cups, they can also be formed in one of the following ways:

- As soon as the warm cookies are firm enough to work with, invert a cookie and immediately bend 1 inch (2.5 cm) of the edge up 45° to form a shallow hexagonal basket; the top of the cookie will face out.
- Fold the warm, soft cookies over the back of a small bowl or jar and press into shape with your hands (Figure 13-21).
- Use 2 large brioche molds to make the cups by placing one mold inside the other, with the cookie pressed between them as shown at left in Figure 13-21.

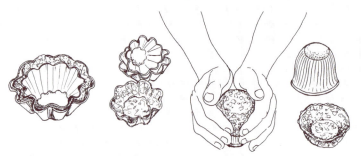

FIGURE 13-21 **Forming Florentina cups by pressing the soft cookies between 2 identical molds; folding the soft cookie over the back of a small inverted mold and shaping it by hand**

Shaping the cookies with the brioche molds or over the back of a small bowl will result in fairly uniform baskets. The ladle method produces a more free-form shape.

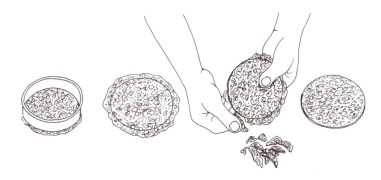

inches (13.7 cm) in diameter to cut out the center of the cookie to the correct size. Pull the baking paper back on the pan (so you can continue to use the cardboard for the next batch), let the cookies cool, then break off the excess from the outside (Figure 13-22).

VARIATION
COCOA-NIB FLORENTINA CUPS (Color Photo 43)

Add 4 ounces (115 g) cocoa nibs at the end of Step 1, before chilling the batter.

Florentina Cones yield: 30 cones (Color Photo 27)

> 1 recipe or 1 pound 10 ounces (740 g)
> Florentina Cups batter (page 687)

1. Draw 30 circles, 3½ inches (8.7 cm) in diameter, on baking paper. Invert the papers on sheet pans.

2. Divide the Florentina batter into 2 equal pieces. Using flour if needed to prevent the mixture from sticking, roll each piece into a rope 11¼ inches (28.1 cm) long. Cut each rope into 15 equal slices, ¾ inch (2 cm) each. Place a Florentina slice in the center of each circle, spread, bake, and trim as directed in the recipe for Florentina Cups (page 687).

3. Return the trimmed cookies, a few at a time, to the oven for a few minutes to soften. Place the cookies, top-side down, on the table and immediately roll them around cream horn molds or other cone-shaped molds; you need 3 or 4 molds to work efficiently. Press the seam together between the mold and the table to be sure the cones will not unroll. Let cool sufficiently before removing the forms so the Florentina cones do not collapse.

CHEF'S TIP
The procedure can be simplified by using Flexipan No. 1299. Omit Step 1. Center a slice of Florentina mixture in each indentation of the pan. Press the slices into the pan gently; you do not need to spread the batter out as directed, the pan takes care of shaping the batter into smooth even circles as it bakes. After the cookies have baked and cooled, place them on a sheet pan lined with baking paper, warm them, and shape as directed in Step 3 (it is not necessary to trim Florentinas baked in a Flexipan; the edges will be perfectly smooth).

Florentina Cookies for Marco Polo

yield: 16 cookies, 9 × 1½ inches (22.5 × 3.7 cm), and 16 cookies, 4½ × 1½ inches (11.2 × 3.7 cm) (Color Photo 86)

> ½ recipe or 12 ounces (340 g) Florentina Cups
> batter (page 687)

1. Draw 2 rectangles measuring 10 × 18 inches (25 × 45 cm) on a sheet of baking paper. Invert the paper on a sheet pan. Divide the Florentina batter between the rectangles and spread or pat it within the lines. Wet your fingers or the palette knife to keep the batter from sticking.

2. Bake at 375°F (190°C) for about 12 minutes or until light brown. Carefully slide the baking paper onto a sheet of corrugated cardboard or your worktable. Using a sharp knife, trim the rectangles to make them 9 inches (22.5 cm) wide. Cut crosswise every 1½ inches (3.7 cm) to make 12 strips measuring 1½ × 9 inches (3.7 × 22.5 cm) from each rectangle. Cut 8 of the 24 strips in half crosswise to make 16 large and 16 small cookies. Reheat the Florentina as needed during this process to keep it from breaking.

3. Place the cookies in the oven just long enough to soften. Drape the pieces, top-side up, over a can or other round object 6 inches (15 cm) in diameter and let stand until firm.

Florentina Twists yield: approximately 20 decorations

> ¼ recipe or 6 ounces (170 g) Florentina Cups
> batter (page 687)

1. Draw a rectangle measuring 7 × 16 inches (17.5 × 40 cm) on a piece of baking paper. Invert the paper, place the Florentina batter on top, and pat or spread it to form a rectangle within the lines. Wet your fingers or the palette knife to keep the batter from sticking.

2. Place the paper on a sheet pan and bake at 375°F (190°C) for approximately 10 minutes or until the Florentina batter turns a light caramel color. Slide the paper off the pan onto the tabletop. Trim just enough from the long sides to make them even.

3. Cut the strip across into wedges measuring approximately ¾ inch (2 cm) at the wide end and ¼ inch (6 mm) at the narrow end, as shown in the illustration. Let the sheet cool and harden, then separate the wedges and place them on a paper-lined sheet pan. A few at a time, return the wedges to the oven just long enough to soften them.

4. One at a time, twist each wedge into a spiral (Figure 13-23). Store the Florentina twists in an airtight container.

FIGURE 13-23 Twisting a softened wedge-shaped Florentina cookie to make a Florentina Twist

92. Ruby Pears with Verbena Bavarois and Port Wine Reduction

(clockwise from top left) **93. Example of chocolate casting (painting) 94. Example of cocoa painting 95. Chocolate boxes with**

(clockwise from top left) **97. Assorted truffle display 98. Pulled, Blown, and Cast Sugar showpiece 99. Marzipan elephant birthday cake 100. Marzipan monkey birthday cake**

(clockwise from top left) **102. Traditional Gingerbread House   103. Traditional Gingerbread House II   104. Santa's Gingerbread Chalet   105. Traditional Gingerbread House III**

(clockwise from top left) **106. Marzipan Pig with Two Santas 107. Marzipan Pig with Two Santas II 108. Chocolate Chalet with White Chocolate and Pistachio Pâté and Bitter Chocolate Sauce**

(clockwise from top) **109. Brandied Gingerbread Cake 110. Persimmon Cream Slices with Cookie Christmas Trees and Cranberry Coulis 111. Persimmon Dome Cake with Gingerbread Lattice**

112. Lemon Verbena–Scented Fruitcake, Soft Gingerbread Cake, Dresdener Stollen

113. Pig's Head Bread Loaf and Dinner Rolls

114. Bûche de Nöel Slices with Pomegranate Sauce and Star Fruit

115. Christmas Cookie Ornaments, Chocolate Snow Hearts, Cinnamon

116. Yule Log (Bûche de Nöel)

117. Christmas Tree Pastries, Yule Log Pastries, Holiday Candle Pastries

Hartmund Florentina Garnish yield: 1 pound (455 g) or 1¼ cups (300 ml)

A few years ago, while I was teaching a dessert course in Columbus, Ohio, I had the pleasure of dining at Hartmund Handke's excellent restaurant, Handke's Cuisine. Chef Handke is one of the few certified Master Chefs cooking in the United States.

These decorations will take on a slightly different — and more attractive — look if you allow the paste to rest for a day after making the batter; it does not need to be refrigerated. This gives the nuts the time they need to absorb moisture. If you need to warm the paste to soften it to a workable consistency, some of the butter may separate. Adding approximately 1 tablespoon (15 ml) heavy cream and stirring over low heat for a few seconds will bring it back together.

4 ounces (115 g) unsalted butter

4 ounces (115 g) granulated sugar

4 ounces (115 g) or ⅓ cup (80 ml) light corn syrup

4 ounces (115 g) finely ground hazelnuts *or* almonds (blanched or natural)

1. Combine the butter, sugar, and corn syrup in a saucepan. Bring to a boil, stirring constantly. Continue to cook for 1 minute after the mixture begins to boil — start timing when the syrup is bubbling rapidly throughout the entire mass.

2. Remove from the heat and stir in the nuts. Set aside to cool, preferably for 24 hours.

3. Spread the paste on sheet pans lined with baking paper or on Silpats, making the desired shape and size or as instructed in individual recipes.

4. Bake at 375°F (190°C) for approximately 6 minutes or until the paste turns golden brown and has caramelized. Remove from the oven, if applicable, and shape the decorations as soon as they are cool enough to handle.

VARIATION

HAZELNUT COOKIE WAFERS yield: approximately 60 to 80 cookies

1. Make the recipe for Hartmund Florentina Garnish, using ground hazelnuts, and allow the paste to rest for a minimum of 6 to 8 hours to set up and become firm.

2. Using a small amount of flour to prevent it sticking, roll out the paste on a Silpat or baking paper to make an 11-inch (27.5-cm) square; this will ensure the correct thickness. If the paste is too soft to roll out, it probably was not cooked long enough or was not cooked at a full boil. Scrape it off the mat, recook, and cool again.

3. Cut out cookies with a plain round cutter, 1 to 1½ inches (2.5 to 3.7 cm) in diameter, and place them, staggered, on sheet pans lined with Silpats or baking paper. Space the cookies well apart, as they will spread to slightly more than double in size. Combine the scraps and reroll until all of the paste is used.

4. Bake at 375°F (190°C) for approximately 8 minutes or until the cookies are golden brown.

Several dessert presentations in this text require sifting cocoa powder or powdered sugar over the base of a dessert plate in a precise pattern. This technique often presents a challenge, especially in the case of large designs, where the rim of the plate may prevent you from laying the template flat against the base of the plate. In this case, not only is it difficult to make well-defined shapes but it is hard to avoid getting the cocoa powder or powdered sugar on the rim of the serving plate. These problems can occur when streaking chocolate over the base of the plate as well. Using a modified disposable pie tin, as a template itself or as a frame in conjunction with a cardboard template, is an easy and inexpensive solution (see page 552 for another way to mask the plate rim when piping lines of chocolate).

Select a disposable aluminum pie tin with a base that will sit flat against the base of the serving plates you are using. You can either cut the desired design out of the base of the pie tin (shown at top left in Figure 13-24) or cut away part or all of the bottom of the pie tin (shown at top center) depending on the size and shape of the template to be used, leaving a frame that can be used to hold various templates, attaching them as needed. Cutting the design out of the base of the pie tin can be difficult because the sides of the pan get in the way and, because you must apply much more pressure on the utility knife to cut through aluminum than through cardboard, it is difficult to make smooth, rounded edges. The advantage, however, is that a template cut directly from the pie tin is significantly more durable, so it can be used for a long time.

When streaking chocolate, you may need to extend the protection of the rim of the plate by taping a ring of baking paper to the sides of the pie tin, as streaking sometimes extends beyond the edge of the plate. A paper plate with a sloping edge can be used instead of a pie tin. These plates are easier to cut but are not, of course, as sturdy.

USING A PIE TIN TEMPLATE

1. Using a felt-tip pen, trace the desired design on the base of the pie tin and cut it out with a utility knife.

2. Place the pie tin on the base of the dessert plate and sift powdered sugar or cocoa powder on top. Remove the pie tin carefully.

3. To make an overlapping design, follow Steps 4 and 5 in the following instructions.

USING A PIE TIN HOLDER WITH A CARDBOARD TEMPLATE

1. Trace the desired template and cut it out of cardboard from a cake box. Tape the template to the bottom of the pie tin frame (Figure 13-24).

2. Place the pie tin right side up on the dessert plate and sift cocoa powder or powdered sugar on top (Figure 13-25).

3. Carefully remove the frame (Figure 13-26).

4. To make an overlapping design, such as a powdered sugar shape over a cocoa powder

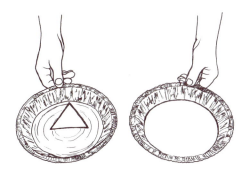

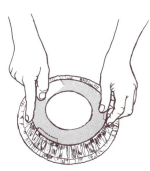

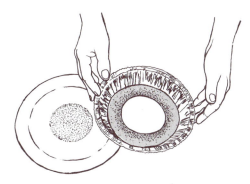

FIGURE 13-24 **Left to right: A template cut directly from the bottom of a pie tin; the entire base of a pie tin removed to hold a cardboard template; a cardboard template being attached to a bottomless pie tin holder**

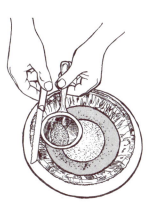

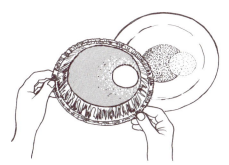

FIGURE 13-25 **Sifting cocoa powder over a dessert plate with the pie tin holder and template set on the plate**

FIGURE 13-26 **Removing the template and holder**

FIGURE 13-27 **Attaching toothpicks to the base of a second template to hold it just slightly above the cocoa powder design when it is placed on the plate**

FIGURE 13-28 **Lifting the template and holder off the plate after sifting powdered sugar over the second template**

design, tape toothpicks around the edge of the frame of the second template (Figure 13-27). This will hold the second template just slightly above the plate and prevent it from smearing the first design.

5. Carefully set the frame on the plate and sift powdered sugar (or cocoa powder) over the top. Remove the frame (Figure 13-28).

This versatile decorating paste can be formed or made into almost any shape you like. Tuile decorating paste consists of only four ingredients in equal weights — butter, sugar, egg whites, and flour. Due to the gluten in the flour, the shapes may shrink just a little during baking, but they will do so evenly all around, so provided it is taken into consideration where it will matter, the shrinkage does not cause a problem. The apparent solution to avoiding or reducing shrinkage is to reduce the gluten strength of the flour (replacing a portion of the flour with starch), but this option is not viable because, the baked pieces would become too fragile. To avoid developing the gluten any more than necessary, take care not to overmix the batter once the flour has been incorporated.

Tuile means "tile" in French. Thin, curved tuiles (a classic French cookie) are said to resemble roof tiles made in a half-sphere shape. Tuile decorating paste is also called *pâte à cigarette,* from its use in making the familiar thin, tube-shaped cigarette cookies, also known as *pirouettes,* which are usually decorated by dipping the ends in chocolate. Finally, it is also known as *tulip paste,* a name that no doubt comes from its well-known application whereby the paste is spread into circles, 7 to 8 inches (17.5 to 20 cm) in diameter, on Silpats or greased and floured sheet pans, and the flexible, warm cookies are then sandwiched between two bowls to form tulip-shaped cups. These are typically used as containers for sorbet or ice cream. The classic tuile cookie and the traditional tulip-shaped containers have given way to new, intricate modern designs.

In the recipes in this book that call for tuile decorating paste, you first need to trace and cut out a template from cardboard or plastic to use in creating the desired shape. Some of the templates in this book are specifically designed to coordinate with the presentation for a particular recipe, but many generic shapes may be purchased from suppliers. These templates are available in stainless steel, aluminum, or plastic, and while obviously more durable than a template made from cardboard (the metal templates will last forever), they are relatively expensive, as they are almost always imported from Europe.

Tuile paste decorations are easiest to make using Silpats. If you do not have them, grease the backs of even sheet pans very lightly, coat the pans with flour, then shake off as much flour as possible. Spread the paste onto the Silpats or prepared pans, spreading it flat and even within the template (Figure 13-29). Be careful when you pick up the template from the pan after spreading the paste. Hold down the opposite end with your spatula as you lift the template to avoid disturbing the paste (Figure 13-30). Specific templates and instructions are given with individual recipes.

FIGURE 13-29 **Spreading tuile decorating paste flat and even within a template**

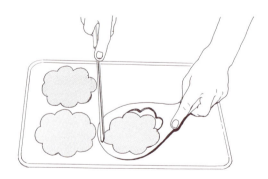

FIGURE 13-30 **Holding down the opposite side of the template as it is removed to prevent distortion**

Vanilla Tuile Decorating Paste yield: 2 pounds (910 g) or 3¼ cups (780 ml)

8 ounces (225 g) unsalted butter, at room temperature

8 ounces (225 g) powdered sugar, sifted

1 cup (240 ml) egg whites, at room temperature

1 teaspoon (5 ml) vanilla extract

8 ounces (225 g) cake flour, sifted

1. Cream the butter and powdered sugar together. Incorporate the egg whites, a few at a time. Add the vanilla. Add the flour and mix just until incorporated; do not overmix.

2. Stored covered in the refrigerator, tuile decorating paste will keep for one week; it may be frozen for longer storage. Allow the paste to soften slightly after removing it from the refrigerator, then stir it smooth and into a spreadable consistency before using. If the paste is too soft, the edges of the tuile decorations will be ragged and unprofessional-looking. If this happens, chill the paste briefly.

Chocolate Tuile Decorating Paste yield: 2 pounds (910 g) or 3¼ cups (780 ml)

8 ounces (225 g) unsalted butter, at room temperature

8 ounces (225 g) powdered sugar, sifted

1 cup (240 ml) egg whites, at room temperature

1 teaspoon (5 ml) vanilla extract

6 ounces (170 g) bread flour, sifted

2½ ounces (70 g) unsweetened cocoa powder, sifted

1. Follow the procedure for Vanilla Tuile Decorating Paste, sifting the flour with the cocoa powder in Step 1 before adding it to the paste. Store and use as directed in Step 2.

Cookie Butterflies yield: about 50 large butterflies or 75 small butterflies (Color Photo 2)

Cookie butterflies are among the easiest tuile paste decorations to produce because they require little contact with the hot cookies as they are formed — the V-shaped support does the job for you (see "Making a V-Shaped Support," page 698). When a butterfly is placed next to an edible flower, a mint sprig, or a piece of fruit, it not only gives the dessert height but also adds a touch of elegance and beauty to the presentation. Cookie butterflies should always be thin and fragile, like real butterflies. If the paste is spread too thick, the decorations will look clumsy and the desired effect will be lost.

¼ recipe or 8 ounces (225 g) Vanilla Tuile Decorating Paste (above)

1 teaspoon (2.5 g) unsweetened cocoa powder

1. Make either of the cookie butterfly templates (Figure 13-31 or Figure 13-32) as instructed in the recipe you are using. The templates, as shown, are the correct size. Trace the drawing, then cut the template out of cardboard that is 1/16 inch (2 mm) thick; cake boxes are ideal.

2. If you do not have Silpats, lightly grease the backs of clean, even sheet pans, coat with flour, then shake off as much flour as possible.

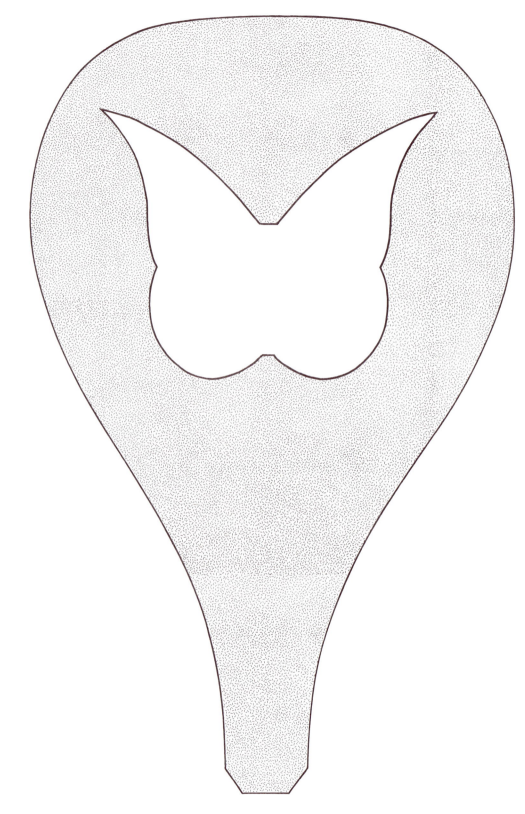

FIGURE 13-31 The template for large cookie butterflies

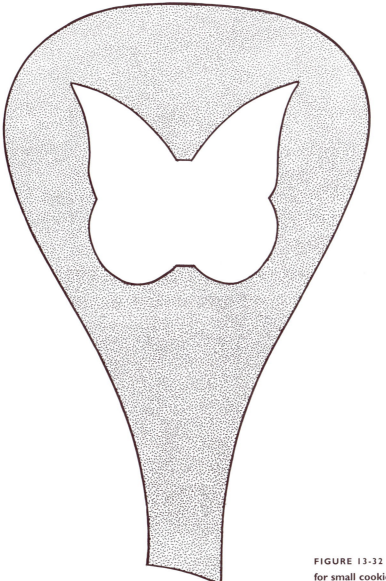

FIGURE 13-32 **The template for small cookie butterflies**

3. Mix the cocoa powder into 2 tablespoons (30 ml) tuile paste, stirring until smooth. Place in 2 piping bags.

4. Spread the plain tuile paste flat and even within the butterfly template on the Silpats or prepared pans (see Figures 13-29 and 12-30, page 694); do not form more than 12 butterflies per pan.

5. Pipe 3 dots of cocoa-colored paste in descending size on each wing, with the largest dot at the bottom (see Chef's Tip).

6. Bake the butterflies, 1 pan at a time, at 400°F (205°C) for approximately 6 minutes or until the cookies begin to develop a few brown spots. Leave the pan in the oven with the door open. Starting with the cookie with the most brown spots, transfer the cookies 1 at a time to the V-shaped form, placing them right-side up and arranging them in the form so they are straight. If you have time and your hands are up to the heat, use your thumbs to quickly press the center of each butterfly body against the box; press toward both sides in an

CHEF'S TIP
You can use the cocoa-colored paste to pipe a body in the center of each butterfly as well as the dots on the wings. In this case, you will need to color twice as much paste.

Making a *V*-Shaped Support

To form the butterflies, you need a *V*-shaped form. If you do not have one, make a form following the directions for the Chalet Support Box (page 475), or make a simplified version as follows. Begin with a strip of corrugated cardboard 16 inches (40 cm) long and 6 inches (15 cm) wide. Make a cut lengthwise down the center of the strip, cutting only halfway through. Bend the cardboard into a *V* shape, placing a strip of tape across the top at each end to make the opening 3½ inches (8.7 cm) wide for the proper angle. To hold the form upright as you work, secure it between the rows of an inverted muffin tin.

outward motion to make the front of the wings spread at a slight angle. Remove the formed cookie butterflies once they have hardened — this only takes a few seconds — and repeat to bake and form the remainder. It is a good idea to make a few more cookie butterflies than you will need to allow for breakage.

Cookie Citrus Rinds and Cookie Figurines

yield: decorations for 16 dessert servings (Color Photo 24)

These long, curling, fanciful shapes are meant to resemble strips of citrus peel removed with a citrus stripper. However, you do not need to limit these decorations to desserts where make-believe citrus peel would be appropriate. They certainly can be used (with or without the addition of grated zest) to dress up a dessert any time you feel like going a little wild with the presentation (which is fun every once in a while).

As you may have experienced, anything made from tuile paste is extremely brittle after baking — to the extent that items can sometimes break seemingly for no reason at all. At the same time, these products are susceptible to moisture and, if they are stored improperly, placed on top of a moist dessert too far ahead of time, or in the case of containers, filled too long in advance, they soften and can collapse. While this softening is normally considered a problem, it occurred to me to try to use it to my advantage, and I came up with the idea of shaping the softened spirals into these eye-catching decorations.

1 recipe Vanilla Tuile Decorating Paste (page 695)	1 tablespoon (18 g) finely grated citrus zest

CHEF'S TIP

If the cookie rinds will not be used until the day after baking, you can omit the softening process. Instead, place them directly on sheet pans lined with baking paper, place another sheet of paper on top, and refrigerate overnight. The cold, damp air in the refrigerator will soften them.

1. If you do not have Silpats, lightly grease the backs of 5 even sheet pans, coat with flour, then shake off as much flour as possible.

2. Stir the citrus zest into the tuile paste and place a portion of the paste in a pastry bag with a No. 1 (2-mm) plain tip. Pipe out spirals, about 6 inches (15 cm) in diameter, onto the Silpats or prepared sheet pans. Do not close the spirals at the ends. Instead, pipe a wavy line, approximately 6 inches (15 cm) long, extending from each spiral (Figure 13-33). Place 6 spirals on each of 3 full-size Silpats or sheet pans. This will give you 2 extra decorations in case of breakage.

3. Using a design such as the one shown on the right in the bottom row in Figure 10-22, page 546, pipe out 36 figurines, 4 inches (10 cm) tall, onto the remaining Silpats or prepared sheet pans. You need 2 figurines per serving; again, this quantity will give you extra.

4. Bake at 400°F (205°C) for approximately 6 minutes or until the tuile paste is golden brown. Set aside to cool (see Chef's Tip).

5. Place a damp towel on the bottom of a sheet pan. Place a sheet of baking paper on top and weigh the corners with forms or coffee cups to prevent the paper curling from the moisture.

6. Carefully transfer the baked spirals (not the smaller figurines) to the prepared pan. If any break as you move them, do not discard the pieces at this point; they may still be usable, unless they have broken in more than 1 place. Invert a second sheet pan on top as a lid.

FIGURE 13-33 **Piping tuile paste into spirals with extended wavy tails for Cookie Citrus Rinds**

7. Return the spirals to the 400°F (205°C) oven for 6 to 8 minutes or until they remain soft and limp after cooling. Transfer the spirals to a sheet pan lined with baking paper. Repeat the softening procedure with the remaining spirals. If they will not be used within the next few hours, store the spirals in the refrigerator. Cover the cookie figurines and store them in a warm, dry place to keep them crisp.

8. Arrange the figurines and cookie rinds on top of dessert servings as specified in individual recipes (see Color Photo 24 for an example).

Cookie Tumbleweeds yield: approximately 20 decorations

These are easy to make and can be used to add a contemporary look to many desserts. Adding the extra butter to the tuile paste makes the decorations a bit thinner and more elegant. Pipe the lines thin and not too close together so the loops and circles do not bake together in the oven; the paste will flow out slightly during baking.

½ recipe **Vanilla Tuile Decorating Paste** (page 695)

1 ounce (30 g) unsalted butter, melted

1. To make a container in which to store the fragile decorations, place a sheet of plastic wrap over an empty cardboard egg carton. If you do not have Silpats, grease the backs of inverted sheet pans, coat with flour, and shake off as much flour as possible.

2. Stir the melted butter into the tuile paste. Place a portion of the mixture into a paper pastry bag and cut a small opening.

3. To make each tumbleweed, pipe out the mixture onto a Silpat or a prepared sheet pan; starting from the center and piping in an unbroken line moving outward, make small overlapping loops and circles until you have gradually formed a lacy decoration approximately 8 inches (20 cm) in diameter (Figure 13-34). Note: The illustration is much smaller than the actual decoration. There

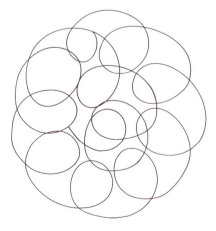

FIGURE 13-34 **The pattern of tuile paste lines piped out to produce Cookie Tumbleweeds**

should be approximately as much uncovered area as there is tuile paste. Place 4 tumbleweeds per full-size Silpat or sheet pan.

4. Bake 1 pan at a time at 400°F (205°C) until golden brown spots appear on 1 cookie, approximately 4 minutes. Leave the pan in the oven with the door open.

5. Using a palette knife, pick up the brownest cookie and quickly gather it into a loose ball in your hands to form a tumbleweed. Place in the plastic-covered egg carton. Quickly repeat with the remaining cookies on the pan.

6. Pipe, bake, and form the remaining cookies in the same way. Store in airtight containers so the decorations remain crisp.

Curly Cues *yield: approximately 70 decorations (Color Photo 86)*

Chances are good you will be a bit frustrated initially when these thin, narrow cookie strips break in your hands as you attempt to form them — but do not give up. Your fingers will soon become used to the heat, allowing you to wind the strips fast enough to keep them from breaking. Remember: If making curly cues were easy, everyone would do it, so these are a great way to show off a little.

Do not attempt to bake more than 6 to 8 cookies at a time, because they bake quickly and you will not have time to form them all before the last few get too dark. You can, as is true of any item made from tuile paste, spread the paste within the template ahead of time and have several pans ready to bake and form in succession. This is a good idea if you need to make a lot of decorations. In this case, have several dowels ready, plan your workspace accordingly, and designate an area where you will place the formed cookies while you shape the remainder.

½ recipe **Vanilla Tuile Decorating Paste** (page 695)	1½ teaspoons (3.5 g) unsweetened cocoa powder

1. Trace the template in Figure 13-35 and cut it out of cardboard that is ¹⁄₁₆ inch (2 mm) thick; cake boxes work fine. The template, as shown, is the correct size for use in this recipe, but you will need to match the dotted lines to join the two halves as you trace it.

2. Use Silpats or lightly grease the backs of even sheet pans, coat the pans with flour, then shake off as much flour as possible. Have ready 2 dowels, ½ inch (1.2 cm) in diameter and 16 inches (40 cm) long; wooden spoon handles are often the appropriate size.

3. Stir the cocoa powder into 3 tablespoons (45 ml) tuile paste until the mixture is completely smooth. Place the paste in 2 or 3 piping bags and cut a small opening in one bag.

4. Spread the vanilla tuile paste flat and even within the template (see Figures 13-29 and 13-30, page 694). Form 6 to 8 cookies on each Silpat or sheet pan. Pipe a straight line of the cocoa-colored paste in the center, down the full length of each cookie.

5. Bake 1 pan at a time at 400°F (205°C) for approximately 2 minutes or until 1 cookie begins to show a few brown spots. It takes a little experience to judge when to begin with the first cookie, and you have to move quickly at this point. If the cookies are overbaked, they will break as you try to form them. However, if the cookies are removed before they show any color at all, they will not become crisp after they cool. Leave the pan in the oven with the door open.

6. Hold the dowel in 1 hand and quickly pick up the darkest cookie strip by the narrow end.

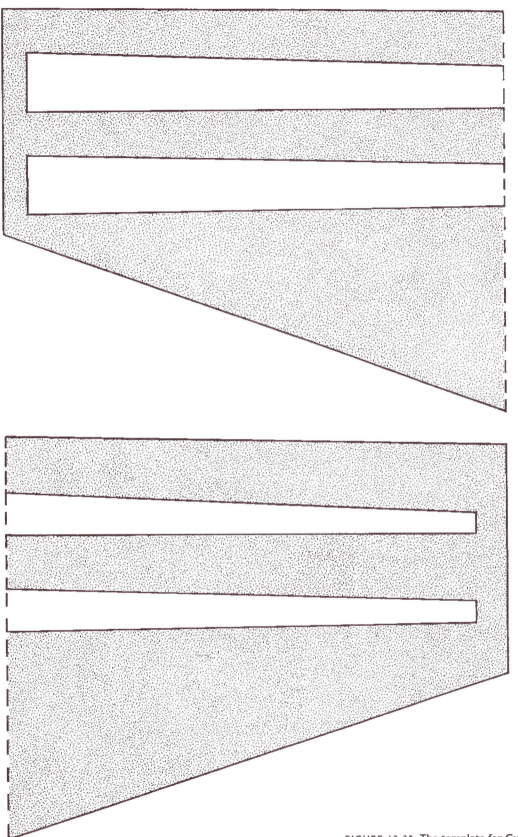

FIGURE 13-35 The template for Curly Cues and
Wavy Tuile Strips. Trace half the template, connect
the dotted lines, then trace the other half.

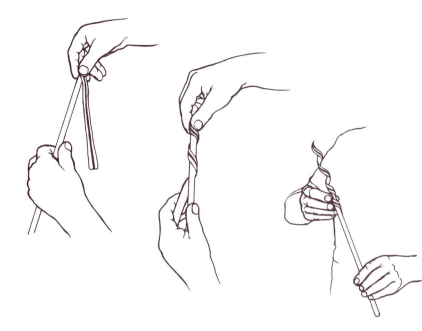

FIGURE 13-36 **Wrapping a soft Curly Cue around a dowel to shape it immediately after removing it from the oven; pulling off the cookie after it has hardened**

CHEF'S TIP
Curly cues can be made without chocolate lines and with reversed colors: Spread Chocolate Tuile Decorating Paste (page 695) within the template and pipe Vanilla Tuile Decorating Paste (page 695) in a line down the center. This variety is a little tricky to bake because the dark batter makes it hard to judge when the cookies are done. To help gauge the timing, place a few sliced almonds on the pan next to the cookies; when the almonds turn golden, the cookies are done. Watching the light lines in the center of the strips is helpful also.

Place the strip at a 45-degree angle to the dowel and quickly turn the dowel as you allow the cookie to wrap around it and form a spiral (Figure 13-36). You can adjust the length and shape of the finished cookie by adjusting the angle at which the cookie falls on the dowel. For example, placing the cookie at close to a 90-degree angle to the dowel produces a short, tightly wound cookie, similar to a telephone cord. Hold both ends of the cookie tightly against the dowel for a few seconds, then slide it off. If you are working with 2 or more dowels, place the dowel holding the cookie on the table with the ends of the cookie underneath, then start to form the next cookie right away.

7. Form and bake the remaining cookies. Stored in an airtight container, the finished curly cues will keep for weeks.

Curved Tuile Wedges yield: approximately 24 decorations (Color Photo 84)

Like the Triangular Tuile Spirals (page 707), these decorations are made with a flat base so they stand straight on the serving plate. However, unlike the spirals, which are designed to sit on top of or next to a dessert, these curved tuile wedges are made to fit over and around a cylindrical dessert, making them both a container and a decoration.

To shape the curved wedges, you will need two plastic tubes or wooden dowels, 2 inches (5 cm) in diameter and 6 to 8 inches (15 to 20 cm) long.

½ recipe Vanilla Tuile Decorating Paste (page 695)

FIGURE 13-37 **The template for Curved Tuile Wedges**

1. Have Silpats ready or grease and flour the back of clean, even sheet pans.

2. Make the template shown in Figure 13-37, page 703. The drawing, as shown, is the correct size for this recipe; however, the temlate is shown in 2 pieces to fit the page. Trace the drawing, matching the dotted lines so the template looks like the small example shown, then cut it out of cardboard that is $^1/_{16}$ inch (2 mm) thick; cake boxes work fine.

CHEF'S TIP

To make an interesting variation of the wedge cookie, as shown in Color Photo 84, make the following changes:

- After spreading the tuile paste and removing the template, place approximately 1 teaspoon (5 ml) additional tuile paste at the slanted edge of the cookie at the end of the long side.
- Using a small offset spatula, spread the paste to the same thickness as the remaining cookie, shaping it into an uneven fanned edge.
- Use a plastic scraper to remove the excess tuile paste so the extension is the same width as the original cookie.
- Bake and shape as directed, but do not overlap the extended edge — leave it flat so it sticks out as a tail on the finished decoration. Store the cookies standing on their base; if stored on their sides, they will roll, and the extension will break off.

3. Spread a portion of the tuile paste flat and even within the template on a Silpat or a prepared sheet pan (see Figures 13-29 and 13-30, page 694; also see Chef's Tip). Do not place more than 4 to 6 decorations per full-size sheet pan because you will not have time to shape more than that before they become crisp.

4. Bake at 400°F (205°C) just until the cookies begin to show a few random brown spots. Leave the sheet pan in the oven with the door open. Quickly pick up a decoration and invert it onto a sheet of corrugated cardboard (see Chef's Tip, page 707) with the short straight side at the base and the long straight side on the left; it will look a bit like the letter *L*. Quickly align the dowel or tube so one end meets the bottom of the left corner of the cookie and the length of the dowel is even with the straight short edge of the cookie. Press the straight short edge against the dowel, then roll the dowel away from you so the cookie wraps around it and overlaps. Be sure to keep the long edge of the cookie even with the end of the dowel to give the decoration a flat, even base.

5. Continue forming and baking the remaining cookies until you have made a few more decorations than you anticipate needing, to give you some insurance against breakage. Store the decorations in airtight containers with a desiccant.

Curvy Tuile Strips   yield: variable (Color Photo 81)

$^1/_4$ recipe Vanilla Tuile Decorating Paste (page 695)	1 teaspoon (2.5 g) unsweetened cocoa powder

1. Have ready a square-notched decorating comb at least 4 inches (10 cm) long, with notches approximately $^1/_4$ inch (6 mm) wide and $^1/_8$ inch (3 mm) deep. You will also need 1 or 2 Silpats.

2. Place 2 tablespoons (30 ml) tuile paste in a small cup and stir in the cocoa powder. Mix until smooth, then put the cocoa-colored paste in 2 piping bags and set them aside.

3. Spread a small portion of the plain tuile paste into a strip, approximately 3 x 12 inches (7.5 x 30 cm) and $^1/_8$ inch (3 mm) thick, on a Silpat (see Procedure 13-3a). Place the decorating comb at the end of the tuile paste strip farthest from you. Using firm pressure on the comb, drag it through the paste to the bottom of the strip, moving it back and forth, side to side, in a smooth, curved motion to produce individual strips with random curves (see Procedure 13-3b).

PROCEDURE 13-3a **Spreading tuile paste on a Silpat**

PROCEDURE 13-3b **Dragging a decorating comb through the paste to form individual curved strips**

PROCEDURE 13-3c **Piping the cocoa-colored dots at each curved bend on the strips**

4. Repeat Step 3 to make as many decorations as required; it is always a good idea to make a few extra.

5. Pipe a small dot of cocoa-colored paste at each curved bend (see Procedure 13-3c).

6. Bake the cookies at 400°F (205°C) for approximately 6 minutes or until the strips turn light brown on the narrower areas. Let the cookies cool, then carefully transfer to an airtight container for storage.

CHEF'S TIP

The technique used to make Curvy Tuile Strips can also be used with tempered chocolate or melted coating chocolate to make impressive chocolate decorations. Follow the procedure, but omit piping the contrasting dots on top. When the chocolate has hardened, remove the strips and store them in a cool location. Try spreading the chocolate on the back of the Silpat, which will give the back (flat) side of the finished decorations an interesting waffle texture.

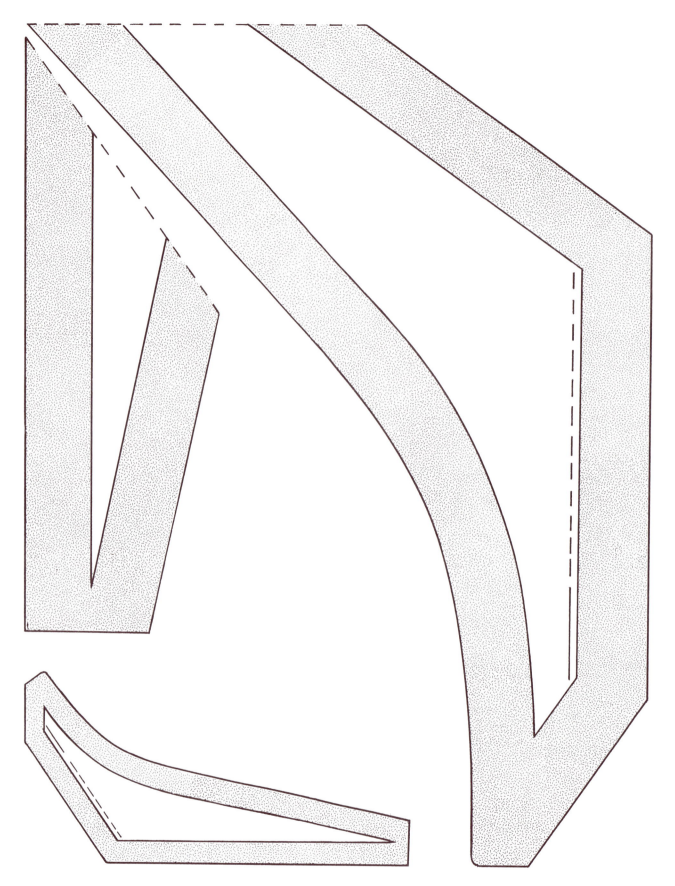

FIGURE 13-38 The template for Triangular Tuile Spirals

Triangular Tuile Spirals yield: approximately 24 decorations (Color Photo 85)

The template for these decorations has a unique design that produces a dramatic curved spiral with a flat base. The base allows the cookie to stand flat on top of a dessert or a dessert plate without either inserting the bottom of the decoration into the dessert or gluing the decoration to the plate with chocolate or some other substance.

To shape the spirals, you will need a cone-shaped mold, 5 inches (12.5 cm) long, 2 inches (5 cm) wide at the wide end, and 1 inch (2.5 cm) wide at the narrow end. If you do not have a mold this size, you can make one for temporary use by cutting the shape out of Styrofoam and covering it with aluminum foil.

½ recipe Vanilla Tuile Decorating Paste (page 695)

1 teaspoon (2.5 g) unsweetened cocoa powder, sifted

1. Have Silpats ready, or grease and flour the back of clean, even sheet pans.

2. Make the template shown in Figure 13-38. The drawing, as shown, is the correct size for this recipe; however, the template is shown in 2 pieces to fit the page. Trace the drawing, matching the edges so the template looks like the small example shown, then cut it out of cardboard that is ¹⁄₁₆ inch (2 mm) thick; cake boxes work fine. The broken line on the template indicates the area that will become the base of the decoration. The longer broken line where the broken line meets the corner of the tip is where you will place the wide end of your molding tool as you begin to form the spirals.

3. Place 2 tablespoons (30 ml) tuile paste in a small cup. Stir in the cocoa powder.

4. Spread a portion of the plain tuile paste on a Silpat or a prepared sheet pan, spreading it flat and even within the template (see Figure 13-29 and 13-30, page 694). Do not form more than 6 decorations per full-size sheet pan; you will not have time to shape more than that before they become crisp.

5. Place a portion of the cocoa-colored paste in a piping bag and cut a very small opening. Pipe a line down the center of each decoration from tip to tip.

6. Bake at 400°F (205°C) until the cookies just begin to show a few random brown spots. Leave the sheet pan in the oven with the door open. Quickly pick up a decoration and lay it flat on a sheet of corrugated cardboard (see Chef's Tip). Place the molding tool on its side, aligning the base of the tool straight on the shorter straight side of the cookie where the flat edge of the cookie meets the corner (indicated by the longer broken line on the template). Pick up the small pointed tip closest to you and wrap it over the top of the molding tool. Then, still working quickly, turn the mold away from you to wrap the cookie around it; keep the straight edge of the cookie aligned with the base of the molding tool until you reach the longer side of the cookie. The cookie should not overlap at any point. Continue forming and baking the remaining cookies until you have made a few more spirals than you anticipate needing, which gives you some insurance against breakage.

CHEF'S TIP
The cardboard helps retain heat and keeps the cookie from becoming crisp too fast. A warm wooden tabletop will do fine as well; avoid marble, which stays cool.

7. Stored in airtight containers, the spirals will stay crisp for several days.

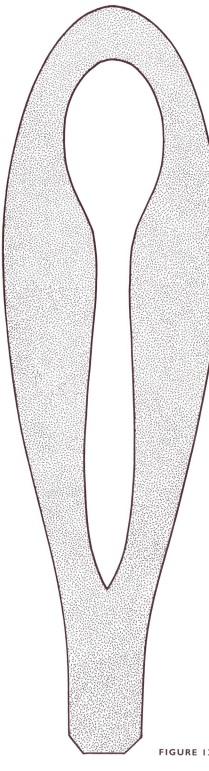

Tuile Cookie Spoons

yield: about 60 spoon decorations (Color Photos 62 and 80)

¼ recipe Vanilla Tuile Decorating Paste (page 695)
½ teaspoon (1.25 g) unsweetened cocoa powder, sifted

1. Make the cookie spoon template (Figure 13-39). The template, as shown, is the correct size for this recipe. Trace the drawing, then cut the template out of cardboard that is ¹⁄₁₆ inch (2 mm) thick; cake boxes work fine.

2. If you do not have Silpats, grease and flour the back of flat, even sheet pans. Have ready at least 2 or, better yet, 4 identical small metal spoons approximately the same size as the template.

3. Mix 1 tablespoon (15 ml) tuile paste with the cocoa powder until completely smooth. Place the cocoa-colored paste in a piping bag.

4. Spread the plain tuile paste onto the Silpats or prepared sheet pans, spreading it flat and even within the template (see Figures 13-29 and 13-30, page 694). Do not spread more than 8 to 10 spoons on each pan or mat or you will not have time to form them all before the small cookies get too dark.

5. Pipe 3 small dots of cocoa-colored paste on the handle of each spoon.

6. Bake 1 pan at a time at 400°F (205°C) for approximately 4 minutes or until a few light brown spots appear on the cookies.

7. Leave the pan in the oven with the door open and remove the cookie spoons 1 at a time. Working quickly, form them by pressing each cookie gently between 2 metal spoons: Center the cookie over 1 spoon, place a second spoon on top, and press together to shape the bowl of the spoon. Repeat to bake and form the remaining spoons. If stored in an airtight container at room temperature, the cookie spoons will keep for several days.

FIGURE 13-39 The template for Cookie Spoons

Tuile Leaves and Cookie Wedges yield: approximately 35 decorations (Color Photo 63)

¼ recipe Vanilla Tuile Decorating Paste
(page 695)

1 teaspoon (2.5 g) unsweetened cocoa powder

1. To make tuile leaves, copy or trace the template in Figure 13-40; for cookie wedges, trace the template in Figure 13-41. Cut out either template from cardboard that is ¹⁄₁₆ inch (2 mm) thick; cake boxes work fine. The templates, as shown, are the correct size for use in this recipe.

FIGURE 13-40 **The template for Tuile Leaves**

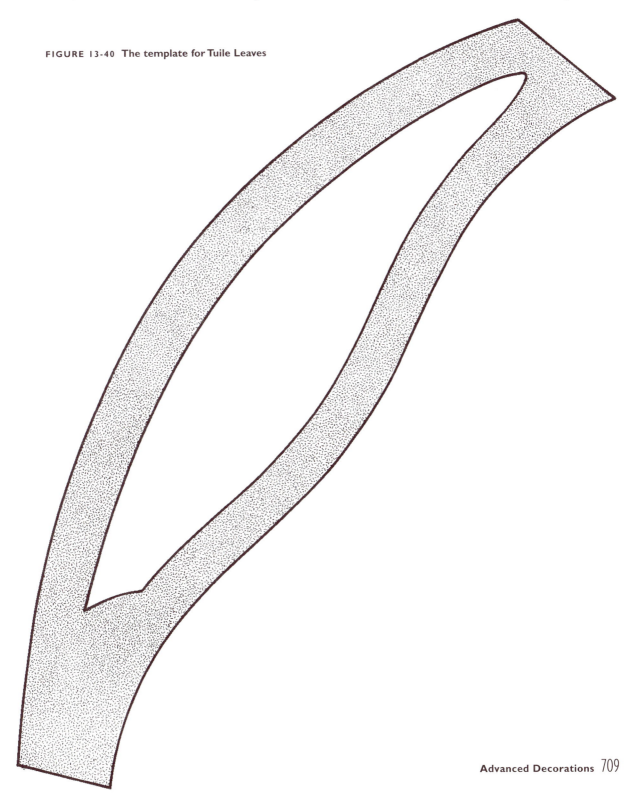

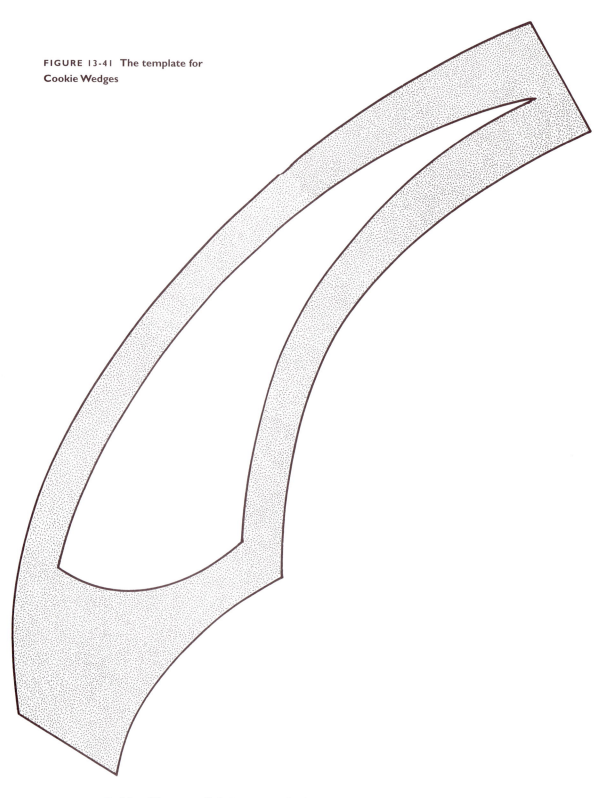

FIGURE 13-41 The template for Cookie Wedges

2. Use Silpats, or lightly grease the backs of even sheet pans, coat the pans with flour, then shake off as much flour as possible. If making cookie wedges or the variation of cookie leaves suggested in Step 5, have ready a standard size rolling pin secured so it does not roll; placing the pin on a damp towel works well.

3. Mix 2 tablespoons (30 ml) tuile paste with the cocoa powder until completely smooth. Place in 2 piping bags, cut a small opening in 1, and set aside.

4. Spread the vanilla tuile paste flat and even within the template on the Silpats or prepared pans (see Figures 13-29 and 13-30, page 694). Do not place more than 4 to 6 per pan, or the last few will be too dark when you get to them. Pipe a straight line of cocoa-colored paste, in the center, the full length of each cookie.

5. Bake 1 pan at a time at 400°F (205°C) for 4 to 5 minutes or until they just begin to turn brown in a few spots and around the edges. Keep the pan in the oven with the door open and remove the cookies 1 at a time. If making tuile leaves, quickly twist each leaf to curve it. Hold the shape for 1 or 2 seconds; then it will be firm enough to keep its shape. For a slightly different look and a faster way to form them, place the leaves on top of the rolling pin at an angle almost parallel to the bias. If making cookie wedges, drape them over the rolling pin at a 45-degree angle as you remove them from the oven. Bake and form the remaining cookies in the same way. Store the decorations in an airtight container.

VARIATION
TUILE MAPLE LEAVES
yield: approximately 35 decorations

These small leaves are fragile and elegant. The thin curved stems give the leaves a realistic appearance but they also break off easily once the cookies are crisp, so handle them with care. Tuile maple leaves make a great accompaniment to soufflés, coupes and baked custards such as crème brûlée and crème caramel.

¼ **recipe Vanilla Tuile Decorating paste (page 695)**

Follow the main recipe, making the following changes:

- In Step 1 make the template in Figure 13-42.

- In Step 2 secure a rolling pin as directed for cookie wedges.

- Omit Step 3.

- In Step 4 do not place more than 6 to 8 cookies per full-size sheet pan.

- Shape the warm baked maple leaves by draping them over the rolling pin straight across or at an angle.

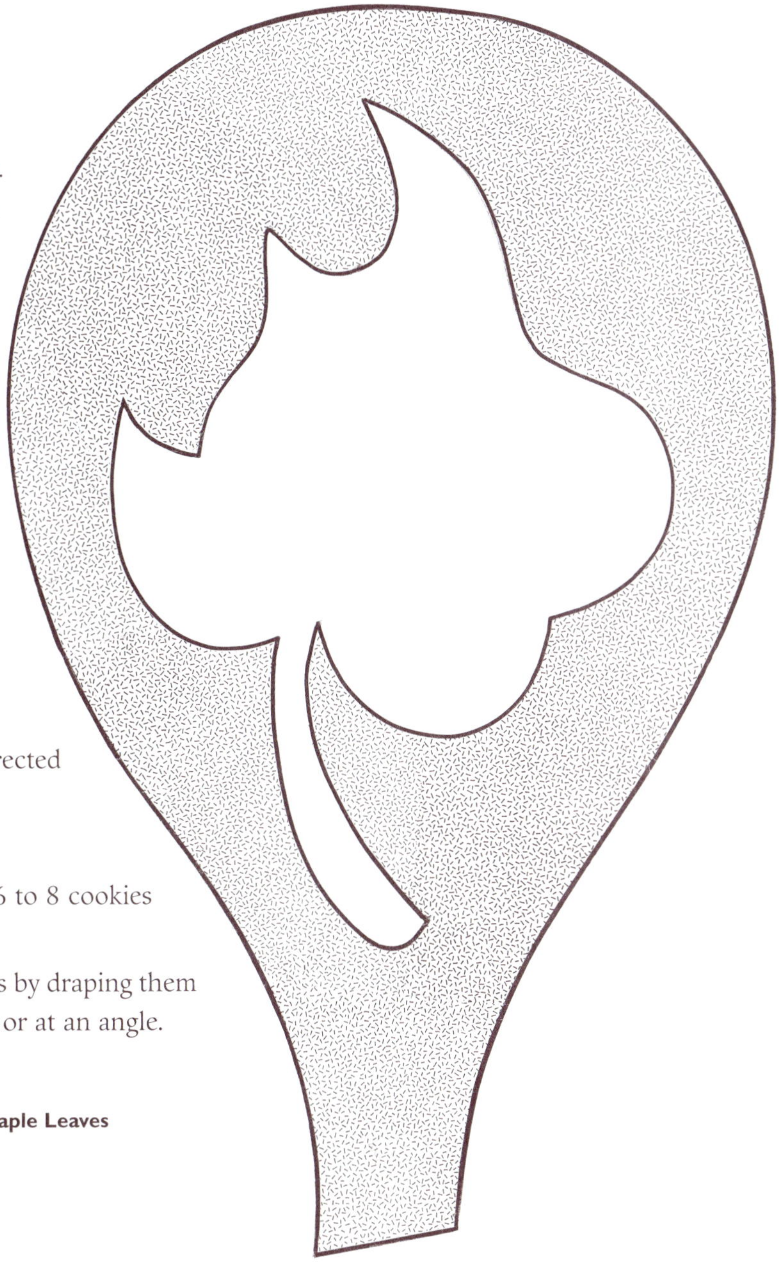

FIGURE 13-42 The template for Tuile Maple Leaves

Tuile Steam Decorations yield: approximately 24 sets of decorations (Color Photo 91)

½ recipe Vanilla Tuile Decorating paste
(page 695)

1. Trace the template in Figure 13-43. The template, as shown, is the correct size for use in this recipe. Cut the template out of cardboard that is ¹⁄₁₆ inch (2 mm) thick; cake boxes work fine. If you do not have Silpats, grease and flour the backs of even sheet pans, then shake off as much flour as possible. Have ready a wavy tool to mold the strips. See "To Make a Tool for Molding Tuile Strips" (page 718).

CHEF'S TIP
You may need to experiment a bit to determine the correct baking time. If the cookies are overbaked, they will not only be too dark, which will detract from their appearance, but also they will break easily when you try to bend them. Conversely, if the cookies are removed before they show any color at all, the strips will not become crisp once they cool.

2. Spread the tuile paste on the Silpats or prepared sheets, spreading it flat and even within the template (see Figures 13-29 and 13-30, page 694). Form 3 to 4 sets of decorations (9 to 12 individual cookie strips) per full-size pan.

3. Bake 1 pan at a time at 400°F (205°C) for 3 to 4 minutes or until a few brown spots appear on the cookies (see Chef's Tip). Remove the sheet pan from the oven. Quickly but carefully place the cookie strips over the wavy molding tool, being certain they fall into the grooves in a straight line, and press down with your fingertips to shape them (see Figure 13-48, page 718). Move the shaped cookies to the side and repeat to form and bake the remaining cookies.

Tuile Symphony of Circles yield: 35 decorations (Color Photo 92)

¼ recipe or 8 ounces (225 g) Vanilla Tuile
Decorating Paste (page 695)

1. Make the template shown in Figure 13-44. The template, as shown, is the correct size to use in this recipe. Trace the drawing, then cut the template out of cardboard that is ¹⁄₁₆ inch (2 mm) thick; cake boxes work fine. If you do not have Silpats, grease and flour the back of flat, even sheet pans. Have ready 3 plain cookie cutters in graduating sizes that match the dotted lines shown in the template. If you do not have cutters of exactly these sizes, choose cutters that will leave a ring of cookie approximately ³⁄₈ inch (9 mm) wide after cutting out the center of the 3 smaller round sections. The 3 smallest cutters in a typical plain cookie cutter set are usually the correct size. Also have ready a round object, 6 to 8 inches (15 to 20 cm) in diameter; a circular stainless steel bain-marie insert works well.

2. Spread the tuile paste on the Silpats or prepared sheet pans, spreading it flat and even within the template (see Figures 13-29 and 13-30, page 694). Do not place more than 4 to 6 decorations per full-size sheet pan.

3. Bake the cookies 1 pan at a time at 400°F (205°C) for a few minutes or just until the paste has set.

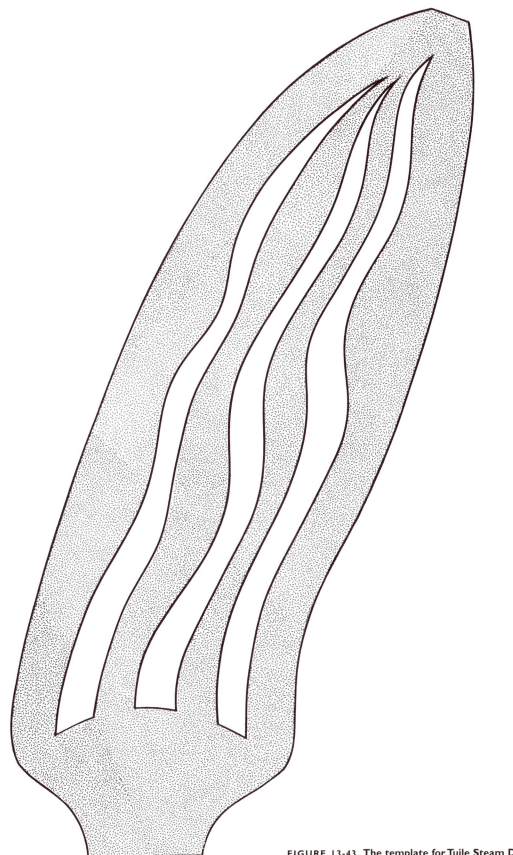

FIGURE 13-43 The template for Tuile Steam Decorations

4. Remove the pan from the oven and use the cookie cutters to quickly cut out the center portion of each of the 3 top round shapes; discard the centers. Leave the large bottom round whole to make the decorations more durable and easier to handle. If the cookies break when you attempt to cut out the centers, they are overbaked.

5. Return the decorations to the oven and continue baking until they just start to turn a pleasant golden brown.

6. Take the sheet pan out of the oven and quickly transfer each cookie to the reserved bain-marie or other appropriate mold, draping each crosswise over the form to curve it. Once the decorations become cool and crisp, store them in an airtight container.

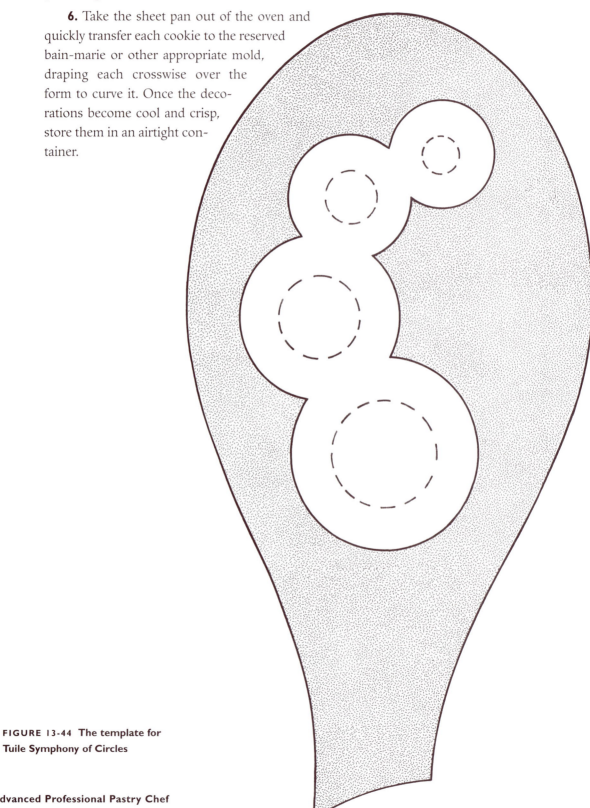

FIGURE 13-44 The template for Tuile Symphony of Circles

Tulips yield: about 25 large cookie shells

½ recipe Vanilla Tuile
  Decorating Paste
  (page 695)

I. Make the tulip template (Figure 13-45). The template, as shown, is the correct size for use in this recipe. Trace the drawing, then cut the template out of cardboard that is ¹⁄₁₆ inch (2 mm) thick; cake boxes are ideal.

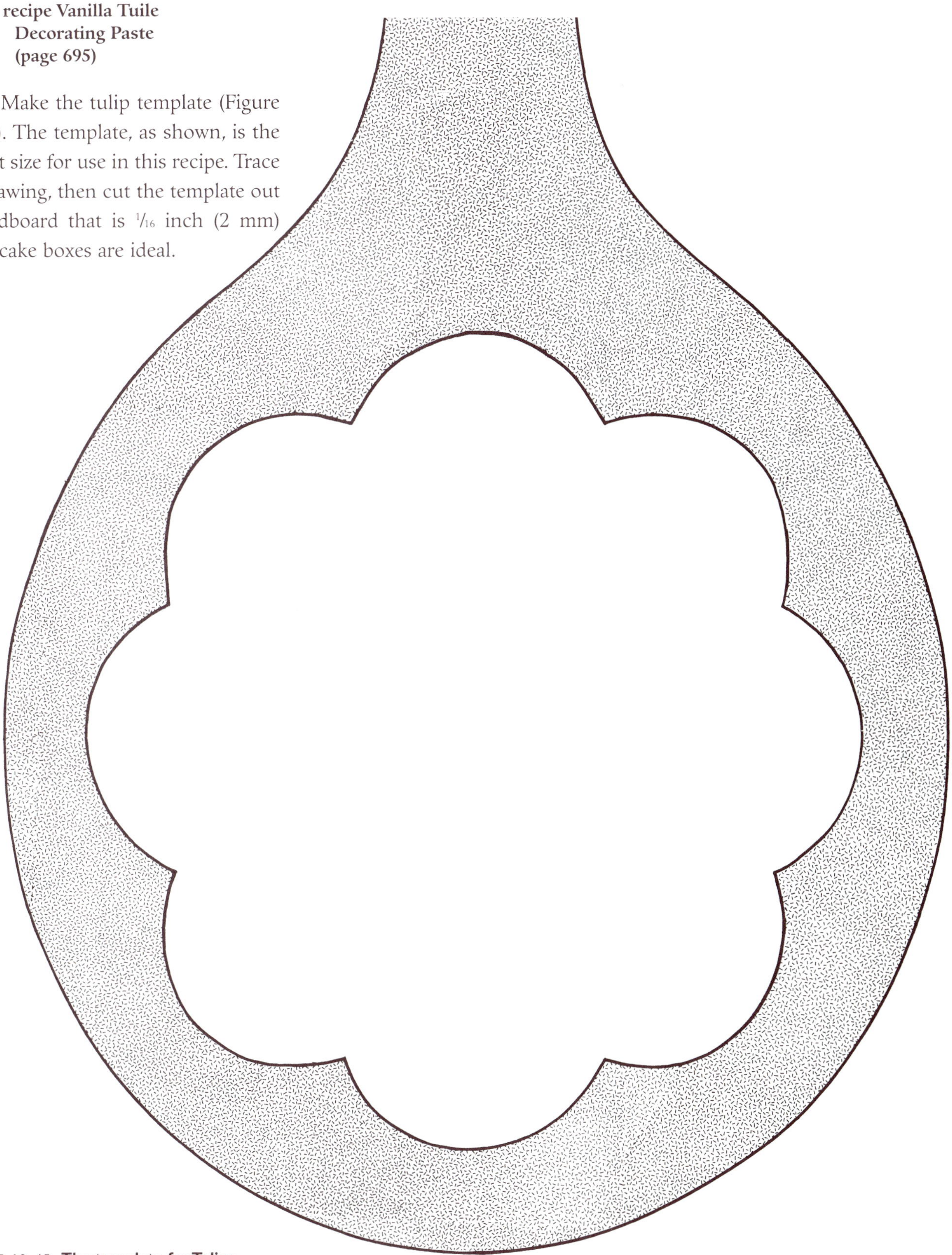

FIGURE 13-45 The template for Tulips

2. If you do not have Silpats, lightly grease the backs of even sheet pans, coat with flour, then shake off as much flour as possible.

3. Spread the tuile paste onto the Silpats or prepared pans, spreading it flat and even within the template (see Figures 13-29 and 13-30, page 694). Do not place more than 4 to 6 cookies per full-size sheet pan or Silpat.

4. Bake 1 pan at a time at 400°F (205°C) for approximately 8 minutes or until a few light brown spots appear on the cookies.

5. Leave the sheet pan in the oven with the door open and remove the tulips 1 at a time. Working quickly, form the shells, brown side out, by pressing each cookie gently over an inverted bowl. Use an object that will leave a 4-inch (10-cm) opening at the top of the finished tulip shell. If you are making quite a few at once, it is faster to form them by pressing a second bowl on top of the shell instead of using your hands; this way, you can go on to forming the next one without waiting for each tulip to become firm (see Figure 13-21 [right], page 688). Bake and form the remaining tulips. Store the cookie shells in airtight containers.

Miniature Tulips yield: about 40 cookie shells (Color Photo 63)

The dots of cocoa-colored paste may be omitted, if desired.

| ¼ recipe Vanilla Tuile Decorating Paste (page 695) | 1 teaspoon (5 g) unsweetened cocoa powder |

I. Make the template in Figure 13-46. The template, as shown, is the correct size required for this recipe. Trace the drawing, then cut the template out of cardboard that is ¹/₁₆ inch (2 mm) thick; cake boxes work fine. If you do not have Silpats, lightly grease the backs of clean, even sheet pans, coat with flour, then shake off as much flour as possible.

2. Color 2 tablespoons (30 ml) tuile paste with the cocoa powder. Place the cocoa-colored paste in 1 or 2 piping bags. Spread the plain tuile paste onto the Silpats or prepared sheet pans, spreading it flat and even within the template (see Figures 13-29 and 13-30, page 694).

3. Pipe a small dot of cocoa-colored paste in each petal of the tuile flowers.

4. Bake 1 pan at a time at 400°F (205°C) for approximately 5 minutes or until a few light brown spots appear on the cookies.

CHEF'S TIP

Another way to form miniature tulips or the miniature tulip crown variation is to use a lime or small lemon to press the cookie into the bottom form instead of using a second form on top. If the fruit is a little smaller than the form, simply roll it around inside until the sides are shaped. If you have a high tolerance for heat, the baked cookies can also be draped over a lemon or lime, then pressed into shape with your cupped hands.

5. Leave the pan in the oven with the door open and remove the cookie shells 1 at a time. Working quickly, form each cookie by pressing it gently between 2 small forms, as shown in Figure 13-21, page 688, in the example on the left (see Chef's Tip). Center the cookie over the form, center a second form on top, and press the center of the cookie into the bottom form to make a tiny cup. It is easiest to work with 2 sets of forms at a time. As you finish forming the second cup, the first cup should be firm enough to remove and set aside. Repeat to form the remaining tulips. Stored in an airtight container at room temperature, the cookie shells will stay crisp for several days.

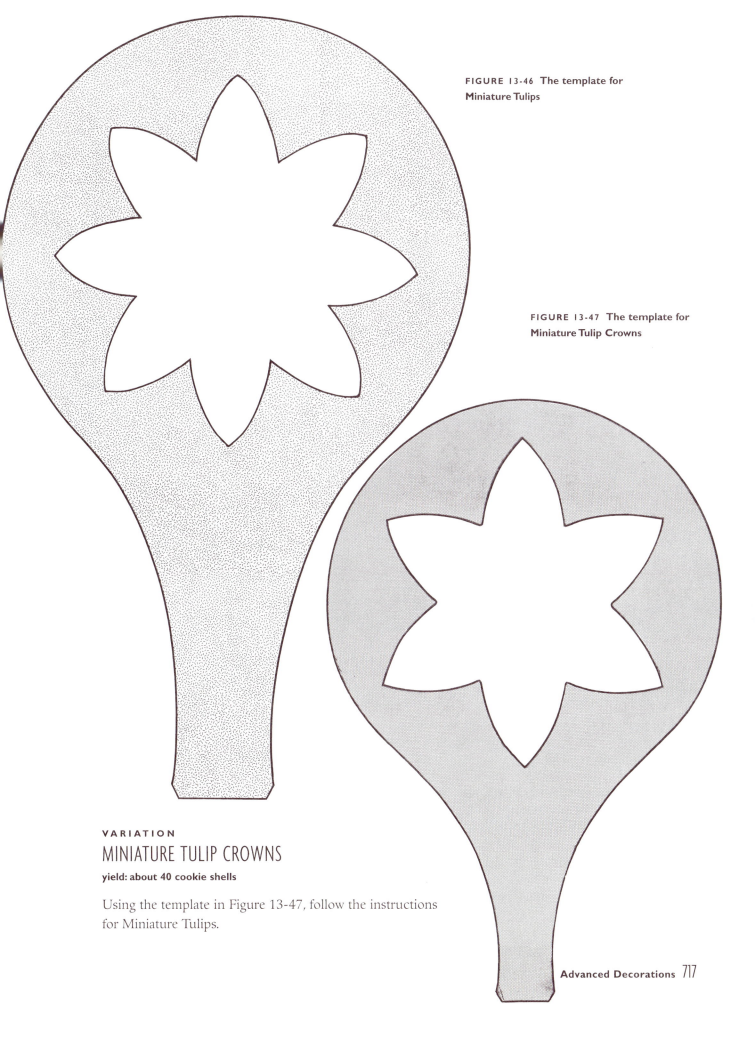

FIGURE 13-46 **The template for Miniature Tulips**

FIGURE 13-47 **The template for Miniature Tulip Crowns**

VARIATION

MINIATURE TULIP CROWNS

yield: about 40 cookie shells

Using the template in Figure 13-47, follow the instructions for Miniature Tulips.

Wavy Tuile Strips yield: approximately 70 decorations

½ recipe Vanilla Tuile Decorating Paste (page 695)

1½ teaspoons (4 g) unsweetened cocoa powder

1. Trace the template shown in Figure 13-35, page 701. The template is the correct size for use in this recipe; however, to fit the page, it is shown cut in half. Cut the template out of cardboard that is ¹/₁₆ inch (2 mm) thick; cake boxes work fine.

2. If you do not have Silpats, lightly grease the backs of flat, even sheet pans, coat with flour, then shake off as much flour as possible.

3. Have ready a curved molding tool to shape the warm cookies as they come out of the oven (instructions follow).

4. Thoroughly mix the cocoa powder into 3 tablespoons (45 ml) tuile paste. Place a small portion of the cocoa-colored paste in a piping bag and cut a small opening. Set aside.

5. Spread the plain tuile paste flat and even within the template (see Figures 13-29 and 13-30, page 694), making 6 to 8 cookies per Silpat or sheet pan. Pipe a wavy line of cocoa-colored paste the length of each cookie.

6. Bake 1 pan at a time at 400°F (205°C) for approximately 2 minutes or until the first cookie shows a few brown spots. Judging the correct baking time may involve trial and error. If the cookies are too brown, they will break as you try to form them; if they are not brown enough, they will not become crisp after they cool.

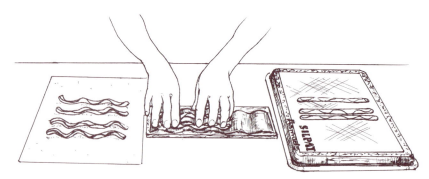

FIGURE 13-48
Shaping the warm tuile strips as soon as they come out of the oven

To Make a Tool for Molding Tuile Strips

As is true of quite a few of the hand tools used in the pastry kitchen these days — PVC pipe, blowtorches, aluminum, and plastic screening — the material used to make this molding tool comes from the hardware store. It is important to note that not all of these materials are considered food grade, and some should be used for showpieces only. In some cases, as is done when using PVC pipe to mold a filling as it sets, the item must be lined with food-grade plastic wrap. The material for this molding tool is aluminum, which is safe for contact with food.

Buy a piece of aluminum corrugated flashing, the type used in combination with corrugated roof panels. Using metal shears, cut off the flat part of the flashing and discard. You need a piece about 10 x 4 inches (25 x 10 cm), but you will have enough material to make 2 tools of this size. You can simply use them as is or, for a more secure base, attach the aluminum to a piece of clear plastic or plywood, ¼ inch (6 mm) thick, the same length and width as the aluminum flashing.

7. Remove the pan from the oven. Quickly and carefully transfer the cookies, 1 at a time, to the wavy molding tool, being certain the cookies fall into the grooves of the mold and are placed on the mold in a straight line. Press down with your fingertips to shape them (Figure 13-48); the cookies will become crisp very quickly. Move the wavy cookies to the side and continue shaping the remaining cookies. If the cookies become too firm to bend, soften them in the oven.

8. Repeat Steps 5, 6, and 7 to form the remaining decorations. Stored in an airtight container, preferably with a desiccant, the tuile strips will stay crisp for weeks.

OTHER DECORATIONS

Chocolate Paper Paste yield: 1 pound 7 ounces (655 g) (Color Photo 90)

Decorations made from this paste acquire a craterlike texture that gives them an interesting and stylish appearance, but this happens only if the paste is spread in a very thin layer. Chocolate paper paste is best suited to free-form shapes. It can be used with a template, but it will not stay in a precise shape, as tuile paste does. While the edges will become ragged, this too can add interest, depending on the look desired. Chocolate paper paste is used for the same applications as Cocoa-Nib Wafer Paste (page 720). It can be used to form dessert containers and can be cut into shapes after baking; these can be left flat or molded into curves, spirals, and so on. Alternatively, the baked sheet can simply be broken into random pieces.

Due to the flour in the recipe as well as the cornstarch in the powdered sugar, decorations made from chocolate paper paste can be made days in advance without having to keep them in an airtight container. If appropriate to the shape you are making, simply placing them on a sheet pan at room temperature will do.

3 ounces (85 g) cake flour	⅓ cup (80 ml) water, at room temperature
11 ounces (310 g) powdered sugar	4½ ounces (130 g) unsalted butter, melted
1¾ ounces (50 g) cocoa powder	

1. Sift the flour, sugar, and cocoa powder together. Gradually stir in the water, then the butter. Continue to stir until you have a smooth, pliable paste. If you do not have Silpats, lightly grease the backs of flat, even sheet pans, coat with flour, then shake off as much flour as possible.

2. Spread the paste in a thin layer on Silpats or the prepared sheet pans, forming the desired size and shape.

3. Bake at 375°F (190°C) for approximately 4 minutes. Chocolate paper paste is dark, so determining when it is finished baking can be difficult. To help you judge, place a few sliced natural almonds on the pan next to the paste: When the almonds are golden brown, the paste is done.

4. Remove the sheet pan from the oven. Wait until the chocolate paper decoration can be lifted from the Silpat

CHEF'S TIP

Chocolate paper paste may be stored at room temperature, covered, for 3 to 4 days. If it becomes too firm to spread in a thin layer, incorporate a small amount of water. If it is refrigerated, allow it to soften at room temperature before using. Do not warm the hard paste over hot water. You may soften the paste in the microwave oven for just a few seconds at a time so none of it melts. If the paste is warmed to the point of melting, it will drastically change in appearance and flexibility after baking.

with the help of a palette knife without breaking, then quickly form it into the desired shape. Because they are so thin, the decorations harden quickly once removed from the heat of the sheet pan.

NOTE: If you are using a dark cocoa powder, the paste may become too thick; stir in a small amount of water to compensate.

Cocoa-Nib Wafer Paste

yield: approximately 25 orange-size half-sphere containers; variable yield for decorations (Color Photo 83)

This is a handsome, tasty, versatile, and trendy decorating material. You could call it the modern version of Florentina paste. Like Florentina paste, cocoa-nib paste flows out as it bakes rather than staying in its original shape the way tuile paste and Hippen paste do. Cocoa-nib paste flows out fairly evenly all around, however, if it is spread into small even circles to begin with — to use for dessert containers, for example. The degree to which the paste flows out, and consequently the appearance and thinness of the finished product, are determined by how thinly the paste is spread on the pan. It should be spread thin enough that small streaks and holes are created as the nibs are dragged through the paste as you work with it. A few tests may be necessary to determine the proper thickness. If you plan to cut the paste after baking — for example, to make straight or curved wedges — do not bake it on a Silpat, as you should not use a knife on the mat.

Judging when the paste is done can be difficult because it is a dark color to begin with, and you cannot wait for it to turn brown as you can with many other recipes. Nor can you judge the doneness by touching it, as you can with a sponge cake, for example. Therefore, it is important that you are familiar with your oven and know it is accurate. Given that, if the decorations look done and have been in the oven the right amount of time, they are probably done. If the baked wafers are any darker than they were when they went in the oven, they are overbaked and will taste bitter. If the decorations are not baked long enough, they will not become firm and hold their shape. A helpful trick, until you get the feel for the baking time, is to put a few sliced almonds on the pan next to the paste; when the almonds just begin to turn golden, the cocoa-nib paste is baked.

You can vary this recipe by adding pine nuts, crushed macadamia nuts, or crushed coffee beans, or you can use any of these in place of the cocoa nibs.

¾ teaspoon (2 g) pectin powder	1 tablespoon (15 ml) heavy cream
6 ounces (170 g) granulated sugar	1 tablespoon (8 g) unsweetened cocoa powder
2 ounces (55 g) glucose *or* light corn syrup	3 tablespoons (24 g) bread flour
6 ounces (170 g) unsalted butter	4 ounces (115 g) cocoa nibs

1. Mix the pectin powder with the sugar. Place in a saucepan with the glucose or corn syrup, butter, and cream. Heat, stirring constantly, until the butter and sugar have melted and the mixture is smooth. Remove from the heat.

2. Mix together the cocoa powder, flour, and cocoa nibs. Combine with the mixture in the pan.

3. Spread the paste in a thin layer the size and shape specified in your recipe on sheet pans lined with baking paper or on Silpats.

4. Bake at 350°F (175°C) for 6 to 10 minutes, depending on the size. Shape as soon as you can lift the baked paste from the pan with the help of a spatula.

5. Store the paste covered in the refrigerator; it will keep for up to 1 month.

Mango Chips yield: variable

2 or 3 firm mangoes, skin on   Simple syrup

1. Place a mango on an electric slicer so the long pit is parallel to the blade. Cut off paper-thin slices until you reach the pit. Turn the mango over and repeat on the other side. Repeat with the other mangoes.

2. Dip each mango slice into simple syrup, letting all of the excess run back into the bowl; place the slices on Silpats.

3. Bake the slices at 250°F (122°C) for 1 to 2 hours or until dried through. The time required will vary depending on the fruit and the oven. When you think the chips are ready, test as follows: Remove 1 or 2 chips and place on a cold surface, such as a marble or metal table. Let stand for about 1 minute, then lift the chip to see if it is crisp. If it is not, return it to the tray and bake the chips a bit longer. It is necessary to test in this manner because the fruit chips are always soft and flexible while warm, even if they have dried all the way. Do not allow the fruit chips to brown at all. If this happens, your oven is too hot.

4. One at a time, remove the sheet pans from the oven; immediately transfer the chips to an airtight container with a desiccant, separating each layer with baking paper. Removing several sheet pans at once is not advisable, as the chips should not stand at room temperature before packaging. If you cannot package them right away, leave them in the oven with the heat off.

Apple or Pear Chips yield: variable (Color Photo 30)

Juice of 1 lemon   4 large green apples *or* 4 firm pears, skin on
1 cup (240 ml) simple syrup

1. Add the lemon juice to the simple syrup.

2. Place an apple or pear lengthwise on an electric slicer so the fruit stem is parallel to the blade. Cut off slices, making them as thin as possible without breaking or tearing. Repeat with the other apples or pears. Discard the end pieces that do not have a complete apple or pear outline.

3. One or 2 at a time, dip each slice into simple syrup, letting the excess run back into the bowl; place the slices on Silpats.

4. Follow Steps 3 and 4 in Mango Chips (above).

Plantain Chips yield: variable

2 firm plantains   Simple syrup

1. Remove the skin from the plantains as follows: Use a sharp knife to cut off both ends so part of the flesh is exposed, then cut lengthwise along the edge of a ridge without cutting into the pulp. Repeat with the adjacent ridge, then use the edge of the knife to lift the cut section of peel and pull it away in 1 piece. Repeat this procedure with each remaining segment of peel or until the remaining skin can be removed in 1 piece.

2. Place a whole plantain lengthwise on an electric slicer. Cut off slices, making them as thin as possible without breaking or tearing. Repeat with the second plantain.

3. One at a time, dip each plantain slice into simple syrup, letting the excess run back into the bowl; place the slices on Silpats.

4. Follow Steps 3 and 4 in Mango Chips (page 721).

Hippen Decorating Paste yield: 3 cups (720 ml) or 1 pound 8 ounces (680 g)

ippen means "wafer" in German. Hippen paste, an old-world decorating medium, can be used to make decorative figurines and dessert containers. It can be spread on a Silpat or a greased and floured sheet pan within a template, or it can be piped out using a pastry bag to make figurines and ornaments. Both the shapes made with a template and the piped ornaments can be formed after baking by rolling them around a dowel, draping them over a rolling pin, pressing them into a mold, and so on. Hippen paste is quite versatile; it can be tinted and is bendable to 360 degrees.

6 egg whites (³⁄₄ cup/180 ml)   ¼ teaspoon (.5 g) ground cinnamon
1 pound 8 ounces (680 g) almond paste   3 drops of lemon juice
1½ ounces (40 g) bread flour   Milk, as needed
½ teaspoon (3 g) salt

1. Add approximately 5 egg whites to the almond paste, mixing them in 1 at a time to avoid lumps. Mix in the flour, salt, cinnamon, and lemon juice. Mix in the remaining egg white. Let the paste rest, covered, for 30 minutes.

2. Adjust the consistency by adding milk, if necessary. For use with a template, the paste should be thin enough to spread easily but should hold the shape made by the template without flowing out once the template is removed. For piped decorations, the paste should be thick enough to hold the shape of the design without changing after it is piped.

VARIATION
HIPPEN MASSE yield: 1 pound 10 ounces (740 g)

his version of Hippen paste differs slightly from the main recipe; it is lighter in color due to the addition of powdered sugar and the subtraction of cinnamon. The extra sugar contributes to quicker caramelization as the paste bakes. It is a good idea to make Hippen masse the day before you plan to use it. If this is not possible, let the paste rest at least 30 minutes before you use it. Because almonds absorb moisture slowly, you will be better able to judge its consistency after it has rested.

3½ ounces (100 g) bread flour

7 ounces (200 g) powdered sugar

10 ounces (285 g) almond paste

¼ cup (60 ml) milk

6 egg whites (¾ cup/180 ml)

1 teaspoon (5 ml) vanilla extract

1. Place the flour, powdered sugar, and almond paste in a mixer bowl and combine using a paddle; depending on the consistency of the almond paste, the mixture may be quite coarse.

2. Slowly incorporate the milk, followed by most of the egg whites, then the vanilla. Scrape down the sides of the bowl from time to time to avoid lumps. Add just enough of the remaining egg white so the paste can be spread. It should hold its shape after being spread within a template.

3. On the back of buttered and floured baking pans or on Silpats, spread the paste within a template as directed in a particular recipe.

4. Bake at 400°F (205°C) until light golden brown. Immediately form as desired.

Lace Cookie Bouquets yield: approximately 15 decorations (Color Photo 82)

This batter is actually a small recipe of Vanilla Tuile Decorating Paste. These lace cookie decorations can also be made with the Seaweed Wafer Decorations batter (page 726), and vice versa. The trick to creating an elegant, lacy decoration is to spread the batter very thin. The paste will, of course, become even thinner once you fold the mat over and make two cookies out of one; in fact, it may be thin to the point where you are unsure if the cookies are going to turn out as they are supposed to. But with practice and by using a quick but gentle touch, you'll find that these decorations are not really difficult to produce. You cannot make these decorations without at least 1 Silpat, and the mat must be fairly new, as any small cut or scratch will create resistance as you remove the baked wafer, and that may cause it to tear.

Cookie bouquets can be made days or even weeks in advance if they are stored, well covered, nestled in a protective egg carton. In fact, I made these at home in California and transported them to New York for a photo shoot. You can see them in a variation of chocolate marquise I did for *Chocolatier* magazine's book, *A Modernist View of Plated Desserts*.

Assembling the fragile cookies on a chocolate platform makes them much easier to handle as well as easier to attach to a dessert during service. Chilling the cookies — for up to 30 minutes, no longer — before standing them on the chocolate bases will make the chocolate set up almost immediately, eliminating the need to hold them in place for any length of time. Another option is to use aerosol chocolate coolant, in which case you do not need to chill the decorations.

4 ounces (115 g) unsalted butter, at room temperature

4 ounces (115 g) powdered sugar, sifted

½ cup (120 ml) egg whites, at room temperature

½ teaspoon (2.5 ml) vanilla extract

4 ounces (115 g) cake flour, sifted

Tempered sweet dark chocolate or melted coating chocolate

1. Cover 1 or 2 cardboard egg cartons loosely with plastic wrap, pushing the film partway into each indentation. Set aside.

2. Cream the butter and powdered sugar together. Incorporate the egg whites a few at a time. Add the vanilla. Add the flour and mix just until incorporated; do not overmix.

3. If not proceeding to make decorations, store the paste, covered, in the refrigerator; it will

PROCEDURE 13-4a **Spreading a round of paste on one side of a Silpat**

PROCEDURE 13-4b **Folding the mat in half and pressing down**

PROCEDURE 13-4c **Opening the mat to show 2 thin rounds**

keep for several weeks. Allow it to soften slightly after removing it from the refrigerator, then stir it smooth and into a spreadable consistency before using.

4. Spread a small portion of the paste into a round, 5 to 6 inches (12.5 to 15 cm) in diameter, at a short side of a Silpat (see Procedure 13-4a). Fold the opposite (empty) side of the mat on top and press down lightly (see Procedure 13-4b). Unfold. You should now have 2 thin, non-uniform rounds, 1 on each side of the mat (see Procedure 13-4c).

5. Bake at 400°F (205°C) for approximately 3 minutes or until the first sign of color appears on a cookie. Leaving the sheet pan in the oven with the door open, run a metal trowel or palette knife underneath 1 cookie and quickly pick it up by its center; hold it upside down and gather the center to form it into a bouquet shape. Set it, right-side up, in the prepared egg carton. Form the second cookie in the same manner. Repeat spreading, baking, and forming until you have made a few more decorations than you need; this allows for breakage. Place the cookies in the refrigerator just long enough for them to become cold.

6. Pipe 4 ovals of chocolate, 1 inch (2.5 cm) long and spaced 4 inches (10 cm) apart, on a sheet of baking paper. Wait until the chocolate begins to set, then stand a cookie bouquet on each oval at a 45-degree angle so when it is placed on top of the angled cut of the marquise, it will appear to stand straight. If you are making these decorations to use on another dessert, you will most likely want to attach them to the bases standing straight. Repeat to create bases on the remaining bouquets. Store the decorations in an airtight container. The thin cookies will soften rapidly if exposed to moist air.

Mango or Strawberry Wafer Decorations yield: variable

I used to call these decorations *fruit leather* because they are a little chewy, but although they are prepared in much the same way, these are not the same as the thin sheets of dehydrated fruit sold rolled up as a snack food — these wafers are crisp.

This medium can be used in many ways to make interesting and tasty garnishes. While still warm from the oven, the fruit paste can be formed into a container in the same manner as Florentina Cups (page 687), or it can simply be rolled into a loose ball, as is done to garnish the Lemongrass Parfait (Color Photo 84). The containers are particularly appropriate holders for sorbet made from the same fruit. Furthermore, being fat-free, the fruit wafers make a good choice to add interest to a light dessert presentation.

You cannot make these wafers without at least one Silpat, and the mat must be fairly new, or at least in good condition, because any small crack, nick, or cut will create resistance as you peel the wafer away, and it will break. Even if your Silpats are in perfect shape, you will undoubtedly break quite a few of these decorations while you are developing a feel for the technique, especially if you are trying to shape them. But don't give up — it is simply a matter of spreading the puree so the layer is not only very thin but also perfectly even, so it will bake uniformly. After you get that part down, you just need to play with the oven temperature a little because the wafers can overbake very quickly. Cooking them too long or with the heat too high not only makes them hard to work with but also decreases their appeal; the color becomes brownish instead of retaining the natural look of the yellow mango or the reddish-pink strawberry. On the other hand, if the wafers are underbaked, they will be too wet to peel off the mat; even if you do manage it, they will never become crisp. This is one of those techniques that requires practice to perfect.

If you are using purchased unsweetened or lightly sweetened fruit puree (which works fine for either flavor), you may need to add simple syrup. Two to 3 mangoes or 2 pints of strawberries yield about 20 average-sized garnishes.

Perfectly ripe mangoes or small, sweet, perfectly ripe strawberries	**Raspberry juice, as needed, if using strawberries**
Lime juice, if using mangoes	

1. If using mangoes, remove the peel and the pits. Puree the fruit with a little lime juice ($\frac{1}{2}$ lime per 2 or 3 mangoes) to make it completely smooth. If using strawberries, puree the fruit and, if necessary, add a little raspberry juice to improve the color. Strain out the seeds, if desired, but retain the other solids so you are not left with only the juice.

2. Spread either fruit puree on a Silpat in a very thin layer, forming whatever shape is desired.

3. Bake at 300°F (149°C) until the puree turns golden brown in a few spots. Remove the pan from the oven and let the wafers cool just until you can peel them off the Silpat with the help of a spatula. Then, working quickly, shape the wafers as desired; drape them over a rolling pin to make a tuile shape or press them into the bowl of a ladle to make a dessert container, for example. You may, of course, leave them flat. Store in airtight containers with a desiccant.

Red Pepper Sails yield: variable (Color Photo 71)

2 medium red bell peppers	2 ounces (55 g) powdered sugar, sifted
Vegetable oil	2 teaspoons (5 g) bread flour

1. Coat the peppers with vegetable oil and place on a sheet pan. Use a blowtorch to blacken the skin, turning the peppers to cook all sides. If you are making more than a single recipe, bake the peppers at 450°F (230°C) until blackened, turning them once or twice. Wrap the peppers in a moist towel or place them in a plastic bag and set aside to cool to room temperature.

2. Peel the peppers; remove the seeds and stems. Puree the roasted pepper flesh in a food processor, then force the puree through a fine mesh strainer.

3. Stir the powdered sugar and flour into the puree.

4. Spread the batter thinly and evenly on Silpats in free-form shapes measuring approximately 2 × 3 inches (5 × 7.5 cm) each.

5. Bake at 200° to 250°F (94° to 108°C) until the decorations are dry and slightly brown at the edges. Use a thin spatula to remove them from the Silpat as soon as possible. Place the decorations on a flat surface to cool; be careful, as they are quite fragile. Alternatively, the warm decorations may be molded in the same way as tuile paste as soon as they are removed from the Silpat. Store in airtight containers.

Seaweed Wafer Decorations yield: approximately 30 wafers, 6 × 4 inches (15 × 10 cm)

These decorations — thin, crisp, and unusual-looking — add a futuristic appearance to any dessert presentation. They add a tasty textural contrast when paired with soft desserts such as Bavarian creams or custards, cakes, and frozen creations. As with several recipes in this section, you cannot make these wafers without at least one Silpat. The mat must be fairly new, or at least in good condition, because any small crack, nick, or cut will create resistance as you peel the wafer away, breaking it. The thin, lacy nature of these wafers makes them particularly fragile. The wafers are a little easier to handle when made with the larger amount of flour specified but, unfortunately, that also makes them less delicate.

Leaving the decorations flat is obviously the quickest and easiest production method. It is simple enough to stand a flat wafer upright in a dessert or to attach a wafer to the back of a dessert for the same look; this makes for a striking display when the light catches the thin, irregular holes. With only a little more effort, the wafers can be curved in the same way as tuiles by draping them over a round object after removing them from the oven.

8 ounces (225 g) powdered sugar, sifted	2 to 3 ounces (55 to 85 g) bread flour, sifted
3 ounces (85 g) unsalted butter, at room temperature	¾ cup (180 ml) strained orange juice, at room temperature
2 egg whites, at room temperature	

1. Stir the powdered sugar into the soft butter and beat for a few minutes until light and fluffy.

2. One at a time, stir in the egg whites, then the flour. The paste should be smooth. Stir in the orange juice, continuing to stir until well combined. Do not be concerned about the mixture appearing loose and broken; this is expected and is part of the character of the batter.

3. Spread the batter into thin shapes on Silpats, as directed in individual recipes; they will expand just a little in the oven.

4. Bake at 400°F (205°C) until the pieces begin to show some color, approximately 3 minutes. Remove from the Silpat with the help of a small spatula or palette knife as soon as the pieces can be handled. Shape as instructed in the recipe you are using, or follow the suggestions in the introduction. Seaweed decorations can be made ahead and stored in an airtight container.

Sour Cream Mixture for Piping yield: variable

This method of making a white piping mixture is much easier and quicker than whipping heavy cream and because such a small amount is eaten, the flavor of the sour cream is not noticeable. Instructions for using sour cream mixture in decorating are given on pages 681 to 685.

Heavy cream   **Sour cream**

1. Gradually stir enough heavy cream into sour cream until the mixture is approximately the same consistency as that of the sauce you are decorating.

2. Use as directed in the individual recipe. This mixture will keep for several days in the refrigerator, but it may need to be thinned with additional cream.

CHEF'S TIP
The sour cream mixture and the contrasting sauce must have the same consistency. If the sour cream is too thick, it will not blend with the sauce but will break into pieces instead. If it is too thin, it will run into the sauce and will not form clearly defined lines. The sauce, too, must be of the proper consistency to begin with; if it is too thin, it cannot be decorated at all.

Spanish Caramel-Flavored Tuile Decorations

yield: approximately 20 decorations (Color Photo 1)

These decorations are easy to make, stylish, and modern in appearance — and they taste great, literally melting in your mouth. Unlike a classic tuile batter, this version is too soft to use with a template. Instead, the batter is spread in a very thin layer on greased Silpats. Silpats are not normally oiled — they are made to be nonstick and their purpose is to eliminate the need for greasing a pan or using baking paper — but oil is used on the mats in this recipe to produce a special effect. The fluidity of the batter, in conjunction with the oil and the nonstick nature of the mat, creates a lacy pattern filled with irregular holes. Because the condensed milk contains so much sugar but the overall recipe so little flour (which is also why the decorations are so tasty), the baked decorations will go from crisp to limp very quickly. They should always be stored in an airtight container, even if they will be needed in just a few hours.

2 teaspoons (5 g) cocoa powder *or* ½ teaspoon (.75 g) ground cinnamon (optional)

2 ounces (55 g) bread flour

1¼ cups (300 ml) sweetened condensed milk

Vegetable oil or pan spray

1. If you are using the cocoa powder or cinnamon, mix it into the flour. Gradually add the flour to the milk, stirring until the paste is smooth.

2. Brush vegetable oil lightly over a Silpat or spray the mat with pan spray.

3. Place about 1 tablespoon (15 ml) batter on the mat and spread it into a round approximately 4 inches (10 cm) in diameter. Repeat. Up to 8 decorations, evenly spaced, fit on a full-size mat. The batter should develop irregular holes and tears as you spread it. If this does not occur, help it along by dragging the spatula randomly through the batter to make small holes.

4. Bake at 375°F (190°C) for approximately 6 minutes or until the decorations begin to turn golden brown. Adding cocoa powder or cinnamon makes it harder to judge doneness because the batter is darker; you may have to test a few wafers to determine the correct baking time.

5. Let the decorations cool at room temperature just until firm enough to remove from the Silpat; do not allow them to become crisp. Carefully slide a thin knife or spatula under the wafers and transfer them to a sheet of baking paper. If you plan to form the decorations — by draping them over a rolling pin to make a tuile shape, for example — do so quickly as soon as you remove them from the Silpat. Store the finished decorations in airtight containers with a desiccant.

Tomatillo Lace Decorations yield: 12 decorations (Color Photo 75)

I first saw these decorations being made at a demonstration at Maricuá Centro de Artes Culinarias in Mexico City, and I was quite taken with their elegance and originality. I certainly had my doubts about the use of a cleaning agent in a poaching liquid, but once you get past this oddity, you will see that after the soap does its job, subsequent steps not only whiten the garnish but also remove all traces of soap. Though they are somewhat time-consuming to produce, for an important occasion — especially if you are looking for a south-of-the-border or Southwestern look — these are sure to impress.

12 medium tomatillos

¼ cup (60 ml) dish soap

3 quarts (2 L 880 ml) water

2 tablespoons (30 ml) Tartaric Acid Solution (page 629; see Note)

1 tablespoon (15 ml) vanilla extract

1. Using the point of a sharp paring knife or the tip of a utility knife, cut through the paper-like husk on the outside of each tomatillo, cutting along the large veins that run vertically in about 8 places on each. Begin each cut approximately ½ inch (1.2 cm) from the stem end; cut all the way through the bottom so the husk remains intact at the stem end but the sections at the base are separate. Grasp the stem attached to the husk and firmly pull the husk off of the fruit. Reserve the fruit for another use, if desired.

2. Combine the soap, 1 quart (960 ml) of the water, and the tomatillo husks. Bring to a boil and cook over medium heat for 5 to 10 minutes. The liquid will develop a light green tint. Remove from the heat, strain, and rinse the husks thoroughly under warm running water to remove all of the soap. Use your fingers to remove any remaining skin as you hold the tomatillos under the running warm water. The husks should now consist of only a lacy membrane.

3. Combine the tartaric acid solution, another 1 quart (960 ml) water, and the prepared husks. Boil for 5 minutes. Rinse the husks thoroughly, as in Step 2.

4. Add the vanilla extract to the remaining 1 quart (960 ml) water and bring to a boil. Add the husks, boil for 1 minute, then remove from the heat and leave the husks to soak in the vanilla solution for 5 minutes.

5. Strain, then blot the husks on absorbent paper.

6. To form each husk into an attractive round shape, place them inside rings approximately 1½ to 1¾ inches (3.7 to 4.5 cm) in diameter (you may use cookie cutters or plastic tubes of the appropriate size) and set aside to dry. The decorations will dry in about 30 minutes at normal room temperature. Store in a single layer in an airtight container.

NOTE: The tartaric acid solution will remove almost all of the green color from the tomatillo husks, but they will still have a pale green to ivory hue. To make the garnishes as light in color as shown in the photo, replace the tartaric acid solution with the same amount of bleach. This quantity of bleach added to the water will produce a solution no stronger than that which is commonly used for kitchen sanitation; however, if you are uncomfortable about using bleach here, skip this option. The tartaric acid still produces an impressive garnish.

The templates and illustrations in Figures 13-49 to 13-66 suggest motifs such as Christmas, Valentine's Day, Easter, a child's birthday, and so on. They can inspire you to create your own designs, or they can be used as patterns to press into marzipan, as described in "Designs Pressed into Marzipan to Be Traced Over and/or Filled In with Fondant" (page 677). Once made in this fashion, the stamps can be kept virtually forever to use as needed. You may also want to use the templates to create designs on marzipan by following the instructions for "Tracing onto Marzipan" (page 635). If necessary, enlarge the templates to the appropriate size for the cake you are decorating.

FIGURE 13-49 **A piping design for a child's birthday cake**

FIGURE 13-50 **A piping design for an engagement party or bridal shower cake**

FIGURE 13-51 **A piping design for a baby shower cake**

FIGURE 13-52 **A piping design for a springtime cake**

FIGURE 13-53 **A piping design for a preportioned cake**

FIGURE 13-54 **A piping design for a springtime cake**

FIGURE 13-55 A piping design for a springtime cake

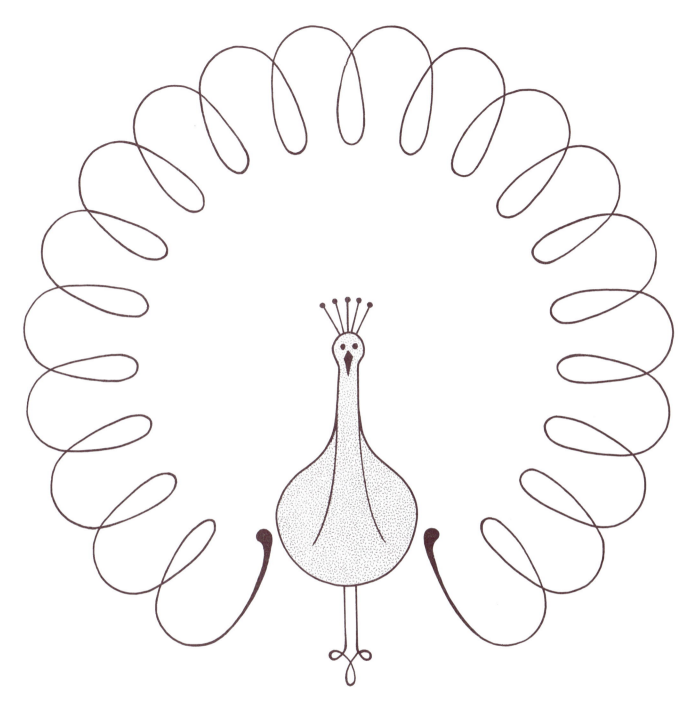

FIGURE 13-56 **A piping design for various occasions. After tracing the outline in dark chocolate, fill in the body of the peacock with light chocolate.**

Aquarius 1-20 to 2-18

Pisces 2-19 to 3-20

Aries 3-21 to 4-19

Taurus 4-20 to 5-20

Gemini 5-21 to 6-21

Cancer 6-22 to 7-22

Leo 7-23 to 8-22

Virgo 8-23 to 9-22

Libra 9-23 to 10-22

Scorpio 10-23 to 11-21

Sagittarius 11-22 to 12-21

Capricorn 12-22 to 1-19

FIGURE 13-57 Piping designs of astrological signs. Enlarging a design 400 percent will make it the correct size to decorate an 8-inch (20-cm) cake. They can also be used at the size shown to decorate an individual pastry or a single cake serving.

FIGURE 13-58 **A piping design for a girl's birthday cake**

FIGURE 13-59 A piping design for a boy's birthday cake

FIGURE 13-60 **A piping design for a Christmas cake**

FIGURE 13-61 A piping design for a New Year's cake

FIGURE 13-62 A piping design for a Valentine's Day cake

FIGURE 13-63 A piping design for an Easter cake

FIGURE 13-64 A piping design for an Easter cake

FIGURE 13-65 A piping design for a Mother's Day cake

FIGURE 13-66 A piping design for a Father's Day cake

IN THIS CHAPTER

Almond Paste	749
Beet Juice	750
Butter and Flour Mixture	750

BUTTERCREAM

Chocolate Buttercream (Italian Method)	752
Vanilla Buttercream (French Method)	752
Vanilla Buttercream (Swiss Method)	753
Cinnamon Sugar	753
Clarified Butter	753
Coffee Reduction	754
Crème Anglaise	754
Crème Fraîche	755
Crepes	755
Crystallized Ginger	756
Candied Citrus Peels	756
QUICK METHOD FOR CANDIED CITRUS PEELS	758

DECORATING SYRUPS

Black Currant Decorating Syrup	758
Green Tea Decorating Syrup	759
Lemon-Vanilla Decorating Syrup	759
Licorice Decorating Syrup	760
Mint Decorating Syrup	760
Orange-Vanilla Decorating Syrup	760
Raspberry Decorating Syrup	761
Red Currant Decorating Syrup	761
Rum Decorating Syrup	762

EGG WASH

Whole-Egg Egg Wash	762
Yolks-Only Egg Wash	763
Egg Wash for Spraying	763

FILLINGS

Calvados Diplomat Cream	764
Calvados Pastry Cream	764
Chantilly Cream	765
Cherry Filling	765
FRESH CHERRY FILLING	766
Chocolate Cream	766
Chunky Apple Filling	767
Classic Bavarian Cream	767
CLASSIC CHOCOLATE BAVARIAN CREAM	768
CREME ANGLAISE-BASED BAVARIAN CREAM	768
Crème Parisienne	768
Diplomat Cream	769
Frangipane Filling	769
Ganache	770
QUICK GANACHE	771
Italian Cream	771
Lemon Cream	771
Lemon Curd	772
Lime Cream	772
Pastry Cream	773
Quick Bavarian Cream	774

GLAZES

Apricot Glaze	774
Chocolate Glaze	774
Chocolate Mirror Glaze	775
Orange Glaze	775
Pectin Glaze	776
Plain Mirror Glaze	776
Red Currant Glaze	777
Graham Crackers and Crumbs	777
Hazelnut Paste	778
Linzer Dough	778
Macaroon Decorating Paste	779
Mascarpone Cheese	779

MERINGUE

French Meringue	780
Italian Meringue	780
Japonaise Meringue Batter	781
Meringue Noisette	781
Swiss Meringue	782
Pâte à Choux	783
Puff Pastry	784
Quick Puff Pastry	788
Plain Cake Syrup	789
Plain Poaching Syrup	789
SPICED POACHING SYRUP	790
Rum Ball Filling	790

SHORT DOUGH

Short Dough	791
Cocoa Short Dough	792
Hazelnut Short Dough	792
Short Dough Cake Bottoms	792
Simple Syrup (28° Baumé)	793

SPONGE CAKES AND CAKE BASES

Sponge Cake	794
Chocolate Sponge Cake	795
Almond Sponge	795
COCOA-ALMOND SPONGE	796
Angel Food Cake	796
Chiffon Sponge Cake I	797
CHOCOLATE CHIFFON SPONGE CAKE I	797
LEMON CHIFFON SPONGE CAKE I	797
Chiffon Sponge Cake II	798
CHOCOLATE CHIFFON SPONGE CAKE II	798
LEMON CHIFFON SPONGE CAKE II	798
ORANGE CHIFFON SPONGE CAKE II	798
Dobos Sponge	799
COCOA DOBOS SPONGE	799
Hazelnut-Chocolate Sponge	800
High-Ratio Sponge Cake	800
HIGH-RATIO CHOCOLATE SPONGE CAKE	800
Ladyfingers	801
CHOCOLATE LADYFINGERS	801
Lemon Ladyfingers	801
Unflavored Yogurt	802
Vanilla Extract	803
Vanilla Sugar	803
White Chocolate Sauce	803
Yogurt Cheese	804
Praline	804

Basic Recipes

Almond Paste yield: I pound 14 ounces (855 g)

Although making almond paste is simple if you have an almond mill, the time involved does not justify the cost savings in today's industry, so it is rarely made in the pastry shop nowadays. The only disadvantage to purchasing a commercial brand is that consistency varies from one brand to another, and you will need to compensate for that in some recipes. Also, some batches may contain tiny specks of almond due to improper milling or specks of brown skin from almonds that were not blanched properly. If you find you cannot produce the specified powdery consistency in Step 1, very finely ground almonds will suffice. The quality of the finished product will not be as good, but the only recipe where this will be noticeable, and in this case should not be used, is Marzipan (page 635).

> 10 ounces (285 g) dry blanched almonds
> 10 ounces (285 g) powdered sugar
> 1¼ cups (300 ml) simple syrup

1. Place the almonds in an almond mill if you have one or in a high-speed food processor and process to a powder (see Note).

2. Add the powdered sugar; then, with the machine running, gradually add the simple syrup until the mixture forms a paste. The amount of simple syrup needed will vary depending on how dry the almonds are. Freshly blanched almonds will need less syrup. Store the almond paste, tightly covered, for up to 1 week at room temperature. Refrigerate for longer storage.

NOTE: If the almonds are not completely dry, you will get a paste at this point rather than a powder. This is fine, provided that the paste is smooth.

Beet Juice yield: approximately 1¼ cups (300 ml)

Beets are among the few red vegetables. They get their color from a group of pigments called *antho-cyanins*. These are the same pigments responsible for most of the color in red, purple, and blue fruits and flowers. Extracted beet juice can be used to color food products as an alternative to artificial red dyes. If added to foods that are too alkaline, however, the color will change from red to purple and begin to fade. Adding an acid will prevent this and will even reverse the effect after it has occurred, changing the purple color back to red.

1 pound (455 g) red beets

1. Wash and peel the beets, then process with a juice extractor (see Note).

2. Store the juice in a plastic squeeze bottle in the refrigerator. It will keep for several weeks.

NOTE: If you do not have a juice extractor, chop the beets and grind in a food processor, or grate them finely. Press the beets against a fine sieve to extract the juice. These alternatives are not as desirable, as they yield less juice and take more time. The freshness of the beets also affects the yield.

Butter and Flour Mixture

Using a butter and flour mixture is a quick and easy way to prepare cake pans, forms, and molds in recipes that direct you to grease and flour the pan. Rather than applying the two separately, you brush on the flour at the same time you grease the pan. This method can save a great deal of time when the task is done over and over throughout the day. Many establishments use commercially produced pan sprays instead; these work fine as well. Although today's equipment is often made from nonstick material, this old-fashioned method will always be needed.

1. Stir together 4 parts melted butter or margarine with 1 part bread flour by volume until blended.

2. Apply the mixture with a brush.

NOTE: The combination can be left at room temperature for up to 1 week. If the mixture is refrigerated, warm it before using (but do not boil) and stir to combine.

Buttercream is indispensable in the pastry kitchen. Its primary use is for filling, icing, and decorating cakes and pastries. Buttercream should be light and smooth and should always be made from high-quality sweet butter. Icings made from all margarine or shortening can be unpleasant to eat — because of their higher melting point, they tend to leave a film of fat in your mouth — but a small amount of margarine or shortening added to buttercream stabilizes it without detracting from the taste. On very hot days or in hot climates, you can increase the ratio of butter to margarine to equal amounts, but only if absolutely necessary to prevent the buttercream from melting.

If you prefer not to use margarine or shortening, another way to stabilize buttercream is to add white chocolate (provided its flavor will be appropriate for the intended use of the buttercream), which is firmer at room temperature than butter. Add 4 ounces (115 g) melted white chocolate for every 1 pound (455 g) butter in the recipe. Because many weddings take place in summer, it is often necessary to display a buttercream-iced cake for several hours in a warm room during the reception. Another trick is to freeze the cake layers, fully or partially, after icing and decorating with buttercream so the cake will stay cold and prevent the buttercream from melting. If you use this method, be certain the cake will have enough time to thaw all the way through before serving time. This method should not be used with cake whose filling will suffer from freezing and thawing.

Buttercream can be stored at normal room temperature for three or four days and in the refrigerator for up to two weeks, and can be frozen for longer storage. Buttercream kept in the refrigerator should be taken out in plenty of time to soften before using. If you need to soften it quickly, cut or break the firm buttercream into small pieces in the same way you would butter when you need to soften it; place in a warm location until partially softened, then warm slightly over simmering water, stirring vigorously, until smooth and shiny. Be careful not to overheat and melt the buttercream; continue to stir after you take it off the heat, because the bowl will stay hot a little longer and can melt the buttercream on the sides. Use the same warming technique to repair buttercream that has broken. Alternatively, place the broken buttercream in a mixer bowl, while mixing at low speed with the paddle attachment, and use a blowtorch to warm the outside of the bowl. When buttercream breaks, it is generally because the butter was too cold when added to the meringue, or because another cold ingredient, such as refrigerated lemon curd, was added. A convenient way to soften buttercream is to microwave it on low; remove the buttercream and stir frequently during the process.

Meringue-based buttercream — that is, soft butter beaten into whipped egg whites and sugar — is probably the type most widely used. This is known as the *Swiss method;* it is quick and easy to make and has a light and fluffy texture. French-method buttercream is made by whipping whole eggs or egg yolks to a thick foam with hot sugar syrup, then whipping in soft butter. Italian-method buttercream is made in the same way, except egg whites are used instead of whole eggs or egg yolks. When you make Italian-method buttercream, you essentially produce an Italian meringue, then whip butter into it. Both the Italian and the French methods produce rich yet light buttercreams.

Chocolate Buttercream (Italian Method) yield: 4 pounds 6 ounces (1 kg 990 g)

To make white chocolate buttercream, substitute melted white chocolate for the sweet dark chocolate in equal amounts. Both white and dark chocolate buttercream can be flavored with hazelnut paste or praline paste. Dark chocolate buttercream is also nice with the addition of coffee reduction to create a mocha flavor.

2 pounds (910 g) unsalted butter, at room temperature

14 ounces (400 g) granulated sugar

1/3 cup (80 ml) water

1 tablespoon (15 ml) light corn syrup

4 whole eggs

2 egg whites (1/4 cup/60 ml)

1 teaspoon (5 g) salt

1 teaspoon (5 ml) vanilla extract

1 pound 8 ounces (680 g) sweet dark chocolate, melted and at 110°F (43°C)

1. Soften the butter, if necessary, then cream until light and fluffy. Reserve.

2. Combine the sugar, water, and corn syrup in a saucepan. Boil to 240°F (115°C), brushing down the sides of the pan. Do not stir.

3. While the syrup is boiling, whip the whole eggs, egg whites, salt, and vanilla just to combine. Remove the syrup from the heat, wait about 10 seconds, then gradually pour the hot syrup into the egg mixture in a steady stream between the whip and the side of the bowl, with the mixer at medium speed. Increase to high speed and whip until completely cooled.

4. Reduce to low speed and gradually mix in the reserved butter. Remove the mixing bowl from the machine. Place one-third of the butter mixture in a separate bowl and quickly mix in the melted chocolate to temper. Still working quickly, add this to the remaining buttercream.

Vanilla Buttercream (French Method) yield: 4 pounds 8 ounces (2 kg 45 g)

1 pound 8 ounces (680 g) granulated sugar

1/2 cup (120 ml) water

12 egg yolks (1 cup/240 ml)

2 pounds (910 g) unsalted butter, at room temperature

2 teaspoons (10 ml) vanilla extract

1. Place the sugar and water in a saucepan. Bring to a boil, stirring to dissolve the sugar. Reduce the heat and boil until the sugar syrup reaches 240°F (115°C).

2. While the syrup is boiling, whip the egg yolks until light and fluffy. Lower the speed on the mixer, then carefully pour the hot syrup into the egg yolks in a steady stream between the whip and the side of the bowl. Whip at high speed until the mixture is cool and light in texture.

3. Turn to low speed and gradually add the soft butter, adding it only as fast as it can be absorbed. Mix in the vanilla.

Vanilla Buttercream (Swiss Method) yield: 5 pounds 4 ounces (2 kg 390 g)

This recipe can be used as a starting point for numerous other flavors. Vanilla buttercream can be flavored with lemon curd, coffee reduction, chestnut puree, hazelnut paste, praline paste, or various liqueurs to use as both a filling and an icing. When using it as a filling only, you can also add chopped toasted nuts or candied fruit. When using fresh fruit with a buttercream filling, it is best to arrange thin slices of fruit on top of a layer of buttercream then cover with additional buttercream, rather than to mix in the fruit directly, both to make uniform, level layers and because the fruit's moisture can cause the buttercream to break.

2 pounds (910 g) unsalted butter, at room temperature

10 ounces (285 g) vegetable margarine, at room temperature (see Note)

1 recipe Swiss Meringue (page 782)

2 teaspoons (10 ml) vanilla extract

1. Thoroughly combine the butter with the margarine. Reserve at room temperature.

2. When the meringue has been whipped to stiff peaks and is lukewarm, lower the speed on the mixer, add the vanilla, and gradually whip in the butter mixture. The butter mixture must not be too cold when it is added, or the buttercream may break.

NOTE: Margarine is used to make buttercream more stable. If you replace the margarine with unsalted butter, you can slowly blend 10 ounces (285 g) melted white chocolate into the finished buttercream to provide further stability.

Cinnamon Sugar yield: 2½ cups (600 ml)

1½ ounces (40 g) ground cinnamon

1 pound (455 g) granulated sugar

1. Combine the ground cinnamon and sugar.

2. Store in a tightly covered container at room temperature.

NOTE: To make a smaller quantity, use 1 part ground cinnamon to 4 parts granulated sugar, measured by volume.

Clarified Butter yield: 12 ounces (340 g)

Clarified butter is butter with the milk solids removed. It has a higher burning point than whole butter, which makes it preferable for sauté work or any time you are cooking foods at a high temperature.

1 pound (455 g) unsalted butter

1. Melt butter over low heat; let it bubble for a few minutes, but do not let it brown.

2. Remove the pan from the heat and let it stand for about 10 minutes.

3. Without moving or disturbing the pan, skim off the foamy solids that have risen to the top. This is easiest to do with a ladle.

4. Carefully ladle or pour the clear butterfat into a clean container, watching carefully so you do not add any of the milky portion that will have collected on the bottom.

5. Discard the milky residue in the bottom of the pan.

Coffee Reduction

This simple method of developing a good, strong coffee flavor can, of course, be modified to your own taste. Start with fresh coffee brewed from top-quality beans; do not use instant coffee.

1. Make coffee 10 times the normal strength.

2. Bring the coffee to a boil in a saucepan and reduce by half.

3. Let cool and use as needed. Store coffee reduction at room temperature for a few weeks, in the refrigerator if it is to be kept any longer.

Crème Anglaise yield: approximately 6 cups (1 L 440 ml)

This classic vanilla custard sauce is prepared using the same basic method and recipe as the custard for vanilla ice cream. I use half-and-half rather than the traditional milk so the chilled sauce can be frozen in an emergency to make ice cream. If you run out of vanilla custard sauce, you can do the opposite and thaw vanilla ice cream. In most cases you will need to thicken it by folding in lightly whipped heavy cream.

This sauce tastes especially nice with apple or pear tarts, and though vanilla is classic, the custard can be flavored to complement many desserts. Like any heated mixture containing eggs, vanilla custard sauce is a perfect breeding ground for bacteria, so follow strict sanitary guidelines.

12 egg yolks (1 cup/240 ml)

10 ounces (285 g) granulated sugar

1 vanilla bean, split lengthwise

1 quart (960 ml) half-and-half

1 tablespoon (15 ml) vanilla extract

1. Combine the egg yolks and sugar in a mixing bowl. Whip until light and fluffy.

2. Scrape the seeds out of the vanilla bean. Add the seeds and the pod halves to the half-and-half. Bring to the scalding point. Gradually pour the hot cream into the yolk mixture while stirring rapidly.

3. Place the mixture over simmering water and heat slowly, stirring constantly, until it is thick enough to coat the back of a spoon. Be careful not to get it hotter than 190°F (88°C), or it will start to curdle.

4. Immediately pour the custard into another container and continue stirring for a few seconds. Remove the vanilla bean halves and discard. Stir in the vanilla extract. Set the sauce aside to cool, stirring from time to time. When cold, store, covered, in the refrigerator. The sauce will keep this way for up to 1 week.

CHEF'S TIP

The sauce can be made up much more quickly if you cook it directly over low heat rather than in a bain-marie. Of course, this is a little trickier. Should you overheat and curdle the sauce, you can usually save it by adding 2 tablespoons (30 ml) heavy cream and processing in a blender, providing the sauce has only curdled and not scorched.

Crème Fraîche yield: 2 cups (480 ml)

1 ounce (30 g) sour cream

2 cups (480 ml) heavy cream

I. Stir the sour cream into the heavy cream. Cover and let stand at 80° to 90°F (26° to 32°C) for 24 hours. An oven with a pilot light, or the top of a stove with pilots, are possible places to maintain this temperature. Store, covered, in the refrigerator.

2. To thicken the cream, whip until you achieve the desired consistency.

Crepes yield: about 40 crepes, 6 inches (15 cm) in diameter

6 ounces (170 g) cake flour

6 ounces (170 g) bread flour

3 ounces (85 g) granulated sugar

2 teaspoons (10 g) salt

6 whole eggs

6 egg yolks (½ cup/120 ml)

6 ounces (170 g) unsalted butter, melted

3 cups (720 ml) warm whole milk

⅓ cup (80 ml) brandy

Clarified unsalted butter

I. Sift the cake flour and bread flour together. Combine with the sugar and salt in a mixing bowl.

2. Lightly beat the whole eggs with the egg yolks just to mix. Gradually stir the eggs into the dry ingredients. Add the melted butter, milk, and brandy. Stir until smooth. If the batter appears broken, the milk was probably too cool. To remedy this, warm the batter over simmering water, stirring constantly until smooth. Let the batter rest at room temperature for 1 hour.

3. Heat 2 crepe pans, each 6 inches (15 cm) in diameter. Brush with clarified butter (see Note); do not use a nylon brush. Using a small ladle, cover the bottom of the pans with a thin film of batter by quickly tilting and rotating them (Figure 14-1). Try to avoid making the batter run up the sides of the pans. Pour any

FIGURE 14-1 Rotating the pan to distribute crepe batter

excess batter back into the bowl. With practice, you will be able to add just the right amount of batter each time.

4. When the bottoms of the crepes have a nice golden brown color, flip them with a spatula and the fingers of one hand, or flip them in the air, if you have the knack. The second side need cook for only a few seconds, until it is no longer sticky; overcooking the crepes will make them dry.

5. Slide the crepes out of the pans and stack them on a plate to prevent their drying out as you make the remaining crepes. Cover once you have a large stack. After you have made a few crepes, adjust the batter, if necessary. If large bubbles form as the crepes cook, the batter is probably too thin, or the pan may be too hot. Thicken the batter by whipping in additional flour. If the batter is too thick and does not pour in a thin film, add milk to thin it. Once you have the batter and the heat adjusted correctly, making a few dozen crepes is easy. If they will not be used within several hours, wrap and store in the refrigerator. Leftover refrigerated crepes are suitable for use in dishes where they will be served hot, but they should not be used in cold dishes because they tend to be a bit rubbery. Wipe crepe pans clean with a towel; do not use water under any circumstances.

NOTE: If you are using properly seasoned crepe pans, you probably will have to grease them for the first few crepes only. In any case, avoid using too much butter, which saturates the crepes and makes them greasy.

Crystallized Ginger yield: about 10 ounces (285 g)

Ginger is rarely crystallized in the professional bakeshop, although the process is quite easy and not time-consuming. As with many homemade foodstuffs, which are free from artificial ingredients, such as coloring, bleaching, and preserving chemicals, the finished product does not look like the familiar commercial product. This crystallized ginger has a much darker color than the commercial golden or tan product you buy.

1 pound (455 g) fresh ginger (see Note)	1 pound (455 g) granulated sugar, plus more for coating
Water	⅓ cup (80 ml) water

1. Peel the ginger and slice ¼ inch (6 mm) thick.

2. Place the ginger slices in a saucepan and add enough water to cover. Simmer over low heat until the ginger is tender, approximately 40 minutes. Drain the ginger, discarding the liquid.

3. Place 1 pound (455 g) sugar in the empty saucepan. Add ⅓ cup (80 ml) water and stir to moisten all the sugar. Bring to a boil, add the drained ginger slices, and boil gently, stirring frequently, until the ginger looks translucent, about 20 minutes.

4. Reduce the heat and simmer until the syrup is quite thick. The sugar syrup is likely to form lumps if you cook it too long. This is all right; however, remove any large lumps that stick to the ginger pieces.

5. Using 2 forks, remove the ginger slices from the syrup and toss them in granulated sugar to coat. Place the pieces in a single layer, spaced well apart, on a sheet pan. Let stand overnight in a warm place. Store the ginger in an airtight container for up to 6 months.

NOTE: Start with ginger pieces that are as large as possible and cut smaller pieces on the bias to make the slices more uniform.

Candied Citrus Peels yield: approximately 2 pounds (910 g)

This recipe should really be titled Sugar Preservation of Citrus Peels because, accurately speaking, the peel must be preserved in syrup before it can be candied. The true procedure for making candied fruit involves covering the exterior surface of sugar-preserved fruit with a thin, crystallized layer of sugar, which prevents it from drying out too rapidly. In this recipe the finished peels are kept in syrup so this is not a concern. These days, most people do not have the time for the rather lengthy process used here and instead purchase prepared candied fruit. The purchased product is convenient but also expensive as it is almost always imported. Though this recipe requires 5 days to complete, it only takes about 30 minutes of your time each day once you have completed the initial steps. Further, as most kitchens have a ready supply of citrus shells that would otherwise be discarded, the only cost other than labor is the sugar. If you need candied peels right away, use the quick-method variation that follows this recipe.

1 pound 10 ounces (740 g) citrus fruit shells, prepared as described in Step 1

1 tablespoon (15 g) salt

20° Baumé Sugar Syrup (recipe follows)

3 ounces (85 g) glucose *or* ¼ cup (60 ml) or 3 ounces (85 g) light corn syrup

1. Cut whole oranges, lemons, limes, or grapefruit in half. Juice the fruit; save the juice for another use and scrape the remaining flesh from the shells. Cut the shells in half again to make quarters.

2. Blanch the shells in boiling water for a few minutes. Pour off the water, add fresh water, and blanch for a few minutes longer. Repeat this step once more to remove the bitter taste from the peels, then drain.

3. Again, add just enough fresh water to cover the fruit shells. Add the salt and simmer until the peels are soft, about 30 minutes. Plunge the shells into cold water to cool. Remove and pat dry. The white part of the peel, the pith, is usually left on but can be removed at this point with a small spoon or a melon ball cutter, if desired.

4. Stack the peels inside one another in a flat, nonreactive pan such as a hotel pan. Weigh them down with a lid (also nonreactive) or plates to prevent them from floating to the surface when you add the syrup. Pour the hot sugar syrup over the peels to cover. Let sit for 24 hours.

5. Pour off the syrup into a saucepan. Boil it until it reaches 24° on a Baumé thermometer (see Chef's Tip); this can be accelerated by adding more sugar to the syrup. When the syrup reads 24°, pour it back over the peels and let stand another 24 hours.

6. Repeat Step 5, bringing the syrup 4° higher each day until it reaches 34° Baumé. This will take 5 days from the day you started. Heat the peels in the syrup to scalding every other day. When the syrup is boiled for the last time, add the glucose or corn syrup to prevent recrystallization. Keep the peels, covered, at room temperature throughout this period.

7. Stored in the thickened syrup, covered, in the refrigerator or at room temperature, the peels will keep for months provided proper sanitation is practiced whenever any of the peels are removed.

CHEF'S TIP

Because the syrup must be at or close to 60°F (16°C) to get an accurate reading, you must remove the pan from the heat when you think it has reduced enough, pour off a little syrup to cool and test, then return the pan to the heat to continue boiling if it has not reduced sufficiently. This can be inconvenient; an alternative is to measure the syrup hot — although not boiling, which can break the Baumé thermometer; however, hot syrup will read 3° lower, so the reading should be 21° in that case.

20° BAUMÉ SUGAR SYRUP yield: 10 cups (2 L 400 ml)

6 cups (1 L 440 ml) water

1 pound 8 ounces (680 g) granulated sugar

1½ cups (360 ml) glucose *or* light corn syrup

1. Combine the water, sugar, and glucose or corn syrup in a saucepan. Heat to boiling and boil for 1 minute.

2. Remove the pan from the heat and skim off any scum that developed on the surface of the syrup. Use hot.

NOTE: This quantity of syrup will probably appear to be a great deal more than you need for the amount of citrus peel you are preparing. You must begin with a large amount because the peels absorb part of the syrup and because the syrup is reduced several times during the preparation process.

VARIATION

QUICK METHOD FOR CANDIED CITRUS PEELS yield: 4 ounces (115 g)

8 ounces (225 g) orange, lemon, lime, or grapefruit peel, removed using a vegetable peeler, without any white pith

2 ounces (55 g) powdered sugar

1. Cut the peels into very thin julienne.

2. Blanch the strips in water for a few minutes to remove the bitter taste. Strain and pat dry with a towel. Spread the peels in a single layer (but not too far apart) on a sheet pan lined with a Silpat or baking paper. Sift the powdered sugar over the top.

3. Dry the peels at 100°F (38°C) for approximately 30 minutes. Move the peels around to make sure all sides are coated with sugar and they are not sticking together.

4. Continue drying the peels about 30 minutes longer. Be careful not to overcook them. When cold, store the candied peels in an airtight container.

DECORATING SYRUPS

Black Currant Decorating Syrup yield: approximately 2 cups (480 ml)

12 ounces (340 g) fresh or IQF black currants   2 cups (480 ml) simple syrup

1. Wash and stem fresh currants. Select and reserve ½ cup (120 ml) small, good-looking currants (see Note).

2. Place the remaining currants in a small saucepan together with the simple syrup. Bring the mixture to a boil and cook for 2 to 3 minutes, until the berries start to crack open.

3. Strain through a fine mesh sieve and discard the solids. Return the liquid to the heat and reduce to approximately 2 cups (480 ml) or the viscosity you desire. (Test the consistency by placing a small amount in the refrigerator to chill, then bringing it back to room temperature; it should hold its shape.)

4. Remove from the heat and immediately stir in the reserved currants. Let cool to room temperature before using.

NOTE: Omit this step if you are using IQF currants because, like most frozen fruit, once thawed, the currants will soften and fall apart. Even when you leave out the decorative currants, the sauce will have a radiant color and unusual taste.

Green Tea Decorating Syrup yield: approximately 2½ cups (540 ml)

2 teaspoons (6 g) unflavored gelatin powder

¼ cup (60 ml) cold water

2 teaspoons (5 g) Japanese green tea powder

2 tablespoons (30 ml) hot water

2 cups (480 ml) simple syrup

1. Sprinkle the gelatin powder over the cold water and set aside to soften.

2. Combine the green tea powder with the hot water and stir to dissolve.

3. In a heavy saucepan, bring the simple syrup to a boil and boil for 3 minutes to reduce it slightly. Pour the syrup into a bowl.

4. Heat the gelatin mixture to dissolve the gelatin.

5. Stir the dissolved gelatin and the tea mixture into the reduced simple syrup. Let the syrup cool to room temperature (or chill a small amount and bring this to room temperature). The syrup should be thick enough to hold its shape. To bring the sauce to the desired consistency, if needed, reduce to thicken it or add a small amount of water to thin it.

6. Store in a piping bottle.

Lemon-Vanilla Decorating Syrup yield: approximately 2 cups (480 ml)

2 teaspoons (6 g) unflavored gelatin powder

3 tablespoons (45 ml) cold water

2 lemons

2 vanilla beans

2½ ounces (70 g) granulated sugar

1½ cups (360 ml) simple syrup

1. Sprinkle the gelatin over the surface of the cold water and set aside to soften.

2. Using a citrus zester, remove the zest from 1 lemon. Chop the zest finely. Extract the juice from both lemons and strain it. Combine the strained juice and the chopped zest; set aside.

3. Split the vanilla beans lengthwise. Scrape out the seeds and rub the seeds into the sugar. Stir the sugar into the simple syrup together with the reserved lemon juice and zest. Save the vanilla bean pods for another use. Bring the syrup to a boil.

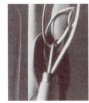

About Green Tea Powder

Imported from Japan, this concentrated product, known as *maccha*, can be used to impart a strong green tea flavor and beautiful celadon green color to syrups, mousses, meringues, and other items without adding extra liquid. Look for it at Asian grocery stores.

4. Heat the gelatin mixture to dissolve the softened gelatin. Stir into the hot syrup. To test the consistency, place 1 teaspoon (5 ml) syrup in the refrigerator; after it has chilled and been brought back to room temperature, the puddle should hold its shape. Adjust as needed by reducing the syrup to thicken or adding a small amount of water to thin.

5. Store in a piping bottle.

Licorice Decorating Syrup yield: approximately 1¼ cups (300 ml)

½ teaspoon (1.5 g) unflavored gelatin powder
⅓ cup (80 ml) water

1½ cups (360 ml) simple syrup
⅓ cup (80 ml) sambuca liqueur

1. Sprinkle the gelatin over the water and set aside to soften.

2. Combine the simple syrup and the sambuca in a saucepan and bring to a boil. Remove from the heat and stir in the softened gelatin; continue to stir until the gelatin is dissolved.

3. Return the pan to the stove and boil the mixture for a few minutes until it thickens. Test the consistency by refrigerating a few drops, then returning them to room temperature. The syrup should hold its shape at room temperature without running.

4. Store in a piping bottle.

Mint Decorating Syrup yield: approximately 1¼ cups (300 ml)

⅓ ounce (10 g) fresh peppermint leaves
1½ cups (360 ml) simple syrup

1 tablespoon (15 ml) green mint liqueur

1. Coarsely chop the mint leaves. Reserve 1 loosely measured tablespoon and place the remainder in a saucepan with the simple syrup and mint liqueur.

2. Bring to a boil and reduce by one-quarter. Test the consistency by placing 1 teaspoon (5 ml) syrup in the refrigerator until chilled, then returning it to room temperature, at which point the puddle should hold its shape. Adjust by reducing the syrup further, if necessary.

3. Chop the reserved mint leaves very finely; set aside.

4. Strain the syrup. Discard the solids and stir in the finely chopped mint. Store, refrigerated, in a piping bottle.

Orange-Vanilla Decorating Syrup yield: approximately 1¼ cups (300 ml)

½ teaspoon (1.5 g) unflavored gelatin powder
⅓ cup (80 ml) water
1 vanilla bean

1 cup (240 ml) simple syrup
½ cup (120 ml) orange juice
⅓ cup (80 ml) orange liqueur

1. Sprinkle the gelatin over the water and set aside to soften.

2. Split the vanilla bean in half lengthwise and scrape out the seeds. Save the empty pod halves for another use. Thoroughly mix the vanilla bean seeds in a small portion of the simple syrup to distribute them and break up any clumps. Mix this into the remaining simple syrup.

3. Combine the vanilla simple syrup, orange juice, and the orange liqueur in a saucepan and bring to a boil. Remove from the heat and stir in the softened gelatin; continue stirring until the gelatin is dissolved.

4. Return the pan to the stove and boil the mixture for a few minutes until it thickens. Test the consistency by refrigerating a few drops, then returning them to room temperature. The syrup should hold its shape at room temperature without running.

5. Store in a piping bottle.

Raspberry Decorating Syrup yield: approximately 1³/₄ cups (420 ml)

1 pound (455 g) fresh or IQF raspberries	1 cup (240 ml) simple syrup
Water, as needed	3 tablespoons (45 ml) raspberry liqueur

1. Puree the raspberries. Strain the puree through a fine mesh strainer to remove the seeds; the result should be approximately 1 cup (240 ml) raspberry juice. If needed, add water.

2. Place the raspberry juice, simple syrup, and raspberry liqueur in a saucepan. Bring to a boil and cook over medium heat until the liquid reduces to a viscosity that will hold its shape when cold and spooned into a puddle; test by placing a small amount in the refrigerator. The puddle should hold its shape when returned to room temperature.

3. Store, refrigerated, in a piping bottle.

Red Currant Decorating Syrup yield: approximately 2 cups (480 ml)

14 ounces (400 g) fresh or IQF red currants	1 cup (240 ml) simple syrup

1. Wash and stem the currants, if using fresh. Combine with the simple syrup in a saucepan and cook over medium heat until the currants start to burst, about 3 minutes.

2. Strain, using the back of a spoon or a ladle to extract as much juice as possible. Discard the solids and return the liquid to the saucepan.

3. Bring to a boil and reduce to approximately 2 cups (480 ml). Test the consistency by placing a small pool of syrup in the refrigerator, then bringing it back to room temperature. Adjust as needed by reducing further or thinning with water. To use, allow to cool to room temperature.

4. Store, refrigerated, in a piping bottle.

> **CHEF'S TIP**
> To make red currant glaze, reduce to 1 cup (240 ml) in Step 3. After cooling to room temperature, force the amount you plan to use through a fine mesh strainer and brush or spread immediately.

Rum Decorating Syrup yield: approximately 1 cup (240 ml)

1½ cups (360 ml) simple syrup
½ cup (120 ml) dark rum

1 vanilla bean

1. Combine the simple syrup and rum in a saucepan. Split the vanilla bean lengthwise and scrape out the seeds. Reserve the vanilla bean pod for another use. Mix the seeds into a small portion of the syrup to distribute them evenly and break up any lumps. Mix this into the remaining syrup.

2. Bring the syrup to a boil and reduce by one-quarter. The syrup should stay in puddles without running when cooled to room temperature and spooned onto the plate; test by placing 1 teaspoon syrup in the refrigerator, then returning it to room temperature.

3. Store the syrup in a piping bottle.

EGG WASH

Egg wash gives a shine to soft breads and rolls, croissants, and puff pastry items. It is also used as a glue to hold pieces of dough together and to make almonds or sugar adhere when sprinkled on a pastry or cookie before baking.

The best shine is obtained from egg wash containing only egg yolks and salt, thinned with a little water or milk. This is not really practical unless you have egg yolks sitting around or have a use for the separated whites. For everyday use, it makes more sense to beat the whole egg with a little salt, but no water or milk (see Chef's Tip). Each of the following recipes will keep for up to 1 week in the refrigerator if kept covered and not left at room temperature for more than just a few minutes at a time when brought out for use.

Whole-Egg Egg Wash yield: 1 cup (240 ml)

4 eggs

½ teaspoon (2.5 g) salt

1. Beat the eggs and salt together until the yolks and whites are combined.

2. Allow to stand 30 minutes before using or, preferably, cover and refrigerate overnight.

About Egg Wash

Although egg wash made from egg yolks alone (no egg whites) produces a deeply colored, shiny surface during baking, using egg yolks alone is too much of a good thing, in most cases. Not only is egg-yolk wash often too thick to be applied in a thin, even layer, the resulting crust can be dark to the point of appearing overbaked. On the other hand, the addition of water and/or milk to egg wash made from whole eggs tones down the coloration. Adding salt to egg wash made from egg yolks, whole eggs, or a combination amplifies the shine on the final product and works to thin the egg wash, which in turn makes it easier to apply correctly. The salt requires some time to break down and thin the egg substance, so its full effect is noticeable only if the egg wash stands approximately 8 hours or overnight (in the refrigerator) before use.

Yolks-Only Egg Wash yield: ¾ cup (180 ml)

8 egg yolks (⅔ cup/160 ml)   3 tablespoons (45 ml) water *or* whole milk

½ teaspoon (2.5 g) salt

1. Beat the egg yolks, salt, and water or milk together until well combined.

2. Cover and refrigerate overnight. If this is not possible, allow the egg wash to stand a minimum of 30 minutes before using.

NOTE: This egg wash might be too strong for items baked at temperatures above 400°F (205°C). The color will be too dark, giving the crust an overbaked appearance. If this is the case, thin further or use whole-egg egg wash.

Egg Wash for Spraying yield: 2 cups (480 ml)

Applying egg wash with a spray bottle powered by compressed air, electricity, or elbow grease instead of a brush (the more typical and time-consuming method) has been common in European bakeries since the early 1960s. The spray technique makes a lot of sense. Not only is it faster but it also produces a smooth, even application. Moreover, because you do not actually touch the product, you do not risk damaging the soft dough. The only disadvantage is that you will, of course, apply egg wash to the sheet pan or baking paper around the items you are spraying, but this small amount of waste is offset by the advantages.

It is a good idea to designate an easily cleaned area of the kitchen for spraying or to place a few sheets of baking paper around your work area to aid in cleanup. For the best result, prepare egg wash for use in a spray bottle a day ahead to give the salt time to make the eggs less viscous. If you are using a power sprayer you will need to double the recipe to have enough liquid to operate the sprayer effectively.

6 whole eggs   ½ teaspoon (2.5 g) salt

4 egg yolks (⅓ cup/80 ml)

1. Combine the eggs, egg yolks, and salt. Process for 10 to 15 seconds in a food processor. Strain through a fine mesh strainer to remove the chalazae (the thick white cords attached to the yolk). Cover the mixture and refrigerate for a minimum of 12 hours.

2. Pour the egg wash into a spray bottle set to fine mist.

3. Holding the bottle about 10 inches (25 cm) above the item to be baked, spray to cover; turn the sheet pan as necessary to ensure even coverage on all sides.

4. To achieve the maximum amount of shine, let the egg wash dry for a few minutes, then apply a second coat.

Calvados Diplomat Cream yield: 9 cups (2 L 160 ml)

2 teaspoons (6 g) unflavored gelatin powder

¼ cup (60 ml) cold water

½ teaspoon (1 g) ground cinnamon

1 tablespoon (15 g) granulated sugar

2 cups (480 ml) heavy cream

1 recipe Calvados Pastry Cream (below)

1. In a bowl large enough to hold the finished filling, sprinkle the gelatin over the cold water and set aside to soften.

2. Combine the cinnamon and sugar. Add to the heavy cream and whip to soft peaks. Set aside in the refrigerator.

3. Stir the Calvados pastry cream until smooth, straining first if necessary.

4. Heat the gelatin mixture over a bain-marie to dissolve. Quickly stir in about one-quarter of the pastry cream; continue to stir until the mixture reaches body temperature. Remove from the bain-marie. Rapidly stir in the remaining pastry cream, then fold in the reserved whipped cream. Use immediately.

Calvados Pastry Cream yield: approximately 2 pounds (910 g)

1 pint (480 ml) whole milk

1 vanilla bean

3 ounces (85 g) granulated sugar

1½ ounces (40 g) cornstarch

3 eggs

⅓ cup (80 ml) Calvados

2 ounces (55 g) unsalted butter

1. Place the milk in a thick-bottomed saucepan. Cut the vanilla bean in half lengthwise and scrape out the seeds. Add the seeds and the pod to the milk. Bring to the scalding point.

2. Keeping an eye on the milk, whisk together the sugar and cornstarch in a bowl. Gradually whisk in the eggs, followed by the Calvados; continue mixing until smooth.

3. Slowly pour about one-third of the hot milk into the egg mixture, whisking rapidly. Pour the tempered egg mixture back into the remaining milk.

4. Return the pan to the stove and bring to a boil over medium heat, stirring constantly. Cook for a few seconds once the mixture reaches the boiling point.

5. Remove the vanilla bean pod. Stir in the butter. Pour the custard into a bowl, cover, and let cool slightly at room temperature, then refrigerate.

Chantilly Cream yield: 6 cups (1 L 440 ml)

Chantilly cream must be refrigerated. It will break if left at room temperature for more than a short period.

1 vanilla bean

1 tablespoon (15 g) granulated sugar

2 cups (480 ml) heavy cream, well chilled

1 teaspoon (5 ml) vanilla extract

1. Cut the vanilla bean in half lengthwise. Scrape out the seeds and thoroughly mix the seeds into the granulated sugar. Save the empty pod halves for another use.

2. Chill the bowl and the whip attachment of an electric mixer. Pour the cream and the vanilla into the bowl. Start whipping at high speed. Add the vanilla-sugar mixture.

3. Keeping a watchful eye on its progress, continue whipping until stiff peaks form or to the consistency specified in the individual recipe. Use as soon as possible.

Cherry Filling yield: approximately 4 pounds (1 kg 820 g)

Because cornstarch will break down and make the filling watery after a few days of storage, pectin powder is used here as well. Be sure to choose regular fruit-canning pectin rather than pure pectin for this recipe.

2 pounds (910 g) drained sweet canned cherries (see Step 1)

3 cups (720 ml) liquid from canned cherries

Simple syrup, as needed

2 tablespoons (30 ml) raspberry juice

2 ounces (55 g) cornstarch

2 ounces (55 g) pectin powder

1. When you drain the juice from the cherries, press the cherries firmly without crushing them. The liquid must be completely drained off, or the filling will be too runny. Measure the liquid; add simple syrup, if necessary, to bring the volume to 3 cups (720 ml).

2. Add the raspberry juice to the cherry liquid. Dissolve the cornstarch in a small amount of the liquid before stirring into the remainder. Mix the pectin powder with the sugar. Blend into the cherry liquid mixture.

3. Bring the sauce to a boil, stirring constantly. Cook over medium heat for about 5 minutes to cook the starch.

4. Remove from the heat; add the drained cherries. Place a piece of baking paper directly on the surface to prevent a skin from forming as the filling cools. Store, covered, in the refrigerator.

FRESH CHERRY FILLING yield: approximately 3 pounds 8 ounces (1 kg 590 g)

2 pounds (910 g) fresh Bing or Lambert cherries

3 ounces (85 g) cornstarch

2½ cups (600 ml) water

1 pound 4 ounces (570 g) granulated sugar

2 ounces (55 g) pectin powder

2 tablespoons (30 ml) raspberry juice

¼ cup (60 ml) lemon juice

1. Wash the cherries and remove the stems. Pit the cherries.

2. Mix the cornstarch with just enough of the water to make a slurry.

3. Combine the sugar and pectin powder. Place this, together with the remaining water, in a saucepan and bring to a boil. Add the cherries and cook gently until tender, 4 to 5 minutes. Strain, reserving the cherries and the syrup separately.

4. Stir the raspberry juice and lemon juice into the reserved cornstarch slurry. Quickly and in a steady stream, stir this into the reserved syrup. Bring the mixture to a boil, stirring constantly. Cook over medium heat for about 5 minutes.

5. Remove from the heat and add the drained cherries. Place a piece of baking paper on the surface to prevent a skin from forming as the filling cools. Store, covered, in the refrigerator.

Chocolate Cream yield: 4 pounds 6 ounces (1 kg 990 g) or 9½ cups (2 L 280 ml)

Chocolate cream is likely to break if the chocolate mixture is too hot; it should be approximately 110°F (43°C). The filling can also break if the cream does not contain at least 36 percent butterfat, but this factor is somewhat harder to control.

5 ounces (140 g) sweet dark chocolate

2 ounces (55 g) unsweetened chocolate

½ cup (120 ml) simple syrup

3 pints (1 L 440 ml) heavy cream

1. Cut the chocolates into small pieces. Place in a bowl and melt over simmering water. Remove from the heat and stir in the simple syrup.

2. Whip the cream until slightly thickened. Be careful: If you overwhip the cream, it will break when you add the chocolate.

3. Place a small amount of the whipped cream in a bowl and quickly fold in the chocolate mixture; do not whisk. Mix in the rest of the cream. If the chocolate cream seems runny, stir it until the consistency becomes firmer.

Chunky Apple Filling
yield: 2 pounds 12 ounces (1 kg 250 g) or 5 cups (1 L 200 ml)

3 pounds (1 kg 365 g) Granny Smith or
    Pippin apples (about 7; see Chef's Tip)

10 ounces (285 g) granulated sugar

¼ cup (60 ml) water

4 teaspoons (20 ml) lemon juice

1. Peel and core the apples. Chop approximately two-thirds of the apples into ½-inch (1.2-cm) cubes.

2. Place the chopped apples in a saucepan with the sugar, water, and lemon juice. Adjust the amount of sugar according to the tartness of the apples and your own taste. Stir to combine and cook over medium heat, stirring from time to time, until the apples have broken down and the mixture starts to thicken.

3. Chop the remaining apples into ¼-inch (6-mm) cubes and add to the mixture on the stove.

4. Continue cooking the filling until the apple chunks are soft and the filling has reached a jamlike consistency, adding a bit more water, if necessary. Let cool at room temperature, then store, covered, in the refrigerator.

CHEF'S TIP

Other good apple choices are Jonathan and Gravenstein. Avoid Red Delicious and Fuji, which are difficult or even impossible to cook down to a saucelike consistency.

Classic Bavarian Cream
yield: 2 quarts (1 L 920 ml)

8 egg yolks (⅔ cup/160 ml)

8 ounces (225 g) granulated sugar

2 tablespoons (18 g) unflavored gelatin
    powder

½ cup (120 ml) cold water

1 vanilla bean

2 cups (480 ml) whole milk

2 cups (480 ml) heavy cream

1 teaspoon (5 ml) vanilla extract

1. Whip the egg yolks and sugar until light and fluffy.

2. Sprinkle the gelatin over the cold water and set aside to soften.

3. Split the vanilla bean lengthwise and scrape out the seeds. Add the seeds and the pod halves to the milk. Bring the milk to the scalding point. Gradually pour the hot milk into the yolk mixture, whipping rapidly. Return the mixture to the heat and bring back to the scalding point, stirring constantly. Do not boil.

4. Remove from the heat and stir in the reserved gelatin. Set aside to cool at room temperature, stirring from time to time.

5. Whip the cream to soft peaks. Remove the pod halves from the custard and discard. Stir in the vanilla extract. When the custard has cooled to body temperature, slowly stir it into the cream.

6. Pour into molds or use as directed in individual recipes.

CLASSIC CHOCOLATE BAVARIAN CREAM

Decrease the gelatin to 4 teaspoons (12 g) and add 8 ounces (225 g) melted sweet dark chocolate when you stir in the gelatin.

CREME ANGLAISE–BASED BAVARIAN CREAM yield: 2 cups (480 ml)

Another popular way of preparing Bavarian cream, and one that is prevalent in professional pastry kitchens, is to make the filling using crème anglaise as the base. This makes particularly good sense if you already have crème anglaise on hand. Even if you do not, should you need both products, this method will save time. Further, the resulting Bavarian cream is richer, as it contains extra egg yolks and half-and-half rather than milk.

1 teaspoon (3 g) unflavored gelatin powder

2 tablespoons (30 ml) cold water

½ cup (120 ml) heavy cream

1 cup (240 ml) Crème Anglaise (page 754), warmed over a bain-marie if not freshly made

1. Sprinkle the gelatin over cold water and set aside to soften.

2. Whip the cream to soft peaks.

3. Heat the gelatin mixture to dissolve the gelatin. Stir the gelatin into the warm crème anglaise, then fold in the whipped cream.

Crème Parisienne yield: 2 quarts (1 L 920 ml) or 4 pounds 8 ounces (2 kg 45 g)

This simple chocolate cream can be used for most of the recipes in this book that call for chocolate added to whipping cream, either as is or, if applicable, with gelatin added. This cream will not break, which can happen when you add warm melted chocolate to whipped cream that is too low in butterfat, because the fat content of the mixture is increased by adding the chocolate to the cream before whipping it. If you are using regular heavy cream (35 percent butterfat), make this the day before (or at least 6 hours before) it is to be used to ensure it will whip to its maximum volume and thickness. However, if it is made with manufacturing cream, which contains 40 percent butterfat, it needs only to be thoroughly chilled before whipping. Either way, crème Parisienne can be stored in the refrigerator, unwhipped, for up to 1 week and used as needed. This can be a real timesaver if, for example, you fill chocolate éclairs or a similar pastry every day.

10 ounces (285 g) sweet dark chocolate

1 quart (960 ml) heavy cream

¾ cup (180 ml) whole milk

3 ounces (85 g) granulated sugar

1. Chop the chocolate into small pieces melt over a water bath and reserve.

2. Bring the cream, milk, and sugar to a boil in a saucepan. Remove from the heat and stir in the melted chocolate. Continue to stir until the chocolate is completely incorporated. (If spots of chocolate persist, strain through a fine strainer.) Cool and refrigerate before whipping (see introduction above).

3. When you are ready to use the filling, whip as you would whipping cream.

Diplomat Cream yield: 2 quarts (I L 920 ml)

Diplomat Cream can be made with or without gelatin, depending on its intended use. In Sweden, when we leave out the gelatin and simply combine pastry cream and sweetened whipped cream, we call it Quick Bavarian Cream. If the gelatin is omitted, the cream should be whipped to stiff peaks rather than soft peaks, as in this recipe. It is also important, in that case, that the pastry cream is not only completely smooth but quite firm to compensate for the missing gelatin. Diplomat Cream made without gelatin is limited in its applications, as it can be used only to fill a premade pastry or shell that will hold it in place. It is perfect for profiteroles and for fruit tartlets, for example, but if it needs to stand alone in a molded cake or pastry — for instance, on a gâteau Saint-Honoré — gelatin is a must.

1 tablespoon (9 g) unflavored gelatin powder	1 vanilla bean
⅓ cup (80 ml) kirschwasser	2½ cups (600 ml) heavy cream
1 small batch or 1 pound 8 ounces (680 g) Pastry Cream (page 773)	1 teaspoon (5 ml) vanilla extract

1. Sprinkle the gelatin powder over the kirschwasser and set aside to soften.

2. Stir the pastry cream to make it perfectly smooth; if necessary, force it through a sieve. Set aside.

3. Split the vanilla bean lengthwise and scrape out the seeds. Add the seeds to the heavy cream; reserve the pod halves for another use. Add the vanilla extract.

4. Whip the cream to soft peaks. Gradually fold the whipped cream into the pastry cream.

5. Heat the gelatin mixture over a water bath to dissolve.

6. Place one-third of the cream mixture in a separate bowl. Rapidly stir in the warm gelatin and kirschwasser. Still working quickly, stir this into the remaining cream mixture.

CHEF'S TIP

If the pastry cream is freshly made for this recipe, make sure it has cooled sufficiently before combining it with the whipped cream, or the mixture may break. Also, heat the gelatin a bit hotter than you normally would because the cream and custard mixture will be very cool. If the gelatin is not hot, it may set up before you can thoroughly mix it in.

Frangipane Filling yield: 4 pounds 10 ounces (2 kg 105 g)

Frangipane is an almond-based filling used in numerous European pastries and tarts. In addition to providing a delicious flavor, the almonds absorb moisture, which helps baked goods made with this filling stay fresh longer than average.

1 pound 14 ounces (855 g) almond paste	2½ cups (600 ml) eggs
6 ounces (170 g) granulated sugar	3 ounces (85 g) bread flour
14 ounces (400 g) unsalted butter, at room temperature	

1. Place the almond paste and sugar in a mixer bowl. Using a paddle and mixing at low speed, gradually add the butter.

2. After all of the butter has been incorporated and the mixture is smooth, mix in the eggs, a few at a time, then the flour. Store the frangipane in the refrigerator. Bring to room temperature to soften, then stir until smooth before using. Use as directed in individual recipes.

NOTE: As with any uncooked filling that contains a large number of eggs, frangipane should be used right away to ensure maximum volume in baked pastries.

Ganache yield: 6 pounds 4 ounces (2 kg 845 g) or 9½ cups (2 L 280 ml)

In its most basic form, ganache is simply equal parts sweet dark chocolate and heavy cream by weight. Other ingredients, such as butter and egg yolks, can be included together with flavorings, if desired. This rich mixture has many uses in the pastry kitchen. It can be used warm as a glaze, for filling and decorating cakes and pastries, and as the filling for a basic truffle. The ratio of chocolate to cream determines the consistency of the product after it cools; in both ganache and Quick Ganache (recipe follows), the ratio is approximately 2:1. Different brands of chocolate, which vary in proportion of cocoa mass, and different types of chocolate — semisweet or bittersweet — will also alter the consistency.

The formula here is ideal if you are adding flavorings containing a high level of moisture (such as spirits and liqueurs) because the fat from the egg yolks as well as the fat in the cocoa butter helps stabilize the mixture. Ganache can easily be adjusted to individual needs. For a firmer ganache, add more chocolate; for a softer ganache, decrease the amount. By not overworking the ganache when adding flavorings or softening it, you will preserve the rich, dark color. If you want a lighter and fluffier ganache, incorporate air by first softening the ganache over simmering water; then, using the paddle attachment, cream for a few minutes.

8 egg yolks (²⁄₃ cup/160 ml)	3 pounds 8 ounces (1 kg 590 g) sweet dark chocolate
8 ounces (225 g) granulated sugar	
2 teaspoons (10 ml) vanilla extract	1 quart (960 ml) heavy cream

1. Whip the egg yolks, sugar, and vanilla until light and fluffy.

2. Chop the chocolate into small pieces, place in a saucepan, and add the cream. Heat to 150°F (65°C), stirring constantly.

3. Stir the hot cream mixture into the egg yolk mixture and keep stirring for a minute or so to make sure the sugar is melted. If you plan to whip air into the ganache, keep stirring at low speed until it is cold, then whip it for a few minutes until light and fluffy.

4. Let the ganache cool and store it in airtight containers to use as needed. Ganache can be stored at room temperature for up to 3 days; it should be refrigerated for longer storage.

NOTE: If a skin or crust forms on the top during storage, pour hot water on top of the ganache, let it stand for 1 minute, then pour the water off. If needed, ganache can be stored in the freezer for months. If the sugar recrystallizes, or if all of the sugar was not dissolved in the first place, heat the ganache in a saucepan over low heat, stirring constantly, until all of the sugar crystals dissolve, around 150°F (65°C).

QUICK GANACHE yield: 6 cups (1 L 440 ml)

This is my version of what is known in the industry as *basic ganache* or *2:1 ratio ganache,* meaning it is made with 2 parts dark chocolate to 1 part heavy cream by weight. If you are in a real hurry, you can leave out both the invert sugar and the butter. I use them to improve the shine when the ganache has cooled and set, making it suitable to use as a glaze, which is frequently done in a pinch.

2 cups (480 ml) heavy cream

2 ounces (55 g) glucose *or* light corn syrup

2 ounces (55 g) unsalted butter

2 pounds (910 g) sweet dark chocolate, chopped into fine pieces

1. Place the cream, glucose or corn syrup, and butter in a saucepan; bring to a boil.

2. Remove from the heat and add the chopped chocolate, stirring constantly until the chocolate is completely melted and the mixture is homogeneous.

NOTE: To make a slightly softer basic ganache — one particularly well suited to use as a glaze — increase the amount of cream by 1 cup (240 ml) to 3 cups (720 ml) total, the glucose or corn syrup by 1 ounce (30 g) to 3 ounces (85 g) total, and the butter by 1 ounce (30 g) to 3 ounces (85 g) total.

Italian Cream yield: 7 cups (1 L 680 ml)

You can enjoy this rich-looking, rich-tasting cream filling while saving yourself calories and cholesterol. Italian cream can be used as a substitute for Quick Bavarian Cream in any of the recipes in this book.

2 cups (480 ml) heavy cream

2 teaspoons (10 ml) vanilla extract

¼ recipe Italian Meringue (page 780; see Note)

1. Whip the heavy cream and vanilla to soft peaks.

2. Fold the cream into the meringue. Refrigerate until needed. Use this filling the day it is made.

Lemon Cream yield: 7 cups (1 L 680 ml)

Finely grated zest of 6 lemons

Finely grated zest of 2 oranges

3 cups (720 ml) lemon juice

½ cup (120 ml) orange juice

2 tablespoons (16 g) cornstarch

1 pound 8 ounces (680 g) granulated sugar

12 eggs

6 ounces (170 g) unsalted butter

¾ cup (180 ml) heavy cream

1. Combine the lemon zest, orange zest, lemon juice, and orange juice. Set aside.

2. Mix the cornstarch into the sugar. Beat the eggs and the sugar mixture for a few seconds, just to combine, in a heavy saucepan made of stainless steel or another noncorrosive material; do not use aluminum. Add the juice and zest mixture, then the butter and heavy cream.

3. Bring to the scalding point, stirring constantly, over medium heat; do not boil. Strain immediately. Use hot, as directed in individual recipes, or cool. Store, covered, in the refrigerator for up to 3 weeks.

Lemon Curd yield: 5 cups (1 L 200 ml)

Lemon curd makes an excellent flavoring or filling and can also be used as a sauce by thinning with lemon juice or simple syrup. You will need approximately 8 medium lemons for the juice in the recipe.

Finely grated zest of 8 lemons
1½ cups (360 ml) lemon juice
8 eggs

1 pound 8 ounces (680 g) granulated sugar
12 ounces (340 g) unsalted butter

1. Combine the lemon zest and juice.

2. Beat the eggs and sugar together in a heavy saucepan made of stainless steel or other non-corrosive material; do not use aluminum. Stir in the lemon zest and juice mixture and then the butter.

3. Heat to boiling over low heat. Cook for a few seconds, stirring constantly, until the curd thickens. Strain immediately, then cool. Stored, covered, in the refrigerator, lemon curd will keep for weeks.

Lime Cream yield: 2 cups (480 ml)

Finely grated zest of 3 limes
1¾ cups (420 ml) freshly squeezed lime juice
  (from approximately 7 limes)
3 eggs

8 ounces (225 g) granulated sugar
2 ounces (55 g) unsalted butter
¼ cup (60 ml) heavy cream

1. Combine the grated lime zest and juice. Set aside.

2. Beat the eggs and sugar together in a heavy noncorrosive saucepan (not aluminum) just long enough to combine. Add the juice and zest mixture, butter, and heavy cream. Bring the mixture to the scalding point, stirring constantly over medium heat. Do not boil.

3. Remove from the heat and strain immediately. Set aside to cool.

4. Stored, covered, in the refrigerator, the lime cream will keep for 2 to 3 weeks. If necessary, thin with water before using.

Pastry Cream yield: 6 pounds (2 kg 730 g)

Making pastry cream is a basic technique that anyone involved with cooking should master, because pastry cream has so many applications. It is a base for soufflés; it is a filling and flavoring for cakes and fruit tarts; it is used to top Danish or other pastries and is perhaps best known as the filling for Napoleons. In the pastry kitchen, a supply of pastry cream should always be in the refrigerator.

Because pastry cream is made with cornstarch to stabilize the eggs, it is in no danger of overheating and curdling — as can happen, for example, with crème anglaise. Of course, you must still watch the heat and stir constantly to avoid burning the custard or having it lump. As eggs are heated their proteins unwind and bind with other proteins resulting in thicker protein strands. The higher the proteins are heated, the more tightly bound the strands become and the thicker they grow. Without the cornstarch in the recipe, eggs brought to the boiling point would essentially form scrambled eggs, and the mixture would be curdled. The cornstarch acts as a barrier — it blocks the protein strands from one another so they are unable to bind.

2 quarts (1 L 920 ml) whole milk

2 vanilla beans

5 ounces (140 g) cornstarch

1 pound (455 g) granulated sugar

1 teaspoon (5 g) salt

6 eggs

6 ounces (170 g) unsalted butter, at room temperature

Small-Batch Pastry Cream
yield: I pound 8 ounces (680 g)

1 pint (480 ml) whole milk

¹/₂ vanilla bean

4 tablespoons (32 g) cornstarch

4 ounces (115 g) granulated sugar

¹/₄ teaspoon (1 g) salt

2 eggs

2 ounces (55 g) unsalted butter, at room temperature

I. Place the milk in a heavy-bottomed saucepan. Split the vanilla bean(s) lengthwise and scrape out the seeds. Add the seeds and the pod halves to the milk and place on the stove. Bring to a boil over medium heat.

2. Keeping an eye on the milk so it does not get too hot or boil over, whisk the cornstarch, sugar, and salt together in a bowl. Gradually add the eggs and mix until smooth.

3. When the milk reaches the scalding point, slowly add about one-third of it to the egg mixture, whisking rapidly. Pour the tempered egg mixture back into the remaining milk.

4. Place over medium heat and cook, stirring constantly, until the mixture comes to a boil and thickens. Boil for a few seconds longer to make sure the raw starch taste has disappeared. Remove the vanilla bean pod(s) and discard. Stir in the butter and continue to stir until it is completely incorporated.

5. Pour the custard into a bowl and cover with a piece of baking paper. When cooled, store in the refrigerator. If made and stored properly, pastry cream will keep fresh for up to 4 days. However, when it is that old, it should be used only in pastries in which it will be baked.

N O T E : If the heat is too high or you are stirring too slowly when the pastry cream reaches a boil, it will lump. If this happens, pass it through a strainer immediately, before it cools.

Quick Bavarian Cream yield: approximately 3 pounds 12 ounces (1 kg 705 g) or 9 cups (2 L 160 ml)

This is not a classic Bavarian cream. In fact, it is closer to a Diplomat cream, but it can be used for many of the same applications and is a real timesaver because it uses pastry cream, a stock item in most pastry kitchens, as a prefabricated base. This eliminates the need to make a custard and wait for it to cool. If you do not have pastry cream on hand, you might want to make Classic Bavarian Cream (page 767) instead. If you are making pastry cream specifically to use in this recipe, make it far enough in advance so it is thoroughly chilled before you combine it with the whipped cream, or you risk breaking the cream.

1½ cups (360 ml) heavy cream

½ teaspoon (2.5 ml) vanilla extract

½ recipe or 3 pounds (1 kg 365 g) Pastry Cream (page 773)

1. Whip the heavy cream and vanilla to stiff peaks.

2. Fold the whipped cream into the pastry cream. Use as directed in the individual recipes.

GLAZES

Apricot Glaze yield: 2 cups (480 ml)

Melted sugar is extremely hot and can cause serious burns, so unless you have a chef's brass fingers, avoid testing the glaze against your skin. Using two spoons is a safer bet.

1 pound (455 g) apricot jam

3 ounces (85 g) granulated sugar

⅓ cup (80 ml) water

1. Place the jam, sugar, and water in a heavy-bottomed saucepan. Bring to a boil over medium heat, stirring constantly.

2. Lower the heat and continue cooking until the mixture can be pulled into a ¼-inch (6-mm) thread between your thumb and index finger or between the back of 2 spoons.

3. Quickly remove the pan from the heat, strain, and use immediately. Store the leftover glaze at room temperature. Reheat the glaze to use again; if it is too thick, add a small amount of water.

NOTE: If you overcook the glaze, it will become too thick to use properly. Unless it has started to caramelize, you can correct this by adding water and cooking to the thread test again.

Chocolate Glaze yield: 4½ cups (1 L 80 ml)

1 pound (455 g) sweet dark chocolate

5 ounces (140 g) unsalted butter, at room temperature

1½ ounces (40 g) unsweetened cocoa powder, sifted

¼ cup (60 ml) dark rum

¾ cup (180 ml) or 9 ounces (255 g) light corn syrup

1. Cut the chocolate into small chunks and melt over hot water. Remove from the heat, add the butter, and stir until the butter is fully incorporated.

2. Stir the cocoa powder into the rum, mixing until smooth. Add the corn syrup, then stir into the chocolate mixture.

3. Let cool, then store in a covered container at room temperature. To use, heat the glaze to the right consistency for the individual recipe. If a skin forms on the surface during storage, pour a little hot water on top, wait a few seconds, then pour the water off.

Chocolate Mirror Glaze yield: ¹/₂ cup (120 ml)

1¹/₂ teaspoons (4.5 g) unflavored gelatin
   powder

¹/₄ cup (60 ml) cold water

¹/₄ cup (60 ml) simple syrup

¹/₂ teaspoon (2 g) unsweetened cocoa powder

1. Sprinkle the gelatin powder over the cold water and set aside to soften.

2. Warm the simple syrup slightly. Add the cocoa powder and mix until completely dissolved.

3. Heat the gelatin mixture to dissolve the gelatin. Stir in the cocoa-flavored syrup. Use as soon as the glaze begins to thicken and work quickly to apply it. If the glaze becomes too thick before you can use it, or if it becomes lumpy, warm it to a liquid, then cool again to thicken.

CHEF'S TIP

If a fatty film develops on the top of the glaze once it has cooled, the chocolate you are using contains too much cocoa butter; it is probably semisweet or bittersweet instead of sweet. Decrease the amount of butter in the recipe to compensate. If you desire a firmer glaze, increase the amount of sweet chocolate in the recipe.

Orange Glaze yield: approximately 1 cup (240 ml)

1 cup (240 ml) orange preserves or
   marmalade

3 ounces (85 g) granulated sugar

¹/₃ cup (80 ml) water

1. Place the preserves or marmalade, sugar, and water in a heavy-bottomed saucepan. Bring to a boil over medium heat, stirring constantly.

2. Reduce the heat to low and continue to cook, stirring from time to time, until the mixture has reduced sufficiently to hold a thread ¹/₄ inch (6 mm) long when pulled between your thumb and index finger or between the backs of 2 spoons.

3. Quickly remove the pan from the heat and strain the glaze. Discard the solids in the strainer. Use the glaze immediately. Store leftover glaze at room temperature. To reuse, add a small amount of water and heat to boiling.

Pectin Glaze yield: approximately 3 cups (720 ml)

Pectin glaze is used in combination with tartaric acid solution, which acts as a catalyst to make the glaze jell and also gives it a slightly tart flavor that especially complements fruit. The ability to jell quickly prevents the glaze from soaking into the fruit; instead, it leaves a thin, shiny coat on the outside. Pure pectin powder can be purchased from a chemical supplier or, in some cases, from a pharmacy.

3 cups (720 ml) water

1 tablespoon (9 g) pure pectin powder (grade USP-NF)

1 pound 6 ounces (625 g) granulated sugar

Tartaric Acid Solution (page 629)

1. Heat the water to the scalding point in a saucepan.

2. In the meantime, mix the pectin powder with 3 ounces (85 g) of the sugar. Whisk into the scalded water, making sure it is thoroughly combined. Bring the mixture to a boil, then stir in the remaining sugar. Return to a boil, but this time check to see exactly when the mixture begins to boil, then reduce the heat and boil for 8 to 12 minutes (see Note). Remove from the heat; let cool.

3. Skim off any foam or scum that appears on the surface. Stored, covered, in the refrigerator, pectin glaze will keep for months at this stage.

4. To set (jell) the glaze, use approximately 4 drops of tartaric acid solution for every 1 ounce (30 ml) pectin glaze; stir in the tartaric acid quickly and use the glaze immediately. The amount required will vary with the consistency of the glaze. The flavor should definitely be tart, but not to the point where it is unpleasant. In addition, adding too much solution, and thereby too much liquid, can prevent the glaze from setting. Add tartaric acid only to the amount of glaze you are ready to use at the moment, because once it is set it is difficult to soften it without the glaze forming lumps. You can keep the glaze from setting up while you are working by stirring it every few seconds.

NOTE: For a quick test, remove 1 to 2 tablespoons (15 to 30 ml) glaze and chill it. Add the appropriate amount of tartaric acid, as described in Step 4. If the glaze does not set properly, bring the solution back to a boil and cook for 1 to 2 minutes. If the glaze sets up too fast or too thick, add a small amount of water. Always test the glaze before applying it to food.

Plain Mirror Glaze yield: 1 cup (240 ml)

1 tablespoon (9 g) unflavored gelatin powder

½ cup (120 ml) cold water

½ cup (120 ml) simple syrup

1. Sprinkle the gelatin over the cold water and set aside until softened. Heat the mixture over a bain-marie until dissolved; do not overheat.

2. Stir the simple syrup into the gelatin mixture. Use the glaze as soon as it begins to thicken. If the glaze becomes too thick before you can apply it, warm it to a liquid and let it thicken again.

Red Currant Glaze yield: 2 cups (480 ml)

1 pound (455 g) red currant jelly   4 ounces (115 g) granulated sugar

1. Place the jelly and sugar in a saucepan. Stirring constantly, bring to a boil over low heat. Keep stirring until all lumps have dissolved.

2. Lower the heat and simmer for a few minutes or until the mixture has a glossy shine. Strain; use immediately. Store leftover glaze in a covered container. Reheat until liquid to use again.

Graham Crackers and Crumbs

yield: 70 crackers, 2 × 2 inches (5 × 5 cm), or 1 pound 8 ounces (680 g) crumbs

I'm sure many of us have, on occasion, found the pantry fresh out of graham cracker crumbs when they were needed for cheesecake. While it is less convenient to make the crackers and crumbs the old-fashioned way, doing so sets you back only about 30 minutes (in an emergency, keep the dough fairly firm to speed the baking and drying process). Once you try these, I think you will find producing your own an advantage in both cost and quality. It is a good idea to keep the crumbs on hand as part of your regular mise en place so they are available when needed. Graham cracker crumbs can be stored at room temperature for several weeks.

6 ounces (170 g) bread flour

6 ounces (170 g) cake flour

2 ounces (55 g) whole wheat flour

2 ounces (55 g) dark brown sugar

1 teaspoon (4 g) baking soda

1 teaspoon (5 g) salt

3 ounces (85 g) unsalted butter, at room temperature

½ cup (120 ml) or 6 ounces (170 g) honey

1 teaspoon (5 ml) vanilla extract

⅓ cup (80 ml) water

GRAHAM CRACKERS

1. Thoroughly combine the bread flour, cake flour, whole wheat flour, brown sugar, baking soda, and salt in a mixer bowl.

2. Using the dough hook, incorporate the butter, honey, vanilla extract, and water. Mix until a smooth and pliable dough has formed, adding more water if necessary. Do not overmix.

3. Using flour to prevent sticking, roll out the dough to a rectangle, 10 × 14 inches (25 × 35 cm). Mark the dough with a docker or the tines of a fork.

4. Cut the rectangle into 2-inch (5-cm) squares. Transfer the squares to a sheet pan lined with baking paper.

5. Bake at 325°F (163°C) for approximately 15 minutes or until dry. Store in an airtight container.

GRAHAM CRACKER CRUMBS

1. Prepare the dough as for graham crackers, but roll it out to ⅛ inch (3 mm) thick.

2. Cut the sheet into small pieces; it is not necessary to measure them. Transfer to a sheet pan lined with baking paper.

3. Bake at 325°F (163°C) until dark golden brown. Let cool.

4. Grind the cooled pieces in a food processor to make fine crumbs. Store in an airtight container.

Hazelnut Paste yield: 1 cup (240 ml)

In most professional operations, this item is typically purchased rather than made. The commercial product is more concentrated, so you may need to decrease the amount specified in the recipes if you substitute purchased paste.

8 ounces (225 g) hazelnuts   ⅓ cup (80 ml) simple syrup

1. Toast the hazelnuts and remove the skins.

2. Process the hazelnuts and simple syrup together in a food processor until the mixture becomes a thick paste. Store in an airtight container at room temperature.

Linzer Dough yield: 1 pound 14 ounces (855 g)

At first glance, this dough appears fairly simple, and although that is true, for the most part, Linzer dough is a bit deceiving in that it can become unusable if you are not careful. It is critical that the hazelnuts be ground to a fine consistency. (If you grind them in a food processor, add half of the sugar to the nuts while grinding to absorb the oil and keep the nuts from turning into a paste.) If the nuts are not ground finely enough, it is impossible to move a rolled sheet of dough without it falling apart. Overmixing the dough will cause the same problem — in this case, a result of incorporating too much air.

6 ounces (170 g) granulated sugar

8 ounces (225 g) unsalted butter, at room temperature

3 egg yolks (¼ cup/60 ml)

8 ounces (225 g) bread flour

2 teaspoons (3 g) ground cinnamon

½ teaspoon (1 g) ground cloves

6 ounces (170 g) finely ground hazelnuts

2 teaspoons (12 g) grated lemon zest

1. Using the dough hook on low speed, combine the sugar, butter, and egg yolks in a mixer bowl.

2. Sift the flour with the cinnamon and cloves.

3. Add the flour mixture, hazelnuts, and lemon zest to the butter mixture; mix just until all ingredients are incorporated and smooth.

4. Cover the dough and refrigerate on a paper-lined sheet pan.

Macaroon Decorating Paste

Prepare the recipe for Small Almond Macaroons (page 57), making the paste a bit firmer by using fewer egg whites. The paste should be soft enough to be piped out without monumental effort, but it should not change shape at all during baking. Macaroon paste should always be baked in a hot oven; follow the directions in the individual recipe.

Mascarpone Cheese yield: I pound 8 ounces (680 g)

Mascarpone cheese is made from fresh cream derived from cow's milk. The cream is reduced to near triple-cream consistency to give the cheese its soft, smooth, rich texture. This cream cheese originated in the Lombardy region of Italy but is now made throughout the country. The flavor of mascarpone blends beautifully with other food, especially fruit. Fresh figs with mascarpone is a classic combination, although tiramisù is probably the mascarpone dessert most people think of first.

Because mascarpone is highly perishable and the imported product is expensive, the time invested in making it yourself is worthwhile.

2 quarts (1 L 920 ml) heavy cream	**1 teaspoon (5 ml) Tartaric Acid Solution (page 629)**

1. Bring the cream to a boil in a heavy oversized saucepan. Boil over medium heat until reduced by one-third to about 5¼ cups (1 L 260 ml). As the cream is reducing, it should bubble but not boil hard; if it reduces too quickly, the fat can separate as it cools (see Note).

2. Remove the pan from the heat, place in an ice bath, and stir the reduced cream until it is cold.

3. Stir in the tartaric acid solution, return the saucepan to the heat, and bring the mixture to 118°F (48°C). Remove from the heat.

4. Line a strainer with three layers of cheesecloth and set it over a bowl or pan to catch the liquid. Pour the cream mixture into the strainer. Cover and refrigerate overnight.

5. Remove the thickened mascarpone from the cheesecloth and discard the liquid in the bowl. If the cheese has not thickened properly, add another ½ teaspoon (2.5 ml) tartaric acid solution, reheat to 118°F (48°C), and repeat Steps 4 and 5. Store, covered, in the refrigerator.

NOTE: If the fat should separate while the mixture is draining, let the mascarpone sit at room temperature for 1 to 2 hours, then blend until smooth in a food processor.

More About Mascarpone
Uses for mascarpone are certainly not limited to dessert. A specialty of Trieste, in the northeast corner of Italy, is a mixture of mascarpone, anchovies, mustard, and spices. Another popular appetizer preparation is a layered torte alternating mascarpone with pesto or smoked salmon.

French Meringue yield: approximately 5 quarts (4 L 800 ml)

French meringue is best for baking *au naturel,* piping into shapes for cookies and dessert shells, mixing with nuts, and use as a cake base. If made and baked correctly, French meringue is tender, light, and fragile. It should be piped or spread immediately after whipping, or the egg whites may start to separate from the sugar; it should then be baked immediately. To guard against salmonella, do not add this type of meringue to fillings that will be eaten raw unless you use pasteurized egg whites. Even then, French meringue is not the best choice as it contains undissolved sugar that gives it a grainy texture when consumed before baking.

2 cups (480 ml) egg whites, at room temperature

3 drops lemon juice *or* Tartaric Acid Solution (page 629)

2 pounds (910 g) granulated sugar

1. In a copper or stainless steel bowl, whip the egg whites with the lemon juice or tartaric acid at high speed until the mixture quadruples in volume and has the consistency of thick foam, 1 to 2 minutes.

2. Still whipping at high speed, gradually add the sugar; this should take about 3 minutes. Continue to whip the meringue at high speed until stiff peaks form. Do not overwhip.

3. Immediately pipe or spread the meringue into the desired shape.

4. Bake at 210° to 220°F (99° to 104°C) until dry, or follow the instructions given in individual recipes.

Italian Meringue yield: approximately 5 quarts (4 L 800 ml)

Italian meringue is a good choice if the meringue must stand for some time before it is used. It is denser than French or Swiss meringue because the egg whites are partially cooked; therefore, it holds up longer before starting to deflate. Italian meringue is also preferable for use in desserts where it is eaten raw, or with only partial further cooking — for example, when added to a filling or when only the outside is browned, as in baked Alaska. When Italian meringue is baked all the way through, it is harder than French meringue and unpleasant to eat.

2 cups (480 ml) egg whites

1 pound 8 ounces (680 g) granulated sugar

12 ounces (340 g) or 1 cup (240 ml) light corn syrup

1 cup (240 ml) water

1. Place the egg whites in a mixer bowl so you will be ready to start whipping them when the sugar syrup is ready.

2. Boil the sugar, corn syrup, and water. When the syrup reaches 230°F (110°C), begin whipping the egg whites at high speed. Continue boiling the syrup until it reaches 240°F (115°C) — the soft-ball stage (see page 827).

3. Remove the syrup from the heat and lower the mixer speed to medium. Pour the syrup into the egg whites in a thin, steady stream between the whip and the side of the bowl; if the syrup hits the whip, it will splatter and cause lumps. Return the mixer to high speed and continue to whip the meringue until it has cooled completely and forms stiff peaks.

NOTE: It is important to use a small pan when making only a quarter-recipe of Italian meringue, or it becomes almost impossible to get an accurate reading from the sugar thermometer because there is so little syrup in the pan. Easier still is to make ½ recipe and discard half of the finished meringue. The cost of the small amount of egg whites and sugar lost is not as valuable as your time.

Japonaise Meringue Batter

yield: enough to form 4 shells, 10 inches (25 cm) in diameter, or 90 shells, 2½ inches (5.6 cm) in diameter

Japonaise meringue is made using the same method as French meringue, but unlike French meringue, which is generally piped into shapes, Japonaise meringue is piped or spread into thin layers to be used as a component of a cake or pastry. It is possible to form the layers with an underwhipped meringue but after baking they will be hard instead of crisp and airy. When used in a cake these underwhipped layers make it impossible to cut the cake without breaking them; when used in pastries, the layers are unpleasant to eat. Be sure to whip the whites to stiff peaks as instructed and take care not to deflate the mixture while forming it.

8 ounces (225 g) finely ground blanched almonds (see Note)	1 cup (240 ml) egg whites
1 ounce (30 g) cornstarch	11 ounces (310 g) granulated sugar

1. Prepare your sheet pans, pastry bag, and a template, if you are using one.

2. Combine the ground almonds and cornstarch; reserve.

3. Whip the egg whites to a foam; they should quadruple in volume. Gradually add the sugar and whip to stiff peaks.

4. Gently fold the almond mixture into the egg whites by hand. Pipe or spread into the desired shape immediately. Bake as directed in individual recipes.

NOTE: If you do not have blanched almonds already ground (almond meal), combine 8 ounces (225 g) whole or sliced blanched almonds with one-third of the sugar and grind together in a food processor to a fine consistency. Process by pulsing on and off to prevent the mixture from heating up and sticking together.

Meringue Noisette

yield: 4 shells, 10 inches (25 cm) in diameter, or about 60 shells, 3 inches (7.5 cm) in diameter

The most efficient way to form the 3-inch (7.5-cm) shells is to spread the meringue over a rubber template made for this purpose. If you do not have a template, draw 30 evenly spaced circles, 3 inches (7.5 cm) in diameter, on a full sheet of baking paper. Place a second sheet of paper on top and pipe out the shells within the circles. Drag the paper with the meringue to a sheet pan. Invert the paper with the drawn circles onto a second pan, and pipe the remaining shells.

4 ounces (115 g) hazelnuts, toasted

1 ounce (30 g) cornstarch

1 cup (240 ml) egg whites

1 pound (455 g) granulated sugar

1 teaspoon (5 ml) vanilla extract

1. Draw 4 circles, 10 inches (25 cm) in diameter, on 2 sheets of baking paper (or follow the directions in the introduction if making the smaller size). Place the papers upside down on sheet pans and set aside.

2. Remove as much skin from the toasted hazelnuts as comes off easily, then grind the nuts to a fine consistency. Combine with the cornstarch.

3. Whip the egg whites to a thick foam; they should quadruple in volume. Still whipping, gradually add the sugar, taking 3 to 4 minutes to add all of it. Continue to whip the meringue until it forms stiff peaks. Add the vanilla. Gently fold the nut and cornstarch mixture into the meringue by hand.

FIGURE 14-2 **Piping meringue noisette batter into a spiral within a circle drawn on a sheet of paper**

4. Place the batter in a pastry bag with a No. 4 (8-mm) plain tip (use a No. 3 [6-mm] tip if making the smaller size). Pipe the batter in a spiral within the 4 circles drawn on the papers, starting in the center and working to the outside (Figure 14-2).

5. Bake immediately at 250°F (122°C) for approximately 1 hour or until dry.

Swiss Meringue yield: approximately 3 quarts (2 L 880 ml)

Swiss meringue can be described as a mixture of French and Italian meringues. Because the egg whites are pasteurized by being heated to 140°F (60°C) with the sugar, this meringue can be eaten raw. It is quicker and easier to produce than its Italian counterpart, but it is not as stable and should be used fairly soon once it has been prepared. It is typically used in buttercream and fillings, but it can also be piped into cookies or made into other shapes, then baked or dried in the same way as French meringue. However, for this use, Swiss meringue should be made with less sugar to ensure better volume and stiff peaks.

2 cups (480 ml) egg whites

1 pound 4 ounces to 1 pound 12 ounces (570 to 795 g) granulated sugar (see Note)

1. Combine the egg whites and sugar in a mixer bowl. Place the bowl over simmering water and heat to 140°F (60°C), whipping constantly to avoid cooking the egg whites.

2. Remove from the heat and whip the mixture at high speed until it has cooled completely.

NOTE: If the meringue is to be piped or spread on top of a dessert, or if it will be dried in the oven, use less sugar to ensure a stiffer and lighter meringue. If the meringue is to be added to a filling or used to make buttercream, use the full amount of sugar.

Pâte à Choux

yield: 5 pounds 8 ounces (2 kg 500 g) or enough for approximately 70 to 100 profiteroles, 1½ to 2 inches (3.7 to 5 cm) in diameter, or about 60 éclairs, 4 to 5 inches (10 to 12.5 cm) long

8 ounces (225 g) cake flour

11 ounces (310 g) bread flour

1 quart (960 ml) water

12 ounces (340 g) unsalted butter

1½ teaspoons (7.5 g) salt

1 quart (960 ml) eggs

1 teaspoon (3.5 g) ammonium carbonate (optional)

Small-Batch Pâte à Choux

yield: 2 pounds 12 ounces (1 kg 250 g) or enough for approximately 35 to 50 profiteroles, 1 to 2 inches (3.7 to 5 cm) in diameter, or about 30 éclairs, 4 to 5 inches (10 to 12.5 cm) long

4 ounces (115 g) cake flour

5½ ounces (155 g) bread flour

1 pint (480 ml) water

6 ounces (170 g) unsalted butter

½ teaspoon (2.5 g) salt

1 pint (480 ml) eggs

¼ teaspoon (1 g) ammonium carbonate (optional)

---

1. Sift the flours together on a sheet of baking paper and reserve.

2. Heat the water, butter, and salt to a full rolling boil, so the fat is not just floating on the top but is dispersed throughout the liquid.

3. Form the ends of the baking paper into a pouring spout. Using a heavy wooden spoon, stir the flour into the liquid, adding it as fast as it can be absorbed. Avoid adding all of the flour at once, which can make the paste lumpy.

4. Cook, stirring constantly and breaking up the inevitable lumps by pressing them against the side of the pan with the back of the spoon, until the mixture forms a mass and pulls away from the sides of the pan, about 2 to 3 minutes.

5. Transfer the paste to a mixer bowl. (If you are making the small recipe, leave the paste in the saucepan.) Let the paste cool slightly so the eggs will not cook when they are added.

6. Using the paddle attachment at low or medium speed, or a spoon if making the small recipe, mix in the eggs, 2 at a time. After the first few eggs are incorporated, add the ammonium carbonate if using. Add as many eggs as the paste can absorb and still hold its shape when piped.

7. Pipe the paste into the desired shape, according to the individual recipe.

8. Bake at 425°F (219°C) until fully puffed and starting to show some color, about 10 minutes (see Note). Reduce the heat to 375°F (190°C) and bake about 10 to 12 minutes longer, depending on size.

9. Let the pastries cool at room temperature. Speeding the process by placing them in the refrigerator or freezer can cause them to collapse.

NOTE: If you experience the problem of the pastries over-expanding in the oven (losing their piped shape), it may be the fault of your oven. Instead of reducing the oven temperature in Step 8, turn the oven off at this point and complete the baking using just the residual heat left in the oven. This will allow the pastries to dry out more gradually.

Puff Pastry yield: approximately 11 pounds (5 kg)

BUTTER BLOCK

4 pounds 6 ounces (1 kg 990 g) unsalted butter, cold

1 teaspoon (5 g) salt

3 tablespoons (45 ml) lemon juice

1 pound 2 ounces (510 g) bread flour

DOUGH

3 tablespoons (45 g) salt

1 quart (960 ml) water

7 ounces (200 g) unsalted butter, melted for Production method; firm for European method

1 tablespoon (15 ml) lemon juice

14 ounces (400 g) cake flour

2 pounds 4 ounces (1 kg 25 g) bread flour

Small-Batch Puff Pastry
yield: approximately 2 pounds 12 ounces (1 kg 250 g)

BUTTER BLOCK

1 pound 2 ounces (510 g) unsalted butter, cold

Pinch of salt

2 teaspoons (10 ml) lemon juice

4½ ounces (130 g) bread flour

DOUGH

2 teaspoons (10 g) salt

1 cup (240 ml) water

2 ounces (55 g) unsalted butter, melted for Production method; firm for European method

1 teaspoon (15 ml) lemon juice

3½ ounces (100 g) cake flour

11 ounces (310 g) bread flour

TO MAKE THE BUTTER BLOCK

1. Work the cold butter into the proper consistency (see Note) with the warmth of your hand. Dissolve the salt in the lemon juice. Mix into the butter together with the bread flour.

2. Shape into a 12-inch (30-cm) square (a 6-inch/15-cm square for the small-batch recipe); refrigerate until firm.

NOTE: The butter block should not be so soft that it is hard to handle; you should be able to transfer the finished block easily from one hand to the other. It should not be so firm that it cracks or breaks if you press on it. Ideally, the dough and the butter block should have the same consistency. A dough that is softer than the butter will be forced to the sides by the firmer butter; a dough that is too firm will force the butter out on the sides. Either will result in poor-quality puff pastry. Remember that the dough needs to rest for 30 minutes; try to time your work so the dough and the butter block are ready simultaneously.

TO MAKE THE DOUGH USING A MIXER (PRODUCTION METHOD)

1. Using the dough hook at low or medium speed, dissolve the salt in the water. Add the melted butter, lemon juice, cake flour, and enough of the bread flour to make a soft, smooth dough; do not overmix. If you add too much flour, the dough will be too glutenous and rubbery.

2. Shape the dough into a tight ball. With a sharp knife, cut a cross halfway into the ball. Let rest for 30 minutes, covered, in the refrigerator.

TO MAKE THE DOUGH BY HAND (CLASSIC EUROPEAN METHOD)

In this preparation method, the ingredients are added in reverse order. You start by using the full measurement of both flours and, instead of adjusting the consistency of the dough with bread flour, adjust the amount of water added at the end. The butter is firm rather than melted. The dough is worked much less and, when finished, should be not soft, smooth, and elastic — quite the opposite.

1. Sift both flours together onto your work surface — preferably a marble slab or table. Cut the firm butter into chunks, place on top of the flour, and, using your fingertips, cut it into the flour, pinching it down until the mixture resembles coarse crumbs.

2. Shape into a mound, make a well in the center, and add the salt and most of the cold water to the well. Stir to dissolve the salt. Using the fingers of both hands, gradually mix the flour and butter into the water. If necessary, gradually add more water to form a dough that holds together but is fairly sticky and rough-looking.

3. Form the dough into a ball, kneading as little as possible. Flatten the dough a little and cut a cross halfway into the ball. Cover and let rest for 30 minutes in the refrigerator.

CHEF'S TIPS FOR WORKING WITH PUFF PASTRY

After you have made perfect puff pastry, there are many things to watch for as you work with it:

- Be careful not to damage the layer structure when rolling the dough. Never let your rolling pin roll over the edge of the dough, which mashes down the sides, and always apply even pressure as you are rolling so the butter is evenly distributed.

- As a general rule, puff pastry dough should rest 5 to 10 minutes between rolling out and cutting. It should then rest an additional 15 minutes after it has been made up (for example, into turnovers) before baking to eliminate shrinkage. If the dough seems particularly rubbery and shrinks back a lot as you roll it, let it rest a bit longer.

- As you cut the dough, hold the knife at a sharp 90-degree angle so the vertical edges of the dough are perfectly straight. This way, the dough will rise straight up in the oven.

- When using egg wash on a product made with puff pastry dough, take care not to let any drip on the side. This can seal the dough to the pan and prevent it from rising.

- Start baking puff pastry in a hot oven. If the oven is not hot enough, you will lose the effect of the steam and the butter will run out of the dough.

- Ideally, puff pastry made according to the recipe in this book is ready to use the day after it is started, with all 4 turns having been made before it is placed in the refrigerator overnight. If the situation demands, the dough can be given 2 turns only, then finished the following day to be ready for use on Day 3. Puff pastry should not be started if time will not permit at least 2 turns before leaving it overnight. The butter layer will be too thick and will break when the dough is rolled out the following day.

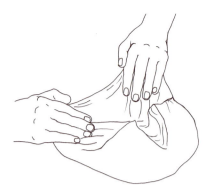

FIGURE 14-3 **Opening a cut ball of dough to make it square**

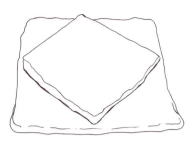

FIGURE 14-4 **Positioning a butter block diagonally on a dough square**

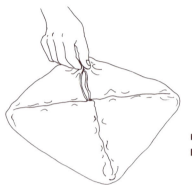

FIGURE 14-5 **Sealing a butter block inside dough**

TO ASSEMBLE

1. Pull out the corners of the cuts to make the dough square-shaped (Figure 14-3).

2. Roll out the opened dough to a square slightly thicker in the center than on the sides and slightly larger than the butter block.

3. Place the butter block diagonally within the square so there are 4 triangles around the sides (Figure 14-4). Fold the dough triangles in so they meet in the center. Pinch the edges together to seal in the butter block (Figure 14-5).

4. Roll the dough into a rectangle ½ inch (1.2 cm) thick. Do not roll the dough wider than a sheet pan is long.

5. Give the dough 4 double turns (instructions follow), refrigerating it for approximately 30 minutes between each turn. Be sure the dough is well covered at all times.

6. After the last turn, roll out the puff pastry to approximately ¾ inch (2 cm) thick. If this is difficult to do, refrigerate the dough for a few minutes to relax the gluten. Place the dough on a sheet pan lined with baking paper, cover, and refrigerate or freeze. Do not keep puff pastry dough in the refrigerator for more than 5 days.

TO MAKE A DOUBLE TURN

1. As carefully and evenly as possible, roll out the dough to a rectangle 30 × 20 inches (75 × 50 cm), or 15 × 10 inches (37.5 × 25 cm) for the small-batch recipe (see Chef's Tip). Arrange the dough with a long side closest to you.

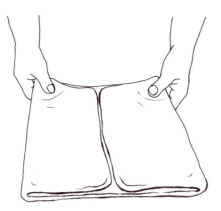

FIGURE 14-6 The first step of a double turn: folding in both short edges to meet at the center

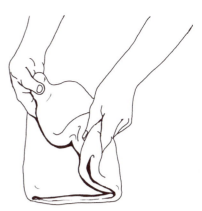

FIGURE 14-7 Completing a double turn: folding the dough in half as if closing a book

2. Make a vertical mark in the center of the rectangle. Fold both ends of the dough in to this mark (Figure 14-6).

3. Brush excess flour from the top of the dough and fold once more, as if you were closing a book (Figure 14-7). The dough now has 1 double turn.

4. Carefully place the dough on a sheet pan, cover, and refrigerate for 30 minutes.

5. When you begin the second double turn, place the dough in front of you so the short ends of the rectangle are on your left and right, opposite to the way the dough lay when you "closed the book" with the first turn. Roll out and turn as above; repeat as you make the remaining turns. After the dough has been given 4 double turns it contains 513 layers of butter and dough.

TO MAKE A SINGLE TURN

1. As carefully and evenly as possible, roll the dough to a rectangle ½ inch (1.2 cm) thick.

2. Divide the rectangle crosswise into thirds by sight alone, or mark the dough lightly with the edge of your hand.

3. Fold one-third of the dough over the middle section (Figure 14-8), then fold the remain-

CHEF'S TIP

When the dough for the small-batch recipe is rolled to make a double turn, it can easily become so thin that the layer structure is compressed and the dough's ability to rise is significantly decreased. A better option is to give the dough 5 single turns, as it does not have to be rolled out as large for a single turn as it does for a double turn. The single turns take slightly less time to complete, and you can be assured of a high-puffing dough at the end. Instructions for making a single turn follow.

Start by rolling the dough to 16 × 12 inches (40 × 30 cm), then make 5 single turns, resting the dough between each turn; the dough does not have to rest as long as for a double turn. When the dough is finished, it will have 487 layers of butter and dough — slightly fewer than with 4 double turns, but more than adequate. The classic French method calls for 1 more single turn, for a total of 6. This final turn requires great care as the number of layers jumps from 487 to 1459, and the layer structure becomes fragile.

FIGURE 14-8 The first step in making a single turn: folding one-third of the dough toward the center

FIGURE 14-9 Completing the single turn: folding the remaining one-third over the folded section

ing one-third over both of them (Figure 14-9), brushing away the excess flour from the inside as you fold. The dough now has 1 single turn.

4. Refrigerate, covered, for 30 minutes.

5. Position the dough so the long sides run horizontally, roll the dough to the same size rectangle as before, and make the second single turn.

6. Chill the dough, covered, for 30 minutes, then repeat the procedure to make the number of turns indicated in the recipe you are using.

Quick Puff Pastry yield: approximately 11 pounds 2 ounces (5 kg 60 g)

If you do not have time to make traditional puff pastry, quick puff pastry (also known as *blitz puff pastry*) is an efficient compromise. You will not get the height of the authentic version, but this recipe can easily be made — from scaling through baking — in 2 hours. It is perfect for lining tart pans or making fleurons and napoleons, when the dough must not puff up too much. In Europe, this type of dough is known as *American puff pastry*. The name came about because the method of making it resembles the technique used to make pie dough — and in Europe, pies are synonymous with the United States.

5 pounds (2 kg 275 g) bread flour

5 pounds (2 kg 275 g) unsalted butter, cold

2 tablespoons (30 g) salt

3 cups (720 ml) cold water

> **Small-Batch Quick Puff Pastry**
> yield: approximately 2 pounds 12 ounces
> (1 kg 250 g)
>
> 1 pound 4 ounces (570 g) bread flour
>
> 1 pound 4 ounces (570 g) unsalted butter, cold
>
> 1½ teaspoons (7.5 g) salt
>
> ¾ cup (180 ml) cold water

1. Place the flour in a mixer bowl.

2. Cut the butter, which should be firm but not hard, into 2-inch (5-cm) pieces (or about half this size for the small-batch recipe). Add to the flour while mixing at low speed with the dough hook; be careful not to knead.

3. Dissolve the salt in the water. Add to the flour and butter mixture and mix just until the dough can be handled. Mix carefully and for only a short time so that lumps of butter remain whole; the dough should look like well-made pie dough.

4. Shape the dough into a square and allow it to rest for 10 minutes. If your kitchen is warm, place the dough on a sheet pan lined with baking paper and let it rest in the refrigerator.

5. Roll out the dough to a rectangle ½ inch (1.2 cm) thick. Give the dough 3 single turns followed by 1 double turn (see single-turn instructions on page 787 and double-turn instructions on page 786). If the dough feels rubbery after you have completed the 3 single turns, let it rest for a few minutes and finish with a fourth single turn rather than a double. Cover and refrigerate.

NOTE: This dough does not need to rest between turns and is ready to use immediately after the last turn. However, after the dough has been rolled, it must rest 20 to 30 minutes before baking to prevent it from shrinking.

Plain Cake Syrup yield: 5 cups (1 L 200 ml)

Plain cake syrup is basically plain poaching syrup without any citric acid. If you have leftover poaching syrup after cooking fruit, keep it on hand to use as cake syrup instead; the subtle flavor from the fruit is a bonus. If the liquid has been reduced significantly during the poaching process, add water accordingly before using. Leftover poaching liquid must be stored in the refrigerator. If you have simple syrup made up, you may use that as a substitute for cake syrup as well. Add ¼ cup (60 ml) water to 1 cup (240 ml) simple syrup. Dilute only the amount required for each use.

1 quart (960 ml) water	1 pound (455 g) granulated sugar

1. Place the water and sugar in a saucepan and bring to a boil. Remove from the heat and let cool.

2. Store, covered, to use as needed. The syrup can be kept at room temperature for several weeks.

Plain Poaching Syrup yield: 5 cups (720 ml)

The basic ratio in poaching liquid is 2 parts water to 1 part sugar by weight. This can be modified depending on the desired sweetness of the finished product. After the first use, the syrup can be used again to poach fruit (you may need to replace the evaporated water) or as cake syrup. After poaching, any fruit that is susceptible to browning should be kept in the syrup until needed to prevent oxidation. Apricots are especially delicate and turn brown quickly. To keep the fruit submerged, place a towel or a sheet of baking paper on top and place a plate on top of that.

1 quart (960 ml) water	½ lemon, cut into wedges
1 pound (455 g) granulated sugar	1 teaspoon (5 ml) vanilla extract

1. Combine all of the ingredients in a saucepan and bring to a boil.

2. Proceed as directed in individual recipes or use the following instructions.

SPICED POACHING SYRUP

Follow the main recipe, but in Step 1, add 6 whole cloves and 1 cinnamon stick.

TO POACH PEARS OR APPLES

1. Peel and core apples or pears. Cut in half, if desired, and add to the poaching syrup in the saucepan. Place a lid or plate that fits down inside the saucepan on top of the fruit to keep it submerged; otherwise, the fruit will bob on top of the syrup and the exposed part will oxidize, turn brown, and not cook.

2. Quickly bring the syrup to a full boil and boil gently for about 5 minutes. Even if the fruit is fairly ripe, the poaching syrup should be brought to a boil so the heat penetrates the center of the fruit, preventing it from becoming brown.

3. Lower the heat and simmer very slowly until the fruit is tender and cooked all the way through. Do not poach the fruit too rapidly, or it will become overcooked on the outside and remain raw inside.

4. To check if pears or apples are done, pinch them gently with your fingers. They should feel soft but not mushy, having about the same amount of resistance as the fleshy part of your hand.

TO POACH PLUMS, PEACHES, APRICOTS, CHERRIES, AND OTHER FRAGILE FRUITS

1. Bring the syrup to a boil, add the fruit, and lower the heat immediately to simmer very gently; do not boil.

2. Cook the fruit until it is tender.

NOTE: Remove peaches after they have cooked for a few minutes. Peel off the skin (pull it away, do not cut into the fruit) with a small, pointed knife, then return them to the syrup and continue cooking until soft.

TO POACH OR RECONSTITUTE DRIED FRUIT

Allow the fruit to soak in cold water overnight, then add the appropriate amounts of sugar and lemon to the water to make a poaching liquid. Poach as directed for fresh fruit.

Rum Ball Filling yield: about 5 pounds 10 ounces (2 kg 560 g) filling

Rum ball filling is an excellent way to recycle good leftover pastries, end pieces, scraps, and other preparations, just as vegetable trimmings, bones, and some types of leftover sauces go into the stockpot in the hot kitchen. Throughout the day in a professional bakeshop, sponge cakes are trimmed to use for decorated cakes, perfectly good cookies and meringues break and cannot be sold, the ends of assembled pastry strips are trimmed before they can be sliced into neat portions, and so on. Rather than throwing these scraps away (although a fair share do get eaten, especially by students who have not yet become as jaded to these treats as long-time professionals), using them to create a moist chocolate and rum–flavored paste that can be made into a variety of pastries is a much more sensible and cost-effective alternative.

However, the rum ball bucket should not be mistaken for a garbage can. Only those scraps that will not spoil within a week or so should be added. No pastry cream or whipped cream should be used, and buttercream or buttercream-filled items should be used only if they are no more than one or two days old. The best kinds of scraps to use are slightly stale cookies, meringues, macaroons, Florentinas, ladyfingers, pastries such as Tosca or Polynées that do not contain buttercream, light or dark sponge cake, and baked short dough cookies or cake bottoms. Danish and other yeast-dough pastries should not be used in a rum ball mixture; recycle them in a bear claw filling.

¾ cup (180 ml) dark rum

6 ounces (170 g) dark raisins

4 pounds (1 kg 820 g) baked pastry or cake scraps (see introduction above)

¼ cup (60 ml) water

5 ounces (140 g) nuts, any variety, crushed fine

12 ounces (340 g) sweet dark chocolate or milk chocolate, melted

1. Heat the rum and raisins slightly; macerate for a few hours.

2. Place the scraps and water in a mixer bowl and mix with a paddle to a smooth consistency. You may have to adjust the amount of water, depending on how many dry items you are using. Mix approximately 10 minutes or until you have a very firm, smooth dough. Add the crushed nuts and the chocolate; mix until combined. Incorporate the rum and raisin mixture.

3. Place on a sheet pan lined with baking paper. Refrigerate the filling until firm before shaping. If it is too soft to work with, add more dry scraps, finely ground, to absorb moisture. If the filling is dry and crumbly, mix in enough buttercream or ganache to bring it to a workable consistency.

Short Dough

yield: 4 pounds 14 ounces (2 kg 220 g), enough to line about 90 tartlet pans, 2½ inches (6.2 cm) in diameter, or 6 tart pans, 11 inches (27.5 cm) in diameter

12 ounces (340 g) granulated sugar

1 pound 12 ounces (795 g) unsalted butter, at room temperature, *or* margarine

2 eggs

2 teaspoons (10 ml) vanilla extract

2 pounds 2 ounces (970 g) bread flour

Small-Batch Short Dough
yield: 2 pounds 6 ounces (1 kg 80 g)

6 ounces (170 g) granulated sugar

14 ounces (400 g) unsalted butter, at room temperature, *or* margarine

1 egg

1 teaspoon (5 ml) vanilla extract

1 pound (455 g) bread flour

---

1. Place the sugar, butter or margarine, eggs, and vanilla in a mixing bowl; mix at low speed with the dough hook just until combined.

2. Add the flour and mix just until the dough is smooth.

3. Place the dough on a paper-lined sheet pan; press as flat as possible so that the dough takes up less space and cools quickly. Cover and refrigerate until firm enough to work with, about 30 minutes.

NOTE: If overmixed, the dough will be difficult to roll out. This is especially true if you use all butter or a large percentage of butter.

Cocoa Short Dough yield: 4 pounds 12 ounces (2 kg 160 g)

8 ounces (225 g) granulated sugar

1 pound 12 ounces (795 g) unsalted butter, at room temperature, *or* margarine

2 eggs

2 teaspoons (10 ml) vanilla extract

2 pounds 4 ounces (1 kg 25 g) bread flour

1 ounce (30 g) unsweetened cocoa powder

> ## *Small-Batch Cocoa Short Dough*
> yield: 2 pounds 6 ounces (1 kg 80 g)
>
> 4 ounces (115 g) granulated sugar
>
> 14 ounces (400 g) unsalted butter, at room temperature, *or* margarine
>
> 1 egg
>
> 1 teaspoon (5 ml) vanilla extract
>
> 1 pound 2 ounces (510 g) bread flour
>
> 2 tablespoons (16 g) unsweetened cocoa powder

1. Place the sugar, butter or margarine, eggs, and vanilla in a mixing bowl. Mix at low speed with the dough hook just until combined.

2. Sift the flour with the cocoa powder, add to the dough, and mix just until smooth.

3. Place the dough on a paper-lined sheet pan; press as flat as possible. Cover and refrigerate.

Hazelnut Short Dough yield: 3 pounds (1 kg 365 g)

8 ounces (225 g) granulated sugar

1 pound (455 g) unsalted butter, at room temperature, or margarine

1 egg

½ teaspoon (2.5 ml) vanilla extract

1 pound 2 ounces (510 g) bread flour

4 ounces (115 g) hazelnuts, finely ground

1. Place the sugar, butter or margarine, egg, and vanilla in a mixing bowl; mix at low speed with the dough hook just long enough to incorporate the ingredients.

2. Add the flour and hazelnuts and mix just until the dough is smooth.

3. Place the dough on a paper-lined sheet pan; press as flat as possible. Cover and refrigerate.

Short Dough Cake Bottoms yield: 1 cake bottom, 10 inches (25 cm) in diameter

9 ounces (255 g) Short Dough (page 791)

1. Work the short dough smooth with your hands, shaping it to a thick circle in the process.

2. Start to roll out the dough to ⅛ inch (3 mm) thick and slightly larger than the size you need. Sprinkle just enough bread flour on the board to prevent sticking. Keep moving and turning the dough over as you roll it, first with your hands and then, as the dough gets thinner, by rolling it up on a dowel. Look closely at the dough as you roll it out. If only the edge of the dough is moving and not the middle, the middle is sticking to the table. Try to roll the dough into the general shape of what you plan to make. Trim the ragged edge that develops when the dough starts to get thin; it often tears away from the dough when you are picking it up or rolling it.

3. When the short dough is ⅛ inch (3 mm) thick, roll it up on a dowel (avoid using a rolling pin) and place on a sheet pan lined with baking paper or a Silpat.

4. Place a 10-inch (25-cm) cake ring or template on top of the short dough and cut around the outside edge; remove the leftover dough. If you cut the dough circle first and then transfer it to the sheet pan, it will probably stretch as you move it, resulting in an oval rather than a circle.

5. Prick the dough lightly so trapped air can escape.

6. Bake at 375°F (190°C) for about 10 minutes.

Simple Syrup (28° Baumé) yield: 3 quarts (2 L 880 ml)

Simple syrup is a useful ingredient to have on hand. If proper hygiene is observed during preparation and storage, it keeps almost indefinitely. Besides everyday uses, such as sweetening sorbets and parfaits, this syrup is used to thin fondant to the proper consistency before it is applied and to thicken chocolate for piping. I also use it as a quick cake syrup by adding ¼ cup (60 ml) water for every 1 cup (240 ml) simple syrup, plus an appropriate liqueur or other flavoring.

2 quarts (1 L 920 ml) water

2 pounds 8 ounces (1 kg 135 g) granulated sugar

2 cups (480 ml) or 1 pound 8 ounces (680 g) glucose *or* light corn syrup (see Chef's Tip)

1. Place the water, sugar, and glucose or corn syrup in a saucepan; stir to combine.

2. Heat to boiling and let boil for a few seconds (see Note).

3. Set aside to cool. Before pouring the syrup into bottles, skim off any scum that developed on the surface. Simple syrup should be refrigerated if kept for more than 2 to 3 weeks.

NOTE: Because it is often impossible to know exactly when the syrup has come to a boil (it would be silly to stand and watch it), do not be concerned about boiling the syrup just a little longer than specified in the recipe; its viscosity will not be adversely affected. However, boiling the syrup for as much as 5 minutes longer than the specified time will increase the Baumé to 30°; 10 minutes of boiling will bring it to 34°. Should this happen, let the syrup cool to approximately 60°F (16°C), use a Baumé thermometer to check the sugar content, and replace the evaporated water as needed to bring it to 28° Baumé. The water you add should first be boiled and then cooled to 60°F (16°C) to get an accurate reading and also to sterilize it so the syrup can be stored. Although it is simple enough to test the Baumé level, this procedure is really practical only for a large batch of syrup.

CHEF'S TIP
To avoid mess when measuring glucose or corn syrup, first weigh the sugar and leave it on the scale, then adjust the scale, make a well in the sugar, and pour the corn syrup into the well until you have the right amount. Glucose is too thick to pour but can easily be scooped with a wet hand. (The glucose or corn syrup is added to prevent the syrup from recrystallizing when stored.) If you are using a small amount of corn syrup in a recipe that does not have any sugar, it may be easier to measure the syrup by volume; both measurements are given throughout this text. Converting dry to liquid ounces is simple for corn syrup: Fluid ounces are two-thirds of dry ounces (for example, 6 ounces by weight = 4 fluid ounces.)

Sponge Cake yield: 2 cakes, 10 × 2 inches (25 × 5 cm)

Butter and Flour Mixture (page 750) *or* cake pan spray

12 eggs

12 ounces (340 g) granulated sugar

1 teaspoon (5 g) salt

8 ounces (225 g) cake flour

4 ounces (115 g) cornstarch

5 ounces (140 g) unsalted butter, melted

1. Brush butter and flour mixture over the inside of 2 cake pans, 10 inches (25 cm) in diameter, or coat the pans with cake pan spray. Reserve.

2. Place the eggs, sugar, and salt in a mixer bowl. Heat over simmering water to about 110°F (43°C), whipping continuously. Remove from the heat and whip at high speed until the mixture has cooled, is light and fluffy, and has reached its maximum volume.

3. Sift the flour and the cornstarch together and fold into the batter by hand (Figures 14-10 and 14-11). Fold in the melted butter. Divide the batter between the prepared pans.

4. Bake immediately at 400°F (205°C) for approximately 15 minutes. Let the sponges cool before removing them from the pans.

FIGURE 14-10 Folding flour into sponge cake batter by moving the hand around the sides of the bowl

FIGURE 14-11 Lifting the mixture from the bottom of the bowl to the top as the flour is incorporated

Chocolate Sponge Cake yield: 2 cakes, 10 × 2 inches (25 × 5 cm)

Butter and Flour Mixture (page 750) *or* cake
    pan spray

12 eggs

12 ounces (340 g) granulated sugar

1 teaspoon (5 g) salt

6 ounces (170 g) cake flour

4 ounces (115 g) cornstarch

2 ounces (55 g) unsweetened cocoa powder

4 ounces (115 g) unsalted butter, melted

1. Brush butter and flour mixture over the inside of 2 cake pans, 10 inches (25 cm) in diameter, or use cake pan spray. Reserve.

2. Place the eggs, sugar, and salt in a mixer bowl. Heat over simmering water to about 110°F (43°C), whipping continuously. Remove from the heat and whip at high speed until the mixture has cooled and is light and fluffy.

3. Sift the flour, cornstarch, and cocoa powder together and fold into the batter by hand. Fold in the melted butter. Divide the batter between the prepared pans.

4. Bake immediately at 400°F (205°C) for approximately 15 minutes. Let the sponges cool before removing them from the pans.

Almond Sponge yield: 2 sheets, 14 × 24 inches (35 × 60 cm), or 2 layers, 10 × 2 inches (25 × 5 cm)

2 egg whites (¼ cup/60 ml)

10 ounces (285 g) almond paste

12 whole eggs, separated

10 ounces (285 g) granulated sugar

1 teaspoon (5 ml) vanilla extract

7 ounces (200 g) cake flour, sifted

1. Gradually mix the 2 egg whites into the almond paste to soften it.

2. Whip the egg yolks with 3 ounces (85 g) of the sugar to the ribbon stage. Add the vanilla. Very gradually, add the yolk mixture to the almond paste mixture; if you add it too quickly, you are sure to get lumps.

3. Whip the egg whites to a foam. Gradually add the remaining 7 ounces (200 g) sugar and whip to stiff peaks.

4. Carefully fold the egg whites into the yolk mixture. Fold in the flour.

TO MAKE SHEETS

1. Immediately spread the batter on paper-lined sheet pans to 14 × 24 inches (35 × 60 cm), taking care not to overwork the sponge.

2. Bake at 425°F (219°C) for approximately 8 minutes or until just done.

NOTE: If the oven is not hot enough or if the sheets are overcooked (and therefore dried out), the sponge will not bend without breaking. To remedy this, place a damp towel on a sheet pan and place the sponge on top with the baking paper next to the towel. Invert a second sheet pan on top as a lid. Place in the oven (400°F/205°C) for 5 to 10 minutes to soften. If the sponge is to be used the next day, follow the same procedure, but soften in the refrigerator instead of in the oven.

1. Line the bottom of 2 cake pans, 10 inches (25 cm) in diameter, with baking paper, or grease and flour the pan bottoms but not the sides. Divide the batter between the pans.

2. Bake at 375°F (190°C) for about 25 minutes or until the sponge springs back when pressed lightly in the middle. When cold, cut the sponge away from the side of the pan with a thin, sharp knife.

VARIATION
COCOA-ALMOND SPONGE

yield: 2 sheets, 14 × 24 inches (35 × 60 cm), or 2 layers, 10 × 2 inches (25 × 5 cm)

Omit 3 ounces (85 g) flour and sift 3 ounces (85 g) unsweetened cocoa powder with the remaining flour.

Angel Food Cake   yield: 1 cake, 10 inches (25 cm) in diameter

Due to the tender and light structure of this cake, it is of the utmost importance that the ingredients are measured precisely and the directions followed exactly. It is also essential to use a tube pan to produce the traditional look and light composition. (You can bake angel food cake in 2 regular cake pans, 9 inches/22.5 cm in diameter, with a fairly good result, but the cakes will not have the same airiness.) The tube pan can be false-bottomed or not, and it does not have to have legs. The legs allow you to invert the baked cake so it cools without falling and, at the same time, they allow air to circulate around the entire cake. Hanging the inverted cake on the neck of a bottle works just as well.

4 ounces (115 g) cake flour, sifted	Pinch of salt
12 ounces (370 g) granulated sugar	2 teaspoons (10 ml) vanilla extract
12 egg whites (1½ cups/360 ml)	Grated zest of 1 lemon
1 teaspoon (2 g) cream of tartar	2 teaspoons (10 ml) lemon juice

1. Line the bottom of a tube pan, 10 inches (25 cm) in diameter, with a ring of baking paper.

2. Combine the flour with half of the sugar. Reserve.

3. Whip the egg whites with the cream of tartar and salt at high speed until they have tripled in volume. Gradually add the remaining sugar and continue whipping until the whites hold soft peaks. Remove from the mixer.

4. Set a sifter on a piece of baking paper. Place the flour and sugar mixture in it. Sift the mixture over the whipped egg whites, a little at a time, and gently fold it in together with the vanilla, lemon zest, and lemon juice. Be sure to fold in the flour-sugar mixture that fell through the sifter onto the baking paper. Place the batter in the prepared tube pan. Tap the pan firmly against the table a couple of times to release any large air pockets.

5. Bake at 325°F (163°C) for approximately 55 minutes or until the cake is golden brown on top and springs back when pressed lightly. Invert the pan onto its legs or over the neck of a bottle to allow air to circulate underneath as it cools upside down.

Chiffon Sponge Cake I yield: 2 cakes, 10 × 2 inches (25 × 5 cm)

The leavening in a chiffon sponge comes from both a chemical agent, baking powder, and the air whipped into the egg whites. This can make it a more practical choice in certain situations than the genoise type of sponge, which does not use a chemical leavener. The vegetable oil contributes moisture and gives the cake a longer shelf life than one made with butter. Further, chiffon cakes tolerate freezing (and thawing) without significant loss of quality.

The popularity of the chiffon method lessened somewhat in the professional industry following the introduction of the emulsifier method, which is even more convenient and practical in a professional setting, although overall flavor is sacrificed, to some extent.

In the following recipes, Chiffon Sponge Cake I is used to create round layers that are to be split and filled. Chiffon Sponge Cake II is used to make sheets. The formulas are fairly interchangeable should you find you prefer one to the other.

²/₃ cup (160 ml) vegetable oil	14 ounces (400 g) granulated sugar
8 egg yolks (²/₃ cup/160 ml)	4 teaspoons (16 g) baking powder
1 cup (240 ml) water, at room temperature	1 teaspoon (5 g) salt
1 tablespoon (15 ml) vanilla extract	8 egg whites (1 cup/240 ml)
14 ounces (400 g) cake flour	

1. Line 2 cake pans, 10 inches (25 cm) in diameter, with circles of baking paper, or grease and flour the bottoms but not the sides of the pans.

2. Whip the vegetable oil and the egg yolks together just until combined. Stir in the water and the vanilla extract.

3. Sift together the cake flour, one-third of the sugar, the baking powder, and the salt. Stir this into the egg-yolk mixture, then whip at high speed for 1 minute. Reserve.

4. Whip the egg whites to a foam. Gradually add the remaining sugar and continue whipping until stiff peaks form.

5. Carefully fold the meringue into the reserved batter. Divide the batter between the prepared pans.

6. Bake at 375°F (190°C) for approximately 25 minutes or until the cakes spring back when pressed lightly in the center.

7. Invert the pans on a rack and allow the cakes to cool in the pans before unmolding.

VARIATIONS

CHOCOLATE CHIFFON SPONGE CAKE I yield: 2 cakes, 10 × 2 inches (25 × 5 cm)

Decrease the cake flour by 3 ounces (85 g) and sift 3 ounces (85 g) unsweetened cocoa powder with the remaining flour.

LEMON CHIFFON SPONGE CAKE I yield: 2 cakes, 10 × 2 inches (25 × 5 cm)

Replace ½ cup (120 ml) water with ½ cup (120 ml) lemon juice. Add the grated zest of 3 lemons together with the water-juice mixture.

Chiffon Sponge Cake II yield: 1 half-sheet pan, 12 × 16 inches (30 × 40 cm)

7 ounces (200 g) cake flour

3 ounces (85 g) bread flour

1 tablespoon (12 g) baking powder

1 pound (455 g) granulated sugar

½ cup (120 ml) vegetable oil

6 egg yolks (½ cup/120 ml)

1 cup (240 ml) water

1 tablespoon (15 ml) vanilla extract

10 egg whites (1¼ cups/300 ml)

½ teaspoon (2.5 g) salt

I. Line the bottom of a half-sheet pan with baking paper or a Silpat. Set aside.

2. Sift the cake flour, bread flour, baking powder, and 12 ounces (340 g) of the sugar together.

3. Combine the oil, egg yolks, water, and vanilla. Mix until well incorporated. Gradually add the dry ingredients and mix until smooth, about 1 minute. Set aside.

4. Whip the egg whites with the remaining 4 ounces (115 g) sugar and the salt until stiff peaks form. Take care not to overwhip. Fold the whipped egg whites into the yolk and flour mixture. Spread the batter evenly over the half-sheet pan.

5. Bake at 375°F (190°C) for approximately 25 minutes or until the sheet springs back when pressed lightly in the center. Dust cake flour lightly over the top of the sheet and invert onto a sheet pan lined with baking paper. When the sheet has cooled slightly, remove from the pan. If necessary, run a thin knife around the inside perimeter before unmolding.

VARIATIONS
CHOCOLATE CHIFFON SPONGE CAKE II

Decrease the cake flour by 2 ounces (55 g) and sift 3 ounces (85 g) unsweetened cocoa powder with the remaining flour.

LEMON CHIFFON SPONGE CAKE II

Replace ½ cup (120 ml) water with the grated zest and juice of 3 lemons (approximately ½ cup/120 ml juice; adjust as desired), combining the juice and zest with the remaining water.

ORANGE CHIFFON SPONGE CAKE II

Replace ½ cup (120 ml) water with the grated zest and juice of 2 small oranges (approximately ½ cup/120 ml juice; adjust as desired), combining the juice and zest with the remaining water.

Dobos Sponge

yield: 3 sheets, 12 × 16 inches (30 × 40 cm), or 6 rounds, 10 inches (25 cm) in diameter and ¼ inch (6 mm) thick

12 ounces (340 g) unsalted butter, at room temperature

12 ounces (340 g) granulated sugar

12 egg yolks (1 cup/240 ml), at room temperature

1 teaspoon (5 ml) vanilla extract

1 teaspoon (5 g) salt

Grated zest of 1 lemon

12 egg whites (1½ cups/360 ml), at room temperature

8 ounces (225 g) sifted cake flour

5 ounces (140 g) finely ground almonds (almond meal; see Note 1)

1. If making sheets, cut 3 sheets of baking paper to 12 × 16 inches (30 × 40 cm). If making rounds for the Dobos torte, follow the directions with that recipe for preparing round templates.

2. Cream the butter with half of the sugar to a light and fluffy consistency. Beat in the egg yolks, a few at a time. Mix in the vanilla, salt, and lemon zest (see Note 2).

3. Whip the egg whites until foamy. Gradually add the remaining sugar and whip until soft peaks form. Carefully fold the whipped egg whites into the yolk mixture.

4. Combine the sifted flour with the ground almonds. Gently fold the flour and almond mixture into the egg mixture.

5. Immediately spread the batter evenly over the 3 sheets of baking paper, leaving ¼ inch (6 mm) paper uncovered around all 4 edges. Drag the papers onto sheet pans. If making rounds, follow the directions in the Dobos torte recipe to shape the batter.

6. Bake at 425°F (219°C) for about 10 minutes or until baked through.

NOTE 1: If you have neither almond meal nor the proper equipment to make it, add part of the sugar from the recipe (taking it away from the amount used in Step 1) to blanched (dry) almonds and process to a fine consistency in a food processor. The sugar will absorb some of the oil released by the almonds and prevent the mixture from caking.

NOTE 2: If the egg yolks are not approximately the same temperature as the butter and sugar mixture, the emulsion will break when they are added. If this happens, warm the broken mixture over a bain-marie, stirring constantly, before folding in the egg whites.

VARIATION

COCOA DOBOS SPONGE yield: 1 sheet, 16 × 24 inches (40 × 60 cm)

Delete 2 ounces (55 g) cake flour and sift 2 ounces (55 g) unsweetened cocoa powder with the remaining flour.

Hazelnut-Chocolate Sponge yield: 2 cakes, 10 inches (25 cm) in diameter

Butter and Flour Mixture (page 750) *or* cake pan spray

14 eggs

12 ounces (340 g) granulated sugar

1 teaspoon (5 ml) vanilla extract

1 teaspoon (5 g) salt

8 ounces (225 g) bread flour

6 ounces (170 g) hazelnuts, toasted and finely ground (see Note)

3 ounces (85 g) sweet dark chocolate, grated

4 ounces unsalted butter, melted

1. Brush butter and flour mixture inside 2 cake pans, 10 inches (25 cm) in diameter, or coat with cake pan spray. Reserve.

2. Combine the eggs, sugar, vanilla, and salt in a mixer bowl. Heat over simmering water until the mixture reaches about 110°F (43°C), whipping continuously. Remove from the heat and whip at high speed until the mixture has cooled and has a light and fluffy consistency.

3. Sift the flour. Mix in the hazelnuts and chocolate, then carefully fold into the batter by hand. Fold in the melted butter. Divide the batter between the prepared pans.

4. Bake immediately at 400°F (205°C) until the cakes spring back when pressed lightly on top, approximately 15 minutes. Allow the sponges to cool completely before removing them from the pans.

NOTE: If you are using a food processor to grind them, add about one-quarter of the sugar to the nuts. The sugar will absorb any oil released by the nuts due to the heat and friction.

High-Ratio Sponge Cake yield: 2 cakes, 10 × 2 inches (25 × 5 cm)

Butter and Flour Mixture (page 750) *or* cake pan spray

14 eggs, at room temperature

1 pound 2 ounces (510 g) granulated sugar

1 pound (455 g) cake flour

2 tablespoons (24 g) baking powder

10 ounces (285 g) emulsified shortening, at room temperature

1 cup (240 ml) whole milk, at room temperature

2 teaspoons (10 ml) vanilla extract

1. Brush butter and flour mixture over the inside of 2 cake pans, 10 inches (25 cm) in diameter, or coat with pan spray. Reserve.

2. Place the eggs, sugar, cake flour, and baking powder in a mixer bowl. Using the whip attachment, stir at low speed until the mixture forms a paste. Add the shortening and whip at high speed for 2 minutes, scraping down the sides of the bowl as needed. Lower the speed and incorporate the milk and vanilla. Continue whipping 1 minute longer.

3. Divide the batter evenly between the prepared pans.

4. Bake at 375°F (190°C) for approximately 20 minutes or until the cakes spring back when pressed lightly in the center.

VARIATION

HIGH-RATIO CHOCOLATE SPONGE CAKE yield: 2 cakes, 10 × 2 inches (25 × 5 cm)

Replace 4 ounces (115 g) cake flour with 4 ounces (115 g) unsweetened cocoa powder.

Ladyfingers yield: approximately 180 cookies, 2 inches (5 cm) long

4 ounces (115 g) bread flour

6 eggs, separated

6 ounces (170 g) granulated sugar

Few drops of Tartaric Acid Solution (page 629) *or* lemon juice

3 ounces (85 g) cornstarch

1. Sift the flour and reserve.

2. Whip the egg yolks and one-third of the sugar at high speed until light and creamy; reserve.

3. Add half of the remaining sugar and the tartaric acid or lemon juice to the egg whites. Whip the egg white mixture at high speed until it is foamy and has tripled in volume, about 2 minutes.

4. Combine the remaining sugar and the cornstarch. Gradually add this to the egg white mixture and whip to stiff peaks.

5. Fold in the reserved egg yolk and sugar mixture, then fold in the sifted flour. Follow the instructions in a particular recipe if not making individual ladyfingers.

6. Place the batter in a pastry bag with a No. 5 (10-mm) plain tip. Pipe cookies, 2 inches (5 cm) long, onto sheet pans lined with baking paper or Silpats (Figure 14-12).

7. Bake at 425°F (219°C) for about 8 minutes or until golden brown. Stored in a dry place, ladyfingers will keep for weeks.

FIGURE 14-12 Piping ladyfingers onto a sheet pan lined with a Silpat; baked ladyfingers after removing them from the oven

VARIATION

CHOCOLATE LADYFINGERS yield: approximately 180 cookies, 2 inches (5 cm) long

Replace 1 ounce (30 g) cornstarch with 1 ounce (30 g) unsweetened cocoa powder.

Lemon Ladyfingers yield: approximately 50 cookies, 4 inches (10 cm) long

8 egg yolks (⅔ cup/160 ml)

6 ounces (170 g) granulated sugar

Finely grated zest of 1 lemon

8 egg whites (1 cup/240 ml)

2 ounces (55 g) cornstarch

5 ounces (140 g) cake flour

Powdered sugar

1. Whip the egg yolks with one-third of the granulated sugar to a stiff ribbon stage; the mixture will be fluffy and light in color. Reserve.

2. Thoroughly combine the lemon zest and the remaining sugar. Gradually adding the lemon-sugar mixture, whip the egg whites to soft peaks. Turn the mixer to low speed, add the cornstarch, then whip at high speed until stiff peaks form.

3. Fold the reserved yolk mixture into the egg whites, followed by the flour.

4. Place in a pastry bag with a No. 8 (16-mm) plain tip. Pipe into cookies 4 inches (10 cm) long on sheet pans lined with baking paper. Sift powdered sugar lightly over the top.

5. Bake immediately at 400°F (205°C) until golden brown.

Unflavored Yogurt yield: 4 cups (960 ml)

Making your own yogurt will take only about five minutes away from your other work while you monitor the temperature of the milk in Step 1. The incubation takes care of itself, thanks to the bacteria cultures *lactobacillus bulgaricus* and *streptococcus thermophilous*. Basically, they consume lactose as a source of energy, thereby producing lactic acid during the incubation period, which, after the pH has reached 4 to 4.5, sets the liquid.

Fermented milk is nothing new. It was almost certainly consumed in some form as early as 6000 B.C., invented most likely by accident and then used as a convenient way to preserve milk. Yogurt made its way to Europe as early as the fifteenth century, but it was not until well into the 1900s that it became fashionable as a health food. Later, plain yogurt was mixed with fruits and flavorings to balance its sourness and became a popular commercial product. Frozen yogurt, which is similar in texture to soft ice cream but generally lower in fat, has been a big seller over the last decade or so. Just how healthy yogurt really is has been the source of debate for a long time. It is, no doubt, a good source of vitamin B, calcium, and protein, but it is, of course, only low in fat if made from low-fat milk to begin with.

5 cups (1 L 200 ml) whole, low-fat, or nonfat milk	¼ cup (60 ml) unflavored yogurt

1. In a thick-bottomed saucepan, heat the milk to a simmer, about 185°F (85°C), stirring frequently. Remove from the heat and let cool to 110°F (43°C; see Chef's Tip).

CHEF'S TIP

If you do not have a dairy thermometer that can be placed in the saucepan, you can make a convenient holder by laying a large spoon across the center of the pan. Place an inverted dinner fork at a 90-degree angle to the spoon with the tines of the fork balanced on the spoon handle. You can now insert your instant-read pocket thermometer through the tines of the fork and let it hang in the milk.

2. Place the yogurt in a mixing bowl, about 9 inches (22.5 cm) in diameter. Gradually stir in the cooled milk, continuing to stir until the mixture is smooth before adding the next portion. Cover the bowl with a plate, wrap 2 or 3 towels around the bowl and the lid, and set aside in a warm location to set the yogurt. This usually takes about 5 hours, depending on the temperature in your kitchen. If this is not 80°F (26°C) or above, and I sincerely hope it is not, place the bowl in a 90° to 100°F (32° to 38°C) oven. You can usually achieve this temperature by turning the oven off and on a few times during the first hour. Do not let the oven get too hot, or you will kill the bacteria.

3. Remove the towels and the plate and cover the bowl with plastic wrap. Store the yogurt in the refrigerator. Use ¼ cup (60 ml) of this batch to make the next batch, and so on.

Vanilla Extract yield: 1 quart (960 ml)

Making your own vanilla extract is as easy as 1, 2, 3 — it merely requires advance planning. The two whole beans added at the end are purely for decoration, but the extract does make a great place to store them.

8 long, soft vanilla beans   **1 quart (960 ml) good-quality vodka**

1. Split 6 of the beans lengthwise, then cut them into small pieces.

2. Put the vanilla pieces and the vodka in a jar with a lid and seal tightly.

3. Let stand in a dark, cool place for about 1 month, shaking the bottle from time to time.

4. Strain the liquid through a strainer lined with cheesecloth.

5. Clean the bottle and return the vanilla extract to the bottle.

6. Add the 2 remaining vanilla beans. Store, tightly sealed.

Vanilla Sugar

Vanilla sugar can be made according to a number of recipes. A simple way that also protects the beans from drying out when stored is to place split or whole vanilla beans in a jar of granulated sugar. The jar should be tall enough to hold the beans standing up and allow room for plenty of sugar around them. Make sure the jar is tightly sealed. Shake it once a day to circulate the sugar and increase the fragrance. After 1 week, the vanilla sugar is ready. As you use the vanilla sugar and the beans, keep adding more granulated sugar and more beans to the jar. Naturally, the more beans you store in the jar relative to the amount of sugar, the stronger the sugar's flavor and fragrance.

White Chocolate Sauce yield: approximately 4 cups (960 ml)

1 cup (240 ml) water   **½ cup (120 ml) glucose *or* light corn syrup**
10 ounces (285 g) granulated sugar   **1 pound 2 ounces (510 g) white chocolate**

1. Combine the water, sugar, and glucose or corn syrup in a saucepan and bring to a boil. Remove from the heat and set aside to cool slightly.

2. Cut the white chocolate into small pieces so it will melt quickly and evenly. Place in a bowl over a bain-marie and make sure the water is simmering, not boiling. Stir the chocolate constantly until it is melted, never letting it get too warm on the bottom and sides of the bowl. Stirring the chocolate constantly during melting is essential. Because white chocolate does not contain any cocoa mass, only the cocoa butter extracted from it, this type of "chocolate" becomes gritty and unusable if overheated.

3. Add the melted chocolate to the warm sugar syrup and stir until combined.

4. Before serving, adjust the consistency as needed. To thicken, warm the sauce lightly and add more melted chocolate. To thin the sauce, add water. White chocolate sauce may be served hot or cold. Store, covered, at room temperature for a few days, or refrigerate for longer storage.

Yogurt Cheese yield: 1¾ cups (420 ml)

While not a true cheese, yogurt (homemade or store-bought) thickened to the consistency of mascarpone can be substituted in some recipes for sour cream, crème fraîche, and cream cheese to reduce fat and calories. The substitution can be made in an equal quantity in recipes where the ingredient is not cooked — for example, Sour Cream Mixture for Piping and Romanoff Sauce, and when crème fraîche is used to accompany a dessert.

2 cups (480 ml) yogurt

1. Place yogurt in a strainer lined with cheesecloth and set the strainer over a bowl to catch the liquid. Cover and refrigerate for 24 hours.

2. Discard the liquid and store the yogurt cheese as you would yogurt.

Praline yield: 1 pound (455 g)

Praline is hard to work with in a humid climate or in wet weather because the sugar starts to break down and the praline becomes sticky. However, sticky praline is suitable to use in making Praline Paste.

4 ounces (115 g) hazelnuts   **8 ounces (225 g) granulated sugar**
4 ounces (115 g) blanched almonds   **1 teaspoon (5 ml) lemon juice**

1. Toast the hazelnuts and remove the skin. Toast the almonds lightly.

2. Lightly oil a marble slab or sheet pan.

3. Caramelize the sugar with the lemon juice to a light golden color. Immediately add the toasted nuts, stir to combine, and pour onto the oiled marble.

4. Let the praline cool, then crush with a dowel or rolling pin to the desired consistency.

PRALINE PASTE yield: 1 cup (240 ml)

Praline paste is used mainly for making candy and for flavoring cake and pastry fillings. As with hazelnut paste, making your own is time consuming, and you will be hard pressed to achieve the same result as the ready-made commercial product. Commercial praline paste is passed through a grinding machine equipped with stone rollers (known as an almond mill), which produces a superior result. Either this recipe or a purchased paste can be used in recipes in this book that call for praline paste.

1 recipe Praline (above)   **¼ cup (60 ml) simple syrup**

1. Crush the praline as fine as possible.

2. Place in a high-speed food processor and process, using the metal blade, gradually adding the simple syrup until the mixture becomes a fine paste. To prepare a small amount, you can use a coffee grinder.

APPENDIX:
WEIGHTS, MEASURES, AND YIELDS

The Metric System	805
Precise Metric Equivalents	806
Precise Metric Conversions	806
Metric and U.S. Equivalents: Length	807
Metric and U.S. Equivalents: Volume	809
U.S. Volume Equivalents	810
Metric and U.S. Equivalents: Weight	811
Temperature Scales	812
Temperature Equivalents	812
Temperature Conversions	815
Volume Equivalents of Commonly Used Products	816
Approximate Prepared Yields of Commonly Used Products	816
Volume Equivalents for Shelled Eggs, Average Size	817
Gelatin Equivalents and Substitutions	817
Yeast Equivalents and Substitutions	818
Gram Weight of Commonly Used Products	818
Volume and Weight Equivalents for Honey, Corn Syrup, and Molasses	818
Calculating a Cake Circumference	819
Cake Pan Capacities by Volume	819
Baker's Percentage	820
Gram Measurements in Rounded Percentages as They Relate to 16 Ounces (1 Pound) as 100 Percent	820
Ounce Measurements in Rounded Percentages as They Relate to 16 Ounces (1 Pound) as 100 Percent	823
High-Altitude Baking	824
Baumé Scale Readings	825
Brix Scale	826
Sugar Boiling Conversions	827

The Metric System

Accuracy of measurement is essential in achieving a good result in the pastry shop. Ingredients are therefore almost always weighed or *scaled,* to use the professional term. The few exceptions are eggs, milk, and water; for convenience, these are measured by volume at the rate of 1 pint to 1 pound, 1 liter to 1 kilogram, or, for a small quantity of eggs, by number. The system of measurement used in the United States is highly complicated and confusing compared to the simple metric system used just about everywhere else in the world. Under the U.S. system, the number of increments in any given unit of measure is arbitrarily broken down into numbers that have no correlation with each other. For example, there are 12 inches in 1 foot, 32 ounces in 1 quart, 4 quarts in 1 gallon, 3 teaspoons in 1 tablespoon, and so on. Adding to the confusion is the fact that ounces are used to measure both liquids by volume and solids by weight; so if you see the measurement "8 ounces melted chocolate," you do not really know if this means to weigh the ingredient or measure it in a cup. This can make a big difference in a particular recipe, as 1 cup (8 liquid ounces) melted chocolate weighs almost 10 ounces. The metric system, on the other hand, is divided into three basic units, one each for length, volume, and weight. (Centigrade and Fahrenheit, the temperature scales, are not part of the metric system.)

Meter is the unit used to measure length. It is divided into increments of millimeters, centimeters, and decimeters.

- 10 millimeters = 1 centimeter
- 10 centimeters = 1 decimeter
- 10 decimeters or 100 centimeters = 1 meter

Meters, centimeters, and millimeters are abbreviated as m, cm, and mm, respectively, throughout *The Advanced Professional Pastry Chef.* The decimeter measure is rarely used in the United States and is not used in this text.

Liter is the unit used to measure volume. A liter is divided into milliliters, centiliters, and deciliters.

- 10 milliliters = 1 centiliter
- 10 centiliters = 1 deciliter
- 10 deciliters or 100 centiliters = 1 liter

Liters, deciliters, centiliters, and milliliters are abbreviated as L, dl, cl, and ml, respectively, throughout the text.

Kilogram is the unit used to measure weight.

- 100 grams = 1 hectogram
- 10 hectograms = 1 kilo
- 1000 grams = 1 kilo

The hectogram is rarely used in the United States. Instead, the kilo is divided into 1000 grams. Kilograms and grams are abbreviated as kg and g, respectively, throughout the text.

The following approximate equivalents will give you a feeling for the size of various metric units:

- 1 kilo is slightly over 2 pounds
- 1 liter is just over 1 quart
- 1 deciliter is a little bit less than ½ cup
- 1 centiliter is about 2½ teaspoons
- 1 meter is just over 3 feet

Units of measure in the metric system are always in increments of ten, making it a precise system and easy to follow once you understand the principles. Nevertheless, many people who did not grow up using this method are reluctant to learn it and think it will be difficult to understand. Reading that there are 28.35 grams to 1 ounce looks intimidating, but this actually shows how the metric system can give you a much more accurate measurement. When measuring by weight any ingredient that is less than 1 ounce, use the gram weight for a precise measurement, or convert to teaspoons and/or tablespoons if necessary.

The equivalency tables that follow have been used to convert the measurements in *The Advanced Professional Pastry Chef* and provide both U.S. and metric measurements for all ingredients in the recipes. However, they do not precisely follow the conversion ratio; instead the tables have been rounded to the nearest tenth. For example, 1 ounce has been rounded up to 30 grams rather than using 28.35 grams which is the actual equivalent; 2 ounces has been rounded down to 55 grams instead of 56.7 grams, and so on. As the weight increases, every third ounce is calculated at 25 g rather than 30 to keep the table from getting too far away from the exact metric equivalent. Preceding these tables are the precise conversion measures, should you require them.

Precise Metric Equivalents

Length

1 inch	25.4 mm
1 centimeter	0.39 inches
1 meter	39.4 inches

Volume

1 ounce	(2 tablespoons) 29.57 milliliters
1 cup	2 dl, 3 cl, 7 ml (237 ml)
1 quart	9 dl, 4 cl, 6 ml (946 ml)
1 milliliter	0.034 fluid ounce
1 liter	33.8 fluid ounces

Weight

1 ounce	28.35 grams
1 pound	454 grams
1 gram	0.035 ounce
1 kilogram	2.2 pounds

Precise Metric Conversions

Length

To convert:	Multiply by:
inches into millimeters	25.4
inches into centimeters	2.54
millimeters into inches	0.03937
centimeters into inches	0.3937
meters into inches	39.3701

Volume

To convert:	Multiply by:
quarts into liters	0.946
pints into liters	0.473
quarts into milliliters	946
milliliters into ounces	0.0338
liters into quarts	1.05625
milliliters into pints	0.0021125
liters into pints	2.1125
liters into ounces	33.8

Weight

To convert:	Multiply by:
ounces into grams	28.35
grams into ounces	0.03527
kilograms into pounds	2.2046
pounds into kilograms	0.4535924

Metric and U.S. Equivalents: Length

In the tables that follow, metric amounts have been rounded to the nearest tenth. These conversions should be close enough for most purposes.

U.S.	Metric	U.S.	Metric
1/16 inch	2 mm	7½ inches	18.7 cm
1/8 inch	3 mm	7¾ inches	19.5 cm
3/16 inch	5 mm	8 inches	20 cm
¼ inch	6 mm	8¼ inches	20.6 cm
⅓ inch	8 mm	8½ inches	21.2 cm
⅜ inch	9 mm	8¾ inches	22 cm
½ inch	1.2 cm	9 inches	22.5 cm
⅝ inch	1.5 cm	9¼ inches	23.1 cm
⅔ inch	1.6 cm	9½ inches	23.7 cm
¾ inch	2 cm	9¾ inches	24.5 cm
⅞ inch	2.1 cm	10 inches	25 cm
1 inch	2.5 cm	10¼ inches	25.6 cm
1¼ inches	3.1 cm	10½ inches	26.2 cm
1½ inches	3.7 cm	10¾ inches	27 cm
1¾ inches	4.5 cm	11 inches	27.5 cm
2 inches	5 cm	11¼ inches	28.1 cm
2¼ inches	5.6 cm	11½ inches	28.7 cm
2½ inches	6.2 cm	11¾ inches	29.5 cm
2¾ inches	7 cm	12 inches (1 foot)	30 cm
3 inches	7.5 cm	12½ inches	31.2 cm
3¼ inches	8.1 cm	12¾ inches	32 cm
3½ inches	8.7 cm	13 inches	32.5 cm
3¾ inches	9.5 cm	13½ inches	33.7 cm
4 inches	10 cm	13¾ inches	34.5 cm
4¼ inches	10.6 cm	14 inches	35 cm
4½ inches	11.2 cm	14½ inches	36.2 cm
4¾ inches	12 cm	14¾ inches	37 cm
5 inches	12.5 cm	15 inches	37.5 cm
5¼ inches	13.1 cm	15½ inches	38.7 cm
5½ inches	13.7 cm	15¾ inches	39.5 cm
5¾ inches	14.5 cm	16 inches	40 cm
6 inches	15 cm	16½ inches	41.2 cm
6¼ inches	15.6 cm	16¾ inches	42 cm
6½ inches	16.2 cm	17 inches	42.5 cm
6¾ inches	17 cm	17½ inches	43.7 cm
7 inches	17.5 cm	17¾ inches	44.5 cm
7¼ inches	18.1 cm	18 inches (1½ feet)	45 cm

U.S.	Metric
18½ inches	46.2 cm
18¾ inches	47 cm
19 inches	47.5 cm
19½ inches	48.7 cm
19¾ inches	49.5 cm
20 inches	50 cm
20½ inches	51.2 cm
20¾ inches	52 cm
21 inches	52.5 cm
21½ inches	53.7 cm
21¾ inches	54.5 cm
22 inches	55 cm
22½ inches	56.2 cm
22¾ inches	57 cm
23 inches	57.5 cm
23½ inches	58.7 cm
23¾ inches	59.5 cm
24 inches (2 feet)	60 cm
24½ inches	61.2 cm
25 inches	62.5 cm
25½ inches	63.7 cm
26 inches	65 cm
26½ inches	66.2 cm
27 inches	67.5 cm
27½ inches	68.7 cm
28 inches	70 cm
28½ inches	71.2 cm
29 inches	72.5 cm
29½ inches	73.7 cm
30 inches (2½ feet)	75 cm
30½ inches	76.2 cm
31 inches	77.5 cm
31½ inches	78.7 cm

U.S.	Metric
32 inches	80 cm
32½ inches	81.2 cm
33 inches	82.5 cm
33½ inches	83.7 cm
34 inches	85 cm
34½ inches	86.2 cm
35 inches	87.5 cm
35½ inches	88.7 cm
36 inches (3 feet/1 yard)	90 cm
36½ inches	91.2 cm
37 inches	92.5 cm
37½ inches	93.7 cm
38 inches	95 cm
38½ inches	96.2 cm
39 inches	97.5 cm
39½ inches	98.7 cm
40 inches	100 cm (1 meter)
40½ inches	1 m 1.2 cm
41 inches	1 m 2.5 cm
41½ inches	1 m 3.7 cm
42 inches	1 m 5 cm
42½ inches	1 m 6.2 cm
43 inches	1 m 7.5 cm
43½ inches	1 m 8.7 cm
44 inches	1 m 10 cm
44½ inches	1 m 11.2 cm
45 inches	1 m 12.5 cm
45½ inches	1 m 13.7 cm
46 inches	1 m 15 cm
46½ inches	1 m 16.2 cm
47 inches	1 m 17.5 cm
47½ inches	1 m 18.7 cm
48 inches (4 feet)	1 m 20 cm

Metric and U.S. Equivalents: Volume

U.S.	Metric	U.S.	Metric
¼ teaspoon	1.25 ml	33 ounces (4⅛ cups)	990 ml (9 dl 9 cl)
½ teaspoon	2.5 ml	34 ounces (4¼ cups)	1 L 20 ml
1 teaspoon	5 ml	35 ounces (4⅜ cups)	1 L 50 ml
1 tablespoon (3 teaspoons)	15 ml (1 cl 5 ml)	36 ounces (4½ cups)	1 L 80 ml
1 ounce (2 tablespoons/⅛ cup)	30 ml (3 cl)	37 ounces (4⅝ cups)	1 L 110 ml
1¼ ounces	37.5 ml	38 ounces (4¾ cups)	1 L 140 ml
1½ ounces (3 tablespoons)	45 ml	39 ounces (4⅞ cups)	1 L 170 ml
1¾ ounces	52.5 ml	40 ounces (1 quart 1 cup)	1 L 200 ml
2 ounces (4 tablespoons/¼ cup)	60 ml (6 cl)	41 ounces (5⅛ cups)	1 L 230 ml
3 ounces (6 tablespoons/⅜ cup)	90 ml (9 cl)	42 ounces (5¼ cups)	1 L 260 ml
4 ounces (8 tablespoons/½ cup)	120 ml (1 dl 2 cl)	43 ounces (5⅜ cups)	1 L 290 ml
5 ounces (10 tablespoons/⅝ cup)	150 ml (1 dl 5 cl)	44 ounces (5½ cups)	1 L 320 ml
6 ounces (12 tablespoons/¾ cup)	180 ml (1 dl 8 cl)	45 ounces (5⅝ cups)	1 L 350 ml
7 ounces (14 tablespoons/⅞ cup)	210 ml (2 dl 1 cl)	46 ounces (5¾ cups)	1 L 380 ml
8 ounces (16 tablespoons/1 cup)	240 ml (2 dl 4 cl)	47 ounces (5⅞ cups)	1 L 410 ml
9 ounces (1⅛ cups)	270 ml (2 dl 7 cl)	48 ounces (1 quart 2 cups)	1 L 440 ml
10 ounces (1¼ cups)	300 ml (3 dl)	49 ounces (6⅛ cups)	1 L 470 ml
11 ounces (1⅜ cups)	330 ml (3 dl 3 cl)	50 ounces (6¼ cups)	1 L 500 ml
12 ounces (1½ cups)	360 ml (3 dl 6 cl)	51 ounces (6⅜ cups)	1 L 530 ml
13 ounces (1⅝ cup)	390 ml (3 dl 9 cl)	52 ounces (6½ cups)	1 L 560 ml
14 ounces (1¾ cups)	420 ml (4 dl 2 cl)	53 ounces (6⅝ cups)	1 L 590 ml
15 ounces (1⅞ cups)	450 ml (4 dl 5 cl)	54 ounces (6¾ cups)	1 L 620 ml
16 ounces (2 cups/1 pint)	480 ml (4 dl 8 cl)	55 ounces (6⅞ cups)	1 L 650 ml
17 ounces (2⅛ cups)	510 ml (5 dl 1 cl)	56 ounces (1 quart 3 cups)	1 L 680 ml
18 ounces (2¼ cups)	540 ml (5 dl 4 cl)	57 ounces (7⅛ cups)	1 L 710 ml
19 ounces (2⅜ cups)	570 ml (5 dl 7 cl)	58 ounces (7¼ cups)	1 L 740 ml
20 ounces (2½ cups)	600 ml (6 dl)	59 ounces (7⅜ cups)	1 L 770 ml
21 ounces (2⅝ cups)	630 ml (6 dl 3 cl)	60 ounces (7½ cups)	1 L 800 ml
22 ounces (2¾ cups)	660 ml (6 dl 6 cl)	61 ounces (7⅝ cups)	1 L 830 ml
23 ounces (2⅞ cups)	690 ml (6 dl 9 cl)	62 ounces (7¾ cups)	1 L 860 ml
24 ounces (3 cups)	720 ml (7 dl 2 cl)	63 ounces (7⅞ cups)	1 L 890 ml
25 ounces (3⅛ cups)	750 ml (7 dl 5 cl)	64 ounces (2 quarts)	1 L 920 ml
26 ounces (3¼ cups)	780 ml (7 dl 8 cl)	65 ounces (8⅛ cups)	1 L 950 ml
27 ounces (3⅜ cups)	810 ml (8 dl 1 cl)	66 ounces (8¼ cups)	1 L 980 ml
28 ounces (3½ cups)	840 ml (8 dl 4 cl)	67 ounces (8⅜ cups)	2 L 10 ml
29 ounces (3⅝ cups)	870 ml (8 dl 7 cl)	68 ounces (8½ cups)	2 L 40 ml
30 ounces (3¾ cups)	900 ml (9 dl)	69 ounces (8⅝ cups)	2 L 70 ml
31 ounces (3⅞ cups)	930 ml (9 dl 3 cl)	70 ounces (8¾ cups)	2 L 100 ml
32 ounces (1 quart)	960 ml (9 dl 6 cl)	71 ounces (8⅞ cups)	2 L 130 ml

U.S.	Metric	U.S.	Metric
72 ounces (2 quarts 1 cup)	2 L 160 ml	101 ounces (12⅝ cups)	3 L 30 ml
73 ounces (9⅛ cups)	2 L 190 ml	102 ounces (12¾ cups)	3 L 60 ml
74 ounces (9¼ cups)	2 L 220 ml	103 ounces (12⅞ cups)	3 L 90 ml
75 ounces (9⅜ cups)	2 L 250 ml	104 ounces (3 quarts 1 cup)	3 L 120 ml
76 ounces (9½ cups)	2 L 280 ml	105 ounces (13⅛ cups)	3 L 150 ml
77 ounces (9⅝ cups)	2 L 310 ml	106 ounces (13¼ cups)	3 L 180 ml
78 ounces (9¾ cups)	2 L 340 ml	107 ounces (13⅜ cups)	3 L 210 ml
79 ounces (9⅞ cups)	2 L 370 ml	108 ounces (13½ cups)	3 L 240 ml
80 ounces (2 quarts 2 cups)	2 L 400 ml	109 ounces (13⅝ cups)	3 L 270 ml
81 ounces (10⅛ cups)	2 L 430 ml	110 ounces (13¾ cups)	3 L 300 ml
82 ounces (10¼ cups)	2 L 460 ml	111 ounces (13⅞ cups)	3 L 330 ml
83 ounces (10⅜ cups)	2 L 490 ml	112 ounces (3 quarts 2 cups)	3 L 360 ml
84 ounces (10½ cups)	2 L 520 ml	113 ounces (14⅛ cups)	3 L 390 ml
85 ounces (10⅝ cups)	2 L 550 ml	114 ounces (14¼ cups)	3 L 420 ml
86 ounces (10¾ cups)	2 L 580 ml	115 ounces (14⅜ cups)	3 L 450 ml
87 ounces (10⅞ cups)	2 L 610 ml	116 ounces (14½ cups)	3 L 480 ml
88 ounces (2 quarts 3 cups)	2 L 640 ml	117 ounces (14⅝ cups)	3 L 510 ml
89 ounces (11⅛ cups)	2 L 670 ml	118 ounces (14¾ cups)	3 L 540 ml
90 ounces (11¼ cups)	2 L 700 ml	119 ounces (14⅞ cups)	3 L 570 ml
91 ounces (11⅜ cups)	2 L 730 ml	120 ounces (3 quarts 3 cups)	3 L 600 ml
92 ounces (11½ cups)	2 L 760 ml	121 ounces (15⅛ cups)	3 L 630 ml
93 ounces (11⅝ cups)	2 L 790 ml	122 ounces (15¼ cups)	3 L 660 ml
94 ounces (11¾ cups)	2 L 820 ml	123 ounces (15⅜ cups)	3 L 690 ml
95 ounces (11⅞ cups)	2 L 850 ml	124 ounces (15½ cups)	3 L 720 ml
96 ounces (3 quarts)	2 L 880 ml	125 ounces (15⅝ cups)	3 L 750 ml
97 ounces (12⅛ cups)	2 L 910 ml	126 ounces (15¾ cups)	3 L 780 ml
98 ounces (12¼ cups)	2 L 940 ml	127 ounces (15⅞ cups)	3 L 810 ml
99 ounces (12⅜ cups)	2 L 970 ml	128 ounces (16 cups/4 quarts/1 gallon)	3 L 840 ml
100 ounces (12½ cups)	3 L		

U.S. Volume Equivalents

3 teaspoons	=1 tablespoon
2 tablespoons	=1 ounce
8 ounces (16 tablespoons)	=1 cup
2 cups	=1 pint
2 pints	=1 quart
4 quarts	=1 gallon

Note: 1 pint (2 cups) of water, or any liquid of similar viscosity, will weigh 1 pound.

Metric and U.S. Equivalents: Weight

U.S.	Metric	U.S.	Metric
½ ounce	15 g	22 ounces (1 pound 6 ounces)	625 g
⅔ ounce	20 g	23 ounces (1 pound 7 ounces)	655 g
¾ ounce	22 g	24 ounces (1 pound 8 ounces)	680 g
1 ounce	30 g	25 ounces (1 pound 9 ounces)	710 g
1½ ounces	40 g	26 ounces (1 pound 10 ounces)	740 g
2 ounces	55 g	27 ounces (1 pound 11 ounces)	765 g
2½ ounces	70 g	28 ounces (1 pound 12 ounces)	795 g
3 ounces	85 g	29 ounces (1 pound 13 ounces)	825 g
3½ ounces	100 g	30 ounces (1 pound 14 ounces)	855 g
4 ounces	115 g	31 ounces (1 pound 15 ounces)	885 g
4½ ounces	130 g	32 ounces (2 pounds)	910 g
5 ounces	140 g	33 ounces (2 pounds 1 ounce)	940 g
5½ ounces	155 g	34 ounces (2 pounds 2 ounces)	970 g
6 ounces	170 g	35 ounces (2 pounds 3 ounces)	1 kg (1000 g)
6½ ounces	185 g	36 ounces (2 pounds 4 ounces)	1 kg, 25 g
7 ounces	200 g	37 ounces (2 pounds 5 ounces)	1 kg 50 g
7½ ounces	215 g	38 ounces (2 pounds 6 ounces)	1 kg 80 g
8 ounces	225 g	39 ounces (2 pounds 7 ounces)	1 kg 110 g
8½ ounces	240 g	40 ounces (2 pounds 8 ounces)	1 kg 135 g
9 ounces	255 g	41 ounces (2 pounds 9 ounces)	1 kg 165 g
9½ ounces	270 g	42 ounces (2 pounds 10 ounces)	1 kg 195 g
10 ounces	285 g	43 ounces (2 pounds 11 ounces)	1 kg 220 g
10½ ounces	300 g	44 ounces (2 pounds 12 ounces)	1 kg 250 g
11 ounces	310 g	45 ounces (2 pounds 13 ounces)	1 kg 280 g
11½ ounces	325 g	46 ounces (2 pounds 14 ounces)	1 kg 310 g
12 ounces	340 g	47 ounces (2 pounds 15 ounces)	1 kg 340 g
12½ ounces	355 g	48 ounces (3 pounds)	1 kg 365 g
13 ounces	370 g	49 ounces (3 pounds 1 ounce)	1 kg 395 g
13½ ounces	385 g	50 ounces (3 pounds 2 ounces)	1 kg 420 g
14 ounces	400 g	51 ounces (3 pounds 3 ounces)	1 kg 450 g
14½ ounces	415 g	52 ounces (3 pounds 4 ounces)	1 kg 480 g
15 ounces	430 g	53 ounces (3 pounds 5 ounces)	1 kg 505 g
15½ ounces	445 g	54 ounces (3 pounds 6 ounces)	1 kg 535 g
16 ounces (1 pound)	455 g	55 ounces (3 pounds 7 ounces)	1 kg 565 g
17 ounces (1 pound 1 ounce)	485 g	56 ounces (3 pounds 8 ounces)	1 kg 590 g
18 ounces (1 pound 2 ounces)	510 g	57 ounces (3 pounds 9 ounces)	1 kg 620 g
19 ounces (1 pound 3 ounces)	540 g	58 ounces (3 pounds 10 ounces)	1 kg 650 g
20 ounces (1 pound 4 ounces)	570 g	59 ounces (3 pounds 11 ounces)	1 kg 675 g
21 ounces (1 pound 5 ounces)	595 g	60 ounces (3 pounds 12 ounces)	1 kg 705 g

U.S.	Metric		U.S.	Metric
61 ounces (3 pounds 13 ounces)	1 kg 735 g		71 ounces (4 pounds 7 ounces)	2 kg 20 g
62 ounces (3 pounds 14 ounces)	1 kg 765 g		72 ounces (4 pounds 8 ounces)	2 kg 45 g
63 ounces (3 pounds 15 ounces)	1 kg 795 g		73 ounces (4 pounds 9 ounces)	2 kg 75 g
64 ounces (4 pounds)	1 kg 820 g		74 ounces (4 pounds 10 ounces)	2 kg 105 g
65 ounces (4 pounds 1 ounce)	1 kg 850 g		75 ounces (4 pounds 11 ounces)	2 kg 130 g
66 ounces (4 pounds 2 ounces)	1 kg 875 g		76 ounces (4 pounds 12 ounces)	2 kg 160 g
67 ounces (4 pounds 3 ounces)	1 kg 905 g		77 ounces (4 pounds 13 ounces)	2 kg 190 g
68 ounces (4 pounds 4 ounces)	1 kg 935 g		78 ounces (4 pounds 14 ounces)	2 kg 220 g
69 ounces (4 pounds 5 ounces)	1 kg 960 g		79 ounces (4 pounds 15 ounces)	2 kg 250 g
70 ounces (4 pounds 6 ounces)	1 kg 990 g		80 ounces (5 pounds)	2 kg 275 g

Temperature Scales

Centigrade Scale

The centigrade scale is the temperature scale used throughout most of the world outside the United States. Temperatures are expressed in degrees Celsius, with 0° as the freezing point of water and 100° as its boiling point. The name *Celsius* comes from the inventor of the scale, Anders Celsius, a Swedish astronomer who developed the system of measurement in 1742. Degrees Celsius are abbreviated as °C throughout this text.

Fahrenheit Scale

The Fahrenheit temperature scale is used almost exclusively in the United States. It was developed in 1714 by German physicist Gabriel David Fahrenheit. The Fahrenheit scale uses 32° as the freezing point of water and 212° as its boiling point. Degrees Fahrenheit are abbreviated as °F throughout this text.

Temperature Equivalents

Fahrenheit	Celsius		Fahrenheit	Celsius
–50°F	–45°C		2°F	–17°C
–45°F	–43°C		5°F	–15°C
–40°F	–40°C		7°F	–14°C
–35°F	–37°C		10°F	–12°C
–30°F	–35°C		12°F	–11°C
–25°F	–32°C		15°F	–10°C
–20°F	–29°C		17°F	–9°C
–17°F	–27°C		20°F	–7°C
–15°F	–26°C		22°F	–6°C
–12°F	–25°C		25°F	–4°C
–10°F	–24°C		27°F	–3°C
–7°F	–22°C		30°F	–1°C
–5°F	–21°C		32°F	0°C (freezing point of water)
–3°F	–20°C		35°F	2°C
0°F	–18°C		38°F	3°C

Fahrenheit	Celsius	Fahrenheit	Celsius
40°F	4°C (yeast is dormant)	128°F	53°C
43°F	6°C	130°F	54°C
45°F	7°C	133°F	56°C
48°F	9°C	135°F	57°C
50°F	10°C	138°F	59°C
53°F	12°C	140°F	60°C
55°F	13°C	143°F	62°C
58°F	14°C	145°F	63°C (yeast is killed)
60°F	16°C	148°F	64°C
63°F	17°C	150°F	65°C
65°F	19°C	153°F	67°C
68°F	20°C (gelatin begins to set)	155°F	68°C
70°F	21°C	158°F	70°C
73°F	23°C	160°F	71°C
75°F	24°C	163°F	73°C
78°F	25°C	165°F	74°C
80°F	26°C (ideal temperature for yeast to multiply)	168°F	76°C
83°F	28°C	170°F	77°C
85°F	29°C (lowest working temperature for tempered chocolate)	173°F	78°C
		175°F	80°C
86°F	30°C (gelatin dissolves)	178°F	81°C
88°F	31°C	180°F	82°C
90°F	32°C (highest working temperature for tempered chocolate)	183°F	84°C
		185°F	85°C
93°F	34°C	188°F	87°C
95°F	35°C	190°F	88°C
98°F	37°C	193°F	89°C
100°F	38°C (lowest working temperature for coating chocolate)	195°F	91°C
		198°F	92°C
103°F	39°C	200°F	94°C
105°F	40°C (working temperature for coating chocolate)	203°F	95°C
		205°F	96°C
108°F	42°C	208°F	98°C
110°F	43°C (highest working temperature for coating chocolate)	210°F	99°C
		212°F	100°C (water boils at sea level)
113°F	45°C	215°F	102°C
115°F	46°C	218°F	103°C
118°F	48°C	220°F	104°C
120°F	49°C	223°F	106°C
123°F	51°C	225°F	108°C
125°F	52°C		

Fahrenheit	Celsius	Fahrenheit	Celsius
228°F	109°C	328°F	164°C
230°F	110°C	330°F	166°C
233°F	112°C	333°F	167°C
235°F	113°C	335°F	168°C
238°F	114°C	338°F	170°C
240°F	115°C (sugar syrup for Italian meringue/soft ball stage)	340°F	171°C
		343°F	172°C
243°F	117°C	345°F	173°C
245°F	118°C	348°F	174°C
248°F	120°C	350°F	175°C
250°F	122°C	355°F	180°C
253°F	123°C	360°F	183°C
255°F	124°C	365°F	185°C
258°F	126°C	370°F	188°C
260°F	127°C	375°F	190°C
263°F	128°C	380°F	193°C
265°F	130°C	385°F	196°C
268°F	131°C	390°F	199°C
270°F	132°C	395°F	202°C
273°F	134°C	400°F	205°C
275°F	135°C	405°F	208°C
278°F	137°C	410°F	210°C
280°F	138°C	415°F	212°C
283°F	139°C	420°F	216°C
285°F	141°C	425°F	219°C
288°F	142°C	430°F	222°C
290°F	143°C	435°F	224°C
293°F	145°C	440°F	226°C
295°F	146°C	445°F	228°C
298°F	148°C	450°F	230°C
300°F	149°C	455°F	235°C
303°F	151°C	460°F	237°C
305°F	152°C	465°F	240°C
308°F	153°C	470°F	243°C
310°F	155°C	475°F	246°C
313°F	156°C	480°F	248°C
315°F	157°C	485°F	251°C
318°F	159°C	490°F	254°C
320°F	160°C (sugar begins to caramelize)	495°F	257°C
323°F	162°C	500°F	260°C
325°F	163°C	550°F	288°C

Fahrenheit	Celsius		Fahrenheit	Celsius
600°F	315°C		850°F	454°C
650°F	343°C		900°F	482°C
700°F	371°C		950°F	510°C
750°F	398°C		1000°F	537°C
800°F	426°C			

Temperature Conversions

To convert centigrade to Fahrenheit, multiply by 9, divide by 5 (centigrade x 9 ÷ 5), then add 32.

Example: 190°C x 9 ÷ 5 = 342 + 32 = 374°F

To convert Fahrenheit to centigrade, subtract 32, multiply by 5, then divide by 9 (Fahrenheit −32 x 5 ÷ 9).

Example: 400°F − 32 = 368 x 5 ÷ 9 = 204.4°C

Volume Equivalents of Commonly Used Products

Product	U.S.	Metric
1 pound bread flour (unsifted)	4 cups	960 ml
1 pound cake flour (unsifted)	4⅓ cups	1 L 40 ml
1 pound cornstarch	3¼ cups	780 ml
1 pound semolina flour	2½ cups	600 ml
1 pound cornmeal	3 cups	720 ml
1 pound butter	2 cups	480 ml
1 ounce butter	2 tablespoons	30 ml
1 pound granulated sugar	2¼ cups	540 ml
1 pound powdered sugar	4 cups	960 ml
1 pound brown sugar	2⅔ cups	640 ml
4 tablespoons table salt	2 ounces	65 g
4 tablespoons kosher salt	1¼ ounces	35 g
1 pound unsweetened cocoa powder	4¾ cups	1 L 140 ml
1 pound honey	1⅓ cups	320 ml
1 pound rolled oats	5⅓ cups	1 L 280 ml
1 pound macaroon coconut	5 cups	1 L 200 ml
1 pound rice (jasmine)	2 cups	480 ml
1 pound peanuts (shelled)	3 cups	720 ml
1 pound pistachios (shelled)	3⅓ cups	800 ml
1 pound hazelnuts (shelled)	3½ cups	840 ml
1 pound almonds (whole)	3 cups	720 ml
1 pound sliced almonds	6 cups	1 L 440 ml
1 pound almonds (slivered)	4 cups	960 ml
1 pound almonds (finely ground)	4 cups	960 ml
1 pound walnuts (shelled, halves)	4½ cups	1 L 80 ml
1 pound pecans (shelled, halves)	4⅓ cups	1 L 40 ml
1 pound pine nuts	3¼ cups	780 ml
1 pound black or golden raisins	2¾ cups	660 ml
1 pound dried currants	2⅔ cups	640 ml

Approximate Prepared Yields of Commonly Used Products

Item	Prepared Yield
1 cup (240 ml) heavy cream whipped to stiff peaks	2 cups (480 ml)
5 pounds (2 kg 275 g/15 medium) whole apples	13¾ cups (3 L 300 ml), chopped or sliced
5 pounds (2 kg 275 g/40 to 60) fresh apricots	12½ cups (3 L), sliced or halved
5 pounds (2 kg 275 g) dried apricots	13¾ cups (3 L 300 ml)
5 pounds (2 kg 275 g) dried apricots, reconstituted	27½ cups (6 L 600 ml)
5 pounds (2 kg 275 g/15 medium) whole oranges	4 cups (960 ml) strained juice
5 pounds (2 kg 275 g/20 to 25 medium) whole lemons	3 cups (720 ml) strained juice
5 pounds (2 kg 275 g/30 to 40 medium) whole limes	2½ cups (600 ml) strained juice
5 pounds (2 kg 275 g) unhulled strawberries	5 cups (1 L 200 ml) strained juice
2 pounds (910 g) raspberries	3 cups (720 ml) strained juice
5 pounds (2 kg 275 g/15 to 20) fresh bananas	10 cups (2 L 400 ml), sliced
1 pound (455 g) frozen blueberries	2½ cups (600 ml)
5 pounds (2 kg 275 g) fresh carrots (without tops)	5 cups (1 L 200 ml), chopped or sliced; 12½ cups (3 L), shredded
5 pounds (2 kg 275 g) fresh cherries	12 to 15 cups (2 L 880 ml to 3 L 600 ml), pitted
5 pounds (2 kg 275 g) whole dates	10 cups (2 L 400 ml), unpitted; 13¾ cups (3 L 300 ml), pitted and chopped
5 pounds (2 kg 275 g) seeded grapes	12 to 15 cups (2 L 880 ml to 3 L 600 ml)
5 pounds (2 kg 275 g/20 medium) fresh peaches	14 cups (3 L 360 ml), sliced; 12½ cups (3 L), chopped
5 pounds (2 kg 275 g/15 medium) fresh pears	10 cups (2 L 400 ml), sliced
5 pounds (2 kg 275 g) fresh plums	10 cups (2 L 400 ml), pitted and quartered
5 pounds (2 kg 275 g) fresh whole pumpkin	5 cups (1 L 200 ml), cooked and mashed
5 pounds (2 kg 275 g) fresh rhubarb	10 cups (2 L 400 ml), chopped and cooked

Volume Equivalents for Shelled Eggs, Average Size

These numbers have been rounded for convenience and ease of multiplication.

Egg Whites

2	¼ cup/60 ml
4	½ cup/120 ml
5	⅝ cup/150 ml
6	¾ cup/180 ml
8	1 cup/240 ml
10	1¼ cups/300 ml
12	1½ cups/360 ml
14	1¾ cups/420 ml
16	2 cups/480 ml

Egg Yolks

3	¼ cup/60 ml
4	⅓ cup/80 ml
6	½ cup/120 ml
8	⅔ cup/160 ml
9	¾ cup/180 ml
10	⅞ cup/210 ml
12	1 cup/240 ml
16	1⅓ cups/320 ml

Whole Eggs

1	¼ cup/60 ml
2	½ cup/120 ml
3	¾ cup/180 ml
4	1 cup/ 240 ml
5	1¼ cups/300 ml
6	1½ cups/360 ml
7	1¾ cups/420 ml
8	2 cups/480 ml
9	2¼ cups/540 ml
10	2½ cups/600 ml
11	2¾ cups/660 ml
12	3 cups/720 ml
13	3¼ cups/780 ml
14	3½ cups/840 ml
15	3¾ cups/900 ml
16	1 quart/ 960 ml

Gelatin Equivalents and Substitutions

- Unflavored gelatin powder and gelatin sheets can be substituted one for the other in equal weights.
- 1 sheet of gelatin (most brands) weighs ⅒ ounce (3 g).
- 1 tablespoon (15 ml) unflavored gelatin powder weighs just under ⅓ ounce (9 g).
- 1 ounce (30 g) unflavored gelatin powder measures 3 tablespoons plus 1 teaspoon (50 ml) by volume.
- A consumer packet or envelope of unflavored gelatin powder weighs ¼ ounce (just over 7 g) and is equivalent to 2½ teaspoons (12.5 ml) when measuring by volume.

Examples of Substituting Unflavored Gelatin Powder in a Recipe That Calls for Sheet Gelatin

Recipe calls for	Use
5 sheets of gelatin	½ ounce (15 g) gelatin powder
5 sheets of gelatin	5 teaspoons (25 ml) unflavored gelatin powder
1 sheet of gelatin	⅒ ounce (3 g) gelatin powder
1 sheet of gelatin	1 teaspoon (5 ml) unflavored gelatin powder

Examples of Substituting Sheet Gelatin in a Recipe That Calls for Unflavored Gelatin Powder

Recipe calls for	Use
1 ounce (30 g) unflavored gelatin powder	10 sheets of gelatin
3 tablespoons (45 ml) unflavored gelatin powder	9 sheets of gelatin
1 packet or envelope of unflavored gelatin powder	2½ sheets of gelatin

Note: When substituting sheet gelatin for powdered, soak the sheets in water as directed on page 8, remove the sheets from the water without squeezing, and melt the sheets in a bain-marie or in a saucepan over low heat. Add to the recipe as directed including whatever liquid was called for to soften and dissolve the gelatin powder.

Yeast Equivalents and Substitutions

- Some nonprofessional recipes specify the amount of yeast in a recipe by the envelope or packet. A consumer packet of active dry yeast weighs ¼ ounce (just over 7 g) and measures 2¼ teaspoons (11 ml) by volume.
- To substitute active dry yeast for fresh compressed yeast, use half the amount of dry yeast by either weight or volume.
- To substitute fresh compressed yeast for active dry yeast, use twice the amount by either weight or volume.
- Dry yeast must always be dissolved in a warm liquid; it cannot be added directly to cold liquid as fresh yeast can.

Examples

Recipe calls for	Use
1 tablespoon (45 ml) fresh compressed yeast	1½ teaspoons (7.5 ml) active dry yeast
1 ounce (30 g) active dry yeast	2 ounces (55 g) fresh compressed yeast
2 tablespoons (30 ml) active dry yeast	4 tablespoons (60 ml) fresh compressed yeast
1 package active dry yeast	½ ounce (15 g) fresh compressed yeast

Gram Weight of Commonly Used Products

Item	Grams per Teaspoon	Grams per Tablespoon
Ammonium carbonate	3.5	10
Baking powder	4	12
Baking soda	4	12
Bread flour	2.5	8
Butter	5	15
Ground cinnamon	1.5	5
Unsweetened cocoa powder	2.5	8
Cornstarch	2.5	8
Cream of tartar	2	6
Granulated sugar	5	15
Grated citrus zest	6	18
Ground spices (except cinnamon)	2	6
Kosher salt	3.5	10
Malt sugar	3	9
Mocha paste	4	12
Powdered gelatin	3	9
Powdered pectin	3	9
Powdered sugar	3	9
Table salt	5	15

Volume and Weight Equivalents for Honey, Corn Syrup, and Molasses

Volume	Weight
¼ cup/60 ml	3 ounces/85 g
⅓ cup/80 ml	4 ounces/115 g
½ cup/120 ml	6 ounces/170 g
⅔ cup/160 ml	8 ounces/225 g
¾ cup/180 ml	9 ounces/255 g
1 cup/240 ml	12 ounces/340 g
1¼ cups/300 ml	15 ounces/430 g
1⅓ cups/320 ml	1 pound/455 g
1½ cups/360 ml	1 pound 2 ounces/510 g
1¾ cups/420 ml	1 pound 5 ounces/595 g
2 cups/480 ml	1 pound 8 ounces/680 g
3 cups/720 ml	2 pounds 4 ounces/1 kg 25 g

Calculating a Cake Circumference

To calculate the circumference (the perimeter) of a cake using *pi* (3.14), multiply the diameter of the cake times *pi* (or simply multiply by 3 and add a little). You may need to calculate the circumference to cut out strips of paper to line the inside of a cake pan, for example, or if you are making a chocolate band to wrap around a finished cake. The chart below shows the basic math using *pi*.

Diameter	Calculation	Circumference
8-inch (20-cm) cake	8 × 3.14 *or* 20 × 3.14	25.02 inches (62.6 cm)
10-inch (25-cm) cake	10 × 3.14 *or* 25 × 3.14	31.4 inches (78.7 cm)
12-inch (30-cm) cake	12 × 3.14 *or* 30 × 3.14	37.68 inches (93.8 cm)

Cake Pan Capacities by Volume

The volume listed for pan sizes below takes into consideration that you would not want to fill the pan to the top with batter. So, more accurately speaking, these numbers are not the precise volume of the pan; they are the amount of batter that would be baked in that size pan.

Pan (all pans are 2 inches/5 cm high)	Volume Size (allowing for expansion in oven)
5 inches (12.5 cm) round	2½ cups (600 ml)
6 inches (15 cm) round	3½ cups (840 ml)
7 inches (17.5 cm) round	5 cups (1 L 200 ml)
8 inches (20 cm) round	6¾ cups (1 L 620 ml)
9 inches (22.5 cm) round	8½ cups (2 L 40 ml)
10 inches (25 cm) round	9 cups (2 L 160 ml)
12 inches (30 cm) round	13 cups (3 L 120 ml)
14 inches (35 cm) round	20 cups (4 L 800 ml)
16 inches (40 cm) round	28 cups (6 L 720 ml)
8 inches (20 cm) square	7 cups (1 L 680 ml)
10 inches (25 cm) square	11 cups (2 L 640 ml)
12 inches (30 cm) square	14½ cups (3 L 480 ml)
14 inches (35 cm) square	22½ cups (5 L 400 ml)

Baker's Percentage

The term *baker's percentage* refers to a mathematical system or formula that is used to compare the proportion of each ingredient to the others in a baking recipe. However, this formula does not take the total of all of the ingredients in a given recipe and express this amount as a 100 percent yield. Instead, flour is always "100 percent" and the other ingredients are calculated in relationship. When using this method, all of the ingredients must be expressed in the same unit (ounces, pounds, etc.). To find the percentage of an ingredient, divide its weight by the weight of the flour, then multiply by 100.

Example:

4 pounds (1 kg 820 g) flour	100 percent
1 pound (455 g) sugar	25 percent
2 pounds (910 g) butter	50 percent
8 ounces (½ pound/225 g) yeast	12.5 percent
1 quart (960 ml/2 pounds/910 g) water	50 percent

The intention of the baker's percentage formula is to provide a tool for comparing the amount of one ingredient to another in a recipe to achieve a better understanding of the particular formula balance. It can also be used to scale a recipe up or down. For a small recipe that you simply want to halve or double, there would be no real advantage to converting all of the ingredients from weight to percentage, multiplying or dividing the percentages, then converting these figures back to pounds and ounces. In a large commercial operation where you are making hundreds of pounds of bread dough, for example, using the percentage method rather than simply multiplying assures that the ingredients will remain in balance. Also, if substitutions are to be made, they can be made based on an equal percentage. A word of caution, however: This is not to say that any recipe can be scaled up or down successfully just by using the correct math!

Gram Measurements in Rounded Percentages as They Relate to 16 Ounces (1 Pound) as 100 Percent

Weight (in grams)	Rounded Percentage	Weight (in grams)	Rounded Percentage	Weight (in grams)	Rounded Percentage	Weight (in grams)	Rounded Percentage
1 g	0%	23 g	5%	45 g	10%	67 g	15%
2 g	0%	24 g	5%	46 g	10%	68 g	15%
3 g	1%	25 g	5%	47 g	10%	69 g	15%
4 g	1%	26 g	6%	48 g	11%	70 g	15%
5 g	1%	27 g	6%	49 g	11%	71 g	16%
6 g	1%	28 g	6%	50 g	11%	72 g	16%
7 g	2%	29 g	6%	51 g	11%	73 g	16%
8 g	2%	30 g	7%	52 g	11%	74 g	16%
9 g	2%	31 g	7%	53 g	12%	75 g	16%
10 g	2%	32 g	7%	54 g	12%	76 g	17%
11 g	2%	33 g	7%	55 g	12%	77 g	17%
12 g	3%	34 g	7%	56 g	12%	78 g	17%
13 g	3%	35 g	8%	57 g	13%	79 g	17%
14 g	3%	36 g	8%	58 g	13%	80 g	18%
15 g	3%	37 g	8%	59 g	13%	81 g	18%
16 g	4%	38 g	8%	60 g	13%	82 g	18%
17 g	4%	39 g	9%	61 g	13%	83 g	18%
18 g	4%	40 g	9%	62 g	14%	84 g	18%
19 g	4%	41 g	9%	63 g	14%	85 g	19%
20 g	4%	42 g	9%	64 g	14%	86 g	19%
21 g	5%	43 g	9%	65 g	14%	87 g	19%
22 g	5%	44 g	10%	66 g	15%	88 g	19%

Weight (in grams)	Rounded Percentage	Weight (in grams)	Rounded Percentage	Weight (in grams)	Rounded Percentage	Weight (in grams)	Rounded Percentage
89 g	20%	129 g	28%	169 g	37%	209 g	46%
90 g	20%	130 g	29%	170 g	37%	210 g	46%
91 g	20%	131 g	29%	171 g	38%	211 g	46%
92 g	20%	132 g	29%	172 g	38%	212 g	47%
93 g	20%	133 g	29%	173 g	38%	213 g	47%
94 g	21%	134 g	29%	174 g	38%	214 g	47%
95 g	21%	135 g	30%	175 g	38%	215 g	47%
96 g	21%	136 g	30%	176 g	39%	216 g	47%
97 g	21%	137 g	30%	177 g	39%	217 g	48%
98 g	22%	138 g	30%	178 g	39%	218 g	48%
99 g	22%	139 g	31%	179 g	39%	219 g	48%
100 g	22%	140 g	31%	180 g	40%	220 g	48%
101 g	22%	141 g	31%	181 g	40%	221 g	49%
102 g	22%	142 g	31%	182 g	40%	222 g	49%
103 g	23%	143 g	31%	183 g	40%	223 g	49%
104 g	23%	144 g	32%	184 g	40%	224 g	49%
105 g	23%	145 g	32%	185 g	41%	225 g	49%
106 g	23%	146 g	32%	186 g	41%	226 g	50%
107 g	24%	147 g	32%	187 g	41%	227 g	50%
108 g	24%	148 g	33%	188 g	41%	228 g	50%
109 g	24%	149 g	33%	189 g	42%	229 g	50%
110 g	24%	150 g	33%	190 g	42%	230 g	51%
111 g	24%	151 g	33%	191 g	42%	231 g	51%
112 g	25%	152 g	33%	192 g	42%	232 g	51%
113 g	25%	153 g	34%	193 g	42%	233 g	51%
114 g	25%	154 g	34%	194 g	43%	234 g	51%
115 g	25%	155 g	34%	195 g	43%	235 g	52%
116 g	25%	156 g	34%	196 g	43%	236 g	52%
117 g	26%	157 g	35%	197 g	43%	237 g	52%
118 g	26%	158 g	35%	198 g	44%	238 g	52%
119 g	26%	159 g	35%	199 g	44%	239 g	53%
120 g	26%	160 g	35%	200 g	44%	240 g	53%
121 g	27%	161 g	35%	201 g	44%	241 g	53%
122 g	27%	162 g	36%	202 g	44%	242 g	53%
123 g	27%	163 g	36%	203 g	45%	243 g	53%
124 g	27%	164 g	36%	204 g	45%	244 g	54%
125 g	27%	165 g	36%	205 g	45%	245 g	54%
126 g	28%	166 g	36%	206 g	45%	246 g	54%
127 g	28%	167 g	37%	207 g	45%	247 g	54%
128 g	28%	168 g	37%	208 g	46%	248 g	55%

Weight (in grams)	Rounded Percentage	Weight (in grams)	Rounded Percentage	Weight (in grams)	Rounded Percentage	Weight (in grams)	Rounded Percentage
249 g	55%	289 g	64%	329 g	72%	369 g	81%
250 g	55%	290 g	64%	330 g	73%	370 g	81%
251 g	55%	291 g	64%	331 g	73%	371 g	82%
252 g	55%	292 g	64%	332 g	73%	372 g	82%
253 g	56%	293 g	64%	333 g	73%	373 g	82%
254 g	56%	294 g	65%	334 g	73%	374 g	82%
255 g	56%	295 g	65%	335 g	74%	375 g	82%
256 g	56%	296 g	65%	336 g	74%	376 g	83%
257 g	56%	297 g	65%	337 g	74%	377 g	83%
258 g	57%	298 g	65%	338 g	74%	378 g	83%
259 g	57%	299 g	66%	339 g	75%	379 g	83%
260 g	57%	300 g	66%	340 g	75%	380 g	84%
261 g	57%	301 g	66%	341 g	75%	381 g	84%
262 g	58%	302 g	66%	342 g	75%	382 g	84%
263 g	58%	303 g	67%	343 g	75%	383 g	84%
264 g	58%	304 g	67%	344 g	76%	384 g	84%
265 g	58%	305 g	67%	345 g	76%	385 g	85%
266 g	58%	306 g	67%	346 g	76%	386 g	85%
267 g	59%	307 g	67%	347 g	76%	387 g	85%
268 g	59%	308 g	68%	348 g	76%	388 g	85%
269 g	59%	309 g	68%	349 g	77%	389 g	85%
270 g	59%	310 g	68%	350 g	77%	390 g	86%
271 g	60%	311 g	68%	351 g	77%	391 g	86%
272 g	60%	312 g	69%	352 g	77%	392 g	86%
273 g	60%	313 g	69%	353 g	78%	393 g	86%
274 g	60%	314 g	69%	354 g	78%	394 g	87%
275 g	60%	315 g	69%	355 g	78%	395 g	87%
276 g	61%	316 g	69%	356 g	78%	396 g	87%
277 g	61%	317 g	70%	357 g	78%	397 g	87%
278 g	61%	318 g	70%	358 g	79%	398 g	87%
279 g	61%	319 g	70%	359 g	79%	399 g	88%
280 g	62%	320 g	70%	360 g	79%	400 g	88%
281 g	62%	321 g	71%	361 g	79%	401 g	88%
282 g	62%	322 g	71%	362 g	80%	402 g	88%
283 g	62%	323 g	71%	363 g	80%	403 g	89%
284 g	62%	324 g	71%	364 g	80%	404 g	89%
285 g	63%	325 g	71%	365 g	80%	405 g	89%
286 g	63%	326 g	72%	366 g	80%	406 g	89%
287 g	63%	327 g	72%	367 g	81%	407 g	89%
288 g	63%	328 g	72%	368 g	81%	408 g	90%

Weight (in grams)	Rounded Percentage	Weight (in grams)	Rounded Percentage	Weight (in grams)	Rounded Percentage	Weight (in grams)	Rounded Percentage
409 g	90%	421 g	93%	433 g	95%	445 g	98%
410 g	90%	422 g	93%	434 g	95%	446 g	98%
411 g	90%	423 g	93%	435 g	96%	447 g	98%
412 g	91%	424 g	93%	436 g	96%	448 g	98%
413 g	91%	425 g	93%	437 g	96%	449 g	99%
414 g	91%	426 g	94%	438 g	96%	450 g	99%
415 g	91%	427 g	94%	439 g	96%	451 g	99%
416 g	91%	428 g	94%	440 g	97%	452 g	99%
417 g	92%	429 g	94%	441 g	97%	453 g	100%
418 g	92%	430 g	95%	442 g	97%	454 g	100%
419 g	92%	431 g	95%	443 g	97%	455 g	100%
420 g	92%	432 g	95%	444 g	98%		

Ounce Measurements in Rounded Percentages as They Relate to 16 Ounces (1 Pound) as 100 Percent

Weight (in ounces)	Rounded Percentage	Weight (in ounces)	Rounded Percentage	Weight (in ounces)	Rounded Percentage	Weight (in ounces)	Rounded Percentage
¼ ounce	2%	4¼ ounces	27%	8¼ ounces	52%	12¼ ounces	77%
½ ounce	3%	4½ ounces	28%	8½ ounces	53%	12½ ounces	78%
¾ ounce	5%	4¾ ounces	30%	8¾ ounces	55%	12¾ ounces	80%
1 ounce	6%	5 ounces	31%	9 ounces	56%	13 ounces	81%
1¼ ounces	8%	5¼ ounces	33%	9¼ ounces	58%	13¼ ounces	83%
1½ ounces	9%	5½ ounces	34%	9½ ounces	59%	13½ ounces	84%
1¾ ounces	11%	5¾ ounces	36%	9¾ ounces	61%	13¾ ounces	86%
2 ounces	13%	6 ounces	38%	10 ounces	63%	14 ounces	88%
2¼ ounces	14%	6¼ ounces	39%	10¼ ounces	64%	14¼ ounces	89%
2½ ounces	16%	6½ ounces	41%	10½ ounces	66%	14½ ounces	91%
2¾ ounces	17%	6¾ ounces	42%	10¾ ounces	67%	14¾ ounces	92%
3 ounces	19%	7 ounces	44%	11 ounces	69%	15 ounces	94%
3¼ ounces	20%	7¼ ounces	45%	11¼ ounces	70%	15¼ ounces	95%
3½ ounces	22%	7½ ounces	47%	11½ ounces	72%	15½ ounces	97%
3¾ ounces	23%	7¾ ounces	48%	11¾ ounces	73%	15¾ ounces	98%
4 ounces	25%	8 ounces	50%	12 ounces	75%	16 ounces	100%

High-Altitude Baking

Because most recipes are developed for use at sea level (including those in *The Advanced Professional Pastry Chef*), when baking at higher altitudes, where the atmospheric pressure is much lower, you must make some adjustments to produce a satisfactory result. Although some experimental baking has to be done to convert a sea-level recipe to a particular local condition and altitude, certain manufacturers supply the rate of adjustment for some of their products.

At high altitudes, the lower air pressure causes water to boil at a lower temperature. Thus, more evaporation takes place while a cake is baking, because the liquid begins to boil sooner. This results in insufficient moisture to fully gelatinize the starch, which weakens the structure. The lower air pressure also causes the batter to rise higher; however, it later collapses due to the lack of stabilizing starches.

It is necessary to make adjustments with cake baking starting at altitudes from 2500 feet (760 m). In general, the changes consist of:

- reducing the amount of baking powder or baking soda
- increasing the amount of liquid, sometimes with additional eggs, egg whites, or yolks
- increasing the flour
- using a higher baking temperature

These changes are applied to a greater degree as the altitude gets higher. Although the changes help protect the shape and consistency of the cake, they reduce its quality and flavor.

Adjustments for specific ingredients are as follows:

Leavening agents—Baking powder or soda, and any other substitute that reacts with heat, must be reduced by 20 percent starting at 2500 feet (760 m) and gradually be reduced up to 60 percent at 7500 feet (2280 m). For example, if a recipe calls for 10 ounces (285 g) baking powder, only 4 ounces (115 g) should be used at 7500 feet (2280 m). In a dark cake or muffin recipe that calls for both baking powder and baking soda together with buttermilk, it is best to change to sweet milk and use baking powder only (add the two amounts together) to save having to convert both leavening agents.

Eggs—At 2500 feet (760 m), add 3 percent more whole eggs, egg whites, or egg yolks. Progressively increase the amount of eggs until, at 7500 feet (2280 m), you are adding 15 percent more eggs. For example, if your recipe calls for 36 ounces (1 kg 25 g) eggs (which is 1 quart/960 ml), you must use an additional 5.4 ounces (150 g) or ¾ cup (180 ml) at 7500 feet (2280 m).

Flour—Beginning at 3000 feet (915 m), add 3 percent more flour, gradually increasing the amount up to 10 percent more at 8000 feet (2440 m). For example, if your recipe calls for 40 ounces (1 kg 135 g) flour, you should use 1¼ ounces (35 g) more at 3000 feet (915 m).

Oven—Starting at 3500 feet (1065 m), increase the baking temperature by 25 percent. For example, if your recipe calls for baking at 400°F (205°C), you should increase the temperature to 500°F (260°C) at 3500 feet (1065 m). The baking time should remain the same as at sea level, but you need to take care not to bake any longer than necessary to prevent the rapid evaporation that takes place at high altitudes.

Storage—Everything dries more quickly in thin air, so to ensure maximum moisture and freshness, cakes should be removed from the pans, wrapped in plastic, and stored in the refrigerator as soon as they have cooled. It is actually preferable not to keep any sponges in stock at high altitudes; instead, make them up as you need them.

Baumé Scale Readings

The Baumé scale of measurement is used to describe the concentration of sugar in a liquid by measuring the density. It is named for a French chemist, Antoine Baumé. Following are the Baumé readings for certain percentages of sugar solutions based on 2 cups (480 ml) water and varying amounts of sugar when the mixture is brought to a boil to dissolve the sugar and the solution is then measured at room temperature (65°F/19°C). When measured hot, the BE° will read 3° lower. If the syrup is boiled for any length of time, these readings will no longer apply because the evaporation that will take place will increase the ratio of sugar to water.

Baumé Readings at Room Temperature for Sugar Solutions Relative to 2 Cups (480 ml) Water

Water	Granulated Sugar	Baumé Reading
2 cups (480 ml)	5 ounces (150 g)	14° (sorbet syrup)
2 cups (480 ml)	6 ounces (170 g)	15°
2 cups (480 ml)	7 ounces (200 g)	17°
2 cups (480 ml)	8 ounces (225 g)	18° (baba syrup)
2 cups (480 ml)	9 ounces (255 g)	20° (candied citrus peel)
2 cups (480 ml)	10 ounces (285 g)	21°
2 cups (480 ml)	12 ounces (340 g)	25°
2 cups (480 ml)	14 ounces (400 g)	27°
2 cups (480 ml)	1 pound (455 g)	28° (simple syrup)
2 cups (480 ml)	1 pound 2 ounces (510 g)	29°
2 cups (480 ml)	1 pound 4 ounces (570 g)	31°
2 cups (480 ml)	1 pound 6 ounces (635 g)	32°
2 cups (480 ml)	1 pound 8 ounces (680 g)	33°
2 cups (480 ml)	1 pound 10 ounces (740 g)	34°
2 cups (480 ml)	1 pound 12 ounces (795 g)	35° (liqueur candies)

Saccharometers that are calibrated to measure density using a decimal scale are becoming more popular. The range of measurement varies with brand and price. A typical range is from 1.1 to 1.4, equivalent to 13° to 37°BE. Following are conversions from Baumé to the decimal system, rounded to the closest even number.

Degrees Baumé	Decimal Reading	Degrees Baumé	Decimal Reading
5°BE	1.03	19°BE	1.15
6°BE	1.04	20°BE	1.16
7°BE	1.05	21°BE	1.17
8°BE	1.05	22°BE	1.18
9°BE	1.06	23°BE	1.19
10°BE	1.07	24°BE	1.20
11°BE	1.08	25°BE	1.21
12°BE	1.09	26°BE	1.22
13°BE	1.10	27°BE	1.23
14°BE	1.11	28°BE	1.24
15°BE	1.12	29°BE	1.25
16°BE	1.12	30°BE	1.26
17°BE	1.13	31°BE	1.27
18°BE	1.14	32°BE	1.28

Baumé thermometer—This tool is also known as a *saccharometer, syrup-density meter, sugar densimeter, hydrometer,* and *Baumé hydrometer.* It is used to determine the concentration of sugar in a liquid, which affects the density of the solution. By technical definition, it is not actually a thermometer because it does not measure heat. However, *Baumé thermometer* is the term typically used in the industry. A saccharometer is a thin glass tube with a graduated scale that ranges from 0° to 50° BE. The weights at the bottom of the saccharometer are precisely adjusted by the manufacturer so that it will read 0° BE when placed in water that is 58°F (15°C). The mixture being measured must therefore be at or close to this temperature (tepid room temperature) for the reading to be accurate. Before using the instrument for the first time, it is a good idea to test it and, if necessary, compensate for any discrepancy, plus or minus, when using it. The weights at the bottom also allow the instrument to remain in a vertical position in the liquid. To use the saccharometer, a high narrow container, preferably a laboratory glass, must be filled with enough of the liquid that is to be measured for the saccharometer to float. The scale is read at the point where the instrument meets the surface of the liquid. For example, if the saccharometer settles at 28°BE, the density of the solution is 1.28, which means that 1 liter (33.8 ounces) of the solution will weigh 1 kg 280 g (2 pounds 13 ounces). The calibration on the scale refers to degrees of Baumé. A list of Baumé readings relative to various levels of sugar concentration appears at left.

Another instrument with a very similar name—*saccharimeter*—also measures sugar concentration in a liquid but does so by measuring the angle through which the plane of vibration of polarized light is turned by the solution. The names of both instruments come from the Greek words *sakcharon* ("sugar") and *metron* ("measure").

Brix Scale

The Brix scale was invented by a German scientist named Adolph Brix. It is used for the same purpose as the Baumé scale: to measure the sugar content in a liquid. The Brix scale is used only with pure sucrose solutions; it cannot be used with other solutions. Both the Brix and Baumé methods use a hydrometer, although, when using the Baumé scale, it is more commonly known as a *saccharometer*. The Baumé scale is expressed in degrees and the Brix scale is based on the decimal system. The Brix scale is calibrated to read 0.1° Brix at 68°F (20°C). A solution containing 20 grams sucrose per 100 grams liquid will read 20° Brix.

The Brix scale is used in the wine-making industry to measure the sugar content in fresh or fermenting grape juice; by farmers, in conjunction with other tools, to measure the sugar-to-acid ratio in determining when to harvest fruits; and in the commercial fruit canning industry in the preparation of sugar syrups.

Following are equivalent measures for degrees Baumé and degrees Brix, with the solution measured at 68°F (20°C).

Degrees Baumé	Degrees Brix	Degrees Baumé	Degrees Brix
5° BE	3.5° Brix	21° BE	37.9° Brix
6° BE	5.4° Brix	22° BE	39.6° Brix
7° BE	7.4° Brix	23° BE	41.5° Brix
8° BE	9.3° Brix	24° BE	43.5° Brix
9° BE	11.3° Brix	25° BE	45.4° Brix
10° BE	14.2° Brix	26° BE	47.4° Brix
11° BE	16.2° Brix	27° BE	49.4° Brix
12° BE	18.1° Brix	28° BE	51.3° Brix
13° BE	20.1° Brix	29° BE	53.3° Brix
14° BE	23.1° Brix	30° BE	55.2° Brix
15° BE	25.0° Brix	31° BE	57.1° Brix
16° BE	27.0° Brix	32° BE	59.1° Brix
17° BE	29.1° Brix	33° BE	61.0° Brix
18° BE	31.1° Brix	34° BE	63.0° Brix
19° BE	33.0° Brix	35° BE	64.9° Brix
20° BE	35.9° Brix	36° BE	66.9° Brix

Sugar Boiling Conversions

If you were to compare the sugar conversion tables in ten cookbooks, you would probably find ten different temperatures and almost as many names used to describe the same stage. Some charts have 14 separate stages, which can really make your head spin! All of these names and stages are, in a way, misleading and unrealistic for use by anyone who does not have years of experience. For example, by the time you have tested and determined that the boiling sugar is at the crack stage, it has probably already reached hard crack. What is important is not what a particular stage is called and how to test for it, but what temperature is required for the sugar syrup based on what it is to be used for. I suggest

you rely on an accurate sugar thermometer rather than your poor index finger and ignore all the different names; however, the testing procedures are listed below should you want to use them.

Special thermometers for boiling sugar are calibrated according to the temperature range needed. Professional thermometers have a wire screen that protects the glass and should be stored hanging up, using the handle that is part of this screen (see "About Thermometers," page 630, for more information). Although centigrade is used more and more for measuring sugar in European countries, I have included the old Réaumur system here because it is still part of the scale on professional European thermometers.

Required Temperature and Testing Procedures for Sugar Stages

Sugar Stage	Fahrenheit Reading	Celsius Reading	Réaumur Reading	Manual Testing Procedure
Thread	215° to 230°	102° to 110°	82° to 88°	Pull a small amount of sugar between your thumb and index finger; shorter or longer threads will form depending on the temperature.
Soft Ball	240°	115°	92°	Place your index finger in ice-cold water, dip it very quickly into the hot syrup, and immediately plunge it back into the ice water. The sugar will fall off your finger and you will be able to roll it into a ball.
Firm Ball	245°	118°	94°	The test is the same as for the soft ball stage, but here the ball will be firmer.
Hard Ball	250° to 260°	122° to 127°	97° to 101°	The test is the same as for the soft ball stage, but here the sugar will be more resistant to forming a ball and the ball will not be malleable.
Small Crack	265° to 270°	130° to 132°	104° to 105°	Dip your finger into ice water and then into the sugar syrup as for the soft ball test; at this stage you will be unable to form the sugar into a ball. The sugar will also show small cracks.
Crack	275° to 280°	135° to 138°	108° to 110°	The test is the same as for the small crack stage, but at this stage, the sugar will break apart.
Hard Crack	295° to 310°	146° to 155°	116° to 123°	The test is the same as for the small crack stage, but at this stage, the sugar will shatter when placed in the ice water.
Caramel	320°	160°	128°	Test by observing the color of the sugar: The syrup will change from amber to golden, and then become light brown.

Acetate/polyurethane strips
  molds, 408
  rings, 135, 164, 238, 376
  sheets, 109, 375, 537–539
  support frame for, 155–157
  tubes, 154, 155, 358
Air pumps, for sugar blowing, 610, 611
Almond(s)
  blanched, 257
  Chocolate Snow Hearts, 456–457
  Doubles, 117
  Fig Logs, 559
  Filling, 161
  Filling, Cointreau-Flavored, Pears
     California with, 302–303
  Finlander Praline, 560
  Florentina Cups, 687–689
  Frangipane Filling, 769–770
  Frangipane Sheet, 115
  Gianduja, 560–561
  Gianduja Bites, 561
  Ice Cream, 257
    Chocolate-Banana Tart with
      Spun Sugar and, 151–152
    and Kadaif Phyllo Nests, Saffron-
      Poached Pears with, 254–257
  Japonaise Meringue Batter, 781
  Joconde Sponge Base I, 670
  Joconde Sponge Base II, 671
  Leaf Croquant, 582–583
  Macaroon Candies, 121
  Macaroons, Small, 57
  Noisette Rings, 105–106
  Nougat for Branchli, 559
  Nougatine, 584–586
  Nougat Montélimar, 586–587
  Opera Sponge, 48
  Paste
    Basic Recipe, 749
    Marzipan, 633, 635
    in Scandinavian cakes, 70
    in sponge cake, 5
  Petit Four Glacés with Apricot Filling
     and Frangipane, 114–115
  Praline, 804
  Sicilian Macaroon Cake, 55–58
  Sponge, 795–796
  Sponge, Cocoa- (variation), 796
  in Triestine Bread, 441–442
  Truffles, 95–96
American wedding cake, 69–70
Angel, Marzipan, 653–655
Angel Food Cake, 796
Anise
  Lemon Parfait, -Scented, with Lemon
     Cookie Tumbleweeds, 375–376

  Springerle, 466–467
Apple(s)
  about, 327
  Caramel-Dipped Wedges, 625
  Chip, Pink Lady Apple and Pear
     Cream with Orange Syrup
     and an, 348–349
  Chips, 721
  Coupe Sweden, 216
  Crème Brûlée, 325–326
  Filling, Chunky, 216–217, 767
  Galette, Caramelized, in Phyllo
     Dough with Kumquat Sauce,
     143–145
  Glacéed, 580–581
  Marzipan, 636–637
  Pink Lady, and Pear Cream with
     Orange Syrup and an Apple
     Chip, 348–349
  poaching, 790
  Tarte Tatin Moderne, 416–421
  varieties, 327
  Wine Cake, 9–11
Apple Cider-Caramel Sauce, 419
Apricot(s)
  Cream Cake, 12–13
  Cream Cake, Contemporary
     (variation), 13–14
  and Fig Tart with Prickly Pear
     Sorbet, 218–219
  Filling, Petits Fours Glacés with
     Frangipane and, 114–115
  Glacéed, 580–581
  Glaze, 774
  Gratin with Sabayon of Muscat
     Wine, 269–270
  poaching, 790
  Sauce, 303
  skins, removing, 270
  Whipped Cream, 13
Asian Pear Tart with Honey-Scented
    Pear Frozen Yogurt, 270–272
Aspic
  Citrus, 314
  Pink Champagne, 384–385
  Pink Champagne, Brandied Cherry
     Ganache Towers with Curvy
     Tuile Strips and, 384
Australian wedding cake, 69
Avocado-Mango Ice Cream, 379
  Baked Plantains in Gingered Meyer
     Lemon Syrup with, 377–378
  Baked Vanilla–Infused Pineapple
     with Mango Fruit Wafer and,
     130–133

Baked Alaska, 220-223
Baked Bananas with Banana-Tofu
    Frozen Yogurt, 273-274
Baked Chocolate Sheet, 355
Baked Plantains in Gingered Meyer
    Lemon Syrup with Avocado-
    Mango Ice Cream, 377–379
Baked Vanilla-Infused Pineapple with
    Mango-Avocado Ice Cream and
    Mango FruitWafer, 130-133
Baker's percentage, 820
Baking paper
  securing on cake ring, 27
  spreading batter, 481
Baklava, 136-137
  with Mascarpone Bavarian and
    Cherry Sauce, 134-137
Banana(s)
  about, 274
  Baked, with Banana-Tofu Frozen
    Yogurt, 273-274
  -Chocolate Mousse Cake Nouvelle
    (variation), 30
  Chocolate Mousse Cake with, 29–31
  -Chocolate Tart with Almond Ice
    Cream and Spun Sugar, 151–152
  Macaroons, 104-105
  Milk Chocolate Marquise with
    Finger Banana Center and
    Red Currant Sauce, 408–410
  Red Banana Truffles in Phyllo
    Dough, 181–183
  Rum Pudding with Brandied
    Whipped Cream and Ginger-
    bread Lattice (variation), 486
  -Tofu Frozen Yogurt, 274
Bannetons, about, 433
Bars, Lebkuchen, 463-464
Basic Bombe Mixture, 206
Basket(s)
  bannetons, about, 433
  Bread, 425-430
  Cherry, with Cherry Compote and
    Black Pepper Frozen Yogurt,
    146-149
  Dacquoise, with Fresh Raspberries,
    Raspberry Sauce, and Mango
    Coulis, 280–282
  Fruit, Global Fresh, with Feijoa
    Sorbet, 289–291
Basketweave pattern, buttercream, 87
Battenburg, 96-97
Baumé scale of measurement, 825
Baumé thermometer, 825
Bavarian Cream
  about, 322-323

Bavarois Filling, 21-22
Blackberry, 366
Blackberry Pastries (variation), 366
Charente Bavarois, 334
Charente Bavarois Cake, 19-22
Charente Bavarois Cake, Moderne
        (variation), 20-21
Citrus, 340
Classic, 767
Classic, Chocolate (variation), 768
Crème Anglaise-Based, 768
in Croquembouche, Individual,
        173-174
Lychee Bavarois, 295-296
Mascarpone, 134-135
Persimmon Bavarois, 479
Quick, 774
Red Currant, 200
unmolding, 323
Vanilla Bean-Lemon Verbena, 60-61
Verbena, 352
White Chocolate Filling, 41-42
White Chocolate Neapolitan,
        360-363
Wine Foam and Blackberry,
        Greystone, 363-366
Bavarois, Charente Cake, 19-22
Bavarois, Charente Cake Moderne
        (variation), 20-21
Bavarois Filling, 21-22
Bear, Marzipan, 637-638
Beet Juice, 750
Beetles
    Chocolate May Beetles, 527-529
    Chocolate May Beetles, Chocolate
        Rum Pudding with, 336-338
Belgian wedding cakes, 70-71
Bénédictine
    about, 226
    Soufflé Glacé, 224-226
Blackberry
    Bavarian, 366
    Bavarian Pastries (variation), 366
    Bavarian, Wine Foam and,
        Greystone, 363-366
    Cake (variation), 54
Black Currant
    Cake, 14-17
    Decorating Syrup, 758-759
    Glaze, 16
    Mousse, 15
    Puree, 16
    Sauce, 391
    Sauce, Caramel-Centered Milk
        Chocolate Mousse with,
        389-391
Black Pepper Frozen Yogurt, 403
    Cherry Baskets with Cherry
        Compote and, 146-149
Black-Tie Strawberries, 236-237
Blood Orange Gratin, 275-276

Bloom
    chocolate, 8
    gelatin, 7
Blown sugar, 610-611
Blueberry
    Financier with Toasted Lemon
        Verbena Sabayon and
        Mascarpone Sherbet, 380-384
    Pirouettes, 137-139
    Sauce, 139
    Soufflé, 369-370
Boiled Sugar. See Sugar, Boiled Sugar
Bombe(s)
    Aboukir, 207-208
    about, 203-204
    Basic Mixture, 206
    Bourdaloue, 208
    Ceylon, 209-210
    Monarch, 211-212
Bourbon Sauce, 182-183
Bow with Ribbons, Pulled Sugar, 608-609
Box(es)
    Caramel, 141-142
        with Caramel-Macadamia Nut
            Mousse, 140-143
        Wild Strawberries Romanoff in, 201
    Chocolate Candy Box, 565-567
    Trio of Chocolates with Marzipan
        Parfait, 187-191
Box forms, 472, 475-476
Braided Stollen, 430-431
Branchli (Branches), 558-559
Brandy(ied)
    Cherry Ganache, 110
    Cherry Ganache Towers with Pink
        Champagne Aspic and Tuile
        Strips, 384-385
    Cherry Mousse, 111
    Gingerbread Cake, 443
    Persimmon Pudding, 486-488
    Pretzels, 117-118
    Traditional Fruitcake, 450-451
    Whipped Cream, 488
    Whipped Cream, Banana Rum
        Pudding with Gingerbread
        Lattice and (variation), 486
Bread(s)
    bannetons, about, 433
    Basket, 425-430
    braided loaves and wreaths, 436
    Chestnut, 432-433
    Lucia Buns, 436-437
    Panettone, 437-438
    Pigs, Whole Large (variation), 440
    Pig's Head Dinner Rolls
        (variation), 439
    Pigs' Heads, Sweet, 438-440
    Stollen
        about, 435
        Braided, 430-431
        Dresdener, 434-435

Swedish Spice (Vörtbröd), 440-441
    Triestine, 441-442
Bread Dough
    Cardamom Yeast, Rich, 437
    Weaver's, 430
    White, 440
Bread Pudding, Chocolate, with
        Cookie Citrus Rind, 152-154
Brix scale, 826
Bubble Sugar, 615-616
    Isomalt, 617
    Twice-Cooked (variation), 616-617
Bûches de Nöel. See Yule Log(s)
Bumblebees, Marzipan, 639
Buns, Lucia, 436-437
Buried Ruby Treasure, 385-389
Butter
    Clarified, 753-754
    and Flour Mixture, for preparing
        pans, 750
    metric/U.S. volume equivalents for, 816
    in sponge cakes, 5
Buttercream
    about, 751
    basketweave pattern, 87
    crumb layer, 84
    drop-loop pattern, 85
    Praline, 176
    Vanilla (French Method), 752
    Vanilla (Swiss Method), 753
    vertical lines, 86
Buttercream in Cakes and Pastries
    Battenburg, 96-97
    Chestnut Puzzle Cake, 22-24
    Chocolate Triangles, 98-100
    Christmas Tree Pastries, 458-459
    Dobos Torte, 34-36
    Marjolaine, 174-176
    Mocha Cake, 45-46
    Mocha Cake, Classic, 46
    Opera Cake, 47-48
    Opera Slices, 106-107
    Queen of Sheba Cake, 50-52
    Raspberry Cake, 52-54
    Strawberry Bagatelle, 58-61
    Strawberry Kirsch Cake, 61-63
    wedding cakes, 84-87
    Yule Log Pastries, 468-469
    Yule Logs, 453-456
Butterfly(ies)
    Chocolate Monarch Ornaments,
        550-552
    Chocolate Monarch Ornaments, in
        Bombe Monarch, 210-212
    Cookie, 695-698

Cage(s)
    Caramel, 618
        Caramel Ice Cream in a, 227
        Forbidden Peach, 164-165
        Half-Sphere (variation), 619

Cages (cont'd)
Simplified, 619
Chocolate, 543-544
Chocolate, Snowbird in a, 413-415
Cake(s), 2-65. See also Cheesecake;
Sponge Cake; Torte(s);
Wedding cakes
Apple Wine, 9–10
Apricot Cream, 12–13
Apricot Cream, Contemporary
(variation), 13–14
Blackberry (variation), 54
Black Currant, 14–16
Caramel, 17–18
Charente Bavarois, 19–20
Charente Bavarois, Moderne
(variation), 20–21
Chestnut (variation), 446–447
Chestnut Puzzle, 22–24
Chocolate. See also Sponge Cake
Chocolate Dome, with Cherry
Sauce and Chocolate Lace,
391-393
Espresso, with Coffee-Bean
Crisps, 401–404
Ganache, 27–28
Mousse, with Banana, 29
Mousse, -Banana Nouvelle
(variation), 30
Mousse, and Frangelico, 24–26
Mousse, and Frangelico,
Contemporary (variation), 26–27
Parisienne, 49–50
Queen of Sheba Base, 51–52
Rounds, Dark Chocolate, 242
Shingle, Dark Chocolate, 32–33
Truffle Batter, 172–173
Truffle, Hot Chocolate, 169–173
Truffle, with Raspberries, 31–32
circumference, calculating, 819
Coconut-Mango, Tropical,
suggestion for wedding cake,
90-91
Coconut, Tropical, 63–65
Cranberry Mousse (variation), 16
Devil's Food, 393
Fillings. See Cake Fillings
Fruitcake
Lemon Verbena-Scented, 449–450
Panforte, 451–453
Panforte, Dark, 453
Traditional, 450–451
Gâteau Malakoff, 36–37
Gâteau Mocha Carousel, 38–39
Gianduja, suggestion for wedding
cake, 89
Ginger, 379
Gingerbread, Brandied, 443
Harlequin, 40–41
Ice Cream, Jamaica, 239–241
Lemon Chiffon, 42–44
Lemon Chiffon Fruit Basket

(variation), 44
Lemon Verbena–Raspberry, sugges-
tion for wedding cake, 89
Macaroon, Sicilian, 55–58
Marjolaine, 174–176
Marquise, Miniature White
Chocolate, 163
Mocha, 45–46
suggestion for wedding cake, 90
Mocha, Classic (variation), 47
Mousse
Black Currant, 14–16
Chocolate, with Banana, 29
Chocolate and Frangelico, 24–26
Chocolate and Frangelico,
Contemporary (variation), 26–27
Cranberry (variation), 16
Kiwi (variation), 197
Round Tropical (variation), 197
Tropical, 195–197
Opera, 47–49
Persimmon Dome, with
Gingerbread Lattice, 484–485
Princess, suggestion for wedding
cake, 90
Queen of Sheba, 50–52
Raspberry, 52–53
Raspberry Nouvelle (variation),
53–54
special-occasion, piping designs
for, 730–747
Strawberry Bagatelle, 58–61
Strawberry Kirsch, 61–63
Tiramisù, suggestion for wedding
cake, 91
Yule Logs (Bûches de Noël),
453–456
Cake Batter
Ladyfinger, 21
Mascarpone Cheesecake, 178
Truffle Cake, Chocolate, 172–173
Cake Fillings. See also Buttercream
Apricot Whipped Cream, 13
Bavarian Cream, Vanilla Bean-
Lemon Verbena, 60–61
Bavarian, White Chocolate, 41–42
Bavarois, 21–22
Black Currant Mousse, 15
Calvados Wine, 11
Caramel Cream, 18
Chestnut Rum, 447
Chocolate
Cognac Cream, 30-31
Dark Chocolate Cream, 26
Ganache, 28
Gianduja Cream, Vanilla-
Scented, 34
Coconut Cream, 65
gelatin in
adding and reheating, 7
powder, 6–7
sheet, 7–8

Kirsch Whipped Cream, 63
Lemon Chiffon, 43
Macaroon-Maraschino Whipped
Cream, 58
Maraschino Cream, 37
Mocha Whipped Cream, 39
Raspberry Cream, 54
Cake frames, making, 59
Cake molds, Flexipan, 6
Cake pans
capacity, calculating, 80–81, 819
preparing, butter and flour mixture
for, 750
size, oven temperature and, 6
Cake rings
acetate/polyurethane strips, 238, 376
baking paper on, 27
size, oven temperature and, 6
Cake stand, for wedding cakes, 84–85
Cake Syrup, Plain, 789
Calvados
Diplomat Cream, 764
Pastry Cream, 764
Wine Filling, 11
Camels, Tuile, 385, 389
Candied Citrus Peels, 756-758
Quick Method for (variation), 758
Candies. See also Chocolate,
Candies; Fruit, Candied
Jellies, Lemon, Raspberry, and
Strawberry (Pâte de Fruit), 591–592
Leaf Croquant, 582–583
Macaroon, 121
Marshmallows, 583–584
Nougatine, 584–586
Nougat Montélimar, 586–587
Candle Pastries, Holiday, 462–463
Candles, Marzipan, 463
Candy thermometer, 570, 631
Cappuccino Mousse, 329
with Sambuca Cream in a
Chocolate Coffee Cup, 328–332
Caramel. See also Caramel Glass
Paste Decorations; Caramelized
Sugar Decorations
Cake, 17–18
-Centered Milk Chocolate Mousse
with Black Currant Sauce,
389–391
Cream, 18
Crème Caramel Nouvelle, 342–344
Croquembouche, Individual, 173–174
Custard, Gingered, 344
Ice Cream, 227–228
Ice Cream, in a Caramel Cage, 227–228
Mousse, -Macadamia Nut, 142–143
Mousse, -Macadamia Nut,
Caramel Boxes with, 140–143
Sauce
Apple Cider-, 419
Clear, 328
Fortified, 19

Caramel Glass Paste, 666
Caramel Glass Paste Decorations
    Boxes, 141–142
        with Caramel-Macadamia Nut
            Mousse, 140–143
        molding blocks for, 141
        Wild Strawberries Romanoff in, 201
    Screens, 666–668
    Screens, Orange-Chocolate Towers
        with Orange Syrup and, 179–181
    Wedges
        Curved, 669–670
        Fluted (variation), 668–669
        Simple (variation), 669
Caramelized
    Apple Galette in Phyllo Dough
        with Kumquat Sauce, 143–145
    Nuts, 626
    Pineapple Barbados, 276–278
    Pineapple with Coconut Ice Cream
        (variation), 278
    Walnuts, 317–318
Caramelized Sugar
    for Crème Brûlée, 326, 341, 489
    for Decorations, 613–614
    for Dobos Torte, 35–36
    Dry Method, 611, 612–613
    pan for, 611–612
    removing from pan, 612
    spreading, 35
    Wet Method, 611, 613
Caramelized Sugar Decorations. *See
    also* Sugar Decorations
    bag for, 615
    Bubble Sugar
        Basic Recipe, 615-616
        Twice-Cooked (variation), 616–617
    Cage(s), 618
        Caramel Ice Cream in a, 227
        Forbidden Peach, 164–165
        Half-Sphere, Using (variation), 619
        Simplified, 619
    Corkscrews, 620–621
    Fans, 627–628
    Fences, 621
    Fruit and Nuts, Caramel-Dipped,
        624–625
    safety precautions, 614-615
    Spheres, 299
    Spiders, 622–623
    Spirals, 623–624
    Spun Sugar (variation), 594
    Sugar Shards, 628–629
Cardamom Yeast Dough, Rich, 437
Carrots, Marzipan, 639–640
Cashew(s)
    about, 166
    Ice Cream, 166–167
    Ice Cream, in Forbidden Peach,
        164–167
Cassata Parfait with Meringue,
    228–231

Casting, Chocolate, 553–554
Cast Sugar
    casting forms, 603
    Figures, 597–604
    repairing breaks, 602
    silicone template, 604
    spraying color, 604
Catalan Custard, 341
    Crème Catalan, Sherry-Poached
        Black Mission Figs with,
        353–354
    Small, 354
Centigrade/Fahrenheit temperature
    equivalents, 812–815
Chalet(s)
    Chocolate, 473–476
    Chocolate, with White Chocolate
        and Pistachio Pâté and Bitter
        Chocolate Sauce, 470–477
    Santa's Gingerbread, 499–503
    Support Box, 475–476
Champagne
    Aspic, Pink Champagne, 384–385
    Aspic, Pink Champagne, Brandied
        Cherry Ganache Towers with
        Curvy Tuile Strips and, 384
    Sabayon, 311
    Sabayon, Fresh Strawberries with, 283
Chantilly Cream, 765
Chardonnay Wine Sauce, 161–162
    Saffron-Poached Date-Stuffed
        Pears with, 158–162
Charente Bavarois, 334
    Cake, 19–20
    Cake, Moderne (variation), 20–21
Charlotte(s)
    about, 321–322
    Charente, 332–334
    Lychee Royal, 294–296
    Lychee, Striped (variation), 296
    Persimmon, 478–479
    Russe (variation), 333
Cheese. *See also* Cheesecake
    Mascarpone, 779
    quark, about, 297
    Yogurt, 804
Cheesecake
    Chèvre, in a Cocoa-Nib Florentina
        Cup with Port-Poached Pears,
        150–151
    Marbled, with Quark Cheese, 297–298
    Mascarpone, with Lemon Verbena
        Panna Cotta, 177–179
    Mascarpone Batter, 178
Cherry(ies). *See also* Kirsch
    Baskets with Cherry Compote and
        Black Pepper Frozen Yogurt,
        146–149
    Brandied, and Chocolate Pastries,
        Petite, 109–111
    Brandied, Mousse, 111
    Compote, 149

Filling, 765
Filling, Fresh Cherry (variation), 766
Ganache, Brandied, 111
    Ganache Towers, with Pink
        Champagne Aspic and Curvy
        Tuile Strips, 384–385
    guinettes, about, 388
    Guinettes, Sauce, 388
    Jelly Centers, Ruby Fruit, 387
    Jubilee, 232
    Maraschino Cream, 37
    Maraschino-Macaroon Whipped
        Cream, 58
    poaching, 790
    Sauce, 230
    Sorbet, Double Cherry, 306–307
    Tuile Spoons, 388
Chestnut(s)
    about, 433
    Bread, 432–433
    Cake (variation), 446–447
    canned purée, about, 478
    Mont Blanc with Pomegranate
        Seeds and Vanilla Curly Cues,
        477–478
    Puree, 445
    Puzzle Cake, 22–24
    removing shells, 432
    Rum Filling, 447
    Rum Torte, 444–445
Chèvre Cheesecake in a Cocoa-Nib
    Florentina Cup with Port-
    Poached Pears, 150–151
Chiffon Cake
    Lemon, 42-44
    Lemon Fruit Basket (variation), 44
    Sponge I, 797
    Sponge II, 798
Children, Marzipan, for the
    Traditional Gingerbread
    House, 656–657
Chips
    Apple or Pear, 721
    Mango, 721
    Plantain, 722
Chocolate. *See also* Chocolate
    Decorations; Tempered
    chocolate
    Bavarian Cream, Classic (variation), 768
    Bread Pudding with Cookie Citrus
        Rind, 152–154
    Buttercream (Italian Method), 752
    Cake. *See also* Chocolate, Sponge
        Dome, with Cherry Sauce and
        Chocolate Lace, 391–393
        Espresso, with Coffee-Bean Crisps,
        401–404
    Ganache, 27–28
    Gianduja, suggestion for wedding
        cake, 89
    Mousse, with Banana, 29

Chocolate (cont'd)
    Mousse, -Banana, Nouvelle
        (variation), 30
    Mousse, Chocolate and Frangelico,
        24–26
    Mousse, Chocolate and Frangelico,
        Contemporary (variation),
        26–27
    Parisienne, 49–50
    Queen of Sheba Base, 51–52
    Rounds, Dark, 242
    Shingle, Dark, 32–33
    Truffle Batter, 172–173
    Truffle, Hot Chocolate, 169–173
    Truffle, with Raspberries, 31–32
  Candies
    Branchli (Branches), 558–559
    Chocolate Candy Box, 565-567
    Fig Logs, 559
    Gianduja Bites, 561
    Hazelnut Cinnamon Ganache,
        561–562
    Mimosa, 564
    Orange Creams, Chocolate-
        Covered, 562
    Pistachio Slices, 564–565
    Praline, Finlander, 560
    Pralines, Marzipan, 563
  and Cherry Pastries, Petite
        Brandied, 109–111
  Coconut Tropicana Pastries,
        100–101
  dipping pastries in, 94–95
  Fillings
    Bavarian Cream, Classic, 768
    Chocolate Cream, 766
    Cognac Cream, 30–31
    Crème Parisienne, 768
    Dark Chocolate, 157–158, 356
    Dark Chocolate Cream, 26
    Dark Chocolate Mousse, 335
    Ganache, 28, 770
    Ganache, Quick (variation), 771
    Ganache, Spiced, 412–413
    Gianduja Cream, 393
    Gianduja Cream, Vanilla-
        Scented, 34
    Light, 158
    Marquise, 395
    Milk Chocolate, 356, 416
    Orange-, 181
    White Chocolate, 356
    White Chocolate Bavarian, 41–42
    White Chocolate Mousse, for
        Teardrops, 336
    White Chocolate Treasure,
        386–387
  fondant, making, 679
  Ganache
    Brandied Cherry, 111
    Brandied Cherry Towers with
        Pink Champagne Aspic and

    Curvy Tuile Strips, 384–385
  Cake, 27–28
Filling, 28, 770
Hazelnut Cinnamon, 561–562
  Quick (variation), 771
  Rounds, 152
  Spiced Filling, 412–413
  Spiced, and Tea Ice Cream
    Marco Polo, 410–413
  Towers, 154-158
Gianduja, 560–561
Gianduja Bites, 561
Glaze, 774–775
  Dark, 393
  Mirror, 775
  Opera, 49
  hardening, 396
  history of, 505–507
Ice Cream
  Cocoa Nib-White Chocolate,
    397–398
  Cocoa Nib-White Chocolate,
    with Chocolate Lace Igloo
    and Tuile Polar Bear, 396–399
  Coffee-Scented, 223–224
  White Chocolate, 217
  White Chocolate, Gingered
    (variation), 217
Ladyfingers (variation), 801
Macadamia Morsels, -Filled, 118–119
Marquise
  Milk Chocolate, with Finger
    Banana Center and Red
    Currant Sauce, 408–410
  with Passion Fruit Parfait and a
    Lace Cookie Bouquet, 394–396
  White Chocolate, Miniature, 163
medicinal properties of, 507–508
melting, tips for, 511
Mousse
  Dark Chocolate Filling, 335
  Raspberry-White Chocolate, 347
  in Ribbon Teardrops, 334–336
  Rum-Scented, 101
  White Chocolate Filling for
    Teardrops, 336
  White Chocolate and Pistachio,
    with Chocolate Lace, 357–360
Pâté, White Chocolate and
    Pistachio, 472–473
Pâté, White Chocolate and
    Pistachio, Chocolate Chalet
    with Bitter Chocolate Sauce
    and, 470–477
production of, 508–511
quality of, 508
Rum Ball Filling, 790–791
Rum Pudding, 337
Rum Pudding with Chocolate May
    Beetles, 336–338
Sauce, 413
  Bitter Chocolate (variation), 413

  Bitter Chocolate, Chocolate
    Chalet with White Chocolate
    and Pistachio Pâté and,
    470–477
  Hot Fudge, 254
  for Piping, 681
  White Chocolate, 803
Sheet, Baked, 355
Snowbird in a Chocolate Cage,
    413–415
Snow Hearts, 456–457
Soufflé (variation), 368
Sponge, 795
  Bittersweet, 33–34
  Chiffon (variations), 797, 798
  Hazelnut-, 800
  Low-Cholesterol (variation), 294
Strawberries, Black-Tie, 236–237
Tart, -Banana, with Almond Ice Cream
    and Spun Sugar, 151–152
Terrine, Triple Chocolate, 354–356
Terrine, Triple-Chocolate,
    Miniature, 192–193
Towers, Ganache, 154–158
Towers, Orange-, with Orange
    Syrup and Caramel Screens,
    179–181
Triangles, 98–100
Trio of Chocolates with Marzipan
    Parfait, 187–191
Truffle Cream, Wild Honey, 169
Truffles
  Dark Chocolate Espresso, 190
  Milk Chocolate, 191
  White Chocolate with Praline,
    190–191
Tuile Decorating Paste, 695
Tulip with Mango Coulis,
    Macadamia Nut Ice Cream in
    a, 243–245
Chocolate Decorations. *See also*
    Tempered chocolate
  Black-Tie Strawberries, 236–237
  Boxes, Chocolate Candy Box,
    565–567
  Boxes, Cupid's Treasure Chest,
    345–347
  Chalets, 473–476
  Chalet with White Chocolate and
    Pistachio Pâté and Bitter
    Chocolate Sauce, 470–477
  Cigarettes
    with Coating Chocolate, 516–517
    with Tempered Chocolate, 517
    Two-Toned, 518
  Cocoa Painting, 555
  Corkscrews, 519
  Cornets, Striped Chocolate, 535
  Cups
    Coffee Cup, Cappuccino Mousse
    with Sambuca Cream in a,
    328–332

Coffee Cups, 330–332
  Striped Chocolate, 536–537
  Striped Chocolate, with Tuile
    Steam Decorations, 415–416
Cutouts, 520–521
decorative strips, 375
Fans (Ruffles), 521–522
Fences, 476–477
Figures, Hollow, Using Molds,
  555–556
Figurines, Piped, 545
Goblets, 522–523
Goblets, Marbled or Multicolored,
  524
Honeycomb Decor, 534–535
instant-set method, 515–516
Lace, 525
  Chocolate Dome Cake with
    Cherry Sauce and, 391–393
  Igloo, Cocoa Nib-White
    Chocolate Ice Cream with a
    Tuile Polar Bear and, 396–399
  Igloos, 526
  White Chocolate and Pistachio
    Mousse with, 357–360
Leaves, 527
May Beetles, 527–529
May Beetles, Chocolate Rum
  Pudding with, 336–338
Modeling Chocolate, 541–542
Molded chocolate strips, 540
Molds, Hollow Figures Using,
  555–556
Noodles, 529–530
Patterned Sheets, 537–540
  Marbleized Chocolate, 539–540
  with Wood Grain, 537–539
Piped
  Cages, 543–544
  Cage, Snowbird in a, 413–415
  Casting, 553-554
  Chocolate for, 543
  designs, 546–549
  Figurines, 545
  instant-set method, 515–516
  letters and numbers, templates for,
    550
  Monarch Butterfly Ornaments,
    550–552
  Plates, Decorating with, 552-553
  Streaking, 553
Ribbons, 530–531
Roses, 542
Shavings, 531–532
Shingles, 532
Sprayed, 556–558
  Chocolate Solution for, 557-558
  Cocoa Solution for, 558
Streaking, 553
streaking with pie tin template, 692
Teardrops, Translucent, 419–420, 421
Twirls, 533–534

Wedding Cake Ornament, 88
Chocolate funnel, about, 679
Chocolate Paper Paste, 719–720
Christmas Cookie Ornaments, 457–458
Christmas Tree(s)
  Cookie, 482–484
  Pastries, 458–459
Chunky Apple Filling, 216–217, 767
Cigarettes, Chocolate. See Chocolate
  Decorations, Cigarettes
Cinnamon
  about, 56
  Hazelnut Ganache, 561–562
  Macaroon Cake, Sicilian, 55–57
  Semifreddo Venezia with Coffee
    Bean Crisps, 233–234
  Stars, 460
  Sticks, Cookie, 420–421
  Sugar, 753
Circles, Chocolate Cutouts, 520-521
Citrus
  Aspic, 314
  Cream, 340
  Cream with Pink Grapefruit and
    Orange, 338–340
Citrus Peels, Candied, 756-758
  Quick Method for (variation), 758
Citrus Rind(s), Cookie, 698
  Chocolate Bread Pudding with,
    152–154
  Frosted Minneola Tangelo Givré
    with Toasted Meringue and,
    283–285
Clarified Butter, 753-754
Classic Bavarian Cream, 767
Classic Chocolate Bavarian Cream
  (variation), 768
Classic Mocha Cake (variation), 47
Cocoa
  folding into plain batter, 46
  Hot Fudge Sauce, 254
  metric/U.S. volume equivalent for, 816
  Painting, 555
  Painting Showpiece, Pastillage
    Display Stand for a, 590–591
  Short Dough, 792
  sifting with pie tin template and
    holder, 692–693
  Solution for Manual Spray Bottle,
    172, 558
  Sponge, 4-5
    -Almond (variation), 796
    Dobos (variation), 799
    Opera, 49
Cocoa Nib(s)
  about, 509
  Florentina Cups (variation),
    689
  -Macadamia Decorations, 197
  Wafer Paste, 720–721
  White Chocolate Ice Cream, 397
    with a Chocolate Lace Igloo and

Tuile Polar Bear, 396–399
Coconut
  about, 64
  Cake, -Mango, Tropical, suggestion
    for wedding cake, 90–91
  Cake, Tropical, 63-65
  Chocolate Tropicana Pastries,
    100–101
  Coupe Hawaii, 213-214
  Cream Filling, 65
  Ice Cream
    Caramelized Pineapple with
      (variation), 278
    Fresh, 214
    Quick (variation), 214
    in a Red Pepper Tuile with
      Strawberry Salsa and
      Tomatillo Lace, 399–401
  Mirror Glaze, 65
  products, 65
Coffee. See also Mocha
  Chocolate Cake, Espresso, with
    Coffee-Bean Crisps, 401–404
  Chocolate Ice Cream, Coffee-
    Scented, 223
  Coupe Bavaria, 213
  Cups, Chocolate, 330–332
  Mousse
    Cappuccino, 329
    Cappuccino, with Sambuca
      Cream in a Chocolate Coffee
      Cup, 328–332
    Hazelnut, Frozen, 234–236
    -Hazelnut Filling, 235–236
    Reduction, 754
    Syrup for Opera Cake, 49
    Tiramisù, Miniature, 194
    Truffles, Dark Chocolate
      Espresso, 190
Coffee-Bean Crisps, 403-404
  Cinnamon Semifreddo Venezia
    with, 233-234
  Espresso Chocolate Cake with,
    401–404
Coffee Beans, Marzipan, 640
Coffee Cups, Chocolate, 330–332
Cognac, Chocolate Cream, 30–31
Cointreau
  Almond Filling, -Flavored, Pears
    California with, 302–304
  Pear Sauce, 319
Cold Sabayon, 312
Cold water method, of tempering
  chocolate, 513–514
Colorings
  beet juice, 750
  for boiled sugar, 578
  for cast sugar, 604
  for marzipan, 634
Compote
  Cherry, 149
  Cherry, Cherry Baskets with Black

Compote *(cont'd)*
    Pepper Frozen Yogurt and,
      146–149
    Winter Fruit, in Late-Harvest Wine
      Syrup, 316–318
Cones, Florentina, 689
    Miniature, 193
Confection thermometer, 631
Contemporary Apricot Cream Cake
    (variation), 13–14
Contemporary Chocolate and
    Frangelico Mousse Cake, 26–27
Cookie(s). *See also* Florentina
    Decorations; Ladyfinger(s);
    Petits Fours Sec; Tuile Paste
    Decorations; Tuiles
    Christmas Cookie Ornaments,
      457–458
    Cinnamon Stars, 460
    Cinnamon Sticks, 420–421
    Coffee-Bean Crisps, 403–404
    Florentina, for Marco Polo, 690
    Gingerbread, 461
    Hazelnut Wafers (variation), 691
    Lace Cookie Bouquets, 723–725
    Lebkuchen, about, 465
    Lebkuchen Bars, 463–464
    Lebkuchen Hearts, 464–465
    Lemon-Butter Dough, 458
    Macaroons, Small Almond, 57
    in Meringue Glacé Leda, 247–249
    Snow Hearts, Chocolate, 456–457
    Springerle, 466–467
Cookie Butterflies, 695–698
Cookie Christmas Trees, 482–484
Cookie Citrus Rinds and Cookie
    Figurines, 698–699
    Chocolate Bread Pudding with,
      152–154
    Frosted Minneola Tangelo Givré
      with Toasted Meringue and,
      283–285
Cookie Tumbleweeds, 699–700
Corkscrew pattern, sauce design, 682
Corkscrews
    Caramel, 620–621
    Chocolate, 519
Cornets, Striped Chocolate, 535
Corn syrup, metric/U.S. equivalents
    for, 818
Coulis
    Cranberry, 243
    Cranberry, Persimmon Cream
      Slices with Cookie Christmas
      Trees and, 480–484
    Mango, 244
      Dacquoise Baskets with Fresh
        Raspberries, Raspberry Sauce
        and, 280–282
      Macadamia Nut Ice Cream in a
        Chocolate Tulip with, 243–245

Omelet Pancake with Sautéed
    Star Fruit, Pomegranate Sauce
    and, 300–302
    Passion Fruit, 396
Coupe(s)
    about, 204
    Bavaria, 213
    Belle Hélène, 213
    Hawaii, 213-214
    Melba, 215
    Niçoise, 215-216
    Sweden, 216-217
Crackers, Graham, 777
Cranberry(ies)
    Coulis, 243
    Coulis, Persimmon Cream Slices
      with Cookie Christmas Trees
      and, 480–484
    Mousse Cake (variation), 16
    Puree, 17
Cream. *See also* Bavarian Cream;
    Sour Cream; Whipped Cream
    Caramel, 18
    Chantilly, 765
    Chocolate, 766
    Chocolate Cognac, 30-31
    Chocolate, Dark, 26
    Coconut Filling, 65
    Crème Fraîche, 755
    Crème Parisienne, 768
    Crème Parisienne, in Chocolate
      Cake, Parisienne, 49–50
    Diplomat, 769
    Diplomat, Calvados, 764
    Frangelico, 26
    Gianduja, Vanilla-Scented, Filling,
      34
    Hazelnut Nougat, 103
    Italian, 771
    Italian, Sambuca-Scented,
      Kardinals with Fresh Fruit
      and, 291–292
    Lemon, 771–772
    Lime, 772
    Maraschino, 37
    Panna Cotta, Lemon Verbena, 178
    Persimmon Slices with Cookie
      Christmas Trees and
      Cranberry Coulis, 480–484
    Pink Lady Apple and Pear, with
      Orange Syrup and an Apple
      Chip, 348–349
    Raspberry, 54
    Truffle, Wild Honey, 169
Crème Anglaise
    Basic Recipe, 754
    Bavarian Cream, Crème Anglaise-
      Based, 768
    with liqueur soufflé, 368
Crème Brûlée
    Apple, 325-328

    on a Caramel Spider with a Sugar
      Shard, 341-342
    Catalan, 340-341
    Pumpkin, 488–489
    Vanilla-Bean Custard, 328
Crème Caramel Nouvelle, 342-344
Crème Catalan, Sherry-Poached
    Black Mission Figs with,
      353–354
Crème de Cassis, Panna Cotta
    (variation), 178
Crème Fraîche, 755
Crème Parisienne, 768
    in Parisienne Chocolate Cake, 49–50
Crepes
    Basic Recipe, 755–756
    Empire (variation), 280
    Jacques (variation), 280
    Pouches, Lemon Chiffon, 292–293
    soufflés, 325
    Vienna, 279
Crescent Decorations, 381–382
Croquembouche
    about, 70
    Individual, 173–174
Crumbs, Graham Cracker, 777–778
Crystallized Ginger, 756
Cup(s)
    Chocolate Coffee Cups, 330–332
    Chocolate Coffee Cups,
      Cappuccino Mousse with
      Sambuca Cream in a,
      328–332
    Chocolate, Striped, 536–537
    Chocolate, Striped, with Tuile
      Steam Decorations, 415–416
    Florentina, 687–689
    Florentina, Cocoa-Nib (variation),
      689
    Florentina, Cocoa-Nib, Chèvre
      Cheesecake in a, with Port-
      Poached Pears, 150–151
    tuile, about, 694
    Tulips, 715–716
Cupid's Treasure Chest, 345–347
Curd, Lemon, 772
Curly Cues, 700–702
    Vanilla, Mont Blanc with
      Pomegranate Seeds and,
      477–478
Currants, in Bavarois Filling, 21–22
Curved string of hearts pattern, sauce
    design, 682
Curved Tuile Wedges, 702–704
Curvy Tuile Strips, 704-705
Custard(s). *See also* Bavarian Cream;
    Crème Brûlée; Sabayon
    about, 322
    baked, 343
    Catalan, 341
    Catalan, Small, 354

Crème Anglaise, 754
Crème Anglaise, with liqueur
	soufflé, 368
Crème Caramel Nouvelle, 342–344
Crème Catalan, Sherry-Poached
	Black
Mission Figs with, 353-354
Gingered Caramel, 344
Orange, 185
Pastry Cream, 773
stirred, 311, 322
unmolding, 343
Vanilla Sauce, Light, 299

Dacquoise Baskets with Fresh
	Raspberries, Raspberry Sauce,
	and Mango Coulis, 280–281
Dark Chocolate
	Cake Rounds, 242
	Cream, 26
	Espresso Truffles, 190
	Filling, 157-158, 356
	Modeling Chocolate, 541
	Mousse Filling, 335
	Shingle Cake, 32-33
Dark Panforte (variation), 453
Date-Stuffed Saffron-Poached Pears
	with Chardonnay Wine Sauce,
	158–162
Decorating combs, 672, 673
	with frames, 674
Decorating pastes. See Pastes
Decorating Sauces. See Sauces,
	Decorating
Decorating Syrups. See Syrups,
	Decorating
Decorations. See also Caramel Glass
	Paste Decorations; Caramelized
	Sugar Decorations; Chocolate
	Decorations; Florentina
	Decorations; Marzipan
	Decorations; Sponge Sheets,
	Decorated; Sugar Decorations;
	Tuile Paste Decorations
	Apple or Pear Chips, 721
	buttercream designs, 85–87
	Chocolate Paper Paste, 719–720
	Cocoa Nib-Macadamia, 197
	Cocoa-Nib Wafer Paste, 720–721
	Cookie Cinnamon Sticks, 420–421
	Fondant. See Fondant
	Gingerbread Lattice, 485
	Hippen Decorating Paste, 722
	Hippen Masse (variation), 722–723
	Lace Cookie Bouquets, 723–725
	Lace Pâte à Choux, 230
	Mango Chips, 721
	Mango or Strawberry Wafer, 725
	Mango Wafer Orbs, Lemongrass
		Parfait, with Green Tea Syrup,
		Macadamia Nuts and, 406–408

Meringue Mushrooms, 455–456
for modernist desserts, 374–375
with pie tin templates and template
	holders, 692–693
piping. See Piping
Plantain Chips, 722
Puff Pastry Lattice, 178–179
Red Pepper Sails, 726
Royal Icing, 680–681
sauce designs, 681–686
Seaweed Wafer, 726-727
Tomatillo Lace, 728–729
Tomatillo Lace, Coconut Ice
	Cream in a Red Pepper Tuile
	with Strawberry Salsa and,
	399–401
Tuile, Spanish Caramel-Flavored,
	727–728
Weaver's Dough for, 430
for wedding cakes, 75–77, 84–89
Dessert Sampling Platter, 162-163
Devil's Food Cake, 393
Dietary restrictions, wedding cakes
	and, 75
Diplomat Cream, 769
	Calvados, 764
Dobos Sponge, 799
	Cocoa (variation), 799
Dobos Torte, 34-36
Double Cherry Sorbet, 306-307
Double turn, instructions for making,
	786–787
Doughs. See Bread Dough; Pastry
	Dough
Dragonfly, Tuile, 131–133
Dresdener Stollen, 434–435
Drop-loop pattern, buttercream, tips
	for piping, 85

Easter Bunny, Marzipan, 641–642
	Resting and Sleeping (variations), 642
Easter Chicken, Marzipan, 642–643
Eggs
	in high-altitude baking, 824
	metric/U.S. volume equivalents for,
		817
	in sponge cake formula, 4
Egg Wash
	about, 762
	for Spraying, 763
	Whole-Egg, 762
	Yolks-Only, 763
English wedding cake, 68–69
Equipment and tools. See also
		Acetate/polyurethane strips
		bannetons, 433
	decorating combs, 672, 673
	with frames, 674
	Flexipan molds, 6, 392
	fondant funnels, 679
	ladyfinger comb, 19

lattice cutters, 485
marzipan rolling pins, 97
modern techology, 373
molding tool, 718
Othello pans, 108
rings, 135, 164, 238, 376
silk screens, 674
Silpat baking mats, 6, 108, 672, 673
for sugarwork, 570, 605–606
	air pumps, 611
	Baumé thermometer, 825
	Brix hydrometer, 826
	fixative syringes, 604, 607
	sugar pans, 576, 611-612
	sugar thermometer, 570, 631, 827
	warming cases, 609, 610
	thermometers, 570, 630–631,
		802, 825, 827
	wood-graining, 537
Espresso Chocolate Cake with
	Coffee-Bean Crisps, 401–404
Espresso Truffles, Dark Chocolate, 190

Fahrenheit/centigrade temperature
	equivalents, 812–815
Fanned Zinfandel Pears, 319
Fans
	Caramel, 627–628
	Chocolate, 521–522
Feathered two-tone pool pattern,
	sauce, 685
Feijoa Sorbet, 290–291
	Global Fresh Fruit Baskets with,
		289–290
Fences
	Caramel, 621
	Chocolate, 476–477
	in Gingerbread Chalet, Santa's, 500
	in Gingerbread House, 497–498
Fig(s)
	about, 250
	and Apricot Tart with Prickly Pear
		Sorbet, 218–219
	Caramel-Dipped, 624-625
	Logs, 559
	Oven-Braised Black Mission, with
		Honey-Vanilla Frozen Yogurt,
		250–251
	Sherry-Poached Black Mission,
		with Crème Catalan, 353–354
Figures. See also Marzipan Decorations
	Cast Sugar, 597-604
	Chocolate, Hollow, Using Molds,
		555–556
	Cookie Butterflies, 695–698
	Macaroon (variation), 121
	Tuile Camels, 389
	Tuile Polar Bears, 398
Figurines, Chocolate, 545–548
Fillings. See also Buttercream; Cake
		Fillings Almond, 161

Fillings (cont'd)
  Almond, Cointreau-Flavored, Pears
      California with, 302–304
  Apple, Chunky, 216–217, 767
  Bavarian Cream
    Classic, 767
    Classic Chocolate (variation), 768
    Crème Anglaise-Based, 768
    Quick, 774
  Chantilly Cream, 765
  Cherry, 765
  Cherry, Fresh (variation), 766
  Chocolate
    Bavarian Cream, Classic
        (variation), 768
    Cream, 766
    Dark Chocolate, 157–158, 356
    Ganache, 28, 770
    Ganache, Quick (variation), 771
    Ganache, Spiced, 412-413
    Gianduja Cream, 393
    Light, 158
    Marquise, 395
    Milk Chocolate, 356, 416
    Milk Chocolate-Orange Mousse,
        410
    -Orange, 181
    White Chocolate, 356
    White Chocolate Mousse, 336,
        360
    White Chocolate Treasure,
        386–387
  Crème Parisienne, 768
  Diplomat Cream, 769
  Diplomat Cream, Calvados, 764
  Frangipane, 769
  Hazelnut-Coffee Mousse, 235–236
  Hazelnut Nougat Cream, 103
  Italian Cream, 771
  Lemon Chiffon, 293
  Lemon Cream, 771-772
  Lemon Curd, 772
  Lime Cream, 772
  Lingonberry Parfait, 243
  Mascarpone, 194
  Orange-Chocolate, 181
  Orange-Milk Chocolate Mousse,
      410
  Passion Fruit Mousse, 196
  Pastry Cream, 773
  Pastry Cream, Calvados, 764
  Peach Cream, 314
  Persimmon, 482
  Persimmon Bavarois, 479
  Raspberry Mousse, 239
  Rum Ball, 790-791
Financier, Blueberry, with Toasted
    Lemon Verbena Sabayon and
    Mascarpone Sherbet, 380–384
Finlander Praline, 560
Fixative syringes, 604, 607
Flambéed Desserts

Baked Alaska, 220–224
Cherries Jubilee, 232
  rum for, 222
Flexipan molds, 6, 392
Florentina Decorations
  Cones, 689
  Cones, Miniature, 193
  Cookies for Marco Polo, 690
  Cookies, in Spiced Ganache and
      Tea Ice Cream Marco Polo, 410
  Cup(s), 687–689
    Cocoa-Nib (variation), 689
    Cocoa-Nib, Chèvre Cheesecake
    in a, with Port-Poached Pears,
    150–151
    Hartmund Garnish, 691
    Twists, 690
Florentine Torte, 447–449
Flour
  in high-altitude baking, 824
  metric/U.S. volume equivalents for,
      816
  for sponge cakes, 4, 5
Flowers. See also Roses
  Cookie Flower, Rainbow of Summer
      Sorbets in a, 304–307
  fresh, decorating with, 76–77, 666
  Hazelnut, 120
  Magnolia Cookie Shells, Red
      Currant Sorbet in, 307–310
  magnolia shells, making, 246
  Marzipan Forget-Me-Not, 644
  tuile petals, making, 171
  Tulips, 715
  Tulips, Miniature, 716
Fluted Caramel Wedges (variation),
    668–669
Fondant
  Basic Recipe, 578–579
  designs piped onto cake or pastry,
      677
  designs using transfer method,
      677–678
  glazing or icing with, 678–679
  mixer, making in, 579
  ornaments, 676–677
  in Petits Fours Glacés, 111–113
  in Petits Fours Glacés with
      Frangipane and Apricot
      Filling, 114–115
  Rolled, 592
  storing, 113
  thinning to ensure shine, 678
  warming, 114
Fondant funnels, about, 679
Food lacquer, about, 611
Forbidden Peach, 164-167
Forget-Me-Not Flowers, Marzipan,
    644
Fortified Caramel Sauce, 19
Frangelico
  and Chocolate Mousse Cake, 24–26

and Chocolate Mousse Cake,
    Contemporary (variation), 26–27
  Cream, 26
Frangipane
  Filling, 769–770
  Petits Fours Glacés with Apricot
      Filling and, 114–115
  Sheet, 115
French Meringue, 780
French-Method Buttercream, 751, 752
French wedding cakes, 70
Fresh Cherry Filling (variation), 766
Fresh Coconut Ice Cream, 214
Fresh Strawberries with Champagne
    Sabayon, 283
Friandise, about, 111
Frosted Minneola Tangelo Givré with
    Toasted Meringue and Cookie
    Citrus Rind, 283–285
Frozen Desserts, 202-265. See also
    Bombe(s); Coupe(s); Ice Cream;
    Parfait; Sorbet(s); Yogurt, Frozen
  Baked Alaska, 220-224
  composed, about, 204
  Mousse, Hazelnut Coffee, 234-236
  Mousse, Lemon, with Orange
      Syrup and a Tuile Spiral, 405–406
  Mousse, Raspberry with
      Meringues, 237–239
  Semifreddo Venezia, Cinnamon,
      with Coffee Bean Crisps, 233–234
  Sherbet, Mascarpone, 383
  Sherbet, Mascarpone, Blueberry
      Financier with Toasted Lemon
      Verbena Sabayon and, 380–383
  Soufflé Glacé, Bénédictine, 224–226
  Soufflé Glacé, Ginger (variation), 226
Frozen Hazelnut Coffee Mousse, 234–236
Frozen Lemon Mousse with Orange
    Syrup and a Tuile Spiral, 405–406
Frozen Raspberry Mousse with
    Meringues, 237
Frozen Yogurt. See Yogurt, Frozen
Fruit. See also specific fruits
  Candied
    Cassata Parfait, 229–230
    Citrus Peels, 756–758
    Citrus Peels, Quick Method for
        (variation), 758
    Dresdener Stollen, 434–435
    Florentine Torte, 447–449
    Fruitcake, Lemon Verbena-
        Scented, 449–450
    Fruitcake, Traditional, 450–451
    Nougat Montélimar, 586–588
    Panforte, 451–453
    Panforte, Dark (variation), 453
    Praline, Finlander, 560
    Soufflé Rothschild, 370–371
    Swedish Spice Bread, 440–441
    Triestine Bread, 441–442
  Caramel-Dipped, 624–625
  Compote, Winter Fruit, in Late-

Harvest Wine Syrup, 316–318
Coupe Niçoise, 215-216
dried, poaching, 790
Fresh, Global Fresh Fruit Baskets
    with Feijoa Sorbet, 289–291
Fresh, Kardinals with Sambuca-
    Scented Italian Cream and,
    291–292
fresh, preparing, 344
gelatin with tropical fruit, 9
Glacéed, 580–581
Jellies, Lemon, Raspberry, and Straw-
    berry (*Pâte de Fruit*), 591-592
Lemon Chiffon Fruit Basket Cake, 44
poaching, basic directions for, 790
Poaching Syrup, Plain, 789
Poaching Syrup, Spiced, 790
prepared yields for, 816
Salad, 285–286
soufflés, about, 325
Soufflés (variation), 370
Valentines, 287–288
Fruitcake
    Lemon Verbena-Scented, 449–450
    Panforte, 451–453
    Panforte, Dark (variation), 453
    Traditional, 450–451
    as wedding cake, 68–69

Galette(s)
    about, 143
    Apple, Caramelized, in Phyllo
        Dough with Kumquat Sauce,
        143–145
    Classic, 144
Ganache
    Brandied Cherry, 110
    Brandied Cherry Towers with Pink
        Champagne Aspic and Curvy
        Tuile Strips, 384–385
    Chocolate Cake, 27–28
    Chocolate Towers, 154–158
    Filling, 28, 770
    Hazelnut Cinnamon, 561–562
    Quick (variation), 771
    Rounds, 152
    Spiced Filling, 412–413
    Spiced, and Tea Ice Cream Marco
        Polo, 410-413
Gâteau Malakoff, 36–37
Gâteau Mocha Carousel, 38-39
Gelatin
    in Bavarian cream, 323
    powder, in cake fillings, 6–7
    powder/sheet equivalents and
        substitutions, 8–9, 817
    powder, softening, 310
    sheet, in cake fillings, 8–9
    strength of set gelatin (bloom), 7
    with tropical fruits, 9
Gellometer, about, 7
Genoise, baking, 5

Gianduja, 560–561
    Bites, 561
    Cream Filling, 393
    Cream Filling, Vanilla-Scented, 34
    wedding cake suggestion, 89
Ginger(ed)
    Cake, 379
    Caramel Custard, 344
    Crystallized, 756
    Ice Cream, Poached Pears with,
        251–253
    Ice Cream, White Chocolate, 217
    Meyer Lemon Syrup, Baked
        Plantains in, with Avocado-
        Mango Ice Cream, 377–378
    Soufflé Glacé (variation), 226
Gingerbread
    Cake, Brandied, 443
    Cake, Soft, 443-444
    Christmas Cookie Ornaments,
        457-458
    Cookies, 461-462
    Lattice, Banana Rum Pudding with
        Brandied Whipped Cream
        and (variation), 486
    Lattice Decorations, 485
    Lattice, Persimmon Dome Cake
        with, 484–485
    Muffins (variation), 444
    Sponge, 481–482
Gingerbread House
    about, 489
    Chalet, Santa's, 499–503
    larger houses, 498
    lights, adding and connecting, 498
    Traditional, 490–499
        Marzipan Children for the,
            656–657
        Marzipan Santa for the, 660–663
Givré
    about, 284
    Minneola Tangelo, Frosted, with
        Toasted Meringue and Cookie
        Citrus Rind, 283–285
Glacéed Fruit and Nuts, 580–581
Glacés
    Petits Fours, 111–113
    Petits Fours, with Frangipane and
        Apricot Filling, 114–115
Glazes
    Apricot, 774
    Black Currant, 16
    Chocolate, 774–775
    Chocolate, Dark, 393
    Chocolate Mirror, 775
    Coconut Mirror, 65
    Fondant, 578–579
        application instructions, 678–679
    Fruits and Nuts Glacéed, 580–581
    Lemon Mirror, 43–44
    Marble Mirror, 22
    Mirror, Plain, 776

Opera, 49
Orange, 775
Pectin, 776
Red Currant, 777
Global Fresh Fruit Baskets with
    Feijoa Sorbet, 289–291
Gluten, in sponge cake, 4
Goat cheese, Chèvre Cheesecake in a
    Cocoa-Nib Florentina Cup with
    Port-Poached Pears, 150–151
Goblets, Chocolate, 522–523
    Marbled or Multicolored, 524
Goldwasser
    about, 371
    Soufflé Rothschild, 370–371
Gooseberry(ies)
    Cape, about, 365
    Cape, in Wine Foam and Blackberry
        Bavarian Greystone, 363–366
    Sorbet, 306
Graham Cracker Crumbs, 777–778
Graham Crackers, 777
Grape Leaves, Tuile, 364–365
Grapes
    Chardonnay Wine Sauce, 161–162
    Vineyard Barrels, 314-316
Gratin
    Apricot, with Sabayon of Muscat
        Wine, 269–270
    Blood Orange, 275-276
Green Tea
    powder, about, 759
    Syrup, Decorating, 759
    Syrup, Lemongrass Parfait with
        Mango Wafer Orbs, Macadamia
        Nuts and, 406–408
Guinettes Cherries
    about, 388
    Sauce, 388
Gum Paste
    with Gum Tragacanth, 581–582
    Pastillage, 588–589
    Pastillage Display Stand for a
        Cocoa Painting Showpiece,
        590–591

Harlequin Cake, 40–42
Harlequin Soufflé, 369
Hartmund Florentina Garnish, 691
Hazelnut(s)
    about, 119, 236
    Caramel-Dipped, 625
    Cinnamon Ganache, 561–562
    Coffee Mousse, Frozen, 234–236
    Coffee Mousse Filling, 235–236
    Cookie Wafers (variation), 691
    Cuts, 119
    Flowers, 120
    Gianduja, 560–561
    Meringue, Nut, 176
    Meringue Noisette, 781–782
    Noisette Rings, 105–106

Hazelnut(s) *(cont'd)*
 Nougat Cream, 103
 Nougat Montélimar, 586–587
 Nougat Slices, 102–103
 Paste, 778
 paste in sponge cake, 5
 Praline, 804
 Praline Buttercream, 176
 Praline, Finlander, 560
 Pralines, Marzipan, 563
 Queen of Sheba Cake Base, 51–52
 Short Dough, 792
Hearts
 Chocolate Cutouts, 520–521
 Chocolate Snow Hearts, 456–457
 Cupid's Treasure Chest, 345–347
 Fruit Valentines, 287–288
 Lebkuchen, 464–465
 Ruby Pears with Verbena Bavarois
  and Port Wine Reduction, sauce
  design, 349–352
 Strawberry, 122–123
 Truffle Cake, Hot Chocolate,
  sauce design, 169–173
 Valentine's Day, 197–200
Hearts with stems pattern, sauce design,
 684–685
Hearts with weave pattern, sauce design,
 683–684
High-altitude baking, 824
High-Ratio Sponge Cake, 800
 Chocolate (variation), 800
Hippen Decorating Paste, 722
Hippen Masse (variation), 722–723
Holiday Candle Pastries, 462–463
Hollow Chocolate Figures Using
 Molds, 555–556
Honey
 Baklava, 136-137
 metric/U.S. equivalents for, 816,
  818
 Pear Frozen Yogurt, Honey-
  Scented, 272
 Truffle Cream, Wild Honey, 169
 Truffle Symphony, 167–169
 -Vanilla Frozen Yogurt, 276
Honeycomb Chocolate Decor,
 534–535
Honey Mandarin Sorbet, 216
Hot Chocolate Truffle Cake, 169–173
Hot Fudge Sauce, 254
Hungarian, Dobos Torte, 34-36

Ice Cream
 Almond, 257
 Almond, Chocolate-Banana Tart
  with Spun Sugar and,
  151–152
 Almond, and Kadaif Phyllo Nests,
  Saffron-Poached Pears with,
  254–257
 Avocado-Mango, 379

Avocado-Mango, Baked Plantains
 in Gingered Meyer Lemon
 Syrup with, 377–379
Avocado-Mango, Baked Vanilla-
 Infused Pineapple with
 Mango Fruit Wafer and,
 130–133
Baked Alaska, 220–223
Bombe
 Aboukir, 207–208
 Bourdaloue, 208
 Ceylon, 209–211
 Monarch, 211
Cake Jamaica, 239–241
Caramel, 227–228
Caramel, in a Caramel Cage, 227
Cashew, 166
Cashew, in Forbidden Peach,
 164–167
Cherries Jubilee, 232
Chocolate
 Cocoa Nib-White Chocolate,
  397–398
 Cocoa Nib-White Chocolate,
  with a Chocolate Lace Igloo
 and Tuile Polar Bear, 396–399
 Coffee-Scented, 223
 White Chocolate, 217
 White Chocolate, Gingered
  (variation), 217
Coconut
 Caramelized Pineapple with
  (variation), 278
 Fresh, 214
 Quick (variation), 214
 in a Red Pepper Tuile with Straw-
  berry Salsa and Tomatillo
  Lace, 399–401
Coupe
 Bavaria, 213
 Belle Hélène, 213
 Hawaii, 213–214
 Melba, 215
 Niçoise, 215–216
 Sweden, 216–217
Ginger, Poached Pears with, 251–253
Macadamia Nut, 245
Macadamia Nut, in a Chocolate
 Tulip with Mango Coulis, 243–245
Mango, 246
 Avocado, Baked Plantains in
  Gingered Meyer Lemon
  Syrup with, 377–378
 Avocado, Baked Vanilla-Infused
  Pineapple with Mango Fruit
  Wafer and, 130–133
 with Chiffonade of Lemon Mint
  and a Chocolate Twirl, 245–246
Meringue Glacé Leda, 247–249
Peach, 212
Pistachio, 207–208
Plum, 262–263

Plum, Vacherin with, 261-264
Rum-Raisin, 249
Strawberry, 222-223
Tea, and Spiced Ganache, Marco
 Polo, 410–413
Tea, Sun-Brewed Jasmine, 209–210
Vanilla, 172
Vanilla, in Hot Chocolate Truffle
 Cake, 169–173
Vanilla, and Hot Fudge Sauce,
 Profiteroles with, 253–254
Icing. *See also* Royal Icing
 Fondant, 578–579, 678–679
Igloo(s), Chocolate Lace, 526
 Cocoa Nib-White Chocolate Ice
  Cream with a Tuile Polar Bear
  and, 396–399
Individual Croquembouche, 173–174
Instant-set method, for chocolate
 decorations, 515–516
Isomalt
 about, 617
 Bubble Sugar, 617
Italian Cream, 771
 Sambuca-Scented, Kardinals with
  Fresh Fruit and, 291–292
Italian Meringue, 780-781
Italian-Method Buttercream, 751, 752
Italian wedding cakes, 71

Jamaica, Ice Cream Cake, 239–241
Japanese wedding cakes, 72
Japonaise Meringue Batter, 781
Jasmine Tea Ice Cream, Sun-Brewed,
 209–211
Jellies, Lemon, Raspberry, and Straw-
 berry (*Pâte de Fruit*), 591–592
Jelly, Passion Fruit, 196
Jelly Centers, Ruby Fruit, 387
Jelly Roll
 Apple Wine Cake, 9–11
 Lychee Charlotte Royal, 294–296
 Lychee Charlotte, Striped
  (variation), 296
Joconde Sponge Base I, 670
Joconde Sponge Base II, 671

Kadaif Phyllo Nests, 257
 Saffron Poached Pears with
  Almond Ice Cream and, 254–257
Kardinals with Sambuca-Scented
 Italian Cream and Fresh Fruit,
 291–292
Kirsch
 kirschwasser, about, 63
 Strawberry Cake, 61–63
 Whipped Cream, 63
 Whipped Cream, in Strawberry
  Pyramids, 185–187
Kiwi(s)
 Mousse Cake (variation), 197
 Sauce, 309–310

Tropical Surprise Packages, 258–261
Kumquat(s)
    Gingerbread Cake, Brandied, 443
    Sauce, Caramelized Apple Galette
        in Phyllo Dough with, 143–145

Lace Decorations
    Chocolate, 525
        Chocolate Dome Cake with Cherry
            Sauce and, 391–392
        Igloo, Cocoa Nib-White
            Chocolate Ice Cream with a
            Tuile Polar Bear and, 396–399
        Igloos, 526
        White Chocolate and Pistachio
            Mousse with, 357–360
    Cookie Bouquets, 723–725
    Pâte à Choux, 230
    Tomatillo, 728
    Tomatillo, Coconut Ice Cream in a
        Red Pepper Tuile with
        Strawberry Salsa and, 399–401
Ladyfinger(s)
    Basic Recipe, 801
    Batter, 21
    Bavarois Charente Cake, 19–21
    Charlotte Charente, 332–333
    Chocolate (variation), 801
    Gâteau Malakoff, 36–37
    Lemon, 801-802
Ladyfinger comb, about, 19
Lattice cutters, about, 485
Lattice Decorations
    Gingerbread, 485
    Gingerbread, Banana Rum
        Pudding with Brandied
        Whipped Cream and
        (variation), 486
    Gingerbread, Persimmon Dome
        Cake with, 484–485
    Puff Pastry, 178–179
        Mascarpone Cheesecake with
            Lemon Verbena Panna Cotta, 177–179
Leaf Croquant, 582–583
Leaves
    Chocolate, 527
    Marzipan Rose, 644–645
    Tuile, 709–711
    Tuile Grape, 364
    Tuile Maple (variation), 711
Lebkuchen
    about, 465
    Bars, 463–464
    Hearts, 464–465
Lemon
    -Butter Cookie Dough, 458
    Chiffon Cake, 42–44
    Chiffon Cake, Fruit Basket
        (variation), 44
    Chiffon Filling, 43, 293
    Chiffon Pouches, 292–293
    Cream, 771-772

Curd, 772
Jellies (Pâte de Fruit), 591–592
Ladyfingers, 801–802
Mirror Glaze, 43–44
Mousse, Frozen, with Orange
    Syrup and a Tuile Spiral, 405–406
Parfait, Anise-Scented, with Lemon
    Cookie Tumbleweeds, 375–376
Syrup, Gingered Meyer Lemon,
    Baked Plantains in, with
    Avocado-Mango Ice Cream,
    377–379
Syrup, -Vanilla Decorating,
    759–760
Lemongrass Parfait, 407-408
    with Green Tea Syrup, Mango
        Wafer Orbs, and Macadamia
        Nuts, 406–408
Lemon Verbena
    about, 351
    Bavarian Cream, -Vanilla Bean, 60–61
    Bavarois, 352
    Bavarois, Ruby Pears with Port
        Wine Reduction and, 349–352
    Fruitcake, -Scented, 449–450
    Panna Cotta, 178
    Panna Cotta, Mascarpone
        Cheesecake with, 177–179
    -Raspberry Cake, suggestion for
        wedding cake, 89
    Sabayon, 381
    Sabayon, Toasted, Blueberry
        Financier with Mascarpone
        Sherbet and, 380–383
Licorice Decorating Syrup, 760
Light Chocolate Filling, 158
Light Desserts, 266–319
    Apricot Gratin with Sabayon of
        Muscat Wine, 269–270
    Bananas, Baked, with Banana-Tofu
        Frozen Yogurt, 273–274
    Blood Orange Gratin, 275–276
    Cheesecake, Marbled, with Quark
        Cheese, 297–298
    Crepes Vienna, 279
    Dacquoise Baskets with Fresh
        Raspberries, Raspberry Sauce,
        and Mango Coulis, 280–282
    Fruit Baskets, Global Fresh Fruit,
        with Feijoa Sorbet, 289–291
    Fruit Compote, Winter, in Late-
        Harvest Wine Syrup, 316–318
    Fruit Salad, 285–286
    Fruit Valentines, 287–288
    Givré, Frosted Minneola Tangelo,
        with Toasted Meringue and
        Cookie Citrus Rind, 283–285
    Kardinals with Sambuca-Scented
        Italian Cream and Fresh Fruit,
        291–292
    Lemon Chiffon Pouches, 292–293
    Lychee Charlotte Royal, 294–296

Lychee Charlotte, Striped
    (variation), 296
Oeufs à la Neige with Caramelized
    Sugar Spheres, 298–300
Omelet Pancake with Sautéed Star
    Fruit, Pomegranate Sauce, and
    Mango Coulis, 300–302
Pears California with Cointreau-
    Flavored Almond Filling,
    302–303
Pears, Zinfandel-Poached, with
    Honey-Scented Pear Frozen
    Yogurt, 318–319
Pear Tart, Asian, with Honey-
    Scented Pear Frozen Yogurt,
    270–273
Pineapple Barbados, Caramelized,
    276–278
Sabayon, 311–312
Sorbet, Feijoa, Global Fresh Fruit
    Baskets with, 289–290
Sorbet, Red Currant, in Magnolia
    Cookie Shells, 307–310
Sorbets, Rainbow of Summer, in a
    Cookie Flower, 304–307
Soufflé, Salzburger, 312
Sponge Cake, Low-Cholesterol,
    293–294
Strawberries, Fresh, with
    Champagne Sabayon, 283
Vineyard Barrels, 314–316
Yogurt Creams, Strawberry-Peach,
    313–314
Light Vanilla Custard Sauce, 300
Lime Cream, 772
Lingonberry Parfait, 241–243
Linzer Dough, 778
Liqueur Soufflé, 367–369
Low-Calorie Desserts. See Light
    Desserts
Low-Cholesterol Chocolate Sponge
    Cake (variation), 294
Low-Cholesterol Sponge Cake,
    293–294
Lucia Buns, 436–437
Lychee
    Barvarois, 295–296
    Charlotte Royal, 294-296
    Charlotte, Striped (variation), 296

Macadamia Nut(s)
    about, 244
    Caramel-Dipped, 625
    -Caramel Mousse, 142–143
    -Caramel Mousse, Caramel Boxes
        with, 140-143
    Chocolate-Filled Morsels, 118–119
    -Cocoa Nib Decorations, 197
    Ice Cream, 245
    Ice Cream in a Chocolate Tulip
        with Mango Coulis, 243–245
    Lemongrass Parfait, with Green

Macadamia Nut(s) *(cont'd)*
    Tea Syrup, Mango Wafer Orbs
      and, 406–408
Macaroon(s)
    Almond, Small, 57
    Bananas, 104–105
    Candies, 121
    Cinnamon Stars, 460
    Figures (variation), 121
    Paste, Decorating, 779
    paste, in Scandinavian cakes, 70
    Sicilian Cake, 55–58
    Snow Hearts, Chocolate, 456–457
    Whipped Cream, -Maraschino, 58
Magnolia Cookie Shells, Red Currant
    Sorbet in, 307–310
Malakoff, Gâteau, 36–37
Mango
    Chips, 721
    -Coconut Cake, Tropical, suggestion
      for wedding cake, 90–91
    Coulis, 244
      Dacquoise Baskets with Fresh
        Raspberries, Raspberry
        Sauce, and, 280–281
      Macadamia Nut Ice Cream in a
        Chocolate Tulip with, 243–245
      Omelet Pancake with Sautéed
        Star Fruit, Pomegranate Sauce
        and, 300–302
    Ice Cream, 246
      Avocado, 379
      Avocado, Baked Vanilla-Infused
        Pineapple with Mango Fruit
        Wafer and, 130–133
      Avocado, Baked Plantains in
        Gingered Meyer Lemon
        Syrup with, 377–378
      with Chiffonade of Lemon Mint
        and a Chocolate Twirl, 245–246
    Wafer Decorations, 725
    Wafer Orbs, Lemongrass Parfait,
      with Green Tea Syrup,
      Macadamia Nuts and, 406–408
    Wafers, Baked Vanilla-Infused
      Pineapple with Mango-Avocado
      Ice Cream and, 130–133
Maraschino
    Cream, 37
    -Macaroon Whipped Cream, 58
Marbled Cheesecake with Quark
    Cheese, 297–298
Marbled Goblets, 524
Marbleized Chocolate, 539–540
Marble Mirror Glazes, 22
Marco Polo
    about, 411
    Florentina Cookies for, 690
    Miniature, 164
    Spiced Ganache and Tea Ice
      Cream, 410–413
Marjolaine, 174–176

Marquise
    Chocolate, with Passion Fruit
      Parfait and a Lace Cookie
      Bouquet, 394–396
    Milk Chocolate, with Finger
      Banana Center and Red
      Currant Sauce, 408–410
    White Chocolate, Miniature, 163
Marshmallows, 583–584
Marzipan. *See also* Marzipan in
    Cakes and Pastries;
    Marzipan Decorations
    Basic Recipe, 635
    cocoa painting on, 555
    coloring, 634, 655
    designs pressed into, 677–678
    making, 633–634
    Parfait, 190
    Parfait, Trio of Chocolates with,
      187–191
    Pralines, 563
    rolling out, 634
    rolling pins for, 97
    storage of, 634
    tracing onto, 635–636
Marzipan in Cakes and Pastries
    Battenburg, 96–97
    Chocolate Triangles, 98–100
    Christmas Tree Pastries, 458–459
    Harlequin Cake, 40–41
    Italian wedding cakes, 71
    Opera Cake, 47–48
    Opera Slices, 106–107
    Petits Fours, 115–116
    Petits Fours Glaces, 111–113
    Petits Fours Glacés with
      Frangipane and Apricot
      Filling, 114–115
    Princess Pastries, 125–126
    Queen of Sheba Cake, 50–51
    Raspberry Cake, 52–53
    Strawberry Bagatelle, 58–60
    Strawberry Kirsch Cake, 61–62
    Valentine's Day Hearts, 197–200
    Yule Log Pastries, 468–469
    Yule Logs, 453–456
Marzipan Decorations
    Angel, 653-655
    Apples, 636–637
    Bumblebees, 639
    Candles, 463
    Carrots, 639–640
    Children for the Traditional
      Gingerbread House, 656–657
    Coffee Beans, 640
    Easter Bunny, 641–642
    Easter Bunny, Resting and Sleeping
      (variations), 642
    Easter Chicken, 642–643
    Forget-Me-Not Flowers, 644
    Oranges, 645
    Pears, 645

    Piglet, 646–647
    Pig with Two Santas, 657–660
    Pig, Whimsical (variation), 648–649
    Polar Bear, 649–650
    Rose Leaves, 644–645
    Roses, 651–653
    Santa's Head, 503
    Santa for the Traditional
      Gingerbread House, 660–663
Mascarpone
    about, 779
    Basic Recipe, 779
    Bavarian, 134-135
    Cheesecake, with Lemon Verbena
      Panna Cotta, 177–179
    Cheesecake Batter, 178
    in Cheesecake Mixture, 151
    Filling, for Tiramisù, 194
    Sherbet, 383
    Sherbet, Blueberry Financier with
      Toasted Lemon Verbena
      Sabayon and, 380–383
Measurement. *See* Metric/U.S.
    equivalents; Weights and
    measures
Melba Sauce, 215
Meringue(s)
    Baked Alaska, 220–224
    base, cooking, 376
    Cassata Parfait with, 228–231
    Chocolate Truffle Cake with
      Raspberries, 31–32
    Dacquoise Baskets with Fresh
      Raspberries, Raspberry Sauce,
      and Mango Coulis, 280–282
    Forbidden Peach, 164–167
    French, 780
    Fruit Valentines, 287–288
    Gâteau Mocha Carousel, 38–39
    Glacé Chantilly (variation), 264
    Glacé Leda, 247–249
    Hazelnut Cuts, 119
    Ice Cream Cake Jamaica, 239–241
    Italian, 780–781
    Japonaise Batter, 781
    Kardinals with Sambuca-Scented
      Italian Cream and Fresh Fruit,
      291–292
    Macaroon Cake, Sicilian, 55–58
    Mushrooms, 455–456
    Noisette, 781–782
    Nut, 176
    Nut, in Marjolaine, 174–175
    Oeufs à la Neige with Caramelized
      Sugar Spheres, 298–300
    Raspberry Mousse, Frozen, with,
      237–239
    Salzburger Soufflé, 312
    Swiss, 782
    Toasted, Frosted Minneola Tangelo
      Givré with Cookie Citrus
      Rind and, 283–285

Vacherin with Plum Ice Cream, 261–263
Metric system, 805-806
Metric/U.S. equivalents
    for commonly used products, 816
    for eggs, 817
    for gelatin, 817
    for honey, corn syrup, and molasses, 818
    length, 806, 807–808
    precise conversions, 806
    volume, 806, 809–810, 816, 817, 818
    weight, 806, 811–812
    for yeast, 818
Meyer Lemon Syrup, Gingered, Baked Plantains in, with Avocado-Mango Ice Cream, 377–379
Mignardise, about, 111
Milk Chocolate
    Filling, 356, 416
    Marquise with Finger Banana Center and Red Currant Sauce, 408–410
    Modeling Chocolate (variation), 541
    Mousse, Caramel-Centered, with Black Currant Sauce, 389–391
    -Orange Mousse, 410
    Truffles, 191
Mimosa, 564
Miniature Florentina Cones, 193
Miniature Marco Polo, 164
Miniature Palm Leaves, 122
Miniature Palm Trees, 255–256
Miniature Tiramisù, 194
Miniature Triple-Chocolate Terrine, 192
Miniature Tulip Crowns (variation), 717
Miniature Tulips, 716–717
Miniature White Chocolate Marquise, 163
Mint
    Chiffonade of Lemon Mint, Mango Ice Cream with a Chocolate Twirl and, 245–246
    Decorating Syrup, 760
Mirror Glaze
    Chocolate, 775
    Coconut, 65
    Lemon, 43–44
    Marble, 22
    Plain, 776
Mocha
    Cake, 45–46
    Cake, Classic (variation), 47
    Gâteau Carousel, 38-39
    suggestion for wedding cake, 90
    Whipped Cream, 39
Modeling Chocolate
    Dark Chocolate, 541
    Milk Chocolate, (variation), 541
    White Chocolate, 542
Modernist desserts, 375–421
    about, 373–375

Brandied Cherry Ganache Towers with Pink Champagne Aspic and Curvy Tuile Strips, 384–385
Buried Ruby Treasure, 385–388
Chocolate Cake, Espresso, with Coffee-Bean Crisps, 401–404
Chocolate Cups, Striped, with Tuile Steam Decorations, 415–416
Chocolate Dome Cake with Cherry Sauce and Chocolate Lace, 391–393
Chocolate Marquise with Passion Fruit Parfait and Lace Cookie Bouquet, 394–395
Cocoa Nib–White Chocolate Ice Cream with a Chocolate Lace Igloo and Tuile Polar Bear, 396–398
Coconut Ice Cream in a Red Pepper Tuile with Strawberry Salsa and Tomatillo Lace, 399-401
Financier, Blueberry, with Toasted Lemon Verbena Sabayon and Mascarpone Sherbet, 380–383
Lemongrass Parfait with Green Tea Syrup, Mango Fruit Leather and Macadamia Nuts, 406–408
Lemon Mousse, Frozen, with Orange Sauce and a Tuile Spiral, 405–406
Lemon Parfait, Anise-Scented, with Lemon Cookie Tumbleweeds, 375–376
Marquise, Milk Chocolate, with Finger Banana Center and Red Currant Sauce, 408–410
Mousse, Caramel Centered Milk Chocolate, with Black Currant Sauce, 389–391
Plantains, Baked, in Gingered Meyer Lemon Syrup with Avocado-Mango Ice Cream, 377–379
Snowbird in a Chocolate Cage, 413–415
Spiced Ganache and Tea Ice Cream, Marco Polo, 410–413
Tarte Tatin Moderne, 416–421
Molasses, metric/U.S. equivalents for, 818
Molded chocolate strips, 540
Molding blocks, making, 141
Molds, Hollow Chocolate Figures Using, 555–556
Monarch Butterfly Ornaments, Chocolate, 550–552
    in Bombe Monarch, 210
Mont Blanc with Pomegranate Seeds and Vanilla Curly Cues, 477–478
Mousse. See also Mousse Cake
    about, 323-324
    Black Currant, 15
    Cappuccino, 329

Cappuccino, with Sambuca Cream in a Chocolate Coffee Cup, 328–332
Caramel-Macadamia Nut, 142–143
Caramel-Macadamia Nut, Caramel Boxes with, 140–143
Cherry, Brandied, 111
Chocolate
    Dark Chocolate Filling, 335
    Milk Chocolate, Caramel-Centered, with Black Currant Sauce, 389–391
    Orange-Milk Chocolate, 410
    in Ribbon Teardrops, 334–336
    Rum-Scented, 101
    White Chocolate Filling, 336, 360
    White Chocolate and Pistachio, with Chocolate Lace, 357–360
Frozen
    about, 205, 324
    Hazelnut Coffee, 234–236
    Lemon with Orange Syrup and a Tuile Spiral, 405–406
    Raspberry, with Meringues, 237–239
    Hazelnut-Coffee Filling, 235–236
    Orange-Milk Chocolate, 410
    Passion Fruit Filling, 196
    Raspberry Filling, 239
    Raspberry-White Chocolate, 347
Mousse Cake
    Black Currant, 14–16
    Chocolate, with Banana, 29–31
    Chocolate-Banana Nouvelle (variation), 30
    Chocolate and Frangelico, 24–26
    Chocolate and Frangelico, Contemporary (variation), 26–27
    Cranberry (variation), 16
    Kiwi (variation), 197
    Round Tropical (variation), 197
    Tropical, 195–197
Mousseline Sauce, 338
Muffins, Gingerbread (variation), 444
Multicolored Goblets, 524

Nectarine
    Sorbet (variation), 307
    Sorbet, White, 307
Noisette Rings, 105–106
Noodles, Chocolate, 529–530
Nougat
    about, 587
    for Branchli, 559
    Hazelnut Cream, 103
    Hazelnut Slices, 102–103
    Montélimar, 586–587
Nougatine, 584–586
Nut(s). See also specific nuts
    Baklava, 136–137
    Caramel-Dipped, 624–625

Nut(s). *(cont'd)*
  Caramelized, 626
  Florentine Torte, 447–449
  Gianduja, 560–561
  Glacéed, 580–581
  Meringue, 176
  metric/U.S. volume equivalents for, 816
  Nougat Montélimar, 586–588
  Panforte, 451–453
  Praline, 804
  Praline, Finlander, 560
  removing skin from, 626
  Rum Ball Filling, 790–791
  in sponge cake, 5
  Stollen, Dresdener, 434–435
  Sugar-Coated (variation), 627

Oeufs à la Neige with Caramelized Sugar Spheres, 298–300
Omelet Pancake with Sautéed Star Fruit, Pomegranate Sauce, and Mango Coulis, 300–302
Opera Cake, 47–49
Opera Glaze, 49
Opera Slices, 106–107
Opera Sponge, 48
  Cocoa, 49
Orange(s)
  Blood Orange, in Chocolate Bread Pudding with Cookie Citrus Rind, 152–154
  Blood Orange Gratin, 275-276
  Chiffon Sponge Cake (variation), 798
  -Chocolate Filling, 181
  -Chocolate Towers with Orange Syrup and Caramel Screens, 179–181
  Creams, Chocolate-Covered, 562
  Custard, 185
  Givré, Frosted Minneola Tangelo, with Toasted Meringue and Cookie Citrus Rind, 283–285
  Glacéed, 580
  Glaze, 775
  Marzipan, 645
  -Milk Chocolate Mousse, 410
  Sauce, 278
  Sauce, Bitter Orange (variation), 278
  Sorbet, Honey Mandarin, 216
  Syrup
    Decorating, 760–761
    Orange-Chocolate Towers with Caramel Screens and, 179–181
    Pink Lady Apple and Pear Cream with an Apple Chip and, 348–349
  Tartlets, Walnut-, 126–127
Othellos, 107–108
Othello Sponge Batter, 108
Oven-Braised Black Mission Figs with Honey-Vanilla Frozen Yogurt, 250–251

Oven temperature. *See* Temperature

Palm Leaves, Miniature, 122
Palm Trees, Miniature, 255–256
Panettone, 437–438
Panforte, 451–453
  Dark (variation), 453
Panna Cotta
  Lemon Verbena, 178
  Lemon Verbena, Mascarpone Cheesecake with, 177–179
Parfait
  about, 205
  Cassata, with Meringue, 228–231
  Lemon, Anise-Scented, with Lemon Cookie Tumbleweeds, 375–376
  Lemongrass, 407–408
  Lemongrass, with Green Tea Syrup, Mango Wafer Orbs, and Macadamia Nuts, 406–408
  Lingonberry, 241–243
  Marzipan, 190
  Marzipan, Trio of Chocolates with, 187–191
  Passion Fruit, 220
  Passion Fruit, Chocolate Marquise with a Lace Cookie Bouquet and, 394–396
  Rum, 241
  Strawberry, Wild, 264–265
  Tamarind, 261
  Tamarind, in Tropical Surprise Packages, 258–261
Parisienne Chocolate Cake, 49–50
Passion Fruit
  Coulis, 396
  Jelly, 196
  Mousse Filling, 196
  Parfait, 220
  Parfait, Chocolate Marquise with a Lace Bouquet and, 394–396
Pastes
  Almond, 5, 633
    Basic Recipe, 749
  Caramel Glass, 666
  Chocolate Paper, 719–720
  Cocoa-Nib Wafer, 720–721
  Dark Modeling Chocolate, 541
  Gum, with Gum Tragacanth, 581–582
  Hazelnut, 778
  Hippen Decorating, 722
  Hippen Masse (variation), 722–723
  Macaroon Decorating, 779
  Milk Chocolate Modeling Chocolate (variation), 541
  Pastillage, 588-589
  Praline, 804
  in Scandinavian cakes, 70
  Tuile Decorating, Chocolate, 695

  Tuile Decorating, Vanilla, 695
  White Modeling Chocolate, 542
Pastillage, 588–589
  Display Stand for a Cocoa Painting Showpiece, 590–591
  Gum Paste with Gum Tragacanth, 581–582
Pastry(ies), 92–127. *See also* Cookie(s); Pastry Dough; Petits Fours; Petits Fours Sec; Phyllo Dough; Tarts
  Battenburg, 96–97
  Blackberry Bavarian (variation), 366
  Candle, Holiday, 462–463
  Chocolate and Brandied Cherry, Petite, 109–111
  Chocolate Coconut Tropicana, 100–101
  Chocolate Triangles, 98–100
  Christmas Tree, 458–459
  dipping in chocolate, 94–95
  Hazelnut Nougat Slices, 102–103
  Macaroon Bananas, 104–105
  Noisette Rings, 105–106
  Opera Slices, 106–107
  Othellos, 107–108
  Pigs' Heads, Sweet, 438–440
  Princess, 125–126
  Tartlets, Walnut-Orange, 126–127
  Truffles, Almond, 95–96
  Yule Log, 468–469
Pastry Cream, 773
  Calvados, 764
Pastry Dough
  Lemon-Butter Cookie, 458
  Linzer, 778
  Pâte à Choux, 783
  Puff Pastry, 784-788
  Puff Pastry, Quick, 788–789
  Short Dough
    Basic Recipe, 791
    Cake Bottoms, 792–793
    Cocoa, 792
    Hazelnut, 792
Pâté
  White Chocolate and Pistachio, 472–473
  White Chocolate and Pistachio, Chocolate Chalet with Bitter Chocolate Sauce and, 470–477
Pâte à Choux
  Basic Recipe, 783
  Croquembouche, Individual, 173–174
  Lace Decorations, 230–231
  Profiteroles with Vanilla Ice Cream and Hot Fudge Sauce, 253–254
  Screen, for Hazelnut Nougat Slices, 102–103
Pâte de Fruit, 591–592
Peach(es)
  Coupe Melba, 215

Cream Filling, 314
Forbidden, 164–167
Ice Cream, 212
poaching, 790
Sorbet (variation), 307
Yogurt Creams, Strawberry-, 313–314
Pear(s). *See also* Prickly Pear
about, 252
Asian
about, 271
Pear Tart with Honey-Scented Pear
Frozen Yogurt, 270–272
California with Cointreau-Flavored
Almond Filling, 302–303
Chips, 721
Coupe Belle Hélène, 213
Fanned Zinfandel (variation), 319
Frozen Yogurt, Honey-Scented,
272
Asian Pear Tart with, 270-272
Zinfandel-Poached Pears with,
318-319
Glacéed, 580
Marzipan, 645
and Pink Lady Apple Cream with
Orange Syrup and an Apple
Chip, 348–349
Poached
with Ginger Ice Cream, 251–253
Port-, Chèvre Cheesecake in a
Cocoa-Nib Florentina Cup
with, 150–151
Saffron-, with Almond Ice Cream
and Kadaif Phyllo Nests,
254–257
Saffron-, Date-Stuffed, with
Chardonnay Wine Sauce,
158–162
Zinfandel-, with Honey-Scented
Pear Frozen Yogurt, 318–319
poaching, 790
Ruby, with Verbena Bavarois and
Port Wine Reduction, 349–352
Sauce, Cointreau, 319
Pecan(s)
Baklava, 136–137
Dresdener Stollen, 434–435
-Raisin Soufflé, 370
Traditional Fruitcake, 450–451
Pectin Glaze, 776
Persimmon(s)
about, 487
Bavarois, 479
Charlotte, 478-479
Cream Slices with Cookie
Christmas Trees and
Cranberry Coulis, 480–484
Dome Cake with Gingerbread
Lattice, 484–485
Filling, 482
Pudding, 486–488
Petite Chocolate and Brandied

Cherry Pastries, 109–111
Petits Fours
about, 111
Basic Recipe, 115–116
coating with fondant, 678–679
Glacés, 111–113
Glacés with Frangipane and
Apricot Filling, 114–115
Sponge, 113
Viennese, 124–125
Petits Fours Sec
about, 116
Almond Doubles, 117
Brandy Pretzels, 117–118
Chocolate-Filled Macadamia
Morsels, 118–119
Hazelnut Cuts, 119
Hazelnut Flowers, 120
Macaroon Candies, 121
Macaroon Figures (variation), 121
Miniature Palm Leaves, 122
Strawberry Hearts, 122–123
Three Sisters, 123–124
Viennese Petits Fours, 124–125
Photo transfer sheets, decorated
sponge sheets using, 675
Phyllo Dough
about, 135
Apple Galette, Caramelized, in,
with Kumquat Sauce, 143–145
Asian Pear Tart with Honey-
Scented Pear Frozen Yogurt,
270–272
Baklava, 136–137
Baklava with Mascarpone Bavarian
and Cherry Sauce, 134–137
Banana Truffles, Red Banana in,
181–183
Chocolate-Banana Tart with
Almond Ice Cream and Spun
Sugar, 151–152
kadaif, about, 159, 254
Kadaif Nests, 257
Kadaif Nests, Saffron-Poached
Pears with Almond Ice Cream
and, 254–257
Pears, Date-Stuffed Saffron-
Poached, with Chardonnay
Wine Sauce, 158–162
pouches, 292
Pigs
about, 659
Marzipan
Piglet, 646–647
with Two Santas, 657–660
Whimsical (variation), 648–649
Pig's Head Dinner Rolls
(variation), 439
Sweet Pigs' Heads, 438–440
Whole Large Pig Pastries
(variation), 440
Pineapple(s)

about, 277
Barbados, Caramelized, 276-278
Caramelized, with Coconut Ice
Cream (variation), 278
Coupe Hawaii, 213-214
in Feijoa Sorbet, 290–291
Vanilla-Infused Baked, with
Mango-Avocado Ice Cream
and Mango Fruit Wafer,
130–133
Pink Lady Apple and Pear Cream
with Orange Syrup and an
Apple Chip, 348–349
Piped Chocolate Decorations. *See*
Chocolate Decorations, Piped
Piping
buttercream, 86-87
chocolate, 543
Chocolate Sauce for, 681
designs for special-occasion cakes,
730–747
fondant, 676–678
meringue, 262, 264, 280–281, 287
royal icing, 680-681
sauces, 145, 162–163, 182, 282,
681–686
Sour Cream Mixture for, 727
templates for, 546–550
whipped cream, 126, 262
Pistachio(s)
about, 359
Baklava, 136–137
blanching and crushing, 182
Blueberry Pirouettes, 137–139
Ice Cream, 207–208
Nougat Montélimar, 586–587
Red Banana Truffles in Phyllo
Dough, 181-183
Slices, 564–565
and White Chocolate Mousse with
Chocolate Lace, 357–360
and White Chocolate Pâté, 472–
473
and White Chocolate Pâté,
Chocolate Chalet with Bitter
Chocolate Sauce and, 470–477
Plain Cake Syrup, 789
Plain Mirror Glaze, 776
Plain Poaching Syrup, 789
Plantain(s)
about, 378
Baked, in Gingered Meyer Lemon
Syrup with Avocado-Mango
Ice Cream, 377–378
Chips, 722
Plated Desserts. *See also* Custard(s);
Frozen Desserts; Light Desserts;
Modernist Desserts; Mousse;
Soufflé(s)
Apple Galette, Caramelized, in
Phyllo Dough with Kumquat
Sauce, 143–145

Plated Desserts (cont'd)
Baklava with Mascarpone Bavarian and Cherry Sauce, 134–137
Banana Rum Pudding with Brandied Whipped Cream and Gingerbread Lattice (variation), 486
Blueberry Financier with Toasted Lemon Verbena Sabayon and Mascarpone Sherbet, 380–383
Blueberry Pirouettes, 137–139
Bread Pudding, Chocolate, with Cookie Citrus Rind, 152–154
Bûche de Noël Slices with Pomegranate Sauce and Star Fruit, 469–470
Buried Ruby Treasure, 385-389
Caramel Boxes with Caramel-Macadamia Nut Mousse, 140-143
Cheesecake, Chèvre, in a Cocoa-Nib Florentina Cup with Port-Poached Pears, 150–151
Cheesecake, Mascarpone, with Lemon Verbena Panna Cotta, 177–179
Cherry Baskets with Cherry Compote and Black Pepper Frozen Yogurt, 146–149
Cherry Ganache Towers, Brandied, with Pink Champagne Aspic and Tuile Strips, 384–385
Chocolate Chalet with White Chocolate and Pistachio Pâté and Bitter Chocolate Sauce, 470–477
Chocolate Ganache Towers, 154–158
Chocolate Marquise with Passion Fruit Parfait and a Lace Cookie Bouquet, 394–396
Chocolates, Trio of, with Marzipan Parfait, 187–191
Crème Brûlée, Pumpkin, 488–489
Croquembouche, Individual, 173–174
Dessert Sampling Platter, 162–164
Forbidden Peach, 164–167
Honey Truffle Symphony, 167–169
Marjolaine, 174–176
Mont Blanc with Pomegranate Seeds and Vanilla Curly Cues, 477–478
Mousse Cake, Kiwi (variation), 197
Mousse Cake, Tropical, 195–197
Orange-Chocolate Towers with Orange Syrup and Caramel Screens, 179–181
Pears, Date-Stuffed Saffron-Poached, with Chardonnay Wine Sauce, 158–162
Persimmon Charlotte, 478–479
Persimmon Cream Slices with

Cookie Christmas Trees and Cranberry Coulis, 480–484
Persimmon Dome Cake with Gingerbread Lattice, 484–485
Persimmon Pudding, 486–488
Pineapple, Baked Vanilla-Infused, with Mango-Avocado Ice Cream and Mango Fruit Wafer, 130–133
Red Banana Truffles in Phyllo Dough, 181–183
Strawberries Romanoff, 183–185
Strawberries Romanoff in Caramel Boxes, Wild Strawberries, 201
Strawberry Pyramids, 185–187
Tart, Chocolate-Banana, with Almond Ice Cream and Spun Sugar, 151–152
Triple Treat, 191–194
Truffle Cake, Hot Chocolate, 169–173
Valentine's Day Hearts, 197–200
Plates, decorating
with piped chocolate, 552–553
with sauces, 681–686
with sprayed chocolate, 556–557
Plum(s)
canned, 263
Ice Cream, 262–263
Ice Cream, Vacherin with, 261–264
poaching, 262–263, 790
Sauce, 263
Poached Fruit
Apple Crème Brûlée, 325–328
basic directions for, 790
Compote, Winter Fruit, in Late-Harvest Wine Syrup, 316–318
Coupe Belle Hélène, 213
dried fruit, 790
Figs, Sherry-Poached Black Mission Figs with Crème Catalan, 353–354
Peach, Forbidden, 164–167
Pear Tart, Asian, with Honey-Scented Pear Frozen Yogurt, 270–272
Pears, California, with Cointreau-Flavored Almond Filling, 302–303
Pears, Fanned Zinfandel (variation), 319
Pears, Poached, with Ginger Ice Cream, 251–253
Pears, Port Wine-Poached, Chèvre Cheesecake in a Cocoa-Nib Florentine Cup with, 150–151
Pears, Ruby, with Verbena Bavarois and Port Wine Reduction, 349–352
Pears, Saffron-Poached, with Almond Ice Cream and Kadaif Phyllo Nests, 254–257
Pears, Saffron-Poached, Date-Stuffed, with Chardonnay

Wine Sauce, 158–162
Pears, Zinfandel-Poached, with Honey-Scented Pear Frozen Yogurt, 318–319
Plain Poaching Syrup, 789
Saffron Poaching Liquid, 160
Spiced Poaching Syrup (variation), 790
Tarte Tatin Moderne, 416–421
Polar Bear(s)
Marzipan, 649–650
Tuile, 398
Tuile, Cocoa Nib-White Chocolate Ice Cream with a Chocolate Lace Igloo and, 396–399
Pomegranate Sauce, 302
Bûche de Noël Slices with Star Fruit and, 469–470
Omelet Pancake with Sautéed Star Fruit, Mango Coulis and, 300–302
Pomegranate Seeds, Mont Blanc with Vanilla Curly Cues and, 477–478
Portion funnel, about, 679
Port Wine
-Poached Pears, Chèvre Cheesecake in a Cocoa-Nib Florentina Cup with, 150–151
Reduction, 352
Reduction, Ruby Pears with Verbena Bavarois and, 349–352
Powdered sugar, sifting with pie tin template and holder, 692–693
Praline(s)
Basic Recipe, 804
Buttercream, 176
Buttercream, in Marjolaine, 174–176
Finlander, 560
Marzipan, 563
Paste, 804
White Chocolate Truffles with, 190–191
Pretzels, Brandy, 117–118
Prickly Pear
juice, 219
Sorbet, 219
Sorbet, Apricot and Fig Tart with, 218–220
Princess cake
about, 72
suggestion for wedding cake, 90
Princess Pastries, 125-126
Profiteroles
Croquembouche, Individual, 173–174
with Vanilla Ice Cream and Hot Fudge Sauce, 253–254
Prunes, Glacéed, 580–581
Pudding
Banana Rum, with Brandied Whipped Cream and Gingerbread Lattice (variation), 486

Chocolate Bread, with Cookie
    Citrus Rind, 152–154
Chocolate Rum, with Chocolate
    May Beetles, 336–338
Persimmon, 486–488
Puff Pastry
    Basic Recipe, 784–788
    Cookie Cinnamon Sticks, 420–421
    Galette, Classic, 144
    by hand (European method), 785
    Lattice Decorations, 178–179
    using a mixer (production method),
        784
    Palm Leaves, Miniature, 122
    Quick, 788–789
    working with, 785
Pulled Sugar
    aerating, 605
    Bow with Ribbons, 608–609
    equipment, 605–606
    Rose, 606–607
Pumpkin Crème Brûlée, 488–489
Puree
    Black Currant, 16
    Chestnut, 445
    Cranberry, 17

Quark Cheese, Marbled Cheesecake
    with, 297–298
Queen of Sheba Cake, 50–52
Quick Bavarian Cream, 774
Quick Coconut Ice Cream, 214
Quick Ganache, 771
Quicklime, in sugarwork, 572–573
Quick Puff Pastry, 788–789
Quick Vanilla Sugar, 435

Rainbow of Summer Sorbets in a
    Cookie Flower, 304–307
Raisin(s)
    macerating, 241, 249
    Panettone, 437–438
    -Pecan Soufflé, 370
    Persimmon Pudding, 486–488
    Rum Ball Filling, 790–791
    Rum Parfait, 241
    Rum-Raisin Ice Cream, 249
    in Stollen, Braided, 430–431
    in Stollen, Dresdener, 434–435
Raspberry(ies)
    about, 53
    Cake, 52–54
    Cake, Nouvelle (variation), 53–54
    Chocolate Truffle Cake with, 31–32
    Cream, 54
    Dacquoise Baskets with Raspberry
        Sauce, Mango Coulis and, 280–281
    Jellies (Pâte de Fruit), 591–592
    Lemon Verbena-, suggestion for
        wedding cake, 89
    Mousse Filling, 239
    Mousse, Frozen, with Meringues,

237–239
Sauce, 173
Sauce, Dacquoise Baskets with
    Fresh Raspberries, Mango
    Coulis and, 280–282
Sauce, Melba, 215
Syrup, Decorating, 761
Rectangles, Chocolate Cutouts, 520–521
Red Banana Truffles in Phyllo Dough,
    181–183
Red Currant(s)
    Bavarian Cream, 200
    frozen/frozen juice, 310
    Glaze, 777
    Sauce, 200
    Sauce, Milk Chocolate Marquise
        with Finger Banana Center
        and, 408–410
    Sorbet, 310
    Sorbet in Magnolia Cookie Shells,
        307–310
    Syrup, Decorating, 761
Red Pepper
    Decorations (variation), 401
    Sails, 726
    Shells, 400
    Tuile, Coconut Ice Cream in a,
        with Strawberry Salsa and
        Tomatillo Lace, 399–401
Ribbon-Pattern Decorated Sponge
    Sheets, 672–673
Ribbons
    Chocolate, 530–531
    Pulled Sugar Bow with, 608–609
Rich Cardamom Yeast Dough, 437
Rings, acetate, 135, 164, 238, 376
Ripple pattern, sauce design, 683
Rock Sugar, 596–597
Rolled Fondant, 592
Rolling pins, marzipan, about, 97
Rolls, Pig's Head Dinner (variation), 439
Romanoff Sauce, 253
Roses
    Chocolate, 542
    Marzipan, 651–653
    Marzipan Leaves, 644–645
    piped, 87
    Pulled Sugar, 606–607
Round Tropical Mousse Cake
    (variation), 197
Roux Batter, 189
Royal Icing
    Basic Recipe, 680
    Cinnamon Stars, 460
    cornstarch in, 127, 460
    Gingerbread Chalet, Santa's,
        499–503
    Gingerbread House, Traditional,
        490–499
    ornaments and showpieces, 681
    traced designs on marzipan,
        677–678

uses for, 680
Walnut-Orange Tartlets,
    126–127
Ruby Fruit Jelly Centers, 387
Ruby Pears with Verbena Bavarois
    and Port Wine Reduction,
    349–352
Ruffles (Fans), Chocolate, 521–522
Rum
    about, 338
    Banana Pudding, with Brandied
        Whipped Cream and
        Gingerbread Lattice
        (variation), 486
    Chestnut Filling, 447
    Chestnut Torte, 444–445
    Chocolate Mousse, Rum-Scented,
        101
    Chocolate Pudding, 337
    Chocolate Pudding with Chocolate
        May Beetles, 336–338
    Decorating Syrup, 762
    for flambé, 221
    Ice Cream Cake Jamaica, 239–241
    Jamaican, about, 240
    Parfait, 241
    Pineapple Barbados, Caramelized,
        276–278
    -Raisin Ice Cream, 249
    Rum Ball Filling, 790–791
Rum Ball Filling, 790–791
    in Yule Log Pastries, 468–469
    in Yule Logs, 453–456

Sabayon, 311–312
    about, 311
    Champagne, Fresh Strawberries
        with, 283
    Cold (variation), 312
    Lemon Verbena, 381
    Lemon Verbena, Toasted,
        Blueberry Financier with
        Mascarpone Sherbet and,
        380–383
    of Muscat Wine, Apricot Gratin
        with, 269–270
    Zabaglione (variation), 311
Saccharimeter, 825
Saffron
    about, 161
    -Poached Pears with Almond Ice
        Cream and Kadaif Phyllo
        Nests, 254–257
    -Poached Pears, Date-Stuffed, with
        Chardonnay Wine Sauce,
        158–162
    Poaching Liquid, 160
    -Vanilla Syrup Reduction, 255
Salsa, Strawberry, 401
    Coconut Ice Cream in a Red
        Pepper Tuile with Tomatilla
        Lace and, 399–401

Salzburger Soufflé, 312
Sambuca
    Cream, Cappuccino Mousse with,
        in a Chocolate Coffee Cup,
        328–332
    Cream, Italian Sambuca-Scented,
        Kardinals with Fresh Fruit
        and, 291–292
    Licorice Decorating Syrup, 760
Sampling Platter, Dessert, 162-163
Santa's Gingerbread Chalet, 499-503
Santas, Marzipan
    Head, 503
    Pig with Two Santas, 657–660
    for the Traditional Gingerbread
        House, 660–663
Sauce gun, about, 679
Sauces. *See also* Coulis; Sabayon;
        Sauces, Decorating
    Apple Cider-Caramel, 419
    Apricot, 303
    Black Currant, 391
    Black Currant, Caramel-Centered
        Milk Chocolate Mousse with,
        389–391
    Blueberry, 139
    Bourbon, 182–183
    Caramel
        Apple Cider-, 419
        Clear, 328
        Fortified, 19
    Chardonnay Wine, 161–162
    Chardonnay Wine, Pears, Saffron-
        Poached Date-Stuffed with,
        158–162
    Cherry, 230
        Baklava with Mascarpone
            Bavarian and, 134–137
        Chocolate Dome Cake with
            Chocolate Lace and, 391–393
        Guinettes, 388
    Chocolate, 413
        Bitter Chocolate (variation), 413
        Bitter Chocolate, Chocolate
            Chalet with White Chocolate
            and Pistachio Pâté and, 470–477
        Hot Fudge, 254
        for Piping, 681
        White Chocolate, 803
    Cranberry Coulis, 243
    Crème Anglaise, 754
    Hot Fudge, 254
    Hot Fudge, and Vanilla Ice Cream,
        Profiteroles with, 253–254
    Kiwi, 309-310
    Kumquat, 145
        Apple Galette, Caramelized, in
            Phyllo Dough with, 143–145
    Mango Coulis, 244
    Melba, 215
    Mousseline, 338
    Orange, 278

Orange, Bitter (variation), 278
    Pear, Cointreau, 319
    Plum, 263
    Pomegranate, 302
    Pomegranate, Bûche de Noël Slices
        with Star Fruit and, 469–470
    Pomegranate, Omelet Pancake with
        Sautéed Star Fruit, Mango
        Coulis and, 300–302
    Raspberry, 173
    Raspberry, Dacquoise Baskets with
        Fresh Raspberries, Mango
        Coulis and, 280–281
    Raspberry, Melba, 215
    Red Currant, 200
    Red Currant, Milk Chocolate
        Marquise with Finger Banana
        Center and, 408–410
    Romanoff, 253
    Strawberry, 186-187
    Strawberry Salsa, 401
    Strawberry Salsa, Coconut Ice
        Cream in a Red Pepper Tuile
        with Tomatillo Lace and,
        399–401
    Vanilla Custard, Light, 300
Sauces, Decorating
    Chocolate Sauce for Piping, 681
    corkscrew pattern, 682
    dots, piping, 162-163
    feathered two-tone pool pattern, 685
    fluted circle, piping, 145
    hearts with stems pattern, 684–685
    hearts with weave pattern, 683–684
    ripple pattern, 683
    spiderweb pattern, 683
        spiral, 684
    string of hearts pattern, 682
        curved, 682
        two-tone, 684
    swirled zigzag pattern, 685
    turntable method, 686
    weave pattern, 683
Scandinavian wedding cakes, 70
Screens
    Caramel Glass Paste, 666–668
    Caramel, Orange-Chocolate
        Towers with Orange Syrup
        and, 179–181
    Pâte à Choux, for Hazelnut Nougat
        Slices, 102–103
Seaweed Wafer Decorations, 726–727
Seeding method of tempering
        chocolate, 513
Semifreddo
    about, 234
    Cinnamon Venezia with Coffee
        Bean Crisps, 233–234
Shavings, Chocolate, 531–532
Sherbet, Mascarpone, 383
    Blueberry Financier with Toasted
        Lemon Verbena Sabayon and,

380–383
Sherry-Poached Black Mission Figs
    with Crème Catalan, 353–354
Shingle Cake, Dark Chocolate, 32–34
Short Dough
    Basic Recipe, 791
    Cake Bottoms, 792–793
    Cocoa, 792
    Hazelnut, 792
Sicilian Macaroon Cake, 55–58
Silica gel, in sugarwork, 572
Silk screen
    decorated sponge sheets using a,
        674–675
    decorating marzipan using a, 647
Silpat baking mats, 6, 108, 672, 673
Simple Caramel Glass Paste Wedges,
        669
Simple Syrup, 793
Single turn, instructions for making a,
        787–788
Snowbird in a Chocolate Cage, 413–415
Snow Eggs (Oeufs à la Neige) with
        Caramelized Sugar Spheres,
        298–300
Snow Hearts, Chocolate, 456–457
Soft Gingerbread Cake, 443–444
Sorbet(s)
    Cherry, Double, 306–307
    Coupe Niçoise, 215–216
    Feijoa, 290–291
    Feijoa, Global Fresh Fruit Baskets
        with, 289–291
    Gooseberry, 306
    Honey Mandarin, 216
    Nectarine, White, 307
    Nectarine or Peach (variation), 307
    Prickly Pear, 219
    Prickly Pear, Apricot and Fig Tart
        with, 218–219
    Rainbow of Summer, in a Cookie
        Flower, 304–307
    Red Currant, 310
    Red Currant, in Magnolia Cookie
        Shells, 307–310
Soufflé(s)
    about, 324–325
    Blueberry, 369
    Chocolate (variation), 368
    fruit, about, 325
    Fruit (variation), 370
    Harlequin (variation), 369
    Liqueur, 367–368
    Pecan-Raisin, 370
    Rothschild, 370–371
    Salzburger, 312
Soufflé(s), Frozen (Glacé)
    about, 205
    Bénédictine, 224-226
    Ginger (variation), 226
    liqueur in, 224
    preparing ramekins for, 226

Sour Cream
    Mixture for Piping, 727
    Romanoff Sauce, 253
South African wedding cake, 69
Spanish Caramel-Flavored Tuile
    Decorations, 727–728
Spice(d)
    Bread, Swedish (Vörtbröd), 440–441
    Dresdener Stollen, 434
    Fruitcake, Lemon Verbena-
        Scented, 449–450
    Ganache Filling, 412–413
    Ganache and Tea Ice Cream Marco
        Polo, 410–413
    Gingerbread Cookies, 461–462
    Panforte, 451–453
    Poaching Liquid, 790
Spider(s), Caramel, 622–623
    Crème Brûlée on a, with a Sugar
        Shard, 341–342
Spiderweb pattern, sauce design, 683
    spiral, 684
Spirals, Caramel, 623–624
Spiral spiderweb pattern, sauce design,
    684
Sponge Cake
    Almond, 795–796
    Angel Food, 796
    baking method, 5–6
    Basic Recipe, 794
    Chiffon I, 797
    Chiffon II, 798
    Chocolate, 795
        Bittersweet, 33–34
        Chiffon (variation), 797, 798
        Hazelnut-, 800
        High-Ratio (variation), 800
        Low-Cholesterol (variation), 294
    Dobos, 799
    Dobos, Cocoa (variation), 799
    formula balance, 4
    Gingerbread, 481-482
    half recipe, 24, 46
    Hazelnut-Chocolate, 800
    High-Ratio, 800
    High-Ratio, Chocolate (variation),
        800
    ingredients, 4-5
    Lemon Chiffon (variations), 797, 798
    Low-Cholesterol, 293–294
    Low-Cholesterol, Chocolate
        (variation), 294
    Opera, 48
    Opera, Cocoa, 49
    Orange Chiffon (variation), 798
    Othello Sponge Batter, 108
    Petits Fours, 113
    refrigerated, 186
    skin, removing, 11, 98
    triangle pastries, sponge sheets for,
        98–100
    trimming to fit, 13

    unmolding, 6
Sponge Sheets, Decorated
    freezing, 234
    Joconde Base I, 670
    Joconde Base II, 671
    photo transfer sheets, using, 675
    Ribbon-Pattern, 672–674
    silk screen, using a, 674–675
    Wood-Grain-Pattern, 675–676
Spoons, Tuile Cookie, 708
    Cherry, 388
Sprayed Chocolate, 556-558
    Chocolate Solution for, 557–558
    Cocoa Solution for, 558
Spraying, Egg Wash for, 763
Springerle, 466–467
Spun Sugar, 593–594
    Caramelized (variation), 594
    Caramelized Sugar Spheres, 299
    Chocolate-Banana Tart with
        Almond Ice Cream and, 151–152
    Meringue Glacé Leda, 249
    Snowbird in a Chocolate Cage, 414
    storing, 414
Squares, Chocolate Cutouts, 520–521
Starch, in sponge cake, 4
Star Fruit
    Bûche de Noël Slices with
        Pomegranate Sauce and,
        469–470
    Sautéed, Omelet Pancake with
        Pomegranate Sauce, Mango
        Coulis and, 300–302
Stars, Cinnamon, 460
Steam Decorations, Tuile, 712–713
Stollen
    about, 435
    Braided, 430–431
    Dresdener, 434–435
Strawberry(ies)
    Bagatelle, 58–61
    Black-Tie, 236–237
    Fresh, with Champagne Sabayon,
        283
    Glacéed, 580–581
    Hearts, 122–123
    Ice Cream, 222–223
    Jellies (Pâte de Fruit), 591–592
    Kirsch Cake, 61–63
    Parfait, Wild Strawberry, 264–265
    Pyramids, 185–187
    Romanoff, 183–185
    Romanoff in Caramel Boxes, Wild
        Strawberry, 201
    Salsa, 401
    Salsa, Coconut Ice Cream in a Red
        Pepper Tuile with Tomatillo
        Lace and, 399–401
    Sauce, 186–187
    Wafer Decorations, 725
    Yogurt Creams, -Peach, 313–314
Streaking chocolate

    with pie tin template, 692
    piping, 553
Streusel Topping, 154
    on Chocolate Bread Pudding with
        Cookie Citrus Rind, 152–153
String of hearts pattern, sauce design,
    682
    curved, 682
    two-tone, 684
Striped Chocolate Cornets, 535
Striped Chocolate Cups, 536–537
Striped Chocolate Cups with Tuile
    Steam Decorations, 415–416
Striped Lychee Charlotte (variation),
    296
Sugar. See also Candies; Caramelized
    Sugar; Sugar Decorations
    about, 571
    Baumé scale of measurement, 825
    Boiled Sugar
        Basic Recipe, 575–576
        cleaning the cooking pan, 612
        color, adding to, 578
        Method I, 576–577
        Method II, 577–578
        reheating stored sugar, 576
    boiling conversions, 827
    Brix scale of measurement, 826
    Cinnamon, 753
    functions in pastrymaking, 575
    Ginger, Crystallized, 756
    metric/U.S. volume equivalents for,
        816
    Nuts, -Coated (variation), 627
    for sponge cake, 4
    stages, temperature and testing
        procedures, 827
    sugar beets refining and process-
        ing, 573, 574
    sugarcane refining and processing,
        572–573, 574
    Syrup, 758
    Vanilla, 803
    Vanilla, Quick, 435
Sugar Decorations. See also
        Caramelized Sugar Decorations;
        Fondant; Royal Icing
    Blown Sugar, 610–611
    Bubble Sugar, 615–616
        Isomalt (variation), 617
        Twice-Cooked (variation), 616
    Cast Sugar
        casting forms, 603
        Figures, 597–604
        repairing breaks, 602
        silicone template, 604
        spraying color, 604
    equipment, 570–571, 605–606
        air pumps, 610, 611
        Baumé thermometer, 825
        Brix hydrometer, 826
        fixative syringes, 604, 607

Sugar Decorations (cont'd)
    sugar pans, 576, 611–612
    sugar thermometer, 570, 630–631,
        827
    warming cases, 609, 610
  Fruit and Nuts, Glacéed, 580-581
  Gum Paste with Gum Tragacanth,
    581–582
  ingredients required, 571–573
  Nougatine, 584–585
  Pastillage, 588–589
  Pastillage Display Stand for a
    Cocoa Painting Showpiece,
    590–591
  protecting from moisture, 571–573
  Pulled Sugar
    aerating, 605
    Bow with Ribbons, 608–609
    equipment, 605–606, 607
    Rose, 606–607
    Rock Sugar, 596–597
  Spun Sugar, 593-594
    Caramelized (variation), 594
    Caramelized Sugar Spheres, 299
    Chocolate-Banana Tart with
      Almond Ice Cream and, 151–
      152
    Meringue Glacé Leda, 249
    storing, 414
  storing, 571–572
  Sugar Crystals for, 594–595
  Sugar Crystal Sheets (variation),
    595
  Sugar Shards, 628–629
    Crème Brûlée on a Caramel Spider
      with a, 341–342
    Noncaramelized and Tinted
      (variation), 629
    Sugar Sticks, 595–596
  Sugar lamps, 609
  Sugar pans, 576, 611–612
  Sugar Shards, 628–629
    Noncaramelized and Tinted
      (variation), 629
  Sugar Syrup, 758
  Sun-Brewed Jasmine Tea Ice Cream,
    209–210
  Swedish Christmas, about, 423–424
  Swedish Spice Bread (Vörtbröd),
    440–441
  Sweet Pigs' Heads, 438–440
  Swirled zigzag pattern, sauce design,
    685
  Swiss Meringue, 782
  Swiss-Method Buttercream, 751, 753
  Symphony of Circles, Tuile, 712, 714
  Syrups. See also Syrups, Decorating
    Cake, Plain, 789
    Coffee, for Opera Cake, 49
    Gingered Meyer Lemon, Baked
      Plantains in, with Avocado-

    Mango Ice Cream, 377–378
    Orange, Frozen Lemon Mousse
      with a Tuile Spiral and,
      405–406
    Orange, Orange-Chocolate Towers
      with Caramel Screens and,
      179–181
    Orange, Pink Lady Apple and Pear
      Cream with an Apple Chip
      and, 348
    Poaching, Plain, 789
    Poaching, Spiced (variation), 790
    Saffron-Vanilla Reduction, 255
    Simple, 793
    Sugar, 758
    Wine, Late-Harvest, Winter Fruit
      Compote in, 316–318
Syrups, Decorating
  Black Currant, 758-759
  Green Tea, 759
  Green Tea, Lemongrass Parfait
    with Mango Wafer Orbs,
    Macadamia Nuts and, 406–408
  Lemon-Vanilla, 759–760
  Licorice, 760
  Mint, 760
  Orange-Vanilla, 760–761
  Raspberry, 761
  Red Currant, 761
  Rum, 762
  turntable method, 686

Tabliering method of tempering
    chocolate, 512–513
Tamarind(s)
  about, 261
  Parfait, 261
  Parfait, in Tropical Surprise
    Packages, 258-261
Tangelo Givré, Frosted Minneola,
    with Toasted Meringue and
    Cookie Citrus Rind, 283–285
Tartaric Acid Solution, 629
  with Pectin Glaze, 776
Tart(s)
  Apricot and Fig with Prickly Pear
    Sorbet, 218–219
  Chocolate-Banana, with Almond
    Ice Cream and Spun Sugar,
    151–152
  Pear, Asian, with Honey-Scented
    Pear Frozen Yogurt, 270–273
Tarte Tatin Moderne, 416-421
Tartlets, Walnut-Orange, 126-127
Tea
  about, 210
  Green Tea Decorating Syrup, 759
    Lemongrass Parfait, with Mango
    Wafer Orbs, Macadamia Nuts
    and, 406–408

    Ice Cream, and Spiced Ganache
      Marco Polo, 410–413
    Ice Cream, Sun-Brewed Jasmine,
      209–210
Teardrops
  Ribbon, Chocolate Mousse in, 334–336
  Translucent Chocolate, 419–420
Temperature
  centigrade/Fahrenheit equivalents,
    812–815
  in high altitude baking, 824
  for sponge cake, 6
  for sugar stages, 827
Tempered chocolate, 511–512
  cold water method, 513-514
  curvy strips, 705
  pretempered (direct method), 514
  seeding method, 513
  tabliering method, 512–513
  testing, 514
  warming to working temperature,
    514
Terrine, Triple-Chocolate, 354–356
  Miniature, 192–193
Thermometers
  about, 630–631
  dairy, 802
  sugar, 570, 630–631, 827
  types of, 631
Three Sisters, 123–124
Tiramisù
  Miniature, 194
  suggestion for wedding cake, 91
Tofu-Banana Frozen Yogurt, Baked
    Bananas with, 273–274
Tomatillo Lace
  Coconut Ice Cream in a Red
    Pepper Tuile with Strawberry
    Salsa and, 399–401
  Decorations, 728–729
Tools. See Equipment and tools
Toppings, Streusel, 154
Torte(s)
  Chestnut Rum, 444–445
  Dobos, 34–36
  Florentine, 447–449
Towers
  Cherry Ganache, Brandied, with
    Pink Champagne Aspic and
    Curvy Tuile Strips, 384–385
  Chocolate Ganache, 154-158
  Orange-Chocolate, with Orange
    Syrup and Caramel Screens,
    179–181
Traditional Fruitcake, 450–451
Transfer sheets, 109, 375, 521
Translucent Chocolate Teardrops,
    419–420, 421
Triangles
  Chocolate Cutouts, 520–521
  cutting sponge sheets for, 98–100

Triangular forms, 186, 475–476
Triangular Tuile Spirals, 706–707
Triestine Bread, 441–442
Trio of Chocolates with Marzipan
    Parfait, 187–191
Triple Chocolate Terrine, 354-356
Triple Treat, 191–194
Tropical Coconut Cake, 63–65
Tropical Mousse Cake, 195–197
Tropical Surprise Packages, 258–261
Truffle Cake
    Chocolate Batter, 172–173
    Chocolate, with Raspberries, 31–32
    Hot Chocolate, 169–173
Truffles
    Dark Chocolate Espresso, 190
    Milk Chocolate, 191
    White Chocolate with Praline,
        190–191
Tuile Paste
    about, 694
    Chocolate Decorating Paste, 695
    Spanish Caramel-Flavored, 727–728
    Vanilla Decorating Paste, 695
Tuile Paste Decorations
    about, 694
    Baskets, Cherry, with Cherry
        Compote and Black Pepper
        Frozen Yogurt, 146–149
    Baskets, Global Fresh Fruit, with
        Feijoa Sorbet, 289–290
    in Blueberry Pirouettes, 137–139
    Butterflies, 695–698
    Camels, 389
    Camels, in Buried Ruby Treasure,
        385–389
    Christmas Trees, Cookie, 482–484
    Christmas Trees, Cookie,
        Persimmon Cream Slices with
        Cranberry Coulis and, 480–484
    Citrus Rind, Cookie, 698–699
        Chocolate Bread Pudding with,
        152-154
        Frosted Minneola Tangelo Givré
        with Toasted Meringue and,
        283–285
        in Crème Caramel Nouvelle,
        342–344
    Crescent, 381–382
    Curly Cues, 700–702
    Curly Cues, Vanilla, Mont Blanc
        with Pomegranate Seeds and,
        477–478
    Curved Wedges, 702–704
    Curvy Strips, 704–705
    Curvy Strips, Brandied Cherry
        Ganache Towers with Pink
        Champagne Aspic and, 384–385
    Dragonfly, 131–133
    Figurines, Cookie, 698–699
    Flower, Rainbow of Summer

Sorbets in a, 304–307
flower petals, making, 171
Leaves, 319, 709–711
Leaves, Grape, 364–365
Leaves, Maple (variation), 711
Magnolia Cookie Shells, Red
    Currant Sorbet in, 307–310
magnolia shells, making, 246
molding tool for, 718
Palm Trees, Miniature, 255–256
Polar Bear, Cocoa Nib-White
    Chocolate Ice Cream with a
    Chocolate Lace Igloo and,
    396–399
Polar Bears, 398
Spanish Caramel-Flavored, 727–728
Spiral, Frozen Lemon Mousse with
    Orange Syrup and, 405–406
Spirals, Triangular, 706–707
Spoons, Cherry Tuile, 388
Spoons, Tuile Cookie, 708
Steam, 712, 713
Steam, Striped Chocolate Cups
    with, 415–416
Symphony of Circles, 712, 714
templates for, about, 694
in Tropical Surprise Packages,
    258–261
Tulips, 715–716
Tulips, Miniature, 716–717
Tumbleweeds, Cookie, 699–700
Tumbleweeds, Lemon Cookie,
    Anise-Scented Lemon Parfait
    with, 375–376
Vineyard Barrels, 314–316
Wavy Strips, 718–719
Wedges, 709–711
Wedges, Curved, 702–704
Tuiles
    Caramel-Flavored Decorations,
        Spanish, 727–728
    Red Pepper, Coconut Ice Cream in
        a, with Strawberry Salsa and
        Tomatillo Lace, 399-401
Tulips, Tuile, 715–716
    Chocolate, Ice Cream in a, with
        Mango Coulis, 243–245
    Crowns, Miniature (variation), 717
    Miniature, 716–717
Tumbleweeds
    Cookie, 699–700
    Lemon Cookie, Anise-Scented
        Lemon Parfait with, 375–376
Two-Tone Chocolate Cigarettes, 518
Two-tone string of hearts pattern,
    sauce design, 684

Unflavored Yogurt, 802

Vacherin with Plum Ice Cream,
    261-264

Valentines, Fruit, 287–288
Valentine's Day Hearts, 197–200
Vanilla
    about, 131
    Bavarian Cream, Vanilla Bean-
        Lemon Verbena, 60–61
    Buttercream, 752–753
    Crème Anglaise, 754
    Crème Brûlée Custard, Vanilla-
        Bean, 328
    Curly Cues, Mont Blanc with
        Pomegranate Seeds and,
        477–478
    Custard Sauce, Light, 300
    Extract, 803
    Gianduja Cream Filling, -Scented,
        34
    -Honey Frozen Yogurt, 276
    Ice Cream, 172
    Ice Cream, in Hot Chocolate
        Truffle Cake, 170-173
    Ice Cream and Hot Fudge Sauce,
        Profiteroles with, 253-254
    -Lemon Decorating Syrup,
        759–760
    -Orange Decorating Syrup, 760–
        761
    Pineapple, Baked Vanilla-Infused,
        with Mango-Avocado Ice
        Cream and Mango Fruit
        Wafer, 130–133
    -Saffron Syrup Reduction, 255
    Sugar, 803
    Sugar, Quick, 435
    Tuile Decorating Paste, 695
Verbena. See Lemon Verbena
Viennese Petits Fours, 124–125
Vineyard Barrels, 314-316
Vörtbröd (Swedish Spice Bread),
    440–441

Walnut(s)
    about, 127
    in Baklava, 136–137
    Caramelized, 317–318
    Glacéed, 580
    -Orange Tartlets, 126–127
Warming cases, sugar, 609, 610
Wavy Tuile Strips, 718–719
Weave pattern, sauce design, 683
Weaver's Dough, design, 430
    in Bread Basket, 425–430
Wedding cakes, 67–91
    assembly and decoration, 75–77,
        84–89
    cake combinations, 89–91
    cultural traditions, 68–71
    dietary restrictions and, 75
    flavors, 74, 89–91
    history of, 68
    logistical considerations, 72–79

Wedding cakes *(cont'd)*
  modern styles, 71–72
  order form/contract, 83
  Rolled Fondant in, 592
  serving procedures, 79
  size, 73–74, 80–82
Weights and measures. *See also*
      Metric/U.S. equivalents
  baker's percentage, 820
  Baumé scale, 825
  Brix scale, 826
  cake circumference, to calculate, 819
  cake pan capacity, 80–81, 819
  gelatin equivalents and substitu-
      tions, 8–9, 817
  gram measurements for baker's
      percentage, 820–823
  gram weight of commonly used
      products, 818
  in high-altitude baking, 824
  metric conversions, 806
  metric system, 805–806
  ounce measurements for baker's
      percentage, 823
  prepared yields of commonly used
      products, 816
  temperature equivalents, centi-
      grade-Fahrenheit, 812–815
  volume equivalents (U.S.), 810
  yeast equivalents and substitutions,
      818
Whimsical Marzipan Pig (variation),
      648–649
Whipped Cream
  Apricot, 13
  Brandied, 488
  Brandied, Banana Rum Pudding
      with Gingerbread Lattice and
      (variation), 486
  Kirsch, 63
  Kirsch, in Strawberry Pyramids,
      185–186
  Macaroon-Maraschino, 58
  Mocha, 39
  piping, 126, 262
White Bread Dough, 440
White Chocolate
  Bavarian Cream, Neapolitan,
      360–363
  Filling, 356
    Bavarian, 41–42
    Mousse, 336, 360

Treasure, 386–387
Ice Cream, 217
  Cocoa Nib-, 397–398
  Cocoa Nib-, with a Chocolate
      Lace Igloo and Tuile Polar
      Bear, 396–399
  Gingered (variation), 217
Marquise, Miniature, 163
Mascarpone Bavarian, 134–135
Modeling Chocolate, 542
Mousse Filling, 336, 360
Mousse, and Pistachio, with
      Chocolate Lace, 357–360
Mousse, Raspberry-, 347
and Pistachio Pâté, 472–473
and Pistachio Pâté, Chocolate
      Chalet with Bitter Chocolate
      Sauce and, 470–477
Sauce, 803
Truffles with Praline, 190
White Nectarine Sorbet, 307
Whole-Egg Wash, 762
Whole Large Pig Pastries (variation),
      440
Wild Honey Truffle Cream, 169
Wild Strawberries Romanoff in
      Caramel Boxes, 201
Wild Strawberry Parfait, 264–265
Wine
  Apple Cake, 9–11
  Aspic, Pink Champagne, 384
  Calvados Filling, 11
  Chardonnay Sauce, 161–162
  Chardonnay Sauce, Saffron-
      Poached Date-Stuffed Pears
      with, 158–162
  Foam and Blackberry Bavarian
      Greystone, 363–366
  Port-Poached Pears, Chèvre
      Cheesecake in a Cocoa-Nib
      Florentina Cup with, 150–151
  Port Wine Reduction, 352
  Port Wine Reduction, Ruby Pears
      with Verbena Bavarois and,
      349–352
  Sabayon, 311
  Sabayon, Champagne, Fresh
      Strawberries with, 283
  Sabayon of Muscat, Apricot Gratin
      with, 269–270
  Sherry-Poached Black Mission Figs
      with Crème Catalan, 353–354

Syrup, Late-Harvest, Winter Fruit
      Compote in, 316-318
  Zinfandel-Poached Pears with
      Honey-Scented Pear Frozen
      Yogurt, 318–319
  Fanned (variation), 319
Winter Fruit Compote in Late-
      Harvest Wine Syrup, 316–318
Wood Grain, Chocolate with,
      537–539
Wood-Grain-Pattern Decorated
      Sponge Sheet, 675–676

Yeast equivalents and substitutions, 818
Yogurt
  Cheese, 804
  Creams, Strawberry-Peach, 313–314
  Peach Cream Filling, 314
  Unflavored, 802
Yogurt, Frozen
  Banana-Tofu, 274
  Banana-Tofu, Baked Bananas with,
      273–274
  Black Pepper, 403
  Black Pepper, Cherry Baskets with
      Cherry Compote and, 146–149
  Honey-Vanilla, 276
    Black Mission Figs, Oven-
        Braised, with, 250–251
    Blood Orange Gratin with,
        275–276
    Pineapple Barbados,
        Caramelized, with, 276–278
  Pear, Honey-Scented, 272
    Asian Pear Tart with, 270–272
    Zinfandel-Poached Pears with,
        318–319
Yolks-Only Egg Wash, 763
Yule Log(s) (*Bûches de Nöel*),
      453–456
  Pastries, 468–469
  Slices with Pomegranate Sauce and
      Star Fruit, 469–470

Zabaglione (variation), 311
Zinfandel
  Fanned Pears (variation), 319
  -Poached Pears with Honey-
      Scented Pear Frozen Yogurt,
      318–319